CW00833043

The Alamo Reader
A Study in History

edited by Todd Hansen

STACKPOLE
BOOKS

Published by
STACKPOLE BOOKS
5067 Ritter Road
Mechanicsburg, PA 17055
www.stackpolebooks.com

Printed in the United States of America

10 9 8 7 6 5 4 3 2 1

FIRST EDITION

Library of Congress Cataloging-in-Publication Data

The Alamo reader / edited by Todd Hansen.— 1st ed.
    p. cm.
  ISBN 0-8117-0060-7
  1. Alamo (San Antonio, Tex.)—Siege, 1836—Sources. I. Hansen, Todd.
F390.A36 2003
976.4'03—dc21

                                                                    2003003852

To My Mother

*Whose love and support has opened so many doors
that otherwise would have remained closed.*

And to the Memory of My Father

*Whose remarkable intelligence and limitless curiosity,
combined with a sparkling personal warmth
and a love for his family, will continue
to inspire his children in all their endeavors.*

CONTENTS

PREFACE

While attending the University of Texas at Austin in the late 1980s, I made a pilgrimage to one of my favorite spots, the Alamo in San Antonio. I had grown up with books and films on the astonishing tale of "fighting against hopeless odds" and the "last stand" of heroic figures like William Travis, Jim Bowie, and Davy Crockett. During that visit, a surprisingly simple question came to me: "If everyone was killed inside the Alamo, how do we know what happened?" This question suggested that studying the events of the siege and fall of the Alamo would be highly interesting, and I decided to explore the local reference libraries and archives to find out the basis of our knowledge for what really occurred.

I had been vaguely aware that one woman, Susanna Dickinson (or Dickerson), was one source of the stories. But the narrations I had read were too detailed to have come from a single individual, especially a noncombatant. After some study, I discovered that a lot more is known about the circumstances of the siege and fall than might be expected. I also began to learn something not only of the participants, but of the researchers, recorders, and scholars as well. Additional surprises came along the way. My greatest astonishment, considering that the fall of the Alamo is one of the more dramatic events of American history, came with the realization that some key documents had never been published. A good many others had been reproduced only in very limited editions, which today are nearly as difficult to obtain as the originals. My research revealed abundant source material available only to those lucky few with access to a limited number of libraries and archives, located mostly in Austin.

Those sources that did survive are, in most cases, contradictory, fragmentary, or unclear. So how does one balance such information? This is, of course, no different from the problem any historian, journalist, juror, detective, or even mystery enthusiast faces. How do we know what we know? In the end, the answer must come from a combination of facts and judgment that brings together a sensible and consistent story. Comparing narrative accounts from writers and scholars with the original sources showed that these authors commonly used a cut-and-paste method, taking some specific details while ignoring others from the same source. If their source material is inconsistent, writers must selectively choose those pieces that fit together to make a reasonable, unified picture. In the case of the Alamo, the problem of the sources having mixed inconsistent and contradictory material with likely valid information is especially acute. As a consequence, the Alamo story, as it has been presented in print and in film, has numerous examples of unbalanced—and even biased—use of selected portions of available sources.

This book is as complete a compilation as possible of primary, secondary, and subsequent sources on the actual events of the siege and fall of the Alamo, giving the reader the opportunity to decide how risky to the integrity of the Alamo story such a process might have been. The book also contains a selection of sources for the more general context of Texas in the winter of 1835–36.

The source materials on the siege and fall of the Alamo, which took place from the afternoon of February 23 to the morning of March 6, 1836, are relatively limited. This allows them to be compiled within a single volume, thus facilitating the study of the subject and allowing the interested lay reader to become as fully knowledgeable as the expert.

The broader context in which these events took place can only be partially addressed here. I have included some documents or excerpts that I consider especially significant. For those interested in more background material, the references in the Bibliography will serve as an introduction to the vast amount of material available for more in-depth studies of the history of Texas and its revolution.

Several factors helped ease the compilation of these sources. For example, virtually all the manuscript sources are in Austin, and this proximity of the archives, as well as the enthusiastic assistance of the archivists (especially the Eugene C. Barker Texas History Center), made accessing the original material relatively easy for a historical research project. It was also good fortune that a high proportion of the manuscripts have fairly legible handwriting, not at all a given with manuscript material.

My prime motivation for compiling these documents into a single volume was to provide the reader with an opportunity to compare and assess the many sources as a complete body of work. Because of this prime motivation, my commentaries in this work are not intended to be thorough analyses. It is my hope that readers will take the opportunity to do their own evaluation. The Commentaries mostly give general observations on the various sources and their relationships with other materials in the collection. Further, they tend to concentrate on the rejection of "bad" details, usually meaning inconsistent ones rather than on the often harder task of affirming "good" ones. The "good" details, in the sense of being reasonably or likely true, often are not elaborated upon or even discussed. Several other authors have published good narrative accounts on the events of the Alamo and have already made such selections of "good" details. Many specific details appear in only one other source and thus cannot be cross-compared as a test of validity. It is the reader's call in such cases to accept or not accept them as "facts," based on the general believability and accuracy of the source. It is not the purpose of this book to make final judgments on the validity of most details, and in many cases I do not even comment on them. The main purpose of bringing these documents together is to provide readers with the means to make their own decisions.

While doing my research, I was surprised to realize how much valuable investigative work was left to be done. The studies of the Alamo are incomplete in both identification of source materials and careful analysis of key documents.

My commentaries note several cases where a letter or interview with a more obscure participant could be a significant addition to our understanding. Such documents might already be in an archive, perhaps even known but not widely disseminated. An important interview or letter may be discovered in the back pages of a nineteenth-century local newspaper or might be held in family or private possession. And there likely is significant material, in the form of journals or letters, in Mexico awaiting discovery or translation. Only a handful of the major and minor documents presented in this book have had a truly thorough analysis. More in-depth and careful studies of a number of these documents would be useful additions to the understanding of Alamo events.

As one reads the original documents, a number of additional questions are raised. Did Commander William Barrett Travis even want to be at the Alamo? How was the command shared between him and James Bowie worked out? Was Travis a grandstander who wanted to die in blaze of glory? Did he really draw the line in the dust? How did Davy Crockett die? Where were the rest of the Texans? What kind of military commander was President and Generalissimo Santa Anna? What did the Mexican Army think of the battle? What did the local Hispanic citizens, the Tejanos, think of it?

And to return to the seemingly simple question asked at the start: If everyone was killed inside Alamo, how do we know what happened? What we have for answers are here.

NOTES ON STRUCTURE AND STYLE

A wide range of documents are included in this compilation: transcripts of handwritten letters, diaries and journals, legal testimony, firsthand narratives by participants, secondhand interviews with considerable variability in editorial handling of the original interview, and careful and not-so-careful histories. Letters and other firsthand accounts are considered primary sources. Interviews and other documents where the original information is presented through a second party are considered secondary sources. Accounts written by historians are still another step removed, though the boundaries are blurred when a history is the only source of a particular piece of information or interview. Nearly all the histories included here reflect this ambiguity to some extent.

An identifying system for the nearly three hundred documents is necessary. The outline-based structure used to number these documents, per the List of Documents, gives an immediate sense of the relationship of each particular document to the rest of the collection.

Each document has a header that consists of two or three parts. The first part gives the document number, the original source, the type of source (such as a letter or interview), and the date of the original information. The second part is a formal bibliographic citation for the document quoted in this work. If the reference has the same date as the source and is located in an archive, this means the original or official contemporary copy (such as a letter by a government official) was successfully located. A citation for a newspaper, book, or other printed source implies that the original was not located and a copy—which may or may not be a careful reflection of the original—had to be used. Some other documents are transcripts of original or typed manuscripts, and these also are noted in the citations. The optional third part of the header gives additional facts of interest related to the document. Evaluation and analysis of the documents are reserved for the Commentaries that follow each section.

A number of rules were applied as consistently as possible when transcribing the documents. Secondary sources often have parenthetical or bracketed comments or additions by the original author or editor. Any additions or insertions I have made inside the quotations are italicized and in brackets; all other parenthetical or bracketed material was in the original source. Footnotes from the source for the material quoted here have sometimes been included. Extensive footnotes in secondary sources are sometimes renumbered to start with "1" for the excerpt given here, while isolated footnotes retain their original numbers.

Original spelling has been retained as much as possible; [*sic*] is used only in cases where a typographical error might be assumed. The old style script "fs" in early handwriting is changed to "ss," and this work does not note rubrics after signatures. Italicizing versus underlining tends to follow publishing rules (use of italics), except to retain the flavor of an original manuscript, as in some of Travis's letters. Punctuation tends to follow that of the original documents as closely as possible, but some corrections have occasionally been made in order to make the content clearer. Spaces have been added in a few documents where words were run together and some left-right positioning of text on certain lines have been modified for easier reading. Many original letters left a space between paragraphs and did not indent; these have been closed up and the paragraphs indented.

References in the Commentaries to documents in this collection are denoted by document number so that the reader can immediately refer to these if desired. External references are given by the author, date, and sometimes page numbers in an endnote to that Commentary. These sources may be found in the Bibliography.

Abbreviations that appear frequently are TSLA for Texas State Library, Archives Division (Austin); CAH for the Center for American History (at the University of Texas at Austin); DRT for Daughters of the Republic of Texas Library at the Alamo; and *SWHQ* for the *Southwestern Historical Quarterly*.

LIST OF DOCUMENTS

Introduction: Context of the Texas Revolution
  1.0. Williams, Amelia, 1931, Ph.D. diss, Introduction

1. Sources inside the Alamo
  1.1. William Barret Travis and James Bowie (Travis unless otherwise noted)
    1.1.1. Pre-siege letters
      1.1.1.1. December 17, 1835, to James W. Robinson
      1.1.1.2. "January 17," 1836, to Samuel Houston
      1.1.1.3. January 21, 1836, to William G. Hill
      1.1.1.4. January 28, 1836, to Henry Smith
      1.1.1.5. January 29, 1836, to Henry Smith
      1.1.1.6. February 2, 1836, James Bowie to Henry Smith
      1.1.1.7. February 12, 1836, to Henry Smith (first from Béxar)
      1.1.1.8. February 13, 1836, to Henry Smith
      1.1.1.9. February 13, 1836, to Henry Smith
      1.1.1.10. February 14, 1836, with James Bowie to Henry Smith
      1.1.1.11. February 15, 1836, to Henry Smith
      1.1.1.12. February 16, 1836, to Henry Smith
      1.1.1.13. February 19, 1836, to J. L. Vaughn
      1.1.1.14. February 19, 1836, testimonial for Felipe Xaimes
      1.1.1.15. February 22, 1836, testimonial for Antonio Cruz
      1.1.1.16. February 23, 1836, to Andrew Ponton
    1.1.2. February 23, 1836, James Bowie to commander of the Army of Texas
    1.1.3. February 23, 1836, with James Bowie to James Fannin
    1.1.4. February 24, 1836, to the People of Texas
    1.1.5. February 25, 1836, to Samuel Houston
    1.1.6. March 3, 1836, to President of the Convention
    1.1.7. March 3, 1836, to Jesse Grimes (?)
    1.1.8. March 3 (?), 1836, to David Ayers (?)
  1.2. Susanna Dickinson (or Dickerson) (Belles, Hannig)
    1.2.1. March 24, 1837, deposition for audited claim of Joshua G. Smith
    1.2.2. Stiff, Edward, 1840, *The Texan Emigrant*
    1.2.3. December 9, 1850, deposition for heirs of David P. Cummings
    1.2.4. November 21, 1853, deposition for the heirs of James M. Rose
    1.2.5. June 30/July 16, 1857, deposition for the heirs of James M. Rose
    1.2.6. March 8, 1860, deposition for the heirs of Henry Warnell
    1.2.7. Morphis, James M., 1874, *History of Texas from Its Discovery and Settlement . . . ,* 174–77
    1.2.8. September 23, 1876, interview for Adjutant General
    1.2.9. N.d. (September 16–30, 1877), interview of Hannig, note on "Ross"
    1.2.10. March 14, 1878, interview in *San Antonio Express*, February 24, 1929
    1.2.11. *Daily Express*, April 28, 1881
    1.2.12. c. 1883 interview in Green, Rena Maverick, ed., 1921, *Memoirs of Mary A. Maverick, Arranged by Mary A. Maverick and Her Son Geo. Madison Maverick*

John Sutherland's account
- Document 1.7.1.2. Sutherland Journal map, n.d., John S. Ford Papers, CN#11506, CAH.
- Document 1.7.1.3. Sutherland rough map, n.d., from Annie Sutherland, ed., 1936, *The Fall of the Alamo*, CN#11507, CAH.

Sánchez plan
- Document 2.7.1. Sánchez-Navarro y Estrada, Capt. José Juan (1836), "Ayudentía de Inspección de Nuevo León y Tamaulipas," vol. 2, CN#01579a, b, CAH.

Labastida plat
- Document 2.8.1. Labastida plat, n.d. (1836), CN#01625, a, b, CAH.

Jameson plat
- Documents 4.2.1.4. De Zavala, Adina, 1917, *History and Legends of the Alamo and Other Missions in and around San Antonio*, 26–30, San Antonio: Published by Adina De Zavala, CN#11508, CAH.

Giraud map
- Document 4.2.2.1. Giraud, François P., 1849, "Book 1, Survey of the City of San Antonio, Texas, Starts Dec. 7, 1847, Francis Giraud, Surveyor, Book 1 of 2," 114–15 from the Office of the County Clerk, Bexar County.
- Document 4.2.2.2. Texas Title Company, n.d. (before 1913?), "5053 LDF" in Historic Sites/Alamo/Maps, Abstract of Title Collection, NCB115 Texas Title Co., 1905 Jan. 17, #5053, CN02.015, DRT.
- Document 4.2.2.3. *San Antonio Light*. February 12, 1912, p. 2, copy of map in Historic Sites/Alamo/Maps, CN00.014, DRT.

Williams plats
- Document 4.2.3.2. Yoakum, Henderson, 1855, *History of Texas from Its First Settlement in 1685 to Its Annexation to the United States in 1846*, vol. 2, between 76 and 77, New York: Redfield, CN#11509, CAH.
- Document 4.2.3.3. McArdle, H. A., n.d., "McArdle's sketch Based on Potter's Description of Alamo," Colquitt (Oscar Branch) Papers, Oversize Box, CN#11152, CAH.
- Document 4.2.3.4. Williams, Amelia, 1931. A critical study of the siege of the Alamo and of the personnel of its defenders, plat C, Appendix II, Ph.D. dissertation, University of Texas, Austin, CN#09226, CAH.

Potter map
- Document 5.1.7. Potter, Reuben M., January 1878. The fall of the Alamo, *Magazine of American History* 2:1, CN#09185, CAH.

CAST OF CENTRAL PLAYERS

Allen, John L. Apparently the last courier from the Alamo.

Almonte, Juan Nepomuceno. Colonel and personal aide to Santa Anna.

Alsbury, Juana. Resident of San Antonio and survivor of the siege and fall of the Alamo.

Barsena, Andrés (also spelled as Andrew Barcena). Resident of San Antonio, with Bergara the first to reach Gonzales with news of the fall of the Alamo.

Becerra, Francisco. Sergeant in the Mexican Army.

Ben. Servant to Santa Anna in San Antonio, then escorted Susanna Dickinson to Gonzales after the fall of the Alamo.

Bergara, Anselmo (or Borgara). Resident of San Antonio, with Barsena the first to reach Gonzales with news of the fall of the Alamo.

Bonham, James. Texas officer and last known defender to enter the Alamo; rode in on March 2 or 3 and died with the rest of the defenders three days later.

Bowie, James. Colonel in the Texas Army and commander of the volunteers in San Antonio. Co-commander with Travis in the Alamo until he became incapacitated by illness about the second day of the siege.

Candelaria, Madame. Claimed late in life to have been in the Alamo during the fall.

Caro, Ramón Martínez. Secretary to Santa Anna during the Texas campaign and a strong critic afterward.

Convention. A meeting held at the beginning of March 1836 to consider independence for Texas. A Declaration of Independence was adopted and a new government was established prior to disbanding because of the rapid advance of Santa Anna's forces after the fall of the Alamo.

Cós, Gen. Martín Perfecto de. Brother-in-law of Santa Anna and in command of government forces in San Antonio in late 1835. Forced to surrender to rebel forces in December 1835 and paroled back to Mexico, returned to San Antonio with reinforcements, and participated in the final attack on the Alamo.

Council. A ruling body of the provisional government of Texas in late 1835 and early 1836 prior to the Texan Declaration of Independence in early March 1836.

Crockett, David. Former Tennessee congressman as well as a famous public figure in the United States. After defeat for reelection, went to Texas, where he became informally one of the leaders of the Alamo defenders.

Dickinson (Dickerson), Almeron. Alamo defender and a captain of artillery; husband of Susanna Dickinson.

Dickinson (Dickerson), Susanna. Wife of Almeron Dickinson and survivor of the siege and fall of the Alamo. With Joe, brought the first confirmation of the fall to Gonzales. Later Mrs. Joseph Hannig.

Esparza, Enrique. Son of an Alamo defender and, as a young boy, survivor of the fall.

Fannin, James W. Colonel in the Texas Army and commander of about four hundred men at La Bahia, Goliad. This was the largest force on the Texas side at the start of the siege, and Travis's primary hope for reinforcements.

Filisola, Vicente. General and second in command to Santa Anna during the Texas campaign. After Santa Anna's capture at San Jacinto, obeyed his commander's orders for the withdrawal of the Mexican forces from Texas

Hannig, Mrs. Joseph. See Susanna Dickinson.

Highsmith, Benjamin. A courier from the Alamo. Gave depositions in the 1890s.

Houston, Samuel. General and commander-in-chief of the Texas Army, later the first president of the Republic of Texas.

Jameson, Green B. Alamo defender and engineer; source of the last maps of the Alamo prior to the siege.

Joe. Slave of William Travis and survivor of the final attack. Accompanied Susanna Dickinson to Gonzales with the first report on the fall of the Alamo.

Johnson, Francis W. Colonel in the Texas Army and commander at the surrender of General Cós at San Antonio in December 1835. The following month with Colonel Grant led a Texas force in a disastrous attack on the Mexican forces at Matamoros.

Labastida, Ygnacio de. Chief engineer of the Mexican Army.

Loranca, Manuel. Sergeant in the Mexican Army.

Menchaca, Antonio. Resident of San Antonio.

Neill, James. Colonel in the Texas Army and commander of the Alamo until replaced by Travis in early February 1836.

Nuñez, Félix. Sergeant in the Mexican Army.

Oury, William. Courier from the Alamo. Later, one of the first settlers in Tucson, Arizona.

Peña, José Enrique de la. Colonel in the Mexican Army.

Pollard, Amos. Alamo defender and surgeon for the fort.

Potter, Reuben M. Published the first systematically studied history of the siege and fall of the Alamo, probably the best done in the nineteenth century.

Robinson, James W. Replacement governor of the provisional government of Texas when Henry Smith was deposed in late January 1836.

Rodríguez, J. M. Resident of San Antonio.

Rose, Louis (also Lewis or Moses). Claimed by William Zuber to have been in the Alamo until shortly before its fall; source of Travis's alleged last speech and drawing of the line in the dust.

Ruiz, Francisco Antonio. Alcalde, or mayor, of San Antonio during the siege; ordered by Santa Anna to dispose of the defenders' bodies after the fall.

Sánchez Navarro, José Juan. Captain and an inspector general in the Mexican Army; was in the battle of Béxar with General Cos in December 1835, as well as the siege and fall of the Alamo.

Santa Anna, Antonio López de. President of Mexico and general in command of the Texas campaign. Commanded the Mexican forces at the Alamo and was captured by the Texans at the battle of San Jacinto on April 21.

Seguín, Juan N. Colonel and perhaps the most important Tejano leader in the Texas Revolution. In the 1840s, went over to the Mexican side, perhaps due to false accusations.

Sesma, Joaquín Ramírez y. General and commander of the Mexican cavalry.

Smith, Henry. Governor of the provisional government of Texas in early 1836 until deposed by the Council in late January.

Smith, John W. ("Red"). Twice a courier from the Alamo, and led the reinforcements from Gonzales in the fort on March 1. Later mayor of San Antonio.

Soldana, Rafael. Captain in the Mexican Army.

Sutherland, John. Courier from Alamo on first day of siege.

Tornel y Mendívil, José María. Mexican secretary of war during the Texas campaign and a strong supporter of Santa Anna.

Travis, William Barrett. Colonel in the Texas Army and commander of the Alamo throughout the siege.

Urissa. Colonel in the Mexican Army.

Urrea, José. General in the Mexican Army and in command of the forces east of San Antonio that captured Goliad and later executed Fannin and his men.

Yoakum, Henderson. Historian and personal friend of Sam Houston. His history of Texas was published in the 1850s, the most important up to that time.

Zuber, William. First reported on the story of Louis (Moses) Rose in the 1870s, and later a major contributor to stories on Texas history.

Context of the Texas Revolution

The scope of this book covers the events of the siege and fall of the Alamo, which occurred from the afternoon of February 23 to the morning of March 6, 1836, in San Antonio de Béxar (or Béjar), Texas. But these events standing in isolation would be somewhat sterile, and some understanding of the larger context of the Texas Revolution is desirable to enrich one's appreciation for the material and the story. Having a summary of the broader context is also useful where the events are referred to in the transcribed documents that follow.

For an overview of events leading to the Texas Revolution, I turn to the foremost scholar on the Alamo. In 1931, Amelia Williams completed her Ph.D. dissertation, entitled "A Critical Study of the Siege of the Alamo and of the Personnel of Its Defenders." This is a fundamental work upon which all subsequent scholarship and popular accounts are heavily dependent, either directly or indirectly, and it will be used a number of times throughout this book. This dissertation is so important because Williams culled the vast amount of original source material—including tens of thousands of Texas General Land Office documents—to locate those relevant to the Alamo studies. The task of all later writers, therefore, has been significantly easier by comparison, since they could start with the documents she had located or identified. Though there have since been important discoveries of source materials, it is still true that a large proportion of all relevant material was identified by her. Furthermore, Williams's analyses of the sources are as thoughtful as any done and so can still give insight for evaluation of the original references. It is a natural starting point to use her (unpublished) introductory chapter to give the background context of the Texas Revolution.

1

Document 1.0. Amelia Williams, dissertation, 1931.

Williams, Amelia. 1931. A critical study of the siege of the Alamo and of the personnel of its defenders. 1–36. Ph.D. diss., University of Texas at Austin.

The heart of this dissertation was published in four parts in the *Southwestern Historical Quarterly*. Not previously published, to the best of my knowledge, are the "Introductory Background" section and two of the five Appendixes (see 5.2.1), so they are reproduced in large part at the appropriate places in this book. This introduction was extensively footnoted, but unlike most other documents in this book, the footnotes are not included with this transcription due to length. While Williams raises deep, fundamental issues, such as racism, slavery, and the history of the Mexican government, including the role of the general and president Santa Anna, these subjects are too broad and cannot be tackled on any significant scale in this work; therefore, this summary will have to serve as only an introduction.

INTRODUCTORY BACKGROUND

The siege and fall of the Alamo is the most dramatic and the most generally known of any single event in Texas history. The very completeness of the Mexican victory, the stubborn defense of the fort by the gallant Travis and his brave men, are deeds that have so stirred human imagination and sympathy that practically all the world has heard the story of this heroic feat in the cause of Texas liberty. And today whenever the name *Texas* is called, it is likely to bring back to memory a Texas orator's brief but graphic account of this heroic tragedy: "Thermopylae had her messenger of defeat, but the Alamo had none." To defend a post till the last drop of life's blood is spent, has, for ages, been a figure of speech to express extreme resoluteness. The Texans did the thing itself at the Alamo, and a cause for which nearly two-hundred men literally fought till they died, is one to stimulate the imagination and to enlist the sympathetic admiration of mankind. It is not, however, the purpose of this study to stress the dramatic element of the subject, nor to paint a word picture of that brief but awful carnage of March 6, 1836. That service has already been rendered and with great skill. Rather, the purpose of this study is to construct from all sources, now available, a clear, unimpassioned account of that event, and to compile as complete and correct a list as possible of the names of the men who fell with Travis. In order that the significance of the fall of the Alamo may be clearly and fully appreciated, it seems fitting and necessary to give a brief review of conditions that antedated and led up to the Texas Revolution of 1835–1836, of which movement the siege and fall of the Alamo was but one episode.

In 1800, Napoleon Bonaparte regained Louisiana from Spain and reunited it to France under the pledge that it should never again be alienated; but in 1803, it was sold to the United States "with the extent it had in the hands of Spain, and that it had when France possessed it," a provision that left the problem of actual delimitation to later negotiations. Thus the question of boundary soon came into prominence and continued to be a matter of dispute until 1819, when the United States, in negotiations which resulted in the purchase of Florida, gave up all claim to Texas lying west of the Sabine river. But long prior to this event, the population of the United States had been moving westward, and after the American Revolution, this advance had gone on with ever increasing momentum. As early as 1785, we find the cross-boundary horse-trader, Philip Nolan, in Texas, where he was killed in 1801. He was followed by a group of adventurers whom Spain was ever on the alert to circumvent, but who, after all, were men of no great political importance, like Sibley, Banks, and Davenport. Then came the more dangerous lot, whose projects, although they did have political significance, were abortive; these were men such as Aaron Burr, Magee, and Long. In the face of this westward movement on the part of the Americans, the Spaniards in Mexico became troubled. They feared American aggression into their rich mining districts, and as early as 1806, the relations between the United States and Spain were at the breaking point over the boundary between Louisiana and Mexico. For a time war seemed inevitable, for Spain stubbornly claimed that her territory extended to the Arroyo Hondo, a creek seven miles east of the Sabine river, while the United States contended that its boundary reached the Sabine if not the Rio Bravo. War was averted by a personal agreement between General Wilkinson, the American official in command of the Mississippi valley, and the Spanish officials in Mexico. By this arrangement the Neutral Ground, a sort of no man's land, was created between the Arroyo Hondo and the Sabine river. It was agreed that in this strip of territory neither country should exercise authority, consequently it was devoid of law and government and it became the refuge of desperadoes and criminals of every type. This condition of affairs held for fifteen years, that is, until Spain and the United States ended it by the negotiations of 1819. During this time many of the men from the Neutral Ground drifted into east Texas and made illegal settlements. Thus it was that conditions engendered in this lawless land, were partly responsible for the Fredondian Rebellion, the catastrophe that first aroused the suspicions of Mexico against her Anglo-Saxon settlers.

From 1808 to 1821, Mexico was fighting her war for independence from Spain. During this struggle the United States sympathized with Mexico and helped her in an indirect way, for while American pirates under the leadership of Jean Lafitte harried all commerce on the Gulf, they practically destroyed that of Spain. Upon gaining her independence in 1821, Mexico set up an empire with Iturbide on the throne. This new emperor's career was short and stormy, and by 1823 another revolution had upset his throne and had driven him from the country. But before that fleeting empire's laws were entirely suspended, a colonization grant had been made to the Austins to settle families from Louisiana in Texas under the empresario system. The Mexicans now declared for a republic. But what kind of a republic? Should it be federal, or centralized? Over this fundamental point of difference, two bitterly opposed political parties developed, the Federalists and the Centralists. These two parties were destined to keep Mexico in the throes of revolution, and her government in chaos for

more than half a century, but in 1824, the Federalists won the argument temporarily and adopted a federal constitution, closely patterned after that of the
United States. In order to establish this constitution, however, an almost exactly
opposite process from that developed by the United States in the adoption of its
government was used. In Mexico the highly centralized nation had to disinte-
grate itself so that states could be created. The states, thus created, then feder-
ated into a union. The public lands, the possession of the central government,
were distributed among the various states for administrative control. Then,
from 1824 to 1825, colonization laws—both state and federal—were enacted
which opened up the unsettled lands of Mexico to foreign colonization on very
liberal terms. Both the nation and the states cordially invited settlers to come;
land was granted almost free for the taking, the governments pledging to the
settlers a guarantee of safety and security of person and of property. Moreover,
the newness of the land and the lack of developed resources made it seem reasonable, also, that these newcomers should be free for a period from taxation
and tariff duties. Accordingly, they were granted immunity from these contributions for a period of seven years. Indeed, the only requirements demanded
were: (1) that the immigrants be Catholics, or willing to become such; (2) that
they show certificates of good character and habit; (3) and that they take the
oath of allegiance to the newly established republic. The avowed object of the
government in making these laws was "to control the savage Indian and to
build up a strong, productive frontier that would serve as a sort of buffer territory between Mexico and the United States, to ward off the cupidity of the latter." To these ideas was joined the notion that the plains of Texas were barren of
real value, and that the gain that Mexico would derive from settling them with
Americans and other foreigners would be a return of protection for nothing
invested. Whatever of self-deception, or of true policy there may have been concerning the matter, these laws were the letting down of barriers that permitted a
perfect flood of immigration that had dammed itself against the eastern border,
to overflow into Texas. Sooner or later these hardy, adventurous frontiersmen,
under some pretense, legalized or otherwise, would have possessed themselves
of these coveted lands anyway, but the Mexican colonization laws of 1823–1825
certainly hastened the process of the taking. By 1834, flourishing settlements
had been planted from the Sabine to the Colorado, and in this year, Colonel
Juan Almonte, whom the federal government had sent to inspect these colonies,
reported a population of 36,300, of whom 21,000 were civilized and 15,300 were
Indians—10,800 savage and 4,500 friendly. Kennedy and Yoakum both think
that Almonte's estimate of the colonial population is too low, and they declare
that at this time the Anglo-American population in Texas aggregated 30,000,
exclusive of more than 2,000 negroes. Dr. Barker practically agrees with this
estimate, for in speaking of the number of colonists he says: "My impression,
derived from a somewhat minute acquaintance with the field, is that the total
population in 1835, when the Texas revolution began, was around 30,000—men,
women, and children." Although a few of these immigrants had come from

Europe, the majority were from the United States, and no doubt a considerable number had arrived after Almonte's report was made.

They settled under two systems: (1) the independent colonist, by which system each settler got his grant of land directly from the government and had all transactions concerning it with the government; (2) the empresario system by which empresarios or land agents, got from the government permission to settle, at their own expense, a given number of families on unoccupied lands. For each hundred families settled, the empresario was given for his own use five square leagues of land (22,142 acres) of grazing quality, and five labors (885 acres) of arable land. During the colonial period, twenty-six empresarios took out grants. By far the most conspicuous of these men was Stephen F. Austin, whose first grant—as has been stated above—was made by the Spanish government in 1821, ratified by the empire under Iturbide, and reaffirmed by the republic. Under the colonization laws of the republic he took out several other grants, and in all brought in more than fifteen hundred families. Austin was the leading figure of the whole colonization period, and by his wonderful sagacity, his diplomatic genius, and his long and patient service, he well deserves the title "Father of Texas."

For the most part, the early Texans were typical American frontiersmen, hardy, bold, aggressive, self-reliant men, engaged chiefly in farming and cattle raising. There were to be found, however, in every settlement, a few professional men—especially doctors and lawyers—as well as shop-keepers, tavern-keepers, horse-traders, and others who could live by supplying the needs of a simple agricultural community. The opinion, commonly held in the United States and in Europe, that the Texans were all criminals and fugitives from justice, was erroneous. These men were industrious, and on the whole, their morality ranked high. They were not very religious, however, according to the ordinary interpretation of the word. To enter the country required a certificate of Catholic faith, but there were few true Catholics among them. They as well as their leader, Austin, interpreted this governmental requirement liberally. In a manifesto issued to his colonists Austin said: "I wish the settlers to remember that the Roman Catholic is the religion of this nation. We must respect the Catholic religion." So after having furnished a certificate of Catholic faith, the colonists were very apt to practice none. They had taken the oath of allegiance to the Mexican government, and the majority of them honestly meant to be loyal to their adopted country. They appreciated their beautiful and rich lands, given to them on such liberal terms; at the same time they fully realized that only by their own trials, privations and hard work had they built their homes and changed wastes, valueless before their coming, into prosperous farms and ranches. They attended to their own business and did not participate in the muddle of Mexican politics, since the seat of their state government was far removed at Saltillo, and local government was slow in being organized, and was poorly established. The central government was in constant turmoil, being now under the control of the Federalists, and next year, or, perhaps, next month, under that of the Centralists.

The Mexicans were not prepared for the complexities of federal government. For more than three centuries their political training had been under the highly centralized system of one of the most absolute monarchies of Europe, and so they should not be too severely blamed because they did not immediately learn the meaning of democracy, for even to their educated men—men who professed republican principles, and who were leaders of the Republican party—"self government, freedom of speech, of the press, and of conscience," were but sweet-sounding phrases of whose practical application they knew next to nothing. But, although the Texans took little part in Mexican politics, they had not left behind them their democratic principles and ideals. To them self-government, liberty, freedom of conscience and of speech were as necessary as the air they breathed; moreover, the conditions of their life forced them to be self reliant. They were ready to conform to laws in the making of which they had had a voice, or in which they saw justice and equity. They had come to Texas confidently expecting that a republic which modeled its constitution on that of the United States, would practice the free institutions which it proclaimed, and so they stubbornly refused to accept the principles of centralism that were set up in the face of the constitution of 1824. Furthermore, these colonists were of Anglo-Saxon descent, and [*the attitude of some was that*] it is the nature of the Anglo-Saxon man to refuse to be dominated by an inferior race. Long before 1836 the[*se*] settlers had come to consider the Mexicans an inferior race, to despise them as they did Indians and negroes, and to ignore Mexican law.

This difference of race, of language, of ideals, of laws, this general lack of understanding between the two peoples, developed conditions bound to produce conflict—and it started early. As early as 1827 or 1828 the Mexicans were already suspicious and jealous of the rapid increases and prosperity of the American settlers. Trouble had arisen over land grants. Notorious for this trouble were the grants made to Edwards in 1825. Before the year had passed, this empresario quarreled with many early settlers already living on his lands before he took out the grant, but who had not made the proper arrangements with the government to secure title to their holdings. Edwards refused to recognize the titles of these colonists. This squabble over land titles was followed by disputes over supposed usurpations of the powers of the state by this empresario. The result of the matter was that Victor Blanco, the vice-governor—then acting as governor—banished Edwards from Texas in 1826. This disturbance brought on the ill-fated Fredonian rebellion, led by Edwards who drew some of the Cherokee Indians into his scheme by a proposal to divide Texas between the new state (Fredonian Republic) and the red men. Edwards had taken it for granted that the other colonists would support him. Instead, the Austin settlers joined the government forces to quell the insurrection; the Indians were separated from the project and the leaders were forced to flee. Austin then secured amnesty for those who would surrender. Nothing had been gained. It is true that the bulk of the American colonists had proved their loyalty to the adopted country, but the thing looked bad. The Mexicans had a just cause for suspicion and mistrust. Thoroughly frightened by the Fredonian Rebellion, because it showed to what lengths many of the American settlers outside Austin's colony would go to effect their ends, the Mexican authorities decided that they would have to adopt a policy of repression if Mexico were to remain dominant in Texas. Accordingly two acts, hateful to the colonists, were passed in order to check, or to stop immigration from the United States. The first was the Emancipation Act of 1829, urged by Tornel, and the other was the decree of April 6, 1830, proposed by Alaman. After the senate had refused to pass an emancipation bill, Tornel persuaded President Guerrero to issue this emancipation decree of 1829. It aimed to limit the growth of farming immigration by forbidding the settlers to possess slaves. But owing to the firm and friendly co-operation of the local Mexican officials at San Antonio with Austin, this decree was soon set aside, so far as it concerned Texas. It seems that the Mexicans were not so averse to the condition as to the word *slavery,* so when the slavery question again became the target for Mexican opposition, the Texans continued to import Negroes but called them "indentured servant." Thus while the development of the slavery system in Texas was checked, it was never absolutely abolished at the hands of the Mexican owners of Texas. Neither was the settlement of Texas a preorganized plot of the "slavocracy," as several American writers have claimed. The slave question at this time was merely an economic incident in the internal history of Texas.

Another thing that kept the Mexicans suspicious of the loyalty of the colonists—and they cannot be blamed for this—was the repeated proposals of the United States to buy Texas. To Mexican statesmen it seemed a grave error and a real danger to continue to permit the influx of great numbers of Americans into a territory so eagerly desired by their mother country; hence this decree of April 6, 1830, proposed by Lucas Alaman. This law, in general terms: (1) encouraged colonization of Mexicans in Texas; (2) forbade the importation of slaves; (3) ordered independent settlers, not on regular grants, to be ejected; (4) required passports for entrance from the northern frontiers; (5) prohibited emigrants from settling in Mexican territory contiguous to the nation from which they had come, and moreover, all contracts not already completed and not in harmony with the law should be suspended. Although it was never efficiently enforced, it did materially check immigration, and it aroused a tremendous amount of ill feeling. General Terán himself was sent to enforce it. His plan was to establish a number of military posts within supporting distance of each other, and to introduce large numbers of Mexican colonists. These colonists were absolute failures, and concerning the soldiery in the new garrisons, Bancroft says, "they were for the most part convicts and the worst class of men in Mexico." Yet such soldiers were designed to enforce the unpopular decree by keeping out all illegal immigration. But the Mexican government finally realized that the law was an impossible measure, and it was rescinded in 1834. It had served little purpose except to arouse the indignation of the American settlers against the Mexican Government, and to cause them to manifest a resentment that bordered on rebellion.

It will be remembered that an Act of September, 1823, had exempted the settlers from duty on certain necessary articles for a period of seven years. This exemption had led to much abuse. Smuggling was popular and wholesale, so when in 1831, the term of the exemption expired, there was wide-spread dissat-isfaction at the enforcement of the payment of duties. The Kentucky adventurer, Bradburn, sent by the Mexican government to Anahuac, was particularly obnoxious to the Texans, because of his arbitrary methods of assisting George Fisher, the collector of customs, at that port. The outrages of Bradburn and of his soldiers were many: (1) He pressed supplies for his garrison, and used slave labor in the erection of military buildings without compensating the owners of the slaves; (2) he encouraged a spirit of revolt among the slaves by telling them that it was the intent of the law to make them free; (3) he harbored two run-away slaves from Louisiana, enlisted them in his detachment, and refused to surrender them to the owner, who demanded them; (4) he arrested several of the colonists on various pretexts and held them in the guard house for military trial. The trouble culminated in an uprising of the colonists under the leader-ship of John Austin; and this disturbance finally resulted in Bradburn's being removed from his command, in the prisoners being released to the civil authori-ties for trial, and in the payment for private property that had been appropri-ated [*i.e., slaves?*]. The garrison declared for Santa Anna and left to join the Liberal Army. Colonel Mexia was sent from Mexico to investigate the affair; but Stephen F. Austin who was returning from Mexico, came on the same ship with Mexia, and succeeded in convincing him that the Texans were not to blame. The colonists, in the meantime fearing the consequences of their actions, had held a meeting and had declared for Santa Anna—at this time the leader of the Mexi-can Republicans—and for the constitution of 1824. So, Mexia finding the Texans pacified, loyal and properly enthusiastic for his chief, induced most of the sol-diers in the Texas garrisons to adopt the cause of Santa Anna, now leading a revolution against the president, Bustamante, and carried them off, leaving Colonel Piedras, at Nacogdoches, as the only adherent to the Centralist admin-istration in Texas. Piedras, also, soon surrendered to the new movement. Thus in 1832, all Mexican troops were taken from Texas, except a few soldiers, left at Bexar and Goliad to protect these places against Indians. The collectors of cus-toms also withdrew, unable, so Filisola states, "to endure the untamable spirits of the inhabitants."

There was yet another cause for conflict between Mexico and her American colonists. In 1824, Texas had been joined to Coahuila, and this union had contin-ued to be a source of growing aggravation to the Texans. In the first place this dual state was administered by a large Mexican majority, since of the twelve members of the single house of the state legislature nine were allotted to Coahuila and only two to Texas. Then, too, the capital, Saltillo, was so far removed that the Texans experienced great inconvenience in transacting the legal business necessary for their welfare. This condition of things kept ever prominent the question: "What is to be the future of Texas? Shall it remain a province of Mexico, subject to the hazards of an ill-defined, arbitrary jurisdiction by military officers? Shall it seek to become an independent nation? Or shall it ask for annexation to the United States? Piedras, Bradburn, Teran, Filisola and other intelligent Mexican officials in Texas, honestly believed that there was a strong sentiment throughout the American settlements for separation from Mexico. The colonists, no doubt, did discuss this question among themselves. There was a good deal of loose talk on the part of hot-headed persons on both sides of the American boundary line that did much to stir up the desire for independence, and many were in favor of breaking away, but the great majority of Texans were loyal and sincerely desired to remain a part of Mexico, and in 1832, there is good evidence of a strong sentiment against independence.

But the Texans did want separation from Coahuila, and they meant to have it, for they believed that as a separate state they could set up a local government that would give them the political freedom for which they were trained and for which they longed. Accordingly, a call was made for a convention to meet at San Felipe, October 1, 1832. The reasons for the meeting as stated in the call were: (1) to check current misrepresentations concerning the desire of the Texans for independence; and (2) to devise means for quelling the frequent Indian raids. Fifty-six delegates, representatives of all the district except Goliad, assembled. In the course of a six days' session it adopted resolutions: (1) to provide for the collection of customs until the government could send out new collectors; (2) to ask for a grant of land for schools; (3) to ask for a reform of the tariff; (4) to pray for the repeal of the law of April 6, 1830; (5) and to petition for separate statehood. It also appointed a central committee to correspond with local committees and to keep them informed concerning questions of general interest, and to call, if need be, another meeting.

Conditions did not improve and another convention was called to meet April 1, 1833. The delegates were elected in March and the convention duly assembled on the day appointed. The petitions to the central government were about the same as those adopted by the Convention of 1832, but this body, in addition, drew up and adopted a tentative constitution for the proposed new state, as well as an address to the Mexican Congress praying for its approval.

Austin and two others were appointed to carry these resolutions to Mexico. Only Austin went. He arrived on July 18, 1833, to find that Santa Anna, the President, had retired to his country home, leaving the government in the hands of the Vice-president, Gómez Farías. Although a strong federal-republican by profession, Farías opposed separate statehood for Texas. After waiting long for a hearing, Austin wrote a letter, October 2, 1833, to be circulated among all the ayuntamientos, in which he advised the settlers to proceed with the formation of a state under the law of May 7, 1824, even though Mexico should refuse assent. The ayuntamiento of Bexar, to whom the letter was addressed, seeing in it intemperance if not treason, and fearing to involve themselves in trouble, sent this letter to the authorities of the national government. By that time Austin had finally effected the abrogation of the hated eleventh article of the Law of April 6, 1830, and feeling that was all he would be able to accomplish, was returning home when he was arrested and carried back to Mexico City. By the thirteenth of February, 1834, he was incarcerated in a dungeon of the old inquisition building, where he was kept in close confinement for three months. He was never given a trial but was held a prisoner, part of the time under bail, till July 1835.

The state government was in a chaotic condition due to a squabble between the cities of Saltillo and Monclova over the capital, but, during 1833–1834, the legislature passed a number of state laws beneficial to Texas, so the tension in that quarter was somewhat relieved. Among these new laws were measures creating several new municipalities, thus making the local condition somewhat better. Texas was divided into three executive departments, each under a *jefe politico* who was to act as the direct representative of the government within the department. Two of these new departments were American in population and in them the English language was made co-ordinate with the Spanish for legal usage. A new judicial system was also adopted, which gave the Texans the right of trial by jury. That this system was never set up was due largely to subsequent events.

In May, 1834, Santa Anna succeeded in dissolving the National Congress and many of the state legislatures; he then made himself dictator through the work of a council, subservient to his bidding. When Austin was given a hearing in November of 1833, he had plead eloquently the cause of Texas, urging the repeal of the Act of April 6, 1830 and for separation from Coahuila. As has been stated, the council had consented to abrogate the law of April 6, 1830, provided no good reasons could be found for continuing it. The dictator and council now, in 1834, definitely decreed that this law should be repealed, but that Texas could not have separate statehood; furthermore, Santa Anna decided to send 4,000 soldiers to San Antonio "to protect the coast and frontier." This decision caused grave apprehension in Texas; and by the time that Austin was released in July, 1835, he had become thoroughly convinced of the futility of hoping for stable conditions in Texas under the operation of the existing Mexican government.

Austin arrived in Texas in September, 1835, to find a revolution brewing. There had been a good deal of local squabbling during his absence. Two strong parties had developed among the Texans since 1832. One, the peace party was composed of the conservatives. These were the calm-minded men who believed with Austin in "ironing out" their differences and in conciliating the Mexican officials, thereby remaining loyal to their adopted country; the other, the war party, composed of the Hotspurs of the colonies, wanted to fight for what they regarded as their rights. The peace party was undoubtedly in the saddle during the middle and latter part of the summer of 1835. Nevertheless there was need for concerted action, and so a number of local meetings were held in order to discuss the situation. The most noteworthy of these meetings was the one at Columbia where it was decided to make a call for a general *consultation* to meet at Washington [*on the Brazos, eastern Texas*], October 15. When Austin arrive in the colonies, a dinner was given in his honor at Brazoria. The truth is the Texans were somewhat doubtful of his approval of their doings, and they were eager to know his attitude toward the condition of affairs. They greatly rejoiced that he favored the calling of the General Consultation, and on September 12, a Committee of Vigilance and Safety was organized at San Felipe with him as a member. From this time till the revolution was well advanced he was at the head of affairs. His motto seems to have been, "Texas first—under Mexico if possible—but always Texas."

At this point it is well to remember that when Santa Anna became dictator and dissolved Congress, Texas and Zacatecas were the only states to protest and to resolve to make a stand for a republic under the constitution of 1824. Both these states again sent up protests when the law of March 31, 1835, regulating the militia was enacted. Zacatecas flatly refused to obey; whereupon Santa Anna marched some three or four thousand troops against that state, and on May 10, in a bloody battle, followed by a brutal butchery, Zacatecas was utterly crushed. Now, General Cos with an army fresh from victory, was on his way to force the Texans to obey the laws which they had been either evading or disregarding. The Texans were now facing a question that had to have a speedy and a determined answer. Should they, too, submit to the tyranny of Centralism? Should they yield to the will of the Dictator; give up their arms and suffer their country to be garrisoned with strong military posts? Should they weakly consent to live under the rule and sway of the military? They must do this or they must prepare for war, and prepare without delay, for the enemy was advancing upon them. In the face of such an alternative war was inevitable.

The first clash came over a cannon at Gonzales on October 2. In pursuance of the Mexican policy to disarm the Texans, Ugartechea had demanded the gun. The Texans refused to give it up. The engagement that resulted was rather trivial, but it ended in victory for the Texans. Six days later, October 8, the fort at Goliad was attacked and taken by the Texans. On the 28th of the same month, Bowie and Fannin with a small company met, near Mission Concepción, a body of Mexicans, and completely routed them, killing about one hundred and capturing their field pieces.

On October 4, Austin had sent out a circular letter to the committees of safety, announcing that war had been declared against military despotism. On the eighth he sent out a general appeal for volunteers, appointing Gonzales as army headquarters. Men flocked to Gonzales and by the 13th there was a small army of 350 men. These men now marched to within eight miles of Bexar, and there pitched camp to await reenforcements. With the exception of the battle at Concepción—just mentioned—there was no fighting, worthy the name, till December. By that time Austin had left the army and General Burleson was the ranking officer.

Burleson had an army of about 800 men, divided into two divisions, commanded by Colonel F. W. Johnson and Benjamin R. Milam. They led their divisions to Bexar and stormed the town between the 5th and 10th of the month, and compelled General Cos [*in the defensively reinforced Alamo mission*] to surrender. After some haggling over the details, articles of capitulation were signed, allowing the Mexican officers to retain their arms and private property, on their promise to retire "into the interior of the republic" and not to oppose in any way the re-establishment of the Constitution of 1824. The 600 convicts who had arrived at Bexar as reenforcements to Cos, just before the surrender, were to be taken back beyond the Rio Grande, accompanied by a small escort of armed soldiers. The rest of the Mexicans were free to remain in Texas or to go with Cos as they pleased; private property was restored to its owners; private citizens were not to be molested; and Texas was to furnish Cos with provisions "at the ordinary price of the country." Cos's losses are [*not*] now known, exactly, but they were relatively large. The Texan loss is given as one officer, Milam, and a private killed, and four officers and twenty-one wounded.

Having given up their munitions of war, Cos and his soldiers were allowed to retire, under parole, beyond the Rio Grande. Thus by December 15, 1835, the Alamo, destined ere long to be the scene of the tragical events of our main narrative, was in the control of the Texans, and was occupied by their volunteer army.

CHAPTER 1

Sources inside the Alamo

At about 2 P.M. on the afternoon of February 23, 1836, the Mexican Army under Gen. Antonio López de Santa Anna entered San Antonio de Béxar and besieged the semiruined mission popularly called the Alamo. This old mission had been converted into a fortress by the Mexican general Cós in late 1835, when he was besieged by the rebel Texan forces. After his surrender, the Texans further improved the fortifications in anticipation of an attack. Inside the Alamo on February 23, there were approximately 150 men with perhaps 10 to 20 women and children. On March 1, a group of 32 men penetrated the Mexican lines and reinforced the besieged defenders. A couple days later, James Bonham also rode through the lines into the Alamo. On the thirteenth day, at dawn on March 6, the Mexican Army swept over these defensive works and killed the defenders. The legend of the siege and fall of the Alamo began.

The joint commanders inside the Alamo were William Barret Travis and James Bowie, though because of illness, Bowie played a small role during the actual siege. The personality of Travis is a central component in why this battle became so famous in American history. Consequently, the first section of the documents presented here will start with some pre-siege correspondence of Travis (and Bowie) before continuing on in the next section with those of the siege itself.

A surprising number of (apparent) noncombatants were in the Alamo and survived the actual fall. Susanna Dickinson and Travis's slave Joe are the most important, because their accounts were the primary sources for most early narratives of the siege and fall. Much later, the remembrances of Juana Alsbury and Enrique Esparza became important in twentieth-century versions of the story.

Three documents are presented next that are concerned with reputed sources inside the Alamo, defenders David Crockett, Isaac Millsap, and Willis Moore. The first two raise the issue of whether and how outright fraudulent material can appear in response to a famous event of considerable popular interest. The commentary for these two documents will discuss some of the reasons

13

why these are commonly rejected. The Moore document demonstrates that important sources once existed but have not (yet?) been found or recorded.

Another class of inside eyewitnesses to some of the events of the siege were the couriers sent out by Travis for assistance. There were a surprisingly large number, but it is a frustrating group in that only John Sutherland and Juan Seguín wrote of their experiences. Sutherland's account is perhaps the single most important source narration of the entire event, yet because of limited publication, the most authentic version has been practically unavailable to interested lay readers. The couriers John Smith, James Allen, William Oury, and Benjamin Highsmith told others a little of their stories in later years. More biographical information has been included in these sections than is typical in the hope that the information might lead to discoveries of additional documents.

The most vivid and dramatic story of the Alamo is that of Travis drawing a line in the dust and asking those to cross over who were willing to stay, fight, and die. This story comes to us thirdhand, from a reputed account by a "Moses" Rose to the parents of William Zuber, first published in 1873. For over sixty years, the story was too good and the evidence too weak to be accepted by professional scholars. Then, astonishingly, a few lines in a county journal reversed this assessment for many to a likelihood of the story being fundamentally true. Consequently, the documents relating to Louis Rose of Nacogdoches and their connection to the Zuber story are especially interesting, controversial, and among the more extensive included in this collection.

The historian has to evaluate false and inaccurate claims as well. The presence of Madam Candelaria in the Alamo was widely reported in her later years but is even more widely disallowed now. Nonetheless, some writers have continued to use specifics originating in her accounts to describe events in the Alamo. The documents relating to these accounts are presented here, as only by comparing them together with the others will the inconsistencies and contradictions become apparent. She serves as an example of when the scales of truthfulness must weigh against someone's claim.

The chapter concludes with some of the mysteries and unknowns relating to those inside the Alamo, and a brief synopsis of the enormous effort, particularly by Amelia Williams, to identify the defenders.

1.1.1.1.   Travis, letter, December 17, 1835.

Travis, William B., to James W. Robinson. December 17, 1835. Mirabeau Buonaparte Lamar Papers, #271. TSLA.

The original is unclear in some places, so the reading of some words follows
Gulick et al. (1968, 1:264–65).

Mill Creek, Decr. 17th 1835.

Hon. James W. Robinson

Dear Sir—I have understood, though not officially that the General Council
have done me the honor to appoint me first Major in the Artillery Regt. I feel
highly sensible of this mark of distinction & I return my sincere thanks to the
honorable body over which you preside for the honor they have intended me;
yet believing that I could not be so useful in the artillery as elsewhere, I beg
leave to decline the office or if I have been commissioned to resign the same.
You will do me a favor by communicating this to the council, although I am
sensible that it is not regular, that I should make this communication until I
should have been officially notified of my appointment. I have taken the liberty
of making this request of you, in order that the Genl. Council may make
another appointment immediately to prevent delay in the organization of the
Regular Army which Texas has to look to for her ultimate defense, I would
thank you to put Francis W. Johnson in nomination for the office of Major in the
artillery to fill the vacancy. He is an old settler & has many claims to the favorable consideration of the council. I understand that he commanded in the storm
of San Antonio after the death of the lamented Milam—.

I hope the council will take measures to fit out an expedition immediately
to take the port & city of Matamoras—I refer your Excellency to a letter I have
just written to Mr. Hanks of the Military Com. for my views on this [*word
unclear*] subject; and I hope you will agree with me—

I intend to join the expedition, if one is gotten up, unless prohibited by
superior orders, & I will execute to the best of my ability any command which
the council may see proper to confer on me.

With considerations of high respect
I have the honor to be
&c. &c.
W. B. Travis

P.S. This letter is entirely private & not intended to be read to [*or "at"*] the
Council, therefore I will thank you to make the requested communication verbally—

If it is necessary for my resignation to be in writing I can make it when I
return to Town, which will be in a few days—

Travis

1.1.1.2. Travis, letter, "January 17," 1836 (inaccurate date).

Yoakum, Henderson. 1855. *History of Texas, from Its First Settlement in 1685 to Its Annexation to the United States in 1846.* 2:59. New York: Redfield.

Yoakum must have erred in the date of this letter, as Travis did not leave for San Antonio for several days (see the next two documents). Probable dating is discussed in the commentary. The original was not located.

The volunteers at Bexar had been promised their pay monthly, which not receiving, they gradually abandoned the service, until there were but eighty troops left. Governor Smith, on being informed of this fact, removed Colonel Travis from his position as superintendent of the recruiting-service, and despatched him, with a small force, to Bexar. Shortly after his arrival, Colonel Neill retired to his home. Colonel Travis called for five hundred more troops, "mostly regulars."—"Militia and volunteers," said he, "are but ill suited to garrison a town." He also asked for money, provisions, and clothing. "Enthusiasm," he justly remarked, "may keep up an army for a few days, but *money,* and money alone, will support an army for regular warfare."*

* Travis to Houston, January 17, 1836: MS.

1.1.1.3. Travis, letter, January 21, 1836.

Mixon, Ruby, ed. August 1930. William Barret Travis; his life and letters. Master's thesis. Mixon (Ruby) Papers, CAH.

Mixon's thesis also served as a convenient check on the reading of all the Travis correspondence when the original manuscripts were not completely clear.

San Felipe, January 21, 1836.—

Dear Hill:

I have this day sent you orders about contracting with McKinney for our uniforms and equipment. I wish you would attend to it immediately. I spoke to him about my uniform, which I have written to him to purchase. I am ordered off to the defense of San Antonio, which is threatened with an attack from the enemy. I shall leave in two days. Do all you can to make recruits and get the cavalry on foot.

I remain,
Yours in haste,
Travis

[To W. G. Hill, Velasco.]

[Undated clipping from the *Houston Post,* found in Miles S. Bennet's Scrap Book, Cuero, Texas. Copy furnished writer by E. W. Winkler, University of Texas.]

1.1.1.4. Travis, letter, January 28, 1836.
Travis, William B., to Henry Smith. January 28, 1836. Adjutant General
(RG-401), Army Papers—Correspondence, TSLA.

Head Quarters—Campt at Burnam's, Colorado
Jany 28ᵗʰ 1836—

Communication,
To His Excellency Henry Smith
Governor of Texas—
Sir—In obedience to my orders I have done every thing in my power to get
ready to march to the relief of Bexar, but owing to the difficulty of getting
horses, provisions &c. and owing to desertions &c. I shall march to-day with
only about thirty men, all regulars except four. I shall however go on & do my
duty, if I am sacrificed, unless I receive new orders to counter march. Our affairs
are gloomy indeed—The people are cold & indifferent—They are worn down &
exhausted with the war, & in consequence of dissentions between contending &
rival chieftains, they have lost all confidence in their own Govt. & officers. You
have no idea of exhausted State of the country—Volunteers can no longer be
had or relied upon—A Speedy organization, classification & draft of the Militia
is all that can save us now. A regular army is necessary—but money, & <u>money</u>
only can raise & equip a regular army—Money must be raised or Texas is gone
to <u>ruin</u>—Without it—war cannot be again carried on in Texas—The patriotism
of a few has done much; but that is becoming worn down—I have strained
every nerve—I have used my personal credit & have neither slept day nor night,
since I reced [*sic*] orders to march—and with all this exertion, I have barely been
able to get horses & equipment for the few men I have—Enclosed I send you a
list of men who deserted on the roads from Washington & San Felipe to this
place. I understand from rumor that His Excellency the Commandant General,
Saml. Houston is gone to San Felipe—Will you be good enough to show this
communication to him & request him to write me—as I wish to be in communication with him—

I have the honor to be
your Excellency's—<u>obt</u> <u>Sert</u>
W. Barret Travis
Lt. Col. Comdt

List of deserters on the road from San Felipe—
A. White
John Cole
From Washington—
——Baker—with a roan horse saddle & Bridle—
Andrew Smith—with a sorrel horse
saddle & Bridle—Blanket—Gun & shot pouch

——Ginnings with a Dun horse—saddle & Bridle—valued at $150—
W<u>m</u> Smith
Solomon Bardwell
Alfonso Steele
——Wiley.

Reported by Seargeant [*sic*]
J. G. Smith—Jany 27th 1836.
W. B. Travis
Lt. Col. Comdt.

[*Cover is noted "<u>Private</u>"*]

1.1.1.5.   Travis, letter, January 29, 1836.

Travis, William B., to Henry Smith. January 29, 1836. Adjutant General (RG-401), Army Papers—Correspondence, TSLA.

Burnam's Colorado; Jany 29th 1836—
To His Excellency Henry Smith Governor of the State of Texas,
    Sir: This will be handed to you by Capt. Jackson, who will explain to you the situation of things here—I leave here with the troops under Capt Forsythe, but shall await your orders at Gonzales or some other point on the road—I shall however keep the 30 men of Forsyth's company in motion towards Bexar, so that they may arrive there as soon as possible—
    Not having been able to raise 100 volunteers agreeably to your order, & there being so few regular troops together, I must beg that your Excellency will recall the order for me to go on to Bexar in command of so few men—I am willing, nay anxious to go to the defence of Bexar, and I have done every thing in my power to equip the Enlisted men & get them off—But Sir, I am unwilling to risk my reputation (which is ever dear to a soldier) by going off into the enemie's country with such little means, so few men, & them so badly equipped—In fact there is no necessity for my services to command these few men—The company officers will be amply sufficient—They should at all events be sent to Bexar or the frontier of Nueces—They may now go on to San Antonio under command of Capt. Forsyth where they can be employed if necessary, & if they are not needed there they may be sent to San Patricio or some other point—I am now convinced that none but defensive measures can be pursued at this inclement season—If the Executive or the Major Genl. desire or order it, I will visit the Post of San Antonio or any other, for the purpose of consulting or communicating with the officers in command there—or to execute any commission I may be entrusted with, but I do not feel disposed to go to command a squad of men, & without the means of carrying on a campaign—Therefore I hope your Excellency will take my situation into consideration, & relieve me from the

orders which I have heretofore received, so far as they compel me to command in person the men who are now on their way to Bexar—Otherwise I shall feel it due to myself to resign my commission. I would remark that I can be more useful at present, in Superintending the recruiting services—I have the honor to be your Excellency's friend & obt. s<u>ert</u>.

W. Barret Travis.
Lt.-Col. Comdt of cavalry.

1.1.1.6.   Bowie, letter, February 2, 1836.

Bowie, James, to Henry Smith. February 2, 1836. Adjutant General (RG-401), Army Papers, TSLA.

Bejar 2^d Feby 1835 [1836]

To His Excy. H Smith
Dear Sir
In pursuance of your orders I proceeded from San Felipe to La Bahia and whilst there employed my whole time in trying to effect the objects of my mission. You are aware that Genl Houston came to La Bahia soon after I did, this is the reason why I did not make a report to you from that post. The Comdr. in Chf. has before this communicated to you all matters in relation to our military affairs at La Bahia; this makes it wholly unnecessary for me to say any thing on the subject. Whilst at La Bahia Genl Houston received despatches from Col Comdt. Neill informing that good reasons were entertained that an attack would soon be made by a numerous Mexican Army on our important post of Bejar. It was forthwith determined that I should go instantly to Bejar; accordingly I left Genl Houston and with a few very efficient volunteers came on to this place about 2 weeks since. I was received by Col Neill with great cordiality, and the men under my command entered at once into active service. All I can say of the soldiers stationed here is complimentary to both their courage and their patience. But it is the truth and your Excellency must know it, that great and just dissatisfaction is felt for the want of a little money to pay the small but necessary expenses of our men. I cannot eulogise the conduct & character of Col Neill too highly: no other man in the army could have kept men at this post, under the neglect they have experienced. Both he & myself have done all that we could; we have industriously tryed all expedients to raise funds; but hitherto it has been to no purpose. We are still labouring night and day, laying up provisions for a seige, encouraging our men, and calling on the Government for relief.

<u>Relief</u> at this post, in men, money, & provisions is of <u>vital</u> importance & is wanted instantly. Sir, this is the object of my letter. The salvation of Texas depends in great measure in keeping Bejar out of the hands of the enemy. It serves as the frontier picquet guard and if it were in the possession of Santa

Anna there is no strong hold from which to repell him in his march towards the
Sabine. There is no doubt but very large forces are being gathered in several of
the towns beyond the Rio Grande. And late information through Senr Cassiana
& others, worthy of credit, is positive in the fact that 16 hundred or two thousand troops with good officers, well armed, and a plenty of provisions, were on
the point of marching, (the provisions being cooked &c) A detachment of active
young men from the volunteers under my command have been sent out to the
Rio Frio; they returned yesterday without information and we remain yet in
doubt whether they entend [sic] an attack on this place or go to reinforce Matamoras. It does however seem certain that an attack is shortly to be made on this
place & I think & it is the general opinion that the enemy will come by land.
The Citizens of Bejar have behaved well. Col. Neill & Myself have come to the
solemn resolution that we will rather die in these ditches than give it up to the
enemy. These citizens deserve our protection and the public safety demands
our lives rather than to evacuate this post to the enemy.—again we call aloud
for <u>relief</u>; the weakness of our post will at any rate bring the enemy on, some
volunteers are expected: Capt Patton with 5 or 6 has come in. But a large reinforcement with provisions is what we need.

James Bowie

over

I have information just now from a friend whom I believe that the force at
Rio Grande (Presidia) is two thousand complete; he states further that five thousand more is a little back and marching on, perhaps the 2 thousand will wait for
a junction with the 5 thousand. This information is corroberated [sic] with all
that that [sic] we have heard. The informant says that they intend to make a
decent [sic] on this place in particular, And there is no doubt of it.

Our force is very small, the returns this day to the Comdt. is only one hundred and twenty officers & men. It would be a waste of men to put our brave
little band against thousands.

We have no interesting news to communicate. The army have elected two
gentlemen to represent the Army & trust they will be received.

James Bowie

1.1.1.7. Travis, letter, February 12, 1836.

Travis, William B., to Henry Smith. February 12, 1836. Secretary of State (RG-307), Records—Domestic Correspondence, TSLA.

The report of Smith in the postscript is undoubtably the one of February 3 that appears as document 4.5.26.

Commandancy of Bejar
February 12th 1836

To
His Excelly. H. Smith
Governor of Texas
Sir

You have no doubt already received information, by Express from La Bahia, that tremendous preparations are making on the Rio Grande & elsewhere in the Interior, for the Invasion of Texas—Santa Ana by the last accounts was at Saltillio, with a force of <u>2500</u> men & Gen. Sesma was at the Rio Grande with about <u>2000</u>—He has issued his Proclamation denouncing [*obviously, "announcing" was meant*] vengiance [*sic*] against the people of Texas—and threatens to exterminate every white man within its limits.—This being the Frontier Post nearest the Rio Grande, will be the first to be attacked.—We are illy prepared for their reception, as we have not more than 150 men here and they in a very disorganisd State—Yet we are determined to sustain it as long as there is a man left, because we consider death preferable to disgrace, which would be the result of giving up a Post which has been so dearly won, and thus opening the door for the Invaders to enter the Sacred Territory of the Colonies—We hope our Countrymen will open their eyes to the present danger, and wake from their false security—I hope that all party dissentions will subside, that our Fellow Citizens will unite in the Common Cause and fly to the defense of the Frontiers.—

I fear that it is useless to waste arguments upon them—<u>The Thunder of the Enemy</u>s <u>Cannon and the pollution of their wives and daughters—The Cries of their Famished Children, and the Smoke of their burning dwellings, will only arouse them.</u>—I regret that the Govt. has so long neglected a draft of the Militia which is the only measure that will ever again bring the Citizens of Texas to the Frontiers.—

Money, Clothing and Provisions are greatly needed at this Post for the use of the Soldiers.

I hope your Excelly. will send us a portion of the Money which has been received from the U.S. as it cannot be better applied, indeed we cannot get along any longer without Money, and with it we can do every thing.

For Gods sake, and the sake of our Country, send us reinforcements—I hope you will send [*"us at le" crossed out*] to this Post at least two companies of Regular Troops.—

Capt. Allen⁵ Corp. under Lt. Thornton, now at Goliad, and the Company of Regulars at Copano under command of Lt. Turner, might well be ordered to this Post, as they could reach here in 4 days on foot.—

In consequence of the sickness of his family, Lt. Col. Neill has left this Post, to visit home for a short time, and has requested me to take the Command of the Post.—In consequence of which, I feel myself delicately and awkwardly situated—I therefore hope that your Excelly. will give me some definite orders, and that immediately—

The Troops here, to a man, recognize you as their legitimate Govᵣ, and they expect your fatherly care & protection.—

In conclusion let me assure your Excelly. that with 200 men I believe this place can be maintained—& I hope they will be sent us as soon as possible. Yet should we receive no reinforcements, I am determined to defend it to the last, and should Bejar fall, Your Friend will be buried beneath its ruins.

I have the Honor to be Your
Most Obt. Vy humble St.
W. Barret Travis
Lt. Col. Comdt

P.S. I enclose you a Report of J. W. Smith⁵, as public Store Keeper, under Johnson & Grant—then reappointed [*tear in original, Mixon has "by Col. Neill—"*] Smith was absent at the time my Reports were forwarded, which accounts for the delay of this—

W. B. T.

1.1.1.8.   Travis, letter, February 13, 1836.

Travis, William B., to Henry Smith. February 13, 1836. Adjutant General (RG-401), Army Papers—Correspondence, TSLA.

Bejar Feby 13ᵗʰ 1836—

To His Excellency Henry Smith,

Dear Sir, I wrote you an official letter last night as Comdt of this Post in the absence of Col Neill; & if you had taken the trouble to answer my letter from Burnam's, I should not now have been under the necessity of of [*sic*] troubling you—My situation is truly awkward & delicate—Col Neil left me in the command—but wishing to give satisfaction to the volunteers here & not wishing to assume any command over them I issued an order for the election of an officer to command them with the exception of one company of volunteers that had previously engaged to serve under me. Bowie was elected by two small company's; & Since his election he has been roaring drunk all the time; has assumed all command—& is proceeding in a most disorderly & irregular manner—interfering with private property, releasing prisoners sentenced by court martial & by the Civil Court & turning every thing topsy turvey.= If I did not feel my honor & that of my country compromitted [*sic*] I would leave here instantly for some other point with the troops under my immediate command as I am unwilling to be responsible for the drunken irregularities of any man. I hope you will immediately order some regular troops to this place—as it is more important to ocupy this Post than I imagined when I last saw you—It is the key of Texas from the Interior without a footing here the enemy can do nothing against us in the Colonies <u>now</u> that our coast is guarded by armed vessels—I do not solicit the command of this Post but as Col Neill has applied to the Commander in chief to be relieved & is anxious for me to take the command, I will do it if it be your orders for a time until an artillery officer can be sent here. The citizens here have every confidence in me, as they can communicate with me & they have shown every disposition to aid me with all they have—We much need money—Can you not send some? I read your letter to the troops & made a speech & they received it with acclamation—Our Spies have just returned from Rio Grande—The enemy is there one thousand strong & is making every preparation to invade us. By the 15th of March I think Texas will be invaded & every preparation should be made to receive them. E. Smith will call on you & give you all the news—So will Mr Williams the Bearer of this—

In conclusion, allow me to beg that you will give me definite orders—immediately—

> I have the honor to
> be&c,
> W. Barret Travis

P.S. This is a private letter & is directed to Nibbs for fear it may fall into bad hands.

> Travis

1.1.1.9.   Travis, letter, February 13, 1836.

Travis, William B., to Henry Smith. February 13, 1836. Adjutant General
(RG-401), Army Papers—Correspondence, TSLA.
The enclosed statement of Crockett referred to is not with the original or other-
wise known.

Head Quarters
of Cavalry—
Bejar Feby. 13/36

To
His Excelly. H. Smith Govr
of Texas—
Sir,
    I herewith transmit to you the Sentence of a Court-Martial, in the Case of D.
H. Barre, and other documents relative to the same, which will speak for themselves—I also enclose to you, the statement of Col. D. Crockett relative to the
release of S'd Barre, who refused to comply with the conditional order for his
release.
    I make no comments upon the late transactions here, as your Excelly. will
be able to Judge from the enclosed impartial statements.

I have the honor to be
Yr. Excy. Most Ob. St.
W. Barret Travis.
Lt. Col. of cavalry

1.1.1.10.   Travis and Bowie, letter, February 14, 1836.

Travis, William B., and James Bowie, to Henry Smith. February 14, 1836. Documents for the History of Texas, 1824–1838 (BANC MSS P-O 110), The Bancroft
Library, University of California, Berkeley.

Commandancy of Bejar
His Excelly H. Smith
February 14th 1836
Govr of Texas.—

Sir:
    We have detained Mr. Williams for the purpose of saying that this Garrison
is in a very destitute situation—We have but a small supply of Provisions, and
are without a Dollar—We therefore beg leave to call the attention of your
Excelly. to the wants of this Post, as we learn that 20,000 Dollars have been sent

to Copano for the use of the Troops there, we think it but just that you should send us at least 5000 Dollars, which we understand you have at your command.—

We have Borrowed 500 Dollars here, which has long since been expended, and besides which, we are greatly in debt, and our credit is growing worse daily—It is useless to talk of Keeping up this Garrison any longer without money, as we believe that unless we receive some shortly, the men will all leave.—

From all the information we have received, there is no doubt but that the enemy will shortly advance upon this place & that this will be the first point of attack. We must therefore urge the necessity of sending reinforcements as speedily as possible, to our aid.—

By an understanding of to-day Col. J Bowie has the command of the volunteers, of the Garrison & Col W. B. Travis, of the Regulars & volunteer Cavalry.

All general orders, and correspondence, will henceforth be signed by both, until Col. Neill[s] return—

—We have the Honor to be your Excelly

Most Ob[t] St[s]
W. Barret Travis
comdt of cavalry
James Bowie
Comandant of voleters [*volunteers*]
at Bexar

1.1.1.11. Travis, letter, February 15, 1836.

Travis, William B., to Henry Smith. February 15, 1836. Secretary of State (RG-307), Executive Record Book (Consultation, General Council, 11/7/1835–3/16/1836), 236, TSLA.

Bexar Feby 15 1836

To His Excellency H Smith
Govenor of Texas.
Sir

I take pleasure in introducing to your acquaintance & friendly notice my friend and your namesake Erastus Smith who has proven himself to be the bravest of the Brave in the cause of Texas[;] in time of need Texas ought to befriend and protect him and his helpless family[.] He will give you the news relative to Every thing here and upon him you may rely.

Your friend
W. Barret Travis

1.1.1.12. Travis, letter, February 16, 1836.

Travis, William B., to Henry Smith. February 16, 1836. Secretary of State
(RG-307), Records—Domestic Correspondence, TSLA.
Note section 4.2 for discussion of the Jameson plats.

Commandancy of Bejar
Feby 16th 1836—

To His Excellency Henry Smith—Governor of Texas.

Sir—Enclosed I send you the report of the Engineer of this Post Mr Green B.
Jameson, together with a Plan or Demonstration of the Alamo & its present
State of defence. I hope they will meet your approbation as Mr G. has shown
himself industrious & attentive in his department—and seems willing to do
every thing in his power to serve the state—

I have nothing of interest to communicate that has transpired since my last.
I must however again remind your Excellency that this point is the key of Texas
& should not be neglected by the Government [underline is not in same pen].
Men, money and provisions are needed—with them this post can & shall be
maintained & Texas (that is) the colonies, will be saved from the fatal effects of
an Invasion.

Respectfully
Your obt Sert
W. Barrett Travis.

1.1.1.13. Travis, letter, February 19, 1836.

Travis, William B., to J. L. Vaughan. February 19, 1836. Typescript copy in Biographical and Historical Files under Travis, W. B., TSLA.

Commandancy of Bexar
Feby 19/ 36

Capt. J. L.Vaughan
Army of Texas
Sir

You are hereby required to proceed forthwith on the Recruiting Service—
You will take up the line of march from the Town of Rio Grande, from thence to
Pictis, thence to San Juan de Mat, thence to Aguaverde, thence to San Fernando,
thence to Laredo, thence to Revilla, thence to Alcantro, thence to Rinosa, thence
to Comargo, from thence to Florido, & thence to Mataroras [sic] where you will
make your Headquarters until you receive further orders,—

You will make regular reports from all the places above named,—and make as many recruits as possible at each place—taking care that when you shall have form(e)d a company to forward the same to this post,—and proceed to recruit other companies as fast as possible,—

Enclosed you have the General Instructions for the recruiting Service, by which you will be govern'd in all cases,—

You have been selected for this Service on account of your distinguished public Services, your well known patriotism, daring valor, firmness and perserverence—It is therefore expected and required that this order will be executed with promptness and dispatch, <u>&</u> it is hoped & confidently believed that my expectations will be fully realized.

> I have the Honor to be
> Yr. Most Ob. St.
> Warren Barret Travers [*sic*]
> (scroll)

P.S.
The situation of enemy must not be lost sight of, you must report weekly in relation to him—

1.1.1.14. Travis, testimonial, February 19, 1836.

Travis, William B. February 19, 1836. Republic Claims, AU-Xaimes, Felipe—OS; 813; R:130 Fr:0606-0606, TSLA.

The Provisional Government of Texas
To Felipe Xaimes D[r]
1835—To 65 head of cattle killed as Beeves by the Army under General Austin & others at/12—per head——$780.00

I do hereby certify that from the declarations of J. N. Seguin, Luciano Navarro, Green B. Jameson, & Ignacio Herera & others, the above account is just & true in my opinion—Besides the party interested, has not chage [*charged*] the yearlings that were killed of his, but has only charged the grown cattle—He is said to be a good man & was actually engaged in the Service of our army for a short time [&] gave of his Beeves freely of his own acord—Bejar, 19th of February 1836—

> W. Barret Travis
> Lt.Col. Comdt.

1.1.1.15. Travis, testimonial, February 22, 1836.

Travis, William B. February 22, 1836. Republic Claims, AU-Cruz, Antonio; 4469; R:023 Fr:0013-0013, TSLA.

This document is from a certificate by Juan Seguín that Antonio Cruz supplied forty "fanegas" of corn to the Federal Army of Texas, and that he was a volunteer in November and December 1835. Both a Spanish original and an English translation are in the files, with the following text at the end of the original.

I certify that from the Statement of Captain Seguin & the best information, I can get, Antonio Cruz was one of those who entered Bennimendi's [*Verrimendi's*] house in the storm of this Town & was one of the few Mexicans who rendered us essential service in the late campaign—I give this certificate because I think a distinction ought to be made between those who lost property while in our service & those who were against us or were neutral—

                    Bejar Feby 22nd 1836—
                    W. B. Travis.
                    Lt.Col. Comdt

1.1.1.16. Travis, letter, February 23, 1836.

Travis, William B., to Judge Andrew Ponton. February 23, 1836. Thomas W. Streeter Collection, Yale Collection of Western Americana, Beinecke Rare Book and Manuscript Library, Yale University Library.

Originally published in the *Telegraph and Texas Register*, February 27, 1836. Facsimiles were published in Brown (1895, 128) and Eberstadt (1957, 31:151).

                    Commandancy of Bejar, 1836.
                    Feby 23rd 3 o'clock P.M.
To Andrew Ponton judge & to the Citizens of Gonzales—

The enemy in large force is in sight—We want men & provisions—Send them to us—We have 150 men & are determined to defend the Alamo to the last—

                    Give u [*us*] assistance—
                    W. B. TRAVIS
                    Lt-Col. Comdt

P.S. Send an express to San Felipe with the news—night & day—
                    Travis.

Commentary

Travis and Bowie Pre-siege Correspondence (1.1.1.1–1.1.1.16)

In reviewing the letters of Travis prior to the start of the siege of the Alamo, one is struck by a number of points. First and foremost, it seems he wanted to be almost anywhere but commanding the garrison at the Alamo. Second, he expressed a continual concern for money and men. And third, he evidenced a certain fatalism or sense of being "sacrificed" even before he arrived at the Alamo.

In his letter of December 17, 1835 (1.1.1.1), Travis wanted to decline an appointment as major in the Artillery Regiment. This is more than a bit ironic, as the artillery was the central defense at the Alamo a few months later. Instead, he expressed interest at being in some command position as part of an expedition to Matamoros. This expedition was an offensive move by the Texans, eventually undertaken by Dr. James Grant and Francis W. Johnson, one motivation of which was to acquire the large trade income of the port city. It was a fiasco for the Texans, because San Antonio was stripped of men and horses for the move, the leadership in Texas became politically fragmented and militarily impotent, and the Mexican Army annihilated the forces that went south.[1] References to it will reappear numerous times in documents in this work.

By January 21 (1.1.1.3), Travis had received orders to go to San Antonio, but on the twenty-eighth, he discussed the difficulty in getting the men together. Here he wrote, "if I am sacrificed," but he appeared equally concerned for the general organization and especially funding for a regular army. A day later, January 29, he was so discouraged that he asked for his orders to be changed on the threat of resigning his commission. Thus, practically every letter prior to his arrival in San Antonio indicated he did not want to go there.

Every letter from San Antonio pleaded for men, money, and provisions. But he made clear right away, in his letter of February 12 (1.1.1.7), that the place had to be defended and he was "determined to defend it to the last."

One item of significance for the approaching crisis was the tension, apparently quickly resolved between February 12 and 14 (1.1.1.10), between Travis and Bowie due to the split command between the regulars and the volunteers. However, this was the only time the two commanders did jointly sign an order per their agreement, and a later memo of Bowie to the commander of the Army of Texas on February 23 (1.1.2) might have been a unilateral action.

Also of interest is the extent of intelligence concerning the Mexican Army's preparations for attack into Texas, also addressed in the letter of February 12. This is worth comparing with other accounts that describe the near total surprise of Santa Anna's arrival (e.g., see Sutherland, section 1.7.1).

In this same period, the important Jameson plans or plats were sent (1.1.1.12, see also section 4.2). These indicate the efforts that must have taken place to assess the defensibility of the Alamo, and they gave a final, pre-siege look at the fort.

A peculiar error in sources is apparent in Henderson Yoakum's dating of a letter from Travis as January 17 (1.1.1.2). It seems probable that this was sent from San Antonio sometime between February 3, when Travis arrived there (see 4.5.27), and February 12, when he received more definite word of the pending invasion. The tone sounds similar to that of his February 12 letter, but the information is different, and it would appear to be a little prior to this one (1.1.1.7, also note letter of January 28/1.1.1.4). The previous commander, J. C. Neill, left on February 11, which is a possible date.

The February 2 letter of James Bowie (1.1.1.6) is of interest for what it does *not* say, specifically that he did not elaborate on the orders Gen. Samuel Houston gave him in La Bahía concerning the Alamo. According to later accounts of Houston's, Bowie was ordered to blow up the Alamo and abandon San Antonio. This will be reviewed in more depth in the commentary to the section on other Pre-siege Correspondence (4.5), particularly on Houston's letters of January 17, 1836. (4.5.13–14).

Two memos supporting claims by Felipe Xaimes and Antonio Cruz (1.1.1.14–15) are of interest in comparison with Travis's letter of March 3 (1.1.6), complaining of lack of support from the citizens of Bexar.

The pre-siege selections end with a hastily scribbled note (1.1.1.16) to the town of Gonzales announcing the arrival of the Mexican Army, with a call for assistance. And so the next phase of the Alamo story—the siege and defense—began.

---

1. For the story of Grant's expedition, see Filisola 1985, 183–90, and Davis 1998, 491 on.

1.1.2. Bowie to commander of the Mexican Army of Texas, message, February 23, 1836.

Jenkins, John H., ed. and trans. 1973. *The Papers of the Texas Revolution, 1835–1836.* 4:414. Austin: Presidial Press, Brig. Gen. Jay A. Matthews Publisher.

This is a translation from the Archivo General de Mexico Papers, University of Texas at Austin, which are typed transcriptions of the Spanish texts. The response appears later, as document 2.1.1.2. The original is in the Thomas W. Streeter Collection, Yale University Library. An early printed copy of both documents is in *El Mosquito Mexicano*, March 22, 1836. The actual manuscript is in two handwritings; most of the letter is in a neat script, but the autograph and title, "Comd de los Volentares De Bexar," is in a second, very shaky hand. A facsimile is in Daughters of the Republic of Texas, 1986, *The Alamo Long Barracks Museum*, 58.

Commander of the Army of Texas:

Because a shot was fired from a cannon of this fort at the time that a red flag was raised over the tower, and a little afterward they told me that a part of your army had sounded a parley, which, however, was not heard before the firing of the said shot. I wish, Sir, to ascertain if it be true that a parley was called, for which reason I send my second aid, Benito Jameson, under guarantee of a white flag which I believe will be respected by you and your forces. God and Texas!

> Fortress of the Alamo, February 23, 1836
> James Bowie
> Commander of the volunteers of Bexar to the
> Commander of the invading forces below Bejar.

1.1.3. Travis and Bowie to James Fannin, letter(?), c. February 23, 1836.

Foote, Henry Stuart. 1841. *Texas and the Texans.* 2:224. [Philadelphia]: Thomas, Cowperthwait & Co.

The Commandant at *Fort Defiance* [*Fannin at Goliad*] had received the express of Travis and Bowie requesting his aid, on the 25th of February. It had been drawn up, of course, in most earnest terms, and concluded as follows: "We have removed all our men into the Alamo, where we will make such resistance as is due to our honour, and that of the country, until we can get assistance from you, which we expect you to forward immediately. In this extremity, we hope you will send us all the men you can spare promptly. We have one hundred and forty-six men, who are determined *never to retreat*. We have but little provisions, but enough to serve us till you and your men arrived. We deem it unneccessary to repeat to a brave officer, who knows his duty, that we call on him for assistance."

1.1.4.   Travis, public pronouncement, February 24, 1836.

Green, Michael R., ed. April 1988. To the people of Texas and all Americans in the world. *Southwestern Historical Quarterly*. 91:492–93.

This, the most famous and dramatic document from the Alamo, is reviewed in depth in an article by the reference archivist at the Texas State Archives, where the original is preserved. The article includes a facsimile of the original as well as detailed information on the messengers Albert Martin and Launcelot Smithers. The article also includes extensive footnotes, which should be read by those interested in knowing more about the details and personalities associated with this message.

Commandancy of the Alamo
Bejar, Fby 24th 1836—

To the People of Texas & all Americans <u>in the</u> <u>world</u>—
Fellow citizens & compatriots—
I am besieged, by a thousand or more of the Mexicans under Santa Anna—I have sustained a continual Bombardment & cannonade for 24 hours & have not lost a man—the enemy has demanded a surrender at discretion, otherwise, the garrison are to be put to the sword, if the fort is taken—I have answered the demand with a cannon shot, & our flag still waves proudly from the walls—<u>I shall never surrender or retreat. Then,</u> I call on you in the name of Liberty, of patriotism & & [*sic*] every thing dear to the American character, to come to our aid, with all dispatch—The enemy is receiving reinforcements daily & will no doubt increase to three or four thousand in four or five days. If this call is neglected, I am determined to sustain myself as long as possible & die like a soldier who never forgets what is due to his own honor & that of his country—

<u>Victory or Death</u>

William Barret Travis
Lt. Col. comdt
[rubric]

P.S. The Lord is on our side—when the enemy appeared in sight we had not three bushels of corn—We have since found in deserted houses 80 or 90 bushels & got into the walls 20 or 30 head of Beeves—

Travis
[rubric]

[*Addressed:*]
To
The People of Texas
and
All Americans
[*Endorsements:*]
send this to San Felipe by Express night & day—
Since the above was writen [*sic*] I heard very heavy Canonade during the whole day[;] [*I*] think there must have been an attack made upon the alamo[.] We were short of Amunition when I left[.] Hurry on all the men you can in haste

Albert Martin
[rubric]

When I left there was but 150 determined to do or die[;] tomorrow I leave for Bejar with what men I can raise [*& we?*] will be [*on our way in*] at all events—
Col Almonte is there[;] the troops are under the Command of Gen Seisma.
N b I hope Every one will Randeves at gonzales as soon as poseble as the Brave Solders are suffering[;] do not neglect the powder is very scarce and should not be delad one moment.

L. Smither
[rubric]

1.1.5.   Travis to Samuel Houston, letter, February 25, 1836.

Arkansas Gazette. April 19, 1836. Little Rock.
Mixon, Turner, and Jenkins gave the date of this newspaper article as April 12, while Williams and Lord correctly stated April 19.

Jonesborough, 29th March, 1836.

DEAR SIR—I hand you a copy of two letters recently received by express from the interior of Texas. To use the language of one of our correspondents, the atmosphere of Texas is becoming "devlish dark." if these letters should be found to contain any thing new or interesting, give them a place in your paper.

Copy of a letter from W. B. TRAVIS, commandant at Bexar, to Gen. S. Houston.

HEAD QUARTERS, FORT OF THE ALEMO [sic]
Bexar, Feb. 25th 1836.

To Major General SAMUEL HOUSTON,
Commander in Chief of the Army of Texas.

SIR—On the 23d Feb. the enemy in large force entered the city of Bexar, which could not be prevented, as I had not sufficient force to occupy both positions. Col. Batres, the Adjutant Major of President General Santa Anna, demanded a surrender at discretion, calling us foreign rebels. I answered them with a cannon shot: upon which the enemy commenced a bombardment with a five-inch howitzer, which, together with a heavy cannonade, has been kept up incessantly ever since. I instantly sent expresses to Col. Fanning, at Goliad, and to the people of Gonzales and San Felipe. Today at 10 o'clock a.m. some two or three hundred crossed the river below, and came up under cover of the houses, until they arrived within point blank shot, when we opened a heavy discharge of grape and canister on them, together with a well directed fire from small arms, which forced them to halt and take shelter in the houses about 90 or 100 yards from our batteries. The action continued to rage for about two hours, when the enemy retreated in confusion, dragging off some of their dead or wounded. During the action the enemy kept up a constant bombardment and discharge of balls, grape and canister. We know, from actual observation, that many of the enemy were killed and wounded—while we, on our part, have not lost a man. Two or three of our men have been slightly scratched by pieces of rock, but not disabled. I take great pleasure in stating, that both officers and men conducted themselves with firmness and bravery. Lieut. Simmons, of cavalry acting as infantry, and Capts. Carey, Dickinson and Blair, of the artillery, rendered essential services, and Charles Despallier and Robert Brown gallantly sallied out and set fire to the houses which afforded the enemy shelter, in the face of the enemy's fire. Indeed the whole of the men, who were brought into action, conducted themselves with such undaunted heroism, that it would be injustice to discriminate. The Hon. David Crockett was seen at all points, animating the men to do their duty. Our numbers are few, and the enemy still continues to approximate his works to ours. I have every reason to apprehend an attack from his whole force very soon; but I shall hold out to the last extremity, hoping to receive reinforcements in a day or two. Do hasten on aid to me as rapidly as possible; as from the superior numbers of the enemy, it will be impossible for us to keep them out much longer. If they overpower us, we fall a sacrifice at the shrine of our country, and we hope posterity and our country will do our memory justice. Give me help, oh my country! Victory or death!

W. BARNET [sic] TRAVIS, Lt. Col. Com.

1.1.6.   Travis, letter, March 3, 1836.

Telegraph and Texas Register. March 12, 1836.

This is one of the most informative of all documents to survive the siege. A possibly independent copy of the letter is in TSLA, Secretary of State (RG-307), Series 64/Proceedings/3/1–3/17/1836. Except for trivial punctuation differences, the content is identical except for two minor words noted.

LETTER
FROM COL. TRAVIS
TO THE PRESIDENT OF THE CONVENTION.
COMMANDANCY OF THE ALAMO
BEJAR, MARCH 3, 1836.

Sir—in the present confusion of the political authorities of the country, and in the absence of the commander-in-chief, I beg leave to communicate to you the situation of this garrison. You have doubtless already seen my official report of the action of the 25th ult., made on that day to Gen. Sam. Houston, together with the various communications heretofore sent by express. I shall therefore confine myself to what has transpired since that date.

From the 25th to the present date, the enemy have kept up a bombardment from two howitzers, (one a five and a half inch, and the other an eight inch,) and a heavy cannonade from two long nine pounders, mounted on a battery on the opposite side of the river, at the distance of four hundred yards from our walls. During this period the enemy have been busily employed in encircling us with intrenched encampments on all sides, at the following distances, to wit,—in Bejar, four hundred yards west; in Lavilleta, three hundred yards south; at the powder house, one thousand yards east by south; on the ditch, eight hundred yards north-east, and at the old mill, eight hundred yards north. Notwithstanding all this, a company of thirty-two men, from Gonzales, made their way into us on the morning of the 1st inst. at 3 o'clock, and Col. J. B. Bonham (a courier from Gonzales) got in this morning at 11 o'clock, without molestation. I have so fortified this place, that the walls are generally proof against cannon balls and I still continue to intrench on the inside and strengthen the walls by throwing up the dirt. At least two hundred shells have fallen inside of our works without having injured a single man: indeed, we have been so fortunate as not to lose a man from any cause, and we have killed many of the enemy. The spirits of my men are still high, although they have had much to depress them. We have contended for ten days against an enemy whose numbers are variously estimated at from fifteen hundred to six thousand men, with Gen. Ramirez Siezma and Col. Batres, the aid de camp of Santa Ana, at their head. A report was circulated that Santa Ana himself was with the enemy, but I think it was false. A reinforcement of about one thousand men is now entering Bejar from the west, and I think it more than probable that Santa Ana is now in town, from the rejoicing we hear.

Col. Fannin is said to be on the march to this place with reinforcements; but I
fear it is not true, as I have repeatedly sent to him for aid without receiving any.
Colonel Bonham, my special messenger, arrived at La Bahia fourteen days ago,
with a request for aid; and on the arrival of the enemy in Bejar ten days ago, I
sent an express to Col. F., which arrived at Goliad on the next day, urging him to
send us reinforcements—*none have yet arrived.* I look to the *colonies alone* for aid:
unless it arrives soon, I shall have to fight the enemy on his own terms. I will,
however, do the best I can under the circumstances; and I feel confident that the
determined valor and desperate courage, heretofore evinced by my men, will
not fail them in the last struggle; and although they may be sacrificed to the
vengeance of a gothic enemy, the victory will cost the enemy so dear, that it will
be the worse for him than a defeat. I hope your honorable body will hasten on
reinforcements, ammunition and provisions to our aid, as soon as possible. We
have provisions for twenty days for the men we have: our supply of ammunition is limited. At least five hundred pounds of cannon powder, and two hundred rounds of six, nine, twelve, and eighteen pound balls—ten kegs of rifle
powder, and a supply of lead, should be sent to this place without delay, under
a sufficient guard.

If these things are promptly sent and large reinforcements are hastened to
this frontier, this neighborhood will be the great and decisive battle [*"battle"* not
in TSLA RG-307 copy] ground. The power of Santa Ana is to be met here, or in
the colonies; we had better meet them here, than to suffer a war of desolation to
rage in our settlements. A blood-red banner waves from the church of Bejar,
and in the camp above us, in token that the war is one of vengeance against
rebels; they have declared us [*"as" in TSLA copy*] such, and demanded that we
should surrender at discretion, or that this garrison should be put to the sword.
Their threats have had no influence on me, or my men, but to make all fight
with desperation, and that high souled courage which characterizes the patriot,
who is willing to die in defence of his country's liberty and his own honor.

The citizens of this municipality are all our enemies except those who have
joined us heretofore; we have but three Mexicans now in the fort: those who
have not joined us in this extremity, should be declared public enemies, and
their property should aid in paying the expenses of the war.

The bearer of this will give your honorable body, a statement more in detail
should he escape through the enemies lines.

God and Texas—Victory or Death!!

Your obedient ser't
W. BARRETT TRAVIS.
Lieut. Col. Comm.

P.S. The enemies troops are still arriving and the reinforcement will probably amount to two or three thousand. T.

Convention Hall, Sunday morning.
10 o'clock, March 6, 1836.

On the arrival of the express with the letter, of which the above is a copy, the Convention was called together, and being called to order, on motion it was read; whereupon Mr. Pmer [*Parmer*] moved the house that one thousand copies be printed for circulation, by the Editors, Messrs, Baker and Bordens of San Felipe, which was agreed to.

H. S. Kimble, *Secretary.*

1.1.7. Travis to Jesse Grimes (?), letter, March 3, 1836.

Telegraph and Texas Register. March 24, 1836. San Felipe.
Yoakum (1855, 2:79) notes that he got this letter from Jesse Grimes, who therefore must have been the friend.

COPY

Of a letter written by Col. Travis to a friend, dated from the Alamo, March 3d.

Dear Sir—do me the favor to send the enclosed to its proper destination instantly. I am still here, in fine spirits, and well to do. With 140 men I have held this place 10 days against a force variously estimated from 1500 to 6000, and I shall continue to hold it till I get relief from my countrymen, or I will perish in its defence. We have had a shower of bombs and cannon balls continually falling among us the whole time, yet none of us have fallen. We have been miraculously preserved. You have no doubt seen my official report of the action of the 25th ult. in which we repulsed the enemy with considerable loss: on the night of the 25th they made another attempt to charge us in the rear of the fort; but we received them gallantly, by a discharge of grape shot and musquetry, and they took to their scrapers immediately. They are now encamped under entrenchments, on all sides of us. * * * * *

All our couriers have gotten out without being caught, and a company of 32 men from Gonzales got in two nights ago, and Col. Bonham got in to-day by coming between the powder house and the enemy's upper encampment. * * * * *

Let the Convention go on and make a declaration of independence; and we will then understand and the world will understand what we are fighting for. If independence is not declared, I shall lay down my arms and so will the men under my command. But under the flag of independence, we are ready to peril our lives a hundred times a day, and to dare the monster who is fighting us under a blood-red flag, threatening to murder all prisoners and to make Texas a waste desert. I shall have to fight the enemy on his own terms; yet I am ready to do it, and if my countrymen do not rally to my relief, I am determined to perish in the defence of this place, and my bones shall reproach my country for her neglect. With 500 men more, I will drive Sesma beyond the Rio Grande, and I will visit vengeance on the enemies of Texas, whether invaders or resident Mexican enemies. All the citizens that have not joined us, are with the enemy fighting against us. Let the government declare them public enemies, otherwise she is acting a suicidal part. I shall treat them as such, unless I have superior orders to the contrary. My respects to all friends, and confusion to all enemies. God bless you.

Your friend
W. BARRET TRAVIS.

1.1.8.   Travis to David Ayers (?), letter, March 3(?), 1836.

Texas Monument. March 31, 1852. La Grange.
This Travis letter is commonly thought to have been written March 3, to go out of the Alamo with his other final messages. This newspaper reference came from Turner (1972), and Tinkle (1958, 116) stated that the original letter still exists, but he did not say where.

From the Victoria Advocate.

MESSRS. EDITORS:—Among the most interesting reminiscences of 1836, which I have seen, is a note addressed by Col. Travis, from the Alamo, to a gentleman in Washington County, who had charge of his son. It ran thus:

"Dear Sir:—Take care of my little boy. If the country should be saved I may make him a splendid fortune. But if the country should be lost, and I should perish, he will have nothing but the proud recollection that he is the son of a man who died for his country.

Yours, &c.,
WM. B. TRAVIS."

It was written on a scrap of yellow wrapping paper, and seemed to have been done in great haste. The paper is torn and ragged, and the date quite effaced. It was transmitted by that last courier, who brought the news, that "the summons to surrender had been answered with a cannon shot, and the flag of Travis still waved on the walls." When the courier was about to depart on this dangerous errand, the hero snatched a hasty moment from the restless duties of his dreadful post, to dispatch this last note on his private business. He could never have supposed that it would reach the public eye. Plain and unvarnished, its hurried diction breathes the heroic tone of that mighty spirit.

R. MONON.
Goliad, Jan. 29, 1852.

Commentary

Travis and Bowie Siege Correspondence (1.1.2–1.1.8):

The primary comment on the all-important siege letters of Travis is to note his flair for dramatic expression. He clearly wanted to address the broadest possible audience, and he had a capability for succinct yet catchy phrasing, which served no small role in creating the fame of the Alamo. A modern reader might accuse him of hyperbole except for the proof by his actions that he fully meant "Victory or Death!" It must be recognized, however, that he failed in his own primary purpose. He wanted and begged for reinforcements, but the only response to these calls was thirty-two men who arrived from the nearby town of Gonzales.

The care given to factual detail is to be expected, as another key purpose of these letters was to report on the military activities to his commanders—both civilian and military. These details are valuable military intelligence, so we should expect them to be accurate and consistent. Certainly, they appear complementary when we compare the March 3 letters with those of February 24 and 25. They can also be compared for consistency with the Mexican sources, especially the Labastida plat (2.8.1) and other maps, which are discussed later. A general review of military details follows section 5.2. The details given by Travis do appear consistent with those in other reliable documents.

In his letters of March 3 (but compare with 1.1.1.14 and 1.1.1.15), Travis was critical of the Hispanic or Tejano citizens of San Antonio who had not joined them. This reveals a certain amount of prejudice on Travis's part, as it has been well established (see sections 1.10 and 1.11) that several more than the count of three people that he gave were in the Alamo throughout the siege, as well as Juan Seguín and a companion sent out as a courier early on. Williams points out the differences in attitudes, as evidenced by Bowie's February 2 letter (1.1.1.6), echoed earlier on January 28 by J. C. Neill (4.5.23).[1] Creed Taylor (in DeShields, 2.11.1 below) gives an even stronger opposing perspective. Lon Tinkle suggests that Travis's anger at the Tejanos was a transfer of anger at the lack of response by the Texans to his call for assistance.[2]

Most writers especially admire the courage of those Tejanos who joined the rebel forces. They not only were subject to execution as traitors along with the rest, but in all probability would have had much fewer options for sanctuary or escape had Santa Anna successfully reconquered Texas.

Bowie's note to the Mexican camp of February 23 is curious in that it was not a joint document with Travis, as agreed per their letter of February 14 (1.1.1.10). In addition, Almonte's journal (2.2.1), discussed by Texas archivist Michael Green, states that Travis sent Albert Martin to the Mexican camp the same day after Bowie had sent Green (Benito in Almonte's journal) Jameson with the note.[3] If we accept Almonte's statement, then one must likely conclude that Bowie and Travis had not resolved their problems of joint command. If Almonte's statement is incorrect, then a simpler possibility is that on the frenzied afternoon of February 23, Bowie was responding to the Mexican Army's initial volley, while Travis was otherwise occupied with preparing the defense (see the Lewis account in Potter 5.1.7). Almonte's journal, being his private journal only accidentally made public, is an unusually reliable source, so one should not readily reject his statement for the sake of simple explanations.

Of course, Travis's subsequent letters, after the one to Fannin (1.1.3), also were not jointly signed with Bowie. The explanation in these cases was likely Bowie's illness, which incapacitated him very early in the siege. The actual handwriting of the signature of the February 23 Bowie note (in a separate hand than the body of the note) is shaky, even in comparison with his autographs of February 2 (1.1.1.6) and 14 (1.1.1.10). Most writers take this as strong evidence that his illness was rapidly developing on the twenty-third.

The "enclosed" in Travis's March 3 letter to Grimes (1.1.7) is most likely to be the short note to David Ayers that follows (1.1.8).[4] There are, however, other possibilities. Mary Austin Holley indicated that it might have been a letter to a fiancée named Rebecca Cummings.[5] If so, such a letter is unknown. A less romantic candidate is Travis's account book, which covered the period from January 21 to February 17, 1836.[6]

As a final comment on this set of documents, a good deal of drama has developed over the Travis letters of March 3 in conjunction with the Moses (Louis) Rose story. As an extreme example, it was called "the most pathetic day in history" by Sidney Lanier in 1873.[7] The heart of this drama is the image of a hopeless situation. After a careful reading of these letters, it seems that this is a bit overdone, or at least so on this date. Clearly, Travis is discouraged by the lack of reinforcements—especially from Fannin—and recognizes that time is running out, but he is still looking for reinforcements and thinks they can still be in time. He makes the point in his letter to the Convention that the messengers and the Gonzales group have gotten out and in without casualties. His state of mind is important in the chronology of Louis Rose, and a subject discussed in greater detail later (section 1.8).

---

1. Amelia Williams, *SWHQ* 36:275, 37:10/note 31.
2. Tinkle, 144.
3. Green in *SWHQ* 91:499.
4. For review of the Ayers notes, see Williams 1933–34, 37:24, n. 57.
5. For Holley story, see Williams 1933–34, 37:87, nn. 26, 27.
6. Chariton, 89–93.
7. Williams, 37:31 and Dobie per 1.8.3.1.

1.2.1.   Susanna Williams, formerly Dickinson, deposition, March 24, 1837.

Republic Claims (Audited Claims and Republic Pensions groups). AU-Smith, Joshua G., #810; R:098 Fr:0041. TSLA.

This claim's cover notes that it was for services in the military from January 8, 1836, for one month and twenty-six days—to March 6. It was cited by Amelia Williams from the Controllers Military Service Record (CMSR) #810 in support of Joshua G. Smith as a defender.

Republic of Texas
County of Brazoria
This day personally appeared before me W. C. Patton, an acting Justice of the peace for s.d [*"said"*] County M^{rs}. Suzana Williams, the late M^{rs}. Dickinson who was in the Alamo at the time of its fall and made oath that she was personally acquainted with a Joshua G. Smith of Co^{l.} Travis, Corps of Cavalry that she believes, he was, one of the Co^{ls} staff. She saw him the day before the fall of the Alamo and she believes he was killed in s.d place, he was a man of about five feet nine inches in height spare made Dark hair eyes & complexion, and appeard to be between twenty five and thirty years, of age. this the 24th day of March 1837

Sworn to and Subscribed
Susannah Williams
this the day and year
above written
W C. Patton, J.P.

1.2.2.   Susanna Dickinson, interview, 1840.

Stiff, Edward. 1840. *The Texan Emigrant.* 312. Cincinnati: George Conclin.

During part of my sojourn in Texas, Mrs. Dickinson resided at Houston, and feeling as I did a melancholy interest in her history, I was introduced by a friend and had different and repeated conversations with her, touching the events at the Alamo and her own forlorn and distressing situation there. It was not however to be expected that she could detail very correctly every occurrence, and feelings of delicacy forbid me to enquire particularly respecting her treatment while a prisoner in the Mexican camp. She corrobrated [*sic*] in substance the foregoing letters from Col. Travis, and was positive, that every man in the garrison was slain, and among the number her own husband and only friend, except one helpless child now at the time I write about five years old; with this infant

and Col. Travis' black man she was escorted to the Texan head quarters, then at
Gonzales on the Gaudalope River, Santa Anna sending his own servant to assist
her safe.

1.2.3.   Susanna Belles, formerly Dickinson, deposition, December 9, 1850.

Cummings, David P. Court of Claims File C-1936. Archives and Records Division, Texas General Land Office, Austin.

The former Mrs. Dickinson gave depositions in the Court of Claims records of the General Land Office for the heirs of three of the Alamo defenders. This and the next three documents give details not otherwise available.

State of Texas
County of Harris
Personally appeared before the undersigned Chief Justice in and for the County
Aforesaid Susan Belles formerly Susana Dickenson and widow of Almorian
Dickenson dce[d] (one of the defenders of the Alamo under Col Travis) to me personally and and [sic] well known who being duly Sworn deposith and Sayeth,
that David P Cummings and others with him came to and joined the Garrison
about three or four weeks before the taking of the Same by the Mexicans and
that the Said David P Cummings there Perished with the ballance of his companions in Arms: And deponent further Sayeth that She has a distinct recollection of the Said David P Cummings from his having been a Surveyor and from
his having in company with Others on permission went to the Cibolo to Survey
their Head-Rights and from his returning in a few days in Compliance with an
order (sent by express) from Co[l] Travis; and also from his having boarded with
her and of her taking care of his clothes.

Susana Belles

Sworn to and Subscribed before me
this 9th day of December AD 1850.
As witness My hand and Official Seal
at Houston the day & date aforesaid—

Harry H Allen
Chief Justice of Harris County

1.2.4.   Susanna Belles, formerly Dickinson, deposition, November 21, 1853.

Rose, James M. Court of Claims File C-7115. Archives and Records Division, Texas General Land Office, Austin.

The body of the text seems to have "Dickenson," while the line before her mark, written in a different hand, reads "Dickerson."

State of Texas

County of Harris

Personally appeared before me Suzannah Bellows heretofore widow Dickenson who being duly sworn deposith and Saith: that some time during the years 1835 or 6. I lived with my former husband Almeron Dickenson in the town of San Antonio in the Said State of Texas and that I was acquainted with a man by the name of Rose who with David Crocket [*sic*] was frequently an inmate of my house, and that when the Army of Mexico advanced upon the town Said Rose Crocket and all the Americans took refuge in the Alamo, and as deponent believes [?] were all masecurd: Said deponent did not know the Christian name of Said Rose, but remembers his personal appearance; that he was a man of some 30 years of age medium height fair skin disposd to freckle sandy or light hair; Blue or gray eyes, broad Shoulders and inclined to round or stoop, and would weigh probably 150 to 160 pounds—and that She knew no other man by that name: and furthermore that she believes that he is the man who came to Texas with Crocket as he seemed to be his friend and companion.

Sworn to & Subscribed)	Suzannah - Bellows
Before me this 21ˢᵗ day of)	heretofore widow Dickerson
November A.D. 1853)	her mark X
F. Castanie [?]	
notary public Harris co,—	

1.2.5.   Susanna Belles, formerly Dickinson, deposition, July 16, 1857.

Rose, James M. Court of Claims File C-7115. Archives and Records Division, Texas General Land Office, Austin.

The questions for this deposition appear on a previous page and are here inserted within < >.

The State of Texas—Caldwell County

Answers to the Interrogatories—hereto prefixed—propounded to Susannah Bellows in behalf of the Heirs of James M Rose.

<1. When did you emigrate to Texas?>

To Inter. 1ˢᵗ. In the year 1833.

<2. Did you reside in the City of San Antonio De Bexar in the year 1835 & 1836? If yea, were you residing there when the Mexican Army advanced upon that city in 1836?>

" " 2ⁿᵈ. Yes _ Yes.

<3. During your residence in San Antonio De Bexar, did you know a person of the name of Rose at that time with the Texas Army & if yea did the said Rose join the late David Crockett to engage in the War between Mexico and Texas? Do you remember his Christian name?>

" " 3ᵈ. Yes _ he did _ James.

<4. At the time the Mexican Army advanced upon San Antonio De Bexar, did the said Rose, with David Crockett & the other Americans take refuge in the Alamo and at that time was he the only person of the name in the Texas Army?>

" " 4th. He did _ was the Only man in the army by the name of Rose that I knew of.

<5. During your residence in San Antonio De Bexar was the late David Crockett and the said Rose inmates of your house? If yea—were they on friendly terms?>

" " 5ᵗʰ. Yes _ So far as I knew they were.

<6. State the age and personal appearance of the said Rose—the manner by which he came to his death and the facts you know in regard to that person.>

" " 6ᵗʰ. He was about 35 or 40 years of age—He was of medium height, heavy set, rather full square face, very quick spoken—he fell with the rest of the defenders of the Alamo—during the siege I saw Rose often, and upon one occasion heard my husband Capt Dickinson speak to Rose of a narrow escape he (Rose) had made from a Mexican officer upon their first attack.

her
July 16, 1857.   Susannah x Bellis
                                  mark

1.2.6.   Susanna Hannig, formerly Dickinson, deposition, March 8, 1860.

Warnell, Henry. Court of Claims File C-8490. Archives and Records Division, Texas General Land Office, Austin.

On the application of the heirs of Henry Wornell [sic] decˢ for Bounty & Donation lands.

Personally appeared before me the undersigned authority, Mrs Susannah Hunneck, alias Dickinson, who on oath says; I was in the Alamo prior to, and at its fall, on 6th March 1836, and knew a man there by the name of Henry Wornell; and recollect distinctly having seen him in the Alamo about three days prior to its fall; and as none escaped the massacre, I verily believe he was among the unfortunate number who fell there, so bravely in the defence of their country. I recollect having heard him remark that he had much rather be out in the open prairie, than to be pent up in that manner. Said Wornell, was a man of rather small stature, light complexion and I think red or Sandy hair.

	her
Subscribed by making her mark	Susannah x Hunneck
and sworn to before me, this	mark
8th March 1860.	
W. J. Hotchkiss	
Com. of Claims	

1.2.7. Susanna Hannig (Dickinson), interview before 1874.

Morphis, James M. 1874. *History of Texas from Its Discovery and Settlement . . .* 174–77. New York: United States Publishing Co.

Aside from quotation marks, it is not clear from the book's layout when the testimony of Mrs. Hannig ends and further text by Morphis continues. The last definite first-person statement is that about Crockett, fourth paragraph from the end of this excerpt.

I will now describe the memorable FALL OF THE ALAMO as related to me by Mrs. Susan Hannig, formerly Mrs. Dickinson, who witnessed it.

"On February 23d, 1836, Santa Anna, having captured the pickets sent out by Col Travis to guard the post from surprise, charged into San Antonio with his troops, variously estimated at from six to ten thousand, only a few moments after the bells of the city rang the alarm.

"Capt. Dickinson galloped up to our dwelling and hurriedly exclaimed: 'The Mexicans are upon us, give me the babe, and jump up behind me.' I did so, and as the Mexicans already occupied Commerce street, we galloped across the river at the ford south of it, and entered the fort at the southern gate, when the enemy commenced firing shot and shell into the fort, but with little or no effect, only wounding one horse.

"There were eighteen guns mounted on the fortifications, and these, with our riflemen, repulsed with great slaughter two assaults made upon them before the final one.

"I knew Colonels Crockett, Bowie and Travis well. Col. Crockett was a performer on the violin, and often during the siege took it up and played his favorite tunes.

"I heard him say several times during the eleven days of the siege: 'I think we had better march out and die in the open air. I don't like to be hemmed up.'

"There were provisions and forage enough in the fort to have subsisted men and horses for a month longer.

"A few days before the final assault three Texans entered the fort during the night and inspired us with sanguine hopes of speedy relief, and thus animated the men to contend to the last.

"A Mexican woman deserted us one night, and going over to the enemy informed them of our very inferior numbers, which Col. Travis said made them confident of success and emboldened them to make the final assault, which they did at early dawn on the morning of the 6th of March.

"Under the cover of darkness they approached the fortifications, and planting their scaling ladders against our walls just as light was approaching, they climbed up to the tops of our walls and jumped down within, many of them to immediate death.

"As fast as the front ranks were slain, they were filled up again by fresh troops.

"The Mexicans numbered several thousands while there were only one hundred and eighty-two Texans.

"The struggle lasted more than two hours when my husband rushed into the church where I was with my child, and exclaimed: 'Great God, Sue, the Mexicans are inside our walls! All is lost! If they spare you, save my child.'

"Then, with a parting kiss, he drew his sword and plunged into the strife, then raging in different portions of the fortifications.

"Soon after he left me, three unarmed gunners who abandoned their then useless guns came into the church where I was, and were shot down by my side. One of them was from Nacogdoches and named Walker. He spoke to me several times during the siege about his wife and four children with anxious tenderness. I saw four Mexicans toss him up in the air (as you would a bundle of fodder) with their bayonets, and then shoot him. At this moment a Mexican officer came into the room, and, addressing me in English, asked: 'Are you Mrs. Dickinson?' I answered 'Yes.' Then said he, 'If you wish to save your life, follow me.' I followed him, and although shot at and wounded, was spared.

"As we passed through the enclosed ground in front of the church, I saw heaps of dead and dying. The Texans on an average killed between eight and nine Mexicans each—182 and 1,600 Mexicans were killed.

"I recognized Col. Crockett lying dead and mutilated between the church and the two story barrack building, and even remember seeing his peculiar cap lying by his side.

"Col. Bowie was sick in bed and not expected to live, but as the victorious Mexicans entered his room, he killed two of them with his pistols before they pierced him through with their sabres.

"Cols. Travis and Bonham were killed while working the cannon, the body of the former lay on the top of the church.

"In the evening the Mexicans brought wood from the neighboring forest and burned the bodies of all the Texans, but their own dead they buried in the city cemetery across the San Pedro.

1.2.8. Susanna Hannig (Dickinson), interview, September 23, 1876.

Hannig, Mrs. Joseph. September 23, 1876. Adjutant General (RG-401), Strays—Alamo Dead and Monument. TSLA.

During the period of 1875 to 1878, the adjutant general's office conducted an investigation to identify the defenders of the Alamo. The referenced "Strays" file is a compilation of the investigation, while some of the original documents were located in other files. The Hannig documents do not identify who took her testimony.

Austin, Tex. Sept. 23. '76

Called on Mrs. Susanna Hannig, whose husband Joseph Hannig is living with her. She was at the sacking of the Alamo in 1836, 6th Mch; was then in her 15th year; was then named Susannah Dickerson wife of Lieut Almarion Dickerson, and her maiden name was Susanna Wilkenson. Her parents were in Williamson Co. Tenn. Her husband was one of the Killed. They had one child, a daughter, who, then an infant, was with them in the Alamo; This daughter maried [*sic*] John Menard Griffith, a native of Montgomery Co. Texas, by whom she had 4 children, all of whom are living. She died in Montgomery Co. Tex about the year 1871.

The Mexicans came unexpectedly into San Antonio & witness & her husband & child retreated into the Fort. Enemy began throwing bombs into Fort, but no one hurt till the last day, i.e. the assault, except one horse killed. Had provisions enough to last the beseiged 30 days. Among the beseiged were 50 or 60 wounded men from Cos's fight. About 18 cannon (she believes) were mounted on parapet & in service all the time. The enemy gradually approached by means of earth-works thrown up. Besieged were looking for reinforcements which never arrived. The only outsiders who succeeded in coming into Fort were 3 of our spys who entered 3 days before the assault & were all killed.

Dr. Horace Alsbury (bro. of Perry Alsbury of S.A.) retreated into the Fort for protection with his Mexican wife & sister-in-law. He left, unknown to witness, & the two women escaped to the enemy & betrayed our situation about 2 days before the assault—

On morning of 6th Mch. about daylight enemy threw up signal rocket & advanced & were repulsed. They rallied & made 2^{d} assault with scaling ladders, first thrown up on E. side of Fort. Terrible fight ensued. Witness retired into a room of the old church & saw no part of fight—Though she could distinctly hear it. After the fall she was approached by a Col. (?) Black (an Englishman) an officer in the Mexican service) who sheltered her from Mexican injury & took her in a buggy to Mr. Musquez, a merchant in town, where she staid till next day, when she was conducted before Santa Anna who threatened to take her to Mexico with her child; when Almonte, his nephew, addressing his [*"him in"* intended?] English, pleaded for witness, saying he had been educated in N. O. & had experienced great kindness from Americans. Witness was thus permitted to depart to her home in Gonzales. Col. Travis commanded the Fort. She [*The*] only man witness saw killed was a man named Walker from Nacidoches, who was bayonetted & shot. She knew John Garnet from Gonzales, who she is certain was killed though she did not see it. After her removal to Musquez's, she expressed a wish to visit the scene of carnage, but was informed by the people of the house that it would not be permitted as the enemy was then burning the dead bodies—and in confirmation thereof, she was shown a smoke in the direction of the Alamo.

She knew Col. Bowie & saw him in the Fort, both before & after his death. He was sick before & during the fight, and had even been expected to die.—

Col. Crockett was one of the 3 men who came into the Fort during the seige & before the assault. He was killed, she believes.

A negro man named Joe, was in the Fort, & was the slave & body-servant of Col. Travis. After the fall of the Alamo, Jo was forced by the Mexicans at the point of the bayonet to point out to them the bodies of Col. Travis & Col. Crockett among the heaps of dead—Jo was the only negro in the Fort. The witnesse's infant was the only child in the fort. The witness & the two Mexican women already mentioned were the only women in the fort.

The witness has had no children in her present marriage.

1.2.9.   Susanna Hannig (Dickinson), interview, c. September 1877.

Hannig, Mrs. Susanna. n.d. (September 16–30, 1877). Adjutant General (RG-401), General Correspondence, 8/1/1877–3/16/1878, TSLA.

On the evening previous to the massacre, Col Travis asked the command that if any desired to escape, now was the time, to let it be Known, & to step out of the ranks. But one stepped out. His name to the best of my recollection was Ross. The next morning he was missing—During the final engagement one Milton, jumped over the ramparts & was killed—

Col. Almonte (Mexican) told me that the man who had deserted the evening before had also been Killed & that if I wished to satisfy myself of the fact that I could see the body, still lying there, which I declined.

Mr[s]. S. A. Hannig

1.2.10. Susanna Hannig (Dickinson), interview and photograph, March 14, 1878.

San Antonio Express. February 24, 1929. Society and Fashions, 1.

SURVIVED ALAMO MASSACRE; HER FIRST PICTURE IN PRINT
Dusty Attic Brings Forth Epic Story of Mrs. Dickinson.
Her Photo Found by History Professor.

From a dusty attic and the dime print of an old newspaper, published 50 years ago, there has come to light a letter written by the late Charles W. Evers, journalist, of Northern Ohio, in which a story of more than passing interest to San Antonio is recounted as another anniversary of her historic day of days, March 6, 1836, draws near.

Mr. Evers, along with other interesting experiences of a trip he was making in Southwest Texas in the '70s, tells of an interview he had with Mrs. Dickinson, who with her little child were the only white survivors of the Alamo massacre. A copy of Mr. Evers' published letter, originally written to his own newspaper in Ohio, has come into the possession of his daughter, Mrs. May Evers Pumphrey of San Antonio. Mrs. Pumphrey has also obtained an authentic picture of Mrs. Dickinson, through the courtesy of Dr. Charles W. Ramsdell, department of history, University of Texas, whose wife is a descendant of Mrs. Dickinson. This picture appears for the first time in print with the following excerpts from the letter, which are self-explanatory:

Austin, Texas, March 14, 1878.

". . . For one of the most pleasing incidents of my stay in Austin I am indebted to Col. Dupre, editor of the Austin Statesman, who kindly drove out with me two miles on a short visit to one of the most historic and to me interesting women of today. I refer to Mrs. Dickinson, now Mrs. J. W. Hannig, the only white survivor of the Alamo massacre, over forty years ago. We were made welcome at her beautiful home, which is on one of those commanding locations for which Austin is noted, overlooking the city and surrounding country. . . .

"Mrs. Hannig is an intelligent woman of excellent memory, and is perhaps not far from 60 years of age, although but few gray hairs are yet noticeable on her head. She engaged readily in conversation about that dark episode in her history which robbed her of her husband and partially of her reason for a time. As she conversed she seemed at times to stop as if in a sudden reverie or dream and I fancied I saw almost a wild light dancing in her eyes for a moment, and it would not be strange, for her recital of the events of that awful day will excite the most stolid listener. If Mrs. Hannig was so inclined or if her circumstances required it (happily they do not) she could go on the lecture platform and draw crowded houses in any city in the United States.

"She expressed a wish to see Frank Mayo, whom she heard was playing 'Davy Crockett' in Texas. She was, of course, well acquainted with Crockett and saw the noble manhood and devotion of himself and comrades through all those eventful 13 days preceding the final, bloody culmination. Her husband, Lieutenant Dickinson, acted during the siege as a sort of nurse and doctor among the men, and she often aided him in caring for the sick and wounded. She was then a young woman and had a child one or two years old, which some writers have stated was killed in his father's arms: This statement, she says, is incorrect, as well as the story that some of the Texans begged for quarter. She says that only one man, named Wolff [?], asked for quarter, but was instantly killed. The wretched man had two little boys, aged 11 and 12 years. The little fellows came to Mrs. Dickinson's room, where the Mexicans killed them, and a man named Walker, and carried the boys' bodies out on their bayonets.

"The room had become dark with smoke and to this circumstance, and the intervention of the Mexican colonel, Almonte, who was educated in New Orleans, and could speak English, and who drove the blood-thirsty Mexicans from her room, she feels indebted for her life. She was shot through the leg between the knee and ankle, but her little child was unhurt. The last she ever saw of her husband he rushed into the room and said, "My dear wife, they are coming over the wall, we are all lost!" He embraced her and the babe, saying "May God spare you both!" then drew his sword and went out. His body when found was riddled with bullets, and later burned by the inhuman victors with the rest of the slain.

"Mrs. Dickinson's escape was almost as thrilling as her capture. Santa Anna tried to persuade her to go to Mexico and take the child. He seemed fearful of the effect of her horrible story among the Texans, and he seemed also afraid to murder her. She states that when she came to her right mind and the reality of her situation stared her in the face, she broke down with grief and for several days her emotion was beyond control.

"Finally, under the persuasion of Almonte, Santa Anna, at her own earnest solicitation, consented to send her, under escort to her friends in the direction of Goliad. When out of the camp a few miles the cowardly Mexican cavalry deserted her, probably fearing the vengeance of Deaf Smith and his scouts. She made her way through the prairie on a pony, carrying the child, scarcely knowing where she was going as the country was entirely wild, when to her great fright a human being raised his head from the tall grass and spoke to her. It was the negro, Ben [sic], Colonel Travis' servant. He had escaped from the Mexicans and was nearly frightened to death lest the mounted woman might prove to be a Mexican who would recapture him. Ben was overjoyed to find Mrs. Dickinson and trudged along beside the pony, but would take to the tall grass every time any suspicious circumstance occurred. While on the journey they saw two horsemen in the distance, Ben took to the grass and urged Mrs. Dickinson to do so, saying they were Comanches, but she refused to turn aside, declaring she would as soon perish one way as another. As the horsemen approached Ben discovered that they rode with martingales and again he became wild with joy knowing they were white men. It proved to be Deaf Smith and Captain Carnes of the scouts. General Houston had heard the cannonade and sent his scouts to reconnoiter and report. She told me that General Houston wept like a child as he held her hand and heard the terrible fate of the brave defenders of the Alamo.

"I can convey nothing of the interest given to this story by Mrs. Hannig with all its thrilling details. To the credit of the State of Texas it may be said that this widow of a brave soldier was remembered with a magnificent gift in land, and it is my humble wish that she be spared many long years to enjoy her beautiful, peaceful home."

C. W. E.

Mrs. Dickinson's home in Austin stood on what is now the corner of Duval and East 32d Street. A lovely, modern house occupies the site at this time.

[*Two photos are here reproduced of the front of the Alamo and Mrs. Dickinson, with the following inscriptions:*]

The Alamo. The lower window on the right opens into the little room occupied by Mrs. Dickinson during the siege.

Mrs. Dickinson, from an old ambrotype belonging to one of her descendants in Austin, Texas.

1.2.11.   Susanna Hannig (Dickinson), interview, 1881.

Daily Express. April 28, 1881. 4. San Antonio.
A heavily edited version of this account was published as an obituary a few years later when Susan Hannig died and was reprinted in Brogan (1922).

THE SURVIVOR OF THE ALAMO
After a Lapse of Forty-Five Years Visits the Old Scene.
How the Cradle of Texas Liberty Was Rocked,
and How the Lone Star State Was Born.

THE EXPRESS representative yesterday enjoyed a most pleasant visit to the Alamo. It was not his first visit there by any means. The grey walls of the old structure have been familiar to him for many years, but the visit yesterday was rendered the more enjoyable from the fact that the party with whom the reporter made this visit was quite a noted one. It consisted of Mrs. Susan J. Hannig, of Austin, the only survivor of the massacre at the fall of the Alamo; Mrs. Rebecca Black, the grand-niece of Deaf Smith, the famous Texas spy; Col. H. R. Andrews, vice-president of the G. H. & S.A. railway, and lady; Bishop Quintard, of Tennessee; Dean Richardson, of St. Mark's cathedral, and two little nieces of Mrs. Hannig.

AN ERRONEOUS IMPRESSION
exists, which is that the Alamo had no survivor. Thermopylae's field of blood left one man to tell the story of the terrible struggle—how Spartan courage met the hosts of Xerxes, and it is said that the Alamo left no one to tell the story of her fall. This is correct, so far as manly courage goes, but there was a brave woman left to give to the present the details of its horrors. Her name is Mrs. Hannig. Some have doubted that this was true—that Mrs. Hannig was really at the Alamo during that immortal contest when Travis, Crockett and Bowie fell, and the name of the Alamo became perpetuated to all ages. But those who are skeptical on this point would doubt no more should they accompany the aged lady to the scene, and hear her tell of the bloody struggle that marked the experience of her presence there in 1836.

AFTER A LONG ABSENCE,
indeed, after the lapse of forty-five years, Mrs. Hannig yesterday returned to the old scene. She is a Tennessean by birth, is now sixty-six years of age, and when the Alamo fell lost her husband, Capt. Dickinson. Just before the Mexicans arrived, headed by Santa Anna, she was, together with her child, at the Musquiz house, near Main Plaza. The enemy appeared first in swarms early in the morning in the southwestern suburbs of the city. Their forces were from ten to thirteen thousand strong. As soon as they were announced to be coming, her husband rode up to the door of her abode and called to her to seize her child and take refuge in the Alamo. She mounted the bare back of the horse he rode, behind his saddle, and holding her child between her left arm and breast, soon reached the old church. An apartment was assigned her, while her husband turned away, after an embrace and a kiss, and an eternal adieu, to meet his obligations to his fellowmen and his country. By this time

THE MEXICAN BUGLES WERE SOUNDING
the charge of battle, and the cannon's roar was heard to reverberate throughout the valley of the San Antonio. But about one hundred and sixty sound persons were in the Alamo, and when the enemy appeared, overwhelmingly, upon the environs of the city to the west, and about where the International depot now stands, the Noble Travis called up his men, drew a line with his sword and said: "My soldiers, I am going to meet the fate that becomes me. Those who will stand by me, let them remain, but those who desire to go, let them go—and who crosses the line that I have drawn, *shall* go!" The scene is represented by Mrs. Hannig to have been grand—in that its location was above the results and influences of ordinary sentiment and patriotism, and bore the plain tige [*sic*] of that divinity of principle which characterizes the acts of the truly noble and the brave.

THE HEROES DEFIED THE MEXICANS,
though the former were but a handful and the aztec horde came on like the swoop of a whirlwind. Organized into divisions, they came in the form of a

semi-circle that extended from northeast to southwest, but the strongest attack was from about where the Military plaza is and from a division that marched up from the direction of the Villita. Three times they were repulsed, and the two cannon, planted high upon the ramparts, carried dismay with their belches of fire and lead. There was indeed a resolution to

BATTLE TILL THE END

And that fated end came, and brought with it horrors of which even the vivid conception of Crockett could not have dreamed. Mrs. Hannig says there was no second story to the Alamo at that time—it was all one floor. She can give but a little of the struggle, as she was in

A LITTLE DARK ROOM

in the rear of the building. The party yesterday entered this apartment, and even with a candle could scarcely see each other's faces. The old lady recognized almost every stone, however, and the arch overhead and the corners she said, with tears in her eyes, came back as vividly to memory as though her experiences of yore had been but yesterday. She showed the reporter where her couch had stood, and the window through which she peeped to see the blood of noble seeping into the ground, and the bodies of heroes lying cold in death. It was in this room that she saw

THE LAST MAN FALL,

and he was a man named Walker, who had often fired the cannon at the enemy. Wounded, he rushed into the room and took refuge in a corner opposite her own. By this time the Alamo had fallen and the hordes of Santa Anna were pouring over its ramparts, through its trenches and its vaults. The barbarous horde followed the fated Walker, and, as Mrs. Hannig describes the scene, "they shot him first, and then they stuck their bayonets into his body and raised him up like the farmer does a bundle of fodder with his pitchfork when he loads his wagon." Then she says they dropped the body. They were all bloody, and crimson springs coursed the yard. The old lady says she doesn't know how it all happened, yet she tells a great deal. What became of her husband, Al Marion Dickinson, she cannot tell, but saw him last when he went from her presence with gun in hand to die for his country. She says that for a while

SHE FEARED HER OWN FATE,

but soon was assured by an English colonel in the Mexican army that the Mexicans were not come to kill women but to fight men. Through the intervention of Almonte she was permitted to leave the city on a horse and carry her child with her. Before she left, however, she was conveyed back to the Musquiz place, her home before the time that she was a widow, and the terrible fate which met the followers of Travis, Bowie and Crockett came on. After leaving on the horse, she proceeded a short distance beyond the Salado, when she met with Travis's servant, who had escaped from the guard and was lurking in the brush. The servant recognized her and followed after her. It may be here remarked, incidentally, that there were in the Alamo at its fall about seventy five men who had been wounded in the fight with Cos, and they were all killed, outright, in spite of their pleadings. The servant of Travis followed her for some time, and when about fifteen miles distant three men were observed approaching. The heart of the woman did not quail, but the servant feared Indians. Said she, under these circumstances: "This is a bald prairie, and if it is an enemy we must meet them face to face." But the apprehensions of the party were assuaged when it was discovered that the dreaded forms were Deaf Smith, Robert E. Handy and Capt. Karnes, sent out by Gen. Sam. Houston to ascertain the condition of the garrison of the Alamo. It was a meeting of friends, and soon Mrs. Dickinson, now Mrs. Hannig, reached Gonzales. Her subsequent history would require too much space to be given.

THE REVIEW OF THE ALAMO
was truly interesting, and the reporter could not keep pace with her recitals of experiences there in the long ago. It was asked whether the men who defended the Alamo were drunk, as some have published, when the fight came on, covertly to defeat the effect of the noblest of human contests for liberty. Mrs. Hannig declared that any such assertion would be an insult to common patriotism, and condemned it. She had never seen either Travis, Crockett or Bowie under an liquored influence, and deprecated any impression of such nature as might come abroad. At the time of the fatal rencounter [sic], all were ready for the fray, and all prepared to die for the nationality of the republic of Texas.

TRUE WOMANLY COURAGE
is exemplified by the conduct of Mrs. Hannig. She loved her own, and that was the child she hugged to her bosom. Her life had been endangered, and they wanted to take her child away from her, but she would not concede, and so she subjected herself to trials, looking consequences squarely in the face, and knowing the firmness would be bound to bring about her ultimate vindication.

A FEW PLEASANT MOMENTS
were spent by the party after the old Alamo had been inspected, and its scenes revived by the only present survivor, when Mr. Grenet's best was produced—not his best beer—but his best of Mumm's celebrated wine. And when this little party dissolved, it was with more than one regret, and will never be forgotten.

1.2.12. Susanna Hannig (Dickinson), interview, c. 1883.

Green, Rena Maverick, ed. 1921. *Memoirs of Mary A. Maverick, arranged by Mary A. Maverick and Her Son Geo. Madison Maverick.* 135–36. San Antonio: Alamo Printing Co.
Entry starts with the unclear line "gal one Maverick 4 30 Hill"

MRS DICKINSON'S STORY OF THE "FALL OF THE ALAMO."
Mrs. Dickinson told Dean Richardson of St Marks Episcopal Church the following story of the "Fall of the Alamo", several times; once when the transfer of the Alamo property from the Church to the State was about to be made (1883). At this time, she walked with him and a party of others to an inner room in the Alamo, and pointed it out as the one in which she and the Mexican women were asked to stay, and where they were when the Alamo fell.

The first attack of the Mexicans was over, and all seemed peaceful, when one day Lieutenant Dickinson came hurriedly up to their home on Main Plaza, saying:

"Give me the baby; jump on behind me and ask me no questions."

They galloped down to the crossing, at the point where the "Mill Bridge" now is, but not in time to escape being fired at by the incoming Mexicans: however, they succeeded in crossing and hastened over to the Alamo.

Mrs. Dickinson said she saw no fighting—only the noise of the battle reaching her and the few Mexican women inside the Alamo.

On the day of the fall, Sunday, her husband kissed her good-bye in the morning, and she never saw him again.

Probably she and the Mexican women, who were her companions, saw the bayoneting of the last American; when the shooting was over, a soldier crawled into the room where they were, not to seek refuge, but to carry out an order previously given, and generally understood, which was that if the garrison fell someone was to try to fire the powder supply; and this man named Evans, wounded and spent with weariness, was killed while making his painful way to the powder room.

One of the Mexican officers, always thought by Mrs. Dickinson to be General Almonte, Chief of Staff to Santa Anna, who spoke broken English, stepped to the door of the room in which the women were, and asked:

"Is Mrs. Dickinson here?"

As she feared to answer and kept quiet, he repeated:

"Is Mrs. Dickinson here? Speak out, for it is a matter of life and death."

Then she answered, telling who she was, and he took her in charge over to Main Plaza. Here she and her child were held and cared for some days, when she was given a horse and a bag of provisions and told to go. She and her baby and a colored manservant journeyed safely eastward to the town of Washington, then the Capital, where she lived some years, later returning to visit in San Antonio.

1.2.13.   Susanna Dickinson, narrative, ca. 1901.

Burleson, Dr. Rufus C. (probable author) N.d. (c. 1901). "MRS. DICKENSON." Typed manuscript in the Williams (Amelia Worthington) Papers, CAH.

This appears to be a manuscript copy of "The Old Guard" biography of Susanna Dickinson in Georgia J. Burleson. 1901. *The Life and Writings of Rufus C. Burleson.* 735-41. He is also named as the author by an accompanying letter of Samuel Asbury to Amelia Williams in the same collection of documents. There is no significant variation between the copy used here and the published work.

MRS. DICKENSON
The Heroine of the Alamo

The Heroine of the Alamo and her husband, Lieutenant Dickenson, were born in Pennsylvania and brought up in the "City of Brotherly Love". But when the cry came from 60,000 Texans, struggling for freedom against 8,000,000 Mexicans, Lieutenant Dickenson said, "I must respond to freedom's call". His young wife said, "I will go with you my husband". [*The paper continues with a description of events in Texas leading up to and the start of the siege, with similar sentiment.*]

. . . During these thirteen days and nights our Heroine of the Alamo displayed a courage that eclipsed the heroism of the Spartan mothers. For though her little daughter was only six weeks old, she cooked the food, prepared the bandages, washed and bound up the wounds, and by her words and heroic bearing cheered on the soldiers. What mother on earth ever was called to listen alternately to the roar of the connon [*sic*] and the groans of the dying and the pitiful cry of her innocent babe? She saw the gashed bosom of her husband pouring out his life blood. She caught his dying accent:

"God, bless you, wife, I am dying; take care of our babe". She has often told me of the solemn hour when the heroic Travis drew a long line with his sword and said, "Now soldiers, every man that is resolved never to surrender, but if need be to die fighting, let him cross over this line," and the 182 heroes leaped over the line at once. But the heroic Bowie, lying on his pallet of straw emaciated with consumption, could not stand up, but cried aloud, "Boys, do take me over that line, for I intend to die fighting," and his companions carried him over amid the wildest shouts of applause.

[*A general description of the morning of March 6 is then given, without anything specifically from Dickinson.*]

At twilight's solemn hour our Heroine with a woman's instinct took her babe in her arms and a picher [*sic*] of water, and visited the bleeding soldiers to see if any dying hero needed a cup of water or wished to send some message of love to mother or wife or sister, far away. She found the dead bodies of Travis, Bonham and Bowie, all weltering in blood. She found Crockett lying dead in a little confessional room in the Northeast corner of the Alamo, with a huge pile of dead Mexicans lying around him.

The horrors and outrages of that night exceeded in blackness the horrors of the day. But let them not blacken the pages of history but remain hid till the Judgment Day, when God will have them and all the dark deeds of earth painted and hung up in the Judgment halls to rebuke the folly of those men who say there ought to be no hell.

[*The narrative continues with postbattle events and tells of Susanna Dickinson being sent to Houston to spread terror among the Texans. The author also gives an account of his ministry and describes meeting Mrs. "Bells" and later Hannig, formerly Dickenson, in 1849 and again in 1862. These stories do not, however, add anything of significance to the story of the Alamo.*]

1.2.14.   Dickinson grandchildren, interviews, c. 1929.

Williams, Amelia. April 1934. A critical study of the siege of the Alamo and of the personnel of its defenders. *Southwestern Historical Quarterly* 37:16–17, n. 42; 32, n. 66; 79, n. 1; 109, n. 7; 171–72, n. 32; 258; 271.

Williams interviewed Susanna Dickinson's grandchildren, Susan Sterling and A. D. Griffith, who passed on oral information from their grandmother. These selections are from multiple chapters of Williams's dissertation and several issues of the *Southwestern Historical Quarterly (SWHQ),* which means that some of the repetitions and inconsistencies (as in the spelling of Susanna's last name—see section 4.4.4) because of the separation in text and in the time of writing are not as obvious in the original. Most of the quotes are footnotes from *SWHQ* 37; the excerpts are preceded by the page numbers on which they appear and the original footnote numbers. In these quotations, first person is typically Williams and third person refers to the grandchildren, unless they are quoting their grandmother, Susanna. Another reference to the grandchildren is in Williams and Barker (1938, 1:362–65).

[37:16–17]

[42]It seems to be pretty generally agreed by historians that Bowie's malady was typhoid-pneumonia; ten different authorities have been found who make the statement. "Mrs. Alsbury's Account of the Alamo Siege," to be found in *Ford's Journal* (MS.) [*document 1.4.1 below*], University of Texas Archives, says that when Bowie realized that he had typhoid fever, he had his cot carried to a "small room of the low barracks on the south side," hoping to prevent the spread of the disease among the soldiers of the Alamo; but she also states that at "lucid moments when the fever was somewhat abated, his soldiers would bring his cot to the main building, where he would talk with them and urge that they remember that Travis was now their commander." This same story was told to me by Mrs. Susan Sterling who had it from her grandmother, Mrs. Dickinson.

[37:32]

[66]Vincente Filisola, *Guerra de Tejas* (1849), II, 9–14. Here Filisola does not record Travis's proposal to surrender as an official report, but rather as a rumor. Mrs. Dickinson, Morphis, *History of Texas*, 175, says "that on the night of the fourth of March a Mexican woman deserted us, and going over to the enemy informed them of our inferior numbers." Mrs. Susan Sterling, the granddaughter of Mrs. Dickinson, told me that her grandmother always said that this Mexican "woman traitor" was Mrs. Horace Alsbury, and that Mrs. Dickinson would never remain in the same house with Mrs. Alsbury—"not even for an hour"—in post-revolutionary days. Mrs. Sterling lived in Austin, Texas, until August, 1929, when she died at the age of 83. My findings concerning Mrs. Alsbury will be given at another place in the narrative.

[37:79]

[1]See Mrs. Alsbury's "Account of the Siege of the Alamo," to be found in John Ford's Journal, Archives of the University of Texas. In my talks with Mrs. Susan Sterling, she told me that her grandmother, Mrs. Dickinson, verified Mrs. Alsbury's statements concerning Bowie's influence over his men. [*This note is in reference to Bowie having his cot taken to his men, as noted in 37:16–17, n. 42, above.*]

[37:109]

. . . Mrs. Dickenson, one of the survivors of the massacre, told that Colonel Crockett was very popular with all the soldiers at the Alamo and after the siege began, constantly cheered and encouraged the men. She also said that Crockett often "played tunes on his fiddle" when the fighting was not brisk; and that sometimes he played in competition with John McGregor's bag-pipes.[7]

[7]Mrs. Susan Sterling, a granddaughter of Mrs. Dickenson, lived in Austin till August, 1929. She told me that in her childhood she spent much time with her grandmother, who told and retold to her many stories of the Alamo. The one story that never failed to amuse her was the account of the musical contest between David Crockett and John McGregor.

[37:171–72]

[32]Mr. A. D. Griffith, a grandson of Mrs. Dickenson, now lives at Austin. Until August, 1929, his sister, Mrs. Susan Sterling, lived with him. She is now dead. It has been my privilege to visit these old people—both past eighty—and to hear from them some of the stories their grandmother was wont to tell them concerning the Alamo disaster. Mrs. Sterling spent most of her young life in her grandmother's home and could retell many of the stories that she had heard from Mrs. Dickenson. Mrs. Dickenson always thought that she owed her life to the intercessions in her behalf of her friend, Mrs. Ramón Musquiz. On March 4, after Santa Anna had held his council of war, the population of Bexar who were friendly to the Texans were greatly grieved and terribly excited and frightened,

because of Santa Anna's determination to annihilate the fortress. Ramón Musquiz was the political chief at Bexar, a Mexican official, but a friend to the Texans. Mrs. Musquiz and Mrs. Dickenson had been intimate friends, so upon learning of the inevitable disaster that would befall the Alamo, Mrs. Musquiz went herself to Santa Anna and pleaded with him to spare Mrs. Dickenson and her baby. After considerable hesitation he promised her that no woman in the fort should be harmed intentionally. So after the men had all been slain, an officer came to the church where the women were and asked: "Is there a Mrs. Dickenson here?" At first Mrs. Dickenson feared to answer, but the officer continued, "If you value your life speak up." She then stepped forward with her child in her arms. Some soldiers, who a short time before had killed Jacob Walker at her feet, started to seize her, but the officer commanded, "Let her alone, the General has need of her." Nevertheless, as she followed the officer across the church, a shot, fired at random, or intentionally, took effect in the calf of her right leg, causing a very bloody and painful wound. At Santa Anna's headquarters, where she was carried, this wound was carefully dressed and tended. Santa Anna seemed to admire the little girl, Angelina, and expressed deep compassion for her, begging that he be permitted to adopt her and educate her as one of his own children. He repeatedly urged this, arguing that without husband, and impoverished as she was, the mother would not be able to train and educate the child as she deserved to be, while as his daughter she would have every advantage that money could procure. Needless to say the widowed mother scorned such a proposal declaring that she would "crawl and work her fingers to the bone to support the babe, but that she had rather see the child starve than given into the hands of the author of so much horror."

[*37:258, entry under Alamo defender Robert Evans*]
. . . Mrs. Susan Sterling told me that her grandmother, Mrs. Dickerson, said that when the fighting came into the old chapel Robert Evans seized a torch and tried to set fire to several hundred pounds of powder that was stored in the little ante-room on the north side of the chapel, but a Mexican officer saw what he was trying to do and shot him dead when he was within a foot of the powder. The powder was some that Cos had left at the Alamo in December, 1835. It was so badly damaged that it was useless in guns, but Travis and his men had agreed to explode it in the event that the fort was taken by the Mexicans. Morphis, *History of Texas*, 138, tells this same story. Mrs. Sterling said that her grandmother described Robert Evans as black-haired, blue-eyed, nearly six feet tall, and always merry.

[*37:271, entry under Alamo defender John McGregor*]
. . . In 1926, Mrs. Susan Sterling, a granddaughter of Mrs. Dickerson, retold to me many of the stories that she as a child and young woman had heard from her grandmother concerning the fall of the Alamo. One story that always amused her was Mrs. Dickerson's account of John McGregor and his bagpipes.

She said that when the fighting would lull, and the Texans had time for rest and relaxation, John McGregor and David Crockett would give a sort of musical concert, or rather a musical competition, to see which one could make the best music, or the most noise—David with his fiddle, and John with his bagpipes. She said McGregor always won so far as noise was concerned, for he made "strange, dreadful sound" with his queer instrument.

1.2.15. Susanna Hannig (Dickinson, or Dickerson), interview, c. 1876.

Elgin, John E. September 23, 1936. "Reminiscences of the Story of the Alamo." Typed manuscript, autographed and notarized, in De Zavala (Adina Emilia) Papers, CAH.

REMINISCENCES OF THE STORY OF THE ALAMO
By Captain John E. Elgin.

I had known Mr. Hanig [sic], he was my most intimate friend, I succeeded him as Grand Commander of Knight Templars of Texas; and was well acquainted with Mrs. Hanig, (the former Mrs. Almeron Dickinson, widow of Lieutenant Dickinson who was killed at the Alamo on March 6, 1836). I was a frequent visitor at the Hannig home at Austin, and have vivid recollections of Mrs. Hannig giving me gingercake and other goodies when I was a boy. I had remembered hearing Mrs. Hannig speak of her experience in the Alamo during the Siege and Fall in 1836.

In later years, in 1876, when I was leaving for a trip to San Antonio, I called on Mrs. Hannig and asked her to give me some details about the Alamo as I intended to visit it and wanted to reconstruct for myself the picture of that memorable event.

I asked her to tell me about James Bowie. She said she never saw James Bowie after he was taken sick—that he was in another part of the Alamo—she understood in the hospital of the Fort—in the upper southwest corner room of the main two-story stone building of the Fort. She was in one of the north rooms of the Church with her babe,—with some of the other women and children. Her husband, Lieutenant Dickinson, was in charge of one of the cannon placed on top of the rocks at the rear of the Church, and which were fired over the roofless wall to the east. The body of the roofless Church was filled with stones and debris on which large trees were growing. Mrs. Dickinson said that she came out of her room several times during the siege and climed [sic] over the rocks up to her husband's position at the top of the east wall of the Church for a visit with him. She remembered distinctly, she said, seeing the enemy's cavalry moving about in every direction.

She said she could tell me nothing of the fighting at the time of the assault, as she was huddled with her babe in one of the north rooms of the Church and could see nothing of the main conflict, but that she heard the din of the battle, the shrieks of the wounded and dying which were terrifying and paralyzing.

She also told me of Lieutenant Dickinson jumping down off the rocks in the Church and rushing into the room and embracing and kissing here and the babe "goodbye" saying: "The Mexicans have broken into the patio, I must go and help the boys." She never saw him again.

As the firing ceased, some Mexican soldiers rushed into her room, she said, snatched off the blanket with which she had covered herself and babe, and seeing no men hidden there, rushed out again. After a few minutes other men, with officers, entered, and found her and led her out of the Fort.

Later, Santa Anna himself, she told me, mounted her on a horse with all the politeness of a French dancing master, and sent her to Gonzales with her babe. He gave the child a bright Mexican silver dollar.

Pablo Diez, an old Mexican whom I knew well, and whose little place I had bought, told me that when he was a boy about 17 he lived in the country. Hearing the cannonading in March 1836, when it ceased, he came to the town to see what had happened. He was impressed and forced to go out and cut brush to be used to burn the bodies of the Alamo heroes. Pablo Diez also told me that each of the children who had been in the Alamo were given a bright silver dollar by Santa Anna.

OTHER INTERESTING MATTER.

Judge A. W. Terrell, of Austin, told me that the Alamo ditch was opened July 4th, 1776. He said that he found this statement in some old manuscripts he was studying in a trial of a case in San Antonio, in which he was substituting for Judge Devine. When the 4th of July arrived, and the trial of the case was not completed, a discussion was had as to whether or not a recess should be taken for the 4th. It seems the attorneys could not agree. Judge Terrell then made the statement that in the old manuscripts he had discovered the statement that the old Alamo ditch was opened on that date in 1776, and inasmuch as this was an anniversary of great importance on many counts, he ruled that the recess should be taken in celebration.

I was told that the Alamo Lodge, York Rite Masons, was organized in the main, two-story stone building of the Alamo Fort in its southwest corner—in the room used as the hospital of the Fort, in 1836—Under the tower room where the flag floated. In the year. [*sic*]

John E. Elgin

Subscribed and sworn to before me at San Antonio, Bexar County, Texas, on the 23rd day of September, A.D. 1936.

Mina Derrick

[*Seal*]   Notary Public in and for
Bexar Co., Texas

1.2.16.   Susanna Dickinson, oral tradition, n.d.

McGregor, T. H., to Ed Kilman. January 21, 1942. Kemp (Louis Wiltz) Papers, CAH. Typed transcript.

This relates to an artifact, a ring reportedly given to Angelina Dickinson by Travis, now on display at the Alamo. Gale Shiffrin (1992) published a narrative of the history of the ring and the rather sad life of Angelina.

T. H. McGREGOR
Lawyer
506 Littlefield Bldg.
Austin, Texas
January 21, 1942.

Mr. Ed. Kilman,
c/o Houston Post,
Houston, Texas.
My dear Ed:

Sorry that I missed you when in my office inquiring about the Travis ring.

I am writing you at once because it seems you were mis-informed as to the attitude of the Daughters of the Texas Revolution as to this ring. It has never been tendered them, they have never refused it for any reason, nor commented on its origin.

The tradition of the ring is that it belonged to Travis, and that at the fall of the Alamo it was tied with a string around the neck of the Babe of the Alamo, the Dickinson girl. Prior to the Civil War she lived in Galveston and was friendly with Jim Britton who at that time was connected with the operation of a train. She gave the ring to Britton. Britton had been raised at Lebanon, Tennessee, and has been an associate and close friend of Paul F. Anderson, a brother of my Mother and the late Mrs. S. S. Ashe of Houston. On the breaking out of the War Anderson and Britton returned to Lebanon when Anderson became a Captain and Britton a Lieutenant of the "Cedar Shags", a company in Baxter Smith's Fourth Tennessee Regiment which was brigaded with the Texas Rangers. Anderson afterwards became a Colonel and Britton a Captain in the Confederate Army. Anderson had a younger brother who was a Junior Lieutenant under Britton[,] DeWitt Anderson. Britton gave the Travis ring to DeWitt Anderson who wore it until his death in 1902 at Marianna, Arkansas, at which time the ring came into my possession. I have heard DeWitt Anderson, Captain S. S. Ashe, and others frequently speak of the history of this ring. After the War Colonel Paul Anderson died at Helena, Arkansas, in 1878 of yellow fever. Britton returned to Texas, lived at Sherman, and formed a partnership with Colonel Lyons, father of the late Cecil Lyons of Sherman. They became contractors and erected many buildings in Texas, among others, the Court House in Harris County, which was replaced by the present Court House in Houston.

Before the present Railroad Commission was created Britton was appointed by a governor of Texas—which one I do not remember—as a perfunctory Railroad Commissioner. He resigned because he said he had nothing to do and no power to do it with. He died in Sherman, Texas, in the late 80's. He was either buried in Sherman or in Lebanon.

Several years ago Mrs. Golman of Austin, a Daughter of the Texas Revolution, knowing the history of this ring borrowed it from me and exhibited it in some way, with the details of which I am not familiar. She returned the ring to me as she had agreed to do and it was never either tendered to, commented upon or refused by the Daughters of the Texas Revolution. I gave the ring to my son, Douglas W. McGregor, U.S. District Attorney in Houston, with a statement as to its history. I know he will be glad to show you the ring.

With best regards, I am

Yours, etc.

T. H. McGregor

Commentary

Susanna Dickinson (1.2.1–1.2.16)

The first problem concerning Susanna Dickinson is the "true" version of her last name—Dickinson, Dickerson, and other variants have all been commonly used. Williams (1.2.14) changed her usage from the first to the second in the course of writing her dissertation because of additional evidence she found during her research. It is not at all a straightforward question to answer, especially since she was illiterate (as shown by the depositions, 1.2.4–1.2.6), and her accounts are secondhand at best. As they make a secondary but interesting ministudy, documents and analyses are discussed in a special section (4.4.4) below. Dickinson is typically used in this book only because it has been the most prevalent in published works.

The documents of Susanna Dickinson provide contradictory and inconsistent material. It is not known whether her memory was unclear from one interview to another, or whether the various interviewers used an excess of editorial license. This was perhaps more common in the nineteenth century than is acceptable by modern journalistic standards.

Certain key events or elements appear several times in this set of Dickinson interviews and depositions: being taken to the Alamo by her husband, staying in a small room, Walker's death, conversation after the Alamo's fall with an English-speaking person, and meeting with Travis's servant (euphemism for slave) after she was freed. It seems reasonable that these were particularly memorable events for a young mother coming through a battle and captured by an opposing army, and therefore it seems probable that these are authentic events.

The main nineteenth-century interviewers—James Morphis, in 1874 (1.2.7); the Adjutant General, in 1876 (1.2.8); Charles Evers, in 1878 (1.2.10); the reporter for the *Daily Express,* in 1881 (1.2.11); and Dean Richardson and Mary Maverick, in 1883 (1.2.12)—consistently give accounts of these key events. They are also supported by the Williams interviews with the Dickinson grandchildren (1.2.14). There can be little question (only Evers omits the story) that she remembered clearly the rush of Almaron Dickinson riding up to the house to fetch her as the Mexican forces entered San Antonio, and her riding horseback behind him to get into the Alamo. Nor can there be a question of her being in a room in the church during the fall; all the accounts agree on this. The impression that the room was small and dark seems vivid as well, especially in the haunting account of her visit to the Alamo in 1881. Every account also includes the killing of a defender in her room, four of the five identifying the individual as Walker.

These sources all agree, though not explicitly in Evers's account, that an English-speaking officer played a memorable role in Dickinson's postbattle experience. The details differ, however. In the Morphis interview, she was approached while in the Alamo by an English-speaking Mexican officer. The Adjutant General account and the *Daily Express* reporter have an English officer in the Mexican Army in the Alamo, and Almonte supporting her in front of Santa Anna. Evers makes no comment about the postfight inside the Alamo, but has Almonte persuading Santa Anna to release her. Finally, Richardson and Maverick have Almonte in the Alamo without an interview in front of Santa Anna. On the whole, it seems most likely that Susanna Dickinson, who had to be in fear of her life as the battle ended, had a sense of being saved by an English-speaking Mexican officer. We probably should credit Almonte with translating to Santa Anna on her behalf. It is less clear, but not improbable, that he or another English-speaking officer was the first to approach or rescue her after the fall.

Another consistent event, not in Morphis but included in Stiff (1840), is her meeting with Travis's servant or slave on the "bald prairie." He should likewise be memorable as the first companion from the Texan side that she'd had after the battle, and while she was defenseless in a desolate, uninhabited region.

Another detail noted by several sources (Morphis, Adjutant General, and the *Commonwealth* article in 1.3.4) is that the attack was twice repulsed, but the third time succeeded. It must be accepted from the descriptions and logic that Dickinson would not have been in a position to actually observe the Mexican attacks, but it is also probable that she could have deduced what was going on from the sounds—especially since she was very close to the chapel cannons. This consensus is strongly supported by the Elgin account (1.2.15) as well. Visual details, such as the assault troops carrying ladders, are much less likely to have come from her, unless she had heard some yelling about them during the attacks.

There are various details throughout the documents that are unsupported by a broad consensus, but that we may reasonably accept. For example, it is likely she was wounded (Morphis, Evers, Williams) while leaving the Alamo. Other accounts that may be considered reliable are those of Crockett playing his fiddle or violin (Morphis, Williams); that the Alamo had provisions for a month (Morphis, Adjutant General, confirming Travis's report on March 3, document 1.1.6, that he had twenty days' provisions); that numerous defenders were still recovering from wounds incurred while fighting Cos (Adjutant General, *Daily Express*); and that Santa Anna offered to care for Angelina (Adjutant General, Evers, Williams). More problematical is the entry of three spies into the Alamo three days before the fall (Morphis, Adjutant General), but one could speculate that this was all she knew of Gonzales's thirty-two men entering at that time.

Even the isolated elements, described in only one source, might be accurate, and perhaps accepted, as long as they are not contradictory to the main independent sources. Some examples include Warnell wanting to be out on the prairie rather than pent up in the Alamo, and Dickinson seeing the body of Crockett after the battle.

A particular caution, however, is the extent to which such a detail makes a good story. In this respect, the story from Richardson and Maverick of Evans being killed while trying to explode the powder supply seems a little too dramatic, as well as isolated from the other accounts, to be readily accepted. This incident appears to be a substitute for the death of Walker, which was described consistently in earlier accounts, and the fact that it was recorded only in one of the later interviews arouses suspicion. On the other hand, it was noted in the earliest newspaper accounts (4.1.1) for which she was a source and was supported by the Williams interviews of Susanna's grandchildren (1.2.14).

We should note her denial of perhaps the most bizarre story of the Alamo. Some Mexican (e.g., de la Peña, 2.9.1) and American accounts reported that in the final moments of the attack, her husband climbed to the top of the chapel with their son and leaped to his death. Houston's first reports (e.g., 3.5.2) did pick up the story from local Tejano sources, so we know the story circulated immediately after the battle. It continued to be repeated many times throughout the nineteenth century. For example, the local artist Theodore Gentilz repeated the story in his notes, and one of his paintings showed Dickinson and child being taken to Santa Anna and executed on the general's direct order.[1] No incontrovertible document known contradicts her statement that she only had a single daughter who survived the battle with her. Consequently, the "Dickinson leap" story is an example of a tale that has no justifiable basis and yet, probably due to the appeal of its dramatic elements, continued to have a life of its own.

Perhaps the most surprising of the more ambiguous elements in these documents are the inconsistencies in the last meeting with her husband. One would expect this to be one of the clearest memories, yet the sources do not agree. Morphis, Evers, and Elgin have Almaron rushing in for a final farewell after the Mexican Army was overrunning the walls. The *Daily Express* reporter has the last meeting on the first day of the siege, which is highly improbable. Richardson and Maverick record the last meeting on the morning of the fall but before the attack, while the Adjutant General doesn't note it at all. A possibility is that the sheer emotional trauma of her experiences overwhelmed her memory. Another possibility is that it might have simply been a neglected topic of discussion by the last three. Therefore, I would lean toward accepting a final scene something like that of Morphis and Evers, and the more matter-of-fact, less melodramatic description given by Elgin seems the most believable. Furthermore, it is possible that such a final farewell occurred. The outer part of the mission walls was overrun before the last stand in the chapel—where both of them were located and exactly as stated in the Elgin account—so there was a realistic opportunity for such a meeting.

There must be differences in the relative quality of the sources, which should caution one from answering these questions on a simple majority-rules basis. We can easily be frustrated with Edward Stiff (1.2.2) who, only a few years after the events, had repeated conversions with her but passed on almost no information. The reputed account of her minister, Dr. Burleson (1.2.13), has far more serious problems. The florid prose immediately suggests he was more interested in a dramatic narration than in forwarding facts given by Mrs. Belles/Hannig. But the strange story of Susanna Dickinson walking among the dead at twilight is so far removed from the possible events as to raise serious doubts about the whole narration—the battle was over in the morning, the bodies cremated by dusk, and where was the Mexican Army supposed to be while she was wandering around? This account must be labeled as totally unreliable.

Because he has been used extensively and uncritically, a more serious and difficult question is the reliability of James Morphis's details. He includes several details within his report of her interview that she would not have been a party to. It is unlikely she knew or even cared about (though she might have heard later) the number of Mexican troops, the number of cannons at the Alamo, the number of killed, or how the bodies of Travis and Bonham were found. There is no possibility that she observed the details of the final assault as Morphis states. It is, in fact, unclear at what point the Dickinson narration ends, the last first-person statement being that of observing Crockett lying dead. It is also far-fetched that she would express herself in terms like "inspired us with sanguine hopes of speedy relief, and thus animated the men to contend to the last." In all, Morphis must be used with much more caution than earlier writers, since he is clearly using other accounts and his own editorial flair to "improve" the narration.

An element in three of the accounts relates to a Mexican woman or women in the Alamo as well. Morphis has an unidentified woman deserting to the enemy and reporting the inferior numbers of defenders, and the Adjutant General identifies two women—Dr. Alsbury's wife and his sister-in-law—as escaping. This belief was passed on to Williams by Susanna's grandchildren. Richardson and Maverick give the Mexican women as Dickinson's companions through the siege and fall. It is hard to come to a firm conclusion about these versions, but weighing the relative unreliability of Morphis against the more sensible Richardson and Maverick version given at a later time, after Mrs. Alsbury's account was likely to be more widely known, gives weight to the latter. Susanna Dickinson might not have seen or noticed Mrs. Alsbury just before or after the fall, and therefore honestly believed—incorrectly—that Mrs. Alsbury had fled the Alamo. She may only have noticed the entry of a small number of the thirty-two Gonzales men, which implies she observed isolated events during the siege. In addition, that any possible deserter would have influenced Santa Anna's decision to attack is very open to question. A further discussion must wait until Mrs. Alsbury's account is presented (section 1.4).

It is difficult to make sense of some details. The Adjutant General commented that Mrs. Dickinson wished to return to the "scene of the carnage." Perhaps she expressed a wish to see her husband's body?

The deposition regarding Joshua G. Smith (1.2.1) has been frequently overlooked; only Williams and later Albert Curtis seem to have noted it.[2] It is of more general interest in that it records her name in 1837 as Williams (no relation to the scholar), which implies an early remarriage often overlooked in her biographies. It is also curious that the original "signature" is not an "X" for her mark, as on the later General Land Office depositions. It seems more likely that this document was a copy, though the signature of Patton appears original, than other possibilities, such as that the claim was fraudulent.

The depositions in the General Land Office are in a category of their own. They were done early, twenty years prior to most interviews, and have a practical, matter-of-fact tone that gives a sense of accuracy that the later interviews lack. Because of them, we know for a fact that Dickinson was illiterate. More importantly, we can see how clear her memory was by comparing the descriptions of James Rose in the depositions of 1853 and 1857. She did not know his first name in the first, but she did in the second. In the first deposition, she described his physical appearance as younger, perhaps not as heavy, and gave details of his complexion and eye color, whereas she described his face shape and speech mannerisms in the second. She clearly associated him with Crockett and identified him as a resident or visitor in her home prior to the siege. Finally, she provided us with the memorable image from Henry Warnell, and one of the few insights into the mental state of the defenders (which must have been a common feeling in the Alamo), "that he had much rather be out in the open prairie, than to be pent up in that manner."

Long after the other Dickinson documents, and ninety-three years after the event, Amelia Williams interviewed Dickinson's grandchildren. In most cases, these interviews stand to support common elements in earlier interviews: Walker's death, being saved by an English-speaking officer, being wounded in the leg, and Santa Anna offering to adopt Angelina. One particularly interesting new detail is the explanation that the appearance of the English-speaking officer was due to intervention by Musquiz with Santa Anna prior to the final assault. This is a believable explanation of why someone called for her by name after the battle had ended. Two additional stories supported were the Crockett-McGregor musical battles—with the fiddle losing to the bagpipes—and Bowie's interactions with his men while sick.[3]

The account recorded by Elgin in 1936 avoids the melodramatic prose of the nineteenth-century interviewers, while remaining consistent with relevant portions of the story. For example the description of cannons being on top of a ramp inside the chapel is not a commonly reported detail in 1936. Consequently, it is easier to accept the unique description of her visits to her husband during the siege at his position on top of the wall. As a whole, this account can be taken very seriously. The Pablo Diez mentioned by Elgin appears to be a different person from the one in the Díaz accounts below (3.7.2, 3.7.4).

The final document of the Dickinson collection (1.2.16) is an example of a long oral tradition. Confirming the validity of such traditions, in this case the history of the "Travis ring," on display at the Alamo (as well as the "Dickert rifle," in 4.4.5.1), presents the historian with special difficulties. First and foremost is the problem of checking any claims of facts. Another is the possibility of additions or distortions to the story as it was retold. Still another is that one of the people who were links in the story's narrative chain might have had ulterior motives to make more of the artifact than it deserved. On the other hand, much important history has been preserved only through oral tradition, and it has been shown that such traditions can be accurately passed down even for centuries, archeological verification of details in the Homeric stories being perhaps the most spectacular example. This particular tradition of the Travis ring has some specific counterpoints to these concerns. First, the story (and with it the ring) has a well-defined, believable, and partially verifiable provenance. The story (with the ring) passed from Susanna Dickinson to Angelina Dickinson to James Britton to his commanding officer Lt. DeWitt Anderson to nephew T. H. McGregor to son Douglas McGregor to the Alamo. Only the Britton-to-Anderson transition lacks an apparent reason as to how and why the ring was transferred. Another important point is that the ring was a gift, so there was not a financial incentive to elaborate the final story. Finally, it is not inconsistent with well-established facts. In summary, the story has neither fundamental proof that it is true nor fundamental problems that indicate it is false.

An important issue that can only be raised for now is the significance of the undated Adjutant General document (1.2.9) about the attempted escape of a defender named Ross, and the follow-up story in the *Daily Express* about Travis drawing a line in the sand to cross. This story will be examined after the introduction of the Rose documents (section 1.8).

Another vital document not yet presented is the first published account of the fall in the *Telegraph and Texas Register* on March 24, 1836 (4.1.1). Susanna Dickinson unquestionably was one of the key sources for this account, but one cannot estimate to what extent without seeing many more documents from other sources, particularly Joe (1.3) and Barsena and Bergara (3.4), along with the specifically Dickinson documents in this section (especially 1.2.8 and 1.2.11). Another thirdhand newspaper account is by William Parker, from the *Mississippi Free Trader and Natchez Gazette* of April 29, 1836 (4.1.6), and still another possible interview from 1838 was by Milledge Bonham (5.1.8.1).

A final issue is how Susanna Dickinson's horrible experiences might have affected her mental state and thereby her later memories. Evers states that the episode "robbed her of her husband and partially of her reason," and Elgin records that "she heard the din of the battle, the shrieks of the wounded and dying which were terrifying and paralyzing." A logical analysis of sources such as the above likely underestimates the difficulty for anyone to retain a clear and accurate recollection of such a situation. Dickinson observed very violent, bloody scenes in a fight in which her husband was killed. Few people likely would have retained the sane and sensible mental state implied in several of these accounts, and therefore we are lucky to have as much information as we do. Susanna Dickinson must have been unusually tough to have gone through such an emotional trauma and still have survived psychologically as well as she did.

1. Gentilz's notes on the "Dickinson leap" are on the same page as the Cruz y Arocha interview, document 3.6.1; the painting is reproduced in Kendall and Perry 1974.
2. Curtis 1961, 57.
3. The papers of Amelia Williams in the Center for American History have notes on the interviews with these two grandchildren in Alamo Research/Dickinson & Other Survivors, Williams (Amelia Worthington) Papers, CAH. The notes include some early history of Almaron Dickinson and his bride prior to the battle, information about the grandchildren, and some material concerning Mrs. Alsbury and Rose.

1.3.1.   Joe, newspaper report, 1836.

Commercial Bulletin. April 11, 1836. New Orleans.
Reprinted (without attribution) in the April 23, 1836, *Port-Gibson Correspondent.*

Extract of a letter from a friend to the Editor.

AT WHARTONS PLANTATION, 31st March, 1836.

The garrison of the Alamo of Bexar have immortalized themselves. Col. Travis, who commanded, was a man of transcendent talents. He has a little son 6, or 7 years of age, who will live, I hope, to avenge the death of his sire. The Hon. David Crockett died like a hero, surrounded by heaps of the enemy slain. Col. James Bowie was sick and unable to rise. He was slain in his bed: the enemy allowed him a grave—probably in consideration of his having been married to a Mexican lady, a daughter of the late Gov. Berrimundi. The enemy had made daily and nightly attacks upon the place for ten days. The garrison was exhausted by incessant watching; at last the enemy made a final assault with 4000 men, half an hour before daylight, on the morning of the 6th instant. It was dark, and the enemy were undiscovered until they were close to the walls, and before the sentinels had aroused the garrison, the enemy had gained possession of a part of the ramparts. The garrison fought like men who knew there was but brief space left them in which to avenge the wrongs of their country's possession. When driven from the walls by overwhelming numbers, they retired to the barracks, and fought hand to hand and man to man, until the last man was slain—no, there was one man yet left; a little man named Warner had secreted himself among the dead bodies, and was found when the battle was over, and the dead men being removed without the walls of the fort. He asked for quarter; the soldiers took took [sic] him to Santa Anna, who ordered him to be shot. The order was executed, and his body was taken out and burnt with the heroes who deserve as bright a remembrance as those who died on the pass of Thermopylae.

I learnt these facts from a negro boy, the servant of Col. Travis, whose life was spared—probably in consideration of his kindred blood. There was a woman in the fort—a wife of a Lieut. of artillery. She was taken, and suffered from the Mexican officers the most odious pollution that ever disgraced humanity. She barely escaped with life—but is diseased, and in a situation exciting pity and horror.

There is no tidings from Col. Fannin. Alas, that science and talents and bravery should fall before brute number! His wife is here with three infant daughters.

From your friend.

1.3.2. Joe, newspaper report, 1836.
Memphis Enquirer. April 12, 1836.
This is one of two versions reproduced here; the other (1.3.3) follows. Both this and the *Columbia Observer* for April 14 refer to an Extra for the *Memphis Enquirer* of April 6 that was not located. Presumably this April 12 article is a reprinting.

FALL OF SAN ANTONIO AND ITS ONE HUNDRED AND EIGHTY SEVEN GALLANT DEFENDERS.

This melancholy intelligence is confirmed. Geo. C. Childress, Esq. late editor of the Nashville Banner, is now by our side, having left Washington, on the Brassos, on the 19th March. Mr. Childress in conjunction with Mr. Hamilton from Texas is on a mission to Washington, D.C. authorized and accredited by the new government to open negotiation with the Government of the United States, for the purpose of obtaining a recognition of the Independence of Texas.

The subjoined statement of the fall of San Antonio we have from the lips of Mr. Childress, who received it personally from the servant of the gallant Travis who fell fighting from the ramparts of the Alamo. This servant was the only being left to tell the mournful fate of the Spartan band. He arrived at Washington, and gave the sad intelligence to the governor and council in the presence of Mr. Childress. The negro is intelligent, and known to be faithful and honest.

San Antonio fell on Sunday morning the 6th of March, after 8 days siege by night and day. SIXTEEN HUNDRED of the Mexicans killed in the siege, is the imperishable monument left to their memory of ONE HUNDRED AND EIGHTY-SEVEN Texians—we may say AMERICANS. History affords no parallel. Since the defence of Thermopylae by the brave Leonidas, the world has witnessed no instance of valor so intrepid, as displayed by the heroes of the Alamo. Not one was taken alive! After eight days and night's [*sic*] constant fighting, besieged by four thousand effective troops commanded by daring officers, the last one of the noble band poured out his blood with sword in hand upon the rampart defended with such desperation.

The servant of the lamented Travis, says his master fell near the close of the siege. That the Texians had picket guards stationed some hundred yards around the Alamo, (as the fort of San Antonio is called,) and upon its walls; that on Sunday morning about 3 o'clock the guard upon the wall cried out, "Col. Travis the Mexicans are coming!" Whether the picket guards were asleep or killed is not known; they were not heard, if they sounded any alarm. The Mexicans were encamped around the Alamo, out of the reach of its cannon. Col. Travis sprang from his blanket with his sword and gun, mounted the rampart, and seeing the enemy under the mouth of the cannon with scaling ladders, discharged his double barreled gun down upon them; he was immediately shot, his gun falling upon the enemy and himself within the fort.—The Mexican General *leading* the charge mounted the wall by means of a ladder, and seeing the bleeding Travis, attempted to behead him; the dying Colonel raised his sword and *killed him!* The negro then hid in one of the apartments of the fort, until the spirit of bravery was entirely quenched, when he heard a voice inquiring if there "were no negroes here." The negro replied, "yes here's one" and came out; a Mexican discharged a gun at him, but did him no injury; another ran his bayonet at him, injuring him slightly, when the Mexican officer speaking English interposed and saved him. This officer conversed freely with the negro as also did Santa Anna; this general was there, and made the negro point out Col. Travis; by which conversation he knew his master had killed the general leading the siege, as their blood then congealed together. The body of Col. Travis and his little yet great band were burnt by order of Santa Anna. The lady of Lieut. Dickinson was within the fort and begged to share the honorable fate of her husband; Santa Anna, honor to his name, —thrice honor to his name, here proved himself a soldier, and protected her; he replied "I am not warring against women." He sent her away with the servant who carried this news, and who left her safely near Washington. He has raised the blood red flag of extermination and no quarters, and swears he will not stop until he has planted his banner upon the capitol of our Washington, if, he understands, our government in the least abets the Texans. If his bones bleach upon any other field than that of Texas, our prophesy fails. Instead of marching against the colonies in the interior, he is now storming Laberdee, (Goliad) defended by a strong fortress with a garrison of about 700 brave Texians, commanded by Col. Fanning, a daring and intrepid officer, who it is tho't, will give Santa Anna a "fanning" that he little anticipates. Mr. Childress says there are now at least 5000 Texian soldiers in the field. And we are also happy to state on his assertion that the government is amply supplied with provisions and ammunition, and money. A negotiation has been effected in New Orleans by the government for $250,000: he also says that many other loans have been offered the government. Santa Anna has threatened the destruction of New Orleans as a "nest of pirates."

Below we give all the information we can obtain upon this exciting subject. . . .

[*The article continues with reports on the Texas situation in general; the fallen at the Alamo, not included here, as there is no eyewitness connection; and letters from Gen. Samuel Houston.*]

1.3.3.   Joe, newspaper report, 1836.

National Intelligencer. April 30, 1836. Washington, D.C.

This is another version of the preceding *Memphis Enquirer* article (1.3.2). It is included here, as there is some variation that might be from the original April 6 Extra.

THE CAPTURE OF ALAMO, (IN TEXAS.)

Further particulars.—The Memphis (Tennessee) Enquirer, Extra, of April 6th, furnishes some additional particulars of this bloody affair. They were stated to the editor by Col. George C. Childress, (late editor of the Nashville Banner,) who had just returned from Washington, in Texas, and had derived them from the intelligent negro, the servant of the brave Travis, who, with Mrs. Dickinson, were the only persons, it will be remembered, whose lives were spared to tell the dreadful tale, and from whom alone authentic information can ever be obtained. The negro states that the attack was suddenly made at 3 o'clock in the morning, after 14 days' siege. It was unexpected, as no alarm, except a single voice crying out "Col. Travis, the Mexicans are coming!" was heard from the guard on the wall—the picket guard, from whom nothing was heard, having probably been killed. Col. Travis sprang from his blanket with his sword and gun, mounted the rampart, and seeing the enemy under the mouths of the cannon with scaling ladders, discharged his double-barrelled gun down upon them; he was immediately shot, his gun falling down upon the enemy, and himself within the fort. The Mexican General leading the charge mounted the walls by means of a ladder, and, seeing the bleeding Travis, attempted to behead him; the dying colonel raised his sword and killed him! The negro then hid in one of the apartments of the fort, until the spirit of bravery was entirely quenched, when he heard a voice inquiring if there "were no negroes here." The negro replied, "yes, here's one," and came out; a Mexican discharged a gun at him, but did him no injury; another ran his bayonet at him, injuring him slightly, when the Mexican officer, speaking English, interposed and saved him. The officer conversed freely with the negro, as also did Santa Ana; this General was there, and made the negro point out Col. Travis; by which conversation he knew his master had killed the General leading the siege, as their blood then congealed together. The body of Col. Travis, and his little yet great band were burnt by order of Santa Ana. The lady of Lieut. Dickinson was within the fort, and begged to share the honorable fate of her husband; Santa Ana, honor to his name—thrice honor to his name—here proved himself a soldier, and protected her; he replied, "I am not warring against women." He sent her away with the servant who carried this news, and who left her safely near Washington. He has raised the blood red flag of extermination and no quarters, and swears he will not stop until he has planted his banner upon the Capitol of our Washington, if he understands our Government in the least abets the Texians. If his bones bleach upon any other field than that of Texas, our prophecy fails.

1.3.4.   Joe, newspaper report, 1836.

Commonwealth. May 25, 1836. Frankfort, Kentucky.
The photocopy for this document is unclear in spots, but the sense is clear.
Based on the next document (1.3.5), the author must be William Gray.

LETTER FROM TEXAS
Correspondence of the Fredericksburg Arena.

Groce's Retreat, March 20th, 1836

I sent you an uninteresting scrawl under yesterday's date, not expecting to
have an opportunity of writing to you again so soon. But persons are continually coming and going here. Some are every day starting to the United States to
raise men, and money, or provisions for the aid of Texas. May success attend
their efforts. The members of the Government are dilligent [*sic*] in their new
duties, and they are likely to have enough to do.

I have this day had an interesting treat. It was the examination of Joe, the
black servant of the lamented TRAVIS, who was in the ALAMO when it was
taken. He is about 21 or 22 years of age. He is the only male of all who were in
the Alamo, when attacked, that escaped death, and he, according to his own
account escaped narrowly. I heard him interrogated in the presence of the Cabinet. He related the affair, as far as known to him, with much modesty apparent
candour, and remarkable distinctness for one of his class. The following is, as
nearly as I can recollect, the substance of his statement. You will find it in part a
repetition of what has been already told—but it corrects the previous statements in some points.

The Garrison was much exhausted by hard labour and incessant watching
and fighting for thirteen days. The day and night previous to the attack, the
Mexican bombardment had been suspended. On Saturday night, March 5, the
little Garrison had worked hard, in repairing and strengthening their position,
until a late hour. And when the attack was made, which was just before day-
break, sentinels and all were asleep, except the officer of the day who was just
starting on his round. There were three picket [*these two words uncertain*] guards
without the Fort; but they too, it is supposed, were asleep, and were run upon
and bayonetted, for they gave no alarm that was heard. The first that Joe knew
of it was the entrance [*this word uncertain*] of Adjutant Baugh, the officer of the
day, into Travis' quarters, who roused him with the cry—"the Mexicans are
coming." They were running at full speed with their scaling ladders, towards
the Fort, and were under the guns, and had their ladders against the wall before
the Garrison were aroused to resistance. Travis sprung up, and seizing his rifle
and sword, called to Joe to take his gun and [*word unclear*]. He mounted the
wall, and called out to his men—"*Come on Boys, the Mexicans are upon us, and
we'll give them Hell.*" He immediately fired his rifle. Joe followed his example.

The fire was returned by several shots, and Travis fell, wounded, within the wall, on the sloping ground that had recently been thrown up to strengthen the wall. There he sat, unable to rise. Joe, seeing his master fall, and the Mexicans coming over the wall and thinking with Falstaff that the better part of valor is discretion, ran, and ensconsed [*sic*] himself in a house, from [*this word uncertain*] the loop holes of which, he says, he fired on them several times after they had come in.

Here Joe's narrative becomes somewhat interrupted; but Mrs. Dickenson, the wife of Lt. D., who was in the Fort at the time, and is now at San Felippe, has supplied some particulars, which Joe's state of retirement prevented him from knowing with perfect accuracy. The enemy three times applied their scaling ladder to the wall; twice they were beaten back. But numbers and discipline prevailed over valor and desperation. On the third attempt they succeeded, and then they came over *"like sheep."* As Travis sat wounded, but cheering his men, where he first fell, General Mora, in passing, aimed a blow with his sword to despatch him—Travis rallied his failing strength, struck up the descending weapon, and ran his assailant through the body. This was poor Travis' last effort. Both fell and expired on the spot. The battle now became a complete *melee.* Every man fought for "his own hand," with gun-butts, swords, pistols and knives, as he best could. The handful of Americans, not 150 effective men, retreated to such cover as they had, and continued the battle, until *only one man,* a little weakly body, named Warner, was left alive. He, and he only, asked for quarter. He was spared by the soldiery: but, on being conducted to Santa Anna, he ordered him to be shot, which was promptly done. So that not *one white man,* of that devoted band, was left to tell the tale.

Crockett, the kind hearted, brave DAVID CROCKETT, and a few of the devoted friends who entered the Fort with him, were found lying together with 24 of the slain enemy around them. Bowie is said to have fired through the door of his room, from his sick bed. He was found dead and mutilated where he had lain. The body of Travis too, was pierced with many bayonet stabs. The despicable Col. Cos, fleshed his dastard sword in the dead body. Indeed, Joe says, the soldiers continued to stab the fallen Americans, until all possibility of life was extinct. Capt. Baragan was the only Mexican officer who showed any disposition to spare the Americans. He saved Joe, and interceded for poor Warner, but in vain. There were several Negroes and some Mexican women in the Fort. They were all spared. One only of the Negroes was killed—a woman—who was found lying dead between two guns. Joe supposes she ran out in her fright, and was killed by a chance shot. Lieut. Dickerson's child was not killed, as was first reported. The mother and child were both spared and sent home. The wife of Dr. Aldridge and her sister, Miss Navaro, were also saved [*these two words uncertain*] and restored to their father, who lives in Bejar.

After the fight, when they were searching the houses, an officer called out in English "are there any negroes here?" Joe then emerged from his concealment, and said, "Yes, here's one." Immediately two soldiers attempted to despatch him—one by discharging his piece at him, and the other by a thrust of the bayonet. He escaped with a scratch only from the steel, and one buck shot in his side, which, however, did little damage. He was saved by the intervention of Captain Baragan, who beat off the soldier with his sword.

The work of death being completed, the Mexicans were formed in hollow square, and Santa Anna addressed them in a very animated manner. They rejointed [*this word uncertain*] to it with loud rings [*this word uncertain*]. Joe describes him as a light built, slender man, rather tall—sharp, but handsome and animated features; dressed very plainly; somewhat *"like a methodist* [*this word not complete*] *preacher,"* to use the negro's own words. Joe [*"was"? word not readable*] taken into Bejar, and detained several days. He was given [*this word uncertain*] a grand review of the army after the battle, and was told [*this word uncertain*] there were 6,000 [*first digit uncertain*] troops under arms. He supposes that there were [*these two words uncertain*] that many. But those acquainted with the ground [*"on" missing?*] which he says they formed, think that not half of that number could be formed there. Santa Anna took much notice of him, and questioned him about Texas and the state of the army.—Among other things, he asked if there were many soldiers from the United States in the army, and if more were expected? On being answered in the affirmative, he sneeringly said he had men enough to *march to the city of Washington if he chose.*

The slain were collected in a pile and burnt.

Thus perished this gallant and devoted band of men, sacrificed by the cold neglect—the culpable, shameful neglect—of their countrymen. Who can read the stiring [*sic*] appeals and calls for help from the despairing Travis, and the bitter reproaches that burst from him but a day or two before the massacre, without feeling the blood rush to his face with shame for Texas—shame for the hundreds and thousands that might have gone up to the rescue—but they would not. Texas will take honor to herself for the defense of the Alamo, and will call it a second Thermopylae, but it will be an everlasting monument of national disgrace. "If my countrymen," says he, on the 3d March, "do not rally to my relief, I am determined to perish in the defence of this place, and my bones shall reproach my country for her neglect." Poor fellows—the immolation of a thousand lives cannot restore your gallant spirits, or remove the stigma that your sacrifice has left on the Nation escutcheon.

1.3.5.   Joe, journal entry, 1836.

Gray, William F. 1909. *From Virginia to Texas, 1835, Diary of Col. Wm. F. Gray . . . ,* 136–42. Houston: Gray, Dillaye & Co.

That this is nearly identical with the preceding letter, published in the *Commonwealth* of Frankfort, Kentucky, indicates that it must be a true diary entry of that time. Entries from prior and subsequent days identify his location as being at the home of Jared Groce, a wealthy planter who supported the revolution (1.3.6 following).

Sunday, March 20, 1836.

This morning Messrs. Zavalla, Ruis and Navarro arrived. The cabinet are now all here, except Hardiman.

The servant of the late lamented Travis, Joe, a black boy of about twenty-one or twenty-two years of age, is now here. He was in the Alamo when the fatal attack was made. He is the only male, of all who were in the fort, who escaped death, and he, according to his own account, escaped narrowly. I heard him interrogated in presence of the cabinet and others. He related the affair with much modesty, apparent candor, and remarkably distinctly for one of his class. The following is, as near as I can recollect, the substance of it:

The garrison was much exhausted by incessant watching and hard labor. They had all worked until a late hour on Saturday night, and when the attack was made sentinels and all were asleep, except one man, Capt. ———, who gave the alarm. There were three picket guards without the fort, but they, too, it is supposed, were asleep, and were run upon and bayonetted, for they gave no alarm. Joe was sleeping in the room with his master when the alarm was given. Travis sprang up, seized his rifle and sword, and called to Joe to follow him. Joe took his gun and followed. Travis ran across the Alamo and mounted the wall, and called out to his men, "Come on, boys, the Mexicans are upon us, and we'll give them *Hell.*" He discharged his gun; so did Joe. In an instant Travis was shot down. He fell within the wall, on the sloping ground, and sat up. The enemy twice applied their scaling ladders to the walls, and were twice beaten back. But this Joe did not well understand, for when his master fell he ran and ensconced himself in a house, from which he says he fired on them several times, after they got in. On the third attempt they succeeded in mounting the walls, and then poured over like sheep. The battle then became a *melee.* Every man fought for his own hand, as he best might, with *butts of guns,* pistols, knives, etc. As Travis sat wounded on the ground General Mora, who was passing him, made a blow at him with his sword, which Travis struck up, and ran his assailant through the body, and both died on the same spot. This was poor Travis' last effort. The handful of Americans retreated to such covers as they had, and continued the battle until one man was left, a little, weakly man named Warner, who asked for quarter. He was spared by the solidery [*sic*], but on being conducted to Santa Anna, he ordered him to be shot, and it was done. Bowie is said to have fired through the door of his room, from his sick bed. He was found dead and mutilated where he lay. Crockett and a few of his friends were found together, with twenty-four of the enemy dead around them. The negroes, for there were several negroes and women in the fort, were spared. Only one woman was killed, and Joe supposes she was shot accidentally, while attempting to cross the Alamo. She was found lying between two guns. The officers came around, after the massacre, and called out to know if there were any negroes there. Joe stepped out and said, "Yes, here is one." Immediately, two soldiers attempted to kill him, one by discharging his piece at him, the other with a thrust of the bayonet. Only one buckshot took effect in his side, not dangerously, and the point of the bayonet scratched him on the other. He was saved by Capt. Baragan. Besides the negroes, there were in the fort several Mexican women, among them the wife of a Dr. ——— and her sister, Miss Navarro, who were spared and restored to their father, D. Angel Navarro, of Bejar. Mrs. Dickenson, wife of Lieut. Dickenson, and child, were also spared, and have been sent back into Texas. After the fight was over, the Mexicans were formed in hollow square, and Santa Anna addressed them in a very animated manner. They filled the air with loud shouts. Joe describes him as a slender man, rather tall, dressed very plainly—somewhat *like a Methodist preacher,* to use the negro's own words. Joe was taken into Bejar, and detained several days; was shown a grand review of the army after the battle, which he was told, or supposes, was 8,000 strong. Those acquainted with the ground on which he says they formed think that not more than half that number could form there. Santa Anna questioned Joe about Texas, and the state of its army. Asked if there were many soldiers from the United States in the army, and if more were expected, and said he had men enough to march to the city of Washington. The American dead were collected in a pile and burnt.

A list of those who fell in the Alamo, March 6, 1836, as far as they are known:

> David Crockett, Tennessee.
> Col. Wm. B. Travis.
> Col. Bowman.
> Col. James Bowie, Tennessee.
> G. Washington, Drum Major.
> Adjt. I. Baugh, Virginia, New Orleans Greys.
> Capt. S. C. Blair, Artillery, Ireland.
> Capt. Carey, Ireland.
> Capt. Baker, Mississippi.
> Capt. Wm. Blazeby, New Orleans Greys.
> Capt. Harrison, Tennessee.
> Capt. Forsayth, New York.
> Lt. John Jones, New Orleans Greys.
> Lt. Kimble, Gonzales.
> Lt. Dickenson, wife and child.
> Lt. Robt. Evans, Master of Ordnance, England.

Lt. Williamson, Sergt. Major, Philadelphia.
Dr. Mitchison, Civil Engineer.
Dr. Pollard, Surgeon.
Dr. Thompson, Tennessee.
Charles Despalier, Aide to Travis.
Elliot Melton, Quartermaster.
——— Anderson, Quartermaster.
Major G. B. Jamison, Kentucky.
Col. J. B. Bonham, Alabama.
——— Robinson, Scotland.
——— Nelson, Charleston, S.C.
——— Nelson, Austin's clerk.
Wm. Smith, Nacogdoches.
Lewis Johnson, Mina.
E. P. Mitchell, Georgia.
——— Thruston.
——— Moor, Mississippi.
Christopher Parker, Mississippi.
——— Hieskell, Nacogdoches.
——— Rowe, Nacogdoches.
John M. Hays, Tennessee.
——— Stewart.
James Blair, Nacogdoches.
William Simpson.
Albert Martin, Gonzales.
David Wilson, Nacogdoches.
Wm. Howell, New Orleans Greys.
Charles Smith, Bastrop.
J. McGregor, Scotland.
——— Rusk.
Col. ——— Hawkins, Louisiana.
Samuel Holloway, Texas.
——— Browne, Travis' Company.
——— Smith, Travis' company.
——— Browne, Philadelphia.
——— Henderson.
Wm. Wells, Tennessee.
Wm. Cumming, Pennsylvania.
——— Battentine, Pennsylvania.
R. W. Valantine, Pennsylvania.
R. Cockran, Boston.
Capt. Robt. White.
Sergt. Isaac White, Harris, Ky.
——— Sterne.

—— Jackson, Ireland.
—— McAfferty.
Wm. D. Southerland, Navidad.
Three Taylors, Trinity.
—— Taylor, Little River, Texas.
R. M. Kinney, Bastrop.
S. B. Evans, Tennessee.
Tom R. Miller, Gonzales.
Wm. R. King, Gonzales.
J. Kane, Gonzales.
Wm. Durduff, Gonzales.
Geo. Tomlinson, Gonzales.
Dan'l Jackson, Sailor.
John C. Goodrich, Tennessee.
Wm. Marshall, New Orleans Greys, Arkansas.
Jon'a Lindley, Tennessee.
Micajah Autry, Tennessee.
Jas. Sewall, Nacogdoches.
John Wilson, Nacogdoches.
A. C. Grimes, Alabama.
Jas. C. Day, Nacogdoches.
Tapley Holland.
James George, Gonzales.
—— Bailey, Logan County, Kentucky.
—— Cloud, Logan County, Kentucky.
—— Lewis, Philadelphia.
—— Stockton, Virginia.
—— Thomas, Tennessee.
—— Bowen, Tennessee.
—— Bailiss, Tennessee.
—— Crawford, Kentucky.
—— Devault, Missouri, Plasterer.
—— Dewell, Blacksmith.
Jas. Kinney.
—— Warner.
John Garvin, Missouri.
—— Wornell.
Capt. —— Gilmore, Tennessee.
—— Smith, Tennessee.
Spain Summerlin, Tennessee.
—— Thompson, Tennessee.
—— Pollard.
—— Nelson, New Orleans Greys.
—— Butler, New Orleans Greys.

Wm. Ellis.

Jos. Shead.

Sam'l Holloway, New Orleans Greys.

—— Ballard.

—— Spratt.

Jacob Dust, Gonzales.

Christopher Parker, Mississippi.

—— Robbins, Kentucky.

John Flanders.

Isaac Ryan, Opelousas.

David Murphy, Tennessee.

Jon's Lindley, Illinois.

Jas. Ewing.

Jas. Stewart, Nacogdoches.

Robt. Cunningham.

Francis Desooks, Storekeeper.

—— Lynn, Drum Major.

John Balone.

—— Burns, Ireland.

John Burnell.

Geo. Neggin.

F. Desanque, Philadelphia.

John —— (clerk in Desanque's store).

Robt. Musselman, New Orleans.

Robt. Crossman, New Orleans.

Richard Starr, England.

J. G. Ganett, New Orleans.

J. G. Dinkin, England.

Rob. B. Moore, New Orleans.

Wm. Lynn, Boston.

—— Hutchinson.

Wm. Johnson, Philadelphia.

Dan'l Bourne, England.

—— Ingram, England.

Charles Lanco, Denmark.

Capt. A. Dickerson, Gonzales.

Geo. C. Kimble, Gonzales.

Dophin Floyd, Gonzales.

Thos. Jackson, Gonzales.

Geo. W. Cottle, Gonzales.

Andrew Kent, Gonzales.

Isaac Baker, Gonzales.

Jesse McCoy, Gonzales.

Claiborne Wright, Gonzales.

Wm. Fishback, Gonzales.
———— Millsap, Gonzales.
Galby Fuqua, Gonzales.
John Davis, Gonzales.

1.3.6.   Joe, biographical sketch, 1981.

Drake, David. 1981. "Joe" Alamo hero. *Negro History Bulletin.* April-May-June:
34–35. Copyrighted and reprinted with permission from the Association for the
Study of Afro-American Life and History (ASALH), Inc., Washington, D.C.
    As Joe is among the most important sources for narratives of the actual fighting
during the fall of the Alamo, this biographical sketch is of sufficient value to reprint
here.

"JOE" ALAMO HERO

The story of the Alamo is well known to most Americans. Texans, especially,
hold its memory precious to their heritage. What is not so well known is that a
black man known only as "Joe," a manservant to the commanding officer of the
Texas forces at the Alamo, was the sole adult male survivor of the final assault
on the old San Antonio mission on March 6, 1836.

    That the sole adult male survivor of the Alamo should be a black slave is
ironic, since slavery was one of the issues of the war between Mexico and Texas
(Mexico had forbidden slavery by law since 1821, but the Texas colonists
insisted upon their right to own and import slaves).

    Joe was born into slavery somewhere in the southern United States around
1813. His earliest years are lost to obscurity, but it is evident that he was taken
to Texas at some time before he reached the age of twenty-one. In February of
1834 he was sold to William Barret Travis, a young Alabaman who had come to
Texas in support of the revolution against Mexico and would eventually command the Texas defenders of the Alamo in their heroic but ill-fated stand. Travis
wrote from San Felipe in 1835, "I have had Joe for the year; I cannot now say,
whether I will sell him or not."[1] Joe was not sold, however, and thus through an
accident of fate wound up at the Alamo.

    The events leading to the siege of the Alamo are too familiar to be repeated
here. During the siege, from February 23 to March 6, 1836, Joe "earned his
spurs" fighting the Mexican forces as a full-fledged member of the garrison.

    On the morning of March 6, the Mexicans began their final assault. At the
first sound of the bugles, Joe rushed to the north battery and kneeled with his
shotgun to meet the onslaught. Vastly outnumbered and virtually out of ammunition, the Texans were unable to prevent the enemy from scaling the walls of
the fort. From the corner of his eye, Joe saw Colonel Travis suddenly knocked
backward, mortally wounded in the head.

Within minutes, the Mexicans were teeming within the walls of the Alamo. Joe fled to the barracks and found shelter in a small room, where he reloaded and continued firing. When his ammunition was exhausted, he crouched down and waited to meet the invaders hand-to-hand.

He did not have to wait long. An ominous hush had fallen over the mission; the massacre was over. Joe heard a voice calling out (in Spanish), "Are there any Negroes here?" Striding forth from his shelter, Joe announced, "Yes, here is one." Unarmed and outnumbered, he could not have known what to expect.

Immediately, two Mexican solders tried to kill him; one by firing his musket at him, and the other with a thrust of his bayonet. Joe was only slightly wounded by both attackers. A piece of buckshot lodged in his side and he suffered a minor scratch from the bayonet on his other side. A Captain Baragan, however, ordered Joe's life spared, perhaps thinking to hold him for interrogation. Only later did Joe learn that he was the only adult male to survive the siege.

Joe was taken into Bexar before the Mexican general, Santa Anna, who questioned him about Texas and the state of its army. For the sake of propaganda, the general had his troops pass in review before the young black man, who later estimated their numbers to be approximately 8,000. Santa Anna's motives were obvious: Joe was spared and shown an impressive display of the Mexican troops in the hope that he would return to the Texas army and tell them that any further resistance to such eminently superior forces would be futile. Such was not to be the case, however.

Freed by Santa Anna, Joe hastily made his way to the temporary revolutionary capitol of Washington-on-the-Brazos. At the home of Jared Groce (an affluent planter and supporter of the revolution), he recounted the story of the Alamo to the patriots gathered there and was said to have ". . . related the affair with much modesty, apparent candor, and remarkably distinctly. . . ."[2] While Joe did not downplay the size of the Mexican army, neither did he describe it as superlatively as Santa Anna would have hoped. When he was asked which of the Texans had killed the most Mexicans, he replied, "Colonel Crockett had the biggest pile."[3]

Penniless and homeless, Joe sought employment in Washington-on-the-Brazos and eventually went to work for a John Rice Jones in connection with the liquidation of William Barret Travis' estate. The relationship evidently was not a happy one; on April 21, 1837, Joe and a fellow employee appropriated two horses and headed east. Upon discovering the pair had departed, Jones attempted to catch up with them. Failing this, he ran the following advertisement in the *Telegraph and Texas Register* from May 26 through August of 1837:

"Fifty Dollars will be given for delivering to me on Bailey's Prairie, seven miles from Columbia, a Negro man named Joe, belonging to the succession of the late Wm. Barret Travis, who took off with him a Mexican and two horses, saddles and bridles. This Negro was in the Alamo with his master when it was taken; and was the only man from the colonies who was not put to death; he is about twenty-five years of age, five feet ten or eleven inches high, very black and good countenance: had on when he left, on the night of the 21st of April ult. a dark mixed sattinet round jacket and new-white cotton pantaloons. One of the horses taken is a bay, about 14+ hands high very heavy built, with a blaze in his face, a bushy mane and tail, and a sore back; also the property of said succession; the other horse is a chestnut sorrel, about 16 hands high. The saddles are of Spanish from [form] but of American manufacture, and one of them covered with blue cloth. Forty dollars will be given for Joe and the small bay horse (Shannon) and ten dollars for the Mexican, other horse and saddles and bridles. If the runaways are taken more than one hundred miles from my residence, I will pay all reasonable travelling expenses, in addition to the above reward.

JOHN R. JONES, Ex'r of W. B. Travis Bailey's Prairie, Mary 21st, 1837."[4]

In fairness to Joe, the horses, saddles and bridles were part of the late Colonel Travis' estate; as the only Texas survivor of that estate, Joe could hardly be labeled a thief for using the horses, especially when one learns of his destination.

Some weeks later, Joe arrived on foot at the Travis family home in Conecuh County, Alabama. He had lost or abandoned the horse and Mexican companion at some early point in his journey. A Travis family historian stated, "This Negro claimed to have walked all the way from Texas to Conecuh County, to have had to swim the Mississippi River and endure many hardships to bring the tale of Travis' death to his people. The family here received the first news of the Alamo from this Negro. . . ."[5]

Joe remained in southern Alabama for the remainder of his life. According to the same Travis family historian, ". . . the Negro mentioned above, who himself was an Alamo hero, is buried in an unmarked grave near Brewton . . ."[6] (Brewton is roughly 64 miles northeast of Mobile).

Joe's last name remains a mystery. Initially, it may have been "Mansfield," the name of his owner before Travis. It is most probable that he used the name "Travis" after the Colonel's death; however, Alabama census records of the time merely counted "Free Colored Persons" without listing their names. It is thus unlikely that this riddle will ever be solved.

No accounts exist of Joe's later years. One can easily picture him as an older man with grandchildren on his knees, enthralling them with his true tales of the Alamo. Conversely, as with many reluctant heroes, he may have chosen to put the past quietly behind him. In any case, his presence and his bravery are well documented. His is an inspiring story, too often overlooked in the record of Texas history.

1 Letter from William Barret Travis to David G. Burnet, February 5 [?], 1835. Archives, Texas State Library, Austin, Texas.
2 Col. William F. Gray, *From Virginia to Texas, 1835* (Houston, 1909), 136–37. (Diary, published posthumously.) [*Document 1.3.5 above.*]
3 Mary Helm, *Scraps of Early Texas History* Austin, B. R. Warner, 1884), 56. [*See document 2.12.3 below, attributed to Ben.*]
4 *Telegraph and Texas Register,* May 26 through August 1837, various pages. Barker Texas History Center, General Libraries, University of Texas at Austin.
5 Ed Leigh McMillan, "Memorandum with Regard to William Barret Travis," August 24, 1957. State of Alabama Archives and Department of History, Montgomery, Alabama (Unpaged).
6 Ibid.

Commentary

Joe (1.3.1–1.3.6)

For Joe's accounts, we basically have no primary sources but three secondary ones: an unknown in the *Commercial Bulletin,* two versions from George Childress, and two of William Gray. The biographical sketch primarily used the third source.

The *Commercial Bulletin* source is of little value. A careful reading reveals that all the details except two are included in the other sources, though this does indicate that the writer did at least hear Joe's account. Of the two exceptions, one is wrong—Bowie was not allowed a grave—and the other, an implied assault of Susanna Dickinson, no doubt comes from Houston's letter (3.5.5) and is unrelated to anything Joe would have observed. A little emotive prose is the only other contribution this writer gives.

Of the George Childress versions, the *Memphis Enquirer* (1.3.2) included more details than the *National Intelligencer.* The latter is given only as a comparison since the original April 6 source was not located and there are a few differences, such as a fourteen-day siege rather than eight. Comparison of Childress to the Gray accounts, however, gives us only a few possible additional facts from Childress: the casualties of the two sides, the hundred yards' distance at which the picket guards were stationed, Travis using a double-barreled gun, and Mrs. Dickinson asking "to share the honorable fate of her husband." This might be attributed to her, but only the last of this list is a detail likely to have been of much interest or known to her, and it is inconsistent with the Dickinson sources. The details about the pickets and Travis's gun would possibly, even likely, have been observed by Joe, and so may be authentic. The specificity of details does strongly indicate that Childress also must have heard Joe's account.

William Gray's account is the most detailed and precise of the interviews with Joe. The contemporary newspaper and diary accounts are powerful supports of the authenticity of facts and time frame of his information. A close comparison of the

Commonwealth article with the diary shows that the newspaper article has several details not in the diary: Joe's age; the identification of the officer of the day (or night) at the time of the attack as an Adjutant Baugh, and his cry to Travis; that Mrs. Dickinson is the source for stating that two attacks were beaten back before the third was successful; the condition of the bodies of Bowie and Travis; and specifics of Joe's interview with Santa Anna after the battle. On the other hand, with the exception of the list of defenders and confirmation that Gray was at Groce's, the diary does not give any details not in the newspaper. We can conclude, therefore, that the *Commonwealth* letter is the definitive document for the account of a key source, Joe, in our knowledge of the actual fall of the Alamo.

Some details of the *Commonwealth* article—for example, the incident of Travis killing General Mora, which is attributed to Mrs. Dickinson—will be discussed further with the March 24 account in the *Telegraph and Texas Register* (4.1.1).

Author William Davis notes that Susanna Dickinson and Joe were likely in the same room when their earliest interviews took place, and therefore could have "cross-fertilized" each other's accounts to a degree not fully appreciated.[1]

In addition to the narrative of the fall, Gray is important for confirming the presence of Mrs. Alsbury (Aldridge in Gray), her sister, plus other Mexican women and African-Americans. Their presence was commonly overlooked in most early accounts of the siege.[2]

Another possible source by Mary Helm is attributed by Drake to Joe (footnote 3 of 1.3.6). I attribute this account to Ben (2.12.3), servant of Colonel Almonte. The original individual is not identified, and the comments on Crockett recorded by Helm match more closely those of Ben.[3]

With the matter-of-factness and careful details of the accounts by Joe, I must agree with the other writers that he was intelligent and narrated his experiences with "modesty, apparent candor, and remarkably distinctly" in comparison with most other eyewitnesses who gave accounts on the fall of the Alamo.

---

1. Davis 1997, 17–19
2. See Jackson c. 1997 and February 1998 for a recent study of the various possible black participants.
3. There is also an account derived from Joe in a history by Niles and Pease (1837, 328), but it has little new information, and the phraseology that Joe "relates these few facts with great apparent simplicity and truth" indicates that they used Gray's version.

1.4.1.   Juana Alsbury, interview, unknown date.

Alsbury, Mrs. Horace, as interviewed by John S. Ford. Manuscript account (Ford's handwriting) in the John S. Ford Memoirs, 102–4, CAH.

Juana Alsbury's interview is one of the rare eyewitness accounts from inside the Alamo. This document has been widely paraphrased in numerous narrative accounts, but remarkably it was not printed verbatim, as far as I could discover, until 1981 in the *Alamo Lore and Myth Organization* (3:37), and not in a widely available printing until 1995, when Timothy Matovina published it in *The Alamo Remembered*.

MRS. ALSBURY'S RECOLLECTIONS OF THE ALAMO

Iuana, the daughter of Angel Navarro, and a niece of Col. Jose Antonio Navarro, when very young was adopted by Gov. Veramendi, who had married her father's sister. Senorita Iuana married a Mexican gentleman, Don Alejo Perez, by whom she had a son, Alejo, who is a respectable citizen of San Antonio. The elder Perez died in 1834, and his widow married Dr. Horatio Alexander Alsbury early in 1836. It must be remembered that, Col. James Bowie married the daughter of Gov. Veramendi, consequently his wife was the cousin and the adopted sister of Mrs. Alsbury. This accounts for her being in his charge and in the Alamo.

When the news of Santa Anna's approach, at the head of a considerable force, was verified in San Antonio, Dr. Alsbury proceeded to the Brazos river to procure means to remove his family, expecting to return before Santa Anna could reach the city. He failed to do so; and his wife went into the Alamo where her protector was, when the Mexican troops were near by. She was accompanied by her younger sister, Gertrudis.

Col. Bowie was very sick of typhoid fever. For that reason he thought it prudent to be removed from the part of the buildings occupied by Mrs. Alsbury. A couple of soldiers carried him away. On leaving he said: "Sister, do not be afraid. I leave you with Col. Travis, Col. Crockett, and other friends. They are gentlemen, and will treat you kindly." He had himself brought back two or three times to see and talk with her. Their last interview took place three or four days before the fall of the Alamo. She never saw him again, either alive or dead.

She says she does not know who nursed him after he left the quarters she occupied, and expresses no disbelief in the statement of Madam Candelaria. "There were people in the Alamo I did not see."

Mrs. Alsbury and her sister were in a building not far from where the residence of Col. Sam Maverick was afterwards erected. It was considered quite a safe locality. They saw very little of the fighting. While the final struggle was progressing she peeped out, and saw the surging columns of Santa Anna assaulting the Alamo on every side, as she believed. She could hear the noise of the conflict—the roar of the artillery, the rattle of the small arms—the shouts of the combatants, the groans of the dying, and the moans of the wounded. The firing approximated where she was, and she realized the fact that, the brave

Texians had been overwhelmed by numbers. She asked her sister to go to the door, and request the Mexican soldiers not to fire into the room, as it contained women only. Senorita Gertrudis opened the door, she was greeted in offensive language by the soldiers. Her shawl was torn from her shoulders, and she rushed back into the room. During this period Mrs. Alsbury was standing with her one-year-old son strained to her bosom, supposing he would be motherless soon. The soldiers then demanded of Senorita Gertrudis: "Your money and your husband." She replied: "I have neither money nor husband." About this time a sick man ran up to Mrs. Alsbury, and attempted to protect her. The soldiers bayoneted him at her side. She thinks his name was Mitchell. After this tragic event a young Mexican, hotly pursued by soldiers, seized her by the arm, and endeavored to keep her between himself and his assailants. His grasp was broken, and four or five bayonets plunged into his body, and nearly as many balls went through his lifeless corpse. The soldiers broke open her trunk and took her money and clothes, also the watches of Col. Travis and other officers.

A Mexican officer appeared on the scene. He excitedly inquired: "How did you come here?" "What are you doing here any how?" "Where is the entrance to the fort?" He made her pass out of the room over a cannon standing nearby the door. He told her to remain there, and he would have her sent to President Santa Anna. Another officer came up, and asked: "What are you doing here?" She replied: "An officer ordered us to remain here, and he would have us sent to the President."—"President! the devil. Don't you see they are about to fire that cannon? Leave." They were moving when they heard a voice calling—"Sister." To my great relief Don Manuel Perez came to us. He said:—"Don't you know your own brother-in law?" I answered: "I am so excited and distressed that I scarcely know anything." Don Manuel placed them in charge of a colored woman belonging to Col. Bowie, and the party reached the house of Don Angel Navarro in safety.

Mrs. Alsbury says to the best of her remembrance she heard firing at the Alamo till twelve o'clock that day.

She says the name of the girl Gen. Santa Anna deceived by a false marriage was—[blank in the original]

She describes Col. Bowie as a tall, well made gentleman, of a very serious countenance, of few words, always to the point, and a warm friend. In his family he was affectionate, kind, and so acted as to secure the love and confidence of all.

[Ford adds another paragraph extolling Bowie's virtues.]

1.4.2.   Juana Alsbury, petition, 1857.

Alsbury, Juana Navarro. November 1, 1857. Petition to Senate and House of Representatives, TSLA.

The handwriting and signature of this document are very neat. It is no doubt a formal copy done by an official scribe.

The State of Texas   San Antonio
County of Bexar   Nov. 1st 1857
To the Honorable the Senate and House of Representatives of the State of Texas. The petition of Juana Navarro Alsbury respectfully represents that during the war with Mexico she was in the Alamo at the time of its fall. She was then the wife of Dr Alexander Alsbury, who was taken prisoner on the 11th day of September 1842 and Carried into Captivity by Genl Adrian Woll. That during the siege of the Alamo She was ever ready to render and did render all the service she Could towards nursing and attending upon the sick and wounded during said siege, which lasted some 12 or 14 days. At the time when the place was stormed and Carried by the enemy she and an only sister and a Mrs Dickinson were the only females in the Garrison. That all the property she had to wit her Clothing, money, and jewels were seized and taken by the enemy—that subsequent to that time her husband the said Dr Alsbury was taken a prisoner at the time above stated and Confined in the Castle of Perite in Mexico over 18 months. That upon his return to this Country he accompanied the American Army across the Rio Grande during the war between the United States and Mexico, and in the year 1846 was killed by the Mexicans some where between Camargo and Saltillo. That since that time your petitioner has Continued to reside and still does reside in Bexar County, that she is a native of said County—that she is now getting old with an only son. That she is extremely poor with hardly the means of subsistence—she therefore prays the honorable Legislature will take her case into Consideration, and in view of all the Circumstances allow her some compensation for her losses, and whatever they may think proper to bestow in this her time of necessity

Juana Navarro Alsbury

1.4.3.   Juana Alsbury, obituary, 1888.

San Antonio Light. July 25, 1888. Reprinted 1908 in "10 and 20 Years Ago in S.A." Clipping in file on Historic Sites Alamo Survivors, DRT.

10 AND 20 YEARS AGO IN S.A.
From S.A. Light Files

July 25, 1888

Mrs. Juana Perez died here yesterday at a ripe old age. She was one of the survivors of the massacre of the Alamo. She was a niece of Gov. Verimendi. Her first husband was a Perez, but she later married Dr. Alsbury. Fearing an invasion, Dr. Alsbury placed her in the Alamo under the protection of Col. James Bowie, who had married her adopted sister, a daughter of Gov. Verimendi. Besides Mrs. Perez and Madame Candelario, who was nursing Bowie, there were six more Mexican women and three Mexican men in the Alamo. The men were all murdered and the women were treated to great indignity. All the women are now dead except Madame Candelario and a Mrs. Losoyo living near the southern portion of the city, and another woman south of the city.

1.4.4.   Mrs. Alsbury, oral tradition, c. 1870s?

Perez, Alijo. N.d. Rough notes on interview with son of Mrs. Alsbury in Folder 3/Descendants of Gregorio Esparza, De Zavala (Adina) Papers, CAH.

This document is extracted from rough notes on an interview by Adina De Zavala with the son of Mrs. Alsbury, who was also an Alamo survivor, though only a year or a year and a half old at the time of the battle. The rather difficult-to-read notes also include other circumstances relating to Mrs. Alsbury and some of the others in the Alamo. It is unclear whether the "I knew him well" statement on Brigidio Guerrero comes from Perez or De Zavala.

Perez was only 1 yr old. He was not born when father died—My mother used to tell me that when they took the Alamo, that they went after any one in shape of a man—they went after a boy that when the soldiers made for the boy [,] the boy got hold of my mothers shoulders behind her and used her as shield saying dont let them kill me and she with the baby in arms, but they thrust the bayonet between her arms and over her shoulders and run him threw and held him up on the bayonets & he was one of the Losoya's. Bigido Guerro [*sic*] they say he used to say that he escaped under some mattresses, I knew him well . . .

1.4.5.   Mrs. Alsbury, oral tradition, c. 1880s.

Maverick, Mary A. N.d. (1898). *The Fall of the Alamo.* N.p.
This account was rediscovered and reprinted in Groneman (1996).

Mrs. Allsbury [*sic*] went into the Fort with Bowie to care for his comfort, he
being in feeble health, and having had to resign command to Colonel Travis.
Mrs. Allsbury told me that the women and children (i.e. her son, 8 years, and
her sister 13 [*)*], and Mrs. Dickenson and babe fled to Colonel Bowie's room
when the soldiers entered the old church—this room was upstairs. She saw the
Mexican soldiers enter, bayonet Bowie, then while he still lived, carry him upon
their bayonets into the Plaza below, and there toss him up and catch him upon
the bayonets 'til the blood ran down upon their arms and clothes. Then a Mexican cavalry officer dashed in amongst the butchers, with drawn sword. Lashing
them right and left and forced them to desist. I am sorry I have forgotten this
officer's name. It should be recorded. Mrs. A. herself and children, were taken
care of by Sergeant Perez of the Mexican army, who was a brother of her first
husband. Mrs. A. died here in 1887.

1.5.1.1.   Esparza, Francisco, deposition, 1859.

Esparza, Gregorio. August 26, 1859. Court of Claims File C-2558. Archives and
Records Division, Texas General Land Office.

The State of Texas
County of Bexar
Before me Sam[l]. S. Smith, Clerk of the County Court of Bexar County personally appeared Francisco Esparza a Citizen of Bexar County to me personally
known, who bing [*sic*] by me first duly sworn upon his Oath saith that the late
Gregorio Esparza was his Brother; that said Gregorio Esparza about the middle
of October 1835. entered the Texas service as a Volunteer and as such volunteer
soldier he entered Bexar between the mornings of the 5th and 10th December
1835. with the American forces; he remained in Bexar until the approach of
Gen[l]. Santa Anna when he entered the Alamo, when he was killed with Cols.
Travis, Crockett, Bowie and the other Americans. After the fall of the Alamo I
applied and obtained permission from Gen[l]. Cos to take the body of my Brother
(Gregorio Esparza) and bury it. I proceeded to the Alamo and found the dead
body of my Brother in one of the Rooms of the Alamo, he had received a ball in
his breast and a stab from a Sword in his side. I, [*"took his body" crossed out*] in
company with two of my brothers, took his body, and we proceeded and
interred it [*in*] the burying ground (Campo Santo) on the west side of the San

Pedro Creek, where it still lies. My Brother at the takin [*sic*] of Bexar was under the command of Col. Juan N. Seguin and Capt. Don Manuel Flores and a member of their company. I was in service at the time of the Storming of Bexar, the company to which I belonged the Local Presidial company of Bexar, and the soldiers of the company of the Alamo, were under the Capitulation of Genl. Cos, allowed to remain in Bexar with their families, I remained with my family, as I was born here, and had always lived here; When Santa Anna arrived here in Feb. 1836. he gave orders that all those who were the local Soldiers at the Capitulation of Genl. Cos, should hold themselves in readiness to join the army for action service, but [*as*] he never called us away from our homes I remained here, when Santa Anna's Army went into the interior of Texas, and I am now fifty four years of age and have lived here ever since, and done and performed all the duties of a good citizen, as all my nighbors [*sic*] can testify. I mention these facts to show the reason why permission was given me to bury the body of my Brother. The legal heirs of my said Deceased Brother, Gregorio Esparza, are as follow "To Wit." Enriquez Esparza; Manuel Esparza; and Francisco Esparza his sons, who are living now in Attascoso County together at their Ranches.

Sworn Soand	his
subscribed, he	Francisco + Esparza
making his mark for	mark
signature declaring his	
inability towrite this	

26th day of August 1859. And I do hereby certify . . . [*There follows a fairly long statement from the clerk that Francisco Esparza is personally known and had the deposition read to him before making his mark. The year in this deposition on first reading appears to be 1839, but taken with other documents in the file, and closely examining the script of the apparent "3," establishes that it was in fact a "5."*]

1.5.1.2.   Villanueva, Candelario, deposition, August 26, 1859.

Esparza, Gregorio. August 26, 1859. Court of Claims File C-2558. Archives and Records Division, Texas General Land Office.

The State of Texas.
County of Bexar.
Before me Saml. S. Smith, Clerk of the County Court of said county personally appeared Candelario Villanueva a citizen of Bexar County to me personally known who being by me first duly sworn upon his Oath saith that he was a member of Capt. J. N. Seguins Company in 1835. & 1836. that he entered Bexar

between the mornings of the 5ᵗʰ and 10ᵗʰ of Decʳ. 1835. with the American forces; that the late Gregorio Esparza was also a Soldier of Capᵗ. J. N. Seguins Company and he did enter Bexar with the American forces and actually assisted in the reduction of Bexar and that he remained therein till after the capitulation of Genˡ. Cos. Subsequently after the storming of Bexar the said Gregorio Esparza remained at Bexar until the approach of Santa Anna's Army when he went into the Alamo with the Americans. I remained at Bexar and when Santa Anna's troops were entering the town I started with Col. Seguin for the Alamo, when we were on the way Col. Seguin sent me back to lock his house up[.] whilst performing that duty Santa Annas' [*sic*] Soldiers got between me and the Alamo and I had to remain in the Town during the siege and assault of the Alamo. After the fall of the Alamo I went there and among the dead bodys of those lying inside of the rooms I recognized the body of Gregorio Esparza; I also saw the dead bodies of Antonio Fuentes; Toribio Losoyo, Guadalupe Rodríguez and other Mexicans who had fallen in the defense of the Alamo, as also the bodies of Col. Travis, Bowie, Crockett and other Americans that I had previously known. I saw Francisco Esparza and his brothers take the body of Gregorio Esparza and carry it off towards the Campo Santo for interment; the bodies of the Americans were laid in a pile and burnt. I remained in Bexar until the return of Capᵗ. Seguin and his companions after the battle of San Jacinto when I rejoined his company—I afterwards entered the Regiment of Col. J. N. Seguin as a regular Soldier, about the 1ˢᵗ of November 1836. as a member of Capt. Antonio Menechaca's Company. The heirs of said Gregorio Esparza are his sons Enriquez, Manuel & Francisco Esparza, now being in Atascoso County.

Sworn so and subscribed he   his
making his mark for signature   Candelario + Villanueva
declaring his inability towrite,   mark
before me this 26ᵗʰ day of

August 1859. And I do hereby certify . . . [*There follows a statement from the clerk, similar to that in prior document, that Candelario Villanueva is personally known and had the deposition read to him before making his mark.*]

1.5.2.   Enrique Esparza, interview, 1901.

San Antonio Light. November 10, 1901.
A rough draft and a clean, handwritten copy of the statement of paragraphs 9
through 13 are in De Zavala (Adina) Papers, CAH.

ANOTHER CHILD OF THE ALAMO
Miss DeZavala Discovers a Man Who Was in the Fort When It Fell—His Father
Among the Massacred

History says that only a woman and one child escaped from the massacre of the
Alamo, but a San Antonio lady has made the discovery that history is wrong
and that two children, whose parents were Texas soldiers, escaped, besides a
number of others who were non-participants.

The lady in question is Miss A. De Zavala, [*grand*]daughter of the first vice
president of the Republic of Texas. The child of the Alamo No. 2 is now an old
man, bowed with the weight of years, but his intellect is still as good as ever and
Miss De Zavala expects to glean some very valuable data from him. He is a resident of this city and says he was only eight years of age at the time of the
famous massacre, but he remembers vividly the scenes of carnage and bloodshed and relates them in a plain matter of fact way, without embellishment or an
attempt at personal aggrandizement.

He is a Mexican and has kept silent all these years because he did not know
the value of his testimony or think any thing about the famous battle through
which he went when he received his baptism of blood and fire. It was only accidentally that he was discovered by Miss De Zavala and she considers her find a
remarkable one.

She says he told her things about the siege and fall of the famous "Cradle of
Texas Liberty" that convinces her beyond doubt that he is no impostor. He has
also given her data on things that occused [*sic*] inside the famous old fort
which history has always been at a loss to accurately chronicle and related other
things which were not known to have occurred, but which are considered to
have been feasible, and she has written a few of them for the Light, enough to
show that her protege is not faking or shamming. Miss De Zavala's article was
handed the Light yesterday and besides the statement that this man was in the
Alamo, her article says that there were a number of others who also were there
and not massacred. They were Mexican refugees, however, and Miss De
Zavala's recent find and the original Child of the Alamo are the only known
ones to escape, whose father's were of the doomed Texas garrison.

This man whom Miss De Zavala has discovered is Don Enrique Esparza
and his photograph[,] which she also handed the Light, shows him to be a man
of apparently more than ordinary intellect, a strong, robust, honest looking old
fellow. His father, he says, was a Texas soldier, who fell in the defense of the
sacred fort. Notwithstanding this, he says his father's body was not burned

with the other slaughtered Texas patriots, but that a friend in the Mexican army secured it and that it was interred. He gives the names of the others who were in the Alamo and among them are some families yet known in this vicinity. The Alsbury family is mentioned for one. Grand children of this family reside in or near San Antonio. Tom is a farmer east of the city and Perry lives here, having until recently been on the city carpenters force. It has always been known that an Alsbury was in the garrison and this man's familiarity with this and other subjects known already, convinces Miss De Zavala that he is not an impostor, and that he knows whereof he speaks.

Esparza tells Miss De Zavala that he and the other Mexicans who escaped from the butchery of Santa Ana's [*sic*] hordes were concealed in two store rooms in the courtyard of the Alamo proper, in front of what is left of the old building, and that these rooms were on each side of the main entrance gate which led into the court from the outside. He also says the walls were surrounded on the outside by a ditch "as deep as two men" and that a drawbridge spanning this moat afforded the means of ingress and egress to and from the place. It is known that such a wall and moat did exist and Esparza's apparent familiarity with this is another proof of the genuineness of his story.

Another thing. Miss De Zavala and numerous other students of Texas history have contended all along that Madam Candaleria, the old Mexican woman who recently died, claiming to have been in the Alamo when it fell, was really not there. Miss De Zavala even says Madam Candaleria did not herself claim to have been in the Alamo at its fall until a few years before her death. Esparza says she was not there. She had been in it frequently before it fell, he says, and was there immediately afterward, but was not present when the actual fall of the Alamo and massacre of its patriotic defenders occurred.

Miss De Zavala's statement regarding her find, as handed the Light, is as follows:

"Don Enrique Esparza, who is still living, was an eye-witness to some of the most tragic scenes of the past century. He was a child of eight at the time of the massacre of the Alamo. His eyes are bright and his memory clear. He had the advantage of a good education and is most entertaining.

"His father, too, lived in terrible days—was captured as a child by the Comanche Indians and was ransomed after he was grown by Col. [*José Francisco? per Matovina*] Ruiz and brought back to San Antonio. The families of both parents of Esparza were well-to-do and intelligent people and chose to fight for freedom and the Constitution of 1824.

"Early in '36 they were warned by letters from Vice President De Zavala, through Capt. [*Francisco? per Matovina*] Rojo, that the Mexican hordes were coming and advised to take their families to a place of safety. No wagons were obtainable, and so they waited. On the morning of Feb. 22, John W. Smith, one of the scouts, galloped up to Esparza's house bearing the news that Santa Anna was near—would be upon them by night. What should they do? was the question. Fly they could not! Should they try and hide or go into the fortress of the

Alamo? The Alamo was decided upon by the mother, as there her husband would be fighting for liberty. There they carried in their arms their most precious possessions—going back and forth many times, 'till at sunset the mother, Mrs. Anita Esparza, with her last bundles and her little daughter and four sons, passed across the bridge over the acequia into the court-yard of the Alamo, just as the trumpet's blare and noise of Santa Ana's [sic] army was heard. Within the Alamo court-yard were also other refugees who were saved—Mrs. Alsbury and one child and sister, Gertrudes Navarro, Mrs. Concepcion Losoya, her daughter and two sons, Vitonna de Salina and three little girls, Mrs. Dickinson and baby (hitherto believed to have been the only ones who escaped alive), and an old woman called Petra.

"No tongue can describe the terror and horror of that fearful last fight! The women and children were paralized [sic] with terror and faint from hunger when the Mexican soldiers rushed in after the fall of the Alamo. A poor paralitic [sic] unable to speak to them and tell that he was not a belligerent, was murdered before their eyes, as was also a young fellow who had been captured some time previous and confined in the Alamo. Bigido Guerrera [sic], a youth, was saved as he managed to say he was not a Texan, but a Texan prisoner.

"A Mexican officer, related to some of the refugees, arrived just in time to save the women and children—but they were subjected to terrible usage and horrible abuse. Finally, some one obtained safe conduct for them at about 2 o'clock on the morning of the 7th to the house of Gov. Musquitz [*Ramón Múquiz, per Matovina*], on Main plaza. Here the famished prisoners were served with coffee by the Musquitz domestics. At daylight they were required to go before Santa Ana [sic] and take the oath of allegiance. Each mother was then given a blanket and two dollars by Santa Ana [sic] in person. The only two who escaped this additional humiliation were the two daughters of Navarro, who were spirited away from Musquiz's house by their father [*uncle, per Matovina*]— Jose Antonio Navarro. The body of Esparza's father, who was butchered with other Texans, was obtained by his brother who was in the Mexican army, and was buried in the San Fernando Campo Santa, and thus he has the distinction of being the only Texan who escaped the funeral pyre."

Miss De Zavala thinks that from what she can glean from Esparza, she can add much valuable information to history about the fall of the Alamo, of which very little is now authentically known. No Texas history mentions the escape of anyone from the Alamo but Mrs. Dickinson and child, and the San Antonio lady's discovery is of great value. She has been a worker in the interest of Texas history since childhood, and has already published and edited some very important articles. She is the daughter of the first vice president of the Texas Republic, president of the local chapter of the Daughters of the Republic and a teacher in the local schools.

[*Three remaining paragraphs discuss the activities of the Daughters of the Republic and Adina De Zavala, including marking the site of the Veramendi house, the old mill from which Milam made his march, and the discovery of paintings in an old mission.*]

1.5.3.   Enrique Esparza, interview, 1902.

Barnes, Charles M. November 22, 1902. The story of Enrique Esparza. *San Antonio Express.*

This article was reprinted nearly verbatim in the March 7, 1904, *San Antonio Express.*

THE STORY OF ENRIQUE ESPARZA
SAYS THAT HE WAS IN THE SIEGE OF THE ALAMO.
Is Seventy-four Years Old and Tells an Interesting Tale
of That Memorable Massacre and Scenes Leading Up to It.

[*The article gives five paragraphs of background on Esparza similar to that in the previous document (1.5.2) before continuing with his story of the Alamo. It is available complete in Matovina.*]

ESPARZA'S STORY.

"My father, Gregorio Esparza, belonged to Benavides' company, in the American army," said Esparza, "and I think it was in February, 1836, that the company was ordered to Corpus Christi. They had gotten to Goliad when my father was ordered back alone to San Antonio, for what I don't know. When he got here there were rumors that Santa Ana [*sic*] was on the way here, and many residents sent their families away. One of my father's friends told him that he could have a wagon and team and all necessary provisions for a trip if he wanted to take his family away. There were six of us besides my father; my mother, whose name was Anita, my elder sister, myself and three younger brothers, one a baby in arms. I was eight years old.

"My father decided to take the offer and move the family to San Felipe. Everything was ready, when one morning, Mr. [*John*] W. Smith, who was godfather to my younger brother, came to our house on North Flores street, just above where the Presbyterian Church now is, and told my mother to tell my father when he came in that Santa Ana [*sic*] had come.

"When my father came my mother asked him what he would do. You know the Americans had the Alamo, which had been fortified a few months before by General Cos.

"'Well, I'm going to the fort,' my father said.

"'Well, if you go, I'm going along, and the whole family too.'

"It took the whole day to move, and an hour before sundown we were inside the fort. There was a bridge over the river about where Commerce Street crosses it, and just as we got to it we could hear Santa Anna's drums beating on Milam Square; and just as we were crossing the ditch going into the fort Santa Anna fired his salute on Milam Square.

"There were a few other families who had gone in. A Mrs. Osbury [*sic*] and her sister, a Mrs. Victoriana, and a family of several girls, two of whom I knew afterwards; Mrs. Dickson [*Dickinson*], Mrs. Juana Melton, a Mexican woman who had married an American, also a woman named Concepcion Losoya and her son Juan, who was a little older than I.

"The first thing I remember after getting inside the fort was seeing Mrs. Melton making circles on the ground with an umbrella. I had seen very few umbrellas. While I was walking around about dark I went near a man named Fuentes who was talking at a distance with a soldier. When the latter got nearer he said to Fuentes: 'Did you know they had cut the water off?'

"The fort was built around a square. The present Hugo-Schmeltzer building is part of it. I remember the main entrance was on the south side of the large enclosure. The quarters were not in the church, but on the south side of the fort, on either side of the entrance, and were part of the convent. There was a ditch of running water back of the church and another along the west side of Alamo Plaza. We couldn't get to the latter ditch as it was under fire and it was the other one that Santa Anna cut off. The next morning after we had gotten in the fort I saw the men drawing water from a well that was in the convent yard. The well was located a little south of the center of the square. I don't know whether it is there now or not.

"On the first night a company of which my father was one went out and captured some prisoners. One of them was a Mexican soldier, and all through the siege he interpreted the bugle calls, on the Mexican side, and in this way the Americans kept posted on the movements of the enemy.

"After the first day there was fighting every day. The Mexicans had a cannon somewhere near where Dwyer Avenue now is, and every fifteen minutes they dropped a shot into the fort.

"The roof of the Alamo had been taken off and the south side filled up with dirt almost to the roof on that side so that there was a slanting embankment up which the Americans could run and take positions. During the fight I saw numbers who were shot in the head as soon as they exposed themselves from the roof. There were holes made in the walls of the fort and the Americans continually shot from these also. We also had two cannon, one at the main entrance and one at the northwest corner of the fort near the post office. The cannon were seldom fired.

REMEMBERS CROCKETT

"I remember Crockett. He was a tall, slim man, with black whiskers. He was always at the head. The Mexicans called him Don Benito. The Americans said he was Crockett. He would often come to the fire and warm his hands and say a few words to us in the Mexican language. I also remember hearing the names of Travis and Bowie mentioned, but I never saw either of them that I know of.

"After the first few days I remember that a messenger came from somewhere with word that help was coming. The Americans celebrated it by beating the drums and playing on the flute. But after about seven days fighting there was an armistice of three days and during this time Don Benito had conferences every day with Santa Anna. Badio [*Juan A. Badillo, per Matovina*], the interpreter, was a close friend of my father and I heard him tell my father in the quarters that Santa Anna had offered to let the Americans go with their lives if they would surrender, but the Mexicans would be treated as rebels.

"During the armistice my father told my mother she had better take the children and go, while she could do so safely. But my mother said:

"'No, if you're going to stay, so am I. If they kill one, they can kill us all.'

"Only one person went out during the armistice, a woman named Trinidad Saucedo.

"Don Benito, or Crockett, as the Americans called him, assembled the men on the last day and told them Santa Anna's terms, but none of them believed that anyone who surrendered would get out alive, so they all said as they would have to die any how they would fight it out.

"The fighting began again and continued every day, and nearly every night. One night there was music in the Mexican camp and the Mexican prisoner said it meant that reinforcements had arrived.

"We then had another messenger who got through the lines, saying that communication had been cut off and the promised reinforcements could not be sent.

THE LAST NIGHT

"On the last night my father was not out, but he and my mother were sleeping together in headquarters. About 2 o'clock in the morning there was a great shooting and firing at the northwest corner of the fort, and I heard my mother say:

"'Gregorio, the soldiers have jumped the wall. The fight's begun.'

"He got up and picked up his arms and went into the fight. I never saw him again. My uncle told me afterwards that Santa Anna gave him permission to get my father's body and that he found it where the thick of the fight had been.

"We could hear the Mexican officers shouting to the men to jump over, and the men were fighting so close that we could hear them strike each other. It was so dark that we couldn't see anything, and the families that were in the quarters just huddled up in the corners. My mother's children were near her. Finally they began shooting through the dark into the room where we were. A boy who was wrapped in a blanket in one corner was hit and killed. The Mexicans fired into the room for at least fifteen minutes. It was a miracle, but none of us children were touched.

"By daybreak the firing had almost stopped, and through the window we could see shadows of men moving around inside the fort. The Mexicans went from room to room looking for an American to kill. While it was still dark a man stepped into the room and pointed his bayonet at my mother's breast, demanding:

"'Where's the money the Americans had?'

"'If they had any,' said my mother, 'you may look for it.'

"Then an officer stepped in and said:

"'What are you doing? The women and children are not to be hurt.'

"The officer then told my mother to pick out her own family and get her belongings, and the other women were given the same instructions. When it was broad day the Mexicans began to remove the dead. There were so many killed that it took several days to carry them away.

"The families with their baggage were then sent under guard to the house of Don Ramon Musqui [*Musquiz*], which was located where Frank Brothers' Store now is, on Main Plaza. Here we were given coffee and some food, and were told that we would go before the president at 2 o'clock. On our way to the Musqui house we passed up Commerce street, and it was crowded as far as Presa street with soldiers who did not fire a shot during the battle. Santa Anna had many times more troops than he could use.

"At 3 o'clock we went before Santa Anna. His quarters were in a house which stood where L. Wolfson's store now is. He had a great stock of silver money on a table before him, and pile of blankets. One by one the women were sent into a side room to make their 'declaration' and on coming out were given $2 and a blanket. While my mother was waiting her turn Mrs. Melton, who had never recognized my mother as an acquaintance, and who was considered an aristocrat, sent her brother, Juan Losoya, across the room to my mother to ask the favor that nothing be said to the president about her marriage with an American.

"My mother told Juan to tell her not to be afraid.

"Mrs. Dickson was there, also several other women. After the president had given my mother her $2 and blanket, he told her she was free to go where she liked. We gathered what belongings we could together and went to our cousin's place on North Flores street, where we remained several months.

1.5.4.   Enrique Esparza, interview, 1907.

Barnes, Charles Merritt. May 12:14 and 19:47, 1907. Alamo's only survivor. *San Antonio Daily Express.*

The first article includes a photograph of Esparza, the second a picture of Santa Anna's headquarters in San Antonio. The copy available had tears or spots that made a few words unreadable. A condensed version of this interview was reprinted with some analysis by Jim Hutton in the *San Antonio Express-News,* June 9, 1991, 1-M.

[*May 12, 1907, article*]

ALAMO'S ONLY SURVIVOR

Enrique Esparza, Who Claims to Have Been There During the Siege, Tells the Story of the Fall.

(Copyrighted May, 1907, by Charles Merritt Barnes)

At 707 Nogalitos Street there stands a small cottage, covered with madlera and trumpet vines which cling to its caves and cluster along its porch. Roses and myrtle grow beside and in front. Nearby figs and other fruits grow, while all about is green and shady, or tinted with the blooms of fragrant and many colored flowers that grow there in profusion.

This humble cottage shelters the only living human being now claiming to have been within the walls of the Alamo when it was besieged by Santa Anna's horde and fell under their deadly fire. Although confessing that 82 years have passed since he was born, he is yet hale and strong. He owns the small suerte of land on which his lowly home stands and when I saw him this week, with a team he was tilling its soil. His name is Enrique Esparza. The story he tells is marvelous. He speaks English admirably and nothing he says is marred but is emphasized by his mode of speech. This is his story.

"All of the others are dead. I alone live of they who were within the Alamo when it fell. There is none other left now to tell its story and when I go to sleep my last slumber in the Campo de los Santos, there will then be no one left to tell.

"You ask me do I remember it. I tell you yes. It is burned into my brain and indellibly [*sic*] seared there. Neither age nor infirmity could make me forget, for the scene was one of such horror that it could never be forgotten by any one who witnessed its incidents.

"I was born in one of the old adobe houses that formerly stood on the east side of what we then called El Calle de Acquia or the street of the acquia or ditch, but now known as Main Avenue. The house in which I was born was but a short distance north of Salinas Street. I am the son of Gregorio Esparza.

"You will see my father's name on the list of those who died in the Alamo. This list is at Austin. It is on the monument in front of the Capitol. That monument was built there in honor of those who fell with the Alamo. I have made several pilgrimages to it just to read the inscription and list of names, because my father's name is on the list. There is no monument here to those who fell in the Alamo and died there that Texas might be free. There are none here with the means to do so who have ever cared enough for those who died there to mark the spot where their bodies were buried. Though this be so, those who died there were all brave, both men and women.

"My mother was also in the Alamo when it fell, as were some of my brothers and a sister. My mother's maiden name was Anna [or Aana] Salazar. She told me I was born in the month of September and in the year 1824.

WENT INTO THE ALAMO

"I was then a boy of twelve years of age; was then quite small, and delicate and could have passed for a child of eight. My father was a friend and comrade of William Smith. Smith had expected to send my father and our family away with his own family in a wagon to Nacogdoches. We were waiting for the wagon to be brought to town. My father and Smith had heard of the approach of Santa Anna, but did not expect him and his forces to arrive as early as they did. Santa Anna and his men got here before the wagon we waited for could come.

"My father was told by Smith that all who were friends to the Americans had better join the Americans who had taken refuge in the Alamo. Smith and his family went there and my father and his family went with them.

"Santa Anna and his army arrived at about sundown and almost immediately after we sought refuge in the Alamo. Immediately after their arrival Santa Anna's personal staff dismounted on Main Plaza in front of the San Fernando church. Santa Anna went into the building at the northwest corner of Main Plaza which was since been superseded by that now occupied by S. Wolfson. That building had been occupied by the Texans and before them by the soldiers of Mexico and still earlier by the soldiers of Spain. It had been a part of the presidio, or old fort, and the part where the officers had the headquarters. The Texans had left this structure and gone over to the Alamo because the latter offered more advantages for defense.

"I have often heard it said that Santa Anna immediately upon his arrival in San Antonio dismounted in the West side of Military Plaza and hitched his horse to an iron ring set into the wall of the old building where the Spanish Governors dwelt and where the combined coats of arms of Spain and Austria form the keystone of the arch above its portal. This is not so. I saw Santa Anna when he arrived. I saw him dismount. He did not hitch the horse. He gave the bridle reins to a lackey. He and his staff proceeded immediately to the house on the Northwest corner of Main Plaza. I was playing with some other children on the Plaza and when Santa Anna and his soldiers came up we ran off and told our parents, who almost immediately afterwards took me and the other children of the family to the Alamo. I am sure of this for I saw Santa Anna several times afterward and after I came out of the Alamo.

WITHIN THE WALLS OF THE ALAMO

"It was twilight when we got into the Alamo and it grew pitch dark soon afterward. All of the doors were closed and barred. The sentinels that had been on duty without were first called inside and then the openings closed. Some sentinels were posted upon the roof, but these were protected by the walls of the Alamo church and the old Convent building. We went into the church portion. It was shut up when we arrived. We were admited through a small window.

"I distinctly remember that I climbed through the window and over a cannon that was placed inside of the church immediately behind the window. There were several other cannon there. Some were back of the doors. Some had been mounted on the roof and some had been placed in the Convent. The window was opened to permit us to enter and it was closed immediately after we got inside.

"We had not been in there long when a messenger came from Santa Anna calling us to surrender. I remember the reply to this summons was a shot from one of the cannon on the roof of the Alamo. Soon after it was fired I heard Santa Anna's cannon reply. I heard his cannon shot strike the walls of the church and also the convent. Then I heard the cannon within the Alamo buildings, both church and convent, fire repeatedly during the nights. I heard the cheers of the Alamo gunners and the deriding jeers of Santa Anna's troops.

"My heart quaked when the shot tore through the timbers. My fear and terror was overwhelming but my brave mother and my dauntless father sought to soothe and quiet my brothers and myself. My sister was but an infant and knew naught of the tragic scenes enacted about us. But even child as I was I could not help but feel inspired by the bravery of the heroes about me.

WOULD HAVE FOUGHT ALSO.

"If I had been given a weapon I would have fought likewise. But weapons and ammunition were scarce and only wielded and used by those who knew how. But I saw some there no older than I who had them and fought as bravely and died as stolidly as the adults. This was towards the end and when many of the grown persons within had been slain by the foes without. It was then that some of the children joined in the defense.

"All who had weapons used them as often as they had the chance to do so, shots were fired fast. Bullets flew thick. Both men and women fell within the walls. Even children died there. The fighting was intermittent. We must have been within the Alamo ten or twelve days. I did not count the days. But they were long and full of terror. The nights were longer and fraught with still more horror. It was between the periods of fierce fighting and all too short armistice that we got any rest.

"Crockett seemed to be the leading spirit. He was everywhere. He went to every exposed point and personally directed the fighting. Travis was chief in command, but he depended more upon the judgment of Crockett and that brave man's intrepidity than upon his own. Bowie too, was brave and dauntless, but he was ill. Prone upon his cot he was unable to see much that was going on about him, and the others were too engrossed to stop and tell him.

Although too weak to stand upon his feet, when Travis drew the line with his sword Bowie and [*sic; asked*] those around him [*to*] bring his cot across the line.

" I heard the few Mexicans there call Crockett 'Don Benito.' Afterward I learned his name was David, but I only knew him as 'Don Benito.'

THOSE WHO LEFT.

"One day when I went to where Bowie was lying on his cot I heard him call those about him and say:

"'All of you who desire to leave here may go in safety. Santa Anna has just sent a message to Travis saying there will be an armistice for three days to give us time to deliberate on surrendering. During those three days all who desire to do so may go out of here. Travis has sent me the message and told me to tell those near me.'

"When Bowie said this quite a number left. Travis and Bowie took advantage of this occasion to send out for succor they vainly hoped would come to the Alamo and those within before it fell. William Smith and Alsberry [*sic*] were among those who were sent for succor then. Seguin claimed also to have been so sent. Among the surnames of those I remember to have left during the time of this armistice were Menchaca, Flores, Rodriquez, Ramirez, Arocha, Silvern. They are now all dead. Among the women who went out were some of their relatives.

"Rose left after this armistice had expired and after the others had been sent for succor. Rose went out after Travis drew the line with his sword. He was the only man who did not cross the line. Up to then he had fought as bravely as any [*word unreadable, one?*] there. He had stood by the [*one word unreadable*].

"Rose [*went?*] out during the night. They opened a window for him and let him go. The others who left before went out of the doors and in the daytime. Alsberry left his wife and sister-in-law there. His sister-in-law afterwards married a man named Cantu. She and Mrs. Alsberry stayed in the Alamo until it fell. They feared to leave, believing the Mexicans under Santa Anna would kill them.

"Bowie asked my father if he wished to go when the armistice of three days was on. My father replied:

"'No. I will stay and die fighting.' My mother then said:

"'I will stay by your side and with our children die too. They will soon kill us. We will not linger in pain.'

"So we stayed. And so my father died, as he said, fighting. He struck down one of his foes as he fell in the heap of slain.

HOW THE END CAME.

"The end came suddenly and almost unexpectedly and with a rush. It came at night and when all was dark save when there was a gleam of light from the flash and flame of a fired gun. Our men fought hard all day long. Their amunition was very low. That of many was entirely spent. Santa Anna must have known this, for his men had been able during the day to make several breeches [*sic*] in the walls. Our men had fought long and hard and well. But their strength was spent. Many slept. Few there were who were awake. Even those on guard besides the breeches in the walls dozed. The fire from the Mexicans had slacked and finally ceased. Those who were awake saw the Mexican foeman [*sic*] lying quietly by their camp fires and thought they likewise slept. But our foes were only simulating sleep, or if they slept, were awakened by their savage chief and his brutal officers.

"After all had been dark and quiet for many hours and I had fallen into a profound slumber suddenly there was a terrible din. Cannon boomed. Their shot crashed through the doors and windows and the breeches in the walls. Then men rushed in on us. They swarmed among us and over us. They fired on us in vollies. They struck us down with their escopetas. In the dark our men groped and grasped the throats of our foemen and buried their knives into their hearts.

A BOY HERO.

"By my side was an American boy. He was about my own age but larger. As they reached us he rose to his feet. He had been sleeping, but like myself, he had been rudely awakened. As they rushed upon him he stood calmly and across his shoulders drew the blanket on which he had slept. He was unarmed. They slew him where he stod [*sic*] and his corpse fell over me. My father's body was lying near the cannon which he had tended. My mother with my baby sister was kneeling beside it. My brothers and I were close to her. I clutched her garments. Behind her crouched the only man who escaped and was permitted to surrender. His name was Brigido Guerrera [*sic*].

"As they rushed upon us the Mexican soldiers faltered as they saw a woman. My mother clasped her babe to her breast and closed her eyes. She expected they would kill her and her babe and me and my brothers. I thought so too. My blood ran cold and I grew faint and sick.

"Brigido Guerrera plead for mercy. He told them he was a prisoner in the Alamo and had been brought there against his will. He said he had tried to escape and join Santa Anna's men. They spared him. They led him out, an officer going with him.

"They took my mother, her babe, my brothers and I to another part of the building where there were other women and children all huddled. Another of the women had a babe at her breast. This was Mrs. Dickinson. There was an old woman in there. They called her Donna Petra. This was the only name I ever knew her by. With her was a young girl, Trinidad Saucedo, who was very beautiful. Mrs. Alsberry and her sister were there also and several other women, young girls and little boys. I do not remember having seen Madam Candalaria there. She may have been among the women and I may have been [*sic; not?*] noticed her particularly. She claimed to have been there and I shall not dispute her word. I did not notice the women as closely as I did the men.

FIRED AFTER ALL WERE KILLED.

"After the soldiers of Santa Anna had got in a corner all of the women and children who had not been killed in the onslaught, they kept firing on the men who had defended the Alamo. For fully a quarter of an hour they kept firing upon them after all of the defenders had been slain and their corpses were lying still. It was pitch dark in the Eastern end of the structure and the soldiers of Santa Anna seemed in fear to go there even after firing from the Constitutionalists from there had ceased. Santa Anna's men stood still and fired into the darkness and until some one brought lanterns.

"The last I saw of my father's corpse was when one of them held his lantern above it and over the dead who lay about the cannon he had tended."

CHARLES MERRITT BARNES

[*Caption of photograph: ENRIQUE ESPARZA, Who Lives Here Now, Says He Was in the Alamo When Santa Anna's Men Siezed (sic) It.*]

[*May 19, 1907, article*]
ALAMO'S ONLY SURVIVOR
Enrique Esparza Continues His Story of Its Siege and Fall.
Copyrighted by Charles Merritt Barnes, May, 1907

Continuing his narration relative to the capture of the Alamo and the incidents connected with it, especially his own personal experiences and those of members of his family who he says were with him, Don Enrique Esparza further said:

"It has been stated that one of the women who claims to have been in the Alamo during its siege and capture, has also claimed that she brought water into the Alamo from the ditch outside. This is not true. When we got into the Alamo, which was before access to the ditch had been entirely cut off by the soldiers of Santa Anna, such occurrance [*sic*] had been foreseen and forestalled by inmates of the Alamo chapel. They had already sunk a well in the church and the water therefrom was then being drunk by the occupants instead of the water from the ditch. A number of cattle had also been driven into the court of the Convent. These latter furnished food for the besieged up to the day of the fall of the Alamo. I do not recollect the inmates having suffered for either food or water during the entire period of the siege. The only article that was scarce was ammunition. This got scarcer and scarcer each day, with no chance or hope of replenishing.

TELLS HOW CROCKETT DIED.

"The old Convent had been used for barracks by Bowie, Travis and Crockett's men and was so used until the besiegers had driven them to seek final refuge in the chapel after a number of breeches [*sic*] had been made in the Convent wall. Communication was constantly kept up between the Convent and the church building. This was done through a door connecting them. I was in the Convent several times, but stayed most, and practically all, of the time in the church, as it was considered safest. Crockett who, as I said before they called Don Benito, went often into the Convent and stayed there for some time. But he was every-where during the siege and personally slew many of the enemy with his rifle, his pistol and his knife. He fought hand to hand. He clubbed his rifle when they closed in on him and knocked them down with its stock until he was over-whelmed by numbers and slain. He fought to his last breath. He fell immedi-ately in front of the large double doors which he defended with the force that was by his side. Crockett was one of the few who were wide awake when the final crisis and crash came. When he died there was a heap of slain in front and one [*sic*] each side of him. These he had all killed before he finally fell no [*sic; on*] top of the heap.

"Travis spent most of his time directing the firing from the roof of the church. He too, seemed not only dauntless but sleepless. He encouraged the gunners. Whenever a good shot was made with the cannon he commended them. He told them where to aim and when to fire efficaciously, the cannon fire from the roof of the church being most of the time under his direct personal supervision. Crockett and he both, however, looked after the cannonading from the Convent as well, both making repeated visits to the locality and at frequent intervals.

"Bowie, although ill and suffering from a fever, fought until he was so severely wounded that he had to be carried to his cot, which was placed in one of the smaller rooms on the north side of the church. Even after he was confined to his cot he fought, firing his pistol and, occasionally, his rifle at the enemy after the soldiers of Santa Anna had entered the church and some of them got into his room. He loaded and fired his weapons until his foes closed in on him. When they made their final rush upon him, he rose up in his bed and received them. He buried his sharp bowie knife into the breast of one of them as another fired the shot that killed him. He was literally riddled with bullets. I saw his corpse before we were taken out of the building.

WOMEN WHO NURSED BOWIE.

"Mrs. Alsbury and my mother were among those who nursed and ministered to his wants. Mrs. Alsbury was near him when he was killed, while my mother and I were in the large main room of the church and by the cannon near the window where my father fell.

The shot and shells tore great holes in the walls. They also sawed out great jagged segments of the walls [?] of both the Convent and the church. The roof of the Convent was knocked in, the greater part of it falling, as also did a con-siderable portion of the roof of the church. Nearly one-half of the walls of the Convent were knocked off.

ALAMO CHURCH BURNED.

"Some time after it had been repaired after the siege and capture of Santa Anna's army, the Alamo church was almost entirely destroyed by fire. This was along about the time of the Civil War. The Convent portion escaped this visitation of conflagration, which did not therefore cause any change in the Convent's appearance. The entire aspect of the church of the Alamo was changed when it was repaired after this fire. Originally towers surmounted the northwest and southwest corners of the church, these towers resembling those of the Concepcion mission. Its sweeping curved facade that now appears on the front was not there originally. Its roof was arched within, but flat on top.

"There was no tower then on the Convent building, but later the United States Quartermaster, while it was occupied as a warehouse, erected a room in the southwest corner of the Convent and above the original walls which it surmounted. This room, which he used for his office, was reached by a stairway whose steps were placed on the southwest side of the Convent building.

GRENET ADDED THE SECOND STORY.

"When the Convent property became the mercantile establishment of the late Honore [?] Grenet, he added the second story which is of lumber. He placed the present woodwork that forms it there. When he first built it, he put up a wooden turret above the second story's center. From this turret projected wooden cannon to give it a martial appearance that it never had possessed before. The room erected by the United States Quartermaster, whose name I believe was Raiston, was made of stone. Its roof was shingled. Originally the large doors that occurred at frequent intervals along the west side of the Convent building had carved arches above them. It was Grenet, I believe, who altered these to flat arches, as they now are. If the Convent ever had towers, as the church had, they disappeared before I ever saw the structure.

"Of course I do not mean to say what may have been the appearance of either the Convent or the church before my memory and recollection of them commences. I do not question the statement of any one regarding their appearance when first built. I have already appeared before a committee of the Texas Legislature and testified in regard to the appearance of both portions of the Alamo according to my first recollection of them. I do not now care to enter any controversy over the structure.

"At the time the question of purchasing the church portion was pending I was living in Pleasanton. I was sent for to testify before a committee of the Legislature which was then investigating the matter and considering the purchase of the property. I do not know, and never asked why, the Convent portion was not purchased when the purchase of the church portion was made, nor why the purchase of the Convent was delayed until it was purchased by Miss Driscoli, now Mrs. Sevier, and when the shjboleth [sic] and slogan was:

"Save the Alamo!"

"Although I do not remember to have seen any one killed in the Convent, because I was not in there when they were, I am told and believe that many of the defenders of the Alamo perished there.

TAKEN OUT OF THE ALAMO.

"But to return to the story of the fall of the Alamo. After all of the men had been slain, the women and children were kept huddled up in the church's southwest corner in the small room to the right of the large double door of the church as one enters it. A guard was put over them. They were held there until after day-light when orders were given to remove them. We were all marched off to the house of Senor Musquiz. Here all of the women were again placed under guard. Musquiz owned a suerte on South Alamo Street not very far from where the Beethoven Hall now is. My mother and father were well acquainted with the Musquiz family. At about 8 o'clock we became very hungry, up to then not hav-ing been given any food. My mother, being familiar with the premises, began to look about for food for herself and children as well as her other comrades. While she was doing so Musquiz told her that it was dangerous for her to be moving about and leaving the place, and room in which she was under guard. She told him she did not care whether she was under guard or not, she was going to have something to eat for herself, her children and her companions whom she intended to feed if Santa Anna did not feed his prisoners. Musquiz admonished her to silence and told her to be patient and he would get them some food from his own store.

"After urging my mother not to leave the room, Musquiz disappeared and went to his pantry, where he got quite a quantity of provisions and brought them to the room in which the prisoners, some ten or a dozen in number, were and distributed the food among them. There was some coffee as well as bread and meat. I recollect that I ate heartily, but my mother very sparingly.

"We were kept at Musquiz's house until 3 o'clock in the afternoon when the prisoners were taken to Military Plaza.

ESPARZA BEFORE SANTA ANNA.

"We were halted on the plaza and in front of the place were Wolfson's store now is. Mrs. Alsbury and her sister, Mrs. Gertrudes Cantu, were the first ones to be taken before Santa Anna. He questioned them and after talking with them for a few minutes, discharged them from custody and they left. Mrs. Cantu afterwards removed to the Calaveras where she married and resided up to the time of her death.

Mrs. Dickinson, the wife of Lieutenant Dickenson [*sic*], the woman whom I told you, like my mother, had a babe at her breast, was the next to be sum-moned before Santa Anna. He spent some time in questioning her after which he dismissed her.

"My mother was next called before the dictator. When she appeared before him my baby sister pressed closely to her bosom, I with my brother followed her into his presence. My brother was clinging to her skirt, but I stood to one side and behind her. I watched every move and listened to every word spoken. Santa Anna asked her name. She gave it. He then asked.

"'Where is your husband?' She answered, sobbing:

"'He's dead at the Alamo.'

"Santa Anna next asked where the other members of the family were. She replied a brother of my father's, she was informed, was in his (Santa Anna's) army. This was true. My father had a brother whose name was Francisco Esparza, who joined the forces of Santa Anna. It was this brother who appeared before Santa Anna later and asked permission to search among the slain for my father's corpse. The permission was given. My uncle found my father's body and had it buried in the Campo Santo where Milam [or Milarn?] Square is now. I did not get a chance to see it before it was buried there, as the burial, as all others incident to that battle, was a very hurried one. It is probable that my father was the only one who fought on the side of the Constitutionalists, and against the forces of the dictator, whose body was buried without having first been burned.

"Santa Anna released my mother. He gave her a blanket and two silver dollars as he dismissed her. I was informed that he gave a blanket and the same sum of money to each of the other women who were brought from the Alamo before him.

"I noticed him closely and saw he was the same officer I had seen dismount on the Main Plaza about sundown of the night when I went into the Alamo. After our release we went back to our home and my mother wept for many days and nights. I frequently went to the Main Plaza and watched the soldiers of Santa Anna and saw him quite a number of times before they marched away towards Houston where he was defeated. He had a very broad face and high cheek bones. He had a hard and cruel look, and his countenance was a very sinister one. It has haunted me ever since I last saw it and I will never forget the face or figure of Santa Anna."

CHARLES MERRITT BARNES

[*Caption of photograph: WHERE SANTA ANNA HAD HIS HEADQUARTERS WHEN HERE.*]

1.5.5.   Enrique Esparza, interview, 1911.

Barnes, Charles Merritt. March 26:26, 1911. Builders' spades turn up soil baked by Alamo funeral pyres. *San Antonio Express.*

This is a section from a longer article (3.7.7) relating to the ashes of the Alamo defenders.

The sites of the two pyres have been pointed out to me by several persons, three of whom saw them when the bodies were being burned and before the ashes had been scattered and the fragments removed. These three persons are all living today. One of them is Enrique Esparza, who states he was a child 8 years old when the siege and fall of the Alamo took place, and that he was in the Alamo with his parents and one of his brothers. He said that his father and the brother mentioned were killed in the Alamo and his mother and he was [*sic*] taken before Santa Ana after it had fallen. Esparaza [*sic*] says that Mrs. Dickenson, the wife of Lieutenant Dickenson, who became a mother during the siege and was taken with her infant to Santa Ana at the same time as also was Mrs. Alsberry [*sic*] and several other women and children.

Santa Anna gave each of the women two silver pesos, or Mexican "dobe" dollars when he ordered their release. Esparza says:

"After this we went to look for the body of my father and my brother, but when we got to the Alamo again all of the bodies had been removed and taken to the Alameda. They were put in two piles, one on each side of the Alameda, and burned, both Mexicans and Americans, and my father and brother were among them, but we could not find them in either pile, for the soldiers would not let us get close enough to examine or claim them.

"They set fire to them and burned them. My mother placed her mantilla before her face and ran screaming from the scene, dragging me by the hand with her. After the bodies were burned we went back several times to the two places until all of the fragments had been removed and the ashes had been scattered in every direction.

1.5.6.   Enrique Esparza, interview, early 1900s?

Driggs, Howard R., and Sarah S. King. 1936. *Rise of the Lone Star*. 213–31. New York: Frederick A. Stokes Co.

This generally overlooked account was partially included in Bill Groneman's *Eyewitness to the Alamo* (1996, 180–87). Groneman noted that King was a longtime principal of the Bowie School, and that her mother was quoted in 1917 as having heard the Alamo story from Esparza. He also points out that the use of Esparza's name as Gregerio is unexplained (likely a confusion with his father's name?). The early portion of this account is not directly related to the battle, but it is included for the portrait of life among the poor of San Antonio de Bexar just prior to the Texas Revolution.

CHAPTER XIII

ESPARZA, THE BOY OF THE ALAMO, REMEMBERS

The principal of the Bowie School one day introduced to her pupils an old Mexican gentleman. The colorful zarape round his shoulders, and the large Mexican hat in his hand emphasized the picturesque.

"Buenas dias, *niños*," he greeted them.

"I am so glad you could come, Señor Esparza," said the teacher as she extended her hand in welcome. Then to the eager group of young Americans: "this, boys and girls, is the man of whom I was just speaking, Señor Gregerio Esparza—the boy of the Alamo. Won't you be seated, Señor?'"

The aged Mexican made a graceful bow, took the proffered chair, and looking over his eager, youthful audience, said, "It gives me great pleasure to see so many bright faces."

"You speak English!" exclaimed one of the girls.

Señor Esparza's black eyes twinkled. "Why not, señorita? I have lived for many years with my American friends. We should know the same language. But before the Americans came we learned how to use the Spanish tongue; so I think in Spanish, and my English words are a little mixed. You must pardon an old man.

"I had many hardships and not the chance for school—not even one day. I did learn by myself to read and to write, and then studied from my children's books. Now I read many hours a day. It is about all an old man can do. I am now over eighty years old and may soon leave my Texas land. While I live I want to tell of my people and of their part in winning the liberty of Texas. Some of us helped the Texans, and it took brave men to face Santa Anna and his resources. We were less than one to a hundred. It shows what right can do against might with the trust in God."

"Do you love Texas more than Mexico?" asked some one.

Señor Esparza shrugged his shoulders and said: "My people have been here—forever. No one counted the ages. We were Indians. Then the Spanish came and other nations. Many of my people are of mixed blood. I am of Indian and Spanish blood. The Indians were the first Americans. We are proud of that ancestry. I know nothing of Mexico but from the tales of old men and what I read in books. My father was killed in the Alamo. He stood by the side of Travis. I saw him die for Texas. I am proud to be a Texan and an American.

"We were of the poor people. There were little riches, and to be poor in that day meant to be very poor indeed—almost as poor as the Savior in his manger. We were not dissatisfied with it. We were very contented. We lived not as the people now live, always seeking happiness in pleasures and much money. There were other things worth while—time to eat and sleep and look at growing plants. We had happy hearts in stout bodies—fresh air aplenty and wild freedom.

"Of food we had not over much—chili and beans, beans and chili. Sometimes my uncle went on a hunt, and then we had venison and buffalo meat; but the Indians were bad and often drove the buffalo far away. Deer along the San Antonio River were as many as the hairs on my head. We planted beans and pumpkins to grow on the walls of the old Alamo. Our jacalita leaned against the ruins—the old wall that came across the Plaza.

"Some of the jacals had a fireplace and chimney. Our chimney was a smoky one, so my mother cooked outside most of the time. It was very pleasant along the acequia—clear sky and clear water. Most of the time we ate and slept outdoors. We were very free and very happy—until my father died in the Alamo. Then we saw and heard much we can never forget.

"The Alamo was old and gray and tumbling when I first remember. It was very large. Near the west walls the good Padres had built houses for the tame Indians. Many years had passed after they had gone. From the tumbling stones of these buildings we built our jacalita. The old wall of the Alamo made one side of it. Our roof was of tula that grew along the river bank, and sometimes of short grass.

"My father would hunt and fish and farm. The church allowed us some rich land not far from the Alamo. The Indians would steal our animals—often our cows, but we did not worry. We lived in peace until General Cos came with his army to drive the Texans out of our country. The Texans were our friends. We were glad when they came and drove Cos and his soldiers out of San Antonio.

"My mother sold many tamales and beans to the Texans. I helped her to carry the earthen jars full of food. It was a heavy task at times. One day while I was carrying a jar along the big log that made a foot-bridge over the San Antonio River, I slipped and fell into the deep water. Señor Bowie jumped in and brought me out. I could swim from the time I was four years old, but this day I think I struck the log in falling for my head was bloody. I was very fond of Señor Bowie after this.

"My father became a Texas soldier. He belonged to the Benavides company. He was promised much land. He was given a little money—not much. Mother used it to buy some food. She had to work very hard to feed the hungry mouths of her children.

"After Cos left San Antonio, the Texas soldiers taught me a queer tune and some words I did not understand. It was like this:

> 'We are the boys so handy,
> We'll teach Santa Anna to fear
> Our Yankee Doodle dandy.'

I was a very small Mexican boy. When I would sing the song the soldiers would laugh and give me centavos.

"We were poor people but we had many friends. Señor Bowie, Señor Smith, and the rich Señor Navarro. I played with the Smith and the Navarro children. Señor Bowie had no family. His wife, the beautiful Ursula Veremendi, and their two children had died. He was a sad man. One day Señor Bowie said to my father, 'Give me Gregorio. I will send him to the United States to school.'

"My father shook his head, and my mother said, 'It is not the will of God, Señor. Gregorio is our son. The United States is far off and is very different. There Gregorio would be like a bird in a gilded cage. We are plain people, Señor, you know—not in your class.' My mother thought that one's place in life was the will of God and it was wicked not to be content. 'Maybe,' as the Americans say, she was right. Now life is hurry, hurry. There is no time to count our blessings. We want more and more—An old man wanders. My life has been long and much time for thinking—Where was I, Señorita?"

"You were telling us of your childhood, Señor."

"Si—Señorita,—forgetfulness—pardon."

"What kind of clothes did you wear?" came a guiding question.

"Not very much and very cheap. A white cotton blouse and cotton pants tied together with rawhide string—no hat, no shoes."

"Was the old Alamo used for worship?" asked some one.

"No, the Alamo was in ruin. It had been that way even before my mother was born. We went to church at San Fernando in San Antonio. The Alamo was almost out in the country. The rich people lived around the Plaza and along the San Pedro River that winds through the town. The poor lived around the Alamo. There were just a few houses between the Main Plaza and the Alamo.

"We thought the Plaza very big and fine. Adobe houses were built all around it, and a grand market place was in the middle of the square. The Indians came here to trade. They brought skins of the deer and the buffalo. The ranchmen brought hides to sell for leather. The hides were worth more than the beef. I have seen hides on the Plaza as high as an adobe house. People came to San Antonio on horseback or in ox-carts and camped on the Plaza.

"On Sunday around the San Fernando Cathedral it was very gay. After mass and vespers there was talking, walking and dancing on the Plaza. The priests lived near San Fernando and sometimes the tame Indians came from the San Jose Mission. They came to mass at the cathedral—Apache, Comanche, Lipans—a few, not many, and old."

"'You cannot tame an Indian, a rabbit or a parrot'—Señorita—'tis a wise Mexican saying.

"We had many saint days. Then we would visit for a long time with relatives and friends. I had many cousins. We would meet and play together. Then we would join in the fiesta around San Fernando. One time we rode from that Alamo in an ox-cart to the Cathedral to see the Pastores. It was very grand to ride and to see this blessed Shepherd Play. The altar to the Christ Child was bright with many candles. All over the Plaza shone candles—the houses were all covered with lights—in remembrance of the 'Light of the World.'

"The first 'villa' in Texas was around the San Fernando Cathedral. After the Americans came we called it all—as far as the Alamo—San Antonio de Bexar.

"As I told you the Alamo was left and it fell into ruins. When the Texas soldiers came and drove Cos away, they camped round the old Mission. I heard some of them say it was too big; they did not have enough men to hold it. I thought that the Texans could do anything. There seemed to be many, many men in the fortress when they gathered there; but they were only a few when we think of Santa Anna's army. Anyway I was sure that these brave men could whip Santa Anna and all his men.

"There was great cheering when Señor Crockett came with his friends. He wore a buckskin suit and a coonskin cap. He made everybody laugh and forget their worries. He had a gun he called 'Betsey.' They told me that he had killed many bears. I knew he would kill many of Santa Anna's soldiers.

"One thing that frightened me was the cannon the Texans brought. They placed these big guns on the top of the thick walls and pointed them every way. The noise they made was terrible to me.

"Santa Anna had many men and much 'thunder.' I mean powder. The Indians called it 'thunder.' A man told my mother he was like a king with much power and many servants. It was said he ate from plates made of silver and gold. I could not believe that, but I have read from books it is true. He was very proud. He said that the Texans could not get away from him. A Mexican woman told this to the men at the Alamo.

"One day Santa Anna demanded that the Texans surrender. Colonel Travis answered with a shot from one of the big cannons. Then Santa Anna ran a blood-red flag to the top of the tower of the Cathedral of San Fernando. Some one said that this meant he would kill every one on the side of the Texans. The Texans did not seem to be excited. At night they would sing and dance. No fighting came for several days.

"Travis was a brave leader. He had been asked by Señor Bowie, who was ill, to take command. Father would rather follow Bowie, because they were friends. I saw Señor Bowie while he was ill. The soldiers let me go about among them.

"This good friend did not forget us. When the mothers and children fled to the Alamo, Señor Bowie had driven in some beeves and found some corn. He gave part of this food to us. We were too scared to think much of eating, but mother made some atole, a sort of mush, for all the children. She ground the corn and boiled it and almost poured it down our throats. Mother was a sensible woman and kept her head. Some of the other women were almost helpless.

"When the trumpets of Santa Anna were heard, we had rushed to the Alamo. When father told her she had better go to a safer place, she said, 'No; if you are to die, I want to be near you!' We gathered up the few things we had—a metate, two chairs, four skins and some cooking utensils. In one bundle was my baby sister. My small brothers and I carried what we could. I was the oldest—nine years.

"We all went into a small store room near the monastery. Here we slept on hay and under hay. With us were other Mexican mothers and children. The women helped by grinding corn and cooking for the men. Mrs. Dickerson and her baby were with us. She seemed not to know what to do in this condition. I heard mother say, 'povrecita,' and take the lady some food.

"At first we got our water from the ditch in front of the Alamo. Later the enemy cut off this supply and we had to use an old well.

"One night father captured a Mexican who was prowling round, and kept him a prisoner. He was one of Santa Anna's soldiers. During the siege he would tell the Texans what the bugle calls of the enemy meant. I heard that this poor fellow was afterwards killed because Santa Anna thought he was a deserter.

"Then came the days of the terrible fighting. It was all so frightful—but what could one do except just watch and wait? The roof of the old Alamo was off. Along the south side was a dirt wall or embankment up which the Texans would run and fire. Some of them were killed when they did this—Lieutenant Dickerson was among these. His sorrowful wife and babe were left with us.

"Señor Crockett seemed everywhere. He would shoot from the wall or through the portholes. Then he would run back and say something funny. He tried to speak Spanish sometimes. Now and then he would run to the fire we had in the courtyard where we were to make us laugh.

"When Señor Smith came from Gonzales with the band of men he had gathered, there was great shouting. The Texans beat drums and played on a flute. Colonel Travis sent Señor Smith off again to get more men.

"Captain Seguin was also sent for help. I saw him go. The way I remember was he rode Señor Bowie's horse. We were afraid he could not get by Santa Anna's soldiers. They were getting closer and closer to the Alamo. Afterwards I heard that the Captain was stopped by them, but he said he was a Mexican rancher. This was true; and they let him go. He tried to gather men to get back to help the Texans; but the ways were long in those days, and not many men to get. Before he and Señor Smith could return, the battle was all over.

"One brave man that did get back was Señor Benham. He had been sent to Goliad to get Fannin to send help. He rode right past the sentinels of Santa Anna. They fired, but he escaped. My mother knelt and said her beads and thanked the good God. Señor Benham had a white handkerchief tied to his hat. If he was shot while trying to get back to his friends in the Alamo, this handkerchief was a sign he had seen Fannin. Benham came through the danger unharmed. He was one of the great heroes that fell there fighting for liberty.

"At times Señor Travis looked very sad and stern. One day he said to Bowie, 'Help will come.' But help did not come. When he felt that they must fight it out alone, he gave his men a chance to say whether they would stay by him to the end. I saw him draw the line with his sword, and heard him say, 'All who are willing to die cross this line.' I think all jumped across. Señor Bowie said, 'Boys, lift my cot across that line.'

"My heart was in my mouth. My eyes were like coals of fire; but I would stay and listen. Some blame the great Bowie and Travis and Crockett because they did not hasten away. Can men do more than give their lives, Señorita? I heard a great man tell that these heroes of the Alamo saved Texas. If Santa Anna had not been stopped there, he would have marched over all Texas before an army could be gathered to defeat him. This sounds right to me. I did know that these men were heroes.

"At last there came fire and guns and bayonets with many men. The soldiers of Santa Anna scaled the walls to be met by the fighting Texans. It was early morning. I ran out to the courtyard from a deep sleep. I was fastened to the ground. The Texans killed many of Santa Anna's men, but more and more kept coming up the ladders. My father was killed. The brave Travis while shooting a cannon was shot down. I wish I could tell you all the great bravery of these few Texans fighting against that host. It would take great words like in your Bible and in your songs. I do not know these words.

"Santa Anna's men broke down the outside wall and came into the courtyard. The Texans went to the second wall and fought them back. They clubbed with their rifles, and stabbed with their bowie knives. At last the few Texans that were left drew back into the monastery and shot the enemy as they came into the courtyard.

"The women and children had hidden themselves where they could. I crawled under the hay. I would open my eyes and shut them again. I could not keep myself from looking and hearing. The awful sights still come to my eyes and the sounds ring in my ears. The soldiers of Santa Anna came on thick as bees. Inch by inch they gained ground, but for every Texan they killed five of them fell. Poor fellows—many of them cared not to fight. It was the will of their tyrant leader. Mexico builds not one statue to Santa Anna. It is a lesson to all. He was a self-seeking, cruel ruler.

"I did not stay in the courtyard. I was afraid. Long before this I had heard Señor Bowie tell Señor Smith, 'We must hold the Alamo. We must keep Santa Anna back from Gonzales. If we don't even the women and children will be murdered.' I had kept close to Señor Bowie. He knew my language and I could feel his strength. Though he was ill I felt he would yet find a way to overcome Santa Anna. When he and the other brave fighters were slain fear seized me.

"I hid with other frightened children and their mothers. Some of Santa Anna's men shot into the room. One boy was killed, but the rest of us escaped alive. We could see little in the dark corner where we had huddled. As soon as it was light enough, some of the soldiers came searching though the rooms.

"One of them put his bayonet against my mother and said, 'Where is the Texans' money?'

"'If they had money, find it,' she said.

"The soldier struck her and I screamed. An officer appeared and ordered the soldier to go and leave the women and children alone.

"When it was broad daylight, the families were sent to the home of Don Musquiz at the southwest corner of Main Plaza. A servant there gave us coffee and tamales. We were very hungry. That afternoon we were taken before Santa Anna. He had his headquarters on the Plaza. I saw a pile of silver on the table where he sat.

"Mrs. Dickerson was more excited than any of the other women. My mother was very quiet and very sad, but not afraid of Santa Anna. I was scared. The Texans had told me that he would cut off my ears if he ever caught me. I did not cry out, but I clung to my mother. Santa Anna, I remember, was dressed up very fine and he had a pleasant voice; but he looked angry. He thought us traitors. He was kind to Mrs. Dickerson, at least his voice sounded different when he spoke to her.

"He asked the Mexican women, 'Why do you fight your countrymen?'

"'They are not our countrymen,' my mother answered; 'we are Texans.'

"'I suppose if I let you go you will raise your children to fight Mexico.'

"'Yes,' my mother said. Her sorrow over the death of my father had made her not afraid to die, I think.

"'You ought to have your ears cut off,' he replied.

"This made me and the other children scream.

"'Get the mob out!' Santa Anna said. 'Give each woman two dollars and a blanket.'

"The officer led us away. As we were going out he said in a low voice, 'Vamonos.' We did.

"Mrs. Dickerson sat there before Santa Anna when we left. She was crying. Señor Travis had a negro slave named Joe, who was also standing there. We heard afterwards that Santa Anna sent Mrs. Dickerson on a horse to Gonzales with Joe to help her along. Deaf Smith and some of Houston's scouts met her on the way. After hearing the sad story from her, some of them hurried on to Gonzales with the news.

"We stayed in San Antonio with my uncle. He had taken no part in the war. He was too old. Uncle found my father's body among the slain and buried it. It took three days for the soldiers of Santa Anna to gather up their dead and bury them. In after years I was told that six hundred of them had been killed by the one hundred and eighty-two Texans who died fighting at the Alamo."

"Did you see them burn the bodies of these Texans, Señor Esparza?" some one questioned.

"No, but I heard that they did burn the bodies. Later, when Santa Anna had been defeated, I learned that Captain Seguin had come to San Antonio and gathered up the ashes of these brave men and given them honorable burial near the spot where they had died fighting for freedom. Alcalde Ruiz helped to burn and bury many of the bodies.

"After the battle of the Alamo we moved away to San Pedro Creek. I was frightened until Santa Anna had left San Antonio. He did not stay long. We were all happy when he was beaten in battle by General Houston.

"The old Alamo was left in ruins. It stood like a haunted place—full of many memories for me."

"Do you know how many Mexicans were in the Alamo fighting as Texans against Santa Anna?' came a question.

"I heard Guerrero, an old man, tell that the names were Fuentes, Loyosa, Jimenes, and my father; also Captain Badilla of Nacogdoches. Guerrero was there too, I was told, but escaped because he said he was a prisoner of the Texans. It is a sin for a man to carry a lie to his grave.

"There was a monument made and the names on it were many, but I heard that no Mexican name was cut in the marble. My father and other Mexicans died for Texas. These of English tongue could do no more, so why not every name? Yet I blame no one. It was thought by too many that all people with dark faces and foreign tongues were wicked like the cruel Santa Anna.

"That is not so. Many of my people loved liberty just as did the Americans who came to help settle Texas. I am glad to tell this story of the Mexicans who gave their lives for freedom. It is good to come and tell it to you American boys and girls.

"Gray hairs cling to old memories. I live by the soil and with the soil. I talk to few about the Alamo and the old days. Some believe me not; some know it all. I talk now and then to friends of understanding and sympathy."

Commentary

Juana Alsbury and Enrique Esparza (1.4, 1.5)

Little commentary is necessary on Juana Alsbury's account. Her presence in the Alamo is attested to by Dickinson, Gray, and Barnard (1.2.8, 1.2.11, 1.3.4, 1.3.5, 4.3.10). However, some other Dickinson accounts (see commentary to section 1.2) stated that Alsbury left before the fall, and even betrayed the fortress. Both Joe (1.3.4) and Esparza (1.5) support her presence throughout the siege, as do her own 1857 petition (1.4.2) and the account of her son (1.4.4). Amelia Williams reviews the documentation and concludes—to my satisfaction as well—that she was present through the siege and the fall.[1]

SIGNIFICANT INTERVIEWS OF ENRIQUE ESPARZA (I.E)

S.A. Light 1901 (1.5.2)	S.A. Express 1902 (1.5.3)	S.A. Express 1907 (1.5.4)	Driggs & King 1936 (1.5.6)
Siege Events			
Pre-siege			
			1, 2. (After description of life in San Antonio.) Texas soldiers said not enough men to hold Alamo. Many men in fortress.
			3. Cheering when Crockett came, wearing buckskin suit and coonskin cap. {G}*
		8. Family entered by Church over a cannon (stayed there most of the siege). [B]*	
1. Family stayed in two storerooms by main gate	11. Family stayed near entrance		17. Family stayed in small storeroom near monastery.
2. Moat and drawbridge at entrance.	12. Ditch in back and west side (not the moat).		19. First got water from ditch.
3. De Zavala warned them.	2. Rumors in town of Santa Anna.	3. Awaiting wagons.	15. Gathered up few things.
4. No wagons available.	3. Awaiting wagons.	4. Smith and father heard of approach.	14. Rushed to Alamo when trumpets heard.
5. Smith told family.	5. Smith told Anita.	5. Smith's family also went into Alamo. {E}*	15. Anita insisted on staying with Gregorio.
6. Anita decided to enter Alamo.	6. Anita insisted on entering Alamo.	7. Saw Santa Anna dismount. {E}	18. Mrs. Dickerson and baby with them. {E}
		6. Went in after sundown.	
7. Back and forth several time to Alamo.	7. Took whole day.		
Siege of the Alamo			
		10. Surrender demand replied to by cannon shot. {G}	6, 7. Santa Anna said Texans couldn't get away. Surrender demand replied to by cannon shot. {G}
			8, 9. Blood-red flag on cathedral, Texans not excited, sang and danced, no fighting for several days. {G}

SIGNIFICANT INTERVIEWS OF ENRIQUE ESPARZA (1.E)

S.A. *Light* 1901 (1.5.2)	S.A. *Express* 1902 (1.5.3)	S.A. *Express* 1907 (1.5.4)	Driggs & King 1936 (1.5.6)
Siege Events			
Siege of the Alamo (continued)			
	9. Melton and umbrella.		
	10. Fuentes and water.		
	13. Well used for water.	28. Well used for water.	20. Later got water from well.
	14. Mexican prisoner identified bugle calls.		21. Mexican prisoner identified bugle calls.
	15. Firing every day.		23. Days of terrible fighting.
	16. Chapel roof off, dirt ramp inside.	9. Some cannons on roof of church. {B}	24. Roof of old Alamo was off, embankment to wall, Dickerson killed here.
			4, 5. Frightened by cannons. Santa Anna had much "thunder."
	17. Few cannons.		12, 13. Bowie gave them beeves and corn, mother made a mush.
		29. Cattle furnished food. {G}	
		11. Some children fought.	
	18. Crockett slim man with whiskers.	12. Crockett leading spirit (also note 31, 32 below).	26. Crocket seemed everywhere, made them laugh.
	19. Crockett led, never saw Travis and Bowie.	14. Travis depended on Crockett; Bowie ill. {G}	10. Travis brave leader, asked by Bowie to take command. {G}
		16. Bowie visited while ill.	11. Father would rather follow Bowie; visited him while ill.
		33. Mrs. Alsbury nursed Bowie. {G}	
	20. Help coming (Williamson?).		28. Seguin sent for help, used Bowie's horse. {G}
			31. Travis looked sad and stern; said to Bowie, "Help will come." {G}
			27. Great shouting when Smith came from Gonzales; Smith sent out again for more men. {G}

SIGNIFICANT INTERVIEWS OF ENRIQUE ESPARZA (I.E)

S.A. *Light* 1901 (1.5.2)	S.A. *Express* 1902 (1.5.3)	S.A. *Express* 1907 (1.5.4)	Driggs & King 1936 (1.5.6)
Siege Events			
Siege of the Alamo (continued)			
	21. Armistice of 3 days, Crockett negotiated.	17. Armistice 3 days per Bowie.	
	22. Anita insisted on staying.	20. Anna insisted on staying.	
	23. Trinidad Saucedo left during armistice.	18. A number left during armistice.	
	24. Men called by Crockett last day.	15. Travis drew line, Bowie carried across. {G}	32. Travis drew line, Bowie carried across. {G}
		19. Rose left at night. {G}	
	25. Reinforcements came to Mexican Army (Travis letter?).		
	26. Messenger got through lines (Bonham?).		29, 30. "Benham" got back from Goliad; white handkerchief sign he had seen Fannin. {G}
	27. Gregorio with Anita last night.		
		21. Men fought long and hard, ammo low.	
Fall of the Alamo			
		22. Waked by terrible din.	33. Fire and guns and bayonets, in early morning awakened from deep sleep.
			34. Texans killed many.
			36. Santa Anna's men broke down outside walls; Texans went to second wall and fought back. {G}
			37. Texans retreated into monastery, fired into courtyard. {G}
		13. Women and children died.	

SIGNIFICANT INTERVIEWS OF ENRIQUE ESPARZA (I.E)

S.A. Light 1901 (1.5.2)	S.A. Express 1902 (1.5.3)	S.A. Express 1907 (1.5.4)	Driggs & King 1936 (1.5.6)
Siege Events			
Fall of the Alamo (continued)			
			38, 39, 40, 41. Women and children hid themselves, Enrique crawled under hay; soldiers thick as bees; Enrique afraid when Bowie and others killed.
10. Paralytic killed in front of them.	29. Boy killed.	23. Boy killed standing in front.	42. Santa Anna's men shot into room, one boy killed.
11. Prisoner also killed.	(Note 14 above.)		22. Prisoner killed because thought a deserter.
12. Brigidio Guerrera saved.		25. Brigidio Guerrera saved.	56. Guerrero was there, too, saved because said he was prisoner of the Texans.
	28. Never saw father again.	24. Father died near them, mother next to him. {E}	35. Father killed (possibly close to them?).
		27. Last sight of father at cannon. {E}	
		30. Crockett led in fight, fought to end (insertion). {G, B}	
		31. Travis on roof of church. {B}	35. Travis killed while shooting cannon. [G]
		32. Bowie in church. {B}	
		34. Roof of convent and church fell in. {B}	
		35. Tower still existed. {B}	
		36. Later history of church included purchasing church portion. {B}	
		37. In Church at end. {B}	
After the fall			
13. Saved by officer; terrible treatment of women and children.	30. Soldiers wanted money; saved by an officer.		43. Soldiers demanded money; saved by an officer.
	32. Santa Anna had more soldiers than needed.		

SIGNIFICANT INTERVIEWS OF ENRIQUE ESPARZA (I.E.)

S.A. Light 1901 (1.5.2)	S.A. Express 1902 (1.5.3)	S.A. Express 1907 (1.5.4)	Driggs & King 1936 (1.5.6)
Siege Events			
After the fall (continued)			
14. To Musquiz house, served coffee.	31. To Musquiz house, served coffee and food.	38. Taken to Musquiz house, Musquiz fetched coffee and food.	44. Taken to Musquiz, gave us coffee and tamales.
15. Oath of allegiance.	33. Declaration made.		45, 49. Taken before Santa Anna, pile of silver on table; he questioned Anita, then gave them $2 and blanket.
16. Received blanket & $2 from Santa Anna.	34. Received blanket and $2.	39. Interview with Santa Anna, received blanket and $2.	47, 48. Santa Anna dressed very fine, looked angry; kind to Mrs. Dickerson.{E}
17. Two daughters of Navarro spirited away.	35. Melton asked Anita about Anglo husband.		
			46, 50, 51. Mrs. Dickerson more excited than other women, crying when Enrique left; Joe with her. [E]
—De Zavala to glean information.			52. Stayed with uncle; found father's body and buried it.
			53, 54. 600 Mexicans killed, 182 Texans; latter buried by Seguin, former by Ruiz. {G}
The Esparzas			54. Fuentes, Losoya, Jimenes, father, Captain Badilla of Nacogdoches fought as Texans against Santa Anna.
—Enrique eight years old.	—Enrique eight years old.	—Enrique twelve years old. [E]	16. Enrique nine years old.

SIGNIFICANT INTERVIEWS OF ENRIQUE ESPARZA (I.E)

S.A. Light 1901 (1.5.2)	S.A. Express 1902 (1.5.3)	S.A. Express 1907 (1.5.4)	Driggs & King 1936 (1.5.6)
Siege Events			
The Esparzas (continued)		1. Enrique spoke English.	—Enrique learned to read and write; also numerous details on life in San Antonio; knew Bowie, Smith, Navarro.
	1. Father in Benavides company, ordered back from Goliad (contradicted by 1.5.1.2?).		
8. Family: daughter and 4 sons.	4. Family: 1 sister and 3 brothers.	2. Family: sister and brothers.	16. Family: brothers and baby sister.
9. Others in Alamo Alsbury and child Gertrudes Navarro Concepcion Losaya, daughter, and 2 sons Victoriana de Salina and 3 girls Dickinson and girl Petra	**8. Others in Alamo** Alsbury Alsbury sister Concepcion Losaya and 1 boy Victoriana and several girls Dickinson Juana Melton	**26. Others in Alamo** Alsbury Alsbury sister Dickinson and babe Donna Petra	

*[G],[B], [E] are for "general knowledge," "building," and "extra," as explained in text of commentary.

Her account is centered on only those events she was likely to have personally experienced. The most vivid details are those under the most stressful, and therefore most memorable, personal experiences. A more subtle point is that she does not claim an especially significant role—which would be an unlikely possibility for any real survivor from either inside the Alamo or in the Mexican Army. In some accounts later in this book, the participants' own claims of special significance are the first indicator that the accounts are faulty. There are no apparent internal inconsistencies or contradictions with other reasonable external sources. We can, therefore, accept this story as one of the more reliable of the Alamo.

The story attributed to Alsbury by Maverick (1.4.5) has considerable discrepancies with the Ford version (1.4.1) for such a short text. The image of Bowie being bayoneted sounds rather like Maverick confused a recollection of Alsbury with some of the Dickinson accounts (e.g., 1.2.7, 4.1.6). Consequently, one need not take seriously the claim that Alsbury was with Dickinson, or believe that this account locates Bowie or the place of his death.

The presence of Madame Candelaria alluded to by Alsbury needs more indepth study and is reviewed later (section 1.9). This person is an example of someone who did claim, unlike Alsbury, an especially important role in the events.

The narrations of Enrique Esparza are more problematic. Some details are attributed to him that he would have been unlikely to have experienced. His story was not discovered until quite late, when he was an old man. The interviews are inconsistent with one another. But on closer examination, several things lend support to his accounts, and they make a useful study of sources.

The first question to ask is whether Esparza was actually there. The events narrated, which he personally would have experienced, do seem real and are not contradictory to those described in other material. So from the accounts themselves, one is inclined to accept his story as authentic. It is hoped, though, that a confirmation of some sort will turn up—specifically, at least one early statement that Gregorio Esparza's wife Anita (or Anna) was one of the women in the Alamo, in which case one could assume his children were as well—particularly since his story became known so long after the event. Ideally, such confirmation should be from a time early enough, by the 1860s or '70s, that it could have been contradicted by people still alive who would have known if it was unlikely or impossible. In this light, the lack of specific information on the family in key Texas General Land Office documents (1.5.1.1, 1.5.1.2) is disappointing.[2] These documents are depositions and awards for land for the services of Gregorio Esparza in the Texas Revolution, and they well document his presence and death in the Alamo. For example, his brother Francisco Esparza and Candlario Villanueva testified that they actually located his body in one of the Alamo rooms after the battle. The presence of the family in the Alamo is not noted. This detail was not the issue of interest—only the presence of Gregorio Esparza was—but one might expect it to have been incidentally recorded.

One particularly curious omission is found in the responses of Gregorio Hernandez and Capt. Don Manuel Flores in 1858 to the question "How do you know that he was at the Alamo with Travis & then killed?" Gregorio Hernandez replied, "Because his Wife, his children, and his relations have told me that they recognized his body after the fight, applied for it, obtained it, and gave it a Christian burial." Manuel Flores replied, "I know that he was at the Alamo and fell with Travis, the same that any one knows that Travis fell then, because I have been told so by men and women who saw him enter the walls, and never saw him afterwards, and by his relations who buried his body."[3] In both cases, the family is cited only in connection with the postbattle recovery of the corpse. It would seem that their presence with Gregorio inside the Alamo should have been important support for the claim of his services, and therefore stated. On the other hand, there might have been legal constraints on testimony when Gregorio Esparza's family were the potential beneficiaries. These cited documents are not all inclusive, and I believe a more thorough study of source material on the Esparza family could be a useful addition to Alamo scholarship.[4]

A first reading of the three key newspaper interviews of Enrique Esparza (1.5.2–1.5.4) might seem quite confusing because of the inconsistencies. A more careful study, however, reveals that the problematic details fall into relatively few groups in the 1907 interview. These three interviews were separated by some time— over which an eighty-year-old man was unlikely to keep track of what he said—and probably done by at least two interviewers. Perhaps the clearest way to study these is by the side-by-side comparison that follows. The specific details or observations are broken out individually, numbered by their original order in the particular account, and reordered into an approximately chronological arrangement. They can then be aligned to see how details match across accounts. A fourth narration, from Driggs and King (1.5.6), recorded under quite different circumstances and published years later, is also included.

Several observations and conclusions can be drawn from this matrix. First, essentially every detail in the first interview, from 1901, is reflected in some fairly consistent fashion in one of the later interviews. The variations are reasonable over a six-year period for someone in his eighties. In addition, these are reasonable events for the young Enrique both to have experienced and to have remembered. Nor are they at odds with accounts from others.

Second, is that the same qualities in general can be said about the additional details of the second interview, from 1902. The seemingly incidental, unimportant details such as Mrs. Melton with her umbrella and Fuentes talking to someone else about the water being cut off (items 9 and 10 in the second column of the table) are things that likely would impress a young boy. Even further weight can be given this interview as it was in a different newspaper and in a somewhat different style, and therefore was probably done by a different journalist.

It is only with the third interview of 1907 that significant problems arise. They are, however, limited to three basic categories. These are designated as G for "general knowledge," B for "building," and E for "extra."

"General" items are those that appear nearly universally in the secondhand histories. These included Travis's cannon-shot reply to the demand for surrender (10), the cattle supplying food (11), Travis's leadership and Bowie's illness (14,16,33), and the drawing of the line and Rose's escape (15,19). It is more likely that a young non-participant would not have been personally knowledgeable about such details. In particular, details on the death of Crockett, Travis, and Bowie are quite unlikely to have been observed by a young noncombatant, while they are highly likely to have been asked of him in later years. On the other hand, Charles Merritt Barnes should have been well aware of such details (e.g., note interviews 3.7.2, 3.7.5), and the addition of such information to an (apparent) interview was common in the earlier sources, such as Dickinson's. Therefore, there is nothing remarkable about these items—most likely they were simply not Esparza's but added by Barnes to flesh out the story.

The "building" items all are linked in some way to the actual convent and church. It perhaps is of some significance that it was around this time (1900–14) that major efforts were made over control of the chapel (now known as the Alamo Shrine) and to save the Long Barracks and convent structures from demolition. Adina De Zavala (1.5.2) played a major role in these efforts, and it is explicitly stated that she planned to glean further information from Esparza.[5] It is therefore reasonable to assume that there was motivation to link the Alamo stories to these physical structures in order to obtain publicity for preservation efforts. Therefore, taking the speculation a step further, Barnes likely relocated the family from Low Barracks near the gate to the church (8,37), Travis's post to the roof (31), and put Bowie in a room inside (32). Some errors then were introduced into the interview, such as a roof on the church (34) and that the towers still existed (35). This possibility does not require deliberate involvement by De Zavala or distortions by Barnes, but rather could be due to answers to innocently leading questions being misinterpreted. This would be even easier if the interview was through a translator. For example, virtually all the "building" group details could be simply explained if Barnes in his interview was saying "church" to mean the "chapel," while Esparza thought "church" meant "mission." The latter term would have encompassed the entire original system of building and walls, which Esparza would remember and Barnes would not, so there would have been no intentional distortions. A hint that this is possible is in Esparza's using a distinctly different word, "monastery," in the Briggs and King interview.

Another, more general, point is that Esparza's descriptions of the physical layout of the Alamo complex are consistent with the early plans rather than the limited portion of the mission extant since the mid-nineteenth century. If one compares his descriptions with others, say that of Eulalia Yorba in 1896 (3.7.1), it is apparent that Esparza (unless he was well coached) had a clearer sense of the original than other reputed eyewitnesses.

The "extra" category consists of items that are harder to explain: the Smith family joining the Esparzas in the Alamo (5), Enrique in the plaza watching Santa Anna dismount (7), and the death of Gregorio (24, 27). There is no evidence that the Smith family was in the Alamo, and the earlier accounts imply that Enrique spent most of February 23 moving things with his family into the Alamo, and that he never saw his father again once the attack started on March 6. Finally, Enrique's age at the time of the battle is correctly given as eight in the first two interviews, but as twelve in the third.[6] It might be assumed that someone, Barnes or Esparza, got carried away with his story in 1907, and that these are likely bogus details.

An additional Esparza document from 1911 (1.5.5) supports this assumption. The details in this claimed interview are simply bizarre. Now it is claimed that Enrique was in the Alamo with a brother, who was killed; his father was no longer the only defender to have been buried; he and his mother returned to the site of the funeral pyres to look for the bodies, where she had an emotional fit; and Susanna Dickinson gave birth in the Alamo. Practically every detail is at variance with Esparza's (and other) earlier accounts—and Barnes must share responsibility, as two of the prior interviews were his. The typographical errors in the original also suggest that this was a very sloppily done article. One can only conclude that Esparza or Barnes had a catastrophic loss of memory or ceased caring in this narration. Another possibility, more remote but not impossible, considering the sloppiness of the text, is that someone else less knowledgeable put the story together and credited Barnes. It is interesting, however, that Enrique's age at the siege returns to being eight years old.

At first, one might be highly skeptical of the Driggs and King (1.5.6) narration. This is an informal transcript of a school talk perhaps not recorded until published nearly twenty years after Esparza's death. But when the details are compared with the newspaper interviews, the similarities and differences become much more striking and support acceptance of this account. The number of differences in the account immediately indicate this is not a disguised paraphrase of an earlier interview, and therefore is independent.

Those items marked "general" in the table for this interview include a number of items not recorded earlier, but they can be explained by the increasing awareness of Esparza of the Alamo story since 1901. By the time of this talk, Esparza is likely to have been something of a spokesperson for the Alamo story for years, he had learned to read and write, and questions from the students likely covered commonly known aspects of the story. As a consequence, it does not seem unreasonable that Esparza had been influenced by general accounts of the fall and had incorporated them into his story. Thus one should not take the inclusion here of these details, such as the Rose story, as definite independent confirmation that they happened.

The only "extra" details that are new to this account and do not match other sources all relate to Susanna Dickinson. One very inconsistent detail is her physical presence with the Esparza family. However, once again Esparza could well have been asked numerous times about her presence and have been misunderstood on this point.

Around half the Driggs and King interview consists of these "general" and "extra" details. The remaining portions are quite consistent with the newspaper interviews. Considering the drastically different circumstances in recording this version, the similarities are in fact remarkable. Therefore, this account also appears to be a valid independent version of Esparza's story.

The items not designated in one of the above three groups are consistent or reasonable. All these interviews are significantly more consistent than those of Dickinson (1.2), who is known to have been in the Alamo. Thus it appears that we still have the identifiable core of an authentic story. Here again, the most vivid details are of events and situations that were likely to be stressful and therefore the most memorable. In particular, any details that relate to Esparza's mother and her reactions would be natural recollections of a (self-admittedly) very frightened youth. Together, these consistencies seem overwhelming support for the validity of the Esparza story in general.

There are a few remaining specific items worth noting. One is that Esparza seemed to have a real impression of an otherwise undocumented and therefore unsupported three-day armistice; he mentions it in 1902 and again in 1907. Another is that the 1902 account may indirectly reflect some interesting events that are known from other sources: Williamson's encouragement to Travis (4.3.4 vs. 20 in second column); reinforcements arriving in Mexican camp (1.1.6 and 2.5.1 vs. 25); and the impact of Bonham's arrival with the bad news from Fannin (1.1.6 and 5.1.8.8 vs. 26).

The story in both Alijo Perez (1.4.4) and Esparza that Brigidio Guerrero surrendered and was not executed is interesting and has been raised in later versions. Esparza's accounts give real support to this possibility, which is reviewed in more depth in section 1.10.2.

The possibility that Dickerson is the correct name for Almeron and Susanna (see 4.4.4) is supported by Esparza in Driggs and King. The name is recorded everywhere as "Dickerson (sic)."

Another possibility raised in Driggs and King (item 54; note section 1.11) is that a previously overlooked Tejano defender of the Alamo is a Captain Badilla of Nacogdoches.

In summary, I join most scholars in accepting Enrique Esparza as an authentic source from inside the Alamo. His experiences are well recorded, provided one excludes or uses with considerable caution those details that fall into the "general," "building," and "extra" categories of the 1907 and Driggs and King interviews. I do not believe Esparza himself is responsible for most of these additions to his 1907 story. The remaining details provide a vivid and highly useful addition to the Alamo story. To put it even more strongly, I believe that the consistency of details recorded by different people over many years would be near impossible if Esparza had not been in the Alamo at the fall.

1. Williams in *SWHQ* 37:169, n. 20. In Alamo Research/Dickinson & Other Survivors, Williams (Amelia Worthington) Papers, CAH, Williams transcribes a different view in a letter of Mrs. James McKeener of July 25, 1893.
2. There are other depositions for Gregorio Esparza in the Texas General Land Office File C-2558, e.g., Bounty Certificate 1577 and Donation Certificate 572. These are consistent with the two cited here.
3. Also in file C-2558, per n. 2.
4. See, e.g., Williams in *SWHQ* 37:257 and 49:636; also Hutton (June 9, 1991).
5. See also Ables 1967 for an account of De Zavala's role in saving the Alamo structures.
6. A DRT manuscript by Etna Scott (1984) documents that Enrique was born in 1828 and therefore eight is the right age.

1.6.1.   David Crockett, reputed autobiography, 1836.

Smith, Richard Penn (putative author). 1836. *Col. Crockett's Exploits and Adventures in Texas . . . Written by Himself.* iii–iv, 13–14, 182–83, 188–89, 191–92, 199,
200–202. Philadelphia: T. K. and P. G. Collins.

Stories from this account have been used in numerous narratives (and later
movies) of the nineteenth and twentieth centuries, and so have some literary interest.
The inclusion of these selections and their validity are discussed in the commentary.

[*Preface, iii–iv*]

COLONEL CROCKETT, at the time of leaving Tennessee for Texas, made a
promise to his friends that he would keep notes of whatever might occur to him
of moment, with the ulterior view of laying his adventures before the public.
He was encouraged in this undertaking by the favourable manner in which his
previous publications had been received: and if he had been spared throughout
the Texian struggle, it cannot be doubted that he would have produced a work
replete with interest, and such as would have been universally read. His plain
and unpolished style may occasionally offend the taste of those who are stick-
lers for classic refinement; while others will value it for that frankness and sincerity which is the best voucher for the truth of the facts he relates. The
manuscript has not been altered since it came into the possession of the editor;
though it is but proper to state that it had previously undergone a slight verbal
revision; and the occasional interlineations were recognised to be in the handwriting of the Bee hunter, so frequently mentioned in the progress of the narrative. These corrections were doubtless made at the author's own request, and
received his approbation.

[*The survival of the manuscript was attributed to its being found in the trunk of
General Castrillon after the battle of San Jacinto.*]

[*Chapter 1, 13–14*]

It is a true saying that no one knows the luck of a lousy calf, for though in a
country where, according to the Declaration of Independence, the people are all
born free and equal, those who have a propensity to go ahead may aim at the
highest honours, and they may ultimately reach them too, though they start at
the lowest dowel of the ladder,—still it is a huckelberry [*sic*] above my persim-
mon to cipher out how it is with six months' schooling only, I, David Crockett,
find myself the most popular bookmaker of the day; and such is the demand for
my works that I cannot write them half fast enough, no how I can fix it. This
problem would bother even my friend Major Jack Downing's rule of three, to
bring out square after all his practice on the Post Office accounts and the public
lands to boot.

I have been told that there was one Shakspeare [*sic*] more than two hundred
years ago, who was brought up a hostler, but finding it a dull business, took to
writing plays, and made as great a stir in his time as I do at present; which will

go to show, that one ounce of the genuine horse sense is worth a pound of your book learning any day, and if a man is only determined to go ahead, the more kicks he receives in his breech the faster he will get on his journey.

[*Chapter 13, 182–83*]

I write this on the nineteenth of February, 1836, at San Antonio. We are all in high spirits, though we are rather short of provisions, for men who have appetites that could digest any thing but oppression; but no matter, we have a prospect of soon getting our bellies full of fighting, and that is victuals and drink to a true patriot any day. We had a little sort of convivial party last evening: just about a dozen of us set to work, most patriotically, to see whether we could not get rid of that curse of the land, whisky, and we made consider-able progress; but my poor friend, Thimble-rig, got sewed up just about as tight as the eyelet-hole in a lady's corset, and little tighter too, I reckon; for when we went to bed he called for a boot-jack, which was brought to him, and he bent down on his hands and knees, and very gravely pulled off his hat with it, for the darned critter was so thoroughly swiped that he didn't know his head from his heels. But this wasn't all the folly he committed: he pulled off his coat and laid it on the bed, and then hung himself over the back of a chair; and I wish I may be shot if he didn't go to sleep in that position, thinking every thing had been done according to Gunter's late scale. Seeing the poor fellow completely used up, I carried him to bed, though he did belong to the Temperance society; and he knew nothing about what had occurred until I told him next morning. The Bee hunter didn't join us in the blow-out. Indeed, he will seldom drink more than just enough to prevent his being called a total abstinence man. But then he is the most jovial fellow for a water drinker I ever did see.

[*188–89*]

February 22. The Mexicans, about sixteen hundred strong, with their Presi-dent Santa Anna at their head, aided by Generals Almonte, Cos, Sesma, and Castrillon, are within two leagues of Bexar. General Cos, it seems, has already forgot his parole of honour, and has come back to retrieve the credit he lost in this place in December last. If he is captured a second time, I don't think he can have the impudence to ask to go at large again without giving better bail than on the former occasion. Some of the scouts came in, and bring reports that Santa Anna has been endeavouring to excite the Indians to hostilities against the Texi-ans, but so far without effect. . . .

February 23. Early this morning the enemy came in sight, marching in regu-lar order, and displaying their strength to the greatest advantage, in order to strike us with terror. But that was no go; they'll find that they have to do with men who will never lay down their arms as long as they can stand on their legs. We held a short council of war, and, finding that we should be completely sur-rounded, and overwhelmed by numbers, if we remained in the town, we con-cluded to withdraw to the fortress of Alamo, and defend it to the last extremity. . . .

[*191–92*]

February 24. Very early this morning the enemy commenced a new battery on the banks of the river, about three hundred and fifty yards from the fort, and by afternoon they amused themselves by firing at us from that quarter. Our Indian scout came in this evening, and with him a reinforcement of thirty men from Gonzales, who are just in the nick of time to reap a harvest of glory; but there is some prospect of sweating blood before we gather it in. . . .

[*199*]

March 2. This day the delegates meet in general convention, at the town of Washington, to frame our Declaration of Independence. That the sacred instrument may never be trampled on by the children of those who have freely shed their blood to establish it, is the sincere wish of David Crockett. . . .

[*200–202*]

March 4. Shells have been falling into the fort like hail during the day, but without effect. About dusk, in the evening, we observed a man running toward the fort, pursued by about a dozen Mexican cavalry. The Bee hunter immediately knew him to be the old pirate who had gone to Goliad, and, calling to the two hunters, he sallied out of the fort to the relief of the old man, who was hard pressed. . . . By this time we reached the spot, and, in the ardour of the moment, followed some distance before we saw that our retreat to the fort was cut off by another detachment of cavalry. Nothing was to be done but to fight our way through. . . . But we did not escape unscathed, for both the pirate and the Bee hunter were mortally wounded, and I received a sabre cut across the forehead. The old man died, without speaking, as soon as we entered the fort. We bore my young friend to his bed, dressed his wounds, and I watched beside him. He lay, without complaint or manifesting pain, until about midnight, when he spoke, and I asked him if he wanted any thing. "Nothing," he replied, but drew a sigh that seemed to rend his heart, as he added, "Poor Kate of Nacogdoches!" His eyes were filled with tears, as he continued, "Her words were prophetic, Colonel;" and then he sang, in a low voice that resembled the sweet notes of his own devoted Kate,

> *"But toom cam' the saddle, all bluidy to see,*
> *And hame cam' the steed, but hame never cam' he."*

He spoke no more, and, a few minutes after, died. Poor Kate, who will tell this to thee!

March 5. Pop, pop, pop! Bom, bom, bom! thoughout the day.—No time for memorandums now.—Go ahead!—Liberty and independence for ever!

[Here ends Colonel Crockett's manuscript.]

1.6.2.   Isaac Millsap, reputed letter, March 3, 1836.

Millsap, Isaac. March 3, 1836. Courtesy of Special Collections, University of
Houston Libraries.

A facsimile of this letter is reproduced in Daughters of the Republic of Texas
(1986b). Serious questions have been raised as to whether this is a forgery, discussed
by Curtis (March 1989a, 109). The large number of misspellings are per the original.

Bexar, Mar 3, 1836

My dear dear ones

We are in the fortress of the Alamo a ruined Church that has most fell
down. The Mexcans are here in large numbers they have kept up a constant fire
since we got here. All of our boys are well & Capt. Martin is in good spirits.
Early this morning I watched the mexcans drilling just out of range they was
marching up and down with such order. they have bright red & blue uniforms
and many canons. Some here at this place believe that the main army has not
come up yeth. I think they is all here even Santana. Col. Bowie is down sick and
had to be to bed I saw him yesterday & he is still ready to fight. He did't know
me from last spring but did remember Wash. He tells all that help will be here
soon & it makes us feel good. We have beef & corn to eat but no coffee, bag I
had fell off on the way here so it was all spilt. I have not see. Travis but 2 times
since here he told us all this morning that Fanning was going to be here early
with many men and there would be a good fight. He stays on the wall some but
mostly to his room I hope help comes soon cause we cant fight them all. Some
says he is going to talk tonight & group us better for defense. If we fail here get
to the river with the children all Texas will be before the enemy we get so little
news here we know nothing. There is no discontent in our boys some are tired
from loss of sleep and rest. The mexcans are shooting every few minutes but
most of the shots fall inside & do no harm. I dont know what else to say they is
calling for all letters, kiss the dear children for me and believe as I do that all
will be well & God protects us all.

Isaac

If any men come through there tell them to hurry with powder for it is
short I hope you get this & know—I love you all

1.6.3. Willis Moore, evidence for lost letter(s), March 3, 1836.

Moore, Willis A. September 22, 1856. Court of Claims File C-5893, Texas General Land Office.

Documents in support of this "Statement of Evidence" included apparently lost letters from Moore—one from the Alamo on March 3, 1836.

Statement of Evidence Case of Heirs of Willis A Moore.

Submitted September 22nd 1856

No 1. Letter from W. A. Moore dated San Antonio de Bexar December 28. 1835

No 2. Letter form W. A. Moore dated San Antonio de Bexar January 13. 1836

No 3. Letter form W. A. Moore dated San Antonio de Bexar March 3. 1836

No 4. Copy of "Raymond Times" of 23 April 1836 containing list of those persons who fell at the "Alamo" under Col. Travis

No 5. The affidavit of Sam[l]. T. King relative to the "Raymond Times" (the copy dated Apl 9. 1836 alluded to in the affidavit is missing from some cause—it will be supplied however should it be deemed essential)

No 6. The affidavit of Stratford Hamon relative to the heirs of W. A. Moore.

No 3. also contains the affidavit of Dan[l] Black relative to his acquaintance with W. A. Moore &[c]. &[c]. &[c].

To the Hon J. C. Wilson

Commissioner &[c]. &[c]. &[c].

Sir,

The above statement together with the evidence there alluded to, is submitted on behalf of the heirs of Willis A. Moore who are resident of the State of Miss'ippi. It is thought that it is such testimony as will prove satisfactory under Art. 1897 Hart. Dig. The applicant, who is W[m]. H. Moore a brother of Willis A. Moore can prove his identity and residence as required by Sec 9. of the "Act to ascertain the legal claims for money and land against the State" if further proof than that already embraced in affidavits No. 3 and 5 should be required under the regulations of your office. As this application is for the Bounty, donation and Headright lands to which Willis A. Moores heirs are entitled under the several laws Hart. Dig. Arts. 1886 (& supplementary / 1897)—1834—2323, it is thought that in view of Art. 2323 and the fact of your office being supplied with copies of the rolls of "Fannin, Ward Travis Grant and Johnson", the 3rd Regulation of your office does not apply to this class of cases.

Respectfully submitted

N. C. Raymond

Atty for heirs

of Willis A. Moore

Commentary

Other Defenders (1.6)

The book *Col. Crockett's Exploits and Adventures in Texas . . . Written by Himself* has routinely been dismissed by historians, and yet it still occasionally has been used to add some "color" to the story of the Alamo. Some believe it was dismissed without sufficient reasons, but they do not give sufficient reasons for retaining it as a possible source. The book has value in the literary history of the United States, as it reflects a literature widely popular in its time, and some of the excerpts are given to illustrate this style.[1] But blatant contradictions with known facts are quickly apparent: Santa Anna known by the defenders to be within two leagues of Bexar on February 22 before entering on the twenty-third; thirty men from Gonzales arriving on February 24; and a fight outside the walls on March 4 (though it does give a literary opportunity to describe the death of one of the central figures of the story). Most egregious, however, is the instantaneous announcement of the Texas Declaration of Independence on March 2 from a location 180 road miles away. In this case, from such internal evidence alone, it is easy and safe to conclude that the literary device of presenting fictional characters as an authentic autobiography or firsthand narrative is not new.

There is also solid external evidence that identifies Richard Penn Smith as the author for Crockett's own publisher, Carey and Hart, who then disguised their role by giving a fictional company name of T. K. and P. G. Collins of Philadelphia as the publisher.[2] Of course, they wished to cash in on the renewed interest of the public due to the death of a celebrity.

An interesting question for the reader to consider is whether some modern biographical writings do not maintain any higher standards. In a case of similar nature, the first question to ask is whether the profit motive of an author or publisher is more important than the reliability of the facts. The technique and motive demonstrated by *Col. Crockett's Exploits and Adventures in Texas . . . Written by Himself* are still quite applicable today.

The questions regarding the letter of Isaac Millsap are more serious, in particular whether this letter is a fraud. Curtis (March 1989a and 1989b) discusses in two articles the forgery of Texas documents in the 1960s. In the article titled "Highly Suspect," the questionability of this particular letter is considered. Most of the Curtis review centers on the deceptive reproduction of valuable authentic documents, such as the Texas Declaration of Independence, as originals. The Millsap letter was unknown until the early 1960s, so even its authenticity can be questioned. On one hand—and unlike the reputed Crockett book—the letter is not inconsistent with known information of the events. But the absence of provenance for this letter should be disturbing. It appeared on the market in the 1960s, and there is no record of it for the previous 120-plus years. Curtis goes further in pointing out handwriting similarities with documents of an accepted forger, stylistic elements that are from later periods, unlikely descriptions of the Alamo chapel and Mexican soldiers, and the lack of any substantive information not available in Walter Lord's book. Wallace Chariton (1992, 187) also cites Texas Archivist Michael Green that the signature does not appear to match one other known autograph.[3] The entire subject of fraudulent documents becomes more significant in the case of the de la Peña diary (section 2.9) because of the relative importance in understanding the events, so this particular document is not studied here in further depth.

A definitive answer should now be technologically available through ion-diffusion analysis or other, more recent techniques, says Curtis, but at a significant cost. The value of the Millsap letter, if genuine, is limited to adding a personal note to the story of the Alamo where very little such material survived. It does not add or detract in a significant way from our knowledge of the event as a whole. The University of Houston, the current owners of the original, have to decide if that potential value is worth the financial investment to obtain a definitive answer by such tests.[4]

The supporting documents submitted by the heirs of Willis A. Moore (1.6.3) are part of the clear evidence that on March 3, letters were sent out from the Alamo. This point was picked up in the Millsap letter and is a somewhat neglected subject. It is discussed further in the commentary to the Sutherland account (1.7.1). The referenced letters from Willis Moore are not found in the General Land Office files, and according to the staff there, "evidence submitted" might mean only that the documents were shown, but not necessarily that any copies were ever made.

---

1. E.g., Myers (1948, reprint 1973, 142–46), though he gives more credence to the work than I think is warranted.
2. The evidence for the forgery of the Crockett book is presented in Shackford 1956, 273–81, and Shackford and Folmsbee 1973, v, xvii–xix.
3. Chariton, 187.
4. Gracy (2001, 271) indicates that some tests on the iron in the Millsap letter's ink have been done, which is consistent with the letter being a twentieth-century forgery. See Whitfield and Dalton 2002 for a discussion of a controversy that can still arise even from physical tests.

1.7.1.1. John Sutherland, narrative, soon after 1860?

Sutherland, Dr. John S. N.d. (after 1860) "The Alamo," in the John S. Ford Papers. 18–55. CAH.

This handwritten manuscript in the John S. Ford Papers is one of the single most important documents on the Alamo because of extensive indirect use by later writers of narrative accounts. It has been generally assumed that this manuscript is the original Sutherland account, but for reasons given in the commentary, the relationship of this Ford version with the original Sutherland account is more complicated. Nonetheless, and despite its significance, this Ford version of the Sutherland account is not readily available, as it was printed fully only in a rare pamphlet by Annie Sutherland (a granddaughter) in 1936, and in earlier abbreviated and/or edited forms by Ford in 1896 and James DeShields in 1911. Page numbers in the original Ford manuscript are included to help locate text. The date of composition of the Sutherland original is after Yoakum (1855) and Ruiz (1860) were published. A hand-drawn plan of the Alamo appears on page 17 of the Ford manuscript, just prior to this manuscript, and is first referenced here on page 30. The plan itself follows as the next document. What is probably a more direct but also fragmentary copy of the original Sutherland account transcribed by Amelia Williams is presented at the end of this section.

[*p. 18*]

The Alamo By Dr. Sutherland

In 1835 I visited Texas with a view of making it my home, and it was my lot to witness her in that struggle with the tyrranical [*sic*] power of Mexico which terminated in securing to her the liberties we now enjoy.

Having acknowledged allegiance to the Provisional Government [*of Texas*], and enlisted in the service of the army fore [*sic*] one month, &c. I proceeded, in company with Capt. Wm Patten, and ten others to San Antonio, which place we [*three words erased*] we reach about the eighteenth of January, 1836. From that time until the twenty-third of February I was cognizant of all that occurred of importance with the Garrison [of the Alamo], and remember well its hopes, ["*its*" *erased*] fears, and anxieties for the safety of the country, and her interests.

I propose to state such facts as came within my own personal knowledge up to the time of my departure from Bexar, and such information as I have derived from the statements of others who were witnesses of the siege and fall.

How I escaped the fate of my comrades, being crippled by my horse falling on me, will appear in its proper connection with the other incidents which I purpose to relate. I have frequently conversed at length with one who was in the Alamo for some days whilst the siege was going on, and with others who were there during the whole of it, and witnessed its beginning, its progress, and its unfortunate termination. The first alluded to was John W. Smith, whose name not only stands prominently connected with this tragic affair, but deserves a conspicuous place in a great portion of the history of our country. The latter were those who were spared from the massacre, Mrs. Dickin [*Dickinson*] [*p. 19*] and Col. Travis' servant. I had also an interview with Col. Almonte,

Gen. Santa Anna, and his private secretary, all of whose accounts agree with each other, whenever they relate to the same incidents, and with the other three mentioned, as well as my own knowledge of what took place whilst I remained at San Antonio. I should not under ordinary circumstances be disposed to credit these Mexican authorities, for they are not always reliable when left to stand upon their own merits, but since they agree substantially with other witnesses upon whom we may safely rely there can be no good reason why their statements should not be adopted as true. These statements being made separately, and at different times, and corroborating such other as they do, build a weight of evidence which is not to be obtained from any other source, and which seems substantial and conclusive.

Though many years have elapsed since the Alamo fall, I have never, until recently, thought it necessary for me to publish any thing in regard to it, supposing the facts would appear from some other source substantially correct. But since several conflicting accounts have been published, some of which differ widely from my own knowledge of facts, I have deemed it my duty to history, to the children of the worthy [*some words erased*] patriots, to work out and publish my version of the last noble struggle of the gallant Travis and his noble band.

When reaching San Antonio we found the force then in a manner destitute. Grant and Johnson had left but a short time previous with their companies— taking with them almost every[*thing? Word ending with "ing" lost in tear of page*] in the shape of supplies, and more than their share of a scant llowance [*sic*] of clothing, blankets, and medicines. The Government [*p. 20*] of course, at that day were not able to meet their demands. They lived upon beef and corn bread. The former they obtained from the numerous stocks of cattle in the country, and the latter from the few farmers who raised it by irrigation in the vicinity of the town. But the consumption of these commodities, at Bexar, had been so rapid for some months past that both were becoming scarce, and not easy to be obtained. They were also out of money. They were all volunteers, and had their own resources upon which they had relied most of the time, even now exhausted. There being no treasury they, of course, had not received anything in the shape of pay. A small amount was [*two words erased*] obtained from a few individuals, from time to time, and distributed amongst those in the greatest need, but the liberality of of [*sic*] these few soon reduced them to a like degree of want. This state of affairs, together without any prospect of relief, was fast bringing about dissatisfaction among the men. Col. James C. Neill, who was there in command, readily foresaw that something must be done, and that too without delay, or his position would be abandoned, and left subject to be retaken by the enemy should they return. He therefore determined to procure, if possible, a portion of a donation of five thousand dollars, which had been made to the cause of Texas by Harry Hill, of Nashville, and accordingly left Bexar, about the twelfth or fifteenth February for that purpose.

About this time there were frequent rumors of an invasion of the country, but being generally of an unauthorized character, but little notice was paid to them. It was generally believed that the terms upon which Cos had been permitted to return to Mexico would be complied with by him, and that his defeat would serve as a warning to Santa Anna, and induce him to postpone operations until the summer.

By Col. Neill's absence Col. James Bowie was left in [*p. 21*] command, but he was shortly after taken sick and confined to his bed. In a few days however Col. Travis reached Bexar, and by the request of the Governor accepted the command. Travis had been commissioned a Lieut. Colonel, and ordered to raise a regiment of men for the regular service, but owing to the distracted state of the public mind, and the embarrassing condition of [*word erased*] affairs generally, he had been unable to do so. In the meantime rumors of a suspicious character reached him, that the country would be invaded much sooner than had been expected. Regarding the maintenance of the position at Bexar as of vital importance to the country, and knowing the inadequacy of the forces there to do it, he set out forthwith to join them. On his route he enlisted, about twenty men, with which number he reached Bexar a few days after Col. Neill's departure.

Col. David Crockett arrived a few days later, with twelve others, direct from Tennessee. Crockett was immediately offered a command by Col. Travis, and called upon by the crowd for a speech. The former honor he would not accept, but mounted a goods-box on the civil plaza, amidst prolonged cheers of the people. The applause, however, was followed by profound silence, when the full-toned voice of the distinguished speaker rose gradually above the audience, and fell with smooth and lively accent upon the ears of all, it's [*sic*] sound was familiar to many who had heard it in days past, while the hearts of all beat a lively response to the patriotic sentiments which fell from his lips. Frequent applause greeted him, as he related in his own peculiar style, some of those jolly anecdotes with which he often regaled his friends, and which he only could tell with appropriate grace. He alluded frequently to his past career, and during the course of his remarks stated, that, not long since [*p. 22*] he had been a candidate for Congress in his native State, and, that during the canvass he told his constituents that "if they did not elect him, they might all go to ———— and he would go to Texas." After which he concluded, in substance, as follows:—"And, fellow citizens, I am among you. I have come to your country, though not I hope, through any selfish motive whatever. I have come to aid you all that I can in in [*sic*] your noble cause. I shall identify myself with your interests, and all the honor that I desire is that of defending, as a high private, in common with my fellow-citizens, the liberties of our common country"

This made many a man Col. Crockett's friend, who had not known him before.

The strength of the Texicans at Bexar now consisted in one hundred and fifty-two men. Eighty of those were a party of the original garrison, who had not caught the Matamoros fever; twenty-five had returned with Col. Bowie from Goliad. Col. Travis had brought with him about twenty. Col. Crockett twelve, Capt. Patten eleven. These detachments, with their respective commanders, make the number. A few days after their concentration, some twenty Mexicans of the City joined them, increasing the number to one hundred and seventy-two.

It is, perhaps, proper to notice that very few of the Mexican citizens of the Republic were friendly to the cause of Texas. Some were openly hostile, and had gone to Mexico to join Santa Anna, while a majority occupied a kind of half-way ground, yet eager to follow the dominant party. It was said that between a thousand and fifteen hundred of them joined Santa Anna, during his stay in Bexar, and whilst on the march from that place to the Colorado.

Of the one hundred and seventy-two men [*p. 23*] now at San Antonio some twenty-five or thirty were on the sick list, and suffering through want of medical aid. The Surgeon of the command, Dr. Pollard, had consumed his stock of medicines, and no others were to be obtained in the country. In this emergency I was requested to take charge of the sick, and appropriate a small quantity of medicines I had brought with me to their necessities. I did so, and [*"finally" erased, then rewritten*] finally succeeded of relieving most of them. A few, however, did not recover entirely. One of which was Col. Bowie, whose disease being of a peculiar nature was not to be cured by an ordinary course of treatment.

Having taken this hasty view of the manner in which Col. Travis and his command were brought to Bexar, and of their necessitous [?] circumstances all the while, I will notice briefly the operations of the enemy.

Although the frequent rumors of an immediate invasion, which reached us, failed to arouse the mass of our population to a sense of danger, they were not without their effect upon some, who notwithstanding the fancied security of the majority, realised the danger of a surprise, and the insecurity of our interests, and were disposed to contribute their efforts to prevent being taken unawares. One of these was Capt. Juan N. Seguin, who though he has since been charged with hostility to the Texas cause, certainly did not manifest it at the time of which I am speaking. He manifested every desire [*two words erased*] for the success of our cause. He was then a citizen of San Antonio, and believing that the conditions upon which Cos had been allowed to return to Mexico would be of no avail. And that his inglorious surrender would but exasperate Santa Anna, and cause him to strike an early blow upon the rebellious province, used the precaution to station a spy upon the Rio Grande, with orders to report to him immediately any movements which [*p. 24*] indicated an advance [*word(s) erased*]. This spy was a young man by the name of Blaz Herrera, a cousin of Col. Seguin's. He remained at his post some time before any signs of a suspicious character were discovered. About the eighteenth of February, however, Santa Anna commenced to cross the river [Rio Grande], with an army of five thousand men. Herrera made some inquiry as to their numbers, plans, &c, without being suspected of his motives. According to his instructions he set out post haste for Bexar, where he arrived about dark, on Saturday evening the twentieth, and reported his discoveries to his employer. Col. Seguin immediately informed Col. Travis of what he had learned, and assured him of his confidence in Herrera. About nine o'clock that night a council of war was held in Col. Travis' room. Herrera was brought before it, and required to report what he had seen. He reported that he had seen the army crossing the river, and through inquiry ascertained that, the main body of the force, numbering thirty-five hundred, would travel slowly, but that the cavalry, fifteen hundred strong in number, would make a forced march for the purpose of taking the Texians by surprise. This created some considerable discussion. Some held that it was more authentic than any[thing] that had reached them before, whilst a majority declared it was only the report of a Mexican, and entitled to no more consideration than many others of a like character that were daily harangued throughout the country. The council adjourned without coming to any conclusion as to whether it was necessary to give any heed to the warning or not.

In justice to the incredulous part of the council, I will remark that, such was the universal distrust of Mexican authority that, no report coming from it ever received due consideration. So many false alarms had been given by [p. 25] a degraded class of "Greasers" continually passing to and fro, through the west, that no credence was given to any rumor, however plausible, and no danger apprehended. Many had persuaded themselves, that Santa Anna would never attempt to conquer Texas, and the most general reply to any argument, to the contrary was that, he was afraid to meet us. "He knew better." A majority believed that Cos' defeat would have the effect to intimidate him, and, if not to deter him from an invasion altogether, at least induce him to postpone it till a late day. This will relieve Travis of the charge, which has been urged against him that, he manifested a want of subordination in neglecting scouting service. He only reached San Antonio, as we have seen, two days before this report, and that being the extreme western part where information from Mexico was most likely to arrive first, to find such an opinion prevailing, it was almost an unavoidable conclusion that he would fall into it. Until Col. Neill's departure Deaf Smith had been a regular scout, but they too entertained the common belief, or they would have never left their post.

The night and following day [after the arrival of Herrera] passed as usual, without the occurrence of anything worthy of notice. The little excitement which was created passed off, as fast as the report which produced it became more and more discredited. The twenty-second passed likewise. On the morning of the twenty-third the inhabitants were observed to be in quite an unusual stir. The citizens of every class were hurrying to and fro, through the streets, with obvious signs of excitement. Houses were being emptied, and their contents put into carts, and hauled off. Such of the poorer class, who had no better mode of conveyance, were shouldering their effects, and leaving on foot.

These movements solicited investigation. Orders were issued [p. 26] that, no others be allowed to leave the city, which had the effect to increase their commotion. Several were arrested, and interrogated, as to the cause of the movement, but no satisfactory answer could be obtained. The most general reply was, that they were going out to the country to prepare for the coming crop. This excuse, however, availed nothing, for it was not to be supposed that every person in the city was a farmer. Col. Travis persisted in carrying out his order, and continued the investigation. Nine o'clock came, and no discoveries were made. Ten o'clock in like manner passed, and finally the eleventh hour was drawing near, and the matter was yet a mystery. It was hoped by Col. Travis that his diligent investigation, and strict enforcement of the order prohibiting the inhabitants from leaving the city, would have the effect to frighten them into a belief that, their course was not the wisest for them to pursue; that, he, provoked by their obstinacy in refusing to reveal the true cause of the uneasiness, would resort to measures, which might be more distasteful than any which would probably follow an open confession. But in that he was disappointed. The treacherous wretches persisted in their course, greatly to his discomfiture all the while.

Finally he was informed, secretly, by a friendly Mexican, that the enemy's cavalry had reached the Leon, eight miles from the city, on the previous night, and had sent a messenger to the inhabitants, informing them of the fact, and warning them to evacuate the city at early dawn, as it would be attacked the [*word erased*] next day. He stated further that, a messenger had arrived, a day or two before, and that, it had been the purpose of the enemy to take the Texians by surprise, but in consequence of a heavy rain having fallen on the road, their march was impeded, and they were unable to reach the place in time. Notwithstanding this statement seemed altogether plausible, and to substantiate the statement [*p. 27*] the report [*sic; "statement" on the previous page should have been crossed out*] given by Herrera three days before, yet it wore the [*word erased, then rewritten*] countenance of so many of their false rumors that it was a matter of doubt that there was any truth in it.

Col. Travis came to me forthwith, however, and informed me what he had learned, and wished to borrow a horse of me to send out to the Salado for his "caballado" that he might start out a scout through the country. As I had two, of course, he obtained one, when a runner was started forthwith. In company with Col. Travis, and at his request, I proceeded to post a reliable man on the roof of the old Church, as a sentinel. We all three went up, but being unable to make a [*word(s) erased except beginning "a"*] any discoveries. The Colonel and myself returned. The sentinel remained at his post with orders to ring the bell, if he should discover any sign, which he might deem ominous.

Col. Travis went to his room, and I to the store of Capt. Nat Lewis, who requested me to assist in taking an inventory of his goods, saying that he had some suspicioun [*sic*] that they would soon be taken from him. We proceeded to the task, but had not been long engaged, when the sentinel rang the bell, and cried out "the enemy are in view." I immediately went out, and ran across the plaza toward the church, when a considerable crowd soon gathered around. Col. Travis was also there. Several persons ran up to the sentinel's post, and not being able to see anything justifying the cry, halloed that it was a "false alarm," and that they "believed the whole tale was a lie," and "our fears useless." The sentinel exclaimed, with an oath, that "he had seen them," and "that they had hid behind a row of brushwood." The crowd disbanded, the greater part discrediting the report altogether.

I then proposed to Col. Travis, that, if any one, who knew the country, would accompany me, I would go out, and [p. 28] ascertain to a certainty the truth or falsity of the whole. John W. Smith was soon at hand. When we started, taking the Suredo road, I remarked to Travis, just as I mounted my horse, that "if he saw us returning in any other gait than a slow pace, he might be sure that we had seen the enemy." This arrangement proved of some benefit. A moderate gait soon brought us to the top of the slope, about a mile and a half west of town, where we were not surprised to find ourselves within one hundred and fifty yards of fifteen hundred men, well mounted and equipped. Their polished armor glistening in the rays of the sun, as they were formed in a line, behind the chaparral and mezquite [sic] bushes mentioned by the sentinel. The commander riding among the line, waving his sword, as though he might be giving directions to the mode of attack. We did not remain long watching their movements, but wheeled around, and started full speed back to town. In consequence of a heavy rain, through the previous night, the road was quite muddy, and my horse being rather smoothly shod, began to slip and scramble, stopped at the end fifty yards, where with a tumbling somersault, he pitched my gun out of my hand, throwing me some distance ahead of him, and followed himself, rolling directly across my knees. Smith dismounted, and pulled him off me, but being slightly stunned, he made no effort to rise, but lay perfectly still, holding me fast beneath him. Afer [sic] some moments he managed to get up, when by the assistance of Smith, I did likewise. When I picked up the pieces of my gun, which was broken off at the breach, Being again mounted, we resumed our gait, and were not long getting to town.

On reaching the civil plaza we met Col. Crockett, who informed us that, Col. Travis had removed his headquarters, together with the entire force, from the city to the Alamo. Smith here left me, and [p. 29] and [sic] went to his house.

On learning the result of our scout Col. Crockett returned with me. We crossed the river at the ford, in the river below, and on our way up to the fort, we met Capt. Dimmitt and Lieut. Nobler [spelling of names uncertain]. The former inquired where we were going. I told him. When he remarked that "there were not even enough at Bexar to defend the place, that it was bound to fall; and insisted that I should go with him" Saying he "would see me safely out." Then we would go and bring reinforcements to the garrison." I replied that "I should go, and report to Col. Travis, and could not [word erased] say, that I could accompany him even then." As we rode on he remarked that he would wait for me down the street at his house. It was not until attempting to dismount, in front of Travis' room, that I was sensible of the extent of the injury caused by the fall of my horse. On alighting from the saddle my knee gave way, and I fell to the ground. By the assistance of Col. Crockett I got up and went to Col.

Travis' room. Where we found him writing a despatch. He had watched our movements, and by this time no longer doubted that the enemy was upon him. I informed him of our discoveries, and of the accident which happened to me, and added that, "if I could be of any benefit to him I was at his service." He replied that he wished me to go forthwith to Gonzales, and rally the settlers, if possible to his relief. Col. Crockett, yet standing by, remarked to him "Colonel, here am I, assign me a position, and I am and my twelve boys will try to defend it." Travis replied that he wanted him to defend the picket wall extending from the end of the barracks, on the south side, to the corner of the church.

At this time the Texians had well nigh consumed anything they had on hand in the way of provisions. Grant and Johnston had left them but a small supply of coffee [*p. 30*]. Sugar, and salt, which had long since disappeared, and none of these necessaries were to be found, though they might have had ever so much money with which to buy them. Their meats they obtained by driving the beef from the prairie, just as they needed it, and as they never had more at one time than would serve more than twenty-four hours; so it happened they were in need just at that time. They were out of corn of which they made their bread, and had no money to purchase more. Though Travis afterwards thought that The Lord was on his side upon the promise that "he would provide for the upright," if he had claimed his favor under the circumstances it would have been upon the score that:—"He chasteneth whom he loveth." While they were retiring from the city to the Alamo, they met twenty or thirty beeves beeves [*sic*] coming down the Alamo street [*the previous line has broken inserts and words; the order is given that makes the most sense*] now Commerce Street, towards the river, when all hands gathered around them, and drove them into the Alamo. They als [*sic*] got their bread by chance. During the hurry, and excitement of the day, a number of Mexican "jacales," near the Alamo, had been vacated. In these they found some eighty or ninety bushels of corn. These were their supplies during the siege.

So soon as the Texians entered the Alamo, they set about preparing for its defence. The beeves were secured in a pen on the north east side of the fortress, designated on the Diagram by Y. [*Not on diagram, however. Rather, "cattle pen" is written*] The corn was stored away in some of the small rooms of the barracks. They did not obtain water from the small canal which runs near, but dug a well within the walls. There being no portholes in the wall, it was necessary for them to make an arrangement by which they could shoot over it. This was done by throwing up an embankment against it on the inside. This being done they proceeded to make other arrangements necessary. Their guns were placed upon the wall, as soon as possible. Of these they had [*p. 31*] some thirty or forty pieces of various calibres, amongst them was an eighteen pounder. Most of these they had taken from the enemy, in December previous, when Cos surrendered. Though they had so many they were not all mounted. I dont [*sic*] think more than about twenty were put to use during the siege. They had also obtained from the same source a considerable number of muskets, swords, and bayonets;

together with any amount of ammunition, which came in play, for of their own they had but a small supply. All were armed with good rifles, single barrel pistols, and good knives. Their powder they kept in a small room in the South West corner of the church, which was covered over with a arched roof of stone, and plastered perefectly [*sic*] tight, so as to make it proof against sparks of fire from the enemy's shells.

So soon as Travis ascertained that the enemy were upon him he sent despatches to Col. Fannin then at Goliad, representing [*word not clear*] to him his condition, and requesting assistance, as speedily [*word(s) erased*] as it could be sent him. This despatch was borne by a young man by the name of Johnson, and not by J. B. Bonham as stated in some accounts. On the twenty-third, when Almonte arrived at Bexar Bonham was absent from the city. He had visited Texas with a view of purchasing land, and had not attached himself to the army, though he held himself in readiness to serve the country whenever an emergency occurred. At the time the cavalry arrived he was prospecting the country in the vicinity of San Antonio, and on hearing the report of cannon in the city, started on the return. On the way near the Salado he met Johnson with the despatch to Fannin, and learned the cause of the cannon fire. He put spurs to his horse and made his way into the walls of the Alamo.

Between three and four o'clock P.M. I started, as requested by Col. Travis, for Gonzales. I first rode down the river, a short distance, thinking to [*p. 32*] meet Dimmitt, but he had gone, taking the easier Goliad road. On coming near the ford I fell in with J. W. Smith, also on his way to Gonzales. We halted, and were paralyzed for a moment when we saw the enemy march into the Military Plaza in regular order. While we sat on our horses, for a moment, watching their movements, Cap. Nat Lewis came to us on foot. He too was bound for Gonzales with as much of his valuables as he could carry in his saddle-bags, thrown across his shoulder; leaving the remainder in his storehouse, a contribution to the enemy.

We soon parted, Capt Lewis taking one direction, Smith and myself another. Thinking the Mexicans might have seen us going [*word erased*] off, and pursue us, we took the old Goliad road, which runs directly south for some distance, after going about half a mile we turned due east into mezquite and chaparral brush, following the winding paths that led through it. We crossed the Gonzales road between the city and Powderhouse Hill, about one mile east of town. Turning eastward over the hill, we saw three men riding in the distance [*word(s) erased*] across the Salado, about a mile and a half from us. We suspected [*handwriting changes at this point*], that they might be a scouting party of the enemy, attempting to cut off any one leaving the city, we kept on our course rather bearing around them to the left.

On reaching the Salado, my injured leg began to stiffen and to give me such pain that I thought of turning back, and should have done so if Smith had not urged me on, believing that the enemy [*p. 33*] had by [*"this" written and crossed out*] that time surrounded the fort; for a few minutes had passed since we had heard a cannon shot; After resting a moment; and filling our gourds, for which we had just paid a Mexican, whom we met, a dollar, we went on, continuing parallel with the road, and about a mile from it. After riding about [*some words erased and written over*] sixteen miles, dark came upon us, when my pains now became so acute that I was forced to stop. We [*handwriting changes again, perhaps to a third hand; the original hand returns on p. 39; spelling becomes more inaccurate as well*] spread our blankets upon the ground, and ourselves upon them, and being somewhat relieved of my sufferings I was soon asleep.

By daylight on the morrow we were again in the saddle, and on our way to Gonzales, where after a hard days ride, and anything else than an agreable one to myself, we arived about four oclock PM.

So soon as we entered the town, we [*word erased*] made known our mission, and sint notice to all the neighbouring settlements with the news of the enemiy's arrival. Calling upon the citizens to come immediately to the relief of the beseiged. This was on Wednesday the [*word erased*] twenty fourth. By Saturday we succeded in getting [*half a line blank*] twenty five men who were placed under the command of Ensign Kimble. These were principally from the town of Gonzales, men of families and her best citizens. They started for San Antonio on Saturday about two oclock P.M. with John [*p. 34*] W Smith acting as guide. On the Cibolo they increased their force to thirty two, which number reached Bexar about one oclock A.M. on Tuesday, the [*word erased*] twenty ninth. On reaching the suburbs of the City they were approached by a man on horseback, who asked in English "Do you wish to go into the fort jentlemen." "Yes" was the reply. "Then follow me" said he, at the same time turning his horse into the lead of the company. Smith remarked "Boys, it's time to be after shooting that fellow." When he put spurs to his horse, sprung into the thicket, and was out of sight in a moment, before a gun could be got to bear on him. Some supposed from his fluency in the English language that this was Genl Woll, who was [*word(s) erased*] Englishman in the Mexican service.

The little band proceeded silently, in single file, towards the fort, but were soon to be saluted again, though not in so friendly a manner. Notwithstanding Smith had taken the precaution to dispatch a messenger ahead, there seems to have been some misunderstanding as to the direction from which they should approach the walls, for the sentinel not being aware of their presence, fired upon them without hailing. The ball took effect in the foot of one of the men. The mistake was soon rectified, when all went in without further mishap.

This accession to the Garrison counting Smith and Bonham increased its original strength to two hundred [*pp. 35, 36 crossed out*] and six, but Capt Patton having left the City, and Johnson and myself having gone with dispatches, left the actual number now within the walls, two hundred and three. [*two lines erased*]

Most of those were wearied and worn by the constant duties of the fort, while the remainder suffered from the fatigue of several days' travel. Their condition was not, indeed, the most desirable in which to sustain a siege against a force so greatly their superior in point of numbers. Some have supposed that Travis and his men, were greatly deficient in desipline and a Knowledge of the arts of war generally. [*half a line blank*] That they knew little of military tactics is quite true, but that they were proficient in the use of arms were as well unsaid. [*half a line blank*] As no pioneer, frontiersman, ever knew anything better than how to use his arms—his daily and nightly companion. That none knew better how to handle them than the Alamo men, their work during this siege, and on the 6th of March will forever attest. Some of them were fair artillerists [*p. 37, marked up but not changed*].

Having followed this noble band of patriots to Bexar, and seen them united in that almost hopeless struggle for the defence of this remote outpost as it then was, I will return to consider the movements of the enemy.

After the entrance of the Cavalry into the city which was effected without resistance, Some few minutes passed when a white flag was seen descending Commerce Street. Maj Morris and Capt Martin were commissioned to meet it, and confer with its bearer's. This meeting took place on a small foot bridge which led from the Alamo to the city, crossing the river just above the one which now crosses on Commerce street. An unconditional surrender was demanded in the name and by the authority of Col Almonte, which being reported to Col Travis, was answard by a Cannon Shot from the walls of the Alamo at a group of the enemy which had haulted on Main Plaza, at the enterance of Commerce Street

This was the shot that was heard by Bonham, Smith and myself, the gun which opened that desperate strugle, which said to the foe your demand is insolent, we are not here to surrender, nor to retreat, but to fight you, though you be a million, and if need be to die here, sword in hand.

Col Almonte proceeded at once to arrange his forces to the best advantage, and to commence the siege. His main force was stationed at a point [*p. 38*] on the hill east of the Alamo, and about one thousand yards from it. Though my informants were of course unable to ascertain the exact disposition which was made of the numerous small divisions which seemed to be maneuvering around in every direction. This position was assumed by Almonte for the purpose of cutting off supplies for the besieged, and of guarding against surprise by any large reinforcement which might be coming on the Gonzales road, near which his incampment was made. They seem to have desired that all the Texians that might have been absent from the city at the time of arrival, and such other persons around Bexar, as were friendly to their cause, and had not gone into the Alamo, might do so, that the slaughter might be the greater, flattering themselves with the delusion, that it would be but an easy matter to take it when their main force should arrive, even against a force twice as strong, as that which it now contained. Their conduct towards Mr Bonham indicates this idea. Whilst going into the fort as before mentioned, he passed their sentinel without being halted or molested. They paid no attention to him. This may not have been the case, and perhaps it is presuming too much upon Mexican vanity.

Yet the idea is supported by many incidents of this war which warrant the conclusion that, Santa Anna regarded the Subjugation of the Texians as a matter of
easy conquest.

The siege though at first opened with considerable [*p. 39*] vigour, was not
for some hours carried on with very great severity. Towards night frequent
Skermishes took place between the Texians and detachments of the enemy
which moved up from almost every direction. These seldom if ever occurred
without damage to the assailants, whilst the Texians lost not a man. [*Handwriting reverts to original, probably Ford's, with a separate sheet incorporated on the page.*]

After dark the Texians tore down, and carried into the fort, several
"jueahes" [*spelling unclear*] [huts] which stood in two rows, near S.E. and S.W.
Corners of the wall. These constituted their firewood of which they had need
only for the purpose of cooking.

During the night the siege grew heavier, and on the following day more
vigorus still. The skirmishes became more frequent. Larger forces were [*word
erased*] employed, and nearer approaches made. This, however, was but the
more fatal to the enemy for the Texians had only to stand at their position, and
drop them as fast as they came in their reach [*word erased*] of their good "old
Kentucky rifles."

We are not to suppose that these assaults were made with a view of storming the fort, for they were generally made by small forces, varying perhaps
from one [hundred] to two hundred men in each. Almonte seems to have feared
the result of an assault, was with his whole force, well disciplined as [*word
erased, possibly Travis*] they were. They even doubtless intended merely to keep
the garrison constantly harrassed and on its guard, and thereby so weary it out
by fatigue and the want of sleep, as to render the storming the easier, when the
main body of the army should arrive. Nor was this plan a useless one as will
eventually appear.

[*p. 40*] With regard to the time of Santa Anna's arrival at San Antonio there
is also some difference of opinion between our historians, and indeed they all
seem to speak positively with regard to it, as though there could be no room to
doubt as to their correctness. Those from whom I derived my information were
of opinion widely different [*words erased*] from any of them, and though they
made no positive assertion in regard to its truth entertained no doubt with
regard to it. The following circumstances seem to merit some consideration in
determining the time of this event.

During the twenty-third the siege, as before remarked, continued with
increasing severity. An incessant bombardment was kept up day and night,
while a hail of bombs and cannon balls was poured within the walls, and,
strange as it may seem, without the loss of one of the besieged. The garrison
replied with great vigor, from their guns mounted around the walls. Thus it
continued from day to day, until the morning of the Third of March, when, if
there was any change, the bombardment increased in severity. Indeed the din
and roar of the artillery had become a monotony, which [*word erased*] though it

was kept up by the enemy, with great loss to them, was nevertheless, fast subduing the physical strength, and vigor of the garrison, their number being insufficient to man the walls [*word erased*] [*p. "40" continued on separate sheet*] detail—every man was required at his post—and sleep was out of the question. About midday on the third of March, whilst the Texians were at their posts, maintaining their position against the charges of the enemy, as usual, a hidious yell was raised by the population of the town. The cry "Santa Anna," "Santa Anna," [*sic*] shouted throughout the city. This attracted the attention of all, when a large body of the enemy were seen entering the streets of the City on the west side. The buildings were at that time so low that the entire City could be viewed from the Alamo. The besiegers for a while slackened the vigor of their operations, and joined in the general rejoicing.

This incident was related to me by J. W. Smith, Mrs. Dickinson, and Travis' [negro] boy, all at different times, and in substance the same. To consider it singly, without any connection [*word erased*] in the others of a like bearing, would be to consider the whole in mystery, unless there were no assertions [*word erased*] that Santa Anna's arrival took place before that time, in which case it would at once fix the time of that event on the third of March. But as it is we could not account for it in any [*word erased*] way. This we must do, we must give it a place somewhere. It was the opinion of Mr. Smith and the other persons mentioned that, neither Santa Anna, nor his main force, were at San Antonio at any time during the siege, before this event took place, and that opinion is supported by some very strong circumstancial evidence. First, [*word erased*] is it not reasonable to suppose that so large a body of men could not have been in and about the city during the siege, without being seen from the Alamo, the country around being comparatively open, unless they concealed them [*words missing in tear?*] [*p. 41*] during the day, and if they had arrived at any time before, why should [*word erased*] such a parade, the like of which had not occurred before, be made on them at this late day. Again we could have no good reason for supposing that Santa Anna would have encamped around the walls of the Alamo, for nearly two weeks, with an army of five thousand men, and have made no effort to take it, especially when he must have been aware of the importance of an early blow. The question might be asked here, [*word(s) erased*], if he knew so well the importance of haste in his movements, why did he not attack the fortress as soon as he reached it, instead of waiting nearly three days? To which I would answer, that his men had just been on a heavy march, and that he might have doubted the result of an assault with jaded troops, while good judgement counseled a few days rest, and further [*unclear word(s), possibly "as such"*] time was necessary for reconnoitering the position for a proper disposition of the column for an assault.

Furthermore there can be no sufficient reason why the demand of a surrender should have been made in the name of Col. Almonte, if the General-in-chief had been present himself. Almonte told me, in person, that Santa Anna did not reach Bexar until after he did, though he did not state the exact day. Whether these circumstances are sufficient to fix the time on the third of March or not, they certainly have their bearing, and are entitled to proper consideration.

After the salutations and rejoicings of citizens were concluded, the besiegers resumed their operations, and prosecuted the siege with renewed violence. Perhaps a few of Santa Anna's troops assisted them. Though the main part took a position on the old Goliad [*unclear word, probably "road"*], half a mile from the Alamo, where they no doubt rested, for no assault for the purpose of storming the fort was made until the sixth of March.

[*p. 42*] By this time nearly all of the Mexicans, who had joined the garrison at the beginning of the siege, had left it. They had joined believing that Travis would receive re-inforcements sufficient to enable him to maintain the fort, when they would be on the safe side, but being disappointed in this their hearts failed in view of the fate which they must unavoidably suffer should they stand up to their first resolves. They knew both the weakness of the garrison and the strength of the enemy. Only three of them remained true to our cause. These desertions left the number of the Texians one hundred and eighty-six, counting John W. Smith, who had remained, since his entrance on the twenty-ninth, to take his chance with the rest.

One would suppose that this little band of men became aware of their inadequacy to maintain their position, and that emotions of despair began to invade their hearts. For eight days and nights they had been constantly on duty, without sleep, on scant rations. They had anxiously expected the hour when assistance would reach them, that hour, which alas, they were never destined to hail. Now they were wearied and worn down by their constant vigilance, yet soon to be called upon to resist a force more than sixteen times their equals in number. What dark emotions they must experience in this extremity. All the sacred associations of the past crowded upon them, whilst the embittering prospects of the future silently admonished them, that they [*word erased*] would never witness that glorious dawn which should hail their country, free and independent of despotic sway. But it was not theirs to falter. Their rights were seized by the oppressive arm of a tyrant, and they were called upon to rescue them from his grasp. The fondest endearments [*word unclear, probable reading*] of time sustained and buoyed them, and though they should perish, and their names be forever consigned to oblivion, the noblest [*p. 43*] considerations of chivalry and honor still pressed upon them, and demanded a sacrifice at their hands, which the All-wise dispenser [*word unclear, probable reading*] of events, for purposes of his own wisdom allowed that they should make, and for which thoughts the dearest that humanity could bestow, they should receive the richest reward of a grateful people. It was this consideration that upheld them. That pride of character, love of home and country, the true soldier's noblest attributes, enabled them to sustain with cheerfulness, if possible, their position, in this their hour of extremity. It was thus [?] surrounded with the enemy, and awaiting the hour of attack, not knowing how soon it might arrive, Travis addressed a letter to the Convention, and several others to private individuals, amongst which was a note to his friend in Washington country. Who as he reads it does not feel something of that spirit possessed by its author, and whose heart does not swell with increased sympathy, and feel for that officer, this noble man, and his compatriots, that they can never repay the debt of honor she owes to their sacred memory. These letters from Travis, and quite a number of others [*word erased*] from his comrades to their relatives were sent out on the night of the Third of March, by John W. Smith, who reached Gonzales on the following day, about three o'clock P.M. Immediately on his arrival there he represented to the citizens the perilous condition of their countrymen at Bexar, assuring them that, Travis and his men must inevitably perish, unless assistance was despatched in the greatest possible haste. He announced that if one hundred men could be raised, that they would be sufficient to sustain the fort, at least until others could reach it, and that he would start with them, as guide, as soon as they could get ready. In a short time he was informed that the number desired could not be raised, but that fifty could and would be ready very soon. The following night passed, and he was again informed that, some of the fifty had declined going, but that twenty-five men were [*p. 44*] available, and would be at his service the next day. Saturday finally came, when owing to some unspeakable cause they were yet unable to set out. After much hurry and confusion, and consequently further delay, Sunday morning found them <u>enroute</u> for Bexar, well equipped, with good arms, and ten days provisions. [*word erased*] Travis' supply of beef and corn had well nigh given out, and when Smith left the fort, his order was that, every man who came to his assistance should bring ten days' rations; saying that he would fire the eighteen pounder three times a day—at morning, noon, and night—so long as the Alamo stood. The gun was fired regularly, and was distinctly heard at Gonzales.

Santa Anna having his position below the Alamo, as mentioned, immediately set about making preparations for the assault. New batteries were erected, which opened heavily upon the Alamo, whilst his men were plainly seen from the church, making ladders for storming the walls. All necessary arrangements being made, the main part of the division rested from the fatigue of their march, awaiting the time of attack, which was, probably, not yet determined. The siege was continued with great violence. Harrassing the Texians constantly on every side, while the heavy batteries, lately erected, thickened. "The showers of bombs and cannon balls which had been continually pounding [*this word unclear, probable reading*] amongst them." The Texians replied vigorously, with rifle and cannon, and made great slaughter amongst their enemies.

About ten o'clock on Saturday night all firing ceased. The besieging forces were withdrawn, and the batteries hushed. The thunder of artillery was now succeeded by a universal stillness which reigned throughout the citadel. Not even the tread of a sentinel around the walls broke upon the waiting senses of the [*p. 45*] little band within. Silence, darkness, reigned within and without the Alamo. The moon had retired from the heavens, whilst the dim light of the stars now shut out by a vail of smoke and mist which settled above. A gloomy pall now enwrapped the walls of the Alamo—fit emblem of the melancholy which hung above the inmates.

This cessation was not without intended effect. In no great while after it took place the, [*word unclear, possible reading "honest"*], vigilant eyes of the Texians were closed in sleep. For more than eleven days and nights they had been constantly at their posts, partaking of food only at such intervals as were allowed them. A few cooked the corn and beef for the rest, who took it from their hands at the wall. Coffee would indeed have been a boon to them. Yet they had no stimulant. However coffee could not have sustained them long for their physical strength began to fail for the want of rest, and artifice could have resisted the power of nature for a short time. Their number having been too small for a part to sustain the defense while the remainder were at rest, they had seldom enjoyed it, and an opportunity being now offered it is not surprising their energies yielded, and the drooping spirits sought repose. Yet they did not leave their posts, but lay near the wall, with their arms beside them. The rough ground upon which they had stood, for nearly two weeks, was to their wearied limbs as an easy couch. They lay unconscious of aught that pertained to life, relieved of the recollections of the past, the anxities of the present, and the mingled forebodings of the future. The heavings of their slumbering spirits was the only sound that broke upon the gloom and darkness of the scene, whilst none were disturbed from their repose save perhaps a dreamer, pierced by a visionary [*word erased, probably "shadow"*] gleam of the future [*"of that future" crossed out*] which awaited him.

Prior [*word unclear, probable reading*] day light dawned on the following morning the enemy advanced, stealthily upon the stronghold, in hopes to complete the [*word unclear, something like "escalude" or "escapade"?*] before the garrison was aroused, but they were [*p. 46*] disappointed. Being discovered by a wakeful sentinel the alarm was given, when the Texians were at their posts in a moment. Yet the Mexicans had arrived so close to the walls that there could be no halting, [*words erased*] saving more than to advance the more [*unclear, probable reading, with following word erased*] rapidly. The ordnance on the walls and rifles both opened upon them with such severity that they were forced to give way. A brief interval passed, and they summoned their stifled courage for a second effort, which though vigorous was also repulsed, without damage to the garrison. By this [*time*] the darkness, which had, hitherto, enveloped all things, began to recede before the approaching light of day. This enabled the enemy to operate to more advantage. They rallied their broken columns, and made a third charge, which proved successful. This time they reached the walls, erected their scaling-ladders, and as Travis' boy "Joe" expressed it "commenced pouring over the walls like sheep." The Texians met them with the sword, and many a one as he leaped from the wall fell lifeless upon the ground. There it was that those hardy sons of freedom felt the responsibility which rested upon them.

They knew well the strength of the enemy, and divined that surrender or defeat meant death. Resistance until death was the motto of each, and none knew the limit of his strength.

The conflict continued some time near the outer barrier, but the area became so [*word unclear, something like "smuoded"?*] that the Texians found it advantageous to retreat near the wall of the long barracks, where the enemy fell in heaps. Finally their number became so diminished that, they retired into the church, and rooms of the barracks. Here each stood as a lion in his lair; piling his assailants at his feet as they advanced upon him, but they too followed their comrades, one by one, until all had shared the same fate.

The struggle did not last longer than half an hour, yet in that half hour, more blood was drawn, perhaps, than ever issued [*p. 47*] before at the hands of the same numbers in the same length of time, and under like circumstances. Travis, and his boy, cut their way through the thickest of the ranks of the enemy, and finally came near the north east corner of the church, where Travis seeing that the enemy were still rushing over the wall, mounted it, cheering his men to the conflict. After discharging his pistol, he continued the slaughter with his sword, dealing blow after blow, as fast as they loosed their holds [*they*] tumbled to the ground beneath him. But he was not long to occupy so conspicuous a place, receiving a ball through the head, he fell on the inside. His boy, ever faithful, had continued near him, doing good service, but seeing the fate of his master, and thinking that all was, of necessity, lost, concealed himself in one of the small rooms of the barracks, where, after the action was over, he and another man were found by an officer. The former's life was spared, because he was a negro. The latter was promised protection, if he would show the bodies of Travis and Bowie, which he did, but Santa Anna soon rode within the walls, and seeing him asked:—"What's that fellow doing here?" On being informed of the condition upon which he had been spared, he replied "that they had no use for any such men," and ordered him shot. A file of soldiers executed the order at once.

So soon as the bodies of Travis and Bowie were shown by the man [*words erased*] they were brutally mutilated by the sword and bayonet. Col. Bowie, being yet sick, was confined to his room, marked K on the diagram, which he had occupied from the beginning of the siege. It was there while suffering the torture of disease, unable to lift his head from his pillow, that he was butchered. He was shot several times through the head, his brains spattering upon the wall near his bed-side.

[*p. 48*] Note Being informed of this circumstance by Mrs. Dickinson, and Travis' boy, I had some curiosity to see the place, and when in Bexar, nearly two years after the fall, I visited the room which Col. Bowie had occupied, and in which he was killed. When upon examination I found the stain of his brains yet upon the wall, precisely as it had been represented to me, by the persons mentioned. The stain remained upon the walls of the room until they were replastered. I frequently visited the place, and pointed out the spot to others. The room has since been demolished, together with the walls which Travis defended, and the barracks all are gone. The Vandal [*this word unclear*] hand of progress has done its work. The Old Church alone, where Dickinson fell, remains, and the wandering tourist is pointed to this room or that, within it, and told that here or there, is where the noble Travis, or Bowie, or Crockett, fell, where in truth they fell not in the Church at all, but as I have said, on ground outside. While the truck-cart of [*word erased*] traffic rumbles over the identical ground that drank in the life-blood of those devoted men.

*   *   *   *   *

Near the picket-wall, reaching from the corner of the barracks to the South West corner of the church, lay in one promiscuous heap, disfigured in their mingled gore, twenty-five of the enemy, and Davie Crockett, with his twelve "Tennessee boys." They had bravely defended their position during the whole siege.

Capt. Dickinson commanded a gun, which bore from the small window in the east end of the church. It was in the second story, and there being no floor overhead, he erected a scaffold for the gun to stand upon. It was in the church that he fell. The story that he killed himself and child, by springing from the window of the church, is a romance. I know what part of the house his wife [*p. 49*] occupied at the time. She told me however that he fell as stated. They had but one child. That is still living. Some time ago a donation was made to her by our Legislature as "The Child of the Alamo."

Capt Dickinson was a brave, noble man, well worthy the distinction shown him in electing him to the command of the Artillery, in the absence of Col. Neill, who had been the principal officer in that department.

With regard to the number of persons, who were found alive after the action, I have never learned that there [*were*] more than eight, Mrs. Dickinson and child. The man who was shot by order of the Commander-in-chief, Travis' boy, two Mexican women, and their children. One of these was Mrs. Dr. [*sic*] Alsbury of San Antonio. These persons were all treated with civility by the victors, except those who vainly trusted to the grace of one who knew but little of such a virtue.

The number of Texians who fell in the Alamo was one hundred and eighty-five. John W. Smith having gone out on the Third. This agrees with Ruiz's account, which says that, the numbers burnt was one hundred and eight-two, of course [*word unclear, probable reading*] exclusive of the three Mexicans who fell with them.

Though the numbers of the Texians is thus easily ascertained, with regard to the loss of the enemy, at their hands, [*word(s) erased*] unfortunately there is some discrepancy. Mr. Yoakum records it at five hundred and twenty-one killed, with a like number wounded. Mr. Potter about five hundred killed and wounded. Mr. Ruiz says it was estimated at sixteen hundred. Indeed it excites no surprise that the authorities differ so widely about a matter which it seems ought to be free from all doubt. We know not why, and perhaps will never know. Yet it is nevertheless a satisfaction to know that the question may yet be settled.

The messenger, who was sent by the Navarro family at [*p. 50*] San Antonio to Col. Seguin at Gonzales, four days after the fall, reported the enemy's loss to have been about fifteen hundred. Mrs. Dickinson, and Travis' boy, on their arrival at Gonzales, six days after the fall, reported the same. But there is another witness, whose statement, I think, is more conclusive still, since his information was of an official character, and more definitive. I allude to the private Secretary of Gen. Santa Anna, whose name I do not remember. During my interview with this man, on the Brazos, I requested Capt. Patton to ask him, how many men they had brought to San Antonio, and what was their loss there? He did so, and I received substantially these words in reply:—"We brought to San Antonio five thousand men, and lost during the siege fifteen hundred and forty-four of the best of them. The Texians fought more like devils than men." Santa Anna and Almonte both were present at the time, and, if the statement had deviated far from the truth, for it certainly [*word unclear, something like "derogated"*] sufficiently from their soldiery [*qualifications*] for them to have denied it, without scrupling to [*word erased*] question the veracity of their fellow. The question however arises, Did he mean that fifteen [*hundred*] and forty-four men were <u>lost to the</u> service—some killed, and some permanently wounded or did he allude to the latter. Mr. Ruiz says, "Santa Anna's loss was estimated at 1600 men.", which would leave us yet in the dark did he not indicate plainly from another remark that he meant the killed only. Speaking of one charge made by the Toluca battalion, [*he says*]:—"They commenced to scale the walls and suffered severely. Out of 800 men, 130 only were left alive," by this remark the former is relieved of mystery, showing that he meant to say that sixteen hundred was about the number killed, for if 670 men fell out of one battalion, in one assault, the number slain during the entire siege must have been fully as great [*in proportion*].

This clears the matter of all doubt, for if Ruiz came by <u>estimate</u> so near to the number, as ascertained by actual count, it at once [*p. 51*] shows that Santa Anna's Secretary did not allude to the wounded, but meant that fifteen hundred and forty-four was the number actually slain. Now his statement being thus definite, and corroborated by those of Mrs. Dickinson, Travis' boy, the messenger to Col. Seguin, and als [*sic*] by Ruiz, who buried the dead, it is no longer a matter of doubt that he spoke truthfully, and we must accept fifteen hundred and forty-four, as the number slain.

I never learned how many of the enemy were wounded. Dr. Jack Shackleford, who was taken prisoner at Goliad, where Fannin surrendered, and afterwards was sent to Bexar to administer to their necessities, told me that there was a great many, though he did not state the exact number.

The action being over, and the unholy appetite of the enemy having been satisfied in the remains of the victims, Santa Anna ordered the slain of his ranks hauled to the graveyard, which was done, but there not being sufficient room to bury them all, some were thrown into the river.

After the Mexicans had been separated from the heaps of slain, wood was procured, and the bodies of the Texians collected for burning. They were then made into a heap, alternate layers of each being placed together, and kindling distributed throughout the whole. The pile being completed, about five o'clock in the evening, it was lighted. Thus was reared the altar upon which the heroic sons of freedom were [*word(s) erased*] conscrated to their country. As the flames crackled and increased, the smoke of the sacrifice ascended on high, invoking the wrath of the Almighty upon the oppressors, and while the rising incense floated around the throne of Heaven, the retributive arm of offended justice was lifting the sword of vengeance which fell upon them at San Jacinto.

[*p. 52*] The pile being consumed, such of the bones of the Texians, as remained, lay for nearly a year upon the ground, while the ashes floated upon the breeze that found the sacred spot. There was no friend to collect and preserve these relics of the brave. They were scattered about on the grounds unnoticed by an ungrateful populace who knew not how to appreciate their value. On the twenty-fifth day of February, 1837, they were collected by Col. Juan N. Seguin and command, and placed in a rude but substantial coffin, and interred with military honors, in what was then a peach orchard near the scene of the last struggle. The place is now an enclosed lot. Nothing remains to designate the exact spot where they lay, though there are persons yet living who might find it. A small, but elegant monument, made from the stones [*words "of the stones" erased*] of the Alamo, is preserved at the State Capitol. Stands as a monument of their death.

It is proper to state that efforts were made by some in behalf of Travis, though many were tardy in their movements. Capt. P. Dimmitt after leaving San Antonio on the twenty-third February, went forthwith to his residence, near [*word(s) erased*] Texana, where he raised a small company, and started on the return, but on reaching Gonzales, about a week after the fall, and finding that the town was on fire, and that Gen. Houston had retreated on the previous night, [*words erased*] He returned home.

John W. Smith, after starting with the second squad of recruits on Sunday morning, the sixth [*of March*] rode rapidly, and came within a short distance of Cibolo, where not hearing the gun of the fortress, he stopped and remained until the next morning, when he proceeded to the Cibolo, about twenty-three miles from Bexar. The signal gun being still silent, he became satisfied that, the Alamo had fallen, and remained there until Wednesday morning, when he sent eight men, as scouts, toward the city. They had only gone about six miles, when they met the advance of [*p. 53*] the enemy, who pursued them. Being well mounted they made good their escape. Smith retreated forthwith, reaching Gonzales on Thursday evening.

On Friday night Mrs. Dickinson and Travis' boy also reached that place, confirming the fact indicated by the silence of the signal gun, which few had been willing to believe.

Of those who fell in the Alamo, on the sixth of March, the proportion was about equal between the Texians and volunteers who had lately arrived from the United States, and other countries. The former were colonists, who had long enjoyed the rights guaranteed them by the Constitution of 1824, and were willing that instrument should govern them without modification, but to be deprived of representation in the councils of the government was a wrong to which they had never been subjected, and a usurpation to which they would never submit. These colonists were from all parts of Texas, as then settled. The numbers from each [section] I am unable to say. I may say, however, that Gonzales county suffered more than any other. Being nearer to Bexar than any other American settlement. Such of her [word(s) crossed out] inhabitants, as responded to Travis' calls, were enabled to reach the scene of action sooner than any others. Many of her best citizens, some of them with large families to support, fell on this gloomy Sabbath. It was said that no less than thirty-three widows were left in the town of Gonzales and vicinity, in a manner destitute.

John Sutherland.

[p. 54]

Remarks

The account given by Dr. Sutherland is worthy of all commendation. He was for awhile a participant in the defense of the Alamo, and was disabled by the fall of a horse. Anything he professes to have seen may be believed with sincerity. The information he derived from others is, in general correct. The tone of his [word erased] article is entirely patriotic, and it is to be regretted that other men of Texas, who saw service during the struggle of Texas for independence, left nothing behind them of a character similar to the writing of Dr. Sutherland. He has written what he considered true. He deserves credit, and the thanks of every true hearted Texian, for the light he has thrown upon one of the most remarkable contests of the present age, in which less than two hundred Texians fought six thousand Mexicans, from the twenty-third day of February till the sixth day of March.

In regard to the presence of Gen. Santa Anna and his entire command during the main part of the engagement there appears to be little doubt. Sergeant Becerra says:—"Gen. Santa Anna's army numbered about four thousand men. He determined to take the Alamo by storm, but concluded to await the arrival of Gen. Tolza [or Golza?] with 10 [number unclear] thousand men." Again:—"On the third day of March Gen. Tolza arrived." Hence the display mentioned by Dr. Sutherland.

There were two forts built by the Mexicans against the Alamo. The first was disliked by Gen. Santa Anna. The other is mentioned in [Gen. erased] Santa Anna's general order for the assault. He directs that "the attack columns shall be stationed within gunshot of their first line of of [*sic*] intrenchments, for the purpose of making the assault to be directed to given by His Excellency, which will be the sounding of the bugle from the North battery." Hence he is known to have been present. Forts and batteries are not built in a day.

A letter published in the Matamoros <u>Mercurico,</u> states that Gen Santa Anna arrived at San Antonio on February twenty-seco[*nd.*] He issued a proclamation from "the camp on the Nueces Ri[*ver*] [*p. 55*] February 17 [*tear in page, unknown if any word missing*]

The fact of the [*missing word(s) due to tear*] of Gen. Santa Anna at San Antonio during the whole conti[*missing, probably something like "nuation of the"*] siege is borne out by Sergeant Becerra in his account, and is generally admitted. The fact that less than two hundred Texians stopped the "Napoleon of the West'" and his army, for twelve days; killed and wounded two thousand five hundred of them, challenges the operations of any similar numbers of civilized men since the world began.

These remarks have not been made with a view to call in question any position assumed by Dr. Sutherland, but to show he was not in possession of facts which would have led him to form other conclusions.

His account of the fall of the Alamo stands almost alone as the statement derived from one of that meritorious band of [*word erased*] patriotic heroes, who by an accident escaped the fate of his comrades, and lived to tell of how they fought and fell.

[*A different hand, apparently that of the second scribe, continues*] Gen Woll of the Mexican army was reported to be a German, and not an Englishman as Dr. Sutherland believed.

Dr. Sutherland lived in Wilson county, Texas. He was held in high repute by his acquaintances. He died several years since. He left behind him several children who are highly respected by all who know them.

1.7.1.2.   Ford/Sutherland? map, n.d.

Sutherland, John (probable). N.d. In John S. Ford Memoirs. 17. Center for American History.

This map is hand-drawn and appears just after the Francisco Becerra account (2.10.1) and just before the John Sutherland narration (1.7.1.1). As it is referred to in the latter document (for the first time on manuscript page 30), it is apparent that it is primarily a supplement to Sutherland's account. There is no explicit statement whether it is primarily Sutherland's or Ford's creation.

Walls of the church A—of solid masonry—4 feet thick—one story high with upper windows.

Long Barracks E—2 stories high—with flat terace [*sic*] roof—covered with thick coat of Cement.

The outer walls 6 to 8 feet high 2-3/4 thick—

The u[s]-designate doorways—M—the gateway entering of the main area. "F"—arched door way though the barracks.

Cannon were mounted all around the outer wall & one small piece at an upper window at "B."

The well was dug after the siege commenced.

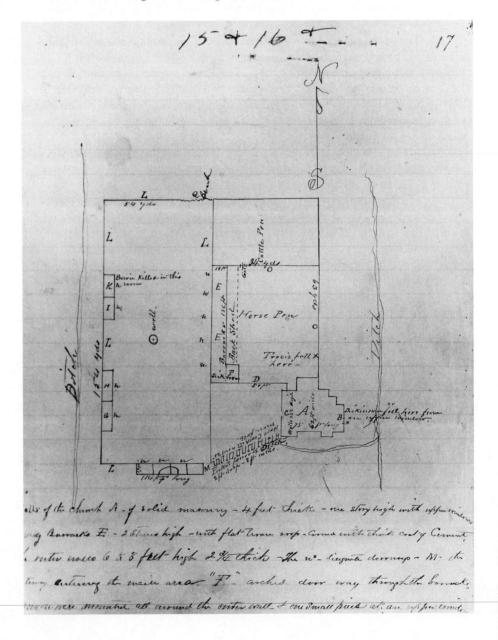

1.7.1.3. Ford/Sutherland? map, n.d.

Sutherland, John (probable) in Annie Sutherland. *Fall of the Alamo*. Frontispiece. San Antonio: The Naylor Co. 1936.

This map was in the Frontispiece of the first full printed version of the Sutherland account, as edited by his granddaughter, Annie B. Sutherland, in 1936. The only indication of source is also the John S. Ford Papers at the "State University Library at Austin." The possible relationship with the map above (1.7.1.2) is discussed in the commentary. Another copy is in the Williams Papers/Photographs and Pictorial Materials and appears to be from a manuscript sheet rather than the book. It is reasonable to guess that Williams obtained her copy directly from Annie Sutherland.

PEN SKETCH MAP OF THE WALLS AND GROUNDS SURROUNDING
THE ALAMO AS THEY WERE IN 1836, BY DR. JOHN SUTHERLAND.

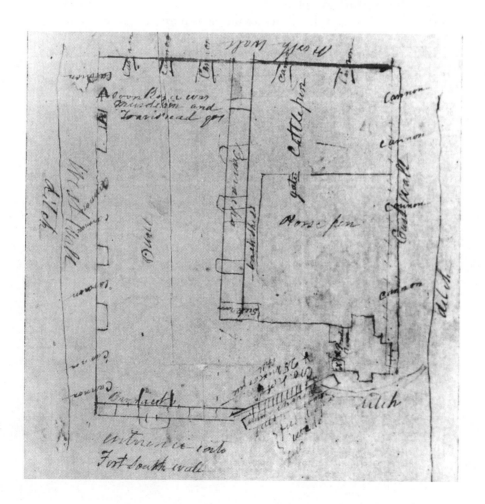

1.7.1.4.   John Sutherland, audited claim, 1836.

Sutherland, John. N.d. (c. November 1, 1836). Republic Claims. AU-Sutherland, John; 1262; R:102 Fr:0300-0311. TSLA.

This document is particularly useful in comparing the dates on which Sutherland said in 1836 that he was in San Antonio (at least to February 19) and Gonzales (February 25) with those he gave in his story in 1860, in which he supposedly left San Antonio on February 23 with the initial information of the arrival of the Mexican Army. It was first noted by Curtis (1961, 21–22). Both *do* as well as ditto marks appear to have been used to indicate *ditto*.

THE REPUBLIC OF TEXAS

1836	In account with John Sutherland Jr. Dᴿ.		
25 Jany	for cash paid at Kents for the use of Troop to reinforce		
	Colᵒ Neil at San Antonio	P	13.50
26 —	do — At Jo MCoys for the Same purpose	P	1.25
27 —	do — Gonzales—corn & Bord [?] at Hensleys	P	16.25
1 Feby	do — at San Antonio corn & Grass	P	.37-1/2
2 —	do — " do — corn & Wood	P	3.00
3 —	do — " do — " Grass	P	1.25
5 —	do — " do — " " & bread		1.75
6 —	do — " do — " " & candles	P	1.50
7 —	do — " do — " " & bread	P	1.75
8 —	do — " do — " " "		1.25
9 —	do — " do — do — " "		1.25
10 —	do — — do — do — " "		1.00
11 —	do — — — do ——— "		1.00
12-13-14+15ᵗʰ	do — — — do — ea day/[?]		4.00
19	do — — — do —	P	3.00
	hay for horses to date	P	2.50
25 —	do — at Gonzales paid for corn	P	2.50
	do — Bill at Smiths $3.50 & coffee $2.00	P	5.50
3 March	— — corn	P	2.00
8 —	— — "	P	2.00
(cash paid for a horse and taken into the Service of)			
in Feby (the Govt by Col. Travis at the time of the arrival of the enemy)			
	(at San Antonio)	P	40.00
	cash advanced to pay troops in San Antonio	P	25.00
8 March	—cash for coffee at Gonzales	P	2.00
13 to 16	Expenses from Gonzales to Washington		5.00
17	" at Washington attending on the Executive		2.00
17 to 20 inclusive cash paid Mʳ Groce attending on do			10.50
	Expenses at Harrisburg as clerk do do		
	to April 6ᵗʰ		<u>10.50</u>

		150.62-1/2
cash paid for a double Barrel Shot gun lost	P	
in the fall of Alamo		35.00
amount assumed for a Gouger [?] & furnished		
Wm Wills who fell in the Alamo	P	20.00
one horse Saddle & bridle valued at one		
hundred & Seventy five dollars & received		
into the public Service by John W. Smith as per		
annexed receipt		$175.00
		$400.62-1/2
Deduct amt for horse, auditted for		175
		$225.62

Personally appeared before me Wm H. Patton and being duly sworn says he was at San Antonio during the last winters while Dr Sutherland was there, and that he knows of Dr Sutherland having paid the several sums in the annexed account which are marked with the letter P. for the use and sustenance of the Garrison at Bejar, and that [*he*] fully believes that all of the sums were paid for the purpose stated,

W H Patton

Columbia
Nov 1.st 1836 Sworn to and defend[?] before

A. Brigham Auditor

[*The next document in the file is an April 9, 1836, valuation of the horse, saddle, and bridle of $175 as noted above and autographed in two places by John W. Smith. Further documents in the Audited Claims files for Sutherland include three autographs by Sutherland himself.*]

1.7.1.5.   John Sutherland, petition, pre-1846.

Sutherland, John. N.d. (before 1846). Memorial no. 128. TSLA.

The cover of the first, undated memorial identifies this as "No. 128." No date is given in the files, though it dates prior to December 1845, when Texas became a state.

To the Honorable the Congress of the Republic the petition of John Sutherland respectfully sheweth that he arrived in the republic about the latter end of the year 1835. That in January of 1836 he entered the Service of his adopted Country under the command Capt William Patton that he served faithfully and was honourably discharged and his cirtificate of discharge is now on file in the war department at the city of Austin

your petioner would further represent to your honourable body that he subsequently brought his family into the Country and landed at the town of

Matagorda on the Eighth day of January 1838 and has ever since resided in the Country with his family your petitioner beg leave to state that upon the opening of the land office he appeared before the board of land commissioners in the County of Colorado and after making all the proof which the law required he received a cirtificate of head right for one Leage and Labour of land to which he was justly entitled

your petitioner would further represent that for some cause unknown to your petitioner the traveling board of land commissioners failed to recommend his claim for pattent thereby depriving him of his just rights vested in him by law.

your petitioner would therefore request of your honourable body to pass a bill for his relief requiring the Commissioner of the General Land office to issue a pattent for his head right the same as though the same had been recommencd by the traveling board of land commissioners and as in duty bound your petitioner will ever pray.

John Sutherland

1.7.1.6. John Sutherland, petition, 1854.

Sutherland, John. January 11, 1854. Memorial no. 131. TSLA.
The cover for the second memorial gives it as "No. 131." The key portion of this memorial was first reprinted in Groneman (1996) from a transcription in the Williams Papers.

To The Hon. Legislature of the State of Texas
I came to Texas in December 1835. and on the 12th day of Same month, took the Oath of Allegiance & became citizen; in company with William Wells who fell in the Alamo on the Sixth day of March following we joined the Army about the first of January with Capt Wm H. Patton, and was in the Service at the time of the fall of the Alamo. I escaped the ["fall" crossed out] masscre by being Sent by Col. Travis to Gonzales with the express to urge the citizens to his relief. On the morning of the commencent of the Seige, I was Sent out by Col. Travis with John W. Smith to reconniter the enemy whom the Col had learned was in the neighborhood, of San Antonio—we found the enemy about one and a half miles from town, and in running in my horse fell, pitching me over his head and falling on my thights, So injured my right knee & left arm as to render me unfit for the duties of the fort, being able to ride the Col^n. Sent me as above Stated to Gonzales, to urge the Settlers & Send express to abtain relief—a few days after Genl. Sam Houston came to Gonzales—and on the Same day we received the news through a friendly Mexican, Sent by Col. Navaro of the fall of the Alamo. being yet unable to use my left arm (from the fall before Stated) he gave me a furlough for eight days (which furlough is Still in my posseon at

home)—during my furlough I visited the convention then Sitting at Washington—when I was taken from the Army by President David G. Barnett & Secretary Carson as their private Secretary—For the above Services I have never
received any land—Such as bounty or donation as was Granted to those who
partisipated or performed like Services John Sutherland

[*The statement was notarized on January 11, 1854. An additional page has the following.*]

This is to certify that I have been intermilly [*intimately?*] acquainted with
D^r. John Sutherland for the last 35 years and from the time of his arrival in
Texas to the present day. and that he has sustained himself as a Gentleman in
every respect, and that he has always been ready to do his duty as a soldier, and
also as private Secretary to the President David G. Burnett during his term of
office

Austin Jany 1854   Bery. J. White

I certify that I have known Dr. Southerland since 1836, and have ever
esteemed him as a gentleman.

                                        A. Turner

Austin Jan. 14, 1854

1.7.1.7.   John Sutherland, draft account, n.d.

Sutherland, John. N.d. "Fall of the Alamo." General/Accounts of Siege and Fall
of Alamo, Williams (Amelia Worthington) Papers, CAH.

This long, complicated document apparently recorded a collection of manuscript pages of multiple versions of the Sutherland account. It was transcribed by
Amelia Williams and first noted in print by William Davis in 1997. It consists of fifty
pages of typed transcripts that are thoroughly mixed and fragmentary. Many pages
start or end in midsentence, with the previous or subsequent page missing from the
set. There is textual evidence that many, quite possibly all, of the pages predate the
Ford manuscript. Because of the complexities of this document, it is likely of more
interest to the specialist rather than the general reader.

Here the pages have been reordered into three general groups. The first section
is a "polished text" most likely written in response to the original publication in
1860 of Reuben Potter's account, and includes comments on Sutherland's personal
experiences. The second has "firsthand fragments" of Sutherland's personal experiences at the Alamo. The third has "additional fragments," which include some of
Sutherland's later experiences or general discussion of the story. At least some of the
fragments appear to be draft material used by the polished text and therefore earlier.
The general discussions include a number of critiques of Potter's early account that
were not incorporated in the Ford version. The reordering in this edition has been
done to reconnect the various fragments into a best guess at the placement in the
original composition(s). The interested reader might well improve the ordering.

In summary, I believe the original Sutherland account likely underwent multiple rewritings and replacements, then random sheets got worn out or lost over time,
and the entire set became misordered. Either the original or this collection by

Williams, rather than Ford, was also the apparent source for the Driggs and King chapter on Sutherland (1936, 199–212). Fortunately for further study, Williams apparently recorded the pages exactly as they had survived (though undoubtedly with added typos). Her transcript must have been done some time after completion of her thesis in 1931, since this version is not referenced there, which raises the possibility that the originals she worked from may still be found. There are a few minor hand corrections to the typed transcripts, which are not explicitly noted in this copy, and a few excess spaces have been eliminated. I consider it more important than ever to retain virtually all the idiosyncratic punctuation, capitalization, and spelling exactly as they appear, as these characteristics might give indications as to what might be original versus errors in transcription.

Individual sheets in this document may or may not have page number(s). In the following transcript, either the page number(s) on the sheet (sometimes more than one is designated) or "n.p." (no page number) is given first, followed by a slash and the current position of the sheet within the fifty pages of the typescript held by the Center for American History. I have reordered them here, but this reordering is only a best judgment. The first several pages of the manuscript are a "polished" text, starting with p. 1/1, though there is also handwritten at the top "pp. 1–12." In those cases where the narrative links to the Ford version (document 1.7.1.1), the Ford manuscript page number is given after a second slash. There is no line break between pages that are continuous, but there is a line break if no connection between pages was made.

[*p. 1/1*]

"The fall of the Alamo"

To the Editor of "The Alamo Express"

I have just Seen a pamphet purporting to give a correct account of the fall etc. From the writers own account, it is evident, the information he has collected, (being intirely obtained from a defeated band of Mexican Officers, and Mexican Soldiers, & a Servant(who had been a Sargent in the army) and that, at the time of the fall he, the writer, lived in Matamoras in Mexico, and enjoying all the rights of the Mexican Citizen in that county [*country*], and for months, after the engagement;—it is hardly to be presumed, he could have had access to the best Sources for information: Indeed, it Seems all the information he has on the Subject, of the invasion, is gathered from the Mexicans pryor to, and after the fall, and after the return of the army to Mexico. The writer of the pamphet, says, "At the beginning of the invasion, the Mexican officers speak of their numbers as 10,000 strong, after its failure, Santa Anna in his letter to Genl Jackson refered to his invading force as having numbered Six thousand, this is the usual Mexican Style as overating as a threat, before action, and underrating as an apology after defeat." (pencil insertion after word "Collected" in fourth line above: "is incorrect, It appears that he was at the time of that melancoly event, a resident of M. a citizen of Mexico &

[*p. 2 /2*]

that what he details as facts with regard to the undesired altogether from a defeated band of Mexican officers & soldiers") I cannot See after the writers admission as above quoted, as being the character of Mexican Officers; how he could undertake to Say, his is the most relyable history of the account of the fall of the Alamo. I do not suppose the writer ever coversed with either of the persons who escaped the slaughter of the Alamo, or he would [*not*] have come to the conclusion set forth in the pamphet.

In the first page he says, "Among the facts which have been perverted by both sides, (and I would say by the author of the pamphet) is the number of Mexican troops ingaged in the assault and in the campaign. The whole force with which Santa Anna invaded Texas in 1836 probably amount to about Seven thousand five hundred men." This probably is about the true number.

The main of our historians' facts, as to <u>dates</u> and <u>numbers</u> are conjectures, founded upon reports of Mexican Officers & Soldiers before their interence, and after their return from Texas. Our historian Says "Genl Bradburn was of opinion that three hundred men in that action wast lost to the service counting with the Killed, these bearing wounds or were permanently disabled." he continues,— "This agrees, with Other most reliable estimates, Anselmo Borgora, a Mexican who first reported the fall of the Alamo to Genl. Houston, at Gonzales and who left San Antonio on the evening after it Occured, Stated that the assaulting force
[*p. 3 /3*]
amounted to 2,300 men, of whom 521 were Killed, as many wounded"? the loss, however is evidently exagerated, because it is simply ["]incredible" See note page 13 of Pamphet—and on page 4 "This is the usual Style of underrating after defeat" I agree with the writer of the pamphet, that his Sources for correct information, has been very uncertain, to enable one to give impartial history; but I do not agree that any relyance is to be placed in his traditionary history, derived as it is, at this late day, from Mexican Officers, Some of whom were never in the State or country untill long after the battles were fought and, who "usually underrated their forces when defeated".

Our Writer Seems not to have informed himself, as to who had the command of the Alamo branch of the Army. Col. James C Nail [*Neill*] was the Commander, by leave of absence, Col. Jas. Bowie, was entitled to the command; but owing to Sickness previous to the commencement of the Seige;, he requested in presence of the writer of this, Col Travis (who had but recently arrived at San Antonio) to take the command, which he did. Hence the charge against Col Travis is in error and uncalled for, "The neglect of Scouting Service, before refered to, indicates great lack of Subordination for Travis, who, during the seige of Bexar had been the efficient head of that brance of duty, must have been aware of its importance." If the writer of the pamphet had have Known, the history of his having the command as Stated before, I think he would not
[*p. 4 /4*]
have cast Such reflection upon that brave man. Col. Nail had had one of the most reliable men in Texas in that Service: to wit "<u>Deaf</u> Smith" than whom, one more reliable could not be found, I think in any country; but, he had leave of Absence at the Same time with Col Nail. When they left it was hardly expected

that an invading army would Soon return, as but Shortly before Col Cass [*Cos*] had been whiped and Surrendered, and permitted to leave for Mexico, with his men—upon parroll of honor never again to return to Texas as an invader. Until Col Nail & Smith left regular Scouts had been kept out, and when they left, Capt (now Col) John N Seguin, (than whom Texas had no better friend) had a reliable relative—a cousin, staying on the Rio Grand, to give notice of any movement going on, like marching forces to invade us. And on Saturday the 20th Feby he came up to Larado in three days, to let us Know that Santa Anna was then crossing the River with five thousand Soldiers for San Antonio. Between 8 & 9 OC at night a councel of war was called; and the writer of this was present; when our Spye reported the fact of the Mexicans, then crossing the River, and that a forced march of the Cavalry would be made to take the town by Surprize,—that there were 1500 Cavalry. Note this was the 20th Saturday February; And, That on tuesday 23rd they came into town. The night previous, the 22nd, they got within eight miles of the city and into camp on the Leon Creek. Some of our men did, and others did not believe, Capt Seguin's Cousins report, but the Seguin family and connections believed, and

[*p. 5 /5*]

left next morning (Sunday) on the retreat towards Gonzales. The cavalry came to the creek (8 miles) from town) incamped and expected to have come in Monday night (22) and to have taken the town by surprise but a heavy rain through the day made the road so muddy that they were prevented getting in.

On tuesday, the Mexican population was in complete commotion, very early in the morning. Such as had carts were loading up with their house-hold dunnage; those who had none, were taking their effects upon there backs; and numbers had already left for the country before the cause was assertained. All parties were completely in motion. This commotion created an inquiry into the cause of such unusual Stir. The most common reply was, That they were going out on to there ranches to commence preparation for the coming crops, but the great hurry and stir, was so unusual, that not much reliance was given to there Statements—.In fact one Lady of Wealth Mrs Roman Musques (whose husband was then supposed to be piloting the Mexican Army, (he being unfriendly to the American cause) was stopped & detain for some hours, and finally, allowed to leave the City with her Carts,—through the interposition of Capt P. Dimit, who persuaded the Officers to let her off, owing to her peculiar situation, as not being in a condition to witness a fight. Although her husband might be an enemy, and with the Mexican Army, by this time it was generally believed the enemy was near by. It was during this stir, and commotion, & investigation, that Col Travis was notified by a friendly Mexican of the

[*p. 6 /6*]

enemies Cavalry being on the Leon and that the citizens of town had been notified the overnight, to leave early the next morning as the town or the Americans would be attacked the next day.

The writer of this in company of Capt Nat Lewis, and a Mexican of whom (the writer) had brought a league of land on the Madina had mounted Our horses to go out and examine the land (not habing Seen it before purchasing) when Capt Lewis was Summoned to give evidence in a case then on trial; this detained us Some hours, before Capt Lewis was at liberty to go. About this time Col. Travis was notified by a friendly Mexican of the Mexican Cavalry being on the Leon. (This last sentence is marked out in pencil.)

The reader will excuse the writer of this, for the following; and he would not wish to be thought egotistic; for a connected chain of the events of the times compells the introduction of Some of his own History. When the Col ascertained the Near approach of the enemy to the city, he appointed the writer, Officer of the day, to Keep a centinall constantly on the top of the Old church, (the ascent of which, made by a scaffle way, leading from the ground to the top of the chuch, which had been erected by the Mexicans, during the Seige, when Col Cass Surrendered to the Americans in december previous. (during which Seige Col. Benj'm R Milam was shot through the head, in the back yard of the Verimenda house, while Superintending, the digging of a dictch to the River, through which to carry water to the Americans, who had cut there way, through the back walls into the buildings

[*p. 7 /7*]

fronting the Civil Plaza.) The writer accompanied the centenel and had not left the top of the church, more than thirty or forty minutes, when the centinel rang the church Bell, and called out "The enemy is in view" At which ring of the Bell the Cavalry filed off to the right of the road, behind a musquite Grove, which hid them from of view of the men, who, ran to the top of the church to see them. The men not being able to See them through the mesquite bushes, hallowed, "its a falls alarm"; But the Centinel insisted that he had Seen them, "and that they were hid by the Musquite bushes." Much excitement now prevailed, and the writer proposed to Col Travis, If any one who Knew the country would accompany him, he would go and See to a certainty; when John W. Smith volunteered to accompany; We Started after arranging, that, if they Saw us returning in any gate, but a walk with our horses, it should be certain, we had seen the enemy. About one & a half mile west from the City on ascending hill, we came in full view of the Cavlry: we immediately wheeled back, and in running down the hill, the writers horse began to Slip, and finally fell within. . . . ;

[*"(end p: 12)" handwritten below*]

[*p. "—for page 8—" /43/Ford pp. 25–26. This begins a group of "firsthand fragments" that relate to Sutherland's personal experiences on February 23–25.*]

The Mexican population was in (great) commotion, verry early in the morning. Such as had carts, were loading all their houshold dunnage, those who had none were taking there effects upon their backs, and numbers had already left for the Country, before the caus was assertained, all parties were completely in motion. This commotion created an enquiry into the caus of Such unusual Stir, the most common reply was that, they were going on to there Rances to commence preparation for a coming crop; but the great hurry, and Stir, was So unusul, that not much reliance was given to there Statements. In fact, one lady of wealth, Mrs. Ramon Musques, whose husband was then Supposed to be piloting the Mexican Army, he being unfriendly to the Americans, was stopped & detained for Some hours, but finally allowed to leave the City, with her carts—through the interposition

[n.p./42]

(of Capt) P. Dimet, who persuaded the Officers (to let) her off, owing to her peculiar Situation, (as not) being in a condition to witness a (fight). although her husband might be an enemy and with the Mexican Army, for by this time it generally believed the enemy was near by. It was during this Stir, and commotion, and investigation, that Col Travis was notified by a friendly Mexican of the enemies Cavalry being on the Leon, and that the Citizens of Town had been notified the over night to leave early, the next morning as the town or Americans would be attacked in that day.

The writer of this, in company of Capt Nat Lewis and a American, of whom the writer had bought a League of Land on the Madena, had mounted Our horses to go Out and examined the land (not habing Seen it before purchasing) when Capt Lewis was Summoned to give evidence in a case then on trail: this detained us Some hours, befor Capt Lewis was at liberty to go.

(See marginal . . .)

[n.p./33/Ford p. 27]

out their way the back walls into the building fronting the Civil plaza). The ——— had not left the top of the church more than thirty or forty minutes when the Centinel rang the church Bell and Called out "They enemy is in view," at which ring of the bell, the Cavalry filed off to the right of the road, behind a musquite grove, which hid them from view of the men who ran to the top of the church to See them. the men not being able to See them through the musquite, hallowed "Its a fals alarm," but the centinel insisted that he had Seen them & that they were hid by the Musquite bushes." Much excitement now Prevailed & the writer proposed to Col Travis if any one who Knew the county would accompany him, he would go and See to a certainty. When John W. Smith volunteered

[n.p./34 /Ford pp. 28–33]

to accompany, we Started after arranging that if they saw us returning in any gate but a wald [walk] with our hoses [horses], it Should be certain we had Seen the enemy. About one & a half mile from the City west on ascending hill we came in full view of the Cavalry; we immediately wheeled back & in runing down the hill, the writers horse began to Slip and finally fell, within about three hundred yards of thy enemy, but, the fall was not observed by them as the musquite & ridge was between us. Mr. Smith dismounted & pulled him off my

Knees, we immediately mounted again & loped into town & fond Col Travis
with the men had gon over the river to the Alamo. On our return to Col Travis
head quarters on the Civil Plaza, we met Col David Crocket,

[*n.p./35*]

on hose back, going out to reconoiter, he returned with—the Alamo. on dis-
mounting my Knee gave way, & I fell. From the fall of my horse in the run, my
Knee, left arm and neck was So injured as to render me unfit for fort duty, the
Col then requested me to go to Gonzales & to rally the Setters to come to his
relief—John W. Smith whose family had left for Gonzales some days before
accompanied me there. Capt Nat Lewis started at the same time on foot. In two
hours after reaching Gonzales we had Started expreses in every direction,
where there were Settlers, this was Wednesday evening 24th by Saturday John
W Smith Started back with 25 men for the Alamo, the men were under command of Ensign Kimble of the ranger they added to there number on the Cibolo
Seven more in all thirty two. (32) Making now no

[*p. 21 (1)/37/Ford p. 32*]

While we yet stood viewing them, Capt Nat Lewis Came to us, on foot,
Upon inquiry we assertained that he too was bound for Gonzales, wit as much
of his valuables as he could carry in his Saddle-bags, which he had on his
shoulder leaving the rest in his store house, a contribution to the enemy.

We soon parted, Capt Lewis taking one direction and me another, E'er we
started the idea struck in that the enemy might espy us as we rode off and, sus-
pecting our purpose, pursue us.

We therefore thought it wise to be a little careful, Accordingly we sat out on
the Goliad road which ran directly south for some distance. After going about
half- a mile we change our course, turning due east, into a thicket of mesquite
and Chapparal which was only to be gone through by following a few winding
paths leading occasionally in the direction which we had started. Meandering
this (swamp) brush-wood around we finally crossed the Gonzales road,
between the city and Powder House ("Magazine" crossed out), and about a
mile due east of the former. We now struck east again ("across the hill" crossed
out) and thought to bear around ("turn back" crossed out) into the Gonzales
road ("and go in haste" crossed out), but on reaching ("Salado and about two
miles farther in the distance, on the hill" crossed out) across the bow of the hill,
we espied ("three suspicious looking" crossed out) Salado and about a mile and
a half from us, three persons riding out on the road, ("towards the city," crossed
out) we at once suspicioned . . .

[*p. 1st /29. This begins another group that is "other fragments."*]

The fall of the Alamo (is important) from it's intimate connection (with the
life of) our republic, and it's well know (effect) upon her after career, deserves
(one of the most) prominent places in her (history and in) some respects, it is
one of the (greatest events) that has ever occurred upon (Texas) territory from

it's earliest existance (when) we have any account down to (the present) time, and when we revert to it, and (contemplate) the sacrafice, we are (caused) to regret that it's history as given us by our historians is so unreliable. Though much that has been published with regards to it, has the semblance of authenticity yet there is a part that is clothed in the garb of fiction. Prejudice and partiality have ever taken an active part in writing the history of all new countries, and especially when in the absence of well known facts, they have been able to furnish a plausible substitute and prepossess the world in favor of an idea having perhaps no other foundation upon which to rest than (mere) imagination. Ours has been (written and) it has but too often shared (the common) fate. Though some of it's (story is) founded upon supposition, a (great part) is derived from it's enemies, (and is recorded) with doubt. The fall (of the Alamo) . . .

[*p. 2nd/30/Ford p. 18 starts midway down this page*]

Seems to have suffered as much, if not more at their hands, than any other event in our history. Indeed they have furnished the principal, if not the only accounts that have been adopted. With these we would certainly have to be content if there were no better to be obtained, but when we remember that there were persons at Bexar who witnessed the affair, and who were friends to our country and our cause, would it not appear more becoming a grateful people, more just, more magnanimour [*sic*] to them, than to cast their evidence aside as worthless, and search the fabulous legends of those abandoned wretches, whose malignity is only equalled by their total disregard of the truth. The heart of the Texian must answer in the affirmative.

In 1835 I visited Texas with a view of making it my home, and it was my lot to witness her in that strugle with the tyranical power of Mexico which terminated in securing to her the liberty which she now enjoys.

Having acknowledged allegiance to the provissional government, and enlisted in the service of the Armory, I proceeded in company with Cap't Wm Patton and ten others to San Antonio, which place we reached about the 18th Jan'y. From that time untill the 23rd of Feb'y I was cognizant of all that occurred of importance within the garrison, and remember well it's hopes, fears and anxieties for the safety of their country and her interests.

[*p. 4/31/Ford pp. 19–20*]

conclusive, that it would seem useless to discredit it. (this last phrase has been scratched out)

Though some years have elapse since this event took place, I have never untill recently thought it necessary to publish any thing in regard to it supposing that the facts would appear substantially the same from some other source, But since several conflicting accounts, some of which differ widely from that which I have always understood to be the correct one, I deem it my duty to the country, to the children of those unfortunate men and to History whatever facts

I may be able to state with regard the last strugle of the gallant Travis & his men. (Scratched out—"to make known these facts with regard the last strugle of these fathers in defence of their rights, which the had been accustomed to enjoy and to cherish as the safe-guard of all happiness,")

I will not however attempt a minute detail of every circumstance pertaining to it though I should be pleased to do so, I desire only to contribute my mite for the benefit of the future historian, and in doing this will give a summary account of the whole, stating the facts as they came to me at that time, supported by as strong circumstancial evidence as I may deduce, and leave the reader to judge of it's correctness by the authority given.

Upon our arrival at San Antonio we found the forces there in a manner helpless, Grant and Johnson had left but a short time previous with their companies, taking with them almost everything in the way of supplies, even more than their share of a scant allowance of clothing, blankets, and the government

[*p. 4 (continued)/32*]

(if it may be called by that name, had failed to meet their necessities. They lived upon . . .

[*p. (25)/22*]

the fate of my comrades in the manner before related; <u>not</u> <u>being</u> able to do Fort duty. Judge Murphree was perhaps out of the city at the Coming in of the Mexican Cavalry, and commencement of the Siege. Capt Lewis left as before Stated. and my movement, to Some extend is, stated in this communication. <u>Secondly,</u> I obtained information in regards to the siege, and final Fall from the Messenger whom Navaro sent to Capt J N. Seguin and Don Erasmus (his Father) and families at Gonzales, whose Statement is coroborated by Mrs. Dickenson with whom I was acquainted, and at the time, (Col Almonte came in with the Cavalry), bording at Capt Dickensons. As also Col Travis Servant man, all the persons here mentioned agreed in their Statements, as to the comencement and prosecution

[*p. (26)/23*]

of the seige to its final fall. as well as to the number slain—they said about fifteen hundred Thirdly: there statements are also corobared by Santa Annas private Secretary (as to the number slain in all) who was taken at the Battle of San Jacinto, and kept with Santa Anna, and Col Almonte untill the following December when Genl Houston (then President of the Republic of Texas) sent an Escot with them by way of Washington City on their return to Mexico. The Seige commenced as b [*sic*] before Stated by the <u>Cavalry,</u> on the 23rd of February (1836) and daily charges, and nightly alarms, were made, but they were as often repulson by Our Rifles with loss to the beseigers, without the loss of a man on our part (so says the first witness) but after Santa Anna arrived on the 3rd of March on the 4th (Friday) the bombardment & firing was incessant untill Saturday night, about 10 OC. All firing ceased,—a dead *[p. (27)/24]*

Calm ensued, and not one of Our Men had fallen as yet. about day break on Sunday morning 6th March the Scaling ladders were placed around the Alamo walls, and the Mexicans rushing over, into the wall enclosure, when Our Men, were aroused from the rest and Slumber which followed the cessation of bombardment during Friday-friday night & Saturday till 10 OC at night; the fight became general throughout the Alamo. but lasted, Only a Short time, the Alamo had Faller! [*sic*] and <u>one</u> <u>hundred</u> & <u>eighty</u> <u>seven</u> as noble and as brave men as ever took up Arms in the cause of Freedom

---

See Travis letter in a note on the bottom of the Pamphet, page 6, dated March the 3rd he says "with a hundred and forty five men I have held this place ten days against a force variously estimated from 1500 to 6000 men, I shall continue

[p. (28)/25]

to hold it, till I get relief from my country men, or I will perish in its defence. We have had a shower of Bombs and cannonballs continually a falling among us all the time, yet none of us have fallen. We have been miraculously preserved." Our writer would here seem to doubt the Statement of Travis. Official report under his own hand, to his claim I can here him, "Travis must have alluded to the Original force of the garrison before the arrival of the Gonzales company. If its full number was 156, eleven men must have been, non effective from Sickness or wounds as none had been killed." the writer on the Same page says, "No assault was attempted as has often been asserted, till the final Storming of the place." I would like to Know who is to believed, Our writer of the Pamphlet, or Col. Travis" for Travis says, "We have had a shower of bombs and cannonball, continually falling among us the whol time." Who is entitled to the most confidence? when I left the Alamo there was 145 men, 110 of which, was on the sick list—Smith pit-oled in 32 on Monday night 2nd March, as before stated

[p. (25)/18]

Our historian Says: "I was a resident of Matamoras when the events happened, and for Several Months after the invading Army returned thither, I had opportini- for Obtaining the Kind of information refered to, which few persons, if any, Still living in Texas have possessed; and I have been urged to publish what I have gathered on the Subject, as by means of it an interesting fragment of history may be Saved"—<u>See</u> <u>page</u> <u>1st</u> <u>Pamphlet</u> The writer of the Pamphlet goes on and with his uncertain information undertakes to establish the fact, that the force engaged in the Seige has been much over—ated, Seeming desirrious to <u>detract</u> <u>from</u> <u>the</u> <u>Noble</u> <u>little</u> <u>band</u> of Soldiers, as well as their esteemed commander—Col. Travis, and to elevate, those officers, of whom he obtained *[p. (26)/19]*

his "historical facts," The writer is of opinion there could not have been more than twenty five hundred men all told, who came to or were engaged at San Antonio, under Santa Anna.—Page 13 the Pamphlet Says, "the number of Mexicans wounded according to various accounts, largely exceeded that of the Killed; and the estimated made of both, by inteligent men who were in the action, and whose candor I think could be relied on, rated there loss at one hundred & fifty to two hundred Killed, and from three to four hundred wounded." Now the writer would ask, whose account is most to be relied on? Santa Anna's Private Secretary, or the above Statement "150 to 200" Killed & 3 to 400 wonded—the secty says fifteen hundred & forty four— (1554) which would be most likely to Know & tell the truth? Now the Mexican who hunted

[p. (27)/20]

them out, (whose name the writer cannot call) reports, as the writer has been informed, there were about Sixteen hundred taken out by him and if there was only the one third of Santa Annas army (7500) ingaged in the San Antonio fight and the Killed & wounded counting either estimate; Santa Anna must have drawn largely upon the Mexican citizen of San Antonio, (Which we have no account of). For he as before Stated Sent Genl Coss with five hundred troops the upper rout by Bastrop to Stimulate the Indians to cut off the retreat of the families and after Sending Mrs. Dickenson & child & Travis's Servant to Gonzales to Genl Houston's Army he Sent one thousand or more to the Colet to cut off Col. Fannin's retreat, he still had a goodly number left to pursue our people on their retreat; say—

[p. (28)/21]

not less than eight hundred to a thousand, for when he recalled Coss from the upper rout he had about fourteen hundred in the Battle of San Jacinto—

The Diagram is correct but the writer is not well informed as to details. R represents an entrenchment running from the South west angle of the chappell to the gate. "This work was not manned against the assaut." Now this work or space was stopped by a double row of Picket, with a pitt its whole length eight feet wide & eight feet deep ever kept full of water from the ditch, running by the chappell—this ditch was made by the Mexicans during the seige, when Coss surrendered.

In page 11 "Bowie had been severly hurt by a fall from a platform, and when the attack came on, was confined to his bed in an upper room of the Barrack marked P. he was there Kill on his couch.

[p. (29)/26]

but not without resistance; for he is said to have shot down with his pistols one or more of the enemy as they entered the chamber." Strange account; this, may or may not have been the fact. When the writer left Col Travis with the express for Gonzales, Col Bowie was then occupying the same room with him;

and Mrs. Dickenson, Col. Travis's Servant told the writer he was Killed in the Sam room, Shot in the head—that his blood & brains when shot spattered on the wall near by his bed—and that over a year after the writer saw the stain yet on the wall, and it continued untill it was whitewashed orplatered [*or plastered*]. that room It was letter K as laid on the Diagram, instead of P Col Travis fell from the wall O near the chappel—after shooting down some & cutting others
  [*p. (30)/27*]
  down Others with his Sword, he fell, being Shot in the head, his Servant was by his Side,—finding all lost retreated into a room from whence he was taken by an officer and protected and Saved Col Crocket and his twelve Tennessee boys, (as he called them) fell on the line marked R he and his twelve friends and about twenty five Mexican lay cross & Pile together on R which was assigned to his defence, in the writers presence, they there fell as reported by Col Travis boy, in front of the chappel.
  Captain Dickenson's Child was not Killed as the pamphet says but is Still living and maried, and by reference to the acts of the legislature of Texas you will find one for her relief of Six hundred and forty acres of land as donation by the State to her as the child of the Alamo!

  [*n.p./39/Ford pp. 35–36*]
  Plazas, to the Alamo, when——lace, it is true, the army was ——sions, both meat and corn, a——found on the Alamo side of the river——70 to 80 bushells corn, in the building—by the Alamo which they Secured as——before leaving for Gonzales—
  While the American Army was encamped ——the old Mill above the— the Mexicans in the city were in the habit of viewing them from the Steeple of the Old Church, which had large openings or windows arched over with Stone— the gunner was ordered to direct a 12lb. Shot at the crowd in the steeple he did so and struck the Arch overhead and as was reported afterwards and Several person felled by the falling of the Arch Stones,—a Second Shot was fired and the ball carried away half its bulk in the upper side of the first hole from which time there was no more looking out from that position—this does not look like "the men were unskilled in there use" as the writer say on page 8 of his Pamphlet.

  [*p. (23)/16*]
  than Outside, (and I may add than Officers engaged in defeats and disapointed expectations) for it was asserted by Mexican authority that, the Old Texians were to be driven from the country and their places filled by Mexican families; and circumstances Seem to favor the belief that this was their intentions; for with each branch of the army; they had families traveling.
  There are many incidents connected with this little history, which the writer, might mention, which is interesting to himself but, may not be to others; and it may be the writer has already trespassed upon your patience. The writer

will now undertake to State Some facts in & about the Alamo—The Pamphlet writer says in the first page of his book "The fall of the Alamo, whose

[p. (24)/17/Ford p. 47, similar to last part]
"whose tragic results are so well Known was an action whose details, So far as the final assault is concerned, have not been fully or correctly given in any of the current histories of Texas. The reason is obvious, when it is remembered, that not a single combattent from within survived to tell the tale, while the official reports of the enemy were neither circumtial nor reliable." Now how our historian could undertake to give a correct, or even to approximate near to a correct account from his own admitted unreliable character, of the Sources of his information is passing strange.
Col. Travis's Servant was perhaps as good & faithful Soldier & fighter as any man in the Alamo fighting by the Side of his Master, till he fell and found all was lost. he then secreted himself in a room, and spared "to tell the tale" So Mrs. Dickenson

[n.p./47]
the commencement and prosecution of the Seige, to its final fall., as well as to the number slain. their statements are also coroborated by Santa Annas private Secretary, who was taken at the battle of San Jacinto and Kept with Santa Anna & Col Almonte until the following december, when Genl Houston Sent an Escort with them by way of Washington City on their return to Mexico. The Seige comenced, as before Stated, with Cavalry on the 23rd February 1836; and, dailey charges, & nightly alarms were made, but they were as often repulsed by Or rifles, with loss to the beseigers—without the loss of a man on our part, untill the fatal 6th of March, when all fell! these facts are Stated by the three first person named, to wit, the Mexican, who Said he was Sent by Navan to notify

[n.p./46/Ford p. 50]
Capt Seguin, and his Father, Don Erasmus & their (cousin) who all being our friends retreated to Gonzales,—the story by Mrs. Dickenson & Col Travis's servant, who all agree as to the Slain during the Seige to be about <u>fifteen hundred</u> received their information from the Army, whilst prisononers understood the Mexican language and and [*sic*] it is presumable would give as correct an account, and I should much sooner <u>believe them</u> than Genl Bradburn, (a notorious enemy & not on the land of Texas at the time) and other interested and defeated parties who as the writer of the Pamphlet admits is the usual Style of underating as an apology after defeat. And further, what I conceive to be the best coroborating testimony of
[n.p./45]
the private Secretary of Santa Anna while he was..ssioner on the Brassos river near Columbia, and under the charge of Capt Wm H Patton—(who was my Capt while in the army at San Antonio)—I asked the secretary throu Capt

Patton, how many men they had brot on to San Antonio? and how many they had lost during the Seige? he answered that they had brot to that point (San Antonio) five thousand men, and that they had lost fifteen hundred & forty four of there best troops during the Seige, and that "the Americans fought more like devils than men"—He (the secty) coroborates the Statement of our people saved from the massacre in the Alamo, that the incessant Bombardment and frequent charges commenced friday 4th March, which continued unceasingly untill 10 O.C. Saturday night when all firing ceased!

[n.p./38]
before we crossed the Salado—commenced firing—and was—Kept up day & night with many faint—rge—no doubt with the view of Keeping—men on constant duty—and fatigue   D. Crocket had been requested to take command but refused at the time Col Travis acepted, remarking at the time I have come to assist Travis as a high Private. "That me and my Tennessee boys, have come to Help Texas as privates—and will try to do our duty"—

Col Travis told me at the time I lef him he had in the Alamo about 40 Mexicans we went in with him but I learned afterwards by Mr. Smith who had brot out the express they had all left the Alamo, fearing there would not be Sufficient reinforcements of Americans to defend it.

The writer Says on page 5 no regular Scouting Service had been Kept up from Travis, port—In this I the writer is, entirely mistaken as Shown in this Statement heretofrom: the enclose North of the church marked D.O.D. had another enclosure North of it which was the Slaughter pen or used as Such on this occasion, into which cattle was driven, which

[p. (21)/12/Ford p. 45]
All became a dead calm (Statement of the three first parties) and at day light Sunday morning, the scaling ladders were around the walls of the Alamo, and the Soldiers rushing over, to within the walls, when the Slaughter Commenced, which lasted but a short time! "The Alamo had fallen." There was only one American Soldier alive, he was fond secreted in a room and promised his life if he would skin [note, "skin" is probably a misreading of the handwriting for "show"] the bodes of Bowie & Travis.—he did so, when the Mexicans Officers mutilated their bodies, by cutting and hacking them to pieces, with Swords & spears—After Santa Anna rode in to the Alamo, to See the work of death, which he had produced, he discovered the young man, he asked what that fellow was doing there? he was answered by an Officer, "That his life should Spared
[p. (22)/13]
if he would skin the bodies of Bowie & Travis; his reply was we have no use for such men, have him shot". A file of men was ordered to do the deed! He was Shot! the writer of this would now ask in all candor, if any thing of a reliable history could be expected, the material for which, is derived from such unreliable Sources as defeated Mexican Officers and Sordiers, which the Author

of the Pamphlet admits (on page four) that they do not report the truth when
they are defeated. Is it not most likely our own people, whose lives were
Spared, and, who witnessed the whold Seige & fall, and heard the Sad tale of
their own loss and head them recounting all the bloody Seens! I repeat, is it
most likely, they would approximate nearer the truth?

[*p. (45)/28/Ford p. 47*]
(Rode into) the Alamo to See the work of death, whi [*which*] had produced
and more, by large odds, of his own men, than of the Americans he discovered
the young man, he asked "what that fellow was doing there," he was answered
by an Officer that his life should be spared if he would skin the bodies of Bowie
and Travis; his reply was "we have no use for such a man, have him shot" A file
of men was Ordered to do the deed! he was shot!

[*n.p./36*]
all in the Alamo at the fall One hundred & eighty seven men; forty of which
when the writer left were on the sick list. (Col Bowie with the sick) On Monday
night W. Smith Piloted the 32 men through the enemies centinals on the Powder
house hill, into the Alamo. There was great rejoicing, on account of the reinforcements of the army. on the Thursday following 3rd March Santa Anna
reached San Antonio with thirty five hundred Infantry; When Santa Anna
arrived with his division of the army, the shouts in the City was distinctly heard
at the Alamo, Santa Anna! Santa Anna! he directly commenced making Scaling
ladders—which was Seen from the Alamo—When Col Almonte arrived on the
23rd February, he Started a flag to Col Travis, which was met by one from
Travis, carried by Maj. Morris & Capt Martin, the flags
[*pp. (13) & (14)/8/Ford p. 37*]
met on the footbridge leading from the city to the Alamo (there was no
waggon bridge then) Col Almonte demanded an unconditional surrender,—
upon the report of Norris & Martin of the terms to Col Travis he answered by
the fire of cannon at a group standing on the Civil Plaza at the enterence of
Commerce Street,—It was supposed some were cut down judging from the
commotion created—After John W Smith left Gonzales on Saturday, with the 25
men before named, we received a letter from Col Fannin at Goliad stating he
had Sent Capts Desock and Chenowith with a co of men to Seguins Rancho on
San Antonio river to get provisions & beef to bring to the Seguin crossing of
Cibolo and had crosses over the San Antonio river at Old Goliad three hundred
men with cannon to join any troops from Gonzales: urging all to come on that
could; this letter was dated & the hour in the day given. On Sunday morning
the writer in Company of Dr Alsbury & ten other Americans crossed the
Guardaloup River at Gonazales & fell in with and waited on Capt John N
Seguin, who with twenty four of his men were getting ready to go on to meet
Col Fannins division, but Capt Seguins men detained so long in getting ready
that we failed overtaking Smith with the 25 men alluded to before at the Cibolo

crossing. this we reached on Monday night after dark 7 Smith left there at Sun
Set, then into the Alamo that night. We waited on Col Fannins divison until
wednesday night, (mid night. we retreated; expecting to meet reinforcement,
but were disappointed,—we got back to

[*pp. (15) & (16)/9*]

Gonzales on Thursday 3rd March. (the day Santa Anna reached San Antonio & commences making scaling ladders, thursday night Col Travis called for
some one to volunteer with express to the people notifying the arrival of Santa
Anna with his Infantry (3500) W Smith arrived at Gonzales on Friday, having
arranged with Col Travis, to fire the 18 lb cannon three times a day, morning
noon, & night, so long as the fort lived. On Sunday he started to the Alamo
again with twenty five more men with Capts Desock and Chenowith but failed
to hear the token guns, he stoped on the Cibolo till wednesday morning, he
hearing no guns when he sent eight men to reconniter towards San Antonio,
when, about six miles, they met the advance of Santa Annas Army—who gave
chase, they all got back to Gonzales on Fridy—here Santa Anna sent a head of
his to Genl Houstons army sending a portion to cut off Col Fannins retreat &
another portion he sent under Genl Coss in the upper country, by Bastrop, to
start the Indians to head, and cut off the retreating families; but Providing
[*Providence*] Sent a rain even floods of water which obstructed their march and
Santa Anna Sent for Coss to come down to Aid in the his attack upon Genl
Houstons Army which made at San Jacinto the result of which is well known

The Author of the pamphlet will perhaps wish to Know how I obtained my
information in regard to Alamo history. and I feel that he

[*n.p./49*]

right & proper he should be informed—

and 1st It was my lot to be one of that Army, and the only one now living,
and escaped the fate of my comrades in a manner before related, being able to
do fort duty & being able & on horse back was Sent by the Col to Gonzales/
and my after movements is to some extent in this communication. Secondly I
obtained information in regards to the seige & final fall from the Messenger
whom Nevan Sent to Capt John N. Seguin's family instead of Genl Houston at
Gonzales; whose story is coroborated with Mrs. Dickenson with whom I was
acquinted some and at the time of Col Almonte's coming with the cavalry,—
bording at Capt Dickensons; as also of Col Travis's Servant man. All the persons
here mention agree in there Statement as to

[*pp. (17) & (18)/10*]

to come on that could; this letter was dated and the hour of the day given.
On Sunday morning, the writer, in company of Dr. Alsbury and ten Others,
Americans, crossed the Guardalupe River at Gonzales, and fell in with, and
waited on Capt. John N Seguin, who, with twenty four of his men, were getting
ready to gon to meet Col. Fannins division but Capt Seguin and men detained
So long in getting ready, that we failed overtaking Smith, who left the evening

before, with 25 men allude to befor; The Cibolo Crossing, we reached, on Monday night, after dark; and Smith left there at Sun Set, and with 6 other men went into the Alamo, that night. We waited on Col Fannins devision, until Wednesday night. (Mid night) We retreated expecting to meet reinforcements, but was disappointed; ;we got back to Gonzales on thursday 3rd of March (The day Santa Anna reached San Antonio, and commenced making scaling ladders. On our return to Gonzales, we met another letter from Col Fannin, dated the same day of the first, but one hour after, the former; Stating, a council of War had been called, and determined, not to Send any reinforcements To Travis, that they would have use for all there Troops: they recrossed the River to Old Goliad. The Same day we got back to Gonzales, Capts Desock and Chenoworth, being notified by one of Seguins men, of the Ranch that the army (Mexican) had heard of their getting provisions and had sent a party after them; they left, and in their flight, fell in with Seguins men waiting for Fannin, and they too, got back to Gonzales on the same day we did. Thursday night Col Travis called for some one to volunteer to go

[*pp. (19) & (20)/11*]

with express to the people notifying the arrival of Santa Anna with his Infantry (3500) Mr. J. W. Smith came forward, and arrived at Gonzales on Friday; having arranged with Col Travis, to fire the 18 lb cannon three times a day,—morning, noon and night, So long as the Fort lived. On Sunday he started to the Alamo, again with twenty five more men, with Capts. Desock and Chenoworth but failed to hear the token guns; He stopped on the Cibolo, till Wednesday morning, he hearing no Guns, when he sent eight men to reconnoiter, towards San Antonio. When about Six miles, they met the advance of Santa Annas Army; who gave chase. They all got back to Gonzales on Friday. Hear Santa Anna Sent, a head of his—to Genl Houstons Army Mrs. Dickerson and child, and Col Travis' servant; After, sending them off, <u>out of sight</u>, he divided his army, sending a portion to cut of Col Fannins retreat, and another portion he sent under Genl Coss in the upper country, by Bastrop to start the Indians to head and cut off the retreating families: But Providence Sent a rain, even floods of Water, which obstructed their march and Santa Anna Sent for Coss to come down and aid in his attack upon Genl Houstons Army which was made at San Jacinto. The result of which is matter of history, and well Known. The Author of the panphlet [*sic*], will perhaps wish to Know, how I obtained my information in regards to the Alamo, History, and I feel that it is right and proper he should be informed

And first, it was my lot to be one of that Army, and the only one now living, except the Honbl David Murphree, who now lives in Victoria county on Prices Creek

[*n.p./44*]

return to Gonzales we met another letter from Col Fannin dated same day of the first but one hour after the former letter, Stating a council of War had been called—and determine not to send any reinforcements to Travis—that they would have sue for all their troops, the recross the river to Old Goliad—

The Same day we got back Gonzales Capts Desock & Chenowith, being notified by one of Seguins men, that the army had heard of there getting provisions at Seguins, and Sent a party after them, they left and in their flight fell in with Capt Seguin & men waiting for Fannin and they two, got back to Gonzales on the Same day we did.

("2500" written on margin)

[n.p./48/Ford p. 32]

it was not Known at that time, the Mexican army had been divided it was assertained by Jack Tilley, who had fallen into the enemies hands, he professed to be much pleased, as to haven taken by his friend (the Mexican), he spoke their language well, and was well acquinted with the country—the made him a Spye & furnished a fine horse for to ride he went in and out days and learned the whole desposition of S. A.s Army, after crossing the Brazos River, he escaped to Genl Houstons Army, and communicated the whole information which led to S A whereabouts and numbers

(21)

and one other American was a Merchant in San Antonio at the time and escaped leaving on foot, with his Saddlebags on his Shoulder, leaving a handsome Stock of Merchandize, a total loss, to wit, Capt Nat Lewis now a citizen of San Antonio. I escaped the fate of my comrades in the manner before related, not being able to do Fort duty, I—Murphree was perhaps out of the city at the commencement of the Seige—Capt Lewis left as before stated

[pp. (21) & (22)/14]

When Santa Anna with the remnant of his Army (which was now but small after Sending off the two divisions before named,) Moved on toward Gonzales, where the small force under Genl Houston was concentrating; mark Santa Anna did not divid his Army as above related until he had sent Mrs. Dickerson & child & Travis' servant to Genl Houstons Army. When they left San Antonio for Houstons, Santa Ann had some three thousand men, beside families (as reported by the prisoners sent to Genl Houston—) when Genl Houston received this report from the prisoners his force was but small, perhaps not exceeding four hundred—consequently he took up the line of retreat no doubt, under the belief, Santa Annas whole force, was on there march for him at Gonzales—It may not be out of place here to state, that when the writer of this had taken the oath of alegiance to Texas at San Philipe De Austin in December, Stephen F. Austin had just been at the consultation (then in session at San Philipe) appointed Genl Agent went on to the "Old State" to solicit men and means, to defend Texas; and that Gentl Houston was "Elected Commander in Chief." We go an account of Coss' surrender on the 12th. On the 14 of december when about starting to San Antonio to join the Texas Army in company with others, Genl Houston informed me he had just ordered the army there to fall back to the white settlement, and that we need not go on to San Antonio, as the Army would have left before we reached that point. The Army, however did not leave as ordered, and a call for volunteers was made by those Commanding at San Antonio to Keep possession of the place, until regulars

[*pp. (22) continued & (23)/15*]

could be had to defend the country. In January I joined with others under Capt Wm H Patton for one month supposing, that would be time to get regulars to answer the call, I would further remark I met Genl Houston at Gonzales after the Convention at Washington, which declared our Independence of Mexico; he told me had just ordered Col Fannin to retreat from Goliad to East of the Guardalupe River.

[*n.p./41/Ford p. 53, and this page continues past the end of his version*]

——that place, confirming the fact————nal gun, which but few had——

——fell in the Alamo on the 6th of——the propotion was about equal between the Texians, and ——who had lately arived from the United States & other countries. The former——admits, who had long enjoyed the rights garranteed to——by the Constitution of 1824, and who were willing that instrument should govern them, without modification, but for a Despot to assert their inferiority, and deprive them of representation in the Councils of the Government, was a wrong to which they had never been subjected, and a usurpation to which they would never Submit.

These colonists were from all parts of Texas, a number of which represented each I am unable to say, I may State however that Gonzales County sufferred more than any other, Being the nearest to Bexar, than any other, which contained American Settlements, Such of her inhabitants as responded to the call for assistance, were ennabled to reach the scene of action sooner than those from any other quarter. Many of her best citizens, Some of them poor, with large families to support, fell on this gloomy Sabbath, No less than thirty three widows were left in the town of Gonzales and vicinity, in a manner destitute, helpless by that fall. Indeed no event in the history of our Country is frought with more untimely disaster, or, in some respects, none with more melancolly results, Yet it is gratifying to Know that those

[*n.p./40*]

who mourned the lost a brother, a son, or a father, were not left altogether comfortless, the proud recollection that their sacrafice was not in vain, was some consolation in the hour of bereavement, and now as they visit the old fortress and with sad hearts survey the rude wall of the buildings which remain, and fancy the particular Spot which absorbed the blood of a dear one, there is an addition consolation in the reflection that they are not with sympathy, that

[*p. 46/50*]

their country men also have come to sorrow for the loss of those so devoted devoted to the common weal, independant of their own interests, Those noble spirits Knew nought of vanity, they were Stangers to the selfish lusts of Ambition. They sought neither emulation, nor distinction, nor the empty praises of mankind. "Liberty or death" was the moto, not only of Travis, but of all, and when the alternative threatened them, they feared it not, but with a consciousness of rectitude forsook their homes with all their sacred endearments, and seized the sword in defence of the former Texas may never forget that (in pencil "Sad but glorius") Sacred day, She may revel in the enjoyment of her Liberties but those liberties (in pencil "which wherever obtained the world over") are stained with the blood of heroes, whose mouldering relics will claim their reward.

As remarked before I have not pretended to give a full and precise detail of this event, my object being only to State the facts as they came to me that the historian who may hereafter compile a correct history of our country, may have as much light upon this part as possible. In many instances I have not taken the pains to designate the points where this account differs with those which have preceeded it, presuming that all who may see this will have seen the others,

If this skitch shall succeed in clearing away some of that cloud of mistery which has hitherto hung around that portion of our countrys history to which it relates, I will have accomplished all that I desired.

(in pencil "John Sutherland")

Commentary

John Sutherland (1.7.1.1–1.7.1.7)

The John Sutherland account is justifiably one of the most widely used for narrative accounts of the siege. The level of detail in Sutherland's personal experiences gives a vividness and richness to the events not obtainable through any other document. The account is also important for being an indirect source for the people he identifies as having interviewed: Susanna Dickinson, Joe, John W. Smith, Colonel Almonte, Santa Anna, and Caro, Santa Anna's private secretary.

The original of the Sutherland account has not been located, but it is available in two later versions: one in the John S. Ford Papers (1.7.1.1) and the second in the Amelia Worthington Williams Papers (1.7.1.7), both in the Center for American History.

Virtually all modern Alamo narrative accounts have used the Ford version directly or indirectly. Ford's original manuscript is a handwritten insertion of about forty pages in his memoirs. Ford was a notable figure in his own right—a Texas Ranger and a colonel in the Civil War—who became interested in gathering accounts of Texas history.[1] Based on a comment in the Annie Sutherland book, Ford was a friend of either John Sutherland himself or a family member who held the original Sutherland manuscript prior to 1896. An edited version of this account was first printed in pamphlet form by John Ford in 1896. The story became much more widely known when published by James DeShields in the February 5 and 12, 1911, issues of the *Dallas Morning News*, which did not give the source for the manuscript, claiming in fact that it was "never before published."[2] The complete account was printed for the first time, again privately in pamphlet form, by Dr. Sutherland's granddaughter Annie Sutherland in 1936. Therefore, it is somewhat difficult to consult, and surprisingly, it has not yet had an in-depth scholarly study. The more detailed commentary given below is intended only to be an initial discussion of the documents.

Amelia Williams preserved an alternate copy of the Sutherland account. William C. Davis, first in 1997 and then in 1998 in *Three Roads to the Alamo,* was the first to pay attention to a typescript of the Sutherland story in the Williams papers.[3] He noted several instances of different wording that indicate that this version may have come from the original Sutherland manuscript, and that Ford's version has been reworked and (consistent with the above comments) additions made. As central as the Sutherland account has been to the Alamo narratives of the twentieth century, Davis's work reinforces the long-standing need for a thorough, comprehensive, and exhaustive study of Sutherland. The Williams copy has been reproduced here by reordering and collating the pages into a less random mix, and cross-referenced when applicable to pages in the Ford manuscript. Some additional observations are made after considering the Ford version.

Analogous relationships between the two apparently Sutherland-based maps (1.7.1.2, 1.7.1.3) are also discussed.

One totally contrary opinion on Sutherland is by Lindley (1989), who attacked his basic character and claims of service at the Alamo. Lindley's two arguments on the latter point seem to be that Sutherland made no such claim prior to 1854 (1.7.1.6), even when he had a chance to do so, an argument that would effectively dismiss all the evidence for essentially all the possible couriers in this entire section, and by a microscopic study of the expense claim (1.7.1.4) that considers missing ditto marks in the third column for February 11 through 19 as significant.[4] To me, the reasoning seems underwhelming. Furthermore, the internal consistency of the Sutherland account, as well as the lack of a reasonable motive for creating such an extensive hoax (it was not done for money or land at the time it was initially written, after Potter's account of 1860), lends support to the basic validity of the Sutherland story. A thorough study of Sutherland, including consideration of inconsistent information among sources and versions rated important in Lindley's study, remains to be done. The reader is invited to draw his or her own conclusions using directly the material presented.

A study of the physical text of the Ford version is necessary to understanding this exceptionally important manuscript. Annie Sutherland noted the family belief that it was a loan to John Ford that should have been returned. However, most of the handwriting appears to be that of Ford's, and so I believe this manuscript could be a copy made for his records from the presumably missing original.

There are three different types of handwriting noted where the changes occur on pages 32, 33, and 39. The different scribes were not independent of each other; two of the three transitions occur in midsentence, while at the third transition, two sheets were cut and fitted together to make the standard size. Throughout the text in the first handwriting, there are also inserts in brackets in the original that would not make sense unless it was a copy. The "Remarks" on the last two pages are also in the same first handwriting. On the other hand, there are erasures and additions that appear to be compositional editing as if this were an original draft—though the editing could be Ford's rather than Sutherland's. Another important clue is that most pages have imprinted in the upper left corner an emblem of a capitol building with "Congress" over it, and the writings by the three hands avoid this part of the page. Ford was elected to Congress in 1844 and to the State Senate in 1857; Sutherland apparently was not an elected official.[5] Clearly, an unambiguous sample of John Sutherland's handwriting would clarify the penmanship in this document. Specifically, there are three Sutherland autographs in the Audited Claims records.[6] Other letters in the Dimitt (Philip) and Sutherland (John) Papers (CAH) have signatures that do not match the one on the last page of the Ford manuscript. A letter by John S. Ford to Adina de Zavala of September 13, 1892, has a signature that is a better match to the handwriting of this one.[7] On this evidence, I believe the Ford manuscript is not the original Sutherland manuscript, but a copy made by Ford.

One possible scenario is that Ford took a somewhat rough original by Sutherland and edited it into a more polished form. Later, some worn or damaged pages were recopied by others, possibly Ford family members with access to the manuscripts. The first part of this argument is weakened, however, by the careful bracketed comments and a number of insertions (not noted in this transcript) added to the text as if making corrections to an original draft. Another possibility is that Ford interviewed Sutherland and wrote down a verbal report, but comments in the fifth paragraph (page 19) about wanting to publish, a desire of Sutherland's supported by the Foreword in Annie Sutherland's printed edition, make this less likely. A more detailed analysis of the physical text would be a useful and important next step in historical scholarship. The most important point is that the content reflects a unified style and manner of expression, regardless of the particular handwriting, which supports belief that the source is common throughout. In other words, I am convinced this is an authentic narrative from Sutherland himself, regardless of the history or the scribes of Ford's physical manuscript.

Turning to the content, one source Sutherland gave was Susanna Dickinson. However, the authentic Dickinson elements as discussed in section 1.2 are basically missing, while some battle details attributed to her (such as casualties) are questionable. In fact, there is little in this account not attributed to her in the *Telegraph and Texas Register* article (4.1.1) or in Morphis (1.2.7), widely disseminated later, after Sutherland's death. The location of Bowie is one detail that might be from direct talks with Susanna Dickinson, but as a resident of San Antonio, Sutherland apparently knew Mrs. Alsbury (1.7.1.1, p. 49; 1.7.1.7, pp. (17) & (18)/10), who was a more likely source.

Similarly, there is not too much new, beyond the *Telegraph and Texas Register* article, in what could have come from Joe. There is a more elaborate account of Travis's death, in that Travis moved during the battle a significant amount—from the north wall to the northeast corner of the church (compare with 1.3.4). This was highly unlikely, though, as there were buildings, walls, and some of the Mexican Army in the way of such a move—so this seems to be a narrative "improvement" on the original, much simpler, version that had Travis killed at his post.

The relative lack of new information from Susanna Dickinson or Joe is not, however, an argument against the value of Sutherland's account. When Sutherland wrote his account in about 1860, it is unlikely that he had ready access to the 1836 *Telegraph and Texas Register* or to the other sources of Susanna Dickinson or Joe to fill in his story. His consistency with these sources gives some support to the idea that his narrative was independent. It is much more possible that he attended or even participated in the original interviews in Gonzales or Washington-on-the-Brazos when the two survivors arrived, which were then published in the newspaper two weeks later.

Sutherland gave a few military details, which are reviewed later in a general survey, but specifics on the positioning of troops were not his interest and so were not an important part of his contribution.

He cited Yoakum (5.1.5), Ruiz (3.1.1), and Potter (5.1.7, though Sutherland would have read the earliest version of 1860), and some passages are likely to have been used from these sources, such as those on the burning of the bodies from Ruiz or general activities outside the Alamo, but a great deal of the narrative does not seem to be dependent on these authors.

In checking additional details against letters available to modern readers, there are some discrepancies. For one, Neill is said to have left the Alamo to obtain money (1.7.1.1, p. 20) while Travis (1.1.1.7) stated that he left to take care of family problems. Another is that Santa Anna was not likely to attack soon (p. 25), while letters of both Neill (4.5.10, 4.5.11, 4.5.21, 4.5.23) and Travis (1.1.1.7, 1.1.1.8) indicate a higher level of concern over the pending invasion. Sutherland had Bowie too sick to command before Travis arrived in Bexar (p. 21), certainly not true per Travis's letter of February 13 (1.1.1.8) and his joint letter with Bowie (1.1.1.10). The February 13 letter also establishes that Travis did not arrive as late as February 18, implied (p. 25) from his arriving two days before the report from Herrera on the twentieth. This last point invalidates Sutherland's argument that Travis could not be blamed for the failure to scout the enemy's movements. This statement also has Crockett arriving on the twentieth, two days after Travis (p. 21), thereby reaching San Antonio much too late. The concluding point to make on these discrepancies, however, is raised in the "Remarks" (p. 54): that they relate mostly to information derived from others and do not reflect on those Sutherland professed to have seen. If one can concede that his memory of dates twenty-five years earlier, such as the arrival of Travis and Crockett, was a little off, then his descriptions of events are not grossly contradictory with those in other sources.

With all the above possible sources taken into account, the majority of the narrative remains as original material. Sutherland was quite clear when describing incidents from personal experience, and any well-described scene in the Alamo after his departure can be assumed to have come from John W. Smith. Consequently, he combined the accounts of two exceptionally involved participants who did not otherwise make their experiences available. Sutherland's highest value is that his accounts provide us a sense of events in San Antonio just before the siege, details of his actions on February 23, and descriptions of the activities of John W. Smith, particularly in returning to the Alamo with thirty-two men from Gonzales. Without Sutherland, these specifics all would have been lost from the Alamo story. There is an additional value: Whereas most of the other direct participants gave only bare facts (or claimed facts), Sutherland had a desire for the reader to picture the events unfolding, to feel like a participant. In this, as well as the other contributions, the value of his narrative is unmatched.

The map (1.7.1.2) in the Ford memoirs is somewhat problematic. The Becerra account (2.10.1) is a printed newsletter, inserted just prior to this page, whereas this map and legend were hand done. It is immediately followed by the manuscript of the John Sutherland account. Stylistically, it is dissimilar to the handwritten portions of the Ford manuscript, including the section on Sutherland, but it (or some map) is referenced in the account for the first time on page 30 of the manuscript. An index for the letters on the map is not included. It seems most likely that it was prepared for the Sutherland account, but by whom? One obvious possibility is that the map was Ford's (or Sutherland's) own effort to piece together the various interviews conducted. Or perhaps someone with later access to the manuscript created or recopied it. The map is directly linked to the story in noting where Travis, Bowie, Crockett, and Dickinson fell. The first three of these men, at least, were almost universal elements in the secondhand versions of the battle. Finally, an index is apparently missing, as several letters on the map are not identified in the short index on the same page as the map.

One aspect of this map gives a possible clue to its origins. There are only two blocks shown of the buildings backing on the west wall of the plaza. Other maps, presented later, indicate that almost the entire wall had such structures. In 1846, Sgt. Edward Everett of the U.S. Army did a map of the structures existing at that time, which also shows two portions still standing on the west side, with a third close to the northwest corner.[8] Sutherland's and Everett's structures also match closely for the south/low barracks and the east/long barracks buildings. This suggests that this map was based on recollections in 1846 or just after, as within a few years they were not depicted on the Giraud map, and new structures were being built along the location of this wall.[9] The fact that this was well before the 1860s, when the Sutherland account was written (since Ruiz, Yoakum, and Potter were among his sources), supports that the map was made by Sutherland rather than by someone else much later, when these partial structures would have been unknown. On the other hand, the identifying letters on the Sutherland map are nearly identical to that of Potter's (5.1.7), with the obvious change being a reversal of letters on the west and south structures. So the map could be based on Sutherland's recollections but modified using Potter's.

Adding further to the mystery is the map reproduced as Sutherland's in Annie Sutherland's 1936 publications (1.7.1.3). Clearly this is different and much cruder. She did not state explicitly where it came from; her only discussion relates to the manuscript in the Ford papers, and she said nothing of the map. The account and the Ford map are similar in the notation on the northwest corner, "Room Bowie was murdered in—and Travis' headqrs," as well as several of the other labels, such as "Backshed," "Horsepen," "Cattlepen." The blocks of rooms on the west side are different, the notation that Travis fell in the northeast corner of the chapel is missing, and cannons are individually located. An obvious possibility is that this is from the original manuscript, which Ford then reworked using Potter's map along with Sutherland's account into the version included in his memoirs.

Three Sutherland claims or petitions (1.7.1.4, 1.7.1.5, 1.7.1.6) between 1836 and 1854 are indirect support to the Sutherland account by recording his activities at San Antonio and Gonzales. His claim in 1836 establishes an active involvement with Neill and Travis, as well as the support of the garrison in San Antonio. For example, his claim that he supplied a horse to Travis "at the time of the arrival of the enemy" directly supports his story years later (1.7.1.1, p. 27). On February 19, he was still conducting routine business in San Antonio by buying hay for horses, while his purchase of corn in Gonzales on the twenty-fifth, two days after the start of the siege, similarly is consistent with the description in his later narrative (1.7.1.1, p. 33).[10]

The Williams version of the Sutherland account has a considerably wider scope of narrative content than what is included in the Ford version. Sutherland discussed other recently published (1860) accounts, defended the actions of Travis, recalled conversations with Nat Lewis, and described activities after he got to Gonzales. There are also several passages of indirect material that are not a narration of events and apparently were not of interest to Ford. The style in much of the fragments is less smooth than in Ford, and the multiple fragments imply various stages of a work in progress.

A direct comparison between the Ford and Williams versions is interesting and shows that there is additional information in the latter. The Williams version is much more of a reaction to Potter, and a number of passages debate or critique items in Potter. In addition, there is much more material of general activities in Texas, particularly of post-Alamo actions. Of special interest is the details on the correspondence from Fannin received at Gonzales, and the consequent delay in additional relief forces with Seguín and Sutherland (pp. (13) & (14)/8/Ford p. 37; pp. (17) & (18)/10).

Of particular interest here is when the Ford version has expanded the original information. What are only two paragraphs in Williams (designated n.p./34/Ford pp. 28–33) become five pages in Ford, where we get a lot more on the activities of Sutherland, Travis, and Crockett on February 23. The return of John W. Smith to the Alamo is also expanded in Ford from the Williams fragments.

Some specific details are part of larger debates. Sutherland noted in one place that Travis told him he had 40 Mexican volunteers (n.p./38), which tends to support accounts that a number might have left the Alamo during the course of the siege. Another issue concerning the total number of Alamo defenders (see section 1.11) depends in part on the sick list and whether Travis counted them in his letter of February 23 (1.1.1.16) stating that he had 150 men. Sutherland implied that the sick were included in Travis's count (p. 28)/25, though the 110 given must be an error; n.p./36 has 40). Finally, he located Bowie in a room on the west that he visited later (p. (29)/26). Sutherland is unique in giving this location (discussed in the commentary in 5.2) and might well have been unaware that Bowie was probably relocated during the siege. What is of special interest here is that he also stated that Travis shared the same room at the time Sutherland left for Gonzales. This might, therefore, be the one bit of evidence for locating Travis's room. The location Sutherland identified is not unreasonable, as it is toward the north end of the mission courtyard and thus not too distant from the cannon where Travis fought and fell.

The Williams transcript must have been done after 1931, since it was not used in her dissertation. Driggs and King have a paraphrase of the Sutherland account that includes material in the Williams version but not the Ford version.[11] Their source was another granddaughter, Sarah Sutherland, who is described as having a treasured old manuscript written by her grandfather. This could explain where Williams got the material she transcribed, as well as raise the hope that if fragments of the actual Sutherland manuscript still existed in the 1930s, they might still be in existence today.

A final comment on the Sutherland story is on a very interesting remark he made (p. 43 in Ford/1.7.1.1): "These letters from Travis, and quite a number of others from his comrades to their relatives were sent out on the night of the Third of March, by John W. Smith." But no unquestionably authentic letters other than those of Travis are known! Millsap's reputed letter (1.6.2) is the only other one, and it is not thought to be authentic (the comment is echoed in Millsap's statement "they is calling for all letters"). As for the Sutherland quote, he personally knew and talked to Smith about the Alamo, and it is hard to believe that none of the defenders sent letters similar in tone to Travis's (and Millsap's). By March 3, the situation to the defenders was clearly more dangerous than at the start of the siege, and so they certainly would have wanted to communicate with their loved ones at home. This could be their last chance. We also know that Crockett (4.5.9), Cummings (4.5.30), and others were writing to their families before the siege about their experiences in Texas. If they wrote during the siege, where might their letters be?

Even stronger evidence is the document in the General Land Office files for Alamo defender Willis A. Moore (1.6.3). This is a "Statement of Evidence" that lists documents to support the claim from a brother, William H. Moore, on behalf of the heirs. Item 3 on this list is a "Letter from W. A. Moore dated San Antonio de Bexar March 3, 1836." Frustratingly, none of the listed documents, including this letter, are in the files. According to the staff of the General Land Office, the letters might only have been shown and not submitted or copied, and therefore no transcript ever existed in the files. To my knowledge, the original of this letter has never been located anywhere by historians.

Such letters are perhaps the most glaring missing components on the history of the Alamo. That originals exist in private hands or in archives, without being widely disseminated or commonly known to historians and students, is possible. It is more likely that a future historian or student, perhaps through a local historical society in the eastern states, may locate an additional letter or letters that were reproduced by an obscure newspaper years after the fall of the Alamo.

---

1. See Hughes 1964.
2. DeShields 1935, 134–50, also includes material from the 1911 *Dallas News* version.
3. Davis 1998, 718, n. 56; 719–20, n. 67; 722, n. 105.
4. Lindley 1989, 18, 19.
5. Biographical files, Ford, John S., and Sutherland, John, CAH.
6. Republic Claims, AU-Sutherland, John; 1262; R:102 Fr:0303 & 0306, TSLA.
7. Biographical Files, Ford, John S., CAH.
8. The Everett map is reproduced in Schoelwer (1988, 446), Fox (1976, 17), and Hard (1994, 10).
9. See, e.g., Arthur T. Lee's elevation of about 1848–49 in Schoelwer (1988, 449).
10. On the other hand, note that Lindley (1989) believes the first and third claims help prove just the opposite conclusion.
11. Driggs & King 1936, 199–212.

1.7.2.1.   Juan Seguín, lost letter, 1836.

Gray, William F. 1909. *From Virginia to Texas, 1835, Diary of Col. Wm. G. Gray . . .* 131. Houston: Gray, Dillaye & Co.
This refers to a letter of Juan Seguín otherwise unknown.

In the afternoon [*of Tuesday, March 15th*], while the convention was sitting, a Mr. Ainsworth, from Columbia, arrived and brought news that an express had arrived below, with the intelligence that an attack had been made on the Alamo, which was repulsed with great loss to the enemy. The rumour was doubted, on account of the circuitous route by which it came. All hoped it true, but many feared the worst. In half an hour after an express was received from General Houston, bringing the sad intelligence of the fall of the Alamo, on the morning of the 6th. His letters were dated on the 11th and 13th, and a letter from John Seguin, at Gonzales, to Ruis and Navarro, brought the same account. Still some did, or affected to, disbelieve it.

1.7.2.2.   Juan Seguín, memoirs, c. 1858?

Seguín, John N. N.d. (c. 1858). "Personal Memoirs of John N. Seguín." Typed manuscript in the Juan N. Seguin Papers. CAH.
This is a personal autobiographical statement by one of the more interesting figures associated with the Alamo. This version is translated from the original in the TSLA. The memoirs are also included, with footnoted references, in Teja (1991), along with many supporting documents.

PERSONAL MEMOIRS OF JOHN N. SEGUIN
From the year 1834, to the retreat of General Woll from the City of San Antonio in 1842. Printed at the Ledger Book and Job Office, 1858.

PREFACE
A native of the City of San Antonio de Bexar, I embraced the cause of Texas at the report of the first cannon which foretold her liberty; filled an honorable situation in the ranks of the conquerors of San Jacinto, and was a member of the legislative body of the Republic. I now find myself, in the very land, which in other times bestowed on me such bright and repeated evidences of trust and esteem, exposed to the attacks of scribblers, and personal enemies, who, to serve political purposes, and engender strife, falsify historical facts, with which they are but imperfectly acquainted. I owe it to myself, my children and friends, to answer them with a short, but true exposition of my acts, from the beginning of my public career, to the time of the return of General Woll from the Rio Grande, with the Mexican forces, amongst which I was then serving. . . .

[*Seguín continues on with how he was attacked and insulted by political enemies, resulting in his exile. The memoirs start chronologically in October 1834, when he was the political chief of the Department of Bejar, and continues up to the capture of San Antonio by the Texans in December 1835, which included actions taken with Bowie. Following is the narrative relating to the Alamo period, when he commanded a company of volunteers in the Texas Army.*]

I was detailed to forage for the army, and was successful in doing so, returning to the camp with a liberal supply of provisions. Our camp was shortly moved to within one mile of the Alamo, whence we proceeded to the "Molina Blanco," and established headquarters. On the 11th of December we entered the city, and after having taken possession of the houses of the Curate Garza [*or Carza*], Veramendi, Garza, Flores, and others, we obliged the enemy to capitulate and withdraw towards Laredo.

After the capture of San Antonio, Captain Travis' company and mine were detailed to go in pursuit of the Mexican forces, and capture from them a cavallado which they had in the Parrita, Laredo road; we succeeded, taking nearly one hundred head of horses, which were sent to San Felipe de Austin, for the benefit of the public service. I was afterwards detailed to the ranches on the San Antonio river, to see if I could find more horses belonging to the Mexican troops.

On the 2d of January, 1836, I received from the Provisional Government the commission of Captain of Regular Cavalry, with orders to report to Lieutenant-Colonel Travis in San Antonio.

On the 22d of February, at 2 o'clock P.M. General Santa Anna took possession of the city, with over 4000 men, and in the mean time we fell back on the Alamo.

On the 28th, the enemy commenced the bombardment, meanwhile we met in a Council of War, and taking into consideration our perilous situation, it was resolved by a majority of the council, that I should leave the fort, and proceed with communication to Colonel Fannin, requesting him to come to our assistance. I left the Alamo on the night of the council, on the following day I met, at the Ranch of San Bartolo, on the Cibolo, Captain Desac, who, by orders of Fannin, had foraged my ranch, carrying off a great number of beeves, corn, &. Desac informed me that Fannin could not delay more than two days his arrival at the Cibolo, on his way to render assistance to the defenders of the Alamo. I therefore determined to wait for him. I sent Fannin, by express, the communication from Travis, informing him at the same time of the critical position of the defenders of the Alamo. Fannin answered me, through Lieutenant Finley, that he had advanced as far as "Rancho Nuevo," but, being informed of the movements of General Urrea, he had countermarched to Goliad, to defend that place; adding, that he could not respond to Travis' call, their respective commands being separate, and depending upon General Houston, then at Gonzales, with whom he advised me to communicate. I lost no time in repairing to Gonzales for further orders. General Houston ordered Captain Salvador Flores with 25 men of my company to the lower ranches on the San Antonio river, to protect the inhabitants from the depredations of the Indians.

Afterwards, I was ordered to take possession, with the balance of my company, of the "Perra," distant about four miles on the road to San Antonio, with instructions to report every evening to head-quarters. Thus my company was forming the vanguard of the Texan army, on the road to San Antonio.

On the 6th of March, I received orders to go to San Antonio with my company and a party of American citizens, carrying, on the horses, provisions for the defenders of the Alamo.

Arrived at the Cibolo, and not hearing the signal gun which was to be discharged every fifteen minutes, as long as the place held out, we retraced our steps to convey to the General-in-Chief the sad tidings. A new party was sent out, which soon came back, having met with Anselmo Vergara [sic] and Andres Barcena, both soldiers of my company, whom I had left for purposes of observation in the vicinity of San Antonio; they brought the intelligence of the fall of the Alamo. Their report was so circumstantial as to preclude any doubts about that disastrous event.

[*Seguín continues with the retreat of the Texas Army, the battle of San Jacinto, and eventual problems after the war with "jealousy evinced against me by several officers," which happened to include John W. Smith. Eventually he joined the Mexican forces in 1842.*]

1.7.2.3. Juan Seguín, testimony, 1860.

Seguín, Juan N. November 22, 1860. File C-6073, testimony for the heirs of Andres Nava. General Land Office, State of Texas.

This is a sample, along with the testimonies of Susanna Dickinson (1.2.2–1.2.5), of the General Land Office documentation for heirs of the Alamo defenders. These files are the most important sources for confirming the identities of Alamo defenders and were a major portion of Amelia Williams's dissertation. Although not all such documents are reproduced in this collection, this one is particularly worth including, as it comes from a major participant. The others signed by Seguín (e.g., see 1.11.3 on Damacio Jimenez) are particularly important for identifying the Tejanos who fought for Texas.

The State of Texas   County Court
County of Bexar   November Term AD 1860
On this 22d day of November AD 1860 personally appeared in open court Juan N. Seguin who being duly sworn deposeth and Saith that he witness was well acquainted with Andres Nava previous to the 2n March 1836, that Said Nava was born in Texas in the city of San Antonio a free white man of Mexican blood, that he did not leave the country during the spring of the year 1836 to avoid a

participation in the struggle, that he did not refuse to participate in the war and that he did not aid or assist the enemy, that Said Andres Nava Served in the company commanded by present deponent that he was domiciled and resided continuously in Bexar County from the date of the declaration of Independence up to the time of his death that he was Killed in the alamo on the 6^{h}, March 1836, when the Same was taken by the Mexican Army and to the best of the Knowledge and belief of witness, Said Andres Nava during his life time never received any valid tittle patent certificant or warrant in virtue of Said claim nor his heirs since his death; that he believes the same to be a just and standing claim in favor of said heirs, witness was residing in Bexar County at the time of the accruel [*sic*] of the right of Andres Nava that he was acquainted with Said Nava previous to 2^{n} March 1836, witness has always resided in Bexar county since the accruel of said claim or right up to 1842, from that time to 1848 he lived in Mexico that he is acquainted with Saml A Maverick, Judge Ths L Devine Jno M Carolan Judge John H Duncan prominent citizens of Bexar county—

sworn so and subscribed   Juan N. Seguin
in open court this 22^{n}
day of November AD 1860.

[*uncertain signature, something like "Sam P Pinick"*]
[*uncertain lettering, something like "CIKCCBCo"?; could be ClkCCBCo, for "Clerk, County Court, Bexar County"*]

1.7.2.4.   Juan Seguín, interview, 1887.
Clarksville Standard. March 4, 1887.

Col. Juan N. Seguin

A representative of the Times called on the venerable Col. Juan N. Seguin, sole surviving captain of the Texan army participating in the battle of San Jacinto. Col. Seguin was born in San Antonio, October 29th, 1806, and is consequently 80 years of age. He comes of pure Castilian descent, his ancestors being of the first colony that came from the Canaries to San Fernando, as San Antonio was first called. He would easily pass now for a man of 60, so gently has time indented its furrows upon his brow and face, although his hair is snow white. In personal appearance Col. Seguin is about five feet, eight inches tall, and, rather heavy doubtless weighing 170 or 180 pounds. His complexion is fair, his features regular, and the general expression of the countenance indicating firmness and gentleness of heart. As a commander his force must have lain rather in persuasion, and the love of his men, than in the exercise of stern power, as was

largely the case with General Ross. His manner is dignified yet kindly and confidential, and tears came to his eyes as he dwelt upon the stirring scenes of
1836, and he inquired of his friends of that period, and of their descendants. Of
those known to the writer only one survives: Mr. Thomas O'Connor, of Refugio;
and as the old veteran inquired of John J. Linn, Edward Linn, John S. Menefee,
and others, the answer was: "Dead!" In many respects Colonel Seguin was a
unique figure in the Texas Revolution, siding as he did against the majority of
his countrymen. That he was actuated by the purest of patriotic motives there
can be no doubt, and equally as true is it that he contributed his full share in
achieving the independence of Texas. He was shut up in the Alamo by the
encircling lines of Santa Anna's army, and was the fourth, and last messenger
sent out by Travis for aid, Major Red [*likely John W. Smith, also known as "Colorado" or "Red" Smith*] being the only one so sent whose name he could recall.
The message was verbal, directing Col. Fannin, at La Bahia (Goliad) to march to
his rescue. His egress from the beleaguered Alamo was under the friendly cover
of darkness, and was attended with great danger, as the fort was entirely surrounded, and bombs were bursting all around. He, however, stealthily made his
way through the Mexican lines afoot, and often upon all fours. A horse was
procured at a ranch, and he rode night and day until La Bahia was reached, and
faithfully delivered the message to Col. Fannin, Col. Seguin says Fannin said it
would be impossible for him to comply, as Gen. Urrea was then near his position. Being unable to re-enter the Alamo, and fortunately for him, Col. Seguin
went to Gonzales, at which point was Gen. Houston and the Texan army. Here
he organized his company, a brave and gallant band of Mexicans who did their
whole duty at San Jacinto. [*The article continues with the friendship of Seguín with
Houston, his later political career (the uncontroversial portion), and something on his
grandson and son. It ends with the following:*] Col. Seguin has never received any
material recognition of his services to Texas, though no one is more deserving
than he. He will go to Austin as soon as his son returns from Mexico, and the
good citizens of the capital city should extend to him the freedom of the same,
and accord him all the distinguished honors so manifestly due a venerable and
illurtrious [*sic*] patriot of the Texas revolution.—[Laredo Times.

1.7.2.5.   Juan Seguín, letter, June 7, 1890.

Seguín, Juan N., to W. W. Fontaine. June 7, 1890. W. W. Fontaine Papers. CAH.
The original letter of Seguín, on the letterhead of "Guillermo M. Seguín," must have been dictated. The body of the letter is in a fine hand, while the signature is in a different, shaky pen that appears to have been written by someone in his old age. The transcript reflects the number of misspellings and inconsistencies, e.g., the name of Santa Anna. The letter apparently remained unpublished until 1991 in Teja's book.

Nuevo Laredo June 7th 1890
William Winston Fontaine
Austin

My dear sir:

Your favor of the 26th May ult° to hand and contents carefully noted. In answer, I beg to state, that I am glad to be able to be of service to you, in the recollection of those days of glory long past, but not forgotten.

Santana's army was drawn up before Bexar on the 22nd day of Fe'by. 1836.

Col. Travis had no idea that Santa ana with his army, would venture to approach the city of Bexar, (now San Antonio) and for this reason, only a watch was kept on the church tower that existed where today stands the cathedral of San Fernando; this watchman was an American, whose name I do not now remember. About three o'clock in the afternoon, he sent a messenger stating that on the road to Leon, he saw a moving body which appeared like a line of troop[s] raising the dust of the road. Upon the receipt of this notice John W. Smith a carpenter (alias "el colorado") was sent to reconoiter, and returned in the evening, about five o'clock saying "there comes the Mexican army composed of cavalry, infantry and artillery"! In the act of the moment, Col. Travis resolved to concentrate all his forces within the Alamo, which was immediately done. As we marched "Potrero street" (now called "Commerce") the ladies exclaimed "Poor fellows you will all be killed, what shall we do?["]

Santana occupied the city of Bexar at about seven o'clock in the afternoon of that same day and immediately established the siege of the Alamo which at first was not rigurosly kept as the sons of a widow named Pacheco, one of whom was named Esteban, took me my meals, and by them we were enabled to communicate with those external to the Alamo.

The day following the arrival of Santa Ana, the bombardment was vigorously commenced and lasted three days. Finding ourselves in such a desperate situation, Col. Travis resolved to name a messenger to proceed to the town of Gonzalez and ask for help—thinking that Sam Houston was then at that place. But, as to leave the fortification at such a critical moment was the same as to encounter death, Santana having now drawn as it were a complete circle of iron around the Alamo, no one would consent to run the risk, making it necessary to decide the question by putting it to vote; I was the one elected. Col. Travis opposed my taking this commission, stating that as I was the only one that possessed the Spanish language and understood mexican customs better, my presence in the Alamo might become necessary in case of having to treat with Santana. But the rest could not be persuaded and I must go. I was permitted to take my orderly Antonio Cruz and we left eight o'clock at night after having bid good bye to all my comrades, expecting certain death. I arrived safely at the town of Gonzalez, and obtained at one [*once*] a reinforcement of thirty men, who were sent to the Alamo, and I proceded to meet Sam Houston.

When the notice of the arrival of the thirty men was given to Santana, it is said, he gave orders, to allow them entrance stating that he would only have that many more to kill.

In the city of Bexar at the time of which we speak, there were no others by the name of Seguin than my father Don Erasmo Seguin and myself. My father was then Judge of the Probate Court and I was commander of the 4th department of the West, with headquarters in Bexar.

Even though there may have been a misunderstanding between Bowie and my father, the forces of Col Travis did not reah [*reach*] the Medina then.

Col. Bougham was about six feet in height, thin, fair complexion, brown hair, gray eyes, he was not vicious, and of very honorable conduct as I knew.

I have an oil painting of my likeness presented to me by Gen Houston in the year 1838 and as we have no photographer in town and my pecuniary resources are very limited I can not afford to have the painting sent some where else to have a picture taken from it. This picture to which I refer, and the one you may now see in the House of Congress there, were taken at the same time.

Any other data you may desire in reference to those days long past, I will glady endeavour to give you to the full extent that my old age will permit me.

> Beleive me dear sir
> Yours respect.
> Juan N. Seguin

1.7.2.6. Juan Seguín, oral tradition, 1997.

Jackson, Ron. 1997. *Alamo Legacy: Alamo Descendants Remember the Alamo.* 65–67, 167. Austin: Eakin Press.

This account of Juan Seguín begins by telling of his friendship with David Crockett, something of their discussions relating to the Texas Revolution, and the beliefs of Juan and his father, Erasmo, about the situation with Mexico. It continues with the following incidents involving Seguín and Crockett.

Seguin and some of his loyal *vaqueros* were busy training the new recruits how to ride horses like Mexicans so they would be on equal terms with the professionally schooled Mexican cavalry.

Crockett called out to Seguin and jokingly told him he was wasting his time training men to ride and shoot at the same time. The Mexican *soldados*, Crockett hollered, will all be on foot.

Seguin politely corrected his friend, noting the number of Mexican cavalrymen would be much larger than those of the foot *soldados*.

"Well," Crockett replied, "how in tar nation do you know that?"

"Mexican men in Mexico are generally shorter than the Mexican *Tejano*,"
Seguin explained. "So they put the shorter men on horseback and the long-
legged men on foot so as to keep a steady march."

Laughter erupted from the walls of the Alamo.

"Hey, Seguin," Crockett shouted, "you've been out in the sun too long.
You're beginning to sound like you're from Tennessee."

"I think that was a compliment, but in case it wasn't, the truth of the matter
is I'm not teaching these men to ride. I'm teaching these beautiful mustangs.
They will be turned loose tomorrow in the path of the oncoming Mexican
Army. They will gallop up to the Alamo and abruptly stop within a hundred
paces, just long enough for you to be able to get off a good shot."

Laughter again broke out from Crockett and others listening. Crockett's
voice then became stern.

"Look here, Seguin," Crockett said, "I'm glad that you brought up the subject of shooting. I do believe we should put all curiosities aside by having ourselves a good ol' turkey shoot. So as soon as this little conflict is over, all of
Texas will know that a Tennessean is the best marksman."

"Yes," Seguin replied, "and all of Tennessee will know that a Texan is not
only the best horsemen, but also the best marksman."

Crockett smiled. "Tomorrow will bring the light of truth."

$$*\quad*\quad*\quad*\quad*$$

Lieutenant Colonel Travis was again looking for a volunteer courier. Travis
previously made this request seven times, and each time one brave man
stepped forward. None of them had returned. The Mexican lines were apparently too strong to break through.

This time, no one volunteered for Travis' call.

Travis pondered his next move, and concluded there was one man in the
ranks who was best suited for his latest assignment. He called on Captain
Seguin to ride to Goliad.

Seguin, Travis reasoned, had the best chance to secure help for the besieged
garrison. Seguin knew the language. He knew the hostile Texas terrain. And,
most of all, there was no one better on the back of a horse.

Travis was certain Seguin could break through the Mexican lines unharmed
and reach Col. James Fannin at Goliad. Ride for Goliad, Travis asked Seguin,
and recruit any and every man to help defend the Alamo.

Seguin hesitated. Not out of fear, but honor.

Travis listened as the brave *Tejano* tried to explain his position. Seguin told
Travis he represented all Texans—native or not—and that he felt bound to fin-
ish the fight he had helped start. Futhermore, Seguin concluded, "My prize
horse was shot and I have no horse to ride."

Jim Bowie, a trusted friend of Seguin, interrupted.

"Amigo," Bowie said to Seguin, "you have complimented me on my horse on many occasions. My horse is yours to ride. Ride like the wind. Recruit any and all help possible to help save the day."

Seguin nodded in agreement.

Bowie's horse was retrieved and saddled for Seguin, who received his final instructions from Travis. Goodbyes were now in order.

Crockett was the last to shake Seguin's hand. Saying goodbye was tough, but Crockett, as usual, found the words. He wished his new friend good fortune and safety.

As Seguin straddled Bowie's horse, Crockett reached up and shook Seguin's hand one last time and said, "Don't you forget, we still have a shooting match to attend to. So don't go and get yourself killed."

Raising his hand in the air, Crockett gave Bowie's horse a swift swat on the rump and shouted, "Open the gate for there goes a brave and true Texan!"[12]

Seguin made it safely through the Mexican lines, and immediately rallied reinforcements to ride to the aid of his friends in the Alamo.

By February 28, Seguin was camped on the Cibolo River waiting to join Col. James W. Fannin and his forces from Goliad. They waited in vain. Fannin never came, and Seguin soon heard news of the Alamo's fall.

Seguin left no doubt about his feelings towards the men at the Alamo.

On year later, on February 25, Seguin shared those feelings at a burial ceremony in Bexar for the Alamo's defenders. He eloquently stated that the defenders "chose to offer their lives to the ferocity of the enemy."

---

[12] Albert Seguin-Carvajal Gonzales, letter to author, 6 July 1995. Gonzales opened his letter with, "My maternal grandmother, Maria Lucrecia Seguin-Carvajal Ramirez . . . was handed down the following story by word of mouth." Gonzales is a great-great-great-grandson of Juan Seguin.

1.7.2.7.   Juan Seguín, letter, March 13, 1837.

Seguín, Juan N., to Albert Sidney Johnston. March 13, 1837. Mrs. Mason Barrett Collection of the Papers of Albert Sidney Johnston, Special Collections, Tulane University Library, New Orleans.

This letter was first quoted by Sibley (1996, 272–80). The original is in English, so it is likely to have been drafted by an aide and signed by Seguín. The future Confederate general Albert Sidney Johnston was at this time the commander of the Army of Texas, and Seguin sent him a report on his activities around San Antonio. After a couple paragraphs discussing other actions, he reported the following.

In conformity with the orders from Genl Felix Huston dated some time back, I caused the honors of war to be paid to the remains of the Heroes of Alamo on the 25th of Feb[y] last. The ashes were found in three heaps. I caused a coffin to be prepared neatly covered with black, the ashes from the two smallest heaps were placed therein and with a view to attach additional Solemnity to the occasion were carried to the Parish Church in Bexar whence it moved with the precession at 4 O'Clock on the afternoon of the day above-mentioned. The Procession passed through the principal street of the city, crossed the River, and passing through the principal avenue arrived at the spot whence part of the ashes had been collected, the procession halted, the coffin was placed upon the spot, and three volleys of Musquetry was discharged over it by one of the Companies, proceeding onwards to the second spot from whence the ashes were taken where the same honors were done and thence to the principal spot and place of interment, the Coffin was then placed upon the large heap of ashes when I addressed a few words to the Battallion and assemblage present in honor of the Occasion in the Castillian language, as I do not possess the English, Major Western then address the concourse in the latter tongue, the coffin and all the ashes were then interred and three volleys of Musquetry were fired over the grass by the whole Battallion with an accuracy that would do honor to the best disciplined troops. We then marched back to quarter in the City with Music and Colors Flying. Half-hour gun[s] were not fired because I had no Powder for the purpose, but every honor was done within the reach of my scanty means. I hope as a whole my efforts may meet your approbation.

1.7.2.8.   Juan Seguín, newspaper account, 1837.

Telegraph and Texas Register. March 28, 1837. San Felipe.
This is the official account of the funeral for the Alamo defenders. It is reprinted with commentary in Sibley 1966, 272–80.

In conformity with an order from the general commanding the army at head quarters, Col. Seguin, with his command stationed at Bexar, paid the honors of war to the remains of the heroes of the Alamo; the ashes were found in three places, the two smallest heaps were carefully collected, placed in a coffin neatly covered with black, and having the names of Travis, Bowie and Crockett, engraved on the inside of the lid, and carried to Bexar and placed in the parish church, where the Texian flag, a rifle and sword were laid upon it for the purpose of being accompanied by the procession, which was formed at 3 o'clock, on the 25th of February; the honors to be paid were announced in orders of the evening previous, and by the tolling knell from day-break to the hour of interment; at 4 o'clock the procession moved from the church in Bexar, in the following order:

Field officers; staff officers; civil authorities; clergy; military not attached to the corps, and others.

Pall	I Coffin	I Pall	[*lettering is vertical*
bearers.	I containing	I bearers.	*in the original*]
	I the ashes	I	

Mourners and relatives; music; battalion; citizens.

The procession then passed through the principal street of the city, crossed the river, passed through the principal avenue on the other side, and halted at the place where the first ashes had been gathered; the coffin was then placed upon the spot, and three volleys of musquetry were discharged by one of the companies; the procession then moved on to the second spot, whence part of the ashes in the coffin had been taken, where the same honors were paid; the process[i]on then proceeded to the principal spot, and place of interment, where the graves had been prepared, the coffin had been placed on the principal heap of ashes, Col Seguin made the following address, in his native tongue, the Castillian.

Companeros de armas!—Estos restos que hemos tenido el bones des conducir en nuestros hombros, son de los valientos heroes que murieron en el Alamo. Si mis amigos ellos prefirieson morir mil vecesq rendirla servir el yugo del triano. Que examplo tan brillante? Digno de anotarse en las paginas de la historia. El genio de la libertad pareso estarto viendo en su clevado trono de donde con semblonte alagueno nos aenealo diciendo—hai tencis a vuestros hermanos Travis, Bowie, Crockett, y otros, vanos a quienes su valor los coloia ec el numero de mis hero erues. Si soldaros y conciudadanos estos son los actos meritorios a quienes el reves de la fortuna en la presente compario entrego mi cuerpo ala ferocia de mis enemigos, los cuales baabaramente semejandolos a las brutos fueror estados de pies y amastrados hasta esta punto en donce fueror reducidos a cenizos, yo os conebido a que poniendo per testigo los venerable restos de nuestros dignes, nos companeros digamos al mundo entro. Tejas sura libre, independieube o pereceremos cos gloria en los combates.

[TRANSLATION]

COMPANION IN ARMS!!! These hallowed relics which we have now the melancholy tasks of bearing onward to consign to their kindred earth, are all that remains of these heroic men who so nobly fell, valiently defending yon towers of the Alamo! If they, my brave associates, preferred rather to die a thousand times, than basely to bow down under the vile yoke of tyranny, what a brilliant, what an illustrious example have they bequeathed to us! How worthy to illumne with unchanging splendor the ever glowing pages of history! Even now the genius of liberty is looking down from her lofty seat, smiling with approbation upon our proceedings, and calling to us in the names of our departed brethren, Travis, Bowie, Crockett, and their iron-hearted band—bids us in imitating their mighty deeds, to secure, like them, a high place upon the scroll of immortality. Since then, soldiers and fellow-citizens, undying fame is the glorious reward of those who fell in this noble contes[*t*] cheerfully will I encounter the formidable dangers which fortune can crowd in the path of glory, in the noble attempt to achieve my country's independence, or regardless of whatever indignity the brutal ferocity of my enemies, may offer to my lifeless body, joyfully perish on the field of battle, shouting the warcry of these heroes; God and liberty, victory or death!!

Major Western then addressed the assemblage in the following words:

FELLOW SOLDIERS AND CITIZENS—Honors are due the brave! Upon us has devolved the duty of doing military honors to the immortal heroes of the Alamo, the bravest of the brave—a band of choice spirits who preferred death to slavery, and whose deeds of valor stand unparalleled on the pages of history.

Friends and compatriots—The spontaneous tear of sorrow I perceive glistens in every eye; but weep not the untimely fate of departed worth; for although in those ashes before us we behold naught but the tangible remains of a Travis, a Bowie, a Crockett, and their heroic companions, now mere dust returned to mother earth; their souls are with God in the regions of bliss, their memory is engraven on the heart of every votary of freedom throughout the universe, and their names are inscribed on the brightest shaft on the pinnacle of the temple of fame, lasting as time and imperishable as adamant.

Companions in arms!—At this moment and while we are performing this act of our sacred obligations to the valiant slain, the genius of liberty is hovering o'er this spot and with smiles of approbation at this grateful tribute of respect, beckons us onward to similar sacrifices at her shrine, and points to us the path to glory. Let us then, my brave fellows, upon this hallowed ground pledge ourselves to honor her call; let the noble acts of the illustrious dead stimulate us to vie with them in valor, and let our motto be—liberty! Texas free or death.

The coffin and all the ashes were then interred, and three volleys of musquetry were fired by the whole battalion.

JOHN N. SEGUIN, *Lieut. Col. Comm'dt*

Thus have the last sad rites of a christian burial been performed over the remains of these brave men. In after times, when peace shall have returned to smile upon our prosperous country, a towering fabric of architecture, shall be reared by their grateful countrymen above their ashes—designating Bexar as the monumental city of Texas, where long after the massive walls of the Alamo have crumbled into dust, the votaries of freedom shall yearly assemble to celebrate at *this tomb of heroes,* the mighty achiev[*e*]ments of the unreturning brave.

1.7.2.9.   Juan Seguín, letter, March 28, 1889.

Seguín, Juan N., to Hamilton P. Bee. March 28, 1889. Photocopy in manuscript files, TSLA.

A photocopy of the original of this letter, in Spanish, is also in the file.

Laredo de Tamaulipas March 28, 1889
Mr. Hamilton P. Bee
San Antonio

My dear Sir and friend

I hasten to answer your pleasant letter of the 9. inst. which I have not done before because of poor health.

The remains of those who died at the Alamo were ordered burned by order of General Santa Anna, and I ordered that the ashes be deposited in an urn and that a grave be opened in the Cathedral of San Antonio, close to the Presbytery, that is, in front of the altar railings, but very near the altar steps.

That is all I can tell you with reference to this affair.

I remain your friend and servant,
Juan N. Seguin

If you are the son of the man who was Secretary of War during the period of the Republic of Texas [*Barnard E. Bee*], I can never forget him, and I offer you my friendship.

Seguín

1.7.2.10.   Juan Seguín, proclamation, 1836.

Seguín, Juan, translated by John Wheat. N.d. (June 21, 1836). Archivo Historico Militar, Expediente 1149:45. Bancroft Library, University of California, Berkeley.

This document, undated in the original in the Mexican archives, was included in Teja 1991, 143 (Appendix 29), from *Telegraph and Texas Register*, September 21, 1836.

Citizen Juan Nepomuceno Seguin, Colonel in the Federal Army of Texas, to the inhabitants of Béxar

Fellow Citizens: Due to the movements of the war, I must leave to join the head-quarters of my army. With this move, I will leave this place, but before I do so I need your help to drive the cattle out of these fields and keep them where the enemy cannot make use of them. I do not doubt that for this act, you will gladly present yourselves and will give to the Supreme Government of Texas proof of your allegiance to our just cause and to the beloved liberty that we seek. But if, on the contrary, you do not provide this small service, it will be an unmistakable proof of your disaffection, which will be most disappointing to the same Supreme Government. It will have to treat you, not as Texanos, but perhaps as enemies. Do not be deceived by the notion that we lack the strength to defend against war; time will tell you the contrary and will show you that Texas will be free.

Fellow Citizens: Your conduct on this day will determine your fate with the high government of Texas. If you stay coldly waiting, if you do not abandon the city, and if you do not head for the interior of Texas so that your army might help you, you will doubtlessly be treated as true enemies and you will suffer the consequences. Native reason *(razón de nacimiento)* and the great friendship that I profess for you make me wish for your happiness, and therefore I will speak with the truth that is characteristic of me.

Bexaneños: Lend all the cooperation you can and soon you shall enjoy your liberty and your prosperity, as your fellow countryman and friend desires for you.

Juan N. Seguin
Colonel in Command

Commentary

Juan Seguín (1.7.2.1–1.7.2.10)

Juan N. Seguín was one of the outstanding leaders at the time of the Texas Revolution and has one of the more interesting biographies. As described in an unquoted section (since it doesn't relate to the Alamo) of his memoirs (1.7.2.2), he was accused in 1842, while mayor of San Antonio, of collaborating with the enemy during an attack into Texas by a Mexican army and was forced to flee into exile for a number of years. His fascinating career takes us too far afield from the siege of the Alamo to explore much further, though a short summary by Williams and Barker is included as a footnote to document 3.5.4. Jesús F. de la Teja's recently published *A Revolution Remembered: The Memoirs and Selected Correspondence of Juan N. Seguín*, gives a biographical sketch, an edited version of the memoirs, and translations of a number of important supporting documents, and it should be referred to for a more in-depth look at Seguín.

He played an important role in the Alamo story. According to Sutherland (1.7.1.7, pp. 23–24), Seguín's testimony for Anres Nava (1.7.2.3), and Damacio Jimenez (1.11.3), Seguín had recruited a personal force of local Mexican-Americans, or "Tejanos," from San Antonio to serve on behalf of the Texas Revolution. He also sent out some spies, who warned of Santa Anna's movements (1.11.2, 3.2.1, 3.3.1).[1] Several of his men fell at the Alamo. Others fought at San Jacinto. This exceptional and brave group richly deserves more attention.[2]

Unfortunately, there are problems with Seguín's narration of events. In his memoirs (1.7.2.2), he has Travis with him in San Antonio in pursuit of Mexican forces at a time when Travis was not in San Antonio. Later, on January 2, he is ordered to report to Travis at San Antonio. Document 1.1.1.3 indicates that Travis did not get his orders for San Antonio until the end of January (he was in the Bexar area earlier in 1835). Santa Anna entered the city on February 23, not the twenty-second, and the bombardment started right away, rather than on the twenty-eighth. Leaving the Alamo, Seguín traveled to Gonzales, where he met Gen. Sam Houston and was ordered back to San Antonio on March 6. Sections 3.4 and 3.5 show that Houston arrived at Gonzales on the eleventh, just in time to receive the news that the Alamo had fallen. The Alamo signal gun fired three times a day, not every fifteen minutes. And Seguín implies that he took Arocha Cruz with him out of the Alamo (1.7.2.4), while Cruz himself said that he met Seguín with a horse outside the Alamo (3.6.1).

Furthermore, Seguín's letter late in life to Bee (1.7.2.9) raises serious questions about his memory at that time. The issue of the burial of the ashes of the Alamo defenders is discussed below. The point to be made here is that this 1889 letter is quite contradictory to his 1837 versions.

That's the bad news. But it does not mean one has to dismiss everything from Seguín. First, he is known to have been a participant in the circumstances he described. He accurately, even to Fontaine in 1890, reflected the surprise of the Mexican arrival at San Antonio and identified John W. Smith as being a scout. The recollection to Fontaine that the bombardment started almost right away is more consistent with other sources. Though some of the rationale for his being a messenger could have been self-serving (e.g., "to leave the fortification at such a critical moment was the same as to encounter death"), the opposition of Travis, on the basis of Seguín's knowledge of language and customs, has a ring of truth. In addition, his descriptions of the start of the siege and his departure from the Alamo are relatively consistent over the thirty-plus years between the memoirs, the *Clarksville Standard* interview (1.7.2.4), and the Fontaine letter. They also are consistent with his interviews with Reuben Potter (5.1.7), sometime toward the end of this period. His commitment and courage at this time were never questioned, even later in the 1840s, when many believed him a traitor to Texas.

These accounts make much more sense if it is assumed that he had a poor sense of time, and hence the dates are not reliable. Viewing the narrations as a string of events without specifying particular times makes them much more believable and consistent. One can then appreciate more the specifics, the foremost being his selection as a messenger, for which he is the only source.

Another possible source is included from a compilation by Ron Jackson of family oral traditions from both sides of the fight, titled *Alamo Legacy* (1.7.2.6).[3] The book includes several dozen accounts that, Jackson noted, vary widely in quality. Though some are likely not authentic, but were derived primarily from earlier published sources, there is little reason to doubt that numerous stories could and would have been passed down over the years through the families of the Alamo participants. The Seguín account is included here because it gives some details of the siege and can be reviewed against the other Seguín accounts. The majority of oral traditions as recorded by Jackson concern either the participants prior to reaching the Alamo or the news of the defenders' death reaching the families. They are, therefore, more of value to the human-interest side of the Alamo rather than to the narrative of the battle itself.

One set of documents in this section relate not directly to the battle of the Alamo, but to the burial of the ashes of the defenders. This topic was reviewed in some depth by Marilyn McAdams Sibley in the *Southwestern Historical Quarterly.*[4] The first selection is a manuscript letter of March 13, 1837, to Albert Sidney Johnston (1.7.2.7), the future Confederate general. This closely matches the printed account in the *Telegraph and Texas Register* of March 28, 1837 (1.7.2.8), both of which are powerful contradictions to Seguín's letter to Hamilton Bee in 1889 (1.7.2.9). While his letter to Bee claims that the ashes were interred in the cathedral, contemporary reports have them ceremoniously interred in an orchard. These early documents are also consistent with the later accounts of the San Antonio residents (Sutherland, 1.7.1.1/p. 52; Rodriquez, 3.3.1; others in 3.7.7). It seems that the story Seguín gave to Bee can be rejected, though the only thing really wrong with the Bee version is the ashes stopping at the church rather than going back out for burial where the bodies were burned.

It is possible that the problem is in the Bee letter itself rather than in Seguín's recollection—that it might be fraudulent in some fashion. The signatures on the original Bee and Fontaine letters appear to be the same, however, so the idea that the Bee letter was from someone else forging Seguín's narration seems unlikely. Another idea is that Seguín was responding to leading or distorted questions and did not realize the inconsistent implications of his reply. Some, such as Adina De Zavala, believed that Seguín buried some ashes both in the church and outside the near cremation site, and that therefore there is less contradiction between the two versions than appears on the surface.

It might be time for further analysis of this subject, particularly as there are other worthwhile documents that have gotten little or no attention. "The Burial Place of the Alamo Heroes," written by Louis W. Kemp circa 1937, is a very thorough survey of nineteenth- and early-twentieth-century references.[5] An excerpt from Creed Taylor's "The Life of Creed Taylor," written circa 1907, disagrees at least in spirit, if not in substance, with Seguín's versions.[6] A location for one pyre is shown approximately to the east-southeast of the Alamo on the Sánchez map (2.7.1). Nor have writers considered the local Tejano accounts with Charles Barnes that Timothy Matovina published in 1995 (especially 3.7.7). Finally, it appears that no one has carefully laid out the various accounts on a historical series of San Antonio maps to see if any insights can come from a two-dimensional analysis.

It is surprising that the mid-nineteenth-century Texans did nothing about establishing a monument or memorial on the site of interment. Yet considering the divergent information available, starting with that supplied by Juan Seguín himself, one need not be surprised if no ultimate resolution is achievable.

Though the final document (1.7.2.10) in this section appears to be from June 21, after the period of the siege of the Alamo, it is included because it shows Seguín's attitudes and strong support toward the cause to which he gave so uninhibitedly.[7] It is, therefore, to those interested in the role of the Tejanos in the Texas Revolution, particularly revealing about their attitudes and dedication. To put it simply, such a document would have been a death warrant should Seguín have fallen into the hands of Santa Anna's forces.

Another interesting aspect of this proclamation is what it implies about the relative efficiency of the Mexican intelligence. That such a document (soon after San Jacinto) showed up in the Mexican archives is curious. There is even a possibility that the document is the original; the signature is similar—though not identical—to those in the much later Fontaine and Bee letters.

1. Also see Williams in *SWHQ* 36:385–87, 37:242–43.
2. For further study on Seguín's men, Lozano's *Viva Tejas* (1985), Poyo's *Tejano Journey, 1770–1850 (1996)*, and Canales's *Bits of Texas History*, Part 2 (1957) are starts. The Republic Claims files, which have just become easily accessible and open up possible new sources, have supporting statements from 1874 by Juan Seguín and/or Antonio Menchaca for services by additional individuals: Julian Dias/R:212 Fr:0469-0471, Agustin Bernal/R:202 Fr:0688-0690, and Miguel Benites/R:202 Fr:0565-0566.
3. Also Jackson 1997.
4. Sibley in *SWHQ* 70:272–80; also Williams in *SWHQ* 37:173–75, nn. 35, 38; Kemp c. 1937.
5. Kemp copy in Folder 7/Muster Rolls and Other Lists of Defenders of the Amelia Williams Papers, CAH.
6. Creed Taylor copy in Defenders Burial Site/Alamo/Historic Sites/San Antonio Clipping Files, DRT; original apparently is in TSLA.
7. Per Teja, 1991, 143 and verified in the *Telegraph and Texas Register* for September 21, 1836, 20. In a section of Seguín's memoirs not quoted here, he stated that he left San Antonio on June 24 because of a false rumor of a Mexican force marching back into Texas.

1.7.3.1.   John W. Smith, article, 1902.

Zuber, William. P. January 1902. Notes and fragments: Last messenger from the Alamo. *Texas Historical Association Quarterly* 5:263–66.

This analysis of John W. Smith's movements while carrying Travis's last message of March 3, 1836, is a follow-up of the discussion Zuber published on Louis Rose (1.8.1.4).

NOTES AND FRAGMENTS.

"LAST MESSENGER FROM THE ALAMO."—*The Proceedings of the Tenth Annual Meeting of the Daughters of the Republic of Texas* contains an article under this caption, by their excellent historian, Mrs. Adele B. Looscan, who therein infers that the messenger, Capt. John W. Smith, left the Alamo "in the evening of the 3d of March, in all likelihood after dark"; which inference conflicts with my conclusion in the QUARTERLY of July, 1901, that he left after midnight on the morning of the 3d, therefore before the departure of Rose on the afternoon of that day, and that his silence concerning Travis's speech does not tend to disprove Rose's statement.

The inference that Smith left the Alamo late in the evening of March 3d is drawn from two considerations: first, Travis's remark in the dispatch borne by Smith, and dated March 3d,—"Col. J. B. Bonham got in this morning at eleven o'clock"; and secondly—another inference—that Smith made all necessary changes of horses on the way.

I believe that my note in the QUARTERLY of October, 1901,—*The Escape of Rose from the Alamo*,—proves that Travis, being weary and pressed for time, made a blunder (surely not an extraordinary one), and that his meaning was 'yesterday morning,' 'last evening,' or 'tonight.' If so, the above quoted inference rests solely on another inference.

The nature of Smith's route to Washington proves the impracticability of his changing horses on the way. Though I believe that there was a standing government ordinance to keep relays of horses on express routes, none were kept. I carefully read the proceedings of the governor and the council every week in the *Telegraph and Texas Register* till my departure for the army, on March 6, 1836; but I never saw therein any statement that such relays were established anywhere. This neglect resulted from two causes: the poverty of the government, and the impracticability of keeping relays on parts of the routes from Bexar and Goliad. The road from Bexar to Gonzales did not then, as later, lead by the present town of Seguin, but the eastern part of it lay southwest of the Guadalupe River, the entire distance being estimated at seventy miles; and, if I was not misinformed, the first dwelling thereon was that of Mr. Bateman, a little way off the road, in the edge of Guadalupe bottom, west of the ferry at Gonzales. The only two families that had, at different times, tried to settle on that long and lonesome trail had been murdered or driven away; one by Indians, the other by Mexican robbers.

The estimated distance from Gonzales to Moore's Ferry (the present town of La Grange), on the Colorado, was forty-five miles. The first dwelling on that road was that of Mr. Berry, four miles east of Gonzales; the second was that of Mr. McClure, on Peach Creek, ten miles from that town; and the third house was a small one-room cabin, near the west bank of the Colorado, and less than a hundred yards above the ferry, with one door, no window, and no fire-place. When I visited this house in March, 1836, it was unoccupied,—the families in that section all having left home in "the Runaway Scrape." I judged that it had been occupied by a lone man, employed by Col. John H. Moore to keep the ferry;—the colonel's residence, across the river, being too distant for travelers to call a ferryman thence.

From Moore's Ferry to Washington, the distance was said to be sixty-five miles. Settlers dwelt along the whole extent of this part of the route; the average distance between dwellings being probably two Spanish leagues, and the settlements being very thin toward the Colorado, but gradually becoming thicker toward Washington.

From Gonzales to Washington, the grass on the uplands, and the wild rye and cane in the bottoms, were so bountiful as to keep all horses and cattle in fine condition during the entire year. Hence all grades of horses, when not kept at home for immediate use nor ridden abroad, ran at large, on the range. This alone was sufficient to deter a courier from relying upon chances to exchange horses on his way. Moreover, good roadsters—then termed "American horses"—could not often be bought at less than two hundred dollars each, and never less than one hundred and fifty dollars; while Mexican ponies were purchasable at from twenty-five to forty dollars each. Nearly all settlers on the route, being financially straitened, owned only the cheap class of horses, which, though able to travel twenty-five or twenty-eight miles per day, would fail within a few hours if ridden at the rate of thirty-five miles per day. It is almost certain that this was the condition of every settler between Gonzales and the Chriesman settlement,—about ninety-eight miles from that town, and within twelve miles of Washington. I knew of only four settlers within twelve miles of Washington who probably each owned one or two "American horses" that a courier could have obtained, if they were not out on the range nor in use abroad. These four gentlemen were Col. Horatio Chriesman, Capt. James G. Swisher, Judge John P. Coles, and Dr. A. C. Hoxey.

Considering the nature of Smith's route, and the condition of the settlers thereon, he could not have changed horses before reaching Gonzales, seventy miles distant from San Antonio. There he might, possibly, but not certainly, have effected an exchange, but under risk of obtaining an untried horse, that might soon have failed. Thence to the Chriesman settlement, ninety-eight miles, there was no probability of a desirable change; and thence to Washington, twelve miles, there was a second uncertain possibility for an exchange. Thus no courier could reasonable expect to change horses on that route.

The biography of Guy Morrison Bryan, in the October QUARTERLY, 1901, supplies an authentic illustration of the difficulty then generally experienced in changing horses by couriers, and substance of which I here repeat. A few days before Smith's departure, Travis dispatched a messenger to San Felipe, bearing a letter, in which he announced the siege of Bexar by the Mexican army, and called for help. The authorities at San Felipe forwarded that letter by another courier to Brazoria and Velasco. This courier proceeded in haste to the residence of Josiah H. Bell, near Columbia, where he and his horse arrived, both broken down; and the school-boy, Guy Bryan, relieved him by bearing the letter, on fresh horses, to its destination.

I am sure that almost or quite every citizen between the Alamo and Washington would have taken the greatest pleasure in exchanging horses with Captain Smith when he bore that dispatch from Travis,—if he had had a horse at hand suitable for such use; but, as I have shown, such was not the case.

Several of the heroes of the Alamo had ridden thither on excellent saddle-horses; and, these being useless in the fort, their owners were willing to lend them to any messenger that Travis might send out. Hence Smith's only *sure* plan to perform his journey in the shortest time practicable was to mount one of the best horses in the Alamo, purposing to ride him moderately all the way to Washington. So I conclude that I am correct in assuming that he could not have performed the trip in less than four days; and therefore that, as he arrived at Washington on the sixth, he left the Alamo soon after midnight on the morning of March the third.

I deem the time of Smith's departure from the Alamo a subject of special importance, because it directly bears upon the proof of the reality of Travis's speech as orally reported by Rose and published by me.

W. P. ZUBER

1.7.3.2.   John W. Smith, dissertation, 1934.

Williams, Amelia. April 1934. A critical study of the siege of the Alamo and of the personnel of its defenders. *Southwestern Historical Quarterly.* 37:304.

A summary of available material, from Williams's "Annotated List of Couriers from the Alamo."

John W. Smith was twice a messenger from the Alamo. He first went out on February 23, in company with Dr. John Sutherland. These two men carried the first message to Gonzales. This is a fact that is accepted by all Texas historians, as is also the fact of common information that Smith served as guide to the Gonzales band who reinforced Travis on March 1. Smith again left the Alamo on the night of March 3. He carried Travis's last dispatches and was the last courier to leave the doomed fortress.

[*footnote:*]"John Sutherland's Account of the Fall of the Alamo," *Dallas News*, February 5, 1911. See also *John S. Ford's Journal*, Volume I, University of Texas Library. John W. Smith's name should be second in the list of couriers that was presented in Chapter IV of this study, on page 164 of *Southwestern Historical Quarterly*, XXXVII.

1.7.3.3.   John W. Smith, article, 1972.

Turner, Martha Anne. 1972. *William Barret Travis: His Sword and His Pen.* 232–33. Waco: Texian Press.

A summary of available material, more recent than that of Williams in 1.7.3.2. After a narrative of Travis writing his last messages, Turner concludes with the following text.

Observing that Smith was preparing to leave the Alamo, other defenders quickly scrawled messages for him to take out to their loved ones and friends. Who knew—it could be the last time.

When Travis finished he found Smith awaiting for him in the plaza. Giving Smith his packet of letters, he suddenly thought of things he had omitted but had intended to include. He told Smith to remind the reinforcements to bring at least ten days' rations. Then, still maintaining a calm unequaled in any crisis, he informed Smith—almost as an afterthought—to tell the people that every morning at daybreak he would fire a cannon as a sign that he still held the fort, but when the cannon was heard no more, its silence would signify that the Alamo had fallen.[5]

There are different versions of how Smith succeeded in getting through the Mexican cordon. One is that he slipped through the northern postern as others had before. When he was ready the postern swung open and a few Texans rushed out of the Alamo, manuevered their way toward the sugar mill, and engaged the enemy in a feint to distract attention. With the Mexican guns spitting replies and the patrols rushing to the spot, Smith got through unnoticed and was quickly swallowed up in the darkness of midnight.[6]

Other accounts assert that Smith crawled out after dark on his hands and knees. One records that he went through an irrigation canal in this manner and succeeded in escaping Mexican fire.[7] The other says that he crawled stealthily upon his hands and knees through a secret tunnel that extended from the fort eastward.[8] In this case there had to be a confederate awaiting with a horse at the other end of the tunnel. If less plausible than the first version, these two means of escape were not impossible. An old tradition has it that all of the old missions were connected by underground tunnels.[9]

---

[5] Williams, "A Critical Study of The Siege of The Alamo . . . ," 136. Some authorities assert that Travis said he would fire the cannon three times a day, morning,

noon, and night, as long as the Alamo held. However, this is not likely since ammunition was scarce and the three detonations could have been misunderstood as part of the cannonading of regular warfare.

6 Lord, *A Time to Stand*, 141.
7 Williams, "A Critical Study of The Siege of The Alamo . . . ," 134.
8 Stephen Gould, *Alamo Guide*, 18. See also Williams, "A Critical Study of the Siege of the Alamo . . . ," 136. Ruby Mixon likewise concurs in "William Barret Travis, His Life and Letters:"—"Smith left the Alamo at midnight, and crawled stealthily upon his hands and knees until he was safely beyond the Mexican lines."
9 Williams, "A Critical Study of The Siege of The Alamo . . . ," 136.

1.7.4.1.   James L. Allen, biographical sketch, 1894.

Memorial and Genealogical Record of Southwest Texas. 1894:402-3. Chicago: Goodspeed Bros. (Listed as James S. Allen.)

J. S. [*sic*] ALLEN. He whose name heads this sketch, comes of historic stock for he is the second cousin of the famous General Ethan Allen of Revolutionary fame, and consequently is a descendant of a good old New England family whose settlement in this country antedates the War of Independence by a number of years. James S. Allen was born in Kentucky in 1815, a son of Samuel and Mary (Lemme) Allen, natives of Virginia and Kentucky, respectively, and grandson of the Virginian, Richard Allen, and great-grandson of Rev. John Allen, who was a native of Massachusetts, and an own cousin of Gen. Ethan Allen. Rev. John Allen moved to Virginia, and began operating a mill, but during the great American Revolution he and two of his sons were in the colonial army under General Washington, the two latter of whom were killed in battle. Another son, Richard, was too young to enter the service of his country, so was detailed to run the mill, and furnish flour to the colonial troops. Years afterward he moved to Kentucky with quite a party of his wife's relations—the Gatewoods—and made a location in the vicinity of Lexington, where he lived to the ripe old age of 106 years. Samuel Allen, his son, and father of the subject of this sketch, resided in the Blue Grass State all his life, was in the Indian Wars with Gen. W. H. Harrison, and was in the battle of the River Thames, when the great Chief Tecumseh was killed, and always said that one Whitaker did the deed. The latter and the great chief were lying about fifteen feet apart, and fired at each other at the same time, both being killed. Samuel Allen died in 1838 and his wife in 1833, having become the parents of seven children, several of whom are still living in Missouri, the subject of this sketch being the eldest of the family. J. S. Allen, the subject of this sketch, received a good collegiate education in Missouri, his alma mater being Marion College but, his initiatory education was received in his own home. He began life for himself by coming to Texas with the other students of Marion College, for the purpose of entering the army in 1835, and upon their arrival at Houston were mounted by General McKinney, and Mr. Allen selected a valuable race-horse as his mount. As he was young and slight he was detailed as courier, and on this work he was sent to San Antonio and was in the Alamo with Travis, at the beginning of the siege. He was sent out by Travis to try and get word to the people at Gonzales in the hope of relief. In this desperate endeavor his race horse was his salvation, for he charged through the Mexican lines and was a target for a thousand guns, but miraculously escaped in safety, and in about two days reached Gonzales, but there no relief could be obtained. He was later in operation as scout with "Deaf" Smith, and burned bridges behind the Mexicans, on the advance to San Jacinto, and before they could reach the field the battle had been fought. In a few months Mr. Allen returned to his home in Missouri, but two years later returned to the "Lone Star State," and became a ranger in Captain Bell's company, and was in battle with the Indians at Corpus Christi. Later he made a settlement at Indianola, gave his attention to the stock business, and eventually became Mayor of the city and Justice of the Peace. At the opening of the Civil War he was Assessor and Collector of the county, and was captured and taken to the fort at Pass Cavallo, from which he made his escape and went to Port Lavaca, and in 1865 came to the place where he now resides. He is the owner of a fine farm of 260 acres, with 100 acres under cultivation, is a substantial and progressive citizen, and has taken quite an active part in the affairs of his adopted State, is a citizen of integrity and is highly esteemed. He has a pleasant and comfortable home, which has become widely known for the hospitality which is extended to all. Mr. Allen was married in 1849 to an estimable lady who died in 1869, having become the mother of seven children, four of whom are living: Mary Louisa, wife of Joseph Cunningham; Cora, wife of a Mr. Everhardt (both of whom are dead), their two daughters being reared by Mr. Allen; Amelia, (deceased); Julia, (deceased); W. J., who is married and has three children; Sterling Price, who is married and has two children, and Robert Lee. Mr. Allen is a worthy member of the Baptist Church, and socially a Mason.

1.7.4.2.   James L. Allen, newspaper article, 1932.

Davis, Robert H. Bob Davis uncovers an untold story about the Alamo. *Star-Telegram*. February 28, 1932. Oils, Auto and Features: 16. Fort Worth.

BOB DAVIS UNCOVERS AN UNTOLD STORY
ABOUT THE ALAMO

Here is another untold Texas tale—*The Last Man* to Leave the *Alamo* Before Its Fall—as told by *Robert H. Davis,* the world's most widely traveled newspaper correspondent . . . Davis' source of information was a *native Texan,* a Houston lawyer whose parents were Texas pioneers . . . Intimate episodes into the life of *Woodrow Wilson,* as told to Bob Davis by *Jesse Jones* of Houston will appear later.

By Robert H. Davis.

HOUSTON—After a lapse of 96 years there now comes to light a new chapter that has to do with the fall of the Alamo, that historic shrine at San Antonio de Bexar, where 182 Texans under command of Lieutenant Colonel Travis, besieged by 6,000 Mexican under Santa Anna, were driven to bay and massacred to the last man on the date of March 6, 1836.

"Thermopylae had its messenger of defeat, the Alamo had none," the line taken from a speech made by Col. Edward Burleson of the First Texas Volunteers under Sam Houston, sums up the tragedy. However, the details of the conflict, which has no parallel in the whole record of hand to hand engagements, still emerge from the misty past and from time to time revive the drama.

This new chapter, presented for the first time, is best told in the words of F. C. Proctor, a Texan born, who has practiced law throughout Texas for half a century. Here is his story:

"About 30 years ago," said he, "I represented the defendants in a suit brought in the Federal Court at San Antonio by the heirs of Asa Walker to recover a tract of land granted to them by the Republic of Texas, by virtue of the fact that Walker had been killed in defense of the Alamo. The defendants claimed title through a sale of this land in an administration had upon his estate. The issue was whether this administration was valid and whether there was a debt that justified the opening of an administration upon his estate and sale of property thereof to pay a debt. In a musty old file in the probate records of Washington County, Texas, there was found proof of the existence of this debt, and incidentally in the form of a letter, evidence of the most gallant declaration that my perusal of Texas history has disclosed. This proof was in the form of a letter from Asa Walker to William W. Gant. Here is the epistle in full:

"MR. GANT—I take the responsibility of taking your overcoat and gun—your gun they would have anyhow, and I might as well have it as anyone else. If I live to return I [*the line "Sam Houston and Santa Anna was" inserted here, no doubt by mistake*] leave you my clothes to do the best you can with. You can sell them for something. If you overtake me you can take your rifle and I will trust to chance. The hurry of the moment and my want of means to do better are all the excuse I have to plead for fitting out at your expense. Forgive the presumption and remember your friend at heart.

"'A. WALKER.'

"History records that Walker reached the Alamo and joined the Texans under command of Travis. Tradition has it that he was the last man killed. Clutched in his hands was the gun borrowed from his friend William Gant. The barrel was empty, a result of firing the last shot. The stock of the weapon he had used as a club. At the feet of Asa Walker, in a semicircle, lay seven dead Mexicans. Walker, upon departing for the Alamo, announced that if deprived of his arms he would fight the enemy with his fists. The mortal clay that fell under his rifle butt proves that Asa kept his promise."

Attorney Proctor left his chair, walked to an open window of his office on the twentieth floor of an office building that towers above Houston and looked out upon a peaceful and prosperous land.

"Asa Walker did not die in vain," said he. "More is the pity that his coming to Texas, as he did in 1835 from Columbia, Tenn., with his friend Gant he should have been cut down the following year. Among the papers filed in the case was a note for $37.87-$^1/_2$ for transportation from Tennessee to Texas, paid by Gant. There was also a claim of $35 for the rifle and $10 for the overcoat. The letter that I have quoted was the particular and important evidence upon which Judge T. S. Maxey, a Cleveland appointee, and the best trial judge that I ever appeared before, rendered a decision for the defendants. In reaching a conclusion Judge Maxey said that he had tried very hard to find a way to award the land to the plaintiffs, because obviously they had not had the benefit of the bounty that the republic intended for them, and that the land had been sold to pay a trifling debt; but it was nevertheless an honest debt, and that title had passed from the plaintiffs. Consequently he had no option other than to decide for the defendants. The law was clear. Gant, after the death of Walker, served in Capt. J. Valder's company at the Battle of San Jacinto, where the Mexicans were defeated by Sam Houston and Santa Ana was taken prisoner. Subsequently William Gant was elected to the House of Representatives from Washington County, from the First to Fourth Congresses, inclusive. He died in what is now known as Grimes County, October, 1840, and is buried at Navasota, in a grave suitably marked by the Texas Historical Board.

"In connection with the Walker-Gant case, it is a curious coincidence that while presenting my argument before the Federal Court justice at San Antonio I could see, past Maxey, through an open casement the very room on the second floor of the Alamo, where March 6, 1836, Asa Walker, after accounting for seven of the enemy, fell and died. I shall never forget the sensations I experienced on that occasion. An extraordinary link between the quick and the dead."

COUNSELLOR PROCTOR turned from the open window and came back to his desk. "Have you," he asked, "ever heard the stroy [sic] about a man by the name of Allen, who according to his own statement was the last man to leave the Alamo alive?"

"To whom did he make the statement?" I asked.

"To me," replied Mr. Proctor, "and in the presence of my father. I was 14 at the time—more than 50 years ago—and I am still of the conviction that what Judge Allen related to me is true. You are welcome to the facts, if interested."

"Has the story been published?" I inquired, with professional caution warm on the trail of a second Alamo chapter from the one source.

"Not to my knowledge," said he, "nor have I ever imparted the information to any one who would be likely to give it circulation in print."

"When I was a boy," said Judge Proctor, "in my fourteenth year, there came to the office of my father at that time a practicing lawyer in Cuero, Texas, a

Judge Allen, justice of the peace at Hocheim, De Witt County. That was in 1866, the thirtieth anniversary of the fall of the Alamo, with which appalling massacre many then living Texans were familiar, although specific particulars were beginning to fade into the fog of hearsay and exaggeration. Occasionally an old-timer would contribute some information and the Alamo tragedy would be reopened. Evidently Judge Allen aroused the curiosity of my father, who, calling me into the presence of his visitor, said in substance: "This gentleman will tell you a very interesting bit of Texas history, which I want you to remember all of your life. Listen attentively and mentally store away what you hear.["] The earnestness with which he spoke served to sharpen my wits. I shall not attempt to quote Justice Allen in exact terms. His narrative, told with great deliberation and addressed specifically to me, set forth the fact that on the afternoon of March 5 Lieutenant Commander Travis called for a volunteer who would leave the Alamo, proceed to Goliad, 200 miles away, and ask Colonel Fannin to hasten with his command in the aid of his countrymen. Allen told me he was selected from among the many who volunteered to make the attempt for the reason that he had a very fleet mare. After nightfall, mounted bareback, his horse wearing a bridle only, with his arms about the animal's neck, and bending low the better to conceal himself, he dashed through the Mexican lines in an endeavor to execute his mission; that after hard riding he arrived at Fannin's headquarters near Goliad about March 8, and found Fannin unable to comply with the call from the Alamo. Believing that he could get some assistance from the town of Gonzales, Allen hastened on to that point where he arrived on March 11 and learned that Anselmo Borgara, a friendly Mexican, had reported the fall of the Alamo as of March 6; that the Texans, 182 in all, had been massacred to the last man. He further reported that 521 Mexicans had been killed and as many wounded.

"In the light of that statement, the last man to leave the Alamo, and obviously the last man to see Travis' intrepid command alive, was Allen. I recall this story, told me 50 odd years ago, as though it were yesterday; also my father's declaration that Judge Allen was an entirely truthful man. I have never seen any account of this in any Texas history. I am of the conviction that Allen told the truth. That it was not recorded at the time is probably due to the turbulence then existing. Upon learning of the advance of the enemy, Gen. Sam Houston, stationed at Gonzales, set fire to the town, ordered Fannin to evacuate Goliad March 11 and to fall back to Guadalupe, Victoria. For some reason or other Fannin delayed and on March 18 found himself face to face with General Urrea; a matter of 200 Texans against 1,300 Mexicans. A fight ensued. On the 20th of March, with no hope of victory and the outlook desperate indeed, Fannin capitulated on terms that seemed mutually satisfactory. Arms delivered up by the Texans were sealed with the understanding that they would be returned upon the release of the prisoners. This appeared to be the final act in what the Texans called the 'Battle of Coleto,' but on March 27, 390 prisoners under escort of Urrea's men were marched from the fort at Goliad, taken a few leagues out of town in three separate groups and shot to death, among them Colonel Fannin, whose body was thrown into a ditch. By the direct orders of Gen. Santa Anna more than 700 Texans had been massacred during a period of 30 days. It is a curious circumstance that of this number a majority of them were seen in the flesh by Allen but a few days prior to their destruction. First the Alamo occupants to whose aid Fannin did not come. Second, Fannin's company at Goliad."

"DID you," I asked, "attempt at any time to verify the statement made by Judge Allen to you in 1866?"

"Yes," replied Mr. Proctor, "but not until I reached middle manhood did the matter seem to be important. Dec. 28, 1926, I wrote a letter to Mr. Sam C. Lackey of Cuero, Texas, in which I asked him whether or no Judge Allen left any memoranda stating his connection with the Texas Revolution. He in turn wrote Mrs. Mary L. Cunningham of Yoakum, daughter of Judge Allen, to which she replied as follows:

"Dear Mr. Lackey: Your letter of January receive in regard to Mr. Proctor's letter. I can verify every word of same as truth. I heard my father often repeat this story to his friends and his children, and would be glad to give any particulars or information if you wish to send someone to interview me, and to make affidavit as to the truth of Mr. Proctor's statement. I am sorry to say that no written notes were left by my father. Yours truth [sic], Mrs. Mary L. Cunningham, Yoakum, Texas, Jan. 6, 1927."

"It would seem to me," said Mr. Proctor, "that the story Judge Allen told me 50 years ago [actually, there are 66 years between 1866 and 1932] and repeated to his children in after years is amply substantiated by this letter from his daughter. At all events, I give it to you for what it is worth, believing in my heart that it should be incorporated in the history of Texas and given in posterity as a new chapter in the Fall of the Alamo, where the spirit of Texas is enshrined forever more."

(Copyright, 1932, Robert H. Davis.)

1.7.4.3. James L. Allen, biographical papers, 1932.

Pittman, B. N. Biographical Files, Allen, James L. CAH.

This file contains some biographical papers, mostly transcripts, sent to Dr. E. C. Barker by Allen's granddaughter, along with the cover letter that accompanied this material. The first transcript enclosed is of the Davis article, presented as document 1.7.4.2 above, followed by a transcript of the biographical sketch, document 1.7.4.1 above. The last transcript is an obituary published presumably in the *Hochheim Herald*. A copy of the original newspaper was not located. The cover letter and the obituary are presented here, along with some notes from Amelia Williams.

Hochheim, Texas
April 4, 1932
Dr. E. C. Barker
Austin, Texas

My dear Dr. Barker:

On request, I am sending you material that I have compiled on the life of my grandfather, Judge James L. Allen.

I shall send this in the three sections that I have this material at present in order that you may be able to select from this what you care to use.

First, an article in a Houston paper, which caused me to think my grandfather's record should be incorporated in the Texas History. This article was written by Robert H. Davis from a conversation with Mr. F. C. Proctor and verified by my aunt, Mrs. J. F. Cunningham.

Second, I found, since writing you, an old Texas History also containing biographical histories and genealogical records of many leading men and prominent families of South West Texas, in which I found a record of my grandfather.

Third and last, the death record taken from a home town newspaper, was written by J. F. Cunningham, a son-in-law.

My father, W. J. Allen, Hochheim, is the only living child of Judge James L. Allen. He who is now seventy-seven years of age, can verify these statements.

We shall be glad to answer any questions that we can. Thank you.

Respectfully yours
Mrs. B. N. Pittman

BNP:RCW

III.

DEATH OF JUDGE JAMES L. ALLEN—APRIL 25, 1901

The long, useful and eventful life of Judge James L. Allen, the hero of two wars, came peacefully to a close at his residence five miles west of Yoakum on April 25, 1901. Judge Allen was born January 2, 1815, in old Kentucky but his parents moving to Missouri when he was quite small he was reared and educated in the latter state until he was about 17 years of age, when he came to Texas and joined Capt. Hays' company, who, with a band of heroic men, were fighting the Indians, during which time he performed many heroic acts and had several narrow escapes. The struggle for freedom of Texas from Mexico soon afterwards becoming a vital issue he joined the Texas band and being brave, judicious and trusty he was used as a messenger, which seems to have saved him, first from the fate of the Mier prisoners, and, second, when the Alamo was surrounded, the same trusty messenger was mounted and dispatched to advise General Houston, who was then stationed near Gonzales, of their perilous condition. Dashing through the Mexican raids midst a rain of bullets, defying danger, he sped on but ere assistance could come his comrades were butchered. After the close of the Mexican war he cast his lot with the colony of old Indianola, at which place in 1848 he married Miss Frederica M. Menchan, who preceded him in 1869, by whose side he now rests. Eight children were born of this union, four of which survive him, towit [sic]: W. J., S. P., R. E. L. and Mrs. J. F. Cunningham. During his residence at Indianola he was honored by his fellowmen by the important offices of county judge, mayor and justice of the peace and during the civil war he served as assessor and collector, and owning to the depreciation of confederate money the state taxes were required to be paid in gold or silver, and as many could not get the hard money and as generosity was characteristic of the man, he exchanged with many, which afterwards proved that he was more generous to his friends than just to himself. He also served as enrolling officer and government yard master during the civil war. As has been said of him "he was intensely southern."

When the Yankee soldiers landed at Indianola and required all to take the oath of allegiance, he refused, for which he was placed under guard on Saluria island, from which place he escaped by swimming the bayou under fire of the gunboat. He again reached home and made his way into the interior, carrying out his determination to never surrender his allegiance to the southern cause. Of the many noble deeds that will ever survive in the memory of the citizens of Indianola is this: During the yellow fever scourge, when Judge Allen without fear of death or hope of reward, for many weeks gave his time, talent and strength to caring for the sick and burying the dead, during which time he lost a brother but never relaxing until it entered his own household, when he went home to nurse his then oldest daughter, the present Mrs. J. F. Cunningham. We learn that Judge Allen was an active member of the Masonic freternity [sic] at Indianola and was ever an advocate of its principle, but never affiliated after moving to this section in 1867, where he lived a quiet and unassuming life, mingling little in society but keeping well posted on the current issues of the day and ever being outspoken in what he believed to be for the best. We extend thanks to Mr. J. F. Cunningham for notes from which we have been able to give this brief sketch of our venerable neighbor.

(This article was taken from a local newspaper, April 28, 1901.)

[*With these transcripts are the following notes, clearly from Amelia Williams.*]

Appendix I, List 4B

Probable Messengers.

James L. Allen. Ione Wright (San Antonio de Bexar, 56) says that Mrs. Sam Bennett of Cuero, Texas, told her that the last messenger from the Alamo, sent out by Travis to Houston, was James L. Allen. In answer to my request for further information concerning this man, Mrs. Bennett wrote me that Mr. Peter Fagan, a first cousin of Sam Houston, and one of the first settlers of DeWitt's colony, told her that Allen carried the last message from Travis to Houston. Fagan said that he knew Allen well both prior to 1836 and afterward. The Land Office records do not show that James L. Allen ever received any land for his services in the Texan army. This fact, however, is not proof that he did not serve in the Texan army, though most of those who did were eager to get the lands due them. (Siege and Fall of the Alamo, 391)

Dear Dr. Barker:

The paragraph above represents about all that I was able to find concerning James L. Allen during my study of the Alamo problem. You notice that I put this name on the probable list of messengers in my last thesis. In the M.A. thesis I had this name on the certified list, but Mr. D—— criticised that list severely and adversely. He thought that my evidence was too meager to justify my putting James L. Allen and several others on the verified list of messengers. I decided that he was probably right about it, for my evidence was rather slim, so I put them on the probable list in my final work. It seems, however, that Allen's name should be on the certified list.

A. W. W.

1.7.4.4.   James L. Allen, dissertation, 1934.

Williams, Amelia. April, 1934. A critical study of the siege of the Alamo and of the personnel of its defenders. *Southwestern Historical Quarterly.* 37:304.

A summary of available material, from Williams's "Annotated List of Couriers from the Alamo."

Allen, James L. This man came to Texas in the late days of 1835. He, along with other newly arrived soldiers, was equipped and mounted by the firm of McKinney and Williams and sent to various commands. Young Allen was given a very fleet horse and was sent to Travis at San Antonio. As he was young and slight he was detailed on the courier squad. His biographers[24] all claim that he was one of the last, if not the last messenger, sent out by Travis. He became a settler

of Indianola, and there served as county judge, town mayor, and later as justice
of the peace, and during the Civil War he served as assessor and collector of
taxes.

---

[24] See the letter and enclosures from Mrs. B. N. Pittman to Dr. Eugene C. Barker,
April 4, 1832 [sic; 1932], University of Texas Archives. Mrs. Pittman is a grand-
daughter of James L. Allen, her father W. J. Allen, is his only living child. Also
see: *Memorial and Genealogical Record of Southwest Texas* (published by Goodspeed
Brothers, Chicago, 1894); Notice of *Judge James L. Allen's Death*, Hochheim Herald,
April 28, 1901; Ione Wright, *San Antonio de Bexar*, 56. All these sources give defi-
nite information concerning James L. Allen having been a courier from the
Alamo in 1836. [*A copy of the* Hochheim Herald *was not located.*]

1.7.5.1.   William Oury, manuscript biography, c. 1930.

Smith, Cornelius C., Sr. N.d. (c. 1930). "A History of the Oury Family." 8–12.
Cornelius C. Smith Papers, MS 738. Arizona Historical Society, Tucson.

This typed biography of an Alamo courier by his grandson was given to the
Arizona Historical Society in 1932. Another carbon of the same document was sup-
plied by another grandson, William O. Smith, to the librarian of the University of
Texas at Austin in 1930, who had a typed copy made, now in the CAH.

WILLIAM SANDERS OURY

The subject of this sketch, William Sanders Oury, without doubt, is the most
interesting of the entire Oury family. His life was one of energetic action,
thrilling and romantic. William was the oldest of a family of nine children, and
was born in Abingdon, Virginia, August 13, 1817. His father, Augustus Oury,
was a land owner and planter, whose father was George Oury. When William's
father, Augustus, pioneered to Missouri, in 1833, William, an adventurous lad,
like the famous Kit Carson, whom he later knew well, went to Texas. No doubt
the influence of his father's friend, Stephen Austin, was the loadstone [sic]
which drew him to the American colony, which was soon to be the lone star
republic.

The life of Wm. Sanders Oury as a subject for romance and literature is one
of the most interesting that can be imagined. His escape from the massacre of
the Alamo, and the drawing of a white bean as one of the Mier prisoners, are
but two of many thrilling incidents of an eventful and active career. The Society
of the Daughters of the American Revolution has recently decided that his was
the most interesting of the lives of the pioneers of Arizona, and has so reported
to its headquarters in Washington, D.C., so that this fact may be entered on its
records, since it collects and keeps such data.

He seemed truly to bear a charmed life and died peacefully at his home in
Tucson, Arizona, March 31, 1887, at the ripe age of seventy years. He was a

friend and associate of Travis, Bowie, Crockett, Kit Carson, and others well known to fame in the Southwest.

In an endeavor to get at some of the facts of Mr. Oury's life, some years ago, I wrote his sister, Mrs. Mary Anne Pettibone, of Louisiana, Pike County, Missouri, who was a great aunt of mine—I quote from her reply. "My father took his family to Missouri in 1833—and later to Texas, on the invitation of Stephen Austin, who was our neighbor and friend in Wythe County, Virginia. On arrival in Missouri brother William went to Texas. He had many adventures, and was one of the messengers of the Alamo sent out by Travis; he belonged to the Texas Rangers; was in the battles of San Jacinto and Monterey, and his commanding officer, Capt. Gillespie (Ad Gillespie, for whom Gillespie County, Texas, is named) was killed right by his side in the latter fight."

In the war between Texas and Mexico, we find him as a member of the little force commanded by the gallant and lamented Travis, the hero of the Alamo; rather the chief of that band of immortal heroes who perished there.

It will be remembered that Santa Ana marched into San Antonio, or Bexar, as it was then called, on February 23, 1836, and that Colonel Travis retired with his command to the Alamo, which, although strongly built, was originally designed for a mission, not a fortress. The walls were plain stone-work; the main one, a rectangel [sic] 190 feet by 122 feet. There were fourteen pieces of artillery—four on the side towards San Antonio, four facing the north, two on the southeast corner, and four defending the gate facing the bridge across the San Antonio river. The place was well supplied with water, but was lacking in men, provisions, and ammunition.

Santa Ana demanded a surrender without terms, and received for answer a defiant shot from the improvised fort. The Mexicans, more than 4,000, then hoisted a red flag on the church in Bexar, and began the attack. That Travis understood his perilous position is evidenced by the number of messages he sent out asking for aid. For the sake of accuracy, it is well to speak of these various messages, and, where it can be done, to give the names of the bearer or bearers.

While on the Colorado, enroute to San Antonio, Travis sent two messages asking for reenforcements. The first was to Governor Smith, on January 28, 1836, no bearer's name given; the second, also to Governor Smith, was sent January 29th, and carried by Captain Tom Jackson.

After Travis arrived at San Antonio and before he went into the Alamo he sent messengers calling for reenforcements on February 12, 13 and 16. Travis retired from his camp into the Alamo between February 16, and 23, and on the 24, and 29; and again on March 3, sent out messengers.

The message of February 13, was to Governor Smith and was carried by E. E. (Erasmus or Deaf) Smith; a second message, on the same day, to Governor Smith, was carried by a man named Williams. On February 16, Mr. Maverick carried out a dispatch. On February 24, Albert J. Martin or Juan Seguin carried

the famous "Victory or Death" message; and on March 3, John W. Smith carried
the last appeal out of the Alamo.

It is seen from the above that February 12, and 29, still remain as dates on
which dispatches were carried from San Antonio and the Alamo; and that the
names of the carriers of these two appeal[s] for help are not given in any history
or account of the fall of the Alamo, or of the days just prior to, or after that disaster.

It is believed that the foregoing is as accurate an account of the appeals sent
by Travis as can be found, and it was compiled from various historical works on
the subject; from voluminous correspondence with Miss Katherine Elliott,
Archivist of the Texas State Library; with Prof. E. W. Winkler, of the University
of Texas; and from the statement of William Oury, who says, "I know messages
were carried from Travis on the Colorado; from his camp at San Antonio; and
from the Alamo; and I was sent out with one a few days before the massacre."
There is then only this conclusion to come to: The carrier of the message of February 12, is unknown; and Wm. S. Oury carried out the one of February 29—the
words," a few days before the massacre" made this certain.

The original garrison of Bexar under Travis consisted of himself and 139
men. Early in February, he was joined by Davy Crockett, and 12 men, and on
March 1, by Capt. Albert Martin with 32 men, making a total of 186. Capt.
Albert Martin is the same who it is supposed by some historians carried the
famous "Victory or Death" message. After delivering the message, Martin,
some historians say, returned, to the Alamo with 32 men and there perished.
Other historians and writers say Seguin carried this message, so that the point
is yet a moot one. Oury would have been among the slain of the Alamo but for
the fact that he could not return to the beleaguered church, having been sent
with dispatches to Sam Houston, with whom he saw Santa Ana captured either
on the day of the fight at San Jacinto, or the day following, April 21 or 22, 1836.

In 1855, the capitol building of the state of Texas was burned to the ground,
and all actual military records lost, but I have recently been able to ascertain the
following concerning part of Mr. Oury's record from the Comptroller's Military
Service Records; and the General Land office of the State of Texas; and, in addition, some data from the War Department at Washington:

From the Comptroller's Record: Certificate No. 2332 of June 14, 1837, signed
by J. Snively, Acting Secretary of War, states, "William S. Oury, a private of Company "D." R.I., has pay due him from November 5, (1836) to May 31, 1837, and
$24.00 bounty." Certificate No. 6155 of January 1, 1838, states: "William S. Oury
a Corporal in Company "D" First Regiment of Infantry is entitled to pay,
rations, and clothing from date of his furlough May 28, 1837—J. Moncour, Captain." This service, of course, was in the army of Texas, and incomplete since
nothing is said of Mr. Oury's service prior to November 5, 1836.

From the General Land Office of Texas, we have the following: "A survey
of 640 acres was made in Polk County on August 15, 1838, by virtue of Certificate 111 issued by the Board of Land Commissioners of Harrisburg County to

William S. Oury, and field notes for this survey were filed in this office, July 7, 1854, but the certificate did not accompany the same, and in fact was never returned to us, and in consequence on account of the failure to return the certificate within the time required by law, the survey became forfeited and the land has been other wise appropriated. This is the only return in the name of William S. Oury."

Texas soldiers who fought in the war for Independence were entitled to 640 acres of land, but William S. Oury, after going to California in 1849, never returned to Texas to claim his, hence the forfeiture, as stated above.

[*The biography continues with Oury's later extensive experiences in Texas, Mexico, California, and Arizona.*]

1.7.5.2.   William Oury, dissertation, 1934.

Williams, Amelia. April 1934. A critical study of the siege of the Alamo and of the personnel of its defenders. *Southwestern Historical Quarterly.* 37:309.

Part of the analysis of Alamo couriers, with bibliographical references.

William S. Oury was sent out of the Alamo with a message to Houston on or about February 29.[41]

[41] Colonel W. O. Smith, Q.M.C., U.S. Army, San Antonio, Texas, the grandson of William Sanders Oury, has presented to the University of Texas a biography of his grandfather. This sketch delineates a very remarkable career of a very remarkable man. The most interesting part of this biography for this study is that it proves that William S. Oury was a messenger from the Alamo in 1836. See also C.M.S.R., Nos. 2332, 6155; Bounty warrant Harris III; and *San Antonio Express,* October 20, 1930.

1.7.5.3.   William Sanders Oury, published biography, 1967.

Smith, Cornelius C., Jr. 1967. *William Sanders Oury: History-Maker of the Southwest.* 19–27. Tucson: University of Arizona Press.

This is an extension of document 1.7.5.1, per the first footnote at the bottom of this document. The original source manuscript by Cornelius Smith, Sr., might be in the Carlisle Barracks Library, Pennsylvania, but I was not able to confirm its whereabouts.

William Sanders Oury went into the Alamo on February 23, to leave it as a courier one week later, just a few days before the tragic climax of events. Bill's entry into the Alamo coincided with the arrival in San Antonio of General Santa Anna and his troops. Abruptly at this point, the casual visits of the garrisoned

Texans to the village ceased, and before another day passed, frightened refugees were streaming out of San Antonio on horseback, oxcart, and on foot.

The Alamo was now a forlorn little island of resistance surrounded by the infantry, artillery, and lancers of Mexico, some 4000 strong. Long afterwards, Bill Oury would tell his grandson at Fort Lowell, Arizona: "There was no getting out now; we would fight until the last."

Memories of the Alamo

Bill Oury in later years remembered the long infantry columns of Santa Anna's army advancing upon San Antonio, the clattering artillery caissons jolting along, and the spear-tips of the lancers dancing in the sun. He remembered the cannon balls smacking into the walls, and the hard work he had done making parapets for the Alamo's own batteries. He remembered the sleepless nights, and the cold, and the ration of beef and corn. He remembered Davy Crockett and his mountain songs, and Colonel Bowie, sick in the little room by the main gate, and Colonel Travis in his dirty homespun clothing. Bill remembered the couriers leaving for Goliad, and Gonzales, and Washington, and he remembered the Mexican campfires winking brightly in the cold Texas nights. But most of all, he remembered the Alamo, the grimy, terrible, wonderful, Alamo where he lived for seven long days. He would remember it all the days of his life.

[*Two paragraphs describing the Alamo follow.*]

Bill said he didn't "think much of the place," but that it "would have to do."[1]

And so the beleaguered men started "making it do." One of the first things to do was to erect parapets along the walls for the cannon, and for the riflemen. This was done primarily on the north wall, against the palisade on the southeast side of the fort, and at key places elsewhere for the placement of the cannon. Parapets were not needed on the west side; the men could take the prone position on the rooftops there although the small lip of protection afforded to a prone rifleman was very small indeed. In the chapel, a scaffold was erected to serve as a catwalk for riflemen. Here and there baffles of cowhide and earth blocked off key doors and passage ways.

It had been reported earlier that the Alamo had twenty or more cannon. There may have been that number, but recent sources inform that only fourteen were serviceable and were used during the siege.[2] There were four four-pounders at the palisade, and two guns of undisclosed size in the lunette just outside the main gate. All of these guns pointed south, or southeast. The eighteen-pounder, heavier than anything the Mexicans had, was placed upon an earthern [sic] ramp at the juncture of the south and west walls. In the chapel, a dirt ramp had been built to a height of some twelve feet. On its top, facing north, east, and south were three twelve-pounders.

Over on the west wall, somewhat near the center, was a single twelve-pounder. The north wall had three eight-pounders.

The Alamo had fourteen guns all told; not a very convincing battery when compared with the artillery Santa Anna would bring into play. Bill remembers "dragging these guns around," and probably sweating like a horse as he helped run them up the ramps to the firing platforms.

Asked about the rifles, Bill said he thought they were "mostly percussion caps," but that there may have been "a few flintlocks there too."

Queried about the number of defenders, Bill was understandably vague, putting his answer at "something over a hundred." Actually, there were "about 150" men there at the start, though even that figure is debatable.[3] [*The narrative continues with material apparently from other sources and no quotes or observations from Oury.*]

The Siege Begins

The first day of the siege was a busy one. Jim Bowie seemed to be everywhere, directing things with a firm hand. Parapets were going up, cannon balls being stacked beside fieldpieces, stores being put away in safe places, and the livestock being led into the enclosures behind the hospital. With great good fortune, foraging parties had secured eighty bushels of corn and thirty beeves; these were now brought in and added to the stores. Out in the courtyard, some riflemen were molding bullets from whatever odd pieces of lead they could find about the place. Into the general work of preparing for siege, Bill Oury threw himself with a will. "I helped wherever I could, watering the horses, pulling the guns in place, and running little errands for Colonel Bowie."[4]

[*The narrative continues with Travis's messages.*]

On the twenty-fourth the defenders suffered a real setback. In helping to pull one of the cannon into place, Jim Bowie was badly injured. The gun-carriage toppled over upon him, crushing him to the ground. He was placed tenderly upon a rude couch and given the best care possible in the circumstances. Thereafter, he was out of active engagement until the end, all command passing over to his co-equal James [*sic*] Barrett Travis. Bill Oury did not see Bowie under the cannon, but remembered the Colonel "sick in the little room by the main gate."[5]

[*The narrative continues about further messages and their reception outside, then of digging a well inside the courtyard.*]

But things were tightening up in other ways. The Mexicans numbered in regiments outside the walls, and could cannonade by day and harass by night. The defenders, 150 strong, were forced to stay right at their posts. There was no relief for anyone. Sleep was a luxury, and might be had only in the shortest catnap on the walls. Bill spoke of this to his grandson years later saying: "we were all tired; I didn't sleep much all the time I was there."[6]

[*There is further narration of the siege and Travis's attempts to get help. Oury's story resumes on the twenty-ninth.*]

It was that night, and just a little later on, as Bill remembered it, that someone called out his name in the dark. He was hunched over his place on top of the artillery barracks, and climbed down a ladder to follow the man to Travis' room on the west wall. He remembered that it was cold, and he shivered as he walked along. Ushered into the room, he stopped before Travis, seated at a table in the far end of the room. There were no formalities. He was asked if he could ride through the lines for help; he said he "thought he could. Yes sir, I'll try."[8] And that was it. Travis told him to find General Houston, and tell him the whole story.

Bill was instructed to find General Houston "wherever he may be." Neither Travis, Oury, nor anyone else in the Alamo knew where Houston was. He had been seen last in Refugio; by now he might be anywhere in the sparsely settled countryside. Travis had a hunch that the general might be in Gonzales, and added: "You might try there first." There was some talk about sending Bill to Washington-on-the-Brazos, Goliad, or on the Refugio, some twenty miles south of Goliad. In the end, the Goliad-Refugio route was ruled out. Also, Washington was 150 miles away as the crow flies, and time was running out. Besides, Gonzales was on the way to Washington, about halfway; Bill could ride on the Brazos if he had to.

Bill went to the animal pen to select his horse. It was black-dark, and the feeble light from his lantern cast its rays but a few feet. There were only a few beasts milling around as he approached, and one looked about the same as another. Throwing a saddle on his horse and adjusting the saddle bags, he led the mount to the gate on the south wall. No one said anything to him as he left, and he eased out into the night. He decided to sneak his way slowly and quietly at first, lest he rouse some Mexican sentry or patrol. The hard riding could come later. Clearing the lunette, he wheeled his horse sharp left and walked it past Davy Crockett's palisade, the baptistry, and then headed due east for Gonzales, seventy miles away.

Young, imaginative, riding through the enemy lines at night, Bill remembered that he thought every sound in the velvety darkness announced the presence of a Mexican. His heartbeats grew louder in his ears, and even the soft clop of the horse's hooves on the ground sounded like cannon shots. Yet he saw no one and was never challenged. With the first rays of dawn he gave his horse the spurs, keeping up a gruelling [sic] pace until he dashed into the main street of Gonzales on the afternoon of March first. Bill had no way of knowing that on the same day he left the Alamo, Houston was riding out of the wilderness and into the muddy little main street of Washington,[9] where two days later he signed the Declaration of Independence and on March 4 was appointed Commander-in-Chief of the Armies of the Republic.[10] Bill may or may not have gone on to Washington but he was in Gonzales when Houston arrived there on March 11.[11] He made the long retreat with Houston's column to Buffalo Bayou, and there fought in the Battle of San Jacinto on April 21, 1836.

[An earlier footnote discusses the primary source:] Cornelius C. Smith (Sr.). "A History of the Oury Family," (unpublished manuscript in possession of the author) . . . An early version of this manuscript was given by my father to the Arizona Pio-

neers' Historical Society in 1932, and forms a part of the library of that institution. My father had added considerable information to this early draft, and was
still working on the manuscript at the time of his death in 1936. The study is
almost wholly reminiscent in character, and reflects the author's memory of the
stories related to him by his grandfather, William Sanders Oury. In those areas
where documents are available to authenticate the manuscript, I have cited them,
and in several instances reproduced them for inclusion in the Appendix. With
but a few minor exceptions all statements of fact have been verified, a factor
which attests to the general soundness of the paper. It is an important source, and
is quoted frequently in the chapters of this book.

[1] Smith, "A History of the Oury Family," *op. cit.*, p. 4.
[2] John Myers, *The Alamo,* (New York: Bantam Books, 1960), p. 124.
[3] *Ibid.,* p. 126. [*Discussion of the number of defenders.*]
[4] Smith, *op. cit.,* p. 7.
[5] *Ibid.*
[6] *Ibid.,* p. 9.
[8] Smith, *op. cit.,* p. 7.
[9] Marquis James, *The Raven.* New York: Blue Books Inc., 1929, p. 226.
[10] *Ibid.*
[11] Smith, "A History of the Oury Family," *op. cit.,* p. 12.

1.7.6.1.   Benjamin Highsmith, interview, 1897.

Sowell, A. J. 1900. *Early Settlers and Indian Fighters of Southwest Texas.* 9–10.
Austin: Ben C. Jones & Co.

After the surrender [*of General Cos in December 1835*] many of the Texans went
back home, thinking the war was over. Colonel Fannin had been sent to La
Bahia, or Goliad, before the taking of San Antonio, and was in command there.
Col. James Neill was placed in command of the Alamo until relieved by Col.
William B. Travis. Mr. Highsmith stayed in the Alamo with Colonel Travis until
the approach of Santa Anna from Mexico with a large army, and he was then
sent by his commander with a dispatch to Colonel Fannin ordering that officer
to blow up the fort at Goliad and come to him with his men. Mr. Highsmith was
gone five days, and on his return Santa Anna's advance of 600 cavalry was on
the east side of the river, riding around the Alamo and on the lookout for messengers whom they knew the Texan commander was sending from the doomed
fort.

Mr. Highsmith sat on his horse on Powderhouse Hill and took in the situation. The Mexican flag was waving from the Church of Bexar across the river,
and the flag of Travis from the Alamo. The country was open and nearly all
prairie in the valley around San Antonio, and objects could be seen some distance from the elevated points. There was a great stir and perceptible activity in
the town, and the forms of some of the doomed men at the Alamo could be
plainly seen as from the walls of the fort they watched the Mexican cavalry.

The daring messenger saw there was no chance for him to communicate with his gallant commander, and slowly rode north towards the San Antonio and Gonzales road. The Mexican cavalrymen saw him, and a dense body of them rode parallel with and closely watched him. Finally they spurred their horses into a gallop and came rapidly towards him. Highsmith took one last look towards the Alamo and the trapped heroes within, and then, turning his horse east, dashed off towards Gonzales. He is the last man alive to-day who talked with Bowie and Travis at the Alamo. The Mexicans pursued Uncle Ben six miles—two miles beyond the Salado Creek—and then gave up the chase. He went on to the Cibolo Creek, eighteen miles from San Antonio, and then halted on a ridge to rest his horse. While here his quick ear caught the sound of cannon as the dull boom was wafted across the prairie. The siege and bombardment of the Alamo had commenced. Mr. Highsmith thinks that David Crockett went into the Alamo with George Kimble, A. J. Kent, Abe Darst, Tom Jackson, Tom Mitchell, Wash Cottle, and two 16-year-old boys named Albert Fuqua and John Gaston. Crockett had a few men who came with him to Texas, and some think he did not come by Gonzales, but straight across from Bastrop to San Antonio. The men mentioned above all came from Gonzales and were led by Captain Kimble. The names are not all given here. There were thirty two of them in all. They came down the river in the night and fought their way into the Alamo by a sudden dash.

1.7.6.2.   Benjamin Highsmith, depositions, 1900.

Highsmith, Benjamin. March 1900. Depositions in the case of Malone et al. v. Moran et al. No. 3644, 43rd District Court of Parker County, Weatherford, Texas.

Information from these two depositions, taken for the referenced case, became widely available when used by McCall (1911, 14:325–56 [ref. also April 1902, 5:355]). Some spaces have been added to separate words that were run together in the original typed record.

[*First deposition*]
No. 3644.
S. C. Malone, et al. I
vs. I SUIT PENDING IN DISTRICT COURT, PARKER COUNTY,
A. O. Moran, et al. I TEXAS.
Sirs:

You will take notice that five days after service hereof we shall apply to the Clerk of the District Court to take the depositions of Ben H. Highsmith, who resides in Uvalde County, Texas, and W. F. Cleveland of Harlan, Shelby Co., Iowa, and J. S. Collins, who resides in Omaha, Douglas County, Nebraska, in answer to the accompanying interrogatories, to be read in evidence in behalf of intervenors and of defendants Wm. Osborne and J. H. Sears, on the trial of this cause.

F. C. Highsmith and G. A. McCall,

Attorneys for Intervenors and defendants Osborne and Sears,

To the Plaintiffs, or Messrs. Kimbell Bros. & Blackmon, and the defendants, or Messrs. Haney & McKenzie, and A. H. Culwell, their attorneys of record.

INTERROGATORIES TO BE PROPOUNDED TO HIGHSMITH:

1. State your name, age and place of residence?

Ans. My name is Benjamin F. Highsmith. My age, to my nearest birthday, September 11th, 1900, is 84 years. I live in Bandera County, Texas, about three miles northwest of my post-office, Utopia, Uvalde County, Texas.

2. If you state that you reside in Texas, state how long you have there resided. State when you came to Texas, and why, and state the different places if any you have lived in since the [*sic*]. State fully.

Ans. I crossed the Sabine River and came into the State of Texas on December 24th, A.D. 1823, and have resided continuously in Texas ever since I came to the State; this constitutes a residence in the State of 76 years past. I came to Texas with my father and his family, because he, with his family, moved from Missouri to Texas. I first lived at Manton's Spring, formerly known as Castleman's Spring, about three miles northwest of La Grange, Fayette County, Texas, where I lived up to 1829. In 1829, I moved to old Caney, in Matagorda County, Texas, and in the spring of 1830, I moved to Cedar Lake, in same county. Then in the fall of 1830, I moved to the town of Matagorda, in same county, where I lived until October 1833. In October, 1833, I moved to Bastrop County, Texas, and lived there until January, 1882, when I moved to Sabinal Canon, Bandera County, Texas, and have resided there up to the present time.

3. Were you or not a soldier in the war between Texas and Mexico? If yea, what command did you serve, and how long were you in the service?

Ans. I was. I joined John Alley's Company the 20th day of September, A.D. 1835, in which company I remained until after the siege of San Antonio; then after taking San Antonio by the Texan Army from the Mexican General Cos, about half of the Texan army went home, the other remaining half garrisoned "The Alamo." I remained in the Texan Army until Annexation, say from September, 1835, until May, 1845.

4. If you state in answer to preceding interrogatories that you were a soldier in the war between Texas and Mexico, state whether or not you were present at the siege of the Alamo? If yea, state in what command you were; state how long you were there; state whether you were there during the whole siege? State whether or not you left the Alamo during the siege; if so, under what circumstances, and why? State fully.

Ans. I was present at the siege of "The Alamo". I belonged to the half of Capt. John Alley's company that remained in the army, and as no officers of Alley's old company remained, we were subject to Travis' command. I remained in "The Alamo" from the fall of San Antonio to the 24th day of February, A.D. 1836. I was not present during the whole siege. On the 24th day of February, A.D. 1836, the last date above given, Travis sent me with an express to Fannin at La Bahia. I went alone.

5. If in answer to the preceding questions, you state that you left the Alamo during the siege, state whether or not you ever attempted to return to the Alamo during the siege? State what, if anything, you did in this regard? State fully.

Ans. I did attempt to return to "The Alamo" during the siege. On the first day of March, 1836, on my return, I came in sight of the city of San Antonio. I did not go in, because I could see that the Alamo was surrounded by Mexican cavalry. I then went to Gonzales to Houston's army, and joined it.

6. State whether or not you knew a man by the name of Malone at the siege of the Alamo?

A. I did know a man named Malone at the siege of the Alamo.

7. If in answer to preceding question you state that you did know such a man by the name of Malone at the siege of the Alamo, state if you recollect where you first met him? State in whose command he was? State if you know his name or initials?

Ans. I first met Malone in San Antonio. I think he belonged to Capt. Cary's company. His name was Wm. T. Malone.

8. If you state that you knew a man by the name of Malone at the siege of the Alamo, state when and where and under what circumstances you last saw him. State if you know where he was when you last saw him? State fully.

Ans. I left him in the Alamo, when I went to La Bahia with the express. I do not recall any particulars under which I last saw him. I only know that he remained in the Alamo when I was sent to La Bahia.

9. State if you know what became of the defenders of the Alamo. State fully.

Ans. They were all killed. There were no survivors.

His
(Signed)   Ben. F. X Highsmith
Mark

(Endorsed:

No. 3644. S. C. Malone, et al., vs. A. O. Moran, et al. Interrogatories to Ben H. Highsmith and W. F. Cleveland and J. S. Collins. Filed Mch. 10, 1900. Geo. Tummins, Clerk.)

[*Second deposition*]

S. C. Malone, et als.	I	No. 3644. Suit pending in the District Court
vs.	I	of Parker County, Texas.
A. O. Moran, et als.	I	

CROSS INTERROGATORIES PROPOUNDED TO THE WITNESS
BEN. H. HIGHSMITH, OF UVALDE COUNTY, TEXAS.

X.1. When and where [*were*] you born? When did you first come to Texas?

Ans. I was born in Lincoln county, Missouri, on the eleventh day of September, A.D. 1817.

X.2. If you say that you were a soldier in the war between Texas and Mexico, then state in what company you served, who was your captain? Give the names of the members of your company, or names of as many as you can, with whom you served. Give the name and address of any living person who was with you or who knows that you served in the war between Texas and Mexico.

Ans. I served in Capt. John Alley's company. Frank W.White was lst Lieutenant; D. B. Kent, Andrew J. Sowell, Sr., Wash Cottle, Ike Aldridge, R. W. Ballentyne, Henry Biggs, Richard Andrews, Winslow Turner, Richard Highsmith, John McGehee, privates, are about all I now recollect. None of my comrades at that time are to my knowledge alive.

X.3. When and where did you inlist in this war? How long did you serve? What battles did you participate in?

Ans. I enlisted in Gonzales, Texas, 20th day of September, 1835. From this date to May, 1845, I was in the Battle of Velasco, in May, 1832, the Battle of Gonzales, Oct. 2nd, 1835. The Battle of Concepcion, Oct. 28th, 1835. The Grass Fight, Nov. 15th, 1835. The Siege of San Antonio, Dec. 5th, 1835. The Battle of San Jacinto, Apr. 21st, 1836. The Battle of "The Salado", Sep. 11th, 1842. The Battle of "The Hondo", Sept. 17th, 1842.

X.4. Where you at the siege of Bexar, if so, in what company did you serve?

Ans. I was at the siege of Bexar, or the siege of San Antonio, and served in Capt. John Alley's company.

X.5. If you were at the siege of Bexar, then state where you went from there. Is it not a fact that most of the companies were disbanded immediately after the capture of Bexar, and did not nearly all of the men who engaged in that siege return to their homes after the capture of that place?

Ans. After the capture of San Antonio by the Texan Army, I went into the Alamo. About half of the Texan Army went home. I with the other half went into the Alamo, and we garrisoned it.

X.6. Did you see and know W. T. Malone at the siege of Bexar; if yea, in whose company was he then serving?

Ans. I did. To the best of my recollection he was in Carey's company.

X.7. Did you know Capt. T. L. F. Parrott? Was he at the siege of Bexar? Was Ben Milam or J. C. Neill at that siege? Did you see David Crockett at the siege of Bexar?

A. I did. He was. They were both there. Milam was killed there. David Crockett was not there. He was then in Tennessee.

X.8. If you say that you were at the siege of the Alamo, then state when you entered that place, on what day of what month of what year, and in what company, how long you remained there, and when you left, if you did leave?

Ans. We entered the Alamo on the 10th day of December, 1835. I belonged to Capt. John Ally's [*Alley's*] Company. I remained there until Feby. 24th, 1836, when I was sent with an express by Travis to Fannin at La Bahia.

X.9. Did you enter the old fort or was you only in the town? Had the Mexican army reached San Antonio when you entered the fort, or when you left there. Why did you leave the Alamo? Where did you go? Who sent you? Who went with you?

Ans. We entered the old fort. They had not reached San Antonio when I left with the express to Fannin. I left to carry an express from Travis to Fannin at La Bahia. No one went with me.

X.10. When and how did you learn of the fall of the Alamo? Where were you when you received the news?

Ans. We learned of it by Mrs. Dickerson & Travis' negro boy coming in. I was at Gonzales, Texas, with Houston's army.

X.11. If you have said that you knew a Malone serving at the siege of the Alamo, then please describe minutely his personal appearance. What was there about him that would cause you to remember him so distinctly? How did you happen to become so well acquainted with this Malone, or know him so well that you are now able to give his initials and describe his personal appearance?

Ans. That is hard to do after a lapse of so long a time. As well as I can recollect, he was a man about 5 feet 10 in. high, square-built, weighed about 160 lbs., dark eyes and dark hair. He looked to be somewhere between 20 and 25 years of age. I was with him every day, while I was there. There was nothing that I remember peculiar about his personal appearance.

X.12. Can you describe the personal appearance, or give the initials of any other person who served at the Alamo?

Ans. I can.

X.13. How many rooms on the ground floor of the Alamo? How many on the second floor? How many doors on the south side of the old fort?

Ans. I never counted the rooms. I do not know. I do not know.

X.14. Why is it that you have never contributed all the information which you possessi [*sic*] with reference to this important event to the world before now? Do you not know that the Alamo Monument Association, a chartered institution under the laws of the State of Texas, the Texas Historical Association, have for several years been making diligent effort to gather every fragment of information or facts connected with the Fall of the Alamo?; that John Henry Brown, Yoakum, Thrall, and other historians, spent years gathering information on this subject? Why have you not spoken?

Ans. I have told lots of people about it. I know nothing about these associations. I do not know what efforts these historians put forth to obtain information. I have spoken whenever I have been asked.

X.[*15.*] Do you belong to the association of Texas vetrans [*sic*]; if so, when did you join? What is your present post-office address?

Ans. I do. I joined in Houston, Texas, in 1874. My present post office address is Utopia, Uvalde County, Texas.

X.16. Are you related to F. C. Highsmith, one of the attorneys for the defendants in this case? If so, how are you related?

Ans. F. C. Highsmith and I are second cousins.

X.17. Have you received any letter from any person connected with this case with reference to your testimony; if so, from whom were said letters? Please attach same to your answers and mark same for identification, or if lost, then please state the contents as near as you can, of each letter you have received on this subject.

Ans. I have received no letters from any one in reference to my testimony in this case.

X.18. Who is present while your deposition is being taken? Who has talked with you about the matter prior to your answering these questions? What memoranda have you referred to to assist your memory; who furnished same?

Ans. No one but the notary public, who is taking the deposition and myself. A Mr. Kimball came to see me about the matter, and I had a talk with him. He said he was from Groesbeck, Limestone County, Texas. I have had no memoranda. No one has furnished me with any memoranda. I have depended alone upon my memory.

X.19. Who has read the questions to you? Has no one made any suggestions to you while your deposition are [*sic*] being taken? Have the parties present been wholly silent and made no remark or suggestion as to how you should answer these questions and in no way any assistance.

Ans. No one but the notary public taking the deposition. No one. No one has made any remarks or suggestions as to how I should answer these questions, and in no way I have I had any assistance.

X.20. Have you ever before answered interrogatories in any case where you testified about being at the siege of the Alamo, or about what you knew of that siege, if so in what case was it, where was it tried, give the style of the suit and the date of your testifying.

Ans. I have not.

X.21. Are you in any way related to, or did you know A. M. Highsmith?

Ans. A. M. Highsmith was my father. I never knew of any other A. M. Highsmith except a son of mine who is dead.

His

(Signed)   Ben F. X Highsmith

Mark

Subscribed by affixing mark, the witness being unable to write, and sworn to before me, on the day & at the place, first aforesaid, namely, at Utopia, Uvalde Co., Texas, on April 2nd, A.D. 1900.

Geo. A. Barker, N.P.,

(SEAL)   In and for Uvalde County, Texas.

Kimbell Bros. & Blackmon,
Attorneys for Plaintiffs.

Endorsed:

S. C. Malone, et als., vs. (No. 3644) A. O. Moran, et als. Cross interrogatories propounded to the witness, Ben H. Highsmith. Filed March, 15, A.D. 1900. Geo. Tummins, Clerk.

THE STATE OF TEXAS
COUNTY OF PARKER.

I, Geo. Tummins, Clerk of the District Court of Parker County, Texas, do hereby certify that the above and foregoing is a true and correct copy of the Direct and Cross Interrogatories to the witness Ben H. Highsmith, now on file in said court, in cause No. 3644.

Given under my hand and seal of said Court, at the office in the Town of Weatherford, this the 15th day of Mch. A.D. 1900.

Geo. Tummins,
Clerk Dist. Court Parker C.T.

1.7.7.   Other couriers, dissertation, 1934.

Williams, Amelia. April 1934. A critical study of the siege of the Alamo and of the personnel of its defenders. *Southwestern Historical Quarterly.* 37:304–12.

This is a synopsis of the documents on other couriers not already quoted in documents above. It is also a comparison of the extent of Amelia Williams's analysis relative to earlier research, such as Yoakum (5.1.5) and Potter (5.1.7).

a. Annotated List of Couriers from the Alamo
[*for those not already included above*]

———— *Johnson.* Dr. John Sutherland says that at the same time that he and Smith were sent to Gonzales with the note to Andrew Ponton, a young man named Johnson was dispatched to Fannin to announce the arrival of the Mexicans at Bexar and again to ask for help.[27] I have not been able to ascertain the Christian name of this man.

Smithers, Lancelot. Among the papers of the late C. H. Raguet of Marshall, Texas, there are letters which prove that Lancelot Smithers was a messanger [*sic*] from the Alamo, sent out on February 23, 1836. The first of these letters reads:

Gonzales, Feby, 24, 1836

To All the Inhabitants of Texas:

In a few words there is 2000 Mexican soldiers in Bexar, and 150 Americans in the Alamo. Sesma is at the head of them, and from the best accounts that can be obtained, they intend to show no quarter. If every man cannot turn out to a man every man in the Alamo will be murdered.

They have not more than 8 or 10 days provisions. They say they will defend it or die on the ground. Provisions, ammunition and Men, or you suffer your men to be murdered in the Fort. If you do not turn out Texas is gone. I left Bexar on the 23rd. at 4 P.M.

By Order of
W. V. [*sic*] Travis
L. Smithers[28]

Upon receipt of this message, Colonel Henry Raguet, chairman of the *Committee of Vigilance and Safety at Nacogdoches,* sent it on to Dr. Sibley who was "Chairman of the Committee of Vigilance and Safety for Texas Affairs at Nachitoches." Colonel Raguet says:

As Chairman of the Committee of Vigilance and Safety of this place, I beg to enclose to you a copy of a letter from Colonel Travis, the commanding officer of the Post at San Antonio, by which you will perceive the situation of our brave countryman and his small but patriotic band on the frontier. In addition to this astounding intelligence we have information which cannot be doubted, that Mexican troops are pouring in from all quarters, with the determination to make simultaneous attacks on various points, thereby compelling the troops of this unfortunate country to defend with a mere handful of men, those posts on the maintenance of which our existence as a people depends. Our situation, as you perceive, is truly critical; nothing, in fact, can save us but a continuance of your generous aid which has already been extended to us with a liberality unprecedented in any country and which never can be obliterated from the memory of a grateful, oppressed and struggling country people. We implore you, therefore, by every thing you hold dear—by your "happy homes and altars free"—to make one more effort on our behalf to save us from the devouring grasp of a ruthless tyrant, and to enable us to live in peace and happiness in the land of our adoption.

We earnestly beg you to give publicity to this statement to every well-wisher to our cause, to communicate the intelligence to our friends in New Orleans. I assure you that the truth of this message may be relied on. . . .

Your friend
Henry Raguet
Chairman Com. Vig. and Safety.[29]

In addition to these letters from the *Raguet Papers* there is further proof that Smithers was zealous in transmitting messages from the Alamo. It is clear that Travis's letter of February 24, the letter that Albert Martin brought out, passed through his hands, for on the back of that letter, under Martin's note, Smithers wrote:

I hope that every one will Rondives (sic) at Gonzales as soon as possible as these brave soldiers are suffering. Don't neglect them. Powder is very scarce and some should not be delayed one moment.

L. Smithers[30]

Martin, Albert. Albert Martin carried out on the night of February 24, the famous letter addressed "To the People of Texas and All Americans in the World." On the back of that letter he wrote in pencil:

Since the above was written I have heard a very heavy cannonade during the whole day. I think there must have been an attack made upon the Alamo. We were short of ammunition when I left. Hurry on all the men you can get in haste.

Albert Martin[31]

Martin sent this dispatch on to San Felipe while he scoured the country round about Gonzales for soldiers who would go to succor Travis. It is well known that he commanded the little band that entered the Alamo on March 1.

Highsmith, Benjamin F. This man was sent out on the night of February 24, with a second message to Fannin.[32]

Bonham, James Butler. James Butler Bonham was twice a messenger from Travis to Fannin. He first went out before the arrival of the Mexicans, that is on February 16, 1836.[33] He returned to the Alamo on February 23, after the arrival of the Mexicans,[34] but was sent out again on, or about February 27 (date not certain), and returned again on March 3.[35]

[*A brief discussion on Juan N. Seguín follows next based on Potter and Seguín's memoirs (1.7.2.2). It is not included as it does not add additional information to that already quoted above.*]

Antonio Cruz y Arocho [*or Arocha, in two other places*] left the Alamo with Juan N. Seguin on the night of February 29.[37]

Alexandro del la Garza was one of the nine soldiers who went to the Alamo with Travis under the immediate command of Captain Juan N. Seguin. Seguin told Potter that this man was sent out as a messenger (see note under Juan Abamillo). The records do not give the date on which Garza left the Alamo, but the inference is that he did not go with Seguin and Arocha or that fact would probably have been mentioned by Seguin, either in his *Memoirs* or in his letter to Potter.

Byrd Lockhart went form the Alamo "just before the fall," to try to hurry reinforcements and to bring in supplies for the soldiers.[38]

Andrew Sowell accompanied Byrd Lockhart.[39]

Baylor, John W. The date upon which Baylor was sent out from the Alamo is not ascertained. Mrs. Mary Austin Holley wrote a letter to her daughter on March 24, 1837 (see Mrs. Holley's MS. notes and letters, University of Texas Archives), from Mobile, Alabama. In this letter she wrote:

Mrs. Baylor's oldest son was a cadet of West Point. He joined the army of Texas and was with Travis at the Alamo, but was sent out on some service and thereby escaped the massacre at the time of its fall. He was then with Fannin's corps but was one of those who escaped the massacre; and after these perils, he died ingloriously of disease soon afterwards. His whole soul was devoted to Texas, so his sister says.

Mrs. Holley's information was not quite accurate concerning Baylor's service at Goliad, for *Memorial*, No. 37, File 5, shows R. E. Baylor, a nephew of John W. Baylor, petitioning for land due his uncle for his services in the Texan army. In his affidavit he says:

> Dr. John W. Baylor of Alabama enlisted in Captain Dimmitt's Company, Octoer [*sic*] 5, 1835. He was at the taking of Goliad, the storming of Bexar, and later participated in the battle of San Jacinto. He died a short time after this battle at his home in Cahaba, Alabama, being at the time of his death on furlough.[40]

Another fact that makes it believable that Mrs. Holley was correctly informed about Baylor's being a messenger from the Alamo is that Dimmitt and a squad of his soldiers were a part of the force at the Alamo when the Mexicans arrived. Dimmitt left with Nat Lewis soon after the arrival of the enemy at Bexar, but his soldiers remained at the Alamo and died there. So Mrs. Holley's letter is fairly conclusive information concerning this matter.

Brown, Robert. It is certain that this man either died at the Alamo or was sent out as a messenger, for on February 25, Travis, in his letter to Houston (see Chapter II of this study, 28–29), gives him especial mention for bravery in going out under the enemy's fire to set fire to jacals that were giving cover to the Mexican sharpshooters. The registers at the Land Office list but one Robert Brown in the Texan army in 1836, and his certificates—Miliam 257, 409, and I Bexar 343—show that he was a single man who came to Texas in October, 1835, and that he rendered service during the San Jacinto campaign by guarding baggage at Harrisburg. My research through other sources has not discovered any Robert Brown who died at the Alamo, so my supposition is that at some time after February 25, 1836, the Robert Brown, mentioned by Travis, was sent out as a messenger, and that he later participated in the San Jacinto campaign. No other information concerning this name has been found, but it certainly belongs on the list of verified Alamo victims, or here on this list of Alamo couriers.

b. Annotated List of Men Who Were Probably Couriers from the Alamo

Captain William Patton carried a company of soldiers to the Alamo on January 18, 1836. He left the Alamo either immediately after or immediately before the arrival of the Mexican forces. The exact date of Patton's departure from the fortress was not ascertained, but very probably he should be on the roll of messengers.

Simpson, W. K. This name appears on the Alamo monument and on many other lists of Alamo victims, but the Bounty and Donation certificates, issued to the heirs of William K. Simpson for land due him, cites service at Goliad with Fannin. On the muster rolls of Fannin's men the name is W. R. Simpson. The records at the Land Office, and the C.M.S.R., as well as other documents, show that there were several William Simpsons and one Wilson Simpson in the Texan army in 1836. Among the C.M.S.R. there was a document, unnumbered and unclassified, a requisition on the Provisional Government of Texas for $31.60 to be paid for beeves bought by Francis DeSauque to be delivered to William Simpson. Since we know beyond doubt that DeSauque left the Alamo on, or about February 22, for the purpose of gathering food supplies for the fort; and since Simpson's name appears on most all of the lists of Alamo dead, and since a man of the same name died at Goliad, the inference is that William K. Simpson left the Alamo with DeSauque, and that cut off from the Alamo, they joined Fannin at Goliad. At any rate, both these men died with Fannin and his men. DeSauque, certainly, Simpson, probably, was a messenger from the Alamo. They left the fort, however, the day before the investment began, a fact that should possibly exclude their names from the list of messengers.

De Sauque, Francis. See notes on William K. Simpson; also under Francis DeSauque, List 2d.

Henry Warnell's (Wornell) name appears on the verified roll of Alamo victims, because of the preponderance of evidence found, saying that he died at the Alamo, but Court of Claims Voucher No. 1579, File (S-Z), states that he was sent from the Alamo with a message, that he was severely wounded as he tried to make his escape, that he managed to evade the enemy and succeded [*sic*] in carrying his message on to Houston, but that he died within a few weeks from the effects of his wounds. See note under this name in the verified list of Alamo victims.

Navan, Gerald. In a letter from Green B. Jameson to General Sam Houston, January 18, 1836, Army Papers, Texas State Library we find this paragraph:

I have one other subject which interests me some; to ask of you, if it is not too late, that is to recommend to your notice Capt. G. Navan, who is clerk in my department, for the appointment of suttler of this Post as he is in every way qualified to fill the office. I know of no man who merits it more than he does, as an evidence of his patriotism he has absented himself from his family when he was also receiving a salary of 1800$ per annum to aid us in our difficulties.

I did not discover whether or not Gerald Navan received the appointment as suttler of the post, but his name is on the return that Neill made to the Provisional Government when he left the Alamo on February 14, 1836. On that list this man is designated as "engineer of dept." The editors of the *Telegraph and*

Texas Register, in the issue of March 24, 1836, state that John W. Smith and Mr. Navan had helped to compile the list of Alamo victims that was published in that issue.

Bastian, Samuel G. Johns Henry Brown, *Indian Wars and Pioneers of Southwest Texas,* 137–38, tells of one Samuel G. Bastian who published his reminiscences in a Philadelphia newspaper in 1891. In these reminiscences Bastian [*sic*] claimed that he was one of the couriers sent from the Alamo on February 23, with a message to Gonzales. Brown denounces Bastian's account as "notoriously false," and one is inclined to think that Brown may be right, for Travis would hardly have sent Bastian to Gonzales on the same day that Sutherland and Smith were sent there. Moreover, no evidence can be found at the Land Office, or in other official documents that have been examined during the work of this study, which show that any man by the name of *Bastian* was in the Texas army in 1836. This is not proof, however, that the statement in his reminiscences that he was a courier from the Alamo is not true, so I include his name in this list of probable messengers. I do not think the evidence is conclusive enough to place it on the list of messengers that I consider verified.

---

27 "John Sutherland's Account of the Fall of the Alamo," *Dallas News,* February 5, 1911. Also *John S. Ford's Journal* (MS.), Library of the University of Texas.

28 I am indebted to Mrs. C. H. Raguet for the privilege of quoting these letters, which are among the papers of the late C. H. Raguet of Marshall, Texas.

Colonel Henry Raguet, the grandfather of Mr. C. H. Raguet, was chairman of the "Committee of Vigilance and Safety" at Nacogdoches in 1836. The letter bearing Smither's signature is marked "copy of a letter from Gonzales, February 24, 1836, by order of W. B. Travis, calling for aid to the Alamo." And below this is, "Nacogdoches No. 2." Evidently Andrew Ponton sent this and other messages from the Alamo to as many places as possible.

29 It appears that this letter was the first draft of the one that was really sent to Dr. Sibley, for several sentences in this one are marked out. They refer to letters from "Col. Fannin published in the newspapers of this place."

30 Travis's letter of February 24, 1836, is in the archives of the Texas State Library. The notes—in pencil—on this letter seem to show that Albert Martin gave it to Smithers to carry on, probably to San Felipe, but that Smithers, in turn, gave it to some one else.

31 *Ibid.* [*Travis's letter of February 24, 1836, is in the archives of the Texas State Library.*]

32 G. A. McCall, "William T. Malone," *Texas Historical Quarterly,* XIV, 326.

33 See Travis's letter of March 3, Army Papers, Texas State Library. (See Chapter II, 22–24.)

34 "John Sutherland's Account of the Fall of the Alamo," *Dallas News,* February 5, 1911. Also *John S. Ford's Journal* (MS.), Archives of the University of Texas.

35 D. G. Wooten (ed.), *Comprehensive History of Texas,* I, 645. This reference is to Seth Sheppard's account of the fall of the Alamo. He says that Bonham was sent out to Goliad and returned by way of Gonzales, and he makes it clear that this trip was after the siege of the fortress was in progress.

37 *Ibid.* [*R. M. Potter, "The Fall of the Alamo," 9. Reprint from the* American Historical Magazine, January, 1878.]

38 A. J. Sowell, *Rangers and Pioneers of Texas,* 136, 143, tells that Byrd Lockhart and Andrew Sowell were sent out by Travis "just before the fall of the fortress" to get supplies.

[39] *Ibid.* A. J. Sowell furthermore states that Andrew Sowell left the Alamo so short a time before the fall that all his friends thought that he was a victim of the massacre, and this became so generally believed that his name was placed on the first Alamo monument.

[40] See also Harriet Smither (ed.), *Journal of the Fourth Congress,* I, p. 270.

Commentary

Other Couriers (1.7.3–1.7.7)

The significance of the surviving Alamo couriers lies not only in their actual participation in the events of the siege, but also in that they are the only other possible sources, besides the surviving women and children, regarding the activities inside the Alamo. Unfortunately, only John Sutherland and Juan Seguín are known to have written firsthand accounts of their experiences. One can always hope additional material may show up from the others, such as in a letter in private hands or a newspaper report. Consequently, more biographical information is given for these individuals than is typical in this selection of documents on the chance that this might lead to further discoveries.

Little direct information is given of John W. Smith's experiences except as incorporated in John Sutherland's account (1.7.1.1). The lack of a thorough interview with one of the most involved individuals on the Texan side of the Alamo is regrettable. The Zuber paper (1.7.3.1), however, adds information about the region between San Antonio and Washington-on-the-Brazos that is of significance in understanding the couriers' experiences and challenges. The real reason Zuber wrote the article is to link Smith to the Louis Rose story, which is reviewed in the next section. The excerpts from Williams (1.7.3.2) and Turner (1.7.3.3) on Smith's participation are taken from modern studies.[1]

The late recognition of the role of James L. Allen (1.7.4.2) as the last messenger from the Alamo is surprising. Later in life he was well known in his Texas community, yet his story did not reach a wider audience until the twentieth century. Despite the absence of a detailed interview or narration of his experiences, independent evidence exists to corroborate this story.[2] The fact that Allen was inside the Alamo for twelve of the thirteen days of the siege makes this a special case where one hopes a letter or report will surface, perhaps inside or on the back page of a rare nineteenth-century newspaper, such as one from Indianola.

The Davis article in the *Star-Telegram* has some specific points worth noting. One is the historical curiosity that U.S. half-cent coins existed at that time (and up to the 1850s). A more directly relevant item is the Walker story, which is not documented as to the source ("history records" is not a useful citation) and rather sounds like a "for dramatic effect" revision and embellishment of Dickinson's story of Warner. The comment that Allen heard of the fall of the Alamo through Anselmo Bergara relates to the possible significance of sources in the vicinity (reviewed in 3.4). The Allen biography (1.7.4.1) and obituary (1.7.4.3) have some variations in details, but they are not seriously inconsistent with each other or the Davis article. It does seem strange and is disappointing, however, that the Davis article is the only one that notes Allen's late— i.e., the last—departure from the Alamo.

The Oury material is striking in how late some original material can show up, based on recollections by a grandson of his grandfather's stories. The manuscripts by Cornelius C. Smith, Sr., now in archives, are disappointing in the lack of narrative details. At the time of writing, however, Smith was more interested in facts of general family history than in anecdotes of specific events. A non-Alamo example of this in another section of this manuscript is that Smith (c. 1930, 92) described his own army career in terms of rather routine positions he held, such as quartermaster, then mentioned without elaboration that he was awarded the Medal of Honor for valor.[3] As for the basic Alamo story, it is not clear which message Oury would have taken. The only message known to Houston (1.1.5) was that of February 25, whereas February 29 is the better-documented date that Seguín was sent out. The February 25 letter would have been unknown if the *Arkansas Gazette* had not printed it right away, and thus the lack of evidence for another letter carried by someone else does not mean one did not exist. Travis might have sent out other couriers besides Seguín on the twenty-ninth (though it seems unlikely), or Oury may have been off by a day or two in his recollection and carried the February 25 letter.

The account by Cornelius C. Smith, Jr., contains a number of details of the defenders' immediate experiences. For example, it shows how hard the men had to work in building or repairing Cós's parapets for the cannon and rifle men and running errands. The lack of sleep left a strong impression as well. Other accounts (e.g., Sutherland, 1.7.1.1/pp. 35 & 42, and *Telegraph and Texas Register,* 4.1.1) also noted the hard work being done by the defenders during the siege. Some of the narrative details not specific to Oury in this book, such as David Cloud as sentinel or Bowie's injury from a cannon, were probably extracted from Lon Tinkle's book.[4]

The case of Benjamin Highsmith as an Alamo courier demonstrates how it can be surprisingly difficult to get a clear answer to a simple question. That he was a courier for Travis is accepted, but it is unclear whether he was a pre-siege courier or left during the siege. Historians, such as Williams (1.7.7) and Groneman, have come to opposite conclusions.[5] Their sources apparently go back to the two reproduced here. The Sowell account (1.7.6.1), on careful reading, is ambiguous. It sounds like Highsmith left before the siege and arrived back at the same time the siege started, but all that is really said was that Santa Anna's cavalry was patrolling the east (Alamo) side of the river; it could have been some days after the start of the siege (February 23) as well. One expects much more precise answers in legal depositions (1.7.6.2), and the answers to questions 4 and 5 on the first deposition seem clear: Highsmith was present at the siege and left February 24. But then, to question 9 of the second deposition, the answer given was that the Mexican Army had *not* reached San Antonio when Highsmith left. Highsmith either had both the date and the intent of the questions wrong in the first deposition or should not have had the word "not" in the answer to question 9 in the second deposition. Without additional evidence independent of these two sources, it seems a judgment call as to what was intended. My guess is that the first deposition has the most weight, and therefore he claimed to be a courier during the siege. It is also unclear how a deposition can be notarized on April 2, but apparently be certified by the county clerk on March 15 of the same year.

The timing of Highsmith's arrival back in Bexar is also linked to the movements of James Bonham, and this is addressed further in the documents and commentary relating to John Henry Brown (5.1.8). But with additional reasons given there, the circumstances and date of Highsmith's arrival at Bexar still remain unclear.

Another reputed courier, Nathaniel C. Lewis, was reported as having slipped into the Alamo with supplies and is said to have "probably" been the last to leave before the fall.[6] However, both Sutherland and Menchaca (1.7.1.1, p. 32 of Ford version; 3.2.1) had him heading out of town on foot when the Mexican Army arrived, and therefore the report is highly unlikely. They are indirectly supported by a letter of Reuben Potter to William Steele of July 29, 1876, that says, "Mr. Nat Lewis of San Antonio once told me of a member of the garrison, an Irish Captain, named Ward, who he said was the only officer he saw at his proper post, and perfectly collected, when the first alarm of the enemy's approach was given; for Mr. Lewis happened to visit the fort that morning."[7] Possibly the error was due to a misreading of Lewis for Alamo defender James L. Ewing in an earlier work.[8]

The Williams summary (1.7.7) of the remaining "satisfactorily documented" or possible couriers completes the list of the possible direct participants for whom there are basically no known narratives of their experiences. If the list is even close to accurate, one must be struck by the number of times Travis sent for help, especially to Fannin and as commented by Ehrenberg (4.3.9).[9] The Smithers study included as a part of this document also gives information on how Travis's calls for help were received. Smithers brings in a bit of later tragedy as well, as he was killed in the Mexican War and Juan Seguín was falsely accused as being responsible.[10]

---

1. Biographical details on John W. Smith, by his grandson John B. Barnhart, are in the *San Antonio Express* for October 28 and November 11, 1906. Documents relating to his service as military store keeper in Bexar are in the Republic of Texas/Audited Claims (4.5.26, below) and R:091 Fr: 0009-0019.
2. Including indirect support noted below in the commentary to 4.3.5.1, also discussed in Lord 1968, 23. There was also a public debt claim in the Republic Claims, PD–Allen, James R:149: Fr:0535-0537, that was paid for service in 1836, but no information is given on what the service was or whether the claimant was this James L Allen.
3. Smith, Sr., 92.
4. Smith, Jr., 1967, 23; and Tinkle 1958, 9, n. 58, 158.
5. Groneman 1990, 61.
6. Webb 1952, 2:53; see also note in *SWHQ* 98:189–90, n. 17.
7. Adjutant General (RG-401), General Correspondence, TSLA.
8. Chabot 1937, 328.
9. Also Williams in *SWHQ* 37:164, n. 10
10. Teja 1991, 99.

1.8.1.1.   Louis (Moses) Rose, published account, 1873.

Zuber, William P., and Mary Ann Zuber. 1873. An escape from the Alamo. *Texas Almanac:* 80–85.

This was the original publication of the most famous story of the Alamo.

AN ESCAPE FROM THE ALAMO.
PRAIRIE PLAINS, GRIMES COUNTY, TEXAS, May 7th, 1871.

Editor Texas Almanac:

I regard the following account worthy of preservation, as it embraces a report of the last scene in the Alamo that has ever been made known to the survivors of those who fell in that fortress.

Moses Rose, a native of France, was an early immigrant to Texas, and resided in Nacogdoches, where my father, Mr. Abraham Zuber, made his acquaintance in 1827. I believe that he never married. My father regarded and treated him as a friend, and I have often heard him say that he believed Rose to be a man of strict veracity. In 1830, I saw him several times at my father's residence, in what is now San Augustine county. He was then about forty-five years old, and spoke very broken English.

Rose was a warm friend of Col. James Bowie, and accompanied or followed him to the Alamo in the fall of 1835, and continued with him till within three days of the fall of the fort.

During the last five days and nights of his stay, the enemy bombarded the fort almost incessantly, and several times advanced to the wall, and the men within were so constantly engaged that they ate and slept only at short intervals, while one body of the enemy was retiring to be relieved by another, yet they had not sustained a single loss.

The following is the substance of Rose's account of his escape and the circumstances connected therewith, as he related them to my parents, and they related them to me:

About two hours before sunset, on the third day of March, 1836, the bombardment suddenly ceased, and the enemy withdrew an unusual distance. Taking advantage of that opportunity, Col. Travis paraded all of his effective men in a single file; and, taking his position in front of the centre, he stood for some moments, apparently speechless from emotion. Then, nerving himself for the occasion, he addressed them substantially as follows:

MY BRAVE COMPANIONS—Stern necessity compels me to employ the few moments afforded by this probably brief cessation of conflict in making known to you the most interesting, yet the most solemn, melancholy, and unwelcome fact that perishing humanity can realize. But how shall I find the language to prepare you for its reception? I cannot do so. All that I can say to this purpose is, be prepared for the worst. I must come to the point. Our fate is sealed. Within a very few days—perhaps a very few hours—we must all be in eternity. This is our destiny, and we cannot avoid it. This is our *certain* doom.

I have deceived you long by the promise of help. But I crave your pardon, hoping that after hearing my explanation, you will not only regard my conduct as pardonable, but heartily sympathize with me in my extreme necessity. In deceiving you, I also deceived myself, having been first decieved [*sic*] by others.

I have continually received the strongest assurances of help from home. Every letter from the Council and every one that I have seen from individuals at home, has teemed with assurances that our people were ready, willing, and anxious to come to our relief; and that within a very short time we might confidently expect recruits enough to repel any force that would be brought against us. These assurances I received as facts. They inspired me with the greatest confidence that our little band would be made the nucleus of an army of sufficient magnitude to repel our foes, and to enforce peace on our own terms. In the honest and simple confidence of my heart, I have transmitted to you these promises of help, and my confident hopes of success.—But the promised help has not come, and our hopes are not to be realized.

I have evidently confided too much in the promises of our friends. But let us not be in haste to censure them. The enemy have invaded our territory much earlier than we anticipated; and their present approach is a matter of surprise. Our friends were evidently not informed of our perilous condition in time to save us. Doubtless they would have been here by the time they expected any considerable force of the enemy. When they find a Mexican army in their midst, I hope they will show themselves true to their cause.

My calls on Col. Fannin remain unanswered, and my messengers have not returned. The probabilities are that his whole command has fallen into the hands of the enemy, or been cut to pieces, and that our couriers have been cut off.

I trust that I have now explained my conduct to your satisfaction, and that you do not censure me for my course.

I must again refer to the assurances of help from home. *They are what deceived me, and they caused me to deceive you.* Relaying upon these assurances, I determined to remain within these walls until the promised help should arrive, stoutly resisting all assaults from without. Upon the same reliance, I retained you here, regarding the increasing force of our assailants with contempt, till they outnumbered us more than twenty to one, and escape became impossible. For the same reason, I scorned their demand of a surrender at discretion, and defied their threat to put every one of us to the sword, if the fort should be taken by storm.

I must now speak of our present situation. Here we are, surrounded by an army that could almost eat us for a breakfast, from whose arms our lives are, for the present, protected by these stone walls. We have no hope of help, for no force that we could ever reasonably have expected, could cut its way through the strong ranks of these Mexicans. We dare not surrender; for, should we do so, that black flag, now waving in our sight, as well as the merciless character of our enemies, admonishes us of what would be our doom. We cannot cut our way out through the enemy's ranks; for, in attempting that, we should all be slain in less than ten minutes. Nothing remains then, but to stay within this fort, and fight to the last moment. In this case, we must, sooner or later, all be slain; for I am sure that Santa Anna is determined to storm the fort and take it, even at the greatest cost of the lives of his own men.

Then we must die! Our speedy dissolution is a fixed and inevitable fact.— Our business is, not to make a fruitless effort to save our lives, but to choose the manner of our death. But three modes are presented to us. Let us choose that by which we may best serve our country. Shall we surrender, and be deliberately shot, without taking the life of a single enemy? Shall we try to cut our way out through the Mexican ranks, and be butchered before we can kill twenty of our adversaries? I am opposed to either method; for, in either case, we could but lose our lives, without benefiting our friends at home—our fathers and mothers, our brothers and sisters, our wives and little ones. The Mexican army is strong enough to march through the country, and exterminate its inhabitants, and our countrymen are not able to oppose them in open field. My choice, then, is to remain in this fort, to resist every assault, and to sell our lives as dearly as possible.

Then let us band together as brothers, and vow to die together. Let us resolve to withstand our adversaries to the last; and, at each advance, to kill as many of them as possible. And when, at last, they shall storm our fortress, let us kill them as they come! kill them as they scale our wall! kill them as they leap within! kill them as they raise their weapons, and as they use them! kill them as they kill our companions! and continue to kill them as long as one of us shall remain alive!

By this policy, I trust that we shall so weaken our enemies that our countrymen at home can meet them on fair terms, cut them up, expel them from the country, and thus establish their own independence, and secure prosperity and happiness to our families and our country. And, *be assured,* our memory will be gratefully cherished by posterity, till all history shall be erased, and all noble deeds shall be forgotten.

But I leave every man to his own choice. Should any man prefer to surrender, and be tied and shot; or to attempt an escape through the Mexican ranks, and be killed before he can run a hundred yards, he is at liberty to do so.

My own choice is to stay in this fort, and die for my country, fighting as long as breath shall remain in my body. *This will I do, even if you leave me alone.* Do as you think best—but no man can die with me without affording me comfort in the moment of death.

Col. Travis drew his sword, and with its point traced a line upon the ground, extending from the right to the left of the file. Then, resuming his position in front of the centre, he said, "I now want every man who is determined to stay here and die with me to come across this line. Who will be first? March!"

The first respondent was Tapley Holland, who leaped the line at a bound, exclaiming, "I am ready to die for my country!" His example was instantly followed by every man in the file, with the exception of Rose. Manifest enthusiasm was universal and tremendous. Every sick man that could walk arose from his bunk and tottered across the line. Col. Bowie, who could not leave his bed, said, "Boys, I am not able to come to you, but I wish some of you would be so kind as to remove my cot over there." Four men instantly ran to the cot, and, each lifting a corner, carried it across the line. Then every sick man that could not walk made the same request, and had his bunk removed in like manner.

Rose, too, was deeply affected, but differently from his companions. He stood till every man but himself had crossed the line. A consciousness of the real situation overpowered him. He sank upon the ground, covered his face, and yielded to his own reflections. For a time he was unconscious of what was transpiring around him. A bright idea came to his relief; he spoke the Mexican dialect very fluently, and could he once get safely out of the fort he might easily pass for a Mexican and effect an escape. Thus encouraged, he suddenly aroused as if from sleep. He looked over the area of the fort; every sick man's berth was at its wonted place; every effective soldier was at his post, as if awaiting orders; he felt as if dreaming.

He directed a searching glance at the cot of Col. Bowie. There lay his gallant friend. Col. David Crockett was leaning over the cot, conversing with its occupant in an undertone. After a few seconds Bowie looked at Rose and said, "You seem not to be willing to die with us, Rose." "No," said Rose, "I am not prepared to die, and shall not do so if I can avoid it." Then Crockett also looked at him, and said, "You may as well conclude to die with us, old man, for escape is impossible."

Rose made no reply, but looked up at the top of the wall. "I have often done worse than to climb that wall," thought he. Suiting the action to the thought he sprang up, seized his wallet of unwashed clothes, and ascended the wall. Standing on its top, he looked down within to take a last view of his dying friends. They were all now in motion, but what they were doing he heeded not. Overpowered by his feelings he looked away and saw them no more.

Looking down without, he was amazed at the scene of death that met his gaze. From the wall to a considerable distance beyond the ground was literally covered with slaughtered Mexicans and pools of blood.

He viewed this horrid scene but a moment. He threw down his wallet and leaped after it; he alighted on his feet, but the momentum of the spring threw him sprawling on his stomach in a puddle of blood. After several seconds he recovered his breath, he arose and took up his wallet; it had fallen open and several garments had rolled out upon the blood. He hurriedly thrust them back, without trying to cleanse them of the coagulated blood which adhered to them. Then, throwing the wallet across his shoulders he walked rapidly away.

He took the road which led down the river around a bend to the ford, and through the town by the church. He waded the river at the ford and passed through the town. He saw no person in town, but the doors were all closed, and San Antonio appeared as a deserted city.

After passing through town he turned down the river. A stillness as of death prevailed. When he had gone about a quarter of a mile below the town his ears were saluted by the thunder of the bombardment, which was then renewed. That thunder continued to remind him that his friends were true to their cause, by a continual roar, with but slight intervals, until a little before sunrise on the morning of the sixth, when it ceased and he heard it no more.

At twilight he recrossed the river on a footlog about three miles below the town. He then directed his course eastwardly towards the Guadalupe river, carefully bearing to the right to avoid the Gonzales road.

On the night of the third he traveled all night, but made but little progress as his way was interrupted by large tracts of cactus or prickly pear which constantly gored him with thorns and forced him out of his course. On the morning of the fourth he was in a wretched plight for traveling, for his legs were full of thorns and very sore. The thorns were very painful, and continued to work deeper in the flesh till they produced chronic sores, which are supposed to have terminated his life.

Profiting by experience, he traveled no more at night, but on the two evenings following he made his bed on the soft mesquit [sic] grass. On the sixth of March he crossed the Guadalupe by rolling a seasoned log into the water and paddling across with his hands. He afterwards crossed the Colorado in the same manner.

He continued his journey toilsomely, tediously and painfully for several weeks, in which time he encountered many hardships and dangers which from want of space can not be inserted here. He finally arrived at the residence of my father on Lake Creek, in what is now Grimes county.

My parents had seen, in the Telegraph and Texas Register, a partial list of those who had fallen at the Alamo, and in it had observed the name of Rose. Having not heard of his escape they had no doubt that he had died with his companions. On his arrival my father recognized him instantly, and exclaimed, "My God! Rose, is this you, or is it your ghost?" "This is Rose, and not a ghost," was the reply.

My mother caused her washing servant to open Rose's wallet, in her own presence, and found some of the garments glued together with the blood in which they had fallen when thrown from the Alamo.

My parents also examined his legs and by the use of forceps extracted an incredible number of cactus thorns, some of them an inch and a half in length, each of which drew out a lump of flesh and was followed by a stream of blood. Salve was applied to his sores and they soon began to heal.

Rose remained at my father's between two and three weeks, during which time his sores improved rapidly, and he hoped soon to be well. He then left for home. We had reliable information of him but once after his departure. He had arrived at his home in Nacogdoches, but traveling on foot had caused his legs to inflame anew, and his sores had grown so much worse that his friends thought that he could not live many months. That was the last that we heard of him.

During his stay at my father's Rose related to my parents an account of what transpired in the Alamo before he left it, of his escape, and of what befell him afterwards, and at their request he rehearsed it several times. Most of the minutia here recorded were elicited by particular inquiries. In the following June I returned home from the Texas army, and my parents several times rehearsed the whole account to me. At the request of several persons I have here honestly endeavored to make a faithful record of the same.

Before doing so I refreshed my memory with repeated conversations with my only living parent, Mrs. Mary Ann Zuber, now in her seventy-eighth year, and since the first writing I have read this account to her, and corrected it according to her suggestions.

Of course, it is not pretended that Col. Travis' speech is reported literally, but the ideas are precisely those he advanced, and most of the language is also nearly the same.

Hoping that this letter may meet your approval and be interesting to your readers, I am, gentlemen, most respectfully, your humble correspondent.

W. P. ZUBER

PRAIRIE PLAINS, GRIMES COUNTY, TEXAS, May 9, 1871. I have carefully examined the foregoing letter of my son, William P. Zuber, and feel that I can endorse it with the greatest propriety. The arrival of Moses Rose at our residence, his condition when he came, what transpired during his stay, and the tidings that we afterwards heard of him, are all correctly stated. The part which purports to be Rose's statement of what he saw and heard in the Alamo, of his escape, and of what befell him afterwards is precisely the substance of what Rose stated to my husband and myself.

MARY ANN ZUBER.

1.8.1.2. William Zuber, letter, 1877.

Zuber, William P., to Gen. William Steele. September 14, 1877. Adjutant General (RG-401), General Correspondence, TSLA. There is a transcript in Adjutant General (RG-401), Strays—Alamo Dead and Monument as well.

Zuber was sensitive to criticism of his famous story of Travis's last speech and the line in the dust, and he wrote five responses describing the process of writing the original account to the 1873 *Texas Almanac*. Three have been published (1.8.1.4, 1.8.1.5, 1.8.1.6), but apparently the next two documents transcribed here (1.8.1.2, 1.8.1.3) have not. They are of special interest in that they show the extent to which he went to reconstruct the story of his parents, and were written earlier than the published accounts.

Iola, Grimes County, Texas; September 14th, 1877.
General William Steele:
Dear Sir:
Your favor of the 29th of August came to hand a few days ago; & I take great pleasure in complying with your request, to the best of my ability.

I believe that I shall be able to assist you in making a few, (though *very few,*) corrections to the published lists of the martyrs of the Alamo: but I must defer this task to a future letter; as this will necessesarily [*sic*] be too long without it.

I must confine this letter to Rose, who escaped from the Alamo. In 1871, I wrote a tolerably lengthy account of the escape of Rose, & of his travels from the Alamo to the residence of my father, in what is now Grimes County. To this account, I supplied quite a number of notes of explanation; showing, as I belived [*sic*], that some parts of the narrative, which, at first view might appear incredible, were, in reality, very reasonable statements. Said account was designed for publication in the Texas Almanac: but, judging it too lengthy for an insertion in that periodical, I withheld it; & yet have the manuscript in possession. I hower [*however*] prepared a condensed copy thereof, without notes; which, with my mother's certificate, was published in the Texas Almanac for 1873. That copey [*sic*], I believe, contains all the important information which I am able to give on the subject: & I therefore respectfully refer you to it.

But, to clear away some apparent doubts which seem to have arisen, I deem it proper to furnish you with some additional particulars.

But, in the first place, please permit me to digress a little. On the night of the 13th of March, 1836, Captain, (afterwards Lieutenant Colonel,) Joseph L Bennett, with his company, (afterwards Captain Gillaspie's [*sic*] Company,) encamped on the east bank of the Colorado river; very near the site of the present town of LaGrange. I was a private in said company, kept a diary, & witnessed & noted what I am now about to state.

On that night, about nine oclock, Colonel J C Neil rode into camp, &, in a conversation with Captain Bennett, confirmed the rumor which we had heard, that the Alamo had fallen. He had borne an express from Colonel Travis to San Felepe [*sic*] or Washington, & was returning; when, on the 7th of March, I believe, at the ford of the Cibolo, between Gunzales [*sic*] & San Antonio, he met Mrs Dickerson & her infant, & Colonel Travis's servant, Joe. They, then & there, informed him of the slaughter of his brave companions in arms. They stated to him, that they had, three days prior to the final assault, been sent for safety, into the city, & placed under the care of the priest; who prepared a place for Mrs Dickerson & her babe, in the upper part of the church; probably the cupola or belfry; where he concealed them in safety, till the fort had fallen, & the fighting had ceased. Of course, Colonel Neil returned with Mrs Dickerson, to the Colorado. He first went to Bastrop, to inform the citizens of the great calamity, & was proceeding down the river, for the same purpose.

I have made the foregoing digression, to explain my reasons for holding that Mrs Dickerson may be mistaken in the time of Rose's escape. As to General Almonte's remark, that Rose was killed, & Mrs Dickerson could see his body, if she wished, I presume he would have made the same remark of any other man in the Alamo. I think his meaning was equivalent to this. "Every man in the Alamo has been killed. Not one has escaped. You can see the bodies of all; or of any one of them, if you wish."

But I must return.

Moses Rose, in 1836, was, as I suppose, about fifty years old. He went to the Alamo in company with Colonel James Bowie, to whom he was a devoted friend. He escaped, according to my information, on the afternoon or evening of the third day of March, 1836. He was a citizen of the town of Nacogdoches.

On his way home, from the Alamo, the first place on which he found the inhabitants at home, was the residence of a Mr Leaky [or Laky, *uncertain loop in the "L"*], in Washington County. His legs were full of cactus thorns, & very sore; & he was greatly worn by traveling on foot. He asked, & obtained, of Mr Leaky, permission to remain & rest for a while. He related, to Mr Leaky & family, the particulars of what he last saw in the Alamo, & of his escape; in which they seemed to take great interest. He remained there two days; enjoying the hospitalities of house-room & board; & sleeping on his own blanket.

On the second evening, two men, whom Rose had never seen or heard of before, & who seemed to be utter strangers to the family, came to Mr Leaky's, & spent the night. Mr Leaky entertained them, with an account of Rose's adventures; in which they seemed to take great interest. On the next morning, on their departure, they asked Mr Leaky to walk with them. He went, & remained out about an hour; during which time, they told him that they were from Nacogdoches; that they knew that old Frenchman Rose, well; that it had not been more than ten days since he had left Nacogdoches; that he had never seen the Alamo; that he was an old lying impostor, who made his living by traveling, & telling big lies, to excite sympathy: & advised Mr Leaky to ship him immediately. So saying, they mounted their horses, & rode away.

The object of those men, of course, is not known: but I conjecture that they were destitute of principle, & paid this slander to Mr Leaky, as a substitute for coin, in settling their bill of fare.

Mr Leaky walked into the house, related to Rose what the men had told him, said that he believed them, & ordered him to leave his house, without delay. Rose took up his wallet, & departed, without making any reply, & persued [*sic*] his journey.

This piece of bitter experience determined Rose never again to tell any person that he had escaped from the Alamo. He traveled, painfully & tediously, from Mr Leaky's to the Brazos. While so doing, he was over-taken & passed by several squads of deserters from the Texas army. One of the first men who thus passed him, told him of an imposter, by name of Rose, who pretended to have escaped from the Alamo; who had been imposing himself on Mr Leaky; but who had just been detected, & driven away. Before reaching the Brazos, he heard the same story repeated half a dozen times. But he was very careful not to tell any person that he was the man, that he had been to the Alamo, or that his name was Rose.

He arrived at my father's residence, in what is now Grimes County, in a condition which satisfied all who saw him, beyond a doubt, that his statement was true. He was then with his friends, who knew him well, & would not doubt his word. He knew this well; & told his story repeatedly, to our family & friends, without reserve; but always said that he never expected to tell it after leaving that place. My father had become acquainted with him, at Nacogdoches, 1827, & knew him well. The whole family had also become acquainted with him, in what is now San Augustine County, in 1830. My father vouched for him, as an honest, truthful man.

During his stay at my father's, I was in the Texas army, (though not quite sixteen years old,) & did not see him.

He remained at my father's about two weeks; & left for Nacogdoches. After that, we never heard of him but once. That was shortly after his arrival at home. He was then in wretched health, & was not expected to live long.

Unfortunately, most of the persons who saw Rose at my father's, in 1836, are now dead. I can not say that more than two such persons now live. One of these is my dear old mother, now eighty four years old: & the other is my sister, Mrs. Mary A D Edwards, wife of Dr J R Edwards, who was then but ten years old. They both live in one house: that of my brother-in-law, Dr. Edwards, in Roan's Prairie, Grimes County. I deem it more than probable, however, that Mr M L Kennard, of Roan's Prairie, Grimes County, & Mr A D Kennard, jr. & Mr D P Hadley, of Johnson County, also saw him there. The Post office address of my mother, Mrs. M A Zuber, of my sister, Mrs M A D Edwards, & of Mr M L Kennard, is Roan's Prairie, Grimes County; of Mr A D Kennard, jr., Covington, Hill County; & of Mr D P Hadley, Cleburn, Johnson County.

I believe Rose's unfortunate experience at Mr Leaky's, & his early death, after arriving at home, are the causes which prevented his escape from becoming known & published, shortly after it occurred. Had I not made it public, the probability is, that this escape, like many other events that ought to have been recorded in history, would have been buried in oblivion.

I will here remark, that Rose was endowed with an extraordinary memory, & rehearsed his story, repeatedly, in my mother's presence; that my mother, at that time, was blessed with the most vivid memory, which I have ever known any person to possess; & repeated Rose's story, in my presence, till I could rehearse it, as well as she; that my own memory was almost as good as my mother's; & that I believe this coincidence of three good memories, has preserved the escape of Rose from the grave of forgetfulness.

One feature in my "Escape from the Alamo," (see Texas Almanac, 1873,) I must confess, gives it the appearance of fiction. That is, Travis's address to his companions in arms. This certainly needs an explanation; which I now give.

[Second Sheet.]

Rose was, if I am not mistaken, but a poor scholar, if a scholar at all. Yet he distinctly remembered the substance of Colonel Travis's speech, & rehearsed it often, before my father's family; not in the form of a speech,—but disconnectedly, & in very bad English. My mother often repeated it in my hearing; not in the form of a speech, nor yet after the manner of Rose: but she simply told, in her own language, the substance of what she had learned from Rose, that Travis had said.

When I wrote my article, I thought it best to reduce that address to the form of a speech; & I did so. Having been somewhat personally acquainted with Travis, & having read printed copies of most of his dispatches from the Alamo, I thought myself able to put it in Travis's own style; & I am not without a confidence, that, to a considerable extent, I succeeded in doing so.

That speech, however, contains one paragraph, which I did not get from Rose. I found a deficiency in the material of the speech, which, from my knowledge of the man, I thought I could supply. I accordingly threw in one paragraph, which I firmly believe to be characteristic of Travis; & without which, the speech would have been incomplete. I distinguished said paragraph, by inserting it between brackets: & it was excepted in my mother's certificate. But, bothe [sic] the distinction & the exception, were omitted by the printer. That one paragraph contains every word of fiction in my article in the Almanac.

In conclusion, please permit me to explain, that the object of the foregoing lines is,

First, to establish the following facts; to wit;
1. That, on the afternoon of the third day of March, 1836, Travis, in a formal address, explained to his command, their real situation; & offered to every man who might be disposed to accept it, an opportunity to risk the chances of surrender or escape:
2. That every man, with but one exception, determined to remain & die in the fort, & sell his life as dearly as possible:
3. That Rose alone accepted the offer, & effected his escape:
4. That my mother received the above facts from Rose, & imparted them to me.
5. That my account of said facts, is correct: &,

Secondly, To explain the reason why the task of publishing those facts, devolved upon me.

Earnestly desiring that this letter may prove satisfactory, & sincerely craving your pardon pardon [sic] for its too great length, I am, Dear Sir, your most ob'd't s'v't. W. P. Zuber

P.S. Please inquire after me, of Col H H Boone, Attorney General, & of Col H W Raglin, of the Comptroller's Department; &, if not too much trouble, of Dr George M Patrick, Dr D C Dickson, & Mr Franklin Brigance; all of Anderson, Grimes County.

1.8.1.3.   Zuber, manuscript undated (c. 1890s?).

Zuber, William P. N.d. "Biographies of Texas Veterans." In William P. Zuber Papers, 1524–34, CAH.

Though this account is in the first person, the actual manuscript is apparently a copy by his daughter S. P. Mize (see the W. P. Zuber biography in the same document, especially her note on page 1,537). Zuber's "Biographies . . ." is a 1,699-page manuscript prepared from the late 1880s on and is worth noting in its own right by students of Texas history.

An Account of the adventures of Moses Rose,
Escape From The Alamo.

Moses Rose was a native of France; he had been a soldier in Napoleon's army in the invasion of Russia and the retreat from Moscow. He was one of the early settlers at Nacodoches [*sic*], Texas, and that was his home, as long as he lived. Mr. Frost Thorn, of Nachitoches, Louisiana, generally kept four wagons running between the two towns, carrying cotton and other produce to Nachitoches and returning with goods for Nacogdoches. He arranged with settlers on the road to repair his wagons, and supply his teamsters with provinder [*sic*] and provision's, on short credit. Rose's duty was to bear the money and to pay the debts thus contracted. At the same time, he carried the mail between the two towns on private contract, there being no Government mail on this route. Hence, I infer that he was trustworthy. My father visited Texas in 1827, and became acquainted with Rose at Nacogdoches. He also knew him later, and believed him to be an honest truthful man. I also knew him in what is now San Augustine County in 1830. He was a close observer, and had a retentive memory. In 1836, when Santa Anna invested the Alamo, Rose was one of its inmates. His name was on the earliest published list of the men who fell in the Alamo, and on the Alamo monument which stood in the vestibule of the old Capitol at Austin. On the afternoon of March the 3rd, when Travis explained the situation and urged the impossibility of escape, but gave permission to as many as so preferred to try to escape, Rose was the only man that availed himself of the permission, having climbed the wall he threw down his wallet of clothes on the outside; it fell in a poodle [*sic*] of blood, and some of the garments fell out in to the blood. He leaped after it, took it up, replaced the spoiled garments without cleaning them, and walked away. To avoid the Mexican army, he went through the city. He went down the river to the ford, waded it, and passed through the town, through the old plaza. The doors in the town, so far as he saw, were all closed, and saw not one person. Before crossing the river he had passed a Mexican picket guard, but they had not hailed him. These were the last persons that he saw till after he crossed the Colorado. (The city of San Antonio did not then extend to the Alamo, nor to the river near the fort, but was in the bend of the river, on the west side, a mesquit thicket intervening between the town and the

fort. From Rose's description of his route from the fort through the town, I easily recognized it in 1842. His passing a picket guard without being hailed seems
to explain the cause of the short cessation of the bombardment. I judge that it
was a ruse to try to draw the men out of the fort in an attempt to retreat, that,
unprotected by the walls, they might easily be slaughtered on open ground, if
such was the fact, it is almost certain that Santa Anna judged that Travis would
first send out men to examine the several Routes, to see whether there was or
was not some way to avoid the enemy, and that he set pickets on all the routes
to report what they might see, instructing them if they should see one or two
men to let them pass, to raise an alarm.)

Having passed through the town, he went down to the river. When he was
about a quarter of a mile below the town, the bombardment of the fort was
renewed. About three miles below the town, at dusk of the evening, he crossed
the river on a foot-log. Then, avoiding the roads he directed his course as best
he could across the prairie toward the Guadaloupe river. During the night of
the 3rd, he could not keep his course, but wandered till daylight. In the darkness he often came into contact with beds of prickly pears, hundreds of whose
long, curved, barbed thorns so gored his legs that he was lame till after he had
crossed the Brazos. At daylight, the sound of the Mexican artillery, and the
smoke arising there-from, admonished him that he was yet within about three
miles of the fort. Warned by this experience, he traveled no more by night. He
did not want to pull the thorns from his legs, but hurried on towards the east.
On the night of the 4th, he slept on the prairie and that on the 5th in
Guadaloupe bottom On the morning of the 6th, being no swimmer, he rolled a
seasoned log in the river, seated himself astride it (securing his wallet of clothes
by placing it under him on the log,) and paddled across the river with his
hands, though the current bore him far down the stream. (He afterward crossed
the Colorado, and probably the Brazos, in the same manner.) On landing, after
ascending a bluff, he found himself at a deserted house, in which he found
plenty of provisions and cooking vessels. There he took his first nourishment
after leaving the Alamo. Travel had caused the thorns to work so deep in his
flesh that he could not bear the pain of pulling them out, and he had become
lame. There he rested two or three days, hoping that his lameness would subside, but it rather grew worse. Thenceforth, he traveled on roads, subsisting, on
provisions which he found in deserted houses. The families were retreating
before the threatened advance of the enemy, and between the Guadaloupe and
Colorado every family on his route had left home. Between the Colorado and
the Brazos he found only one family at home. With them he stayed during a
considerable time; but probably from want of knowledge or skill, they did nothing to relieve his sore legs. While he was with them, two travelers, of whom he
had no previous knowledge, called and lodged during the night. The landlord
intertained [sic] them with an account of Rose's escape. They seemed to be
much interested in the account; but on the next morning, just as they were leaving, they obtained a private interview with the landlord, and told him that they

lived in Nacogdoches and knew this Frenchman, Rose; that he was a man of very bad character, that he was an imposter, and had never seen the Alamo, and that he (the landlord), for the honor of his family, ought to ship him immedi- [*"ately, ought" crossed out in the original*] I judged that they themselves were bad men, and tendered this pretended friendly advice to their landlord, hoping, thereby, to induce him not to charge them for their lodging. After their departure, the landlord told Rose what the men had said of him, and said that he believed them; and that the best thing Rose could do for himself was to leave immediately. Rose returned not a word, but immediately departed. His sensibility was deeply wounded, and he determined never again to tell that he had been in the Alamo. This was during Houstons retreat from the Colorado, and several squads of deserters from the army overtook and passed Rose. The first of those told him that an imposter by the name of Rose had imposed himself upon an old gentleman as having escaped from the Alamo, but that two men from Rose's home had informed the old gentleman of the imposition, and that he had promptly driven the imposter from his premises. Succeeding squads told the same story, and before reaching the Brazos, Rose heard this caricature of part of his own history four times, but did not tell any of his informants that he was the man, nor that his name was Rose. Years later, I learned that the report of his reputed imposition preceded him to Nacogdoches, and that several malicious persons there circulated the slander. I further learned that, not able to disprove it by eyewitnesses, he was ever averse to talking on the subject. This reticence, though natural to a slandered man who could not positively prove his innocence, was imprudent. The people of Nacogdoches knew that he had been in the Alamo, but his sullenness excited a suspicion that he was not merely an imposter, but a deserter and traitor. As I shall yet show, he at one place exhibited conclusive evidence of his innocence, yet his stubborn reticence caused his adventures to be forgotten, and this, I judge, was what prevented his escape from being recorded in the early histories of Texas.

After crossing the Brazos, Rose found several families at home, and from them obtained direction to my fathers residence. My parents had seen in the "Telegraph and Texas Register" the name "Rose, Nacogdoches," on the earliest published list of part of the men who had fallen in the Alamo; therefore when Rose came in, my father was frightened, and said,—"Rose, is this you or your Ghost?" Rose arrived in a pitiable condition. The thorns had worked very deep in his flesh, and rendered him so lame that he walked in much pain and his steps were short and slow. Rose remarked to my father that "it was he, and not his ghost." Of course he was feverish and sick. Moreover he had not changed his apparel since leaving the Alamo.

My father supplied him with a clean suit, and my mother had a servant to wash his clothes. When the servant in my mothers presence, opened the wallet, the first garments that she took out were those which had fallen out into the puddle of blood when thrown from the wall of the Alamo and the clotted blood which had dried in the wallet had glued them together. My parents occupied parts of two or three days picking thorns from his legs with a pair of nippers. My mother made a supply of salve which, being daily applied to his sores, healed them rapidly.

After resting a few days, and becoming easy, Rose dispensed for the time with his premeditated reticence and freely related to my parents the history of his escape, the circumstances connected there-with, and his travel from Alamo to their house. At their request he repeated it often, till my mother could have repeated it as well as he. Rose stayed with my parents a week or two, and then resumed his journey to Nacogdoches. I was then in the army, and of course did not see Rose. But after my return, my mother repeated his story to me, and I like her and my father, wished to know it well. At my request she repeated it often to me, till I became familiar with it. God had endowed my mother with close observation and extraordinary memory, and I had inherited them. Hence what Rose had stated became stamped upon her memory and mine. I admired the sentiments of Travise's [sic] speech even as they had come to me third handed, and not in the speakers own language. I I [sic] regretted the apparent impossibility of the speech being preserved for posterity. In 1871, I determined to commit it to paper, and try by rearangement of its disconnected parts to restore its form as a speech. I enjoyed a slight personal acquaintance with Col Travis, had heard repetitions of some remarks as a lawyer before the courts, and had read printed copies of some of his dispatches from the Alamo. After refreshing my memory by repeated conversations with my mother, I wrote the sentiments of the speech in what I imagined to be Travises style, but was careful not to change the sense. I devoted several weeks of time to successive rewriting and transpositions of the parts of that speech. This done, I was surprised at the geometrical neatness with which the parts fitted together.

1.8.1.4.   Louis (Moses) Rose, analysis, 1901.

Zuber, William P. July 1901. The escape of Rose from the Alamo. *Quarterly of the Texas State Historical Association.* 5:1–11.

The importance of Zuber's story justifies reproducing his own analysis done "in self-defense."

THE ESCAPE OF ROSE FROM THE ALAMO.[1]
W. P. ZUBER.

I wish to say something in self-defense and for the truth of history, concerning my published account of the escape of a man whose name was Rose from the Alamo, March 3, 1836. The occasion of what I have to say is that I have been reliably informed that my account of that escape has been contradicted. I have not seen any published contradiction of it by any reliable authority, neither do I know of any reliable person who has publicly contradicted it; yet I am led to believe that such contradictions, though unreliable, have made an impression upon the minds of some well meaning persons. Therefore I feel called upon to present the case more fully.

It should be remembered that I learned the facts, though secondhand, from Rose himself. He recited them to my parents, who, in turn, recited them to me.

I must admit that, after years of reflection, I arrived at the opinion that in my first writing on this subject as published in Richardson's *Texas Almanac* for 1873 I erred in stating Rose's service in the French army; and I wish to explain how I did so. My father was then afflicted with deafness, and was very liable to misunderstand many things that were told to him. Learning that Rose had served in Napoleon Bonaparte's army, he understood him to say that he had served under that general in Italy, as well as in Russia, and so I then stated; but my mother, whose hearing was unimpaired, did not hear him say that he had served in Italy, though she did hear him say that he had served in the invasion of Russia, and on the retreat from Moscow. On later reflection, I infer that my father was mistaken regarding the service in Italy. Remembering his habits, I now believe that Rose told him something which he had learned of the Italian campaign, and my father inferred that he had served in it also. I also believe that I would have done better to omit Rose's estimate of the number of slain Mexicans that he saw near the Alamo, when he looked down upon them from the top of the wall. Of course, being horrified at the hopeless condition of the garrison, as Travis had just explained it, he saw what appeared to him a great number, and he had no leisure even to *think* of counting them. He only said that they *seemed to be so many.* The rest of his statement was all repeated to me by my mother, and I vouch for its correctness. In my account of this escape in Mrs. Pennybacker's *History for Schools,* I have made the needed corrections, and I affirm that I believe my entire statement in the excellent little book to be correct.

Now, were I to admit Rose's entire statement to be false, yet I would contend that no person is now able to disprove it. The Alamo was not in 1836, as now, in the heart of the city of San Antonio, but a considerable distance from it. The town then covered about one-half of the peninsula formed by the horse-shoelike bend of the San Antonio river; and that the west end of it was farthest from the fort, while the east end, next to the fort, was uninhabited and covered by a dense mesquite thicket, which obstructed the view between the town and the fort. The view between the fort and the small suburb of Laveleta was likewise obstructed. This was the situation when I explored part of the ground in 1842. During the siege, though the people in the town heard the reports of firearms, as used by the besiegers and the besieged, none of them could see what was done about the fort without needlessly risking their own lives, which they probably had no inclination to do. The men in the fort (all but Rose), were killed, none surviving to tell the story. Mrs. Dickinson and Travis's negro were shut up in the rooms, and could not see what was done outside the fort, nor much that was done in it. None of the Mexicans knew all that was done, and the official reports of the Mexican officers were not distinguished for veracity.

Then, how can any person at this late period disprove Rose's statement of what occurred about the fort?

I must notice an error which has been thrust into history, which seems to have been relied upon as a disproof of Rose's statement. That is, that, prior to March 3d, 1836, no Mexican soldier had approached within rifle-shot of the Alamo.[2] But both probabilities and facts are against this assertion. We know that Santa Anna, during his Texas campaign in 1836, perpetrated some gross blunders; but, to say that he stormed the Alamo without first having it closely reconnoitered to obtain, so far as practicable, a knowledge of the strength of its walls and of the condition of its defenders would be to accuse him of incredible stupidity, and to say that he delayed doing so till after the ninth day of the siege would be an accusation to the same effect. To my mind, it would be clear without positive evidence that, for this purpose, before the ninth day he sent scouting parties even to the ditches which surrounded the walls. As such approaches *could not be* made in daylight, they were of course made in the night, when but few persons even in the Mexican army were aware of them, excepting those who participated in them. And, of course, the watchful inmates must have slain a large number of those who thus approached.

But we are not without positive evidence that such approaches were made. At least, I have it. Colonel Travis had not leisure to write everything in his dispatches, and of course he sent out as couriers some of his most reliable men, who would state facts and nothing else. His last courier, sent out on March 3d, 1836, who arrived at Washington-on-the-Brazos on the morning of March 6th, stated to members of the Convention then sitting in Washington, that the enemy had more than once approached to the walls of the fort. Of course, I infer that the courier meant that they approached to the brinks of the ditches which were as near toward the walls as they could proceed. On the next day, March 7th, Dr. Anson Jones, afterward President of the Republic, passed through Washington, halting there; and several members of the Convention repeated to him what the courier had told them of such approaches. On the night of the same day, Dr. Jones arrived at the residence of Mr. A. D. Kennard, Sr., twenty-three miles east-northeast of Washington, and stayed there till after breakfast on the next morning, March 8th, 1836, when he repeated to several other gentlemen what had been told by the courier to members of the Convention, and by them to him, of several approaches by the enemy to the walls of the Alamo. He did not say how often they had approached, but his expression was "more than once." Dr. Jones does not tell this in his *Republic of Texas;* nevertheless, I was then at Mr. Kennard's, en route, as I thought, for the Alamo, and I heard him repeat this statement.[3] Thus we have excellent positive evidence that, before the 3d of March, 1836, some Mexican soldiers did, more than once, approach within rifle-shot of the Alamo, and nearer than that.

Rose left the Alamo on the afternoon of March 3d, and historians say that the courier, Captain Smith, left on the *night* of the 3d. If it were certain that Smith left on the night *following* the 3d after Rose left, this would prove Rose's statement to be false; for Smith said nothing of Travis's speech. But Smith certainly left before that night. I have no doubt that he left on the 3d, and in the night; but his departure evidently was on the *morning* of the 3d, between midnight and daybreak—say, soon after midnight. He could not have escaped the vigilance of the Mexican guards earlier than about midnight, as they were on strict watch for men from the Alamo. But suppose he left about midnight *following* the 3d. Then he would have, at most, three days in which to ride to Washington, where he arrived on the morning of the 6th. The distance from San Antonio to Washington was one hundred and eighty miles, and to cover this distance in three days would have required him to go sixty miles per day; but he could not have ridden at that rate during three successive days, without great danger of breaking down his horse. Suppose, however, that he left soon after midnight on the *morning* of the 3d. This would give him four days in which to ride the one hundred and eighty miles; that is, forty-five miles per day, which is reasonable. So I opine that Smith certainly left before the delivery of Travis's speech.[4]

I have now to refer to a striking instance of interpolation in a history by an officious publisher or printer. I have no doubt that the historian Thrall was a truthful and conscientious gentleman, but evidently he sometimes relied too much upon his memory in stating historical facts; and his publisher or printer added to his mistakes. This is demonstrated in a passage, in which it is said:

"Travis now despaired of succor; and, according to an account published in 1860, by a Mr. Rose, announced to his companions their desperate situation. After declaring his determination to sell his life as dearly as possible, and drawing a line with his sword, Travis exhorted all who were willing to fight with him to form on the line. With one exception, all fell into the ranks; and even Bowie, who was dying with the consumption, had his cot carried to the line. The man who declined to enter the ranks that night made his escape. [This tale is incredible, since he reported large pools of blood in the ditch, close to the wall, when no Mexican had then approached within rifle shot.]"[5]

This passage is evidently the work of more than one writer. Had its authors *intended* to embrace as many errors as possible within a given space, they could scarcely have crowded more into a paragraph of the same length. The statement referred to was not published in 1860, nor by a Mr. Rose. The man who declined "to enter the ranks" (that is, to cross the line) did not wait till that night to make his escape. That statement did not mention a ditch. And Mexican soldiers had, more than once, "approached within rifle-shot" of the fort, and nearer than that. Rose was the author of that statement, which he made orally, but not its writer or publisher; moreover, it was not written till 1871, and it was first published in Richardson's *Texas Almanac* for 1873.

But Mr. Thrall is responsible for only the first three errors, to wit: those relative to the date and publisher of the statement and the time of the man's escape. These are comparatively unimportant.

The last three errors are between brackets, showing that, without authority from Mr. Thrall, they are interpolated by the publisher or printer. They are the assertion that Rose's statement "is incredible"; the allusion to a ditch; and the assumption that "no Mexican had then approached within rifle-shot." It is fortunate for Mr. Thrall that the authors of these eccentricities relieved him of the responsibility for them, by inserting them between brackets.

Mr. Thrall himself, in effect, gave full credit to Rose's statement, as is evidenced by a passage in his biography of Col. James Bowie, the facts of which he could have obtained from no other source than Rose's statement, as first published by me. In it he says:

"During the siege, when Travis demanded that all who were willing to die with him defending the place should rally under a flag by his side, every man but one promptly took his place, and Bowie, who was sick in bed, had his cot carried to the designated spot."[6]

But even here is an instance of our historian's too great reliance upon his memory, though the mistake is in a mere want of precision. Travis requested all his comrades who would stay with him and die fighting not to "rally under a flag by his side," but to step across a line which he had drawn with his sword.

It may be thought that, under such excitement as Rose must have suffered before leaving the Alamo, his memory must have been blunted. On other subjects, it may have been blunted; but, as to the substance of Travis's speech, which he afterwards repeated in his manner, the excitement only sharpened his memory. That speech was a sudden revelation to him, and every idea expressed thereby sank deep into his soul and stamped its impression there.

With the explanations already given, it does seem to me that, without further comment, every item in Rose's narrative ought to be accepted as quite reasonable and credible; but, as some persons seem determined to discredit it, and I know not what points may yet be assailed, I prefer to subject it to a severe sifting.

Rose was in the Alamo a short time before it fell. While the mass of his contemporaries lived, this was acknowledged even by those who affected to discredit the rest of his statement, and none but two unnamed tramps are known to have asserted otherwise. In evidence of this fact, and of the consequent inference that he was one of the men who perished in that fort, his name was on the first partial list of those heroes, including only seventeen, which was published soon after the fall of the Alamo, in the *Telegraph and Texas Register,* at San Felipe. It was also on the more extensive list in Richardson's *Texas Almanac* for 1860, on page 82; and it has been further recognized by the inscription of his name on two Alamo monuments, one of which yet stands; that is, the one in the porch of the old capitol at Austin, which was destroyed by fire in 1881, and the present one in front of the new capitol. In the three lists first mentioned, the Christian name is omitted. The two printed lists named him as "—Rose, Texas," that is, of Texas; and on the destroyed monument it was simply "—Rose." Yet, no one who knew the author of the narrative under consideration doubted that he was the man referred to, and I am sure that he was the only Rose in the Alamo. On the new monument now standing, the name is inscribed "Rose, J. M.," for J. M.

Rose. It is on the fourth pillar, the first name after that of David Crockett.[7] I understood his name to be Moses Rose; but by whom or why the "J" is now prefixed is unknown to me. I know that he was generally understood to be in the Alamo when last heard of before its fall. However, he was not one of the heroes who died in defense of that fortress, and his name ought to be erased from the monument.

Colonel Travis was known to be an apt extemporaneous speaker; and I judge that all who knew him believed that, if any man could, under the trying circumstances, deliver such a speech as Rose affirmed that he delivered in the Alamo on March 3d, 1836, Travis was the man. I do not doubt that, to one unaware of the known facts, it would seem a high pitch of absurdity to believe that, under such circumstances, any man could deliver such a speech. Yet it would seem more absurd to believe that one hundred and eighty men would stay in a fort, and die fighting in its defense, rather than surrender or retreat; yet more absurd that they would die without first mutually pledging their honor to do so; and equally absurd that any orator could, by a speech, induce them so to pledge themselves. But it would be far more absurd to believe that they would make this pledge without being induced to do so by such a speech. Nevertheless, we know that, whether such an appeal was made to them or not, and whether they so pledged themselves or not, they did stay, fight, and die. Knowing this, we must pronounce Rose's account of that speech and of that mutual pledge reasonable and credible.

Is it incredible that, when all the other men in that little garrison covenanted to stay there and fight to the death, Rose alone declined to do so, and resolved on an attempt to escape? I believe that a majority of men will admit that, if similarly situated, they might do as Rose professes to have done. Is it incredible that, to disencumber himself for descending from the top of the wall on the outside, he threw down his wallet of clothes, which fell into a puddle of blood, part of which adhered to some of his garments, and on drying glued them together? My mother saw her black servant-girl, Maria, take those garments out of the wallet and find them so glued. On leaving the fort, he did not attempt to go east through the Mexican army, by which he would have been killed or captured, but went west, through San Antonio; then south, down the San Antonio river, about three miles; then east, through the open prairie, to the Guadalupe [sic] river, carefully avoiding roads after leaving San Antonio, from fear of encountering Mexican scouts. Is this incredible? Any prudent man would have traveled the same route. Is it incredible that he saw no person in San Antonio; but, so far as he saw, all doors in the town were closed? The danger of the time was sufficient to cause the people of the town to keep themselves shut up in their houses. Is it incredible that, after leaving San Antonio, he saw no person till after crossing the Colorado, and only one family at home between the Colorado and the Brazos? His road down the San Antonio river did not then lead by any residence; nor did it till more than six years later. There were then no residences between San Antonio and the Guadalupe excepting a few ranches on the Cibolo, and avoiding roads he passed between these. All families on the Guadalupe had left on the "Runaway Scrape" excepting those of De Leon's Colony, which was below his route, and the people of Gonzales, which was above it.[8] After resting three days on the Guadalupe, and proceeding slowly, on account of his lameness, to the Colorado, he arrived at that river after nearly all the people between it and the Brazos had left home; and only one family remained on his route between those two rivers. I could name that family; but, for personal reasons, I prefer not to do so unless it shall become necessary. Is it incredible that, in his haste to get away from danger, he traveled all the first night out, but was bewildered and made but little progress? Is it incredible that, in his attempt to travel during that night, his legs were gored by hundreds of the large cactus thorns which abound in that region? Is it incredible that he did not take leisure to relieve himself of them till they had worked so deep into his flesh that he could not bear the pain of drawing them out? My parents drew those thorns from his legs with nippers. Is it incredible that he crossed rivers by rolling seasoned logs into the streams, seating himself upon them, and paddling across with his hands? Other men who could not swim have done so, and why not he? Is it incredible that, after traveling two days without food and being hungry, sore, lame, and weary, he rested three days at an abandoned house at which he found plenty of provisions? Is it incredible that he rested during some time with the only family that he found at home west of the Brazos? Is it incredible that two unknown men, professing to live in Nacogdoches, spent a night with that family, and, when about to leave, drew the landlord out where Rose could not hear them and told him that they knew Rose to be an impostor, who had never seen the Alamo, and advised him to send him away immediately? The landlord told many persons that they did so. It is not incredible that honorable men residing at Nacogdoches would then be traveling in that abandoned region, from which the Texas army was retreating, and to which the Mexican army was advancing. Had their purpose been, as they professed, to confer a favor upon the landlord, they would have tendered their advice in Rose's presence. What could they have intended? The only conceivable object was to gain the landlord's favor, and thereby save their bill for accommodations. Is it incredible that the landlord did as those tramps advised him to do so? It is surprising, yet true. He, as well as Rose, said that he did so; and he said so boastingly to many persons. Is it incredible that a man of very tender sensibility was so wounded and discouraged by such treatment that he resolved never again to say that he had been in the Alamo? Such a resolve was foolish, and injurious to himself, yet he said that he had made it, and I believe that generally he had stood to it. Is it not probable that his subsequent reticence on this subject was what prevented his statement from being inserted in the early histories of Texas? Is it incredible that, his rash resolve notwithstanding, when he found friends who had seen his name on a partial list of the heroes of the Alamo, who believed his report, and who kindly ministered to his affliction, he, at their request, narrated to them his escape and journey to their residence?

Finally, is it incredible that, yielding to their importunities, he repeated his story to them till they knew it by heart?

Now, I have directed attention to about all the notable items of Rose's narrative. And when they are compared, which one of them is absurd or incredible? To my mind, every statement therein is reasonable and credible; yet to some minds his story may seem too much like truth to be accepted as such.

My writing down of Rose's narrative was incidental to a more important purpose, which was to preserve the substance of Colonel Travis's speech to his fellow-heroes of the Alamo, on March 3d, 1836. Rose's disconnected recitals of that speech, my mother's repetition of them to me, and my many rewritings of the same, by which I compiled the disconnected parts into a connected discourse, all are explained in my account of the adventures of Rose, in the revised edition of Mrs. Pennybacker's *History of Texas for Schools*, pp. 183–188, especially pp. 187–188. The speech itself, as compiled by me, fills a foot-note in the same book, pp. 139–140. The first issue of the revised edition contains one misprint, p. 139, which has been corrected in subsequent issues. It represents Travis as saying that the enemy outnumbered the defenders "two to one." The correction is "twenty to one."

Now, I think I have fully explained this affair; and what is the conclusion? One of two hypotheses is evidently a fact. Rose's statement is either true or false. If it be false, who fabricated it? The guilt would rest upon one of three persons; that is, upon Rose, upon my mother, or upon myself. Rose, being illiterate, could not possibly have manufactured what is represented to be Travis's speech. I do not believe that my mother could have done so, if she would; and I am sure that she would not. I do not know that I could have done so, if I would, and I would not have perpetrated such a fraud,—to save my own life. My sole purpose was to perpetuate the memory of what I knew to be of great historical importance; that is, the substance of Colonel Travis's speech to his comrades in the Alamo, and to show how I learned it. If I have succeeded, I have done well; and, if I have failed, I enjoy the consolation of knowing that my failure is in a just and truthful cause. If the present generation and posterity refuse to do me justice, God will award it to me in the day of final account. But I am not distressingly anxious for what the world may say about my veracity, for I believe that my reputation as a truthful man is well established; and, even should I be mistaken on this point, I have a clear conscience, and this is better than all things else on earth.

---

[1] Read at the annual reunion of the Texas Veterans and the Daughters of the Republic at Austin, April 22, 1901.

Among the details of the defense of the Alamo, as it is frequently described, is a speech by Travis in which he tells his companions how desperate their case is, and at the conclusion of which he draws a line on the ground with his sword, and asks all who are willing to stay and die with him to cross it and stand beside him. The authority for this is the story told by Rose to the parents of Captain Zuber, repeated by them to himself, and first published by him in *The Texas Almanac* for 1873.—EDITOR QUARTERLY.

[2] Rose asserted in the story of his escape that when he left the Alamo he saw numbers of dead Mexicans laying near the walls.—EDITOR QUARTERLY.

[3] During many years I was ignorant of the identity of this courier, but I have learned from Bancroft's history that he was Capt. John W. Smith (Bancroft's *North Mexican States and Texas*, Vol. II, p. 213, foot note 26). It was this same Capt. John W. Smith who piloted Capt. Albert Martin's company into the Alamo on the night of March 1, 1836. (Ibid., p. 209.) His bearing Travis's last dispatch preserved his life. He was an honorable citizen of San Antonio, and represented Bexar district in the Texas Senate in 1842.

[4] In the letter carried by Smith Travis says, "Col. J. B. Bonham * * * got in this morning at eleven o'clock." See Foote's *Texas and the Texans*, II, 220.—EDITOR QUARTERLY.

[5] Thrall's *History of Texas*, p. 242.

[6] Thrall's *History of Texas*, p. 506.

[7] See Scarff's *A Comprehensive History of Texas*, Vol. I, p. 710.

[8] Our little army was then meeting at Gonzales, and for the time protecting that town.

1.8.1.5.   Louis (Moses) Rose, published defense, 1901.

Zuber, William P. October 1901. Letter in "Notes and Fragments." *Texas Historical Association Quarterly* 5:164.

"THE ESCAPE OF ROSE FROM THE ALAMO."—The editorial footnote (on page 5, Vol. V, No. 1, of the QUARTERLY) to the article bearing this title is correct, to wit: "In the letter carried by Smith [dated March 3d, 1836], Travis says, "Col. J. B. Bonham * * * got in this morning at eleven o'clock." I remember to have read the letter, as it was printed in hand bill form, not many days after it was written. I should have noted this myself, but happened not to think of it. Yet, considering the circumstances under which Travis wrote, it does not disprove my position that he wrote it after midnight, on the morning of March 3d.

It is very probable that Travis had not slept since Bonham's arrival. Under such circumstances it is not uncommon for persons, conversing or writing, to make such blunders as to say this morning or this evening for yesterday morning, or for last evening or tonight. It is not unreasonable to infer that Travis, being weary, made such a blunder; and, as he was unquestionably pressed for time, failed to discover the blunder, or had not leisure to correct it. The distance which Smith rode after the writing proves this hypothesis to be correct. A ride of one hundred and eighty miles in three days is more than man or horse could perform.

My inference is that Bonham arrived at eleven o'clock on March 2nd;—more probably p.m. than a.m., as he could escape the vigilance of the Mexican guards and scouts more easily in the night than in daylight.

W. P. ZUBER

1.8.1.6.   Louis (Moses) Rose, published defense, 1902.

Zuber, William P. July 1902. Rose's escape from the Alamo. *Southwestern Historical Quarterly.* 6:67–69.

ROSE'S ESCAPE FROM THE ALAMO.—I have been advised by a friend whose position entitles his opinion to high respect, that it is incumbent upon me to answer the question as to why the narrative of this escape was not published before 1873, and I do so according to my knowledge of the subject.

I have elsewhere explained what I believe to be the cause of the silence, till that date, of others on this subject.[1] Therefore, it remains only to explain why I did not publish the facts sooner.

Be it remembered that my account of Rose's escape and journey was not the *principal* purpose of my article in the *Texas Almanac* for 1873; that story was merely incidental to, and in proof of, my version of the substance of Colonel Travis's last speech to his comrades. The compilation of that speech was a work of much study and long deliberation, besides repeated conversations with my mother, to refresh my memory. Though I often thought of the speech, and wished that it could be rescued from oblivion, I did not, till 1871, believe that I or any other person could perform such a task.

In 1871, after much reading of early events in Texas—mainly in Richardson's *Texas Almanac*—I experienced a phenomenal refreshment of my memory of what I had seen, heard, and read of during my earlier life. Among other things, I recovered scraps of Travis's speech, as Rose had disconnectedly repeated them to my parents, and they had likewise repeated them to me. I then felt that I owed to posterity the duty of preserving all that I could of that speech. By the assistance of my mother, whose memory was yet bright, I committed to writing all that we could remember of the speech, according to our recollection of its substance; but its parts were disconnected, and we did not think that they included all that Travis said. Then I wished so to arrange the parts as to approach, as nearly as possible, toward their proper connection. Accordingly I rewrote and transposed the parts many times, and the result was the speech as it was afterwards published. My success was as much a surprise to me as it could be to any one else.

Having reproduced Travis's speech, as nearly as it could be done, it was necessary that I should explain how I had obtained it. This explanation consisted in Rose's statement in full. To repeat this was comparatively an easy task, as his narrative was one of successive events which he stated in the order of their occurrences and was easily remembered. I accordingly wrote his full statement, embracing the speech, and this was the form in which both the speech and the narrative was first published. I hoped to have my article published in the *Texas Almanac* for 1872; but it was not ready in time for that year. It was published in that for 1873, which was the last issue of the valuable annual.

On request of Mrs. Pennybacker I prepared for her use separate copies of
my versions of Travis's speech and Rose's escape and journey to my father's
residence, both of which are inserted in her *History of Texas for Schools*.[2]

Summary (Here I condense my explanation to twenty words): Prior to 1871,
I did not believe that the substance of Colonel Travis's last speech could be rescued from oblivion.

W. P. ZUBER

---

[1] See Mrs. Pennybacker's *New History of Texas for Schools,* revised edition, pp.
185–187; also THE QUARTERLY for July, 1901, pp. 9–10.
[2] Revised edition, pp. 139–140, 183–188.

1.8.1.7.   William Zuber, letter, 1904.

Zuber, William P., to Charlie Jeffries. August 17, 1904. Inventing stories about
the Alamo. In J. Frank Dobie. 1939. *In the Shadow of History*. 42–47. Austin: Texas
Folk-Lore Society Publications no. 15.

This letter of Zuber's does not directly relate to the Rose story, but it is cited in
discussions on Zuber's veracity and is also a possible source for an account by General Cós.

INVENTING STORIES ABOUT THE ALAMO
W. P. ZUBER TO CHARLIE JEFFRIES

FROM my earliest years I read everything I came across in any way pertaining
to the Alamo; the appetite has never slackened. As a youth I would occasionally
come across something, maybe a work of fiction, maybe something that pur-
ported to be straight history, painfully at variance with what Anna J. Pennybacker had taught us. So one day I decided to write William P. Zuber, about the
last representative of the Texans who had fought in the Revolution and a man
whom I considered as being intelligent with first-hand information. I asked him
about Rose's escape from the Alamo, his estimate of the casualties on both sides
during the battle, and whether he knew any surviving Mexicans. If he did
know any survivors, my notion was to hunt them up and get whatever they
had to say. The letter that follows came in reply to my inquires.

Iola, Texas, August 17th, 1904.

Mr. C. C. Jeffries,
Winkler, Texas.
My Dear Sir:

Your letter of the 4th instant has been to hand during several days, but
recent absence and ill health have delayed my reply till now.

My conviction is that every one of our 181 men in the Alamo fought till
slain, unless we except Colonel James Bowie, who being prostrate with pneu-

monia, and not able to rise, was murdered in his cot after the rest were all killed, and who it was said that, from his cot, he fired two effective shots from his pistols at his murderers. I do not believe that any one of them surrendered or asked for quarters, for they all knew that the Mexicans would not spare the life of a man. It is not probable that any one of the Mexicans who stormed the fort now lives.

The storming of the Alamo was brisk work. The assault was made at dawn, and by a little after sunrise every defender was slain.

I happen to know how some of the absurd stories of alleged Alamo incidents originated. On the night of March 13, 1836, Captain Joseph L. Bennett's company, including myself, being en route for the Alamo, camped on the edge of the Colorado bottom, east of the river, where the town of La Grange now is. Just at dusk of evening, Colonel J. C. Neill rode into our camp and informed us of the disaster. His statement was that on the 8th of March he was en route from Gonzales to the Alamo. I did not understand his purpose, but I now judge that it may have been to resume command of the garrison. On that day (March 8) at the Cibola he met Mrs. Dickinson, who was in the fort when it fell; but being a noncombatant, and shut up in a room, was not killed. There she told him of the lamentable event, and he returned toward the east. He seems to have passes Gonzales without halting to inform General Houston, our little force at that place, nor the people of the town of the great calamity. I know not why, for while he was stating the facts to us—at that precise moment—Mrs. Dickinson was stating the same to General Houston at Gonzales, 45 miles nearer than our camp to the Alamo. He did not dismount at our camp, but, after delivering the sad news to us, he rode away.

Just as Colonel Neill rode into our camp, four young men arrived from the settlement around Bastrop. They had assisted their families to start on "the runaway scrape," and were proceeding down the Colorado to join a company of volunteers for the army—so they said. They camped at my mess-fire, opposite the side occupied by us. We all sat up late talking of the sad news brought by Colonel Neill, and one of the four young men entertained us with recitals of many alleged incidents of the fall of the Alamo. I was a lad, and believed all that he said; of course inferring that he had seen Mrs. Dickinson, and learned the facts from her.

On the next morning, soon after early breakfast, they left us, but, before their departure, I asked one of the gassy man's comrades where they had seen Mrs. Dickinson. He replied that they had not seen her at all.

"Then," said I, "how did you learn so much about the fall of the Alamo?"

"We never heard of it," said he, "till our arrival here last night, and know no more about it than you know."

"Why," said I, "one of your comrades told us last night of many incidents of that event. How did he learn them?"

"Oh!" said he, "you ought not to listen to him. He talks to hear himself talk; and spins yarns as fast as he can talk."

I was astonished. I had been badly gulled and was ashamed of my credulity. But some members of our company treasured the gasser's scraps of intelligence, and after we joined the main army repeated them to others, who repeated them again, and thus they were broadly distributed. After the battle of San Jacinto, some of our men repeated them interrogatively to prisoners, inquiring if they were true, and many of them, to seem intelligent, confirmed them, answering in effect, "Yes, that is true. I saw it." These yarns spread from mouth to ear, as facts, among the prisoners, and even some of their generals utilized them in modified form in efforts to prove themselves innocent of the outrages perpetrated by their countrymen. I refer especially to the yarns of one idle talker, because I witnessed them, but doubtless others did likewise, with similar results.

I recite one of the gasser's yarns as a sample of the whole, and give it, as I remember it, nearly in his own words. He said substantially: "The Texans all fought bravely, till all but six were killed. Then the six called for quarters, but were answered, 'No quartero.' Then the six fought till all but one were killed. Then the one cried for quarters, surrendered, and was conducted to Santa Anna, who ordered his soldiers to execute him. Then six Mexicans formed a circle around him, each drove his bayonet into him, and the six lifted him, on their bayonets, above their heads." I repeat the substance of this yarn, because, after being repeated with several variations, it found its way, in one form, into Mexican history, and thence into a footnote into Bancroft's *History of Texas*.

Another version of this story—referring to the six men—is that, after the battle, some washerwomen discovered six men hiding under a bridge and reported them; they were conducted to Santa Anna, and an officer begged him to spare their lives, but he caused them to be executed immediately.

The Mexican general, Cos, while a prisoner, referring to the one man, applied the story to himself—doubtless in hope thereby to mitigate his condition as a captive. He stated it to the late Dr. George M. Patrick, late of Anderson, Texas. I state his recital as Dr. Patrick stated it to me. When the Mexican prisoners were quartered at Anahuac, in 1836, Dr. Patrick visited them and obtained an interview, through an interpreter, with General Cos. He asked Cos if he saw Colonel David Crockett in the Alamo, and if he knew how he died.

Cos replied: "Yes, sir. When we thought that all the defenders were slain, I was searching the barracks, and found, alive and unhurt, a fine-looking and well-dressed man, locked up, alone, in one of the rooms, and asked him who he was. He replied: 'I am David Crocket [*sic*], a citizen of the State of Tennessee and representative of a district of that State in the United States Congress. I have come to Texas on a visit of exploration; purposing, if permitted, to become a loyal citizen of the Republic of Mexico. I extended my visit to San Antonio, and called in the Alamo to become acquainted with the officers, and learn of them what I could of the condition of affairs. Soon after my arrival, the fort was invested by government troops, whereby I have been prevented from leaving it.

And here I am yet, a noncombatant and foreigner, having taken no part in the fighting.'

"I proposed [Cos is narrating] to introduce him to the President, state his situation to him, and request him to depart in peace, to which he thankfully assented. I then conducted him to the President, to whom I introduced him in about these words: 'Mr. President, I beg permission to present to your Excellency the Honorable David Crockett, a citizen of the State of Tennessee and Representative of a district of that State in the United State Congress. He has come to Texas on a visit of exploration; purposing, if permitted, to become a loyal citizen of the Republic of Mexico. He extended his visit to San Antonio, and called in the Alamo to become acquainted with its officers and to learn of them what he could of the condition of affairs. Soon after his arrival, the fort was invested by Government troops, whereby he has been prevented from leaving it. And here he is yet, noncombatant and foreigner, having taken no part in the fighting. And now, Mr. President, I beseech your Excellency to permit him to depart in peace.'

"Santa Anna heard me through, but impatiently. Then he replied sharply, 'You know your orders'; turned his back upon us and walked away. But, as he turned, Crockett drew from his bosom a dagger, with which he smote at him with a thrust, which, if not arrested, would surely have killed him; but was met by a bayonet-thrust by the hand of a soldier through the heart; he fell and soon expired." This story by Cos, though a gross falsehood, shows what Santa Anna would have done if it were true.

Exposure of the origin of some of the myths related of the fall of the Alamo shows how easily the lies of idle talkers may find their way into history; but the truth alone is vastly wonderful. Some of our historians seem reluctant to tell the whole truth from fear of being discredited. My estimates are that the defenders of the Alamo numbered 181 men; that their assailants outnumbered them more than twenty to one, and that the loss of the latter during the siege of thirteen days, including the final assault, was nearly or quite one thousand men. All reliable reports of the battle concur in the idea that not one Texan of the 181 escaped or surrendered, or tried to do so; but every man of them died fighting.

Yours truly
W. P. ZUBER

1.8.2.1.   Lewis (or Louis?) Rose, claim, 1837.

Rose, Lewis (or Louis?). June 20, 1837. Nacogdoches First Class #312, Archives and Records Division, Texas General Land Office, Austin.

This is the one definitive document for the existence of a Lewis Rose in Nacogdoches associated with Frost Thorn. It is a printed form with the specifics, identified by underlining, filled in by hand in the blanks. The name "Lewis" is a natural anglicization of the French "Louis."

Republic of Texas)

County of Nacogdoches.)

BE IT KNOWN, That, on this <u>twentieth</u> day of <u>June</u> one thousand eight hundred and thirty-<u>seven</u> and of the Independence of Texas the <u>Second</u> Before <u>me</u> <u>Charles</u> <u>S</u> <u>Taylor</u> <u>Chief</u> <u>Justice</u> <u>of</u> <u>the</u> <u>County</u> <u>Court</u> <u>and</u> <u>Ex</u> <u>officio</u> <u>notary</u> <u>publick</u> <u>together</u> <u>with</u> <u>the</u> <u>under</u> <u>signed</u>——— witnesses, personally appeared <u>Lewis</u> <u>Rose</u> <u>of</u> <u>Said</u> <u>County</u> who declared that for and in consideration of the sum of <u>Five</u> <u>hundred</u> Dollars, to <u>him</u> in hand, paid by <u>Frost</u> <u>Thorn</u>——— the receipt of which is hereby acknowledged, as well as for divers other good causes and considerations <u>him</u> thereto moving <u>he</u> <u>hath</u> nominated, constituted, and appointed the said <u>Frost</u> <u>Thorn</u> <u>his</u> true and lawful attorney, for <u>him</u> and in <u>his</u> name, (or in the name of the said <u>Frost</u> <u>Thorn</u>——— or in the name of any one to whom the said Attorney may see proper to sell and transfer the after-mentioned LAND,) to apply for, receive an order of Survey, have located, Surveyed and laid off, and obtain Patents or Title for <u>the</u> <u>third</u> <u>part</u> <u>of</u> <u>a</u> <u>League</u> <u>of</u> [*sic*]——— of Land to which the said <u>Lewis</u> <u>Rose</u>——— **is entitled as a resident citizen, of Texas,** on the day of the DATE OF THE DECLARATION OF INDEPENDENCE and for the said <u>Lewis</u> <u>Rose</u> and in <u>his</u> name, (if the Patent of Said Land be issued in <u>his</u> name,) to sell, alien, convey, receive payment for, and good and bona fide Titles, to make to any one, the said Attorney may see fit, for the said <u>Third</u> <u>of</u> <u>a</u> <u>League</u> of Land; And on or more Attorneys or substitutes, under <u>him</u> to appoint, with the like power and for the same purpose this power of Attorney, to be forever irrevocable, and law to the contrary notwithstanding.

And said <u>Lewis</u> <u>Rose</u> acknowledges <u>himself</u> held and firmly bound unto <u>Frost</u> <u>Thorn</u> <u>his</u> <u>heirs</u> <u>and</u> <u>assigns</u>——— in the just and full sum of <u>Five</u> <u>Thousand</u> Dollars, for the true payment of which <u>he</u> binds <u>him</u> <u>self</u> <u>his</u> heirs, Executors and Administrators, jointly, severally, firmly, by these presents, to be void; on condition the said <u>Lewis</u> <u>Rose</u>——— shall made to the said <u>Frost</u> <u>Thorn</u> <u>his</u>——— heirs, or assigns, good, lawful and sufficient Title for the aforesaid <u>Third</u> <u>of</u> <u>a</u> <u>League</u> of Land, so soon as a Patent is issued for the same, and shall do and perform all things which may be necessary to be done, on <u>his</u> part, to vest in the said <u>Frost</u> <u>Thorn</u> <u>his</u>——— heirs and assigns, good and lawful Titles for the said Land.

In testimony of all which, the said <u>Lewis</u> <u>Rose</u> hath hereunto set <u>his</u> hand and affixed <u>his</u> Seal, in presence of the undersigned, on the date first aforesaid.

his

Lewis **x** Rose {Seal}

Mark

Chal. S. Taylor

Asst witness   C J of the County

Tho J Rusk   *[unclear title, "C. &*

                 Ex ofo N P"?]   Asst Witness

                                 P. H. Carraway

                                 [unclear, maybe "Jr"?]

1.8.2.2.   Lewis (or Louis?) Rose, depositions, 1838.

Rose, Lewis (or Louis?). 1838. Exerpts of testimony for heirs of M. B. Clarke, John Blair, and Marcus Sewell. "Proceedings of the Board of Land Commissioners." Nacogdoches County, County Clerk's Office.

These simple entries are remarkably important Alamo documents, as they independently validate the underlying basis of William Zuber's story. The three presented here are the most significant of a number of entries in Nacogdoches County records; the others are included in the next document, by Robert Blake (1.8.2.3). The column headings are given first, followed by the row entries, which are indented.

No Sppls

    203 John Forbes adm^{n} of M. B. Clarke dead

Witnesses

    J W Burton

    Absalom Go'sony [?] &

    Stephan Rose

Testimony

    1st Stated he knew applicant in the Summer of 1835, left this place for San Antonio thinks he is since dead 2^{n} States left here for the army in the Alamo—3 States he saw him a few days before fall of the Alamo—A single Man

           Certificate Issued the 6th Febry 1838 *[parenthetical in margin]*

Decision

    Entitled to one Third of a League of Lands.

Remarks

    [left blank]

    Sppls

    254 The Heirs of John Blair dcd by J Lee [?] administrator

Witnesses
    Elisha Roberts &
    James Carter &
    Lewis Rose
Testimony
    1st Knew him as a resident 8 or 11 years ago 2nd States he Knew him 8
years—left him at San Antonio 3r left him in the Alamo 3 March 1836
                    Certificate Issued 7th Febry 1838 [*parenthetical in margin*]
Decision
    Entitled to one third of a league of land.
Remarks
    [*left blank*]

Sppls
    579 The Heirs of Marcus Sewell by Johnl. McDonald administrator,
Witnesses
    Johnl Dorset [?],
    Adolpshus Sterne [?] &
    L Rose
Testimony
    1st W. Knew him 3 years ago understood he fell in the battle of the Alamo
    2nd Knew him before the 2 May 1835 understood he fell in the battle of the
    Alamo 3^{d} Knew him in the Alamo and left him there 3 days before it fell
Decision
    [*left blank*]
Remarks
    [*left blank*]

1.8.2.3. Louis (or Lewis, Moses) Rose, analysis, n.d.(1940).

Blake, Robert B. N.d. (1940). "Documents from Nacogdoches County Records
Relating to Moses (Louis) Rose." Typed manuscript in the Robert Bruce Blake Collection. LXI:126–40. CAH.

This is a portion of Robert Blake's massive effort to transcribe the Nacogdoches
County records, in the process of which he discovered the evidence for the existence
of Louis Rose and of his presence in the Alamo shortly before its fall. This material
apparently is unpublished. Blake's original footnotes are inserted in lines in the text,
included here in brackets but not italicized. In some cases, they appear a line or two
after the entry to which they refer. Many additional items relating to Rose that document his presence in Nacogdoches are included in the collection by Blake but are
not reproduced here.

ROSE AND HIS ESCAPE FROM THE ALAMO.

For sixty-seven years the account given by Rose of the last speech of Colonel
Travis to his companions in the Alamo has been the storm-center of criticism

among Texas historians. No corroboration by survivors was possible, and after a time the more conservative historians began to regard the account as a figment of the imagination—some attributing it to the fertile imagination of William P. Zuber, others to the romancing of the old Frenchman.

But the speech itself so reflects the known characteristics of William Barret Travis, that the story would not down [*die*], though under a cloud of suspicion. When I began to discover corroboration of Rose's story in the official records of Nacogdoches county, and to tell others of what I was finding, I met with the same incredulous smile, but continuing my search, first among the official records, and then in traditions of the past, I believe I am able at this time to at least prove that Moses Rose was a man of flesh and blood, and that he escaped from the Alamo on March 3, 1836, and at least render it probable that Zuber's account of Rose's story was about as correct as traditional history can ever be.

In presenting to the State Historical Association the result of my research, I would like to begin with that part of this narrative which preceded the narrative of Rose.

At the outset, I might first state that the old Frenchman's real name was Louis Rose, and the Moses was his nickname, though the records of the Nacogdoches County Board of Land Commissioners indicate that he was probably better known to the clerk of that body by his nickname than by the name of "Louis," as he names his [*sic*] as "Stephen Rose" in Rose's testimony concerning M. B. Clark. [Proceedings Nacogdoches County Board of Land Commissioners, #203—John Forbes Admr. of M. B. Clark, decd.]

For corroboration of Zuber's statement that Louis Rose was a Frenchman, we must rely mainly upon tradition handed down here in Nacogdoches, that he was a Frenchman and spoke very broken English. The next statement of Zuber is that he "was an early immigrant to Texas, and resided in Nacogdoches, where my father, Mr. Abraham Zuber, made his acquaintance in 1827." In support of that, I shall first refer to the Certificate of Character issued by John M. Dor, primary judge in Nacogdoches, August 25, 1835, which states that he was a "resident in this country since the year 1827." Also the testimony of Louis Rose himself before the County Board [University of Texas Transcript of Nacogdoches Archive, Volume 80, page 89.] of Land Commissioners in the case of Antonio Chirino, where Rose testified in February, 1838, that he "knew applicant twelve years, resides here since." [Proceedings Nacogdoches County Board of Land Commissioners, #245, James Carter Ass. of Antonio Chirino.]

The next statement by Zuber is: "I believe that he never married;" and again referring to John M. Dor's Certificate of Character, he says of Rose, "unmarried, without family." This is further confirmed by the power of attorney from Louis Rose to Frost Thorn for "one-third part of a league of land to which the said Louis Rose is entitled as a resident citizen of Texas on the day of the date of the Declaration of Independence," and the same statement in the deed from Rose to Frost Thorn, both being dated June 20, 1837; also by the award of the Land Commissioners, and of the patent from the Republic of Texas to Frost Thorn, assignee of Lewis Rose. [Deed Records Nacogdoches Country,

Texas, Volume U, page 363–4. Deed Records Nacogdoches County, Texas, Volume C, page 364–5. Deed Records Nacogdoches County, Texas, Volume I, page 107–8. Proceedings Nacogdoches County Board of Land Commissioners, #244, Frost Thorn, Ass. of Lewis Rose.]

The next statement of Wm. P. Zuber is to the effect that "My father regarded Rose to be a man of strict veracity;" and in that regard I again refer to Rose's Certificate of Character, in which Dor says, "I, the undersigned, certify that the Citizen Louis Rose is a man of very good morality, habits and industry, a lover of the constitution and laws of the country and of the Christian religion." It might be contended that this is simply a form that was followed by the Primary Judge in all those certificates; but upon the subject of the credibility of Rose as a witness, as bearing upon the probable truth of his narrative, I should like to dwell at some length at this point.

The Board of Land Commissioners in Nacogdoches County for 1838 was composed of Dr. James H. Starr as chairman, with Adolphus Sterne and William Hart as associates—three of the very highest type of men. Of the first two, nothing further need be said than to name them—they are too well known to the people of Texas; of the third member, I might simply say that he was the second chief justice of Nacogdoches county, and a man of the same high type as were Dr. Starr and Adolphus Sterne, men well qualified to pass upon the credibility of the witnesses who appeared before them.

Speaking of the duties of the members of the Board of Land Commissioners, and of his experiences in particular, Dr. Starr, in his autobiography says: "The office was of much responsibility, and the duties of extremely difficult performance; especially in Nacogdoches County, which embraced the most populous region of Eastern Texas, including a large number of native Mexicans. Many citizens, especially Mexicans, had already received their headright grants from the former government; but it so became known to the board that numerous persons of this class were fraudulently presenting claims for certificates. 'Americans,' (as citizens of the United States were called) were mainly the original instigators of these attempts, bribing the applicants to give false testimony, and agreeing to purchase their certificates when issued. By severe scouting the Nacogdoches Board met with gratifying success, in detecting and defeating the attempted frauds; though on more than one occasion threatened with violence, by men of mob power, (some of them men of prominence) whose applications by the score or more had been rejected." ["Some Biographical Notes of Dr. James H. Starr, of Texas," printed for private distribution at Marshall, Texas, 1917.]

One of the instances referred to by Dr. Starr was evidently that of General James Smith, who filed a bunch of twenty-four applications, most of which were transfers from Jasper county and elsewhere to Nacogdoches county, supported by written depositions taken before Charles C. Grayson, justice of the peace, and the notation made by the board to each of these applications is: "Rejected on ground that the witnesses are unknown to the Board." James Reily had filed an even greater number, soon after Gen. James Smith filed his, and when this action of the Board was made known, Reily refused to present any evidence to the board, and relied upon the District Court on appeal, and in most of these cases the certificates were granted by the district court. Dr. Starr and his associates always insisted on having witnesses who were known to the members of the Board, and upon whom they could intelligently pass as to their credibility.

Louis Rose appeared before the Board of Land Commissioners as a witness for sixteen several [sic] applicants for certificates and in two instances, the only corroborating witnesses were Mexican citizens. In other cases the corroborating witness was Adolphus Sterne, a member of the board. In no instance was the testimony of Rose rejected as lacking in credibility.

Continuing our examination into that part of the narrative for which Zuber is responsible, he says: "Rose was a warm friend of Col. James Bowie, and accompanied or followed him to the Alamo in the Fall of 1835 and continued with him till within three days of the fall of the Fort." Again examining the records here for data concerning the time of Rose's departure for San Antonio, that date can be very accurately determined from the records. John Durst, on May 8, 1834, deeded to Louis Rose 100 acres of land "in consideration for services rendered," and this land was transferred to Vicente Cordova in Nacogdoches on October 24, 1835. (Nacogdoches Archives #32, office of County Clerk, Nacogdoches, Texas.) Referring to the Nacogdoches Archives now on file in Austin, we find a "List of the effects of the citizen Louis Rose that by order of the Alcalde interino [sic] Citizen George Pollitt, the which [sic] were delivered to Citizen Vicente Cordova as security for an account and obligation which the aforesaid Cordova holds of the said Rose, which effects were sold at public auction at the exact end of one month, by which they were to cover the obligation and debt that on this date has been presented." Dated November 7, 1835. [University of Texas Transcript of Nacogdoches Archives, Volume 82, pages 62–3.] This was an auction sale of the household and personal effects of Louis Rose, and was evidently sold after Rose's departure, which was between October 24th and November 7th, 1835, and probably immediately after obtaining the necessary funds from Vicente Cordova on October 24th.

Before taking up the career of Louis Rose in the Alamo, and afterwards, I should like to make reference to some source material having to do with his occupation and every-day life. One of these is the Journal of Frost Thorn's mercantile establishment in Nacogdoches, which covers the period of December, 1833, and January and part of February, 1834. During this period I have noted seventeen entries on the books of Frost Thorn and most of which was for cash drawn for wages, he being a log cutter and hauler for Frost Thorn's sawmill near Nacogdoches. One item is "To 1 Cast Steel Axe, $4.00." Three charges are for whiskey, one being for one gallon, and three bought within a space of about one week, indicating that he probably drank rather heavily at intervals. On February 7, 1834, he is charged with "Sundries for Spanish Woman, $1.00."

Naturally, there is nothing on the records in Nacogdoches concerning Rose's career from the time of his leaving Nacogdoches until the time of his leaving the Alamo. For that reason, I shall next take up the evidence as to the date of his leaving the Alamo, and for this purpose must again refer to the proceedings of the Nacogdoches County Board of Land Commissioners. Taking these applications in the order in which they appear on the docket of that Board, in the case of F. H. K. Day, Lewis Rose testified that he "died with Travis in the Alamo." While in the application of John Forbes, Administrator of M. B. Clark, Rose "states he saw him a few days before the fall of the Alamo." In the application of the "Heirs of John Blair, decd., by J. Lee, administrator," the testimony of Louis Rose is even more specific, when he states that he "left him in the Alamo 3 March, 1836." Again, in the case of Chas. Haskel, Rose testified that he "knew him four years, supposes him killed in the Alamo." In the application of "The Heirs of David Wilson," Rose testified that he "knew him before the 2nd May 1835, was in the Alamo when taken." And finally, in the application of "The Heirs of Marcus Sewell," Louis Rose stated that he "knew him in the Alamo and left him there three days before it fell." [Proceedings Nacogdoches County Board of Land Commissioners #125 F. H. K. Day by Moses L. Patton and the Heirs of Henry Teal, assignees. Ibid. #203 John Forbes Admr. of M. B. Clark, decd. Ibid. #254 The Heirs of John Blair decd. by J. Lee, Admr. Ibid. #269 George Pollitt Admir. of Charles Haskel. Ibid. #427 The Heirs of David Wilson by George Pollitt, Admr. Ibid. #579 The Heirs of Marcus Sewell by John McDonald, Admr.]

Zuber fails to state what time Rose reached his father's home in what is now Grimes county, though two hundred miles of wandering over a strange country, on foot and grievously wounded by the cactus thorns, must have occupied at least eight or ten days. It is stated that Rose remained at the Zuber home recuperating for two or three weeks, and then proceeded toward Nacogdoches. Taking up the evidences in Nacogdoches again at that point, the first we see of him back at home is an account on the general ledger of Logan & Raquet's mercantile establishment, page 58, under date of May 10, 1836, amounting to $20.75. [Probate Records Nacogdoches County, Estate of William G. Logan, Inventory of the Estate.] The next record showing Louis Rose's presence in Nacogdoches is the record of the power of attorney and deed executed by Rose to Frost Thorn for his one-third league certificate, already referred to, which was executed in Nacogdoches on June 20, 1837. Following that are his sixteen appearances before the Nacogdoches County Board of Land Commissioners during the Spring of 1838. Turning then to the records of the criminal court of Nacogdoches county, we find the account of an examining trial of one Francisco Garcia for an assault to murder committed upon Louis Rose; the evidence in the case showing [Cause No. 65—Republic of Texas vs. Francisco Garcia—Examining Trial Papers, in Archives of Stephen F. Austin College, Nacogdoches, Texas.] that the Mexican was crazy drunk at the time of the assault, and probably did not know what he was doing; Rose's testimony being: "I was starting about my own business. A man at Thorn's yard called after me; supposed he was groggy and did not answer; the man was the prisoner. Prisoner ran after me, came near the graveyard, presented a pistol. I threw down my axe, took hold of the pistol to prevent his shooting me. Prisoner let go of the pistol and took up my knife which I had thrown down. When he took the knife he rushed upon me with the knife. I then snapped pistol at him. He went to cutting me with the knife and I shot the pistol at him. He wounded me in the back. After I shot him, he caught hold of me and threw me down. I escaped from him and ran. I wounded him with the knife. When he came to me he said, 'Stop! I want to kill you.'"

There is also the record of the Court in this case, showing the indictment, continuance and final quashing of the indictment because it was faulty in form. [Complete Records District Court Nacogdoches County, Volume A, page 253.]

On December 5th and 17th, 1839, and again on January 3rd, 1840, Rose is again shown as a witness before the Nacogdoches Board of Land Commissioners, indicating that Louis Rose probably at that time lived in what is now Cherokee county. [Proceedings Nacogdoches County Board of Land Commissioners, #348, 2nd Class—John Gilliland, December 5, 1839. Ibid. #443, 2nd Class—Stephen Richards, December 17, 1839. Ibid. #627, 2nd Class—David Musick—January 3, 1840.]

The last record evidence concerning Louis Rose is from the Account of James H. Starr, administrator of Estate of Kelsey H. Douglass, filed August 1, 1842, showing Louis Rose's note, received June 14, 1842, for $7.75, with $1.09 as the amount of interest received on the account for which the note was given. [Probate Court of Nacogdoches County, Record of Accounts of Executors and Administrators, Book A, pages 24-25.]

This completes the record evidence to be considered in our sketch of Louis Rose. The traditional evidence concerning the last eight of [or] ten years of Rose's life, was obtained in the main from Mr. R. L. Brown of Nacogdoches, Texas, who had heard some of the anecdotes related by Mr. Sam Reid, son of one of the early settlers of Nacogdoches, as well as the account of Rose's last days as related to him by his step-grandmother, who was a daughter of Aaron Ferguson, with whom Louis Rose lived during the last years of his life; and before taking up the traditional evidence, I should like to review Rose's career down to his return to Nacogdoches about May 1, 1836, after his escape from the Alamo.

Rose was probably born in France about 1785. He was an enthusiastic follower of the "Little Corporal," in his triumphant invasion of Russia; endured the hardships of the disastrous retreat from Moscow, through the snow and intense cold of the Russian winter of 1812; doubtless following the vicissitudes of Napoleon Bonaparte's career to its disastrous termination on the field of Waterloo. My surmise then is that Rose attached himself to the band of refugees under command of General Lallemand, seeking a home in the New World. Instead of proceeding with Lallemand to the settlement on Trinity River, Rose probably came to Louisiana, remaining there until Haden Edwards recruited men in November, 1826, for the Fredonian Rebellion, when he came to Nacogdoches—1826 being the date he came to Nacogdoches according to his own testimony. [Proceedings Nacogdoches County Board of Land Commissioners, #245, James Carter Ass. of Antonio Chirino.]

After the Fredonian fiasco, Rose remained in the neighborhood of Nacogdoches, probably living the greater part of the time among the Mexican population until the Battle of Nacogdoches, on August 2nd, 1832, when Adolphus Sterne and James Carter became acquainted with him. Especial significance is [Proceedings Nacogdoches County Board of Land Commissioners, #244, Frost Thorn, Ass. of Lewis Rose.] attached to their statement that they became acquainted with Rose in 1832, because the little band of seventeen Texans who captured the entire Mexican garrison on August 3rd, 1832, was led by James Carter and piloted by Adolphus Sterne.

Following the Battle of Nacogdoches, and his definite alignment with the American element there, Louis Rose became a more definite fixture in Nacogdoches county, or Department as it was then known. John Durst employed him in the operation of his saw-mill near the site of the Old Presidio, east of the Angelina River; and Frost Thorn at his saw-mill south of Nacogdoches. [Nacogdoches Archives #32, Office of County Clerk of Nacogdoches County, Texas. Frost Thorn's Journal for December, 1833, and January and February, 1834. (Original owned by J. R. Gray, Nacogdoches.)]

Soon after the departure of Thomas J. Rusk's company for the siege of Bexar, about the middle of September, 1835, the old roving "soldier of fortune" spirit was again aroused in Rose. October 7, 1835, he borrowed what money he could from Vicente Cordova, who was later to head the Cordova Rebellion, pledging his household goods and personal belongings as security for the loan. Needing still more cash, he sold his Walke ranch west of the Angelina river to the same party, purchasing his necessary supplies, horse, etc., he left Nacogdoches during the latter part of October, 1835, headed for Bexar, probably in company with other volunteers from Nacogdoches.

During the tedium of the siege of Bexar, many of the volunteers from Nacogdoches returned to their homes, dissatisfied with the inaction; but Rose and many others remained until the capture of the city, when he and more than a score of other Nacogdoches volunteers were left with the garrison there, afterwards retiring to the Alamo upon the approach of Santa Anna's army.

Louis Rose was always ready to stay with his comrades as long as there was a chance of victory, but like the typical soldier of fortune, when the situation became absolutely hopeless, as disclosed by Travis to his men on March 3rd, 1836, he was ready to beat a retreat, as his hero had done in Moscow in 1812.

I feel it useless to follow Rose through the siege of the Alamo, his escape to the home of the Zubers near the Brazos, and on to Nacogdoches, where he arrived about the first of May, 1836; and will now undertake to relate some of the anecdotes and traditions of his later years.

Soon after the Revolution, Louis Rose operated a meat market, located about half a block east of the Old Stone Fort, facing the narrow street or alley, now known as Commerce street. Across the alley was the old Mexican bull-pen, where bull-fights were held in the early days, enclosed with a high board fence. Mr. Sam Reid relates two incidents which occured [*sic*] during the operation of that market, which are indicative of the temperament of Rose. Mr. Reid stated that one day John R. Clute, who had come to Nacogdoches from New York prior to the Revolution, and was a well-known character here following the Revolution, dropped into Rose's market to raise a rough house and complain of some unusually tough beef he had gotten there. Rose became enraged at Clute's complaint, turned around to get a loaded shot-gun hanging on the wall of the market, when his customer, seeing what Rose was reaching for, leaped for the street, vaulted the high fence around the bull-pen and disappeared before Rose could fire. Moses turned, placed the gun back on the rack and said, "Oh, well; he has gone; I will let him go." Mr. Reid further stated that he had on several occasions heard the acquaintances of Rose ask him: "Mose [*sic*], why didn't you stay there in the Alamo with the others?" and his invariable reply was: "By god, I wasn't ready to die."

On another occasion described by Mr. Reid, when a customer was complaining of the toughness of his beef, he grabbed the man, siezed [*sic*] a Bowie knife, sharp as a razor, lying on his cutting block, and drew it across the customer's stomach, cutting entirely through his clothing, though barely drawing blood from his body, and Rose told him, with an oath, "If you come in here complaining again, I'll cut you half in two."

Rose is described by those who knew him as being illiterate, and he always signed his name with his mark. Tradition states that he was of a restless, roving disposition; never remaining in one employment for very long at a time. During the early forties he is said to have left Nacogdoches, first going to Natchitoches, Louisiana, and finally drifting to the home of Aaron Ferguson, near Logansport, Louisiana.

Aaron Ferguson's daughter—the step-mother of Mr. R. L. Brown's mother, who married a man by the name of Walker—re-remembered Rose, seeing him many times on her visits to her father's home, after her marriage and removal to Harrison county, Texas. this daughter stated that the old man was a great deal of trouble during the latter years of his life, because of the chronic sores caused by the cactus thorns in his legs, picked up during his flight from the Alamo, as described by W. F. Zuber at a later date; and that for some time prior to his death, at the age of sixty-odd years, he was bed-ridden by reason of those chronic sores.

A few days ago I stood in the old abandoned Ferguson cemetery, overgrown with trees, and with scores of graves, marked only by a slight depression in the earth, with very few of the graves marked with a headstone, though the grave of Aaron Ferguson, who died in 1861, is marked with a marble slab; and wondered which depression might mark the last resting-place of the soldier of fortune.

East of the cemetery about two hundred fifty yards, is the site of the old Aaron Ferguson home, on which now stands a small house, built of logs, and covered over during the last few years with boards, thought by some to be the original home of Aaron Ferguson, where Louis Rose passed his last days, probably dreaming of the days when he followed the conquering Napoleon; forgotten by the world, with not even a bounty or donation warrant from the Republic of Texas for his services.

In my opinion, the most enduring monument to the memory of Louis Rose is his account of the last great speech of Colonel William Barret Travis to his comrades in the Alamo. Probably Rose was peculiarly fitted to carry this speech to the people of Texas, because of the fact that he could not read and write, and had, for that reason, trained his memory to retain what he heard.

R. B. Blake.

1.8.2.4.   Louis (or Lewis, Moses) Rose, article, n.d. (1940).

Blake, Robert B. N.d. (1940). Robert Bruce Blake Collection. LXI:176-77. CAH. This is an introduction to the published article by William Zuber included in 1.8.1.4 and addressing the "fascinating sports of the historian."

CHASING A TRADITION TO ITS LAIR

One of the most fascinating sports of the historian is that of tracing a tradition to its origin, and although one may find its origin in the wild romancing of its author, such as Washington's cherry tree myth, there is a certain satisfaction in arriving at the truth, the goal of the true historian, even at the expense of a beautiful drama. But when it is found that folk-lore and tradition meet on a common ground of origin with source material of history, it is an especially gratifying discovery.

Tradition, founded upon facts, is often of more value to the historian than is source material, for tradition is usually the composite view of many people, as the story passes from mouth to mouth, possibly adding a little here and taking away a little there to please the fancy of the teller of tales, yet retaining the essence of the story from generation to generation. On the other hand, source material may lead us into gross error in the most essential details; thus the participants in a battle, on opposite sides of the conflict, may write accounts that seem to describe entirely different events, and in order to arrive at the facts, we must get the composite view of many eye-witnesses.

It has been the privilege of the writer to engage in one of these interesting searches among the early records of Nacogdoches county for evidence concerning the story of Moses Rose and his escape from the Alamo during the siege.

[*Paragraphs one, two, and four of the document above, 1.8.2.3, repeated here, then continues on with Zuber's article.*]

1.8.3.1.   Louis (or Lewis, Moses) Rose, analysis, 1939.

Dobie, J. Frank. 1939. The line that Travis drew. *In the Shadow of History.* 9–16. Austin: Texas Folk-Lore Society Publications no. 15.

Though primarily a literary rather than a history treatise, this analysis is one of the most thoughtful summaries of the publications of the Rose/Zuber story and its reception by professional historians. In addition, it is worth considering Dobie's reflections on the broader perceptions and the impact of this great drama.

ROSE AND HIS STORY OF THE ALAMO

I

THE LINE THAT TRAVIS DREW

BY J. FRANK DOBIE

In 1873 the *Texas Almanac* published W. P. Zuber's narrative, "An Escape from the Alamo," to which was appended a statement from his mother verifying the account. It sets forth how a man named Rose appeared at the Zuber home in Grimes County some days after the fall of the Alamo. He was in a pitiable plight physically, starved, his legs full of thorns, his wallet clotted with blood. The Zubers were good Samaritans to him. He told them how in the Alamo on the night of March 3, 1836, Travis had made a remarkable speech to his men; how at the end of it he had drawn a line across the dirt floor with his sword and invited all who would stay, fight, and die to cross over; how all went over, Bowie being carried on his cot, except Rose himself; how he climbed the wall, threw his wallet on the ground, where it soaked up Mexican blood, and how he then got through the cordon of Mexicans and made his way east afoot.

Up to the year 1873, the chronicles of Texas contained no mention of an escape from the Alamo, though the name of Rose had been set down, both in print and in stone, as one of the men who died in the Alamo. Up to this date also, the chronicles of Texas contained no intimation of the speech made by Travis or of the line drawn by his sword. The personal experiences of Rose on his fear-hounded walk across a wide land either uninhabited or now deserted by families who had joined in the Runaway Scrape still makes good reading—a kind of parallel to John C. Duval's *Early Times in Texas*—the story of his escape from Goliad. But this part of the Zuber—or Rose—narrative is minor compared to the speech of Travis, the drawing of the line, and the crossing of the men to his side, four of them bearing the cot on which the shrunken lion Jim Bowie lay.

Here was indeed something new, dramatic and vital to inflame the imagination of the Texas people—a people who, though towers may rise higher than the Tower of Babel to mark the San Jacinto Battlefield and though monuments commemorating events and personalities of history may sprinkle the roadsides from Red River to the Rio Grande, cherish the Alamo as they cherish no other spot either in Texas or in the world beyond. The story seized not only the popular mind; it seized the imagination of story-tellers, poets and historians.

In the very year it was published, Sidney Lanier, a visitor in San Antonio, wrote for the *Southern Magazine,* an essay on "San Antonio de Bexar," which was later included in his *Retrospects and Prospects* and then popularized over Texas by inclusion in William Corner's *San Antonio de Bexar, 1890,* which remains the best history of the city to have been published. Writing on the fall of the Alamo, Lanier comes to Travis's speech and gesture with these words: "On the 3rd of March a single man, Moses Rose, escapes from the fort. His account of that day must entitle it to consecration as one of the most pathetic days of time."

In 1874 or 1875, hard upon the appearance of the Zuber narrative and the refinement that Lanier gave it, Morphis repeated the story in his *History of Texas.* But Thrall's history, which appeared in 1879, gave it only scant mention, along with a slur upon its validity.

The medium that gave the story its widest vogue was Mrs. Anna J. Hardwick (Mrs. Percy V.) Pennybacker's *History of Texas for Schools.* No publisher would take the book, and she and her husband issued it themselves, the first edition appearing in 1888. During the next twenty-five years it went into six editions and "several hundred thousand copies were sold, chiefly for use in Texas schools."[1]

To quote from the 1888 edition of this work, which for a quarter of a century gave the school children and also teachers attending the state normals their chief education in Texas history: "On March 4 [*sic*], the Mexicans kept up a terrible cannonade. Just before sunset, this suddenly ceased, and Santa Anna ordered his men to withdraw some distance from the Alamo. The weary Texans who, for ten days and nights, had toiled like giants, sank down to snatch a few moments' rest. Travis seemed to know that this was the lull before the last fury of storm that was to destroy them all; he ordered his men to parade in single file. Then followed one of the grandest scenes history records. In a voice trembling with emotion, Travis told his men that death was inevitable, and showed that he had detained them thus long, hoping for reinforcements.

"When Travis had finished, the silence of the grave reigned over all. Drawing his sword, he drew a line in front of his men and cried: 'Those who wish to die like heroes and patriots come over to me.' There was no hesitation. In a few minutes every soldier, save one, had crossed. Even the wounded dragged themselves across the fatal mark. Colonel Bowie was too ill to leave his couch, but he was not to be deterred by this. 'Lads,' he said, 'I can't get over to you, but won't some of you be kind enough to lift my cot on the other side the line?' In an instant it was done."

In the revised edition of 1895 of the Pennybacker history (and also in the editions of 1898 and 1900) the story of Rose and of the Travis speech was included with extensions, Zuber at the invitation of the author adding many details. Scholars from the first had taken exception to the narrative, generally dismissing rather than discussing it. In Volume 5 (1901–1902) of the *Quarterly* of the Texas State Historical Association Zuber made three contributions in defense of the story; in Volume 6 he made another.

In 1903 Garrison's history appeared—without allusion to Rose or Travis's speech. Doctor George P. Garrison, Professor of History in the University of Texas, became the critic for Mrs. Pennybacker. The very much revised edition of her history that appeared in 1908 omitted, as if it had never appeared, the tale that Zuber ascribed to Rose. In 1913 the Pennybacker history, which had been used so long that some of the men and women who studied it in school saw their own children using it, was supplanted by *A School History of Texas,* by Barker, Potts, and Ramsdell. This kept its place in Texas schools until displaced in 1932 by Clarence A. Wharton's *Lone Star State,* now in use. I wonder if leaving out all reference to Rose and the Travis speech in this book cost Clarence Wharton a twinge.

On page 120 of the first edition of the Barker, Potts and Ramsdell history, under the caption, in black letters, "Some Old Errors," the Rose narrative is bowed out. As Eugene C. Barker has remarked, "Until scientific scholars correct history it is an illusion, and after they write it, it remains an illusion."

The latest study—the most searching that has ever been made—of the battle of the Alamo and the lives of participants, the treatise by Amelia Williams,[2] sums up the matter by saying: "Historians have been divided in their opinion concerning this story, the most careful students have discredited it. At best they consider it a legend, plausible perhaps, but almost certainly the creation of a vivid imagination."

But what makes history, whether authenticated or legendary, live is that part of it that appeals to the imagination. Amid many imagination-rousing facts connected with the siege and fall of the Alamo—the superlatively moving letter written by Travis; the picture of Crockett playing his fiddle to cheer the boys up; Bowie on his cot with pistols and Bowie knife; Bonham dashing back from liberty to die with his comrades; the final charge of Santa Anna's men to the strains of the death-announcing *deguello;* the extermination of a hundred and eighty-odd Texans at the hands of an army numbering perhaps five thousand, of whom more than fifteen hundred were killed before the last free man in the walls of the old mission went down; the one sentence entitled to immortality that Texas can claim: "Thermopylae had her message of defeat, the Alamo had none"—amid these and other facts no circumstance has appealed more to popular imagination than the story of how Travis drew the line and invited individuals of the little group to choose between life and immortality. Rose in choosing life got something of the other also, doomed like Carlyle's Doctor Guillotin to wander "a disconsolate ghost on the wrong side of Styx and Lethe."

I was sixteen or seventeen years old when for the first time I went to San Antonio and entered the Alamo, though I had lived all my life not much over a hundred miles away. As I walked through the low door with my father and mother and came into the darkling light of the ancient fortress—ancient for

Texas, and a fortress and not a church for Texans—I looked first for the place where Travis drew the line. I never enter the Alamo now but that I think of the line.

It is a line that nor [neither] all the piety nor wit of research will ever blot out. It is a Grand Canyon cut into the bedrock of human emotions and heroical impulses. It may be expurgated from histories, but it can no more be expunged from popular imagination than the damned spots on Lady Macbeth's hands. Teachers of children dramatize it in school rooms; orators on holidays silver it and gild it; the tellers of historical anecdotes—and there are many of them in Texas—sitting around hotel lobbies speculate on it and say, "Well, we'll believe it whether it's true or not."

Could Rose with his "broken English," no matter how good his memory, have transmitted the Travis speech as we have it from Zuber, who wrote it down thirty-five years after Rose had given it to Zuber's parents, who in turn repeated it to him? Zuber frankly said that he was transmitting only approximation. But it was the kind of speech that the inward-burning Travis might have made, the Travis who wrote "I shall never surrender nor retreat," "I am determined to sustain myself as long as possible and die like a soldier," and whose rubric was "Victory or Death." And for Travis to have drawn the line would have been entirely natural, the more natural because of the fact that in both history and fiction Rubicon lines have repeatedly been drawn for fateful crossings. Because an act has precedent is no reason for denying it. History is sprinkled with momentous sentences spoken by military men at crucial hours. These men about to die in the Alamo must have been conscious of doing a fine and brave thing. Travis certainly thought that he was acting a part that the light of centuries to come would illumine. To have imagination is no reflection on integrity. A magnificent gesture does not abnegate sincerity. Not everything orally transmitted is *mere* legend; there is traditional history as well as traditional folk-lore.

For hundreds of thousands of Texans and others who could not cite a single authenticated word spoken in the Alamo or a single authenticated act performed by a single man of the besieged group—for these hundreds of thousands of human beings the gesture and the challenge made by William Barrett Travis are a living reality—almost the only personal reality of the Alamo. In a book of reminiscences written by an old cowpuncher of Montana I came only yesterday upon this passage: "The Alamo had fallen. Brave Bob Travis, that drew the dead line with his sword, lay cold in death at the gate."[3] In the "chronicles of wasted time" Travis's dead line belongs as inherently to Texas as William Tell's apple belongs to Switzerland, or as dying Sir Philip Sidney's generosity in refusing a drink of water so that a wounded soldier whose "necessity was greater" might sup it, belongs to England.

For this noble and moving tradition I would register a feeling of gratitude to Louis, or Moses, Rose—a character that from Zuber's narrative and R. B.

Blake's study, following this, emerges strangely vivid, even while shrinking and striking back in this, to him, always foreign and bullying world.

Yet it is the thing created and not the creator that the world remembers. Nothing could make a creator happier. Rose has been forgotten, will continue to be forgotten. That line that Travis drew cuts out and off everything else. To illustrate the forgetting and the remembering, too, I will quote from a book dealing with San Antonio, written by an informed newspaper man thirty years ago.

"In the Chapel, sick almost unto death, Bowie lay on a cot, prone and unable to rise. Travis with his sword drew a line across the space in front of where his forces had been assembled. . . . He said: 'All who wish to leave, stand in their places. All who wish to remain and fight to the end cross over this line and come to me.' All but one crossed over to him. Bowie had his cot lifted and brought over. Rose was the only man who did not cross that line. . . . During the night Crockett lifted Rose up and helped him out of one of the windows. Rose was never heard of after. Probably he perished miserably, butchered before he had gone many yards from the shadow of the structure in which his comrades remained. No one knows his fate, or, if so, it has never been told."[4]

But nobody forgets the line. It is drawn too deep and straight.

Reading the documented historians, you'd think nothing could be so unless it happened. I think Travis made the speech. He certainly made it according to something that the historians might well use—in proper place—to the advantage of truth. In My Ireland Lord Dunsany found it necessary to quote a fictional character in order to reveal a historical truth. I want to quote Lord Dunsany himself: "I look, in fact, as much for Ireland in the Irish mind as I do in the Irish fields. Much may pass over a field and leave no trace, but what wonderful tracks we may see where a fancy has passed over the mind."

---

[1] From an interview with Mrs. Pennybacker published in the Dallas *News*, April 20, 1934.

[2] "A Critical Study of the Siege of the Alamo and of the Personnel of Its Defenders," by Amelia Williams, published in five chapters in the *Southwestern Historical Quarterly*, Vols. 36-37, 1932–1934.

[3] *We Pointed Them North*, by E. C. Abbott and Helena Huntington Smith, New York, 1939, 259.

[4] *Combats and Conquests, or Immortal Heroes*, by Charles M. Barnes, San Antonio, 1910, 33–34.

1.8.3.2. Louis (or Lewis, Moses) Rose, analysis, 1961.

Lord, Walter. 1961. *A Time to Stand.* Appendix, "Riddles of the Alamo," 201–4. New York: Harper & Brothers. Reprinted 1978. Lincoln: University of Nebraska (Bison Book).

Did Travis Draw the Line?

Ever since William Zuber launched the story in 1873, historians have pondered over his tale of Colonel Travis' last appeal to his garrison. Did Travis really draw a line on the ground with his sword, ask all who were with him to cross, and give any others the chance to escape? Did Louis Rose really hang back—the only man in the Alamo who preferred to live? Did he really vault the wall and escape?

There were so many things wrong with the account, few scholars took it seriously for years. At best it was secondhand hearsay: Rose was illiterate and Zuber's parents, who heard him tell the story, never wrote it down. William Zuber himself was an incorrigible raconteur—another of his tales had a Mexican tearing Jim Bowie's tongue out.

Worst of all, the story just didn't fit the known facts: (1) Only one Rose was listed in the Alamo, and that was generally understood to be James M. Rose, ex-President Madison's nephew and an impeccable hero. (2) Travis had not lost all hope on March 3—his letters that day were full of high spirits and detailed instructions on what the relief force should bring. (3) John W. Smith, who left the Alamo later that night, never mentioned the speech or the line.

Nor, in fact, did any of the survivors, until long after the Zuber story was published. Then, versions by Enrique Esparza and Mrs. Dickinson began to appear . . . but obviously with heavy and not very skillful editorial assistance. In 1881, for instance, Mrs. Dickinson had the story backward—the line was to be crossed by anyone who wanted to leave. Far worse, she had it all happening on the first day of the siege.

Then in 1939 came a thunderbolt. R. B. Blake, a conscientious office worker long interested in the Zuber story, uncovered some amazing evidence in the Nacogdoches Country Courthouse. It showed convincingly that there was indeed a Louis Rose, that he had been in the Alamo during the siege, and that his testimony was accepted by the local Board of Land Commissioners in deciding claims filed on behalf of six different Alamo victims. On Claim No. 254 by the heirs of John Blair, for instance, Rose testified, "Left him in the Alamo 3 March 1836."

So Rose was there. But did he leave under the dramatic circumstances described by Zuber? Freshly uncovered information suggests that he did. This consists of a formal statement, never published, given by Mrs. Dickinson to the State Adjutant General, who was trying to develop a more definitive list of Alamo defenders. Dated September 23, 1876, part of her statement declares:

On the evening previous to the massacre, Colonel Travis asked the
command that if any desired to escape, now was the time, to let it be
known, and to step out of the ranks. But one stepped out. His name to
the best of my recollection was Ross. The next morning he was missing.

Of course, she did say "Ross," not "Rose." But letters and spelling meant
nothing to Mrs. Dickinson, who couldn't read or write. At this distance, her
statement looks good enough—especially since there was no "Ross" in the
Alamo. Nor does it seem damaging that her statement postdated the Zuber
story by three years. It doesn't have ring of a coached remark; and Mrs. Dickinson, who was exasperatingly uninterested in her historic role, didn't have it in
her to take off all alone on a flight of fancy.

But the statement does throw great light on another point raised by Zuber's
critics: How could Travis have drawn the line on March 3, when his letters were
still so hopeful and John W. Smith never mentioned it at all? The answer: It
didn't happen on March 3—it happened, as Mrs. Dickinson testified, on the
evening of March 5. By then the picture had entirely changed. Moreover, the
later date would fit perfectly with the course of battle on March 5, when Mexican fire did taper off around sunset.

All that's needed is to allow Rose the same leeway on dates as everyone
else in the Alamo story. In the true frontier spirit, none of them cared very
much—who ever saw a calendar? Ramón Caro said Santa Anna arrived on February 26; Seguín said February 22. Travis himself gave two different dates for
the arrival of the Gonzales men.

So Rose was there and Rose fled—but still, did Travis draw the line? In her
statement to the Adjutant General, Mrs. Dickinson didn't mention it. Now a
recently uncovered Zuber letter casts further doubt on the story. He too was
writing the Adjutant General about this time, apparently because his account
had come under such heavy fire. In a letter dated September 14, 1877, Zuber
acknowledged that he had made up Travis' speech completely, although it was
based on information supplied by Rose. Moreover, Zuber admitted that he
invented one paragraph which did not come from Rose at all: "I found a deficiency in the material of the speech, which from my knowledge of the man, I
thought I could supply. I accordingly threw in one paragraph which I firmly
believe to be characteristic of Travis, and without which the speech would have
been incomplete."

Zuber never said what the passage was, but the omission itself is significant. The line was the crux of the whole speech—the center of all the controversy. If his concoction ('without which the speech would have been
incomplete") was not the line, it seems he would have said so, for this was the
one thing everyone wanted to know.

Summing up his account of the speech, Zuber said all he was trying to do
was show "That on the afternoon of the 3rd day of March 1836, Travis in a formal address explained to his command their real situation and offered to every

man who might be disposed to accept it an opportunity to risk the chances of surrender or escape."

Again, no mention of the line. But perhaps it was just as well. If Zuber was hiding a gentle fabrication, he was also protecting a shining legend—and what harm in a legend that only serves to perpetuate the memory of valor and sacrifice? As matters stand, there's still room to speculate, and every good Texan can follow the advice of J. K. Beretta in the *Southwestern Historical Quarterly:* "Is there any proof that Travis didn't draw the line? If not, then let us believe it."

Commentary

Louis (Moses) Rose (1.8)

The Zuber/Rose documents leave one with an idiosyncratic view—what one focuses on is strongly dependent on one's own preferences to validate or deny a story. Both Dobie and Lord are good summaries for their respective purposes.

The eight Zuber documents (1.8.1.1–1.8.1.7) are all useful to review, as each has a different motivation and therefore emphasis. The original 1873 account, as Zuber states many times, was written to "recover" the final speech of Travis. The 1877 letter was intended to give more details on the circumstances of Rose and his story to validate the Travis narrative. By the time Zuber wrote the Rose biography, he felt that Rose himself was worth additional attention, and he apparently had recovered a number of details about the Frenchman from people who had met him. By 1901, the story had been widely disseminated and criticized, especially concerning its use in the Pennybacker school text editions, and Zuber felt the need for a detailed response and analysis to address those criticisms. Also, by this time, Zuber had become a leader among those interested in Texas history and thus had a much broader view of the significance of the Rose story. The fifth and sixth documents address some specifics relevant to the story—details on the arrival of Bonham and the delay in publication of the original 1873 account. The seventh gives us Zuber's perspectives on false stories. The eighth is so focused on John Smith and the route from San Antonio to Washington on the Brazos that it is basically independent of the Rose story and therefore was included under the Smith documents above.

The disclosures of Robert Bruce Blake are so significant that it is worth recalling the weaknesses in the Zuber/Rose story that caused earlier historians to reject it— and rightfully so, without the Nacogdoches evidence. It is clear from Zuber's own account that he *worked* at reconstructing the story, and this makes one question how much of a tendency he may have had to fill in the blanks, consciously or subconsciously.

One bothersome trend is the readiness with which Zuber contributed additional details or substories over the years as specific parts of the narrative were criticized.

In 1877, he had Mrs. Dickinson and Joe (1.8.1.2) being sent into San Antonio three days before the fall as an explanation for her giving a different date for Rose's escape. And incidentally, this passage clearly shows that he was aware of the adjutant general's interview with Mrs. Dickinson (1.2.8, 1.2.9). He was prompt to explain away (in 1.8.1.3) the two individuals at Leaky's who discredited Rose, without having any better basis of his own to judge. Still later, in 1901 (1.8.1.4), he used his father's deafness to explain some discrepancies, dismissed the possibility that Rose was confused with the statement that "excitement only sharpened his memory," and gave a rather reaching paragraph discussing the documented presence of a Rose from Nacogdoches by arbitrarily dismissing the possibility—true, as it turns out—of a second Rose being in the Alamo. And it would leave any careful reader cold to hear that Zuber had "a phenomenal refreshment" of his memory to re-create the story (1.8.1.6).

The fundamental problem is that the entire story is too good. It was very hard—unreasonable, in fact—for pre-1939 historians to consider this account as anything beyond a marvelous literary accomplishment. If such a great story were true, they asked, why hadn't it appeared long before?

A possible early record from Williams is that Dickinson's grandson A. D. Griffith had heard the story from his uncle J. D. Griffith and Capt. Frank Dupree by the 1860s or as early as 1852.[1] W. T. Neblett and his sister Mary Neblett Brown, neighbors of the Zubers, also wrote Williams that they had heard the story earlier than 1871.[2] There are other records, not seen by Blake, of services by Lewis Rose for October 1836 and in 1838—also including his testimonies to the Board of Land Commissioners—in the Republic Claims files, but these do not cover the period of interest here.[3]

Zuber is supported by another manuscript letter in the Texas State Library from Rufus Grimes to E. M. Pease of July 20, 1876.[4] The letter concerns Grimes's brother Albert and Tapley Holland, both Alamo defenders. Rufus Grimes supported Zuber's veracity and noted that Zuber had told him many other interesting statements from Rose that were not included in the reproduction of Zuber's article in Morphis (5.1.6), though unfortunately Grimes doesn't give any further elaboration.

Zuber also made telling points in support of his narrative. The original account (1.8.1.1) notes near continuous fighting and Mexican advances to the walls of the Alamo, which were inconsistent with published accounts on the siege up to that time. However, his 1901 defense (1.8.1.4) sounds true when he noted that Santa Anna must have reconnoitered and tested the fortress with small groups through the siege. The discussion about John W. Smith (1.7.3.1) makes a strong case for Smith's departure prior to the Travis speech, even if we hold to the March 3 date for Rose's departure. In the 1901 defense, he continued with a long—and cleverly constructed—list of questions prefaced by "Is it incredible that . . ." to which we must answer no. I agree with Zuber that the speech and events portrayed are not, in fact, incredible under the circumstances.

Perhaps Zuber was at his strongest when he stated that "Travis was the man" to make such a speech (1.8.1.4). We have seen in Travis's letters, some of which would not have been available to Zuber, something of his mind and mode of expression. Zuber asserted that Rose's account of the speech and pledge was reasonable and credible, that he was able to catch the substance of Rose's accounts. As Zuber pointed out, if the speech were a fraud, it must have been perpetrated by Rose, Mary Zuber, or himself. We can readily agree with Zuber that neither Rose nor Mary Zuber were likely to be the inventors. Clearly, we have a world-class story here. We have to acknowledge Travis, who clearly showed such capabilities in his letters, as being the most able of the two possible sources of originating such dramatic, even epical, expressions.

Historians must hold to higher standards, however. That something *could* have happened, as Zuber stated, is not evidence that it *did*. What was missing for sixty years was positive, independent evidence that at least some portion of the story did happen. With the location of the Nacogdoches documents, one can give far more weight to Zuber's assertions on the believability of much of the story.

One must be impressed with Blake's study of the Nacogdoches materials. He did an exceptional bit of analysis (1.8.2.3) by taking the Zuber account and discussing almost line by line how the county documents support or are at least consistent with the story. He was even able to establish that there was a lack of documentation in Nacogdoches corresponding to the time Rose would have been in San Antonio. Blake rightly recognized and elaborated on the membership of the Board of Land Commissioners. These were highly respected individuals, well known in their community, and therefore their acceptance of Rose's testimony is quite significant. Rose's function as a regular witness establishes a high level of authority for his testimony, and thus indirectly for the Zuber account. Rarely has such an important story as Zuber's been as well supported after the original publication as by Robet Blake's studies.

Walter Lord's book *A Time to Stand,* certainly one of the finest narrative interpretations of the Alamo story, was thoroughly researched and made careful use of original sources. His chapter on "Riddles of the Alamo" is also an exceptional case of Alamo source analysis. His evaluation of the heart of the Rose story (1.8.3.2) is the best overview to date.

As a counterpoint to these conclusions, Thomas Miller did not accept the evidence of Louis Rose (1.8.2.2, 1.8.2.3) as being definitive. Miller, an authority on the General Land Office documents, stated, "Students of Texas land grants are aware that the county boards of land commissioners were residents of the county and the applicants were their friends and neighbors and they were usually very generous in granting headrights."[5] Consequently, he does not accept the evidence to add M. B. Clarke, and does not believe that any of the testimony by Rose substantiates the Zuber story. But Miller does not address the actual land commissioners in Nacogdoches who were hearing this testimony, which Blake does, or acknowledge the high improbability that Zuber could have known of such testimony as an independent check on the Rose story. Therefore, I find Miller's conclusion unconvincing.

Another point critics of Zuber make is that he unquestionably was, in Lord's words, an "incorrigible raconteur." Some go further and believe he invented such stories as that of Cós (1.8.1.7, though Zuber himself rejects this account) and of Saldigua (2.17.2). Groneman reasonably describes the Saldigua account as the product of "lurid imagination."[6] I certainly agree, but I have seen no real evidence that Zuber invented these stories as opposed to simply passing them along. In the same work, Gronemen himself reproduces a number of clearly bogus accounts for the sake of thoroughness, and perhaps Zuber was not much different.

We are still left with Lord's question, "Did Travis draw the line?" There is little I would add to Lord's analysis. I would not, however, agree with him that the validity of the line was the only issue in 1877 when Zuber wrote his letter to the adjutant general. At that time, the entire account would have been questioned, and the specific act of drawing the line was not necessarily as central a focus as it was later. Lord also points out the quite real possibility of Rose having left March 5 rather than the third. He does not discuss that Rose's story explicitly notes his hearing the bombardment the morning after he left the Alamo, while it is much vaguer for subsequent days. Rose must be mistaken in saying he heard the bombardment after the first morning if he left the fifth, so the vagueness at least keeps this possibility alive.

Zuber never made it clear which paragraph he added (1.8.1.2, 1.8.3.2). No doubt it is too petty to put much weight on the literal count in Zuber's statement that he added one paragraph that was missing, while the description of Travis's line covers three.[7] Perhaps it is a little less petty to note that he attributed the one added paragraph explicitly to Travis's speech itself rather than the surrounding narrative, which includes the drawing of the line. Is it, however, more significant that in 1877, Zuber still had his original manuscript, which would have answered many of these questions, but it is not now found with his other papers? Zuber's list "to establish the following facts . . ." in 1877 also does not include the line. On the other hand, in his 1901 article, Zuber still explicitly stood by that specific portion of his story right after he quoted another historian with a different version that did not include the line (1.8.1.4, the text footnote with number 6 and just after).

As long as there is room to speculate, which the Rose story will always have, I might as well do so too. Some of the fourteen paragraphs of the Travis speech are a bit uneven in tone and therefore could be potential candidates for Zuber's insertion. However, the one paragraph of the complete narrative that least fits for me is the one on Rose's thoughts while standing alone after his decision. Would Rose really have been that self-reflective? If he hadn't, would Zuber have felt the need to express the reflections of an individual who had just made such a significantly contrary choice to that of his companions? If this were the case, I would have to theorize that Zuber was referring to the entire story when he wrote about "Travis' speech," not just the specific text on what Travis said, when he noted that there was a missing piece. Nonetheless, this is my candidate for the added paragraph.

In the end, perhaps Dobie (1.8.3.1) was closest to the truth. We know that for the defenders, the line had to be there, and crossed, at least in a figurative sense, regardless of what literally happened. Thus we can also ask, does it really matter? What does matter is that we are left to wonder, as Zuber noted (1.8.1.4), whether we ourselves would have chosen Rose's way out. Seldom does history—or life—offer such clear, decisive options. It is the choice that all but one of the defenders made that has led to the major fascination with the Alamo story.

1. Alamo Research/Dickinson & Other Survivors, Williams (Amelia Worthington) Papers, CAH.
2. General Correspondence: 1935, which has three letters in April 1935 on the family recollections, Williams Papers, CAH.
3. Republic Claims R:003 Fr:0541, R:088 Fr:0324, R:091 Fr: 0144–0145, R:104 Fr:0043, TSLA.
4. In Adjutant General (RG-401), Miscellaneous Papers, TSLA.
5. Miller 1964, 62, footnote for M. B. Clark. Other difficulties in using land office documents are demonstrated in Miller 1967.
6. Groneman 1996, 87, 141.
7. Chariton 1992, 196–97, makes the same point. He also speculates that Rose left after the final assault began (189–90).

1.9.1.   Madame Candelaria, newspaper interview, 1890.

Corner, William, ed. 1890. *San Antonio de Bexar.* 117–19. San Antonio: Bainbridge & Corner.

Madame Candelaria claimed to have been a survivor of the fall of the Alamo, but this has not been accepted by most twentieth-century historians. The key published interviews are included here for comparison.

Señora Candelaria

On Saturday, March 17th 1888, St. Patrick's Day: I believe, I went with a friend (who took his Photographic Camera along for he had the amatuer [*sic*] craze) and Mr. ———, who was an acquisition on account of his fluent knowledge of the two languages, Spanish and English, to call on the old, very old, Señora Candelaria. Our interview lasted for upwards of an hour and knowing but little or nothing of Spanish myself I asked her through Mr. ——— a few questions that I thought would elucidate what some deemed to be obscure pretentions [*sic*]. The result of this and other later interviews are here given, and the reader must judge for himself the value of the statements and evidence. She is at least a very old and interesting person, lively and full of the recollection and reminiscences of the men and the stirring times of the Texan Revolution.

I asked her was she inside the fortifications of the Alamo during the fight? She answered unhesitatingly "Yes." Was she in the Alamo Church building during the last stand? She replied as before without reflection that she was, in those moments she was nursing Colonel James Bowie who was in bed very ill of typhoid fever, and that as she was in the act of giving him a drink of water the Mexican soldiery rushed in, wounding her in the chin—showing an old scar— and killing Bowie in her arms. She demonstrated this scene in quite an active fashion and showed us exactly how she was holding Bowie, her left arm around his shoulders and a drinking cup in her right hand.

I next asked her what was done with the bodies of the Texans? She said all were cremated. With the bodies of the dead Mexicans? All were cremated. Were there many American families living in San Antonio then? Some, but they all fled or the men took refuge within the Alamo. Did she know Mrs. Dickinson? Yes, but not well. She adopted an expression of considerable repugnance at this question, and said with some snap that Mrs. Dickinson hated Mexicans. Perhaps Mrs. Dickinson has some reason to do so! I was particular to ask her about a child of Mrs. Dickinson and she said that the husband of Mrs. Dickinson was fighting as one of the defenders of the Alamo and that when he saw the cause was lost he hastened down from the walls and took his son, a little child, and tied him around his waist in front of him, got to the top of the wall at the front of the Church and jumped down among the fighting Mexicans below and both were killed. This is very dramatic but it is not I believe elsewhere recorded. Being anxious to know about the daughter of Mrs. Dickinson I asked her if she had not heard that such a child had escaped the massacre with her mother. She believed she said, that Mrs. Dickinson had taken a daughter with her in her flight, she had been told so at any rate.

She said that she recollected David Crockett before the fight. But she could not have known him well, for Crockett was only in San Antonio a few weeks before he lost his life in the Alamo. The rest of the Texans she did not know so well. Most of these men came to San Antonio just previous to the siege. She did not know anything of Ben Milam who was killed in the Veraméndi House at the storming of San Antonio in December, 1835. She had not heard of him nor was she aware that he was buried on Milam Square, and that there was a stone to his memory there, though her house and jacal were almost within a stone throw of the place.

I then asked her age. The old lady said one hundred years and three months, holding out three very wrinkled fingers. Her hands were large for a Mexican. She looked quite the age she said, or older, for that matter, great deep ridges, wrinkles and furrows of skin on her face and hands as "brown as is the ribbed sea sand." She was almost toothless, very little hair of a light yellowish color. Never suffered any sickness, quite active, alert and quick to perceive and understand. A cigarette smoker. Her eyes she feared were beginning to fail her; they were rheumish with red circles underneath.

My friend next interviewed her with his camera and took two excellent negatives in different positions. I then asked her a question upon a matter which had puzzled me and which puzzles me still, though she had a ready answer to it as she had for any other asked. She informed me that the water from the Acequia was used constantly by the defenders of the Alamo during the siege. I naturally asked why the besiegers did not cut off the water or divert it and so distress those within? She said the Indians at the Missions would not have allowed this!

She remembered perfectly that there was a roof formerly to the Alamo Church prior to the siege, but that it was destroyed during the siege by the cannonading.

She had given, when her memory was better, full dispositions and statements of all her recollections to Major Teel, and that he held the same. As to Mr. Gentilz's picture that was compiled from her personal descriptions and recollections. It was very good: that it was an exact representation of the Alamo as it was at the time of its fall, and that it gave a fair idea of the fight.

She mentioned Mr. John Twohig, saying that she knew him "Como mis manos,"—"Like my hands," which is a favorite idiom of the old woman. "Visitors come every day to see me to hear my story of the Alamo."

Returning to the subject of David Crockett, the old Señora said he was one of the first to fall; that he advanced from the Church building "towards the wall or rampart running from the end of the stockade, slowly and with great deliberation, without arms, when suddenly a volley was fired by the Mexicans causing him to fall forward on his face, dead."

She was quite anxious to remember everything. With reference to a man whom many regard to be an imposter, and of whom no one has ever gleaned anything authentic, Señora Candelaria said she could endorse him as another child of the Alamo. She remembered his frightened condition during the bombardment. "He clutched her dress as children do," trying to hide his face.

Such are her recollections; the reader must make many allowances. So long and active a life as hers must be crowded—more—overcrowded, and jumbled with the multitude of things to remember.

On other occasions, in April of this year, I revisited her twice with a good interpreter as a companion, and she said: "My maiden name was Andrea Castañon. I was born on St. Andrew's day, in November, 1785, at Laredo. I am 105 years old. I have been twice married; my first husband was Silberio Flores y Abrigo; my second was Candelario Villanueva,* but I am called familiarly Señora Candelaria.

I may add that I read to my companions these interviews at the dates of our visits. I wrote them from notes taken at the time upon arriving home, and my companions subscribed to every particular.

---

* I find the following in the County Records—ED
   "I do solemnly swear that I was a resident citizen of Texas at the date of the Declaration of Independence. That I did not leave the country during the Campaign of the spring of 1836 to avoid participation in the War, and that I did not aid nor assist the Enemy: that I have not previously received a title for my quantum of land, and that I conceive myself to be justly entitled under the Constitution and laws to the quantity for which I now apply. April 29th, 1837. CANDELARIO VILLANUEVA."

1.9.2.   Madame Candelaria, newspaper interview, 1892.

San Antonio Express. March 6, 1892.
   Matovina (1995, 52–53) notes that Madame Candelaria's proper name was Andrea Castañón Villanueva, and she was married to Candelario Villanueva (1.5.1.2). He also says she was 88 (born in 1803), rather than the 107 claimed, at the time of this interview.

FALL OF THE ALAMO

HISTORICAL REMINISCENCES
OF THE AGED MADAME CANDELERIA.

**Her Statement as to the Manner of Bowie's Death Differs
from That in Histories—An Anniversary Event.**

[*Article starts with four paragraphs summarizing the siege and fall. The article also includes an etching portrait of her.*]
   The name of Madam Candeleria [*sic*] is a household word in San Antonio. She is without doubt the oldest living native of Texas, being 107 years of age as

is shown by the certificate of the priest who administered to her spiritual wants in her childhood. This certificate is in Spanish and its authenticity cannot be disputed. The aged heroine lives in a typical Mexican house on South Laredo street, where she is visited by hundreds of tourists and old friends in the course of a year. On this day, the anniversary of the fall of the Alamo, it is befitting that a sketch of Madame Candeleria, who was in the midst of that stirring historical affair, be given. In order to secure a statement from her own lips a reporter for the EXPRESS in company with an interpreter visited her yesterday.

When the unpretentious dwelling of the centenarian was entered she rose from her comfortable chair and extended a cordial greeting to the visitors. The more than one hundred years that have passed over her head have not affected her voice in the least and she speaks the soft, musical Spanish language with a force and warmth that is entertaining and faultless in expression. In response to an inquiry of the reporter she stated that she was born on November 30, 1785 at Laredo, Tex., and the priest's certificate bears out her statement.

"My father said he was the tailor of Ferdinand VII and after my birth I lived several years at Laredo with my parents. There were only a few houses there at that time and they were mere jacales covered with hides. I was first taken by my father to Rio Grande City and then to Zarragosa. After living there a few years I lived in various places in what is now the state of Coahuila, but which was at that time embraced in the state of Texas. I afterward lived in Nacogdoches, and in 1820, came to San Antonio. This was a mere village at that time and was occupied by General Bustamanto and his troops."

In relating her reminiscences of the fall of the Alamo Mme. Candeleria stated that she was called upon a few days before the fatal attack was made to nurse Colonel Bowie, who was very sick of typhoid fever.

"Santa Anna made the attack," she continued, "on March 6. The Alamo was filled with Texans, a number of women being among them. Colonel Bowie died in my arms only a few minutes before the entrance to the Alamo by the soldiers. I was holding his head in my lap when Santa Anna's men swarmed into the room where I was sitting. One of them thrust a bayonet into the lifeless head of Colonel Bowie and lifted his body from my lap. As he did so the point of the weapon slipped and struck me in the jaw," and here the aged heroine showed the scar of the wound which she had received.

During her recital of this exciting experience she made numerous expressive gesticulations, swaying her body to and fro in a highly dramatic style.

In conclusion Madame Candeleria stated that she was never sick in her life and never took a particle of medicine of any kind. She has never even so much as had a touch of headache. Her father lived to the extreme age of 130 years and her mother 120 years.

1.9.3.   Madame Candelaria, obituary, 1899.
San Antonio Daily Express. February 11, 1899. 5.

THE LAST VOICE HUSHED
DEATH OF MADAM CANDELARIA YESTERDAY
Death Came At the Age Of 113 Years—Sketch Of the Last Survivor
Of the Fall Of the Alamo

Madame Candelaria Villanueva, the most interesting woman in Texas from a historic standpoint, the last survivor of the battle of the Alamo, perhaps the oldest woman in the world, and the sponsor and foster mother of twenty-two orphan children, died at 2:20 o'clock yesterday afternoon.

The deceased had been ill about ten days. Death was due to old age. She died at the home of her daughter, Mrs. Francisco Flores Pacheo, at 419 [?] South Concho street.

The residence is a wooden cottage and presents an unpretentious, homelike appearance. There are two large trees in the front yard. There are five rooms in the house.

Madame Candelaria lost consciousness twenty-four hours before she passed away. Just before she became unconscious she said: "Why is it that God punishes me and does not take me away when I suffer so? I have never done any one any harm and have always tried to do good. I wish God would take me."

These were her last words.

When she died yesterday afternoon she was surrounded by her immediate family and relatives.

[*Following are five paragraphs about her family and funeral, including a statement by her son that he refused "a fabulous sum" to take his mother "to the Atlanta Exposition to show her as the only remaining survivor of the battle of the Alamo."*]

Ten years ago a committee of old citizens called on Madame Candelaria and promised when she died to see that a valuable monument was erected over her grave. Most of them are now dead. Deputy County Clerk Juan Barrera said last evening:

"Madame Candelaria was with our family from 1830 to 1836 [*probable dates; not clear in photocopy*]. I was a baby then and she was my nurse. She told my parents that she was in the Alamo battle and that Bowie died in her arms. She said that she helped wash and prepare the dead for burial, and that Santa Ana burned them afterwards. When I was a lad I frequently saw a wooden monument upon which was inscribed: 'Here lied the heroes of the Alamo.' This monument stood about where the St. Joseph's Catholic Church now stands."

[*Nine more short paragraphs follow on her funeral arrangements, Alamo, birthdate, family, and life.*]

The deceased claimed that on [*only*] a short time before the battle of the Alamo she saw Santa Ana, the Mexican general, come into the city in disguise. She said that he drove a mule and was apparently selling hay, while getting his plans of the battle mapped out. It was her idea that he did the work himself, not wishing to entrust so important a duty to any of his aides.

She always contended that James Bowie, the famous scout, died of pneumonia the day before the battle of the Alamo. She had nursed him and after the massacre with the dead and dying all around her she fell upon his body and entered heartrending pleas to the Mexican soldiers not to take his body, explaining that he had not died in battle, but had died a natural death and was therefore entitled to a regular burial.

While she was entreating and pleading one of the Mexican soldiers drew his bayonet, striking her on the chin and the right wrist. The scars of the wound made at that time she will carry with her to the grave. It is said that the same bayonet went through Bowie's body.

After Madame Candelaria had been silenced Bowie was taken out of the Alamo and burned on a rude funeral pyre. She was not massacred. A squad of Mexican soldiers were placed over her and later one of the Mexican generals came in and withdrew them. Her life had been spared because of her nationality.

[*The remaining six paragraphs continue with later events, such as being put to hard labor by the Mexican Army, treating the sick during a smallpox epidemic, cooking for prominent Texans, raising twenty-two orphans, and giving money to stranded "forty-niners." The article ends by noting, "She had been visited by thousands of people . . . from one to twenty-five visitors a day" and received a $12 monthly pension from the state of Texas. The article also includes a sketch portrait.*]

1.9.4.   Madame Candelaria, newspaper interview, about 1898.

San Antonio Light. February 19, 1899. 6.

There are quite a number of typos, inconsistencies, and misspellings in this document, and Madame Candelaria is most often rendered as Madam Candaleria.

ALAMO MASSACRE
AS TOLD BY THE LATE MADAM CANDALERIA
**Her Vivid Story of the Great Battle, Where 177 Brave Men
Met Death as True Heroes—Colonel Bowie Died
in Her Arms—Blood Was Ankle Deep.**

The St. Louis Republic recently published a lenghty article about the late Madam Candaleria and the Battle of the Alamo, which will prove of interest to San Antonians:

Old Madam Candaleria says that she has heard and read a hundred different descriptions of the battle of the Alamo, and that not one is correct. Although she is now in her one hundred and sixteenth year, her health is good, and her mind is perfectly clear as to events that transpired in the early part of the century. Her great age and the conspicuous and heroic part that she enacted during the famous siege of the Alamo are matters that are well authentic and beyond all question of doubt. A few years ago the Texas Legislature appointed a committee to wait upon this very remarkable woman and investigate all the facts connected with her claims upon the gratitude of the state. After examining many witnesses, and looking over the records preserved in the old missions, they reported that no doubt could exist as to the fact that Madam Candaleria was inside of the walls of the Alamo engaged in nursing Colonel James Bowie at the time the battle was fought, and further declared that they believed she was born in the year A.D. 1782. Acting upon this report, and promptly by a commendable desire to promptly recognize and reward the services of one who had done so much to aid in the establishment of the old republic, the legislature granted a pension of $100 a year to this heroic old lady.

Mme. Candaleria is still alive, and living in a small adobe house at 611 Laredo street, San Antonio. Nothing pleases her better than to receive a visitor who manifests interest in her story of the fall of the Alamo. She is totally blind, and though rather feeble and somewhat slow and hesitating in the use of the English language, she manages, through rapid and emphatic gestures, occasionally assisted by a Spanish girl who is constantly by her side, to give an attentive listener a very impressive description of one of the most remarkable battles ever fought in the history of the world.

Mme. Candaleria is a born revolutionist, and during the whole of her long life she has been in sympathy with every people who were struggling for freedom. She has kept well posted concerning the progress of the war in Cuba, and so eager she has been for the success of the revolution that she has frequently sent small sums of money to the Cuban junta in New York.

Not long ago, when she received a check for her pension, she told her grand-daughter to go to one of the stores and purchase her a pair of shoes. When the young girl was getting ready to obey the request some one happened to say something about the Cuban war. The old lady sprang up on the side of her cot and excitedly exclaimed: "Never mind the shoes, send $2 to the Cubans; I can go barefooted until next pay day.["] This little act is characteristic of her whole life. She is a lover of justice and charitable to a fault. A young lady who was present during my visit, said: "They call for [*sic*] her the mother of the waifs and the strays, and those who have known her a long time say that she has raised about forty children, though she never had but two of her own."

Though every drop of her blood is Spanish blood, she has never loved Spain, from the fact that her father's family was forcibly moved to Texas from the Canary islands about the middle of the last century for the purpose of carrying out a colonization scheme, concerning which her poeple were never consulted.

She married a revolutionist, who embraced the first opportunity to show his hatred of the mother country.

He fought with Perry, Mina, Magee, and Toledo.

Mad. Candaleria was with the Americans at the terrible battle of the Median, where 800 revolutionists charged a whole Mexican army, and she saw 707 of these fall dead and wounded upon the bloody field. Here her husband was wounded, and a flame of bitter hatred against Mexico ever afterwards burned fiercely in her breast.

In 1836 she kept a hotel in San Antonio, and her house was always at the disposal of Houston, Austin, Travis, Lamar and such other daring spirits as were at that time committing themselves to the cause of Texas freedom. All of the old warriors knew her well, and all of them admired her many fine traits of character, and her patriotic devotion to the sacred principles, for maintenance of which many of them afterwards sacrificed their lives. James Bowie had been living in San Antonio for several years, where he was very popular with all classes. The Mexicans, who were still attached to the old country, hoped that he would embrace their cause, from the fact that he had married a beautiful Mexican girl. But the alarm was no sooner sounded than this man of peerless valor offered his services to Texas. When Santa Anna suddenly appeared on the prairies, in sight of San Antonio, at the head of a veteran army of 10,000 men, Colonel Bowie was very sick. Hopeful as all are who are afflicted with consumption, he still felt himself able to discharge the duties of a soldier. He went to the Alamo and declared that he would fight as a private. It was not long before he was confined to his cot. General Houston wrote a letter to Mme. Canaleria, which she still possesses, asking her to look after his friend Bowie, and nurse him herself. All save Bowie himself realized that the hero was in the last stages of consumption.

When Santa Anna invested the city and drew a cordon of troops around the Alamo, Mme. Candaleria was inside of the walls. She might easily have returned to her home, but her heart was with the patriots, and she determined to remain with them and share their fortunes. Bowie grew worse every day. He was never able to sit up more than a few moments at any period during the time that the battle was going on. He occupied the little room on the left of the great front door, and Mme. Candellario sat by his side. When the firing grew hot he would ask his faithful nurse to assist him to raise himself to the window. He would aim deliberately and after firing would fall back on his cot and rest. One evening Colonel Travis made a fine speech to his soldiers. Mme. Candaleria does not pretend to remember what he said, but she does remember that he drew a line on the floor with the point of his sword and asked all who were willing to die for Texas to come over on his side. They quickly stepped across the line but two men. One of these sprang over the wall and disappeared. The other man was James Bowie. He made an effort to rise, but failed, and with tears streaming from his eyes, he said: "Boys, won't none of you help me over there?" Colonel Davy Crockett and several others instantly sprang towards the cot and carried the brave man across the line. Mme. Candelleria noticed Crockett drop on his knees and talk earnestly in low tones to Colonel Bowie for a long time. "At this time," says the heroic old lady, "we all knew that we were doomed, but not one was in favor of surrendering. A small herd of cattle had been driven inside of the walls, and we had found a small quantity of corn that had been stored by the priests. The great front door had been piled full of sand bags, and there was a bare hope that we might hold out until General Houston sent a re-enforcement.

"There were just 177 men inside of the Alamo, and up to this time no one had been killed, though cannon had thundered against us and several assaults had been made. Colonel Travis was the first man killed. He fell on the southeast side near where the Menger hotel stands. The Mexican infantry charged across the plaza many times, and rained musket balls against the walls, but they were always made to recoil. Up to the morning of the 6th. of March, the cannon had done us little damage, though the batteries never ceased firing. Colonel Crockett frequently came into the room and said a few encouraging words to Bowie. This man came to San Antonio only a few days before the invasion. The Americans extended him a warm welcome. They made bonfires in the streets, and Colonel Crockett must have made a great speech, for I never heard so much cheering and hurrahing in all my life. They had supper at my hotel and there was lots of singing, story telling and some drinking. Crockett played the fiddle and he played well if I am any judge of music. He was one the strangest-looking men I ever saw. He had the face of a woman and his manner was that of a young girl. I could not regard him as a hero until I saw him die. He looked grand and terrible standing in the door and fighting a whole column of Mexican infantry. He had fired his last shot, and had no time to reload. The cannon balls had knocked away the sand bags, and the infantry was pouring through the breech, Crockett stood there swinging something bright over his head. The place was full of smoke and I could not tell whether he was using a gun or a sword. A heap of dead was piled at his feet, and the Mexicans were lunging at him with bayonets, but he would not retereat an inch. Poor Bowie could see it all, but he could not raise up from his cot, Crockett fell and the Mexicans poured into the Alamo."

On the morning of the 6th of March, 1836, General Santa Anna prepared to hurl his whole force against the doomed fort. The duguelo was sounded and Mme. Candaleria says that they all very well understood what it meant, and every man prepared to sell his life as dearly as possible.

The soldiers with blanched cheeks and a look of fearless firmness, gathered in groups and conversed on low tones. Colonel Crockett and about a dozen strong men stood with their guns in their hands behind the sand bags at the front. The cot upon which Colonel Bowie reposed was in the little room on the north side, within a few feet of the position occupied by Crockett and his men.

These two brave spirits frequently exchanged a few words while waiting for the Mexicans to begin the battle. "I sat by Bowie's side," says Mme. Candaleria, "and tried to keep him as composed as possible. He had a high fever and was seized with a fit of coughing every few moments. Colonel Crockett loaded Bowie's rifle and a pair of pistols and laid them by his side. The Mexicans ran a battery of several guns out on the plaze and instantly began to rain balls against the sand bags. It was easy to see that they would soon clear every barricade from the front door, but Crockett assured Bowie that he could stop a whole regiment from entering. I peeped through the window and saw long lines of infantry, followed by dragoons, filing into the plaza, and I notified Colonel Crockett of the fact. 'All right,' said he. 'Boys, aim well!' The words had hardly died on his lips before a storm of bullets rained against the walls and the very earth seemed to tremble beneath the tread of Santa Anna's yelling legions. The Texans made every shot tell, and the plaza was covered with dead bodies. The assaulting columns recoiled, and I thought we had beaten them, but hosts of officers could be seen waving their swords and rallying the hesitating and broken columns.

"They charged again, and at one time, when within a dozen steps of the door, it looked as if they were about to be driven back, so terrible was the fire of the Texans. Those immediately in front of the great door were certainly in the act of retiring when a column that had come obliquely across the plaza reached the southwest corner of the Alamo and bending their bodies, they ran under the shelter of the wall to the door. It looked as if a hunder bayonets were thrust into the door at the same time, and a sheet of flame lit up the Alamo. Every man at the door fell but Crockett, I could see him struggling with the head of the column, and Bowie raised up and fired his rifle. I saw Crockett fall backwards. The enraged Mexicans then streamed into the building firing and yelling like madman. The place was full of smoke, and the death scream of the dying, mingled with the exultant shouts of the victors, made it a vertiable hell. A dozen or more Mexicans sprang into the room occupied by Colonel Bowie. He emptied his pistols in their faces and killed two of them. As they lunged towards him with their muskets I threw myself in front of them and received two of their bayonets in my body. One passed through my arm and the other through the flesh of my chin. Here, senor, are the scars; you can see them yet. I implored them not to murder a sick man, but they thrust me out the way and butchered my friend before my eyes. All was silent now. The massacre had ended. One hundred and seventy-six of the bravest men that the world ever saw had fallen, and not one had asked for mercy. I walked out of the cell, and when I stepped upon the floor of the Alamo the blood ran into my shoes."

1.10.1.   Alamo Survivors, analysis, 1946.

Williams, Amelia. April 1946. *Southwestern Historical Quarterly*. 49:634–37.
This is an overview of all survivors of the fall of the Alamo. No account has
been located for those survivors not already included in documents above.

Questions on the Alamo are recurrent in the office. The following inquiry is
somewhat typical and, as Dr. Amelia Williams's reply is quite meaty, it is a pleasure to make the information generally available in the Texas Collection. Miss
Williams' doctoral dissertation was, "A Critical Study of the Siege and Fall of
the Alamo." Portions of the study were published in the Quarterly between
July, 1933, and April, 1934.

Colonel Gerald E. Cronin, 426 South Main Street, Milford, Michigan, writes
as follows:

While stationed at Laredo, Texas, in 1914 or 1915, I dimly recall reading an
article in one of the San Antonio papers concerning an aged woman who, as an
infant, had survived the Alamo battle.

Recently reading Herbert Gorman's *The Wine of San Lorenzo*, I noted that he
makes this alleged survivor into a boy.

I would deeply appreciate if you would set me right on this matter. (1) Was
there any survivor of the Alamo? (2) If so, what was his or her name and when
and where did he or she die?

Dr. Williams's reply is as follows:

So far as I know, my thesis, "A Critical Study of the Siege and Fall of the
Alamo and of the Personnel of its Defenders," contain[s] citations of all the reliable sources, both original and published, concerning the various aspects of the
Alamo story. My bibliography is somewhat long. Since my information that
answers the questions asked by Colonel Cronin is gathered from many sources,
I make the above statement. However, I shall also cite a few specific sources that
deal partially with the questions asked. They are as follows:

1. ORIGINAL SOURCES.
    a. Bounty and Donation Certificates—General Land Office of Texas.
    b. Court of Claims Files—General Land Office of Texas.
    c. Headright Certificates—General Land Office
    d. Comptroller's Military Service Records, Texas State Library.
    e. Petitions and Memorials—Texas State Library.
    f. Financial Papers—Texas State Library.
2. PRINTED SOURCES
    a. *The Lamar Papers.*
    b. Gray, F. W., *From Virginia to Texas.*
    c. *The Austin Papers.*
    d. *The Southwestern Historical Quarterly*—Volumes used, I to XXIII.

e. *Texas Almanac,* 1856–1873.

f. Barnes, C. M., *Combats and Conquests of Immortal Heroes.*

g. Caro, Ramon Martinez, *Veradera Idea de la Primera Campana de Tejas y Suceses ocurridos despues de la Accion de San Jacinto,* (Mexico, 1837).

h. Clairborne, Airie M., *The Story of the Alamo.*

i. Corner, William, *San Antonio de Bejar.*

j. Filisola, Vicente, *Memorias para la Historia de la Guerra de Tejas*—two volumes.

k. Linn, John J., *Reminiscences of Fifty Years in Texas.*

l. Rodrigues, J. M., *Memories of Early Texas.*

m. Winkler, E. W., *The Alamo.*

n. Wright, Ione, *San Antonio, Historical, Traditional, Legendary* (and scores of other printed sources that deal in scrappy manner with subjects desired).

3. NEWSPAPERS

a. *Telegraph and Texas Register,* March 12, 24, 1836; March 28, 1837; March 23, 1842; July 26, 1843.

b. *El Correo Atlantico,* April 11, 18, 1836; June 13, 1836.

c. *Austin City Gazette,* April 14, 1841; July 17, 1874.

d. *San Antonio Express,* November 24, 1901; May 12, 1907; February 18, 1912; September 8, 1912, etc.

e. *El Mosquito Mexicana,* (Garcia Library) April 5, 1836.

All the sources that I have investigated—original documents as well as printed accounts—agree in saying that there were fifteen or more women and children in the Alamo at the time of its fall on March 6, 1836. Most of these were San Antonio citizens who took refuge within the Alamo when the Mexican army arrived at San Antonio on February 22, 1836. Most of the women and children belonged to the defenders of the fortress.

I was never able to verify by name all these women, but for the following women I was able to find considerable information: (1) Mrs. Almeron Dickinson and her fifteen-month-old daughter, Angelina. Angelina was subsequently known in Texas as the "Babe of the Alamo." Almeron Dickinson was a captain in command of the artillery force at the Alamo. Mrs. Dickinson lived until the 1880's (I do not recall the date of death and do not have notes available). Angelina married the son of an old Texas family by the name of Frank Griffith. This couple had three children, two sons and a daughter.

(2) Mrs. Horace Alsbury, formerly Mrs. Alijo Perez, born Juana Navarro, daughter of José Angel Navarro II, the only member of the large Navarro family not loyal to the Texan cause. At the time of the siege of the Alamo, José Angel Navarro II was an officer in Santa Anna's army. His wife had died when his two daughters were small children. His sister, Mrs. Juan Martin Veremendi, had adopted the children and had reared them as her own children. Mrs. Alsbury

had married Dr. Horace Alsbury in January, 1836. When it was certain that Santa Anna was marching into Texas with a large army, Dr. Alsbury left his family—his wife, her eighteen-month-old son, Alijo Perez, and her fifteen-year-old sister, Gertrudis Navarro—in the care of James Bowie, while he (Dr. Alsbury) went to East Texas to prepare a place of safety for them. James Bowie looked upon these Navarro girls as if they were his own sisters, for they were first cousins and foster sisters of his deceased wife, Ursula Veremendi. So when the Mexican army arrived in San Antonio, February 22, 1836, he took them into the Alamo with him, and they were there during the siege and fall. In 1842, Dr. Horace Alsbury was killed, and soon afterward his wife married again, this time to Juan Perez, a cousin of her first husband. I did not trace her career further. Gertrudis Navarro married one Juan M. Cantu, a wealthy and influential Mexican. She lived out her life in Mexico.

(3) Another woman definitely known to have been within the Alamo fortress at the time of its fall was Mrs. Gregorio Esparza with her four children. Her son Enrique was nearly nine years old at the time. He grew to manhood and lived in San Antonio, Texas, to be an old man. He was intelligent, received a fair education, and was considered an honest, honorable citizen. He was frequently interviewed by newspaper men. The San Antonio *Express*, May 12, 1907, carries the story he told of his recollections of the fall of the Alamo. The Bounty and Donation Certificates, Bexar No. 1183, Travis No. 762, and the Court of Claims Applications No. 572, File (D–G)—all in the General Land Office of Texas, give full accounts of Gregorio Esparza and his family. Gregorio Esparza was one of the Alamo victims.

(4) Mrs. Toribio Losoya—later Mrs. Milton—and her three children were in the Alamo. Her husband was a Texas soldier and died in the defense of the fort.

(5) I have also verified the fact that Trinidad Saucedo and Dona Petra (a very old woman) were also in the fort. I know nothing about them afterwards.

(6) Madam Candalaria, a Mexican woman of worthy service during the 1840's in San Antonio, as nurse during epidemics of smallpox, always claimed that she also was in the Alamo during its siege and fall. She gave many interviews to newspaper men and anyone who would hear her. Her stories varied from time to time. In her old age she settled on the story that she was in the Alamo to nurse James Bowie, and that he was killed as she raised him in her arms to give him a drink. Documents of 1836 do not bear out this story. It seems that she went into the Alamo (only sixteen years old) with her lover, Antonio Cruz y Arocha, a young Mexican of high birth, a member of Juan Seguin's company, and that when Travis sent him out as a messenger, February 29, 1836, he took his sweetheart with him. But the old lady always claimed that she was at the Alamo during the massacre. Texas gave her a pension for her services. She deserved the pension for her service as a nurse in San Antonio, even if she was not at the Alamo when it fell. Since her story was believed by many who had never investigated earlier documents, I tell it here.

Besides these women and children, two negro slave boys were left alive after the massacre. Joe, the servant of Travis, and Sam, Bowie's man. Then, too, there was old Anselmo Borgarra who claimed that he was Travis's bodyguard during the final assault, although he was never a combatant against the Mexicans. It was Borgarra who first reached Gonzales with the news of the Alamo disaster.

I have never read *The Wine of San Lorenzo,* but I suspect that the boy immortalized was Enrique Esparza.

The old woman, about whom Colonel Cronin remembers to have read in a San Antonio paper, was probably Madam Candalaria, or it may have been Mrs. Dickinson. Mrs. Dickinson was frequently interviewed by writers. It was not she herself, however, but her daughter Angelina who was the child of the Alamo.

1.10.2.1. Brigidio Guerrero, petition, January 4, 1861.

Guerrero, Brigidio. January 4, 1861. Court of Claims Voucher File #3416. General Land Office, Texas.

This excerpt records the claim of Brigidio Guerrero that he was in the Alamo at the time of the fall. The referenced file includes four other documents, the second of which follows next.

To the Hone. the County Court of Bexar County
Your petitioner Brigidio Guerrero of the county of Bexar and State of Texas—respectfully represents unto your Hone Court that he was born in the year 1810 and is at present fifty years of age, that at the date of the declaration of Independence he was a resident citizen of Texas and a Single man over 17 years of age as as [sic; and as] Such Justly entitled under the Constitution and laws of the Republic of Texas to a first class head right certificate for one third of a league of land which he has never received nor any part there of[.] your petitioner further represents and affirms on oath that far from leaving the country to avoid a participation in Struggle, far from refusing to participate in the war, he was one of those who entered the Alamo under Col Travis, in February 1836 that he was one of the defenders of that place that he remained there up to the last moment and that when after the storming of the place by the Mexican army he saw that there was no hope left, he had the good fortune of saving his life by concealing himself, he and perhaps one other man an American being the only survivors of that awful butchery[.]

Petitioner since that time has always resided either in the city of San Antonio or on the ranchos situated in the vicinity of that place and he believes that under the existing laws of the state of Texas he is justly entitled to claim against the state of Texas his aforesaid Headright certificate as well for his military services, his ignorance of the English language and his rights prevented him from applying before for the same. He therefore prays your Honᵉ Court to receive this his application for a first class headright certificate for one third of a league of land and permit him to prove the Justice of his claim by the Testimony of credible witnesses and made all proofs required by law in order that a certificate for the Land claimed may issue in his favor

And as in duty bound will pray—

sworn so and	his
subscribed in open	Brigidio + Guerrero
Court this 4 day	mark
January AD 1861.	
Sam S. Smith	
CRKCCBCo	

1.10.2.2. Brigidio Guerrero, petition, January 5, 1861.

Brigidio Guerrero. January 5, 1861. Testimony of Eugenio Munos. Court of Claims Voucher File #3416. General Land Office, Texas.

This document is the second of five documents in the referenced Court of Claims file to support the claim of Brigidio Guerrero. The third is the deposition by Juan Garcia that follows, and the two remaining are court documents recording the examination of Guerrero, Munos, and Garcia on December 30, 1860, and the formal recording of the application on February 2, 1861.

The State of Texas	County Court
County of Bexar	December Term AD 1860

On this 5ᵗʰ day of January AD 1861 personally appeared in open court Ugenio Munos who being duly sworn deposed and Said that he witness the applicant Brigido Guerrero previous to the declaration of Independence in the city of San Antonio, that in the beginning of the Year 1836 applicant was attached to the person of Col Bowie and was employed in procuring cattle for the support of the Garrison at the Alamo at the beginning of the Seige [*sic*] that Applicant to the Knowledge of witness was in the alamo at the time it was attacked[.] witness knows the above facts from the fact that his house was convenient to the alamo and which was destroyed by order of Col Travis[.] witness learned by public notoriety that applicant saved his life after the Alamo was taken as also he saw the applicant a few days after and since then applicant has resided either in the city of San Antonio or the county of Bexar continuously without interruptions, applicant was a resident citizen of the country a Single man over

17 years of age, a free white man of Mexican origin and is now fifty years old or thereabout, and that [*t*]he witness conceives applicant justly entitled to a First Class headright certificate for one third of one league of land, which he has never received or any part thereof to witnesses knowledge. Witness was a grown up a man at the time of the seige of the alamo and has a perfect recollection of the occurrances [*sic*] which took place at the time and is now over forty years old and is well acqueunted [*sic*] with Sam A Maverck Sam S Smith Judge Tho J Devine Francis Guilbeen Francis Giraud, as also several other prominent citizens of Bexar county and that applicant is the same person of whom he gives testimony

	his
sworn so and sub-	Eugenio + Munozs
scribed in Open Court	mark
This 5th day of January	
A.D. 1861. Sam S. Smith	
CR.KC.C.B.Co.	

1.10.2.3. Brigidio Guerrero, petition, January 4, 1861.

Brigidio Guerrero. January 4, 1861. Testimony of Juan Garcia. Court of Claims Voucher File #3416. General Land Office, Texas.

The State of Texas	County Court
County of Bexar	December Term AD1860

On this 4th day of January AD 1861 personally appeared in open court Juan Garcia who being duly sworn deposed and Said that [*t*]he witness became acquainted with the applicant Brigidio Guerrero in the latter part of the year 1835. At the Storming of the Alamo it was of public notoriety that applicant went in there with the Americans but witness does not know in what capacity and it was also of public notoriety that applicant made his escape after the alamo was taken by the Mexicans and consequently escaped the massacre of that day, that at the date of the declaration of Independence 2n. March 1836 applicant was a Single man over 17 years of age he being now over fifty years old, that applicant is a free white man of Mexican origin and that he has resided ever since witness became acquainted with him either in San Antonio or Bexar county, and that to the best of witensses [*sic*] Knowledge applicant never received his granturn [*sic*] of land which in the opinion of witness he is entitled viz one third of a league of land, that witness knows all the above facts from personal knowledge being always intimate with applicant and his family which consists of his wife and three or four children one of whom is married, and that applicant is the same person of whom he testifys [*sic*] witness is acquainted with Sam A Maverick Sam S. Smith Judge Th⁵. I Devine Judge Jno. H. Duncan Francis Guilbean Francis Giraud as well as many other prominent citizens of Bexar county

sworn So and	his
subscribed in	Juan + Garcia
Open Court this 4ᵗʰ	mark
day of January 1861.	
Sam S. Smith	
CRKCCBCo	

1.10.2.4. Brigidio Guerrero, sworn statement, 1874.

Guerrero, Brigidio. October 27, 1874. Republic Claims, PE-Guerrero, Brigido [*sic*]; 996; R:218 Fr:0178, TSLA.

The State of Texas Before me the undersigned
County of Bexar authority personally came and
appeared Brigido Guerrero to me well known born in Tallemango Mexico who being by me duly sworn deposed and declares that he is 64 years of age that he emigrated to Texas in 1832 that he has lived in Texas up to the present time that he served as a volunteer with many other Mexican citizens of San Antonio and the Missions that he was camped at the old Mill above and near San Antonio with the Texian troops and that he aided the same in capturing San Antonio in December 1835 that he participated in the siege of San Antonio at that time that he remained with the Texian troops until they were disbanded or returned to their homes affiant further says that he is the identical Brigido Gueriero [*sic*] he represents himself to be

his
Brigido X Guerrero
mark

Sworn so and subscribed before me on this the 27ᵗʰ day of October AD 1874 and to certify which I hereinto sign my name and affix the impress of my official seal at Office in San Antonio on the day and Year first hereabove written
Jno. [?] Rosenheimer
Notary Public Bexar County

1.10.2.5. Brigidio Guerrero, testimony, 1874.

Guerrero, Brigidio. October 29, 1874. Testimony of Remigio Casanova. Republic Claims, PE-Guerrero, Brigido [*sic*]; 996; R:218 Fr:0184, TSLA.

The State of Texas   Before me the undersigned
County of Bexar   authority personally came and
appeared Remigio Casanova of said State and County to me well known who being by me duly sworn deposes and declares that a few days after the battle Concepcion he saw Brigido Guerrerro in the camp with the Texians there stationed near the battle ground and that he had arms in his hand and appeared to be acting as a soldier and affiant further says that he subsequently and about that time saw Brigido Guerrero with the Texian troops camped at the leodite [?] on the East side of the San Antonio River above and near San Antonio and that he remained with the Texian troops until the fall of the Alamo in March 1836

his

Remigio X Casanova

mark

Sworn to and subscribed before me on this the 29th day of October AD 1874

Geo. W. Caldwill

Notary Public

BC.

1.10.2.6. Brigidio Guerrero, published account, 1882.

Gould, Stephen. 1882. *The Alamo City Guide, San Antonio, Texas. Being a Historical Sketch of the Ancient City of the Alamo and Business Review* . . . 21–22. New York: Macgowan & Slipper, Printers.

This excerpt is an early published record for Brigidio Guerrero's claim.

In one of the rooms of the Alamo were three non-combatants: Mrs. Dickinson and her infant daughter (Mrs. Alsbury), and a negro servant of Colonel Travis. Mrs. Dickinson, now Mrs. Hanning, alone survives, and resides in Austin. Her infant daughter afterwards married, and was the mother of A. D. Griffith, who resides in Yarrelton, Milam county, in this State. She died in 1868. It is related that the last Mrs. Dickinson saw of her husband, Captain Dickinson, was when he rushed into her room and said: "My dear wife, they are coming over the wall; we are all lost. He then silently embraced her and their babe, and said: "May God spare you and our dear baby." He drew his sword and went out, and his body was afterwards found riddled with bullets. In the fall of 1878, an aged

Mexican by the name of Brigido Guerrero applied to the County Court of Bexar county for a pension as a survivor of the Alamo. His story is that he was one of the soldiers under Colonel Travis, and continued to fight until the enemy had entered the enclosure. Seeing that further resistance was useless he entered the room in which were the women, and was concealed by them under some bedding, where he remained until night, and then made his escape. Although he has steadfastly maintained the truth of this story since 1843, his veracity is doubted by many of the early inhabitants. At any rate, the evidence he offered the court was so strong that he was placed on the pension list, and to the present writing has received aid from the State.

1.10.3.   Henry Warnell, deposition for heir, 1858.

Anderson, Henry. Deposition, July 30, 1858. Court of Claims File #8490, General Land Office, Texas.

This deposition raises the possibility of one Alamo defender having survived the fall by a few months. There are a number of documents in this Court of Claims File #8490 (e.g., 1.2.5) that primarily establish a son John as the heir and that Henry Warnell was an Alamo defender. One description in these documents is that he was about five foot three and 120 pounds, had red hair with fair skin and freckles, and was quite a talker and an extravagant tobacco chewer. The validity of this particular claim with respect to the others in the file is discussed in the commentary.

To the Hon. Edmond Clark,
Commissioner of Claims
Austin, Texas.
The undersigned would respectfully represent that Henry Warnell was a soldier under Travis—at the massacre of the Alamo, in the year 1836, in the struggle for Texan Independence; that he was wounded at the said massacre but made his escape to Port Lavacca, where he died in less than three months from the effects of said wound.—That he was a single man, and as such entitled to receive a Headright, of one third of a League, a Bounty of 1920 acres, and Donation of 640 acres. Respectfully submitted.

Henry Anderson
Agent for the Heirs

Sworn to and subscribed before me. In witness whereof I have herein to subscribe my name and affixed the impress of my official seal, at office in Belknap, this 30th day of July A.D. 1858.

James H. Swindells.
Notary Public
Young Co. Texas.

1.10.4.   Possible survivors, newspaper account, 1836.

Arkansas Gazette. March 29, 1836.

Lord (5.2.2) notes that the end of this article suggests that there might have been other survivors from the fall.

LATE FROM TEXAS—San Antonio safe—*Gen. Cos again defeated*—By a gentle-man who arrived here yesterday morning, direct from New Orleans, which place he left on the 17th inst., we learn, that the Louisiana Advertiser, of that morning, contained news, derived from the Captain of a vessel from a Texas port, which he left on the 6th inst., that Gen. Cos had again been defeated at San Antonio—that he had attacked that post with 1000 men, and after a sharp con-test, had been compelled to retire with the loss of 500 men killed. He then retreated across the river, with the remnant of his troops, and was pursued by 800 Texian troops. Col. Travis' force in the garrison, it was said, amounted to 150 men—their loss not ascertained.

If this intelligence be true, as we hope it is, it will inspire the Texian troops with fresh vigor; and the Mexican troops, having received so signal a defeat in the commencement of the campaign, will be proportionally disheartened, and will probably fall as easy prey to the victorious arms of the revolutionists.

———

LATER—*San Antonio re-taken, and the Garrison massacred*—Just as our paper was ready for press, a gentleman who arrived this morning, from Red River, informs us that, on Thursday night last, he spent the night, on the Little Mis-souri, with a man and his family, who had fled from the vicinity of San Antonio, after that post was besieged by the Mexicans. This man, he says, informed him, that, on his arrival at Nacogdoches, he was overtaken by two men (one of them badly wounded), who informed him that San Antonio was re-taken by the Mex-icans, and the garrison put to the sword—that, if any others escaped the general massacre, beside themselves, they were not aware of it.

We give the above report, precisely as it was communicated to us by our informant, who was recently a citizen of this county, and is a man of veracity. We hope it may be unfounded—but fear that our next accounts from that quar-ter will confirm it.

1.11.1.   Williams, dissertation, 1931.

Williams, Amelia. January 1934. A critical study of the siege of the Alamo and of the personnel of its defenders. *Southwestern Historical Quarterly* 37:159–61.

The most difficult task accomplished in Williams's dissertation was verification, to the extent possible, of the identity of the defenders. For the complete documentation and analysis for each individual, her complete thesis must be consulted, but her roster at least is worthwhile here. The name of John M. Hays, of Tennessee, is missing from this list but included in the detailed documentation. A more recent version of her analysis is Groneman 1990.

2. Roster of the Victims

Travis never made a complete return to the Texan government of his forces at the Alamo,[5] whatever muster-rolls he may have used in his command of the fort were apparently destroyed by the Mexicans after they took possession of it. The roster of the Alamo dead, therefore, must necessarily be a reconstruction. Many attempts have been made to compile it, but no complete or accurate roll has ever been made, probably no absolutely accurate roster of those brave men will ever be made; however, the list of 187 names which follows, compiled from an exhaustive study of all available sources, is, I believe, as nearly complete and accurate as it is possible to make it. In addition to this verified list, I present two lists. One is a list of five names of men who *probably* died at the Alamo, the other, of six names, is of men who *possibly* died there.[6] There is some evidence that these ten [*sic*] men died at the Alamo, but it is not sufficiently clear to justify my putting them on the verified roll.

a. Victims of the Alamo Massacre Verified by Reliable Documents
[*reformatted table*]

Abamillo, Juan	Blair, Samuel C.	Carey, William R.
Allen, R.	Blazeby, William	Clark, Charles H.
Andross, Miles De Forest	Bonham, James Butler	Cloud, Daniel William
Autry, Micajah	Bowie, James	Cochran(e), Robert
	Bowman, Jesse B.	Cottle, George Washington
Badillo, Juan Antonio	Bourne, Daniel	
Bailey, Peter James	Brown, George	Courtman, Henry
Baker, Isaac G.	Brown, James	Crawford, Lemuel
Baker, William Charles M.	Brown, Robert (?)	Crockett, David
	Buchanan, James	Crossman, Robert
Ballentine, John J.	Burns, Samuel E.	Cummings, David P.
Ballentine, Robert W.	Butler, George D.	Cunningham, Robert
Baugh, John J.		
Bayliss, Joseph	Campbell, Robert	Damon (Daymon), Squire
Blair, John	Cane (Cain), John	

Darst (Durst, Dust), Jacob C.

Davis, John
Day, Freeman H. R.
Day, Jerry C.
Dearduff, William
Dennison, Stephen
Despallier, Charles
Dickerson, Almaron
Dillard, John H.
Dimkins, James R.
Dover, Sherod J.
Duel (Dewell), Lewis
Duvalt (Devault), Andrew

Espalier, Carlos
Esparza, Gregorio
Evans, Robert
Evans, Samuel B
Ewing, James L.

Fishbaugh (Fishback), William

Flanders, John
Floyd, Dolphin (Ward)
Forsyth, John Hubbard
Fuentes, Antonio
Fuqua, Galba
Furtleroy, William H.

Garnett, William
Garrand, James W.
Garrett, James Girard
Garvin, John E.
Gaston, John E.
George, James
Goodrich, John Calvin
Grimes, Albert (Alfred) Calvin

Guerrero, Jose Maria
Gwin (Gwynne) James C.

Jackson, William Daniel
Jackson, Thomas
Jameson, Green B.
Jennings, Gordon C.
Johnson, Lewis
Johnson, William
Jones, John

Kellogg, Johnnie
Kenney, James
Kent, Andrew
Kerr, Joseph
Kimbell, George C.
King, John G.
King, William P.

Lewis, William Irvine
Lightfoot, William J.
Lindley, Jonathan L.
Linn, William
Losoya, Toribio D.

Main, George Washington

Malone, William T.
Marshall, William
Martin, Albert
McCafferty, Edward
McCoy, Jesse
McDowell, William
McGee (McGhee), James

McGregor, John
McKinney, Robert
Melton, Eliel
Miller, Thomas R.
Mills, William
Millsaps, Isaac
Mitchasson, Edward F.
Mitchell, Edwin T.
Mitchell, Napoleon B.
Moore, Robert B.
Moore, Willis A.

Reynolds, John Purdy
Robinson, Isaac
Roberts, Thomas H.
Robertson, James
Rose, James M.
Rusk, Jackson J.
Rutherford, Joseph
Ryan, Isaac

Scurlock, Mial
Sewell, Marcus L.
Shied, Manson
Simmons, Clelland
  (Cleveland) Kinloch
Smith, Andrew H.
Smith, Charles S.
Smith, Joshua G.
Smith, William H.
Starr, Richard
Stewart (Stuart), John W.

Stockton, Richard L.
Summerlin, A. Spain
Summers, William E.
Sutherland, William D.

Taylor, Edward
Taylor, George
Taylor, James
Taylor, William
Thomas, B. Archer M.
  (B.A.M.)

Thomas, Henry
Thomson, John W.
Thompson, Jesse G.
Thruston, John M.
Trammel, Burke
Travis, William Barret
Tumlinson, George W.

Walker, Asa
Walker, Jacob

Musselman, Robert

Ward, Michael W.

Warnell (Wornel), Henry

Hannum, James

Harris, John

Harrison, Andrew Jackson

Harrison, William B.

Haskell (Heiskill), Charles M.

Hawkins, Joseph (M.)

Hendricks, Thomas

Herndon, Patrick Henry

Hersee (Hersey), William

Holland, Tapley

Holloway, Samuel

Howell, William D.

Nava, Andres

Neggan, George

Nelson, Andrew M.

Nelson, Edward

Nelson, George

Northcross, James

Nowlan, James

Pagan, George

Parker, Christopher A.

Parks, William

Perry, Richardson

Pollard, Amos

Washington, Joseph G.

Waters, Thomas

Wells, William

White, Isaac

White, Robert W.

Williamson, Hiram J.

Wilson, David L.

Wilson, John

Wolfe, Antony

Wright, Clairborne

Zanco, Charles

———, John

b. Men Who Were Probably Alamo Victims

Anderson, George Washington

Burnell, ——— (John)?

Kedison, ———

Ingram, ———

Robbins, ———

c. Men Who Were Possibly Alamo Victims

Ayers, ———

George, William

Jackson, John

Olamio, George

Spratt, John

Warner, Thomas S.

---

[5] This statement is verified by the fact that after the fall of the Alamo, the government was unable to produce a muster roll of the victims, so various interested persons began trying to compile one. See William Gray, *From Virginia to Texas,* 138; also, the *Telegraph and Texas Register,* March 24, 1836. Travis's neglect to make a return of his men to the government was probably due to the chaotic conditions of that government and to the fact that, prior to the beginning of the siege, the command at the Alamo was a dual one.

[6] Chapter V repeats these rolls with annotations and with a description of the principal documents used. I also describe my method of handling the documents.

1.11.2.   Reuben Potter, letter, 1874.

Potter, Reuben, to Gen. William Steele. July 10, 1874. Adjutant General (RG-401), General Correspondence, TSLA.

Additional correspondence from Potter that relates to the Alamo, such as the one of July 7 referenced in the first sentence, can also be found in the Adjutant General's files in the 1874–76 period. Some readings of the handwriting follow a transcript in the Williams Papers, CAH, from the *Austin State Gazette* of July 17, 1874 (citing in turn a printed source coming from the *Telegraph,* though the newspaper and city were not identified).

Office of the Port Qu^r. Master

Fort Wood, N.Y.H.—July 10th 1874

General,

Referring to y^r. letter of the 27th of last month, & mine of the 7th of this, I have the honor to inclose to you herewith a copy of the two groups of names borne by McShields of the Alamo monument, as shown by the lithograph mentioned in my former letter. Finding that I have five copies of that print, I send you one of them by the same mail, though in a separate packet. That alone would put you in possession of the list, but I give it also in this, that one duplication may replace the other, in case of miscarriage.

The Alamo monument was made in 1841; and, as I have understood, the names of the ill fated garrison were obtained by the artist from M^r. Sutherland, then well known as a member of the Congress of Texas from the lower Colorado. As the same family name occurs on the monument, that gentleman may have had a kinsman in the garrison. It has been asserted that the monumental muster roll is the most full and accurate of any extant; but of this I have doubts. It certainly does not name all who fell with the Alamo; & I think it probable that a more correct list could be obtained from the archives of the War Office of the Republic of Texas. I have seen in some printed book such a muster roll, probably from that source, which I know to have been more complete in some particulars. I regret that I can not call to mind in what wor[k] I saw it. I expected to find it in Yoakum's history of Texas, but am disappointed; and I think it may have been in a number of the Texas Almanac. Whatever book it was in, you probably have the original of that roll among the old records of your office.

It may be that the repair provided for by the Legislature of Texas contemplates only the restoration of obliterated names; but it has occurred to me that it might give an opportunity, not again to be had, for supplying what the artist omitted, if the omission can be well ascertained.

The first group in the inclosed copy contains (88) eighty eight names,—the other (74) seventy four,—making (162) an hundred & sixty two; and, by adding those of the four leaders, given more prominently on the monument, we have a total of (166) an hundred & sixty six. This is more than the garrison numbered before the reinforcement of (32) thirty two men from Gonzales won its way in, five days before the assault, and is less than it counted after that entrance. The original force, as reported by Travis in a letter dated two days later, was (145) an hundred and forty five, and the aforesaid accession must have raised it to (177) an hundred and seventy seven. -x- [*footnote at bottom of page:*] -x-Yoakum/Vol. II, p. 78. states that the reinforcement "made the effective force under Travis on[e] hundred & eighty eight." This cannot be made out if Travis's report of the previous number be correct. [*end of footnote*] In that letter of the 3ᵈ. of March, Travis states that none had yet fallen, and we have no evidence that any fell before the final assault. The number, therefore, is not likely to have been much varied by casualties. Mʳ. King, who lived a few miles above Gonzales, as I have always understood, lost more than one son in the massacre. They went in with the reinforcement; yet the monument mentions the name of "King" but once. I hence infer that the Gonzales men are not included in the stone record. A part of them *may* be: the monument tells of three brothers, named Taylor, which ha[s] the tint of neighborhood muster. There were two Evanses among those who fell, thought the monument names but one. Of those two, who were both in the printed list, I have seen one, a lieutenant, was a son of Musgrove Evans Esq., and a grandson of General Jacob Brown U.S.A.,—the other, who was the master of ordnance, was an Irishman.

From what I have stated, it might be inferred that the original of the monumental roll was set down, (as the latter now stands) before the last doomed number was made up and shut in. Southerland's memorandum may have enumerated the garrison as it existed a short time before the siege commenced, when it comprised only Bowie's command, which occupied the fort before Travis arrived. The latter who was a Lieut. Colonel of regular cavalry, was assigned to the post by the Provisional Government; but Bowie, who had been elected a Colonel of volunteers, claimed to rank him. They acted in conflict during the first two or three days of the siege, when the dispute about command was cut short by an illness, which prostrated Bowie. Travis took in with him the skeleton of this imaginary half regiment of cavalry, consisting of Captⁿ. Juan Sequin and nine recruits, all men of San Antonio. One of the latter, Sergeant Alexandro de la Garza, was sent out as a courier to the Provisional Government, and Private Antonio Cruz Arocha, accompanied Seguin when the Captain was sent out on the night of the 29ᵗʰ—February, upon a mission to Fannin for aid. The remaining seven of those Mexicans, though ignored by the monument, perished in the slaughter of the 6th . of March. Their names, as given to me by Seguin in 1860., were as follows:—Sergeant Badillo.—Corporal Antonio Fuentes,—and privates Gregorio Esparza,—Torivio Losoya,—Andres Nava,— One eyed Guerrero,—and Almillo.—As they were the only enlisted men in the garrison, and the only soldiers of Travis's own corps, they merit oblivion as little as the volunteers they died with.

As you have alluded to my rumored share in originating this monument, it may not here be amiss to state in what my limited claim to it consists. I suggested the first crude idea for such a memento, made from the stones of the

Alamo, and furnished some of the inscriptions and devices. In 1841, I found in San Antonio a man named Nangle, a lapidary of unusual skill, then engaged in making from the materials above mentioned, for sale, diverse small tokens, such as vases and pipes, & candlesticks. I advised him to construct a monument of size suitable for a decoration of the interior of some public building, and offer it for sale to the Government of Texas, unless he should prefer to make a present of it by way of advertising his artistic ability.

[*Potter goes on in three paragraphs to describe the details of the 1841 monument and its disposition.*]

Texas no doubt has now too much need, in matters of necessity, for all the means she can raise, to spare more than a trifle to the memory of dead heroes; but, should she ever be able to afford it, I trust she will some day call to mind the neglect in which the remains of Travis & his band have so long lain. But it may already be too late to mark properly the spot where their ashes were buried by Colonel Seguin in 1837; for I doubt if the locality can now be identified. It might, with diligent search, have been found twelve or fourteen years ago, but I fear it has by this time been built over and irrecoverably lost.

If I have given you more details than your inquiry called for, my excuse must be that anything which throws light on the most remarkable defense in our history, and on its only memento must be of interest to every old resident of Texas.

I have the honor to be most respectfully y. obo'se'

Reuben M. Potter
Capt &
a.u.g.w
Ft. Wood

To
Br. Genl. Wm. Steele—
Adjt.Gen'l.—State of Texas,
Austin, Texas.

1.11.3.   Defender identity, analysis, 1992.

Casso, Raul, IV. July 1992. Damacio Jimenez: The lost and found Alamo Defender. *Southwestern Historical Quarterly* 96:87, 90, 92.

The article reviews the nature of Texas land records and the discovery of the key documents, along with numerous footnotes on sources. A facsimile of the referenced affidavit by Juan Seguín is included in the article on page 89. The summary presented here was verified with the original entries in the Headright Book 2, 370–73, in the Office of the County Clerk, Béxar County. Casso's summary is accurate, though "Gimenes" might be a more literal rendition of the name, as the entry is in the "G" section of the Headright Book 2 Index and the niece's name, "Gertrudes," has the same leading letter.

[*p. 87*]

It is truly surprising that the identity of an unknown Alamo defender may still come to light over 150 years since the fall of the Alamo. Such is the case of Damacio Jimenez, who died defending the Alamo on the morning of March 6, 1836. Although he remained unknown until 1986, Damacio Jimenez is now recognized as the 189th Alamo defender, the 9th of Mexican heritage.

Damacio Jimenez's participation in the Battle of the Alamo became known when this author discovered a petition for a quantity of land that had been filed in the courts of Bexar County in 1861 by Damacio's niece and nephew, Gertrudes and Juan Jimenez. Although Juan and Gertrudes' petition was never decided upon because of their failure to pay filing fees, they—perhaps unwittingly—provided a record of Damacio Jimenez's contribution to Texas's independence.

[*p. 90*]

In the petition, Damacio is said to have "attached his fortune to that of the celebrated Col. [William] B[arret] Travis . . . [and] he continued to serve under Col. Travis and entered with him the Alamo [sic] where he fell a victim of his devotion to his country."

The petition was supported by affidavits from Col. Juan N. Seguin and Mr. Cornelio Delgado. Both affiants, as the court's minutes state, were examined separately. Col. Seguin attested to the fact that Damacio was one of his volunteer soldiers and states that he saw Damacio in the Alamo as he (Seguin) left the Alamo as a messenger for Travis. Mr. Cornelio Delgado was a member of the "party engaged in the burying of the dead [soldiers]," and he identified Damacio's corpse among the fallen. Presumably, Cornelio Delgado was among those San Antonians ordered by General Santa Anna to collect and dispose of the bodies of soldiers killed in the battle.

[*Footnote, p. 92*]

---

[28] . . . Damacio Jimenez's name was finally read at the Alamo roll call on March 6, 1987—151 years after his death in that famous battle.

Commentary

Madame Candelaria and Others inside the Alamo (1.9–1.11)

We need not spend too much additional time on Madame Candelaria's accounts. These stories have two fundamental problems: They are quite inconsistent with each other, and they are full of details that are simply wrong. Whether they are deliberate fabrications or a result of poor journalism, her narratives are simply so unreliable that we must reject them as sources. Other printed versions of her stories are available as well, but these accounts add little that is new or consistent with what is presented here.[1]

The first indication that one should be skeptical of her accounts is that she assigns herself a significant role—particularly that of being with Bowie at his death. Though not impossible, such a special role in any account can be motivated by wanting to make an entertaining and sellable story rather than reflecting actual facts.

The most obvious examples of inconsistencies are variations in the details surrounding Bowie's death. Corner's version (1.9.1) has her giving him a drink of water as the Mexican soldiers rushed in; the *San Antonio Express* version of 1892 (1.9.2) says Bowie died a few minutes before the soldiers entered; the *San Antonio Daily Express* of 1899 (1.9.3) reports that he died of pneumonia the day before the fall; and the *San Antonio Light* (1.9.4) has Bowie emptying two pistols at the soldiers. The two accounts of Crockett's fall in Corner and the *Light* are equally inconsistent, one having him among the first to fall, and the other with Travis the first to fall and Crockett as the last after a carefully detailed fight.

Among the details that are simply wrong, Corner's interview quotes Madame Candelaria as saying that during the siege, the defenders were allowed to use water from an external source and there was a roof on the Alamo Church. The *Daily Express* says that she washed and prepared the dead for burial and that a disguised Santa Anna entered San Antonio alone prior to the siege. The *Light* reports that Bowie went to the Alamo declaring that he would fight as a private (compare with 1.1.1.8). Careful reading shows that the *Light* also apparently places all the action of the final battle within and around the chapel, as if she were unaware of the fighting at the outer plaza walls and the Long Barracks.

The narratives also have numerous examples of events she would not have been likely to see. Could she really have been in a position—as per the *Light* account—to watch Crockett's last stand, and would she have had her head so exposed while a volley of bullets was flying?

It is clear what she gained from claiming to be an Alamo survivor from the references to many visitors, who likely would have tipped her, and the pension she received from the state of Texas. James DeShields's narration also supports this conclusion (2.11.1).[2]

It can thus be concluded that her accounts are of no value to our understanding. This conclusion is not new or original. Virtually every historian who has examined her accounts has concluded the same. But the documents were worth considering here because others have taken, in isolation, one or two of the versions and incorporated the material into narratives of the events. Any such usage should be considered faulty scholarship.

Williams's discussion (1.10.1) of survivors of the fall of the Alamo is essentially an appendix to her thesis, as she had not earlier dealt with this subject in depth. More recently, Groneman and Ragsdale have written more about the individuals involved, but not as critically as done by Williams.[3] Groneman generally did not cite all his sources, and Ragsdale accepted Madame Candelaria. I have already argued (in section 1.5) that though sources on the presence of the Esparza family are not as definite as I would like, the interviews are conclusive in establishing the presence of Enrique Esparza. Williams included Mrs. Toribio Losoya, while Ragsdale had the mother-in-law Concepción Losoya as a survivor. Williams also included Sam, Bowie's slave. The Becerra account (2.10.1) additionally gives a thirdhand account of Bowie's cook, Bettie, and another man named Charlie. Both Groneman and Ragsdale included a number of interesting personal details on the lives of the various survivors.

Of the people noted by Williams, there are no known accounts of Gertrudis Navarro, Mrs. Alsbury's younger sister, who moved to Mexico later, or Mrs. Toribio Losoya, who was later Mrs. Milton. There is some confusion about Sam. Williams's source was an undated (c. 1910s?) *San Antonio Light* article, "Conquering Santa Anna: Defied after Alamo," by Bess Carol, who in turn cited the Esparza accounts.[4] Still earlier sources allude to a "Sam," who appears to have been confused with Almonte's orderly, Ben (2.12), or with "Travis' servant," Joe.[5] Dr. Barnard's journal entry for May 17 does note that slave of Bowie in the Alamo when it was stormed (4.3.10). Perhaps Sam was a real person and later in the nineteenth century became confused with Ben or Joe, or maybe he was a misidentification of one of these two. I lean to the latter, but further study is warranted.

The story that Brigidio Guerrero (or Guerrera) was a defender who surrendered and survived is especially intriguing. It likely originated with Guerrero's own 1861 Court of Claims petition (1.10.2.1, 1.10.2.2, 1.10.2.3) and pension claims (1.10.2.4, 1.10.2.5), and was reported by Gould (1.10.2.6). The Esparza (1.5.2, 1.5.4, 1.5.6) and Alijo Perez/Adina De Zavala (1.4.4) documents support the story. One significant Mexican source, Colonel Almonte (2.2.1), also lends support to the possibility of such a survivor. As far as scholars go, Williams (1.10.1) did not include Guerrero. Lord (5.2.2) accepted the claim, citing Esparza, Almonte, and a petition to Béxar County in 1878. Groneman asserted that he was a survivor without discussion or citation, apparently based on the statement made in 1861.[6]

An examination of Béxar County records was done by Jake Ivey, who located a claim by Guerrero as early as 1838, though it did not explicitly state that he served in the Alamo under Travis.[7] This claim was rejected for unspecified reasons.[8] The appeal was also unsuccessful.[9] Guerrero's 1878 testimony reported by Gould is also reflected in the *Dennison Daily News* for October 4, 1878.

For now, I follow Lord—whose sources in turn followed the 1861 Court of Claims documents—in believing it a reasonable possibility that Brigidio Guerrero was in the Alamo and survived the fall. Should this be true, then Guerrero could be a source for the fall of the Alamo through Barsena and Bergara (section 3.4) to the *Telegraph and Texas Register* (4.1.1).

The story that Henry Warnell (1.10.3) survived the battle as either a courier per Williams or a defender per Lord (5.2.2) is curious, as both cited the same document as a source—General Land Office Court of Claims voucher no. 1579 of July 30, 1858.[10] The excerpted deposition from Henry Anderson states that Warnell was "wounded in the said massacre," implying that he was wounded in the fall rather than as a courier, and escaped to die a few months later. A possible scenario might be that several defenders fled the mission once the walls were overrun and were hunted down by Santa Anna's cavalry in the open field (Sesma 2.3.1). It is not an impossibility that one person could have escaped, and there is weak support by Brigidio Guerrero above (1.10.2.1). Nonetheless, there does not appear to be any compelling basis for believing the statement. The balance of the numerous documents in the Court of Claims file are to establish the claim of a John Warnell as the only son and heir, while the names or relationships of the heirs being represented in this earlier statement are conspicuously missing. As the document is quite inconsistent with the others of the file, it is possible that this was a fraudulent claim. Something more supportive is necessary before giving the story much weight.

Another suggestion that others could have survived the fall comes from the *Arkansas Gazette* for March 29 (1.10.4). The first part of this article includes a report illustrative of the way rumors circulate quickly around a kernel of truth. The untrue claim that Cós was repulsed might well have been based on a considerable elaboration of the initial investment of the Alamo and the minor attacks that occurred in the first few days. The accurate information on Travis's force (150 men) indicates that this rumor might have originated with some valid source of information. The second part notes the intriguing thirdhand story of a couple survivors of the fall. The newspaper itself does not make excessive claim for the validity of the story, and Lord (5.2.2) could not help wondering whether there was something to it.[11] The main constraint to accepting this story is the timing: Is it reasonable that two survivors of the fall, one badly wounded, could have made it all the way to Nacogdoches, and their story to Little Rock, Arkansas, two weeks ahead of the authentic news of the fall? The definitive reports, which came primarily via Susanna Dickinson to Sam Houston to New Orleans newspapers to Little Rock, were in the *Arkansas Gazette* of April 12, 1836 (2.17.1, 4.1.4.2).[12] I have to be skeptical.

Williams also noted a claim, apparently per Linn (3.4.3), by Anselmo Borgarra that he was a noncombatant in the Alamo. This also is of some significance in considering possible sources for the earliest accounts of the battle when discussing these documents (section 3.4, 4.1.1). I think it most likely that Linn simply confused Anselmo Bergara with Brigidio Guerrero.

Two other accounts of reputed survivors, included in Groneman (1996), are not presented here. The first is of William Cannon in a letter of June 9, 1893, to Texas governor J. S. Hogg.[13] In the original typed account, Madame Candelaria is a participant with Cannon in about half the story—as shown above, reason enough to reject the entire narrative. In the portions not involving Madame Candelaria, Cannon stated he was a brother of Susan Dickinson, whose father, mother, older brother, and two sisters were also in the Alamo prior to the fall. The balance of the account has equally unsupported (per section 1.2) and inaccurate information. Furthermore, a comparison of the far more sophisticated style and expression of this claim with a handwritten original letter by Cannon of August 3, 1892, in the same file indicates, though the signature appears the same, that Cannon himself could not possibly have been the direct author of the June 9, 1893, account. The earlier letter is by a barely literate person. Groneman believed that the letter was an attempt by Cannon (or, more likely, someone close to him) to obtain money for his services. Indirectly, the story did have some benefit, as it was in response to this claim that W. P. Hardman and E. Malloch (4.4.4.6 to 4.4.4.8) presented some information on the accurate spelling of Dickerson versus Dickinson.

The second omitted account is an interview with Charles Bledsoe.[14] Bledsoe described the entire action as having taken place inside the roofed chapel, as if unaware of the larger complex that existed in 1836 or the unroofed condition of the chapel. This is the same problem as in the accounts of Madame Candelaria and Félix Nuñez (2.14.1). He also described several skirmishes with Mexican troops on the way to the Alamo that do not fit with the movements of the Mexican Army. Groneman noted the entire lack of evidence that Bledsoe and his two uncles included in the story were in the Alamo. Again everything in this story is flatly contradicting to other versions.

These two spurious accounts were not included here because, unlike the Crockett (1.6.1) and Madame Candelaria (1.9) stories, they have not entered the Alamo literature as having merit, nor do they have literary interest.

The identification of the defenders in the Alamo was a massive effort. Few people who haven't read Williams's dissertation and tracked back some of her references can appreciate the extent of her contribution and the care that went into deriving an accepted list. Her effort started by studying the muster rolls and various nineteenth-century lists. She was the first to appreciate the value of the General Land Office files and to extensively use them, examining about a hundred thousand documents.[15] Some of the early lists of defenders, such as those in Gray (1.3.5) and *Telegraph and Texas Register* (4.1.1), are included in this collection. These lists were collated and thoroughly checked against later witnesses' testimonies and claims in the various General Land Office and county records, and her work is the basis of all subsequent studies. It is also likely that her dissertation helped motivate the construction, after nearly a hundred years of delay, of the monument to the defenders in front of the Alamo.

Since 1934, there have been a handful of modifications to the list of defenders. Williams herself added William Wills, based on a probate record, though she also thought it was somewhat meager proof.[16] Lord modified her list by deleting Sherod Dover, José Maria Guerrero (whom he equated with Brigidio Guerrero, 1.10.2), Toribio

Domingo Losoya (but note 3.1.2), John G. King, and John Davis; and adding M. B. Clark, who was one of the defenders for whose heirs Louis Rose testified. Later, Lord also found an analogous probate record for James Tylee.[17] Thomas Miller did a careful reexamination of the General Land Office documents cited by Williams, and agreed with Lord's corrections. He also deleted George Brown, James McGee, James Robertson, and Jesse Thompson, and considered uncertain Jesse Bowman, Jerry Day, James Hannum, and John Wilson. These conclusions were in part due to documents in Williams's citations missing. Earlier he thought Thomas Hendricks should be deleted, but he included Hendricks as a defender in his later article.[18] The list kept by the Daughters of the Republic of Texas at the Alamo now has 189 names. It is nearly the same as Williams's list of 188 (including John M. Hays), with the addition of M. B. Clark, Damacio Jimenes, James Tylee, and William Wills; and the omission of Sherod Dover, Thomas Hendricks, and John G. King. They also have Richard W. Ballantine rather than Williams's Robert, and William B. Ward rather than Michael W.

Deciding on the identity of defenders is a judgment call. Williams's decision on William Wills was based on meager evidence, but she had a better right than anyone to decide it was adequate. A similar statement can be said for Lord's decision on James Tylee. No effort is perfect, and Miller carefully reviewed the Williams citations to come to different and reasonable conclusions in the cases noted.

The files in the archives have undergone major reorganizations, and as a consequence, additional evidence has been found that caused earlier conclusions to be modified, but some of the documents and files located earlier were not found later. This problem has occurred in a number of cases of citations by different researchers, and it might be due to documents being filed very differently, misfiled, or even removed from the archives.

Whether Thomas Hendricks should be deleted is still up to question. He was eliminated by Miller earlier, but apparently some missing documents were found by the time of his more detailed study, and I did not locate further information.

Williams included Toribio Loyosa in part because his name was on a list by Juan Seguin to Reuben Potter.[19] Miller reviewed the General Land Office files for Toribio Loyosa, but didn't notice the Seguin list. Losoya's presence is strongly supported by Ruiz (3.1.2), but Miller has four other sworn statements indicating that he was discharged in October 1836 and was alive in 1855. Lord (5.2.2) said he was not in the Alamo. The latest word on the subject was by Jake Ivey, who reviewed the history of the Losoya family and concluded that Lord confused the record of Toribio with that of his uncle Domingo, who did not fight in the Alamo but was among the most dedicated Tejano fighters on behalf of the Texas Revolution.[20]

The letter of Potter to Adj. Gen. William Steele (1.11.2) is included for several reasons. It is one of the earlier efforts to resolve in a coherent way the questions associated with the identities of the Alamo defenders that arose from the original lists and muster rolls. The letter also gives secondhand information from Juan Seguín on the identity of his men at the Alamo, and adds details on Seguín's mission as a courier to Fannin. Potter also noted that the burial location of the defenders' ashes was in 1874, probably irrevocably lost.

Casso's (1.11.3) new discovery of Damacio Jimenez, as well as giving us an additional Alamo defender, also indicates by the fifty-five-year separation how difficult it has been to extend Williams's work through documented sources.

Although Thomas Lloyd Miller did not accept the Nacogdoches testimony of Louis Rose (1.8.2.2 and 1.8.2.3) as being as definitive as I do (or as Blake or Lord did), Miller is one other scholar besides Williams who systematically surveyed and reviewed the General Land Office records for information on the identities of participants in the key battles of the Texas Revolution. Thus his opinion on the defenders for whom Rose testified should not be ignored.

There are still opportunities for more research and review in this area. Potential topics for further research are Williams's twelve "probable" and "possible" victims, and the Miller lists.[21] There are additional names in the Republic Claims, such as a Washington Anderson, that were not included for lack of sufficient evidence.[22]

Recent studies are considering the possibility that there were significantly more defenders, perhaps over 250, reflecting the Mexican accounts of Almonte (2.2.1), Sesma (2.3.1), de la Peña (2.9.1), and Loranca (2.13.1).[23] These sources merit attention. There also may have been defenders whose heirs did not pursue any documented activity and thus would have been missed.

On the other hand, a much higher numbers of defenders would require additional explanations for the count given in Travis's letter of February 23 (1.1.1.16) and put considerably less weight on the accounts of Ruiz (3.1.1), Caro (2.5.1), and Filisola (2.6.1). Unlike Williams's use of explicit documentation, later arguments to increase the count to include individually undocumented defenders are more speculative.

It should be clear, as stated by Williams, Lord, Miller, and others, that we cannot expect to ever achieve a final resolution on exactly who were the Alamo defenders.

---

1. E.g., the *Southern Messenger* of February 16, 1899, and the *Dallas Morning News* of March 9, 1930.
2. See also Williams in *SWHQ* 37:170, n. 27.
3. Groneman 1990a and Ragsdale 1994.
4. Alamo Research/Dickinson & Other Survivors, Williams (Amelia Worthington) Papers, CAH.
5. Brown 1887, 332.
6. Groneman 1990a, 55–56.
7. Ivey 1982b. He also clarified the past confusion of Brigidio with José Maria Guerrero, who was a participant in the siege of the Alamo when it was held by Cós in December 1835, e.g., General Land Office claim of July 6, 1881, #RV 1384.
8. In Headright Book 1, 89, Office of the County Clerk, Béxar County.
9. In Book A, 36–37, Office of the County Clerk, Béxar County.
10. Williams in *SWHQ,* 37:311; see also 37:283 n. 22. General Land Office Court of Claims voucher no. 1579 of July 30, 1858, is now included as part of the general file #8490.
11. Also Lord 1968, 24.
12. Chariton 1992, 30–32, speculates that the two people in Zuber's story at Mr. Leaky's (1.8.1.2) could have been these two.
13. The typed original of Cannon's letter is in TSLA Claimaints to Property files. The file includes Governor Hogg's related letter of July 7, 1893, to General Hardeusau, along with the apparently original earlier letter of Cannon of August 3, 1892. In the same file

are a number of follow-on letters from several people, including one from Susan Sterling—granddaughter of Susanna Dickinson—dated February 17, 1926, disagreeing
with the Cannon claim. This claim was published in Lindley 1994, 4–7; and Groneman
1996, 211–17.

14. Groneman 1996, 141–43: source is *San Antonio Express* for August 23, 1904.
15. Nichols 1959.
16. Letter August 25, 1949, in William Wills, Alamo Defenders file, DRT.
17. Lord 1961, 213–19. Letter regarding Tylee, dated May 18, 1965, is in James Tylee,
Alamo Defenders file, DRT.
18. Miller 1964, 1971, on the Tejano defenders. The Hendricks comment is c. 1956,
though not published until 1967.
19. Letter of E. M. Pease to William Steele, July 14, 1876. The reference was transposed to
an Austin paper by the time of publication in *SWHQ* 37:237–38, n. 1, but Williams's
rough notes make clear the correct reference: Transcript in Folder 1/Correspondence
and Accounts, rough notes in Folder 1/Muster Rolls and Other Lists of
Defenders/Williams Papers, CAH.
20. Ivey 1982b.
21. Williams in *SWHQ* 37:286–91, and Miller 1964.
22. Republic Claims/Unpaid Claims, UN-Anderson, Washington R:248 Fr:0167, TSLA.
23. Also see Hardin and Lindley per *Austin American-Statesman* of March 12, 1996; and
Davis 1998 731 n. 95; 736 n. 105.

CHAPTER 2

Sources in the Mexican Camp

A study of the other side of the battle of the Alamo requires examining a more diverse and perhaps more difficult set of documents. A number of sources are available, written by various participants at various levels in the Mexican Army. These accounts should be looked at carefully, as many are the results of retrospective thinking with ulterior motives. In particular, less than seven weeks after the fall of the Alamo (April 21), the Mexican Army was crushingly defeated at San Jacinto, and Santa Anna and his senior officers were captured or killed. The blame and accusations among the leaders in the aftermath are apparent in many narratives of the earlier event. Another motivation in many accounts was a desire to tell the Texans, who were now holding them captive and even threatening their lives, what they wanted to hear. Therefore, some of the details may have been answers to leading questions. These are not straightforward documents to be accepted at face value.

This chapter starts with the accounts of President and General Santa Anna himself. These range from being exceptionally useful, such as his actual order for the final assault and his victory announcement, to being exceptionally self-serving. In some cases, the reader learns more of Santa Anna's character than of the events of the Alamo.

The next documents presented are those of other senior leaders in the Mexican Army: Santa Anna's military aide, Col. Juan Nepomuceno Almonte; Gen. Juaquín Ramírez y Sesma, commander of the cavalry; and other reports from the military archives, including those of Santa Anna's brother-in-law Martín Perfecto de Cós, Santa Anna's personal secretary Ramón Martínez Caro, and the second in command of the Texas campaign, Gen. Vincente Filisola. These accounts are of high interest because of the authors' important positions and the circumstances under which they were written. Almonte's account was a personal and private diary that survived and became public only by accident; Sesma's is an official report only five days after the fall; Cós's and others' are official military reports also near in time to the events; Caro's is an attack on Santa Anna that contradicts and perhaps gives some balance to Santa Anna's claims; and Filisola's is a comprehensive history of the entire campaign making extensive use of available sources.

Next follows a group of documents from senior but not highest-ranking officers: Adjutant Inspector José Juan Sánchez (or Sánchez-Navarro); the Labastida plat, or map, by the chief engineer of the Mexican Army; and Lt. Col. José Enrique de la Peña. Sánchez and de la Peña were not senior enough to need to be defensive about the conduct of the Texas campaign, and therefore their accounts were less motivated by self-justification. These documents are full of specific details of the siege and battle, and being by direct participants, they are the most valuable we have from the Mexican side. A different issue to consider here, however, is the authenticity of the manuscripts.

The final collection of accounts consists of those from individuals of lower rank or position: Sgt. Francisco Becerra; Capt. Rafael Soldana; Colonel Almonte's orderly Ben; Sgt. Manuel Loranca; Sgt. Félix Nuñez; Captain Urissa; an unidentified source in *El Mosquito Mexicano;* an anonymous deserter in the *Arkansas Gazette;* fifer Apolinario Saldigna; and Sgt. Santiago Rabia. The first three are relatively consistent with the other accounts and so add to our understanding of the events. The next three are still fairly extensive accounts, but they are more problematical due to inconsistencies. The last three have fewer new details but still should be considered.

2.1.1.1.   Santa Anna to Sesma, military orders, December 7, 1835.

Filizola, Umberto, ed. and trans. August 1939. Correspondence of Santa Anna during the Texas campaign, 1835–1836. 30, 3–4. Master's thesis, University of Texas at Austin.

These orders from Santa Anna to his cavalry leader are of special interest here because of his instruction 9.

[TO GENERAL JOAQUIN RAMIREZ Y SESMA,
GIVING HIM SPECIFIC ORDERS ON THE MILITARY STRATEGY
TO BE EMPLOYED; OTHER INSTRUCTIONS.]

Army of Operations

General D. Joaquín Ramírez y Sesma, who has been entrusted with the command of the 1st brigade to aid Béjar or to fight the besiegers, will observe the following:

[*Instructions 1–7 regard actions to be taken from Laredo to Béjar under various contingencies, including whether the enemy should advance to meet Sesma before Béjar or should entrench in the missions of Espada and Concepción. The last two instructions become more significant in what actually happens the following February.*]

8. If the enemy were to remain in one of the missions named, or in some other place which they might have fortified, you will try, before attacking, to examine it [the place] well until there is no more doubt about its real condition, and nothing will be undertaken if there are no certain facts of a successful outcome, which is a decisive defeat, as any upset would be irreparable in those lands so distant from aid; for the same reason nothing should be left up to fortune.[13]

9. The foreigners who are making war against the Mexican nation, violating all laws, are not deserving of any consideration, and for that reason no quarter will be given them. This order will be made known to the troops at an opportune time. They have, with audacity, declared a war of extermination to the Mexicans, and they should be treated the same way.

Not being able to foresee all the situations in which the General of the 1st Division might find himself, it is up to his valor and skill to prepare for them, charging him above all not to undertake any action whatsoever, without being certain of a successful ending. Although not because of this must he fail to take advantage of any opportunity that might present itself of carelessness or cowardice on the part of the enemy.

> General Headquarters of San Luis Potosí.
> December 7, 1835.
> Antonio López de Santa Ana.
> [To General Joaquín Ramírez y Sesma]

---

[13] The distance from Monclova to the Rio Grande is 240 miles, and from there to Béjar, about 300 more. No supplies could be secured in these 540 miles, and water was found only at infrequent intervals.

2.1.1.2.   Santa Anna/José Batres to James Bowie, letter, February 23, 1836.

Jenkins, John H., ed. and trans. 1973. *The Papers of the Texas Revolution, 1835–1836.* 4:415. Austin: Presidial Press.

This is in response to Bowie's query in document 1.1.2. Jenkins's original source was located in Archivo General de Mexico, Secretaria de Guerra y Marina 334:48, CAH. A microfilm of a manuscript copy is in Archivo Historico Militar, Expediente 1897:9, UC Bancroft Library. The transcript in the former has a little more text and so appears to be from a different and more complete original than the latter.

As the Aid-de-Camp of his Excellency, the President of the Republic, I reply to you, according to the order of his Excellency, that the Mexican army cannot come to terms under any conditions with rebellious foreigners to whom there is no other recourse left, if they wish to save their lives, than to place themselves immediately at the disposal of the Supreme Government from whom alone they may expect clemency after some considerations are taken up. God and Liberty!

Jose Batres to James Bowie

This is a copy, Jose Batres
General Headquarters of the San Antonio de Bejar
Feb. 23, 1836

2.1.1.3. Santa Anna, military report, February 27, 1836.

Filizola, Umberto, ed. and trans. August 1939. Correspondence of Santa Anna during the Texas campaign, 1835–1836. 70–73. Master's thesis, University of Texas at Austin.

A microfilm of the original letter to Tornel is in Archivo Historico Militar, Expediente 1897:1–2, UC Bancroft Library, with a copy, also apparently signed by Santa Anna (the copy sent to Filisola?), in 1897:7–8. The transcript appears in Archivo General de Mexico, Secretaria de Guerra y Marina 334:45–46, CAH. The version in Filizola, and therefore the reprint in Jenkins, missed a detail in the second paragraph that the city was occupied on the twenty-third "at 3 p.m." The expression is in the originals and in the version published in Santos 1968.

[TO GENERAL FILISOLA, ADVISING HIM OF A LETTER
WRITTEN TO THE MINISTER OF WAR AND MARINE
PERTAINING TO THE BEGINNING OF THE SIEGE OF THE ALAMO.]

Army of Operations
Most Excellent Señor:
Today I am writing the Most Excellent Señor the Minister of War and Marine the following:
"Most Excellent Señor:
"On the 23rd of this month I occupied this city,[1] after some forced marches from Río Grande, with General D. Joaquín y Sesma's division composed of the permanent battalions of Matamoros and Jiménez, the active battalion of San Luis Potosí, the regiment of Dolores, and eight pieces of artillery.
"With the speed in which this meritorious division executed its marches in eighty leagues of road, it was believed that the rebel settlers would not have known of our proximity until we should have been within rifle-shot of them; as it was they only had time to hurriedly entrench themselves in Fort Alamo, which they had well fortified, and with a sufficient food supply. My objective had been to surprise them early in the morning of the day before, but a heavy rain prevented it.

"Notwithstanding their artillery fire, which they began immediately from the indicated fort, the national troops took possession of this city with the utmost order, which the traitors shall never again occupy; on our part we lost a corporal and a scout, dead, and eight wounded.

"When I was quartering the corps of the division a bearer of the flag of truce presented himself with a paper, the original which I am enclosing for your Excellency, and becoming indignant of its contents I ordered an aide, who was the nearest to me, to answer it, as it is expressed by the copy that is also enclosed.[2]

"Fifty rifles, of the rebel traitors of the North, have fallen in our possession, and several other things, which I shall have delivered to the general commissary of the army as soon as it arrives, so that these forces may be equipped; and the rest will be sold and the proceeds used for the general expense of the army.

"From the moment of my arrival I have been busy hostilizing the enemy in its position, so much so that they are not even allowed to raise their heads over the walls, preparing everything for the assault which will take place when at least the first brigade arrives,[3] which is even now sixty leagues away. Up to now they [the enemy] still act stubborn, counting on the strong position which they hold, and hoping for much aid from their colonies and from the United States of the North,[4] but they shall soon find out their mistake.

"After taking Fort Alamo I shall continue my operations against Goliad and the other fortified places, so that before the rains set in, the campaign shall be absolutely terminated up to the Sabine River, which serves as the boundary line between our republic and the one of the north.

"Your Excellency will do me the favor of telling everything to the President-Interim for his knowledge and satisfaction, and so that he may give me the orders that he sees fit."

And I transcribe it for your Excellency's knowledge, and for the troops that are under your immediate orders.

For God and Liberty. General Headquarters of Béjar. February 27, 1836.

Antonio López de Santa Ana.

Most Excellent Señor General of Division, D. Vicente Filisola, Second in Command of the Army of Operations.

---

[1] A good description of the siege which ended with the fall of the Alamo can be found in Bancroft, *op. cit.*, II, 201–15, and also in Filisola, *Memorias*, II, 178–88, 193–208. [*Note document 2.6.1 in this work.*]

[2] The surprise attack failing, Santa Anna sent Alamonte, with a flag of truce, toward the Alamo. Two of Travis' officers came out to parley. On their return to the Alamo, the Texans fired a cannon as an answer to the demand of the Mexican leader to surrender.—J. C. Valades, *Santa Anna y la guerra de Tejas*, 198.

[3] Colonel D. Juan Bringas, Santa Anna's aide, was ordered on the 29th or 30th to go to meet General Gaona's division, to pick the best companies, and by forced

marches to return to Béjar. They arrived on the 4th and on the 5th the order of attack was given.—R. M. Caro, *Primera campaña de Tejas*, 8, 9.

[4] Santa Anna in his Manifiesto says that it is well known that Travis' soldiers at the Alamo, Fannin's at Perdido, the riflemen of Dr. Grant, and even Houston and his troops at San Jacinto, with a few exceptions, came from New Orleans and other points of the United States, solely for the purpose of aiding the Texas Revolution.

Thirty-two men from Gonzáles entered the Alamo on March 1, 1836, at three o'clock in the morning, after the siege had begun, and two days later J. B. Bonham, who had gone to Goliad for aid before the approach of the enemy, arrived without mishap. The siege began on February 24, 1836, yet the Texans sallied out the next two nights to burn some houses that served as cover for the enemy and to obtain wood and water, without loss.—Bancroft, *op. cit.*, II, 209. Caro claims that from February 26 to March 5, twenty-nine Texans entered the Alamo, four one night, and a group of twenty-five during the day.—Caro, *op. cit.*, 9.

2.1.1.4.   Santa Anna, military order, February 27, 1836.

Filizola, Umberto, ed. and trans. August 1939. Correspondence of Santa Anna during the Texas campaign, 1835–1836. 74–75. Master's thesis, University of Texas at Austin.

There is also a third short letter by Santa Anna of this same date, unrelated to the Alamo, transmitting to Tornel a dispatch from Urrea in Archivo Historico Militar, Expediente 1904:31, UC Bancroft Library, and also published in Borroel 2001, 2:27 from transcripts in CAH.

[TO GENERAL FILISOLA, URGING HIM TO MAKE HASTE WITH
THE BRIGADES, AND TO HASTEN THE COMMISSARY
AND THE TREASURY.]

Army of Operations
Excellent Señor:

Under separate cover your Excellency will see the conditions which the first division maintains in front of the enemy, and the necessity which exists that you make the army brigades move with celerity, as up to the present they are moving very slowly.[1]

Your Excellency will command the Purveyor General to gather all the food supplies and to march immediately, avoiding any delays that might hamper the services of the Nation, as these troops are lacking in food.

Your Excellency will also order that the Treasury, with the Commissary, take the lead with forced marches, and escorted by a convoy, as there is a very urgent need for money.

Your Excellency will order that two or three half *cargas* of salt come with the Treasury, since there is not a single grain here, and it is needed very much.

I trust that your Excellency will act with your usual efficacy and promptness so that these dispositions be fulfilled, as all are urgent.

For God and Liberty. General Headquarters of Béjar. February 27, 1836. Antonio López de Sta. Ana.

Most Excellent Señor General, D. Vicente Filisola, Second in Command of the Army of Operations.

---

[1] The brigades could not march faster because of lack of water, and if they had doubled their marches, a tenth of the supplies and troops would have been left behind.—Filisola, *Memorias*, II, 387.

2.1.1.5. Santa Anna, military order, February 29, 1836.

Filisola, Gen. Vicente 1987. *Memoirs for the History of the War in Texas.* Translated by Wallace Woolsey. 2:172–73. Austin, TX: Eakin Press.

This letter is to General Sesma, when he moved into position on the road to Gonzales to prevent reinforcements to the Alamo during the siege.

Béxar, February 29, 1836

My esteemed friend. Having been informed of the news that you have sent me, I have this to say: It is a very good idea for you to go out in search of the enemy since they are so close by. However, I consider it necessary for you to take with you the Jiménez battalion, and at the same time ten boxes of cartridges for your guns; ammunition always stands one in good stead. Try to fall on them at dawn in order that you may take them by surprise.

"In this war you know that there are no prisoners.—Your most affectionate friend who sends your greetings.—Antonio Lopez de Santa Anna.—General Don Joaquín Ramírez y Cesma."

2.1.1.6. Santa Anna, military order, March 3, 1836.

Urrea, José. 1838. *Diario Militar del General José Urrea durante la Primera Campana de Tejas.* 54–55. Translated by Adam Lifshey. Victoria de Durango, Mexico: Manuel Gonzalez.

This and the next document regard two letters from Santa Anna on his policy for treatment of prisoners, written while preparing for the final assault on the Alamo.

NUM. 2

Army of Operations.—From the correspondence from Your Excellency dated the 27th of the last month, which I have received today, I have learned with satisfaction of the triumph that the national arms under the command of Your Excellency have obtained over the rebel colonists in the village of San Patricio.

This event is owed, without doubt, to the appropriate measures and activity taken by Your Excellency, and therefore I give to you the most expressive thanks in the name of the Supreme Government, hoping that Your Excellency communicates them to the brave men who accompany you. This very day I passed on Your Excellency's original document to His Excellency, the interim president, for his satisfaction.

I am likewise informed that Your Excellency is occupied in pursuing the foreigner Dr. Grant, and I do not doubt that he will be soon taught a lesson, as he deserves.

Regarding the prisoners that Your Excellency speaks of in the aforementioned correspondence, I ought to remind you of the instructions from the Supreme Government that the foreigners who have invaded the republic and who are caught with arms in hand should be treated or judged like pirates; and since in my opinion the Mexican who commits treason by uniting with adventurers of that sort, loses the rights of citizens according to our laws, the five prisoners of whom Your Excellency speaks should be treated like [the foreign invaders].

Your Excellency can advance up to Goliad, as I anticipated in my correspondence of the 27th of last month, taking advantage of the opportunity for a group to intercept the provisions that the enemy should be receiving from the Río de la Vaca, according to my information, with which Your Excellency can provide for that division. Your Excellency also can take the cattle of the rebel colonists and whatever else they own for the subsistence of the troops.

I hope that Your Excellency advises me ahead of time the day you will be coming to Goliad [to meet me], so that I can anticipate this and reinforce it [Goliad] with a section of infantry and artillery.

I am currently readying the assault on the Alamo, the place to which the enemy has fallen back, and very soon they will experience the punishment that is duly merited to them.— God and liberty. General quarters of Bejar, 3 March 1836.—Antonio Lopez de Santa Anna.—Señor General Don José Urrea, commander of the division of operations around Goliad.

2.1.1.7.   Santa Anna, military order, March 3, 1836.
United States Magazine and Democratic Review. October 1838. 143.

In a series of orders from the Commander-in-Chief, is the following:

"In respect to the prisoners of whom you speak in your last communication, you must not fail to bear in mind the circular of the Supreme Government, in which it is declared, that foreigners invading the Republic, and taken with arms in their hands, shall be judged and treated as pirates; and as, in my view of the matter, every Mexican guilty of the crime of joining these adventurers loses the rights of a citizen by his unnatural conduct, the five Mexican prisoners whom you have taken ought also to suffer as traitors.

GENERAL QUARTERS, BEJAR, *March 3d, 1836.*

ANTONIO LOPEZ DE SANTA ANNA.

To GENERAL URREA, *Commander of the Division of Operations upon Goliad.*

In a private letter, of the same date, addressed to me by the same, is the following paragraph:

"In regard to foreigners who make war, and those unnatural Mexicans who have joined their cause, you will remark that what I have stated to you officially is in accordance with the former provisions of the Supreme Government. An example is necessary, in order that those adventurers may be duly warned, and the nation be delivered from the ills she is daily doomed to suffer.["]

2.1.1.8. Santa Anna, military order, March 5, 1836.

Texas Almanac. 1870. 37–38.

This is the general order for the attack on the Alamo. The source for this version is "Translated from General Filisola's 'Memoirs on the Campaign of 1836, in Texas.'" A microfilm of the original is in Archivo Historico Militar, Expediente 1897:4–5, with an official copy in 1897:10–11, UC Bancroft Library. A typed transcript is in the Archivo General de Mexico, Secretaria de Guerra y Marina 334:52–54, CAH.

ARMY OF OPERATIONS

GENERAL ORDERS OF THE 5TH OF MARCH, 1836.

2 o'clock P.M.—Secret

To the Generals, Chiefs of Sections, and Commanding Officers:

The time has come to strike a decisive blow upon the enemy occupying the Fortress of the Alamo. Consequently, His Excellency, the General-in-chief, has decided that, tomorrow, at 4 o'clock A.M., the columns of attack shall be stationed at musket-shot distance from the first entrenchments, ready for the charge, which shall commence, at a signal to be given with the bugle, from the Northern Battery.

The first column will be commanded by General Don Martin Prefecto [*sic*] Cos, and, in his absence, by myself.

The Permanent Battalion of Aldama (except the company of Grenadiers) and the three right centre companies of the Active Battalion of San Luis, will compose this first column.

The second column will be commanded by Colonel Don Francisco Duque, and, in his absence, by General Don Manuel Fernandez Castrillon; it will be composed of the Active Battalion of Toluca (except the company of Grenadiers) and the three remaining centre companies of the Active Battalion of San Luis.

The third column will be commanded by Colonel José Maria Romero, and, in his absence, by Colonel Mariano Salas; it will be composed of the Permanent Battalions of Matamoros and Jimenes.

The fourth column will be commanded by Colonel Juan Morales, and, in his absence, by Colonel José Miñon; it will be composed of the light companies of the Battalions of Matamoros and Jimenes, and of the Active Battalion of San Luis.

His Excellency the General-in-chief will, in due time, designate the points of attack, and give his instructions to the Commanding Officers.

The reserve will be composed of the Battalion of Engineers and the five companies of Grenadiers of the Permanent Battalions of Matamoros, Jimenes and Aldama, and the Active Battalions of Toluca and San Luis.

This reserve will be commanded by the General-in-chief, in person, during the attack; but Colonel Agustin Arnat will assemble this party, which will report to him, this evening, at 5 o'clock, to be marched to the designated station.

The first column will carry ten ladders, two crowbars, and two axes; the second, ten ladders; the third, six ladders; and the fourth, two ladders.

The men carrying ladders will sling their guns on their shoulders, to be enabled to place the ladders wherever they may be required.

The companies of Grenadiers will be supplied with six packages of cartridges to every man, and the centre companies with two packages and two spare flints. The men will wear neither overcoats nor blankets, or anything that may impede the rapidity of their motions. The Commanding Officers will see that the men have the chin-straps of their caps down, and that they wear either shoes or sandals.

The troops composing the columns of attack will turn in to sleep at dark, to be in readiness to move at 12 o'clock at night.

Recruits deficient in instruction will remain in their quarters. The arms, principally the bayonets, should be in perfect order.

As soon as the moon raises, the centre companies of the Active Battalion of San Luis will abandon the points they are now occupying on the line, in order to have time to prepare.

The cavalry, under Colonel Joaquin Ramirez y Sesma, will be stationed at the Alameda, saddling up at 3 o'clock A.M. It shall be its duty to scout the country, to prevent the possibility of an escape.

The honor of the nation being interested in this engagement against the bold and lawless foreigners who are opposing us, His Excellency expects that every man will do his duty, and exert himself to give a day of glory to the country, and of gratification to the Supreme Government, who will know how to reward the distinguished deeds of the brave soldiers of the Army of Operations.

(Signed)   JUAN VALENTINE AMADOR.

A certified copy:
BEXAR, March 6th, 1836,

(Signed)   RAMON MARTINEZ CARO,
Secretary

2.1.1.9.   Santa Anna, military report, March 6, 1836.

El Nacional, Suplemento al Numero 79. Translated by John Wheat. 1836. Mexico.
This printed journal or broadsheet presents several letters from the army in Texas, including 2.1.1.8 and 2.1.1.10 quoted here from other sources. This, apparently the first letter of Santa Anna on March 6, had not been previously printed, as far as I could discover, until Borroel did so in 1998 (Borroel 1998b, 59). I have also included the editorial introductions for this important source of the Santa Anna correspondence. Jenkins (1973, 4:501) mistakenly attributed a March 3 letter to this source. A third letter from Santa Anna of this significant date regarding San Patricio is in Archivo Historico Militar, Expediente 1898:3, UC Bancroft Library.

EL NACIONAL.
SUPPLEMENT TO NUMBER 79.
OFFICIAL NEWS OF TEXAS.

The official reports and other documents that we insert below need no comment. They tell of deeds, deeds whose intrinsic glory and heroism words cannot amplify. If Divine Providence destined General ITRUBIDE to achieve the independence of Mégico, doubtless that same [Providence] has chosen General SANTA-ANNA to avenge the outrages perpetrated on this privileged country, to establish and assure in it the peace and order that we sorely need, and even to destroy that hatred that the destructive spirit of factionalism has spread among the sons of the same family: He is the IRIS [i.e. mediator, peacemaker] of the Mexican people. . . .

If the resistance of the ungrateful colonists has been tenacious and stubborn, they have faced Mexicans whose patriotism and courage were superior to the afore-mentioned qualities, as they have experienced in every encounter they have had, and will continue to discover if they are not chastised by the blows they have received.

So as to delay no further this *Supplement,* we concluded by beseeching the sovereign congress to pass as soon as possible a law that will stipulate the honorable and due reward that should go to the individuals who have distinguished themselves so valiantly in the national [i.e. civil] war into which we have been provoked by the ingratitude and treachery of the colonists of Texas. Everything is deserved by those who have given and continue to give so many days of glory to the nation. LONG LIVE THE INTREPID GENERAL SANTA-ANNA, LONG LIVE THE VALIANT GENERAL URREA; LONG LIVE THE INVINCIBLE MEXICAN ARMY!

The Editors.

MINISTRY OF WAR AND MARINE.
Central Section.—First Desk.
Personal Ministry of the President of the Mexican Republic, General-in-Chief of the Army of Operations.—Sr. General Don José María Tornel.—Béjar, March 6, 1836.—My Esteemed Friend.—By the official report I am sending you, you

will learn of the most complete victory that our national arms have just
achieved over the adventurers who were manning the fortress of the Alamo,
which will weigh extraordinarily in the ending of the war in this part of the
republic. The battle was extremely bloody, because the enemy was determined,
and our soldiers are valiant by nature, especially when they fight against foreigners and defend the rights of the nation. How I would have enjoyed it had
the unjust enemies of the army witnessed the marvelous spectacle this morning!
And by the reports I am sending you from General Urrea, you will learn also of
the victories that he has won against forces led by Dr. Grand [sic] at San Patricio
and Lipantitlán, in one of which this leader was killed. All goes well, and our
enemies both internal and foreign can do no more than gnash their teeth.==I
will closed, because there is no need for more, by wishing you congratulations
as your most affectionate friend and sure servant, w[ho] k[isses] y[our]
h[and].—*Antonio López de Santa Anna.*

This is a copy. Mégico, March 21, 1836.—*Juan L. Valázques de León.*

[*The supplement continues with transcripts of letters by Santa Anna and General
Urrea regarding the actions of the latter's army at San Patricio, then Santa Anna's
order of March 5 for the attack on the Alamo similar to that above, followed by his second letter of March 6 describing the victory, as per the next document, and finally the
Williamson letter, presented as document 4.3.4.*]

2.1.1.10. Santa Anna, letter, March 6, 1836.

Texas Almanac. 1870. 40–41.

The source for this victory message is "Translated from General Filisola's
'Memoirs on the Campaign of 1836, in Texas.'" The much older version is used here
instead of the more recent Filisola edition edited and translated by Woolsey, as this
would have been the translation used by nineteenth-century historians. A microfilm
of an official copy, signed by Santa Anna, is in Archivo Historico Militar, Expediente
1897:8–9, UC Bancroft Library. A transcript is in Archivo General de Mexico, Secretaria de Guerra y Marina 334:49–51.

ARMY OF OPERATIONS

Most Excellent Sir—Victory belongs to the army, which, at this very
moment, 8 o'clock A.M., achieved a complete and glorious triumph that will
render its memory imperishable.

As I had stated in my report to Your Excellency of the taking of this city on
the 27th of last month, I awaited the arrival of the 1st Brigade of Infantry to
commence active operations against the Fortress of the Alamo. However, the
whole Brigade having been delayed beyond my expectation, I ordered that
three of its Battalions, viz.; the Engineers—Aldama and Toluca—should force
their march to join me. These troops, together with the Battalions of Matamoros,

Jimenes, and San Luis Potosi, brought the force at my disposal, recruits excluded, up to 1400 Infantry. This force, divided into four columns of attack and a reserve, commenced the attack at 5 o'clock A.M. They met with a stubborn resistance, the combat lasting more than one hour and-a-half, and the reserve having to be brought into action.

The scene offered by this engagement was extraordinary. The men fought individually, vieing with each other in heroism. Twenty-one pieces of artillery, used by the enemy with the most perfect accuracy, the brisk fire of musketry, which illuminated the interior of the Fortress and its walls and ditches—could not check our dauntless soldiers, who are entitled to the consideration of the Supreme Government and to the gratitude of the nation.

The Fortress is now in our power, with its artillery, stores, &c. More than 600 corpses of foreigners were buried in the ditches and intrenchments, and a great many who had escaped the bayonet of the infantry, fell in the vicinity under the sabres of the cavalry. I can assure Your Excellency that few are those who bore to their associates the tidings of their disaster.

Among the corpses are those of Bowie and Travis, who styled themselves Colonels, and also that of Crockett, and several leading men, who had entered the Fortress with dispatches from their Convention. We lost about 70 men killed and 300 wounded, among whom are 25 officers. The cause for which they fell renders their loss less painful, as it is the duty of the Mexican soldiers to die for the defence of the rights of the nation; and all of us were ready for any sacrifice to promote this fond object; nor will we, hereafter, suffer any foreigners, whatever their origin may be, to insult our country and to polute [sic] its soil.

I shall, in due time, send to Your Excellency a circumstantial report of this glorious triumph. Now I have only time to congratulate the nation and the President *ad interim,* to whom I request you to submit this report.

The bearer takes with him one of the flags of the enemy's battalions, captured to-day. The inspection of it will show plainly the true intention of the treacherous colonists, and of their abetors [sic], who came from the ports of the United States of the North.

God and Liberty!

HEADQUARTERS, BEXAR, March 6th, 1836.

      (Signed)   ANTONIO LOPEZ DE SANTA ANNA.

To His Excellency the Secretary of War and Navy, Gen. Jose Maria Torne.

2.1.1.11. Santa Anna, public proclamation, March 7, 1836.

Telegraph and Texas Register. October 11, 1836. San Felipe, Texas.
A microfilm of this document, signed by Santa Anna, is in Archivo Historico
Militar, Expediente 1900:5–6, UC Bancroft Library.

Shortly after the taking of the Alamo, Santa Anna sent with Mrs. Dickinson several proclamations, calculated to intimidate as well as to allure the unwary to
acquiescence in his measures respecting what were then termed colonies.

ARMY OF OPERATIONS

The General-in-Chief of the Army of Operations of the Mexican Republic,
to the Inhabitants of Texas:

CITIZENS! The causes which have conducted to this frontier a part of the Mexican army are not unknown to you: a parcel of audacious adventurers, mali-
ciously protected by some inhabitants of a neighboring republic, dared to
invade our territory, with an intention of dividing amongst themselves the fertile lands that are contained in the spacious department of Texas; and even had
the boldness to entertain the idea of reaching the capital of the Republic. It
became necessary to check and chastise such enormous daring: and in consequence, some exemplary punishments have already taken place in Saint Patrick,
Lipantitlan and this city. I am pained to find amongst those adventurers the
names of some colonists, to whom had been granted repeated benefits, and who
had no just motive of complaint against the government of their adopted country.—These ungrateful men must also necessarily suffer the just punishment
that the laws and the public vengeance demand. But if we are bound to punish
the criminal, we are not the less compelled to protect the innocent. It is thus that
the inhabitants of this country, let their origin be whatever it may, who should
not appear to have been implicated in such iniquitous rebellion, shall be
respected in their persons and property, provided they come forward and
report themselves to the commander of the troops within eight days after they
should have arrived in their respective settlements, in order to justify their conduct and to receive a document guaranteeing to them the right of enjoying that
which lawfully belongs to them.

Bexarians! Return to your homes and dedicate yourselves to your domestic
duties. Your city and the fortress of the Alamo are already in possession of the
Mexican army, composed of your own fellow citizens; and rest assured that no
mass of foreigners will ever interrupt your repose, and much less, attack your
lives and plunder your property. The supreme government has taken you
under its protection, and will seek for your good.

Inhabitants of Texas! I have related to you the orders that the army of operations I have the honor to command comes to execute; and therefore the *good*
will have nothing to fear. Fulfill always your duties as Mexican citizens, and

you may expect the protection and benefit of the laws; and rest assured that you will never have reason to report yourselves of having observed such conduct, for I pledge you in the name of the supreme authorities of the nation, and as your fellow citizen and friend, that what has been promised you will be faithfully performed.

ANTONIO LOPEZ DE SANTA ANNA.

Head-Quarters, Bexar, March 7, 1836.

2.1.2. Santa Anna, printed defense, 1837.

Castañeda, Carlos, trans. 1928. Manifesto relative to his operations in the Texas campaign and his capture, by Santa Anna. *The Mexican Side of the Texan Revolution, by the Chief Mexican Participants.* 5–6, 10–15. Dallas: P. L. Turner Company.

MANIFESTO
WHICH
GENERAL ANTONIO LOPEZ DE SANTA-ANNA
ADDRESSES TO
HIS FELLOW-CITIZENS
RELATIVE TO HIS OPERATIONS
DURING THE TEXAS CAMPAIGN
AND HIS CAPTURE 10 OF MAY 1837[1]

THE MEXICAN SIDE OF THE TEXAN REVOLUTION

Never has the ambitious thought of obtaining universal approval for my actions entered my mind; nor have I been so pusillanimous that the fear of the disapproval of a few, or even of many, could have prevented me from acting in a certain way when convinced, even though erroneously, of the propriety of my action. In the palace of Mexico as in this humble hut, in the midst of the applause of a free people the same as amidst the insolent hisses of the Texans who loudly called for my death, I have realized that my conduct would always be criticized, for who has not at least one enemy if fate has raised him above his fellow-citizens and placed him in the public eye? I was not surprised, therefore, to see the triumphs of Béxar and the Alamo tainted by the tireless and venomous tooth of that envy which I have always despised, nor the defeat of San Jacinto horribly portrayed by the unfaithful and disloyal brush of an unjust animosity; much less was I surprised that by these means a great part of a nation, zealous as it should be of its honor and anxious that the cost of sustaining it should be reduced to a minimum, should have been made to doubt the propriety of my war measures if not to condemn them outright. But my misfortune having reached its limit, this ill opinion has gone one step further, and, although I expected as much, it has been all the more painful to me. Thus, when I placed foot upon the soil of my native land, evoked as it were from the grave, after having suffered for its cause, the most sacred of causes, a painful imprisonment, a cruel separation, a great misfortune, the judgment of my compatriots would like to banish me. This ill-deserved judgment has not failed to inflict a mortal wound to my heart, in spite of the fact that I recognize its noble origin in some cases. Still I expected, yea, I flattered myself in the midst of my sorrows, that I would obtain the compassion of my compatriots and that upon hearing me they would accept my justification.

[*Santa Anna continues with a narration of his misfortune, honor, military achievements ("Some journalists had tried to compare my campaigns to those of Napoleon . . ."), and difficulties in raising troops and money. He then starts his narrative of the campaign.*]

I went to Mexico, therefore, in November, 1835, to take charge of a war from which I could have been excused, for the fundamental law of the country offered me a decorous excuse that my broken health made all the more honorable. Nevertheless, aware of the adverse circumstances I have expressed, I still desired to try to serve my country. In a few days I gathered six thousand men, clothed and equipped. At the cost of immense sacrifices, rising above obstacles that seemed insuperable, this force set out from San Luis towards the end of December, 1835. The difficulties arising from the need of securing food supplies sufficient for the army while crossing four hundred leagues of desert lands, and those attendant upon its conveyance, as well as the transportation of the other equipment, arms, munitions, etc., were all difficulties that, though not pressing at the time of organization, were, nevertheless, of the utmost importance, particularly since the cost of transportation was extremely high in that long stretch. Hospitals had to be located and protected; a great number of rivers had to be crossed without bridge equipment, without even a single boat; the coast had to be watched and the ports kept open to receive provisions and to prevent the enemy from receiving reenforcements or from retreating—all of this with only one serviceable war vessel—and lastly, we had to raise a reserve force to come to our help in case of a reverse, a frequent occurrence in war, when, in order to complete the number of those deemed necessary for the campaign, we had had to use raw recruits.

When a general is given command of an army and everything that is necessary is furnished to him and placed at his disposal, he should be held strictly responsible if he departs from the established rules of war. The government has said, and with truth, that all the resources at its command were placed at my disposal in this campaign, but these being so few, could it have given me many? Could they have been sufficient to carry on a war according to usage when all those resources which are necessary for such an undertaking were practically lacking? The army under my command consisted of only six thousand men when it left Saltillo[2] and of these at least half were raw recruits from San Luis,

Querétaro and other departments, hastily enlisted to fill the ragged companies. The people of Nuevo León and Coahuila, at the instigation of their worthy and patriotic governors, donated food supplies to the army. These, added to those that were brought, made a considerable amount that in a country so vast, where all transportation is done on mule back, was extremely embarrassing to me, although indispensable for our needs. In order to transport it, I made use of extremely heavy ox-charts, a means of transportation never used by armies but which because of the lack of the necessary equipment, and in spite of the most active efforts made to secure it, I was obliged to use. Our needs had been foreseen and that was all that could be done, for to meet them all was an impossibility. The great problem I had to solve was to reconquer Texas and to accomplish this in the shortest time possible, at whatever cost, in order that the revolutionary activities of the interior should not recall that small army before it had fulfilled its honorable mission. A long campaign would have undoubtedly consumed our resources and we would have been unable to renew them. If the only four favorable months of the year were not taken advantage of, the army, in the midst of the hardships of a campaign, would perish of hunger and of the effects of the climate, upon those who composed the army under my command, who were accustomed to a more temperate climate. In order that the soldier by means of repeated marches and frequent battles should forget the immense distance which separated him from his family and home comforts; in order that his courage might not fail; and, in short, to maintain the morale which an army obtains from its activity and operations, it was of the utmost importance to prevent the enemy from strengthening its position or receiving the reenforcements that the papers from the North asserted were very numerous. In a word, the government had said to me that it left everything to my genius, and this flattering remark became an embarrassing truth, making it necessary in this campaign to move with all diligence to avoid the many difficulties that delay in action would undoubtedly bring about. This realization established the norm for all my operations and I always tried earnestly to shorten them. Had we been favored by victory to the last, this policy would have shown a surprised world our occupation, in sixty days, of a territory more than four hundred leagues in extent and defended by the enemy.

Béxar was held by the enemy and it was necessary to open the door to our future operations by taking it. It would have been easy enough to have surprised it, because those occupying it did not have the faintest news of the march of our army. I entrusted, therefore, the operation to one of our generals, who with a detachment of cavalry, part of the dragoons mounted on infantry officers' horses, should have fallen on Béxar in the early morning of February 23, 1836. My orders were concise and definite. I was most surprised, therefore, to find the said general a quarter of a league from Bexar at ten o'clock of that day, awaiting new orders. This, perhaps, was the result of inevitable circumstances; and, although the city was captured, the surprise that I had ordered to be car-

ried out would have saved the time consumed and the blood shed later in the
taking of the Alamo.

Having taken Béxar and the proceeds of the small booty having been sold
by the commissary department to meet its immediate needs, all of which I communicated to the government (Document No. 4 [*letter/testimonial by José López to
Santa Anna on April 5, 1837.*]), the enemy fortified itself in the Alamo, over-look-
ing the city. A siege of a few days would have caused its surrender, but it was
not fit that the entire army should be detained before an irregular fortification
hardly worthy of the name. Neither could its capture be dispensed with, for bad
as it was, it was well equipped with artillery, had a double wall, and defenders
who, it must be admitted, were very courageous and caused much damage to
Béxar. Lastly, to leave a part of the army to lay siege to it, the rest continuing on
its march, was to leave our retreat, in case of a reverse, if not entirely cut off, at
least exposed, and to be unable to help those who were besieging it, who could
be reenforced only from the main body of the advancing army. This would
leave to the enemy a rallying point, although it might be only for a few days.
An assault would infuse our soldiers with that enthusiasm of the first triumph
that would make them superior in the future to those of the enemy. It was not
my judgment alone that moved me to decide upon it, but the general opinion
expressed in a council of war, made up of generals, that I called even though
the discussions which such councils give rise to have not always seemed to me
appropriate. Before undertaking the assault and after the reply given to Travis
who commanded the enemy fortification, I still wanted to try a generous measure, characteristic of Mexican kindness, and I offered life to the defendants
who would surrender their arms and retire under oath not to take them up
again against Mexico. Colonel Don Juan Nepomuceno Almonte, through whom
this generous offer was made, transmitted to me their reply which stated that
they would let us know if they accepted and if not, they would renew the fire at
a given hour. They decided on the latter course and their decision irrevocably
sealed their fate.[3]

On the night of the fifth of March, four columns having been made ready
for the assault under the command of their respective officers, they moved forward in the best order and with the greatest silence, but the imprudent huzzas
of one of them awakened the sleeping vigilance of the defenders of the fort and
their artillery fire caused such disorder among our columns that it was necessary to make use of the reserves. The Alamo was taken, this victory that was so
much and so justly celebrated at the time, costing us seventy dead and about
three hundred wounded,[4] a loss that was also later judged to be avoidable and
charged, after the disaster of San Jacinto, to my incompetence and precipitation.
I do not know of a way in which any fortification, defended by artillery, can be
carried by assault without the personal losses of the attacking party being
greater than those of the enemy, against whose walls and fortifications the
brave assailants can present only their bare breasts. It is easy enough, from a

desk in a peaceful office, to pile up charges against a general out on the field but this cannot prove anything more than the praiseworthy desire of making war less disastrous. But its nature being such, a general has no power over its immutable laws. Let us weep at the tomb of the brave Mexicans who died at the Alamo defending the honor and the rights of their country. They won a lasting claim to fame and the country can never forget their heroic names.

The enemy, discouraged by this blow that left fateful memories, fled before our forces . . .[*The narrative continues on with the rest of the campaign in Texas.*]

---

[1] This *Manifiesto* was first printed at Vera Cruz, 1837, by Antonio María Valdés. It was reprinted by Genaro García in *Documentos para la Historia de México*, XXIX. This reprint was used for the present translation, though the text was verified with the first edition in the García Collection, University of Texas.

[2] Many years later, while in exile, Santa Anna said, referring to the number of men, "I gathered and organized the expeditionary army of Texas, consisting of eight thousand men, in the city of Saltillo." *Diario de mi vida politica y militar* in *Documentos para la Historia de Mexico*, II, 33.

[3] "To the proposals to surrender he replied always that every man under his command preferred to die rather than surrender the fort to the Mexicans." Genaro García, *Documentos*, II, 34.

[4] "Not one remained alive but they disabled over a thousand of our men between dead and wounded." *Ibid.*, 35.

2.1.3.1. Santa Anna, letter, October 24, 1836.

Winkler, Ernest William, ed. 1911. *Secret Journals of the Senate, Republic of Texas, 1836–1845.* 13–5. Austin: Austin Printing Company, for the Texas Library and Historical Commision.

These transcripts are mainly included for the footnotes, which review correspondence from Santa Anna soon after the time of the Alamo. The original Santa Anna letter with an official translation can be examined in the Texas State Library Archives.

To His Excellency Gen[era]l Sam Houston.

Orazimba, Oct. 24 1836.[1]

Much Esteemed Sir:

I enclose you the original answer of President Jackson to my letter of July 4th in order that you may be informed of its contents.

The communication from the Government of Mexico, referred to by Gen[eral] Jackson, stating that *no act of mine while a prisoner would be obligatory upon the authorities of the Nation,* emphasizes what I have repeatedly stated that my presence in the Cabinet of Mexico is necessary and indispensable, and that anything I do or write from here would be unimportant after the retreat of the Mexican Army to the other side of the Rio Bravo del Norte. It is necessary, my dear Sir, to be convinced at once that delay in fulfilling the treaty of May 14th results in nothing but the injury of all parties concerned. The independence of Texas would by this time have been recognized, or on the point of being so recognized, if the commotion at Velasco had not hindered my departure, after if had been so directed by the proper authority. The time lost is precious and perhaps will not return. Put away then unjust mistrust as unworthy of the offenders as of the offended. The acts of my public life shall not be stained by an unworthy act either in prosperity or in misfortune.

The reasons above stated persuade me that any thing I could write to the Mexican Minister in the United States would be useless; and to save time I could proceed to Washington, for there is no doubt that an interview with Gen[era]l Jackson would be beneficial to all.

Consider what is best, and you may depend on the approval of your friend and humble servant,

Ant. Lopez de Santa Anna

P.S.

I have discussed fully with General Austin and Col[onel] Bee the importance of my visit to Washington, preferring this certain communication to paper. Wherefore I refer to these gentlemen for any information upon this subject.

L. de S[an]ta Anna

Whilst the clerk was reading the accompanying documents Mr. Everitt submitted a resolution calling for all the documents referred to by Gen[eral] Santa Anna.

Resolved That the President be Requested to send to this house Translations of all documents connected with the communication of Santa Anna not hitherto sent.[2]

When the Message and documents was laid on the Table [sic].

And the doors of the Senate opened.

Columbia Oct 26 1836

A Message[3] was rec[eive]d from the president with closed doors

On motion of Mr. Everitt it was ordered that all the rooms adjoining the Senate Chamber be cleared whenever the Senate is in secret session Carried

Message[4] Rec[eive]d from the President

Executive Department
Columbia 26th Oct. 1836

To the honorable
The Senate
Gentlemen,

In accordance with your resolution of yesterday, requesting to be furnished with the translations of all the documents, connected with the communication of Santa Anna, which have not heretofore been sent to you, I have the honor to transmit the entire series of communications accompanying this Message.[5]

Those parts of the correspondence which have eminated [*sic*] from the late Government ad interim, are in the English language and those eminating from the President Santa Anna, in Spanish. The difficulty of procuring them to be translated, the length of time which would be required to transcribe them and the scantiness of clerical aid in this department, have induced me to submit to you the Originals belonging to the files of my office. These I intend to recall to their appropriate place and supply you with authenticated copies.

The method will be the most speedy and best adapted to hasten your action upon those interesting subjects now under your consideration; and I trust that therefore, a literal compliance with your resolution, will be dispensed with in this instance, as the defect arises from absolute necessity.

Sam Houston

---

[1] Translation from original letter in Mexican Diplomatic Correspondence. Texas State Library.

[2] MS. Resolution in Papers of First Congress, First Session.

[3] Message has not been found.

[4] A space was reserved for this message in the secret journal, but was not filled in. The copy here printed has been taken from the original manuscript message.

[5] As the "communications accompanying this message" were not enumerated and are not filed with the message, there is no means of identifying them. However, as the question submitted to the senate was, Shall Santa Anna be released, the following documents were probably among them:

1. Orders from Santa Anna to General Filisola, three in number and dated April 22, 1836. Printed in *Telegraph and Texas Register*, September 6, 1836.
2. Letter from Santa Anna to General Filisola, transmitting a copy of the treaty of May 14, 1836. Printed in *Telegraph*, August 23, 1836.
3. General Filisola's ratification of the treaty of May 14, 1836, dated May 26, 1836. Printed in Yoakum's *History of Texas*, II 529.
4. Letter from Santa Anna to President Burnet, dated June 9, 1836, protesting against the nonfulfillment of treaty stipulations and his retention as a prisoner. Printed in *Telegraph*, October 4, 1836.
5. Letter from President Burnet to Santa Anna, dated June 10, 1836, replying to Santa Anna's protest. Printed in *Telegraph*, October 4, 1836.

2.1.3.2.   Santa Anna, letter, 1874.

Santa Anna to H. A. McArdle. Dr. Plutarco Ornelas, trans. March 19, 1874. In H. A. McArdle. *Companion Battle Paintings.* Vol. 1, *Dawn at the Alamo.* TSLA.

The original letter of Santa Anna and translations by Dr. Ornelas, the Mexican consul in San Antonio (September 30, 1899), and Mose Austin Bryon (n.d.) are in a scrapbook of background correspondence and other material McArdle assembled in preparation of his large painting *Dawn at the Alamo,* still on display in the legislative chambers at the Texas state capitol.

Mexico March 19 1874

Mr. H. A. McArdle
Independence, Texas
My Dear Sir

Answering your favor dated the 4th of January I will state: that regarding the capture or restauration [*sic*] of the Alamo Fortress in April, 1836, there is little to add to what was then given out in the official reports and to what is generally known. Nevertheless, in order to gratify your wishes I will add that said deed of arms was a bloody one owning [*sic*] to the fact that Travis, Commanding the forces of the Alamo, refused to enter into any adjustments and his replies were insulting making it necessary to storm the fortress before it was reinforced by Samuel Houston who was coming to its relief with a respectable amount of troops. The obstinacy of Travis and his soldiers was the cause of the death of all of them, because none of them wish to surrender. The struggle lasted more than two hours from the time the Mexican soldiers saved [scaled] those stone walls climbing them with courage—I will be glad if this explanation satisfies your wishes and that it may show you my good will to serve you as your most attentive and devoted servant.

A. L. de Sta Anna

2.1.3.3.   Santa Anna, memoirs, 1874.

Watkins, Willye Ward, trans. 1922. Memoirs of General Antonio López de Santa Anna. 90–93. Master's thesis, University of Texas at Austin.

This translation is noted to be from the manuscript in Santa Anna's own hand, dated February 12, 1874, still in the Benson Library at the University of Texas at Austin. The complete translation with footnotes was published by Ann Fears Crawford in 1988, as *The Eagle: The Autobiography of Santa Anna.*

In the year 1835 the colonists of Texas (citizens of the United States), in possession of the vast and rich lands which the Mexican Congress with unbelievable imprudence had given them, and, on pretext that other privileges which they solicited were not granted them, declared themselves in open revolution, pro-claiming independence.[1] They soon received aid without any difficulty from New Orleans, Mobile, and other points in the United States; and the filibusters joined in such numbers that the Commanding General of the State of Texas, Don Martín P. de Cos, found himself in a perilous situation in San Antonio de Bexar and was force to capitulate, thus leaving the colonists and filibusters owners of all the state.[2]

The government, zealous as it should be in the fulfillment of its duties, declared that it would sustain the integrity of the national territory at all costs. It was necessary to undertake a difficult campaign immediately; accordingly, a capable general who could take charge of this was sought. At my fiery age, being dominated by a noble ambition, I staked my pride on being the first who should go to the defense of the independence, of the honor, and of the rights of the nation, undeterred by any difficulties. Impelled by these principles, I took charge of this campaign, preferring the vicissitudes of war to the seductive and coveted [*substituted for the word "avaricious," which was crossed out*] life of the palace. Congress named as President *ad interim,* General of Division Don Miguel Barragán. I assembled and organized the expeditionary army of Texas in the City of Saltillo—8,000 men in number with corresponding material [*sic*]. A seri-ous illness confined me to my bed for two weeks; however, after my recovery, not another day was lost. The march was slow because the material for the most part, consisted of carts drawn by oxen; the rivers were crossed on rafts con-structed in the absence of bridge material. The lack of other things increased the penalties of the desert. It suffices to say that plants supplied the provisions of the campaign, and wild animals completed the ration of the soldiers. Notwith-standing, nothing was to be complained of. For its valor and constancy, that army well deserves national gratitude.

The filibusters who believed that the Mexican soldiers would not return to Texas were greatly surprised on seeing us and ran frightened to the fortress of the Alamo (solid handiwork of the Spaniards). On that day the fortress had mounted eighteen guns of different caliber and a garrison of 600 men whose commander was named N. [*sic*] Travis, of great renown among the filibusters.[3] To the propositions which were made to him, he always replied *that before sur-rendering the fortress to the Mexicans his men preferred to die.* He was confident that aid would come soon.

The so-called General Samuel Houston, in a letter which was intercepted, said to the famous Travis: *"Take courage and hold out at all risk as I am coming to your aid with 2,000 splendid men and eight well manned cannons."*[4] This information being acquired so opportunely, it was impossible not to take advantage of it. I immediately ordered the assault, since it was not fitting to delay it one day more. The filibusters, in compliance with their purpose, defended themselves obstinately; not one gave any sign of wishing to surrender; with ferocity and valor, they died fighting. I was obliged to call in the reserve to decide a struggle maintained so stubbornly for four hours. Not one was left alive. But among us they put out of battle more than a thousand, dead and wounded. The fortress presented a frightful sight; it would have moved a man less sensitive [than I].[5] Houston on learning the fate of his comrades marched rapidly.

General Don José Urrea, with the brigade at his command, completely defeated Colonel Facny [Fannin] in the Llano del Perdido.[6] Facny was occupying the town of Goliat [Goliad] and came out to meet Urrea with 1,500 filibusters and six pieces of artillery.[7] Urrea announced his triumph and in a despatch stated in conclusion: "Since the adventurers who entered Texas armed in order to further the revolution of the colonists are outside of the law, the prisoners have been shot." This was based on the law of November 27, 1835, in compliance with which the war with Texas was waged without quarter.[8]

---

[1] The Texans had taken up arms in defense of the Constitution of 1824, and it was not until March 2, 1836, that they declared their independence from Mexico.—Garrison, George P. *Texas* (Boston, 1903) 189–214.

[2] December 11, 1835.—Garrison, op. cit., 193.

[3] According to Fortier and Ficklen (*Central America and Mexico*, 311), fourteen guns had been mounted at the Alamo and a garrison of 150 men under William B. Travis. The number was later increased to 183. See Garrison, op. cit., 298.

[4] Search has been made in histories, biographies of Samuel Houston, and in manuscript material in the Texas State Library, pertaining to this period, but no reference to such a letter has been found. Vicente Filisola (*Memorias para la Historia de la guerra de Texas* (Mexico, 1849), *Segunda parte*, 387) states that news was received on February 28, that 200 men were coming from Goliad to the aid of the Alamo. Santa Anna admits having written his Memoirs "without other aid than his taxed memory."

[5] Martínez Caro (*Verdadera idea de la Primera Campana de Tejas* (Mexico, 1837), 9) states that five men were found hiding by General Castrillón and brought into Santa Anna's presence. The latter reprimanded Castrillón severely and turned his back, *"a cuya accion, los soldados auneue ya formadas, cargaron sobre ellos hasta concluirlos."* [*"...while the soldiers stepped out of their ranks and set upon (the prisoners) until they were killed,"* per 2.5.1.]

[6] Bancroft (*North Mexican States and Texas* (San Francisco, 1889 II, 231) refers to this engagement a few miles from Goliad as the battle of the Encinal del Perdido.

[7] According to Garrison (op. cit., 206) Fannin had 400 men.

[8] Santa Anna evidently refers to the *Circular de la secretaria de guerra* of December 30, 1835. *"Se trata y castigue como a piratas a los extranjeros que introduzcan armas o Municiones por algun puerto de la republica."* [*The aliens who introduce weapons or munitions through any port of the republic shall be treated and punished as pirates.*] See Arillaga, José, *Recopilación de Leyes* (Mexico, 1836) 677–679.

Commentary

Santa Anna (2.1)

One cannot read these Santa Anna documents without being struck by their self-serving nature. Here was an individual who felt that he never made a mistake, and that whatever unfortunate incidents he was involved in were due to failures by others.

Santa Anna's orders (2.1.1.1) to his cavalry commander, General Sesma, set the tone for the future campaign at Béxar. His direct order that no quarter be given to the enemy—specifically the foreigners, rather than the Tejanos—anticipated the execution of all military prisoners who fell under his control, particularly at San Patricio and Goliad.

His actions were often contradictory. He emphatically ordered Sesma to not attack an unknown position of the enemy "until there is no more doubt," yet said Sesma must not "fail to take advantage of any opportunity that might present itself." Santa Anna eventually blamed the losses at the Alamo on Sesma (2.1.2) because he obeyed instruction 8 rather than the final comment in this document.

All these documents are, despite their self-interest, valuable for understanding the events of the Alamo by giving or confirming details that would otherwise be unclear, such as that the memo from Batres to Bowie at the start of the siege (2.1.1.2) was dictated directly by Santa Anna (2.1.1.3). He also stated that he fully intended a surprise attack on San Antonio, which was foiled by heavy rain, and that the delay in the final assault was due to waiting for further reinforcements by three divisions of the first brigade (2.1.1.3, 2.1.1.10). Even more interesting is the order that the final assault would be signaled by bugle (2.1.1.8). Joe (1.3.4) believed that the final assault was a surprise, with the outlying sentinels being overrun before they could give the alarm. As this document is the actual attack order, it is unlikely that the attack was an entire surprise to the whole garrison, regardless of whether Joe (or Travis) happened to be asleep at the time of the initial advance. Santa Anna also confirmed (2.1.1.9, 2.1.1.10) that resistance was stubborn, that the attack lasted about one and a half hours, and that the reserve had to be called in. He recalled years later (2.1.3.2, 2.1.3.3) the valor of the defenders.

Santa Anna also mentioned sending a flag to Tornel. This flag is depicted in Lord as that of the New Orleans Greys, hence Santa Anna's comment on the abettors from the United States.[1] Potter (5.1.7) and Williams believed that the flags of the Alamo most likely would have had reference to the constitution of 1824, dismissed by Santa Anna, and therefore were likely to have been destroyed.[2] But the New Orleans Greys flag served a specific propaganda purpose of Santa Anna and hence was preserved.

In his memoirs and other documents, Santa Anna frequently called his enemies in Texas "filibusters," which, according to *Merriam-Webster's Collegiate Dictionary*, was a term used to refer to Americans engaged in fomenting insurrections in Latin America in the mid-nineteenth century. He used this term to include anyone who supported the constitution of 1824. A more negative meaning, which was his normal intended use, is "freebooter," in the sense of a pirate, or "land-grabber." Typically, he was really talking about the immigrants from the United States.

A curious detail raises deeper questions on the preparedness of the Mexican Army. Santa Anna specified (2.1.1.8) that a total of twenty-eight ladders were to be carried for the assault. One wonders how effective an attack on walls with so few ladders for so many soldiers might have been, and furthermore, why they were so explicitly enumerated. This same document also indicates that the soldiers had a low level of training by specifying the use of chin straps for soldiers' hats and even that they should be wearing shoes or sandals.

In another letter (2.1.1.4), Santa Anna cited an urgent need for food and money. It is worth asking how well planned by the army leadership were the logistics, training, and support activities, especially the medical services. When Santa Anna complained later of the difficulties in preparing for the Texas campaign, why did he have to order up food and money at the first significant town he reached in Texas?[3]

One of the most difficult questions of the Alamo story was the extent of Mexican casualties. One extreme, not usually accepted by American scholars, is Santa Anna's report (2.1.1.10) of seventy Mexican dead and three hundred wounded (along with six hundred defenders killed). Even his *Manifesto* of 1837 (2.1.2) suggests that this is low, with a statement that personal losses of the attacking party would be greater than those defending a fortress. Years later (2.1.3.3), he numbered the army dead and wounded at a thousand. This topic is revisited in Appendix B, after more evidence is presented.

Santa Anna's comments on possible reinforcements are of interest. He noted this in several places: during the siege (2.1.1.5), after the fall (2.1.1.10), and in 1874 (2.1.3.2, 2.1.3.3). We know from his letters that Travis was determined to hold the Alamo at all costs, but even the Travis letters of March 3 have some optimism. Did Travis get encouragement and promise of reinforcements? The Rose story suggests he did, and Santa Anna's documents support this idea as well. This question is directly relevant in considering the Robert Williamson letter (4.3.4.1).

El Nacional, Suplemento al Numero 79, is a very early source for the Mexican documents. Considering the nature of the documents, it no doubt served a semiofficial function of forwarding government news. In addition to those quoted here, the other letters of Santa Anna (2.1.1.8, 2.1.1.10) and the Williamson letter (4.3.4.1) are also reproduced, and could quite possibly be the source of some of the Filisola documents (2.6.1). John Jenkins made an unusual mistake in citing a document of Santa Anna's for March 3 that likely is the first one of March 6 (2.1.1.9).[4] The broadsheet must have been published between March 21, which is when the copy was certified, and the end of April, before news of San Jacinto reached Texas. The end of March is the most probable.

The most poignant topic is on Santa Anna's treatment of prisoners. From the start of the siege (2.1.1.2), only unconditional surrender was accepted, but in fact, the policy throughout the campaign (2.1.1.1, 2.1.1.5, 2.1.1.6, 2.1.1.7) was to execute all prisoners.[5] This was amply demonstrated by the execution of four hundred of Fannin's men a few weeks later. In his *Manifesto* a year later (2.1.2), Santa Anna was already trying to minimize blame by saying he offered an amnesty to Travis—something not supported by his claimed agent Almonte (2.2.1). Instead, the conditions for the amnesty sound suspiciously similar to what the Texans gave Cós earlier. By 1874, the entire battle was Travis's fault for not surrendering (2.1.3.2). Santa Anna also bore no responsibility, by hearing after the fact, for the Fannin massacre (2.1.3.3). The various documents referenced, including Santa Anna's own direct military orders of the time, make a lie of his attempted revision of history in his own favor.

His *Manifesto* (2.1.2) presents Santa Anna as a servant or agent prepared to sacrifice for his country rather than, in fact, the military ruler and the only genuine authority in Mexico. He lamented the immense sacrifice and the seemingly insuperable obstacles to launching the Texas campaign. Texas was fertile when colonists were taking it (2.1.1.11), but a desert when he crossed it. This is not to imply that it wasn't a difficult crossing. It was, but this doesn't negate the fact that his statements are contradictory and self-serving. After the fact, he said that a number of his difficulties were due to necessary caution in case of reverses, contradicted by his earlier statements of optimism (2.1.1.3, 2.1.1.4). By 1837, the lack of surprise in taking San Antonio was due to a general, not to the heavy rains (2.1.1.3 vs. 2.1.2). He couldn't wait for a siege of a few days, as "it was not fit that the entire army should be detained before an irregular fortification," and so he avoided recognizing the thirteen-plus days he actually waited before the final attack. The army moved forward "with the greatest silence, but the imprudent huzzas of the men awakened the sleeping vigilance of the defenders of the fort," he wrote in his *Manifesto* (2.1.2), while his order (2.1.1.8) had them blowing a bugle to announce the attack. Finally, there is the lamest excuse a general can make: "Had we been favored by victory to the last, this policy would have shown a surprised world." So might anyone say in defeat!

There are two previously overlooked (not in Jenkins) letters to Tornel from Santa Anna during the siege, dated February 27 and March 6. Both transmit reports of General Urrea, the one of March 6 announcing the victory over Grant at San Patricio.[6]

For interested readers who would like more flavor of this unique personality, Santa Anna's autobiography is now available in a footnoted edition by Ann Fears Crawford.[7]

---

1. Lord 1961, plates; published originally in the *Star-Telegram,* November 12, 1933.
2. Williams in *SWHQ* 37:179–81.
3. Presley 1959 gives a general discussion on this subject, and Borroel's several translations out of de la Peña's papers (see section 2.9.3 and Commentary below) go into considerable detail. All of Castañeda 1928 is interesting and valuable in giving the widely divergent opinions of the senior leaders as to who is at fault.
4. Jenkins 1973, 4:501.
5. Also see Becerra (2.10.1), which includes Santa Anna's proclamation of February 17; and Filisola 1987, 2:167 for the Tornel proclamation of February 18.

6. In the manuscript collection of the Archivo Historico Militar, Expediente 1904:31 and 1898:3 UC Bancroft Library (former is also in Borroel 2001a, 2). Another reputed account not included here is from *Man's Illustrated* magazine by Jackson Burke reprinted by Groneman (1996, 207–8). The story has no relation to the documents presented here. It states that thirty defenders mutinied and were executed, and that the source was Crockett before being executed himself. Groneman points out other indications that the account is fiction, and further attention is unwarranted.

7. Crawford 1988.

2.2.1.   Almonte, journal, 1836.

Asbury, Samuel E., ed. 1944. The private journal of Juan Nepomuceno Almonte, February 1–April 16, 1836. *Southwestern Historical Quarterly* 48:10–25.

As noted in Asbury's introduction, this is from a near contemporary newspaper publication in the *New York Herald*. More of the journal and commentary is included than necessary for the topic of the Alamo siege, but some of the context of the times is valuable, and many of the day-to-day details of the march to Béxar and the siege itself are unique. The journal extends to April 16, just prior to San Jacinto; it is presented here up until Almonte's departure from Béxar on March 18. The *Southwestern Historical Quarterly* transcript is very accurate. It apparently was generated directly from a facsimile of the newspaper now in the Almonte (Juan Nepomuceno) Papers, CAH, complete with notations to the printer. Only minor stylistic differences from the original newspaper publication appear.

Introduction

THE PRESENT publication of Juan Nepomuceno Almonte's[1] Journal is from photostats of the original issues of the New York *Herald*, obtained from the New York State Library, Albany, New York, and the Library of Congress. The *Telegraph and Texas Register*, October 4, 1836, published part three; and about a third of part six was published in William Kennedy's *Texas, 1841*, pp. 218–220. This Journal and other documents were sent to the *Herald* because of its strong support of the Texian cause, and the long friendship of Sam Houston and James Gordon Bennett,[2] the editor and owner. The original documents are lost. The space required for the Journal itself and its accompanying notes limit present notes. Many questions arising remain unanswerable or speculative. The writer welcomes correspondence.

---

[1] Juan Nepomuceno Almonte was born in Valladolid, Mexico, 1804, and died in Paris, France, March 20, 1869. He was reputed to be the son of the patriot Mexican priest Morelos. Almonte was a typical Mexican soldier of fortune and statesman. Educated in the United States, he became a lifelong follower of Santa Anna. In the 1836 campaign against the Texans, his services were manifold—something more than an aide-de-camp's, and more than a confidential secretary's. Almonte's brief, apt style is worthy of note; there is not an ideological phrase in it. For his life, see Appleton's *Cyclopedia of American Biography*, I, 59, and for a more extensive account see Helen Willits Harris, The Public Life of Juan Nepomuceno Almonte, Ph.D. dissertation, The University of Texas, 1935.

[2] James Gordon Bennett, Sr. (1795–June 1, 1872), had established the New York *Herald*, May 6, 1835, a penny daily. He was still "editor, reporter, proof-reader, folder, carrier," etc., in June, 1836, when he published Almonte's Journal in the *Herald* from a cellar at 20 Wall Street. Bennett was a Spanish translator but did not translate this Journal. His staunch support of Texas from the Revolution onward deserves a memorial far more than many who received it. See *Dictionary of American Biography*, II, 195–199.

[The New York Herald, Thursday, June 16, 1836]
IMPORTANT FROM TEXAS.

By the packet ship Nashville from New Orleans, which arrived on Tuesday evening, we have received various documents and papers from Texas and New Orleans—and among them, the original copies of the "PRIVATE JOURNAL OF THE MEXICAN CAMPAIGN AND ITS PROGRESS," by Almonte, together with a "GENERAL ORDER BOOK," both contained in two folio manuscripts and written in Spanish. As soon as the Journal shall be translated, we shall publish it in the *Herald*.

It is a highly interesting and valuable document, and throws a great deal of light on the secret motives and movements of Santa Anna and his generals. The journal is kept by Almonte, who was in this city last summer, and previous to the war and afterwards travelled through Texas as a spy. To his misrepresentations is attributed the campaign altogether.

The Journal or Private Diary commences on the 1st of February, 1836, dated at Sa[l]tillo. Under the date of the "6th March, Sunday," there is an entry describing the assault on the Alamo. It began at 5-1/4 A.M. and continued till 6 o'clock. The journal states that the enemy (The Texians) attempted to escape but were all killed, or put to the sword. Only four women and one negro slave saved their lives. At the close of the entry is the following by way of postscript:

"Our soldiers robbed me.—Almonte."

A great many other curious particulars are told in this journal which will appear in our columns in a day or two.

Meantime we are are [sic] happy to learn that the affairs of Texas are in a most prosperous condition. General Cos and Col. Almonte have been adjudged by a Texian court martial to be shot—Santa Anna's life will be preserved but he will remain a close prisoner of war.—This decision has been made though not yet promulgated.

Both Cos and Almonte deserve their fate. The former was a prisoner to the Texians in the early part of the contest. He was released on his word of honor not to take up arms against them. He broke this honor, and he dies as a traitor ought to do.

Almonte is the same person who was here last summer and secretly furnished or stimulated the Courier & Enquirer to publish articles calling the Texians "rebels" and "insurrectionists." He afterwards went to Texas as a spy. He also deserves his fate.

We further hear *that the gallant Houston will soon be in New York.* His physicians have recommended to him a northern latitude till his wounds are healed. The climate of New Orleans, and the general excitement there, protract his convalescence. He wants retirement and tranquility.

By the next New Orleans packet we therefore expect General Houston, the hero of San Jacinto—a victory unparalleled in ancient or modern times. It is the Marathon of Texas.

[The New York Herald, Wednesday, June 22, 1836]
SINGULAR DISCLOSURE.
JOURNAL OF THE MEXICAN CAMPAIGN—BY ALMONTE,
AID TO SANTA ANNA. PICKED UP ON THE BATTLE GROUND
OF SAN JACINTO BY ANSON JONES.

Annexed will be found a translation of the first portion of the remarkable "Secret Journal" of the recent Mexican Campaign, written by Col. Almonte, aide de camp to General Santa Anna. The original, in the Spanish language, is now in our possession. It was picked up on the battleground of San Jacinto by Dr. Anson Jones, and was sent to us via Galveston Island, on the 12th of May last. The journal was seen and examined by Mr. Childress, the diplomatic representative from Texas, who left this city a few days ago for Washington. The Journal begins as follows:

JOURNAL COMMENCES IN FEBRUARY, 1836.

Feb. 1st.—At 8 A.M.—The President set out from Saltillo for Monclova, passing by way of the Hacienda (farm) of Santa Maria, 6 leagues distant; thence to Carretas, 5 leagues; thence to the Hacienda de Messillas, 5 leagues; making in all 16 leagues of good waggon [*sic*] road. In Carretas there is running water, no pasture, the road passes through high ridges and hills, and with little stone. There is a shorter road to Saltillo from Low Arcos, or a bridge near to the Hacienda of Santa Maria. Mesillas has no running water, but a reservoir; the running water being 1-^{1}/2 leagues distant; there is a large house, corn and corn stalks.

2d.—Started for Anclo at 7-^{1}/2 A.M.—To the reservoir of San Felipe, 7 leagues; road almost level; little stone; the water in the reservoir somewhat scarce; there is some pasture; no house; we encamped in a small valley; there we met the second Division under command of Tolsa; we arrived at 5 P.M. having made a short halt.

3d.—At 8-^{1}/4 A.M.—Started to the Hoya, 8 leagues; no people; well dry; two small poor houses—to Bejar, 6 leagues; very good road; some dry pasture; no water in the road. The Infantry arrived at 7-^{1}/2 P.M. and rested the day following; many soldiers sickened with diarrhoea, and some with blistered feet; plenty of water, but no fodder; corn at 2 rials [reals] the almad [almúd].

4th.—Started at 8 A.M. to the Hacienda de Castaños, 10 leagues; running water, good and abundant; to Monclova, 3 leagues; good road; corn and stalks, but few provisions. From Saltillo to Monclova, according to our account, there are 57 leagues; according to the Itinerary, 52 leagues.

5th—The thermometer at Monclova in the house at 59°; in the afternoon arrived Messrs. Ampudia, Caro, Wall, and Arago; *I wrote to New York;* it rained in the night; stood guard; Mr. Moral arrived.

6th.—In Monclova, thermometer at 59°, cloudy.—The second Division arrived; Flores was ordered to deliver the command of the Division of Gaudalaxara to his next in command; *wrote under dictation of His Excellency the President;* D. Ramon Musquiz left for Sta. Rosa; Arago continues unwell; Moral on guard.

7th.—In Monclova, thermometer 62°, day clear. Orders issued at 6 A.M. the next day; Sr. Mora, assistant guard; I wrote to *   *   *   *   *   *   *   *   *   *   *   *   *   *   *   *   *   *   * the mail from Mexico arrives at Monclova, Tuesday, in the morning, and leaves Wednesday at night.

8th.—Left Monclova at 7-¹/₂ A.M. arrived at the Hacienda de Dos Hermanas and slept there.

9th.—To Lamparos, 5 leagues, (well water); to Laura, 5 leagues, (well water); good roads, all level, and good pasture.

10th.—To the river Sabinas at La Hacienda de Soledad, 5 leagues; to San Juan, also Hacienda, 1 league; to San Jose, 9 leagues; good roads and pasture.

11th.—To the Cabezeras de Sta. Rita, 7 leagues, (running water); to San Miguel de Allende, 4 leagues; good roads and pasture; high hills.

12th.—We arrived at Rio Grande, having left Nava 14 leagues to the left; road good and level; pasture, but no water until reaching the river.

13th.—At the Rio Grande; weather stormy; thermometer 51°; the Americans burnt the bridge over the river Nueces; the Division left the day before under the command of Sr. Sesma.

14th.—At the Rio Grande; the weather moderates; thermometer 46°; our baggage arrived at 6 P.M. after dark.

15th.—At the Rio Grande; weather good; thermometer 56°; fine weather for traveling; *despatched a part of the correspondence.*

16th.—At 4-¹/₂ P.M. started from Rio Grande, after writing until 3 in the afternoon; arrived at La Peña 11 o'clock at night; distance 12 leagues.

17th.—Exceedingly hot at mid-day on the Nueces; from La Peña to La Expantora, 5 leagues; to the river Nueces 1-¹/₂, and to La Fortuga [Tortuga], 3 leagues.

18th.—To La Leona, 8 leagues; to No lo Digas, 4 leagues; no water.

19th.—At the Rio Frio, 5 leagues; found there in the morning the Division of Sr. Ramirez; little pasture; made a new bridge; the division crossed in the afternoon.

20th.—Started for Arroyo Seco, 4 leagues; to Tahuacan, 2 leagues; to Rio Hondo, 2 leagues, making 8 leagues. The night was clear and pleasant, morning cloudy, 72° of Farenheit; day cloudy, misty, no rain.

Thus far to day. We have only a few observations to make.

The publication of this authentic document, will be interesting on many accounts. The question of Texian Independence, is rapidly becoming the absorbing topic of the present day. Mexico, the United States, Great Britain, and France will all take a deep interest in the astounding events of the last six months. The creation of a new nation by the arms of a few brave men, will establish a new principle of action among mankind. The romantic enterprizes [*sic*] of Cortez and Pizarro, are about to be renewed by a different race, and under a new auspices. Religion was the impulse that overthrew the ancient races of this continent, and established a fresh people over their ruins. Liberty is now the watchword, that may drive Spanish superstition and Spanish cruelty, not only from Texas, but from all South America.

Under the date of the 7th, we have left a gap in the Journal. This is done on purpose. In the original, the names are given at full length, to whom Almonte wrote. They are persons now residing in New York and Philadelphia, some of them of great respectability. During their *sejour* in this country, we do not wish to endanger their peace. The intelligence and views which Almonte communicated to them, is also known to persons here. It has a close and intimate connection with various movements of various men and prints both in New York and Philadelphia. Robt. Walsh, the editor of the National Gazette—Charles King, of the New York American—and several other persons have been conspicuous for their sympathy with the enemies of American liberty in Texas. We could a tale unfold, connected with these personages and the Mexican *intriguants* here—but we stop a little while, and give them time to repent. The day will soon be here, when we may feel is our duty to fill up the blank from the original manuscript, which out of generosity and kindness, feelings, very probably, which they cannot appreciate, *is for the present suppressed.*

Another remarkable fact is known. In Almonte's correspondence with persons in New York and Philadelphia, it is certain, that some persons who have been speculating in Texas Land Companies, have been trying to keep on the kindly side of both the chiefs of the Mexican, and those of the Texian armies. They had made arrangements of such a nature, that whatever might be the issue of the contest, they should, like cats, fall on their feet. *The same people have been, and are on the fence.* Has any person in New York or Philadelphia been advancing funds on the Mexican interest? Have such persons refused to aid the Texians? These questions will be solved in proper time.

This portion of the journal brings down the Mexican army to the eastern bank of the Rio Frio, only a short distance from San Antonio. It begins at Soltillo [Saltillo] or Leorna Vicario, in the State of New Leon. The descriptions of the scenery are brief, pithy, and correspond exactly with the accounts we have received personally from travellers. The next portion of the journal will bring us down to the assault of the Alamo.

[The New York Herald, June 23, 1836]
ALMONTE'S JOURNAL

We continue our translations from the "Journal." The first portion was all preparation and diplomacy—this is all war and bloodshed. The account of the investing and storming of the Alamo is quite interesting. To the general reader it will be more pleasant reading than the first part. We have some further remarks to make—but we reserve them for another day.

ALMONTE'S JOURNAL CONTINUED.

Feb.—Sunday 21st—At 7-^{1}/$_2$ A.M. left Aroyo Hondo—weather cloudy— slight showers—not cold—wind south east. To Franciso Perez 4 leagues, (a stream of water very distant, but not on the road) To Arroyo del Chacon, good water, 3 leagues. To the river Median 2 leagues; all good road, but broken by large hills. At ^{1}/$_4$ before 2 o'clock the President arrived. The day completely overcast; the whole division at 5 o'clock, when it commenced raining heavily— all wet but baggage dry, at 12 o'clock at night it cleared some.

Monday, 22d—Commenced cloudy, but cleared at 10 o'clock. The troops cleared their arms and dryed their clothes; no desertions whatever or sickness. We passed the day at Medina to rest the troops. Two men from the Ranchos near Bexar arrived, one menchaca [Menchaca] and another; killed a beef; various other persons came in, reviewed the troops. Sr. Ramirez y Sermer [Sesma], marched to cut off the retreat of the enemy with—dragoons. It was believed the enemy discovered our movements.

Tuesday 23—At 7-^{1}/$_2$ A.M. the army was put in march—To the Potranca 1-^{1}/$_2$ leagues—To the Creek of Leon or Del Medio, 3-^{1}/$_2$ leagues—To Bexar 3 leagues, in all 8 leagues. At half a league, from Bexar the division halted on the hills of Alazan at 12-^{1}/$_2$ o'clock. General Sesma arrived at 7 A.M. and did not advance to reconnoitre because he expected an advance of the enemy which was about to be made according to accounts given by a spy of the enemy who was caught. There was water, though little, in the stream of Las Lomas del Alazan. At 2 the army took up their march, the President and his staff in the van. The enemy, as soon as the march of the division was seen, hoisted the tri-colored flag with two stars, designed to represent Coahuila and Texas. The President with all his staff advanced to Campo Santo (burying ground.) The enemy lowered the flag and fled, and possession was taken of Bexar without firing a shot. At 3 P.M. the enemy filed off to the fort of Alamo, where there was—pieces of artillery; among them one 18 pounder: I[t] appeared they had 130 men; during the afternoon 4 grenades were fired at them. The firing was suspended in order to receive a messenger, who brought a dispatch the contents of which appears in No. 1, and the answer which was given will be found in No. 2. I conversed with the bearer who was Jameson (G. B.) and he informed me of the bad state they were in at the Alamo, and manifested a wish that some honorable conditions should be proposed for a surrender. Another messenger afterwards came, (Martin) late a clerk in a house in New Orleans. He stated to me what Mr. Travis said, "that if I wished to speak with him, he would receive me with much pleasure." I answered that it did not become the Mexican Government to make any propositions through me, and that I had only permission to hear such as might be made on the part of the rebels. After these contestations night came on, and

there was no more firing. In the night another small battery was made up the river near the house of Veremenda. I lodged in the house of Nixon, (Major) with Urriza and Marcil Aguirre. An inventory of the effects taken was made; many curious papers were found. One Smith, carpenter and cabinet maker, they say was the owner of the effects. I did not sleep all night, having to attend to the enemy and the property, the charge of which of which [sic] was entrusted to me; its value was about $3000.

Wednesday, 24th.—Very early this morning a new battery was commenced on the bank of the river, about 350 yards from the Alamo. It was finished in the afternoon, and a brisk fire was kept up from it until the 18 pounder and another piece was dismounted. The President reconnoitered on horseback, passing within musket shot of the fort. According to a spy, four of the enemy were killed. At evening the music struck up, and went to entertain the enemy with *it* and some *grenades.* In the night, according to the statement of a spy, 30 men arrived at the fort from Gonzales.

Thursday, 25th.—The firing from our batteries was commenced early. The General in Chief, with the batallion [sic] de Cazadores, crossed the river and posted themselves in the Alamo—that is to say, in the houses near the fort. A new fortification was commenced by us near the house of McMullen. In the random firing the enemy wounded 4 of the Cazadores de Matamoros battalion, and 2 of the battalion of Jimenes, and killed one corporal and a soldier of the battalion of Matamoros. Our fire ceased in the afternoon. In the night two batteries were erected by us on the other side of the river in the Alameda of the Alamo—the battalion of Matamoros was also posted there, and the cavalry was posted on the hills to the east of the enemy, and in the road from Gonzales at the Casa Mata Antigua. At half past eleven at night we retired. The enemy, in the night, burnt the straw and wooden houses in their vicinity, but did not attempt to set fire with their guns to those in our rear. A strong north wind commenced at nine at night.

Friday, 26th.—The northern wind continued very strong; the thermometer fell to 39°, and during the rest of the day remained at 60°. At daylight there was a slight skirmish between the enemy and a small party of the division of the east, under command of General Sesma. During the day the firing from our cannon was continued. The enemy did not reply, except now and then. At night the enemy burnt the small houses near the parapet of the battalion of San Luis, on the other side of the river. Some sentinels were advanced. In the course of the day the enemy sallied out for wood and water, and were opposed by our marksman. The northern wind continues.

[To be continued.]

[The New York Herald, June 25, 1836]
ALMONTE'S JOURNAL OF THE MEXICAN CAMPAIGN
NO. 3

TAKING OF BEXAR—REINFORCEMENT OF THE ENEMY FROM LA
BAHIA—FIRING FROM THE ALAMO—ALMONTE'S OPINION OF THE
CAMPAIGN—CAPTURE OF SAN PATRICIO—COUNCIL OF WAR ON
ASSAULTING THE ALAMO—SANTA ANNA UNDECIDED.

We continue our translations from this highly interesting document. Some of the
opinions and transactions recorded are quite curious. This portion of the Journal
brings us down to the Council of War at which was deliberated the assault of
the Alamo, in which Travis and his brave companions were massacred.

JOURNAL CONTINUED.

Saturday 27th.—The northern wind was strong at day break, and continued
all the night. Thermometer at 39°. Lieutenant Manuel Menchacho was sent with
a party of men for the corn, cattle, and hogs at the Ranchos (small farms) of
Seguin and Flores. It was determined to cut off the water from the enemy on the
side next to the old mill. There was little firing from either side during the day.
The enemy worked hard to repair some entrenchments. In the afternoon the
President was observed by the enemy and fired at. In the night a courier extraordinary was dispatched to the city of Mexico, informing the Government of
the taking of Bexar, [1] and also to Gen'ls Urrea, Filisola, Cos & Vital Fernandez.
No private letters were sent.

Sunday, 28th.—The weather abated somewhat. Thermometer at 40° at 7 A.M.
News were received that a reinforcement to the enemy was coming by the road
from La Bahia, in number 200. [2] It was not true. The canonading [*sic*] was continued.

Monday 29th.—The weather changed—thermometer at 55°; in the night it
commenced blowing hard from the west. In the afternoon the battalion of
Allende took post at the east of the Alamo. The President reconnoitered. One of
our soldiers was killed in the night. The wind changed to the north at midnight,
about that time Gen. Sesma left the camp with the cavalry of Dolores and the
infantry of Allende to meet the enemy coming from La Bahia or Goliad to the aid
of the Alamo. Gen'l Castrillon on guard.

March 1st.—The wind subsided, but the weather continued cold—thermometer at 36° in the morning—day clear. Early in the morning Gen. Sesma
wrote from the Mission de la Espador that there was no such enemy, and that
he reconnoitered as far as the Tinaja, without finding any traces of them. The
cavalry returned to camp, and the infantry to this city. At 12 o'clock the President went out to reconnoitre the mill site to the north west of the Alamo. Lieut.
Col. Ampudia was commissioned to construct more trenches.—In the afternoon
the enemy fired two 12 pound shots at the house of the President, one of which
struck the house, and the other passed it. [3] Nothing more of consequence
occurred. Night cold—thermometer 34° Farenheit, and 1° Reaumur.

Wednesday, 2d.—Commenced clear and pleasant—thermometer 34°—no
wind. An Aid of Col. Duque arrived with despatches from Arroyo Hondo, date

1st inst.; in reply, he was ordered to leave the river Median, and arrive the next day at 12 or 1 o'clock. Gen. J. Ramirez came to breakfast with the President. Information was received that there was corn at the farm of Sequin [Seguin], and Lieut. Menchaca was sent with a party for it. The President discovered, in the afternoon, a covered road within pistol shot of the Alamo, and posted the battalion of Jimenes there. At 5 A.M. Bringas went out to meet Gaona.

Thursday, 3d.—Commenced clear, at 40°, without wind. The enemy fired a few cannon and musket shots at the city. I wrote to Mexico and to my sister, directed them to send their letters to Bexar, and that before 3 months the campaign would be ended. [4] The General-in-Chief went out to reconnoitre. A battery was erected on the north of the Alamo within musket shot. Official despatches were received from Gen. Urrea, announcing that he had routed the colonists at San Patricio—killing 16 and taking 21 prisoners. [5] The bells were rung. The battalions of Zapaderes, Aldama, and Toluca arrived. The enemy attempted a sally in the night at the Sugar Mill, but were repulsed by our advance.

Friday, 4th.—The day commenced windy, but not cold—thermometer 48°. Commenced firing very early, which the enemy did not return. In the afternoon one or two shots were fired by them. A meeting of Generals and Colonels was held, at which Generals Cos, Sesma, and Castrillon were present; (Generals Amador and Ventura Mora did not attend—the former having been suspended, and the latter being in active commission.) Also present, Colonels Francisco Duque, battalion of Toluca—Orisñuela, battalion of Aldama—Romero, battalion of Matamoros—Arnat, battalion of Zapadores, and the Major of battalion of San Luis.—The Colonels of battalions of Jimenes and San Luis did not attend, being engaged in actual commission. I was called. After a long conference, [6] Cos, Castrillon, Orisñuela, and Romero were of the opinion that the Alamo should be assaulted—first opening a breach with the two cannon of—and the two mortars, and that they should wait the arrival of the two 12 pounders expected on Monday the 7th. The President, Gen. Ramirez, and I were of opinion that that [sic] the 12 pounders should not be waited for, but the assault made.—Colonels Duque and Arnat, and the Major of the San Luis battalion did not give any definite opinion about either of the two modes of assault proposed. In this state things remained—the General not making any definite resolation [sic]. In the night the north parapet was advanced towards the enemy through the water course. A Lieutenant of Engineers conducted the entrenchment. A messenger was despatched to Urrea.

[To be continued.]

Notes

[1] "Taking of Bexar"—this was the first signal victory gained by Santa Anna himself over the Texians. It appears to have cheered up their spirits wonderfully. So overjoyed were they that no private letters were written—no time—all was "pomp and circumstance of glorious war."

[2] La Bahia or Goliad was situated on the west side of the river San Antonio, on the banks of one of whose tributaries is Bexar or the Alamo. Col. Fannin's command was stationed at Goliad—the main Texian army under Gen'l
Houston had retreated at that time to the east of the Colorado.

[3] These twelve pounders came very near levelling San Anna in the dust.
Travis in this showed them good gunnery.

[4] "Wrote to my sister"—"before three months the campaign will be
ended." What a flood of reflections these recorded sentiments of poor Almonte
create! At the last accounts he was a close prisoner of war at Valasco on the
mouth of the Brassos. When his sister hears of his sad fate what a burst of grief
and sisterly affection! Even in the midst of war these sentiments cannot be con-
trouled [sic]. "Wrote to my sister!" This simple passage has raised Almonte
higher in our estimation than all his talents—his brief—energetic mind. He was
the sole cause and occasion of the war in Texas. He stimulated Santa Anna to
that expedition. Standing before the Alamo—measuring over his various fortunes—he exultingly predicts that Texas will be reduced in three months—and
that he will return in triumph to Mexico, where he can embrace with the affection of a brother his beloved sister. With all his errors, Almonte's heart breaks
out in the right spot—honorable to himself and to human nature.

[5] This was their second victory and their ringing the bells is highly characteristic. San Patricio is a small place on the eastern bank of the Rio de las Nueces near the bay of that name. It formed the extreme right of the base of Santa
Anna's operations.

[6] "After a long conference, &c." Here is a remarkable disclosure. Cos who
had been released by the Texians on *parole,* is the first to advise an assault upon
the handful of brave men in the Alamo. Almonte also is for immediate assault.
This disclosure ought to decide the question of life and death as affecting Gen.
Cos. He has justly forfeited his life according to the rules of war.

The next portion will contain a brief and energetic description of the assault
on the Alamo itself.

[The New York Herald, June 27, 1836]
ALMONTE'S JOURNAL—NO. 4

In the annexed portion there are several important particulars, both political
and military.

The assault of the Alamo is very briefly given. It will be observed that
Almonte's account differs very essentially from what we received at the time
through the Texas Papers.

Another point is the account of the news from Mexico of the election of M.
Corro as President *ad interim,* instead of General Bravo, who was the candidate
of Santa Anna. This singular fact shews that during Santa Anna's absence, his
political opponents had gained a majority of votes in the Senate of Mexico. Here
is the germ of the revolution which we expect to hear of every day from Vera

Cruz. A New-Orleans paper, in the Mexican interest, stated very recently that Gen. Bravo was assembling an army of 10,000 men to recapture Texas. We doubt very much the accuracy of such statements, and wait with impatience to hear of the events which must follow Santa Anna's discomfiture at San Jacinto.

JOURNAL CONTINUED.

Saturday, March 5th.—The day commenced very moderate—thermometer 50°—weather clear. A brisk fire was commenced from our north battery against the enemy, which was not answered, except now and then. At mid-day the thermometer rose to 68°.—The President determined to make the assault; and it was agreed that the four columns of attack were to be commanded by Generals Cos, Duque, Romero, and Morales, and second in command, Generals Castrillon, Amador, and Miñon. For this purpose the points of attack were examined by the commanding officers, and they came to the conclusion that they should muster at 12 o'clock tonight, and at 4 o'clock to morrow morning (Sunday, 6th) the attack should be made.

Sunday, 6th.—At 5 A.M. the columns were posted at their respective stations, and at half past 5 the attack or assault was made, and continued until 6 A.M. when the enemy attempted in vain to fly, but they were overtaken and *put to the sword, and only five women, one Mexican soldier (prisoner,) and a black slave escaped from instant death.* On the part of the enemy the result was, 250 killed, and 17 pieces of artillery—a flag; muskets and fire-arms taken. Our loss was 60 soldiers and 5 officers killed, and 198 soldiers and 25 officers wounded—2 of the latter General officers. The battalion of Toluca lost 98 men between the wounded and killed. *I was robbed by our soldiers.*

Monday, 7th.—Commenced with a north wind. A special despatch was received from Gen. Urrea, dated 3d March, from San Patricio, in which he communicated that the preceding day, at a place called Los Cohates, he attacked Dr. Grant and his party, and killed Dr. Grant and 41 of his men, and afterwards 2 out of 5 who fled. There was no loss on our side. By the 14th General Urrea would be in Goliad. The greater part of the 1st brigade arrived under command of General Gaona. The mail arrived from Matamoros and Mexico—dates to the 2d and 3d of February.

Tuesday, 8th.—Fine clear day, but cold. Letters were written to Mexico under date of 6th inst. Commenced blowing hard. I wrote to * * * *. Official reports were forwarded to-day.

Wednesday, 9th. Commenced with a violent north wind, weather not very cold. Generals Filisola, Araga, &c., &c., arrived. Orders to march were given to Gen'l Sesma and Colonel Gonzales. Two persons arrived from the interior to see the President. The wind continued all night.

Thursday, 10th. Day broke mild, but soon the cold north wind commenced blowing, though with clear weather. The cavalry under command of General

Audrade [sic] came in. They were quartered in the Alamo. The Commissary and the Treasury of the Army arrived.

Friday, 11th. Day pleasant, but somewhat windy. Gen'l Tolsa came in with the 3rd brigade, but the divisions of Sesma and Gonzales had already marched with four six pounders and one howitzer. Marches detailed being 9 days to Goliad, 5 to Gonzales and 14 to San Felipe.

Saturday, 12th. Day broke mild—became windy—but clear and temperate. We consumed many fish. Sesma wrote from El Salado, giving the details—Romero likewise. The troops were reviewed in the afternoon in the Square.

Sunday, 13th. Day clear but windy. *Heard mass in the Square.* Very warm in the afternoon. Thermometer 85°. Nothing particular.

Monday, 14th. Cloudy and windy, and warm.—Weather cleared and the wind abated a little. The correspondence from Mexico, Monterey and Matamoros was received, and a despatch from Gen'l Urrea stating that he would be at Goliad the 14th, that is to-day.—Orders to march were issued to the battalion of Tres Villas.

Tuesday, 15th. Windy and warm. The battalion of Queretaro was ordered to march to Goliad, with one 12 pounder and the corresponding munition. To-morrow the two battalions of Queretaro and Tres Villas will march. In the afternoon the courier was despatched to Gen'l Urrea. Accounts came from Gonzales by a Mexican that the *Americans, in number 500 fled as soon as they heard of the taking of the Alamo* and the approach of our troops, leaving their stores and many goods, and throwing two cannon in the water, &c. &c. This was Sunday in the afternoon. The same man said that the Convention had met at Washington and declared the independence of Texas. The battalions of Guerrero and Mexico were ordered to get ready to march to Gonzales to-morrow with about 200 horses selected from Dolores and Tampico. A courier extraordinary arrived with accounts of the sickness of Gen'l Barragar [Barragan] and the election of Mr. Corro as President, ad interim by 27 votes. For Bravo 18 votes, and Parres 8. *This election did not please Gen'l Santa Anna; he preferred Gen'l Bravo.* It is said that Gen'l Michilena voted for Bravo.

Wednesday, 16th. Accounts were received from Gen'l Ramirez—it was determined that Gen'l Tolsa should march with two battalions to Goliad, and he started at 3 o'clock P.M. It was also determined that I should join Sesma. Montoga left with two battalions for Goliad, to reach there in seven days. Wind continues.

[To be continued.]

[The New York Herald, June 29, 1836]
ALMONTE'S JOURNAL—NO. 5

We continue our translations from this interesting journal. Some of the distant papers doubt the authenticity of this curious document. Fools! what do they imagine us to be? The old line newspaper editors in this and every other large city, have entered into a league to discountenance and run down the small daily press. Now it happens that I was for years an editor of the largest paper in the country, and had to cut my connections with these pompous blockheads, because they were too ignorant and too stupid to make any improvement in newspapers, or to know what talent was. The efficiency of the Parisian press of New York, will soon be universally acknowledged.

As to the authenticity of Almonte's Journal, the original went on yesterday to Washington, to be exhibited to his Excellency, the President of the United States.

The following portion brings the Mexican army down to the banks of the Colorado:—

JOURNAL CONTINUED.

Thursday, March 17th.—A Courier Extraordinary was despatched to Tolsa and Sesma, and to Matamoras; one for Mexico will start to-morrow; by it go my letters for Mexico and the United States; I could not start to-day, because the mules did not arrive in time.

Friday, 18th.—At 10 A.M. we started from Bejar; at 3 leagues from Cibelo [Cibolo], we met a solder of the company of Bejar, with dispatches from the President; he said that General Sesma left yesterday (17th) for San Felipe. General Tolsa started this afternoon from Cibelo; it was supposed he will not reach Carrizo; one and a half leagues before reaching Cibelo, we saw a large drove of horses; at half past 5 P.M., we arrived at Cibelo; encamped on the side towards Bexar about 100 yards from the river; on the other side, the grass was burnt, and the track of two persons on foot, who had been down to the river; nothing occurred during the night; we passed Rosio creek and the Tinaja; day windy and rainy.

2.3.1.   General Sesma, military report, March 11, 1836.

Sesma, Joaquín Ramírez y, to Santa Anna; translated by Adam Lifshey. March 11, 1836. Archive General de Mexico, Secretaria de Guerra y Marina, Book 335:166–68. CAH.

This report on the fall of the Alamo by Santa Anna's general in command of the cavalry appears to have been overlooked by historians until William Davis referred to it in his 1998 book, nor was it previously published. This version of the report is from a huge collection of transcripts from several Mexican archives, done in the 1920s and 1930s at the University of Texas under the direction of Carlos Castañeda. A microfilm of the original is in Archivo Historico Militar, Expediente 1149:6–7, UC Bancroft Library.

Guerra. Frac. I. Leg. 2. Op. Mil. Texas. 1836[1]

Section of Austin operations—Your Excellency—Consequent to the high order of Your Excellency that I give you a detailed document as chief of the

Cavalry that operated in the exterior in the assault upon the Alamo fort the 6th of the current month, I have the honor of telling you that situated in the position that Your Excellency had the goodness to anticipate for me, I waited for the moment to fulfill the orders that you communicated to me before our attack columns marched forward to the assault. The enemy was obstinate in its fire and displaced from its first line of fortifications just as Your Excellency predicted, and as many of them believed their retreat was secure they left the fort from the right, and so many came out [from the fort] that they marched organized on the plains trying to take advantage of the nearby *brañal*.[2]

As[3] soon as I observed this, I sent a company from the Regiment of Dolores with my assistants the lieutenant colonel Don Juan Herrera, captain Cayetano Montero, the Superior Lieutenant from Dolores the lieutenant colonel Don Juan Palacios, and second lieutenant Don José María Medrano so that they would harass the enemy from the side of the *brañal*[4] and charge them with valiant officers' short lances/spears, and in this way the troop that they commanded charged [the enemy] and knifed them in moments, without letting the desperate resistance of [the enemy] make them vacillate for a moment. Another group of around fifty men then came from the center of the fort, and I ordered the company of Lancers from the Regiment of Dolores under the orders of Superior Lieutenant Colonel Don Ramón Valera, Lieutenant Don Santos Castillo, and second lieutenant Don Leandro Ramírez, and Don Tomás Viveros, to charge them. And upon seeing this movement, the enemy availed themselves of a trench/ditch and made such a vigorous defense that I had to send Lieutenant D? Dran[co] [sic] with twenty Lancers from Tampico and twelve from Veracruz to help this force which, although it never vacillated, I feared would be repulsed, and [I also sent] the Captain of the Río Grande, Don Manuel Barragan, and the Lieutenant of the same company, Don Pedro Rodríguez, with fifteen men of the same company, in order to defeat[5] the [enemy]. All of these officials executed the movement with such decision and exactitude that some men truly barricaded in that position and resolved to lose their skins only at great expense, were run over in just a few minutes and knifed [to death].

Then the Superior Captains of Lieutenant Colonels of the Regiment of Dolores, Don Manuel Montellano, Don José Fato, and second lieutenant Don José Guijarro, were detained with another company in order to charge those [of the enemy] who were coming off the fort from the left, and who were also killed by these officers and troops upon showing themselves, and whose companions had not exceeded them in anything [in terms of bravura and performance]; like the rest of the cavalry under the orders of Señor General Don Ventura Marar, colonel of the Regiment of Dolores; major sergeant Don Venuto Lopez, Captain Don Antonio Valdez, Lieutenant Don Telesfero Carrio, and second lieutenant Don Manuel Ruis, whom I destined to cover the other flank of the fort, this troop left nothing to desire. Lastly, Your Excellency, the high cavalry fired upon[6] the Alamo fort at a distance of fifteen strides[7] under enemy fire, and has fulfilled the orders that it had, so that I can assure Your Excellency that the troops on this day under my orders have left me nothing to desire.

It is in vain to show Your Excellency the desperate resistance of these men because you were in the middle of the risk dictating my orders and you were a witness who presenced [*observed*] better than any other the deeds of each man. The enthusiasm was so general that it would be impossible to single out anybody without causing offense, and for the same reason I believe that the valiant Officials who have taken part in this memorable and important day are as deserving of the consideration of the Supreme Government as of the gratitude of their fellow citizens. Therefore I will only take the liberty to recommend to Your Excellency the mother of the corporal of the Regiment of Dolores, José Hernandez, who was killed in the charge upon those who availed themselves of the trench, who [the mother] had no other support besides her son and who lives in the village of Santiago Tlaguinterco. With this motive I have the honor of expressing again to Your Excellency the considerations of my singular appreciation and respect.

God and Liberty. Arroyo of Salado.—11 March 1836. Excellent Señor Joaquín Ramíres y Sesma—Excellent Señor General in charge of the Army of Operations, Don Antonio López de Santa Anna.

This is a copy. Mexico,[8] August 23, 1836.

Joaquín Ramírez y Sesma (rubric)

---

[1] The abbreviations "Frac" and "Leg" are of uncertain definition. "Leg." might be short for "legación" (legation, delegation) or "legado" (military chief or testimony) or "legión" (corps of troops).

[2] "brañal" is not a word; the transcript is a misspelling of "breñal" (terrain that is rocky or overgrown with weeds). [*Verified breñal per original in Exp. 1149:6–7.*]

[3] The original text does not have paragraph breaks. They are included here for the sake of easier reading.

[4] Please see footnote #2, breñal is in original transcript.

[5] "Llanqueasen" does not seem to be an actual word, but the meaning here is clear in context.

[6] "circumbalado" seems to be a composite word of "circum" (around) and "balado" (fired)

[7] "posos" is not a word; it may be a misspelling of "pasos" (steps, strides, or paces)

[8] "Mexico" may refer here to Mexico City.

2.3.2.   General Sesma, military report, August 23, 1836.

Borroel, Roger, trans. and ed. 2000. *Field Reports of the Mexican Army during the Texan War of 1836*. Vol. 1, 23–24. East Chicago, IN: La Villita Publications.

Borroel was among the first researchers to begin systematically using the huge collection of transcripts, noted in document 2.3.1, produced under the direction of Carlos Castañeda. His source here is in Book 335.

THE TEXAS ACTIVITY REPORT OF
GENERAL JOAQUÍN RAMÍREZ Y SESMA—
August 23rd 1836

MOST EXCELLENT, SIR: Carrying out the duty with foresight that

Your Excellency had wanted me to do per your letter of the 16th of the present month for an account upon the merited efforts made by the troops that were at Béjar (San Antonio, Texas), the Alamo and the other points that were under my orders. The following is given.

I will say to Your Excellency that in the Occupation of Bejar, I had attended only to the First Division of the Army of Operations. And that I directed everyone to do their duty.

The ones that had distinguished themselves are: Don Juan Morales, Colonel and the commander of the San Luis battalion; The Second Lieutenants of the cazadores (light infantry), from the Matamoros battalion, S. Alonso Gonzales and Don José María Souza, then to the accredited valor of this leader. And to the gallantry of the two cited officers they were able in a few moments to entirely reduced [*sic*] the enemy remaining at the fortification of the Alamo.

During the blockade (the siege of the Alamo) that they had to put up with at this point, before the assault, they had worked with the utmost perseverance. And always at risk was the cited leader, the captain of the cazadores from the Jiménez battalion, Don José Frias; the Lieutenant Colonel of the Matamoros battalion Don Manuel Gonzales, and of equal rank, the commander of the Jiménez battalion, Don Mariano Salas, and the captains of the Dolores regiment (cavalry), Don José Fato and Don Ramón Valera.

In the attack, my division was augmented with units from other brigades and since we took Béjar, I went forth from the Plaza in order to cover and guard the camp.

Commanded the first column was Colonel Morales who was able to give to the Government the dispatch that I carried to His Excellency, the General-President-in-Chief. The second (column) was commanded by General Cós, but his second was General Amador and consequently was able to report with accuracy upon the individuals that were in it. The third was commanded by Colonel Don José María Romero but his second was Mr. Salas who was present in the Army. And the fourth was commanded by Colonel Francisco Duque, whose leader is in this capital. The reserve was commanded by Colonel Don Agustín Amat who was also available in the Army.

On March the 10th, I incline to the General-in-Chief that some units of my division go to Goliad. Therefore, I placed under my orders a section composed of the Matamoros and Aldama battalions; an Active from the Toluca battalion; fifty cavalrymen and two pieces of artillery and with such, I began the march on the 11th of said month.

[*Sesma continues with additional details of the campaign through April 15. Also translated by Borroel, 19, is Sesma's report of March 15 (ref. Jenkins 1973, 5:85) reporting on what he found upon arrival at Gonzales.*]

2.4.1. General Cós, military report, 1836.

Cós, Martín Perfecto de, translated by John Wheat. February 12, 1836. Archivo Historico Militar, Expediente 1904:39–40, UC Bancroft Library.

An untranslated version of this letter was included in Jenkins (1973, 4:304–5) from the Archivo General de Mexico collection, CAH.

Commandancy General and Inspector's Office
Coahuila and Tejas

No. 4

Most Excellent Señor==For many days I have wished to explain to Your Excellency the miserable state of all the individuals employed in the Commandancy General under my command, and I have avoided doing it so as not to burden your attentions, covering their needs in any way possible. But now that I find myself in the same situation as my subordinates, I am sending the present message to Your Excellency and I hope you will attend it in a benign spirit==It is a pity, Your Excellency, that soldiers of our own army, without just reason to disregard their services, not only lack for the basics of their subsistence, but do not even know who can provide it to them, or when. At the same time, they see their comrades paid and seemingly [enjoying] a certain abundance, because it is well known that in the Commandancy General there are more than 100,000 *pesos*==Without making mention of the enormous assets of the presidial companies, such as the one in this city, which have not received their salaries for July, there is no one whose pay is not in arrears. The majority are driven to the painful extreme of turning to charity to satisfy their hunger. Other less unfortunate ones are also prevented by their poverty from continuing their march to Tejas, because their prior duties have exhausted the horses==In view of all this, since I must continue my journey until I catch up to the Most Excellent Sr. General in Chief, I beseech Your Excellency most earnestly to deign to order that all the individuals accompanying me be aided by the treasury of the army with a payment that can be charged to the salaries for the present month, although in my view it would be enough for the señor treasurer to forward the documents presented by the favored ones to the commissioner's office of this department, which is the office that should adjust them==Although I know what I tell Your Excellency in the 1st paragraph—that I find myself in the same situation as my subordinates—I can assure you that it was not personal advantage that motivated me, and to prove it to you I swear that you will not find, even in the budget that is drawn up, the salary that is due me==I repeat to Your Excellency my plea that you attend as much as possible to the presidial troops, who are assigned to different posts and have not supplies or rations for a long time. For all this, you obedient servant will remain deeply [grateful] to Your Excellency==God and Liberty. Monclova, February 12, 1836==Martín Perfecto de Cós==Most Excellent Sr. General Don Vic[en]te Filisola, 2nd in Command of the Army of Operations.

This is a copy. Riogrande, February 24, 1836.

Perf[ec]to de Cós

2.4.2.   General Cós, military report, 1836.

Cós, Martín Perfecto de, translated by Adam Lifshey. February 23, 1836. Archivo Historico Militar, Expediente 1904:28, UC Bancroft Library.

This report summarizes the number of forces from General Cós while bringing up reinforcements to Santa Anna, signed the day the latter arrived in San Antonio. The Battalions of Aldama and Toluca are two of the five (joining those of Matamoros, Jimenez, and St. Luis) that attacked and overran the Alamo less than two weeks after this report was signed. The "Total" column does not include the counts for officers. A fragmentary version of this document was published in Borroel (2001, 3:34) from the CAH transcripts. The original is followed by a transmittal letter by General Cós dated February 25 (Expediente 1904:29) and Santa Anna's receipt of March 18 (Expediente 1904:30).

ARMY OF OPERATIONS

1st INFANTRY BRIGADE

State of the forces of the following Brigades, as to today

CORPS	Colonel	Lt. Colonels	First aides	Captains	Lieutenants	Sub-Lieut.	Sargents	Horn players & Drummers	Corporals	Soldiers	Total
Artillery.	"	"	"	" 1.	"	" 3.	" 3.	" 4.	" 9.	" 47.	" 63.
Batallion of Zapadores.	"	" 1.	" 1.	" 2.	" 3.	" 4.	" 15.	" 16.	" 20.	" 131.	" 182.
Batallion of Aldama.	"	" 1.	" 1.	" 6.	" 6.	" 13.	" 13.	" 34.	" 26.	" 320.	" 393.
Batallion of Toluca.	" 1.	"	"	" 3.	" 10.	" 10.	" 10.	" 24.	" 21.	" 269.	" 324.
Batallion of Querétaro.	" 1.	"	" 1.	" 4.	" 3.	" 10.	" 14.	" 15.	" 30.	" 234.	" 293.
Batallion of Guanajuato.	"	"	" 1.	" 5.	" 9.	" 7.	" 19.	" 10.	" 36.	" 226.	" 291.
Squad of the Batallion of St. Luís.	"	"	"	"	" 2.	"	" 1.	"	" 1.	" 29.	" 31.
Total....	2.	2.	4.	21.	33.	47.	75.	103.	143.	1256.	1577.

ARTILLERY.

12" Cannons	6" Cannons	7" Obiuci [?]
—2.—	—2.—	—2.—

Village of Guerrero, Feb. 22, 1836.=Jo.Bo.Ant. °Gaspra [?].=Mig. [one word uncertain]

Riogrande 23 February, 1836—A Copy

Martin Prefecto de Cos

2.4.3.   General Ampudia, military report, March 6, 1836.

Ampudia, Pedro de, and Mariano Silva, translated by John Wheat. March 6, 1836 (official copy made April 29, 1836). Archivo Historico Militar, Expediente 1655:39. UC Bancroft Library.

This and documents 2.4.4 and 2.4.5 were first discussed in Davis 1998.

No. 1

Permanent <u>artillery</u>   <u>Army</u> of <u>Operations</u>

Report which shows the artillery, arms, munitions, and other articles taken from the enemy.

Rifle cartridges with bullets	14,600	Same for 4[-pounder] cannon	200
Same for 12[-pound] caliber cannon	369	Loaded 7 $^1/_2$ *quintal* grenades	25
Same for 8[-pounder] same	226	Same of same for 7 [*quintales*]	150
Same for 6[-pounder] same	201	Grapeshot in 12[-caliber] balls?	127
Same for 4[-pounder] same	109	Same for 8[-caliber] balls	83
Same for 3[-pounder] same	120	Same for 6[-caliber] balls	159
Same for 2[-pounder] same	93	Same for 4[-caliber] in bags	79
12-caliber bullets	155	Same for 3[-caliber]	20
Same, 8[-caliber]	89	Same for 2[-caliber]	18
Same, 6[-caliber]	198	Kegs of fine powder	3
		Lead in sheets, *arrobas*	2

<u>Mounted</u> <u>Artillery</u>

Of Brass and iron, from calibers of 12[-pounders]
     down to 2 . . . . 21 pieces

Armory

English rifles in usable condition . . . . 216[?]
Small artillery pieces *(esmeriles)* 3
Unattached bayonets. 200

Note: Of the cannons, two have been spiked and one is useless. All the rifles and pistols were given to the troops at the orders of the Most Excellent Señor General in Chief. Fortress of the Alamo, March 6, 1836.==Commanding General==Pedro de Ampudia==Commander of [artillery] park==Mariano Silva.

This is a copy. Méjico April 29, 1836.

José M. Perez
[Rubric]

2.4.4. General Ampudia, military report on munitions fired, March 21, 1836.

Ampudia, Pedro de, translated by John Wheat. March 21, 1836 (official copy made April 29, 1836). Archivo Historico Militar, Expediente 1655:40, UC Bancroft Library.

No. 2

Permanent Artillery   Army of Operations

Report on the consumption of munitions by the aforesaid [artillery] in its batteries during the siege that . . . ? . . . ? . . . ? . . . on the aforesaid fortress_.

For 7 $\frac{1}{2}$-inch mortars

Grenades of 7 $\frac{1}{2}$ inches 32
Same of 7 inches 80
Cartridges for their services 224

Cannons, 2 to 8[-pounder]

Cartridges with flat balls 240
Canisters of grapeshot. 86
Cartridges for their service 86

Cannons, 6[-pounder]

Cartridges with flat balls . . . . 54 [*or 94*]

Rifle Munitions

Cartridges with bullets 36,000
Canisters of grapeshot. 2,800

Headquarters in Béjar, March 21 1836.==Commander of the general [artillery] park==J. M[arí]a de Ortega==*V[ist]o B[uen]o*==Pedro de Ampudia. This is a copy. Méjico April 29, 1836.

José M. Perez
[Rubric]

2.4.5.   Army surgeon, military report, 1836.

Arsoy [?], Mariano, translated by John Wheat. August 1, 1836. Archivo Historico Militar, Expediente 1151:22, UC Bancroft Library.

Borroel (2000, 1:79–80) translated this document from the Archive General de Mexico, Secretaria de Guerra y Marina, Book 335, CAH. This reading of the surgeon's last name is Azsoyo, which is also quite possible in examining the original signature.

Army of Operations   Military Hospital of Béjar

Report showing the number of sick which the aforesaid hospital had, with an expression of the aid they received, how many were saved as a consequence of it, and how many died, as well as the amputations performed and their results.

Ranks	Surgeries	Medications	Total	Recoveries	Losses	On Hand
A General		1	1	1		
Three Commanders	3		3	3		
Three [?] Officers	25		25	21	4	
Troops	380	47	427	288	71	68

Notes: 1st. The number of sick [i.e., wounded] shown in this report are those from the assault on the Alamo, and those resulting from the capture of the Plaza de Béjar by the enemy. The undersigned took care of them with a small supply of medicine and with no other recourse for the sustenance of the former than what was provided by our enemies themselves, because Señor General Don Martín Perfecto de Cós had not been able to carry them when he undertook his retreat.

2nd. The wounded from the Alamo, despite having received no more than a small supply of medicine that was delivered by order of the General-in-Chief, were attended with every care and efficacy by the undersigned and his assistants, as is shown in the recoveries and losses in the preceding report.

3rd. It was necessary to perform two amputations: one with good success, the other with misfortune.

Matamoros, August 1, 1836.

Mariano Arsoy [?]
[Rubric]

2.4.6.　López, military report, 1840.

López, José Beyer, translated by John Wheat. May 12, 1840. Archivo Historico Militar, Expediente 1713:375–84, UC Bancroft Library.

This informative but difficult-to-read document of the names of officers involved in the Mexican Army at Béjar is given here in incomplete form, which it is hoped will motivate further careful study. The portions so uncertain that no translation was attempted are identified by multiple question marks, brackets, and/or underlining. Extra line spacing was also inserted to make groupings, done by vertical lines in the original, more readable.

Report on the señores chiefs and officers belonging to the Army of Operations in Texas who passed review in the month of March of 1836, in the city of San Antonio [de] Béjar.

Permanent Artillery

_.._./.[meaning?]	Sr. Col. Don Pedro de Ampudia	P
_.._./.	Another: Don Estevan B????	P
Attached __??__	Inspection Don José María [?] Ortega	P
	Don Buenaventura Soriano	P
1st C?? of ???	*Alférez* Don Ignacio Segura	P+ [meaning?]
2nd ??? of same	*Alférez* Don José O_??_ Ramirez[?]	P
1st C????	Capt. Don Mariano Silva	P
	I Capt. Don Francisco P__??__	1 In Mexico
	I Lt. Don José M__??_a	P
5th Company	I Another Don Francisco Díaz	P
	I Another, attached Don Pedro Ortiz?	1 At Cópano
	I Sub-lt. Don Juan F_??_s [Torres?]	P+
6th	Sub-lt. Don José Maria Cabello	P
	I Permanent[?] Lt. Don Ignacio A????	P
Company of ???	I Sub-lt. Don A_??_ Maria Lansa [?]	P
	Capt. Don Salvador[?] Mojica	P
	Lt. Don Feliciano[?] Quijano	P
	Capt. Don José Mariano Sotomayor	P

Political Administration ??? and ??? of Artillery

1st Officer	Don Pablo Aquilar	P
2nd same, paymaster[?]	Don Juan Elg__??__	P

| Same, __??__ | Don José Márquez | P |
| Same, 2d interim | Don Antonio <u>Olan</u>[?] | P |

Battalion of Sappers

__..__./.	Lt. Colonel Don Agustin Amat	P
	./. I 1st adjutant Don ??silo Díaz de la Vega	P
	+ I Capt. (attached) Don José Enrique de la Peña	P
__????__	I Another same Don Juan O????	1 in Mexico
	I Sub-adjutant Don __??__ Martínez	1 In Mexico
	I Surgeon Don Juan José <u>Febles</u>?	1 In Mexico
1st Company	Lt. Don José Maria Carrasco[?]	1 in Acapulco
	I Capt. Don Francisco M__??__ga	1 in Mexico
2nd Company	I Lt. Don P__??__ Rosa[?]	P
	I Sub-lt. Don Fran[cis]co M_??_garay	P
	I Lt. Don Miguel A_??_aga	P
3rd Company	I Sub-lt. Don José María __??__	P
	I Lt. Don José Maria <u>Heredia</u>?	P
4th Company	I Sub-lt. Don José María Gard_??_	P
	Capt. Don José María <u>Ricoy</u>?	P
5th Company	Sub-lt. Don José María <u>Torres</u>?	P
Attached, __??_ _??_	Don José Ignacio B__??__	P

Permanent Battalion of Guerrero

__..__./.	I Col. Don Manuel Céspedes	P
	I Lt. Col. Don Ignacio <u>Peñalta</u>?	P+
P_??__	I 1st Adjutant Don Marano <u>Garcia</u>?	P
	I 2nd same Don José María Puelles	P
	I Sub-adj. Don Ignacio <u>Menteaguda</u>?	In San Luis Potosi
Company of Grenadiers	I Capt. Don <u>Néstor</u>? G__??	P
	I Lt. Don Pío Aguilar	P
	I Lt. Don José Maria Silva?	P
	I Sub-lt. Don Basilio <u>Ospina</u>?	P
1st Company	I Another, Don Manuel María <u>Pérez</u>?	P
	I Same, second[?] Don Mariano Villa	P

	I Lt. Don Mariano Ola_??_an	P
2nd Company	I Sub-lt. Don Trinidad <u>Santiestevan?</u>	P
	I Another, Don José Vázquez	P
	I Capt. Don José Benito? Rosas?	P
3rd Company	I Lt. Don <u>Romualdo?</u> Maceda	In San Luis Potosi
	I Sub-lt. Don Mariano Chávez	In Leóna Vicario

<u>General</u> <u>Army</u> <u>Headquarters</u>

<u>Quartermaster-General</u>

<u>General</u> <u>Staff</u>

General Don Juan Arago	P+
./. Colonel Don Juan Amador	P

Mexico City, May 12, 1841

> José Reyes López
> [Rubric]

2.5.1.   Caro, published account, 1837.

Castañeda, Carlos, trans. 1928. A true account of the first Texas campaign and the events subsequent to the battle of San Jacinto, by Ramón Martínez Caro. *The Mexican Side of the Texan Revolution.* 93–94, 99–104, 107, 152–53. Dallas: P. L. Turner Company.

The original of this translation is *Verdadera Idea de la Primera Campaña de Tejas y Sucesos Ocurridos* . . . , published in Mexico in 1837. Caro was Santa Anna's secretary, and his lack of enthusiasm for his former boss is obvious from the first sentence.

The evident artfulness of the communications addressed to the supreme government by His Excellency, Antonio López de Santa Anna, on the 20th of February and the 11th of March of the present year, is in keeping with his well-known character of duplicity. It confirms the opinion in which he is generally held as a result of the many deceits he has practiced upon the nation.

The daring boldness with which he claims, before the whole world, that he obtained his liberty unconditionally; that he did not compromise either the honor, the independence, or the integrity of the territory of the nation in the agreements signed; that he has made no promises either to individuals or to any government in the treaties he concluded; and that he would have endured a thousand deaths before consenting to any such terms, either deliberately or by force, is an insult to the good judgment of the generous people whom he addresses. Such an insult deserves to be exemplarily punished in order to satisfy, as justice demands, national honor so basely sacrificed and outraged.

Many of the acts that must be investigated are still enveloped by a mysterious veil. When this is removed, we shall see if the loan negotiated in San Luis was a slanderous invention. We shall see whether the misappropriation of national funds in various ways; the so-called armistice that has been the source of untold misfortunes; the massacres of Refugio, Goliad, and the Alamo; the shameful treaties—one secret and one public—so eagerly agreed to, and as a result of which the cabinet of Texas placed His Excellency on board the *Invincible*; his promise to lend his support to obtain the recognition of Texas independence and the admission of the two commissioners that were to accompany him—Zavala being one of them—; and the official letter of July 4th to the President of the United States that reveals the degrading depths to which he descended in his desire to obtain his freedom, forgetting his honor and tarnishing that of his country, were slanderous inventions or facts. . . .

[*Caro continues his Introduction in much the same vein, without further mention of the Alamo. The main text begins a narrative of the Texas campaign, along with his more detailed commentary on Santa Anna's actions. We pick up the narrative before he leaves Mexico.*]

During the first days of February the army set out for Monclova together with His Excellency. He remained there only a few days, for on the 9th he set out with his staff and 50 mounted men for Río Grande for the purpose of joining the brigade of General Ramírez y Sesma which was there. Before leaving, he issued orders setting the time and the manner of the departure of the second and third brigades and of the cavalry. At the same time he ordered that the troops should be placed on half rations of hard-tack and that each man be allowed one *real* a day. The officers were to provide themselves with their necessary supplies out of their regular pay, without receiving an extra campaign allowance.

I have been unable to find out the reason for this unjust and mysterious order, unjust because it marks the beginning of the privations of the soldiers, just as they set out on their long march over deserts,[1] in the middle of the winter, which is very severe in those regions, without sufficient clothes, particularly among the wretched recruits who in the main were conscripts and were practically naked; mysterious because in San Luis Potosi the Commissary General of the Army, Colonel Ricardo Dromundo, brother-in-law of His Excellency, had been given the necessary funds for two months' provisions and supplies for 6,000 men. What became of these provisions and supplies? When we arrived in Monclova the said Commissary was already there. If he had secured the supplies that he was supposed to get, why, then, was the soldier put on half rations of hard-tack?[2] From this time dates the discontent that began to permeate all ranks and which increased notably after the desert was reached and the sad perspective of advancing farther and farther without the relief of the hospital corps that had set out from the capital became apparent. This corps was never seen by the army. During the entire campaign the army had to depend on medical students and a small and inadequate supply of drugs secured at Saltillo, whose cost did not exceed 300 *pesos*. Thus the munition wagons and the gun

carriages had to be used to carry the numerous patients. On more than one
occasion, General Ampudia and I were obliged to put in the wagons (though
already filled to capacity) some of the dying wretches we found on the road. I
remember particularly, the General must remember him too, a poor wretch
whom we found, at the point of death, unable to move, loaded down with his
gun and pack. We placed him in one of the wagons, but he expired before the
day's journey was over. Of course, he, like many others, received no spiritual
consolation. Such was the sad spectacle offered by the army on its march. In
fact, only the heroic constancy and the unlimited endurance so often displayed
by the Mexican soldier succeeded in overcoming the disheartening spectacle
presented to their eyes.

His Excellency finally reached Río Grande. There he found the brigade of
General Ramírez y Sesma which he ordered to proceed to San Antonio de
Béxar. The general-in-chief, his staff, and the 50 mounted men of his escort followed a few days later. We overtook the brigade before it reached Béxar, about
two days' journey from that place, and His Excellency took over the command
in order to enter the city, which he did on the 26th of February, without encountering any resistance on the part of the Americans. According to the citizens of
the place, the enemy, which numbered 156, took refuge in the so-called fortress
of the Alamo[3] the moment they saw our troops approaching. On the following
day, His Excellency placed a battery of two cannons and a mortar within 600
paces of the fort and began a bombardment, taking possession at the same time
of several small isolated houses that were to the left. These were nearer to the
enemy's position and were occupied by our troops who suffered the loss of several killed and wounded in the operation. Around the fortress there were
ditches which were used by the enemy to fire upon our troops, while our soldiers, in order to carry out their orders to fire, were obliged to abandon the protection that the walls afforded them, and suffered the loss of one or two men,
either killed or at least wounded, in each attempt to advance. During one of our
charges at night, His Excellency ordered Colonel Juan Bringas to cross a small
bridge with five or six men. He had no sooner started to carry out his instructions than the enemy opened fire upon this group and killed one man. In trying
to recross the bridge, the colonel fell into the water and saved himself only by a
stroke of good luck.

On the 29th or 30th, His Excellency sent Colonel Bringas to meet the
brigade of General Gaona with instructions for him to send, by forced marches,
the picked companies of his brigade. These arrived in Béxar on the 4th of
March. The following day the orders for the assault which was to take place on
the 6th were issued.

It has already been stated that when we entered Béxar we were assured by
the citizens that there were only 156 Americans. In the time intervening
between our entrance into the city and the day set for the assault, the enemy
received two small reenforcements from González that succeeded in breaking
through our lines and entering the fort. The first of these consisted of four men

who gained the fort one night, and the second was a party of twenty-five who introduced themselves in the daytime. Two messengers succeeded in leaving the fort, one of whom was the Mexican, Seguín. The entry of these reenforcements and the departure of the messengers were witnesses by the whole army and need no particular proof.[4] At the time of the assault, therefore, the enemy's force consisted of 183 men.

Early in the morning of the 6th the four attacking columns as well as the reserve took up their respective positions as assigned by the general order of the 5th, a copy of which was transmitted to the supreme government. From this it will be seen that our force numbered 1400 men in all. At daybreak and at the agreed signal our whole force moved forward to the attack. The first charge was met with a deadly fire of shot and shell from the enemy, the brave colonel of the Toluca Battalion, Francisco Duque, being among the first who fell wounded. His column wavered as a result of his fall, while the other three columns were held in check on the other fronts. His Excellency, seeing the charge waver, gave orders for the reserve to advance. The brave General Juan Valentín Amador, General Pedro Ampudia, Colonel Esteban Mora, and Lieutenant-Colonel Marcial Aguirre succeeded in gaining a foothold on the north side where the strife was bitterest, which encouraged the soldiers in their advance and resulted in their capture of the enemy's artillery on that side. The enemy immediately took refuge in the inside rooms of the fortress, the walls of which had been previously bored to enable them to fire through the holes. Generals Amador and Ampudia trained the guns upon the interior of the fort to demolish it as the only means of putting an end to the strife.

On the opposite side, where there was another entrance to the enemy's stronghold, the resistance was equally stubborn, but Colonels Juan Morales and José Miñón, commanding the attacking column, succeeded in overcoming it. Though the bravery and intrepidity of the troops was general, we shall always deplore the costly sacrifice of the 400 men who fell in the attack. Three hundred were left dead on the field and more than a hundred of the wounded died afterwards as a result of the lack of proper medical attention and medical facilities in spite of the fact that their injuries were not serious. This is a well-known fact, as stated before, which made the fate of those who were instantly killed or mortally wounded enviable to those who lingered in pain and suffering without the proper comfort or relief. The enemy died to a man and its loss may be said to have been 183 men, the sum total of their force. Six women who were captured were set at liberty.[5] Among the 183 killed there were five who were discovered by General Castrillón hiding after the assault. He took them immediately to the presence of His Excellency who had come up by this time. When he presented the prisoners, he was severely reprimanded for not having killed them on the spot, after which he turned his back upon Castrillón while the soldiers stepped out of their ranks and set upon the prisoners until they were all killed.[6]

[*Caro continues with reports from General Urrea and discusses Santa Anna's involvement in the massacre at Goliad. Before continuing on to San Jacinto, he has a paragraph relating to the Alamo.*]

In the meantime, the public sale of the goods and supplies taken from the enemy,[7] who had hurriedly taken refuge in the Alamo the moment we entered Béxar, continued. This sale was conducted by two members of the commissary department of the army under the supervision of the Commissary.

[Caro makes an additional comment on the tactics of Santa Anna with respect to the Alamo.]

Let us pass rapidly over the *Manifesto* until we reach the time of our stop in Béxar to which I have previously referred. The events of this period though transcendental and numerous, are made still more important by what he says in his *Manifesto* regarding them. "Having occupied Béxar, etc, the enemy retired to the fort of the Alamo, which dominates the city. With a siege of a few days, it would have been forced to surrender." Our entry into Béxar took place on the 23rd of February, and the assault was made on the 6th of the following March. Was not the fort besieged for twelve days by more than 600 men under General Sesma? If the siege had been prolonged a few more days, it would likely have surrendered. Why didn't we wait? Did we not stay in that city until the end of the said month after the assault was made? What advantage was gained by the brigades of Gaona and Sesma as a result of their having set out a few days before that of His Excellency? The first of these, whose objective was Anahuac, was detained at the Colorado by the enemy, while the second whose goal was Nacogdoches lost its way in the desert just beyond Bastrop. Such were the advantages of the so much praised triumph of the Alamo! One hundred and eighty-three unfortunate wretches who were sacrificed there cost us the lives of over 400 Mexicans! He [General Santa Anna] would have us believe that "life was guaranteed to the enemy on condition that they surrender their arms and take an oath never to take them up again against Mexico." There never was such a promise made. From the moment we entered Béxar, the enemy was asked to surrender at discretion to which the enemy never consented. Let them deny this fact if they dare; let them deny the fact that a red flag was raised on the steeple of the cathedral of that city as a sign that no quarter would be granted and the everything would be carried by fire and sword.

---

[1] From Monclova to Río Grande is more than 80 leagues and from there to Béxar almost 100. No supplies can be secured in all this distance, for even water is scarce and found only at long intervals that have to be covered by forced marches.

[2] It should be kept in mind that before leaving Monclova His Excellency said that supplies would be found at Rio Grande. No supplies were found there. The reader can imagine the horrible distress of the troops, confronted with the necessity of continuing the march over a distance of more than 100 leagues of desert to Béxar.

[3] A mere corral and nothing more, built about 500 paces from the town, on the opposite side of the San Antonio River. The town is named after the river. Many of the walls of the fort are of adobe.

[4] It is to be kept in mind that the reenforcements succeeded in entering the fort and the messengers in leaving it through no lack of vigilance, for 600 men, cavalry and infantry, surrounded it.

⁵ In the report made on that date to the supreme government by His Excellency it is stated that more than 600 of the enemy were killed. I myself wrote that report and must now confess that I put down that number at the command of His Excellency. In stating the truth now, I must say that only 183 men were killed. I call upon the whole army to witness my statement.

⁶ We all witnessed this outrage which humanity condemns but which was committed as described. This is a cruel truth, but I cannot omit it. More cruel falsehoods have been promulgated against my character.

⁷ A miserable prize and the only one taken. Even if it had been distributed among the troops, as it should have been, it would have hardly given each man more than one peso apiece, since the net proceeds did not exceed $2500. The sale took place at the corner of the house occupied by His Excellency.

2.6.1.   Gen. Vicente Filisola, published account, 1849.

Filisola, Gen. Vicente. 1987. *Memoirs for the History of the War in Texas*. Edited and translated by Wallace Woolsey. 2:82–84, 167–81. Austin, TX: Eakin Press.

This is a carefully constructed account of the Texas campaign, including the Alamo, by Santa Anna's second in command at that time. General Filisola followed behind Santa Anna throughout the campaign; Almonte noted that he arrived at San Antonio on March 9. There were two publishers of Filisola's memoirs in 1849: R. Rafael and I. Cumplido. Most of the Woolsey translation is based on the first, but he gave the second version as well for the siege of the Alamo. Filisola included the official count of casualties from Gen. Juan de Andrade.

This document includes two excerpts. The first is General Filisola's description of the Alamo in the section on the earlier siege of Béxar under General Cós in December 1835. This description is important for several reasons. First, it is an independent early account of the Alamo layout. Second, as a general, Filisola was very complete in noting those features important for the defense of the place. Finally, it was General Cós who converted the Alamo from a ruined mission to a fortress. The additions made by him would be in place and would be critical defensive installations (defended by Jameson, Dickinson, Crockett, and Travis) during the siege less than half a year later. The second excerpt then joins Santa Anna at the Alamo.

Downriver [*from Béxar*] in the direction of Goliad on either bank are located a number of fields in cultivation that belong to the people of Béxar. With the passage of time they have also taken over the cultivated lands of the four missions referred to [*Concepcion, San Jose, San Juan, and La Espada*], and even those of Alamo Mission which are upstream from the mission.

All the land surrounding the city and the banks of the river are covered with thick woods and a sort of brush with which the fields have filled up for lack of cultivation. This lends the greatest facility to enemy ambushes and offers a great danger to those people.

To the Northeast of the city, on the left bank of the San Antonio River, and at a distance of some two hundred varas from the bed of the river towards the farthest part of extremity of the half circle which it describes, and within which also is included Béxar, is located the former mission of the Alamo. Its enclosure and church, which have remained, served in the time we are referring to as the barracks of the presidio company which bore the same name. The surface of the site is higher than that of the city and can dominate it easily, but the wall is nothing more than a rectangular quadrangle of eighty Castillian varas on each of the sides of the North and South and ninety-five on the East and West. The walls are no more than two and a half varas high and four thick, made of stone and mud.

The entrance is in the curtain wall that faces the South, about thirty varas from the angle that this one forms with the one on the North, and attached to the curtain wall is located a corral with a wall of the same type as that of the main wall; it is some thirty-four varas long and twenty-four wide. The entrance is through that of the barracks which is formed against the same wall of the enclosure in the inner part. In the South corner of this corral, and on the inside, is built a small house eight varas square, projecting from the corral wall facing the East, in such a manner that with that wall it forms an interior angle.

Next, attached to the South wall of this house is the Church made in the form of a cross from East to West with the door on the West and looking towards the curtain of the main courtyard. The Church is fifty varas long and thirty-five from the part that makes the arms of the cross with the right arm resting against the adjoining house looking to the East. Thus there are two other protruding angles and one recessed, all facing the North and flanking perfectly the walls of the corral and of the main enclosure which look to the East.

This church was never finished and had [*sic*] no roof, but the walls of cut stone and limestone are better preserved. It is joined to the buildings that must have once been destined for the sacristy and for the main quarters of the chaplain or missionary. In the inner part of the wall and attached to it were built several rooms that served for the officers, the guard corps, etc., but these places had scarcely twenty-five square varas.

General Cos filled in the head of the church up to the outer corner and formed with it a platform or earthen mound on which they could place up to three artillery pieces with some inconvenience. Access was by means of a ramp that began at the door of the church. From the corner made by the walls that run to the East and to the South he had them open a ditch and raise diagonally a parapet with a porthole in the middle. The parapet was projected to the South corner which forms the front of the church as it joins the wall that is in the same direction. In the door of the enclosure mentioned there was built also a platform on which could be placed two artillery pieces, with the entrance on the right hand.

In the angle formed by the walls on the West and South he constructed an esplanade or platform to mount a cannon over the wall. In the wall of the West he had built two earthen mounds for two other pieces. A similar platform and also a mound was made in the angle formed with the North wall, and a little more than half way down this facing the East they built another esplanade with portholes and head guards. However, since this wall was in ruins, it was necessary to cover it with pieces of wood five or six inches thick placed horizontally, and supported by the outside part with some straight legs, also of wood.

In the projecting angle formed by the corral with the wall to the Northwest was placed another platform or mound for another artillery piece. Likewise, in this angle as in the principal enclosure on the same side they dug out a ditch of average proportions. It should be noted that all the rest of the wall of the main enclosure as well as of the corral was left without a ditch or walkway for the troops to ascend in order to defend it, although they did make some portholes in the walls so that they might fire through them.

Going from East to West within rifle range of the enclosure described there was a small poplar grove, and at a similar distance there were several mud huts and small houses with gardens at the back which formed a sort of street from North to South. The rest of the fields that surrounded this point within range of cannon fire were completely cleared. Then began the woods, which in general, as we have said, surrounded all of Bexar.

[*Now begins the second excerpt, with Santa Anna at the Alamo.*]

After great fatigue and suffering General Santa Anna finally arrived in the vicinity of Béxar on the twenty-second and without any difficulty whatever he took possession of that city on the twenty-third; in the manner which is explained in his dispatch to the minister of war where he says:

[*Filisola then quotes a letter of February 27, 1836, already presented above as document 2.1.1.3. The following is chapter 26 of the Woolsey translation.*]

The day of the twenty-fourth was spent in reconnoitering the fortifications of the Alamo and the river crossings in order to prepare the operations that were to be taken in sequence until they overcome [*sic*] the colonists, adventurers or bandits that under such a mask had come from the United States to harass a friendly nation that had in no way offended them, which group now found itself shut up in the quarters of the Alamo. With this purpose in mind during the night two batteries were set up, and the next day, the twenty-fifth, at dawn they opened fire on the enemy parapets, which did likewise in the direction of our batteries.

The commander in chief, with the companies of chasseurs from Jiménez and Matamoros crossed the river and took up a position in the houses and huts to the south of the Alamo about half a rifle shot's distance from the enemy parapets. At the same time our men were digging a trench near Mr. Mullen's house. In these operations, with the fierce fire from the enemy, we had one corporal and a chasseur from Matamoros killed, and four wounded, and two more wounded of those from Jiménez. Our fire ceased in the afternoon with the conclusion of the movements that had been decided upon for the moment by the commander in chief. The latter, wishing to step up the action of the taking of the Alamo, that same day issued the following order to General Ganona, commander of the first infantry brigade.

During the night two trenches were constructed adjoining the houses located in the cottonwood grove of the Alamo for the infantry. The Matamoros battalion was established in them for their defense, and the cavalry posted itself on the hills to the east of the fort on the road to the town of Gonzáles and in the vicinity of the former Casa Mata. This operation was completed at eleven thirty at night, and during that time the enemy burned the hay and the wooden houses that were near them or within reach; a brisk norther blew up. The Alamo from then on was surrounded by our troops, with only the north side open.

On the twenty-sixth the norther continued to blow strongly, and in the morning there was a small skirmish between some of the enemy that ventured outside the walls and the advance sentries of the eastern line under the command of General Ramírez y Cesma. Our artillery fire continued, and it was answered only by a shot now and then from their guns. During the night they burned some other straw huts that were built against the walls and tried to obtain water and some wood. They were prevented from doing so by our advance sharpshooters.

On the twenty-seventh there was some fire from both sides, and Lieutenant Menchaca of the presidio guard was dispatched with a party to the ranches in Seguín and Flores to obtain corn, cattle and hogs. An attempt was made to cut off the water to the rebels on the side of the old Mill, but that was not possible. It was noted that they were working incessantly on opening up a ditch on the inside of the parapet with the intention of enlarging it and giving more resistance against our artillery. However, this operation was more harmful than useful to them. Since they had no walkway it was necessary for them on the day of the assault to stand up on it in order to fire with their guns, and thus they presented an immense target for our fire. In the afternoon the enemy became aware of the presidio group as they reconnoitered the points of the line, and they opened fire upon it. During the night the government was advised of the capture of the city in the terms that are included here. That same day General Gaona in Charco de la Peña received the order of the twenty-fifth to advance with the three battalions mentioned there, and these were immediately put on forced march to Béxar.

Since the supplies that had been brought from Río Grande by the first division were about to be exhausted, the commander in chief sent the following communications to General Filisola who was with the rearguard of the army.

[*This letter was presented above as document 2.1.1.4.*]

All these orders were carried out, but it was not possible for the brigades, provisions, etc., to move faster than had been designated for them in the itinerary that was laid out beforehand for the reasons that we have set forth. Also, only at the places that had been indicated for them in the itinerary was there water for the men and animals, and it was not possible to double the days' marches without having all the troops and cargoes scattered.

On the twenty-eighth news was received that two hundred men from Goliad were due to arrive to aid those against the Alamo, and the cannon fire continued almost all day long. On the twenty-ninth the Jiménez battalion was ordered to establish itself to the right of the cavalry, or to the left of the road that runs from the town of González, in order to surround and enclose even more

the Alamo. During the night General Cesma moved in, leaving the field covered, with the approval of the commander in chief. This approval is contained
in the following letter:

[*This letter to General Sesma of February 29, 1836, was presented above as document 2.1.1.5.*]

He marched with a detachment of the Jiménez battalion and another from
the Dolores regiment in the direction of Goliad expecting to meet up with the
reinforcements that he had been told were coming to the aid of that place. However, since he had met no one and had had no news whatsoever concerning the
troops, he returned to his post the next day, and the Jiménez battalion was again
a part of general headquarters.

With our troops now in possession of the city of Béxar the commander in
chief began to put into action his commands beginning on the night of the fifth
of March to undertake the siege and capture of the Alamo if it were possible to
surprise the enemy that were garrisoned there. To this end the general ordered
that four attack columns commanded by their respective leaders—these all of
unquestioned loyalty—should leave the city in greatest silence and order the
operations to begin that same night.

But such was the enthusiasm and excitement of those brave men to meet
up with the enemies of the name and the government of their country, that it
degenerated into a sad and overwhelming lack of discretion of the sort that is
never committed with impunity on such occasions. One of the columns began
to shout "Long live the Republic" in a loud voice. This cry immediately
resounded in the air and awakened the drowsy vigilance of the Texans. Thus
warned of the approach of our army, they prepared to make a desperate
defense and began to train their artillery in such manner their fire shortly
played terrible havoc in our ranks.

Although the bravery and daring of our soldiers hastened to fill in the
ranks, after a long while they began to become disorganized and perhaps
would have retreated if General Santa Anna who was watching had not
ordered the reserves into action. With their support confidence and order were
restored to our men, and the siege was begun. The enemy against whom it was
directed strove to repel this attack with vigorous resistance and fire from all
their arms. They were convinced that they had no other choice than to perish if
only they could overcome us.

Thus, although the Alamo fell, this triumph cost the Mexican army more
than seventy men dead and three hundred wounded. But they avenged with
honor the surrender of General Cos so that the enemy began to fall back before
our arms. They had recourse to the only decision left to them in order to free
themselves, even though this were the most reprehensible—as it no doubt
was—that of laying waste the Mexican villages in order to deprive our army of
all means of subsistence.

The army for its part showed itself as superior in the face of these sufferings just as it did before the fortifications and fire with which those of the
Alamo were defending themselves. In the capture a greater number of our men

died than of the Texans, which was only natural in view of the great advantages that they had with the trenches and the artillery with which they defended themselves. For that reason it was impossible to attack the trenches and silence the fire of the cannon without a great loss among the attackers who had no other wall than their own breasts.

This then is the beginning of the operations of the Texas campaign in the month of March 1836; these were followed by great events, even greater because of their consequences in all that memorable and fateful year.

However, since the first hand accounts from which we have been composing our history come only this far, it is necessary that we continue with the aid of other writers or witnesses who may deserve our confidence. Nevertheless, since we cannot answer for them as for those of the author, it also seems fitting to us to call attention to it. When we again touch on later events in which the author himself took part it will become apparent that the account comes from the same pen as those recorded thus far.

Vicente Filisola, MEMOIRS FOR THE HISTORY OF THE WAR IN TEXAS,
Vol. I, Chapter I, pp. 3–17, Ignacio Cumplido edition,
Mexico City, 1849.

[Translator's Note: Filisola explains that in Chapter 24 of his first edition (R. Rafael) of His MEMOIRS he did not have access to the details of the Battle of the Alamo. Now that he has obtained this material, he wishes to describe the action in more detail.

The translation of Filisola's account (pp. 6–17) begins here.]
In the staff meeting held for this purpose on the afternoon of March 5 several of the officers and leaders were of the opinion that they should have waited to have in hand the 12 caliber pieces that were supposed to arrive on the 7th or the 8th. However, since the commander in chief's mind was made up, and the other officers were of the same opinion, it was agreed, and there were distributed to the participating members of the staff copies of the following plan of attack:

[*The general order of March 5 was presented above as document 2.1.1.8.*]

On that same evening about nightfall it was reported that Travis Barnet (William Barrett Travis), commander of the enemy garrison, through the intermediary of a woman, proposed to the general in chief that they would surrender arms and fort with everybody in it with the only condition of saving his life and that of all his comrades in arms. However, the answer had come back that they should surrender unconditionally, without guarantees, not even of life itself, since there should be no guarantees for traitors. With this reply it is clear that all were determined to lose their existence, selling it as dearly as possible. Consequently they were to exercise extreme vigilance in order not to be surprised at any time of the day or night.

The Mexican troops, at 4:00 A.M. on the 6th, were in their places as had been indicated in the instructions set forth. The artillery, as is gathered from the same instructions, was to remain inactive since they were not scheduled for anything, nor was it impossible in the darkness, and also according to the plans for the troops, to attack on four sides. There could be no artillery fire without blowing their comrades to bits. Thus the enemy enjoyed the advantage of not enduring the artillery fire throughout the whole time of the attack.

Their own artillery was ready and alert so that when the fatal trumpet sounded, there was no doubt that the ultimate scene was at hand—conquer or die. And if there had been any doubt, they were promptly disillusioned by the reckless shouting and *vivas* by the attacking columns as soon as they were seen. They were hit by a hail of shrapnel and bullets that the besieged men let loose on them. The attackers at the first sound of the trumpet were all on their feet at their respective posts with their arms at the ready.

The three columns that attacked on the West, North and East drew back or hesitated a little at the first fire from the enemy, but the example and the efforts of the leaders and officers soon caused them to resume the attack. They did so although the columns of the West and the East found no means of getting on top of the flat roofs of the small rooms, whose walls formed the enclosure, by means of a move to the right and the left simultaneously and unorganized, both swung to the North so that the three columns almost merged into a single mass. Whereupon, with their officers leading them on, they redoubled their efforts to mount the parapet or top of the wall of that front line. They went over finally with General Juan V. Amador being one of the first to reach the goal.

At the same time, to the South Colonels José Vicente Miñón and Juan Morales with their columns skillfully took advantage offered by some small *jacales* with walls of stone and mud which were next to the angle corresponding to the West. By a daring move they seized the cannon which was placed on a platform, as were all the others in the enclosure. They made their way into the fortified area of the quarters, assisting the efforts of General Amador. He had made use of the enemy's own artillery and turned them towards the doors of the small inner rooms in which the rebels had taken cover. From there they opened fire on the troops who were coming down from the parapet to the patio or plaza of the aforesaid enclosure so that all were finally killed by shrapnel, bullets and bayonets. Our losses were great and deplorable. Colonel Francisco Duque was one of the first who fell gravely wounded; from the ground where he lay prostrate, trampled upon by his own subordinates, he continued encouraging the attack. The assault, according to the manner in which it was first set up along the four sides of the enclosure, was very poorly planned and unmilitary. Our own men, in addition to the gunfire from the enemy had to suffer all that from our men themselves from the opposite sides. Since they attacked in a closed column, all the shots, the direction of which was turned somewhat downward, aimed the bullets towards the backs of those ahead of them. Thus it was that most of our dead and wounded that we suffered were caused by this misfortune. It may be said that not a fourth of them were the result of enemy fire. The way their cannon were positioned they were not alongside the wall, nor could they aim their fire against our men once they were surrounded by the wall itself. Nor could they use their rifles thus because the parapet did not have a banquette on the inner side. Consequently it was necessary in order for them to take the offensive to mount the parapet, where as it easily understood they could not remain for a single second without being killed.

Here is a list of our dead and wounded which was made up by General Juan de Andrade according to the accounts from the various corps.

| | Officers | | Troops | | |
Corps	Dead	Wounded	Dead	Wounded	Total
Sappers	1	3	2	21	27
Jiménez	1	3	8	22	34
Matamoros	—	2	7	35	44
Aldama	2	5	9	46	62
San Luis	2	—	7	37	46
Toluca	2	5	18	69	94
Dolores	—	—	1	3	4
Totals	8	18	52	233	311

A large number of wounded died because of poor care and lack of beds, surgical instruments, etc.

All of the enemy perished with only one old woman and a Negro slave left alive. The soldiers spared them out of compassion and because it was supposed that only by force had they been kept in such danger. Of the enemy dead there were 150 volunteers, 32 people of the Town of Gonzalez who under cover of darkness joined the group two days before the attack on the fort, and some twenty people and tradesmen of the city of Bexar itself.

From the manner in which the attack was laid out our losses should have been greater than they were if the pieces of the enemy had [sic] could have been placed in the wall or enclosure. But the rooms of the latter of the inner part would not permit it, and those that were in the right location could fire only to the front. In addition the enemy did not have enough trained men to man the guns because good artillerymen cannot be just jumped up, as is done with rebellions. Furthermore, the instinct of the troops as they attacked, moving to the right and to the left on the North side and the movement made by Miñón and Morales with their column on the West corner of the South side which they attacked, left without a target all the guns that the enemy had located on the other three sides.

In short, be that as it may, the place fell to the possession of the Mexicans, and its defenders were all killed. It is most regrettable that after the first moments of the heat of the battle there should have been atrocious authorized acts unworthy of the valor and resolve with which that operation was carried out, which forthwith left it with an indelible mark for history. These acts were denounced immediately by all who were disgusted upon witnessing them, and afterwards by the entire army who surely were not moved by any such feelings. They heard this with the horror and repugnance in keeping with the bravery and generosity of the Mexicans who can agree only with noble and generous actions. There were deeds that we refrain from relating because of the sorrow that the account of the events would cause us, and which with all good will and the honor of the republic we would wish had never existed. This is like others that preceded these while that poor imitation of a blockade or siege lasted. Although of different sort and purely personal, they did not fail to scandalize and to cost a number of lives and wounded of the most inspired soldiers of the army.

In our opinion all that bloodshed of our soldiers as well as of our enemies was useless, having as its only objective an inconsiderate, childish and culpable vanity so that it might be proclaimed that Béxar had been reconquered by force of arms and that in the attack many men had died on both sides. As we have already stated, the defenders of the Alamo were ready to surrender with only the condition that their lives should be saved.

But let us suppose that such an arrangement had not existed, what would those wretched men do or hope for with more than 5,000 men surrounding them with no means of resistance nor any means of escape by retreat, nor that any friendly force that might have caused the Mexicans to raise the siege to save them, without food to keep them alive in that indefensible location? Even though there had been more than enough of what we had indicated that they lacked, by merely placing twenty artillery pieces properly, that poor wall could not have withstood one hour of cannon fire without being reduced to rubble with the poor quarters inside.

How much more glorious would have been the good name of Mexico if instead of so much blood and so many dead, the lives of the unbridled and ungrateful enemies of the Alamo, as well as of Refugio, Goliad, and Guadalupe Victoria had been saved and the men sent to Mexico to engage in public works that would have in some degree indemnified the expenses that they had caused! And how great would not have been the fame of the same general in chief when without the loss of a single soldier and without any remorse what-soever over the blood spilled later in San Jacinto, if he had brought back to his country that vast territory that the ungrateful protegés were trying to usurp.

Those were the consequences of the executions of the Alamo, of Refugio, Goliad, and Guadalupe Victoria. The rebels saw that with such conduct and design there could be no hope for a peaceful understanding and they had no other way but to conquer, die or abandon the fruits and labors of their fondest dreams that they may have thought to be forever.

Finally, the general in chief gave to the supreme government an account of that episode by means of the note which we insert at this point. In it one can also see in a most positive manner the spirit by which he was motivated for the prosecution of the campaign.

[*The chapter concludes with the victory announcement of March 6, presented above as document 2.1.1.10.*]

2.6.2. Filisola, published account, 1836.

Castañeda, Carlos, trans. 1928. Representation addressed to the supreme government, by Gen. Vicente Filisola. *The Mexican Side of the Texan Revolution.* 169, 170–71. Dallas: P. L. Turner Company.

The original document was published in Mexico in 1836. Not much is said about the Alamo, but a little more background on the consequences of the fall by such a key figure is still useful.

MOST EXCELLENT SIR

VICENTE FILISOLA, general of division, has the honor of addressing Your Excellency with all the respect due the supreme government, to render a true and frank account of his military and political conduct as general-in-chief of the army of operations in Texas.

Sir, the surprise and mortification which I have experienced as a result of the slanderous accusations propagated against me, framed with but little reflection and great levity, entirely erroneous in the main, and inspired by a false and malicious intent, utterly without foundation, are only commensurate with the purity and sincerity of my intentions. These slanders and false accusations have appeared in official communications and in the official *Diario* of the supreme government, the official article of the 15th of last July being particularly offensive.

[*Filisola discusses his situation and responsibilities in some detail to justify his actions in the Texas campaign. The following are his references to the Alamo.*]

First, the defeat of the 21st of last April and the imprisonment of the president, cannot be said to have destroyed the morale of the army, for you cannot destroy that which does not exist. I will, however, relate what was done at this time and not what could or should have been done.

After the capture of the Alamo on the 6th of March and the insignificant advantage gained on the 2nd of that same month by the death of Dr. Grant, 20 adventurers and 3 Mexicans who accompanied him, news of which reached Bexar on the 7th, the president and general-in-chief supposed that the enemy would not dare to show its face again and thought that the war was over.

It is from this false conception and the disdain conceived for the enemy that the misfortunes which we have since suffered have emanated and from which we may still expect many others if we persist in displaying the same carelessness which has been exhibited in considering a question which demands the greatest firmness, circumspection, and judgment.

With this false idea in mind, the president decided that there was nothing to do but to detail the various generals and divisions to occupy the different parts of Texas.

[*Filisola continues on the dispositions of the various forces under Santa Anna's command.*]

If the capture of the Alamo and the unimportant victory of Urrea over Dr. Grant made the general-in-chief think that the war was over, the triumph of

Perdido persuaded him that his presence was no longer necessary in Texas and that he should return to the capital of Mexico, going from Cópano or Matagorda to Tampico and thence overland to San Luis, etc., leaving under my care whatever remained to be done in Texas subject to his instructions.

[*Further orders are detailed.*]

It is very opportune, your Excellency, to state at this point that those of the enemy who were killed at the Alamo and in the various engagements of Urrea were all adventurers who had come from New Orleans after the colonists took Béxar, with the exception of thirty citizens of Gonzales who succeeded in reenforcing Travis the day before the assault, and a few of the leaders. Consequently, the forces of the colonists or inhabitants of Texas remained as yet untouched. . . .

Commentary

Key Senior Officers (2.2–2.6)

These documents by Santa Anna's key senior officers are of high value for the specific information they give. They are particularly strong in presenting military details of the battle and campaign. These details are in large part consistent and probably valid, so only a few general comments follow.

The journal of Almonte (2.2.1) is exceptional because, as Asbury comments, "there is not an ideological phrase in it." It is a day-to-day log with interesting details on what the army was doing and what the conditions and weather were like. Clearly, this is an unusually valuable source for confirming the basic chronology of the Mexican Army.

Almonte's journal shows that the army was getting intelligence on the Texans throughout the campaign—but that it sometimes was not particularly good. On February 22, the Mexicans believed the Texans in San Antonio had learned of their approach. In the entry for the twenty-fourth, a spy, presumably from inside the Alamo, reports on Texan casualties and the arrival of a Gonzales contingent. There is confirmation of Santa Anna's document that the ranches of Juan Seguín and Gaspar or Salvador Flores (4.5.10, 4.5.19) were singled out for a raid on supplies; clearly their support of the Texan cause was reported to the Mexican leaders.[1] The intelligence for the twenty-third was fairly accurate regarding the number of defenders, if the twenty-some on the sick list are allowed for.

Two especially interesting details are the report of two messengers from the Alamo on the twenty-third (presumably one each from Bowie and Travis), and the report that one Mexican soldier (prisoner) inside the Alamo survived. The first point is discussed in the Commentary for Bowie document 1.1.2. An additional comment is that Travis's message through Martin could have been more a personal invitation to Almonte rather than a more formal invitation to negotiate. The claim, however, that

Jameson told Almonte what bad shape the defenders were in seems improbable, at best, so Almonte's (or the translator's) tone in these passages must be considered cautiously. The second point is of interest regarding Brigidio Guerrero and is discussed in the Commentary for section 1.10.2.

Other interesting items are Almonte's recording on February 23 of the tricolored flag with two stars of Coahuila and Texas, and that he supported Santa Anna's casualty figures. The flag is discussed in the Commentary for section 5.2, and the casualties in Appendix B. A final comment is on the original note [4] by Bennett in the *Herald* of June 25, stating that Almonte was the sole cause and occasion of the war in Texas. In her Introduction, however, Williams explained that the war was part of a general consolidation of federal power led by Santa Anna. Almonte's role therefore would have been a supporting one.

The Almonte diary probably was not maintained on a strict daily basis. Two entries appear to have been written after the fact: thirty men arriving from Gonzales (on February 24, actually March 1), and the untrue statement of two hundred reinforcements coming from La Bahia (on February 28). These may have been inserted a few days to a week later. Such insertions might be obvious in the original, but not in the secondhand translation. The last entry in the diary was dated April 16, five days before the diary was lost at San Jacinto, which also indicates that it was not updated daily.

The report by General Sesma (2.3.1) on the activities of the Mexican cavalry the morning of the battle has unappreciated information, because this account has been overlooked until quite recently. Perhaps the strongest impression is a sense of the brutal fighting that took place that morning. Historians have not considered fully, at least until Chariton and Davis pointed it out, the numbers of defenders who might have fallen outside the walls of the Alamo.[2] Of course, the high count could be a self-serving exaggeration, but this military report is probably not as politically motivated as Santa Anna's version (2.1.1.10). On the other hand, it is improbable a significant fraction of the defender had time or position to get away from the escalating fight inside the Alamo plaza once the walls were breached. Sesma's account also implies that an organized retreat, after the outer defenses were overrun, into the surrounding brush might have been planned ahead of time by the Alamo officers.

The Archivo Historico Militar; Archivo de la Secretaria de la Defensa Nacional deserves much more attention. This is a collection of ninety-three reels of microfilm of original documents from the Mexican Archives in the Bancroft Library at the University of California at Berkeley. The collection is approximately three hundred thousand pages from about 1724 to 1864, the majority covering circa 1840–57. As an example of the undiscovered material to be mined, several original reports of General Cós, not in Jenkins's *Papers of the Texas Revolution,* are in the file covering his command in San Antonio in the latter half of 1835. Taken as a whole, the collection should also be an unparalleled source for original research into the Mexican side of the Mexican-American War and the annexation of California.[3]

Another underutilized archival resource is the volumes of transcripts done by Carlos Castañeda, and his colleagues and students around the 1930s, now in the collections of the Center for American History at the University of Texas at Austin. These hundreds of pages of material are the often unrecognized source for many of the Mexican documents that have been available since that time. One example is the Sesma letter (2.3.1), which apparently was overlooked in this collection for nearly sixty years and not published until Davis found it in Mexico. Furthermore, in at least one case of the Alamo (2.1.1.2), the CAH transcript appears to be from a more complete original than the manuscript version found in the Archivo Historico Militar collection at UC Berkeley.

The Military Archives of Mexico are only the most obvious locale for additional historical documents, and it is hoped that other provincial, personal, and archival locales will also become available and examined.

The letter from General Cós to General Filisola of February 12, 1836 (2.4.1), is not directly related to the siege of the Alamo. Nevertheless, it should be of considerable interest to those studying the management of the Texas campaign. This letter of Cós is an overlooked statement by a senior commander and is a strong reinforcement of critiques by intermediate-level Mexican officers such as Sánchez and de la Peña (2.7.3, 2.9.1).

Another overlooked statement of Cós (2.4.2) adds some real specific data to the long-standing debate on the number of Mexican troops at the Alamo. Cós here recorded, less than two weeks prior to the fall of the Alamo, an official count of the number of troops for approximately two-fifths of the attacking force. A further analysis of the significance of this specific document to the general question of the total number of troops appears in Appendix B.

The next three documents, military reports regarding the artillery and the hospital, are from the Mexican Archives and were only recently reported by William C. Davis, as paraphrased in *Three Roads to the Alamo*.[4] They give explicit details on the armaments and munitions captured at the fall and the Mexican wounded still in Béxar from the prior December, as well as details of the fight. They are additionally important in that they hint at the untapped records still to be found in Mexico.

The artillery documents (2.4.3, 2.4.4) indicate that Cós left twenty-one bronze and iron cannons sized from two- to twelve-pounders, a figure that validates much later studies (Commentary on 4.4.5.2). What is particularly striking is the large quantity of munitions fired or recovered from the Alamo (though a figure of thirty-six thousand rifle cartridges might be a misreading; Davis gives it as sixteen thousand). Whatever Travis's problems with resupply, his actual available small-arms supply appears to have been plentiful. The one very significant exception, if it represents a complete inventory, is that only three kegs of powder are recorded.

The hospital report (2.4.5) indicates a surprisingly high recovery of the wounded—288 recoveries out of 427 patients—despite the lack of medicine. One possibility, however, is that the most seriously wounded as well as the soldiers immediately killed were never sent to the hospital and thus were not included in this report.

The final document in this section (2.4.6) can make a real contribution in identifying the names of officers on the Mexican side of the battle. This initial effort to transcribe the names is quite fragmentary, and further careful study is necessary to obtain the full value offered by the list.[5]

There are a lot of interesting comments in the Caro account (2.5.1), but considering his extreme anti–Santa Anna attitude, it is hard to know what to make of those that relate to his commander-in-chief. Were his claims of deceit and duplicity by Santa Anna accurate, or did Caro's prejudices highly distort and thus invalidate the record? Either is quite possible, though one is hard-pressed to take Santa Anna's side on anything. Where Caro narrated events not involving Santa Anna, they tend to match well with or complement other accounts, and thus considerable credit can be given to Caro when Santa Anna was not directly involved. Caro's presentation of Santa Anna, however, raises questions about his motivation and why he became so antagonistic. This is a topic too tangential for this selection of documents and must await a future scholarly study.

A few details of interest from the Caro account are a wrong date, February 26, for the start of the siege; a figure very close to most Texan numbers for defenders (thereby indicating either some reasonably good intelligence or an accurate count of the bodies afterward); that his Mexican casualty figures of four hundred include one hundred due to lack of medical care in the army; and his statement that he personally wrote that six hundred corpses of the defenders (in Santa Anna's letter, 2.1.1.10) were found in the Alamo on the direct order of Santa Anna.

General Filisola gave another detailed account (2.6.1, 2.6.2) that appears quite accurate, but with two caveats. First, he was not present during the siege and fall; hence, he depended on other sources for much of what he narrated. This is not too serious, as he was primarily narrating military events that can often be compared with other sources. This possible shortcoming is more than balanced by his comprehensive use of material—more than any other Mexican source—which gives us much that would otherwise have been lost or lack perspective. Second, he was under considerable attack, primarily as Santa Anna's most convenient scapegoat, after the San Jacinto battle for not rescuing the Mexican campaign, but rather withdrawing his troops from Texas (as ordered by the captured Santa Anna). This also is not a serious problem in the selections given on the Alamo, as Filisola was not particularly at odds with Santa Anna over the conduct of this part of the campaign. A very interesting issue, outside the scope of this book though briefly noted below with General Urrea's excerpt (4.4.3.1), is Filisola's conduct in ordering a retreat after San Jacinto.

The Mexican documents presented in this chapter are from a number of different translations, including some from 1870 based on Filisola (2.1.1.8, 2.1.1.10); Woolsey from Filisola in 1987 (2.6.1); and recent translations of *El Nacional, Suplemento al Numero 79* (e.g., 2.1.1.9). A careful study of the originals might establish that *El Nacional* was the source for Filisola's quoted documents as well. Though these various translations vary in expression, the substance of what is reported is consistent.

Filisola also gave a number of details of the locale and the battle (reviewed with the maps in Appendix B). He noted the broken-down mission walls and ad hoc nature of the defenses. He confirmed Almonte's story of a debate on holding off the assault for some twelve-pound cannons to come up March 7 or 8. Almonte, a participant, dated this debate to March 4, whereas Filisola gave it as March 5, no doubt based on the attack order (2.1.1.8). In addition, Filisola also supported Almonte and Caro (as did Sánchez and others) on the neglect of medical services in the Mexican Army, with a consequent increase in casualties after the battle.

Among the more interesting details is the contradiction within the same document (2.6.1) that more Mexican soldiers died than defenders, even though Filisola also basically supported Santa Anna by giving figures of 60 dead and 251 wounded. This suggests that the documents and sources he was pulling from were themselves contradictory. Another curious detail is a report of Travis looking for surrender terms on the evening of March 5. Something like this is also stated by de la Peña in document 2.9.1. Finally, Filisola's opinions on the policy to execute prisoners and the underestimating of the Texan resolve (2.6.2) are worth remembering when evaluating Santa Anna's strategic thinking.

1. Also Tinkle 1958, 122; Teja 1991, 18, 77.
2. Chariton 1992, 27–29; Davis 1998, 736 n. 105.
3. For documents from this collection, the full record designations are XI/481.3/****, where **** is Expediente #. The records were compiled in these Expedientes, or record books, in 1946. The file designations previous to the Expediente numbers for all cited references in this book are from either Fracción 1/a, Legajo #1, 2, or 6; or Operaciones Militares Año de 1836. The numbering system within each Expediente is for each sheet of paper, so there are frequently two pages per sheet number if both sides of the sheet were used. Also note Gracy 2001, 105:278 n. 40 says that Jackson and Lindley located a microfilm collection in the headquarters of the Palo Alto Battlefield National Historic Site in Brownville.
4. Davis 1998, 711 n. 87; 723 n. 8; 730 n. 88; 731 n. 96; 736–37 n. 105; 739–40 n. 22. Microfilms of the originals, difficult to read, are in Archivo Historico Militar, Expediente 1655:39 and 40, and 1151:22.
5. See Borroel 2001, 3:81 for an analogous effort from other sources to individually identify the deaths on the Mexican side.

2.7.1.   Sánchez, map, 1836.

Sánchez Navarro y Estrada, Capt. José Juan. N.d. (c. 1836). Map in "Ayudentía de Inspección de Nuevo León y Tamaulipas," Vol. 2. CAH.

Appendix II of the document 2.7.2 gives the translated captions for the map.

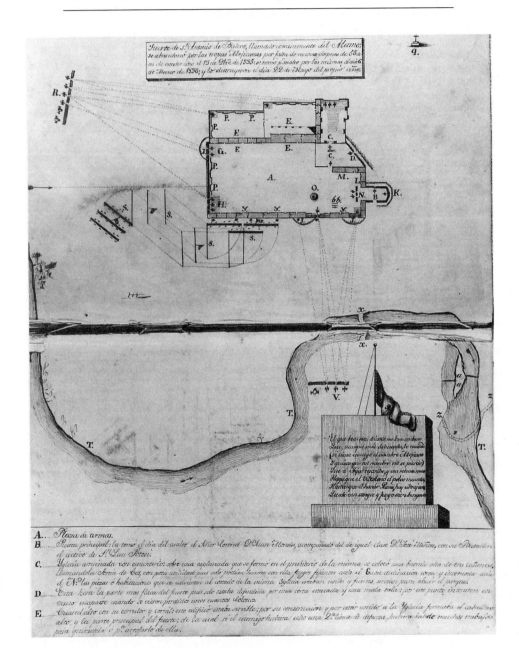

2.7.2.   Sánchez, journal, 1836.

Hunnicutt, Helen, ed. and trans. Summer 1951. "A Mexican View of the Texas War: Memoirs of a Veteran of the Two Battles of the Alamo." *Library Chronicle of the University of Texas* 4:59–74.

This is a translation and commentary of an exceptional manuscript, including a map of the Alamo by Capt. José Juan Sánchez Navarro y Estrada. The original, "Ayudentía de Inspección de Nuevo León y Tamaulipas," Vol. 2, is in the Center for American History at the University of Texas at Austin. Other translations are in the same collection and include "A Mexican Officer's Report of the Fall of the Alamo," an unattributed pamphlet with a reprint and translation of the Alamo plan, and the unattributed "Translation of Sánchez Navarro Papers." A transcription of the Spanish original was published in 1960 by Carlos Sánchez-Navarro as *La Guerra de Tejas: Memorias de un Soldado;* a complete translation was published in 1988 by C. D. Huneycutt.

A Mexican View of the Texas War:
Memoirs of a Veteran of the Two Battles of the Alamo

Among the manuscripts recently acquired by the Archives Collection is a two-volume index to records kept by José Juan Sánchez Navarro during his term of office as Adjutant Inspector of the Departments of Nuevo León and Tamaulipas, entitled *Ayudantía de Inspección de Nuevo León y Tamaulipas.* The file date for each volume is 1831 and 1836 respectively; the period covered extends from April 1831 to November 1839. The contents of the two volumes, in the order recorded, are appended to this article. (Appendix I.)

In the blank pages between the different divisions of the index, Sánchez wrote a detailed account of the two major encounters between the Mexican and the Texas forces in San Antonio de Béxar, in which he participated. The narrative is in the form of a diary and was written on the scene, as is indicated by the following entry:

Today is December 12 [1835]. I was writing this when, by order of the Commandant General, I went to Béxar to compare the invoices for the ponchos, hats, and shoes that I brought from Leona Vicario.[1]

The diary is prefaced by these words:

"All has been lost save honor!" I do not remember, nor am I in mood to remember, what French king said this, perhaps under better circumstances than those in which we are today, the eleventh of December, 1935 [sic; 1835]. Béxar, and perhaps Texas has been lost, although the majority of the faithful subjects the Supreme Government had here for its defense cannot be blamed for such a loss. This is my humble opinion; and to prove it, I shall related the event in so far as it is within my power to do so . . .[2]

His feeling towards the American colonists is bitterly expressed:

We were surrounded by some gross, proud, and victorious men. Anyone who knows the character of the North Americans can judge what our situation must have been![3]

Much as he despised the "norteamericanos," however, Sánchez could take little comfort in the quality of the Mexican leadership. He relates his encounter with Santa Anna in Leona Vicario, February 1836, as follows:

The Most Excellent President, to whom I introduced myself and who recognized me—we were classmates in officers' training . . . has granted the request I made him [to permit me] to return to the Texas campaign . . . There is much activity by way of preparation for this purpose. There are many troops and [there is] much noise; but I see no indications of good political, military, and administrative systems.

His Excellency himself attends to all matters whether important or most trivial. I am astonished to see that he has personally assumed the authority of major general . . . of quartermaster, of commissary, of brigadier generals, of colonels, of captains, and even of corporals, purveyors, *arrieos*, and *carreteros*.

Would it not be better for His Excellency to rid himself of such troublesome work which will occupy his time, which is more needed for the execution of the high duties of his office, by keeping each individual member of the army in complete exercise of his authority according to the provisions of the general ordinances . . . ?

What will become of the army and of the nation if the Most Excellent President should die? Confusion and more confusion because only His Excellency knows the springs by means of which these masses of men called the army are moved. The members of the army in general have no idea of the significance of the Texas war, and all of them believe that they are merely on a military excursion. If, when questioned, one tells the truth about what one has seen there, one is considered a poor soul. As if the enemy could be conquered merely by despising him . . .

Today the Most Excellent President left with his General Staff. He was accompanied by General Cos as far as Santa María. It is said that His Excellency is very economical, even miserly. Those close to him assert that whoever wants to, can make him uncomfortable by asking him for a peso; and they add that he would rather give a colonel's commission than ten pesos. Can all this be true? Even if it is, would it not be better not to mention it? I believe so. But the facts speak for themselves. When we took leave of each other, His Excellency shook my hand and expressed surprise that I was not wearing the insignia of lieutenant colonel, and he told me so.[4]

In Monclova, as the Mexican re-enforcements are on their way to San Antonio, February 1836, Sánchez describes the wretched conditions of the soldiers:

It is pitiful and despairing to go looking for provisions and beasts of burden, money in hand when there is plenty of everything in the commissaries, the *almacenes*, and depots, and to have everyone from the quartermaster general, who is General Woll, and the *jefe politico* to the humblest clerk reply—as if I were a Turk and the supplies I order and for which I offer to pay cash were for the Russians—"We cannot sell that, we cannot let you have it because it is for the army." Consequently, we are perishing from hunger and misery in the midst of plenty.[5]

He is consistently critical of many of the superior officers, particularly of the President and Commander-in-chief of the army.

When we arrived in this city [Monclova], his Excellency the President had left for Río Grande the day before. He is going to Béxar with inconceivable, rather, astonishing haste. Why is His Excellency going in such haste? Why is he leaving the entire army behind? Does he think that his name alone is sufficient to overthrow the colonists?[6]

On the 21st [of March 1836], Fannin and four hundred twenty one prisoners were shot at la Bahía between six and eight in the morning. Sad day! God grant that there may not be another like it! Would it not be well to save the prisoners for the purpose of using them if we should some day suffer reverses?[7]

The Most Excellent President and many of those close to him assert that the campaign is ended; but Generals Filisola, Arago—who is dying—Amador, Andrade, and Cos say that it has hardly started. I am of the opinion of the latter gentlemen. It is reported as a fact that we set fire to all the residences that are not burned by the colonists. I have made many efforts to see what there is by way of a plan for the campaign. I believe there is none; or that if there is one, it is in the mind of His Excellency the President.[8]

If it is true, as is asserted, that an army of four thousand men is coming from Mexico to carry on the Texas campaign, why was the Texas army dissolved and withdrawn? Who or what circumstances can give to the generals, the *jefes*, the officers, and the troops that are coming now for the first time the experience and the practical knowledge of those who have been in Texas previously? Is it possible that we Mexicans must always learn by trial and error? It is indeed dangerous to expose the fate of a nation a second time.[9]

With reference to the recapture of the Alamo by the Mexican forces, Sánchez makes extensive comments:

Long live our country, the Alamo is ours!

Today at five in the morning, the assault was made by four columns under the command of General Cos and Colonels Duque, Romero, and Morales. His Excellency the President commanded the reserves. The firing lasted half an hour. Our *jefes*, officers, and troops, at the same time as if by magic, reached the top of the wall, jumped within, and continued fighting with side arms. By six thirty there was not an enemy left. I saw actions of heroic valor I envied. I was horrified by some cruelties, among others, the death of an old man named Cochran and of a boy about fourteen. The women and children were saved. Travis, the commandant of the Alamo, died like a hero; Buy [Bowie], the braggart son-in-law of Beramendi [died] like a coward. The troops were permitted to pillage. The enemy have suffered a heavy loss: twenty-one field pieces of different caliber, many arms and munitions. Two hundred fifty-seven of their men were killed: I have seen and counted their bodies. But I cannot be glad because we lost eleven officers with nineteen wounded, including the valiant Duque and González; and two hundred forty-seven of our troops were wounded and one hundred ten killed. It can truly be said that with another such victory as this we'll go to the devil.[10]

After the capture of the Alamo, I proposed to the Commandant General, Don Martín Perfecto de Cos, that the valiant officers and soldiers who died in the assault be buried in the cemetery of the chapel of the said fort, that the names of each be inscribed on a copper tablet made from one of the cannons captured to be placed on a column at the base of which these eight line might be written:

Los cuerpos que aqui yacen,
    se animaron
Con almas que á los cielos
    se subieron,
A gozar de la gloria que
    ganaron
Con altas proesas que el
    mundo hicieron
	The bodies that lie here at
	    rest
	Were those of men whose
	    souls elate
	Are now in Heaven to be
	    blest
	For deeds that time cannot
	    abate.

El humano tributo, aqui pa-
    garon;
Al pagarlo la muerte no
    temieron,
Pues muerte por la Patria
    recibida
Mas que muerte, es un paso
    á mejor vida.
	They put their manhood to
	    the test
	And fearlessly they met their
	    fate;
	No fearful end, a patriot's
	    fall
	Leads to the highest life of
	    all.[11]

My suggestion was not approval and I believe that it was not the fault of General Cos. Consequently, I wished to write down the said verses here not so much for the purpose of passing myself off as a poet as to render the due tribute in the only manner within my power to those illustrious, valiant, and untimely victims.[12]

The dead, it appears, were not the only "untimely victims":

There are no hospitals, medicines, or doctors; and the condition of the wounded is such as to cause pity. They have no mattresses on which to lie or blankets with which to cover themselves, in spite of the fact that on entering Béxar, we took from the enemy the remnants of three or four stores and that one has been set up and called the Government Store, where everything is sold at a high price and for cash.[13]

Of his own condition and of the cost of living, Sánchez writes:

I have been sick with rheumatism and misery for twenty-one days. What must be the conditions of others? In Colonel Dromundo's commissary, *piloncillo* sells for one peso, flour for one peso the pound, a tablet of chocolate for two reales, an almud of corn for three pesos, and so on. I am told that only the table of *Señor* Sesma is sumptuous. *Señor* Cos and his adjutants have eaten only roast meat for three days. There is money but there might as well not be any because it is only at the disposal of the Most Excellent President, and His Excellency is annoyed when asked for a peso.[14]

In the entry for April 26, 1836, in Matamoros, Sánchez writes:

Two days ago news was received that His Excellency the President, after having joined his divisions, had left them again and, with very few forces, was pursuing Houston and was on his way to Harrisburg. May God bring His Excellency safely through so daring an undertaking.[15]

In January 1837, the rejoicing which he observed in Leona Vicario over the adoption of the new constitution of 1836 caused Sánchez to pray that it might last longer than the one it was replacing and to state:

Upon leaving, I was assured that it [the new constitution] had the same deficiency as the previous one, that is to say there was no fiscal system. We must not deceive ourselves; as long as the nation does not know the actual amount of its total income and the actual amount of its total and necessary expenditures we shall be walking on precipices and erroneous pathways, we shall contend over false and dubious issues and we shall build without foundations and upon sands. Without removing the causes of evil, we shall never be rid of its pernicious consequences nor find the good way.[16]

The first part of the diary of José Juan Sánchez through April 1, 1836 was published at Mexico City in 1938 by Carlos Sánchez-Navarro under the title *La Guerra de Tejas: Memorias de un Soldado*. From the introduction to this work, and from the internal evidence of the diary, the following facts about his life may be determined.

José Juan Sánchez Navarro was a native of Saltillo. His predecessors distinguished themselves in the field of battle in Spain as early as the thirteenth century. About 1550, Captain Juan Sánchez Navarro migrated to the New World and in 1575, with Alberto del Canto, he founded the *villa* Santiago del Saltillo.

José Juan Sánchez joined the army very young and was made captain after the consummation of independence. He became adjutant inspector of Nuevo León and Tamaulipas April 8, 1831, and was still holding this position during the Texas campaign. As his diary so eloquently testifies, he took an active part in the two major encounters between the Mexican and the Texas forces in San Antonio de Béxar in December 1835 and March 1836, respectively.

[*Sánchez Navarro's further career, including his discouragement with the absence of "good political, military, and administrative systems," is reviewed up to his death while the commandant general of Coahuila in 1849. Appendix I is a listing of the Contents of the Sánchez Index.*]

APPENDIX II: PLAN OF THE ALAMO

On the flyleaves of the second volume, Sánchez drew a plan of the Alamo showing the position of the Mexican forces which recaptured the fort on March 6, 1836.

The caption to this plan reads:

The Fort of San Antonio de Valero, commonly called the Alamo. It was surrendered by Mexican troops for lack of resources the 13th of December 1835 after fifty-five days of constant siege. It was taken by assault by the same [troops] the 6th of March of 1836 and was destroyed the 22nd of May of the same year.

Under the flag with the skull and crossed bones for a device the following lines were written:

*El que bea este diceño no bea
en bano
Que, aunque mál delineado,
le recuerda
(Si tiene en algo el nombre
Mejicano
Y quiere que tal nombre no
se pierda),
Que á Tejas marche, y con
robusta mano
Haga que el vil colono el
polvo muerda,
Hasta que el honor Patrio,
hoy ultrajado,
Quede con sangre y fuego
vien bengado.*

*Let him who sees this crude
device
Remember every patriot must
(If name of Mexican suffice
To proudly bear its fame in
trust)
Return to Texas, seal the
price
Of vile rebellion low in dust,
Until our honor, now out-
raged,
In blood and fire shall be as-
suaged.*[*]

The description written immediately below the sketch and on the following page is as follows:

A. Parade Grounds.
B. Main gate. It was taken the day of the assault by Colonel Don Juan Morales assisted by the [officer] of the same rank, Don José Miñón, and his battalion, the reserve militia of San Luis Potosi.
C. Church in ruins, with a cemetery. On an esplanade formed in the chancel of the same, a high battery of three cannons was set up and named Fortín de Cos. [It was] not very practical because it could be used for firing down only toward the east [and because of] a slight and cumbersome declivity toward the north. The rooms or apartments which appear on the side of the same church were strong and usable and were used for raising the park.
D. This was the weakest part of the fort since it was protected only by a short palisade and a poor barricade of trees. At this point a few colonists tried in vain to escape when they saw all was lost.
E. Tall *cuartel* with a corridor and a corral. This edifice was usable because of its construction and because it was contiguous to the church. It formed the high fortification and the principal part of the fort. If the enemy had made it into a second line of defense, it would have been very difficult to have taken it from them or to have driven them out of it.
F. Barracks for the troops and corral for horses, through which, with the Matamoros and Ximénez Battalions, the colonel of the first [named], Don José María Romero, attacked and entered. This corral and *cuartel*, whose exterior wall was two feet thick and twelve feet high, were protected by the two cannons shown in their [respective] angles toward the north on esplanades one foot [high] and by embrasures.
G. Battery of two cannons called by the Mexicans Fortín de Terán located upon the wall at the height of eleven feet, Mexican vara. The wall was two feet thick; it was reenforced on the outside by a palisade with earth in between which made it five feet thick. Through the said point and through the line which runs toward the center of the other battery, Colonel Duque attacked with his Toluca Battalion; and because he was wounded, General Castrillón continued the attack and entered the fort with the Toluca and the Zapadores [Battalions]. In the esplanade of the said battery, the commander of the colonists, named Travis, died like a soldier.
H. Through this point, called Fortín de Condelle, having the same elevation as the foregoing, General Don Martín Perfecto de Cos attempted to attack with the first column of attack composed of the Aldama Cazadores and fusiliers and one hundred fusiliers of the reserve militia of San Luis. But having lost many men by the sustained firing by the battery and being annoyed by the firing of the Toluca Battalion, he ordered an oblique movement to the right; and since this was executed

promptly and effectively, he flanked the enemy on all sides at the point which he believed the strongest; and he entered the plaza by the postern, over the wall, and by the other points marked by [asterisk].

Y. Rooms which were in the interior [side] of the wall which had loop-holes for rifles toward the outside and the inside.

J. Circular saps with a moat and stockade defending the exterior of the enclosure.

K. Moat defending the main gate.

L. Hospital. In the inner room located in the fore part toward the main gate, the braggart James Wuy [Bowie] died without resisting.

M. Kitchens.

N. Barrier or trench for the defense of the gate.

O. Well dug by the colonists for water.

P. Inner moat and poorly constructed banquette with which the colonists, thinking they were reenforcing part of the fort, weakened it.

Q. Place where the bodies of two hundred fifty-seven ungrateful colonists were burned.

R. Battery for demolition and repercussion set up against the fort at [a distance of] a fusil shot, with which a breach could have been opened in two hours; but it was not ordered to go into action. It was constructed by order of General Amador under the supervision of Lieutenant Colonel Ampudia on the night of the fourth and dawn of the fifth of March. It was manned by the reserve column composed of the Zapadores Battalion and of the companies of grenadiers of the other battalions. It was commanded by His Excellency the President.

S. Position held by the first column of attack under the command of General Cos from three in the morning of the sixth of March, where they remained flat on the ground until five, when they received the signal from the trench to attack. The march and movements made by them before beginning the actual assault are shown.

T. River of San Antonio de Béxar.

V. Battery set up in the City of Béxar since the first of March.

X. Board bridge to facilitate the passage of the people from Béxar to the Alamo.

Z. Ford for vehicles and horses going toward la Villita.

aa. Island which facilitates the crossing of the river by means of two boards.

bb. Three dismounted cannons which were found within the Alamo.

---

[1] *Ayudantía de Inspección de Nuevo León y Tamaulipas,* 1831–1839, 2 vol- 418ff., I:145.

[2] *Ibid.* I:253.

[3] *Ibid.* I:245v.

[4] *Ibid.* II.3–3v.

[5] *Ibid.* II:4.

[6] *Ibid.* II:4–4v.

[7] *Ibid.* II:78v.

[8] *Ibid.* II:79.

[9] *Ibid.* II:93v.
[10] *Ibid.* II:6v.
[11] Translation supplied anonymously.
[12] *Ibid.* II:78.
[13] *Ibid.*
[14] *Ibid.* II:78v.
[15] *Ibid.* II:79v.
[16] *Ibid.* II:111.
[*] Translation supplied anonymously.

2.7.3.   Sánchez, journal, 1836.

Sánchez Navarro y Estrada, Capt. José Juan, translated by John Wheat. N.d. (c. 1836). Journal in "Ayudentía de Inspección de Nuevo León y Tamaulis," Vol. 2. CAH.

This is a translation of the narrative portion of Sánchez's record books. Not included here is his detailed description of the battle of San Antonio in December 1835 from the Mexican perspective.

Capt. José Juan Sánchez-Navarro
Adjutant Inspector for Nuevo León and Tamaulipas

Feb. 21—We passed in sight of the *villa* of Nava* near the Mota del Armadillo [Armadillo Bog]. It rained until we were soaked. We arrived at Rio Grande, presidio 17

When the señor general arrived, the Sr. President had already departed for Béjar with the brigade under the command of Sr. General Sesma

                                          Overleaf 130
(*in this villa was the 1st Brigade of Sr. General Gaona)

                                          From overleaf 130
Everywhere one heard nothing but complaints against the practices of this general, who, according to what they say and we can see, pulls up the reeds and grass without sparing the green vegetation. General Gaona's brigade has arrived and it continued its march with great eagerness. We must acknowledge that the army lacks mobility, and this being of such importance [the army] is at the disposition of teamsters and wagon drivers, upon whom the army's subsistence also depends, [and] though it is carrying innumerable suppliers[?], it suffers from shortages. Let it not be said of us (I speak of the personnel of the Commandancy General) that we are poverty stricken and without pay. When we get a *peso*, we search in vain for corn, firewood, or forage. We find nothing, although we can see it all [around], because they answer with the terrible words, "That is for the army."

26th—From Rio Grande, after crossing the river, to San Ambrosio. It is terribly cold. A scene of total defeat is created by the brigades that are ahead. Everywhere one sees stragglers, dead mules and oxen, broken crates, and abandoned wagons, still with their yokes and straps. <u>Where</u> <u>are</u> <u>they</u> <u>going</u> <u>in</u> <u>this</u> <u>fashion!</u>
.... 4

27th—The north [wind] continues. At La Peña we found General Gaona, who, at the request of the Most Excellent Sr. President, had sent ahead the Sappers, Aldama, and Toluca battalions. <u>The</u> <u>bridge</u> <u>that</u> <u>we</u> <u>had</u> <u>left</u> <u>on</u> <u>the</u> <u>Nueces</u> <u>River</u> <u>was</u> <u>still</u> <u>standing</u> 7

28th—At La Tortuga, shortly before the Cañada del Negro, we caught up with the battalions. 12

29th—We passed through the uninhabited sites of Buena Vista, Arroyo de la Leona [and] No Lo Digas, and arrived at the Rio Frío. Today's march has been very long. The mules and especially the wagons fell behind 17

<u>Month</u> <u>of</u> <u>March</u>

1st—We crossed a dry arroyo and spent the night at Rio Hondo. Here the señor commandant general wanted to push on, but he was dissuaded by appeals, because looking for danger is for the foolhardy 8

Carried overleaf 178

[*new page*]

From overleaf 178

2nd—At noon we arrived at the Chacón, and the troops were given a rest. At 5 in the afternoon, at the Medina River. There the battalions and the señor commandant general made a halt because they had received an order from the Most Excellent Sr. President. [The commandant] went ahead, with six of us as his aides and five soldiers. We crossed the Arroyo de Enmedio, and at 9 in the evening, the León. We could clearly perceive the plaza, in addition to the occasional cannon fire traded with the Alamo, and some grenades hurled from the plaza to the fortress. At 11 we arrived at Béjar. It was not possible to speak with His Excellency. The cold is horrible. On this day we traveled 19

Leagues from Leóna Vicario to Béjar 197

3rd—At ten in the morning, His Excellency the Sr. President went out to inspect the cannons and batteries. He was followed by Sr. Cos, whom I accompanied. Of two of our batteries, one is located on the edge of the city that slopes to the river to the west of the Alamo, served by an 8[-pounder] cannon, 16[-pounder], and one 7[-pound?] howitzer. It is at a distance of about 200 *toesas* [400 yds.] The other is between north and east of said fortress, with four pieces like the previous ones. It would be at a distance of about 150 *toesas* [300 yds.] It is not apparent that the batteries do any serious damage. The enemy does not emerge from behind his parapets. There is a <u>contrast</u> <u>between</u> <u>the</u> <u>efforts</u> <u>that</u>

His Excellency makes to expose himself needlessly to danger (God keep him in his hand) and the care that Sr. General Sesma takes to avoid even those places where there is not danger. Our troops generally perform their duties in the open field.

4th—Inspection such as yesterday. While at the outer trench, His Excellency learned from the mail that I brought him that Sr. General Urrea had defeated the enemy at San Patricio. The man continues to expose himself needlessly to death. The Sappers, Aldama, and Toluca battalions have arrived. There is hunger and cold, but we feel nothing because we are charged with expectations of what we were sent to do. The enemy appears unchanged. One knows there are men in the Alamo only by the cannons and rifles they fire, and because one hears nothing more than the blows of hammers and beams. Vulgar matters: a rumor has spread that [the enemy] has mined the exterior and interior of the fortress, so that we can all go up together if we attack them. It appears that tomorrow a breech will be opened.

5th—In fact, last night our troops worked tenaciously, while our generals were in a meeting. It is said that His Excellency favors an assault, while everyone feels the opposite. A trench was dug between east and north at a distance of half a rifle shot, but this morning at 7[?] it did not operate for even a quarter hour. The assault has been determined. Why is it Sr. Santa Anna always wants his triumphs and defeats to be marked by blood and tears! Sr. General Cos is commanding the 1st column. He has ordered me to go at its head . . . God protect us all!

6th—**Long live the nation. The Alamo is ours!**

At five o'clock this morning, the assault was made in four columns commanded by the señores General Cos and Colonels Duque, Romero, and Morales. His Excellency the Sr. President commanded the reserves. The firing lasted about half an hour. Our commanders, officers, and troops, as if by magic, topped the walls at the same time and rushed in, where hand-to-hand fighting ensued. By 6 in the morning, no enemy was left alive. I saw with envy deeds of heroic valor. Some cruelties horrified me, among others, the death of an old man they called Cocran and that of a boy about 14 years old. The women and children were spared. Travis, the commander of the Alamo, died a brave man. Buy [Bowie], the braggart son-in-law of Beraméndi, like a coward. The troops were permitted to loot. A strong post has been taken from the enemy, 21 [artillery] pieces of various calibers, [and] many weapons and munitions. 257 [enemy] were killed, whose bodies I have seen and counted, but I can feel no joy, because we have lost 11 of our officers, with 19 wounded, among them the valiant Duque and Gonzales. Among the troops [we suffered] 247 wounded and 110 dead. Well could I say, with another victory such as this, the Devil will take us.

Sánchez
[Rubric]

2.8.1.   Labastida plat, map, 1836.

Labastida plat. Original map in CAH.

Astonishingly, the original map prepared in the Mexican camp during the siege of the Alamo has survived.

2.8.2.   Labastida plat, commentary, 1931.

Williams, Amelia. 1931. A critical study of the siege of the Alamo and the personnel of its defenders. Appendix II, 409–10. Ph.D. diss., University of Texas at Austin.

The commentary on this important map, one of three that directly relate to the siege (see also document 2.7.1 and section 4.2), is from the unpublished appendixes of Amelia Williams's original dissertation. The Jameson plats referred to are presented here as documents 4.2.3.2 and 4.2.3.3.

PLAT NO. 2. THE LABASTIDA PLAT

This is a topographical map of San Antonio and environs, made by Ygnacio de Labastida, the chief engineer of the Mexican army of 1836. It was made prior to the capture of the Alamo in March, 1836. The original map, done in water colors, is now in the University of Texas Archives, having been purchased from H. R. Wagner in 1916. It was formerly a document in the <u>Wagner</u> <u>Collection</u> <u>of</u> <u>Mexican</u> <u>Materials</u> now the property of Yale University.

The University of Texas was fortunate to secure this old map, because it is wonderfully interesting and useful in the study of the Texas Revolution. Especially is it valuable for this study because it shows the relative positions of the Alamo, the villita, the city of Bexar, and the surrounding country, thereby enabling the reader to visualize all descriptions of these locations. Note the similarity between this plat and the plate drawn by Jameson, Plans 1, plats A and B.

Translations of explanation:

1. Inscription at the bottom of the map.

Plan of the City of San Antonio de Bexar and fortifications of the Alamo, drawn and colored by Col. Ignacio de Labastida, chief of the engineers of the Army of the North, who dedicated it to his Excellency, General Don Vicente Filisola, chief of the same army.

2. Explanation, written at the side of the map.

A. Entrance.
B. Dwellings of the officers.
C. Guard Room.
D. Artillery.
E. Quarters of the same.
F. Barracks.
G. Park.
H. Interior ditch.
I. High fortifications.
J. Barbette battery.
L. The same in rear.
M. Idem-Iden.
N. Idem, Idem, barbette.
O. Exterior ditches.

2.9.1.   José Enrique de la Peña, journal, c. 1840.

Perry, Carmen, ed. and trans. 1975. *With Santa Anna in Texas: A Personal Narrative of the Revolution, by José Enrique de la Peña.* xi, xiii–xiv, 38–58. College Station: Texas A&M University Press.

Perry notes in her Preface that this document only recently became available, having been repressed by Santa Anna and others because of its critical view of the leadership of the army. This material makes de la Peña potentially one of the most important sources for more general studies on the Mexican Army in the Texas campaign, but only a little is reproduced here, as it digresses further from the Alamo than space allows. The validity of the document has received extensive criticism, especially by Groneman (1994), which is reviewed in the Special Commentary for section 2.9. Four excerpts are included here: two sections of Perry's Preface, the complete text of chapter 4, and a paragraph from chapter 5 that notes another possible significance of the Alamo to the Mexican Army. In this chapter, de la Peña discusses in more specific detail the shortcomings of the army leadership.

[*The Preface starts with a brief introductory paragraph, then addresses de la Peña's significance.*]

Enrique de la Peña's contribution is significant because he was an active participant, an eyewitness and a trained officer, who had advantages in observation and evaluation coupled with an honest objectivity. His rank of lieutenant colonel did not require that he send reports or issue orders during the campaign that later had to be explained or justified, although he frequently was present at closed meetings of his superior officers where important decisions were made.

He was unusually observant and extremely sensitive to his surroundings, interrupting the chain of events to describe in his diary the beauty of the flowers in a prairie, a house, or individual trees. He was also very objective in describing the enemy, pointing out his good qualities with the same detachment with which he deplored the weaknesses in his compatriots. Fortunately his diary has survived in spite of Santa Anna, Filisola, and others who were determined that it be destroyed so that he could not publish it as he had planned.

[*Perry continues with a biographical sketch based on de la Peña's military records. The Preface ends with a discussion of the diary.*]

In 1955 José Sánchez Garza, since deceased, published *La Rebelión de Texas, vol. 1: Manuscrito inédito de 1836 por un oficial de Santa Anna.* He included the diary of José Enrique de la Peña and thirty appendixes, but he deleted, added, and corrected words and sentences, which he felt made the narrative easier to read and to understand.

In this translation we have, with only a few minor exceptions, followed the original manuscript exactly as it was written by José Enrique de la Peña. Where he uses a shortened form of a name (for example, "Sesma" for the more familiar "Ramírez y Sesma") or omits a well-known first name, we have silently amended the text rather than burden the reader with brackets. Likewise, since pronouns cannot perform the same tasks in English as in Spanish, substantives have been introduced where necessary to spare the reader troublesome searches for antecedents. De la Peña spelled phonetically many names and terms that were unfamiliar to him (for example, "Fanning," "stimbot," "Hol Fort"); these have been silently regularized. The many documents de la Peña collected to support his own record, which Sánchez Garza included as appendixes to his edition, have been omitted here but are cited in the footnotes. Many of these documents are held in the Military Archives in Mexico City or in the State Archives in Austin, and copies of some of them are available in the John Peace Memorial Library of the University of Texas at San Antonio. Unless otherwise indicated, the footnotes are the author's own. The text itself has not been edited. If the author sometimes seems to be repetitious, it is because he was so determined that the truth be known and that some action be taken to correct it.

The Sánchez Garza book contains a title page which purports to be from an edition of the de la Peña diary printed in September, 1836, in Matamoros, Tamps., Mexico. However, no copy of this edition could be located either in Mexico or the United States. If indeed this edition ever appeared, it is possible that most or all copies of it were destroyed because of the highly critical nature of its contents.

The de la Peña diary, in the hands of the Sánchez Garza family for many years, was eventually acquired by the late John Peace of San Antonio. Mr. Peace, chairman of the Board of Regents of the University of Texas and an avid collector of Texana, was the moving spirit behind the establishment of the University of Texas at San Antonio.

Shortly before his death in August, 1974, Mr. Peace made the de la Peña diary and related material available to me for the preparation of this book. This valuable collection of documents will be given to the University of Texas at San Antonio, where it will reside in the John Peace Memorial Library. [*Eventually, however, the papers were auctioned off and then donated to the Center for American History.*] It includes all the field notes and the original holograph diary of José Enrique de la Peña, letters, copies of numerous articles he published, and copies of his military records obtained from the Military Archives in Mexico.

CARMEN PERRY

[*Chapter 4*]

Before going on to describe what happened at that post during our sojourn there, we will speak of what happened between the arrival of the First Division and our commander, and our division. The relevant section of the diary is transcribed as follows:

On the 23rd General Ramírez y Sesma advanced at dawn toward Béjar with one hundred horsemen; although he had approached them at three o'clock in the morning, the enemy was unaware of our arrival. The rest of the division came within sight between twelve and one, but by then the enemy had sounded the call to arms and had withdrawn to his fortification at the Alamo. There they had fifteen pieces of artillery,[1] but not all were mounted and ready to use, because of a shortage of cannon balls. They had an eighteen-pounder and an eight-pounder pointing toward the town. After the division had rested for about half an hour at the foot of the Alazán Hill, two miles from Béjar, the president-general mounted his horse and started toward this city with his general staff, three companies of light infantry under command of Colonel Morales, three of grenadiers under command of Colonel Romero, two mortar pieces, and General Ramírez y Sesma's cavalry; he ordered the rest of the division to march with General Ventura Mora to Missión Concepción. The president, unaware upon entering Béjar that the church was abandoned, ordered Colonel Miñón to take it with half the chasseurs. As the column entered the plaza, from the Alamo came a cannon shot from the eighteen-pounder; immediately the artillery commander was ordered to set up two howitzers and to fire four grenades, which caused the enemy to raise a white flag. The firing ceased and Bowie sent a written communication addressed to the commander of the invading troops of Texas, stating that he wished to enter into agreements.[2] The president ordered a verbal answer that he would not deal with bandits, leaving them no alternative but to surrender unconditionally. Then he ordered the placement of the troops, and that they eat and rest, and summoned to Béjar the forces attacking Concepción.

On the 24th at nine o'clock his Excellency appeared and ordered that shoes be distributed in his presence among the preferred companies, and that the frontal advance proceed immediately toward the Alamo and commence the firing, which had been interrupted the previous afternoon. A battery of two eight-pounders and a howitzer was properly placed and began to bombard the enemy's fortification. The enemy returned fire without causing us any damage. On this day, inventories were also taken of stock in the stores belonging to Americans. At eleven, his Excellency marched with the cavalry in order to reconnoiter the vicinity.

On the 25th at nine-thirty his Excellency appeared at the battery and had the column of chasseurs and the battalion from Matamoros march to the other side of the river, he himself following. Our soldiers fought within pistol range against the walls, and we lost two dead and six wounded. During the night some construction was undertaken to protect the line that had been established at La Villita[3] under orders of Colonel Morales. On the 26th, 27th, and 28th nothing unusual happened; the artillery and rifle fire had been brought into play as needed without any misfortune to the division. On the 29th the siege continued, and about seven-thirty at night the enemy killed a first-class private belonging to the first company of the San Luis Battalion, Secundino Alvarez, who on orders of the president had got in close to reconnoiter the Alamo.

On the 1st, 2nd, 3rd, 4th, and 5th of March, the siege continued without anything of note happening, except that on the 2nd the chasseur from San Luis, Trinidad Delgado, drowned, and on the 3rd the sapper battalions from Aldama and Toluca arrived.

On the 17th of February the commander in chief had proclaimed to the
army: "Comrades in arms," he said, "our most sacred duties have brought us to
these uninhabited lands and demand our engaging in combat against a rabble
of wretched adventurers to whom our authorities have unwisely given benefits
that even Mexicans did not enjoy, and who have taken possession of this vast
and fertile area, convinced that our own unfortunate internal divisions have
rendered us incapable of defending our soil. Wretches! Soon will they become
aware of their folly! Soldiers, our comrades have been shamefully sacrificed at
Anáhuac, Goliad, and Béjar, and you are those destined to punish these murderers. My friends: we will march as long as the interests of the nation that we
serve demand. The claimants to the acres of Texas land will soon know to their
sorrow that their reinforcements from New Orleans, Mobile, Boston, New York,
and other points north, whence they should never have come, are insignificant,
and that Mexicans, generous by nature, will not leave unpunished affronts
resulting in injury or discredit to their country, regardless of who the aggressors
may be."

This address was received enthusiastically, but the army needed no incite-
ment; knowing that it was about to engage in the defense of the country and to
avenge less fortunate comrades was enough for its ardor to become as great as
the noble and just cause it was about to defend. Several officers from the
Aldama and Toluca sappers were filled with joy and congratulated each other
when they were ordered to hasten their march, for they knew that they were
about to engage in combat. There is no doubt that some would have regretted
not being among the first to meet the enemy, for it was considered an honor to
be counted among the first. For their part, the enemy leaders had addressed
their own men in terms not unlike those of our commander. They said that we
were a bunch of mercenaries, blind instruments of tyranny; that without any
right we were about to invade their territory; that we would bring desolation
and death to their peaceful homes and would seize their possessions; that we
were savage men who would rape their women, decapitate their children,
destroy everything, and render into ashes the fruits of their industry and their
efforts. Unfortunately they did partially foresee what would happen, but they
also committed atrocities that we did not commit, and in this rivalry of evil and
extermination, I do not dare to venture who had the ignominious advantage,
they or we!

In spirited and vehement language, they called on their compatriots to
defend the interests so dear to them and those they so tenderly cherished. They
urged mothers to arm their sons, and wives not to admit their consorts in their
nuptial beds until they had taken up arms and risked their lives in defense of
their families. The word liberty was constantly repeated in every line of their
writings; this magical word was necessary to inflame the hearts of the men,
who rendered tribute to this goddess, although not to the degree they pretend.

When our commander in chief haughtily rejected the agreement that the
enemy had proposed, Travis became infuriated at the contemptible manner in

which he had been treated and, expecting no honorable way of salvation, chose the path that strong souls choose in crisis, that of dying with honor, and selected the Alamo for his grave. It is possible that this might have been his first resolve, for although he was awaiting the reinforcements promised him,[4] he must have reflected that he would be engaged in battle before these could join him, since it would be difficult for him to cover their entry into the fort with the small force at his disposal. However, this was not the case, for about sixty men did enter one night, the only help that came. They passed through our lines unnoticed until it was too late. My opinion is reinforced by the certainty that Travis could have managed to escape during the first nights, when vigilance was much less, but this he refused to do. It has been said that General Ramírez y Sesma's division was not sufficient to have formed a circumventing line on the first day, since the Alamo is a small place, one of its sides fronting the San Antonio River and clear and open fields. The heroic language in which Travis addressed his compatriots during the days of the conflict finally proved that he had resolved to die before abandoning the Alamo or surrendering unconditionally. He spoke to them thus: "Fellow citizens and compatriots, I am besieged by a thousand or more of the Mexicans under Santa Anna. I have sustained bombardment and cannonade for twenty-four hours and have not lost a man. The enemy has demanded a surrender at discretion, otherwise the garrison are to be put to the sword, if the fort is taken. I have answered the demand with a cannon shot, and our flag still waves proudly over the walls. *I shall never surrender or retreat.* Then, I call on you in the name of Liberty, of patriotism, and every thing dear to the American character, to come to our aid. If this call is neglected, I am determined to sustain myself as long as possible and die as a soldier who never forgets what is due to his own honor and that of his country."[5]

Twelve days had passed since Ramírez y Sesma's division had drawn up before the Alamo and three since our own arrival at Béjar. Our commander became more furious when he saw that the enemy resisted the idea of surrender. He believed as others did that the fame and honor of the army were compromised the longer the enemy lived. General Urrea had anticipated him and had dealt the first blow, opening the first campaign, but we had not advanced in the least during the twelve days that our vanguard stood facing this obstinate enemy. It was therefore necessary to attack him in order to make him feel the vigor of our souls and the strength of our arms. But prudent men, who know how to measure the worth of true honor, those whose tempered courage permits their venturing out only when they know beforehand that the destruction they are about to wreak will profit them and who understand that the soldier's glory is the greater, the less bloody the victory and the fewer the victims sacrificed; these men, though moved by the same sentiments as the army and its commander, were of the opinion that victory over a handful of men concentrated in the Alamo did not call for a great sacrifice. In fact, it was necessary only to await the artillery's arrival at Béjar for these to surrender; undoubtedly they could not have resisted for many hours the destruction and imposing fire from twenty cannon. The sums spent by the treasury on the artillery equipment brought to Texas are incalculable; the transportation alone amounts to thousands of pesos. Either they did not wish or did not know how to make use of such weaponry; had it been judiciously employed, it would have saved us many lives, and the success of the campaign would have been very different indeed.

There was no need to fear that the enemy would be reinforced, for even though reinforcements had entered because of our lack of vigilance, we were situated so as to do battle with any other possible arrivals one by one. We were in a position to advance, leaving a small force on watch at the Alamo, the holding of which was unimportant either politically or militarily, whereas its acquisition was both costly and very bitter in the end. If Houston had not received news of the fall of the Alamo, it would have been very easy to surprise and defeat him.

During a council of war held on the 4th of March at the commander in chief's quarters, he expounded on the necessity of making the assault. Generals Sesma, Cos, and Castrillón, Colonels Almonte, Duque, Amat, Romero, and Salas, and the interim mayor of San Luis were present and gave their consent. The problem centered around the method of carrying it out. Castrillón, Alamonte, and Romero were of the opinion that a breach should be made, and that eight or ten hours would suffice to accomplish this. Field pieces were coming up and Colonel Bringas, aide to the president-general, had left with the idea of activating them. It was agreed to call the artillery commandant and to alert him to this, and although the artillery would not arrive for a day or so, and that solution was still pending, on the 5th the order was given for the assault.[6] Some, though approving this proposal in the presence of the commander in chief, disagreed in his absence, a contradiction that reveals their weakness; others chose silence, knowing that he would not tolerate opposition, his sole pleasure being in hearing what met with his wishes, while discarding all admonitions that deviated from those wishes. None of these commanders was aware that there were no field hospitals or surgeons to save the wounded, and that for some it would be easier to die than to be wounded, as we shall see after the assault.

When in this or some other discussion, the subject of what to do with prisoners was brought up, in case the enemy surrendered before the assault, the example of Arredondo was cited; during the Spanish rule he had hanged eight hundred or more colonists after having triumphed in a military action, and this conduct was taken as a model. General Castrillón and Colonel Almonte then voiced principles regarding the rights of men, philosophical and humane principles which did them honor; they reiterated these later when General Urrea's prisoners were ordered executed, but their arguments were fruitless.

We had no officers of the engineers' corps who could estimate for us the strength at the Alamo and its defenses, because the section in this corps appointed for the army had remained in Mexico; however, the sappers were not lacking in personnel who could have carried out this chore, and, furthermore, information given by General Cos, by wounded officers he had left at Béjar, and by some townspeople of this locality was considered sufficient. The latter made clear to us the limited strength of the garrison at the Alamo and the shortage of supplies and munitions at their disposal. They had walled themselves in so quickly that they had not had time to supply themselves with very much.

Travis's resistance was on the verge of being overcome; for several days his followers had been urging him to surrender, giving the lack of food and the scarcity of munitions as reasons, but he had quieted their restlessness with the hope of quick relief, something not difficult for them to believe since they had seen some reinforcements arrive. Nevertheless, they had pressed him so hard that on the 5th he promised them that if no help arrived on that day they would surrender the next day or would try to escape under cover of darkness; these facts were given to us by a lady from Béjar, a Negro who was the only male who escaped, and several women who were found inside and were rescued by Colonels Morales and Miñón. The enemy was in communication with some of the Béjar townspeople who were their sympathizers, and it was said as a fact during those days that the president-general had known of Travis's decision, and that it was for this reason that he precipitated the assault, because he wanted to cause a sensation and would have regretted taking the Alamo without clamor and without bloodshed, for some believed that without these there is no glory.

Once the order was issued, even those opposing it were ready to carry it out; no one doubted that we would triumph, but it was anticipated that the struggle would be bloody, as indeed it was. All afternoon of the 5th was spent on preparations. Night came, and with it the most sober reflections. Our soldiers, it was said, lacked the cool courage that is demanded by an assault, but they were steadfast and the survivors will have nothing to be ashamed of. Each one individually confronted and prepared his soul for the terrible moment, expressed his last wishes, and silently and coolly took those steps which precede an encounter. It was a general duel from which it was important to us to emerge with honor. No harangue preceded this combat, but the example given was the most eloquent language and the most absolute order. Our brave officers left nothing to be desired in the hour of trial, and if anyone failed in his duty, if anyone tarnished his honor, it was so insignificant that his short-comings remained in the confusion of obscurity and disdain. Numerous feats of valor were seen in which many fought hand to hand; there were also some cruelties observed.

The Alamo was an irregular fortification without flank fires which a wise general would have taken with insignificant losses, but we lost more than three hundred brave men.

Four columns were chosen for the attack. The first, under command of General Cos and made up of a battalion from Aldama and three companies from the San Luis contingent, was to move against the western front, which faced the city. The second, under Colonel Duque and made up of the battalion under his command and three other companies from San Luis, was entrusted with a like mission against the front facing the north, which had two mounted batteries at each end of its walls. These two columns had a total strength of seven hundred men. The third, under command of Colonel Romero and made up of two companies of fusiliers from the Matamoros and Jiménez battalions, had less strength, for it only came up to three hundred or more men; it was to attack the east front, which was the strongest, perhaps because of its height or perhaps because of the number of cannon that were defending it, three of them situated in a battery over the church ruins, which appeared as a sort of high fortress. The fourth column, under command of Colonel Morales and made up of over a hundred chasseurs, was entrusted with taking the entrance to the fort and the entrenchments defending it.

The Sapper Battalion and five grenadier companies made up the reserve of four hundred men. The commander in chief headed this column, according to the tenor of the secret order given for the assault, and its formation was entrusted to Colonel Amat, who actually led it into combat.

This was the general plan, and although there were several minor variations proposed almost all were cast aside.

Our commander made much of Travis's courage, for it saved him from the insulting intimation that the critical circumstances surrounding Travis would have sufficed to spare the army a great sacrifice.

Beginning at one o'clock in the morning of the 6th, the columns were set in motion, and at three they silently advanced toward the river, which they crossed marching two abreast over some narrow wooden bridges. A few minor obstacles were explored in order to reach the enemy without being noticed, to a point personally designated by the commander in chief, where they stationed themselves, resting with weapons in hand. Silence was again ordered and smoking was prohibited. The moon was up, but the density of the clouds that covered it allowed only an opaque light in our direction, seeming thus to contribute to our designs. This half-light, the silence we kept, hardly interrupted by soft murmurs, the coolness of the morning air, the great quietude that seemed to prolong the hours, and the dangers we would soon have to face, all of this rendered our situation grave; we were still breathing and able to communicate; within a few moments many of us would be unable to answer questions addressed to us, having already returned to the nothingness whence we had come; others, badly wounded, would remain stretched out for hours without anyone thinking of them, each still fearing perhaps one of the enemy cannonballs whistling overhead would drop at his feet and put an end to his sufferings. Nevertheless, hope stirred us and within a few moments this anxious uncertainty would disappear; an insult to our arms had to be avenged, as well as the blood of our friends spilled three months before within these same walls we were about to attack. Light began to appear on the horizon, the beautiful dawn would soon let herself be seen behind her golden curtain; a bugle call to attention was the agreed signal and we soon heard that terrible bugle call of death, which stirred our hearts, altered our expressions, and aroused us all suddenly from our painful meditations. Worn out by fatigue and lack of sleep, I had just closed my eyes to nap when my ears were pierced by this fatal note. A trumpeter of the sappers (José María González) was the one who inspired us to scorn life and to welcome death. Seconds later the horror of this sound fled from among us, honor and glory replacing it.

The columns advanced with as much speed as possible; shortly after beginning the march they were ordered to open fire while they were still out of range, but there were some officers who wisely disregarded the signal. Alerted to our attack by the given signal, which all columns answered, the enemy vigorously returned our fire, which had not even touched him but had retarded our advance. Travis, to compensate for the reduced number of the defenders, had placed three or four rifles by the side of each man, so that the initial fire was very rapid and deadly. Our columns left along their path a wide trail of blood, of wounded, and of dead. The bands from all the corps, gathered around our commander, sounded the charge; with a most vivid ardor and enthusiasm, we answered that call which electrifies the heart, elevates the soul, and makes others tremble. The second column, seized by this spirit, burst out in acclamations for the Republic and for the president-general. The officers were unable to repress this act of folly, which was paid for dearly. His attention drawn by this act, the enemy seized the opportunity, at the moment that light was beginning to make objects discernible around us, to redouble the fire on this column, making it suffer the greatest blows. It could be observed that a single cannon volley did away with half the company of chasseurs from Toluca, which was advancing a few paces from the column; Captain José María Herrera, who commanded it, died a few moments later and Vences, its lieutenant, was also wounded. Another volley left many gaps among the ranks at the head, one of them being Colonel Duque, who was wounded in the thigh; there remained standing, not without surprise, one of the two aides to this commander, who marched immediately to his side, but the other one now cannot testify to this. Fate was kind on this occasion to the writer, who survived, though Don José María Macotela, captain from Toluca, was seriously wounded and died shortly after.

It has been observed what the plan of attack was, but various arrangements made to carry it out were for the most part omitted; the columns had been ordered to provide themselves with crow-bars, hatchets, and ladders, but not until the last moment did it become obvious that all this was insufficient and that the ladders were poorly put together.

The columns, bravely storming the fort in the midst of a terrible shower of bullets and cannon-fire, had reached the base of the walls, with the exception of the third, which had been sorely punished on its left flank by a battery of three cannon on a barbette that cut a serious breach in its ranks; since it was being attacked frontally at the same time from the height of a position, it was forced to seek a less bloody entrance, and thus changed its course toward the right angle of the north front. The few poor ladders that we were bringing had not arrived, because their bearers had either perished on the way or had escaped. Only one was seen of all those that were planned. General Cos, looking for a starting point from which to climb, had advanced frontally with his column to where the second and third were. All united at one point, mixing and forming a confused mass. Fortunately the wall reinforcement on this front was of the lumber, its excavation was hardly begun, and the height of the parapet was eight or nine feet; there was therefore a starting point, and it could be climbed, though with some difficulty. But disorder had already begun; officers of all ranks shouted but were hardly heard. The most daring of our veterans tried to be the first to climb, which they accomplished, yelling wildly so that room could be made for them, at times climbing over their own comrades. Others, jammed together, made useless efforts, obstructing each other, getting in the way of the more agile ones and pushing down those who were about to carry out their courageous effort. A lively rifle fire coming from the roof of the barracks and other points caused painful havoc, increasing the confusion of our disorderly mass. The first to climb were thrown down by bayonets already waiting for them behind the parapet, or by pistol fire, but the courage of our soldiers was not diminished as they saw their comrades falling dead or wounded, and they hurried to occupy their places and to avenge them, climbing over their bleeding bodies. The sharp reports of the rifles, the whistling of bullets, the groans of the wounded, the cursing of the men, the sighs and anguished cries of the dying, the arrogant harangues of the officers, the noise of the instruments of war, and the inordinate shouts of the attackers, who climbed vigorously, bewildered all and made of this moment a tremendous and critical one. The shouting of those being attacked was no less loud and from the beginning had pierced our ears with desperate, terrible cries of alarm in a language we did not understand.

From his point of observation, General Santa Anna viewed with concern this horrible scene and misled by the difficulties encountered in the climbing of the walls and by the maneuver executed by the third column, believed we were being repulsed; he therefore ordered Colonel Amat to move in with the rest of the reserves; the Sapper Battalion, already ordered to move their column of attack, arrived and began to climb at the same time. He then also ordered into battle his general staff and everyone at his side. This gallant reserve merely added to the noise and the victims, the more regrettable since there was no necessity for them to engage in the combat. Before the Sapper Battalion, advancing through a shower of bullets and volley of shrapnel, had a chance to reach the foot of the walls, half their officers had been wounded. Another one of these officers, young Torres, died within the fort at the very moment of taking a flag.[7] He died at one blow without uttering a word, covered with glory and lamented by his comrades. Something unusual happened to this corps; it had as casualties four officers and twenty-one soldiers, but among these none of the sergeant class, well known to be more numerous than the former.

A quarter of an hour had elapsed, during which our soldiers remained in a terrible situation, wearing themselves out as they climbed in quest of a less obscure death than that visited on them, crowded in a single mass; later and after much effort, they were able in sufficient numbers to reach the parapet, without distinction of ranks. The terrified defenders withdrew at once into quarters placed to the right and the left of the small area that constituted their second line of defense. They had bolted and reinforced the doors, but in order to form trenches they had excavated some places inside that were now a hindrance to them. Not all of them took refuge, for some remained in the open, looking at us before firing, as if dumbfounded at our daring. Travis was seen to hesitate, but not about the death that he would choose. He would take a few steps and stop, turning his proud face toward us to discharge his shots; he fought like a true soldier. Finally he died, but he died after having traded his life very dearly. None of his men died with greater heroism, and they all died. Travis behaved as a hero; one must do him justice, for with a handful of men without discipline, he resolved to face men used to war and much superior in numbers, without supplies, with scarce munitions, and against the will of his subordinates. He was a handsome blond, with a physique as robust as his spirit was strong.

In the meantime Colonel Morelos with his chasseurs, having carried out instructions received, was just in front of us at a distance of a few paces, and, rightly fearing that our fire would hurt him, he had taken refuge in the trenches he had overrun trying to inflict damage on the enemy without harming us. It was a good thing that other columns could come together in a single front, for because of the small area the destruction among ourselves could be partially avoided; nevertheless, some of our men suffered the pain of falling from shots fired by their comrades, a grievous wound indeed, and a death even more lamentable. The soldiers had been overloaded with munition, for the reserves and all the select companies carried seven rounds apiece. It seems that the purpose of this was to convey the message to the soldier not to rely on his bayonet, which is the weapon generally employed in assault while some of the chasseurs support the attackers with their fire; however, there are always errors committed on these occasions, impossible to remedy. There remains no consolation other than regret for those responsible on this occasion, and there were many.

Our soldiers, some stimulated by courage and others by fury, burst into the quarters where the enemy had entrenched themselves, from which issued an infernal fire. Behind these came others, who, nearing the doors and blind with fury and smoke, fired their shots against friends and enemies alike, and in this way our losses were most grievous. On the other hand, they turned the enemy's own cannon to bring down the doors to the rooms or the rooms themselves; a horrible carnage took place, and some were trampled to death. The tumult was great, the disorder frightful; it seemed as if the furies had descended upon us; different groups of soldiers were firing in all directions, on their comrades and on their officers, so that one was as likely to die by a friendly hand as by an enemy's. In the midst of this thundering din, there was such confusion that orders could not be understood, although those in command would raise their voices when the opportunity occurred. Some may believe that this narrative is exaggerated, but those who were witnesses will confess that this is exact, and in truth, any moderation in relating it would fall short.

It was thus time to end the confusion that was increasing the number of our victims, and on my advice and at my insistence General Cos ordered the fire silenced; but the bugler Tamayo of the sappers blew his instrument in vain, for the fire did not cease until there was no one left to kill and around fifty thousand cartridges had been used up. Whoever doubts this, let him estimate for himself, as I have done, with data that I have given.

Among the defenders there were thirty or more colonists; the rest were pirates, used to defying danger and to disdaining death, and who for that reason fought courageously; their courage, to my way of thinking, merited them the mercy for which, toward the last, some of them pleaded; others, not knowing the language, were unable to do so. In fact, when these men noted the loss of their leader and saw that they were being attacked by superior forces, they faltered. Some, with an accent hardly intelligible, desperately cried, *Mercy, valiant Mexicans;* others poked the points of their bayonets through a hole or a door with a white cloth, the symbol of cease-fire, and some even used their socks. Our trusting soldiers, seeing these demonstrations, would confidently enter their quarters, but those among the enemy who had not pleaded for mercy, who had no thought of surrendering, and who relied on no other recourse than selling their lives dearly, would meet them with pistol shots and bayonets. Thus betrayed, our men rekindled their anger and at every moment fresh skirmishes broke out with renewed fury. The order had been given to spare no one but the women and this was carried out, but such carnage was useless and had we prevented it, we would have saved much blood on our part. Those of the enemy who tried to escape fell victims to the sabers of the cavalry, which had been drawn up for this purpose, but even as they fled they defended themselves. An unfortunate father with a young son in his arms was seen to hurl himself from a considerable height, both perishing at the same blow.

This scene of extermination went on for an hour before the curtain of death covered and ended it: shortly after six in the morning it was all finished; the corps were beginning to reassemble and to identify themselves, their sorrowful countenances revealing the losses in the thinned ranks of their officers and comrades, when the commander in chief appeared. He could see for himself the desolation among his battalions and that devastated area littered with corpses, with scattered limbs and bullets, with weapons and torn uniforms. Some of these were burning together with the corpses, which produced an unbearable and nauseating odor. The bodies, with their blackened and bloody faces disfigured by a desperate death, their hair and uniforms burning at once, presented a dreadful and truly hellish sight. What trophies—those of the battlefield! Quite soon some of the bodies were left naked by fire, others by disgraceful rapacity, especially among our men. The enemy could be identified by their whiteness, by their robust and bulky shapes. What a sad spectacle, that of the dead and dying! What a horror, to inspect the area and find the remains of friends—! With what anxiety did some seek others and with what ecstasy did they embrace each other! Questions followed one after the other, even while the bullets were still whistling around, in the midst of the groans of the wounded and the last breaths of the dying.

The general then addressed his crippled battalions, lauding their courage and thanking them in the name of their country. But one hardly noticed in his words the magic that Napoleon expresses in his, which, Count Ségur assures us, was impossible to resist. The *vivas* were seconded icily, and silence would hardly have been broken if I, seized by one of those impulses triggered by enthusiasm or one formed to avoid reflection, which conceals the feelings, had not addressed myself to the valiant chasseurs of Aldama, hailing the Republic and them, an act which, carried out in the presence of the commander on whom so much unmerited honor had been bestowed, proved that I never flatter those in power.

Shortly before Santa Anna's speech, an unpleasant episode had taken place, which, since it occurred after the end of the skirmish, was looked upon as base murder and which contributed greatly to the coolness that was noted. Some seven men had survived the general carnage and, under the protection of General Castrillón, they were brought before Santa Anna. Among them was one of great stature, well proportioned, with regular features, in whose face there was the imprint of adversity, but in whom one also noticed a degree of resignation and nobility that did him honor. He was the naturalist David Crockett, well known in North America for his unusual adventures, who had undertaken to explore the country and who, finding himself in Béjar at the moment of surprise, had taken refuge in the Alamo, fearing that his status as a foreigner might not be respected. Santa Anna answered Castrillón's intervention in Crockett's behalf with a gesture of indignation and, addressing himself to the sappers, the troops closest to him, ordered his execution. The commanders and officers were outraged at this action and did not support the order, hoping that once the fury of the moment had blown over these men would be spared; but several officers who were around the president and who, perhaps, had not been present during the moment of danger, became noteworthy by an infamous deed, surpassing the soldiers in cruelty. They thrust themselves forward, in order to flatter their commander, and with swords in hand, fell upon these unfortunate, defenseless men just as a tiger leaps upon his prey. Though tortured before they were killed, these unfortunates died without complaining and without humiliating themselves before their torturers. It was rumored that General Sesma was one of them; I will not bear witness to this, for though present, I turned away horrified in order not to witness such a barbarous scene. Do you remember, comrades, that fierce moment which struck us all with dread, which made our souls trem-

ble, thirsting for vengeance just a few moments before? Are your resolute hearts
not stirred and still full of indignation against those who so ignobly dishonored
their swords with blood? As for me, I confess that the very memory of it makes
me tremble and that my ear can still hear the penetrating, doleful sound of the
victims.

To whom was the sacrifice useful and what advantage was derived by
increasing the number of victims? It was paid for dearly, though it could have
been otherwise had these men been required to walk across the floor carpeted
with the bodies over which we stepped, had they been rehabilitated generously
and required to communicate to their comrades the fate that awaited them if
they did not desist from their unjust cause. They could have informed their
comrades of the force and resources that the enemy had. According to documents found among these men and to subsequent information, the force within
the Alamo consisted of 182 men; but according to the number counted by us it
was 253. Doubtless the total did not exceed either of these two, and in any case
the number is less than that referred to by the commander in chief in his com-
muniqúe, which contends that in the excavations and the trenches alone more
than 600 bodies had been buried. What was the object of this misrepresenta-
tion? Some believe that it was done to give greater importance to the episode,
others, that it was done to excuse our losses and to make it less painful.[8]

Death united in one place both friends and enemies; within a few hours a
funeral pyre rendered into ashes those men who moments before had been so
brave that in a blind fury they had unselfishly offered their lives and had met
their ends in combat. The greater part of our dead were buried by their comrades, but the enemy, who seems to have some respect for the dead, attributed
the great pyre of their dead to our hatred. I, for one, wishing to count the bodies
for myself, arrived at the moment the flames were reddening, ready to consume
them.

When calm opens the way for reflection, what sad and cruel thoughts rush
to the sensitive soul contemplating the field of battle! Would anyone be the
object of reproach, who, after having risked his life to comply with his duty and
honor, for a brief period unburdens his feelings and devotes some time to chari-
table thoughts?

The reflections after the assault, even a few days after it had taken place,
were generally well founded; for instance, it was questioned why a breach had
not been opened? What had been the use of bringing up the artillery if it were
not to be used when necessity required, and why should we have been forced
to leap over a fortified place as if we were flying birds? Why, before agreeing on
the sacrifice, which was great indeed, had no one borne in mind that we had no
means at our disposal to save our wounded? Why were our lives uselessly sacrificed in a deserted and totally hostile country if our losses could not be
replaced? These thoughts were followed by others more or less well based, for
the taking of the Alamo was not considered a happy event, but rather a defeat
that saddened us all. In Béjar one heard nothing but laments; each officer who

died aroused compassion and renewed reproaches. Those who arrived later added their criticism to ours, and some of these, one must say, regretted not having been present, because those who obeyed against their own judgment nonetheless attained eternal glory.

All military authors agree that battles should be undertaken only in extreme situations, and I will take full advantage of these opinions; they affirm that as a general rule, so long as there is a way to weaken and overcome the enemy without combat, it should be adopted and combat avoided. Civilization has humanized man and thanks to its good effects the more barbarous methods that were prevalent before, to kill the greatest number of men in the least possible time, have been abandoned; murderous maneuvers to destroy a whole army at a single blow have been discarded. It has been established as an axiom that a general entrusted with the command of an army should devote as much zeal to sparing the blood of his army as to the enemy. The opinion of the military sages, together with that of the moralists, states that the general who is frugal with the blood of his soldiers is the savior of his country, whereas he who squanders and sacrifices it foolishly is the murderer of his compatriots. One of these authors states that Louis XIV, at the time of his death, was inconsolable because of the blood spilled during his reign; that the memorable Turenne, in the last moments of his life, could not be quieted by the priests, in spite of all the consolation religion offers. As a matter of fact, false feelings of glory are not sufficient to suppress the remorse that the useless spilling of blood always brings about. If General Santa Anna were to see gathered together at one place the bodies of all the Mexicans he has sacrificed in all the revolutions he has promoted and in all the ill-directed battles over which he has presided, he would be horrified, no matter how insensitive he may be. The most renowned captains have always feared the day of battle, not so much because of danger to their lives as because of the interests and the soldiers entrusted to their care; but ignorance fears nothing because it foresees nothing. Some of our generals, particularly the conqueror of the Alamo, seemed not to have heeded these authors, for the latter, in his long career, has always separated himself from principles and has cast aside wise counsel. He has acted capriciously, uselessly sacrificing the life of the soldier, the honor and interests of the Republic, and the decorum of its arms, certain that no accounting will be required of him, or else that were this to be brought about, he would be acquitted, as experience has demonstrated. He would certainly act differently were he to be punished for his errors, but since he is lavished with honors even after his defeats, regardless of how shameful these may be, he could care less about losing or winning battles so long as they serve the interest of his party.

The responsibility for the victims sacrificed at the Alamo must rest on General Ramírez y Sesma rather than on the commander in chief. He knew that the enemy was at Béjar in small numbers and in the greatest destitution; he had scarcely had news of our march before our vanguard reached the gates of the city; he ordered the vanguard to surprise the enemy with a force of sixty horsemen, and to effect the march quickly and without the enemy's knowledge; he ordered the officers at the Medina River to yield their own horses to the dragoons that lacked good mounts. When General Ramírez y Sesma sighted the town, the enemy was still engaged in the pleasures of a dance given the night before; he therefore could have and should have prevented their taking refuge in the Alamo. Several came to inform him, indicating to him the points through which he might enter and the orders he should give, and urging him earnestly, but he turned down these recommendations and the repeated requests, conducting himself with extraordinary uncertainty and weakness; we have seen how dearly his indecision was paid for. At the very moment that General Ramírez y Sesma was advised to enter Béjar, there were only ten men at the Alamo, and it would have required an equal number to take it. Had he just placed himself at the bridge over the San Antonio that connects the fort to the city, as he was advised, he would have prevented the enemy from taking refuge there, thus avoiding the painful catastrophe that we witnessed. Later on we shall see how this same general made another great mistake that strongly influenced the fatal outcome of the campaign, and that the commander in chief noticed his lack of skill too late, although it was common knowledge among the expeditionary army, for he had certainly revealed his worthlessness through the censurable conduct we have just described.

[Chapter 5]
The morale of the army had changed completely since the taking of the Alamo, because of the errors committed in that undertaking and the sufferings they were undergoing and had undergone en route; on the march the soldier could count on only half his rations and the officer had only enough pay to provide himself with food, which was sold at prices quoted in gold by the very people who were responsible for providing these necessities. The critical situation in which the army found itself at Béjar and the exasperation of its members is faithfully expressed in several letters of that period, written at that city, and also in various printed articles. Since these documents exist, authenticating the facts, and since no one can label them as false, because they were written by eyewitnesses, I take the liberty here of quoting some passages, obviously with some repetition.

[In addition to the shortage of supplies and pay, the lack of medical assistance to the wounded is also documented.]

---

[1] There were nineteen, of different calibers.

[2] William Barret Travis was commander at the Alamo, James Bowie his second, and a certain Evans a commander of artillery.

[3] A small village near the Alamo and on the left bank of the San Antonio River.

[4] Fannin was still expected to come with aid from Goliad. Not until several days after the Alamo fell was he ordered to Victoria instead. See his letter from Fort Defiance on March 14, 1836, to Colonel A. C. Haton [Albert C. Horton].—Ed.

[5] De la Peña's Spanish translation of the Travis letter is accurate except for three omissions: the reference to Mexican reinforcements in the body of the letter, the

closing words "Victory or Death" and the postscript. The original letter, with those omissions, is used here.—*Ed.*

[6] The disposition of the troops for the assault is specified in the general order of March 5, 1836, marked secret and issued under the signature of Juan Valentín Amador and certified at Béjar, March 6, 1836, by Ramón Martínez Caro, Santa Anna's secretary (see *La Rebelión de Texas*, appendix 8).—*Ed.*

[7] The only flag proved to have flown over the Alamo is that of the New Orleans Greys. It is the one Santa Anna sent home, and it can be seen at the museum in Chapultepec Castle in Mexico City.—*Ed.*

[8] See the accompanying documents, the second of which states exactly the number of losses sustained by us. Most of the wounded died on account of poor care, lack of beds, shelter, surgical instruments, etc., etc. All of the enemy perished, there remaining alive only an elderly lady and a Negro slave, whom the soldiers spared out of mercy and because we had established that only force had kept them in danger. The enemy dead, therefore, were 150 volunteers, 32 inhabitants from the township of Gonzáles who had entered the fort two days before the assault under cover of darkness, and about 20 or so townspeople or merchants from the township of Béjar. [De la Peña included two documents (see *Rebelión de Texas*, appendix 9). The first, an excerpt from Santa Anna's official report of March 6, 1836, states that 600 Texans had been killed, among them Bowie and Travis, and that Mexican losses were 70 dead and 300 wounded, including 2 commanders and 23 officers. The second, Juan Andrade's tabulation of Mexican losses by rank and brigade, lists 8 officers dead and 18 wounded, 252 soldiers dead and 33 wounded [*a typo for 52 dead and 233 wounded, per General Andrade's list in Filisola document 2.6.1*], a total of 311.—*Ed.*]

2.9.2.   De la Peña, analysis, 1994.

Groneman, Bill. 1994. *Defense of a Legend: Crockett and the de la Peña Diary.* ix–xiii. Plano, TX: Wordware Publishing (Republic of Texas Press).

This book-length critique argues that the de la Peña diary is a forgery. Groneman's Introduction is presented here as a lead-in to an extended discussion in the Special Commentary for section 2.9. Three footnotes have not been included.

On October 18, 1975 I attended a book signing party in Rosengren's Book Store in San Antonio, Texas. The party was in honor of Carmen Perry, whose book had recently been published by Texas A & M University Press. The book was *With Santa Anna in Texas—A Personal Narrative of the Revolution by José Enrique de la Peña*, and it marked the culmination of eight years of work for Ms. Perry. It was the translation of the "diary," of de la Peña, an officer who allegedly took part in the Mexican campaign against Texas in 1835–36, and fought in the famous battle of the Alamo. Besides translating the account, Ms. Perry was also partly responsible for the acquisition of the original document by the University of Texas at San Antonio.

In the cool air, hushed tones, and polite banter of Rosengren's, it was difficult to imagine the storm of controversy that this book was causing in Texas history and how it would substantially affect every book and article to be written on the Texas Revolution and the Alamo for years to come. You see, the pleasant tan dust jacket of *With Santa Anna in Texas,* bearing an attractive illustration of the Alamo chapel, concealed a bombshell. The book ran for some 200 pages, but just one paragraph was a controversial one. This paragraph described the death of the legendary American frontiersman and former U.S. Congressman, David Crockett. According to de la Peña, Crockett did not actually die in combat during the Alamo battle, but was taken captive and then executed, minutes later, on the orders of the Mexican commander, Generalissimo Antonio López de Santa Anna. The paragraph reads:

[*Groneman here quotes from Perry the account of the execution of Crockett; see the text in the document 2.9.1.*]

This was heady stuff. Almost everyone knows of the Alamo or at least has a working knowledge of the story. The Alamo was the old Spanish mission in which Lieutenant Colonel William Barret Travis and his small band of Texans made the desperate last stand against a superior force of the Mexican army during the Texas Revolution. Over the years, the Alamo, more than any other battle in American history, has grown to be an almost sacred image, signifying patriotism, determination against overwhelming odds, and the value of sacrifice in the insurance of freedom. The defenders of the Alamo have been elevated to mythological proportions in our national psyche.

The most famous of all of the Alamo's defenders was David Crockett of Tennessee. Everyone from my generation knew that David (Davy) Crockett was "King of the Wild Frontier." We all grew up with the heroic image of him as portrayed by Fess Parker in the Walt Disney television series of the early 1950s. We were all slightly traumatized when Davy (Fess), after only three short episodes, faded from view while swinging his famous rifle, "Old Betsy," at the hordes of Mexican soldiers who were about to overwhelm him at the Alamo. Although we did not actually see him die on screen, we got the message. We were a pragmatic lot, we postwar "baby boomers." At any rate, Crockett went on to become the very symbol of American heroism. But now this! So what if the de la Peña account did not really say that Crockett did anything dishonorable. So what if he was just as dead whether he died while fighting or was executed. So what if there was nothing in the account which said that Crockett did not perform his duty right up until the end. There was just something wrong with it all. After all, the Alamo was the story of men going down fighting against overwhelming odds. It was not the story of men being executed by overwhelming odds. And Crockett was the ultimate symbol of the Alamo itself!

It did not take long for trouble to start. Ms. Perry began to receive crank phone calls and hate mail. She was harassed for the publication of *With Santa Anna,* and her only crime had been to translate from Spanish to English the words of someone else. On the other hand, she did get some support. The Movimiento Estudiantil Chicanos de Aytlan stood solidly behind her and praised her book for destroying long standing myths and legends by scholarly work. She also received the prestigious Summerfield G. Roberts award from the sons of the Republic of Texas. Later, she would have the satisfaction of seeing her book cited in many other works on the Alamo for years to come. In addition, Dan Kilgore, President of the Texas State Historical Association, would come out with his own book three years later, offering a number of "corroborating," witnesses to the de la Peña account.

The reaction to *With Santa Anna*, both positive and negative, is very interesting in light of the fact that it was not the first time that the De La Peña account appeared in book form. Twenty years earlier, in 1955, it had been published in Spanish, in Mexico City, by J. Sanchez Garza, under the title *La Rebelion de Texas—Manuscrito Inedito de 1836 por un Oficial de Santa Anna*. The account, even the infamous paragraph, had already been cited a number of times in books published in the U.S.

So why then was there such a sudden uproar over this account? A great deal has to do with the time and place. *La Rebelion de Texas* was published in Mexico and apparently achieved only limited circulation. Also, 1955 was the height of Crockett's popularity via Walt Disney, and nothing was about to change that for a while; 1975 was quite another matter. The image of Crockett clubbing away at hoards of swarthy men was not that attractive in 1975 after so many Americans had been "clubbed" by other hoards of swarthy men in Vietnam just a few years earlier. Military heroics, even legendary ones from the past, were not especially palatable, and at no other time in our history were we ever more susceptible to a revisionist look at ou[r] heroes. America was also still up to its neck in the Watergate scandal, and the fact that Crockett had served three terms as a U.S. Congressman from Tennessee did not help the matter. Suddenly, in 1975 it became easy to visualize him as a sly politician. It was a time which caused even the most ardent "baby boomers" to become cynics.

Well, for better or worse, the information was there. If de la Peña's account was credible, then even the biggest Crockett fan would have to accept the fact that Crockett was executed. After all, the account did not really tarnish Crockett's image. It only forced us to give up some of our legendary beliefs about him. It was a lesson in maturity as well as history. It would still be some time yet before other writers began to interpret the de la Peña account to mean that Crockett surrendered and then was guilty of some type of cowardice at the Alamo.

At any rate, the story grudgingly became part of the Alamo saga, and it seemed destined to remain as such, barring of course, the discovery of some new, unforeseen information to change things around again.

2.9.3.1.   De la Peña, supporting documents, 1836.

Borroel, Roger, trans. 1997a. *The Papers of Colonel José Enrique de la Peña: Selected Appendixes from His Diary, 1836–1839.* 19–20. East Chicago, IN: La Villita Publications.

A number of articles from the Garza 1955 Mexican edition of de la Peña or in the additional papers that form the De la Peña Papers at the CAH, which complement the diary quoted above, were translated in print by Roger Borroel starting in 1997. This testimonial by Col. Francisco Duque is the first of several following from this set. Borroel's footnotes, which give more context to the people or other documents, are not included in these transcripts. The source of this first document, translated from Garza (1955), is *El Mosquito Mexicano*, February 28, 1837.

ANNEX No. 3
Document III
July 11, 1836

FRANCISCO DUQUE, Colonel of the Toluca active battalion.

CERTIFY: That in the section of the first brigade that I was commanding at Béjar, I restored the battalions of the Zapadores, Aldama, and my own battalion. The lieutenant colonel of the army, Don José Enrique de la Peña discharged the function of his duties with much zeal and energy.

ALSO CERTIFY: That I was appointed to command the second attack column in the assault of the Alamo. I went to receive the final orders of the general-in-chief (Santa Anna), and I presented to him that although Peña was destined to be with the reserve column, I had so much confidence in him and desire[d] that he would accompany me in the attack. His Excellency consented to my request and Peña confirmed that it was a good idea.

He (de la Peña) advanced with the enthusiasm that is so characteristic of him, and he was very calm and cool at the head of the attacking column. When I was wounded in the vicinity of the enemy parapets, he was the only one of my assistants who was able to command in order to summon the leader who was appointed to succeed me.

Peña, then without fear of danger to himself, went from one end of the enemy line to the other extreme end to meet up with General Manuel Fernández Castrillón, who was coming with the rear guard of the reserve column. He (Peña) informed him, notified him, in time, that I would be out of combat because of my wound.

It was necessary to view all of the activity; the cannon fire, the rifle and gunfire that was happening all along the front, when de la Peña made the trip for the second time. In order to evaluate the merit that he acquire[d] in this memorable journey, I can never say enough about this gallant officer. And that, therefore, for the record, I agree with this, given in the City of Matamoros, July 11, of 1836.

FRANCISCO DUQUE
(Signature)

2.9.3.2. De la Peña, supporting documents, 1836.

Borroel, Roger, trans. 1997a. *The Papers of Colonel José Enrique de la Peña: Selected Appendixes from His Diary, 1836–1839.* 21–22. East Chicago, IN: La Villita Publications.

The source of this second document, translated from Garza (1955), also is *El Mosquito Mexicano*, February 28, 1837. It is a testimonial by Lt. Col. Pedro de Ampudia.

ANNEX No. 3
Document IV
June 22, 1836

PEDRO DE AMPUDIA, Lieutenant Colonel and General Commander of the artillery of the Army of Operations in Texas.

CERTIFY: That the captain, with the grade of lieutenant colonel, attached to the engineer corps, Don José Enrique de la Peña, in the deadly assault of the Alamo Fort, he did function as a[n] assistant to Don Francisco Duque, commander of one of the attacking columns. At the height of the strife, he went through and among the gunfire with the object to inform General Don Manuel Fernández Castrillón of his chiefs' (Duque) wound, so that he could replace him, he being the second in command. In accordance, he was already given the command earlier.

This young man (de la Peña) with bravery, climbed, in my sight, the palisade that formed part of the enclosure, and in the interior of the fort (the Alamo), he fulfill[ed] his duty like a good officer.

Furthermore, when we were crossing over the Guadalupe, Colorado, and Brazos Rivers, he worked, and assisted me in all of the hardships and toils with honorable perseverance. Because of his last contribution, by my orders with fifty-seven zapadores (engineers) they pulled out of the mud, the batteries (the artillery) that were stuck among the swamps. And it was during the rainy season among the small streams of the San Bernardo and the Atascocito Rivers.

Finally, his irresistible conduct, together, with his interesting services, Peña has lent these attributes to the campaign in Texas. In my judgement that I have form[ed] of him, he is very worthy of consideration and high regards of the Supreme Government and the classes that make up our society.

General quarter in Matamoros, June 22nd of 1836.

PEDRO DE AMPUDIA
(Signature)

Note [*by Borroel*]—These documents reveal the fact that de la Peña's permanent rank was captain. It seems that when he was assigned to the Zapadores unit, he was give the brevet rank of lieutenant colonel, that he is so well known by. This type of administrative promotion is common among the armies of the world.

2.9.3.3. De la Peña, supporting documents, 1836.

Borroel, Roger, trans. 1997a. *The Papers of Colonel José Enrique de la Peña: Selected Appendixes from His Diary, 1836–1839.* 23. East Chicago, IN: La Villita Publications.

The source of this third document, translated from Garza (1955), also is *El Mosquito Mexicano*, February 28, 1837. It is a testimonial by Col. Agustin Amat.

ANNEX No. 3
Document V—August 17, 1836

The citizen Agustin Amat, colonel of the army, lieutenant colonel and commander of the Zapadores battalion.

CERTIFY: That the lieutenant colonel of the army, Captain Don José Enrique de la Peña, was in command of a section of the force which Colonel Duque was commanding in Bejar. And who carried out his commission with energy and zeal which is so well known about this officer. In the deadly assault of the Alamo Fort on March the 6th of the present year, he was one of the ones that had distinguished himself the most in the attacking column that was commanded by Colonel Duque. He ran two times to the front where the fire was the deadliest in order to communicate an important order. And I can attest to his courage that he has within himself. For he set the pattern of the attack and helped save victims (his fellow soldiers in the attack), the kinds of things that happen in the confusion of an attack.

ALSO CERTIFY: That in the section he was commanding at the Brazos River, he carried out with the same energy, the majority of his orders, and passing by the river where it was very difficult and hard, they (de la Peña and his men) had many fatigues. He also worked with perseverance and constancy. And in the retreat, he helped the commander of the artillery (Ampudia, see Document IV) to pull out the artillery pieces that had been left in the gun pits, with 57 engineers, that I had to leave. And for the record, I agree with this report, given and presented in this City of Matamoros, August 17th of 1836.

AGUSTIN AMAT
(Signature)

2.9.3.4.   De la Peña, supporting documents, 1836.

Borroel, Roger, trans. 1997b. *The Papers of Colonel José Enrique de la Peña: The Last of His Appendixes*, Vol. 2. 31, 33–34. East Chicago, IN: La Villita Publications.

The source of this document, also translated from Garza (1955), is *El Mosquito Mexicano*, September 30, 1836. It is a published statement by José Faustino Moro, first surgeon of the Mexican Army.

ANNEX NO. 11

Gentlemen, editors of the Mercury.—It would be a favour if you would insert in your esteem[*ed*] periodical the official communications and the related document, by whose favour, I will always acknowledge your gracious service.—Jose Faustino Moro.

[*The document includes a letter from an official named Pedro del Villar questioning the conditions of the health services in Béjar, and a longer response from Moro, which includes the following.*]

At the end of April, the commission that was entrusted to me was already concluding. However, I soon found myself not knowing what to do, since no one had order[*ed*] me to communicate afterwards with anybody. Yet, my desire was leading me to San Antonio de Bejar, where I believed I would be useful. I cross[*ed*] without help of any kind, a desert of a hundred or so miles, flooded with savages . . . with the intern I had with me.

I arrive[*d*] in Bejar where I was shocked to find out what all had occurred there. Without having any medical resouces [*sic*] for a bloody hospital, an assault was given (the battle of the Alamo) and there were more than two hundred wounded men as a result of that battle. There wasn't even a place to lay them decently and I soon found myself looking for space and rooms. Furthermore, the infected, wounded patients went walking around and wandering from place to place, thereby increasing their sufferings. And this is only natural, upon reflection, that this would happen in their lamentable condition & situation.

The gentlemen, Hurtado, Reyes and the interns that came with them, did not arrive in San Antonio till many days after the battle. And Mr. Arroyo had exhausted almost all of the medical resouces, what little there was, that I had left him in December of the previous year.

There was no bandages left, neither could he make any because there was no lint for dressing the wounds, for the cures of the wounded. Nothing had been prepare[*d*], and there was a lack of everything that was needed for the wounded. He had order[*ed*] medical supplies many times, but always receive[*d*] a negative answer.

Lastly, the bandages that they gave were a sort of cotton, pernicious, as Your Excellency knows, to the wounded.

Among those that we came across were two leaders and 20 or so officers, to whom not a single intern was able to attend them. Who is to be blamed in the Military Sanitary Corp or is it them that was suppose[d] to put all things in order?

[*Moro continues with more general information on the medical situation in the Texas campaign.*]

2.9.3.5. Andrade, report, 1836.

Borroel, Roger, trans. 1997c. *After the Battle of the Alamo: Documents Published by General Juan José Andrade on the Evacuation of San Antonio de Béjar, Texas, May 1836.* 11. East Chicago, IN: La Villita Publications.

This is not, strictly speaking, a de la Peña document, but it is strongly linked with the related material in the prior documents and thus is included here. Borroel translated this request for supplies from Andrade (1836).

—Document Number 2—
First Request for Supplies
General Andrade to General Francisco Vital Fernández,
General of the Departments of Nuevo León & Tamaulipas

The Most Excellency, Sir, the President General had left this city in order to be able to be at the head of the forces that are marching upon the enemy. In this place they left the wounded and the sick who have no medical resources or supplies. They have consumed so much resources and all of the medicines that you will not find anymore medical supplies here. Therefore I see that this is a matter for Your Excellency in order to prepare a set of rooms for new supplies, and I have requested medical supplies which should consist of the necessary articles without omitting (ilas?) and brandy, and vegetables, proper food for the sick.

A physician of this [*sic*] would be able to provide said medical supplies in his concept of quality and quantity with the thought in mind that there are 150 wounded and 40 sick soldiers to take care of.

Your Excellency, has lent a very praiseworthy service to the nation by his servants in particular. And above all, with humanity, with friendly influence and with badly needed resources, and without them, there would probably be many more victims.

This occasion now gives me the opportunity to complement [*sic*], to offer you my respects.

God and Liberty. City of San Antonio de Béjar, Department of Texas, Mexico, April 10, 1836.—Juan José Andrade.—Sir, Commissary. General of the Departments of Nuevo León and Tamaulipas. (b)

2.9.3.6.   De la Peña, supporting documents, 1836.

Borroel, Roger, trans. 1998a. *The J. Sanchez Garza Introduction to the Rebellion of Texas: The Diary of Lt. Col. José Enrique de la Peña*. 24–25. East Chicago, IN: La Villita Publications.
This is an excerpt from Miguel A. Sanchez Lamego, *Notes for the History of the Engineer Branch in Mexico: History of the Zapadores Battalion* (in Spanish), Vol. 1, Secretary of the National Defense, Mexico City, D.F., 1943. It is part of a history called by Lamego "The Roll Call of the Zapadores Battalion," which he said never had more than two hundred men and officers. There is some earlier history prior to this excerpt.

For the Texas campaign, the personnel that made up the battalion were: Lt. Col. Agustin Amat, commanding; one first assistant, Romulo Diaz la Vega (this was the man who had ordered the Zapadores into the fight at the Alamo); one captain, Jose Maria Ricoy; three lieutenants: Primo Rafael de la Rosa (wounded in the arm at the same battle), Miguel Areizaga and Jose Enrique de la Peña (this last one was attached to the staff); four second lieutenants: Jose Maria Almaraz, Jose Maria Garduno, Juan Alzugaray (who was wounded in the head by cannon fire at said battle) and Jose Maria Torres (he was killed after valiantly planting the Mexican colors during the height of the battle), and 191 troopers. From this personnel, six troopers were left behind in the cities of Queretaro and Aguascalientes . . . leaving with [*them*] two chiefs, eight officers and 185 troopers.

In fact, on the 18th of December, Lt. Col. Amat had sent to the General Director of Engineers, a report on the state of the force. The original document is a part of the records, and it is label[*ed*], D/481.3/1895, from Archivo de Cancelados de la Secretaria de la Defensa Nacional . . . with the following personnel listed in this troop: 6 first sergeants, 10 second sergeants, 18 corporals, 18 band members, and 133 troopers.

The General Juan Jose Andrade, in a letter directed to the Minister of War, dated from the city of Matamoros, July the 8th of 1836, (document s/n.—national service—with a label, D/481.3/1150 of the Archivo de Cancelados de la Secretaria de la Defensa Nacional) in reference to this structure (the Alamo):

". . . it is just a corral, badly made in order to protect the unsheltered men and horses of the Presidial Companies and to save them from surprise attacks from the barbaric Indians on the frontier. . . ."

[*Borroel here gives a quote from Santa Anna with a matching description of the Alamo.*]

—THE DEAD AND WOUNDED OF THE ZAPADORES BATTALION—
—ALAMO—
MARCH 6, 1836

ZAPADORES—dead: 1 chief (leader), 2 trooper, total 3 kia's.
wounded: 3 officers, 21 troopers, total 24 wia's.
Overall total: 27 casualties, killed & wounded.

The three officers wounded are: The Lt. Col. Jose Enrique de la Pena, bruised caused by being hit; the lieutenant with the grade of captain, Primo Rafael de la Rose, he received a profound wound in the arm, and Lieutenant Juan Alzucaray, who was gravely wounded in the head by grape-shot.

[*The document continues with a roll call of the Zapadores Battalion in 1840, at the time of an award of the "Cross of Honor" to the survivors.*]

2.9.3.7.   De la Peña, supporting documents, 1836.

Borroel, Roger, trans. 1999a. *Mexican Battalion Series at the Alamo*. Vol. 1. 15, 18–22. East Chicago, IN: La Villita Publications.

Portions of this account have also been published by McDonald and Young in the Fall 1998 issue of *Journal of the Alamo Battlefield Association*, and in 1999 by Huffines. Borroel also included facsimiles of some pages of the original document. The original is in the De la Peña Papers, CAH.

THE ACTIVE BATTALION OF THE SAN LUIS POTOSI
1st Division of the Operation Against Texas
Itinerary of the Daily Journey Made by the Expressed Corp (452 men) from the City of San Luis Potosi, starting on the 17th day of November, 1835.

[*The account gives brief descriptions of daily activities up to the arrival in Béjar on February 23.*]

23,   At Bejar (San Antonio) The general Ramirez having advanced himself ahead with 100 cavalry in the morning, at which hour the enemy was unaware of our arrival. The rest of the Division came between 12 and 1. But the enemy, having sounded the alarm, retreated themselves to their fortifications of the Alamo. There, they had 15 pieces of artillery, but not all were mounted in a state of services on account of a lack of (cannon) balls . . . a 16 and other 8 (pounder—the size of a[n] artillery piece) bearing at the population (at the city of San Antonio). After the Division had rested a half-hour behind a hill at a half-mile distance, the General-President mounted on a horse, and started towards the city with his General Staff (E.M. in Spanish); 3 (three) companies of cazadores (light infantry) commanded by the Colonel Morales; 3 (three) of grenadiers, commanded by the Colonel Romero; two mortar pieces; the cavalry of General Ramirez; he ordered the rest of the Division to march at the orders of General Ventura Mora, to the rancho (s/b mission) of Concepción. The president, near the outskirts of Bejar, ordered the Colonel Minon, with a half of cazadores to take the Church, ignorant of it being abandoned.

At the entrance of the column at the front, a shot of grapeshot was fire[d] at them from the 16-pounder piece. The artillery commander, Ampudia, was commanded to set up the howitzers, and fire four grenades, which made them (the Alamo defenders) raise up a white flag, which ended the fire. And there came one with an official communication from Bowie (in the manuscript, Bowie is spelled, something like, "Boumarie".) to the commander of the invading troops of Texas, desiring an agreement. The president ordered an answer of words (a verbal reply) that he would not deal with bandits, not giving them [a] choice but to surrender unconditionally. He then ordered the placement of the troops, that they eat and rest, and then ordered back to Bejar all of the troops that had marched to Concepcion.

24,   Inscribed in Bejar. His Excellency arrived at nine o'clock in the morning, he then ordered the distribution of shoes to the preferred companies, in his sight. He then directed, at once, a frontal advance against the Alamo, and started the firing which had been suspended since the previous afternoon. Placed, a battery of two 8 pounders, and a howitzer, and they began to bombard the fortifications of the enemy. The enemy answered with fire, but was not able to cause any "damage", (the word is really, "desgracia" i.e. misfortune). Inventories of the stock of the Americans were taken. At 11 (eleven) in the morning, His Excellency marched out with the cavalry to reconnoiter the area.

25,   Inscribed in Bejar. At 9:30, His Excellency presented himself at the battery, and ordered to march, to the other side of the river, the column of chasseurs and the battalion, Matamoras, he himself following them. Our soldiers fought within pistol range against the parapets (of the Alamo). There was wounded a soldier of the 3rd (company) named, Epitacio Hernandes. The Division had two dead and six wounded. During the night, construction was taken to protect the line that had been made at La Villita, at the orders of Colonel Morales.

26,

27,

28,   (On these days) Nothing of note happen[ed]. The artillery fire, and the rifle fire have been going on this day, satisfied that the objective has been made, without misfortune to any part of the Division.

29,   Inscribed in Bejar. The siege of the Alamo continues. At 7 (seven) thirty on this night, the enemy killed a soldier of the First company ———— (of the San Luis Battalion), Secundino Alvarez, who had moved close to the Alamo on the orders of the President.

March 1, 1836 As usual.

2,   Inscribed in Bejar. The chasseur, Trinidad Delgado, drowned in the river. The siege of the Alamo continues.

3, 4, and 5,   Inscribed in Bejar. The siege continued with out anything of note in these three days. On the third day, the Zapadores, the Aldama, and the Toluca battalions arrived.

—THE BATTLE OF THE ALAMO—

6,   Inscribed in Bejar. At 5:35 in the morning, the bugle sounded
by the orders of the General-President, sounding the agreed signal for the 4
(four) attack columns to began the assault at the Alamo. The fire, the attack and
the defense, was obstinate, it lasted 20 minutes, and at 8:30 in the morning, not
one enemy exists. At 10, the troops began to file back for Bejar. Afterwards, they
began to gather the dead and wounded, resulting in 230 enemy in the class of
the "primeras", (the sense is, the enemy that were killed were of decent quality). And among them were the ringleaders; Boumarie (sic) (s/b Bowie), the
commander of the Alamo; Trevis (sic) (s/b Travis), his Second, and Crookr (sic)
(s/b Crockett) having gotten inside three nights before (the original manuscript
text being 'Crookr habia lagrado meterse tres noches antes'); not any wounded
or prisoners.

************MEXICAN MARTYRS AT THE ALAMO************
Of the Mexican troops . . . dead and wounded; 21 officers, and 295 men
from the troops (the total Mexican casualty count, according to this unit log
book is, 316 personnel).

ROLL CALL OF THE SAN LUIS POTOSI BATTALION
[*An explicit list by rank and individual name is given, totaling nine dead and
thirty-seven wounded. Borroel notes that Andrade's list, quoted by Filisola in 2.6.1, no
doubt used this one for the line of the San Luis Potosi Battalion, which is why they
match exactly. The document goes on to list the various columns, the commanders, and
the sides against which the assault was made—basically the same type of information in
the attack order of Santa Anna. There are not any further specific incidences of the fight
itself. The daily log continues through the Texas campaign until June 15, when the San
Luis Potosi Battalion had retreated to Matamoros, Mexico.*]

Commentary

Sánchez, Labastida Plat, and de la Peña (2.7–2.9)

The journal of Sánchez, the Labastida plat, and the de la Peña account are, as a
group, the most informative documents from the Mexican side. They came from officers who were high-ranking enough to see the broader picture of the events of the
Alamo, but not senior enough to be caught up in the accusations and blame their
superiors faced after the battle of San Jacinto, and therefore their accounts are not a
product of self-justification. In addition, the Sánchez journal and the Labastida plat
appear to have been near contemporaneous with the events described, and the de la
Peña account to have been written soon after.

All three documents, being from individuals in important military positions, have numerous military details. Only a few comments will be made on these here, and details are reviewed in the Special Commentaries following 5.2.

The Sánchez journal (2.7.2, 2.7.3) was written by an important officer with an independent viewpoint. His writings bring into focus what must have been the attitudes and patriotism of an officer of his rank, and reveal the dilemma of a patriotic soldier who sees critical faults in his superiors and in the management of the army.

Of equally high value is his map of the Alamo (2.7.1), which serves as a check on the military details of the siege and fall. It also makes a good complement to the more official Labastida plat (2.8.1, 2.8.2). This Alamo map is one of two in the journal; the second is more polished and likely was reworked from the one presented here (per Schoelwer, 5.2.4).

A careful, documented study of Sánchez was made by Jackson and Ivey (2001), who discussed the confusion among earlier writers regarding his name. In full, it is José Juan Sánchez Navarro y Estrada. Often Sánchez Navarro has been used, and variants in usage led to some confusion among earlier writers about whether the same individual was being referred to. Jackson and Ivey made the telling point that Sánchez himself signed his name without the "Navarro," and typically this book follows their recommendation. They also made a detailed study of the map and the source for Sánchez's early view of the Alamo, including an update of Schoelwer's study (5.2.4). The authenticity of the Sánchez documents is also supported by a review in some detail.[1]

The de la Peña account (2.9.1) is the most detailed narrative from the Mexican side. Carmen Perry noted in her introduction that de la Peña was a lieutenant colonel in the Sapper Battalion, so he had an important perspective on the siege and the final battle. The inclusion of the Travis letter shows that de la Peña's account was written after the fact, when he had other sources available. The extent of details demonstrates, however, that he must have kept a detailed diary at the time. What is most unusual is the personal and even psychological perspective he gave of the battle, writing of the men's emotions and fears, such as their "painful meditations" as they waited to start the attack, and their excitement and self-denying enthusiasm once the battle began. It seems more like a journalist's narration than that of a lieutenant colonel. The description of the confusion, plans gone awry, and difficulties of the actual battle has to be a much more realistic picture than most versions written of any battle.

De la Peña provided a different picture of Travis and the other defenders than in other accounts, depicting them as hoping for quick relief with a promise to surrender if help didn't come. A similar statement, which could be from the same source, was also made by Filisola (2.6.1). De la Peña cited Dickinson and Joe as the sources for this report, but this was not supported by any of their accounts, nor does it seem likely, considering Travis's expressed attitudes. Regarding the promise to surrender, perhaps de la Peña read something of what he wanted to hear into their accounts. The tone in the hope of reinforcements sounds a bit like that in parts of Travis's last speech per Rose. Could that speech be reflected here? If so, de la Peña's only sources would have been Dickinson and/or Joe. De la Peña was unusual among the Mexican writers in explicitly citing survivors as sources, and with his journalistic flair, he was one Mexican officer who might have been genuinely interested in their accounts.

Another different picture is that of David Crockett, "the naturalist," who was not perceived as a direct fighting participant in this account. De la Peña's report of Crockett surrendering after the fall is another confusing and highly controversial subject for special review, which is done in conjunction with the discussion of forgeries (Special Commentary following), the deaths of the Texas leaders, and the subject of casualties (Special Commentaries following 5.2). He also notes the leap of a defender with a small son, without identifying the story with Dickinson (section 1.2). De la Peña, like many sources throughout this work, used both personal observations and second-hand material for his narrative. My belief is that his personal observations are highly relevant, whereas the secondhand material, such as the paragraph on Crockett, might have less significance.

The section on the Alamo ends with a strategic, almost philosophical, overview of the actions at the Alamo. De la Peña was not interested in battles for their own sake, nor the squandering of men and resources without justifiable cause. Like Santa Anna (2.1.2), however, he placed much blame on Sesma for not taking the unprepared Bejar and the Alamo on the first day.

The remarkable fact that a number of important Alamo documents have remained unpublished or untranslated until the last few years has been already noted. An exceptional example of such material is the collection of documents in the 1955 Spanish edition by Garza and also now in the de la Peña papers. Once Perry had published the journal, the significance of the broad collection of additional material was largely overlooked until Roger Borroel started publishing translations in 1997. The next group of documents (2.9.3.1–2.9.3.7) represents the items of specific interest to Alamo studies, but these are only highlights from the abundant material of more general interest to the history of the Texas Revolution.

The first three of this group (2.9.3.1–2.9.3.3) are testimonials by senior officers on behalf of de la Peña. Indirectly, they give a sense of the violence and confusion of the attack. They also show that de la Peña was being modest in his diary when describing in third person the climbing of the palisade wall of the Alamo, when he was in fact one of the leading participants. One also wonders how many other such testimonials and incidental accounts of the battle might still be found in Mexico.

Several of these accounts (2.9.3.4–2.9.3.7) discuss the personnel and casualties in the Mexican Army, which are considered in the Special Commentary following 5.2. The account from the San Luis Potosi Battalion (2.9.3.7) complements the daily log of other sources such as Almonte (2.2.1). It is probable, as seen by comparing the entries for some days, such as February 24 and 25, that de la Peña used this to complement his own narrative. There are no obvious signs of this account being invented, such as the narrator giving himself a central role in the action, and the narrative adds some perspectives "from the trenches." The account supports the deadly reputation of the defenders' rifles by noting the wounded and killed before the final attack. A few features are strange, however. For the entry for February 23, which counts the artillery inside the Alamo, it's a little hard to believe—though not impossible—that such information would have been known in the Mexican camp as soon as the siege started. Such intelligence might have been obtainable from townspeople, though whether it would have reached a more junior officer is questionable. Another item is the knowledge of Crockett, which, if this story is true, makes this the only source from the Mexican Army to take Crockett's identity and significance for granted. Furthermore, the comment that Crockett entered the Alamo three nights before contradicts the notion that the information had come from townspeople, who would have seen Crockett in the weeks prior to the siege.

In addition to these documents directly related to the Alamo, there are a number of others in the de la Peña papers that interested readers and students of the Texas Revolution should consider.

Briefly quoted at the end of the the de la Peña diary (2.9.1) are a few of his criticisms on the leadership and planning in the Mexican Army for the Texas campaign. Everything in de la Peña's writings indicates that he was a very patriotic and professional Mexican officer, and the fiasco of the Texas campaign left him highly critical of the senior leaders and their tactics, such as the executions of prisoners, actions of Santa Anna and Sesma, and Filisola's abandonment of Texas after the defeat and capture of Santa Anna at San Jacinto. He was strongly supportive of Urrea and might have been a key contributor to the Urrea account (4.4.3.1).[2] Concerning the opposite side of the war, he was also sympathetic to Fannin and Ward.[3]

De la Peña's main criticism of Santa Anna's conduct at the Alamo was that the general precipitated the final assault because he did not want the fortress to surrender. He also felt that nothing would have been lost by waiting a couple of days for heavy artillery to arrive that could pound the Alamo into submission. Considering that Santa Anna's uncompromising demand for unconditional surrender made the possibility remote that Travis would surrender, the critique does not seem likely to have been based on any facts known at the time. On the other hand, sources (e.g., 2.2.1) state that the debate of March 4 discussed waiting for additional siege guns to arrive—and clearly the Alamo walls could not have withstood much heavy cannon fire. Thus this critique of Santa Anna's impatience does seem a good point to consider, though not necessarily for the first reason given by de la Peña.

The more general criticism of overall mismanagement of the logistics for the army appears in several of the Mexican accounts (e.g., 2.9.3.4).[4] Unlike such critics as Caro (2.5.1) and Urrea (4.4.3.1), de la Peña goes into considerable detail in reviewing the actions of the senior officers, and therefore gives modern scholars an abundance of material that otherwise likely would have remained unknown. One is struck by First Surgeon Moro's "not knowing what to do" and showing up in Bejar with no specific or stronger orders than that it was, as he said, "where I believed I would be useful" (also 2.9.3.4). This is a general subject that deserves much more attention than can be given here, and the interested reader is referred to all of de la Peña's papers, now translated by Roger Borroel, to explore.

---

1. Groneman (1994) and Lindley (2000) attacked the authenticity of Sánchez as part of a broader effort to challenge the de la Peña account following. The Lindley critique was

well answered by both Zaboly (2001) and Ivey (2001). A discussion of the validity and chronology of Sánchez is also in Davis 1997, 14.
2. Also see Borroel 1998a, vi.
3. E.g., Borroel 1997d, 13. Urrea is also sympathetic in Castañeda 1928, e.g., 235.
4. Also see the Commentary to 2.1; Cós document 2.4.1; Perry's introduction to de la Peña for much more that is not quoted here; Borroel 1997c, 12–15, for an unquoted report to Tornel by Andrade; Borroel 1999b for Lieutenant Colonel de la Portilla's perspective; and Barnard document 4.3.10. DePalo (1997) has published a major and very relevant study of the Mexican Army in general, which includes vivid details on the Texas campaign.

   Castañeda 1928 also gives considerable information and argument on the effectiveness of the opposing armies in the claims and counterclaims of the senior leaders, including Urrea 4.3.1.1 and Tornel 4.3.1.2. For example, Filisola (Castañeda, 190) was very impressed with differences in the Texans' ability with rifles versus his Mexican troops, who had never fired one! Even Santa Anna (Castañeda, 23, 30, 76–78) gives implied support to this point by blaming Cós for not sending him *picked* (emphasis Castañeda's) troops—i.e., trained—rather than ordinary soldiers. More violently argued is the state of morale and capabilities of the army after San Jacinto, especially Filisola versus Urrea (e.g., Castañeda, 178–79, 265–66).

Special Commentary

Forgeries and Historical Documents (2.9)

Because of his detailed and personal reflections, de la Peña's account gives us more insight into the siege and battle for the Alamo than any other account from the Mexican side. Several of its significant points are discussed in the preceding Commentary. Furthermore, his account covers the entire campaign in Texas, so it is of more general significance as well to all students of the Texas Revolution. This document has extraordinary value, *provided it is authentic.*

   Author Bill Groneman published in 1994 his book *Defense of a Legend: Crockett and the de la Peña Diary,* attacking the account on this very point. The fraudulent production of source documents was briefly considered regarding the Crockett and Millsap documents (1.6.1, 1.6.2). But the authenticity of such an extensive and potentially informative source as the de la Peña account is a far more serious matter, and an examination of Groneman's arguments and the issues raised is merited. Groneman's work is therefore the centerpiece of this special commentary.

   One of the first questions Groneman addressed is to what extent we should even care if the de la Peña material is authentic. A considerable part of the Groneman discussion concerns the paragraph describing the possible execution of David Crockett. He notes, "The defenders of the Alamo have been elevated to mythological proportions in our national psyche," and so a death by execution rather than in battle could be a blow to that psyche.[1] This is evidenced by the shameful fact that Carmen Perry, the translator and editor of the first English publication of the central account, received crank calls and hate mail because the Crockett death in de la Peña did not match some popular conceptions (2.9.2). The reactions of these "crazies," as Groneman described them, naturally should not be of relevance in evaluating a historic event. Nor should a fragile psyche, racism, or conformity or nonconformity with accepted opinions be in themselves relevant.[2] The point is to recognize that emotionalism can be a component of studying and drawing conclusions about a popularly engaging event. This is certainly one such event.

As the Crockett death scene is only one paragraph of an entire book, further discussion of this paragraph is reserved for the Special Commentary 5.2. A number of additional points by Groneman relating to the specifics of the story of Crockett's death are included as part of that discussion. My perspective is that a work of such scale as de la Peña's should not stand or fall on the basis of such a limited excerpt, and therefore the two issues of what happened to Crockett in particular and whether de la Peña is a valid source in general properly can be separated. This commentary will focus on general issues and questions valuable in regarding the authenticity of source documents, while in effect using the de la Peña account and Groneman's critiques as illustrations of the broader principles.

I want to make my conclusions, and potential bias, clear from the start. I consider some of Groneman's arguments very weak or invalid, and accept the authenticity of the de la Peña account. Serious efforts and more exhaustive analysis by other scholars discussed below have confirmed this conclusion for many—though apparently not for Groneman. But others of his arguments are quite strong, and his basic issue that the validity of such a document requires careful consideration is correct. Whether or not this account is authentic, the additional textual analyses discussed below are worthwhile, and the general concerns and indicators of authenticity have relevance for other such sources. In short, Groneman asked the right questions, regardless of any shortcomings in his answers.

There are some useful overview questions and issues to be raised that do not give specific weight to arguments either pro or con on the authenticity of this particular account.

The first point to consider is the acceptance of the de la Peña material as authoritative. Groneman rightly stated that justification is called for when an account is considered "the best" or "the most reliable."[3] He asserted that this was not done for the de la Peña account, and I would agree that a careful, detailed study of the entire work remains to be done.

Additional questions concern the identity of the author and whether it is reasonable that he could or would have written such a work. Since 1994, various documents on de la Peña's career have begun to be reviewed and in some cases translated. A summary of the appendixes to the original publication (in Spanish) of portions of de la Peña in Garza (1955) is given by Groneman.[4] These indicate, if nothing else, the complexities of a career in the Mexican Army of the 1820s and 1830s.[5] The other aspect of the authorship question is the purpose of the author. Specifically, is it reasonable that an officer like de la Peña would have written a piece that is so critical of his sponsor and senior officer?[6] Some might say no and therefore question the authorship of the account on this basis. This potential criticism, however, carries much less weight when one sees that de la Peña is quite moderate compared with Caro's diatribe (2.5.1).

Another question is whether this was a daily diary or an after-the-fact account. The extent of day-to-day details implies some sort of diary. On the other hand, there are items that appear to have been written later, including a copy of Travis's letter of February 24, which wouldn't be known on the Mexican side until much later, and a reference to an account of Urrea published in 1838.[7] Of particular interest is an 1839 document of de la Peña's that talks about the execution of defenders but does not mention Crockett.[8] The central question is whether de la Peña's account was based on a diary, with inclusions from other sources a little later. Or were such inclusions from a period later than de la Peña, therefore indicating a forgery? For example, does the exact wording of Travis's message come from a contemporary source or one much later?[9]

In considering possible sources for de la Peña, another caution is necessary. Other documents that may seem to validate de la Peña's account, such as those from Castañeda, Almonte, Andrade, or Loranca, might actually have been source material for a forger.[10]

There are several discussions or arguments used by Groneman, however, that I consider exceptionally weak. First, the Groneman book is to a large extent a single-issue discourse. The issue to him is Crockett's death. As the title *Defense of a Legend* indicates, he seems to believe that the account given by de la Peña—more specifically, one paragraph of the entire book—requires a defense on behalf of Davy Crockett by invalidating the entire work. The question becomes whether the discussion was driven by the desire to know what happened or to simply defend a preconception. Interested readers are referred to his book to make up their own minds.

Groneman seems to consider it highly suspicious that de la Peña's account might not be an actual, spontaneous diary, but used some later-published information to round out the story.[11] Why this is important evidence of fraud is not made clear, at least to this reader. I am left wondering how de la Peña's possible use of such a technique is more questionable on this point than, say, Winston Churchill's multivolume history of World War II, which uses a similar style.

Groneman also claimed that the de la Peña account has misinformation that is "staggering, especially when it focuses on the Alamo," but the items so identified are not unreasonably misinformed. Some examples are the labeling of the Alamo defenders as pirates; the account of Travis's death contradicting Joe's version; Evans being given as the commander of the Alamo artillery—in fact, that Evans was mentioned at all, when he was only noted "in books years *after* the battle"; an incorrect number of survivors (two, "an elderly lady and a negro slave"); and the fact that Crockett is referred to as a casual traveler in Texas, in contrast to Travis's letters.[12]

It is immediately apparent—based on other available documents—that these points were not misinformation from the contemporary Mexican point of view. First, only a few defenders were considered legal immigrants, and the balance were perceived as pirates as per Santa Anna (2.1.1.1, 2.1.1.6, 2.1.1.11, and the proclamation of February 17 in 2.10.1 as well as in de la Peña's account). Second, only if de la

Peña's account of Travis's death matched Joe's (1.3.4)—an account highly unlikely to be available to a Mexican officer—would there be cause for suspicion. Third and fourth, Evans was given as the "master of ordnance" who tried to blow up the powder magazine in the *Telegraph and Texas Register* of March 24, 1836 (4.1.1)—obviously not long after the fact. Fifth, the actual number of survivors—approximately twenty, as Groneman stated—was only determined a century later by the foremost Alamo scholar (1.10.1). *Only* if a (reputed) near-contemporary source differed from (loosely) identifying Susanna Dickinson and Joe—the only two survivors commonly noted at the time—should we wonder if after-the-fact knowledge was being used. Finally, Crockett's role in Texas and the Alamo as described by Travis could not have been known to anyone in the Mexican Army (marginally excepting Almonte, who was the only known officer to have spent significant time in the United States prior to the Texas Revolution). The main point of all this is that the sources referenced in my counterexamples here are commonly available, and the fact that Groneman drew his conclusions without accounting for them indicates that his analysis is incomplete.

This is further reinforced in a chapter questioning the validity of the Sánchez Navarro account, an elevation of the Alamo attributed to Sánchez, and a picture of Travis.[13] In these cases, the scholars who made the documents available or understandable—Hunnicutt (2.7.2) and Schoelwer (5.2.4)—are cited, but there is no analysis of why their acceptance of these documents was wrong.[14] Readers do not learn why one person's opinion (Groneman's) should supersede those of the researchers who put the effort into presenting or analyzing the material in the first place.

An exceptional example is Groneman's rejection of the Zuber/Rose story.[15] This is necessary, from his viewpoint, because Zuber is another source for the possibility that Crockett was executed. Groneman treated the story of Travis's line just as any scholar would have prior to 1940—and before the contributions of Robert Blake, whom he simply ignored. The Rose documents (section 1.8) should make Blake's importance clear, and the portion of any analysis that ignores—some fifty years later—the significance of these discoveries or Blake's contributions must be rejected as inadequate and incomplete.

There is a much broader, subtler, and deeper problem with this type of criticism as represented by Groneman: the imposition of a double standard. In any debate or legal case, a consistent set of standards should be applied to both sides of a reasoned argument. But what is left if the standards applied to critique one side of the argument also make the other side fail? In the case of the Alamo story, secondhand newspaper accounts and long-after-the-fact "interviews" form the backbone of what is known of the events. Groneman makes piecemeal arguments that such sources are too deficient. However, essentially the only materials directly relating to the battle in this *Alamo Reader* that meet such stringent criteria are Travis's letters, Santa Anna's orders, and perhaps Almonte's diary, though this also has evidence of later additions. Groneman sets standards for source material that are too high for the Alamo sources; practically none of the available documents would clear his bar. By these same standards, Groneman would be left with essentially no documents to support his case either, and the best he could say is that little can be said on the Alamo and *nothing* on

Crockett's death. This applying of a double standard, depending on whether the evidence supports or does not support an author's arguments, should be watched for when reading and evaluating any author's conclusions.

Yet Groneman also made strong points on the validity of historical documents, and his points on this general issue should be—and subsequently have been—taken seriously.

The first is that false copies of known authentic documents, such as fake printings of the Texas Declaration of Independence, while they hurt investors who buy such material, do not significantly distort the study of history.[16] Forgeries of manuscripts, letters, or other such source materials that affect our perceptions of history are much more serious. "Over the years, these documents, with little or no provenance, have been regularly cited in historical books and articles, and history has actually been altered due to them."[17] Thus there is a major difference between the Millsap letter (1.6.2)—which would add color but not change the history of the Alamo—and the de la Peña account. The latter is significant enough to become a fundamental part of, rather than an adjunct to, history. Groneman is quite correct in raising concerns that such a document be scrutinized more carefully.

The next point is whether there is a reasonable possibility of forgery, and if so, by whom. Of printed Texas documents, there are examples now known of such forgeries.[18] That a modern forger might have tackled such a manuscript on the scale of the de la Peña account is seriously considered, and a potential forger is identified in John Laflin, who forged Jean Laffite material. Laflin also might have forged the Millsap letter, and therefore the possibility of a more ambitious forgery is raised. Any similarities between the Laffite forgeries and the de la Peña diary must be seriously considered.[19] This was eventually addressed as part of a 2001 study by David Gracy, discussed later in this commentary.

A study of the narration itself might give indications as to the validity of the document—the sort of consideration that allowed us to reject the reputed Crockett account (1.6.1) and the Candelaria stories (section 1.9). An example given by Groneman, which is not demonstrated in the translated selection given here, is an apparent change in the original Spanish of the Alamo account from first to third person.[20] The question this raises is whether that whole section is an insertion. But would it be a forged insertion into an authentic account, an authentic insertion account into a forgery, an authentic insertion (possibly composed at a different time) into an authentic account or a forgery into a forgery? A careful study of other internal indicators, such as the handwriting, the paper itself, watermarks, and the physical condition, is also important.[21] (These were also examined in the study by Gracy.)

Perhaps the most important point of all, and properly a concern in the case of the de la Peña account, is the provenance of a manuscript. Where has the document been since its creation? Is there any independent indication of the existence of the document? For de la Peña at the time of translation by Perry, the provenance was unknown before Garza 1955.[22] The Texas archivist Michael Green is noted to have reservations, "if for no other reason than the considerable vacuum in the provenance of the item."[23] Once again, this issue was eventually examined and documented by

Gracy, who significantly added to our knowledge of the background of the de la Peña material. The trail of the manuscripts is not complete, but several key landmarks between 1840 and the 1950s have now been added.

The above discussion (and Groneman's, for that matter) is mostly limited to the logical consistency of the internal content, rather than presenting external supporting or contradicting evidence. In 1994, James Crisp did one of the more thorough analyses on a controversial Alamo topic, in which he cleared up much of the confusion and inaccuracies in the account of de la Peña.[24] Crisp did a very careful study on the meaning of the original Spanish. Among the most significant contributions is that he found new and abundant material that answered several questions raised by Groneman. For example, a reputed Matamoros 1836 edition, of apparent relevance to the authenticity issue, turned out to be a misunderstanding by modern historians. He also found that there are a number of contemporary references to de la Peña and the existence and development of his journal. This study negates many of Groneman's arguments against the validity of the de la Peña diary that hinge on external evidence. Still, Groneman performed a real service by motivating an in-depth look at this exceptionally important document.[25]

There are two further, more general points to make from Crisp's study. One is that ultimately, real documented information is more important than logical consistency arguments in drawing strong conclusions. The second is that Alamo-related studies of the Mexican sources have been limited because most scholars (including myself) have not been independently competent in Spanish.

A careful study of the physical aspects of the documents was at long last done in 2001 by Gracy and his team.[26] They examined the paper, watermarks, continuity of wormholes and stains through several pages, feathering of the ink on the paper (the ink bleeds into adjacent paper over time), and iron content of the ink, all with respect to what would have been available to de la Peña versus a twentieth-century forger. Other parts of this study examined the handwriting—in particular, comparing it with that of the forger Laflin and with other samples of de la Peña's writing. Broader studies were also done, such as the relative histories of the de la Peña documents and the Laflin career, and numerous other aspects related to the question of authenticity. Simply put, in the end, Gracy concluded that the account of de la Peña is what it purports to be. No matter who might still argue this, the burden of proof has now shifted to the critics to present factual evidence if they want to refute Gracy's conclusions.

Discussions like that in *Defense of a Legend* and this commentary indicate that professional historians have left a lot undone on the topic of the Alamo. Thus lay historians such as Groneman and I are left to try to interpret what happened. Not that historical studies are, or should be, the exclusive domain of professionals. But it is curious that the Alamo, despite its fame, has not yet been thoroughly researched.

---

1. Groneman 1994, xi. Page references in this Special Commentary refer to this book unless otherwise noted. Also, Hardin (1990), in his analysis of the Nuñez document (2.14.1), discusses the emotional context of the Crockett story.
2. Groneman 1994, 40, 41–43.
3. Ibid., 2–3.

4. Ibid., 9–19.
5. There are now a number of translations in Borroel 1998a, and Gracy (2001) finally reviewed many of them.
6. Groneman 1994, 116–17.
7. Ibid., 28–29 (note that de la Peña could well have been a source for Urrea; see also Borroel 1997a, 14; 1997d, ii; 1998a, vi).
8. Ibld., 18 (also Borroel 1997d, 9–10).
9. Ibid., 31.
10. Ibid., 45–47.
11. Ibid., 4, 26–27.
12. Ibid., 4–6.
13. Ibid.: validity of the Sánchez account, 95–98, 101–4; the elevation of the Alamo attributed to Sánchez, 98–101; and a picture of Travis, 104–5.
14. A letter of Bonham's (ibid., 105–6) is also critiqued. In this case, a detailed study has not been done, so Groneman has a free field.
15. Ibld., 65–75.
16. Ibid., 21–24.
17. Ibid., 24.
18. Ibid., 22 (also Curtis 1989b).
19. Ibid.: on scale of de la Peña, 117–19; the forger Laflin, 121–29; Millsap letter, 129–31 (also Curtis 1989b); similarities of the Laffite forgeries, 130–2.
20. Ibid., 8 (though as noted by James Crisp in later reference, we need to be cautious about translations).
21. Ibid., 117, 135–47.
22. Ibid., 32–37 (though note Borroel 1997d, 22, regarding the Lamego publication in 1943 that appears based on de la Peña).
23. Ibid., 39.
24. Crisp 1994, 260–96.
25. Regarding the authenticity of de la Peña, there have been numerous other discussions in print and alternate media beyond what is noted here. For example, a six-part debate between Thomas Lindley and James Crisp, from the 1995–96 *Alamo Journal,* was posted in 2002 on the Internet at http://alamo-de-parras.welkin.org/archives/delapena/delapena1.html. Jackson and Ivey (2001) also addressed a number of criticisms by both Groneman and Lindley. There are others who have been neglected in this overview. The footnotes of the articles cited will lead an interested reader into the various papers of the debate.
26. Gracy 2001, 254–91.

2.10.1.   Francisco Becerra, interview, 1875.

Texas Mute Ranger. April 1882. Manuscript pages 15, 14-1/8, 14-1/4, and 16; or 169–72 of original newsletter. John S. Ford Papers, CAH.

This newsletter article is incorporated in John Ford's biographical manuscript just prior to the account of Dr. Sutherland (1.7.1). Ford is the superintendent referred to in the Introduction; it is less clear whether he is the writer. Becerra's story was first published in *Albert Hanford's Texas State Register for 1878,* 29–30; and this account was first reprinted in 1957 by Canales and again in 1980 by the Jenkins Publishing Co.

FALL OF THE ALAMO.

The article on that subject published in the present number of the Ranger, the writer believes, contains many truths in regard to that memorable and tragical event which have never seen the light.

The "Recollections" were written in 1875, and read to an audience in the Austin Public Library room. They were prepared from copious notes which had been read to Sergeant Becerra in Spanish and English—he spoke both languages—and he endorsed them as a true version of the affair. He was a man of good sense, was an experienced soldier, and frequently employed at Gen. Santa Anna's headquarters. He is dead.

The notes concerning the storming of the Alamo were taken previous to the time the writer came into the possession of the old newspaper, *"El Mercurio."* In that periodical he found Gen. Santa Anna's official order for the attack on the Alamo; and he discovered no reason for changing a single note. The accounts of the operations on the morning of March 6, 1836, did not vary materially. The *"Mercurio"* has been loaned to the Hon. V. O. King, of San Antonio, who is said to be writing a history of Texas.

It was the intention of the writer to prepare and publish "Sketches of Texas History." The "Recollections" would have figured therein. Victor Rose, and other gentlemen, are engaged in the laudable enterprise of furnishing material for some historian to compile a full history of Texas. Some of these gentlemen may consummate such a work, and receive the thanks of old Texians, at least.

With these explanations the Superintendent submits the "Recollections" to the perusal and candid judgment of the readers of the Ranger.

A MEXICAN SERGEANT'S RECOLLECTIONS OF THE
ALAMO AND SAN JACINTO

Francisco Becerra was born in the State of Guanajato [*sic*], Mexico, September 7, 1810. He entered the Mexican service in 1828, and was promoted to first sergeant in 1835. He was in Gen. Sesma's division when Gen. Santa Anna took up the line of march for Texas. He was at the storming of the Alamo, and took part in the battle of San Jacinto. In the latter affair he was wounded and made a prisoner. To avoid the expense of feeding the Mexican prisoners the Texas authorities permitted them to seek employment. Becerra hired to Mrs. Mann, afterwards to Mrs. Long. He lived a number of years with Gen. Lamar. He enlisted in the service of Texas, and was in the campaign of 1839 against the Cherokee and other Indians, which resulted in their defeat and expulsion from Texas. He was also a member of Capt. Mark Lewis's company. In 1849 he joined Capt. Lamar's company, and served during the war between Mexico, and the United States. After the conclusion of peace he settled at Brownsville. During the Confederate war he was a lieutenant in Capt. F.J. Parker's company, and was a strong supporter of the southern cause. Since the war he has been nearly all the while on the police force of Brownsville. More than a year since he received a bayonet wound in attempting to arrest a soldier. He has not recovered from the effects of the wound, and probably never will. He is regarded as an honest man, and possesses the respect and the confidence of all classes of citizens. He is a member of the Cameron County Association of Veterans of the Mexican War.

His details of the events of 1836 may be defective in some particulars. His memory may be at fault after a lapse of thirty-nine years, but he has aimed to tell the truth, that is a merit no one is disposed to deny him. He certainly throws some light on the fall of the Alamo. His narrative will be given as told by himself, and its merits can be judged of by the old men, yet living, who took part in a war which gave an empire to the United States.

THE MARCH UPON SAN ANTONIO.

"President Santa Anna crossed the Rio Grande at Laredo. He was met there by Gen. Cos and the troops he had surrendered at San Antonio. He forced Gen. Cos and his men to return, and thus violate the terms of his capitulation. Cos and his men were averse to so doing. There was no alternative but a compliance with the President's orders, or condign punishment.

"From Laredo Gen. Santa Anna marched up the Rio Grande to a point opposite the town of Presidio de Rio Grande. His object was to unite with a column which had charge of supplies of provision and ammunition. Thence he proceeded to San Antonio. On the march we found the prairies had been fired and the grass burned. The horses of the command in consequence became almost unserviceable. The cavalry were ordered to dismount and lead their horses. The burning of the prairies was attributed, by us, to Deaf Smith.

"Gen. Sesma's division constituted the vanguard of the army. The cavalry, under Col. Mora, was attached to it. On the seventh day's march Gen. Santa Anna came to the front. When he saw the cavalrymen walking and packing their saddles he was very angry. He despatched an orderly for Gen. Sesma. He did not find the general. Col. Mora came and reported. Santa Anna told the colonel he had received those horses in fine condition—they were broken down—the men walking and packing their saddles. He said the colonel might consider himself in arrest, and that he would be sent to the city of Mexico for trial before a court martial. Gen. Castrillon was present, and asked Gen. Santa

Anna how he could blame Col. Mora? He said the enemy had burned the grass, there was no corn for the horses, and how could Col. Mora help it? Gen. Santa Anna revoked the harsh and hasty order.

"On reaching Medina river Santa Anna halted one day to reunite and rest his army. Señor Navarro and a priest met him there. He received them well. The priest told the President there were two hundred and fifty Americans in the Alamo; that they were at a fandango that night, and could be easily surprised. Santa Anna intended to make a forced march for that purpose. A wet norther had been blowing during the day, the Median river had risen suddenly, the ammunition train had been left on the opposite bank, and could not be crossed. His Excellency was very mad, but there was no remedy, and he had to abandon the enterprise. The Median had fallen the next evening, and every thing was passed over safely. The march was resumed the next day.

"Col. Mora was ordered to take the advance, and when near San Antonio to move to the right, cross the river, and take possession of the Mission of Concepción. Santa Anna feared the Texians might abandon the Alamo, and occupy Concepción. He considered the latter place more defensible by a small force than the Alamo.

"When the head of the column rearched [*sic*] the cemetery a cannon shot was fired. Skirmishers were deployed, and pushed into town. They reported having [*portion missing in tear, perhaps "en-"*] countered no resistance. The men [*had?*] on their arms during the night; and we fired one shot which was answered by the Texians. Col. Mora was directed to take position north and east of the Alamo to prevent escape from the fort.

"When the army arrived many inhabitants fled from the city, leaving everything behind them; most of them went to the country. This was later in February. Gen. Santa Anna's army numbered about four thousand. He determined to take the Alamo by storm, but concluded to await the arrival of Gen. Tolza with two thousand men. Santa Anna made the preparatory arrangements during the interval. The first movement was made by the battalion Matamoros which crossed the river and took possession of some houses situated below the Alamo. Their mission was to collect timbers to build a bridge over the San Antonio river. They were in charge of Gen. Castrillon. The Texians fired on them. Gen. Santa Anna and Gen. Minon went to the spot. During these operations an incident occurred not connected with military operations, which will be referred to in another place.

"The next day two companies were sent to make a reconnoisance [*sic*]. They went within range of the deadly rifle; thirty were killed within a few minutes. Gen. Castrillon requested Gen. Santa Anna to withdraw them, if he wished to save any of their lives; the order was given. The main body of the army was still on the south side of the river, but the battalion Matamoros was still under fire. The Texians kept up a steady fire all day, with little effect. That night the battalion Matamoros was sent to reinforce Col. Mora, and to more effectually cover the approaches north and east of the Alamo. They were replaced by Col.

Romero's command. A small work was commenced above the Alamo. The next day the battalion Matamoros was sent to reoccupy position in front of the Alamo. Various movements were made in succession, brisk skirmish fighting occurred, the Texians were invested, and losses were inflicted on the Mexican army. When the small work was finished and inspected it did not suit the commanding general. He ordered another to be constructed nearer the Alamo, under the supervision of Gen. Amador. The working party took advantage of the night to commence. The Texians discovered them, and kept up a heavy fire on them all night. They completed the little fort in due time. Fire was opened from it upon the Alamo.

"On the third of March Gen. Tolza arrived. The greatest activity prevailed in every department. The plan of assault was formed, and communicated to the commanders of corps, and others, on the fifth. On the same day ammunition, scaling ladders, etc., were distributed. Every thing was made ready for the storming. During the night the troops were placed in position. About three o'clock on the morning of the sixth the battalion Matamoros was marched to a [*word ending in "nt" lost in tear, possibly "salient"*] near the river, and above the Alamo. [*Word lost in tear, probably "In"*] their rear were two thousand men under Gen. Cos. Gen. Castrillon commanded this portion of the army. Gen. Tolza's command held the ground below the Alamo. Gen. Santa Anna spent the night in the work near the Alamo. The troops were to march to the attack when the bugler at headquarters sounded the advance. The order delivered by Santa Anna to the commanders was to move in silence, and not to fire a single shot until the trenches of the enemy had been reached. The Mexican troops little thought of the terrible ordeal through which they were about to pass.

THE BATTLE AND THE STORMING

"On the morning of March 6, 1836, at four o'clock, the bugle sounded the advance from the small work near the Alamo. The troops under Gen. Castrillon moved in silence. They reached the fort, planted scaling-ladders, and commenced ascending; some mounted on the shoulders of others; a terrific fire belched from the interior; men fell from the scaling-ladders by the score, many pierced through the head by balls, others felled by clubbed guns. The dead and the wounded covered the ground. After half an hour of fierce conflict, after the sacrifice of many lives, the column under Gen. Castrillon succeeded in making a lodgement in the upper part of the Alamo. It was a sort of outwork. I think it is now used as a lot, or a courtyard. This seeming advantage was a mere prelude to the desperate struggle which ensued. The doors of the Alamo building were barricaded by bags of sand as high as the neck of a man, the windows also. On the top of the roofs of the different apartments were rows of sand bags to cover the besieged.

"Our troops, inspirited by success, continued the attack with energy and boldness. The Texians fought like devils. It was at short range—muzzle to muz-

zle—hand to hand—musket and rifle—bayonet and Bowie knife—all were mingled in confusion. Here a squad of Mexicans, there a Texan or two. The crash of
firearms, the shouts of defiance, the cries of the dying and the wounded, made
a din almost infernal. The Texians defended desperately every inch of the fort—
overpowered by numbers, they would be forced to abandon a room; they
would rally in the next, and defend it until further resistance because [*sic;
became*] impossible.

"Gen. Tolza's command forced an entrance at the door of the church building. He met the same determined resistance without and within. He won by
force of numbers, and at a great cost of life.

"There was a long room on the ground-floor—it was darkened. Here the
fight was bloody. It proved to be the hospital. The sick and the wounded fired
from their beds and pallets. A detachment of which I had command had captured a piece of artillery. It was placed near the door of the hospital, doubly
charged with grape and canister, and fired twice. We entered and found the
corpses of fifteen Texians. On the outside we afterwards found forty-two dead
Mexicans.

On the top of the church building I saw eleven Texians. They had some
small pieces of artillery, and were firing on the cavalry, and on those engaged in
making the escalade. Their ammunition was exhausted, and they were loading
with pieces of iron and nails. The captured piece was placed in a position to
reach them, doubly charged, and fired with so much effect, that they ceased
working their pieces.

"In the main building, on the ground-floor, I saw a man lying on a bed—he
was evidently sick. I retired, without molesting him, notwithstanding the order
of Gen. Santa Anna to give no quarter to the Texians. A sergeant of artillery
entered before I had finally left the room—he leveled his piece at the prostrate
man; the latter raised his hand and shot the sergeant through the head with a
pistol. A soldier of the Toluca regiment came in, aimed his gun at the invalid,
and was killed in a similar manner. I then fired and killed the Texian. I took his
two empty pistols, and found his rifle standing by his bed. It seemed he was too
weak to use it.

"In another room I saw a man sitting on the floor among feathers. A bugler,
who was with me, raised his gun. The gentleman said to him in Spanish:—
"Don't kill me—I have plenty of money." He pulled out a pocket-book, also a
large roll of bank bills, and handed the latter to the bugler. We divided the
money.

"While this was occurring another Texian made his appearance. He had
been lying on the floor, as if resting. When he arose I asked:—"How many is
there of you?" He replied:—"Only two."

"The gentleman, who spoke Spanish, asked for Gen. Cos, and said he
would like to see him. Just then Gen. Amador came in. He asked why the
orders of the President had not been executed, and the two Texians killed. In

answer the bugler exhibited his roll of bank bills, and they were taken from him immediately by the general. In a few moments Gen. Cos, Gen. Almonte, and Gen. Tolza, entered the room. As soon as Gen. Cos saw the gentleman who spoke Spanish he rushed to him, and embraced him. He told the other generals it was Travis, that on a former occasion he had treated him like a brother, had loaned him money, etc. He also said the other man was Col. Crockett. He entreated the other generals to go with him to Gen. Santa Anna, and join with him in a request to save the lives of the two Texians. The generals and the Texians left together to find Santa Anna. The bugler and myself followed them. They encountered the commander-in-chief in the court yard, with Gen. Castrillon. Gen. Cos said to him:—"Mr. President, you have here two prisoners—in the name of the Republic of Mexico I supplicate you to guarantee the lives of both." Santa Anna was very much enraged. He said:—"Gentlemen generals, my order was to kill every man in the Alamo." He turned, and said:—"Soldiers, kill them." A soldier was standing near Travis, and presented his gun at him. Travis seized the bayonet, and depressed the muzzle of the piece to the floor, and it was not fired. While this was taking place the soldiers standing around opened fire. A shot struck Travis in the back. He then stood erect, folded his arms, and looked calmly, unflinchingly, upon his assailants. He was finally killed by a ball passing through his neck. Crockett stood in a similar position. They died undaunted like heroes.

"The firing was brisk for a time. It came from all sides. Gen. Santa Anna, and most of the officers ran. Gen. Castrillon squatted down—so did I. In this affair eight Mexican soldiers were killed, and wounded, by their comrades.

"I did not know the names of two Texians, only as given by Gen. Cos. The gentleman be [sic] called Crockett had a coat with capes to it.

"The Alamo, as has been stated, was entered at daylight—the fighting did not cease till nine o'clock.

"Gen. Santa Anna directed Col. Mora to send out his cavalry to bring in wood. He ordered, that they should make prisoners of all the inhabitants they might meet, and force them to pack wood to the Alamo. In this manner a large quantity of wood was collected. A large pile was raised. It consisted of layers of wood and layers of corpses of Texians. It was set on fire. The bodies of those brave men, who fell fighting that morning, as men have seldom fought, were reduced to ashes before the sun had set. It was a melancholy spectacle.

"There was an order to gather our own dead and wounded. It was a fearful sight. Our lifeless soldiers covered the grounds surrounding the Alamo. They were heaped inside of the fortress. Blood and brains covered the earth, and the floors, and had spattered the walls. The ghostly faces of our comrades met our gaze, and we removed them with despondent hearts. Our loss in front of the Alamo was represented at two thousand killed, and more than three hundred wounded. The killed were generally struck on the head. The wounds were in the neck, or shoulder, seldom below that. The firing of the besieged was fearfully precise. When a Texas rifle was leveled on a Mexican he was considered as good as dead. All this indicates the dauntless bravery and the cool self-possession of the men who were engaged in a hopeless conflict with an enemy numbering more than twenty to one. They inflicted on us a loss ten times greater than they sustained. The victory of the Alamo was dearly bought. Indeed, the price in the end was well nigh the ruin of Mexico.

"During the evening we buried our dead. These were sad duties which each company performed for its fallen members. How many never again responded at roll call! It was a day of bitter strife, of sadness, and sorrow. A triumph which bore bitter fruits.

"Our wounded were placed in houses, and properly cared for.

"On the seventh of March the army rested. On that day a courier arrived from Goliad, bearing a letter from Gen. Urrea, asking for reinforcements. Two battalions were sent to him.

THE INCIDENT.

"During the operations preparatory to the storming of the Alamo I mentioned that the battalion Matamoros was under fire while collecting timbers for a bridge, and that Gens. Castrillon, Minon, and Santa Anna went to them. Gen. Castrillon was in charge of the battalion, and directing the work. Many of the timbers were taken from houses. The General entered a house, and found a lady, and her daughter. The girl was beautiful. The General asked the mother what she was doing there, and if she was not afraid. She told him it was her home, and she had no other place to go; that she was not afraid. She was well bred, and intelligent, though poorly clad.

"Gen. Castrillon related what had happened to the President. Santa Anna was in a great fever to see the pretty girl. He told Gen Castrillon he wanted her, and asked him to carry a message to her mother. Castrillon replied that he was ready to obey any legitimate order coming from Gen. Santa Anna, as the President of Mexico, and the commander-in-chief of the army, but in that particular case he begged to be excused, and requested the President to employ some one else.

"Gen. Santa Anna commanded the lady and her daughter to be taken to his quarters; and Gen. Minon executed the order. He delivered Santa Anna's message to the mother. She replied that she was a respectable lady of good family, and had always conducted herself with propriety; that her deceased husband was an honorable man, and commanded a company in the Mexican service; that President Santa Anna was not her president, and could not get her daughter except by marriage. She was not only inflexible, but defiant. Gen. Minon reported accordingly. He informed Santa Anna, that he had a man in his command, who was well educated, a great rascal, and capable of performing all sorts of tricks, even the personating of a priest. The man was sent for, and was ready to do the bidding of His Excellency. He went to a priest, and in the name of Gen. Santa Anna, President of Mexico, asked for and received vestments, and all else necessary to celebrate a nuptial ceremony according to the rites of the Roman Catholic Church.

"The obsequious pseudo-priest consented to solemnize the marriage in Gen. Santa Anna's quarters. The wedding took place late in February. The honeymoon lasted until the army marched for the Guadalupe river. The deceived and trusting girl was sent to San Luis Potosi in the carriage of Gen. Minon. She was placed in the care of a very respectable family. In due course of time she became the mother of a son. I do not know when she ascertained that Gen. Santa Anna was already a married man, and the father of a family, and that she had been made the victim of a foul and rascally plot. The information came too late, yet its effects must have been crushing upon the unfortunate girl."

IS THE ACCOUNT CORROBORATED?

The narrative of Sergeant Becerra differs from others. Though we must keep in view the fact, that quite all we know of the fall of the Alamo has come from Mexican sources, and has been biased. The massacre created a sensation in the civilized world, and it has been the effort of Mexicans to escape from the effects of a verdict of condemnation which was rendered against them by an enlightened public opinion. Much they have said on the subject has been more in the shape of a plea of justification than a desire to impart the truth.

Sergeant Becerra speaks from no such motives. Since the battle of San Jacinto he has been an American. He has identified himself with the people of Texas—he tells a straight forward tale—attempts to make no concealments—and impresses upon his version the ear-marks of truth told by an honest man.

A short while after the above account had been written Becerra brought to the writer a bound copy of the *Mercurio*, a newspaper published in Matamoros, Mexico by Juan Southwell, in the years 1834-35-36. It contains a great deal of matter which is now historical. The number for February 26, 1835 [sic], gives an English version of Gen. Santa Anna's address to his army while on the march to Bexar:

TRANSLATION.

"The General-in-chief to the army of operations under his command:
COMPANIONS IN ARMS! Our most sacred duties have conducted us to these plains, and urge us forward to combat with that mob of ungrateful adventurers on whom our authorities have incautiously lavished favors which they have failed to bestow on Mexicans. They have appropriated to themselves our territories, and have raised the standard of rebellion, in order that this fertile and expanded department may be detached from our Republic; persuading themselves that our unfortunate dissensions have incapacitated us for the defence of our native land. Wretches! They will soon see their folly.

SOLDIERS! Your comrades have been treacherously sacrificed at Anahuac, Goliad, and Bejar; and you are the men chosen to chastise the assassins.

MY FRIENDS! We will march to the spot whither we are called by the interests of the nation in whose services we are engaged. The candidates for "acres" of land in Texas will learn to their sorrow, that their auxiliaries from New Orleans, Mobile, Boston, New York, and other northern ports (from whence no aid ought to proceed are insignificant, and that the Mexicans, though naturally generous, will not suffer outrages with impunity—injurious and dishonorable to their country—let the perpetrators be whom they may.

ANTONIO LOPEZ DE SANTA ANNA.

Camp on the Nueces River, February 17, 1836."

This proclamation fixes on Gen. Santa Anna the feeling of hostility to Americans which has since prevailed so strongly in Mexico, and which led him to imbrue his hands in American blood.

In order to leave no doubt as to the intention of the government of Mexico, of which Gen. Santa Anna was the head, and the leading spirit, the following document will be quoted:

[*Here is quoted a "Circular" of Tornel, dated December 30, 1836, regarding anti-Mexican activities in the United States, along with comments of actions "against the people of Texas" in April 1836. As they are post-Alamo, they are not included here. Next is quoted the general order for the attack (document 2.1.1.8), misdated March 6 rather than March 5. The article then continues.*]

[N.B.—This order, Becerra said, was issued March 6, 1836, and copied the next day.]

Why was Gen. Santa Anna so careful to prevent the escape of the Texians? Was it because he wished to have the glory of having made all the garrison of the Alamo prisoners of war? No, it was for the purpose of carrying out his sanguinary order of no quarter, of leaving no defender of that fortress to tell the tale of their superhuman efforts to hold the place. He murdered the garrison yet living after he effected an entrance into the forts, and he burned their bodies, thus denying them a christian burial. He stamped upon the war he was waging against Texas the indelible stain of inhumanity, and barbarian cruelty. He was the representative man of the Mexican nation, the head of the Supreme Government, and his acts attached to the Mexican people a fearful responsibility.

Gen. Santa Anna, as long as he was at the head of a victorious army, boldly avowed his acts and justified them. In proof of this we will quote his . . .

[*Following is the "Proclamation" of March 7, 1836 (document 2.1.1.11).*]

The Napoleon of the West came not only as the President of Mexico and Commander-in-chief of her armies, the executor of the national decrees, the dispenser of life and death, but as a judge to decide upon the rights of the people of Texas to their property.

The documents given above were published officially in the *Mercurio* and may be relied on as authentic.

As far as this documentary evidence goes it sustains the views and the allegations of Señor Becerra. He has other endorsers.

Don Lino Ruis, now living in Brownsville, was a resident of Bexar county when the Alamo fell. He was one of the citizens captured by the Mexican cavalry, and compelled to carry wood to the Alamo to burn the corpses of its defenders.

Mr. Nathaniel Mitchell, one of the veterans who fought at San Jacinto, was studying the Spanish language in 1834 and 1835, in the town of San Antonio. His preceptor had two beautiful nieces. He learned that one of them had been fooled by Gen. Santa Anna and sent to San Luis Potosi. He afterwards met with a man who had driven the stage in Mexico for Mr. Jaques. This man saw the girl, and became well acquainted with her. Mr. Mitchell is of opinion that Becerra's account of the false marriage is truthful.

Capt. M. Kenney was in Mexico after our civil war. He was at a theatre where some Americans were performing sleight-of-hand tricks, or giving *seances,* and a Mexican came forward and proposed to do all the Americans had done. He was hissed and hooted off the stage by an indignant audience. Capt. K. inquired the cause. He was told that the said man had once personated a priest, and performed a mock ceremony of marriage between Gen. Santa Anna and a Mexican lady. The Captain did not believe it the case referred to by Becerra, yet the fact is significant.

The *Mercurio* of March 8, 1836, published an extra announcing the fact that when Gen. Santa Anna's army reached San Antonio the people fled from their houses and stores, leaving them open. This accords with Señor Becerra's statement.

William Neale, ex-Mayor of Brownsville, in speaking of Becerra's account of the fall of the Alamo, remarked that he had omitted an incident. Mr. Neale says, at the time the Mexican army, under Gen. Felisola, reached Matamoros, on the evacuation of Texas after the battle of San Jacinto, he was living in the State of Tamaulipas, near the mouth of the Rio Grande. He says a colored woman came with the Mexican troops, called Bettie, who represented herself as the former cook of Col. James Bowie. She hired herself to Mr. Neale, and remained with him for a year or two. She often spoke of the fight of the Alamo. On the morning of March 6, 1836, she was in the kitchen with a colored man, named Charlie; after the resistance of the defenders had ceased a detachment of Mexican soldiers entered the kitchen. Charlie attempted to secrete himself, was found and dragged out. The officer in charge of the men was very small. A soldier made a bayonet thrust at Charlie. The colored gentleman seized the little officer and held him before his own body as a shield—at the same time he backed into a corner. The soldiers made many attempts to bayonet Charlie, and in every instance he skilfully covered himself with the diminutive officer. This lasted for several minutes. The soldiers began to relish the joke, and were laughing. The officer did not feel comfortable. He finally called for a parley. He promised to save Charlie's life, on condition that his precious little person should be deposited on the floor. Charlie acceded, and the treaty was faithfully observed.

Señor Becerra remembered the affair, and said it had escaped his memory.

When some Texas war vessels were cruising near the mouth of the Rio Grande Bettie became afraid they would land, and carry her back to Texas. She left Mr. Neale, and went to Monterey, and he lost sight of her.

Mr. Neale says there was a man with the Mexican troops who insisted that he escaped being killed at the storming of the Alamo. He claimed to have hid himself among some pack saddles and rubbish, that the Mexicans overlooked him, and he finally slipped out of the fort.

This man said he was a German by birth. He lived in Matamoros several years, and gave lessons in fencing. He was a very expert swordsman.

The latter matter is given for what it may be worth.

It would not be a just notice of the fall of the Alamo which omitted the lines of Col. Reuben M. Potter. I have received the impression, and I think from the mouth of that distinguished gentleman himself, that he was in prison in Matamoros at the time the Hymn was written, and had not heard of the battle of San Jacinto. The *Mercurio* has a long notice of Col. Potter's imprisonment. His expressions were prophetic, and no true Texian can read his spirited little poem and repress his emotions. Believing it will strike a chord in every heart in the audience I will recite the . . .

[*Following is the "Hymn of the Alamo" of Reuben Potter.*]

"Remember the Alamo" was the shout which arose above the noise of battle on the plains of San Jacinto. Its import was understood and appreciated by the Mexican soldiery—many of whom denied having participated in that bloody affair. It was heard on other fields. It was a slogan which carried with it a sense of dread, and a feeling akin to fear when it fell from the lips of Texians who were striking for freedom, and for revenge. In process of time the sentiment was adopted by the American people. It animated our troops at Palo Alto, Monterey, Vera Cruz, Cerro Gordo, and in the valley of Mexico. It fired the hearts of the men who triumphed in Chihuahua, amid the golden *placeres* of California, and wherever the starlit banner of our fathers floated over the conquered provinces of Mexico. The sentiment has been transmitted to the present generation. It bids fair to exert a potential influence upon our international affairs.

2.11.1.   Rafael Soldana and others, interview, 1935.

DeShields, James T., ed. 1935. *Tall Men with Long Rifles: The Glamorous Story of the Texas Revolution, as Told by Captain Creed Taylor, Who Fought in That Heroic Struggle from Gonzales to San Jacinto.* 152–67. San Antonio: Naylor Company.

Though Creed Taylor apparently talked with many people about the Alamo, this account is particularly noteworthy for the interview with Capt. Don Rafael Soldana included toward the end of this selection.

[*This account of the Alamo begins with a brief summary of the surrender of Cós and the scattering of the Texans to their homes or with Grant on the Matamoros campaign.*]

With those that remained Travis could maintain but a mere semblance of discipline. These men were volunteers from other states, they had been promised a liberal reward for their services and pay-day had never arrived. They were disheartened, discouraged, unable to get away, and consequently abandoned themselves to all excesses of a military post. Gambling, cockfighting, and fandangos were the popular pastimes, and at roll call of the 150 names on the list very often there were not 25 to answer. Travis was helpless but bore with the insubordination of these men, realizing the importance of holding Bexar and hoping that the clash of authority between Governor Smith and the Council would be adjusted and that troops and supplies would reach San Antonio in time to forestall any attempt of the enemy to retake the place.

The arrogance and tyranny of these men under Travis embittered most of the Mexican population. With most of these men the Mexican was regarded as a common enemy and his property was considered as lawful prey. Grant's followers had despoiled them of all their servicable [*sic*] horses to the extent that when one of Cos' wounded men so far recovered as to be able to undertake the homeward journey, he had to remain, as his friends and sympathizing countrymen in San Antonio could not furnish him a horse to ride out of town. These Mexicans knew of Santa Anna's approach; they knew when his army crossed the Rio Grande; but they kept their own council, trusting to the day when an overwhelming force of their countrymen should drive the obnoxious invaders from their presence. A young Mexican girl who had become the mistress of one of Travis' men told her lover of the approach of the Mexican army but her statement was treated as an idle rumor. Travis had scarcely a sufficient number of horses with which to drive in beef cattle from the range along the San Antonio River and this accounts for the fact that there were no scouts or reconnoitering parties to report the advance of the Mexican army. Early in January Travis had sent a detail as far as 25 miles out in the direction of Laredo with orders to burn all the grass in that part of the country. This order was obeyed and further than that, no precautions were taken against the advance of the invading force.

Witness the consternation of these men when suddenly and without warning they awoke on the morning of February 22nd to behold the Mexican army in battle array at their very doors! The night before, Santa Anna with his army lay in absolute security on the Medina, a few miles from town. His spies entered San Antonio during the night and from their sympathizing countrymen obtained all the information they required. These spies found no picket to challenge their presence and spent most of the night carousing with their newly made friends and on their return were accompanied by several of Cos' convalescent soldiers. When Santa Anna heard their report and finding the way clear he ordered that neither bugle nor drum should sound but that with the utmost silence the army should fall into line and move forward.

Our historians tell us that Santa Anna appeared before the walls of Bexar with an army of 6000 men, the flower of Mexican chivalry, trained officers and seasoned veteran soldiers. Let us examine their statements and, if possible, arrive at just conclusions.

As previously stated, Santa Anna left San Luis Potosi with 6019 men of all arms. His divisions were commanded by the following generals: Mora, Gaona, Tolsa, Andrade, Urrea, besides a number of colonels and captains who held important commands. After leaving San Luis, General Urrea's command was detached and marched to Matamoros, where it crossed the Rio Grande and proceeded to Goliad. Urrea had only 300 in his command when he set out for Matamoros, but before he crossed into Texas his army was strengthened by the addition of other troops and his operations were confined to San Patricio, Refugio and Goliad.

General Gaona's division of 1600 men with two twelve pound cannon and two howitzers did not reach Bexar until the 8th of March, two days after the fall of the Alamo. General Woll arrived on the 10th and Generals Filisola, Arago, and Andrade, with their respective commands reached San Antonio also on the 19th. Just how many troops composed the command of these generals is not known, but 2000 is a reasonable figure and this being a reasonable low estimate and making all the allowances for deaths from disease and hardships and also for the large number of desertions while en route, Santa Anna could not have had much over 3000 effective troops at the Alamo—about half the number usually credited to him by our historians. In his letter to the Secretary of war, written from San Antonio on February 27th, Santa Anna says he reached that place February 23rd with only the division of General Sesma composed of the battalions of Matamoros, Jiminez, the Dolores Regiment and eight pieces of artillery.

"In telling of the siege and fall of the Alamo," says Taylor, "I shall relate only such facts as were told to me by soldiers who took part in the tragedy and citizens who lived in Bexar and were cognizant of all that transpired during those eventful days. True, these were Mexicans but I accepted no narrative as related without corroborative evidence, and the facts herein recorded were substantiated by the statements of a number sufficient to guarantee the veracity of these statements.

"The 24th of February was spent in preparation for the siege and in reconnoitering the Alamo and its fortifications. Santa Anna knew that Travis' only hope was to hold the Alamo until reinforcements, which he expected daily, could reach him. The Mexican general knew as well as Travis, perhaps better, that the latter's only means of relief lay with Fannin at Goliad. His spies and swift couriers kept him posted as to Fannin's movements, his attempt to leave Goliad for Bexar, his signal failure, and his return to La Bahia. Santa Anna knew all this and, furthermore, he knew that Urrea, with a large force, was moving upon Goliad and that it was only a question of time as to the destruction of Fannin's army. Hence, all he had to do was to lay siege to the Alamo and by slow degrees reduce the beleagured [sic] men to a state of starvation and non-resistance, after which the taking of the fortress would be an easy task.

During the night of the 24th, two batteries commanding the Alamo were planted, and at dawn on the morning of the 25th these opened fire on the garrison which in turn responded with vigor. A brisk fire was maintained by both sides during the day until late in the evening firing ceased and a deep silence fell upon the town and fortress. During the night, according to my informant, Juan Ortega, who was a sergeant in the Dolores Regiment, and who died at Brownsville in June, 1862, and his story was corroborated by several others whom I knew personally, two entrenchments were constructed along the alameda of the Alamo and, while details of men were working on these entrenchments, nine men came over from the fortress and asked to be conducted into the presence of Santa Anna. As the General was asleep at that hour and no one cared to disturb his slumbers these were held under guard until morning. Señor Ortega told me that one of these men spoke Spanish sufficiently fluent to make their wants known, but he did not learn whether they were Texans or volunteers. What they said to Santa Anna, when led into his presence, is not known, but it is well attested that they told him where fifty American rifles had been left in town by Travis' men, besides other belongings, all of which were seized by the Mexicans. What became of these traitors I have never been able to learn. Captain Henry Teal, who was one of the commissioners sent by Houston with a copy of the Santa Anna treaty for Filisola's signature and ratification, overtook the retreating Mexican army west of Goliad. He told me, on his return, that he saw four Americans with Filisola's men. They were not soldiers nor were they prisoners, and appeared to be either fugitives or camp followers. He tried to learn something of their identity and of their antecedents, but they refused to divulge anything and tried in every way to avoid his presence. Teal had heard of the desertions at the Alamo and he believed that these four men were of the nine traitors.

"Of the 38 captives taken out and shot at Caralvo in 1846, one of them was evidently an American and John McPeters, of Mustang Gray's company, questioned this man on the way to the place of execution but he denied being other than a 'puro Mexicano.' We were told on the day following that this man was indeed an American, that he was a refugee, and with others had come from San Antonio with the Mexican army when it retreated from Texas, and dared not return to his country.

"The desertion of these nine men at the very beginning of the siege of the Alamo was known to all the Mexicans in San Antonio at the time. Owing to the disrespect touching the rights of property displayed by the Americans after the surrender of Cos and up to the date of Santa Anna's arrival, the Mexican population held the utmost hatred toward them, and when these nine came over to Santa Anna and declared their loyalty and fealty their protestations only served to intensify the contempt of these people. This hatred on the part of the populace was fully displayed when Santa Anna ordered the bodies of the Alamo victims burned, many of those people volunteering to gather wood from a nearby chaparral.

"Another American traitor of whom little is known, was one Davis who belonged to General Sesma's command and was colonel of the Queretaro Battalion and took an active part in the storming of the Alamo. I made diligent inquiry among the Mexicans of my acquaintance but no one could tell me anything other then [*sic*] that Davis was an American and was held in favor by Santa Anna. Juan Seguin held the opinion that he was one of those daring Americans who fought with Peter E. Bean against the Spaniards during the war for Mexican Independence and when that was established he accepted a commission in the army, became a naturalized citizen and remained in the service of his adopted country. Filisola mentions this Colonel Davis but once in his account of the Texas invasion.

"'Thermopylae had its messenger of defeat, but the Alamo had none.' Of course, I was not in the Alamo during the siege and fall, else I would not be here to tell of my humble part in other affairs; and, strictly speaking, the Alamo, unlike Thermopylae, had no messenger of defeat, for certain it is that not one remaining there until the commencement of the final assault escaped or was spared—not one save the few non-combatants, Mrs. Dickenson and babe, Travis' and Bowie's negro servants, and perhaps one or two other servants, to bear to Houston and his little army the news of the bloody tragedy and threats of a like fate.

"I never saw the man Rose, who, it is said, escaped before the Alamo fell; never heard of him until of late years. Of course it is possible that the story is true, but it is more probable that Rose was an imposter and palmed off his story on the confiding Zubers who gave it publicity.

"Another claimant who has succeeded in imposing upon the credulous public and gaining some notoriety was an old Mexican midwife by the name of Candelaria, whose story has found its way into history. She claimed to have been in the Alamo as the nurse of Jim Bowie, when it fell. But, mind you, she did not make this claim till in late years when there were few, if any, of her generation left to refute her pretentions. I knew Madam Candelaria as early as the 50's and, while I knew she had spent her life in San Antonio, I never heard of her being in the Alamo during the fight, until a few years ago. The Madam got to be very old, she needed alms and to that end some enterprising but unscrupulous writer helped to prepare her story. I believe it all a hoax.

"Several aged Mexicans yet survive in San Antonio who claim to have been living there when the siege occurred, among others one Juan Diaz, then a youth, the son of Antonio Diaz, the then trusted custodian of San Fernando Cathedral. Juan Diaz is considered an honorable and reliable Mexican, being a native of San Antonio, a man of some prominence, and he is one of the very few survivors of the Mexican Society. An excellent oil portrait of this venerable Mexican hangs in Benevolence Hall, San Antonio. I give his story in substance as he told it to me, and for what it is worth: 'There was much excitement in town as Santa Anna's great army approached and as a boy I observed what was going on. I witnessed and well remember the wonderful sight as the troops, horse and foot, and artillery, swept into town led by the regimental band playing the liveliest airs, and accompanied by a squad of men bearing the flags and banners of Mexico and an immense image that looked like an alligator's head. The band stopped on Main Plaza and remained there until after the fall of the fort; the artillery was parked where the French building now stands, and the cannoneers had a clear sweep to the Alamo, there being no buildings at that time between it and the cathedral. I knew of the progress of the siege from day to day; watched some of the assaults from a safe vantage point, and then witnessed the final scene of the bloody drama—the burning of the dead. I did not go out to where the dead were burned; I had no desire to see the great funeral pyre, but the odor of it permeated every part of the town. It was sickening, and for weeks and months people shunned the place. Some of the men who witnessed the cremation said that the Texan and Mexican slain were piled in a heap and burned together.'

"Non-combatants who were in the fortress and spared have left very little of the details. Mrs. Susan Dickenson, wife of the brave Lieutenant Almaron Dickenson, said that the final struggle lasted more than two hours; that the noise of the battle was terrific as the desperate fight went on from every direction, and that the bloody scene was sickening and heart rending. It must have been enough to dethrone the poor woman's reason at that hour, and crouched with her babe in a secluded angle of the church, she knew but little of what was going on in and around the old fortress.

"I have talked with a few Mexicans who saw service under Santa Anna and fought at the Alamo. Just before the Civil War a Mexican gentleman was passing through the country going from Matamoros to Austin on some business errand. He was traveling in an ambulance accompanied by three or four companions, and one night he encamped on the San Domingo Creek. Here he was attacked and robbed by outlaws that occasionally infested that section, and during the fight he was shot through the arm below the shoulder. He came next day to my ranch in Wilson county and remained a week, doctoring his wound. He had been a captain in the Mexican army and was at the storming of the Alamo. He related many incidents in connection with the battle, but most of them have passed out of my memory. I remember his effort to say "Crockett" but he invariably pronounced it 'Kwokety.' He said Crockett was the last man slain and that he fought like an infuriated lion. He stated that his last stand was in a small room and with gun in hand he brained every Mexican that tried to enter the door. He used his gun as a club until a shot from just without the door broke his right arm, and his gun-barrel (the stock had been broken off) fell to the floor. Seeing this the Mexican soldiers made a rush into the room with fixed bayonets, but drawing a large knife with his left hand he rushed upon his assailants and parrying their thrusts, killed several before he was finally slain. He said he did not hear of a sick man being bayoneted while helpless on his bed (Bowie) but there was a sick man who got out of his bed when the Mexicans entered the fortress and died fighting with the rest. He also stated that Santa Anna could not have done otherwise than to put the defenders of the Alamo to the sword, since they were in open rebellion, held a government fortress, and had refused all overtures looking to a surrender.

"While guarding prisoners at Saltillo shortly after the battle of Buena Vista I talked with two of them who were at the storming of the Alamo, and their version was along the same lines as that given by the wounded captain at my ranch.

"An old Mexican by the name of Rodriguez, who lived in Bexar all his life, told me that during the siege of the Alamo the Mexican women in San Antonio remained indoors, praying, and when the final assault began on Sunday morning, every woman was on her knees pleading for the repose of the fallen, foes as well as friends. He spoke of one young woman who was enamored of one of the garrison and who went into the Alamo when the carnage had ceased, found the object of her affection among the slain, folded his hands across his breast, wiped the grime from his pallid face, placed a small cross on his breast, and when ordered away, she dipped her handkerchief in his blood and carried it away in her bosom.

"I was told by a number of San Antonio Mexicans that many of Santa Anna's men deserted after the fall of the Alamo. They told their friends that if all Texans fought like those who fell in the Alamo, they could never expect to return to their homes and there were not enough men in all Mexico to subdue *estos Tejanos diablos.*

"We will never know, of course, just how many of the enemy fell in the Alamo siege and fight, but taking statements of Mexican participants themselves and all other evidence, a conservative estimate would be about 1600 to 2000, or about one-half of the besieging force. Speaking of the Toluca Battalion Santa Anna says: 'They commenced to scale the walls and suffered severely. Out of 800 men, only 130 were left alive.' Such was the fearful execution by iron-willed and steady nerved riflemen and gunners, who, cool and fearless, met the legions and sold their lives dearly.

"Of incidents in the final struggle and of closing scenes in the Alamo tragedy, we know nothing except the little that has been told to us by Mexican participants and eyewitnesses.

"Señor Don Rafael Soldana was a captain in the Tampico battalion and led his company in the final charge on the Alamo on that memorable Sabbath morning. I became acquainted with Captain Soldana at Corpus Christi shortly after the close of the Mexican War and from him I heard the story of the last charge. 'During the siege,' said he, 'which began on the 23rd of February, every available means was employed to harass and weaken the defenders of the fortress. One of the measures employed was that of constant alarms during the hours of the night. At intervals, when silence reigned over the Alamo and all was still in camp, the artillery would open, a great shout would be raised by the besieging forces and this uproar, supplemented by volleys of musketry, was intended to make the impression that a night assault had been planned, and also to make it appear to the beleaguered that their expected reinforcements, while trying to make their way into the Alamo, had become engaged with the enemy and were being destroyed. These continued—almost hourly—alarms throughout the night were supposed to keep every American in position ready to repel the attack, thus through loss of sleep and increasing anxiety unfitting him for the final struggle.'

"'These men,' said Captain Soldana, and his story was corroborated by others with whom I talked, 'were defiant to the last. From the windows and parapets of the low buildings, when taunted by the Mexican troops, they shouted back their defiance in the liveliest terms. A tall man, with flowing hair, was seen firing from the same place on the parapet during the entire siege. He wore a buckskin suit and a cap all of a pattern entirely different from those worn by his comrades. This man would kneel or lie down behind the low parapet, rest his long gun and fire, and we all learned to keep at a good distance when he was seen to make ready to shoot. He rarely missed his mark and when he fired he always rose to his feet and calmly reloaded his gun seemingly indifferent to the shots fired at him by our men. He had a strong resonant voice and often railed at us, but as we did not understand English we could not comprehend the import of his words further than that they were defiant. This man I later learned was known as "Kwockey" (Crockett).

"'When the final assault was made upon the walls these men fought, like devils,' continued Señor Soldana. When asked if any begged for quarter he replied by saying that he had never heard that any of them offered to surrender [sic] or that a single man had begged for his life. 'Kwockey' was killed in a room of the mission. He stood on the inside to the left of the door and plunged his long knife into the bosom of every soldier that tried to enter. They were powerless to fire upon him because of the fact that he was backed up against the wall and, the doorway being narrow, they could not bring their guns to bear upon him. And, moreover, the pressure from the rear was so great that many near the doorway were forced into the room only to receive a deadly thrust from that lone knife. Finally a well directed shot broke this man's right arm and his hand fell useless at his side. He then seized his long gun with his left hand and leaped toward the center of the room where he could wield the weapon without obstruction, felling every man that came through the doorway. A corporal ordered the passage cleared of those who were being pressed forward, a volley was fired almost point blank and the last defender of the Alamo fell forward—dead.

"Señor Soldana told me there were three or four Mexicans who went down with Travis in the Alamo. He did not know of any Mexican women being in the fortress when it fell. He had heard that nine men deserted Travis before the Alamo was invested but he did not see them and did not know what became of them."

"A glamor of romance and chivalry hangs around the story of the Alamo and its immortal defenders; and its heroic defense and fall are among the imperishable records of human fortitude and valor in all ages and countries. Travis, Bowie, Bonham, and Crockett were the noble figures in that terrible sacrifice, but every one of the devoted little band, privates as well as officers, deserves to be canonized in the calendar of heroism so long as valor and the deeds of war are esteemed the test of a patriotism that renders life for love of country. They died at the dawn of Sunday, March 6, 1836, and it is a grim irony of their lonely isolation in the hour of doom that they fell beneath the flag of Constitutional Mexico while, unknown to them, their countrymen at old Washington-on-the-Brazos had declared the independence of Texas and raised the banner of the 'Lone Star' just four days before.

"The final assault which began before daylight, ended about sunrise, and then, as some one has so pathetically said, 'A stillness fell upon the scene so profoundly that the drip, drip of heroic blood could be heard.' When all was over Santa Anna strode over the scene and then gave orders for the disposition of the dead. The Mexican officers received burial but most of the Mexican privates were either dumped into the river or burned. The bodies of the Texans were gathered up and carted off a short distance where they were thrown into a heap, alternate layers of wood and bodies being placed together and kindling distributed throughout.

"The pile being completed about five o'clock in the evening, it was lighted. Thus was reared the altar upon which the heroic sons of freedom were consecrated to their country. As the flames cracked and increased, the smoke of the sacrifice ascended on high invoking the wrath of the Almighty upon the oppressors, and while the rising incense floated around the throne of heaven the retributive arm of offended justice was lifting the sword of vengeance which fell so heavily upon them at San Jacinto.

"Thus I have attempted to tell the story of the Alamo, a story that will emblazon the pages of history until the end of time, and the spark of patriotism will always enkindle and thrill at the very mention of that fearful conflict—the warm blood rushing to the heart as one listens to the valorous deeds of those matchless heroes in that unparalleled struggle. Indeed, the story of how Travis and his little band of devoted and defiant comrades offered up their lives, a willing sacrifice and a rich oblation upon the altar of Texan liberty at the Alamo fortress in the historic and blood-stained old town of San Antonio, possesses an interest for the reader over any other chapter in the fiery history of Texas. As boys we all remember the charm that possessed us in reading of the wonderful exploits and chivalric acts of prowess performed by Travis, Bowie, Crockett, Bonham, and others of that dauntless band, especially of Davy Crockett and Jim Bowie whose lifeless and mangled bodies were found with heads [*sic; heaps*] of dead Mexicans piled high around and upon them—so the story always went.

"'Thermopylae had its messenger of defeat; the Alamo had none.' An[*d*] this is true as to actual combatants. But there were a few non-combatants within the walls of the doomed fortress, who witnessed the terrible fight from the first shot to the last sword thrust. These were spared, to carry the news of the tragedy to the world.

"Of all the scenes and incidents connected with the fall of the Alamo, it always seemed to me that the story of Mrs. Dickenson and babe is the most pathetic. True, they were spared from the slaughter, but the horrible scenes of blood and carnage through which that devoted wife and mother passed in the fearful hour must have made an impression that haunted her throughout life and left a sadness that never could be erased from her memory.

"As stated, the only inmates of the doomed fortress spared were a few non-combatants, Mrs. Dickenson and child, Travis' negro Ben, and Bowie's colored servant, and perhaps one or two Mexican women, nurses.

"Mrs. Dickenson, as a young mother, had gone into the Alamo with her husband, Lieutenant Dickenson, and with her baby remained with him to the end. Dickenson was a volunteer from Gonzales, and was one of the dauntless men who stood by Travis, Crockett, Bonham, and others of that 'devoted little band' and went down with them in the holocaust of carnage, fire and death. In telling of the final terrible scenes of that awful combat she could never recount the story without a shudder and without evincing great emotion. Of the last moments she said: 'Finally my husband rushed into the baptismal room of the church, where I stood holding our baby, and exclaimed; "Great God, Sue! The Mexicans are inside our walls! All is lost! If they spare you, save my precious child!" Then with a parting kiss, he drew his sword and plunged into the strife that was raging in the different parts of the fortification. At this moment poor Jim Bowie, sick unto death, attempted to rise from his cot and follow, but was restrained by his Mexican nurse. When the Mexicans poured into the room I closed my eyes and knelt in prayer. There was much noise and confusion as the assailants crowded around Bowie and the poor man met his death fighting to the last breath.' Thus this poor bereft woman, praying and clasping her baby close to her breast in that terrible hour of mortal combat, witnessed the furious and bloody struggle.

[*The narrative continues with an account of the "Babe of the Alamo."*]

2.12.1. Ben, interview, 1838.

Newell, C. 1838. *History of the Revolution in Texas, Particularly of the War of 1835 &*
'36 . . . 87–89. New York: Wiley & Putnam.
In one of the earliest printed histories of Texas, Newell gave his account of
interviews with Ben, the servant to Colonel Almonte.

The storming of the Alamo took place on the morning of the 6th, the second
after the conference of the Mexican officers. The events of that memorable
morning, on which was exhibited perhaps the most obstinate and determinate
valor ever known, have been but very partially related, since not an American
belonging to the fort—except a woman, Mrs. Dickerson, and a negro man, Col.
Travis' servant—was left to tell the tale. The account the most to be relied upon,
and which is undoubtedly substantially correct, is given by a negro man, Ben,
who, at the time of the siege, acted as cook for Santa Anna and Almonte. Ben
had previously been a steward on board several American vessels—had been
taken up at New York, in 1835, by Almonte as body servant—had accompanied
him in that capacity to Vera Cruz, and thence to Bexar. After the fall of the
Alamo he was sent, with Mrs. Dickerson and Travis' servant, to the Texan camp
at Gonzales, and subsequently became cook to General Houston.

"I," says a highly respectable officer of the General's Staff, "had repeated
conversations with Ben relative to the fall of the Alamo. He knew but little. He
stated that Santa Anna and Almonte occupied the same house in the town of
Bexar, and that he cooked for both; that, on the night previous to the storming
of the fort, Santa Anna ordered him to have coffee ready for them all night; that
both he and Almonte were conversing constantly, and did not go to bed; that
they went out about midnight, and about two or three o'clock returned together
to the house; that Santa Anna ordered coffee immediately, threatening to run
him through the body if it was not instantly brought; that he served them with
coffee; that Santa Anna appeared agitated, and that Almonte remarked 'it
would cost them much;' that the reply was, 'it was of no importance what the
cost was, that it must be done.'

"'After drinking coffee,' says Ben, 'they went out, and soon I saw rockets
ascending in different directions, and shortly after I heard musketry and cannon, and by the flashes I could distinguish large bodies of Mexican troops
under the walls of the Alamo. I was looking out of a window in the town, about
five hundred yards from the Alamo, commanding a view of it. The report of the
cannon, rifles, and musketry, was tremendous. It shortly died away, day broke
upon the scene, and Santa Anna and Almonte returned, when the latter
remarked, that 'another such victory would ruin them.' They then directed me
to go with them to the fort, and point out the bodies of Bowie and Travis—
whom I had known—which I did. The sight was most horrid.'"

2.12.2. Ben, interview, c. 1840?

Stiff, Edward. 1840. *The Texan Emigrant*. 313–15. Cincinnati: George Conclin.
Stiff quotes loosely and somewhat inaccurately from the journal of Almonte,
and then without transition goes into an interview with Ben.

The assault took place on the night of the 7th, and some circumstances attending it were narrated to me by a gentleman formally an officer in the Texan army,
which he had obtained from Santa Anna's servant, who after the battle of San
Jacinto was cook for Gen. Houston. The statements of this servant were generally relied on by those who knew him, and he contradicted in the most positive
terms the oft repeated rumor that the dead bodies of the Americans were burnt.
On the night of the 7th, Santa Anna ordered this servant to prepare and keep
refreshments ready all night, and he stated that Santa Anna appeared cast
down and discontented, and did not retire to rest at all. That accompanied by
his private Secretary the General went out about 11 o'clock and did not return
until 3 in the morning; that he served them with coffee of which Santa Anna
took but little, and seemed much excited, and observed, to Almonte, that if the
garrison could be induced to surrender, he would be content; for said he, if they
will not, I well know, that every man before the dawn of day must, unprepared,
meet his God. But what more can I do; my summonses, said he, are treated with
disdain; it appears to me the only alternative presented is to assault the garrison; we cannot delay longer here wasting the resources of the nation and any
termination of the affair will relieve, me of a load of anxiety. He further stated
that at 4 o'clock Santa Anna and other officers left the house, and very soon a
tremendous discharge of cannon told that the work of death was began; he saw
rockets in awful brilliancy blazing through the darkness of the night, and the
walls and grounds of the Alamo reflected the light so that from a window he
could plainly perceive columns of Mexican troops around the fort and ascending the walls on ladders, and that the whole interior of the Alamo was perfectly
illuminated, as he supposed, by the firing of the Americans within; and that the
old servant feelingly remarked that he liked master Santa Anna, but that when
he heard the thunders of the artillery and saw blazing rockets gleaming through
the air, he thought of Master George Washington and old Virginia, and prayed
to God that the Americans might whip.

Before day light the firing had ceased and every thing was again wrapped in
silence and gloom, when Santa Anna and his staff returned, one of them remarking that the victory had cost more than it was worth and that many such would
ruin them. At day light this servant who had seen Col. Crockett at the city of
Washington many years ago, and perhaps Col. Travis and Bowie, was taken to
the fort to designate their bodies; he done so, and found no less than 16 dead
Mexicans around the corpse of Colonel Crockett and one across it with the huge
knife of Davy buried in the Mexican's bosom to the hilt. He stated that these

three bodies were interred in the same grave separate from all the rest, and that he heard the Mexican officers say that their own loss was about 1200 men.

2.12.3. Ben?, possible interview, unknown date.

Helm, Mary S. 1884. *Scraps of Early Texas History.* 56. Austin, TX: B. R. Warner & Co.

This account is attributed to Ben rather than Joe by consistency with the preceding two documents.

When we returned home from a visit to New York, it was about the 15th of January, 1836, giving us plenty of time to get in our spring crops. Some of our friends had not yet returned from the fall campaign of 1835, being detained by sickness. These poor fellows were massacred while prisoners of war with their leader, Colonel Fannin; and San Antonio was taken by an army twenty or more to one, about the same time, and every man put to the sword with no quarter given—all of which is a part of history well known. But there are some items not so well known. A negro man, an officer's servant, was spared to carry the news to the Americans, and when asked which one of our men killed the most Mexicans, replied: "Colonel Crockett had the biggest pile."

2.13.1. Manuel Loranca, interview, 1878.

San Antonio Express. June 23 (or 28), 1878.

The referenced article of the *Corpus Christi Free Press* was not located to be verified.

SANTA ANNA'S LAST EFFORT.

THE ALAMO AND SAN JACINTO.

Narrative of a Mexican Sergeant who belonged to Santa Anna's Army.

[The following narrative, written for the Corpus Christi *Free Press* by an ex-sergeant in the last Mexican expedition under Santa Anna, is full of thrilling interest. It might be appropriately termed a "knapsack sketch." We are assured that the writer (ex-sergeant Manuel Loranca) has his original discharge from the expedition, and, if needed, can be sent to us. We are indebted to D. M. Hastings, Esq., Corpus Christi, who kindly made the translation.—ED. FREE PRESS.]

Manuel Loranca, who in the year 1835, was a Second Sergeant in the Mexican army, makes the following statement of what transpired within his own knowledge after the march from San Luis de Potosi for the campaign of Texas:

On the 25th day of October, 1835, his regiment being the vanguard of the Division under the command of Señor Don Joaquin Remires y Serna [sic; Sesma], marched towards Saltillo, thence to Monterey; from Monterey in the direction of Salevias de Victoria; from Victo [sic] to Lampasas and thence to Laredo, meeting there the Mexican forces retiring under the General Vicente Filisola and Martin Perfecto de Cos. This force came for the purpose of joining the President, Santa Anna, coming from the direction of Candela, for the purpose of opening in form the campaign of Texas.

This division marched immediately as vanguard to the Rio Grande, joined President Santa Anna and the forces brought by him, and followed him to San Antonio de Bexar. We advanced a force to the river Medina, from which point the President dispatched a column of cavalry to attack the Texas forces which were in San Antonio; but these, perceiving the movement, occupied the fort of the Alamo, which being defended by eighteen pieces of artillery, was difficult of assault.

About nine in the morning, the President Santa Anna arrived and joined with his escort and staff the column which was now in the vicinity of San Antonio. We marched upon the place and were received by the fort with one or two cannon shots; those in the Alamo raising a red flag.

Santa Anna then ordered a parley to be sounded, which was answered by the chiefs of the Alamo, and the President commissioned the Mexican Colonel Batress to confer with Bowie and Travis, both Colonels of the Texan forces holding the Alamo. This was on the 26th of February, 1836.

The President Santa Anna proposed to Travis and Bowie that they should surrender at discretion, with no other guarantee than that their lives should be spared. The said Texan chiefs answered and proposed to surrender the fort on being allowed to march out with their arms and go join their government (as they had permitted the Mexican forces under Generals Cos and Filisola when they capitulated to the Texans at the Mission de la Espada and were allowed to march out with their arms, munitions of war, provisions, etc., and join the Mexican army then in the field against Texas), and if this was not willingly conceded to them, they would willingly take all the chances of war.

The bombardment was effectually commenced on the 27th of the same month. During this time the Mexican forces were joined by several bodies of infantry, making about four thousand men.

On the 4th of March, the President Santa Anna called a council of war to consider the mode of assault of the Alamo, and they decided to make the assault on the 6th, at daybreak, in the following manner: On the north, Col. Don Juan Baptisto Morales with the Battalion "Firmas," of San Luis Potosi; on the west, Col. Don Mariano Salas, with the Battalion of Aldama; on the south, Col.

Jose Vicente Minon, with the Battalion of Infantry; on the east, a squadron of Lancers, flanked by a ditch, to cut off the retreat at the time of the assault. These Lancers were commanded by Gen. Don Joaquin Ramires y Serna.

The assault took place at 3:30 a.m. on the 6th, and was so sudden that the fort had only time to discharge four of the eighteen [*"cannon" in page tear*] which it had.

The Fort Alamo had only one entrance, which was on the south; and the approach was made winding to impede the entrance of the cavalry. The Mexican infantry, with ladders, were lying down at musket-shot distance, awaiting the signal of assault, which was to be given from a fort about a cannon-shot to the east of the Alamo, where the President Santa Anna was with the music of the regiment of Dolores and his staff to direct the movements. In the act of assault a confusion occurred, occasioned by darkness in which the Mexican troops opened fire on each other. A culverin, or 10 pound howitzer, fired from the fort, swept off a whole company of the Battalion Aldama, which made the attack on the point toward San Antonio.

After that we all entered the Alamo, and the first thing we saw on entering a room at the right was the corpses of Bowie and Travis. Then we passed to the corridor which served the Texans as quarters, and here found all refugees which were left. President Santa Anna immediately ordered that they should be shot, which was accordingly done, excepting only a negro and a woman having a little boy about a year old. She was said to be Travis' cook.

Sixty-two Texans who sallied from the east side of the fort, were received by the Lancers and all killed. Only one of these made resistance; a very active man, armed with a double barrel gun and a single-barrel pistol, with which he killed a corporal of the Lancers named Eugenio. These were all killed by the lance, except one, who ensconced himself under a bush and it was necessary to shoot him.

There in front of the fosse were gathered the bodies of all those who died by the lance, and those killed in the fort, making a total of two-hundred and eighty-three persons, including a Mexican found among them, who, it appears, had come from La Bahia (Goliad) with dispatches; and here they were ordered to be burned, there being no room in the *campo santo* or burying ground, it being all taken up with the bodies of upwards of four hundred Mexicans, who were killed in the assault.

[*The account continues with the later movements of the army to San Jacinto and the retreat of Filisola after the defeat there.*]

MANUEL LORANCA.

2.14.1.   Felix Nuñez, interview, 1889.

San Antonio Daily Express. June 30, 1889. 3.

A careful and detailed critical review with transcription of this source is by Stephen L. Hardin in the *Southwestern Historical Quarterly* 94, no.1 (July 1990): 65–84. This transcription is from a photocopy of the original newspaper article.

FALL OF THE ALAMO.

One of the Besiegers Tells the Story of the Siege and Final Assault.

FRIGHTFUL SCENES OF CARNAGE—DEATH OF TRAVIS AND THE "MAN IN THE FOX-SKIN CAP."

How the Bodies Were Collected and Burned—Horrible Scenes Depicted by an Eye-Witness

---

[Felix Nuñez is an aged Mexican who has lived in this and adjoining counties since the [y]ear 1837, and has long been noted among his neighbors for his wonderfully retentive memory and power of description. He bears an unexceptional reputation for truth and veracity, and THE EXPRESS has the assurance of many well known and reliable citizens of this county that in what he says he conscientiously endeavors to tell the truth, and that if there are any inaccuracies in his statement they must be attributed to incorrect information received at the time of which he writes. After leaving the Mexican army Señor Nuñez re-entered this country on a passport purchased from a Mexican named Bacca, and issued to him by General Sam Houston. Fearing punishment for his part in the war against the Texans, he lived several years under the name of Bacca. He says he kept the coat of Travis and the papers contained therein secreted about his premises until about eighteen years ago, when he found them so worm-eaten and mouldy that he destroyed the remnants, having all the time feared making his valuable possessions known, but desiring to retain them as mementoes of one of the most tragic battles known to the history of the world. The coat was "home made" of Texas jeans. Nuñez has always been reticent about his part in the war of Texas Independence, but a friend and neighbor for twenty-five years, Professor Geo. W. Noel, to whom THE EXPRESS is indebted for the interesting article to follow, has during that time taken notes of statements made by Nuñez during his periods of confidence, and having secured much information in that way, finally prevailed on the old gentleman to make a corrected statement concerning the thrilling event, and which the professor has translated for THE EXPRESS. Nuñez now lives near Amphion, in Atascosa county.]

[*The article has an artist's rendition of "THE ASSAULT ON THE ALAMO, March 6th, 1836."*]

My name is Felix Nuñez, and I was born in 1804, and am consequently nearly 85 years old. I was forcibly conscripted in 1835 in the state of Guadalajara, Mexico, and was assigned to duty in that division of the Mexican army which was always under the immediate command of President Santa Anna, and, as I was then 32 years of age, you will see that I had a good opportunity for knowing and observing every event that transpired within my sphere from the time of my enlistment until the unfortunate encounter at San Jacinto, April 21, 1836.

General Santa Anna with an army of 7,000 men started from Guerrero, Mexico, about the middle of February, 1836, and though marching on double-quick time we did not arrive at San Antonio until near the end of the month.

There was some delay at El Paso de la Pinta, on the Median, occasioned by the death of a colonel of one of the regiments and a favorite of General Santa Anna, who ordered this officer to be buried with the honors of war. Santa Anna, not wishing to take part in the obsequies of his deceased friend, moved on with his staff and the division of troops under his immediate command, and halted on the Alazan, a little west of the city. Shortly after his arrival at the Alazan he learned that there was a baile (a dance) going to take place in the Domingo Bustillo house, which is just north of the Southern hotel. Obtaining this information, Santa Anna doffed his regimentals and disguised himself as a muleteer and went to the dance. There he learned the exact force and number of the troops that were in the city and all other necessary information, as well, also, the feeling of the citizens in regard to the invasion. The president, being an elegant talker and a very brilliant conversationalist, directed his conversation to the Americans and Mexicans citizens who were in sympathy with the American cause. One of the incidents I recollect distinctly. It was a very heated controversy that took place between Gen. Santa Anna and Señor Vergara, the father-in-law of Capt. Jno. W. Smith (of whom I shall speak again), in which this gentleman gave Santa Anna an unmerciful abusing and hooted at the idea of the Mexicans ever subjugating the Americans. Just after the fall of the Alamo Gen. Santa Anna sent his orderly to Señor Vergara and commanded him to appear before him. Upon being asked if he recollected the conversation with the muleteer he was almost scared out of his wits. He was reprimanded by Santa Anna, who told him to go his way and sin no more. Here the president completely disguised, was talking and chatting in company with some of the Americans who had come over from the Alamo and participated in the festivities of the dance, not even dreaming that they were in such close proximity to the one who would shortly spread before them the last and fatal feast of death.

After the army invested San Antonio and the Americans had retreated to the Alamo, Santa Anna ordered the Americans to surrender. The summons was answered by those of the Alamo by the discharge of a cannon, whereupon Santa Anna caused a blood-red flag to be hoisted from the Cathedral of San Fernando on the west side of the Main plaza, which at that time was in plain view of the Alamo. Simultaneously all the bugles sounded a charge all along the lines of both cavalry and infantry, but this charge was repulsed by the Americans with heavy loss to us. Where-upon the President ordered "sapas" (subterranean houses) to be dug on the north, south and east of the Alamo, which were strongly garrisoned with troops, for the double purpose of preventing re-inforcements from entering the Alamo and to cut the Americans off from water. This completed the cordon of troops which was drawn around the doomed Alamo. And right here let me state that no ingress or egress could have been accomplished from the time our army regularly besieged the Alamo, and there was none, with the single exception of Don Juan Seguin and his company, who were permitted to leave. They were let go from the fact that they were Mexicans and we did not wish to harm them.

There was no Capt. John W. Smith and company, nor no one else ever cut their way through our lines and entered the Alamo, because they would have been cut to pieces in the attempt, for the main object of Santa Anna was to keep the garrison from receiving re-inforcements. And, moreover, there is but one Captain Jonh [sic] W. Smith mentioned about San Antonio and he was mayor of the city at the time of the desperate fight with the Comanche chiefs on the east side of the Main plaza. If he had been in the Alamo he would have been killed, and therefore could not have been mayor of San Antonio afterwards.

The second and third day of the siege resulted with very little variance from the first, to-wit: With heavy losses to our army. This so exasperated Santa Anna that he said, to use his own language, that he was losing the flower of his army, and to see the Alamo still hold out he became terribly enraged, and it was at this time that he made the fatal promise, that he would burn the last one of them when taken whether dead or alive. He immediately called a council of all his officers and proposed another attack on the Alamo in the evening of the third day's siege with his entire force. His cry was: "On to the Alamo." This was met with the cry by the officers and men that: "On to the Alamo was on to death."

A large majority of the officers were in favor of waiting until they could get more heavy cannon and perhaps by that time the garrison would be starved out and surrender and further bloodshed be avoided. But Santa Anna, with his usual impetuosity, swore that he would take the fort the next day or die in the attempt. So on Wednesday, the 6th day of March, 1836, and the fourth day of the siege, was the time fixed for the final assault.

Each and everything pertaining to the final assault underwent the personal supervision of General Santa Anna, to the end that it would be successful. Three of his most experienced officers were selected to assist him in command-ing the assaulting parties. General Vicente Felisola [sic], his second in com-mand, with a thousand picked men took charge of the assault on the east of the Alamo. General Castillior [sic], with a like number, was placed on the south side. General Ramirez Sesma was to have taken command on the west side next to the river, but seeing that President Santa Anna was determined to make the final assault the next day feigned sickness, the evening before, and was put under arrest and started back to the capital. This part of the command then devolved on Gen. Woll, so there was no General Sesma in command of any portion of the army at the fall of the Alamo, nor afterwards. The troops on the north and northwest, 1,500 in number, were commanded by General Santa Anna in person. This made 4,500 men who participated in the engagement. In addition to this, there was a fatigue party well supplied with ladders, crowbars and axes for the purpose of making breaches in the walls, or at any other vulnerable point.

The infantry were formed nearest the Alamo, as we made the least noise. The cavalry was formed around on the outside of the infantry, with special orders from all of the commanders to cut down every one who dared to turn back.

Everything being in readiness just at dawn of day on the 6th of March, and the fourth day of the siege, all the bugles sounded a charge from all points. At this time our cannon had battered down nearly all the walls that enclosed the church, consequently all the Americans had taken refuge inside the church, and the front door of the main entrance fronting to the west was open. Just outside of this door Col. Travis was working his cannon. The division of our army on the west side was the first to open fire. They fired from the bed of the river near where the opera house now stands. The first fire from the cannon of the Alamo passed over our heads and did no harm; but as the troops were advancing the second one opened a lane in our lines at least fifty feet broad. Our troops rallied and returned a terrible fire of cannon and small arms. After this the cannonading from the Alamo was heard no more. It is evident that this discharge killed Travis, for then the front door was closed and no more Americans were seen outside. By this time the court yard, the doors, the windows, roof and all around the doomed Alamo became one reeking mass of humanity. Each one of us vied with the other for the honor of entering the Alamo first. Just at sunrise a lone marksman appeared on top of the church and fired. A colonel was struck in the neck by this shot and died at sundown. This the officers took as an evidence that the Americans had opened a hole in the roof themselves. This proved to be true, for almost in the next moment another American appeared on top of the roof with a little boy in his arms, apparently about three years old, and attempted to jump off, but they were immediately riddled with bullets and both fell lifeless to the ground. With this the troops pressed on, receiving a deadly fire from the top of the roof, when it was discovered that the Americans had constructed a curious kind of ladder, or gangway, of long poles tied together with ropes and filled up on top with sticks and dirt. This reached from the floor on the inside of the church to over the top edge of the wall, to the ground on the outside. As soon as this discovery was made Santa Anna ordered his entire division to charge and make for the gangway and hole in the roof. But most of the soldiers who showed themselves at this place got not into the Alamo, but into another world, for nearly every one of them was killed. We then found out that all the Americans were alive inside of the church. During the entire siege up to this time we had not killed even a single one, except Colonel Travis and the man and boy referred to, for afterwards there were no new graves nor dead bodies in a advanced state of decomposition discovered.

By this time the front door was battered down and the conflict had become general. The entire army came pouring in from all sides, and never in all my life did I witness or hear of such a hand to hand conflict. The Americans fought with the bravery and desperation of tigers, although seeing that they were contending against the fearful odds of at least two hundred to one, not one single one of them tried to escape or asked for quarter, the last one fighting with as much bravery and animation as at first. None of them hid in rooms, nor asked for quarter, for they knew none would be given. On the contrary, they all died like heroes, selling their lives as dear as possible. There was but one man killed in a room, and this was a sick man in the big room on the left of the main entrance. He was bayoneted in his bed. He died apparently without shedding a drop of blood. The last moments of the conflict became terrible in the extreme. The soldiers in the moments of victory became entirely uncontrollable, and, owing to the darkness of the building and the smoke of battle, fell to killing one another, not being able to distinguish friend from foe. General Filisola was the first one to make this discovery. He reported it to General Santa Anna, who at once mounted the walls. Although the voice of our idolized commander could scarcely be heard above the din and roar of battle, his presence, together with the majestic waving of his sword sufficed to stop the bloody carnage, but not until all the buglers entered the church and sounded a retreat, did the horrible butchery entirely cease.

To recount the individual deeds of valor, of the brave men who were slain in the Alamo, would fill a volume as large as the History of Texas; nevertheless there was one who perished in that memorable conflict who is entitled to a passing notice. The one to whom I refer was killed just inside of the front door. The peculiarity of his dress, and his undaunted courage attracted the attention of several of us, both officers and men. He was a tall American of rather dark complexion and had on a long cuera (buck skin coat) and a round cap without any bill, and made of fox skin, with the long tail hanging down his back. This man apparently had a charmed life. Of the many soldiers who took deliberate aim at him and fired, not one ever hit him. On the contrary he never missed a shot. He killed at least eight of our men, besides wounding several others. This fact being observed by a lieutenant who had come in over the wall he sprung at him and dealt him a deadly blow with his sword, just above the right eye, which felled him to the ground and in an instant he was pierced by not less than twenty bayonets. This lieutenant said that if all Americans had have killed as many of our men as this one had, our army would have been annihilated before the Alamo could have been taken. He was about the last man that was killed.

After all the firing had ceased and the smoke cleared away, we found in the large room to the right of the main entrance three persons, two Mexican women named Juana De Melto and La Quintanilla and a negro boy, about fifteen or sixteen years old who told us that he was the servant of Colonel Travis. If there had been any other persons in the Alamo they would have been killed, for General Santa Anna had ordered us not to spare neither age nor sex, especially of those who were Americans or American descent.

On the floor of the main building there was a sight which beggared all description. The earthen floor was nearly shoe-mouth deep in blood and weltering therein laid 500 dead bodies, many of them still clinched together with one hand, while the other held fast a sword, a pistol or a gun, which betokened the kind of conflict which had just ended.

General Santa Anna immediately ordered every one of the Americans to be dragged out and burnt. The infantry was ordered to tie on the ropes, and the cavalry to do the dragging. When the infantry commenced to tie the ropes to the dead bodies they could not tell our soldiers from the Americans, from the fact that their uniforms and clothes were so stained with blood and smoke and their faces so besmeared with gore and blackened that one could not distinguish the one from the other. This fact was reported to Santa Anna and he appeared at the front and gave instructions to have every face wiped off and for the men to be particular not to mistake any of our men for Americans and burn them, but to give them decent sepulture. He stood for a moment gazing on the horrid and ghastly spectacle before him, but soon retired and was seen no more.

When the Americans were all dragged out and counted there were 180 including officers and men. Upon the other hand this four days siege and capture of the Alamo cost the Mexican nation at least a thousand men, including killed and wounded, a large majority of this number being killed. Our officers, after the battle was over, were of the opinion that, if the Americans had not made holes in the roof themselves, the Alamo could not have been taken by assault. It would either have had to have been starved out or demolished by heavy artillery.

After we had finished our task of burning the Americans a few of us went back to the Alamo to see if we could pick up any valuables, but we could not find anything scarcely, except their arms and a few cooling utensils and some clothing. I found Colonel Travis' coat which was hanging on a peg driven to the wall just behind the cannon and from where his dead body had just been dragged away. In the pockets I found some papers that resembled paper money or bonds of some kind. His cannon was standing just as he had left it with its mouth pointing west and not towards the Alamo plaza. We did not use Colonel Travis' cannon, nor even our own, because cannons were almost useless on the day that we made the final assault.

The next movement inaugurated by Santa Anna was to set out for the interior of Texas, and, as I have stated before, that I belonged to the division under his immediate command, I accompanied the invading army and was taken prisoner by the Americans at the Battle of San Jacinto.

After San Jacinto I resolved never to take up arms against my fellowman again and promised myself never to return to the army that had been triumphant in so many hard fought battles—an army that was commanded by (as he always called himself) "The Napoleon of the West," but had just been so completely defeated, nay, annihilated, by a handful of poor undisciplined half-armed Americans.

In conclusion, permit me to state that I have no object in giving this description of the fall of the Alamo only as a response to the solicitations of my friend and benefactor, Mr. G. W. Noel, who has been talking to me occasionally for the last twenty-five years and taking notes for the purpose of writing a true account of the siege and capture as detailed by one of the assaulting party, that those heroic deeds of valor for which his countrymen are so justly famous may be handed down to posterity free from those errors into which some of the historians of Texas have so innocently and unknowingly fallen. And to add solemnity to this occasion and veneration for the "martyred heroes of the Alamo" he has seen fit to make this account public, upon the very spot of ground that was drenched with their blood and at the very place where the air was filled with the fumes of their roasting flesh.

FELIX NUNEZ.

2.15.1.   Colonel Urissa, interview, 1859.

Labadie, N. D., ed. 1859. Urissa's account of the Alamo massacre. *Texas Almanac.* 61–62.

This is part of a longer account of experiences of a veteran of the Texas Revolution.

URISSA'S ACCOUNT OF THE ALAMO MASSACRE.

One day Dr. Phelps being about to leave for his place on the Brazos, requested me to take charge of some eight or nine of the wounded, thus adding to my labors. Among others, he pointed out to me a Mexican officer wounded on the 20th, on whom Dr. Cooper had been attending. Learning that this officer was present at the storming of the Alamo, I desired him to give me a statement of the facts connected with that event, which had happened but a few weeks before, and about which our information was vague and uncertain. He first made some inquiries of the details of the battle of the 21st, the number of killed, wounded, etc., asking the names of the Mexican officers that had been taken prisoners, and that had been killed. "Is General Castrion [*Castrillion*] alive?" said he. "No," said I, "his body has been identified on the battle-field, his breast and both arms pierced with balls." "Poor Castrion," said he, the tears coming into his eyes, "he was a good man. Can you have him buried? He was opposed to Santa Anna exposing himself as he did, by going in advance of his main army; but Santa Anna would not listen to him. When you opened on us on the

20th, I was in the act of putting my foot in the stirrup, when a slug-shot struck my hip, tearing off the flesh, as you see. Santa Anna was near me, but paid no regard to me, as Castrion was then forewarning him of our probable defeat, although young, Castrion was the best general in our army. And as regards the slaughter of the Alamo, Castrion was opposed to putting the men to death. One night, past midnight, when Santa Anna and Castrion were planning an assault, Santa Anna declared that none should survive. It was then inevitable that the fort could hold out but little longer, and Castrion was persuading the commander to spare the lives of the men. Santa Anna was holding in his hand the leg of a chicken which he was eating, and holding it up, he said: 'What are the lives of soldiers more than of so many chickens? I tell you, the Alamo must fall, and my orders must be obeyed at all hazards. If our soldiers are driven back, the next line in their rear must force those before them forward, and compel them to scale the walls, cost what it may.' I was then acting as Santa Anna's secretary, and ranked as Colonel. My name is Urissa. After eating, Santa Anna directed me to write out his orders, to the effect that all the companies should be brought out early, declaring that he would take his breakfast in the fort the next morning. His orders were dispatched, and I retired. I soon after heard the opening fire. By day-break our soldiers had made a breach, and I understood the garrison had all been killed. At about eight o'clock I went into the fort, and saw Santa Anna walking to and fro. As I bowed, he said to me, pointing to the dead: 'These are the chickens. Much blood has been shed; but the battle is over: it was but a small affair.' As I was surveying the dreadful scene before us, I observed Castrion coming out of one of the quartels [*sic*], leading a venerable-looking old man by the hand; he was tall, his face was red, and stooped forward as he walked. The President stopped abruptly, when Castrion, leaving his prisoner, advanced some four or five paces towards us, and with his graceful bow, said: "My General, I have spared the life of this venerable old man, and taken him prisoner." Raising his head, Santa Anna replied, "What right have you to disobey my orders? I want no prisoners," and waving his hand to a file of soldiers, he said, "Soldiers, shoot that man," and almost instantly he fell, pierced with a volley of balls. Castrion turned aside with tears in his eyes, and my heart was too full to speak. So there was not a man left. Even a cat that was soon after seen running through the fort, was shot as the soldiers exclaimed: "It is not a cat, but an American." "What was that old man's name?" said I. "I believe," said he, "they called him *Coket*." At that time, we knew very little of David Crockett, and Dr. Phelps, who was still present at his [*sic*] conversation, knew as little as the rest of us. All I knew was, that I had heard of David Crockett passing through Nacogdoches in the month of February, to join the army, with some fifteen others. But I have never since had any doubt but that Urissa's account gave the fate of Crockett truly. This statement was made some four or five days after the battle of the 21st, and Urissa could have had no motive to misrepresent the facts.

2.16.1.   Unidentified, newsletter account, 1836.

El Mosquito Mexicano, translated by John Wheat. April 5, 1836. 2:108. Mexico.
This letter sounds similar to the writings of Sánchez or Caro. An excerpt (given as April 15) is in Williams, *HQ* 37:35 n. 72; and a different version was published in Rios 1987. Rios's source was Leona Vicario, *Por Extraordinario Llegado del Alamo*, Coahuila y Tejas: Imprenta del Gobierno, 1836. (Additional material from *El Mosquito Mexicano* in support of de la Peña is given in section 2.9.3.)

El Mosquito Mexicano
April 5, 1836

Leóna Vicario, March 16, 1836.
By special [post] arriving from the Alamo today at four in the morning, the following letter has been received.

Béjar, March 7, 1836
"Dear brothers of my heart: Thanks be given to Our Lord God, because the triumphs of our arms multiply. The ungrateful and arrogant colonists, who caused us so many days of anguish in the previous campaign, now have succumbed to the fate that their foolish audacity has dealt them. After thirteen days of continuous cannon fire, it was decided by the most excellent señor president night before last at two in the morning, that the fortification of the Alamo should be assaulted. To this end four columns were prepared, commanded by Sr. General COS and by the señores Colonels Don Juan Morales, Don N. Duque de Estrada, and Romero. I marched under the direct orders of Sr. COS, and therefore I will tell you what I saw up close. After a large circling movement, we stationed ourselves at three in the morning on the north side at about three hundred paces from the enemy fortress. There, rest was given to the column, which consisted of the Aldama battalion and part of the San Luis Potosí. We remained prone on the ground until five thirty (the morning felt very cold), when the call to march sounded, ordered given by His Excellency the Sr. President from a battery where he himself was located, between north and east. Immediately Sr. COS shouted, "Up!" and placed himself at the head of the column. We rushed to the attack, for which purpose we carried ladders, planks, crowbars, picks, etc. Though the distance was short, in crossing it we suffered two cannon volleys of grapeshot that felled more than forty men. The tenacious resistance of our enemies was amazing, as was the steadfast and dauntless [action] of all the señores generals, commanders, officers, and troops. It seemed that the bullets and grapeshot from the cannons and rifles were spent, [bouncing harmlessly off] the breasts of our soldiers, who constantly shouted, LONG LIVE THE MEXICAN REPUBLIC! LONG LIVE GENERAL SANTA ANNA! I assure you that all notion of fright or terror vanished at the sight of so many valiant men who, up ladders, over batteries, through embrasures, and even over one another, overran the defenses. The four columns and the

reserves, as if by magic, climbed the enemy's walls at the same time, and rushed into the grounds after about three quarters of an hour of terrible firing. When that ceased, there ensued a horrible struggle with blades, and then a pitiful but deserved slaughter of the ungrateful colonists, who threw down their weapons and thought to find safety in escape or by hiding. Miserable souls! They no longer exist: They all died, everyone, and up to now I have seen 257 bodies burned (to avoid their putrefaction), without counting those who died earlier during the thirteen day [siege], or those [bodies] being collected of the ones who in vain sought safety in escape. Their commander, named Trawis [sic], died a brave man with carbine in hand behind a cannon. But the perverse braggart Santiago Bowie died like a woman, almost hidden beneath a mattress. On our side, we have many dead officers and troops, and about two hundred wounded, a painful loss, but a small one if one considers the strong position occupied by the enemy and the quality of the latter. Now the outrage that we suffered before is avenged. The Most Excellent Sr. President made a beautiful speech to the entire division inside the Alamo, in sight of the enemy dead, and he has been pleased with everyone's performance.

At San Patricio, Yompson [sic] has died along with sixteen [others], and twenty-three prisoners were taken by the gallant Sr. General Urrea. On the 2nd of the current [month] this same [general] killed 42 of the enemy, among whom were identified Morris and the never-well-thought-of Don Diego Grant.

This deed has been celebrated by this town with the greatest enthusiasm, because in addition to seeing it as such a glorious triumph, which proves the courage and decisiveness of the MEXICAN ARMY, it gives hope for a bright future. The death of the foreigners Trawis, Morris, Grant, and Bowie, principal instigators of the rebellion of the colonists of Tejas and of all the upheavals that this department has suffered, should greatly dishearten their allies. Eternal praise to the immortal SANTA-ANNA and to the generals, commanders, officers, and troops who so heroically have avenged the outrages perpetrated on our great nation! Eternal praise to the valiant General COS, who at the head of the column that made the assault, has vindicated himself so gallantly against the gratuitous and indecent accusations of his unjust enemies.

2.17.1.   Mexican deserter, newspaper report, 1836.

Arkansas Gazette. April 12, 1836. Little Rock.
This article was repeated in *The Advocate*, April 15, 1836, also of Little Rock. A sample of David Crockett's humor happens to be in that paper and is included for extra color.

LATEST FROM TEXAS.—DIRECT.
Mr. JESSE B. BADGETT, who was one of a small party who left Little Rock, for Texas, last fall, and who was a member of the late Convention at Washington,

the Seat of Government of Texas, returned to this place, on Sunday evening last, direct from that country, and has communicated to us the following highly interesting news from the theatre of war.

San Antonio, as heretofore stated, was taken by storm, by an overwhelming force, commanded by Gen. Santa Anna, in person, early on the morning of the 6th ult. The whole force of Col. Travis, at its capture, was only 183 men, (14 of whom were on the sick list, and unable to take part in the battle.) They were ALL SLAIN. The siege lasted 14 days and nights, and, from the best information that could be obtained from a Mexican deserter, the Mexican loss during the siege amounted to 881 killed, and about 700 wounded. The deserter reported, that, at 11 o'clock on the night of the 5 ult., the Mexicans formed, to the number of 3400 infantry, led by Gen. Moro, in four columns, supported by 2000 cavalry, led by Santa Anna, in person, and, at between 3 and 4 o'clock, on the next morning, at a signal given by throwing up rockets from the town, the attack was simultaneously made on all sides of the garrison. The besieged, considering their small number, were well prepared for the assault—every man being provided with at least a brace of pistols and four or five rifles and muskets, all loaded, besides knives—and poured in a most deadly fire on the assailants, with cannon and small arms. The struggle, for a short period, was most desperate, but the garrison could not long sustain the attack of so overwhelming a force. By half an hour before sun-rise, on the morning of the 6th, the gallant spirits who had so bravely defended the post, and killed and wounded more than five times their own number, were numbered with the dead—and Santa Anna, surrounded by his life-guards, made his triumphant entry into the fort. In this assault, the Mexican loss was said to be 521 killed, and nearly the same number wounded.

Col. Travis was killed within the first hour of the storming of the garrison, having first killed, with his own hand, Gen. Moro, who led the storming party, by running him through with his sword. On his fall, the command of the Texians devolved on Adj't Maj. J. J. Baugh, who fell in the course of an hour or two, when the command devolved on Col. David Crockett, who likewise soon fell.

The following are the names of such of the officers who fell in defending San Antonio, as are recollected by Mr. Badgett:

Col. W. B. Travis, commandant; Col. James Bowie, Col. David Crockett, Maj. Green B. Jamison, (formerly of Ky.), Capts. Baugh, of Va., Blair, formerly of Conway county, A. T. Cary of La., Baker of Mississippi, Blasby of the New Orleans Grays, J. G. Washington of Tenn., Harrison of Tenn., Forsyth of N. York, Jones, do. J. Kimble of Gonzales; Lieuts. Dickinson and Evans; Sergt. Maj. Williamson from Philadelphia; Dr. Mitcherson of VA., Surgeon Pollard.

The previous report of the death of Col. JESSE BENTON, is incorrect. Mr. Badgett saw him near Nacogdoches, about the 25th, on his way to Jonesborough, Miller country, in this Territory, where a volunteer company was organizing, and with whom he intended marching for the seat of war.

On the 11th March, Santa Anna marched from San Antonio, with 3000 men, for Laborde (Goliad), which post was defended by Col. Fanning, with about 800 men, with plenty of provisions and ammunition, and who said he could defend his position against any force the Mexicans could bring against him.

On the 12th, Gen. Almonte and Col. Ball (an American) left San Antonio, for Gonzales, with 2000 men, but, after marching 27 miles to the Sea willow river, changed their directions, and bent their course towards Laborde, to assist Santa Anna in reducing that post. From the Sea willow, they sent Mrs. Dickinson, the widow of Lieut. Dickinson, who was killed in the storming of San Antonio, with her child (who was not killed, as previously reported) and servant, to Gen. Houston's camp at Goliad; at the same time Gen. Almonte sent his servant to Gen. Houston, with Santa Anna's proclamation, offering an amnesty to the inhabitants and Texian troops, provided they would yield submission, and give up their arms, to the Mexican authorities. Gen. Houston detained the servant, and sent to the Mexican commander, by a Spaniard, a copy of the Declaration of Independence recently agreed on at Washington.

Mr. Badgett left Washington (Seat of Gov't) on 18th March, and, on the next day, arrived at General Houston's camp, at Beason's Crossing of the Colorado, 90 miles this side of San Antonio, to which point Gen. H. had fallen back from Gonzales, which he burnt before abandoning it. Gen. H. was fortifying his camp, had about 2000 men, and reinforcements were arriving daily. Mr. B. thinks there is no doubt he had a force of at least 4000 men, in a few days after he left his camp.

On the 20th, Mr. Badgett left Gen. Houston's camp, on the Colorado, and, on the next day, reached Washington, where the Convention were still in session, but adjourned on the following day, 22d, after forming a Constitution for the Republic of Texas.

[*The following is from* The Advocate, *April 15, 1836, Little Rock, Arkansas.*]
On Crockett's return to his constituents after his first session in Congress, a nation of them surrounded him one day, and began to interrogate him about Washington, "What time do they dine at Washington, Colonel?" asked one. "Why," said he, "the common people, such as you, here, get dinners at one o'clock, but the gentry and big bugs dine at three. As for us representatives, we dine at four, and the aristocracy and the Senate, they don't get their victuals till five." "Well, when does the President fodder?" asked another. "Old Hickory!" exclaimed the Colonel, (attempting to appoint a time in accordance with the dignity of the station) "Old Hickory! well if he dines before the next day I wish I may be tetotally ———!"

2.17.2   Apolinario [Polin] Saldigua, interview, 1882.

Sowell, A. J. 1884. *Rangers and Pioneers of Texas.* 145–49. San Antonio: Shepard Bros. & Co.

The interview was not located in the cited *Houston Daily Post*, March 1, 1882. Groneman (1996, 83–87) reprinted it with the name Saldigna in a version with differences in both style and some content, such as a more positive identification of Crockett's body. The attributed author is the same William Zuber who is the source for the Rose story (1.8.1).

From the Houston *Daily Post*, bearing the date, March 1, 1882, we get the winding-up scene at the Alamo after the battle. The sketch was written by W. P. Zuber, of Iola, Grimes county. The facts were furnished him by a Mexican fifer, who was in the assault, and is as follows:

"This sketch is an account of the burning of the bodies of the heroes of the Alamo, after the storming of that fortress by the forces of Santa Anna, on the 6th of March, 1836, and includes the murder of Colonel James Bowie. The facts were related to me by the Mexican fifer, Apolinario Saldigua, who was then but sixteen years old, and who was an eye-witness of the scene. He was known in Texas by a contraction of the Christian name Polin, pronounced Poleen, accenting the second syllable. I knew him during several years, and feel that I can safely vouch for him as a truthful boy.

"After the fort (the celebrated church of the Alamo at San Antonio) had been stormed, and all of its defenders had been reported to have been slain, and when the Mexican assailants had been recalled from within the walls, Santa Anna and his staff entered the fortress. Polin being a fifer, and therefore a privileged person, and possibly more so on account of his tender age, by permission, entered with them. He desired to see all that was to be seen; and for this purpose, he kept himself near his general-in-chief. Santa Anna had ordered that no corpses should be disturbed till after he should have looked upon them all, and seen how every man had fallen. He had employed three or four citizens of San Antonio to enter with him, and to point out to him the bodies of several distinguished Texans.

"The principal corpses that Santa Anna desired to see, were those of Colonel W. Barrett Travis, Colonel James Bowie, and another man, whose name Polin could not remember. I asked Polin if the other man's name was Crockett, to which he replied: 'May be so; I can't remember.'

"On entering the fort, the eyes of the conquerors were greeted by a scene which Polin could not well describe. The bodies of the Texans lay as they had fallen, and many of them were covered by those of Mexicans who had fallen upon them. The close of the struggle seemed to have been a hand-to-hand engagement, and the number of slain Mexicans exceeded that of the Texans. The ground was covered by the bodies of the slain. Santa Anna and his suite, for a time, wandered from one apartment of the fortress to another, stepping over and upon the dead, seemingly enjoying this scene of human butchery.

"After a general reconnoitering of the premises, the Dictator was conducted to the body of Colonel Travis. After viewing his form and features a few moments, Santa Anna thrust his sword through the dead man's body, and turned away. He was then conducted to the body of the man whose name Polin could not remember. This man lay with his face upward, and his body was covered by those of many Mexicans who had fallen upon him. His face was florid, like that of a living man, and looked like a healthy man asleep. Santa Anna viewed him for a few moments, thrust his sword through his breast, and turned away.

"The one who had come to point out certain bodies, made a long but unsuccessful search for the body of Colonel Bowie, and reported to Santa Anna that it could not to be found.

"Then a detail of Mexican soldiers came into the fort. They were commanded by two officers, a captain and a junior officer, whose title Polin could not explain to me; but whom I shall for convenience call the lieutenant. They were both quite young men, very fair, and handsome, and so nearly alike in complexion, form, size and features, that Polin judged them to be brothers; the captain being apparently a little older than the other. Polin did not remember to have ever seen them before; was confident that he never saw them afterward; and did not learn their names.

"After the entry of this detail, Santa Anna and his suite retired; but the two officers, with their detail, remained within. The two kept themselves close together, side by side. Polin was desirous to know what was to be done, and remained with the detail; and to enable himself to see all that was to be seen, he kept near the officers, never losing sight of them.

"As soon as the Dictator and his suite retired, the squad began to take up the Texans and to bring them together, and lay them in a pile. I had learned from other prisoners that the Mexicans, at the same time, performed the additional work of rifling the pockets of the slain Texans.

"The two officers took a stand, about the center of the main area. The first corpse was brought and laid as the captain directed. This formed a nucleus for a pile. The bodies were brought successively, each by four men, and dropped near the captain's feet. In imitation of the general, the captain viewed the body of each dead Texan for a few moments, and thrust his sword through him, and then, by a motion of his sword, directed the four men who had brought him, to throw him upon the pile, which pantomime was instantly obeyed.

"When all the Texans had been thrown on the pile, four soldiers walked around it, each carrying a can of camphene, which he spurted the liquid upon the pile. This process was continued until all the bodies were thoroughly wetted; then a match was thrown upon the pile, and the combustible fluid instantly sent up a flame to an immense height.

"While the fluid was being thrown upon the pile, four soldiers brought a cot, on which lay a sick man, and set it down by the captain; and one of them remarked, 'Here, captain, is a man who is not dead.' 'Why is he not dead?' asked the captain. 'We found him in a room by himself,' said the soldier. 'He seems to be very sick, and I suppose he was not able to fight, and was placed there by his companions, to be in a safe place, and out of the way.' The captain gave the sick man a searching look, and said, 'I think I have seem this man before.' The lieutenant replied, 'I think I have too,' and stooping down, he examined his features closely. Then, raising himself up, he addressed the captain: 'He is no other than the infamous Bowie.' The captain then also stooped, gazed intently upon the sick man's face, assumed an erect position, and confirmed the conviction of the lieutenant.

"The captain then looked fiercely upon the sick man and said: 'How is it, Bowie, you have been found hidden in a room by yourself, and have not died fighting, like your companions?' To which Bowie replied, in good Castilian: 'I should certainly have done so, but you see I am sick, and can not get off this cot.' 'Ah, Bowie,' said the captain, 'you have come to a *fearful end*—and well do you deserve it. As an immigrant to Mexico, you have taken an oath, before God, to support the Mexican government; but now you are violating that oath by fighting against the government which you have been sworn to support. But this perjury, common to all your countrymen, is not your only offense. You have married a respectable Mexican lady, and are fighting against her countrymen. Thus you have not only perjured yourself, but you have also betrayed your own family.'

"'I did,' said Bowie, 'take an oath to support the constitution of Mexico; and in defense of that constitution I am now fighting. You took the same oath, when you accepted your commission in the army; and you are now violating that oath, and betraying the trust of your countrymen, by fighting under a faithless tyrant for the destruction of that constitution and for the ruin of your people's liberties. The perjury and treachery are not *mine*, but *yours*.'

"The captain indignantly ordered Bowie to shut his mouth. 'I shall never shut my mouth for your like,' said Bowie, 'while I have a tongue to speak.' 'I will soon relieve you of that,' said the captain.

"Then he caused the four of his minions to hold the sick man, while a fifth, with a sharp knife, split his mouth, on each side, to the ramus of the jaw, then took hold of his tongue, cut it off, and threw it upon the pile of dead men. Then, in obedience to motion of the captain's sword, the four soldiers who held him, lifted the writhing body of the mutilated, bleeding, tortured invalid from his cot, and pitched him alive upon the funeral pile.

"At that moment a match was thrown upon the funeral pile. The combustible fluid instantly sent up a flame to an amazing height. The sudden generation of a great heat drove all the soldiers back to the wall. The officers, pale as corpses, stood gazing at the immense columns of fire, and trembled from head to foot, as if they would break asunder at every joint. Polin stood between them and heard the lieutenant whisper, in a faltering and broken articulation, 'It takes him up—to God.'

"Polin believed that the lieutenant alluded to the ascension, upon the wings of that flame, of Bowie's soul to that God, who would surely award due vengeance to his fiendish murderers.

"Not being able to fully comprehend the great combustibility of the camphene, Polin also believed that the sudden elevation of that great pillar of fire was an indication of God's hot displeasure toward those torturing murderers. He further believed that the two officers were of the same opinion, and thus he accounted for their agitation. And he thought the same idea pervaded the whole detail, as every man appeared to be greatly frightened.

"For the time, Polin stood amazed, expecting each moment that the earth would open a chasm through which every man in the fort would drop into perdition. Terrified by this conviction, he left the fort as speedily as possible.

"On a subsequent day, Polin visited the fort again. It was then cleansed, and it seemed to be a comfortable place. But in a conspicuous place, in the main area, he saw the one relic of the great victory—a pile of charred fragments of human bones."

2.17.3   Sgt. Santiago Rabia, journal, 1836.

Rabia, Santiago, Papers, translated by John Wheat. N.d. (c. 1838). DRT. The original notebooks in the DRT collections were started when Sergeant Rabia was a prisoner on Galveston Island after the battle of San Jacinto. The complete account was first translated in a typescript, also in the DRT Library, by Ned Brierley, trans., 1997, *The Journal of Sergeant Santiago Rabia*, Austin, TX: Texian Army Investigations (copyrighted Thomas Ricks Lindley).

[Santiago Rabia]

We left for Moncloba on the 1st of February of [1]836 and arrived on the 4th. We left for Río Grande on the 8th and arrived on the 12th. We left for San Ant[oni]o Béjar on the 16th and arrived on the 23rd of the month stated above. The enemy was greeted with 3 *granadas* [mortars], lasting alternatively for fifteen days [figuratively, two weeks] and the assault on the fortification of the Alamo was made on the 6th of March, between four and six in the morning. The battalions taking part in the aforesaid assault were the following: _?_adara [or adares? i.e. Zapadores?]==Aldama==Toluca Ma?_ [Matamoros?].....S[a]n Luis. Cavalry: Regiment of Dolores and 2nd _?_ of Tampico. The force that was in the afore-mentioned Alamo consisted of 200 [and] 50 Americans, [and] 4 women. They were all killed, and only one man and the women were spared. The dead and wounded among the Mexican troops were around five hundred men.

Commentary

Other Mexican Sources (2.10–2.17)

As a collection, these documents from Mexican sources come from individuals of lower rank or position than the others presented so far. They are also a far more mixed ensemble in terms of quality, consistency, and difficulty of interpretation, and they range from accounts considered quite reliable, such as those of Ben, to ones that are probably useless or even fraudulent, such as that of Nuñez.

The first account is that of Sgt. Francisco Becerra (2.10.1), who was in the employ of John Ford. John Linn (3.4.3) also reported a Sergeant Becero as a servant of his for several years, though the Linn account seems basically a rewrite of Potter (5.1.7) and Yoakum (5.1.5), with little if any material from Becerra.[1] That Ford is connected with Becerra is important because, due to Ford's stature, this account was more widely disseminated in the late nineteenth century than many in this collection. As noted by Dan Kilgore, this account is important for Bowie's final moments, the execution of prisoners after the battle, and "Dickinson's leap" (which was later ignored).[2]

Becerra's account, however, has a suspicious tendency to answer in some way what the Texans he knew later in life would have questioned him about. Probably every Mexican soldier questioned by a Texan was asked how key leaders like Bowie, Travis, and Crockett died. Becerra supplied a version for all three—a figure in bed clearly suggestive of Bowie, and Travis and Crockett sitting or lying on the floor of an inner room. It is not credible, however, that a soldier would have entered a room with an enemy and retired without at least checking on his condition or whether he was armed, or that Travis and Crockett would not have been doing something more active than what is given in Becerra's description, and separately. In the case of Travis, at least, there are enough other versions to reject this detail on the basis of inconsistency.

Other details of Becerra are also inconsistent. There is described the burning of the prairies before the army reached San Antonio (when the Texans had very little idea of their approach), the capture in San Antonio of the Mission Concepción before the Alamo, the battle lasting until nine in the morning, and Mexican casualties well in excess of what is believable.

These suspicious details, however, are relatively few in comparison with all the details of the entire account. Becerra was at his most vivid and clearest in describing the violence and courage of both sides—which would be the most memorable to a soldier. Nor did he claim a special role in the fighting, which is frequently an indicator of an overactive imagination. Even in the narrative of the two defenders reputed to be Travis and Crockett, the details of the incident are rather clearer than the identification of the individuals, which was given almost as an afterthought. These details easily could have been based on something that actually happened, with the individuals' identification a later "refinement" in response to questioning. The tone throughout is more that of a Texan than a Mexican soldier, indicating that the account was heavily influenced in later years by questioners. Most of what is described seems to be reasonable for a participant to have experienced, but more incidences of the war are described than one might expect from a single participant. A reasonable conclusion, based on this quick look, is that Becerra's account could well be authentic but must be treated with caution on the specifics or where he is not a direct participant. Lord has a contrasting opinion, however, rating him the least reliable of the Mexican sources. The Becerra/Ford account should be a good candidate for a future in-depth study.

Not central to the purpose of this book, but still interesting, is the story of the girl and the false wedding. This account of Becerra's was printed in 1882, long after Santa Anna's enemies had published attacks on his character. For instance, Anne Crawford in *The Eagle: The Autobiography of Santa Anna,* adds a note on a different but similar "lurid" account involving a young girl.[3] This indicates that analogous accusations were circulating about Santa Anna prior to the publication of Becerra.

The narration of Creed Taylor as edited by DeShields (2.11.1), which includes the Soldana account, is of interest in that it gives some additional stories not otherwise recorded. These include the possible desertion of a small group at the start of the siege (though it differs from de la Peña in why citizens carried wood for the cremation of the Alamo defenders), a youthful view by Juan Díaz of the entry of the Mexican Army into San Antonio, possible secondhand comments from Susanna Dickinson, a story from an unidentified Mexican captain, and another local vicinity experience from a Rodríguez (perhaps J. M. Rodríguez in 3.3.1?). As these are stand-alone stories, they cannot be readily compared with other documents (except for another version of Crockett's death) and so can be accepted or rejected as the individual reader sees fit. One seemingly noteworthy entry is the last encounter of Almaron Dickinson with his wife, which seems to confirm a version presented earlier (1.2.7, 1.2.10). The problem with this, though, is that the source might well have been one of those documents, and therefore this story may not be independent. In fact, the wording is essentially that of Morphis, and since DeShields knew of the Zuber/Rose story, we know that the Taylor/DeShields account was written after Morphis was published.

However, one outright error is that Taylor portrays Travis in command in Béxar through January, sending a detail to burn the grass in early January and holding the town during the clash of Governor Smith and the Council, which was later in January. Apparently he was unaware of the prior commander J. C. Neill.

The Soldana story is more significant than the other Taylor/DeShields stories, being about an identified individual and having a longer narrative content. The Soldana story of Crockett's death is curiously like DeShields's earlier unidentified captain, except with the sequence of gun and knife reversed. The report of the "tall man" (Crockett) firing from the parapet during the siege sounds very much like what would be expected of Crockett, from what we know of his personality. Or is it too much so, and therefore the story that was expected of Soldana by his Texan questioners later in his life? Like Becerra, Soldana seems authentic where he is a direct participant in the action, but the extent of such details is rather limited.

The account of Ben by Newell (2.12.1) is unique in tone, and the details also stand isolated from other accounts. The total lack of dramatic embellishment gives considerable weight to the authenticity of the short narrative. Consequently, these accounts are considered important in the discussion of the deaths of Bowie and Travis in the Special Commentary 5.2, especially the detail that Ben was called to identify the bodies by the leaders. If true, this statement contradicts those accounts that have either Bowie or Travis surviving the battle only to be knowingly executed (e.g., Becerra's account above).

The Stiff version (2.12.2) of Ben's story is a little more problematic. Most of the details match the Newell account: the all-night wait with coffee, Santa Anna and Almonte going out and returning at 3 A.M., the firing of rockets, observing by the flash of gunfire the Mexican Army attacking, the concern over the cost of victory, and the identification of Travis and Bowie. Possibly significant is that Stiff includes the identification of Crockett, which suggests a coached addition later on. One anomaly in Stiff is the statement about Travis, Crockett, and Bowie being buried. This need not be particularly significant; it could mean little more than that the bodies were initially moved apart before the funeral pyre was built. My conclusion is that though there are problems with Stiff's editing, Ben himself appears to be an important and reliable source. Nor is Stiff a blind copy of the earlier Newell, and so these interviews do appear to be separate.

The third document by Helms (2.12.3), though somewhat vague, gives support to a secondhand account of Crockett's death by either Ben or Joe. The "negro man, an officer's servant," is not identified and describes both of them. That he "was spared" could mean it was Joe, but the subject matter is quite consistent with the documents of Ben, while not so with those of Joe. Therefore, for now, this source is attributed to Ben. I consider both men among the more reliable sources, so the attribution should not affect the reliability of using this source for discussing Crockett's death in the Special Commentary.

There are all kinds of problems with the Loranca account (2.13.1). He (or the newspaperman) has the name of his own commander as Serna rather than Sesma; Filisola as a co-commander with Cós in Texas in late 1835; the Alamo raising the red flag (the Alamo defenders were going to show no mercy to their besiegers?); Travis proposing to surrender on the same terms as Cós, with those terms allowing Cós to join the army in the field against Texas; and all the refugees being shot except for a woman with a little boy. The Texan casualties number one hundred more than in most other accounts (except de la Peña), with sixty-three fleeing over the walls to be killed by the cavalry. This last detail, however, does reflect the report by Sesma himself (2.3.1). The whole battle description is as if it took place at the main gate and in the immediate buildings inside, rather than the more spread-out barracks, outbuildings, and chapel. And finally, a careful reading makes it apparent that there was no personal involvement by Loranca in the details of the battle. In all, this account must be considered highly doubtful.[4]

The Nuñez account (2.14.1) is full of even worse problems.[5] The idea that Santa Anna would go into San Antonio without taking his army with him is simply unbelievable. Other inconsistent details include the impossibility of ingress or egress from the Alamo; that Seguín's company was allowed to escape, as no harm was wished on them; the impossibility of John Smith being at the Alamo; Filisola and Woll being leaders in the attack; Sesma being arrested and starting back to Mexico the evening before; the Alamo's outer walls being pounded down; and particularly, the siege lasting four days. Even more error-ridden is the account of the actual battle taking place entirely inside the church, which had a roof through which the attackers gained entry, while Santa Anna was giving directions in the middle of the fight. There is no reason why this story should be accepted as having any value.

The Nuñez account is surprisingly rare in that it is one of the few Alamo sources to have been thoroughly reviewed. Any serious student of the Alamo documents must refer to the referenced Stephen Hardin article in the *Southwestern Historical Quarterly* (1990). Though too extensive for inclusion here, the article does a far more complete study of the Nuñez account, with much the same conclusion: that details from Nuñez should not be used without careful justification. Hardin leans heavily on the de la Peña account as a check on facts. He does not use all the available sources reproduced in this collection, however, and I feel that the additional material even more strongly supports skepticism of the Nuñez account. Hardin points out that the significance of Nuñez is that his story has been used, unquestioningly, in popular films about the Alamo, and hence is an important contribution to the public perception of the events. He also gives an overview of why there have been such emotional reactions to the accounts of Crockett's surrender, as discussed in the Special Commentary for section 2.9.

This skepticism of the Nuñez account does not necessarily mean that he was an outright fraud. The concluding paragraph gives a statement on Nuñez responding to a benefactor for the purpose "that these heroic deeds of valor for which his countrymen are so justly famous may be handed down." This could be a possible motivation for heavy distortion by an authentic participant. Nonetheless, the Nuñez story is so far off that he or the newspaper report is essentially useless.

The Urissa, or Urizza, account (2.15.1) also stretches believability. He described himself as a colonel and Santa Anna's secretary, yet went to bed on the eve of the battle and so missed all the action except to enter the Alamo to be yet another witness to the death of Crockett (discussed further in the Special Commentary 5.2). There is an appeal to this account, as it supports the stereotype of Santa Anna as an unfeeling, heartless leader, but this is precisely why one should be suspicious of its validity.

The anonymous author of *El Mosquito Mexicano* (2.16.1) has been suggested by Lord, based on similarity in style, to have been Sánchez (2.7.2, 2.7.3). Davis sees a connection as well, though he also considers the possibility that Sánchez used this account to fill in his journal at a later time.[6] This is certainly a vivid account, and its immediate publication gives it an authenticity unusual among the Alamo documents. The details on casualties are included in a later review of this topic (Special Commentary 5.2). The correlation with Sánchez also comes perhaps from the comment about Bowie's death. Sánchez does refer to Cós a lot, as if he served under him as per the newsletter's account. On the other hand, the anonymous individual is far more generous to Santa Anna and less to the soldiers in the ranks than Sánchez—a feature striking about Sánchez. In summary, this short but seemingly authentic narration gives some real imagery of the battle, but its attribution to a known figure is questionable.

Jesse Badgett, who provided the report from a Mexican Army deserter (2.17.1), was a notable leader in the Texas Revolution. This is a possible check on later sources because of its close publication to the events. The timing of the assault, starting at 11 P.M., is a little different than in Santa Anna's orders, and two figures seem to be given for casualties. Of particular interest is the claimed succession of command within the Alamo from Travis to Baugh to Crockett. What could be the source for this paragraph? The vagueness later in the narrative makes it seem unlikely that Badgett heard Mrs. Dickinson or Joe. Thus one is left to guess whether this is new or invented material. The chances of such an item being known to a Mexican soldier are slim, so this must be treated with some skepticism.

Another document is from fifer Saldigua (2.17.2), which is a composition with the central purpose of giving James Bowie a highly melodramatic closing scene. The story is universally rejected by scholars, because of the unlikelihood that a low-ranking soldier would be allowed a front-row seat in such a drama, and the extent to which such a story is exactly what Texans wanted to hear from Mexican prisoners after San Jacinto. Its one value has been to critics of Zuber, who suggest he invented rather than just repeated it, and therefore cite it as a reason to doubt his story of Moses Rose. Not much evidence has been put forward to support the contention.

The short account of Sgt. Santiago Rabia (2.17.3) has few details that are new, though it does in a small way seem to confirm traditional counts of the casualties on both sides of around two hundred defenders and five hundred attackers.[7] Both Wheat, in the translation given here, and Borroel who gives the notation "200, 50 [?]," think this means there were two hundred plus fifty defenders found respectively inside and outside the Alamo.[8] A less likely reading might be that fifty of the two hundred defenders were thought by Rabia to be U.S. citizens rather than Texans.

1. Linn 1883, 139.
2. Kilgore in the introduction to the Becerra 1980 reprint.
3. Crawford, 277 n. 1 to Chapter 12. Caro in Castañeda 1928, 108 and 111, refers to Santa Anna sending *travelers* (emphasis Castañeda's) in his carriage from Béxar to San Luis and states that "[D]ecency and respect for public morals do not permit further details to be given." This implication was published in 1837.
4. However, an alternate opinion is Davis (1997, 32–33; 1998, 727 n. 19 and 736 n. 105), who considers Loranca "strikingly accurate," apparently because of the similarities to the Sesma account.
5. Nuñez is also used in DeZavala c. 1911, as noted in Groneman 1996, 170.
6. Davis 1997, 14, 16.
7. Also note Jackson (1997, 144–45), who has oral traditions from the Texas campaign by other Mexican soldados as well.
8. Borroel 1997c, 19–20; 1998b, 71–72.

CHAPTER 3

Sources from the Vicinity

The next set of documents comes from sources that were located very close in location or time to the events of the siege or fall. They give more than just insight into the context of the battle; they also supply some details that are secondhand but sometimes reasonable because they possibly were obtained from firsthand sources.

Four individuals given here—Francisco Ruiz, J. M. Rodríguez, Andrés Barsena, and Anselmo Bergara—were physically in San Antonio or the immediate environs during the battle. Ruiz, a city official (alcalde, similar to a mayor) who had to respond to orders of Santa Anna, in particular gives details of the immediate aftermath of the battle. Barsena and Bergara brought the first word of the fall of the Alamo to the Texans.

Antonio Menchaca was another San Antonio resident involved with the Texas Revolution. From him we get a picture of Travis, Bowie, and Crockett a little prior to the beginning of the siege, as well as the action of the Seguín brigade in the immediate post-Alamo army. The account of J. M. Rodríguez, though he was a young boy at the time, portrays the town and people at the time of the battle.

The next section presents the earliest letters of Gen. Samuel Houston after receipt of the news of the fall of the Alamo. Aside from their interest for the broader context of the Texas war, they also serve as a check on the later secondhand versions of Susanna Dickinson's and Joe's experiences.

Early (1840s) interviews of Juana Peña Cruz y Arocha and José Antonio Navarro gives especially early recollections from some of the San Antonio residents. Another reputed eyewitness was Col. R. L. Compton, who was serving in the Texas Army and claimed to have been watching from a house in town.

The section ends with a series of later (1896–1911) newspaper interviews with the few surviving witnesses from the town. The information in these interviews varies widely in quality.

3.1.1.   Ruiz, published account, 1860.

Ruiz, Francis Antonio. 1860. Fall of the Alamo, and massacre of Travis and his brave associates. *Texas Almanac*. 80–82.

Francis, or Francisco, Ruiz was alcalde, a position essentially equivalent to mayor, of San Antonio at the time of the siege. There is a handwritten version of this interview, which possibly could be an earlier copy, in the Gentilz-Fretelliere Family Papers at the Daughters of the Republic of Texas Library at the Alamo. It has the same information except that the statement by Quintero and the lists of privates are not given, and the entry "Davy Crockett, who ranked as a private" is given before Travis. According to John O. Leal (personal communication), now retired from the Office of the County Clerk, Bexar County, the statement was prepared by Francis's son.

FALL OF THE ALAMO,
AND MASSACRE OF TRAVIS AND HIS BRAVE ASSOCIATES.
BY FRANCIS ANTONIO RUIZ—TRANSLATED BY J. A. QUINTERO.

ON the 23rd day of February, 1836, (2 o'clock P.M.,) Gen. Santa Anna entered the city of San Antonio with a part of his army. This he effected without any resistance, the forces under the command of Travis, Bowie, and Crockett having on the same day, at 8 o'clock in the morning, learned that the Mexican army was on the banks of the Medina river, they concentrated in the fortress of the Alamo.

In the evening they commenced to exchange fire with guns, and from the 23d of February to the 6th of March (in which the storming was made by Santa Anna) the roar of artillery and volleys of musketry were constantly heard.

On the 6th of March, at 3 o'clock P.M. [*sic; "A.M." meant*], Gen. Santa Anna at the head of 4000 men advanced against the Alamo. The infantry, artillery, and cavalry had formed about 1000 vrs [*varas*] from the walls of said fortress. The Mexican army charged and were twice repulsed by the deadly fire of Travis' artillery, which resembled a constant thunder. At the third charge the Toluca battalion commenced to scale the walls and suffered severely. Out of 800 men, 130 were only left alive.

When the Mexican army had succeeded in entering the walls, I, with the Political Chief, (Gefe politico,) Don Ramon Murquiz [*or Musquiz*], and other members of the Corporation, accompanied the Curate, Don Refugio de la Garza, who, by Santa Anna's orders, had assembled during the night at a temporary fortification erected in Potrero street, with the object of attending the wounded, etc. As soon as the storming commenced, we crossed the bridge on Commerce street with this object in view, and about 100 yards from the same a party of Mexican dragoons fired upon us and compelled us to fall back on the river and place we occupied before. Half an hour had elapsed when Santa Anna sent one of his aid-de-camps with an order for us to come before him. He directed me to call on some of the neighbors to come up with carts to carry the dead to the Cemetery, and also to accompany him, as he was desirous to have Col. Travis, Bowie, and Crockett shown to him.

On the north battery of the fortress lay the lifeless body of Col. Travis on the gun-carriage, shot *only* in the forehead. Toward the west, and in the small fort opposite the city, we found the body of Col. Crockett. Col. Bowie was found dead in his bed, in one of the rooms of the south side.

Santa Anna, after all the Mexicans were taken out, ordered wood to be brought to burn the bodies of the Texians. He sent a company of dragoons with me to bring wood and dry branches from the neighboring forest. About 3 o'clock in the afternoon they commenced laying the wood and dry branches, upon which a file of dead bodies was placed; more wood was piled on them, and another file brought, and in this manner they were all arranged in layers. Kindling wood was distributed through the pile, and about 5 o'clock in the evening it was lighted.

The dead Mexicans of Santa Anna were taken to the grave-yard, but not having sufficient room for them, I ordered some of them to be thrown in the river, which was done on the same day.

Santa Anna's loss was estimated at 1600 men. These were the flower of his army.

The gallantry of the few Texians who defended the Alamo was really wondered at by the Mexican army. Even the Generals were astonished at their vigorous resistance, and how dearly victory had been bought.

The Generals who, under Santa Anna, participated in the storming of the Alamo, were Juan Amador, Castrillon, Ramirez, Sesma, and Andrade.

The men burnt numbered 182. I was an eye-witness, for as *Alcalde* of San Antonio, I was with some of the neighbors collecting the dead bodies and placing them on the funeral pyre.

Signed,   FRANCISCO ANTONIO RUIZ.

P.S.—My father was Don Francisco Ruiz, a member of the Texas Convention. He signed the Declaration of Independence on the 2d day of March, 1836.

F. A. R.

The foregoing is a correct translation of the original document.

QUINTERO.

A List of those who fell with Travis in the Alamo, at San Antonio de Bexar, March 6th, 1836:

OFFICERS.

W. Barrett Travis, Lieut.-Colonel Commanding.
James Bowie,   "   "
J. Washington, Colonel, Tenn.

Captain —— Forsyth, N. Y.	Adjutant I. G. Baugh.
" —— Harrison, Tenn.	Mast. Ord., Robert Evans, Ireland.
" Wm. Blazeley, La.	Serg't-Major —— Williamson.
" Wm. C. M. Baker, Miss.	Aid to Travis, Charles Despalier.

"   S. B. Evans
"   W. R. Carey, Texas.
"   S. C. Blair,   "
"   —— Gilmore, Tenn.
"   Robert White.
Lieutenant John Jones, La.
"   Almaron Dickinson
George C. Kimbell.

Lieut.-Qr.-Master Elial Melton.
Assistant   "   —— Anderson
"   "   —— Burnell.
Surgeon, D. Michison.
"   Amos Pollard.
"   —— Thompson.
Ensign, Green B. Jemison

PRIVATES.

David Crockett, Tenn.
E. Nelson, S. C.
—— Nelson, Texas.
W. H. Smith, "
Lewis Johnson, Texas.
E. T. Mitchell, Ga.
F. Desangue, Pa.
—— Thruston, Ky.
—— Moore.
Chistopher Parker, Miss.
C. Huskell.
—— Rose, Texas
John Blair, "
—— Kiddeson.
Wm. Wells, Tenn.
Wm. Cummings, Pa.
—— Valentine.
—— Cockran.
R. W. Ballantine.
S. Halloway.
Isaac White.
—— Day.
Robert Muselman, New-Orleans.
Robert Crossman, "
Richard Starr, Eng.
I. G. Garrett, New-Orleans
Robert B. Moore, "
Richard Dimkin, Eng.
Wm. Linn, Mass.
—— Hutchinson.
Wm. Johnson, Pa.
E. Nelson.
Geo. Tumlinson.
Wm. Deardorf.
Daniel Bourne, Eng.

—— Harris, Ky.
John Flanders.
Isaac Ryan, Opelousas.
David Wilson, Texas.
John M. Hays, Tenn.
—— Stuart.
W. K. Simpson.
W. D. Sutherland, Texas.
D. W. Howell, New-Orleans.
—— Butler,   "
Charles Smith.
—— McGregor, Scotland.
—— Rusk.
—— Hawkins, Ireland.
Samuel Holloway.
—— Brown.
T. Jackson, Ireland.
James George, Gonzales.
Dolphin Ward,   "
Thos. Jackson,   "
Geo. W. Cottle,   "
Andrew Kent,   "
Thos. R. Miller,   "
Isaac Baker,   "
Wm. King,   "
Jesse McCoy,   "
Claiborne Wright,   "
Wm. Fishback,   "
Isaac Millsaps,   "
Galba Fuqua,   "
John Davis,   "
Albert Martin,   "
—— John, Clerk to Desangue.
B. A. M. Thomas.
Wm. Fuhbaigh.

—— Ingram, Eng.	John G. King.
W. T. Lewis, Wales.	Jacob Durst.
Charles Zanco, Denmark.	M. L. Sewell.
Jas. L. Ewing.	Robert White.
Robert Cunningham.	A. Devault.
S. Burns, Ireland.	John Harris.
George Neggin, S. C.	Andrew Kent.
—— Robinson, Scotland.	Wm. E. Summers.

3.1.2.   Ruiz, Francisco Antonio, deposition, April 16, 1861.

Ruiz, Francisco Antonio. April 16, 1861. Deposition for the heirs of Toribio Losoya, Court of Claims Voucher File #5027 (or 5026), Texas General Land Office.

This file includes another deposition by Don Agustin Barrero, who states that he saw the body of Toribio Losoya in the chapel after the battle.

The State of Texas) Before me Sam¹. S. Smith
County of Bexar) Clerk of the County Court of
    said county, personally appeared Don Francisco A. Ruiz, a citizen of said County and state to me personally well known who being by me duly sworn upon his Oath saith that during the seige [*sic*] and capture of the Alamo in February & March 1836, by Gen¹. San [*sic*] Anna affiant was Alcalde of the city of San Antonio; that after the fall of the Alamo Gen¹. San Anna sent for affiant, Don Ramón Musquiz and others to identify the bodies of Travis, Bowie and Crockett which was done; that affiant was commanded by Gen¹. San Anna to procure Carts and Men and proceed to so make a funeral pile of the Texans, which order he carried out with much difficulty as there were but few male citizens remaining in the Town, that in collecting the bodies of those that were killed in the Alamo, he recognized the body of Toribio Losoyo, who had fallen fighting with the Americans in defense of the Alamo, that he knew said Toribio Losoyo well he was a native of Texas of Mexican blood, that he was also acquainted with [*sic; "the wife" missing*] of the said Toribio Losoyo, Maria Francisca Curbiere who is still living in Bexar County and is the applicant for the Bounty and Donation of her said late husband That the said Widow Maria Francisca Curbire y Losoyo was born in Texas, and has continuously resided therein all of her life—That he, affiant, is well acquainted with Nat. Lewis, Judge T. J. Devine, Maj. G. T. Howard and all of the principal Citizens of Bexar County.
Sworn so and subscribed
before me this 16ᵗʰ day of   Fran.ᶜᵒ A. Ruiz.
April AD 1861,
Sam S. Smith
CLKCCBCo

3.2.1.   Menchaca, memoirs, 1937.

Menchaca, Antonio. 1937. *Memoirs.* Edited by James P. Newcomb. 2, 22–23. San Antonio: Yanaguana Society.

This is another account by a contemporary resident of San Antonio. The Foreword notes that this was earlier published in the *Passing Show,* San Antonio, Texas, June 22 to July 27, 1907, John B. Carrington, ed., and J. E. Jones, adv. mgr. The original was not located. The Foreword discusses that Menchaca dictated his memoirs to Charles Barnes, and that the manuscript was in the possession of Pearson Newcomb. The Introduction is by James P. Newcomb, written in 1907, and discusses his personal experiences and observations of Menchaca, who was also a personal friend of Sam Houston.

[*The Introduction ends with the following.*]

Some years ago, over a quarter of a century—though, I think, after the civil war—I met Captain Menchaca and our conversation turned upon the discussion of events of early Texas history. When he related in a clear and concise manner many striking circumstances, I suggested that I would like the privilege of transcribing his narrative. Thereupon he volunteered to furnish me the manuscript which he would have properly prepared. In accordance with his promise he handed me a plainly written history of events from the date of his birth to the battle of San Jacinto. I have never used the story and have had little opportunity to examine it critically. It is evident the amanuensis who took down the old Captain's story put it down without coloring, and one regrets that he did not enlarge more fully upon details that are so full of historic and romantic interest.

Neither have I compared the story with the current published history of Texas, particularly that of the important battle of San Jacinto, upon which turned the fate and destiny of the great American republic and brought about the expansion that reached to the waters of the Pacific and the uncovering of the gold fields of California.

I have taken no liberties with the manuscript and give it to you as it is, in all its barrenness of invention and lack of coloring that would be justified for a period fraught with terrible tragedies and wild romance.

JAMES P. NEWCOMB.

[*Menchaca starts his Memoirs with his birth in 1800. The following is his account of the Alamo.*]

On the 26th December, 1835, Dn. Diego Grant left San Antonio, towards Matamoros, with about 500 men, A's and M's of those who had assisted in the siege. They here kept up guards and patrols of night. 250 men went from here to keep a lookout on Cos, who had gone to Mexico, and returning here on the 5th January, 1836. On the 13 January, 1836, David Crockett presented himself at the old Mexican graveyard, on the west side of the San Pedro Creek, had in company with him fourteen young men who had accompanied him from Tennessee, here. As soon as he got there he sent word to Bowie to go and receive him, and conduct him into the City. Bowie and A. went and he was brought and lodged at Erasmo Seguin's house. Crockett, Bowie, Travis, Niell [*sic*] and all the officers joined together, to establish guards for the safety of the City, they fearing that the Mexicans would return. On the 10 February, 1836, A. was invited by officers to a ball given in honor of Crockett, and was asked to invite all the principal ladies in the City to it. On the same day invitations were extended and the ball given that night. While at the ball, at about 1 o'clock, A.M. of the 11th, a courier, sent by Placido Benavides, arrived, from Camargo, with the intelligence that Santa Ana, was starting from the Presidio Rio Grande, with 13,000 troops, 10,000 Infantry and 3,000 Cavalry, with the view of taking San Antonio. The courier arrived at the ball room door inquired for Col. Seguin, and was told that Col. Seguin was not there. Asked if Menchaca was there, and was told that he was. He spoke to him and told him that he had a letter of great importance, which he had brought from P. B. from Camargo, asked partner and came to see letter. Opened letter and read the following: "At this moment I have received a very certain notice, that the commander in chief, Antonio Lopez de Santa Anna, marches for the city of San Antonio to take possession thereof, with 13,000 men." As he was reading the letter, Bowie came opposite him, came to see it, and while reading it, Travis came up, and Bowie called him to read that letter; but Travis said that at that moment he could not stay to read letters, for he was dancing with the most beautiful lady in San Antonio, Bowie told him that the letter was one of grave importance, and for him to leave his partner. Travis came and brought Crockett with him. Travis and Bowie understood Spanish, Crockett did not. Travis then said, it will take 13,000 men from the Presidio de Rio Grande to this place thirteen or fourteen days to get here; this is the 4th day. Let us dance to-night and to-morrow we will make provisions for our defense. The ball continued until 7 o'clock, A.M.

There Travis invited officers to hold a meeting with a view of consulting as to the best means they should adopt for the security of the place. The council gathered many resolutions were offered and adopted, after which Bowie and Seguin made a motion to have A.M. and his family sent away from here, knowing that should Santa Anna come, A. and his family would receive no good at his hands. A. left here and went to Seguin's ranch, where he stayed six days, preparing for a trip. Started from there and went as far as Marcelino to sloop; then three miles the east side of Cibolo, at an old pond at sun up next morning. Nat Lewis, passed with a wallet on his back, a-foot from San Antonio, and A. asked him why he went a-foot and he was answered that he could not find a horse; that Santa Anna had arrived at San Antonio, the day previous with 13,000 men. A asked what the Americans had done. He said they were in the Alamo inside the fortifications. A. asked why N. did not remain there and he answered that he was not a fighting man, that he was a business man. A then told him to go then about his business. A. continued his journey, got to Gonzales, at the house of G. Dewitt, and there met up with Gen. Ed Burleson, with seventy-three men, who had just got there, then, slept. And on the following day, attempted to pass to the other side with families, but was prevented by Burleson, who told him that the families might cross, but not him; that the men were needed in the army. There met up with fourteen Mexicans of San Antonio, and they united and remained there until a company could be formed. The Americans were gradually being strengthened by the addition of from three to fifteen daily. Six days after being there Col. Seguin, who was sent as courier by Travis, arrived there and presented himself to Gen. Burleson, who, upon receipt of the message, forwarded it to the Convention assembled at Washington, Texas. On the following day, the M. Co. was organized with twenty-two men, having for Capt. Seguin; 1st. Lt. Manuel Flores, and A. M. 2nd. Lieut. On the 4th of March, the news reached [*them*] that Texas had declared her Independence. The few that were there, 350 men swore allegiance to it, and two days after, Gen. Sam Houston arrived there and received the command of the forces. When Santa Anna took the Alamo and burned the men that he had killed, he ordered, Madam Dixon [Dickinson] (Travis' servant and Almonte's servant,) a lady whose husband had been killed in the Alamo, with propositions to A. or to those desiring to make Texas their home. The propositions were in these terms: All American Texans, who desires to live in L. will present himself to Gen. Santa Anna, will present his arms, and he will be treated as a gentleman. When the Americans understood what they proposed, they in a voice cried, "General Santa Anna, you may be a good man, but the Americans will never surrender," "go to H... and hurrah for Gen. Sam Houston." On the following day, the Texan spies arrived with the intelligence that the Mexicans were on their way to Gonzales; that they were encamped on th[*e*] Cibolo. On the same day the Americans started for the Colorado river, and slept on Rock Creek. [*The narrative continues with the Texas campaign leading to San Jacinto.*]

3.3.1.   Rodríguez, memoir, 1913.

Rodríguez, J. M. 1913. *Rodríguez Memoirs of Early Texas*. 7–10. San Antonio: Passing Show Printing Co.

A very similar version of this account, but with fewer details, was published in the *San Antonio Express*, September 8, 1912.

War of Independence

My earliest recollection is when I was a boy about six years old. One evening I was coming with my father and mother up Soledad Street, where the Kampmann Building is now, and as we got a little further up the street, we were stopped by a sentry and there were other soldiers there and we saw some breastworks there. General Cos, the Mexican general, my father told me, was in possession of the town. We went a little further down where the present corner of Travis and Soledad Street is. We crossed a ditch on a plank and went up Soledad Street to see my uncle, Jose Olivarri. I heard a great deal of shooting towards the Plaza and my father said that General Burleson of the Texas Army was trying to capture the city. The next day General Cos capitulated and was allowed to take his arms and leave the city.

Ben Milam was killed at the Veramendi House. The arms the Mexicans had were old English muskets that did not reach much over fifty yards. The Texas army used long range flint rifles. Shortly after that, Colonel Travis was put in command with a small garrison and he stayed at the Alamo. Colonel Travis was a fine man of more than ordinary height. I recollect him distinctly from the very fact that he used to come up to our house from the Alamo and talk to my father and mother a great deal. Our house was the first one after you crossed the river coming from the Alamo and Col. Travis generally stopped at our home going and coming. He was a very popular man and was well liked by everyone. My father was always in sympathy with the Texas cause, but had so far not taken up arms on either side.

Soon after this, a report came to my father from a reliable source that Santa Ana was starting for San Antonio with 7,000 men, composed of cavalry, infantry and artillery, in fact a well organized army. My father sent for Colonel Travis and he came to our house and my father told him about this coming of Santa Ana and advised him to retire into the interior of Texas and abandon the Alamo. He told him he could not resist Santa Ana's army with such a small force. Colonel Travis told my father that he could not believe it, because General Cos had only been defeated less than three months, and it did not seem possible to him that General Santa Ana could organize in so short a time as large an army as that. Colonel Travis, therefore, remained at the Alamo, and at the last, Travis told my father, "Well we have made up our minds to die at the Alamo fighting for Texas." My father asked him again to retire as General Sam Houston was then in the interior of Texas organizing an army.

The Mexicans in San Antonio who were in sympathy with the war of Independence organized a company under Colonel Juan Seguin. There were twenty-four in the company including my father and they joined the command of General Sam Houston. My mother and all of us remained in the city.

One morning early a man named Rivas called at our house and told us that he had seen Santa Ana in disguise the night before looking in on a fandango on Soledad Street. My father being away with General Houston's army, my mother undertook to act for us, and decided it was best for us to go into the country to avoid being here when General Santa Ana's army should come in. We went to the ranch of Dona Santos Ximenes. We left in ox carts, the wheels of which were made of solid wood. We buried our money in the house, about $800.00; it took us nearly two days to get to the ranch.

A few days after that, one morning about day break, I heard some firing, and Pablo Olivarri, who was with us, woke me up. He said, "You had better get up on the house; they are fighting at the Alamo." We got up on the house and could see the flash of the guns and hear the booming of the cannon. The firing lasted about two hours. The next day we heard that all the Texans had been killed and the Alamo taken. A few days after that an army consisting of about 1200 men under General Urrea came by from San Antonio on their way to Goliad to attack Fannin. I saw these troops as they passed the ranch.

There has been a great deal of discussion with reference to what had been done with the bodies of the Texans who were slain in the Alamo. It is claimed that Colonel Seguin wrote a letter in which he stated that he got together the ashes in the following February and put them in an iron urn and buried them in San Fernando Cathedral. This does not seem possible to me, because nothing of that kind could have happened without us knowing that and we never heard of any occurrence of that kind. Seguin did not return from Houston's army until my father did, both of them being in the same command, my father a first Lieutenant and he a Colonel. It is true that the bones were brought together somewhere in the neighborhood or a little east of where the Menger Hotel is now and were buried by Colonel Seguin, but that any of them were ever buried in the Cathedral, I have never heard nor do I believe that to be true. The only person I know of being buried in the Cathedral was Don Eugenio Navarro, who was buried near the south wall of the Cathedral near the chancel.

Some days after the Urrea army passed, we heard of the massacre of Fannin's army at Goliad. My mother, along with other loyal families, determined then to move to East Texas, and we started with all our goods and chattels in ox-carts. The Flores and Seguin families were among those who went with us. Most of us traveled in the carts. Horses were very scarce, the army taking nearly all they could find. We had gotten as far as the Trinity river on the road to Nacogdoches where we heard of Santa Ana being defeated and all returned to San Antonio, except our family, who went on the Washington, which was the Texas Capital, as my father was still in the field with Houston's troops.

3.4.1.   Barsena and Bergara, interview, March 11, 1836.

Chabot, Frederick C., ed. 1940. *Texas Letters*. 146–47. San Antonio: Yanaguana Society Publications no. 5.

This document was likely the earliest account of the fall of the Alamo to reach the Texans. I was not able to locate the current location of the original, which was in the Louis Lenz Collection at the time Walter Lord was writing his book *A Time to Stand* in the 1950s.

Copy. Examination of Andrew [sic] Barsena and Ansolma [sic] Bergara. Gonzales, 11 Mar. 1836.

Andres Barsena, says that last Saturday night Anselmo Bergara arrove [sic] at the rancho of Don Jose Flores, where he who declares was and that Bergara informed him that his mother had solicited him Bergara to take her son if he could find him to the Colorado River to avoid the military who was gathering up all they could and making soldiers of them.

Antonio Peres left the rancho of Don Jose Ma. Arocha on Sunday morning last and returned in the evening with the notice that the soldiers of Santa Anna had that morning entered the Alamo and killed all the men that was inside and that he saw about 500 of the Mexican soldiers that had been killed and as many wounded.

Bergara landed at the Rancho Saturday evening and gave no notice of the fall of the Alamo, but that Antonio Peres brought the news to the rancho Sunday evening, and Father Bargara [sic] stated at the rancho that Musquiz had advised him to leave as it was not prudent for him to remain.

Antonio Peres was called to Bejar by Don Louisana Navarro for the purpose of sending him to Gonzales with a letter calling on all Mexicans to come forward and present themselves to the President to receive there [sic] pardon and enter on their own proper pursuits. Antonio refused to come unless Santa Anna would give a passport which could not then be obtained but was promised in three or four days and that on tomorrow if he (Antonio) comes he will leave the rancho for this place.

Gen'l Cos entered Bejar with 700 men (so says Bergara).

Intelligence obtained from friendly Mexicans of Bexar relating to "Fall of the Alamo." This letter is in the handwriting of Col. G. W. Hockley who was stationed at Gonzales, Texas and was dispatched to Gen'l Sam Houston on March 11, 1836. From a photostat of the original, presented to Mrs. Leita Small, Custodian of the Alamo, on March 11, 1939, by Louis Lenz.

3.4.2. Barsena and Bergara, letter, March 11, 1836.

Unknown author, transcribed by E. N. Gray. March 11, 1836. Transcript in Republic of Texas, General File, CAH.

This is another version of the interview recorded in the above document, with a few more details. A copy of the transmittal letter by Dr. E. N. Gray of Houston on July 23, 1930, is in the Williams Papers, Box 2N493/Folder 5, CAH.

Translation

To Senores D— And D—

Gonzales, March 11th. 1836.

Dear Sirs:—

At 4—O'clock this afternoon, Anselmo Bergara and Andrew Bargana [*Barsena*], came to this town with the disagreable intelligence of the taking of the Alamo by Genl. Santa Anna. The event is related in the following manner:—

On Saturday night, the 5th of the present month, he marched his infantry under the walls, and surrounded them with cavalry, to prevent escape in case they should attempt to fly. At daybreak on Sunday morning he planted his ladders, which were carried by the infantry, against the sides of the four walls, and carried the place by assault, with great loss of infantry. All within the Fort perished. Seven of them were killed by order of Santa Anna when in the act of giving up their arms. Travis killed himself. And Bowie was killed while lying sick in bed. The Misses ———— & ————, who were in the Fort, were delivered up to their father.

All the above is derived from what was told to Bergara by D——— on Sunday ["*morning*" *crossed out*] night when he, Bergara, went in from the country. On the morning of the attack he had come hastily out to the country. It must be understood that Bergara remained at large in Bejar thirteen days after the entrance of Santa Anna, and walked about undisturbed by him all that time.

Barcena says that Bergara came to the rancho of my father-in-law, on Saturday night, before the entrance of the troops into the walls, and that he knows nothing about it—only what was told by Antonio Peroz, who came from Bejar (where he had been called by D,L,) on Sunday in the night, who said that <u>he</u> had been in the battle,—that 521 of the infantry were killed and as many more badly wounded.

The contradiction of these two men makes me suspect that they are spys sent by Santa Anna;—because, why should Bergarra [*sic*] fly from Bejar after remaining so many days there undisturbed and enjoying himself? . . .

&c. Vc.

The remainder of the letter is of no public importance.

3.4.3.　　Bergara, interview, 1870s?

Linn, John J. 1883. *Reminiscences of Fifty Years in Texas.* 141. New York: D. & J. Sadlier & Co.

The last words of Travis were, "*No rendirse muchachos!*" I obtained this from "Old Borgarra [*sic*]," who was among them till the last, and who escaped and arrived at Gonzales to give the news, that the "Alamo had fallen." He was an aged man, an admirer of Travis and a friend to Texas, though upon his arrival at Gonzales he was imprisoned as a spy when he gave the information above stated.

3.4.4.   Bergara, interview, 1860s?

Potter, Reuben. 1868. The fall of the Alamo: A reminiscence of the revolution of Texas. *Texas Almanac* 36.

This excerpt is from an early version of document 5.1.7.

. . . The real loss of the assailants in killed and wounded probably did not differ much from five hundred men. General Bradburn was of the opinion that 300 men in that action were lost to the service, counting with the killed those who died of wounds or were permanently disabled. This agrees with the other most reliable estimates.*

---

* Anselmo Borgara, a Mexican, who first reported the fall of the Alamo to General Houston at Gonzales, and who left San Antonio on the evening after it occurred, stated that the assaulting force amounted to about 2300 men, of whom 521 were killed and as many wounded. He had probably either had opportunities of seeing and estimating the bulk of the besieging force, or had his information on this point from those who had a tolerably correct idea of its strength. It probably did not exceed twenty-five hundred men, nor much fall below that number. The loss, however, is evidently exaggerated, because it is simply incredible. We would have to search history closely to find where any troops have carried a fortress with a loss of more than two fifths of that number. If there was any basis for this part of the statement, it is probable that 521 was the entire loss of killed and wounded, which at second hand would become that of killed alone, and then it would be assumed that the number of wounded was equal. General Houston seems to have gathered from this man the idea that Travis had only 150 effective men out of 187.—(Letter of March 11th to Fannin.) But if none had fallen up to the 3d, the effective force could hardly have been reduced so much in the next two days and nights.

3.5.1.   Sam Houston, military order, March 2, 1836.

Telegraph and Texas Register. March 12, 1836. San Felipe.

This transcript is included as it is a contemporary general order of Sam Houston while the siege was under way.

ARMY ORDERS.
Convention Hall, Washington,
March 2, 1836.

War is raging on the frontiers. Bejar is besieged by two thousand of the enemy, under the command of general Siezma [*Sesma*]. Reinforcements are on their march, to unite with the besieging army. By the last report, our force in

Bejar was only one hundred and fifty men strong. The citizens of Texas must rally to the aid of our army, or it will perish. Let the citizens of the East march to the combat. The enemy must be driven from our soil, or desolation will accompany their march upon us. *Independence is declared,* it must be maintained. Immediate action, united with valor, alone can achieve the great work. The services of all are forthwith required in the field.

SAM. HOUSTON,
Comm.-in-Chief of the Army.

P.S. It is rumored that the enemy are on their march to Gonzales, and that they have entered the colonies. The fate of Bejar is unknown. The country must and shall be defended. The patriots of Texas are *appealed to in behalf of their bleeding country.*

S. H.

3.5.2.   Sam Houston, letter, March 11, 1836.

Houston, Samuel, letter to James W. Fannin. March 11, 1836. A. J. Houston Collection, TSLA.

Williams and Barker 1938, 1:362–65, includes two transcripts for a Houston-to-Fannin letter of March 11, 1836. The first is cited from the *Arkansas Gazette,* April 5, 1836, the second from Yoakum 1855, 2:471–72. They included both, as there had been some confusion over the differences between the two published versions. However, their transcript of the *Arkansas Gazette* version has some inaccuracies, especially in the number of miles and the hours in the last sentence of the postscript, and the remaining differences appear to be little more than heavy-handed stylistic editing by one or both early publications. The A. J. Houston Collection has three "official-looking" handwritten copies of this letter; the one not used here gives losses by the Mexican army as 521 rather than 520 and has strike-throughs with corrections in the manuscript.

The order following the postscript and the fact that Fannin was still in Goliad on March 19 to be captured and his command executed form the heart of one of the other key stories of the Texas Revolution, which has continued to be of unending interest through all the years since.

Head Quarters
Gonzales 11th March 1836

To Col. J W Fannin Jr.
Commanding At Goliad
Sir

Upon my arrival here this afternoon the following intelligence was received through a Mexican Supposed to be friendly—which however has been Contradicted in some parts by another who arrived with him—it is therefore only given to you as rumor though I fear a melancholy portion of it will be found true Anselma Bergara states that he left the Alamo. on Sunday 6th Inst and now is three days from Aroaches Rancho That the Alamo was attacked on Sunday morning at the dawn of day by about 2300. men and was Carried a short time before sunrise with a loss of 520 Mexicans Killed And as many wounded. Col Travis had only 150 effective men Out of his whole force of 187. after the fort was <u>Carried</u> seven men surrendered and called for Genl St Anna and for quar-ter= <u>They</u> <u>were</u> <u>murdered</u> by his <u>order</u> Col. Bowie Was Sick in his bed and also murdered.

The enemy expict [*sic*] reinforcements of 1500. men under Genl Cordella, and fifteen hundred reserve to follow them. he also informs that Ugartichea had arrived with Two Millions of Dollars for the payment of the troops &^c &. The bodies of the Americans were burned after the massacre an [*sic*] alternate layers of Wood and bodies laid and set on fire—Lieut. Dickinson who had a wife and child in the fort. after having fought with desperate Courage tied his child to his back and leaped from the top of a two Story building both were killed by the fall. I have little doubt that the Alamo has fallen Whether the above particu-lars are all true may be questionable. You are therefore referred to the enclosed order.

> I am Sir Y^r obt Servt
> Signed —— Sam Houston
> Com-in Chief of the Army.

PS The wife of Lieut Dickinson is now in the possession of one of the offi-cers of St Anna—The men as you will perceive fought gallantly and in Corobo-ration of the truth of the fall of the Alamo I have ascertained that Col Travis intended firing signal guns.—at three different periods each day untill succor should arrive. No Signal guns have been heard since Sunday. and a scouting party have just returned who approached within 12 miles of the fort, and remained there for 48 hours.

> Copy. Head Quarters Gonzales
> 11th March 1836

Army Orders
To Co^l. J. W. Fannin Jr.
Commanding at Goliad.

Sir.—You will as soon as practicable after the receipt of this order fall back upon Guadaloupe Victoria with your command, and such Artillery as can be brought with expedition. The remainder will be sunk in the river.—You will take the necessary measures for the defence of Victoria, and forward one third the number of your effective force to this point, and remain in command untill further orders. Every facility is to be rendered to Women and children who may be desirous of leaving that place.—Previous to abandoning Goliad, you will take the necessary measures to blow up that fortress, and do so before leaving its vicinity.—the immediate advance of the Enemy may be confidently expected—as well as a rise of water.—Prompt movements are therefore highly important

Signed Sam Houston
Commander in Chief of the Army

I Certify the foregoing to be a true copy of the original on file [*in*] the Dept of War

F'eby 1839   Charles Mason
                                   Ch. Clk

3.5.3.   Sam Houston, letter, March 12, 1836.

Houston, Samuel, to Philip Dimmit. March 12, 1836. Thomas W. Streeter Collection, Yale Collection of Western Americana, Beinecke Rare Book and Manuscript Library, Yale University Library.

Head Quarters Texas
12th March 1836

To Capt. P. Dimmitt [*sic*]
Sir.

You are ordered with your command to this place, with all your disposable force, and should there be any companies or Troops. at Victoria, whose services are not indispens[*ible*] to the present emgencies [*sic*] of that section of the frontier; you will notify them, that it is my order for them to repair to this point forthwith. Co^l. J.W. Fannin is ordered to fall back on Victoria; after blowing up LaBahia. You will send expresses to Head Quarters, as often as practicable.

I am yr abt Servt
Sam Houston
Comd^r in Chief of the Army.

Unofficial
Dear Sir.

I am induced to believe from all the facts communicated to us that the Alamo, has fallen, and all our men are <u>murdered!</u> We must not depend on Forts; the roads, and ravines suit us best.

Your friend
12th March 1836 Sam Houston

3.5.4. Sam Houston, letter, March 13, 1836.

Houston, Samuel, to James Collinsworth. March 13, 1836. Facsimile copy in the Madge W. Hearne collection, Letters: Sam Houston 1835–June 1836, TSLA. Also published in Williams, Amelia, and Eugene Barker, eds. 1938. *The Writings of Sam Houston, 1835–1836.* 1:367–70. Austin: University of Texas Press.

The original letter differs from the published transcript in several minor details. The Williams and Barker edition has footnotes that will be of interest to the careful reader. They include details on sources, background information on James Collinsworth and Erastus ("Deaf") Smith, and a reference to Henry Wax Karnes. They are not included here, as they are not directly relevant to the Alamo. However, a summary in a footnote on Juan Seguín is too useful with respect to other Alamo documents to omit.

(Copy) Headquarters Texas
Gonzales March 13th 1836

To Honble Jas Collinsworth.
C.[*hairman of the*] M.[*ilitary*] Committee.
Sir

I have the honor to report to you my arrival at this place, on the afternoon of the 11th Inst., at about four oclck P.M. I found upward of three hundred men in camp without organization, and who had rallied on the first impulse! Since then the force has increased to more than 400. I have ordered their organization to day at 10 oclck A.M; and hope to complete it, and prepare to meet the enemy. The enclosed statement [*document 3.4.1?*], which came here a few moments after my arrival, has induced me to adopt a course very different from that which I had intended, until the information was received; and the inclosed order to Colonel Fannin, will indicate to you my convictions that, with our small, unorganized force, we can not maintain sieges in Fortresses, in the country of the enemy—Troops pent up in forts are rendered useless; nor is it possible that we can ever maintain our cause by such policy. The want of supplies and men, will insure the success of our enemies. The conduct of our brave country men in the Alamo was only equalled by Spartan valor!

I am informed that Colonel Fannin had about seven hundred men under his command and at one time, had taken up the line of march for the Alamo, but the breaking down of a wagon induced him to fall back, and abandon the Idea of marching to the relief of our last hope in Bexar. Since then, he has written letters here, indicating a design to march upon San Patricio and also the occupation of Copano. So that I am at a loss to know where my expresses will find him. From the Colorado I forwarded by this place, an express to him to meet me with all his disposable force on the west side of the Cibello, with a view to relieve Bexar. The news of the fall of Bexar corroborated by so many circumstances, compelled me to change my plan, as the inclosed order will indicate; nor could I rely upon any Cooperation from Colonel Fannin on seeing his various communications at this point. The force under my command here was such as to preclude the idea of my meeting the enemy: supposing their force, not to exceed the lowest estimate which has ever been made of it. My reason for delaying my despatch until the present, was, the assurance of Capt Seguin, that two men had been sent by him to his Rancho, and would return on last night. They have not returned and the belief is, that they have been taken by the enemy or deserted. I am using all my endeavors to get a company to send in view of the Alamo; and if possible, arrive at the <u>certainty</u> of what all believe— its fall! The scarcity of horses, and the repulse of a party of twenty-eight men, the other day, within eighteen miles of Bexar, will I apprehend, prevent the expedition. This moment Deaf Smith and Henry Karnes have assured me that they will proceed in sight of Bexar; and return within three days. The persons, whose statement is enclosed for your information, is in custody; and I will detain them, as spies for the present.

[*Houston goes on to discuss items of importance for the future, his thinking and near-term strategy, but gives no further information on the Alamo, now past.*]

Juan N. Seguin, the son of Erasmo Seguin, was a native Texan, born and reared at San Antonio. The Seguins were always friendly to the American-Texan. While Juan N. Seguin was political chief of the Department of Bexar, he joined the Texan cause in the revolution, and with nine soldiers of his company which he raised for service in the Texan cause, formed almost half of the band of twenty-five that William Barret Travis carried to the Alamo with him on February 2, 1836. Seven of those nine Mexicans died with Travis on the morning of March 6; Seguin and two of his company having been sent out with messages escaped the massacre (see *Southwestern Historical Quarterly*, XXXVII, 243). Immediately he recruited his company, and it became the rear guard of Houston's army on its slow retreat from Gonzales to the field of San Jacinto; Seguin's business on this retreat was to keep the main army supplied with meat and grain and do other scout duty. At San Jacinto his Mexican company was assigned the task of assisting Mosley Baker's company in preventing Santa Anna's army from crossing the Brazos. After San Jacinto, Seguin and his company remained with the Texas Army and became the ninth company of the Second Regiment of volunteers. Seguin himself was raised to the rank of lieutenant colonel and was placed in charge of the second regiment of cavalry stationed at San Antonio. One of the first tasks he was ordered to perform in this new position was to collect the ashes and charred remains of the victims of the Alamo massacre and give them Christian burial. This duty was performed with considerable ceremony; Seguin delivered an address in Spanish, which was followed by another in English by Major Thomas G. Western. After the interment, three volleys of musketry were fired by the whole battalion over the grave into which the ashes had been gathered. (See the *Telegraph and Texas Register*, March 28, 1837; also the *Texas Historical Quarterly*, V, 69; and *The Southwestern Historical Quarterly*, XXXVII, 173–175.) Colonel Seguin represented the Bexar district in the Texas Senate for the Third and Fourth Congresses—Septmber [*sic*] 25, 1837–February 5, 1840—and an interpreter was employed for his benefit, since he did not understand the English language well. He was elected mayor of San Antonio in 1841. Claiming that he had been cheated, mistreated, and his life threatened by a group of Anglo-Texans at San Antonio in 1842, Seguin left Texas and took up his residence in Mexico. It was soon rumored that he had deserted Texas and had gone over to Arista (see *Tele-*

graph and Texas Register, June 15, 1842), and later it was said that he was in Monterrey trying to raise an army to plunder San Antonio. It is true that when General Woll seized San Antonio, September 11, 1842, Seguin ranking as a major, commanded the Mexican cavalry, and it was reported that with his own hand he killed Dr. Launcelot Smithers, McDonald, and McRea. (See Mrs. Mary Maverick's *Memoirs*.) It is evidently true that Seguin had been badly treated by some Americans at San Antonio, but that fact hardly justifies his subsequent conduct. He remained with the Mexican Army and fought against the Americans and Texans at the Battle of Buena Vista; but shortly after this battle he resigned his commission as colonel in the Mexican Army, and with the assistance of some of his American friends, made his way back to Texas. But he was never again happy or contented. In 1858, he published a thin volume of his *Memoirs*, it being, however, merely an effort to explain his past conduct. The last years of his life were spent in the home of his son in Santiago, Mexico. He died in 1889. See the *Texas Historical Quarterly,* XXI, 382, XXVIII, 92, XXXIII, 318. Wooten (ed)., *Comprehensive History of Texas,* I, 205, 316, 394. *Lamar Papers,* II, 14, 44, IV, Part 2, p. 70. Thrall, *Pictorial History of Texas,* 616. Juan N. Seguin, *Memoirs* (1858). Dixon and Kemp, *Heroes of San Jacinto,* 437–438.

3.5.5.   Sam Houston, letter, March 13, 1836.

Houston, Samuel, to Henry Raguet. March 13, 1836. Facsimile copy in the Madge W. Hearne collection, TSLA.

Published in Williams Barker 1941, 4:17–19. As in the document above, the original differs from the published transcript in minor details. The one significant omission is discussed in the commentary.

Gonzales
13th March 36.

My dear Friend

On the 11th Inst I reached this place assured that I would find 700 men— only the rise of 300 unorganized were on the Ground—since then my force has increased to near 500.

A few moments after my arrival the awful news of the fall of the alamo [*sic*] reached us. I [*sic; "A"*] statement will be forwarded from Washington the last [*sic; "with a list"*] of the facts. Our friend Bowie, as is now understood, unable to get out of bed, shot himself, as the soldiers approached it [*"his bed" crossed out*]. Despalier, Parker, and others, when all hope was lossed [*sic*] followed his example. Travis, tis said, rather than fall into the hands of the enemy, stabbed himself.

Our spies have been driven back from within 12 miles of Bexar. They heard none of the previously concerted signals, which were to be given by our friends: all was silen[*t*,] as they report. I will send two spies in a few minutes to view Bexar, and they will report in 3 days.

Co[l] Fannin should have relieved our Brave men in the Alamo. He had 430 men with artillery under his command, and had taken up the line of march with a full knowledge of the situation of those in the Alamo, and owing to the breaking down of a waggon, abandoned the march, returned to Goliad, and left our Spartans to their fate!

We are now compelled to take post on the east side of the Guadeloupe, and must battle if the enemy should press upon us. I am informed that Fannin has upward of 700 men now under his commands. I have ordered Goliad to be blown up and if possible, prevent all future murders where our men have no alternative but to starve in forts, or remain inactive, and useless to the defence of the country. With our force, we can not fight the enemy ten to one, in their own country—where they have every advantage. (It is reported and I do believe that (Labarb) or Ybarbo, who has lately been at San Antonio de Bexar, has gone on to incite the Indians, in the neighborhood of Nacogdoches. Keep an eye to this but be prudent.) Arouse our friends in the States. I would have sent the express as soon as I heard the news from the Alamo, but was assured that two spies were out; and were hourly expected, on whose statement I might place unbounded reliance as to the fate of the Alamo.

The conduct of the General Council and that of their "agent," has already cost us the lives of more than 230 [*brave men*]—Had it not been for that we should have kept all the advantages which we had gained. We must repair our losses by prudence and valour. I have no doubt as to the issue of the contest. I am in good spirits! Tho not ardent!!!

Johnsons & Grants parties are cut off. The enemy at the alamo are said to have loss[d] 521 killed and an equal number wounded—Murdered Americans, 187. One American female the wife of Lieu[t.] [D]ickinson dishonored! Three negroes and Mrs. Dickinson were all in the fort, who [es]caped Massacre as reported! Several Mexic[ans] in the fort were also murdered, and all killed in the fort were burned: The Mexicans killed in the assault were burried [*sic*]—This is the report of the matter in substance!

Tell the Red Landers to awaken and aid in the struggle*!*

Salute affectionately your family, with D[r]. Porter's and all friends. Write to me.

	Ever yrs truly
Co[l] Raguit	Sam. Houston

P.S. Our force tomorrow I hope will be 600 men. I am in great haste—will Major Allen join me? Let the People beware of [*name erased?*] and [*another missing or erased name*]!!! They are enemies to Texas and Liberty! Be vigilant! Major Hockley salutes y[r]self and family. I send a paper to your care!

Ever yours truly

Houston

Raguet

3.5.6.   Sam Houston, letter, March 15, 1836.

Williams, Amelia, and Eugene Barker eds. 1938. *The Writings of Sam Houston,*
1835–1836. 1:373–77. Austin: University of Texas Press.

There are two "official-looking" copies in the A. J. Houston Collection, TSLA, as
well as the source used by Williams and Barker (quoted here to include the footnotes). The cited Executive Record Book they used is likely to be the more accurate
source. Though this account gets a little away from the siege and fall of the Alamo,
it does note the arrival of Susanna Dickinson (Dickerson, see footnote 2 and documents in 4.4.4) and gives a picture of the immediate impact of the news on the Texas
Army.

TO JAMES COLLINSWORTH[1]
Camp at Navadad, March 15, 1836.

To James Collingsworth [*sic*], Chairman of the Military Committee:

Sir,—Since I had the honor to address you from Gonzales, the lady of Lieutenant Dickinson,[2] who fell at the Alamo, has arrived, and confirms the fall of
that place, and the circumstances, pretty much as my express detailed them.
She returned in company with two negroes—one the servant of Colonel Travis,
the other a servant of Colonel Almonte. They both corroborate the statement
first made and forwarded to you. Other important intelligence arrived at Gonzales—that the army of Santa Anna had encamped at the Cibolo on the night of
the 11th inst., after a march of twenty-four miles that day. The army was to
encamp on the 12th at Sandy, and proceed direct to Gonzales. The number of
the enemy could not be ascertained, but was represented as exceeding two
thousand infantry. Upon this statement of facts, I deemed it proper to fall back
and take a post on the Colorado, near Burnham's, which is fifteen miles distant
from this point. My morning report, on my arrival in camp, showed three hundred and seventy-four effective men, without two days' provisions, many without arms, and others without any ammunition. We could have met the enemy,
and avenged some of our wrongs; but, detached as we were, without supplies
for the men in camp, of either provisions, ammunition, or artillery, and remote
from succor, it would have been madness to hazard a contest. I had been in
camp two days only, and had succeeded in organizing the troops. But they had
not been taught the first principles of the drill. If starved out, and the camp once
broken up, there was no hope for the future. By falling back, Texas can rally,
and defeat any force that can come against her.

[*Houston goes on in three more paragraphs to discuss the movements of the army*
and the enemy, deserters, and other logistical details. Then he finishes with the follow-
ing.]

Our forces must not be shut up in forts, where they can neither be supplied
with men nor provisions. Long aware of this fact, I directed, on the 16th of January last, that the artillery should be removed, and the Alamo blown up; but it

was prevented by the expedition upon Matamoras, the author of all our misfortunes.

I hope that our cruisers on the gulf will be active, and that Hawkins[5] and —— —— may meet the notice of the government. Let the men of Texas rally to the Colorado!

Enclosed you will receive the address of General Santa Anna, sent by a negro to the citizens. It is in Almonte's handwriting. Santa Anna was in Bexar when the Alamo was taken. His force in all, in Texas is, I think, only five or six thousand men—though some say thirty thousand! This can not be true. Encourage volunteers from the United States—but I am satisfied we can save the country. Had it not been for the council, we would have had no reverses. We must have the friendship of the Comanches and other Indians.

Gonzales is reduced to ashes!

> Sam Houston,
> *Commanding General.*

---

[1] *Executive Letter Book No. 3,* Texas State Library. Yoakum, *History of Texas,* II, 475–477. C. E. Lester, *Sam Houston* (1837), 83–84.

[2] A few writers of Texas history spell Almeron Dickerson's name correctly, but the majority write it "Dickinson." Several documents to be found among the *Comptroller's Military Service Records,* Texas State Library, show this man's signature as written by himself. It is clearly "Almeron Dickerson," and at the Alamo from January, 1836, to March 6, 1836, he enjoyed the rank of captain of artillery. He is usually called Lieutenant Dickerson, and it is probable that few persons outside the Alamo knew of his raise in rank, but the *Army Papers,* Texas State Library, shows his commission as *captain* of artillery.

[*The remaining footnotes, including #5 for Hawkins, are biographical sketches of three Texans who do not relate to the Alamo, and so are not included here.*]

3.6.1.   Antonio and Doña María Jesusa Peña Cruz y Arocha, interview, c. 1840s?

Matovina, Timothy M. 1995. *The Alamo Remembered: Tejano Accounts and Perspectives.* Translated by Pascal Wilkins. 27. Austin: University of Texas Press.

The source for this interview is the papers of the French artist Theodore Gentilz, Document SM-2, DRT. A portion was also included in Groneman 1994, 113–14, where the name of the wife appears as Juana Peña.

Colonel Juan Nepomuceno Seguín escaped from the Alamo [during] the night by the *acequia* [canal], Cruz was waiting for him with a horse from the *jacal* [hut] [on the] west side in front of the church. Cruz lived in one of the *jacales* in the vicinity of the place of San [Antonio de] Valero. His wife Doña María Jesusa

Peña, could see by a small window all or a good part of what happened. After the firing ceased, Santa Anna got in by the southwest door. A few Texans which were hidden came to kneel down before him, holding each a little white flag (*banderita blanca*). The Mochos [soldiers?] surrounding them were hesitating as to kill them but Santa Anna going by made a signal by his head and sword and immediately they were pierced by bayonets.

3.6.2.   Navarro, José Antonio, interview, 1846.

Gregg, Josiah. 1941. *Diary and Letters of Josiah Gregg.* Edited by Maurice Garland Fulton. 1:231–32. Norman: University of Oklahoma Press. Copyrighted 1941 by the University of Oklahoma Press.

---

*DIARY, SEPTEMBER, 1846

Wed. 23— . . .

Not very long after my arrival at San Antonio de Bexar, I visited Don José Antonio Navarro, who has become somewhat famous—first on account of the active part he took in the Texas revolution and his having been a member of their Congress—and secondly for his connection with the Texas Santa Fé Expedition—his having been taken prisoner at Santa Fé—and his protracted confinement and suffering in the castle of Perote. I found him reclined upon a rude sofa, with his lame leg elevated. Supposing he spoke English, I accosted him in that tongue, but he at once requested I should converse in Spanish, as he spoke very little English. He appeared a very agreeable man, and of far greater intelligence, than is usual among the Mexicans of this region. He conversed with much volubility, and expatiated particularly upon the ways of Texas. He with much justice condemned the wonted temerity of the Texans, which, as he remarked, had cost them a great deal of blood, and most of their defeats. He instanced, in particular, the affair of the Alamo, where 180-odd men undertook to defend it against several thousand. He asserted that Santa Anna at all time left the eastern side of the fortification free, in hopes the Texans would escape—preferring to let them go in peace, to a victory over them which he knew must cost him dearly.

I have several times visited the famous fort of Alamo (or rather its ruins) which stand about 100 yards from the east bank of the San Antonio river, and some 400 yards northeastward of the Public Square of San Antonio. Scattered along below it, on the east bank of the river, are several inferior houses and huts, with perhaps between one and two hundred population, known as the village of the Alamo.

3.6.3.   Col. R. L. Crompton, interview, 1887.

San Antonio Daily Express. March 6, 1887.

FALL OF THE ALAMO.
FIFTY-FIRST ANNIVERSARY OF THAT GREAT EVENT.
Recollections of an Eye-witness of That Massacre—The Hopeless Fight of the Americans Against Mexicans—Heroic Deeds of Crocket [*sic*], Travis and Bowie

To-day is the fifty-first anniversary of the fall of the Alamo, one of the most memorable and disastrous events of the heroic struggle for Texas independence from the tyranny of Mexico. It was there within the old walls now standing upon the eastern edge of Alamo plaza, that Crockett, Travis and Bowie, with but a handfull of Texas patriots struggled manfully against the Mexican legions who swarmed around the walls and only succeeded in gaining an entrance when nearly all the Texans had either been killed or wounded. Not one survived to tell the tale.

Col. R. L. Crompton, of Roxbury, Mass., then in San Antonio, related the following account of the terrible battle recently to a Globe Democrat reporter at St. Louis:

"In the winter of 1834," Col. Crompton began, "I left my home in Massachusetts for the purpose of seeking my fortune in the west. My destination was Lexington, Ky., but while on the Ohio river I fell in with a party of young men who were on their way to join Col. Travis in Texas, and, carried away by their vivid pictures of the life of adventurous excitement that awaited them in that country, I joined their band, without much knowledge as to the right or wrong of the cause which I pledged myself to sustain. We traveled by boat to New Orleans, and there took ship for Galveston. Here we procured horses, and proceeded to join the Texan forces, then operating in the neighborhood of San Antonio de Bexar. Anything less like an army in appearance it would be hard to imagine. Uniform there was none, each dressing to suit his own peculiar fancy, and the men were as various as their attire. A very large percentage had left the States because they had 'met with an accident'—the Texan euphonism [*sic*] for having committed some crime—but the greater number were young fellows who, like myself, had been led into the war by love of change and excitement. So large a proportion of very young men has seldom been found in any military force.

"Shortly after my arrival I attached myself to the command of that magnificent Tennesseean, Col. Milam, and soon became devotedly attached to him. He was a man of splendid character, without the sternness of Travis or the strong flavor of blackguardism that hung about Houston. The latter I knew well, but never liked, although I could not help recognizing his strong qualities. But Milam won all hearts, and many of us thought he was the proper leader of the army.

"As soon as we had gathered sufficient strength we attacked the Mexican forces in San Antonio. They far outnumbered us, and a desperate struggle ensued. For days we fought in the streets and among adobe houses, each of which was a miniature fortress. With picks and spades we dug our way through the walls from house to house, thus avoiding the great loss which would have resulted from any attempt at a direct storm. The fight for the Vera-mendi house was fierce and bloody, but at last we drove the Mexicans out and took possession. But our triumph was soon turned to mourning, for shortly after it was captured the beloved Milam fell dead, shot by a Mexican who lay concealed behind a wall on the opposite side of the San Antonio river. We at length obtained possession of the town, but did not retain it long, as the advance of President Santa Anna compelled us to withdraw, leaving Travis with less than 150 men to garrison the town. I shall never forget the day when young Maverick rode into our camp with news that Travis, refusing to retreat, was shut up in the Alamo and surrounded by an overwhelming force.

"I do not now what madness possessed me, but when I heard that Houston had decided that he was too weak to march to the relief of Travis (as was indeed the case), I determined to gallop to San Antonio, endeavor to steal through the Mexican lines and join my old Kentucky friends, who were nearly all within the garrison walls. I reached San Antonio without difficulty, and found that one assault had already been made, and that the besieged had more than held their own. So far all was well, but in endeavoring to creep between the Mexican pickets I was fired upon and wounded, and owed my escape from death to the darkness. With difficulty I made my way to the house of a Mexican whom I had befriended during our occupation of the city, and he generously agreed to conceal me in his house. A narrow window commanded an excellent view of one front of the Alamo wall, and from this point I could see nearly all of that memorable struggle. Day after day the Mexican fire was kept up, and time after time were their storming columns hurled against the old church wall, which formed the Texan rampart. But nothing could disturb the calm desperation of the defenders, and at the close of each day the Lone Star flag floated as proudly, and, apparently, as securely as ever, from the roof of the mission. The Mexican losses were fearful. Their clumsy escopetas were no match for the long Hawkins rifles in the hands of Kentucky and Tennessee backwoodsmen. Hundreds fell every day, but their loss was little felt in the overwhelming host, while every man of the garrison who died was an irreparable injury. The line along the wall grew very thin, but still there was no thought of surrender amidst that gallant band. At length, when death and wounds had reduced the poor handful to half its original numbers, the Mexicans effected a lodgment in an undefended portion of the wall and poured in by hundreds.

"Although there was no hope of success, the brave Texans fought as steadily and firmly as on the first day of the siege. From room to room went the fight, and the puny Mexicans learned by bitter experience what deadly weapons bowie knife and clubbed rifles were in the hands of desperate Americans. But human endurance has its limits, and at last Santa Anna was the master of the Alamo, but not until the last American lay cold in death. From my window I could hear the shouts and yells and see the struggling figures. When all was over I begged my host to go into the Alamo and bring the news of all that had occurred. He came back in an hour or two and said that such a shambles had never been seen. The dead were heaped in wild confusion all over the building, and the gutters fairly ran with blood. In a room on the ground floor was the corpse of Colonel Bowie, who had been butchered upon his sick bed. Not far from him was found the brave and eccentric Crockett, but the most impressive sight was in a small room in the upper story, where the gallant Travis lay, a bullet hole in his forehead, surrounded by the corpses of fifteen Mexicans who had died by his own hand. Of the Texans not one survived. But they did not die unavenged, as 1600 Mexicans fell before less than 150. It was well said that 'Thermopylae had its messenger of defeat, the Alamo had none.'

"I served through the rest of the war and was at San Jacinto, but after the tale of the Alamo all seems small and petty, and it would be an anti-climax for me to continue my story. But I hope that the memory of our gallant struggle for independence will not be forgotten, for when all is said and done, the virtues of the early Texans far more than compensated for their shortcomings, and their heroism, like charity, covers a multitude of sins."

3.7.1.   Eulalia Yorba, interview, 1896.
San Antonio Express. April 12, 1896, 13.

ANOTHER STORY OF THE ALAMO.
THE BATTLE DESCRIBED BY AN ALLEGED EYE WITNESS.
How Santa Ana's Overwhelming Forces Attacked and Captured the Enemy's Stronghold—The Death of Davy Crockett.

There is now living in the United States but one person who saw the awful conflict. She is Senora Eulalie Yorba, a poor old Spanish woman, who lives in the suburbs at Fort Worth. She was born in 1801, and is therefore nearly 95 years of age. She was 34 when the Alamo was besieged. She lives with her granddaughter's family, and is supplied with a little means of livelihood by the well-to-do citizens of San Antonio and Fort Worth, who take just pride in the memories of the old Spanish woman of the battle at the stone mission. Her mind is very keen on events of sixty and seventy years ago, and she has been sought after by numerous writers of history in the Southwest.

The writer had a most interesting interview with Mrs. Yorba not long ago, and communicated the results to The San Francisco Examiner. Every one in Fort Worth knows where to find her and we were soon at her door. She said:

"I well remember when Santa Ana and his 2000 soldiers on horses and with shining muskets and bayonets marched into the little pueblo of San Antonio. The news ran from mouth to mouth that Col. Travis, Davy Crockett and Col. Bowie and the 160 or so other Texans who had held that locality against the Mexicans for several weeks, had taken refuge in and had barricaded themselves in that old stone mission, which had been used as a crude fort or garrison long before I came to the country. It belonged to Mexico and a few stands of muskets and three or four cannons were kept there.

"When Santa Ana's army came they camped on the plains about the pueblo and a guard was put about the Alamo fort. That was from the last day of February to March 4. Of course, I kept at home with my little boys and never stirred out once, for we women were all terribly frightened. Every eatable in the house, all the cows, lumber and hay about the place were taken by the troops, but we were assured that if we remained in the house no personal harm would come to us.

"Of course, we were hourly informed of the news. We knew that the Texans in the Alamo were surrounded by over 500 soldiers constantly, while 1500 more soldiers were in camp out on the plains. We learned that four days had been given the Texans to surrender. We heard from the soldiers that not one of the imprisoned men had so much as returned a reply to the demand for surrender, and that on the morning of the 6th of March, 1836, Santa Ana was going to bring matters to a crisis with the beleaguered rebels. I never can tell the anxiety that we people on the outside felt for that mere handful of men in the old fort, when we saw armed hostile troops as far as we could see, and not a particle of help for the Texans, for whom we few residents of the town had previously formed a liking.

"The morning of Sunday—the 6th of March—ah! Indeed, I could never forget that, even if I lived many years more—was clear and balmy, and every scrap of food was gone from my house and the children and I ran to the home of a good old Spanish priest so that we could have food and comfort there. There was nothing to impede the view of the Alamo from the priest's home, although I wished there was. The shooting began at 6 in the morning. It seemed as if there were myriads of soldiers and guns about the stone building. There was volley after volley fired into the barred and bolted windows. Then the volleys came in quick succession. Occasionally we heard muffled volleys and saw puffs of smoke from within the Alamo, and when we saw, too, Mexican soldiers fall in the roadway or stagger back we knew the Texans were fighting as best they could for their lives.

"It seemed as if ten thousand guns were shot off indiscriminately as fire-crackers snap when whole bundles of them are set off at one time. The smoke grew thick and heavy, and we could not see clearly down at the Alamo, while the din of musketry, screams of crazy, exultant Mexicans increased every moment. I have never heard human beings scream so fiercely and powerfully as the Mexican soldiers that day. I can compare such screams only to the yell of a mountain panther or lynx in desperate straits.

"Next several companies of soldiers came running down the street with great heavy bridge timbers. These were quickly brought to bear as battering rams on the mission doors, but several volleys from within the Alamo, as nearly as we could see, laid low the men at the timbers and stopped the battering for a short time. Three or four brass cannons were loaded with what seemed to us very long delay and were placed directly in front of the main doors of the mission. They did serious work. Meanwhile, bullets from several thousand muskets incessantly rained like hail upon the building, and went through the apertures that had been made in the wood barricades at the windows and doors. The din was indescribable. It did not seem as if a mouse could live in a building so shot at and riddled as the Alamo was that morning.

"Next we saw ladders brought and in a trice the low roof of the church was crowded with a screaming, maddened throng of men armed with guns and sabers. Of course we knew then that it was all up with the little band of men in the Alamo. I remember that the priest drew us away from the window and refused to let us look longer, notwithstanding the fascination of the scene. We could still hear the shouts and yells and the booming of the brass cannon shook the priest's house and rattled the window panes.

"Along about 9 o'clock, I should judge, the shooting and swearing and yelling had ceased, but the air was thick and heavy with blue powder smoke. A Mexican colonel came running to the priest's residence and asked that we go down to the Alamo to do what we could for the dying men.

"Such a dreadful sight. The roadway was thronged with Mexican soldiers, with smoke and dirt begrimed faces, haggard eyes and wild, insane expression. There were twelve or fifteen bodies of Mexicans lying dead and bleeding here and there, and others were being carried to an adobe house across the way. The stones in the church wall were spotted with blood, the doors were splintered and battered in. Pools of thick blood were so frequent on the sun-baked earth about the stone building that we had to be careful to avoid stepping in them. There was a din of excited voices along the street, and the officers were marshaling their men for moving to camp.

"But no one could even tell you the horror of the scene that met our gaze when we were led by the sympathetic little colonel into the old Alamo to bandage up the wounds of several young men there. I used to try when I was younger to describe that awful sight, but I never could find sufficient language. There were only a few Mexicans in there when we came, and they were all officers who had ordered the common soldiers away from the scene of death, and—yes—slaughter, for that was what it was. The floor was literally crimson with blood. The woodwork all about us was riddled and splintered by lead balls and what was left of the old altar at the rear of the church was cut and slashed by cannon ball and bullets. The air was dark with powder smoke and was hot and heavy. The odor was oppressive and sickening and the simply horrible scene nerved us as nothing else could.

"The dead Texans lay singly and in heaps of three or four, or in irregular rows here and there all about the floor of the Alamo, just as they had fallen when a ball reached a vital part or they had dropped to their death from loss of blood. Of course we went to work as soon as we got to the mission at helping the bleeding and moaning men, who had only a few hours at most more of life; but the few minutes that we looked upon the corpses all about us gave a picture that has always been as distinct as one before my very eyes.

"So thick were the bodies of the dead that we had to step over them to get a man in whom there was still life. Close to my feet was a young man who had been shot through the forehead. He had dropped dead with his eyes staring wildly open and, as he lay there, seemingly gazed up into my face.

"I remember seeing poor old Col. Davy Crockett as he lay dead by the side of a dying man, whose bloody and powder-stained face I was washing. Col. Crockett was about 50 years old at that time. His coat and rough woolen shirt were soaked with blood so that the original color was hidden, for the eccentric hero must have died of some ball in the chest or a bayonet thrust.

3.7.2.   Pablo Díaz, interview, 1906.

Barnes, Charles M. *San Antonio Express.* July 1, 1906, 11.
Several of the open quotes were missing in the original and have been added here. The article includes an etched portrait of Díaz.

AGED CITIZEN DESCRIBES ALAMO FIGHT AND FIRE
Pablo Diaz, Now 90 Years of Age, Relates Story of Alamo
as He Saw It Next Day.
HOW THE RIVER WAS FILLED WITH BODIES

To have seen the ashes of those who were slain in the Alamo is an experience that but few men now living can claim. There is one man living in San Antonio who makes this claim. He does so with all the appearances and indications of his contention being correct. He seems not only to know the place where the heroes' corpses were burned, but gives a vivid description of the occurrence and his experience and positively points out and locates the spot, as well as the one where the few charred bones that were left were interred.

This man is Pablo Diaz. He lives with his niece, Alcaria Cypriana, on the west side of the Alazan Creek near the old San Fernando Cemetery. He is nearly 90 years old. He tells a very interesting story. He says:

"I was born in Monclova, Mex. Myself and my brother, Francisco Diaz, who is my senior by about eight years, had heard a great deal about the beauty of San Antonio. We were both very young then, he in his twenties and I still in my teens. We had both learned the trade of carpenter, and as wages in Monclova were very small we concluded to come here.

"After many narrow escapes we finally reached here in February, 1835. Not very long after our arrival Austin and Burleson with their forces came to the vicinity of San Antonio and located their camp near the head of the San Antonio River, and later at the Molino Blanco. Along about that time Capt. Juan N. Seguin was recruiting a company to join Austin's force of Constitutionalists, as the American colonists were called. Seguin prevailed on my brother, Francisco, to enlist in his company and the latter endeavored to induce me to join them, but I did not. I held that, having been born in Mexico, it was not right for me to take up arms against my native land, but I held that as I was living in this country it was not right for me to fight against it, so I became strictly neutral and took no part on either side.

"I have since regretted, however, that I did not join the Constitutionalists or Texans, for when I saw and realized the cruelties and enormities perpetrated by the invading armies from Mexico and the brutal treatment they accorded to the innocent women and children I could not help feeling ashamed and held aloof. I had not been here very long before General Cos and his army from Mexico came here. I was too young to have been impressed or conscripted into its service.

"I noticed from the time of its arrival the brutality of the soldiers. They, acting under the order from Cos and his subalterns, pressed even the women and children into service to make tortillas and prepare food for the soldiers and in many ways abused the women and were cruel to the children. My brother and I were then working for Don Domingo Bustillos. He was a very powerful and influential man. His home was at the southwest corner of Galen Street and Main Plaza, across the Street from the Cathedral, in the one-story stone building now owned by the Altgelts and occupied as a cigar store and restaurant. When Bustillos realized that we were likely to be impressed into service, either as soldiers or for other purposes, by the invading army, and needing us himself greatly, he sent my brother and I down to the First Mission and put us to work on a building. We were so engaged at the Mission that my brother joined Seguin's company. I was at the Mission when Bowie and his force successfully combatted the Mexican cavalry and artillery sent out there to capture them, and saw Bowie's force take the cannon from the Mexicans and turn their own guns on the Mexicans troops [this is referring to the "Grass Fight" in late 1835, near Mission Concepción]. My brother, Francisco, was with the Texans then.

When Milam Came In.

"I was at the Mission when Ben Milam and Maverick came in and captured San Antonio from Cos on December 7, 1835, but I prudently remained away during the fighting, as I knew if I came in that the Mexicans would make me serve in their ranks, but I came in after the capitulation, and after Milam had been buried within ten feet of where he had fallen. There had been great excitement in San Antonio prior to and during the fighting between the forces of Cos and Milam, but soon after Cos capitulated the city became quiet and remained so for some weeks until Santa Anna, Arredondo and their immense army arrived, although there had been some intermediate skirmishes. The Mexican troops had been quartered in barracks that extended all along the north side of Military Plaza and between Military and Main Plazas, and their barracks extended as far as where Saul Wolfson's store, at the corner of Main Avenue and Main Plaza, now stands. During the fighting the Mexican forces were pressed back by Milam's brave men until they were compelled to cross the river at the ford at Garden street, where the long Garden Street Bridge now stands. Cos then moved his headquarters from Military Plaza to La Villita and not far from the corner of Villita and Presa Streets. It was in a building in the rear of Mrs. Mitchell's residence and on Presa Street, that Cos signed the articles of capitulation to the Constitutionalists, and from whence the latter permitted him and his troops to retire and return to Mexico. Almost immediately adjacent to this now stands, with but slight alteration, the house in which "Deaf" Smith resided for quite a while.

"After Cos surrendered that portion of the army of the Constitutionalists that remained for a while was quartered in the barracks vacated by the Mexicans on Military Plaza, but soon after the arrival of Davy Crockett the small band moved over to the Alamo, because the defenses were better and more substantial than the ones on the West Side of the city. The weakness of the military fortress or Presidio, as it was called, on Military Plaza, had been demonstrated by the facility with which Milam's forces had dislodged the soldiers under General Cos. As soon as the coming of Santa Anna, which had been heralded, was known the Constitutionalists retired to the Alamo and commenced to fortify it. Up to this time it had not been used as a military fortification, but was a church and convent.

"The arrival of Santa Anna was announced by the firing of a gun from in front of the alcalde's house on Main Plaza. His red flag was hoisted over the Cathedral. I heard the gun fired from the plaza and saw the flag floating from San Fernando. From the Mission I could see also the flag of the Constitutionalists floating from the Alamo. The latter flag was not the flag that was afterward adopted by the Texas Republic, with its blue field and single star and a stripe of white and one of red, but was the flag of Mexico under the Constitution and prior to the usurpation and assumption of the Dictatorship by Santa Anna. When Santa Anna hoisted his red flag it was his announcement, that no quarter would be shown those opposing him. This was well understood by those in the Alamo. They knew that unless Houston, on whom they vainly relied, sent them succor they were lost.

Diaz Saw the Terrible Carnage.

"For six days I heard the rattle of musketry and the roar of cannon. I did not dare to leave my refuge near the mission lest I become involved in the terrible slaughter which I knew was going on there. Messengers frequently came out to the mission and told us of the terrible devastation and butchery in progress and of the brave and dauntless defense of the heroic Constitutionalists. The cannon shots became louder and more frequent as Santa Anna's soldiers got closer and closer to the Alamo. Finally, on the sixth day, after a fierce fusillade, there was silence and I saw the red flag of Santa Anna floating from the Alamo where the Constitutional flag before had been. Then I knew that the battle was over, that the invading tyrant and his horde had won and that the price paid for their stubborn defense by the Constitutionalists had been their lives. I had several personal friends among the brave men in the Alamo. One of them was named Cervantes. His descendants lived on the Alameda for many years and some of them are now residing on Losoya Street.

"Next I saw an immense pillar of flame shoot up a short distance to the south and east of the Alamo and the dense smoke from it rose high into the clouds. I saw it burn for two days and nights and then flame and smoke subsided and smoldered. I left my retreat and came forth cautiously, coming along Garden Street to town. I noticed that the air was tainted with the terrible odor from many corpses and I saw thousands of vultures flying above me. As I reached the ford of the river my gaze encountered a terrible sight. The stream was congested with the corpses that had been thrown into it. The Alcade [sic], Ruiz, had vainly endeavored to bury the bodies of the soldiers of Santa Ana who had been slain by the defenders of the Alamo. He had exhausted all of his resources and still was unable to cope with the task. There were too many of them. Nearly 6000 of Santa Anna's 10000 had fallen before they annihilated their adversaries and captured their fortress. I halted, horrified, and watched the vultures in their revel and shuddered at the sickening sight. Then involuntarily I put my hands before my eyes and turned away from the river, which I hesitated to cross. Hurriedly I turned aside and up La Villita and went to South Alamo. I could not help seeing the corpses which congested the river all around the bend from Garden to way above Commerce Street and as far as Crockett Street is now.

"They stayed there for many days and until finally the Alcalde got a force sufficient to dislodge them and float them down the river. But while this was a most gruesome sight, the one I saw later filled me with more horror. I went on to the Alameda. It was then a broad and spacious, irregularly shaped place, flanked on both sides with huge cottonwood trees, from which it gets its name. I turned into the Alameda at the present intersection of Commerce and Alamo Streets. Looking eastward I saw a large crowd gathered. Intuitively I went to the place.

He Saw the Ashes of the Heroes.

"It was just beyond where the Ludlow now stands. The crowd was gathered around the smouldering embers and ashes of the fire that I had seen from the mission. It was here that the Alcalde had ordered the bodies of Bowie, of Crockett, Travis and all of their dauntless comrades who had been slain in the

Alamo's unequal combat to be brought and burned. I did not need to make inquiry. The story was told by the silent witnesses before me. Fragments of flesh, bones and charred wood and ashes revealed it in all of its terrible truth. Grease that had exuded from the bodies saturated the earth for several feet beyond the ashes and smoldering mesquite fagots. The odor was more sickening than that from the corpses in the river. I turned my head aside and left the place in shame."

At this juncture of his story the venerable Patriarch Diaz stopped and pointed out the spot to me. I had got Ben Fisk to interpret the first part of it for me, after which I had asked Diaz to go with me and show me the spot that I might know its exact location. Antonio Perez accompanied us, Fisk being unable to go with us. We left the car at the point indicated by Diaz. He first took us to the old Post House, where it had been stated to me by another person that the bodies had been buried. To this Diaz replied: "The pyre was a very long one, as it had to consume nearly two hundred corpses, and it may be that some of the bodies may not have been burned in the main one, but have been burned on the opposite of the Alameda, but if they were I did not see the ashes. I am not prepared to say there were no bodies burned anywhere but at the spot I shall indicate, and it is not unlikely that they were burned here. It is probable that all of the bodies were not carried away from the Alamo at the same time or the Constitutionalists all separated from the Federals at the same time, so the story that some of the bodies were burned on the south side of the Alameda and where stands the Post House belonging to Dr. Herff Sr. and now called the Springfield House, may be true. But the main funeral pyre was about two hundred yards east of where St. Joseph's Church now stands and just beyond this big red brick house (meaning the Ludlow) and thence for fifty to sixty yards north."

The spot was then pointed out to me by Senor Diaz and I have it now definitely located in my mind. The location is confirmed by Perez, who states that when he was a little boy and used to play on the Alameda he was frequently shown the same spot as the place where the bodies of the Alamo heroes were burned. Perez goes further than Diaz and says that for many years there was a small mound there under which he was told the charred bones that the fire did not consume were buried by some humane persons, who had to do so secretly, and that he was familiar with the spot as the burial place of Bowie and Crockett. Perez states that about thirty years ago these bones were exhumed and place in the Old City Cemetery, the first one located on the Powder House Hill, but that he does not know the part of that cemetery they were placed in. Diaz when told that no monument had ever been erected to the memory of any of the heroes, except the one started, but never completed, that stands above the spot where Milam is finally buried, said: "It is a great shame to be forced to admit that neither the State nor the United States have ever erected a monument. It is to be hoped that a suitable and imposing one may be placed on the

Alameda to mark the place where the bodies of those heroes were burned and I hope you will remember the spot and endeavor to get someone to so mark it."

CHARLES MERRITT BARNES

3.7.3.   María de Jesús Buquor, interview, 1907.
San Antonio Express. July 19, 1907, 3.

WITNESSED LAST STRUGGLE OF THE ALAMO PATRIOTS
Mrs. Maridejesus Buquor of Floresville
Saw Fall of Cradle of Texas Liberty.
WARNED COLONEL TRAVIS OF MEXICANS' APPROACH

To have witnessed the Fall of the Alamo, that historic Cradle of Texas Liberty, and to have personally enjoyed the friendships of such men as Travis, Bowie and Crockett, are honors such as few persons living today can boast and yet there is today down on the narrow little street of this city, known as Arciniega, a little, well-preserved Mexican woman who enjoyed the friendship of these men and who was in San Antonio when the death of Travis and his fellow heroes awakened Texas to a struggle that was to end only with the establishment of her freedom.

Mrs. M. J. Burquor [*sic*], on the tenth of the past month, celebrated her 81st birthday and at the time of the fall of the Alamo was not quite ten years of age. Children in whose veins courses the warm blood of Castile, however, develop at an early age and Mrs. Buquor, in spite of her advanced age at present and her extreme youth at the time of the historic siege, is able to discourse in a very interesting manner concerning the incidents attendant upon the attack on the Texas stronghold by Santa Anna and the Mexican forces.

Was Friend of Heroes.

Sitting on the broad, old fashioned gallery of the house of her daughter, Mrs. Felicia Bledsoe of this city, whom she is here from Floresville to visit, and forming an interesting link between the present and the historic past, she yesterday related memories which rendered realistic the deeds which seem so unreal and far away when read in black and white. Her words transported one to the past and one seems to see Travis and Crockett at the home of her, who was then Maridejesus Dellado [*María de Jesús Delgado, per Matovina*], on the day that Santa Anna marched to San Antonio. Maridejesus steps out into the yard and beholding many men approaching calls to her mother to question her concerning them. It is the Mexican army and Travis and Crockett hastily bid their friends farewell and hastened to the fortress and a glorious death.

Then Mrs. Buquor, for the little Maridejesus was she, gave Travis his first warning of the actual approach of the enemy although, of course, rumors of this enemy's coming had been heard for days. Mrs. Buquor says that this was not the last that she saw of the Texas patriots by any means as for days before the final onslaught by the Mexican troops Travis, Crockett and others of the garrison would wave greetings to their friends in this city and bid them good bye, knowing full well that their doom had been sealed and that death was very near.

During the siege Mrs. Buquor says she and her family as well as the other citizens suffered severe hardships and were harshly treated by the Mexican soldiers from whom they had no protection. The Dellado family, consisting of her mother, father, three sisters, four brothers and herself, she says, was forced to give up their home, which is still standing on the river bank in the vicinity of the electric power house, to the Mexican soldiers. The members of the family sought refuge at the old Arciniega home which stood on the street which now bears its name. Here they were forced to dig and seek refuge in a cellar where they were safe from the bullets which swept the streets of the city at the moments of attack.

Childhood's idea of humor has not wholly departed from the now aged woman for she laughed slightly as she remembered the efforts of an aged, blind woman to get into the cellar and the woman's fall into the same just in time to avoid a bullet which whistled by.

Santa Anna a Lothario.

During the siege, Mrs. Buquor says she saw General Santa Anna many time and she bears testimony to his well known penchant for amours in that she related how he seized a young girl living near her home and held the maiden captive during his stay in the city.

She says that she did not see any of the Texas dead after the final attack but she plainly remembers seeing the smoke arising from the burning bodies of the Texans when their remains were destroyed in this way, a sacrificial fire on the altar of Texas liberty. She, however, fails to remember much concerning the departure of the Mexican troops from the city.

[*The article continues with information on Mrs. Buquor's life and family. It ends with the following paragraph.*]

She is well preserved, in spite of this numerous posterity, and her memory is wonderful considering her age. Save that she is a little confused as to dates, her memory is very clear. She related yesterday the death of seven Texans who tried to make their escape from the Alamo and were killed on the river bank near her house as vividly as if it were an event of the past few days. Another event which she remembered clearly is the killing of a party of Commanche [*sic*] Indians who came to San Antonio on a trading mission and became involved in a quarrel with some officers in the old Military Plaza. The quarrel led to a fight to the death between the Indians and the citizens in which all of the Commanche party were killed. Mrs. Buquor was unable to recall the date of this event but says that it happened a number of years after the Fall of the Alamo. Many other interesting events, clearly allied with the history of the Alamo City, are also recalled by her.

3.7.4.   Juan Díaz, interview, 1907

San Antonio Light. September 1, 1907, 13.

AS A BOY, JUAN DIAZ, VENERABLE SAN ANTONIAN WITNESSED THE ATTACK ON THE ALAMO

When the sun rose Sunday morning, March 6, 1836, a little Mexican boy climbed the ladders that led to the tower of San Fernando Cathedral and watched the gorgeous forces of General Santa Anna as they marched into the city from the westward and halted on Main plaza.

This mite of a boy who watched the invading forces come to San Antonio, led by martial music and flying banners, was Juan Diaz, and he lives today at his home [*at*] 110 Speed street, old and feeble, but still retaining vivid memories of that Sabbath morning when the Mexican army came, the cannonading and subsequent capture of the Alamo, the slaughter of its defenders and the final chapter, the burning of the dead on Alamo plaza, just in front of where the Menger hotel now stands.

Juan Diaz is the son of Antonio Diaz, who, at the time of the fall of the Alamo, was the trusted custodian of San Fernando cathedral. The Diaz family lived near the church, and young Juan played about the yard and the plaza. It was while he was playing with his sisters and some of the neighbor children that the sound of martial music broke on the air. Diaz says he was old enough to know something of what war meant, and that the first thing he did was to send his sisters home. Then he scampered to the tower to watch the army, and later clambered down and stood in awe-struck wonder near the plaza as the big guns of the Mexicans began to roar and boom and send deadly cannon balls hurtling against the solid walls of the sacred Alamo.

"I will never forget how that army looked as it swept into town," said the old man as he told the story of what he knew and saw of the fall of the Alamo to a Light reporter yesterday. "At the head of the soldiers came the regimental band, playing the liveliest airs, and with the band came a squad of men bearing the flags and banners of Mexico and an immense image that looked like an alligator's head. The band stopped on Main plaza and remained there until after the fall of the fort. The artillery was planted where the French building now stands, and the cannoneers had a clean sweep to the Alamo, for at that time there were no buildings between it and the San Fernando cathedral."

Diaz tells how he watched the progress of the battle from a distant point of vantage, how, after the cannon had ceased to boom, he saw the six columns of

Mexican soldiers form in line and go straight for the walls of the Alamo. He was not too far away to see the soldiers go scrambling up and up, only to be hurled back onto their comrades, who, all undaunted, stepped into the breaches and fought their way to the top of the battle-scarred walls.

"I did not go to the plaza when the dead were burned," said Diaz. "I had no desire to see that great funeral pyre, but the odor of it permeated every part of the city. It was sickening, and for weeks and months people shunned the Alamo. Some of the men who went there during the cremation told us that the Texas and Mexican soldiers were all piled in a heap and burned together."

Many of Santa Anna's staff officers had quarters at the San Fernando cathedral and were fed by Diaz's mother. He says the general gave orders that their home was to be safe from the soldiers and that a guard was constantly on watch to see that no damage was done.

The aged Mexican says that for days after the battle there was the most intense excitement, but he asserts that Santa Anna kept his victorious soldiers well under control and that but few cases of damage resulted from their depredations.

[*The article finishes with two paragraphs on Díaz's life and family, along with a photograph.*]

3.7.5.   Juan Antonio Chávez, interview, 1907.

Barnes, Charles M. *San Antonio Express.* December 15, 1907, 54; December 22, 1907, 11.

[*December 15, 1907*]
REMEMBERS EARLY DAYS
Antonio Chavez Tells of the Old Military Plaza and the Many Things That Happened During and Following the Siege of the Alamo.
(BY CHARLES MERRITT BARNES.)

Among the very few who resided here when the tyrant, Santa Anna, made his incursions and created such havoc, is an old citizen whose home is at 229 Obrajo Street, within a very few yards of where he was born. This old resident is Don Juan Antonio Chavez, who was born in the year 1827. He was 10 years old when the tyrant came, and remembers it well. His parents were then living in the house where he was born. Speaking of the coming of Santa Anna, Don Antonio said:

"When Milam and his comrades came into San Antonio from the Molino Blanco, the December previous to the coming of Santa Anna, our home was right in the line of fire between Milam's men and the Mexican army under the command of General Cos. On that occasion we were compelled to flee from home and seek refuge in the country. When we returned we found the house badly shattered with shot and shell. The doors were riddled with bullets and grape shot from the cannon and escopetas [*muskets, per Matovina*] and the rifle balls. Had our family remained some, if not all, would have been killed.

"When Santa Anna was marching on San Antonio, a friend of my father's came and told us there was going to be another very wicked fight. He advised him to leave and go again into the country. The experience my father had during the previous fight between the forces of Milam and Cos induced him to heed the counsel of this friend. My father took the entire family with him to the country several miles away from the city. We remained there until the Alamo had fallen and all of its defenders slain. We did not return for quite a while afterwards. This time our house was not in the line of fire, but we did not know this and it was much safer, anyway, for us in the country.

[*The article continues with stories about Chávez's grandfather, who was captured by Indians and later served as an interpreter, his parents, early families in San Antonio, and some description of the town itself.*]

[*December 22, 1907*]
[*The interview continues with more on early San Antonio and its citizens, then has the following paragraph mentioning the Alamo.*]

Lived under Five Flags.

"I have lived in San Antonio under five different dominions and have seen as many flags float over her citadel and the Alamo since I have been living here. I was born under the Mexican dominion. Its constitutional flag of A.D. 1821, against which Santa Anna contended and prevailed, was floating over the Alamo when he came here in 1836. He captured it together with the Alamo and annihilated its brave defenders. On his arrival the flag he hoisted was the bloody red one. It was the flag of no country. He hoisted it to indicate his intention of giving no quarter.

[*The article ends with a brief history of the Texas Republic, Confederate, and U.S. eras.*]

3.7.6.   Juan Vargas, interview, 1910.
San Antonio Light, April 3, 1910, 34.

THIS MAN WAS OLD WHEN SANTA ANA SPILLED BLOOD IN ALAMO AND BUILT TEXANS'
FUNERAL PYRE

JUAN VARGAS OF SAN ANTONIO
CARRIES WEIGHT OF 114 YEARS

REMEMBERS WELL DESPERATE
CHARGE AGAINST THE ALAMO

**Born January 1, 1796, twenty years after American revolution,
he has seen and participated in more historical events than any man alive—
fought in 1810 for Mexican independence and in 1830 came to San Antonio to
make his home. Five generations of the Vargas family are today alive, the
youngest being Rosa, his 3-year-old great-great-grandchild. His life and experiences related by himself.**

BY LOUIS DE NETTE

Where is the man who, having stepped past the Biblical three score and ten
milestone, believes he is old?

Where is the man who, as he nears the century mark, feels the weight of his
years and believes that indeed he is aged in the land?

All honor to them! They, in their own and other's [sic] estimation, are old.
They may contemplate the past from the lapse of time—

But here, in San Antonio is a man on whose head rests the accumulated
snow's and sunshines of a century and even more—many years more, as many
as make two men's lives.

For Juan Vargas, an Indian of the tribe from which Porfirio Diaz claims
descent, a true descendant of the mighty Aztecs, is the man who has lived in
three centuries and is now over 114 years old.

[*There are three more paragraphs in a similar style, followed by this discussion of
the Alamo.*]

At the Alamo, that shrine, that altar bathed in heroes' blood and strewn
with heroes' clay, Juan Vargas was not far distant. Impressed by Santa Anna, he
was forced to menial tasks about camp and equipage. They did not force him to
fight, for he refused to draw weapons against those with whom he had lived,
and his refusal almost cost him his life.

"Rivers of blood flowed," says the old man, now dim of mind in many
things, but remembering the Alamo as though but yesterday. "Rivers of blood
flowed and the earth ran red. Texans—Americans—gave their lives willingly to
the holy cause. I—known as a Mexican and guarded by Santa Anna's men—
bound up the wounds of the injured of his army and helped to bury the dead.
My life is going. Little longer can I hope to keep this mould of clay animate; the
grave, the crossing to the other side is before me, but over in eternity I shall
carry with me the memory of that fight, of that struggle wherein the Alamo fell
and Texan blood bedewed its floors."

[*Several paragraphs follow on Vargas's earlier biography before arriving at 1836.*]

Storming of the Alamo.

Came rumors of war and then war Texans, chafing under the intolerable rule and despotism of Mexico, declared their independence. Santa Anna, conqueror and self-styled president of Mexico, sent his invincibles to down the spirit and slay the men who thus dared to affront him by seceding from the nominal states of the republic of Mexico.

"I remember," says the aged man, "how the troops of Santa Anna marched into San Antonio de Bexar. I remember how they overawed all, taking what they wanted with no thought of pay. They had come to suppress a rebellion and one way to do it was to take the worldly goods of the rebels. They camped, to uncounted numbers, within the city, close to the Alamo and yet far enough away to escape the leaden hail which the Texans poured into them. As for me, I was with them. They had taken me in passing. I waited on them, performed kitchen and equipage tasks about camp. They said I did not know how to shoot and they would not trust me with a gun. Little did they know that I had fought with Padre Hidalgo and with Iturbide [*during the Mexican fight for independence from Spain.*]

"Thing are dim to me now. As the light of day has gone from my eyes, so the light of memory has left my mind. But never can I forget the battle of the Alamo. I did not fire a shot, neither did I storm the old fort when the Mexicans rushed in to cut to pieces the last remnant of the gallant band. They did their own work, I refusing to go to the Alamo. For this they threatened execution when the day was won, but could not at that time waste a shell on me. One shell might mean victory or defeat. They used their shells on the Texans.

"Back in the camp I heard the roar of the artillery. Shriek of shell mingled with groan of dying; soldiers mutilated and torn stumbled into camp to be bound up; dozens and scores were dragged in with gaping wounds through which their life-blood had trickled; ever and anon the cry of "Muerte a los Tejanos" [*"death to the Texans"*] echoed; carnage and a hell of battle reigned; Mexicans were mowed down as though a scythe passed; the uncounted dead were piled in camp, while [*a*] sort of service was rendered the living by doctors, aided by myself and others who, like me, had been impressed for this service.

"Oh, senor, that day is one to go down in history, for never did patriot band go more willingly to death than did those handful of Texans imprisoned behind stone wall and fighting to the last. And never in history is there recorded a battle in which so few gave death to so many.

"The day after, the piling of these dead in trenches, the absence of humans from San Antonio—ah, but let us pass that, senor, let us pass that. I am old, close to the grave. Excitement is not good for me. I tremble and lose strength."

[*Several more paragraphs follow with few details. De Nette says the rest of Vargas's life is "but one stretch in the memory."*]

3.7.7. Enrique Esparza, Pablo Díaz, and Juan Antonio Chávez, interview, 1911.

Barnes, Charles M. *San Antonio Express.* March 26, 1911, 26.

Five images accompany this article, with the following captions: "East Commerce Street—site of old Alameda" (photo); "The Old Alameda" (an early painting); "Sketch of the Recognition of Travis' Body" (painting); "Place on North side of former Alameda where Alamo Bodies were Burned" (photo); and "Site of Pyre on South Side of former old Alameda where the Alamo Slain were incinerated" (photo).

BUILDERS' SPADES TURN UP SOIL BAKED BY ALAMO FUNERAL PYRES

SITE OF BURIAL OF ASHES OF TRAVIS AND HIS MEN DEFINITELY FIXED

(Copyrighted 1911, by Charles Merritt Barnes)

Where workmen are excavating for the cellar of a new building that will stand on the spot of one of the two funeral pyres whereon the bodies of those slain in the Alamo's defense were consumed, is one of the memorable places of San Antonio, never marked and constantly passed unheeded. Few know that such a prominent event in history was there enacted. It will not be long before this spot and the one where the other funeral pyre was built will be the sites of buildings for commercial purposes and the populace, in all probability, will forget that either place was ever of such historical interest.

The spot where the cellar is being dug comprises one-half of the area on which the first pyre mentioned was located. It is on the north side of East Commerce Street, adjoining the Ludlow House. The building is being constructed by Dr. G. H. Moody. The pyre occupied a space about ten feet in width by sixty in length and extended from northwest to southeast from the property owned by Mrs. Ed Steves, on which the Ludlow House is built, to and through the property that the Moody structure is to occupy, and a short distance out into the street. The other pyre, which was of equal width, was about eighty feet long and was laid out in the same direction, but was on the opposite side and on property now owned by Dr. Ferdinand Herff Sr., about 250 yards southeast of the first pyre, the property being known as the site of the old Post House or the Springfield House.

The sites of the two pyres have been pointed out to me by several persons, three of whom saw them when the bodies were being burned and before the ashes had been scattered and the fragments removed. These three persons are all living today. . . .

[*The rest of this and the next two paragraphs relate to Enrique Esparza, presented earlier as document 1.5.5. The next two sections are the narrative of Pablo Díaz, which is essentially the same as in document 3.7.2. Barnes then gives the story of Juan Antonio Chávez, as follows.*]

THIRD EYE-WITNESS.

Don Juan Antonio Chavez, also living here now, who saw the remnants of the pyres and the fragments of the bodies, was the third eye-witness who showed me the same spots that the other two did and confirmed their stories, all three coinciding.

Antonio Perez and August Biesenbach also showed me the same places and stated they had been the ones whereon the bodies had been burned. Biesenbach said that some of the fragments of heads, skulls, arms and hands had been removed and buried after being buried beneath the pyre at the Ludlow and Moody site. They had been taken many years later to the Odd Fellows Rest, on Powder House Hill, and there given final burial, together with the bodies of several other persons who had been killed or died later, and had first been interred where the Alamo defenders' bodies had been burned.

I went with Biesenbach to the cemetery mentioned and he showed me the place where they were said to have been buried, between two tombs. These two tombs had monuments to people killed in tragic episodes which occurred some years after the struggle at the Alamo, and had no connection with it, but happened to have been buried for some time below the location of one of the pyres. When they were removed some of the fragments of those whose corpses were burned on this pyre may have been found, removed and buried, as stated by Mr. Biesenbach and other credible citizens, between the two tombs in the Odd Fellows Rest.

[*Barnes goes on to discuss the lack of a monument for the Alamo defenders, tells a story about Santa Anna considering giving Crockett a military burial (which there is no basis for believing), and talks about the San Antonio artists Lunkwitz and Gentilz. He then returns to the topic of the pyres.*]

There was an orchard very near the place where the bodies were burned on the south side of the Alameda and it is stated that flames and sparks blowing in the fierce March wind that prevailed a part of the time during the incineration blew the flames into the orchard, injuring many and destroying some of the fruit trees, most of which died soon after.

This fact probably gave rise to the prevalent belief that obtained for many years, that after the bodies were burned none of the fruit trees in the neighborhood would bear and that they as well as the cottonwood trees all died soon after.

It is a fact that there are now no bearing fruit trees within a block of where either of the two pyres were and there are but two of the fifty or more cottonwood trees left that grew originally on the Alameda. Neither of them is within a block of either of the pyres.

[*The article continues with stories of lost treasures, dueling, Crockett's marksmanship, and a claim that the Alamo defenders might have lost due to a lack of ammunition.*]

3.7.8.　Trinidad Coy, interview, 1911.

San Antonio Light. November 26, 1911, 41.

Another recently rediscovered source in Jackson 1997 is this interview with the son of Trinidad Coy, who said he was one of Travis's Tejano soldiers and was captured and spent the siege in the Mexican camp.

New Light on Alamo Massacre

Trinidad Coy Sent Out on Reconnoissance [*sic*], Might Have Been Able
to Avert Disaster Had His Horse been Less Partial to Loco Weed—Information
Which Colonel Travis Needed Formulate Better Plan Never Came.

But for the unguarded action of a farmer's boy, the history of Texas and the map of the United States might today be different.

When Travis, Bowie and Crockett and their band of immortal heroes lay intrenched in the Alamo in April [*sic*], 1836, rumors flew about that Santa Ana and his Mexican troops were on the way to San Antonio. There was no way to trace these reports to any authentic source. But their very persistency gave rise to suspicion and credence in the minds of the brave Texans.

As a consequence Travis, who was at that time in command of the troops at the Alamo, sent out scouts who were to locate the Mexicans under Santa Ana, if possible, and to bring in accurate information as to their whereabouts, and their probable destination, if it were possible, the scouts were to bring in an estimate of the probable force of the Mexican troops, so that action might be taken in accordance with the information so secured.

There is living today a descendant of one of the scouts, from whom this information has been secured. Some of it sheds a new light on the situation that finally culminated in the massacre in the historic little mission on the plaza in San Antonio.

Police Captain Andres Coy is the son of one of the messengers sent out by Colonel Travis.

[*The narrative of Captain Coy's account goes on to tell a fairly extensive story about his father, Trinidad Coy, being sent out on reconnaissance and captured by the Mexican army, in which the accidental feeding of loco weed to his horse plays a key role. The story continues as follows.*]

Called before the commander of the little troop, he explained that he was on his way to a neighboring little town to see a sick sister, that he was in no way connected with the Texas army; that all he desired was permission to depart unmolested.

The Mexican commandant pondered awhile. "Well," he decided, "you may be telling the truth. But I believe that you ate some of the loco-weed that you fed to your horse there in the road. You come with us."

Too Late

They carried him back to the main army. With them, as a prisoner, he was taken to San Antonio. One day they appeared before the city. Coy afterwards learned that their appearance was entirely unexpected. The defenders were taken by surprise.

He was kept in the Mexican camp while preparations were made to attack the band of faithful heroes in the little church. With great avidity he saw the work go forward that was to destroy his comrades, to whom he should have brought word. He cursed the luck that had tied his hands in this important of all important hours.

The preparations of warfare went on. The attack commenced. With unholy joy, he saw the Mexican troops beaten back, only to surge forward again, overpowering the brave defenders by sheer weight of numbers. He longed to join his friends.

Looking hastily about him he saw that the camp was deserted. All the hangers-on had followed the line of soldiery. He worked his bonds against a stone until they parted. He made his way out of the camp, followed a well-known path that led around the city, and in another hour he had arrived at a point in back of the chapel of the Alamo, from where he could join his comrades.

Only a bank of cottonwood trees hid them from his view. He forced his way through the underbrush. The Alamo lay before him. There were no signs of fighting. All was quiet. Only, before his eyes, there rose the heavy black cloud from a smoking pile.

It was the funeral pyre of his friends.

Commentary

Sources from the Vicinity (3.1–3.7)

The Ruiz account (3.1.1) seems matter-of-fact. The details, however, are not all based on his personal knowledge and so should not be viewed in the same light as those that are. He likely would have observed the army entering San Antonio; the exchange of gunfire during the siege; the events of the night of March 5–6; and the preparation of the funeral pyre. It is also believable that he was asked to identify Travis, Bowie, and Crockett after the fall, and that he knew where to find their bodies. On the other hand, he would have had somewhat less knowledge of the Mexican casualties, and he referred to his number as an estimate. The Texan casualty list is not claimed to be his. The most controversial and discussed detail is his statement that he threw bodies of a number of the dead Mexican soldiers into the river. It seems hard to believe from our modern perspective, but his deposition on behalf of the heirs of Toribio Losoya (3.1.2, though other evidence indicates that Losoya did not die in the Alamo; see the Commentary for section 1.11) reaffirms a portion of his story, and the Mexican dead are vividly described by Pablo Díaz (3.7.2).[1]

The Menchaca memoirs (3.2.1) provide some interesting pictures of the pre-siege events, particularly the receipt of intelligence of the Mexican advance on San Antonio. They also relate something of the immediate post-Alamo events in the Texan Army. Some of Menchaca's dates are off—January 13 for Crockett's arrival is too early (see 4.5.8, 4.5.23)—and the thirteen thousand figure for Mexican troops is far too high. On the other hand, the matter-of-fact tone and lack of embellishment in the details support the narrative's authenticity. In his comment on meeting Nat Lewis, Menchaca gave an independent confirmation of a small piece of the Sutherland accounts (1.7.1.1, 1.7.1.7). Overall, this source seems fairly reliable, with respect to events the narrator was personally involved in, and it gives an interesting perspective in the vicinity of the siege.

The account of Rodriguez (3.3.1) likewise seems reliable, recognizing that he was only six or seven years old when the battle occurred. The secondhand account of Revas seeing Santa Anna in disguise is interesting because, if Rodriguez's recollection was correct that he heard it prior to the siege starting, it would establish that story as having circulated very early (e.g., see the unreliable Candelaria and Nuñez stories, 1.9.2 and 2.14.1). Of course, that it circulated early doesn't mean it is any more believable or true. One can ask whether, even farther back in time, all these stories were based initially on the dance described by Menchaca (3.2.1).

The interviews with Barsena and Bergara (section 3.4) are especially significant. Not only did they bring Gen. Sam Houston the first reports on the fall of the Alamo, but they—and indirectly the cited Antonio Peréz (Peres)—are also the only true (not invented or rumored) sources other than Susanna Dickinson, Joe, and possibly Ben for the narratives that were soon circulated in Texas and the United States. The analysis of the important account in the *Telegraph and Texas Register* of March 24 (4.1.1) hinges on what these three could have contributed, and they are revisited in the Commentary for that section.

Although John J. Linn (3.4.3) claimed he talked with participants and is often cited by later historians, essentially all the details he gave are based on Yoakum (5.1.5), Potter (5.1.7), and the *San Antonio Daily Express* (1.2.11), and the *Telegraph and Texas Register* (4.1.1). The excerpt given here is the only clearly new piece of information identified.

Also important are the early letters of Sam Houston (section 3.5), with probable indirect accounts from Susanna Dickinson, Joe, and perhaps Ben, as well as details definitely derived from Barsena, Bergara, and/or Peréz. Information in these documents includes the attackers' losses given as 520 (or 521), Travis's effectives as 150 of 187 men, the execution of seven defenders who surrendered, and Dickinson's leap off the roof. The Houston letters also give an immediate picture of the Texas situation exactly when the news of the Alamo's fall reaches the Texas Army. The strategic thinking of the most important Texas leader is also valuable. One interesting question is whether Sam Houston did order the Alamo blown up, which is addressed in the Commentary after his earlier correspondence is given (4.5.13, 4.5.14). The footnote in document 3.5.4 gives a synopsis of Seguín's role in Texas, and the second footnote in 3.5.6 explains the confusion over spelling of Dickinson's name (more in section 4.4.4).

One letter (3.5.5) makes reference to Susanna Dickinson being "dishonored." She never mentioned this, and all her accounts (section 1.2) indicate that she was well treated, especially by the Mexican officers. On the other hand, this statement less than two days after the news first reached Gonzales, and from such an authoritative source, cannot be dismissed out of hand. If Houston was accurately reporting something told him, one must ask what an 1830s gentleman—in the formal sense— would have meant by the term. Williams and Barker apparently believed it meant raped, as they substituted the sentence with dashes in their 1930s transcript of the letter. A careful reading of all the Houston letters for March 13 and 15 strongly indicates that this statement did not come directly from Dickinson herself. In the letter to Collinsworth of the thirteenth (3.5.4), Houston said he was waiting for two spies sent by Seguín to return and was sending out Deaf Smith and Henry Karnes to gather intelligence. In the letter of interest (3.5.5), also dated the thirteenth, he reported that he was sending two spies in a few minutes, and that he had held up an express waiting for the report of two other spies—presumably the two Seguín sent. There is no explicit mention of the arrival of Susanna Dickinson in this letter, or even that she was not in San Antonio. It was Deaf Smith and Henry Karnes who discovered Dickinson (see 1.2.10 and 1.2.11) and took her to Houston. Finally, in a letter of the fifteenth (3.5.6), Houston told Collinsworth that since he last wrote him on the thirteenth, the lady of Lieutenant Dickinson had arrived. Thus it seems definite that the report of her being "dishonored" was not personally from her—she had not yet arrived in Gonzales.

As neither Hockley nor Houston mentioned this in the reports of the eleventh, one might suspect that Houston was repeating a rumor or misunderstanding that had quickly circulated without basis. Note that the letter also includes questionable accounts of the deaths of the Texas leaders. One possibility is that it was a garbled comment originating from a report from Barsena or Bergara that she had been injured (1.2.10 records that she was hit by a stray bullet in the leg). There was no apparent reason for Houston to immediately drop the story, with its obvious wartime propaganda value, unless Dickinson corrected the report once she personally talked to him.

One source for Alamo accounts not yet fully tapped is the notes by the French artist Theodore Gentilz (3.6.1). Only Kendall and Penny (1974) have published much material on his interviews with Béxar residents in the 1840s. The interview with Antonio and María Jesusa Peña Cruz y Arocha raises some questions. Did the execution of prisoners take place outside the Alamo, where María could have observed them, and did some surrender waving a white flag? She could, of course, have seen and identified as a flag anything light colored, and her account is not at significant variance with the other accounts of the execution of some prisoners. Perhaps some of the defenders who were reported to have jumped the walls after the mission was overrun were the ones killed per the execution accounts—in other words, maybe the incident took place outside the walls rather than inside.

Another early interview, by Josiah Gregg (3.6.2), has a brief comment from José Antonio Navarro that Santa Anna left the east side of the Alamo open, as he preferred to let the defenders escape. It did take some days before the Alamo was completely encircled, and couriers and the Gonzales reinforcements still got through, so Navarro's comment cannot be immediately rejected. As a reason for the encirclement not being tight, though, it is hard to believe that Santa Anna wished anyone to escape. His attitude throughout the Texas campaign was to capture and execute his opponents, and his ordering of Sesma to prevent possible reinforcements (early in the siege, per 2.3.1, and in the final attack, per 2.1.1.8) indicates that Santa Anna was not interested in letting anyone escape or avoiding casualties in his own army.

Crompton's interview (3.6.3) is somewhat disappointing, although it gives interesting insight into the attitudes and motivations of the Americans going to Texas, surprisingly casual in his case, as well as something on the character of various leaders. On the other hand, he was undoubtedly influenced by published histories—proven by his use of the Thermopylae quote—and gave a number of details regarding activities inside the Alamo that he would have gotten secondhand at best. His account is of value mostly for understanding the attitudes of the time rather than for details on specific events.[2]

Around the turn of the century, the local San Antonio newspapers apparently realized that the last eyewitnesses of the events associated with the Alamo soon would be gone. Consequently, several articles appeared with new accounts, such as those of Enrique Esparza (1.5.2–1.5.5). The next collection (section 3.7) is some of the remainder of these interviews. Matovina 1995 gave the first really systematic collection of the local Tejano accounts. Not all are presented in this work, as they do not all give additional details of the actual siege and fall. The interested reader is encouraged to consult Matovina to learn more about the citizens in San Antonio at the time.[3]

Eulalia Yorba (3.7.1), on first reading, appears to have put all the action in the chapel. A stone building is referred to as singular in various places, action on the low roof is mentioned in the battle, and her description of the dead when she entered the Alamo seems to be inside a single structure. Two other details are also unlikely—timbers being brought through the street to break in the door, and an altar observed at the back of the room. The Alamo outer walls were carried by soldiers climbing in the weak, low areas rather than breaking in the main gate, and the attack on the chapel door would not have been visible from outside the mission. An earth ramp covered the back of the chapel, so an altar was not likely to have been visible. Another item of uncertain origin is the report of four days being given for the defenders to surrender. Taken in all, especially the descriptions implying that the battle was restricted to the chapel, these items make the account seem somewhat suspicious. However, a counterpoint has already been noted in the Commentary on the Esparza accounts (section 1.5). Yorba's recollection might have been of the mission, while the interviewer was thinking of only the chapel. For example, her description of "the low roof of the church" might really have been of the low barracks, the part closest and most visible to the town. This structure disappeared long before 1896, and the interviewer could well have been ignorant of its existence. It turns out there is little problem with this account when viewed in the light that all her descriptions refer to the mission in general rather than the chapel in particular.

The Pablo Díaz account (3.7.2) likewise seems reasonable. He seems to have remembered the move to the Alamo defenses from town taking place very late (compare with the work described in the Jameson plats, section 4.2). His mention of the Alamo flag is of interest in that it is one of the few comments recorded by an eyewitness (see 5.2.1.1). He also apparently confirms Ruiz's account (3.1.1) of throwing bodies into the river—unless there is some reason for believing that the story is an invention based on Ruiz. As there is little sign of this, such as a central role for the narrator, I am inclined to accept this story.

The account of María de Jesús Buquor (3.7.3), on the other hand, has serious problems. She took on a central role, telling Travis and Crockett of the approach of the Mexican Army. It is far more probable that they were warned by the bells of the cathedral tower when Sutherland and Smith raced back (1.7.1.1). It is equally unlikely that the townspeople were close enough to identify the defenders on the Alamo walls. The final battle was at nearly point-blank range, so bullets were unlikely to have been sweeping the town streets in the manner described. And the Becerra account (2.10.1) had already been published by Ford, with the story on Santa Anna being "a Lothario" sufficiently titillating that it would have circulated well before this 1907 interview. After these details, there is not much else left for this account to be of any value.[4]

The Juan Díaz account (3.7.4) is suspicious for two reasons. The first is his being on the plaza and hearing the advance of the army by the martial music rather than the warning bells from the cathedral tower, which would have been even more likely to have been remembered by the custodian's son. The second is the clarity with which he saw the six columns of soldiers attacking the walls. The attack mostly took place before dawn, and the lighting, distance, and his position would not have made such details visible. This account could have been based on an authentic experience, but with the story having grown in the imagination.

Juan Antonio Chávez (3.7.5) did not experience much related to the battle, but his account does give us a little more feeling for the town at the time.

The Juan Vargas narrative (3.7.6) has only limited value. There is nothing fundamentally wrong or demonstratively incorrect in what he described, but the descriptions are too vague to add much to our understanding. The description of the battle could apply to any violent conflict; for example, with a few name changes, it could equally describe a World War II battle near an inhabited town. The several qualifications on Vargas's memory suggest an explanation for the vagueness.

A main interest in two of these interviews concerns the final burial location for the ashes of the Alamo defenders. The subject has already been raised in the Seguín documents (1.7.2.7–1.7.2.9; note also "q" on the Sánchez map, 2.7.1). By and large, the Pablo Díaz account (3.7.2) and the Esparza, Díaz, and Chávez interview (3.7.7) are complementary with Seguín's original descriptions of the disposition. The one alternative detail comes from Peréz in 3.7.2 and 3.7.7, supported by Biesenbach in 3.7.7, that at least some of the buried remains were exhumed and reburied in the old city cemetery about thirty years previously. Had this been done, say, in the 1870s or so, one would expect some confirming comment to be in the contemporary San Antonio newspapers. In conclusion, this final Barnes article gives what could be the most definitive information on the location that will ever be obtained.

The account of Trinidad Coy (3.7.8), which could also be placed in the sources from the Mexican camp, would be a unique point of view if true. The story doesn't give any insight into events, but is about an individual's personal reactions to the events. The only real narrative detail relating to the battle is suspicious—Coy escaped while the attack was in progress, circled the Mexican Army as well as the Alamo in an hour, apparently did not realize the Alamo had fallen, and found the funeral pyre. Considering the amount of noise of the battle itself, and the length of time from the start of the battle at 5 A.M. until the townspeople had gathered the wood and lit the funeral pyre late in the afternoon, this story doesn't fit at all well with the known facts. On the other hand, there does seem to be a significant difference in the level of detail and vividness between the early part of the narration, when Coy was doing his reconnaissance—fairly extensive and not quoted here—and the events of the fall of the Alamo, suggesting that the latter portions are heavily edited additions to an underlying valid story.

Some of these interviews discuss the treatment of the Béxar citizens by the Mexican Army. Yorba indicated that they were assured that no personal harm would be done; Pablo Díaz talked of the "cruelties and enormities" of the invading armies; Buquor (whose account I do not accept) claimed severe hardships and harsh treatment; Juan Díaz said the soldiers were kept well under control, with only a few cases of damage; and Juan Vargas reported being pressed into service and threatened. Dr. Bernard also said that the citizens seemed relieved when the troops left on May 25 (4.3.10). This is an interesting question, but this selection of documents is too incomplete to draw any reasonable conclusions.

A general argument on the unreliability of the Anglo-based accounts relative to the Mexican sources was made by Roger Borroel.[5] In particular, he was highly critical of Charles Barnes's editing of various interviews, and noted where he appeared to use the same wording for different interviewees.[6] Per the Commentary on Esparza (section 1.5), I too believe that Barnes added to and modified the material in his interviews. On the other hand, I also feel credit needs to be given to Barnes, as he was the only journalist in early-1900s San Antonio to realize that a unique body of recollections was disappearing quickly and do something about it. Without Barnes, several of these accounts would not exist at all for current commentators to critique.

Taken in all, these "sources from the vicinity" fill in details and context not otherwise available, and add some firsthand drama to the story.

---

1. For a contrary opinion that Ruiz "is completely spurious in nature," see Borroel 1998b, 9–15, and 2002, 211–17.
2. In the (John Salmon) Ford Papers, vol. 1, 129–33, TSLA, Ford rejects the entire account based on a number of specific items.

3. E.g., Matovina 1995: 96–98 (interview of Díaz, October 31, 1909); 106–7 (Díaz/Esparza/Chávez, 8/27/1911); 107–13 (Coy, 11/26/1911); 116–17 (Chávez, 4/19/1914). Another such account is in Groneman 1996, 147 (Félix Rodríguez 5/4/1907).
4. For a totally contrary opinion on Buquor, see Borroel 1998b, 109–10.
5. E.g., see Borroel 1998b, 5–6, 104–6.
6. Borroel 1998b: Díaz, 33–34; Esparza, 43–45; general conclusions, 117–18. Note that Borroel's critiques appear mostly based on a book by Barnes, rather than the interviews cited here.

CHAPTER 4

Other Primary Sources

In addition to the obviously important direct participant accounts already included, there are a number of other primary sources that add information on the siege, the fall, or the immediate context of the battle. Some of these sources are possibly secondhand versions of the eyewitnesses cited earlier and therefore may add something to one's ability to analyze the different narratives.

The first selection of documents is of contemporary newspaper accounts. These versions are basically independent of others and therefore are valuable checks on one another. Some were heavily used by later scholars and writers, and therefore their validity and accuracy are particularly important.

The second selection relates to two key plans produced by Texans of the Alamo and its associated defensive works. The maps come from Alamo engineer and defender Green B. Jameson in 1836, and later, in 1849, from San Antonio city surveyor François Giraud. These documents are significant for understanding the layout, specific events, and military details of the Alamo defense and siege. None of the originals are now available, so their information can be extracted only from second- or thirdhand copies that vary in the details. Another problem is that in 1855 historian Henderson Yoakum, who apparently had plans from both sources available, wrote in his text about the Jameson plats while reproducing in his book the unattributed Giraud map. Consequently, the two sources were confused, and it has only been recently that scholars have untangled the origins of the various copies.

The next selection of documents is that of other near-contemporary sources, such as letters written close to the events by people not immediately in the vicinity of the Alamo. Though less helpful in understanding the direct events at the Alamo, they add to what was heard or perceived about the Alamo at the time.

Other less-contemporary sources include a couple of documents written later by Frank W. Johnson and Mary Austin Holley, which give some additional retrospective insights into the details of the siege and the role of Sam Houston.

549

Other Mexican sources, José Urrea and José María Tornel y Mendívil, flesh out a little more of the broad picture of their side of the war. An additional set of documents is presented on Almaron Dickerson/Dickinson to give a bit of a personal interest to the story, as well as demonstrate the difficulties in answering such a seemingly simple question of how a name is spelled. Two further documents address possible artifacts—a rifle and the cannons—from the battle.

Finally, a number of documents representing pre-siege correspondence establishes the setting, in both circumstances and logistics, for the siege and battle.

4.1.1. Newspaper account, March 24, 1836.

Telegraph and Texas Register. March 24, 1836. San Felipe de Austin.

This is probably the most influential single account of the fall of the Alamo by virtue of being the first in print, its access to authoritative sources, and its near universal dissemination.

MORE PARTICULARS RESPECTING THE FALL OF THE ALAMO.

That event, so lamentable, and yet so glorious to Texas, is of such deep interest and excites so much our feelings that we shall never cease to celebrate it, and regret that we are not acquainted with the names of all those who fell in that Fort, that we might publish them, and thus consecrate to future ages the memory of our heroes who perished at the Thermopylae of Texas. Such examples are bright ones, and should be held up as mirrors, that by reflection we may catch the spirit and learn to fashion our own behaviour. The list of names inserted below, was furnished by Mr. Jno. W. Smith, and Mr. Navon, and as we obtain more we will publish them. To Mr. Smith, who has rendered good service to Texas, and to Judge Ponton are we indebted for the particulars, as communicated to them by Mrs. Dickinson, who was in the "Alamo" during the siege and assault.

At day-break of the 6th inst. the enemy surrounded the fort with their infantry, with the cavalry forming a circle outside to prevent escape on the part of the garrison; the number consisted of at least 4000 against 140! General Santa Ana commanded in person, assisted by four generals and a formidable train of artillery. Our men had been previously much fatigued and harrassed [*sic*] by nightwatching and incessant toils, having experienced for some days past, a heavy bombardment and several real and feigned attacks. But, American valor and American love of liberty displayed themselves to the last; they were never more conspicuous: twice did the enemy apply to the walls their scaling ladders, and, twice did they receive a check; for our men were determined to verify the words of the immortal Travis, "to make the victory worse to the enemy than a defeat." A pause ensued after the second attack, which was renewed on the third time, owing to the exertions of Santa Ana and his officers; they then poured in over the walls, 'like sheep:' the struggle, however, did not even there cease—unable from the crowd and for want of time to load their guns and rifles, our men made use of the but-ends of the latter and continued to fight and to resist, until life ebbed out through their numberless wounds and the enemy had conquered the fort, but not its brave, its matchless defenders: they perished, but they yielded not: only one (Warner) remained to ask for quarter, which was denied by the unrelenting enemy—total extermination succeeded, and the darkness of death occupied memorable Alamo, but recently so teeming with gallant srits [*spirits*] and filled with deeds of never-failing remembrance.

We envy not the feelings of the victors, for they must have been bitter and galling: not proud ones. Who would not be rather one of the Alamo heroes, then of the living of the merciless victors? Spirits of the mighty, though fallen! honours and rest are with ye: the spark of immortality which animated your forms, shall brighten into a flame, and Texas, the whole world, shall hail ye like demi-gods of old, as founders of new actions, and as patterns for imitation!

From the commencement to its close, the storming lasted less than an hour. Major Evans, master of ordnance, was killed when in the act of setting fire to the powder magazine, agreeably to the previous orders from Travis. The end of David Crocket [*sic*] of Tennessee, the great hunter of the west, was as glorious as his career through life had been useful. He and his companions were found surrounded by piles of assailants, whom they had immolated on the altar of Texas liberties. The countenance of Crocket was unchanged: he had in death that freshness of hue, which his exercise of pursuing the beasts of the forest and the prairie had imparted to him. Texas places him, exultingly, amongst the martyrs in her cause. Col. Travis stood on the walls cheering his men, exclaiming 'Hurra, my boys.' till he received a second shot, and fell; it is stated that a Mexican general, (Mora) then rushed upon him, and lifted his sword to destroy his victim, who, collecting all his last expiring energies, directed a thrust at the former, which changed their relative positions; for the victim became the victor, and the remains of both descended to eternal[*l*] sleep; but not alike to everlasting fame.

Travis's negro was spared, because as the enemy said, 'his master had behaved like a brave man;' words which of themselves form an epitaph: they are already engraved on the hearts of Texians, and should be inscribed on his tomb. Col. James Bowie, who had for several days been sick, was murdered in his bed: his remains were mutilated. Humanity shudders at describing these scenes, and the pen, as if a living thing, stops to gain fresh force that sensibility may give way to duty.

Suspended animation has returned to the instrument of our narration, and we continue. Mrs. Dickinson and her child, and a negro of Bowie's, and as before said Travis's were spared.

Our dead were denied the right of Christian burial: being stripped and thrown in a pile, and burned. Would that we could gather up their ashes and place them in urns!

It is stated that about fifteen hundred of the enemy were killed and wounded in the last and previous attacks.

	W. B. Travis, Commandant,
Colonels.	James Bowie,
	David Crocket, of Tenn.
Captains.	Forsyth, of the regular army,
	Harrison, of Tenn.
	Wm. Blazeby, N.O. Grays,

Baker, Miss. volunteers,
Evans,
Carey, militia of Texas,
S. C. Blair, volunteer militia,
Lieut's.   John Jones, N.O. Grays,
J. G. Baugh, N.O.
Rob't Evans, mast. ord. Ireland
    Williamson, serg't major,
Dr. Michison
" Pollard, surgeon.
" Thompson, Tenn.
Chas. Despalier,
Eliel Melton, quartermaster,
    Anderson, assist't qr. mast.
    Burnell,   "   "
Privates.   Nelson,
    Nelson, (cl'k of Austin, mer.)
William Smith, Nacogdoches,
Lewis Johnson. Trinity
E. P. Mitchell, Georgia,
F. Desanque, of Philadelphia,
John (cl'k in Desanque's store,)
    Thurston,
    Moore,
Christopher Parker, Natchez,
    Heiskill,
    Rose, of Nacogdoches,
    Blair,   "
David Wilson, "
John M. Hays, Tenn.
    Stuart,
    Simpson,
W. D. Sutherland, Navidad, Tex.
Doctor Howell, N.O.
    Butler   "
Charles Smith,
    McGregor, Scotland,
    Rusk,
    Hawkins, Ireland,
    Holloway,
    Browne,
    Smith,
    Browne, Philadelphia,
    Kedeson,

Wm. Wells, Tenn.
Wm. Cummings, Penn.
     Voluntine, "
     Cockran,
R. W. Valentine,
S. Holloway,
Isaac White,
     Day,
Robt. Muselman, N.O.
Robt. Crossman, "
Richard Starr, England,
J. G. Ganett, N.O.
James Dinkin, England
Robt. B. Moore, N.O.
Wm. Linn, Boston,
     Hutchinson,
Wm. Johnson, Philadelphia,
     Nelson, Charleston, S.C.
George Tumlinson
Wm. Deardorf
Dan'l Bourne, England,
     Ingram, England,
     Lewis, Wales,
Chas. Zanco, Denmark
James Ewing,
Robert Cunningham,
     Burns, Ireland,
George Neggin
Maj. G. B. Jamieson,
Col. J. B. Bonham, Ala.
Capt. White,
     Robinson, Scotland,
     Sewell, shoemaker,
     Harris, of Ky.
     Devault, of Mo. plasterer,
Janathan Lindley, of Illinois,
Tapley Holland,
     Dewell, blacksmith, N.Y.
James Kinney,
     Cane,
     Warner,
John Garvin, Mo.
     Wornel,
     Robbins, Ky.

Jno. Flanders.
Isaac Ryan, Opelousas,
      Jackson, Ireland
Capt. A. Dickinson, Gonzalez,
Geo. C. Kimball,   "
James George   "
Dolphin Floyd,   "
Thomas Jackson   "
Jacob Durst,   Gonzales,
George W. Cottle   "
Andrew Kent,   "
Thos. R. Miller   "
Isaac Baker,   "
Wm. King,   "
Jesse McCoy,   "
Claiborn Wright,   "
William Fishback, "
    Millsap,   "
Galby Fugua,   "
John Davis,   "
Albert Martin,   "

4.1.2.   Jno. M. Shreve, letter, March 17, 1836.

Commercial Bulletin. April 9, 1836. New Orleans.

We give to-day a communication from Brazoria, Texas, which, in consequence of containing some particulars, not heretofore published, we deem may probably be read with some interest by those of our readers favorable to the cause of Texas.

BRAZORIA, TEXAS, March 17, 1836.

To the Editor of the Commercial Bulletin:

Dear Sir—Desirous of giving the citizens of New Orleans the latest information in regard to the condition of affairs in Texas, and the important events in our war—I enclose you a publication of the Committee at San Felipe, who are acting as a Committee of Vigilance.

The publication will speak for itself. The measure will speak for itself. The measure alluded to in the publication is truly to be lamented. Our force in the Alamo at the time of its being stormed, amounted to one hundred and eighty-seven, every soul of whom was put to death—extending mercy [*word unclear; probably "only"*] to a female, the wife of one who nobly lost his life in the engagement—to tell the melancholy news. The Mexican force was six thousand, having bombarded the Alamo for two days without doing any execution, a tremendous effort was made to take it by storm, which they succeeded in doing after a most sanguinary engagement, lasting near an hour. History, neither ancient nor modern, can give evidence of such bravery and heroism as was evinced on the occasion. No quarters were called for until every soul had perished save seven, who on asking quarters, and being told none could be given, again commenced the work of death, and the last died as did the first, without yielding an inch of ground.

The Alamo was attacked at four different points; the walls being only about breast high, the enemy was enabled to scale them by means of scaling ladders, our force not being sufficient to protect it at all points.

The loss of the enemy was great: 533 killed, 600 mortally wounded, and many slightly.

Thus the garrison which cost us much hard fighting, has been retaken at great cost to Texas, but much greater to the enemy. It is much to be regretted that our force in the garrison was not greater, though it was always supposed to have been sufficient to maintain the post. Texas has to mourn the loss of Wm. B. Travis (in command). The celebrated Col. David Crockett, or Tennessee, was among the slain. His conduct an [sic] the occasion was most heroic; having used his rifle as long as possible by loading and discharging, and the enemy crowding upon the walls, he turned the britch [sic] of his gun, and demolished more than twenty of the enemy before he fell.

Does not humanity revolt at the cruelty of the Mexicans? will [sic] not the indignation of all the world rest upon the head of Santa Anna, who is at the head of the troops, in person. Our army in the field numbers only about 3600, which Gen. Houston is concentrating on the bank of the Colorado, towards which point the enemy are marching, having advanced as far as Gonzales on the Warloop river. It is presumed to be Gen. Houston's intention to give them battle on the Colorado; his force is augmenting daily and will no doubt exceed 4000 before the arrival of the enemy. All is anxiety with us at present, and every man has put his shoulder to the wheel, and are anxiously looking for aid from our brothers in the United States, in addition to what we have already received.

Santa Anna after defeating our out post, (I mean the Alamo.) issued a proclamation offering protection to all who would quietly lay down their arms and acknowledge the established form of government, notifying us that [he] is the chief, and allowed eight days for a reply. Gen. Houston immediately returned an answer that we would not acknowledge the Central form of Government, and that although he had succeeded in defeating our out post, if he will presumed to enter the interior of our colonies, he would repay him ten fold. Our army is still in high spirits and confident of victory. The Convention is still in session, and all things moving on harmoniously. The declaration of independence I presume you you [sic] have received ere this.

Respectfully yours, &c.
JNO. M. SHREVE.

4.1.3.   Andrew Briscoe, letter, March 1836.

New Yorker. April 16, 1836. 60 (page actually reads 50, which is a typo).
This is from a letter of Andrew Briscoe published in the *Louisiana Advertiser* of
March 28, 1836. Neither that newspaper nor the cited *Red River Herald* was located.

From the Louisiana Advertiser March 28.

We are indebted to a gentlemen, passenger on board the steamer Levant,
from Natchitoches, for the annexed letter, giving the particulars of the fall of
Bexar—it is a copy of one addressed to the editor of the Red River Herald:—

"Sir—Bexar has fallen! Its garrison was only 187 strong, commanded by
Lieut. Col. W. Travis. After standing repeated attacks for two weeks, and an
almost constant cannonade and bombarding during that time, the last attack
was made on the morning of the 6th inst. by upwards of 2000 men, under the
command of Santa Anna in person; they carried the place about sunrise, with
the loss of 520 men killed, and about the same number wounded. After about
an hour's fighting the whole garrison was put to death, (save the sick and
wounded and seven men who asked for quarter)—All fought desperately, until
entirely cut down; the rest were cooly murdered. The brave and gallant Travis,
to prevent his falling into the hands of the enemy, shot himself. Not an individual escaped, and the news is only known to us by a citizen of Bexar who came
to our army at Gonzales—but from the cessation of Travis' signal guns, there is
no doubt of its truth. The declaration of independence you have, no doubt
received, and will, in a few days, receive the constitution proposed by the
republic.

Cols. James Bowie and David Crockett are among the slain—the first was
murdered in his bed, to which he had been confined by illness—the latter fell,
fighting like a tiger. The Mexican army is estimated at 8000 men; it may be more
or less."

A. Briscoe

4.1.4.1.   Newspaper account, 1836.

Commercial Bulletin. March 28, 1936. New Orleans.
This article was also reprinted in the *Mississippi Free Trader and Natchez Gazette,*
April 8, and in the *New Yorker,* April 16, in the same article as the previous document.
This issue of the *New Yorker* also records on page 56 the famous quote from David
Crockett that if he were not reelected to Congress, "they might go to * * * *, and I
would go to Texas. . . ."

IMPORTANT FROM TEXAS!
Fall of San Antonio and Massacre of the Texian Troops.

The following important documents were placed in our hands by a gentleman
just arrived from Texas. The news is melancholly [*sic*] indeed; and here is

opened another field of action for the noble hearts now returning triumphant, and covered with laurels won on the banks of the Withlacoochie [*Florida?*], against foes less savage, perhaps, than Santa Ann's merciless Mexican bands.

Our informant met the express bearing the news we give, and from him procured copies to be published for the information of the people on this side of the Sabine whose relations and friends, kin and countrymen, are now the victims of Mexican barbarity. Col. Bowie, it is said, shot himself;—and Col. Travis stabbed himself to escape the cruelties of the enemy. Nobly they fought; dearly they sold their lives, but none escaped of the whole garrison of San Antonio.

[*Following is another copy of Houston's letter to "Fanning" of March 11, presented earlier as document 3.5.2. It is followed by a proclamation "To the People of the United States," by Richard Ellis, president of the Convention, which does not add any additional information on the Alamo. The article then continues with the following.*]

We learn further by the passengers of the schooner Cumanche [*sic*], eight days from Texas, that on the 25th February the Texian Garrison in Bexar, of 150 men, commanded by Lt. Col. B. Travis, was attacked by the advance division of Gen. Santa Anna's army, consisting of 2000 men, who were repulsed with the loss of many killed, between 500 to 800 men, without the loss of one man of the Texians. About the same time Col. Johnson with a party of 70, men while reconnoitering the westward of San Patricio, was surrounded in the night by a large body of Mexican troops. In the morning the demand of a surrender was made by the Mexican commander, unconditionally, which was refused; but an offer of surrender was made as prisoners of war, which was acceded [*sic*] to by the Mexicans: but no sooner had the Texians marched out of their quarters and stacked their arms, a general fire was opened upon them by the whole Mexican force, the Texians attempted to escape, but only three of them succeeded—one of whom was Col. Johnson.

Between the 25th February and 2d March the Mexicans were employed in forming entrenchments around the Alamo and bombarding the place. On the 2d March, Col. Travis wrote that 200 shells had been thrown into the Alamo, without injuring a man. On the 1st March the garrison of Alamo received a reinforcement of 32 Texians from Gonzales, having forced their way through the enemy's lines, making the number in the Alamo 182 men.

On the 6th March about midnight, the Alamo was surrounded by the whole force of the Mexican army, commanded by Santa Anna in person; the battle was desperate until day-light, when only 7 men belonging to the Texian Garrison were found alive who cried for quarters, but were told that there was no mercy for them; they then continued fighting until the whole were butchered. One woman, Mrs. Dickinson, and a negro of Col. Travis, were the only persons whose lives were spared. We regret to say that Col. David Crocket, his companion Mr. Benton, and Col. Bonhan [*sic*] of South Carolina, were among the number slain.—Gen. Bowie was murdered in his bed, sick and helpless.—Gen. Cos on entering the Fort, ordered the servant of Col. Travis to point out the body of his master; he did so, when Cos drew his sword and mangled the face and limbs with the malignant feeling of a Cumanche savage. The bodies of the slain were thrown into a heap in the centre of the Alamo and burned. The loss of the Mexicans in storming the place was not less than 1000 killed and mortally wounded, and as many wounded—making with their loss in the first assault, between 2 and 3,000 men. The flag used by the Mexicans was a blood-red one, in the place of the Constitutional one.

Immediately after the capture, Gen. Santa Anna sent Mrs. Dickinson and the servant to Gen. Houston's camp, accompanied by a Mexican with a flag, who was bearer of a note from Santa Anna, offering the Texians peace and general amnesty if they would lay down their arms and submit to his government. Gen. Houston's reply was, "true, sir, you have succeeded in killing some of our brave men—but the Texians are not yet conquered." The effect of the fall of Bexar throughout Texas was electrical. Every man who could use the rifle and was in a condition to take the field, marched forthwith to the seat of war. It is believed that not less than 4,000 riflemen were on their way to the army when the Cumanche sailed, determined to wreak their revenge on the Mexicans.

Gen. Houston had burnt Gonzales, and fallen back on the Collorado [*sic*] with about 1000. Col. Fanning was in the Fort at Goliad, a very strong position, well supplied with munitions and provisions, with four to five hundred men.

The general determination of the people of Texas is to abandon all their occupations and pursuits of peace, and continue in arms until every Mexican east of the Rio del Norte shall be exterminated.

4.1.4.2. Newspaper account, 1836.

Arkansas Gazette. April 12, 1836. Little Rock.

There are several other articles in this issue related to the fall of the Alamo (e.g., 2.17.1), mostly derived from Sam Houston's reports (section 3.5). This selection immediately follows a transcript of the Briscoe letter (4.1.3) from the *New Orleans Post and Union* of March 28, so it appears to be quoted from that same newspaper. Gaddy 1973, 49, reproduces a nearly identical version of this source from the *New Orleans True American* of about March 28, 1836. Clearly, this *Arkansas Gazette* version originated with the same interview as that of the *Commercial Bulletin* above, but it has a significant modification concerning the death of Crockett. The significance of this is discussed in the Commentary.

FURTHER PARTICULARS.

We learn by the passengers of the schr. Camanche [*sic*], eight days from the *Brazos* river, that the war in Texas has assumed a serious character. Many of those who left this city, determined to lay down their lives in the cause of Texas, have bravely yielded them up at Bexar. Three young men from our office, we learn, are among the slain—the names of Wm. Braseby and Robert Moore have been mentioned to us—that of the other we could not ascertain.

On the 25th of February, the Texian garrison at Bexar, of 150 men only, commanded by Lieut. Col. W. B. Travis, was attacked by the advanced division of Santa Anna's army of about 2,000 men, when the enemy were repulsed with a loss of many killed and wounded, variously estimated from 450 to 600, and without the loss of a man in the garrison.

The great slaughter was ascribed to the fact that every man of the garrison had about eight guns loaded by his side. About the same time, Col. Johnson, while reconnoitering to the westward of San Patricio, with a party of 70 men, was surrounded by a large body of Mexican troops. In the morning the commander sent in a summons to surrender at discretion, which was refused, and an offer to surrender as prisoners of war made. This was acceded to by the Mexican officer; but no sooner had the Texians marched out of their encampment and stacked their arms, than a general fire was opened upon them by the whole Mexican force, when the prisoners endeavored to escape—three only of whom effected it, among them was Col. Johnson and one man who had been wounded.

Between the 25th of February and 2d of March, the Mexicans were employed in forming entrenchments around the Alamo, and bombarding the place. On the 2d of March Col. Travis wrote that 200 shells had been thrown into the Alamo, without injuring a man.

On the 1st of March, 32 men from Gonzales made their entry through the enemy's lines and reached the Alamo—making the whole number in the garrison 182.

On the 6th of March, about midnight, the Alamo was assaulted by the entire force of the Mexican army, commanded by Santa Anna in person. The Mexicans [sic; "Texians"] fought desperately until daylight, when 7 only of the garrison were found alive. We regret to say, that Col. David Crockett and his companion, Mr. Benton, also the gallant Col. Bonham of South Carolina, were of the number who cried for quarter, but were told there was no mercy for them. They then continued fighting until the whole were butchered. One woman, Mrs. (Dickinson) and a wounded negro servant of Col. Travis's, were the only persons in the Alamo whose lives were spared. Gen. Bowie was murdered in his bed, sick and helpless.—General Cos, on entering the fort, ordered Col. Travis's servant to point out to him the body of his master; he did so, when Cos drew his sword and mangled his face and limbs with the malignant feeling of a savage.

The bodies of the slain were thrown into a heap in the centre of the Alamo, and burned. On Gen. Bowie's body being brought out, Gen. Cos said that he was too brave a man to be burned like a dog, then added, *pew no es cosa eschade*—never mind, throw him in. The loss of the Mexicans in storming the place, was estimated at not less than 1,000 killed and mortally wounded, and as many more disabled—making, with their loss in the first assault, between 2,000 and 8,000 killed and wounded. It is worthy of remark, that the flag of Santa

Anna's army at Bexar, was a blood red one, in the place of the old tri-colored flag.—Immediately after the capture of the place, Gen. Santa Anna sent Mrs. Dickinson and Col. Travis's servant to Gen. Houston's camp, accompanied by a Mexican with a flag, who was bearer of a note from Santa Anna, offering the Texians peace and a general amnesty if they would lay down their arms and submit to his government. Gen. Houston's reply was, "True, sir, you have succeeded in killing some of our brave men, but the Texians are not whipped."—The effect of the fall of Bexar throughout Texas was electric. Every man who could use a rifle, and was in a condition to take the field, marched forthwith to the seat of war. It was believed that no, less than 4,000 riflemen were on their way to the army when the Camanche sailed, to wreak their vengeance on the Mexicans, and determined to grant no quarter.

[*The article continues with General Houston burning Gonzales and falling back, and Fannin being in a strong position at Goliad.*]

4.1.5.   Newspaper account, 1836.
Memphis Enquirer. April 5, 1836.

MELANCHOLY NEWS FROM TEXAS.
SAN ANTONIO TAKEN BY THE MEXICANS—
150 TEXIANS SLAIN.

Such is the report that has had current circulation here for the past three days; and we regret to add our painful fears that all is true. The disastrous news has come by different gentlemen and from different parts, all stating the fall of San Antonio and its 150 gallant soldiers. The fort it is said was besieged by Santa Anna with several thousand troops, (some say by Cos who is mortally wounded,) and the Texians fought until but six were left alive; that the Mexicans scaled the walls, and BURNT TO DEATH THE GALLANT SIX that remained. Col. Bowie it is said was sick in his hammock, and was one among the burnt. For humanity's sake we wish not to believe this cruel and horrorful report, but our fears confirm it. It is said the Texians slayed 500 of the enemy. A letter is in town dated at Nacogdoches from Gen. Houston, who gives the amount of what we have stated. He received it from a friendly Mexican who saw the storming of San Antonio. San Antonio has undoubtedly fallen. Col. D. Crockett is among the killed.

4.1.6.   Susanna Dickinson, interview(?), 1836.

Mississippi Free Trader and Natchez Gazette. April 29, 1836.
This account by William Parker, reprinted in full in Jenkins 1973, 6: 121–22, is a possible additional secondhand source for Susanna Dickinson. His "informant" is not identified.

To the Editor of the Free Trader

SIR,—Having just returned from a trip to Nacogdoches, made for the purpose of obtaining information concerning the fate of my son, who fell in defending the Alamo, I take this method to correct the erroneous news in circulation among my fellow citizens, concerning the position of the belligerents of Texas, and concerning the part which the Indian tribes, near the frontiers, are likely to act in this mementuous and exterminating crusade against civil and religious liberty.

[*Parker then gives a fairly extensive report on other events of the Texas Revolution, including activities by the Indians, General Houston and the army, and Fannin.*]

My informant above quoted states, that on his way in, he saw and conversed with Mrs. Dickerson, the widow of one of the gunners at the fall of the Alamo, and the only white person in the fortress at the time of the final catastrophe of this post, who was spared by the enemy, and permitted to return into the American settlements. He says that Mrs. D. informed him, that of the five who, for a moment, survived their companions, and threw themselves on the victors clemency, two were pursued into her room, and subjected in her presence to the most torturing death. They were each raised on the points of the enemies lances, let down and raised again and again, whilst invoking as a favor, instaneous [*sic*] death to terminate their anguish, till they were at last too weak to speak, and then expired in convulsion.

[*Parker continues with rumors of Colonel Ward and infighting in the Texas government.*]

WILLIAM PARKER
Natchez, April 29th, 1836.

4.1.7.   Newspaper account, 1836.

Louisville Daily Journal. July 11, 1836.
This account also appears in the *Washington, D.C., Metropolitan* for July 19, 1836. The original article from the *Xenia Gazette* was not located.

COLONELS CROCKETT AND BOWIE—The following facts, characteristic of the brave and lamented men, which are well authenticated, are extracted from a letter recently received from a friend residing in Natchitoches, Louisiana:

"During the siege of the Alamo, the Mexicans planted a piece of ordnance within gunshot of the Fort, with the intention of commencing a brisk cannonade. Five men successfully stepped forth to fire the gun, and were each marked down by the unerring rifle of Crockett. The consequence was that the gun was abandoned.

"A characteristic fact is also related of Col. Bowie, who formed one of that ill-fated garrison. When the fort was carried he was sick in bed. He had also one of the murderous butcher knives which bears his name. Lying in bed he discharged his pistols and gun, and with each discharge brought down an enemy. So intimidated were the Mexicans by this act of desperate and cool bravery, that they dared not approach him, but shot him from the door—and as the cowards approached his bed over the dead bodies of their companions, the dying Bowie, nerving himself for a last blow, plunged his knife into the heart of his nearest foe at the same instant that he expired. Such are a few of the facts I have learned connected with the fall of San Antonio.—*Xenia (Ohio) Gaz.*

4.1.8. Newspaper account, 1836.

Commonwealth. July 27, 1836. Frankfort, Kentucky.

This account is important for making David Crockett one of the prisoners executed right after the fall. Groneman (1996, 367) located the original article in the *Morning Courier and New York Enquirer* for July 9, 1836, and quoted essentially the same material that is in the first paragraph below.

TEXAS

From the correspondence of the N.Y. Cour. & Enq.

GALVESTON BAY, 9th June, 1836.

Dear Sir:—The fall of the *Alamo* and the massacre, must be fresh in the memory of every American. But I will relate one circumstance, detailed by an *eye witness*, not before known, that will at once establish, (if not before established,) the blood thirsty cruelty of the tyrant, Santa Ana. After the Mexicans had got possession of the Alamo, the fighting had ceased, and it was clear day light, six Americans were discovered near the well yet unconquered, and who were instantly surrounded and ordered by General Castrillon [*sic*] to surrender, and who did so under a promise of his protection, finding resistance any longer in vain—indeed, perfect madness.—Castrillon was brave and not cruel, and disposed to save them. He marched them up to that part of the fort where stood "his Excellency," surrounded by his murderous crew, his sycophantic officers. *David Crockett* was one of the six. The steady, fearless step, and undaunted tread, together with the bold demeanor of this hardy veteran—"his firmness— and noble bearing," to give the words of the narrator, had a most powerful effect on himself and Castrillon. Nothing daunted he marched up boldly in front of Santa Ana, looked him steadfastly in the face, while Castrillon addressed "his Excellency, "Sir, here are *six* prisoners I have taken alive; how shall I dispose of them! Santa Ana looked at Castrillon fiercely, flew into a most violent rage, and replied, "Have I not told you before how to dispose of them? Why do you bring them to me?" At the same time his brave officers drew and plunged their swords into the bosoms of their defenceless prisoners!! So anxious and intent were these blood thirsty cowards to gratify the malignicy of this inveterate tyrant, that Castrillon barely escaped being run through in the scuffle himself.—Castrillon rushed from the scene apparently horror-struck—sought his quarters, and did not leave them for some days, and hardly ever spoke to Santa Ana after. This was the fate of poor Crockett, and in which there can be no mistake. Who the *five* others were, I have not been able to learn. Three wounded prisoners were discovered and brought before "his Excellency," and were ordered to be instantly shot. There are certain reasons why the narrator of these events should not be known. I will only repeat that he was *an eye witness.*

I may tell you more about the Alamo yet, that Travis' boy, Joe, and Mrs. D. had not an opportunity of seeing or knowing. After the fall of the Alamo, and the retreat of Gen. Houston from the Colorado, the people became panic struck, and began to fly in every direction. St. Felipe was evacuated and burnt. All that could get with their families towards the Trinity and Sabine, did so. Some sought one place of refuge—some another. Some took the bottoms and swamps; but all who could get off in the direction of the United States, did so. Some sought the sea-shore; some Galveston Island. Some few families believed there would be safety at *Anahuac.* In fact, they could get no farther. Horses and cattle had given out; some were left in the road; some could not cross the Trinity on account of the overflow. Indeed, the confusion and distress occasioned by the panic created by this blood thirsty monster, Santa Ana, is totally indescribable.

The war between Mexico and Texas is at an end. Santa Ana and suite will soon be at liberty; and the American enemies of Texas, and friends of Mexico, may again be seen arm in arm in the streets of New York, with one of the commanders of the Alamo, the worthy and ——— son of Hidalgo.*

I will give you a few more facts. Six hundred and one dead Mexicans have been counted that were killed in the battle of the 21st April, without taking into considerations those shot in the lake, perhaps 50 or 100 more. There are 630 prisoners that I know of—perhaps 650 in all. We can make out 1300 and odd, dead, wounded and prisoners.—*Thirteen* [*this number not totally cclear*] are supposed to have escaped; Gen. Ball, I have understood gave that account. The Mexican account of the battle is, that we had 6000 Americans, and 2000 Indians, opposed to them in battle! It will never be possible to convince them to the contrary. The balance of Santa Ana's army fled—General Rusk was close in the rear, occasionally cutting off small detachments and harrassing [*sic*] them with his cavalry at every step, until he was ordered to stop, that a treaty had been made. The enemy had passed La Bahia and Bexar, blowing up the Alamo; spiking and throwing the cannon in the river, in his retreat. The Comanche Indians commenced depredating in the rear of the Mexican army as they advanced from

Bexar upon the settlements. All their horses and mules, of which they had many, as well as much baggage, were taken by the Indians. At every step they meet with trouble, and are hurrying with all possible despatch towards the Interior. At the battle of the 21st April, Almonta's [*sic*] and Cos's private journals and letter fell into the hands of the Americans—among them some letters from New York. Some having slips of *newspapers* in them; some letters in English, some in Spanish, &c. &c.!! As they will, in all probability, find their way to New York, you will be enabled to see the effects of Mexican Gold in that great city.

While the Texans were marching towards the Colorado, to meet the Mexicans, meeting hundreds who were flying from their homes; among the rest an aged lady, whose eyes were diffused with tears, and when told to be of good cheer, that the Mexicans would be soon driven out the country, "Ah," replied the old lady, "all the beating you can give the Mexicans now, wont restore *my son who was murdered in the Alamo.*"

[*The article has three more paragraphs: one on additional details of San Jacinto, one on the deaths of Cós and Castrillón during that battle, and a postscript on the death of Fannin.*]

---

* He is said to be the illegitimate son of a Priest named Hidalgo, by an Indian woman.

Commentary

Newspapers (4.1)

The newspaper accounts are all noteworthy for being very early accounts of the Alamo, and therefore important as relatively independent narratives, as well as for their influence on the broader literature that arose later (reference chapter 5).

The most important of all post-fall narratives of the Alamo is that in the *Telegraph and Texas Register* of March 24. This would be the picture of the fall for Texans (and the United States) and the starting point for all later secondhand accounts. As the *Telegraph and Texas Register* was something like a semiofficial organ of the Texas Convention, it was also based on the most authoritative sources known in Washington-on-the-Brazos. The casualty list was particularly valuable for this reason. The sources for this list are given as John W. Smith and a Mr. Navon. Williams (1.7.7) gave a likely identification of the latter as Gerald Navan, a possible courier. His presence at the Alamo was based especially on the Jameson letter of January 18 (4.2.1.1) and the Neill letter of January 23 (4.5.15). As for the narrative, the possible witnesses were Susanna Dickinson, Joe, and Ben, with only Dickinson given explicitly as a source. Being well before San Jacinto, the Mexican sources must be very limited. Also of interest is that Mr. Navon/Gerald Navan and Judge Ponton of Gonzales (note 1.1.1.16) are cited as supplying information, but no additional documents are known related to what they knew. It is possible that further archival searches might turn up additional material by these two.

Study of this narrative indicates that there are more details than the credited sources (Dickinson, Smith, Navan, and Ponton) could have supplied. From Barsena and Bergara (3.4.2) no doubt came the specifics that the attack took place at daybreak of the sixth, with the cavalry forming a circle to prevent escape. They also could be the source for the figure of four thousand Mexican troops, as Houston cited them by saying twenty-five hundred plus fifteen hundred reserves (as opposed to Joe, who gave—a probable reading—six thousand). An examination of the definitive version of Joe's experiences, the *Commonwealth* article of May 25 (1.3.4), shows him as the probable source for the details that Santa Anna personally commanded the attack, the defenders were fatigued and harassed during the siege by bombardment and attacks, Crockett's body was surrounded by piles of assailants, Travis cheered his men and fell when shot, and Bowie was murdered in bed. One of the most memorable expressions, that the Mexican soldiers came over the walls "like sheep," must be from Joe. The end of Crockett and Bowie also matches the account in the *Commonwealth* article. At a minimum, the same details did get into both newspapers, which would be strange if not originated by Joe. The possibility that one paper derived from the other should be unlikely if, as stated, the *Commonwealth* account is from a letter of March 20—prior to the publication of the *Telegraph and Texas Register* version.

Some of the remaining details are more problematic. Susanna Dickinson is explicitly attributed in the *Commonwealth* account as the source for the battle details that the Mexican Army with its scaling ladders was twice repulsed before going over the walls on the third try—"like sheep." But this is information that, as a noncombatant, she was highly unlikely to know, and her later interviews (section 1.2) give little indication that she so claimed. The only aspect of the fighting she might have been aware of is that the attackers were repulsed twice (1.2.8) or three times (1.2.11); it is certainly possible that she could have heard lulls in the noise between the attacks. One other detail, that of Evans being killed while trying to blow up the powder magazine, shows up only in the accounts by Maverick and the grandchildren (1.2.12, 1.2.14). These versions were recorded long after the fact, and this incident could have been inserted because of its original inclusion in the *Telegraph and Texas Register* rather than actually having come from Dickinson. On the other hand, the matter-of-fact interview(s) with granddaughter Susan Sterling tend to support accepting the story. Meanwhile, as reviewed in the Commentary for section 1.2, the incidents that Dickinson most likely did narrate are mostly not included here. The exception is the death of Warner (or Walker). This should not be surprising, as the other incidents she later recalled were more personal and not part of the actual fighting, which is both the focus of this article and more likely to be the subject about which she was first questioned. So one conclusion is that the *Commonwealth* misattributes these battle details to Susanna Dickinson.

In considering other possibilities, the solid, sensible core of Joe's accounts suggests he would not claim some of the information regarding the final fighting and the death of a General Mora—he left the walls as soon as Travis was shot. For the same reason, Ben (2.12) is unlikely to have added any imaginative details. Regarding other sources, one early account by a reputed Mexican deserter (2.17.1) is known, but examination indicates little similarity to the other versions. Another possibility is a Tejano survivor noted by Almonte (2.2.1) and identified by Williams (1.10.1) as possibly being Anselmo Borgarra (or Bergara). If true, the reports of the fall (3.4.1, 3.4.2) would take on special importance—and would explain the details of fighting in these accounts. On the other hand, Barsena (or Bargana) has Bergara coming out of the city on Saturday night, and the identification of a survivor is more likely to be Brigidio Guerrero. In summary, I believe one can be fairly certain that Dickinson is incorrectly named as the source for many of the battle details of the *Telegraph and Texas Register* and the *Commonwealth* articles, and that an additional source other than Dickinson or Joe—either an actual participant such as Guerrero or someone initiating "camp rumors"—was more probably the originator of this information. If a letter by Judge Ponton discussing his interview with Susanna Dickinson from around this time were to be found, it could be a major discovery by clarifying this question.

The letter of March 17 by Shreve in the *Commercial Bulletin* (4.1.2) is an example of another very early account. Comparing it with the *Telegraph and Texas Register* narrative, the tone and several details are different, including the number of casualties and of Mexican troops (six thousand), a two-day siege, and the execution of seven defenders. Hence the *Commercial Bulletin* account was not derived from the earlier newspaper article. Clearly some knowledge of the Barsena and Bergara interviews (3.4.2) is reflected, as the number of defenders is the same and that of the Mexican casualties is very close. They no doubt are also the source for the story of the execution of seven defenders (3.4.2). The *Commonwealth* story of Joe is likewise reflected in the six thousand Mexican troops, the fight lasting about an hour, the attack being made with scaling ladders, and Crockett found among the slain. However, there is the new detail of Crockett fighting first by firing his gun, then with the breech. Who might have observed this? Susanna Dickinson, Joe, or a townsperson removing bodies after the battle? A deserter? Was this detail invented? Here is a case where it is far easier to point out the problems in an account than to arrive at a valid conclusion. Shreve is another person from whom contemporary letters might be an important discovery.

On or around March 27, 1836, the schooners *Levant* (with a letter by Andrew Briscoe) and *Camanche* arrived in New Orleans with some of the first real news outside Texas about the fall of the Alamo. The three articles published immediately thereafter (4.1.3, 4.1.4.1, 4.1.4.2) are useful to compare with each other and with the original reports from Sam Houston in Gonzales (3.5.2). The first observation is that practically all the information on the fall derives from Sam Houston, and therefore Barsena and Bergara (3.4.1, 3.4.2). A related point is that these accounts clearly are not independent, but a retelling of similar information. An insertion into the accounts, not in Briscoe's letter (4.1.3) but added in the New Orleans newspapers, is the story of a major attack on February 25, with the loss of hundreds of Mexican soldiers. This circulated very early, earlier perhaps than Travis's report of March 3 (1.1.6), because Travis made no mention of such an attack.

The variations among these accounts becomes significant, specifically concerning the death of David Crockett. Briscoe (4.1.3) reported that he fell "fighting like a tiger." How would Briscoe have known? This statement could ultimately be derived from Joe's report (1.3.4) of Crockett surrounded by enemies, but it seems unlikely that news from interviews with Joe around March 20 would have caught up with the Houston report of March 11 to arrive in New Orleans on March 27. The *New Orleans Commercial Bulletin* (4.1.4.1) simply records that Crockett was among the slain. The variant of the same interview in the *Arkansas Gazette* (4.1.4.2) quotes (apparently) from the *New Orleans Post and Union,* also duplicated in the *New Orleans True American;* it has a change in the sentence order making Crockett one of the seven who attempted to surrender but continued fighting when told no quarter would be given.[1] This is a suspicious revision, since the overall account is otherwise fairly similar to that reported in the *New Orleans Commercial Bulletin.*

Some other differences between these two versions originating in New Orleans are the *Camanche* being three versus eight days from Texas, and Mexican casualties as 500 to 800 versus 450 to 600. The second version also adds the story of eight guns by the side of each defender and the Cós/Bowie story. The last two items, the addition of new details, suggest to me that the second version is a later, modified form of the first. Another item to note is the misuse of "Mexicans" for "Texians" in the *Arkansas Gazette,* which implies sloppy editing in the second version as well.

These two versions should have been more similar had they been recording the same story coming out of Texas. Authors including Lord (5.2.2) use the account per the second version as support for the possible validity of the Crockett surrender story, but I see it as far more likely that the second version of Crockett's surrender originated in New Orleans or with the editor of the *Arkansas Gazette.* This subject is discussed in broader scope in the Special Commentary on deaths (5.2). For now, the conclusion is that this version inserted an addition into the common account and therefore is suspect.

The *Memphis Enquirer* (4.1.5) gave the first account that Bowie was burned alive (see 2.17.2). Houston is cited as the source, but a check of his reports (section 3.5) shows that the claim is inaccurate, and therefore this account is likely to be the result of journalistic dramatization.

The letter of William Parker (4.1.6) gives a variant of the stories on the death of Walker (section 1.2). In this case, there were two unidentified defenders killed in the presence of Susanna Dickinson. The better-documented interviews show that something like this grim account could have happened. However, that there were two defenders rather than one killed and the lack of identification of Walker suggest that this is not as direct or accurate a recording of a Dickinson interview as those in the earlier section.

The *Louisville Daily Journal* of July 11 (4.1.7) is the earliest account located of Crockett's deadly Kentucky long rifle, an image frequently used by later writers. This account is hard to accept or reject on its own merits. There is no known earlier version to directly validate this, but the events are not improbable and—having been written after San Jacinto—a Mexican captive might have narrated such a story. The qualification to the latter is that very few Mexicans knew (reference Ben, 2.12.1, and Ruiz, 3.1.1), or would care, who Crockett was. So the specific personal identification is more likely to have been made after the fact by the Texans. Nonetheless, the abandonment of artillery within gunshot range of the Alamo defenders is supported by Sánchez (2.7.2), and the story was being told in San Antonio in 1837.[2]

The *Commonwealth* July 27 article (4.1.8) now explicitly makes Crockett one of the prisoners executed right after the fall. There must be some connection to new, post–San Jacinto Mexican sources, as General Castrillión is now identified as having taken the prisoners to Santa Anna (see Dolson's July 19 letter, 4.3.7). This consequently is an important version to consider later (Special Commentary 5.2) in analyzing the death of Crockett. Groneman attributed the story to a reporter named William H. Attree, "known for his flamboyant style and sometimes outrageous stories."[3]

A couple other points concerning this document are also worth noting. One is that Lord considered the unknown eyewitness of the first paragraph to these executions as possibly being Caro (3.5.1), but for reasons that are not obvious.[4] This text is certainly similar to Dolson's letter of July 19 (4.3.7). Finally, it mentions another document that once existed that would be of considerable interest: the private journal of General Cós. That it is unknown implies either that it is a misidentification of Almonte's or that it must have been lost very early.

---

1. *New Orleans True American* is in Gaddy 1973, 49
2. Muir 1958, 113
3. Groneman 1996, 378
4. Lord 1961, 230

4.2.1.1.   G. B. Jameson, letter, January 18, 1836.

De Zavala, Adina. 1917. *History and Legends of the Alamo and Other Missions in and around San Antonio*. 23–26. San Antonio: privately published by author.

Green B. Jameson, the engineer at the Alamo, described in his letter at least a couple of plats he did for the government showing the defenses (a plat is a plan, map, or chart of a piece of land). Only one version is currently known, and it is available in copies only. An analysis of the versions and copies by Williams and Schoelwer follows the letters and maps. The original of this first letter was not located. A note in the Williams Papers, CAH (Alamo Research: Materials relating to defenders, messengers, victims, and survivors of 1836/Folder 1), says a fragment of a letter with Jameson's signature was in the Houston Public Library, but the librarians were not able to locate it (personal communication).

Bexar, January 18th, 1836.

Major General Sam Houston,
Sir:

Believing that a letter will meet you at Goliad, and having had more time to make a better plot of the "Fortress Alamo" at this place have embraced this conveyance, to acquaint you more satisfactorily of the condition and progress of the department, which you have so kindly assigned to me.

I send you herewith inclosed a neat plot [sic] of the fortress exhibiting its true condition at this time, as also an Index being duplicates of my former addressed to you at Washington, added to which is a recapitulation more explanatory, and showing the improvements already made by me

I am now fortifying and mounting the cannon. The 18 pounder now on the N.W.* corner of the fortress so as to command the Town and the country around. [*A footnote at the bottom of the page reads, "*In his plat it is plainly marked on the southwest corner."*]

The officers of every department do more work than the men and also stand guard, and act as patrol every night. I have no doubt but that the enemy have spies in town every twenty-four hours, and we are using our utmost endeavors to catch them every night, nor have I any doubt but there are 1500 of the enemy at the town of Rio Grande, and as many more at Laredo, and I believe they know our situation as well as we do ourselves.

We have received 100 bushels of meal and 42 Beeves which will last us for two months to come, but no other supplies have come to our relief.

You have heard so much about our situation from our Commander that I shall say nothing further on the subject.

We can rely on aid from the citizens of this town in the case of a siege. Seguine [sic] is doing all for the cause he can, as well as many of the most wealthy and influential citizens.

You can plainly see by the plot [sic] that the Alamo was never built by a military people for a fortress, tho' it is strong, there is not a redoubt that will command the whole line of the fort, all is in plain wall and intended to take advantage with a few pieces of artillery, it is a strong place and better it should remain as it is after completing the half moon batteries than to rebuild it. The men here will not labour and I cannot ask it of them until they are better clad and fed. We have now 114 men counting officers, the sick and wounded which leaves us about 80 efficient men. 40 in the Alamo and 40 in Town, leaving all the patrole [*sic*] duty to be done by the officers and which for want of horses has to be performed on foot.

We have had loose discipline untill [*sic*] lately. Since we heard of 1000 to 1500 men of the enemy being on their march to this place duty is being done well and punctually in case of an attack we will all move into the Alamo and whip 10 to 1 with our artillery.

If the men here can get a reasonable supply of clothing, provisions and money, they will remain the balance of the 4 months, and do duty and fight better than fresh men, they have been tried and have confidence in themselves.

I can give you full assurance that so far as I am concerned there shall be nothing wanting on my part, neither as an officer nor as a soldier to promote and sustain the great cause at which we are all aiming, and am at all times respectfully subject to your orders for the verification of which I refer you to my Commander at this place, as well as all the officers and men. I have been much flattered for my exertions at this place. I have more than one time received the vote of thanks of the whole Garrison.

I have one other subject which interests me some; to ask of you, if it is not too late, that is to recommend to your notice Capt. G. Navan, who is clerk in my department for the appointment of Suttler [*sic*] at this Post as he is in every way qualified to fill the office. I know of no man who merits it more than he does, as an evidence of his patriotism he has absented himself from his family when he was also receiving a salary of $1800 per annum to aid us in our difficultues.

> I am with esteem
> Very Respectfully,
> Your obt. servt.,
> G. B. JAMESON.

I will in my next give you a plan of the Town as fortified when we took it. We have too few to garrison both places, and will bring all our forces to the Alamo tomorrow as well as the cannons. In excavating our ditches we can with perfect safety rely on a fall from the two ditches or acqueducts [*sic*] of at least 20 feet, consequently we can make our ditches deep enough with perfect safety, and the earth here is of such a nature that it will not wash, and we can ditch very near the half moon batteries with perfect safety. I will say all that is necessary in my answer to your official letter on this subject. In regard to the ditch we can have a flood gate at the mouth of it, which will answer for keeping in a supply of water in case of a siege, as also by raising, for cleansing the Fortress. I am too much occupied to copy these papers but I shall be able to show you by demonstration when I have nothing else to attend to that I will not be wanting in my abilities as a topographical Engineer.

Respectfully, Your Obt. Servt.

G. B. JAMESON

4.2.1.2.   G. B. Jameson, letter, February 11, 1836.

Jameson, G. B., to Henry Smith. February 11, 1836. Secretary of State (RG-307), Records of the Governor, TSLA.

Bexar February 11th 1836

To His Excellency Henry Smith

Dear Sir

I have been in the field on actual duty more than four Months and have not lost one hour from duty on account of Sickness or pleasure.

But have served my country in every capacity I possibly could when I left home it was with a determination to See Land free & Independent Sink or Swim die or perish. And I have Sanguine hopes of seeing my determination consummated. There is Still a powerful force at Rio Grande Say 2000 certain the last accounts we have is that they were preparing Ferry Boats to March against us we know not when they may come. We are badly prepared to meet them. Though we will do the best we can.

A great number of the volunteers. here will leave to morrow as the end of their second Month is up and no pay no clothes nor no provisions. poor encouragement for patriotic men who have Stood by their Country in the hour of trial. $7" each for 4 months We are now one hundred and fifty Strong Col Crockett & Col Travis both here & Col Bowie in command of the Volunteer forces. Col Neill left to day for home on account of an express from his family informing him of their ill health.

There was great regret at his departure by all of the men though he promises to be with us in 20 days at the furthest. We have nominated two delegates from the Army to represent us in the Convention which I hope will be received as we were not allowed the privilege of voting here they are both Staunch Independence men I damn any others than Such.

I have some improved demonstrations to make & send you of our Fortress whereby fewer men & less artillery will be required in case of a seige [sic] or an attack. Politics are all Strait [sic] here and every man in the Army your friend. I have named to Genl Houston through Col Neill & others that I would like a permanent appointment in the Engineer. Corps. And know that my country will reward me as I may merit Yours Verry [sic] Respectfully

G.B.Jameson

4.2.1.3.   G. B. Jameson, letter, February 16, 1836.

Jameson, G. B., to Henry Smith. February 16, 1836. Secretary of State (RG-307), Records of the Governor, TSLA.

This letter was transmitted by the Travis letter of the same date, 1.1.1.12.

Bexar Febry 16th 1836

To His Excellency Henry Smith
Sir

I have been dilatory in communicating to you the situation as well as the plan of the Fortress whereby you might know our exact state of defense & security in case of a siege from the enemy. Unless through my commander Genl Sam[l] Houston—But will now Send you a complete plan of the same Showing the situation at the time it was surrendered to us. Also Such improvements as we have made, and Such as was contemplated to strengthened, all of which contemplated work is characterised by red ink. Such improvements as we have made in exacting redoubts digging wells & mounting cannon is characterized thus * with red ink—All of which I send you for your information and that of your friends & the friends to our cause and Country—But after seeing the improbability & perhaps the impractibility and impolicy of keeping up a Strong Garrison here, I now submit a further sugestion to you as well as the Commander in Chief, which you will remark to me as you may both think most economical & efficient. The suggestion is, to square the Alamo and erect a large redoubt at each corner Supported by Bastions & have a ditch all around full of water.

When Squared in that way four cannon & fewer men would do more effective service than twenty pieces of artillery does or can do in the way they are now mounted. The mexicans have shown imbecility and want of skill in this Fortress as they have done in all things else—I have seen many fortifications in the U.S. and find that all of the Interior ones are Squares and those of the Forts are generally circular—

Taking into consideration the Security of Forts we have done well in mounting & remounting Guns and other necessary work—If I were ordered to construct a new & effective Fortress on an economical plan I would suggest a diamond & with two acute & two oblate angles—with few men & Guns with a sufficient entrenchment all around. Such a Fortress with projecting redoubts & Bastions would command all points—If you are not too much perplexed with other business I wish you to write me officially on this subject—I beg leave to tender to you my high esteem for your firm & unShaken course pursued since you have had the honor to preside over this state as chief magistrate as also that of the Garrison to which I am attached and assure you that the courses by you pursued has won all Philanthropists to your person & conduct and hope that you may ever retain the same confidences you now hold

and Subscribe my self Yr. Obt. humble Servt.

Verry Respectfully
G.B.Jameson
By David Murphser [?] clk Engineer

4.2.1.4.   After Green B. Jameson, plat or map, 1836.

De Zavala, Adina. 1917. *History and Legends of the Alamo and Other Missions in and around San Antonio.* 26-30. San Antonio: privately published by author.

De Zavala was responsible for the first published version of the Jameson plats. After citing the Jameson letter of January 18 (given separately here as document 4.2.1.1), De Zavala presented the map as follows.

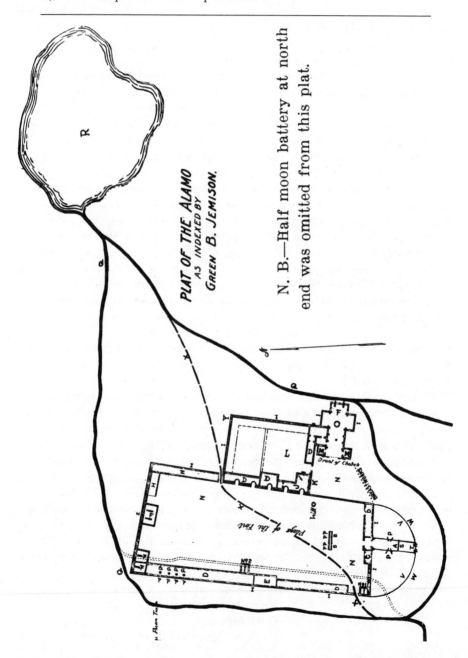

PLAT OF THE ALAMO
AS INDEXED BY
GREEN B. JEMISON.

N. B.—Half moon battery at north end was omitted from this plat.

This same plat and letters were used by H. Yoakum in the preparation of his Texas History, and is referred to in his description of the Alamo as "the plat and letters which lie before me." He sent the sketch on February 12, 1855, to Mr. Francis [*sic*] Giraud asking him to place upon it the measurements—length and thickness of the walls, and to return the sketch to him. He endorsed it: "The enclosed sketch of the Alamo with proposed alterations was drawn by Capt. G. B. Jameson a few days before he was killed at the taking of the Alamo." The plat and key and letters we also copied by Mrs. Mary Jane Briscoe, from papers belonging to Peter W. Gray, in July 1886.

INDEX TO THE PLAN OF THE ALAMO DESIGNATED IN ALPHABETICAL ORDER.

A. Represents the entrance into the Alamo with two cannon

B. Temporary redoubts of stakes on end and rocks and dirt between, the long one is in front of the house in which Col. Mendoza now lies wounded.

C. The Guard House.

D. Soldiers quarters built up of stone houses.

E. Headquarters of Alamo now occupied by 2 wounded officers.

F. Batteries and platforms where cannon are now mounted.

G. Cannon mounted on the ground with ports in the main wall.

H. Soldiers quarters built up of doby [*adobe*] houses and picketed all round as letter B.

I. Strong stone walls without pickets all around.

J. The hospital up stairs in a two story building of stone, the lower story being represented by the letter K. and now occupied as an Armory for our small arms.

L. A large stone quartel for horses adjoining the Church San Antonio, Hospitals and Armory.

M. The Magazine in the Church San Antonio two very efficient and appropriate rooms 10 feet square each, walls all around and above 4 feet thick.

N. All large vacancies inside the walls of the fortress, the Church San Antonio is in the Alamo and forms a part of the fortress and is marked by the letter O.

P. The cannon mounted in the Alamo. Their number corresponding with that of the letters.

Q. The acqueduct as around the fortress by which we are supplied with water, marked with red ink.

R. A lake of water where we contemplate supplying the fortress by ditching from one of the acqueducts laid down.

S. A pass from the present fortress to a contemplated drawbridge across a contemplated ditch inside a contemplated half moon battery as laid down on the plan.

T. A part of said ditch, as well as a trap door across said ditch, which is contemplated to be raised by a tackle from inside the half moon battery.

U. The hinges on which said bridge is to be raised.

V. The half moon battery at each end of the fortress as contemplated.*

W. A 12 feet ditch around the half moon battery as contemplated.

X. The contemplated ditch where we wish the permanent water to pass thro' the fortress and thence to pass out erecting an arch over each place and also a redoubt for a permanent cannon in case of siege.

Y. A ditch passing under the stone wall to the lake marked R.

---

* The editor omitted the half moon battery on the north end of the Plaza of the Fort from the plat shown herewith, as it was thought that it was never completed. It corresponded exactly in construction to the one on the south end as shown in the accompanying plat.

You will perceive in this index that I have always marked the parts of notoriety with more letters and characters than one of the same kind.

The letter D represents a large stone building that will answer for a public store house. The letter V represents a want of provision, munitions and men.

I would recommend that the doby houses, letter H, to be torn down and stone houses erected in their stead. The stone can be obtained out of the old Church San Antonio, which is now a wreck or ruin of a once splendid Church. All we want now is provisions and munitions to stand a siege against an innumerable force tho' we are weak beyond imagination, not being more than 100 strong since Johnson and Grant left, and there could be raised in town 300 men that could besiege us at any time.

4.2.2.1. François Giraud, map, 1849.

Giraud, François P. 1849. "Book 1 Survey of the City of San Antonio Texas, Starts Dec. 7, 1847, Francis Giraud, Surveyor, Book 1 or 2." 114–15. Office of the County Clerk, Béxar County. This is a photocopy from the original book in the Central Mapping Office, City of San Antonio.

Giraud's survey is the one other near-contemporary map of the old mission before the outer walls disappeared for good. It also had the particular advantage of being a surveyed work done by a professional. The original of this map, in book 1, page 114 of a volume once in the San Antonio City Engineers Office, was not found. The Central Mapping Office of the City of San Antonio does have a microfilm of the book done approximately twenty years ago (late 1970s?). At that time, the original map was significantly damaged, with portions missing. A photocopy, apparently when the original was even slightly more damaged, was made by John O. Leal in 1987 and is in the Office of the County Clerk, Béxar County. This photocopy is used here, as it gives a clearer reproduction of the text than does the microfilm in the city office. Either version equally demonstrates the near total loss of information of the map itself. No previous publication of a direct facsimile has been found.

Not transcribed here, but undamaged and quite readable in the copies, is Giraud's narrative description of his survey. As can be read there, the survey and map were done for Samuel A. Maverick and recorded in December 1849. This narrative can be used to check dimensions otherwise missing or unclear.

Villita Ditch — Thence up said Ditch N. 12½° E. 26½ vas — N. 23½° E. 49 vas — N. 50½° E. 84 vad to a stake in the junction of the Ditch, and that running North and West of the buildings of the Mission — Thence down the latter ditch, N. 86° W. 19½ vas hora Willow — N. 81° W. 139 varas to a point in a line with East wall of the old Convent — Thence S. 75½° W. 27¼ vas to the N.W. Corner of the Muralla or outer wall of the Mission, which is about 4 vas from the ditch — Thence keeping down the same ditch S. 64¾° W. 30¼ vas — S. 40½° W. 30 vas & S. 21½° W. 38 vas to a stake on the edge of ditch — Thence with North line of a lot and house of Dᵃ. Jesusita Treviño and going along the North side of Chimney of said house S. 79⅜° E. 25⅓ vas to the Mission Square — Thence along the West side of said Square, N. 8½° E. 22. vas and N. 7⅞° E. 62.80 varas, to the N.W. exterior corner of the Mission wall or Muralla, already mentioned — Thence along North side of said wall S. 75⅞° E. 51.90 vas — Thence running across said wall (which is about 1.08 vara thick) and six varas beyond it, to Cover the building site of Carmel delas Reyes S. 10° W. 7.08 vas — Thence S. 75⅝° E. 20 vas to the N.E. Corner of the Mission Square — Thence along the East side of said Square. S. 10° W. — 52.4 vas to the beginning, but leaving a passage 2 varas wide on the North side of the old Convent, by which access may be had to the yard on the East side of said Convent, from the Square of the Mission

San Antonio
Dec. 1849.

F Giraud Atty S. B.º

Recorded in City Survey Book, pp. 114 & 115. F Giraud

4.2.2.2. François Giraud, map, 1849.

Texas Title Company. N.d. (before 1913?). 5033 LDF, Historical Sites/Alamo/Maps, DRT Library.

This version of the Giraud map may be the most accurate now available of the official record in book 1, page 114, per discussion in the Commentary for section 4.2.

Note: This plat is taken from one recorded in Book 1, p. 114, i n the City Engineer's office, representing a survey of the S. A. Maverick tract made in December, 1849, by F. Giraud, City Surveyor.

4.2.2.3.   François Giraud, map, 1849.

San Antonio Light. February 12, 1912. 2. Copy of map in Historical Sites/Alamo/Maps, DRT Library.

**ALAMO LINES
DEFINITELY
ESTABLISHED**

Two Old Plats Found and They
Agree Perfectly on All Essential Details

EXCAVATIONS VERIFY

Wall Along Houston Street and
One on East Are Modern
and Will Be Razed.

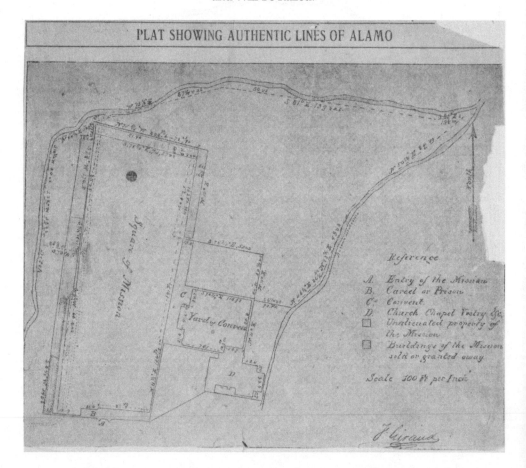

Two plats of the Alamo mission and its purlieus, identical in every essential detail, are now in the hands of J. B. Nitschke, state inspector of masonry, who is in charge of the work of restoring the old mission. One was drawn by Quartermaster-Sergeant, Ruben M. Potter, who was sent to San Antonio in 1841, five years after the famous battle, by the United States war department to investigate the condition of the fort. The other, found among the old archives of the Bexar Abstract company and loaned by H. E. Hildebrand, was compiled by F. Giraud, city engineer, from a drawing made some time in the '40's.

The work of actual restoration will begin this week, probably Wednesday, when Governor Colquitt is expected to be here and personally direct the work. Mr. Nitschke will communicate with the governor tonight, informing him that the excavations have been finished.

Details All Verified
Nearly every dimension given in the diagrams has been verified by actual excavations. To make sure, Mr. Nitschke this morning measured off the lengths of the foundations that have been unearthed, and in every instance the dimensions thus found tallied with those marked on the charts. It was shown that the present wall on the east is of modern construction, as is also the portion of the wall running along Houston street. It has also been established beyond a doubt that the long, narrow building on the Alamo plaza side was the convent. As given in the two plats, the convent was eighteen feet in width by 191 feet in length. In Sergeant Potter's drawing it is shown that the convent was divided into five apartments, each of which had an arched doorway on the Alamo plaza side.

Differ in Small Details
The only differences in the two plats is in regard to the chapel. In F. Giraud's copy the location of two pilasters at the entrance of the chapel is indicated, and a slight offset in the north wall of this building is shown. These small details do not appear in Sergeant Potter's drawing.

The east wall, supposed to have been alongside the Alamo Madre acequia, the source of the mission's water supply, is placed on both charts at a distance of seventy-three feet from the ditch. The foundations of this wall was discovered Saturday, and this morning Mr. Nitschke measured the distance to the ditch on the east and found it to be exactly seventy-three feet.

Is Room for Parking
In the light of this new information the present wall on the east will probably be razed, as will the short wall running along Houston street. The space between the sidewalk along Houston street and the inner wall, the foundation of which was discovered last week and which is shown in the two plats to have been a cattle pen, will probably be parked [sic; parking].

4.2.3.1.   Williams, dissertation, 1931.

Williams, Amelia. 1931. "The Jameson Plats and Letters." A critical study of the siege of the Alamo and of the personnel of its defenders. 397–408 (Appendix II). Ph.D. diss. University of Texas, Austin.

Williams discussed the sources of her documents in the text. However, she was unaware of the Giraud plan as an independent document, so she was misled by Yoakum (4.2.3.2 and 5.1.5) in evaluating the significance of her three plans. Schoelwer corrected the attribution in her article (4.2.4). For the first two of her plats and the Jameson letters, Williams's ultimate sources are reproduced, rather than the copies or tracing used in her dissertation. As noted in her dissertation, Williams had independent access through Adele Looscan to the Briscoe tracing, which she used for her "Plan C," rather than that used by De Zavala for document 4.2.1.4. Therefore, this Looscan/Williams version serves as an alternate to De Zavala's copy.

Williams included transcripts of Jameson's three letters and one from Travis. There are trivial differences in wording and layout between originals or the De Zavala transcript and Williams's version of these letters. She also included a discussion of Jameson, which is still worthwhile. Williams's footnotes, embedded in the text of the dissertation, are here moved to the end.

APPENDIX II. PLANS OF THE ALAMO
PLANS NO. 1. THE JAMESON PLATS AND LETTERS

Green B. Jameson was a young engineer who joined the Texan army at Gonzales, October 18, 1835. He participated in the Storming of Bexar in December 1835, and remained with the Texan forces at San Antonio after that city was wrested from the Mexicans. On February 11, 1836 he applied for and received the appointment as chief engineer of the Texan forces at San Antonio. On February 16, he and Travis both wrote letters to Governor Smith, and both mention enclosing plats of the Alamo. On January 18, Jameson wrote to General Sam Houston and said that he was sending plats that he had made of the Alamo, one of the fort as it was when the Texan forces occupied it, and the other showing improvements that he had made. In this letter of January 18, 1836, he also mentions another plat of the Alamo which he had previously sent to Houston, and writes of changes that he desires to make in the fortress for the sake of more effective defense. He promises to send a drawing to illustrate his ideas concerning these contemplated changes. If the originals of those plats are in existence to day, they cannot be found.[1] There are numerous copies to be found of these plans, however, and two are presented here as Plan A and Plan B.

The Plan A that is presented here is a photostat from Henderson Yoakum's *History of Texas*, Vol. II, between pages 76 and 77. Yoakum there speaks of the plat as "the original plat that lies before me."[2] Evidently Yoakum had access to the plats that Jameson had sent to Houston. The one he presented in his book is clearly the drawing made of the fortress as it was when the Texan forces took possession. One wonders why he did not present both plats, or at least the one showing the improvements that Jameson had made up to February 18, the date of his letter to Houston.

[*Williams's Plan A is presented here as document 4.2.3.2, from the published copy by Yoakum.*]

The Plan B, shown here, is taken from the material on the Alamo, collected by O. B. Colquitt, and presented in his *Message to the Thirty-third Legislature Relative to the Alamo Property.*[3] Colquitt obtained this plan from H. A. McArdle who claims to have copied it from the original plat; but McArdle fails to say to whom he was indebted for the use of the original drawing. I think, however, that he copied his plat from one of the drawings that Jameson sent to Houston. It is the one that shows the improvements that had been made. Comparing this plat with the one used by Yoakum, one readily sees that "R", the earthwork from the southwest corner of the chapel to the south wall of the large area; the gate cut through the northeast corner of the large area; the raised platform for cannon near the centre of the large area; and other minor changes have been added.

[*Plan B is presented here as document 4.2.3.3, McArdle/Colquitt copy.*]

Plat C of this series of Jameson plats of the Alamo, was traced from the original drawing by Mrs. Mary Jane Briscoe for Miss Adina DeZavala. At the time that Mrs. Briscoe took her copy of this plat, the original was among the *Peter W. Gray Papers,* at Houston, but if it still exists it cannot be found. In tracing the plat, Mrs. Briscoe also copied the explanatory indexing from the original document.[4]

[*Plat C is presented here as document 4.2.3.4, another version of Briscoe via Looscan.*]

It is very evident that this drawing is the one that Jameson promises, in his letter of January 18 to send to Houston. It delineates the changes which the engineer was planning to make in the fortress, but it is doubtful whether many of the contemplated improvements were ever begun. If they were begun they were not perfected before the siege was laid. In Potter's plan of the Alamo (see Plat No. 4 of this appendix), which is a reconstruction made several years after the massacre, there is to be noted a "lunett" of guns at the south entrance, but it is by no means so elaborate as the half moon batteries shown in this Plat C. However, this similarity in the plats probably indicates that Jameson succeeded in fortifying the south entrance in a manner somewhat like his contemplated plan, but the halfmoon battery at the north was never constructed. This plat C with its explanatory index also points out the location of 20 guns that were mounted in the fortress during the siege. They are indicated on the drawing by the letter p, and in addition to the 14 plainly shown on Potter's plat, there were one over the hospital, three in the northwest wall, and two on the platform in the south end of the main area.

The index of the plat is as follows:

Plat of the Alamo as indexed by Green B. Jameson
A.   represents the entrance to the Alamo, covered by two cannon, p.p.
B.B. are temporary redoubts of stakes on end and rocks and dirt between.

C̲   is the guard house.

D̲   represents the soldiers' quarters built of stone.

E̲,   headquarters of the Alamo, now occupied by the wounded officers.

F̲,   batteries and platforms where cannon are now mounted. (Note—It was on one of these—north east corner of large area—that Travis is said to have fallen)

G̲.   Cannon, mounted on the ground with ports in the main wall.

H̲,   Soldiers' quarters built up of doby houses and picketed all around as is B.W.

I̲,   Strong stone walls without pickets around.

J̲.   The hospital upstairs in a two-story building of stone, the lower story being represented by K̲ and now occupied as an armory for small arms.

L̲.   A large stone quarter for horses. It adjoins the church, hospitals and armory.

M̲.   The magazine in the church San Antonio de Valero. These are two very efficient and appropriate rooms, each 10 feet square, walls all around and above are 4 feet thick.

N̲.   All large vacancies inside the walls of the fortress. The church San Antonio is within the Alamo and forms a part of the fortress and is marked O.

O̲.   Church of the Alamo.

P̲.   Cannon mounted in the Alamo. Their number corresponds with that of the letters. (21 may be counted).

Q̲.   The aqueduct as around the fortress by which we are supplied with water marked with red ink.

R̲.   A lake of water from which we contemplate supplying the fortress by ditching from one of the acqueducts laid down.

S̲.   A pass from the present fortress to a contemplated draw bridge across a contemplated ditch inside a contemplated half moon battery as laid down on the plat.

T̲.   A part of said ditch as well as a trap door across said ditch which is contemplated to be raised by a tackle from inside the half moon battery.

U̲.   The hinges on which said bridge is to be raised.

V̲.   The halfmoon battery at each end of the fortress as contemplated.

X̲.   The contemplated ditch where we wish the permanent water to pass out, erecting an arch over each place and also a redoubt for a permanent cannon in case of siege.

The letters accompanying this series of plats, are included, because they explain, in part, the plans submitted, and because they throw a light on general conditions at the Alamo just before the siege began. The first letter is from Jameson to Smith, February 11, 1836. It is Jameson's application for the position of chief engineer of the forces at San Antonio, but its importance to history lies in the fact that it gives a pretty clear understanding of the general situation at the post. The second letter presented, is one from Travis to Smith, February 16, 1836. It is included in this appendix to show Travis's opinion of Jameson and his work. The third letter is from Jameson to Smith, February 16, 1836. It discusses plats A and B of this appendix No. 1. And the fourth letter is from Jameson to Houston, January 18, 1836. Among other things, it discusses the contemplated changes to be made in the fortress. Plat C illustrates these changes described in this letter.

The originals of all these letters are among the "Army Papers," State Library Archives; copies may be found at various places. All of them are copied in "Book No. 3," Secretary of State's office. Letter No. 1 is as follows:

[*Jameson's letter of February 11, presented as document 4.2.1.2, is given here.*]

The second letter reads:

[*This document is Travis's letter of February 16, 1836, to Henry Smith, presented as document 1.1.1.12.*]

The third letter—one for Jameson to Smith, February 16, 1836—attempts to explain the plans submitted by Travis. It also throws a strong light on affairs at San Antonio. How scornful Jameson is of Mexicans and their work! How partisan the men of the Alamo seem to have been in Smith's favor! No doubt, this was one reason that Travis sent so many messages to Goliad in vain. Jameson's letter says:

[*Jameson's letter of February 16, document 4.2.1.3, is given here.*]

Previous to the writing of these letters to Smith, Jameson had been in correspondence with Houston. On January 18, 1836, he wrote:

[*Jameson's letter of January 18, document 4.2.1.1. is given here.*]

---

[1] The ones sent to Smith would logically be among either the *Army Papers,* or the *Council and Governor Papers,* State Library. They are not there. The ones sent to Houston may still exist in the possession of the Houston heirs.

[2] Mrs. Fannie D. Yoakum of San Marcos, Texas, tells me that her father-in-law, Henderson Yoakum, lived in her home in the days of his old age. While she lived at Houston, Texas, her home burned, and in this fire, the historian lost two trunks filled with manuscripts and documents of various kinds. She also says that Yoakum and Houston were very intimate friends and near neighbors at Huntsville, Texas, during the time that Yoakum was writing his *History of Texas.* Houston helped in the work of writing the history by putting many valuable documents into his friend's hands, by reading manuscript, and by almost daily conference during the progress of the work.

[3] All the original documents of Governor Colquitt's exhibits to the Thirty-third Legislature are to be found in the Secretary of State's office, in a file box labeled "Alamo." Copies of most of the printed matter of this collection of material may be found in the State Library, and also in the University of Texas Library.

[4] I am indebted for my copy of this plat to Mrs. Adele B. Looscan, daughter of Mrs. Briscoe, and to Miss Adina De Zavala.

[5] [*Footnote 5 in the Williams text that includes this Jameson letter (4.2.3.1) relates to the statement that the 18-pounder is in the northwest corner. The footnote says,*] In the plat it is plainly marked on the southwest corner, and should be so to command the town.

4.2.3.2.   After Giraud?, map, 1855.

Yoakum, Henderson. 1855. *History of Texas, From Its First Settlement in 1685 to Its Annexation to the United States in 1846.* 2:between 76 & 77. New York: Redfield.

The context of this map is discussed by Schoelwer in more detail in document 4.2.4.

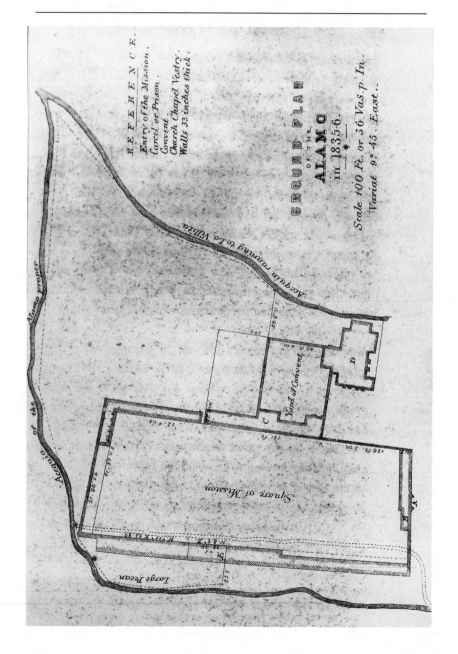

4.2.3.3. After Giraud?, map, 1913.

McArdle, H. A. N.d. "McArdle's sketch based on Potter's description of Alamo." Colquitt (Oscar Branch) Papers, Oversize box, CAH.

The version that Williams included in Appendix II of her thesis as plat B derived from original materials collected by Governor Colquitt and published in 1913. As Williams noted, it was based on information from McArdle and was included in the published booklet on page 155. The Colquitt Papers in CAH appear to have the original, with significant details that are discussed in the Commentary for section 4.2.

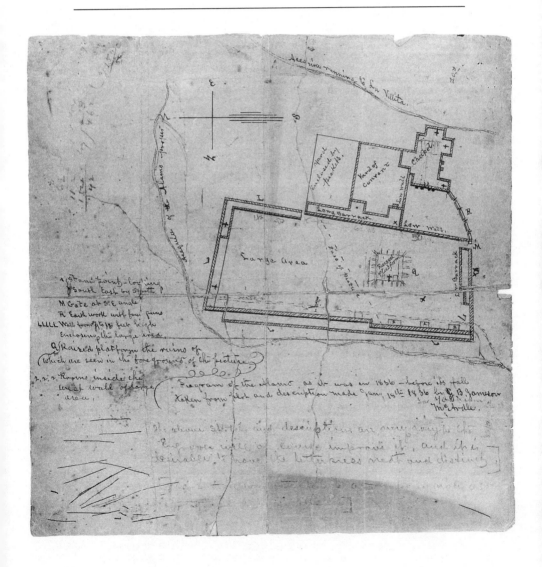

4.2.3.4. After Jameson?, map, c. 1930.

Williams, Amelia. 1931. A critical study of the siege of the Alamo and of the personnel of its defenders. Plat C, Appendix II. Ph.D. diss. University of Texas, Austin.

Williams's plat C is a drawing based on the same source as De Zavala's document 4.2.1.4, which Williams got via Briscoe's daughter Adele Looscan. It is given as a comparison with the De Zalava version.

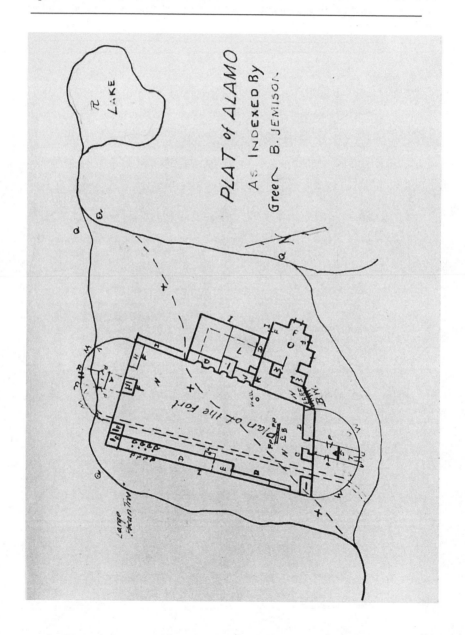

4.2.4.   Schoelwer, analysis, 1988.

Schoelwer, Susan Prendergast. April 1988. The artist's Alamo: A reappraisal of pictorial evidence, 1836–1850. *Southwestern Historical Quarterly*. 91:409–11, 452–54.

Schoelwer updated and corrected some of Williams's dissertation, and presents a more general overview of the maps. Not all footnotes are included in these selections (also 5.2.4 below), which should be consulted for more detailed study.

[*pp. 409–11*]

At present, only one Alamo visual can be conclusively dated prior to the battle: the plan of fortifications (fig. 2) [*4.2.1.4 from De Zavala*] prepared by Alamo engineer Green B. Jameson, who perished with his comrades on March 6, 1836. The production and provenance of this diagram were outlined by Williams in an appendix to her dissertation that was unfortunately never published. According to letters written by Jameson and Alamo commander William Barret Travis, there may originally have been as many as three versions of the Jameson plat: two prepared in January, 1836, and one in February. On January 18 Jameson wrote to Sam Houston enclosing "a neat plat of the fortress exhibiting its true condition at this time," accompanied by an explanation of its features and "improvements already made" by Jameson. In the same letter Jameson also mentions a duplicate copy of this plat, previously sent to Houston at Washington-on-the-Brazos, and promises to prepare for the commander an additional "plan of the Town [as distinguished from the fort, presumably] as fortified when we took it." It is not presently known whether this anticipated plan of Béxar was ever completed, but in February Jameson prepared for Governor Henry Smith "a complete plan" of the "Fortress," with red ink used to distinguish Jameson's improvements from the condition of the fortifications as "surrendered to us." Actually, it is not clear from Jameson's explanation whether the red ink indicated only contemplated improvements, or both contemplated and completed projects: "all of which contemplated work is characterized by red ink, such improvements as we have made in erecting redoubts, digging wells and mounting cannon is characterized thus with red ink." Since Jameson's stated objective was an appointment to the Regular Army Engineer Corps, it would hardly be surprising if he had blurred the distinction between work planned and actually in place. This same red-inked map is also mentioned in Travis's cover letter of February 16, forwarding Jameson's report of the same date to Smith.

Unlike the letters, the originals of the enclosed plats could not be located by Williams in the 1930s, nor have they appeared since. Consequently, we can evaluate the content of this important visual document only through copies, the earliest of which was prepared for Adina De Zavala in 1886 and made public during her turn-of-the-century campaign to preserve the old Alamo *convento* (now the Long Barracks museum). According to De Zavala, the copy was traced by Mrs. Mary Jane Briscoe from an original belonging at that time to Peter W.

Gray of Houston. In publishing the plat in her 1917 *History and Legends of the Alamo,* however, De Zavala deliberately altered it, eliminating "the half moon battery on the north end of the Plaza of the Fort . . . as it was thought that it was never completed." The unaltered version traced by Briscoe evidently remained in either Briscoe's or De Zavala's possession and was later obtained by Williams for her dissertation. Although the plat itself is not dated, the fact that De Zavala published it with Jameson's January 18 letter to Houston (and was apparently unaware of the additional correspondence cited by Williams) suggests that the letter and map shared the same provenance. Because the number of contemplated improvements that the Texans actually completed has always been a significant question for military historians, it is unfortunate that Briscoe did not provide a clear key to Jameson's use of red ink; the index, however, suggests that items "R" through "X," effectively all of the major earth- and waterworks outside the compound walls, were at the time of writing far from complete. Furthermore, Jameson's February letter to Smith shows a distinct decline in enthusiasm for his previous plans. In January the engineer had reported to Houston that the Alamo "is a strong place and better it should remain as it is after completing the half moon batteries than to rebuild it"; in his February report to Smith he proposed remodeling the Alamo as a square fortification with corner redoubts or, even more grandiosely, constructing an entirely "new and effective Fortress on an economical plan."[11]

---

[11] Jameson to Houston, Jan. 18, 1836, Jenkins (ed.), *Papers,* IV, 59 (2nd quotation); Jameson to Smith, Feb. 16, 1836, ibid., 352 (3rd quotation); De Zavala, *History and Legends,* 29 (1st quotation). The most plausible explanation for the disposition of the map sent by Jameson to Houston is that Houston may have later given it to his close friend Henderson Yoakum to aid the latter in preparing his *History of Texas* (1856). Yoakum, before his death in 1855, may in turn have passed the map along to Peter W. Gray, to whom the History was dedicated and in whose papers the map was located thirty years later by Briscoe. Why Yoakum chose to publish another plat (see fig. 23) [4.2.3.2 here] if he had in his possession the original Jameson drawing remains unclear. It is also worth noting that the indices, as transcribed by De Zavala and Williams, do not agree in exact wording, suggesting either that they were paraphrased in transcription or that they were taken from two originally distinct keys prepared by Jameson at separate times.

[pp. 452–54]
[*Previously, Schoelwer noted that Samuel Maverick had purchased land at the northwest corner of the plaza in 1841.*]

Maverick's desire to protect his claim from the army and the Catholic church apparently prompted him to request a land survey, performed in December, 1849, by San Antonio city surveyor François P. Giraud. Because Maverick's property encircled the entire northern end of the old mission, the survey map (see fig. 23) [*actually, the Yoakum map, 4.2.3.2*] provides a detailed, measured plat of the Alamo property. Its distinguishing features are its official survey markings (in directional degrees, *varas,* and feet) and a curious rectangular indentation in the northwest corner of the outer wall. This indentation, which is not corroborated or explained by any other contemporary source, marks the eventual location of Maverick's house and was evidently created for his benefit.

Unfortunately, this 1849 real-estate survey has frequently been confused with Green B. Jameson's 1836 plan of fortifications. It appears initially, with minor additions and refinements, in Henderson K. Yoakum's 1856 *History of Texas* (fig. 23). Although Yoakum's illustration of the survey is not signed or attributed, the author's previous reference to the Jameson letter of January 18, 1836, "with plot and description of the Alamo," apparently misled subsequent historians. Despite clear visual evidence in the plat itself, both Adina De Zavala and Amelia Williams erroneously attributed the Yoakum plan to Jameson. Governor Colquitt, in his 1913 *Message to the Legislature,* apparently unwittingly included two versions of the Giraud plat: the original survey map, plus a second "Diagram of the Alamo as it was in 1836—before its fall," which is said to have been copied by artist Henry A. McArdle "from Plot and description made Jan. 18th, 1836 by G. B. Jameson." McArdle's authorship is confirmed by the large, square "Raised Platform" inserted in the center of the main plaza, a distinctive feature that also looms in the foreground of the artist's epic battle painting *Dawn at the Alamo.* Other aspects of the plan, however, are clearly drawn from the Giraud survey.

Giraud's survey dimensions, as published by Yoakum, were hotly contested by Reuben Marmaduke Potter, Texas Revolution veteran and early historian of the Alamo. In his account "The Fall of the Alamo," first published in 1860 and subsequently expanded for the *Magazine of American History* in 1878, Potter argued that "Yoakum, in his history of Texas, is not only astray in his details of the assault, but mistaken about the measurement of the place." (Yoakum had, in fact, obtained these measurements from Giraud, to whom he had written for information.) "Had the works covered no more ground than he represents," Potter continues, "the result of the assault might have been different." Potter's own plan of the Alamo (fig. 24) [*in document 5.1.7*], offered to correct Yoakum and Giraud's alleged mistakes, was said by the author to have been taken from "actual measurement" made in 1860. Although the outer walls had by then been long demolished, Potter claimed to have been able to "trace [their] extent," based on his "recollection of the locality" as he had seen it in 1841.[65] The conjectural nature of this method is reflected in Potter's outline of the outer compound, which is erroneously drawn as a true rectangle oriented due north. The low barracks appear incorrectly on the outside, rather than the inside, of the south wall. Potter's placement of fourteen guns is also at odds with revolutionary-era battle-field maps. Despite its shortcomings, however, Potter's map has been widely accepted and frequently published. . . .

---

[65] R[euben] M. Potter, "The Fall of the Alamo," *Magazine of American History,* II (Jan. 1878), 2 (quotations), 3; Yoakum, *History of Texas,* II, 76–77. The dimensional error is actually Yoakum's. According to De Zavala, *History and Legends,* 26, the historian had written to Giraud on February 12, 1855, "asking him to place upon [the

sketch] the measurements—length and thickness of the walls, and to return the sketch to him." Yoakum evidently misread the diagram, giving 191 feet (Giraud's measurement of the length of the *convento*) as the length of the entire main compound. In fact, the measurements recorded by Giraud and Potter were almost identical: for the total length of the main plaza, Giraud says 463 feet, Potter gives 462 feet; Giraud says the *convento* was 191 feet long, Potter says 186 feet; both give the width of the west wall as 33 inches. The confusion may arise from Giraud's division of the measurements into segments, some of which he expressed in *varas* (1 *vara* equals 33 $^1/_3$ inches).

Commentary

Other Alamo Plans (4.2)

Green B. Jameson, engineer and defender at the Alamo, and François Giraud, San Antonio city surveyor, are two of the most significant sources for understanding the layout of the Alamo, and therefore are a formal check on specific events and the military details of the Alamo defense and siege. As is seen in the documents of this section, the originals are probably lost for good, and their information can be extracted only from second- or thirdhand copies that vary in details. Furthermore, Yoakum apparently had plans from both sources available and cited the Jameson plats in his text but reproduced in his book the unattributed Giraud map. The resulting confusion took Williams and especially Schoelwer to untangle, but the limitations of the surviving copies leave many questions unanswered.

The Jameson plats are the Texan maps complementary to the Mexican views in the Labastida plat (2.8.1) and Sánchez (2.7.1). Together they make an unusual set by providing the physical layout of a battle as drawn by both sides—and in having survived. The Jameson letters also add the tactical thinking of the Texan engineer. His enthusiasm for adding to and reconstructing the layout ran ahead of the time and resources available to him, and his patriotic spirit in condemning the Mexican work seemingly blinded him to the fact that the Alamo was originally a mission and not a military fortress. But those are secondary issues. The stage on which the battle was to be fought in a few weeks is laid out in detail that is particularly reliable, since this was a military report to senior commanders. The accuracy of the originals would have been limited only by the time and equipment available to Jameson to prepare the drawings.

Some of the confusion surrounding the Jameson plats is due to ambiguity in his letters. According to Jameson's letter of January 18 (4.2.1.1), he was sending either a second map or a duplicate of an earlier one to Houston. This was "of the fortress exhibiting its true condition at this time . . . showing improvements already made by me." Later he continued, "It is a strong place and better it should remain as it is after completing the half moon batteries than to rebuild it." The half-moon batteries are portrayed on Adina De Zavala's plan (4.2.1.4), but these were never completed, as shown, on the Labastida and Sánchez versions. So this January plat must have shown proposed as well as actual defenses. The February 11 and 16 letters (4.2.1.2, 4.2.1.3) are explicit that contemplated improvements are shown in red ink, but—as Schoelwer pointed out—whether completed improvements are also shown the same way is unclear. Also in February, Jameson wrote that the Alamo showed "imbecility and want of skill," and his interests were to completely rebuild it as a very different fortification.

As noted by Schoelwer (4.2.4), the fact that De Zavala included the map (4.2.1.4) with the January 18 letter could indicate the same provenance, but the extent of contemplated changes led her to think the map is the February version. On the other hand, not only was the north half-moon battery not built and so eliminated by De Zavala, but the southern battery protecting the Alamo main gate was also significantly smaller, as shown by the Mexican maps and modern archeologists.[1] Thus the large structures might have been much earlier contemplations than the February 16 map.

The provenance noted by De Zavala and Williams gives another clue to which version this is. They both got their copies from Mary Briscoe, who in turn traced hers from the one in the Peter Gray papers. Peter Gray was a close friend of Yoakum, who was a friend of Houston. Thus the Gray/Briscoe version was more likely from the January 18 plat to Houston rather than the February 16 plat to Smith. The evidence, therefore, is not conclusive but leans toward the Briscoe copy being from the January version of Jameson's plats.

Williams (4.2.3.1) received a sketch by Adele Looscan, daughter of Mary Briscoe, for her plat C (4.2.3.4), which therefore is an alternate reproduction to De Zavala's of the Briscoe copy. It is surprising that information given for the two does not agree more exactly. Aside from trivial wording variations and a couple of parenthetical remarks, Williams has some additions in the index not in De Zavala for items A, H, and O. On the other hand, De Zavala has additions for B, E, W, and Y, as well as a short, three-paragraph narration after the index. Some wording variations between the two are in D, L, and X.

Comparing the two plans themselves, some corresponding differences in the designated indexes are also apparent. The Looscan/Williams plan also shows the plaza as significantly less rectangular than De Zavala's, and the contemplated north half-moon battery was added back in (or more accurately, not removed) as well. Most of these differences are not major, but that they exist at all is a curious inconsistency in what should be two copies of the same Briscoe tracing. One possibility is that the original Briscoe copy was cruder and the layout less precise, with the index as reflected in the Williams version, while De Zavala gave a less exact index and used other maps, such as Yoakum's, to modify the layout to appear more like published versions. She might also have made additions to match its current appearance. Therefore, I speculate that De Zavala's plan is a less precise copy of the original. Because of these difficulties, Schoelwer goes so far as to suggest that Jameson prepared two indexes, and then presumably De Zavala got hold of one and Williams the other. It would be particularly helpful if the Briscoe tracing would come to light to settle these problems.

In the Williams Papers of the CAH is a note from Looscan of June 17, 1930, apologizing for not being able to help further on the Jameson plat, followed by a version of the Williams plat C without information on its provenance.[2] Of particular interest in this small plan is a note pointing to the north half-moon battery, stating: "This north fortification is what I have added to Miss De Zavala's plat. She says it seems right as she recollects this plat, but I am not satisfied with it." The note must be by either Looscan, who was trying to correct the published De Zavala plan based on her personal recollection of the Briscoe copy, or Williams trying to reconstruct the Jameson plat from the information she obtained from De Zavala and Looscan. The handwriting appears to be Williams's. Still another possibility is that Williams was transcribing what she was told verbally by Looscan.

Unpublished notes in both the De Zavala Papers and the Williams Papers give details explaining perhaps why the originals and some secondary copies are now missing. In her papers at the University of the Incarnate Word, De Zavala said that her phone was tapped during her "war" to save the Alamo, and that a number of "things, documents and pictures" were sent to Governor Colquitt and never received or recovered.[3] She was told later that someone connected with the group wishing to tear down the Long Barracks structure was arrested for removing mail from the post office, and she therefore believed a deliberate destruction of her material had occurred.[4] Williams, in a typed note, elaborated on the footnotes in her dissertation, saying that in 1926 she had contacted Fannie Yoakum, who remembered the destruction of her father-in-law's papers in a fire at her home, while before his death Peter Gray told Williams that the plat Briscoe had traced had disappeared from his collection.[5] It is not known for sure whether the original was destroyed earlier, as per Fannie Yoakum's account, and Gray had a careful copy reproduced by Briscoe, or the original disappeared from Gray's collection. The details of Briscoe's copy as described by De Zavala suggest that Gray might have had the original. Meanwhile, no trace of the second Jameson plat has ever been noted since his letter. Regardless of what happened, it appears that a near miracle will be necessary for an original to ever appear. Thus the copies by De Zavala and Looscan/Williams are the best historians may ever have.[6]

Practical military tactics and logistics raise a broader issue with these copies of the Jameson plats. Considering what a mess in personnel, supplies, and money Commanders Neill and Travis had to deal with (as demonstrated in the correspondence in section 4.5), how could Jameson have imagined he would ever have enough men and materials to build such grandiose half-moon structures? Also, considering how few cannons and men they had, wouldn't those large semicircles have *weakened* the defenses by increasing the blind spots in the Alamo's field of fire? What was Jameson thinking?

Jake Ivey has come up with a different hypothesis that addresses these very questions.[7] He raised the possibility that De Zavala, followed later by Looscan, did not actually have the 1886 Briscoe copy in hand to trace, but that their versions were created from memory of the earlier copy. Their sketched proportions might then easily have become too large. In such a case, Jameson himself might have intended and drawn his proposed half-moon batteries basically of the size actually built, as determined by archeology, on the south side at the main gate. In Jameson's letter of January 18 (4.2.1.1), the connection to archeological finds is supported in the postscript that he intended a ditch to be built very close to the half-moon batteries. This possibility also could explain the differences between the De Zavala and the Looscan/Williams versions. Possible direct evidence that this is not just speculation is that Ivey located rough sketches, with smaller batteries, in the De Zavala Papers that might be the "working draft" of the De Zavala version.[8] From my perspective, Ivey's hypothesis, though speculative, solves more problems than it creates.

The François Giraud map of 1849 of the mission complex gives the only professionally surveyed measurements of the entire layout at a period when the outer walls and structures could still be identified, and therefore has irreplaceable value as a check on all other plans.

Schoelwer's review article (4.2.4, see also 5.2.4) helps resolve the confusion between the Jameson plats and the information derived from Giraud. This confusion originated in Yoakum's saying he had the actual Jameson maps at hand and footnoting the Jameson letter of January 18 as a source (5.1.5), while the map (4.2.3.2) actually included in his book was derived from Giraud. This is readily apparent by the notch in the northwest corner of the property, the small main gate, the lack of the palisade wall between the chapel and the low barracks, the four-letter legend (A–D), and the surveyed dimensions (degrees, varas, feet). There is nothing on the reproduced map itself stating the source, so the text discussion naturally misled everyone until the Giraud survey came to light.

The narration of De Zavala suggests one reason for this ambiguity in Yoakum's normally carefully documented work—that as Yoakum was close to publication in 1855, he received the Giraud map and substituted it without changing the text. He might not have even realized that Giraud was giving him an independent 1849 surveyed map rather than just adding dimensions to a copy of Jameson's map. Yoakum's death the following year prevented clarification of which map was used. Then the lack of general knowledge of the Giraud original meant that De Zavala, Governor Colquitt, and Williams had to assume that the various maps they had were all derived solely from Jameson.

Unfortunately, the original Giraud map has not been located. Neither the Central Mapping Office nor the City Architect's Office of San Antonio was able to locate "Book 1 . . . in the City Engineer's office." However, direct copies of the book (4.2.2.1) show that the original had extensive portions missing and the balance damaged in the 1970s and 1980s, and therefore most map information was already permanently lost. Consequently, earlier copies of the map have become much more valuable.

Yoakum's version shows the wall along the side of the Long Barracks as straight, whereas other copies match the original by showing a slight bend north of the actual buildings. Yoakum also has many fewer dimensions than later copies. His legend D for the chapel is one detail that can be directly verified on the San Antonio microfilm. A somewhat different map that came from McArdle was published by Governor Colquitt in 1913 and was reproduced in Williams's dissertation (4.2.3.3).[9]

Other versions, not derived from Yoakum, are in the published version of the 1913 Colquitt report and another reproduced in 1976 by Anne Fox.[10] The Colquitt and

Fox printings have been the most accessible sources for the Giraud map. But rather disconcertingly, these versions do not exactly match. It turns out that a couple other versions, now in the DRT Library at the Alamo, give better insight into the Giraud original(s). One is undated, from the Texas Title Company (4.2.2.2), and the other is from a 1912 issue of the *San Antonio Light* (4.2.2.3).

Following is an analysis of these various copies of Giraud's maps to establish their relationship.

Williams (4.2.3.3) reproduced a version that came through Governor Colquitt from H. A. McArdle, with a number of modifications including a raised platform in the center of the plaza. Schoelwer noted that this was a connection with the McArdle painting, which shows the same feature. Some key features, specifically the palisade wall on the south (R on the map), the main gate on the south misplaced to the southeast corner of the large enclosure (M on the map), and the legends for the buildings, clearly were derived by McArdle from Potter (5.1.7). The primary interest remaining to this version is that Williams had access to the original Colquitt material, not all of which got into the 1913 published *Message to the Thirty-third Legislature Relative to the Alamo Property*. The copy reproduced here, found in the Colquitt Papers in the CAH, appears to be the original received by Governor Colquitt.[11] This identification seems positive because of notations on the back that it is "McArdle's sketch based on Potter's description of Alamo" and on the front "The above sketch and description are very rough, the Engraver will of course improve it, and it is desirable to have the letterpress neat and distinctly." Regardless of these specific details, the map as a whole follows much of the layout of the Yoakum copy, and the original confirms the identification with the notation "Inc Yoakum." Therefore, this ultimately is a Giraud map via Yoakum and modified from Potter, with the raised platform being the only significant new item. McArdle's source for this platform is not clear.

The published Colquitt and Fox versions are very close in general appearance, while they differ in some dimensions. On the west wall, Colquitt has "22.0 vs" while Fox has "22.20 vs"; on the northeast wall, the dimensions are "52.4 vs" compared to "52'4""; and on the east, from the yard to the acequia or stream, they are "S. 73-3/4°E" and "S. 75-3/4°E," respectively. Of these three differences, the last two appear on the city microfilm of the original, but not clear enough to decide which is correct. There are also dimensions for the acequia to the north in the original, but not on either of these copies.

Anne Fox obtained her copy from the Daughters of the Republic of Texas Library at the Alamo.[12] In their Historic Sites/Alamo/Maps files is one by the Texas Title Company (4.2.2.2) that is an exact match of the Fox copy. Furthermore, a comparison with the Colquitt copy indicates that the differences between Colquitt and Fox are in lettering that is somewhat less clear and therefore easier to misread on the Texas Title Company copy. Overall, a visual comparison strongly suggests that the Texas Title Company map was the common source for both Colquitt and Fox, and that the engraver for the printed Colquitt report made the small errors noted. The text of the Colquitt report also includes an abstract to the title of the property prepared by the Texas Title Company that states: "Note.—This plat is taken from one recorded in Block 1, p. 114, in the

City Engineer's office, representing a survey of the S.A. Maverick tract made in December, 1849, by F. Giraud, City Surveyor."[13] Thus it is reasonable to conclude that the Texas Title Company version was an official commission around 1913 by the governor to make an accurate copy of the original.

The same files in the DRT Library include a copy of an article in the *San Antonio Light* for February 12, 1912 (4.2.2.3).[14] This is clearly a Giraud map as well, but with obvious significant differences. A quick examination reveals that the various numbers give many more directional bearings as well as length, which indicates that this version includes more of the surveyor's raw data rather than being a more finished plan such as in the city's "Book 1." Therefore this map is essentially an independent copy recording original survey measurements of Giraud (unless it is derivative of the text in 4.2.2.1). Jake Ivey probably was the first to appreciate the significance of this copy and is preparing an in-depth study to reconstruct the physical layout of the Alamo based on all available information.[15]

Giraud's narrative description of his survey in "Book 1" was still preserved clearly in the facsimile reproductions. It is informative to look at the three sets of numbers across all the copies being discussed. For the west wall, the Texas Title Company map (same as Fox) has "22.20 vs"; this is verified as "22.^{vas}20" on the sixteenth line of page 115 (though it is easy to see how the .20 could have been misread as .0 by Colquitt). This number does not appear directly on the *San Antonio Light* version, so it must be a calculated dimension. Fox and the Texas Title Company's "52'4"" on the northeast wall turns out to be wrong (and Colquitt 1913 right), as "52.4 vas" appears in the fifth line from the bottom of page 115. The *San Antonio Light* number is difficult to read, but it looks likely to be the same. The last number, the bearing of the wall going to the east of the convent yard, is even more curious. Fox and the Texas Title Company have "S. 73-3/4°E," Colquitt 1913 has "75" instead of the "73," *San Antonio Light* is too blurred, and the number on the last line of page 114 doesn't match either—it is "78." So all later versions were wrong here!

Of the many uncertainties associated with the Alamo, the particular questions raised by these plans are among the more intriguing because they seem resolvable to some degree.

---

1. Hard 1994; Ivey 2000. Also note other references in the Commentary for 5.2.3.
2. Looscan, Adele B., to Amelia Williams. June 17, 1930. Correspondence/General 1930–1931. Williams (Amelia Worthington) Papers. CAH.
3. "Desk Diary" in the De Zavala Papers at the University of the Incarnate Word in San Antonio; entry is under November 27, 28, but no year is given.
4. The possible destruction of items in the post office is not as far-fetched as it initially sounds; see Ables 1967 for more on "the second battle for the Alamo." See also De Zavala 1911, which is essentially a pamphlet defending preservation of the Long Barracks.
5. Folder 2/Photographs and Pictorial Material/Williams Papers/CAH.
6. Interested researchers should note that there is additional correspondence in the General Correspondence files, not reviewed here, between De Zavala or Looscan and Williams, in the latter's papers in the CAH, that add additional insight into their contribution to Williams's dissertation.

7. James Ivey, personal communication, letter to the author, April 8, 2002.
8. James Ivey, manuscript in preparation, 2002.
9. See also Colquitt 1913, 155, and Williams 1931, Plan B, Appendix II.
10. Colquitt 1913, 12; Fox 1976, 19.
11. The Texas State Archives was not able to locate a file from the secretary of state's office that might be some of the rest of the extensive material that was part of the 1913 publication. It seems likely that it was divided up sometime after 1931. In addition to the McArdle map, the Colquitt Papers in the CAH have the apparent original plates of other maps and views in Colquitt's report. The Texas State Archives has files on the Alamo Property that perhaps are some originals of Colquitt's written documents.
12. Anne Fox, personal communication, letter to the author, October 15, 1998.
13. Colquitt 1913, 10.
14. The DRT records indicate the Texas Title Company plan might be from 1907. They also hold an official copy of the Giraud plat made by the city engineer in 1885, but dimensions are too faint in reproduction to be readable. The University of Texas Institute of Texan Cultures at San Antonio also has holdings including the *San Antonio Light*.
15. Jake Ivey, personal communication, letters to the author, c. March 20 and April 8, 2002; and manuscript in preparation, 2002.

4.3.1.   Gov. Henry Smith, public appeal, February 27, 1836.

Barker, Eugene, ed. 1929. *Readings in Texas History.* 263. Dallas: Southwest Press.

II. GOVERNOR SMITH'S APPEAL FOR REINFORCEMENTS

[In reply to Travis's note of the twenty-third to Andrew Ponton, thirty-two men marched from Gonzales to support him and, passing through the enemy's lines, entered the Alamo on the night of March 1. Ponton sent the letter to San Felipe, and on February 27, Governor Smith published in handbill form an appeal to the people of Texas for reinforcements.]

Fellow Citizens and Countrymen: The foregoing official communication from Col. Travis, now in command at Bexar, needs no comment. The garrison, composed of only 150 Americans, engaged in a deadly conflict with 1,000 of the mercenary troops of the Dictator, who are daily receiving reinforcements, should be a sufficient call upon you without saying more. However secure, however fortunate, our garrison may be, they have not the provisions nor the ammunition to stand more than a thirty days' siege at farthest.

I call upon you as an officer, I implore you as a man, to fly to the aid of your besieged countrymen and not permit them to be massacred by a mercenary foe. I slight none! The call is upon ALL who are able to bear arms, to rally without one moment's delay, or in fifteen days the heart of Texas will be the seat of war. This is not imaginary. The enemy from 6,000 to 8,000 strong are on our border and rapidly moving by forced marches for the colonies. The campaign has commenced. We must promptly meet the enemy or all will be lost. Do you possess honor? Suffer it not to be insulted or tarnished! Do you possess patriotism? Evince it by your bold, prompt and manly action! If you possess even humanity you will rally without a moment's delay to the aid of your besieged countrymen!

[*Barker adds: "But no response could be made to this appeal in time to save the garrison."*]

4.3.2.   Philip Dimitt, letter, February 28, 1836.

Brown, John Henry. 1892. *History of Texas from 1685 to 1892.* 1:568. St. Louis: I. E. Daniell.

This is in Jenkins 1973, 4:453, which gives the source as the Army Papers, TSLA, but the original was not found. The text is essentially identical to this one, including the parenthetical remark.

. . . From Dimmitt's [*sic*] Point, at the mouth of the Lavaca, on the night of February 28th, Captain Philip Dimmitt wrote to Major James Kerr and a committee on the Lavaca saying:

'I have this moment, 8 p.m., arrived from Bexar. On the 23d, I was requested by Colonel Travis to take Lieutenant Nobles and reconnoitre the enemy. Some distance out I met a Mexican who informed me that the town had been invested. After a short time a messenger overtook me, saying he had been sent by a friend of my wife (Mrs. Dimmitt was a Mexican lady) to let me know that it would be impossible for me to return, as two large bodies of Mexican troops were already around the town. I then proceeded to the Rovia and remained till 10 p.m., on the 25th. On the 24th there was heavy cannonading, particularly at the close of the evening. I left the Rovia at 10 p.m., on the 25th, and heard no more firing, from which I concluded the Alamo had been taken by storm. On the night of the 24th, I was informed that there were from four to six thousand Mexicans in and around Bexar. Urrea was at Carisota, on the Matamoros road, marching for Goliad. If immediate steps are not taken to defend Guadalupe Victoria, the Mexicans will soon be upon our families.'

4.3.3.   Col. James Fannin, letter, February 29, 1836.

Foote, Henry Stuart. 1841. *Texas and the Texans.* 2:225–26. Philadelphia: Thomas, Cowperthwait & Co.

Why Colonel Fannin did not march to Bexar as contemplated, is thus satisfactorily explained, in an official letter to the government, under date of the 29th of February, in which he says: "I have to report, that yesterday, after making all the preparations *possible*, we took up our line of march (about three hundred strong, and four pieces of Artillery,) towards Bexar, to the relief of those brave men now shut up in the Alamo, and to raise the siege, leaving Captain Westover in command of this post. Within two hundred yards of town, one of the wagons broke down, and it was necessary to *double teams* in order to draw the Artillery across the river, each piece having but one yoke of oxen—not a particle of breadstuff, with the exception of half a tierce of rice, with us—no *beef*, with the exception of a small portion which had been dried—and, not a *head* of cattle, except those used to draw the Artillery, the ammunition, &c.; and it was impossible to obtain any until we should arrive at Seguin's Rancho, seventy miles from this place. After crossing the river, the troops encamped. * * * This morning whilst here I received a note from the officer commanding the volunteers, requesting, in the name of the officers of his command, a Council of War, on the subject of the expedition to Bexar, which, of course, was granted. The Council of War consisted of all the Commissioned officers of the command and it was by them unanimously determined that, inasmuch as a proper supply of provisions and means of transportation could not be had; and, as it was *impossible*, with our present means, to carry the artillery with us; and as by leaving Fort Defiance without a proper garrison, it might fall into the hands of the enemy, with the provisions, &c., now at Matagorda, Demit's [*sic*] Landing and Coxe's Point, and on the way to meet us; and, as by report of our spies (sent out by Colonel Bowers, &c.,) we may expect an attack upon this place, it was expedient to return to this post and complete the fortifications, &c., &c. * * * * * I sent an express to Gonzales to apprise the committee there of our return."

4.3.4.1. Robert McAlpin Williamson, letter, March 1, 1836.

El Nacional, Suplemento al Numero 79, translated by John Wheat. 1836. Mexico.
The existence of Alamo documents, including this Williamson letter, in *El Nacional* was first discussed by Streeter (1955–60, #1647). The letter was first published in 1961, without noting the source, in the Curtis book cited in document 4.3.4.2. *El Nacional* gives this as if it were a postscript to Santa Anna's victory letter of March 6 (2.1.1.10) but the original of that letter in the Archivo Historico Militar, Expediente 1899:8–9, does not include it. This is the only correspondence known of any that might have been received at the Alamo during the siege.

The attached documents were found in the bag of the commander of the Alamo fortress, and I send it to Your Excellency so that you might also bring it to the attention of the Most Excellent Señor interim president and make whatever use of them that is seen fit.—*Antonio López de Santa-Anna.*—Most Excellent Secretary of War and Marine, General Don José Maria Tornel/
   This is a copy. Mégico, March 21, 1836.—*Juan L. Valázquez de León.*

Translation of a letter from R.M. Williamson to the leader Barrel [sic] Travis. González.—March 1, 1836.—Sr. Colonel Travis. You cannot know my anxiety, sir. Today makes four full days that we have not received the slightest report regarding your dangerous situation, and therefore we have indulged in a thousand conjectures about it. Sixty men have set out from this municipality and in all human probability they are with you at this date. Colonel Fannin, with three hundred men and four pieces of artillery, has been on the march toward Béjar for three days. Tonight we expect some three hundred reinforcements from Washington, Bastroj [sic], Brazoria, and San Felipe, and no time will be wasted in seeking their help for you. With regards to *the other letter of the same date, let it pass;* today you will know what it means. If the multitude gets hold of it, let them figure it out.—I am your true friend.—R.M. Williamson.—PS.—For God's sake, hold out until we can help you.—I am sending to you with Major Bonham a message from the interior government.—A thousand greetings to all of your people, and tell them to hold firm "for Willis" until I get there.—*Williamson.*—Write us as soon as you can.
   This is a copy. Mégico, March 21, 1836.—*Juan L. Valázquez de León*

4.3.4.2.   Curtis, narrative, 1961.

Curtis, Albert. 1961. *Remember the Alamo*. 42–45. San Antonio: Clegg Co.

Curtis makes clear the significance of the Williamson letter (4.3.4.1) in motivating Travis to hold out. The documentation of the Bexar elections for the Convention representatives is also interesting background and indicates some of the factions among the defenders, so it is presented here as well.

On the very day that Santa Anna began his march for San Antonio, another meeting took place in the large central Alamo courtyard—today's Alamo Plaza—whose purpose was to elect civilian members to the Convention which was to meet at Washington, Texas, on March 1st, 1836, and vote on the question of Texas Independence from Mexico. This document reads as follows: "En la Asamblea de Valero, primero de Febrero, 1836, en el cuartel del Alamo" Antonio Navarro received 65 votes, Erasmo Seguin 60 votes, Francisco Ruiz 61 votes and Gaspar Flores 59 votes. These four San Antonio celebrities were to be sent to the Convention, but later, due to complaints raised by the San Antonio military, only Antonio Navarro and Francisco Ruiz were sent, and Esrasmo [*sic*] Seguin and Gaspar Flores were replaced by the two elected by the military, that is, by Samuel A. Maverick and Jesse B. Badgett, since only four members were apportioned for San Antonio.

The referenced document also mentioned those who "also ran". These included Antonio de Leon, 1 vote; Antonio de la Graza, 1 vote; Jimerson (Jameson?), 1 vote; Luciano Navarro, 2 votes; Miguel Arciniega, 6 votes; Maverick, 2 votes; Pollard, 2 votes; Ramon Musquiz, 1 vote; J. B. Bonham, 1 vote; J. B. Badgett, 3 votes; Jose Maria Salinas, 8 votes; Jose Maria Flores, 1 vote and Juan Angel Seguin, 1 vote.

This historic document was signed with characteristic flourishes called rubrics or paraphs, beneath each signature. Among the San Antonio celebrities who signed this document were Juan Nepomuceno Seguin as Presiding Judge, and eight others whose signatures included Jose Antonio Navarro and Francisco Ruiz who later signed the Texas Declaration of Independence, voted on March 2nd, 1836, and concerning which all Texas historians note that the Alamo heroes had no official knowledge. But certainly the Alamo Defenders had a very good idea that Independence would be declared, and that knowledge, in addition to the several letters brought into the Alamo by Alamo courier James Butler Bonham on March 3rd, 1836, particularly the desperate, tenderly-written plea of the Major of the Ranging Company, Robert McAlpin Williamson, the "Patrick Henry of the Texian Revolution", begging Travis to hold out at the Alamo until reinforcements could reach him, must have convinced Travis and his gallant Alamo defenders to make their supreme sacrifice on March 6th, 1836, the day the Alamo fell.

On the following day, that is February 2nd, 1836, a separate election return for "Béxar", that is San Antonio de Béxar, was announced. The contestants were announced by name and count who "received votes in the assemblies of this municipality, celebrated on the first day of the present month with the aim of naming four delegates invested with ample, full power and without restrictions as to the form of government to be adopted, with the exception that no Constitution which they (the delegates at Washington, Texas, meeting on March 1st, 1836) form will have effect until it is presented (evidently for ratification) to the people and confirmed by a majority of them in the manner prescribed by the same instrument, according to what is provided by the superior order of the 10th of December of the preceding year (1835) issued by the council and the Provisional Government of Texas".

The results of the election held in "Béxar" reads as follows: Antonio Navarro, 46 votes; J. B. Bonham, 1 (actually the count read 9 votes); J. B. Badgett, 3; Francisco Ruiz, 43; Gaspar Flores, 43; Ignacio Herrera, 2; Jose Maria Flores, 1; Jose Maria Salinas, 1; Tamion (name not clear), 1; Luciano Navarro, 2; Miguel Arciniega, 6; (Samuel A.) Maverick, 2 (actually the count was 11); Dr. Pollard, 2 (actually his count was 12).

On this occasion, of the result for "Béxar" (the list of names for those voting in the Assembly of the Alamo fortress is not available), those voting included the later Alamo heroes and Alamo couriers William R. Carey, William Blazeby, James B. Bonham, M. Hawkins, William Linn, B. F. Musselman (Robert?), Joseph Magee and a signature which might be Isaac Ryan (and the Alamo couriers) John W. Smith, (Horace) Alexander Alsbury, Lancelot Smither and a name which might be the San Antonio merchant who employed later Alamo hero John M. Thurston, and the Alamo hero a negro slave John, that is Francis Desangue.

Now for a moment of glory, recall the Alamo heroes, all of them, in their beleaguered fortress, when they received that "lost letter" of the Alamo period, sent to Travis and his gallant heroes on March 1st, 1836, from Gonzales, Texas, written by Major of the Ranging Service, Robert McAlpin Williamson, the "Patrick Henry of the Texas Revolution", and delivered on March 3rd, 1836 by Alamo courier James Butler Bonham. And as you read, do you not agree that this important letter and other documents he carried, reveals Bonham's determination to return to the Alamo and deliberately, with all of the other Alamo heroes, make his supreme sacrifice in the Alamo, the "Texas Hall of Martyrdom", on March 6th, 1836, the day the Alamo fell?

Look, can you not see the tears of Travis and his men rolling down their rugged cheeks, when this precious Williamson letter was read in the council of war in the Alamo, on March 3rd, 1836, "one of the most pathetic days of time", as Sidney Lanier described this day of tragedy bolstered even then by hope of reinforcements?

Then read this tenderly-written "lost letter of the Texian revolution": it is an heirloom of the thirteen days of glory in the Alamo. It reads as follows:

[*A translation of the above document 4.3.4.1 is given.*]

Now you know why Travis and his gallant defenders remained at their posts in the Alamo? They expected reinforcements! Reinforcements which did not come, but the desperate hope for aid must have sustained Travis and his heroic Alamo Defenders! And so the gallant garrison of the Alamo remained.

4.3.5.1.   John Sower Brooks, letter, March 2, 1836.

Barker, Eugene, ed. 1929. *Readings in Texas History.* 263–64. Dallas: Southwest Press.

III. WHY FANNIN FAILED TO REINFORCE TRAVIS

[At the same time that Travis wrote to Ponton he sent a messenger to Fannin at Goliad, asking for assistance. Fannin had some four hundred and twenty men there, and on February 26 he started with most of them for San Antonio, but shortly afterward changed his mind and returned to the fort at Goliad, which he began to strengthen. The account of his movements and the reasons therefore are given in a letter written by his aid, John Sowers Brooks on March 2].

We marched at the time appointed, with . . . nearly the whole force at Goliad, leaving only one Company of Regulars to guard the Fort. Our baggage wagons and artillery were all drawn by oxen (no broken horses could be obtained) and there were but a few yokes of them. In attempting to cross the San Antonio River, three of our wagons broke down and it was with the utmost labor and personal hazard, that our four pieces of cannon were conveyed safely across. We remained there during the day, with our ammunition wagon on the opposite side of the River. During the night, some of the oxen strayed off and could not be found the next morning. Our situation became delicate and embarrassing in the extreme. If we proceeded we must incur the risk of starvation, and leave our luggage and artillery heind [*sic; behind*]. The country between us and Bexar is entirely unsettled, and there would be but little hope of obtaining provisions on the route and we would be able only to carry 12 rounds of cartridges each. Every one felt an anxiety to relieve our friends, who we had been informed, had retired to the Alamo, a fortress in Bexar, resolved to hold out, until our arrival. Yet every one saw the impropriety, if not the impossibility of our proceeding under existing circumstances and it was equally apparent to all that our evacuation of Goliad, would leave the whole frontier from Bexar to the coast open to the incursions of the enemy, who were then concentrating at Laredo and the provisions, clothing, military stores, et cetera, at Dimmitt's Landing and Matagorda, perhaps all that were in Texas, would eventually be lost. Intelligence also reached us that the advance of Santa Anna's lower division had surprised San Patricio about 50 miles in front of our position and put the whole garrison under the command of Col. Johnson to the sword. Five of them have reached this place. Col. Johnson is one of them, and they are probably all that have escaped. Capt. Pearson of the volunteers, was killed with several others, after they had surrendered. The war is to be one of extermination. Each party seems to understand that no quarters are to be given or asked. We held a Council of War in the bushes on the bank of the River; and after a calm review of all these circumstances, it was concluded to return to Goliad, and place the Fort in a defensible condition.

4.3.5.2.   John S. Brooks, letter, March 9, 1836.

Roller, Gen. John E., ed. January 1906. Capt. John Sowers Brooks. *Texas Historical Association Quarterly* 9:190–92.

This is an excerpt from a letter by one of Fannin's captains giving news heard in Goliad about the Alamo. The full letter is naturally of great interest for the events at Goliad in Fannin's command.

Letter to Mr. James Hagarty, New York, U.S.
Fort Defiance, Goliad Texas, March 9, 1836.

My dear friend:—

[*Brooks summarizes in a couple of paragraphs the movements of Fannin's men and the Texas situation in general before coming to more current news.*] In the mean time, the scout who had been sent ahead, returned with information, that Santa Ana had already commenced the concentration of his army on our frontiers. They were rendezvousing at Matamoras, Monclova, Saltillo, Monterey, and Laredo, to the number of from 6 to 10000 men, and designed attacking Bexar and Goliad simultaneously, with two divisions of his army, and marching the third between those points to San Felipe, where he intended fortifying. We immediately apprised Government of these facts, and fell back to Goliad with our small force of 450 men, and commenced repairing the Fort. Bexar was garrisoned by 150 or 200 men; and with this handful of 6 or 700 Volunteers, we are left by the generous Texians, to roll back the tide of invasion from their soil.

On the 23rd ult. the Mexican advance, reached Bexar, and attacked the subsequent morning with 1800 men. The gallant little garrison retired to the Alamo, a fortress in the suburbs, resolved to hold out to the last. The Mexicans made several assaults, and were repulsed with loss at every instance. On the receipt of the intelligence at Goliad, we promptly marched with 320 men and four pieces of artillery, to their aid. In marching a few miles, our oxen became weary, and we were compelled to halt or leave our baggage and artillery. While consulting on what course to pursue, we received news of the successive defeats of the parties of Cols. Johnson and Grant, in Tamaulipas, and of the approach of the lower division of Santa Ana's army on our position at Goliad. A Council of War was held in the bushes, and it was determined to return to the post we had vacated in the morning, as its abandonment would leave the road open to the settlements, and completely uncover our depot of provisions, the only one now in Texas, and consequently the main stay of the Army.

The Mexicans, to the number of 700, are now in San Patricio, about 60 miles in front of our position; and another party of 200 have been discovered within 18 miles of us, between us and Gonzales. Every thing indicates that an attack will be speedily made upon us. Their scouts, well mounted, frequently push up to our walls, and, from the want of horses, we are unable to punish them.

We have again heard from Bexar, Santa Ana has arrived there himself, with 3000 men, making his whole force 4800. He has erected a battery within 400 yards of the Alamo, and every shot goes through it, as the walls are weak. It is feared that Bexar will be taken and that the devoted courage of the brave defenders will be of no avail.

[*Brooks concludes the letter with the "critical situation" in Goliad.*]

4.3.5.3.   John S. Brooks letter, March 10, 1836.

Roller, Gen. John E., ed. January 1906. Capt. John Sowers Brooks. *Texas Historical Association Quarterly* 9:193–94.

This is an excerpt from another letter from Brooks to his father, A. H. Brooks.

Fort Defiance, Goliad, Texas,
March 10, 1836.

My dear Father:—

[*After a couple introductory paragraphs, including the defeat of Grant and Johnson, Brooks continues.*] Scarcely had the intelligence of these disasters to our advance in Tamaulipas reached us, when we were informed by express, that the Mexicans had entered Bexar with an effective force of 1800 men. The garrison there consisted of 156 Americans, who retreated, on the approach of the enemy to the Alamo, a Spanish fortress in the neighborhood, which was immediately invested, and has been vigorously besieged up to the date of our latest intelligence.

Immediately on receipt of the news, we promptly took up the line of march, in order to relieve them. After proceeding three miles, several of our baggage wagons broke down; and it was found impossible, to get the ammunition carts or artillery over the river San Antonio. We accordingly halted. During the night our oxen strayed off. In the morning a Council of War was convened. While it was in session, a courier apprised us, that 650 of the enemy, the same, probably, who had defeated Grant and Johnson, had reached San Patricio on the Neuces [*sic*] and would attack our depot of provisions on the La Baca, and at

Matagorda. With these facts before us, it was concluded to return to Goliad, and maintain that place, which was done.

Thirty two men have cut their way into the Alamo, with some provisions. The enemy have erected a battery of nine pounders within 400 yards of the Fort, and every shot goes through the walls. A large party of the enemy are between this and Bexar, with a design of cutting off reinforcements. Another division of 3000 Mexicans have arrived at Bexar, making their whole force now there 4800 men. The little garrison still holds out against this formidable force. It is said that Santa Ana is himself with the army before the Alamo.

[*Brooks continues with the expectations of the force at Goliad.*]

4.3.6.   Burr H. Duval, letter, March 9, 1836.

Corner, William, ed. July 1897. John Crittenden Duval: The last survivor of the Goliad massacre. *Texas Historical Association Quarterly* 1:48–49.

[The following is a copy of a letter written by Burr H. Duval to his father, William P. Duval, Governor of Florida, dated March 9th, 1836, eighteen days prior to his death at the Goliad massacre, March 27, 1836. This copy is verbatim et literatim. The original is written on cream-laid quarto letter-fly. The edges of the sheet indicate that the paper is hand-made. The hand-writing is good, firm, and neat. The last page contains no part of the body of the letter, but was left blank, as was the early fashion, to form the envelope by folding and to receive the address, post-marks, etc. A copy of the latter is here made at the end of this copy of the letter.]

Goliad, March 9th, 1836.

Dear Father,

It has been some time since I have had an opty. of writing to you, A gentleman leaves here to day for the U. States but have my doubts if he gets fifty miles from this post as we are surrounded by Mexican troops— By last express, yesterday, from San Antonio we learned that their [our[1]] little band of 200 still maintained their situation in the Alamo, the fort outside of the town— They have been fighting desperately there for 10 or 15 days against four or five thousand Mexicans. Santa Anna is there himself and has there and in this vicinity at least six thousand troops— Contrary to the expectation of every one he has invaded the Country when least expected— Not a Texian was in the field, nor has even *one* yet made his appearance at this post— The greater portion of the Mexican troops are *mounted,* and of course have greatly the advantage over us— We now muster at this post 400 strong, and from the preparations we have made shall be enabled to give *any* number a desperate fight— San Antonio I fear has fallen before this;—from its situation and construction, I cannot believe it possible so small a band could maintain it against such fearful odds— D. Crockett is one of the number in the fort— We are expecting an attack hourly. An express yesterday was chased in by 200 cavalry eighteen miles from this— Sixty miles south of this is another party of 650 who have been quartered at San Patricio for some days, waiting reinforcements. Several of our parties of 20 and 30 have been cut off by them—As I anticipated, much dissention prevails among the Volunteers, Col. Fannin, now in command (Gen'l Houston being absent), is unpopular— and nothing but the certainty of hard fighting, and *that shortly*, could have kept us together so long— [*Duval continues with his situation in the army and activities at Goliad and Washington.*]

---

¹ "Our" is written over "their."

4.3.7.   George M. Dolson, letter, July 19, 1836.

Democratic Free Press. September 7, 1836. Detroit.

Thomas Connelly in 1960 did a very careful transcription and analysis of the stories that had Crockett surrendering. He considered it likely that this letter was the basis for many such stories. The original article is extensively footnoted for more detailed research. He modified a few words such as Galveston, Camp Travis for "Trevos," and Jeremiah for "Jervis" Brown. A few words and one sentence were unreadable in my copy from the *Free Press* and therefore are quoted from Connelly; these have been italicized and put in brackets. The letter was partially reprinted in the October 15, 1836, *Springfield (Massachusetts) Republican and Journal.*

Extract from a letter written by Mr. George M. Dolson, an officer in the Texian Army, to his brother in this city; dated

                Glaveston [*sic*] Island, Camp Trevos July 19, 1836.

"In my last letter, dated in May, I gave you some account of the battle of San Jacinto, which took place on the 21st of April, since which time few things of importance transpired here; few as they are, however, they are worth relating, and I will therefore endeavour to sketch the principal movements.

"It appears, from what I can learn, that there was a stipulation or treaty made between the Cabinet, or General Houston, and Santa Anna, by which the latter was to be set at liberty; and for that purpose he was embarked on board the Texian war schooner Invincible, Capt. Jervis Brown, then lying at the port of Velasco, now the seat of government of our new republic, with the intention of taking him to Vera Cruz, where the treaty was to be ratified. But previous to the tyrant's leaving our shores, which he so much stained with the blood of unarmed prisoners of war, the news reached the army like an electric shock. The whole, with one voice as it were, said 'bring him ashore, in irons, and inform the Cabinet that we respect them; but that should it become necessary, the same rifles that poured such a deadly fire on the enemy, are in readiness to treat a domestic foe in the same manner.' The prisoner was accordingly remanded to shore, when, I am told by the officers of the schooner, he swallowed a large quantity of opium for drowning his feelings of remorse, cried like a child, and acted in every manner as though his last ray of hope had deserted him. Conduct ill-becoming as great a man as he is represented to be; but a true index of what he really is—a cold-blooded murderer, and worthy only of the sympathy of cowards and the scorn of great men. His conduct on the following occasion justifies me in branding him with the opprobious epithet of murderer.

"I am employed a considerable part of my time in interpreting Spanish for Colonel James Morgan, commander of this station. He sent for me yesterday and told me there was a communication of importance from one of Santa Anna's officers, which he wished to interpret; accordingly the officer of the day was dispatched for the Mexican officer, who came in in [*sic*] a few minutes, and the Colonel's quarters were vacated of all, save us three. The Mexican was then requested to proceed with his statement according to promise; and he said he could give a true and correct account of the proceedings of Santa Anna towards the prisoners who remained alive at the taking of the Alamo. This shows the fate of Colonel Crocket and his five brave companions—there have been many tales told, and many suggestions made, as to the fate of these patriotic men; but the following may be relied on, being from an individual who was an eye witness to the whole proceedings. The Colonel has taken the whole in writing, with the officer's name attached to it, which he observed to him, if he had the least delicacy, he might omit, but he said he had not and was willing to be qualified to it in the presence of his God, and General Santa Anna, too, if necessary. He states that on the morning the Alamo was captured, between the hours of five and six o'clock, General Castrillon, who fell at the battle of St. Jacinto, entered the back room of the Alamo, and there found Crockett and five other Americans, who had defended it until defence was useless; they appeared very much agitated when the Mexican soldiers undertook to rush in after their General, but the humane General ordered his men to keep out, and, placing his hand on one breast, said, 'here is a hand and a heart to protect you; come with me to the General-in-Chief, and you shall be saved.' Such redeeming traits, while they ennoble in our estimation this worthy officer, yet serve to show in a more hedious [*sic*] light the damning atrocities of the chief. The brave but unfortunate men were marched to the tent of Santa Anna. Colonel Crockett was in the rear, had his arms folded, and appeared bold as the lion as he passed my informant (Almonte.) Santa Anna's interpreter knew Colonel Crockett, and said to my informant, 'the one behind is the famous Crockett.' When brought in the presence of Santa Anna, Castrillon said to him, 'Santa Anna, the august, I deliver up to you six brave prisoners of war.' Santa Anna replied, 'who has given you orders to take prisoners, I do not want to see those men living—shoot them.' As the monster uttered these words each officer turned his face the other way, and the hell-hounds of the tyrant [*despatched the six in his presence, and within six feet*] of his person. Such an act I consider murder of the blackest kind.

Do you think that he can be released? No—exhaust all the mines of Mexico, but it will not release him. The one half, nor two thirds, nor even the whole of the republic, would not begin to ransom him. The combined powers of Europe cannot release him, for before they can come to his release, Texas will have released him of his existence; but I coincide with the secretary of war, as to the disposal to be made of him, that is, to try him as a felon. Strict justice demands it and reason sanctions it.

[*The letter continues with additional news and details in another six paragraphs, which are not included here as they are not related to the Alamo. Dolson notes that he is an orderly sergeant in the Texas Army.*]

Your brother,
GEORGE M. DALSON [*sic*].

4.3.8.   E. M. Pease, letter, January 8, 1837.

Hart, Katherine, and Elizabeth Kemp, eds. July 1964. E. M. Pease's account of the Texas revolution. Notes and documents. *Southwestern Historical Quarterly* 68:85–86.

... The people of Texas having been so fortunate thus far, imagined their Independence already achieved & trusted for security on the weakness and disorder of their enemy, to this apathy is to be attributed the reverses of our arms last spring which came well nigh ruining the country. All volunteers that came in were concentrated at Goliad & Bejar. During the month of January a party of about 100 under the command of Cols [James] Grant & [Francis W.] Johnson made an expedition towards the Rio Grande sometimes called Rio Bravo & sometimes Rio del Norte, meeting with no opposition they became careless & were finally about the last of Feb., suprised [sic] near San Patricio and nearly all destroyed, the few that escaped brought us the first news of the large force that was already upon us & we entirely unprepared. About 500 men at Goliad and 150 at the Alamo were all the forces we had in the field to oppose the progress of 8000. The Militia were called out, they collected but slowly at Gonzales which was the rendezvous, in the meantime one division of the enemy 3 or 4000 strong arrived at Bejar on the 23 of Feb, they summoned our garrison (consisting of 150 under command of Col. W. B. Travis) to surrender or be put to the sword. They answered the summons by the thunders of their artillery. This intelligence aroused the people to a true sense of their danger, they began to rally, 32 men from Gonzales succeeded in getting into the Alamo, not withstanding they were closely invested, this made the number in the Alamo 182. The enemy made frequent attempts to storm the place between the 23 of Feby and 6th of March, but were as frequently repulsed with great loss, our men

were occupied night and day in watching their foe and strengthening the works, the works were large, & required at the least 500 men to man them well, on the night of the 5th they had worked nearly all night upon the Walls until nearly exhausted. They retired to rest about 2 hours before day. That night the enemy had resolved to attack them. The Infantry were drawn out around the Fort, at a distance and the Cavalry out side of them with orders to shoot every man that turned back, thus driving their own forces to the attack, about an hour before day the attack was commenced. It is supposed that our sentinels worn out with fatigue had fallen asleep & were killed at their posts, on the first alarm within the fort, they were on and within the Walls in large numbers, our men were soon rallied, they cleared the yard & the Walls in a few minutes.
"They fought like brave men long & well,
They piled that ground with foes they had slain"
but overpowered by numbers, they sunk with weariness and loss of blood. You have probably read many accounts of that scene, they are all more or less fancy sketches. But one Male escaped to tell the news, he was a servant Boy belonging to Col. Travis. There was also a Mrs. [Almaron] Dickinson, wife of a Lieut. of the garrison, who however saw nothing, shut up in the Fort during the fight. The Boy says, there was one man found alive when the enemy had full possession of the place & he was shot by order of Santa Anna. Travis had said, if they took the fort it should be a defeat to them & it truly was, from the first attack to the fatal morning of the 6th they had not less than 1000 killed, the bodies of our men were burned the same day. I blame not the enemy for the fate of the Alamo, our friends *died nobly, one only survived to ask for quarter & he was refused it.* [*The letter continues with an account of the activities of Fannin, Grant, and Johnson.*]

4.3.9.   Ehrenberg, memoirs, 1843.

Ehrenberg, Herman. 1935. *With Milam and Fannin: Adventures of a German Boy in Texas' Revolution.* Translated by Charlotte Churchill. 154–55. Dallas: Tardy Publishing Co.

Ehrenberg was a German with Fannin, who gives another account complementing those of Brooks and Duval, above.

Discouraging news soon reached us concerning the Alamo. Santa Anna had invested the fortress with seven thousand men and had built around it a line of trenches which every day drew a little closer to the dilapidated walls of the ancient stronghold. There had already been several assaults which the besieged had successfully repulsed, but the defenders were so few they would not be able to hold their own much longer against the overwhelming superiority of the enemy; their defeat was only a matter of time. In the early days of the blockade a night sally could easily have opened a way of escape to the beleaguered garrison; but the volunteers were reluctant to desert the walls so brilliantly wrested from the enemy in a previous campaign.

Almost daily, messengers would risk their lives and slip through the enemy's camp to come to us. With the most earnest entreaties they would also bring us letters from Travis, their commander, from Bowie, and from Crockett. The latter two, famous pioneers from the United States, begged the volunteers at Goliad to help them save the Alamo. But couriers, letters, and supplications all failed to achieve their purpose. Fannin was immovable, for he still cherished the conviction that the volunteers could effect their retreat from the Alamo if they wished to do so. At any rate, this is the only acceptable explanation of his indifference, since it is impossible to believe that he feared to meet Santa Anna's troops when he knew that General Houston was willing to support him.

4.3.10.   Dr. Bernard, journal, 1836 and later?

Bernard, J. H. In Dudley G. Wooten, ed. 1898. *A Comprehensive History of Texas, 1685 to 1897.* Dallas: William G. Scarff. 1:630–31, 632–34.

Wooten included a transcription of the journal of Dr. John (or Joseph?) Bernard, captured with Fannin at Goliad. He and Dr. Shackelford assisted the Mexican Army medical corps, were saved from the Goliad massacre by a Colonel Guerrier, and were later sent to Béxar to help treat the wounded there. The portion of his journal covering the period at Goliad, not included here, is one of the most vivid accounts of that part of the Texas Revolution. On April 16, he states he commenced a regular journal. These excerpts are while he was in Béxar around the time of San Jacinto.

April 21.—Yesterday and to-day we have been around with the surgeons of the place to visit the wounded, and a pretty piece of work "Travis and his faithful few" have made of them. There are now about one hundred here of the wounded. The surgeon tells us that there were five hundred brought into the hospital the morning they stormed the Alamo, but I should think from appearances there must have been more. I see many around the town who were crippled,—apparently two or three hundred,—and the citizens tell me that three or four hundred have died of their wounds. We have two colonels and a major and eight captains under our charge who were wounded in the assault. We have taken one ward of the hospital amputation performed before we arrived, although there are several cases even now that should have been operated upon at the first; and how many have died for the want of an operation it is impossible to tell, though it is a fair inference there are not a few. There has been scarcely a ball cut out as yet, almost every patient carrying the lead he received that morning. In the course of the week after we came in town a party of Comanches were here. They brought in hams and things to trade to the Mexicans, who made much of them and treated them with a great deal of deference. They are large men and very muscular.

Wednesday, April 27.—This evening a family of *rancheros* coming with a cart were attacked two or three miles out (by "Tawakana Indians," as they say), but I suspect them to be the Comanches who left two or three days ago. Two or three men and women were killed, one woman dangerously wounded in the stomach, one slightly in the back, and a girl scalped severely. We have taken them in our care and dressed their wounds. I am told that Indians frequently kill people a few miles out of town. We get on very comfortably here; these people show us much respect and courtesy. We meet with much simple and unaffected kindness of heart from the citizens, particularly the females; we are also well treated by the officers. It is evident they have a high opinion of our skill, and if the surgeons I have seen among them are a fair sample of the medical talent in the nation, I can safely say, without the least spark of vanity, they have reason to think well of us. The surgeon of the garrison came for me the other day to visit his wife, who was in the greatest distress, and he did not know what to do for her. On going to the house I found she had toothache. He amputated a man's leg the day we arrived, and the man died the next day. We have as yet amputated but one, and that patient is doing well. About half a dozen more should have been operated upon, but now they will die anyhow. To-day I got a change of clothing, the first change I've had since coming here. . . .

[*In the entry for May 6, rumors circulated around town of the defeat and capture of Santa Anna. It still took some time before definite news was confirmed.*]

Sunday, 15th.—Nothing more of news. A Mexican surgeon from Nondoya arrived. His name is Hivran, and he seemed something more respectable for a surgeon than the others I have seen. Yesterday I strolled over to the Alamo with the hospital captain (Martinez). They are hard at work fortifying. Went along through some of the old gardens; many of the most beautiful flowers now in bloom. Mulberries are ripening, and the fruit on the big trees begins to appear, but everything of nature's production looks wild and neglected.

Tuesday, 17th.—Dr. Alsbury came in town to-day from General Felisola, now commander-in-chief, with a pass. He (Dr. Alsbury) is son-in-law to Angelo Navarro, with whom I live. His wife and sister, together with a negro of Bowie's, were in the Alamo when it was stormed. He has come in order to look after his family and take them off. He gave us all the particulars of the battle of San Jacinto, the capture of Santa Anna, the retreat of the Mexican army, and the number of volunteers pouring into Texas, stimulated thereto by the fate of Fannin and Travis. Now I am truly revived. Our cause is prospering and the blood of so many heroes has not been shed in vain.

Thursday, 19th.—Dr. Alsbury in his narration related Santa Anna's complimentary speech to General Houston, where he modestly compares himself to Napoleon and Houston to Wellington. There is a sprightly little Frenchman here who is armorer, and I could not forbear relating to him the anecdote. He sprang up in the greatest excitement. "What!" says he, "does Santa Anna compare himself with Napoleon because he can run about with two or three thousand ragged Indians and take a few mud towns? Does he think his greatest exploit will bear any comparison with the least thing ever done by our hero?" He stormed and raved for a considerable length of time before he could cool down, so indignant was he, and was much amused at this idea of the comparison.

Sunday, 22d.—General Andrade has received orders to destroy the Alamo and proceed to join the main army at Goliad. The troops have hitherto been extensively engaged in fortifying the Alamo. They are now as busy as bees tearing down the walls, etc. We were promised our passports a few days ago, but there being some difficulty in getting them, and finding the troops were about retreating from here, we have by means of our friends, Don José Lambardas and Don Ramon Musquiz, induced the commandant to leave us here when he goes out, ostensibly in charge of the sick he is obliged to leave behind. Yesterday Dr. Alsbury took his family out to Calaveras Rancho, on the Goliad Road. Took a horse and some other things of ours to be in readiness for us. The citizens have been packing up and leaving for the past three or four days,—I mean those that are hostile to Texas. Our friends, who are by no means few, are waiting with impatience for the Texan troops to come and take possession. I heard to-day that a party of Texans had been seen about ten leagues off on the Cibolo coming in.

Monday, May 23.—Last evening Colonel Ugartachea came up from Goliad. He appeared pleased to see us and that we had been treated well here; gave us news of our fellow-prisoners; told us that some had run away, some gone to Matamoras, and some had been released.

Tuesday, May 24, 12 M.—The Mexican troops are now leaving town. The last column is this moment crossing the river. Our friends (for some of them have contrived within the month we have been here to wind themselves strongly into our affections) have bidden us *adios,* and a momentary pang was felt at their departure; yet a strong feeling of pleasure pervades the mind, a sense of hilarity, of regaining freedom, of triumph for the success of the cause we had suffered in, for the success of our friends who bring us release from captivity. Here the foes of liberty came and dealt death and destruction to all around. Here they exulted in the carnage and gloried in the conquest of a handful of brave men who, overpowered by numbers, fell as did those heroes of old at Thermopylae. Shades of Crockett, Travis, and Bowie, and your band of noble martyrs for the cause of liberty in Texas, look down upon your enemies, discomfited and routed, retreating ignominiously from the country they had entered with such bravado! So may freedom ever prosper! So may her opponents ever find that defeat and disgrace await them!

Six o'clock P.M.—As the troops left town this morning, a large fire streamed up from the Alamo, and, as soon as they had fairly left, Dr. Shackelford and myself, accompanied by Señor Reriz and some other of the citizens, walked over to see the state in which they left it. We found the fire proceeding from a church, where a platform had been built extending from the great door to the top of the wall on the back side for the purpose of taking up the artillery to the top of the church. This was made of wood, and was too far consumed for any attempt to be made to extinguish it. The walls of the church being built of solid masonry, of course would be but little injured by the fire. The Alamo was completely dismantled, all the single walls were leveled, the fosse filled up, and the pickets torn up and burnt. All the artillery and ammunition that could not be carried off were thrown in the river.

Wednesday, May 25.—We had a heavy shower this morning, attended with much thunder and lighting, which had the very pleasing effect of purifying the atmosphere. Quiet and still to-day. The remaining citizens seem to be relieved at the departure of the troops, with which they have been oppressed for three months. Some of them broke out into transports of joy that made them act quite ludicrously. The grave and dignified person of mine host, Navarro, who is at least forty-five years old and far gone with hydrothorax, was seen capering about the streets like a boy, in a perfect ecstasy of glee. He said that now he should recover his health; that nothing but the impure air occasioned by the residence of the Mexican troops made him sick. Alas! his confidence availed him nothing; he died about two weeks after the troops left. There were three brothers of the Navarros who had families residing in San Antonio. They all treated me with the greatest kindness and affection. The one at whose house I made my home was Angelo. Antonio was a member of the convention which made the declaration of independence, and was with the Texans. The other brother kept himself concealed in the interior. They were all friendly to the Texas cause, and their families were not molested by the Mexican troops; probably money had some agency in securing them good treatment. After sauntering about the Alamo and calling to mind the startling and interesting scenes that have at different times been acted on this little theatre, and the last unparalleled in modern history, which must forever mark this spot as the Thermopylae of Texas; after looking at the spot where it is said that Travis fell and Crockett closed his mortal career, we went to visit the ashes of those brave defenders of our country, a hundred rods from the fort or church to where they were burnt. The bodies had been reduced to cinders; occasionally a bone of a leg or arm was seen almost entire. Peace to your ashes! Your fame is immortal! The memory of your deeds will remain bright and unsullied in the hearts of your countrymen!

Thursday, 26th.—We got ready, took leave of our friends, and about nine o'clock left Bexar.

Commentary

Other Near-Contemporary Sources (4.3)

The collection of near-contemporary sources adds to the context of the battle, and perhaps even some secondhand details to the actual events of the siege and fall. Certainly they give an immediacy to the events around the Alamo.

The appeal of Governor Smith (4.3.1) is of value in seeing how Travis's news of the arrival of Santa Anna's army was announced, and how the government echoed Travis in appealing to courage and patriotism.

The letter of Philip Dimitt (4.3.2) records another action of Travis on February 23 and raises the question of how Travis must have wondered what had happened to his reconnaissance people.[1]

Fannin (4.3.3) was certainly ready with excuses as to why he did not go to Béxar as requested by Travis. Here is a case of a military commander using a council of war as one excuse for taking no action. One must wonder how he had enough supplies for his men in Fort Defiance (the protection of which is cited by Brooks, 4.3.5.2, as a reason not to leave the post), but not enough to travel to Béxar. The documents presented allow a comparison of attitudes on the difficulties of a military campaign: Fannin made excuses like Santa Anna (2.1.2) when events did not work out, whereas Houston's attitudes were quite different (e.g., 3.5.1, 3.5.5, and section 4.5). Houston had no fewer problems than Fannin, yet they did not stop him from pursuing the Mexican forces the next month. Clearly, decisive action was not Fannin's strong suit.

But in all fairness, one should also ask whether Fannin really could have cut his way into the Alamo. It is clear from the Mexican sources (e.g., Almonte, 2.2.1 for February 28, Filisola 2.6.1) that they anticipated a reinforcement, had some intelligence capabilities (at least better than those of the Texans), and would have been prepared. Thus a breakthrough into the Alamo would seem unlikely. In end, perhaps Fannin made the appropriate tactical decision for all the wrong reasons. Might Houston in the same situation have tried something indirect, such as trying to cut Santa Anna's supply lines?[2]

The Williamson letter of March 1 (4.3.4.1, 4.3.4.2) is the one representative of the messages that went the other way—into the Alamo rather than out. Williamson was the commandant of the rangers and a close personal acquaintance of Travis.[3] The letter also lends a little support to the Rose narrative (1.8.1.1) of Travis's last speech, when Travis stated he was misled by promises of help. Santa Anna saved this letter to demonstrate the extent of "treason" and "foreign," meaning U.S., intervention in Texas.

Among the more noteworthy omissions in this work is the absence of any official correspondence responding to Travis. Did Governor Smith or General Houston send any letters to Travis in reply to his appeals? If so, why wouldn't Santa Anna have recorded them as well? One is left only to speculate, as in Curtis, as to any additional encouragement given to Travis and his men.

Lindley pointed out the usefulness of the Williamson letter in establishing the movements of Bonham (section 5.1.8) and other possible couriers.[4] The Williamson letter implies that, as of the first of March, Juan Seguín was the last messenger from Travis to have reached Gonzales.

The papers of Albert Curtis in the DRT deserve more attention. Despite his very limited publications—for the Alamo, only two pamplets published in the early 1960s— he is probably second only to Amelia Williams in the sheer amount of brute labor he expended in researching Alamo documents. Like hers, his papers include hundreds, possibly thousands, of notebook pages of hand-copied transcripts and notes of original material. The papers include a couple boxes of more than a hundred small notebooks filled with detailed notes. It is easy to predict that there is much information to be mined from his research.

Curtis was one of the first to explore in depth the Republic Claims files, long before they were indexed by name to make discoveries far easier. An interesting example is two claims, dated January 18 and c. February 18, for J. H. Nash that were signed by Jim Bowie. Examination of the microfilm records shows that the auditors' certificates for the two claims are still in the files, but the original signed claims are not.[5] Curtis recorded a significant point: that the February Bowie note was not signed by Travis, per agreement (1.1.1.10) of the two commanders.

We are lucky to get an inside look at Fannin's situation from John Sower Brooks (4.3.5.1–4.3.5.3), who died a few weeks later in the Goliad massacre. His letters of March 2 and 10 confirm wagon breakdowns as a key reason the advance stopped, with the additional reason that that night, "some of the oxen strayed off and could not be found." Curiously, his March 9 letter to a friend gives an even weaker excuse: "Our oxen became weary." An important issue raised in these letters is the source of some of the news from Béxar. In the March 9 letter, Brooks knew that Santa Anna himself was in Béxar—something Travis never knew for sure (1.1.5). This suggests that the Texans in Goliad were getting some intelligence from the townspeople of San Antonio. Even more interesting is the comment on March 10 about the thirty-two men from Gonzales getting in. As they arrived in the Alamo on March 1, only John Smith, leaving March 3, and James Allen, leaving March 5, are likely candidates. As Smith left for Washington-on-the-Brazos, arriving March 6 (see 1.7.3.1), he does not seem to have been the source. Thus this independent detail lends strong support to the James Allen story (1.7.4.2) of his going to Goliad as the final messenger from the Alamo.[6]

The letter from Burr Duval (4.3.6) of March 9 likewise independently supports the James Allen mission to Fannin by saying they received an express the prior day. He also had a little different tone than Fannin, being ready and willing to accept a desperate, hard fight.

The George Dolson letter (4.3.7) complements the earlier newspaper article (4.1.7) that identifies Crockett as one of the executed survivors of the fall. An important motivation for this identification, quite apparent in this document, is the desire of one group of Texans to execute Santa Anna. This story clearly supports a "Death to Santa Anna" movement in the Texan Army, discussed in more detail in the Special Commentary on deaths. Kilgore cautioned that this translation could be inaccurate in that Almonte might be referred to as Santa Anna's interpreter in the following sentence, rather than the writer's informant as implied.[7]

The letter of E. M. Pease (4.3.8) is one of the more thoughtful and detailed of the near-contemporary letters. Certainly most of the information is from Joe, and unlike the published documents (see Commentary for 4.1.1), his letters are quite clear that Susanna Dickinson saw nothing of the fighting. There is a suggestion as well of other sources from the Mexican side in the details concerning the preparation for the attack. This letter seems the opposite of the general rule that the farther away from events in time or space, the more wild the stories that creep into a narrative.

The memoirs of Herman Ehrenberg (4.3.9) also note the stream of messengers coming from the Alamo and, curiously, letters from Bowie and Crockett as well as Travis.

The last document in this section is the vivid journal of Dr. J. H. Bernard (4.3.10). There are several items to note in this account. The first is that his estimate of casualties is an important alternative to the very suspect Mexican counts or the uncertain vicinity sources (sections 3.1–3.5). However, one should be cautioned by the terminology he includes on the Alamo: the "Thermopylae of Texas." This and other phrases suggest that Bernard added to his journal from later published works, so not everything stated is necessarily an independent observation. Nonetheless, he was in a unique position as a medical doctor in Bejar, and his assessment deserves serious consideration.

A number of other items in Bernard's journal touch on issues raised in other documents. His comments on the medical care in the Mexican Army reflect the criticisms of de la Peña (2.9.1) and others. The attack by Indians just outside Béxar is a generally unappreciated aspect of the Texas Revolution, illustrating just how close to the frontier one of the major towns of Texas still was at this time. This adds support to the usefulness of Houston's negotiation of a peace treaty with the Comanche back in February (see 4.4.2, 4.5.8). Bernard's journal also confirms the presence of Juana Alsbury and her sister (section 1.4) in the Alamo during the siege, and adds to the story of the Tejanos in Béxar and their attitudes toward both the occupation by the Mexican Army and the Texas Revolution (see Commentary for 1.7.2). Finally, the closing entries provide the first postbattle description of the Alamo at the time the Mexican Army finished its partial demolition and abandonment.

A general issue needs to be raised concerning the selection of documents. A dramatic story like the Alamo spreads quickly and in ever-expanding circles, and I have attempted to identify and include those documents that might contain original information. However, I have not included *every* letter and document, since many simply repeat earlier sources or add rumors. But such a selection is necessarily a judgment call by an editor, and such judgment might be incorrect. It is a universal concern in the study of history that the selection of sources might be incomplete or biased.

Serious students of the Alamo should study compilations such as John Jenkins's *Papers of the Texas Revolution* for those other documents to make their own judgments.[8] The journal of Ammon Underwood, not in Jenkins, is another vicinity source that discusses casualties and notes the arrival in Gonzales of Mrs. "Dickerson" with Joe and Ben (though not by name). The Swisher Memoirs describe the scene in Gonzales of the "mad agony of the widows and the shrieks of the childless and fatherless." Robert Hunter was also in the vicinity when the news arrived.[9]

A letter from E. Thomas, dated March 10, in Jenkins perhaps should have been included. It is an early letter from Goliad that talks about "Davy Crocket" and "James Bowy" fighting like tigers, and says that there was an early major attack on the Alamo that was repulsed. The language is very similar to that in the newspaper accounts of late March (4.1.4.1, 4.1.4.2). Had this letter been published immediately, it might have been the source for portions of those narratives; but Jenkins quoted it from a bookseller's list, implying that it was not commonly known in early Texas and therefore was not a source for other accounts. The letter does suggest that those stories originated in early March in Goliad and were repeated by Thomas and the New Orleans newspapers.

Another letter that just missed the cut is one by Fannin of March 14, which gives no new information but adds at the end an ironic—from Fannin—cry: "Travis and his Rescue!"

---

1. E.g., by Davis 1998, 723 n. 5, 725 n. 29. Chariton 1992, 117–29, studies Dimitt's movements in some detail, and makes an argument that this letter was an alibi and that Dimitt in fact deserted the Texan Army for a couple of weeks.
2. A more generalized study of documents relating to Fannin and his "follies" is in Chariton 1992, 131–45. A report, not specifically helpful for the Alamo story but of interest concerning the reaction in Goliad to Travis's letter of February 24 by J. W. Hassell on February 29, 1836, is in the Hassell Family Papers, CAH.
3. Some background on Williamson is in Barker 1906 and Williams in *SWHQ* 37:82–83.
4. Lindley 1988, 5, 8.
5. Bowie documents are referred to in Curtis 1961a, 13, and should be in the J. H. Nash Republic Claims: Audited: Reel 76: Fr 0686-0690, TSLA.
6. Also discussed by Lord 1968, 23.
7. Kilgore 1978, 36–37.
8. Examples of such cases are J. W. Hassell from Austin colony, February 29, 1836 (Jenkins 1973, 4:459–60); Moseley Baker letter from Goliad, March 8, 1836 (5:22–23); Jos. B. Tatom, March 10, 1836 (5:44); E. Thomas, March 10 (5:45); Fannin, March 11 (5:47); Fannin, March 14 (5:74–75, translated in *United States Magazine and Democratic Review,* October 1838); Goodrich, March 15 (5:80–82); C. B. Stewart, March 16 (5:93); Bowker, March 29 (5:223–25); and so on. A couple additional examples are from W. P. M. Wood, March 10 (*Richmond Enquirer,* May 6, 1836), and Calvin Henderson, March 16 (*New Yorker,* April 30, 1836).
9. Greer 1928; Swisher 1932, 31; Hunter 1936, 13–16.

4.4.1.   Frank W. Johnson, letter, 1873.

Johnson, Francis W., to H. A. McArdle. November 27, 1873. In *Companion Battle Paintings*. Vol. 1, *Dawn at the Alamo*. Scrapbook. 103. TSLA.

Johnson was an earlier commander at the Alamo, hence one of the few who actually knew something of the outfitting of the defenders.

City of Austin
Nov. 27/73.

M. Mᶜ.Ardle, Esq.

Sir:—Yours of Oct. 19th was not received until after it was [*unclear, something like "and vistised"?*], hence the delay on that account as well as not being able to furnish you the information you request as to arms and uniform of the Texan troops. At the fall of the Alamo, if any flag was used it was the Mexican as Col. Travis had not been informed of the declaration of independence, which was made on the 2nd of March, only four days previous to the fall of the Alamo.

The arms used were rifles and muskets.

I have no pictures of those who fell in battle, nor of Santa Anna, though I have and am still trying to get pictures of all who won a prominent part in our revolution. If successful and you are still in want of such, I will give you the benefit of such as I can provide.

Any information I am in possession of is at your service.

Yours Respectfully
J. W. Johnson

4.4.2.   Samuel Houston, interview, 1844.

Holly, Mary Austin. April 7, 1844. In "Notes and items . . . about the persons in the early history of Texas." Mary Austin Holly Papers, CAH.

This astonishingly frank interview of Sam Houston on April 7, 1844, appears in three versions in the Mary Austin Holly Papers. The first is in pencil on 4 3/4-by-7-inch sheets of paper and looks to be her rough handwritten notes. The others are a handwritten prose version, apparently worked up from the rough notes, and an unattributed transcript. The first part of the document below is from the rough and the second from the worked version, but they follow the transcript where the writing is weak. The rough notes have page numbers in the upper right corner; those marked 18 and 19 are in the wrong order and are reversed in this text.

Galveston
Sunday, April 7, 1844

Gen. Houston arrived to day while Church was in — a Salute fired during Services. Returning, found him & Capt. Elliot closeted on business of State — how much affairs of nations depend on individuals! The national existence of Texas, for instance.

Quite a parade at dinner hoe [*sic*], & sautern — 3 German Captains at dinner with Mr. Kleaner, Bremen Consul. proud to dine with the President. Capt Mirtas, who sat next much excited by the dignity — compared Gen Houston to the King of Prussia & Emperor of Russia — European nations different from Republican.

Gen Murphy also came from Houston. Here are three powers at work — Texas-England & U States — quíen sabe?

The President inquired the way to Col. Rhodes — I offered to conduct him — talked all the way of important events of Texan history — "always liked Gen. Austin father & foundation of the Country — had been nothing but [*respect*] for him — Wharton's, & other demagogues made the troubles that led to the premature revolution & consequent troubles!

"I am a peace man — followed the Austin policy — he was forced into war measures by demagogues — I pledged myself to him not to take civil office. Conflicting circumstance forced me to do so, in order to reconcile discordent elements. had I not run, Smith would — enemies of Austin. filled the public with base slanders — charging him with speculation — Subserviency to [*Mexico*] acting for his own interests &c: &c: we always agreed — I followed him to his grave — was one of those rare spirits that come but seldom — a real patriot — not a mere politician few could appreciate his rare qualities — he knew the Mexican character — act slow — must be approached quietly — slowly.

I went in company with Col Hockley and 2 or 3 other to the Frontier — told Cols Johnson — Copane — if they persisted would be cut off — ordered Fanning to retreat — The Alamo to be blown up—no force—no artillery—enemy would surround and cut off retreat — drive away the cattle — stop up the wells — their bones would bleach on the sands — in case of marching to Matamoras.

Went back to Nacogdoches — had to go to the Indians to keep that border in peace — when a boy lived within 11 miles of the Cherokees — they had great confidence in me — I loved them — none could do so well as I, knew them in Tennessee from 12 years old — was in exile with them — naturalized —

Provisional Govt in disorder no Constitution — Travis sending for assistance — none to give — had to make a Constitution without that no better than pirates — signed constitution on my birthday — had a good spree — egg nog — every body — 2 days — bad business — hated it — Report appointed me to command — got to Mr. Millers — had not heard Travis' signal gun that morning — fired an 18 pounder every morning—heard him 200 miles off—marched on.—heard of Travis defeat — great consternation — panic — but 700 men on the Colorado —Travis defeat — 2 men came with the news — ordered them to be put in irons — to be gibbeted next morning though did not doubt the fact — to save further panic — retreated to San Felipe — Sant Ana had crossed the Country below — I pursued — Cut him off at Jacinto

[*The interview continues with further items on people and circumstances, though nothing more relating to the Alamo*]

[*Following is an excerpt from the worked version, which includes additional details such as her reaction to the story. Note that the report of the two men follows Fannin's, not Travis's, defeat in this version.*]

"The Provincial Government was in disorder — we had no constitution. Travis was sending for assistance — had none to give — had to make a Constitution, no better than pirates without one — Signed the Constitution on my birthday and had a great spree on egg nog that lasted two days!!! What, I exclaimed, with so much at stake with such a responsibility could you give yourself to so low a pleasure? I hoped it had been a slander. "It was a bad business — I hated it — and repented of it. They had appointed me to command," — we got to San Millins [*unclear; "William's" crossed out*] — they had not heard Travis' gun that morning which was heard 200 miles — marched on. and heard of his defeat. caused great consternation and panic. I had but 700 men on the Colorado. Then came Fanning's defeat — two men came into camp with the news — I ordered them to be put in irons — to be gibbeted next morning, though I did not doubt the fact. [*The worked version continues with more that is not relevant here.*]

4.4.3.1.　Urrea, published account, 1838.

Castañeda, Carlos, trans. 1928. Diary of the military operations of the division which under the command of general Jose Urrea campaigned in Texas, by Jose Urrea. *The Mexican Side of the Texan Revolution.* 207–8. Dallas: P. L. Turner Co.

This is a selection from Urrea's account published in Victoria De Durango 1838. It is not directly informative on the Alamo, but it is included as a more severe critic of General Filisola and, by implication, his account (2.6.1) would be hard to find. This diary is very detailed on the day-to-day military operations and also gives Urrea's version of such events as the execution of the prisoners in Goliad. Consequently, it is one of the more important documents in a study of the Texas Revolution in its more general scope. Two footnotes are not included in this excerpt.

This is the first time in my life that I appear before the public to engage its attention. I have always prided myself upon making my action speak rather than my pen. I am ignorant of the art of weaving personal eulogies, and I am not acquainted with those fine tactics that convert faults into traits of consummate skill, that clothe mistakes with the mantle of virtue and give gigantic proportions to deeds that hardly rise above vulgar mediocrity, adorning them with assumed splendor. Nor am I accustomed to impute faults to others, reserving to myself their glory and casting upon them my own guilt. This is a favorite practice which, happily or unhappily, I have always ignored.

I tried the means prescribed by law and dictated by honor, addressing to the government a protest. In this I asked that my acts be judiciously examined in order that I might be exonerated or punished as deserved if found guilty. I waited for a long time, provided with the principal proofs for my defense; but, in spite of my repeated and urgent demands, I have not succeeded in getting even an acknowledgment to my communication. The case of General Filisola was being tried at the time and a principle of decorum and consideration, which he did not deserve, made me keep silence that it might not be said I was trying to injure his cause in order to avenge personal insults by his ruin. The said general was exonerated as foreseen by all those who were aware of the influences that were put into play. He first issued a *Representation* to the supreme government in which he insults me, abuses me, satirizes me, and belittles me, forgetting the respect due to authority, to the public, and to himself. He was moved by those principles that once characterized his country and made of its name a synonym for falsehood and calumny. In his military operations he conducted himself in a way that has covered the country with opprobrium and submerged us in untold misfortunes. The remainder of this century will not suffice to repair them. If to-day the republic is vilified and threatened by the ambition of a neighboring nation, if she has sacrificed her sons in vain, if her most beautiful province is lost, if a handful of rebellious foreigners insults her, if her campaign has been unavailing, if part of the army has become demoralized, if the treasury is exhausted, if the public money has been wasted in useless expense, if the people groan overcome by the weight of unbearable economic laws, if the enemy has gained new courage and obtained reenforcements, if it is necessary to undertake a new campaign and to multiply our victims and our sacrifices, if national independence finds itself endangered, if our flag has been insulted, if every branch of society finds itself in turmoil as the result of the lack of means to defray the most insignificant expenses, if internal peace is disturbed and the customs, the morals, and the century itself seem to slip back in our unhappy country, all will be due to General Filisola. The people will point to him as the cruel instrument of their misfortune, not because as Attila or Omar he raised the standard of devastation, but because, by his inaptitude or lack of courage, he opened the flood gates to the torrent of calamities that has swept over us. To have checked it, to have turned defeat into victory and glory, it would have been sufficient for him to have taken the one step that honor and duty prescribed, but he shamelessly disregarded both of them. The precipitate and disgraceful flight which he undertook in Texas while facing a vanquished enemy, a flight he has tried to disguise with the honorable title of a retreat, is the fountain of all our present calamities. It is the seal of national disgrace, a seal impressed upon us by an act of General Filisola that has brought untold misfortunes.

4.4.3.2.   José Maria Tornel Y Mendívil, published account, 1837.

Castañeda, Carlos, trans. 1928. Relations between Texas, the United States of America, and the Mexican Republic, by José Maria Tornel y Mendívil. *The Mexican Side of the Texan Revolution.* 287, 350–52. Dallas: P. L. Turner Co.

The original of this translation was published in Mexico in 1837. As the Mexican secretary of war during the Texas campaign, Tornel naturally gives an exceptionally broad perspective of the war from the Mexican government's—more specifically, Santa Anna's—point of view.

For more than fifty years, that is, from the very period of their political infancy, the prevailing thought in the United States of America has been the acquisition of the greater part of the territory that formally belonged to Spain, particularly that part which to-day belongs to the Mexican nation. Democrats and Federalists, all their political parties, whatever their old or new designations, have been in perfect accord upon one point, their desire to extend the limits of the republic to the north, to the south, and to the west, using for the purpose all the means at their command, guided by cunning, deceit, and bad faith. It has been neither an Alexander nor a Napoleon, desirous of conquest in order to extend his dominions or add to his glory, who has inspired the proud Anglo-Saxon race in its desire, its frenzy to usurp and gain control of that which rightfully belongs to its neighbors; rather it has been the nation itself which, possessed of that roving spirit that moved the barbarous hordes of a former age in a far remote north, has swept away whatever has stood in the way of its aggrandizement.

[*Tornel continues with a more detailed analysis in the same light, then starts his narration of the war itself.*]

The supreme government entrusted the command of the army to His excellency, Antonio López de Santa Anna, President of the Republic. To-day, as then, I still maintain that his appointment was the most advisable at the time. The recent prestige of the glorious victory of Zacatecas was a potent stimulus to the soldier accustomed to follow in the path of glory of an accredited leader. In this campaign dangers and difficulties multiplied them selves with such astounding rapidity that it was most urgent to appeal to the enthusiasm of the masses, for though a furtive passion, it produces happy results when used opportunely. At the generals' council of war which I called in the capital, it was unanimously agreed that the appointment of one so favored by fortune was most desirable.

The general-in-chief arrived in Mexico towards the close of November, proceeding to San Luis Potosi early the following month, after issuing the corresponding orders for the march of the various divisions, the assembling of all army equipment, and the arrangement of everything that was necessary for beginning the campaign. The General displayed the greatest activity while in San Luis, both with regard to the increase of the divisions, the organization of the brigades, and the assembling of supplies and of practically everything that was needed. The government invested Santa Anna with authority to secure funds by pledging the revenue of the nation because the Minister of Finance had found all doors closed to his efforts, and was now at his wits end to secure the necessary resources. The advisability of such a measure was justified, as expected, by the results.

Towards the close of December, our forces assembled at San Luis Potosi, consisting of a little more than 6,000 men, began their march to Béxar, then held by the enemy. The General had deliberately planned to make it the base for his operations out of regard for the fact that being the only city in the territory of Texas whose population was Mexican in its entirety, it could be relied upon to lend that cooperation which can be expected only of friends. It was for this reason that he determined to cross 400 leagues of uninhabited deserts, enduring inconveniences and hardships that might have been avoided by choosing another route. The army underwent great privations during its march and consequently deserves the highest praise for its constancy and resignation, qualities characteristic of the Mexican soldier.

A division of the army was to surprise Béxar early the morning of the 23rd of February, 1836, but for some reason yet unknown the orders of the General were not carried out. It is a fact, however that the failure or the inability to comply with an order so evidently wise, was responsible for the loss of many lives later. On March 6th, at daybreak, the assault was made upon the fortress of the Alamo as agreed in a council of war. The blood of the conquerors and the conquered mingled in the engagement and our soldiers added new laurels to their accredited heroism. Party spirit has underestimated the true merit of the engagement. A fort that has artillery, a defence consisting of two separate walls, and whose capture required the loss of 70 killed and 300 wounded, cannot rightly be called an indefensible position.

[*Tornel continues on with the campaign, basically justifying Santa Anna's actions.*]

4.4.4.1.   Dickinson/Dickerson, signed claim, 1835.

Neill, James C., et al. November 23, 1835. Republic Claims, AU-George, James; 119; R:035 Fr:0191-0197, TSLA.

This is to certify that I demanded and received into the public service; for hauling the the [*sic*] Gonzales Cannon, to Sanantonio: one yoke of oxen, and all necessary geering; belonging to James George—and that Said yoke of oxen, is now so much crippled as to render it unfit for service Novr 23^d 1835

J.C Neill Cap.

We the undersigned do certify that we believe that the yoke of oxen and geering as received into the public service by Captain Neil and belonging to James George was worth Forty five dollars as witness our hands and seals this 23'd Novr 1835

> J.C. Neill Cap
> Wm Barton
> Almeron Dickerson

4.4.4.2.   Dickinson/Dickerson, signed claim, 1835.

Dickinson, Almeron, et al. December 13, 1835. Republic Claims, AU-Tumlinson, George W.; 5273; R:106 Fr:0563-0563, TSLA.

Head Quarters
Dec 13th 1835
Cu Bejar
    This is to certify that George Tumilson entered the volunteer army of Texas on the 2d [?] of Sept as an artilery man under the command of Capt. Dickerson who discharged his duty with honors to himself and was one of the number who charge into Befar [sic] and distinguished himself by his bravery and courage who is this day honorably discharge from further service

Wm J Austin By order   Almeron Dickinson Capt [?]
Aide de Camp   Edward Burleson
                                          Comd in chief

4.4.4.3.   Dickinson/Dickerson, signed claim, 1835.

Dickinson, Almeron, et al. December 13, 1835. Republic Claims, AU-Criswell, William; 268; R:021 Fr:0630-0630, TSLA.

Head Quarters December 13th 1835
    —This is to Certify that Wm Criswell of the Brass Gun [?] Constitution 1824 Entered the Volunteer Army of Texas on the 28 of September—& has discharged his duty with Honor and applause he is also one who So galantly [sic] distinguished himself on the Seige [sic] of Bexar he is hereby Honorably discharged

> Almeron Dickinson Cap
> J.C Neill Coln

By Order

> Edward Burleson
Wm. J Austin   Comd in chief
Aid de Camp

4.4.4.4.   Dickinson/Dickerson, signed claim, 1835.

Dickinson, Almeron, et al. December 18, 1835. Republic Claims, AU-Ware, Joseph; 7688; R:110 Fr:0390-0390, TSLA.

Head Quarters
Dec 18th 1835

Bejar This is to certify that Joseph Ware entered the volunteer army of Texas on the 28 of Sept as an artillery[*man*] and discharged his duty with honour to himself and was on[*e*] of the number who charged into Bejar and distinguished himself by his courage and bravery during the sege [*sic*] under the command of Capt. Dickerson who is this day discharged from further service and is allowed five days to return home.

Almeron Dickinson Capt

By order   Edward Burleson
Wm J Austin   Comd in chief
Aide de Camp

4.4.4.5.   Dickinson/Dickerson, interview, c. 1875.

Strays—Alamo Dead and Monument, File "Josephine Work Box." Adjutant General (RG-401), TSLA. This short note is included in the material gathered in 1875–1876 on Alamo defenders, which includes the interview of Mrs. Hannig in 1.2.8.

Note K—Hannig says name is Almaron Dickerson—See letter of W.P. Hardeman.

4.4.4.6.   Dickinson/Dickerson name, letter, 1875.

Hardeman, William P., to Gen. W. Steele. December 28, 1875. Adjutant General (RG-401), Army Papers/ General Correspondence: December 16–31, 1875, TSLA. This is the original of the letter referred to in the previous document.

Galveston Dec 28th, 1875

Genl. W. Steele
Dear Sir

I think the first name of Lt. Dickinson as published among the Patriots assi- nated [*sic*] at the Alamo—is wrong—my recollection is that his name was Almarion Dickerson his wife is now Mrs Hannig—wife of the Furniture Dealer

of that name on Pecan St—his headright League was located on the St. Marcos—about four miles above the town of Prarie Lea—the map in the land Office
ought to show—his name—the paper stated that the child who escaped was living in Austin—the mother of the child of the Alamo is—If the child is I do not
know—I think she is dead—

Respectfully your friend
W^m. P Hardeman

Dickerson was one of McKean & Mathews Colonists
McKean lives in Seguin.

4.4.4.7.   Dickinson/Dickerson name, letter, 1893.

Hardeman, William P. August 1, 1893. Alamo Papers, Claimants to Property,
TSLA.

Hardeman apparently wrote the letter from which this excerpt is drawn to comment on an earlier letter by William Cannon (discussed in the Commentary for section 1.10) claiming Susanna's maiden name was Cannon.

His statement that Mrs. Dickinson (wife of Lt Dickinson killed in the
Alamo) was a Cannon before she married I know to be utterly false as I knew
her to be Susie Wilkinson when a girl and saw her married to Dickinson at my
fathers house in Harderman County Tennessee about 1831.

4.4.4.8.   Dickinson/Dickerson name, letter, 1893.

Malloch, Lucy Ellen, and E. Malloch. August 8, 1893. Alamo Papers, Claimants
to Property, TSLA.

This additional letter, also in response to the Cannon claim, apparently is from
the McKean family noted in Hardeman's letter above of December 28, 1875.

Prairie Sea Aug' 8 /93

Genl W. P. Hardeman
D^r. Sir

In reply to yours of 2^d inst. have to say that your recollection of the name of
Mrs Dickerson of Alamo fame is altogether Correct. her maiden name was Sus-
sana Wilkerson her Fathers name as you say was James Wilkerson, and she was
own [or "our"] Cousin to my Fathers second wife whose Father was Frank Wilkerson a brother of James Wilkerson. After the fall of the Alamo, during the runaway my Father John C. McKean with his family, got to the Trinity river, at
Robbins ferry. The river was very high and there was. a great number of people
there, with Cattle and wagons waiting for the river to fall. Mrs Dickerson was
there and when She found out, that we were there She came to our camp, and

had much to tell about the Alamo disaster. as well as I can recollect her account agrees in all respects with Texas history. As to the name of Cannon I never heard of it in this conection. and it is no doubt a fabrication, and I think Cannons claims about being in the Alamo and making his escape so, rests on no better foundation.

Respectfully you old schoelmate
Luicy [*sic*] Ellen Malloch
fr E. Malloch

4.4.4.9. Dickinson/Dickerson name, affidavit, 1909.

Brogan, Evelyn. 1922. *James Bowie: A Hero of the Alamo*. 39. San Antonio: Theodore Kunzman.

COPY OF
Affadavit of Mrs. Susan Sterling, Granddaughter of Mrs. A. Marion
Dickinson-Hannig, Made From the Copy of I. D. Afflect, a
Historian of Texas.

San Antonio, Oct. 29, 1909.

To Whom it may Concern:

I, Mrs. Susan A. Sterling, nee Griffith, do hereby confirm that my grandmother's name was Susanna A. Wilkinson, and was the wife of Lieutenant Alman [*sic*] Dickinson, who was killed at the Battle of the Alamo, March 6, 1836, and my mother's name was Angeline Griffith, nee Angeline Dickinson, who was the child inside the Alamo on that memorable date and that I have heard my grandmother, the above mentioned, confirm often that she was in the right hand side upon entering room known as the baptismal room, on the date of March 6, 1836 in the Alamo, known as the Alamo Church where my grandmother told me the last hand to hand fight took place, and was in the same room with James Bowie and his nurse who was wounded at that time.

MRS. SUSAN A. STERLING,
The Granddaughter of
Mrs. Dickinson of the Alamo.

Witnesses:
>   CHARLES WELERT,
>   G.S. RAYMOND
>   MRS. T. J. PARTRIDGE,
>   MRS. SARAH E. EAGER.

My mother at the time of the Siege of the Alamo was 15 months old and was born in Gonzales, Texas, 25th of December, 1834.

4.4.4.10. Dickinson/Dickerson, biography, c. 1939.

Kemp, Louis Wiltz. N.d. (1939). Typescript in "General Biographical Notebook: Ded–Di" of the Kemp (Louis Wiltz) Papers, CAH.

This document is useful for biographical information on Almeron and Susanna, as well as a discussion of the uncertainty of the spelling of Dickerson versus Dickinson. It is particularly helpful for the specifics on dates and documents, hence leaving a good track for anyone who cares to pursue the subject further. Another close copy differing mostly in stylistic details is in the DRT Library at the Alamo.

DICKINSON, ALMERON—Born in Pennsylvania in 1810. In Tennessee he married to Susanna Wilkinson, and of this union one child, Angelina Arabella Dickinson was born. With wife and child he came to Texas in 1831 and settled at Gonzales in the colony of Green De Witt. At the outbreak of the Texas Revolution he entered the army of Texas and he was among those who defended Goliad, [*underneath is "(GONZALES)" in the DRT version*] October 2, 1835, when the first shot of the Revolution was fired. On December 7, 1835, he was elected first lieutenant of artillery and shortly thereafter was stationed at San Antonio, his wife and daughter joining him there. On about February 1, 1836 the officers stationed in the Alamo addressed a petition to the Constitutional Convention, scheduled to assemble at Washington-on-the-Brazos, March 1. Dickinson signed the petition as <u>Almeron Dickinson</u>, Lt. On February 23, 1836 Mrs. Dickinson and daughter entered the Alamo where on March 6, Lieutenant Dickinson was killed. The lives of his wife and daughter were spared.

As Chairman of the Historical Board of the Commission of Control for Texas Centennial Celebrations this writer caused name to be inscribed on the Alamo Cenotaph completed in San Antonio in 1939 as <u>Almaron Dickerson</u> but he has since become convinced that the name should be spelled <u>Almeron Dickinson</u>. Dr. Amelia Williams after an exhaustive study of the Alamo rolls was positive that <u>Almaron Dickerson</u> was the correct spelling and this writer accepted her findings as final. He now, on September 1, 1939, differs with her. Dr. Williams rendered a great service when she corrected the many names that were misspelled, on the original army rolls and it would have been almost a miracle had she made no errors in her painstaking work. The following sketch of Captain Dickinson appears on page 256 of Volume 37 of the Southwestern Historical Quarterly, being a part of "A Critical Study of the Siege of the Alamo" by Dr. Williams.

"Age, 26; rank Captain, immigrated to Texas from Tennessee, resident of Gonzales. Sources: Fannin, 297, 305; I. Gonzales 99; Comptroller's Military Service Records Nos. 13 and 7688. The last document is a soldier's discharge and is signed by 'Almaron Dickerson'" Captain, and William T. Austin, Aide to Col. Burleson. It is dated December 13, 1835. Almaron Dickerson is generally rated as a lieutenant, but he had his commission as a captain of artillery and was in command of the artillery forces at the Alamo. There has been a great deal of confusion concerning the spelling of this man's name. Most of the better Texas historians, Yoakum, Wooten, Brown, Foote, and others spell the name 'Dickinson' others write it 'Dickenson', but Comptroller's Military Service Record No 7688, and an affidavit made by Mrs. Dickerson's last husband, J.W. Hannig, (Miscellaneous Papers of the Adjutant General's Office, State Library, Archives), show conclusively that the name would be written 'Almaron Dickerson'. My own spelling of the name in the previous chapters of this study has not been consistent with this explanation; my only excuse for this discrepancy is that I have only recently found conclusive evidence for the true spelling of the name."

This writer examined Comptroller's Military Service Record No. 7688 mentioned by Dr. Williams and he thinks the signature is definitely Almeron Dickinson.

In the Spanish Archives in the General Land Office, Austin, it is shown that Almeron Dickinson, married, with a family of two, (himself and wife) had arrived at Gonzales, Texas Feb. 20, 1831. On May 5, 1831 Almeron Dickinson received title to one league of land in De Witt's Colony situated in the present county of Caldwell.

The following is from a letter written by Mr. John W. Dickinson of Brownsville, Tennessee, Aug. 8, 1939 to L.W. Kemp, Houston, Texas;

I am advised that you have charge of the preparation of the inscription that is to be placed on the Alamo Memorial now in course of construction.

There may be need for knowing the exact spelling of the name of Almeron Dickinson.

I have the marriage license and marriage bond of Almeron Dickinson and Susanna Wilkinson, and the bond bears the signature of Dickinson, and is spelled thereon as above indicated."

On page 4 of the Army Rolls in the General Land Office, the name appears Almeron Dickinson.

On page 636. Vol. I. of Gammel's *The Laws of Texas* it is shown that on December 7. 1835 Almeron Dickinson was elected First Lieutenant of Artillery by the General Council of the Provisional Government of Texas.

Donation Certificate No. 3002 for 1920 acres of land was issued in the name of Almeron Dickerson [*sic*], April 23, 1838, due him for having served in the army from December 7, 1835 to March 6, 1838 [*sic*], and for having been killed in the service. This certificate is in Fannin County Bounty File No 305 in the General Land Office. In the same file there is an affidavit signed September 25, 1855 by John T. Tinsley and C.E. Dewitt of Gonzales, "Who being duly sworn deposeth and saith that they knew Almeron Dickinson and that he was a resident citizen of the Republic of Texas". Donation Certificate for No 931 for 640 acres of land was issued in the name of Almeron Dickinson, due him for "having been killed in the Alamo the 6th of March, 1836" Headright Certificate No 73 for one labor of land was issued April 12, 1838 in the name of Almeron Dickerson [*sic*]. The certificate is in Gonzales County First Class Headright File No 99. In the file it is shown that William A. Matthews, administrator of the estate, appeared before the Board of Land Commissioners of Gonzales County April 12, 1838, and stated that <u>Almeron</u> <u>Dickerson</u> [*sic*] had arrived in Texas in 1831.

In the Court of Claims Vouchers, M to S in the General Land Office, there is an affidavit signed by her mark by Mrs. Susannah Bellis of Caldwell Country, Texas, July 16, 1857. Mrs. Bellis, formerly Mrs. Dickinson, had submitted a deposition in favor of the descendants of James W. Rose, who, Mrs. Bellis claimed, fell at the Alamo. In answer to one of the questions asked Mrs. Bellis replied "Upon one occasion heard my husband, <u>Capt.</u> <u>Dickinson</u> speak to Rose."

Mrs. Dickinson was married to Francis P. Herring at Houston, Dec. 20, 1838 (<u>Marriage</u> <u>Records</u> <u>of</u> <u>Harris</u> <u>County</u>, A,77). In Harris County Third Class Headright File No 49 there is a certificate for 640 acres of land issued to Francis P. Herring, deceased, July 7, 1845, and delivered to George R. Carodine, to whom Mr. Herring had assigned his rights to the land, September 7, 1839. Thus it is seen that Mr. Herring was alive as late as September 7, 1839 and had died before July 7, 1845. Mrs. Herring on December 7 1847 was married to Peter Bellis (Frequently misspelled "Bellows") by Rev. Charles Gillett, an Episcopal minister (<u>Marriage</u> <u>Records</u> B., 49).

In *The Life and Writings of Dr. Rufus C. Burleson* seven pages, 735 to 741 inclusive are devoted to Mrs. Dickinson. Rev. Burleson stated that he first met the lady, whom he called Mrs. Dickenson, in 1849 while he was pastor of the Baptist Church in Houston. He stated that she was nominally a member of the Episcopal Church but after hearing Dr. Burleson preach had become a Baptist. "At least 1500 people," he said, "crowded the banks of Buffalo Bayou on Sabbath evening to see her baptised." He stated that both Captain and Mrs. Dickinson were born in Pennsylvania and raised in Philadelphia. He said that he performed the ceremonies when the daughter of Captain and Mrs. Dickinson was first married. A separation followed, he said, and the daughter moved to New Orleans, soon to be followed by her mother.

Mrs. Bellis and her second husband were likely divorced, for when on October 13, 1877 the estate of Peter Bellis, deceased, was divided, his nearest kin and heirs were his first cousins, Isaac S. Bishop and Ann E. Alsover, and his second cousins, Edmund S. Bishop, Helen Bishop, John Bishop, Alice Clifton and Emily Young. (<u>Probate</u> <u>Minutes</u> <u>of</u> <u>Harris</u> <u>County</u>. G. p. 533)

In New Orleans, according to Dr. Burleson, Mrs. Bellis met Joseph William Hannig, a most worthy and industrious man who had been sent by Jefferson Davis to establish a workshop for manufacturing munitions of war. In 1857 Mrs. Bellis was living in Caldwell County. In 1862, Dr. Burleson stated, he met her in Austin after her marriage to Mr. Hannig. Hannig located in Austin where he ran a furniture store. He moved to San Antonio where he died June 6, 1883. He was born June 14, 1834.

Mrs. Hannig was born in 1815 and died at her residence at the corner of Duval and East Thirty-second streets, Austin, October 7, 1883 and was buried beside her husband in Oakwood Cemetery, Austin.

[*The manuscript has handwritten notes at the end concerning some of the surviving descendants, added from an immediately following newspaper clipping from the* Austin American, *March 1, 1949.*]

4.4.5.1.   Dickert rifle, oral tradition.

Siegmund, Col. Walter F. September 1, 1947. History of the Dickert rifle used in defense of the Alamo. Typed manuscript with some hand insertions, DRT.

This paper by the donor gives the background for one of the artifacts now on display at the Alamo. The original manuscript is in typed capital letters, with a few handwritten additions or corrections.

HISTORY OF DICKERT RIFLE
USED IN DEFENSE OF THE ALAMO
SAN ANTONIO, TEXAS

On March 6, 1836, after the battle of the Alamo, a Mexican peon hid this "Dickert" rifle away under some debris while completing his military imposed task of carrying out the slain Texans to the funeral pyre in the square. This grisly task done, he stole away with this rifle and later turned it over to Colonel Frederick W. Johnson, an ardent and patriotic member of the Texan army, and later the author of "A History of Texas and Texans."

Colonel Johnson made a visit to the "States" in 1839, no doubt to raise funds, and at that time he presented this famous Dickert rifle to William Carr Lane, the first Mayor of St. Louis, Missouri. Mr. Lane later became Governor of New Mexico. He was born and reared in Fayette County, Pennsylvania and just before his migration west in 1819, married Miss Mary Ewing, daughter of Nathaniel Ewing, a representative of a prominent early American family. Thus, the rifle passed on to the Ewing family.

The Ewing family had a country place at Glencoe, Missouri some fifty miles from St. Louis, from which was take the atmosphere and historical background in Winston Churchill's book "The Crisis".

This Dickert rifle was passed from William Carr Lane, through the Ewing family, to Colonel Walter F. Siegmund, of St. Louis Missouri, who served in the Army on the Texas-Mexican border and in World Wars I and II. It came to him through his uncle Henry Koch, who upon his return from the Civil War became superintendent of the Ewing place at Glencoe. He passed the gun on to Colonel Siegmund through the Colonel's mother. Thus, the rifle has been in the possession of the Carr, Ewing, Koch and Siegmund families continuously from 1839 to 1947, a period of 108 years.

Rifles made by Jacob Dickert are often mentioned in histories, novels, and old public, tax and church records, although the name Dickert is frequently misspelled, appearing as Dickerte, Dickart, Deckard, Deckerd, Dechard, Decherd, Deschert, Digert and other variations. These misspellings can be attributed to the general use of phonetic spelling common in the early days. A list of some of the authors and their books in which reference to the Dickert rifle can be found is Winston Churchill's "The Crossing", Dillin's "The Kentucky Rifle", Davis' "A Forgotten Heritage", Lyman C. Draper's "Kings Mountain and Her Heroes", James R. Gilmore's "Rear Guard of the Revolution", Van Wyck Mason's "Three Harbours", Sawyer's "Firearms in American History", Gardiner's "American Arm Fabricators, Ancient and Modern", and others.

This Dickert rifle was made by Jacob Dickert of Lancaster, Pennsylvania, and is a fine example of a craftsman's work, and shows the skill and patience of a master. He was known as early as 1750 and died in 1822. The overall length of the rifle is sixty inches, the barrel forty-five inches, the bore about .55 caliber, weight $8^1/4$ lbs., and is fitted with a flint lock made by T. Ketland of Birmingham, England between 1750 and 1791. The stock is curly maple with brass and silver trimmings.

It is a matter of record that Dickert rifles were used before, during and after the Revolutionary War. It was the favorite rifle of the backwoodsmen who fought at Kings Mountain, North Carolina; of George Rogers Clark and his men, whose campaign won the territory west of the Alleghenies, north of the Ohio river and east of the Mississippi river in the Revolutionary War; by the backwoodsmen who fought in the Indian wars and later won the Battle of New Orleans in the War of 1812; by the Lewis and Clark Expedition; and in the defense of the Alamo in Texas.

The identity of the patriot who used this Dickert rifle in the battle of the Alamo may never be known, but this long Dickert rifle will remain forever, a mute reminder for future generations of the great sacrifices and glorious deeds of our forefathers to gain life, liberty and the pursuit of happiness for all of us and to ever remind us to remain alert and prepared so that all we now enjoy will not be denied us.

W. F. Siegmund [signature]
COLONEL WALTER F. SIEGMUND

September 1, 1947.

4.4.5.2.   Cannons, newspaper report.

Republic Daily. June 28, 1852. Washington, D.C. 1.

A surprising number of original pieces of artillery from the battle have likely survived. This document is an initial representative of a collection of articles and research on the subject. The paragraph prior to this excerpt quotes from a correspondent of the *Galveston Journal,* which possible source was not verified. Seven or so cannons were discovered or rediscovered on the Maverick homestead adjacent to the Alamo and reported in the *San Antonio Daily Light* and the *San Antonio Daily Express* for August 1 and 2, 1889.

While some laborers were digging a ditch for a fence in the Alamo, in San Antonio recently, they came suddenly upon several pieces of ordnance, since which time thirteen cannons have already been recovered from their hiding place, four of which are copper pieces, and nine iron pieces, from one to twenty four pounders, all spiked, and the trunnious [*sic; trunnions*] and knobs of the cascables [*cascabels*] broken off. An old Mexican woman says they were buried there by the brave men under the command of the noble Travis, Bowie, and Crockett, at the seige [*sic*] of the Alamo in 1836.

Commentary

Other Less-Contemporary Sources (4.4)

Although these documents are a little further separated in time and topic from the battle, they add insight into some more obscure or less central details.

Francis W. Johnson was the Alamo's first commander after its seizure from General Cós (note documents 4.5.2–4.5.4). In the brief letter (4.4.1) included here, he mentioned the outfitting of the Alamo defenders.

The interview by Mary Holly (4.4.2) gives Samuel Houston's recollections from 1844. His blunt honesty in discussing his drunken binge at the time of the Alamo is surprising in a political leader. Another document relating to the slowness of response, not included in this collection, is an affidavit by W. W. Thompson.[1] Thompson claimed that Houston, while on the way to Gonzales, stated that the reports from Travis and Fannin warning of the Mexican attacks were all lies in order to get popular support and delayed two nights and a day in continuing on toward San Antonio. Sam Houston did make enemies and earn critics with his unique character and leadership, but that is too large a subject to discuss much further here.

In fairness to him, it should be pointed out that at the time the siege started, he was negotiating a peace treaty with the Cherokee nation (e.g., 4.5.8, 4.3.10); and the vote on independence didn't come until March 2, so his two-day drunk came too late for any action to affect the outcome at the Alamo.[2] Therefore, his actions, or lack thereof, would not have affected the outcome to the defenders in the Alamo.

A couple short excerpts of published justifications by Urrea and Tornel (4.4.3.1, 4.4.3.2) are not as important to the immediate story of the Alamo as those included above, but they help round out the retrospective look at the campaign by senior Mexican leaders. The document of Urrea (4.4.3.1; as per Commentary for 2.9, de la Peña may be a source for this account) is included as a possible check on Filisola's account (2.6.1). One can safely say that Filisola, whatever his shortcomings, could not have been as responsible for all the disasters as the polemic of Urrea gives him credit for. The lack of balance in this introduction is also indicated by the fact that Urrea neglected to admit that Filisola was ordered by (the captive) Santa Anna to retreat. Later on in the same document, he gives a detailed critique of Filisola and also disclaimed personal responsibility for the execution of Fannin's men at Goliad.[3] Tornel's statement (4.4.3.2) is interesting for the strategic view of the campaign and the carefully worded support for Santa Anna. Both Urrea and Tornel are also important sources for giving additional background that reflects on the limitations to the Mexican Army (see Commentary for sections 2.1 and 2.9). In Urrea's case, the limitations basically consisted of Filisola's actions.

The short excerpts given in this book from Carlos Castañeda's *Mexican Side of the Texas Revolution* (2.1.2, 2.5.1, 2.6.1, 4.4.3.1, 4.4.3.2) only suggest the wealth of valuable information and fascinating extent of opinions and self-defense of the high command of the Mexican Army (see commentary to de la Peña, section 2.9, for example). A particularly interesting issue is Filisola's conduct after San Jacinto. The Mexican leaders give detailed claims and accusations, counterclaims, and self-justifications that would make an interesting study in itself. Castañeda's book is an appropriate starting point for anyone to pursue those areas further.

The next group of documents (4.4.4.1–4.4.4.8) in this section relates to Almeron Dickinson/Dickerson. These documents give an educational example of how difficult resolving such a seemingly simple question as the correct spelling of a name can be. (There is uncertainty as well in the spelling of Almeron versus Almaron versus Almarion.) The Kemp article stating that the correct spelling is "Dickinson" gives a wealth of specific references that an interested scholar can follow up on. Williams's dissertation and later works (3.5.6, footnote 2) give her reasoning that it is "Dickerson."[4]

The problem with Kemp's conclusion is that in examining some of the originals of the cited documents at the Texas State Library, I found that they are more ambiguous than he implied. The script is such that the name can be read either way. The clearest signature I have seen is on the document given here of November 23, 1835 (4.4.4.1), not used by Kemp, and I think it reads "Dickerson." On the other hand, three other signatures of December 13 and 18, 1835 (4.4.4.2, 4.4.4.3, 4.4.4.4) appear to be "Dickinson." Copies of Spanish documents cited by Kemp do read "Dickinson": February 22 (not February 20), 1831, regarding arrival in Gonzales, and May 4 (not May 5), regarding a league of land.[5] Likewise, so do the marriage license and the marriage bond. However, it is not clear to me that any of these handwritten names are signatures by Dickerson/Dickinson himself. The handwriting of each seems to match the handwriting of the surrounding document, which was unlikely to have been filled out by Dickerson.

Another possible counterexample, however, is the apparent original of the Memorial to the President and Members of the the the Convention, c. February 5, 1836 (4.5.27), on which the signature might be "Almeron Dickinson Lut." Other clues are that two individuals who actually knew him are also quoted as saying "Dickerson": J. C. Neill in 1836 (provided Zuber, 1.8.1.2, was accurately recording a conversation) and Benjamin Highsmith in 1900 (provided one can trust the court deposition, 1.7.6.2). There is weak support by Enrique Esparza (1.5.6) as well.

I find the affidavits of Mrs. Dickerson/Bellis (1.2.5) and of her granddaughter Susan Sterling (4.4.4.7) less convincing than one might initially expect. The first concerns James Rose, not Dickinson, and Susanna was unable to read what was written when she made her mark. The Sterling document is primarily concerned with Susanna's maiden name of Wilkinson and gets the first name of Almaron wrong. The affidavit also seems to reflect information recorded in the *San Antonio Express,* specifically concerning Susanna's location in the Alamo and the Madame Candelaria interviews, and Brogan also reprinted a heavily edited obituary of Susanna based on the account of her visit to the Alamo in 1881 (1.2.11, 1.9.2).

In the end, one must consider that Dickinson/Dickerson himself, who may have been barely literate, might have signed both ways, and therefore the later confusion is hardly surprising. A much earlier, yet enlightening, example to modern writers is that three of the four known autographs of William Shakespeare are signatures on each of three pages of his will, and each one is somewhat different. For me, ultimately the weight goes to the November 23, 1835, receipt, the terse note in the "Alamo Strays" file (4.4.4.5), and the associated letters (4.4.4.6, 4.4.4.7) by William Hardeman, further supported by the Malloch letter, who stated that he knew Susanna and her husband from a very early period (despite his use of "Dickinson" in some places). The "Alamo Strays" is part of the research that provided actual interviews with Susanna Hannig (1.2.8, 1.2.9). Here is the only possible word we have from the source, along with some independent collaboration, and thus I believe "Dickerson" is correct. However, insisting on a personal opinion based on ambiguous data seemed pedantic in this case, so the more commonly accepted "Dickinson" has been typically used throughout this work.

The final two documents in this group relate to artifacts that possibly are actual relics of the battle. The first (4.4.5.1) concerns the "Dickert rifle," a gun on display at the Alamo. Written by the gun's last owner, the document relates the oral tradition for the significance of this gun. Consequently, the issues and questions in the earlier discussion on the oral tradition of the "Travis ring" (1.2.16) are equally applicable here. The only additional comment is that the early owners, Francis W. Johnson and William Carr Lane, were prominent historical figures (note 4.4.1, 4.5.1–4.5.4.), and Johnson was also an author. Consequently, one could hope that in their papers are some written records supporting this story. Weaknesses in this story are the lack of specific provenance for owners in the Ewing family and the justification that the gun would go to Henry Koch. But for now, the same conclusion can be drawn, though a bit more tentatively, as for the Travis ring: The story has no fundamental proof that it is true nor fundamental problems that indicate it is false. Further research on the provenance could clarify the validity of the story.

The newspaper report (4.4.5.2) on the discovery of cannons near the Alamo is included to introduce the special topic of the Alamo artillery. The evidence appears strong that some of the cannons located around the Alamo and in La Villita (an "old town" area of modern San Antonio) were in fact the ones used during the siege. These were then rendered militarily useless and dumped into a nearby irrigation ditch by the Mexican Army prior to evacuating the city after San Jacinto (ref. Barnard, 4.3.10). The files of the DRT Library at the Alamo have a number of articles, newspaper clippings, manuscripts, and correspondence that discuss and review the identification of the Alamo ordnance. This is an area of active research by people like Philip Haythornthwaite, Thomas Lindley, Charles Long, William Orbelo, and Kevin Young. Only a very brief synopsis of the subject and their research is given here.[6]

Twenty-one was the best judgment for the number of cannons at the siege of the Alamo, and this is now validated by the records from the Mexican archives (Santa Anna, 2.1.1.10, Sánchez, 2.7.2, 2.7.3).[7] As recorded in the *Republic,* thirteen cannons were discovered in 1852 on the property of Samuel Maverick, located at the northwest corner of the original plaza (ref. Giraud map, 4.2.2). Cannons were also reported as being discovered on the Maverick property in 1871, 1876, and 1889, though it is not apparent to what extent these might have been new discoveries or rediscoveries of some of the original thirteen. A number were unearthed in 1908 when the Gibbs Building was being constructed in the area. At least nine cannons, which can be traced to the Maverick family or the Boynton family (owners of the Gibbs building), have survived. Four others were destroyed. Thus the disposition of a minimum of thirteen of the original twenty-one is documented at some level. Travis's famous eighteen-pounder, which fired the answer to the call for surrender, is likely to be the one later placed outside the Alamo gift shop. In fact, it is probably a French sixteen-pounder—but on an old weight scale that is equivalent to eighteen pounds in the English. The materials on the artillery submitted to the Alamo Library are a good basis for a comprehensive understanding of this aspect of the battle.

1. W. W. Thompson, December 1, 1840, Home Papers, TSLA.
2. Also see Williams in *SWHQ* 37:22 n. 55, and Houston's letter of February 29, 1836, in Jenkins 1973, 4:461 on.
3. Filisola 1985, On Santa Anna's order to retreat, see 234–36; Filisola in Castañeda 1928, 175–76; Urrea in Castañeda 1928, 244–48. Urrea's view on the execution of Fannin and his men is in Castañeda 1928, 234–37.
4. Williams' thesis *SWHQ* 37:256.
5. Citations by Kemp are in DRT.
6. Files on Alamo artillery are in Historic Sites/Alamo/Cannon, DRT. Also see Labadie 1986 for a useful overview of the fortifications and weapons in use at the time of the battle.
7. Also see Lindley 1992, which documents where they came from and explains the variation in count among different sources.

4.5.1.   Francis W. Johnson, letter, December 11, 1835.

Brown, John Henry. 1892. *History of Texas from 1685 to 1892*. 1:417–21. St. Louis: I. E. Daniell.

This is a report to Commander-in-Chief Burleson on the storming of Béxar in December 1835. The Alamo had been occupied and strengthened by the Mexican Army under General Cós. This is the key event that put the Alamo in the Texans' hands and led to Santa Anna's return attack a few months later. Future Alamo defenders were involved as well.

"SAN ANTONIO DE BEXAR, December 11, 1835.
"General Burleson, Commander-in-Chief.

"SIR: I have the honor to acquaint you, that on the morning of the 5th inst., the volunteers for storming the city of Bexar, possessed by the troops of General Cos, entered the suburbs in two divisions, under the command of Colonel Ben. R. Milam. The first division under his immediate command, aided by Major R. C. Morris, and the second under my command, aided by Colonels Grant and Austin, and Adjutant Brister.

"The first division, consisting of the companies of Captains York, Patton, Lewellyn, Crane, English, and Landrum, with two pieces and fifteen artillery-men, commanded by Lieutenant-Colonel Franks, took possession of the house of Don Antonio de La Graza. The second division, composed of the companies of Captains Cooke, Swisher, Edwards, Alley, Duncan, Peacock, Breeze and Placido Benevides, took possession of the house of Verraméndi. The last division was exposed for a short time to a very heavy fire of grape and musketry from the whole of the enemy's line of fortifications, until the guns of the first division opened their fire, when the enemy's attention was directed to both divisions. At seven o'clock, a heavy cannonading from the town was seconded by a well directed fire from the Alamo which for a time prevented the possibility of covering our lines, or effecting a safe communication between the two divisions. In consequence of the twelve pounder having been dismounted, and the want of proper cover for the other gun, little execution was done by our artillery, during the day. We were, therefore, reduced to a close and well directed fire from our rifles, which, notwithstanding the advantageous position of the enemy, obliged them to slacken their fire, and several times to abandon their artillery, within the range of our shot. Our loss during this day was one private killed, one colonel and one first lieutenant severely wounded; one colonel slightly, three privates dangerously, six severely and three slightly wounded. During the whole of the night, the two divisions were occupied in strengthening their positions, opening trenches, and effecting a safe communication, although exposed to a heavy cross fire from the enemy, which slackened towards morning. I may remark that the want of proper tools rendered this undertaking doubly arduous. At daylight of the 6th, the enemy were observed to have occupied the tops of houses in our front, where, under the cover of breastworks, they opened through loop-holes, a very brisk fire of small-arms on our whole line, followed by a steady cannonading from the town, in front, and the Alamo on the left flank, with few interruptions during the day. A detachment of Captain Crane's company, under Lieutenant W. McDonald, followed by others, gallantly possessed themselves, under a severe fire, of the house to the right, and in advance of the first division, which considerably extended our line; while the rest of the army was occupied in returning the enemy's fire and strengthening our trenches, which enabled our artillery to do some execution, and complete a safe communication from right to left.

"Our loss this day amounted to three privates severely wounded, and two slightly. During the night the fire from the enemy was inconsiderable, and our people were occupied in making and filling sand bags, and otherwise strengthening our lines. At daylight on the 7th, it was discovered that the enemy had, during the night previous, opened a trench on the Alamo side of the river, and on the left flank, as well as strengthening their battery on the cross-street leading to the Alamo. From the first they opened a brisk fire of small-arms, from the last a heavy cannonade, as well as small-arms, which was kept up until eleven o'clock, when they were silenced by our superior fire. About twelve o'clock, Henry W. Karnes, of Captain York's company, exposed to a heavy fire from the enemy, gallantly advanced to a house in front of the first division, and with a crowbar forced an entrance, into which the whole of the company immediately followed him and made a secure lodgment. In the evening, the enemy renewed a heavy fire from all the positions which could bear upon us; and at half-past three o'clock, as our gallant commander, Colonel Milam, was passing into the yard of my position, he received a rifle shot in the head, which caused his instant death, an irreparable loss at so critical a moment. Our casualties otherwise during this day, were only two men slightly wounded.

"At a meeting of the officers at 7 o'clock, I was invested with the chief command, with Major Robert C. Morris (late captain of the New Orleans Grays) as second. At ten p.m. Captains Lewellyn, English, Crane and Landrum with their respective companies, forced their way into and took possession of the house of Don Jose Antonio Navarro, an advanced and important position, close to the square. The fire of the enemy was interrupted and slack during the whole night, and the weather exceedingly cold and wet.

"The morning of the 8th continued cold and wet, with but little firing on either side. At nine o'clock the same companies who took possession of Don Jose Antonio Navarro's house, aided by a detachment of the Grays, advanced and occupied the Zambrano Row, leading to the square, without any accident. The brave conduct on this occasion, of William Graham, of Cook's company of Grays, merits mention.

"A heavy fire of artillery and small-arms was opened on this position by the enemy, who disputed every inch of ground, and who, after suffering a severe loss in officers and men, were forced to retire from room to room, until at last they evacuated the whole house.

"During this time our men were re-inforced by a detachment from York's company, under command of lieutenant Gill.

"The cannonading from the camp was exceedingly heavy from all quarters during the day, but did no essential damage.

"Our loss consisted of one captain seriously wounded, and two privates severely. At 7 o'clock p.m. the party in Zambrano's Row were re-inforced by Captains Swisher, Alley, Edwards and Duncan and their respective companies.

"This evening we had undoubted information of the arrival of a strong re-inforcement to the enemy, under Colonel Ugartechea. At half-past ten o'clock p.m. Captains Cook and Patton, with the company of New Orleans Grays, and a company of Brazoria volunteers, forced their way into the priest's house in the square, although exposed to the fire of a battery of three guns, and a large body of musketeers.

"Before this, however, the division was re-inforced from the reserve, by Captains Cheshire, Lewis and Sutherland, with their companies.

"Immediately after we got possession of the priest's house, the enemy opened a furious cannonade from all their batteries, accompanied by incessant volleys of small-arms against every house in our possession, and every part of our lines, which continued unceasingly until half-past six o'clock, a.m., of the 9th, when they sent a flag of truce, with an intimation that they desired to capitulate. Commissioners were immediately named by both parties; and herewith I send you a copy of the terms agreed upon.

"Our loss in this night's attack, consisted of one man only (Belden of the Grays) dangerously wounded, while in the act of spiking a cannon.

"To attempt to give you a faint idea of the intrepid conduct of the gallant citizens who formed the division under my command, during the whole period of the attack, would be a task of no common nature, and far above the power of my pen. All behaved with the bravery peculiar to freemen, and with a decision becoming the sacred cause of liberty.

"To signalize every individual act of gallantry, where no individual was found wanting to himself or to his country, would be a useless and endless effort. Every man has merited my warmest approbation, and deserves his country's gratitude.

"The memory of Colonel Ben R. Milam, the leader of this daring and successful attack, deserves to be cherished by every patriotic bosom in Texas.

"I feel indebted to the able assistance of Colonel Grant, (severely wounded in the first day), Colonel W. T. Austin, Majors S. Morris and Moore, Adjutant Brister, Lieutenant Colonel Franks of the artillery, and every captain (names already given) who entered with either division, from the morning of the 5th, until the day of the capitulation.

"Doctors Levy and Pollard also deserve my warmest praise, for their unremitted attention and assiduity.

"Dr. John Cameron's conduct during the siege and treaty of capitulation, merits particular mention; the guides, Messrs. Erastus Smith, Kendrick Arnold and John W. Smith, performed important service; and I cannot conclude without expressing my thanks to the reserve under your command, for such assistance as could be afforded me during our most critical movements.

"The period put to our present war by the fall of San Antonio de Bexar, will, I trust, be attended with all the happy results to Texas which her warmest friends could desire.

"I have the honor to subscribe myself.

Your most obedient servant
"F. W. Johnson, *Commanding.*"

4.5.2.   Francis W. Johnson, memo, December 17, 1835.

Johnson, F. W. December 17, 1835. Secretary of State (RG-307), Communications Received, TSLA.

Francis W. Johnson wrote this requisition list, intriguing for reasons given in the Commentary, in anticipation of continuing the defense of Bejar (Béxar) and the Alamo.

List of Provisions, Military & Other Stores, required for the use of the Garrisons of Bejar & the Alamo.

Provisions.

250	Bbls Salt beef or Pork
140	Bbls. Flour
4.450	lbs. Coffee
4.500	lbs. Sugar
10	Sacks Salt
1	Bbl. Pepper
10	Bbls. Vinegar

Military Stores &c.

2,000	— 6lb. Cannon Balls
1,000	— 9 lb. D°. D°.
1,000	— 12 lb. D°. D°.
200	— 5^1/2 Inch Shells
200	— Hand Granades
20,000	— 8^{oz} Grape for gantling
12,000	— lbs Cannon Powder
6	— Kegs Rifle — D°
40	— D°. Musket D°.
3	— Tons Lead
100	lbs Pulverized (flour of) Sulphur
200	lbs D°. (fine) Saltpetre

150	lbs Rosin
6	lbs Antimony
2	Demijohns Spirits of Turpentine in a barrel
4	gallons Spirits of Wine for tubes [*or "tribes"?*]
4	Boxes Tin for Cannisters
1.000	Bottoms & Spindles for Grape for 6^s. 9^s. & 12^s. $^1/_3$ of ea —
10	lbs. Marlin for quilting grape
1	Bolt N°. 3 Canvas for D^o.
500	yds Coarse Flannel for Cartridges
100	Sail Needles & 10 lbs twine or Sail thread
1	Ream Coarse blue paper for portfire cases
12	lbs Coarse Wire for Cannon primers
1	Gross of brass scupper nails for Sponges
2	hapers two penny Clouts (nails) for Cannisters
1	Selt gimblets for boring fuses
1	Fuse augur with guage, if possible.
1	Spirit level
1	Gun Quadrant
2	Pair Caliper (bow) Compasses
2	Drawing Knives for making fuses
1	Fine Tennant Saw
2–	$^1/_2$ Inch — 2 one Inch & 1 one & half Inch Augurs

[*writing from here on is in a different hand*]

2–	Screw Wrenches & 2 Hammers
1	Sett of Instruments for making portfires

Blacksmith's Tools

1	Large 36 In. bellows,
1	Mousehole Anvil, & 1 large Strong Vice
2	Sledges & hand hammers in proportion
1	Sett Tonges & Set hammers, punches & all tools required for mounting & bushing artillery.
1	Doz. large Rasps
3	Doz. large Iron files
3	D^o. Common Size D^o
3	Doz. Flat Steel files
3	Doz. CrossCut D^o.
3	Doz. HandSaw files
1	Brace & Crts for boring iron
1	Sett Screw plates from smallest to largest_ with taps & dyes.
1000	lbs. Swedish Iron

100	lbs. English blister steel
25	lbs Cast Steel
1	Stake & Small Tools for a Gun Smith.
1	Bench Vice _
—	

List of Carpenter's tools herewith — Likewise list of provisions.

Head Quarters Bejar Decr. 17^t. 1835

F. W. Johnson
Com. in Chief F. V. A. of T.

P.S.

10	Boxes Sperm Candles
50 D°.	Soap
12	Spades for trenching
2	Reams Commonpaper (foolscap)
1 D°.	letter paper

F.W.J.

4.5.3.   Francis W. Johnson, memo, December 17, 1835.

Johnson, F. W. December 17, 1835. Secretary of State (RG-307), Communications Received, TSLA.

This continues the requisition lists that Johnson requested for Béjar and the Alamo.

Order for clothing —

Bejar 17th Dec^r <u>1835</u>

100	Suits blue clothing for artillery, consisting of blue Jackets, waist-coats, & trowsers —
150	Suits Grey clothing for Infantry, consisting of the same
50	Suits Green [*unclear/smeared word, "Also" or "D°"?*] for Rifle corp. consisting of the same _
600	Check Shirts, 600 Pair Socks (Stout) & 300 pair Shoes of Strong materials —
200	Fur Caps

Head Quarters–
F. W. Johnson
Com. in Chief Fed.
Vol. Army of Texas

4.5.4.   Francis W. Johnson, memo, December 17, 1835.

Johnson, F. W. December 17, 1835. Secretary of State (RG-307), Communications Received, TSLA.

This continues the requisition lists that Johnson requested for Bejar and the Alamo. This document is one of the more uncertain transcriptions, due in part to unclear handwriting and perhaps archaic carpentry terminology.

A List of Carpenters Tools. —
    6 Hand Saws
    l large Task D°.
    1 Small   "   "
    2 W. Compass " [*"W" uncertain*]
    2 long pointers
    2 short D°.
    2 fose plains [*"fose" uncertain*]
    2 [*or 3*] Smoothing D°.
    1 Set Bud plains
    1 D°. Moulding D°.
    on the Gothic order
    2 set of Match plains
    Brace of Bolts
    Plow of D°.
    1 Set framing Chisels
    1 D°. fimser — D°. [*"fimser" uncertain*]
    D°. Goughy
    2 Broad Axes (for Hewing)
    2 Adz's
    1 Set of Augers
    1–12 Inch Trying Square [*"Trying" uncertain*]
    1– 6 D°.–D°.–D°.
    2– 24 D° framing Square
    4 W. Compass [*"W" uncertain*]
    6 Claw Hammers
    6 Chalf ling [*perhaps "Chalk lines"?*]
    1 side filliston
    2– 2 inch Rabbit planes
    1–1 D°.–D°.–D°.
    2– 2 feet Boxwood Rules [*"Rules" uncertain*]
    6 Spoke Sheeves
    6 Wood Rasps & files
    1 Cross - Cut Saw

1 Pit — D°. –
1 Doz. files for each

A^d.Q^m. Bejar Dec. 17t. 1835
F. W. J.

4.5.5.   Provisional Government, report, December, 1835.

Military Affairs Committee to the Provisional Government of Texas. N.d. (c. December 31, 1835). Secretary of State (RG-307), Communications Received, TSLA.
   This is a reaction to Johnson's requests in 4.5.2–4.5.4. The manuscript appears to be a draft; there are several strike-throughs, insertions, and misspellings.

Your Committee to whom was refered the communication of Maj F. W. Johnson to His excellency the P. [*probably "Provisional"*] Governor of Texas & transmitted by him to the Hon<u>ble</u> the Genl. Council, together with accompaying documents containing a list of such articles as is stated to be requisite for the safety, defence & actual wants of the troops at St. Antonio De Bejar, have had the same under consideration of Your Committee, and we would respectfully report to the Hon. The Genl. Council, That the only disposition, which, we could recommend of said documents & to request His Excellency, the P. Governor to order through his proper officer [*or offices*] at Bejar, The Captains of Companies to report Muster rolls of their companies, setting forth the Number of men, for what time they enlisted, when they enlisted, whether in the regular army, or auxiliary corps, and everything relative to their condition & situation—
   Your committee further recommends that His Excellency The Governor be requested to order his proper officer, to report the true conditions of the Ordinance Department at Bejar—how many peices of artillery—the ammunition and supplies of said Department—the tools & instruments necessary for making and repairing fortifications, and every thing connected therewith.
   Your committee recommends this course, because it is impossible for the Genl. Council to order supplies, or make provisions for a Garrison, or any Military—Post, without knowing it's situation & condition in every respect.
   Your committee would further suggest the propriety & necessity of ascertaining from the Officers at Bejar, or Commanding Officer, what companies were at Bejar, when the peace was taken, together with a Muster roll of their Company, if it is possible to be done.
   [*The following is added, with vertical strike-throughs of the entire text.*]
   Therefore be it resolved by the Genl. Council of the Provisional Government of Texas that a copy of this report & resolution be furnished by the Secretary of the Genl. Council to His Excellency the Governor, and that His Excellency the Governor be requested to carry the same into effect.—

4.5.6. Neill, letter, January 1, 1836.

Neill, J. C., to Samuel Houston. January 1, 1836. Adjutant General (RG-401), Army Papers, TSLA.

This letter is by the commander of the forces in Bejar and the Alamo who succeeded Johnson and preceded Travis. It suggests some behind-the-scenes maneuvering related to the command in Bejar.

Bejar 1ˢᵗ January 1836—

General Samuel Houston.

Dear Sir,

The Bearer of this Mʳ. W. S. Blount who bears the express is particularly recommended to you as one whose conduct during the Siege of this place & since that time has been such as entitles him to public attentions, he will receive any appointment, in the regular army & I have no doubt will fill any expectations, he is quite poupular [*sic*] here,

I therefore particularly recommend him to you & Remain with Esteem & Respect

Yours & C—
J.C Neill Let Coln

[*The following is added in a different hand.*]

You are particularly refered [*sic*] to <u>Lieut</u> Blount for information as regards the Conduct of Johnson & Grant at this Garrison of late and any statement on that subject may be relied on G. B. Jameson

4.5.7. Neill, letter, January 6, 1836.

Neill, J. C., to Governor and Council. January 6, 1836. Secretary of State (RG-307), Communications Received, TSLA.

Commandancy of Bejar
To January 6ᵗʰ 1836

The Governor and Council
at San Felipe de Austin
Sirs

Having informed officially the Commander in Chief of the Federal Army of Texas at Washington, the conditions and situation of my command, I deem it my infinite duty to make a corresponding representation to you. Altho So far as regards the Social intercourse desired between the Civil authorities, the citizens, and our army, every thing has been harmonized Since the Command has

devolved upon me to my Complete Satisfaction, and far beyond my most sanguine expectations.

You have doubtless heard from various Sources of the arbitrary rule of the
Aide de Camp of Genl. E. Burliston, F. W. Johnson, and James Grant. The Town
was Surrendered on the 9th Decr and So long as they remained in command
there was not a move made by them to restore or organize harmony or to
reestablish the civil functions of Gov^t which continued up to the 30th retro [?],
and on that day the command devolved upon me, and during that day and the
next through the act of major G. B. Jameson, I had on the first day of this month
all of the civil functions of this department put in power—under the Constitution of 1824, and all things are now conducted on a permanent basis. The Army
aids and Sustains the Civil authority, while the Civil Authority aids us in getting horses and Such Supplies as the greatly impoverished vicinity affords.

It will be appalling to you to learn, and See herewith inclosed our alarming
weakness, but I have one pleasureable gratification which will not be erased
from the tablet of my memory during natural life. That they whose names are
herewith inclosed are to a man those who acted So gallant in the 10 weeks open
field Campaign, and then won an unparalelld [sic] victory in the five days Seige
[sic] of this place—Such men in Such a condition and under all the gloomy
embarrassments surrounding, calls aloud upon you and their Country for aid,
praise, and sympathy.

We have 104 men, and two distinct fortresses to garrison, and about 24
pieces of artillery. You doubtless have learned that we have no Provisions nor
clothing in this garrison Since Johnson and Grant left, If there has Ever been a
dollar Since I have no Knowledge of it. The clothing Sent here by the aid, and
patriotic operations of the Honorable Council, was taken from us by the arbitrary Measures of Johnson and Grant. Taken from men who endured all the
hardships of winter, and who were not even Sufficiently clad for Summer, many
of them have but one blanket, and one Shirt, and what was intended for them
given away to men Some of whom, who had not been in the Army more than 4
days, and many not exceeding two weeks. If a dividend had been made of
them, the most needy of my men could have been made comfortable by the
Stock of clothing and provisions taken from here—

About 200 of the men who volunteered to garrison this Town for 4 months
left my Command, Contrary to my Special orders, and thereby viltiated [*word
unclear*] the policy of their Enlistment, and Should not be entitled to neither
Compensation, nor an honourable discharge, leaving this Garrison destitute of
men, and at all times within 8 or 10 days reach of an overwhelming Enemy, and
at all times great danger was apprehended from want of Civil order and Gov^t
among the lower class of the Mexican Soldiery left behind. They have not Even
left here for our Government an english copy of the Treaty, So (derogatorily
made).

I want here for this garrison at all times 200 men and I think 300 until the
repairs and improvements of the fortification is completed. A chart and index of

which has been sent to Head Quarters at Washington, with the present condition of the Fort, and Such improvements suggested by Mr Jameson as has met my approbation, and I hope will be accorded by my Commander.

As I have Stated to you before our exact Situation here, I Know you will make no delay to amiliorate [*sic*] our condition. The men have not Even money to pay their washing. The hospital is also in want of Stores, and Even the necessary provisions for well men was not left the wounded by Grant and Johnson. Send us money in haste. The men have been here many of them more than three months, and Some of them have not had a dollar during the time.

I shall Say to you as I have said to my Commander in chief; the Services of Major Jameson to this army, and to his Country, cannot be too highly appreciated. The present Army owes in a great part its existence to his exertions and management, and So far as I am concerned in my Command, I assure you I cannot get along without him. I hope he will be continued in the army.

There are many subjects, that owing to the hour of this letter being on the eve of leaving, that has passed my attention of which you Should be advised. And I will from time to time give you Such information as may transpire here, and hope that you will use all the exertions necessary in your power, to Stimulate the men now under my command to remain, and to award to each, and Every one of them, Such praise as your patriotism may dictate, and I particularly recommend to your notice the officers now under my command.

I further add that owing to our having no correspondence with the interior, that we know not what day, or hour, and enemy of 1000 in number may be down upon us, and as we have no supplies of provisions within the fortress we could be Starved out in 4 days by any thing like a close Seige.

I will Say all to you I Know about the feelings of the Citizens of this place on the Subject of Independence—they Know not which hands they may fall into, but if we had a force here that they Knew could Sustain them, I believe they would be $^3/4^{ths}$ Americans and go for Independence and claim all to the Rio del Norte as they Know we want it and will have it—

The extent to which the impressment of Cattle and Horses, has been carried by Johnson and Grant, has been the Cause of great Complai[*nt*] and very much distress among the poorer class of the inhabitants, as Several of them have been deprived of the means of Cultivating their Crop for the Ensuing Season, and which is their only means of Support, owing to their Cattle being taken from them.

I beg leave to tender to his excellency the Governor and the Honorable Council, the high regard I have for their patriotic exertions, in Sustaining the present Federal Army of Texas, in my own name, and also in the name of all those I have the Honor to command at this post. And Subscribe myself

                                J.C Neill [*Lt. Coln?*]
Your ob^t. Servt Commanding

P.S The troops who Engaged to Garrison this place for the term of 4 months, did So with an understanding that they were to be paid monthly, and unless Money comes in time there are Several of them will return home—

I am just informed through a private Source, that there are over thousand Troops now on their march from Laredo towards this place. Should I receive any further information as to their proceedings or dis[*position?*] I will advise you without loss of time by express

> J. C. Neill Lt Coln
> Commanding

4.5.8.   Neill, letter, January 8, 1836.

Neill, J. C., to Governor and Council. January 8, 1836. Secretary of State (RG-307), Communications Received, TSLA.

This letter identifies another concern of this period to the leaders in the Texas Revolution.

> Head Quarters, Comancy [*Commandancy*] of
> Bejar Jan 8t[h]/36 Official

Gov. & Council of <u>Texas</u>
Sirs

We have this morning received an Embassdor [*sic*] from the <u>Camancha</u> [*Comanche*] nation, who informs us that his nation is in an attitude of hostilities towards us-

The[*y*] are, however, willing to treat with us, & propose to concede hostilities for Twenty days, for that purpose, & suggest that each party shall furnish Five Commissioners to form a Treaty of <u>Amity</u>, <u>Commerce</u> & <u>Limits</u>.—I would suggest that Franciso [*Francisco*] Ruis & Don Gasper Flores, of this place, be named as two of the Commissioners, they are familiar with the <u>Camancha</u> character, and have acted in the capacity of Negociators [*sic*] to that nation.—They propose to hold the Treaty at this place, at the time above named and it is hoped that no time will be lost in the completion of an object involving such vital importance—

I remain Your ob[t]. S[t].

> J. C Neill L[t] Coln
> Commanding.

4.5.9.   David Crockett, letter, January 9, 1836.

Crockett, David, to Wily and Margaret Flowers. January 9, 1836. Special Collections Library of the University of Tennessee, Knoxville. Facsimile of original.

This letter was first published in *Dallas News*, June 1, 1913, and also in Folmsbee and Catron 1958, which notes that the original letter still existed in private hands. The letter is also quoted in full—though it differs in some details—by Amelia Williams in *SWHQ* 37:110, where she cited the newspaper date as January 1, although her original notes in CAH (Box 2N492/Folder 3) clearly read "Jun" rather than "Jan." There are numerous misspellings and missing punctuation throughout the letter. "Nacing doches" in the first paragraph is undoubtedly Nacogdoches. Folmsbee and Catron identified "Bordar" and "Chactaw Bro-" as possibly Bois d'Arc Creek and Choctaw Bayou, and they noted that William was his second oldest son and John Wesley was the eldest son.

Saint Agusteen Texas
My Dear Sone & daughter,   9th January, 1836

This is the first I have had the opertunity to write to you with convenience I am now blessed with excellent health, and am in high spirits although I have had many defficulties to encounter I have got through Safe and have been received by everybody with the open cerimony of friendship I am hailed with a harty welcom to this country A dinner and a party of ladys have honored me with an invitation to partisapate both at Nacing doches and at this place The Cannon was fired here on my arivel and I must say as to what I have seen of Texas it the garden spot of the world the best land and the best prospects for health I ever saw and I do believe it is a fortune to any man to come here there is a world of country here to settle

It is not required here to pay down for your League of land every man is entitled to his head right of 4000-428 [*sic*] acres—they may make the money to pay for it on the land I expect in all probilaty to settle on the Bordar or Chactaw Bro- of Red River that I have no doubt is the richest country in the world Good land and plenty of timber and the best springs & good mill streams good range clear water—and every appearance of good health and game plenty—It is in the pass whare the Buffalo passes from North to South and back twice a year and— and bees and honey plenty—I have a great hope of getting the agency to settle that country and I would be glad to see every friend I have settle thare It would be a fortune to them all I have taken the oath of government and have enrolled my name as a volunteer for [*unclear, perhaps "Six"?*] monthe and will set out for the Rio grand in a few days with the volunteers from the United States But all volunteers is intitled to a vote for a member of the convention or to be voted for and I have but little doubt of being elected a member to form the constitution for this province I am rejoiced at my fate I had rather be in my present situation than to be elected to a seat in congress for life I am in hopes of making a fortune yet for myself and family bad as my prospects has been

I have not wrote to William but have requested John to direct him what to do I hope you show him this letter and also Brother John as it is not convenient at this time for me to write them I hope you all will do the best you can and I will do the same Do not be unesy about me I am among friends—I must close with great respects Your affectionate father Farewell. David Crockett
to Wily & Margaret Flowers

4.5.10.   Neill, letter, January 14, 1836.

Neill, J. C., to Sam Houston. January 14, 1836. Adjutant General (RG-401), Army Papers, TSLA.

This letter is known from being published in Brown's 1892 history, but with a number of important lines not included. One is struck by the Travis like tone of Neill's fifth paragraph. Again in this letter, there are a lot of misspellings.

Official   Commandancy of Bexar
                                                   January 14th 1836

Major Genl. Samuel Houston:
Sir/

This is the third official [*letter*] since my command at this place, and they are all of the same nature, complaining of Scarcity of Provisions, Men, and money, and I think we have plenty ordinance [*sic*], Small arms, cannon and musquet cartridges but no rifle powder.

The men all under my command, have been in the field for the last four months, they are almost naked, and this day they were to have received pay for the first month of their last enlistment, and almost every one of them speak[s] of going home, and not less than twenty will leave tomorrow, and leave here only about eighty efficient men under my command, there are at Laredo now 3,000 men under the command of Genl Ramirez, and two other Genls and as it appears from a letter received here last night, 1,000 of them are destined for this place, and two thousand for matamoros, we are in a torpid, defenseless Situation, we have not and cannot get from all the Citizens here, Horses enough Since Johnson and Grant left, to send out (a) patrole, or Spy Company. Capt. Salvador Flores a Mexican, has volunteerd to go with two others as Spies, all the way to Loredo, to learn the Situation of the Enemy, or meet them on the road, and report to us here the movements and distination of the Enemy.

I can Say to you with Confidence, that we can rely on great aid from the Citizens of this town in case of an attack. They have no money here, but Don Jasper Flores, and Louisians [*? probably Luciano; ref. Ragsdale, 32*] Navaro, have offered us all their goods Groceries, and Beeves, for the ade and Support of the army, but men will not be satisfied without some money to pay their little incidental expenses which we must have.

I have sent to the Command of Major Demmitt, Three pieces of artillery, and must have in return three loads of Supplies, asper [*after*] contract with the owners of said waggons.

I hope we will be reinforced in 8 Days here, or we will be overrun by the Enemy, but, if I have only one Hundred men, I will fight one thousand as long as I can and then not surrender—I have sent this day a similar letter to the Governor and Council at San Felipe, learning from Doctor Polland that you would be in Goliad before this letter would come. I hope you will send me one Hundred men from Goliad, unless they have been already sent from some other quarter, as it is absolutely necessary for the support of this place.

Fourteen days has expired since I commenced informing my superior officers of my Situation, and not Even an item of news have I received from any quarter, I hope tomorrow or next day, will bring something good.

There has been a Comancha indian in here, wishing to treat with us a nation, and has Set the 20th April for the purpose of meeting our Commissioners at this place, to Enter into a treaty of Amity, Commerce, and limits with us.

Private
We will learn what Sneaking and Gamboling has been done, to operate against you by J[*ohnson*] & G[*rant*]. You will hear all about the Houston flag, and the Houston House in Bexar, for fear you would be elected Commander of the Volunteer Army. They never would bet it come near an Election, but Shuffled it off, and threw all the army into Confusion Several times, and the responsiblity on the heads of the Several Captains. I am at all times ready to obey the Several orders of my Commander in Chief in a respectful manner and remain with high regard Your ob^t. Servt

"J. C. Neill." Lieut. Col^n. Command^g.

4.5.11.   Neill, letter, January 14, 1836.

Telegraph and Texas Register. January 23, 1836. San Felipe.

COMMANDANCY OF BEXAR
January 14, 1836.

To the Governor and Council, San Felipe de Austin.

Sirs,—I beg to refer you to my official communication, under the date of yesterday, since when, I am sorry to inform you, that our situation becomes such as to be compelled to acquaint you of it by express. There can exist but little doubt that the enemy is advancing on this post, from the number of families leaving town today, and those preparing to follow; among which, is that of John W. Smith, who has this evening engaged wagons to remove his family into the colonies. We are informed that the advance of the enemy is on the Rio Frio, and so situated are we, for want of horses, that we cannot, through our own exertions gain any information, not being able to send out a small spy company. The volunteers that entered for two or four months under Burleson or Johnson, did so with an understanding that they were, for that period, to be paid monthly; which not having been complied with, has weakened me very much, as several left yesterday and to-day and I have not more than seventy-five men fit for duty, and afraid that number will be considerably reduced in a few days. Unless we are reinforced and victualled, we must become an easy prey to the enemy, in case of an attack.

My frequent repetitions of the subject of our distress, and the apprehensions of an enemy, arise partly from the interest I feel for my country, and a wish to preserve those lands she has acquired in the infant stage of her campaign; and being well convinced as above stated, that the enemy may be nearer than rumored, without a power of ascertaining it through our own men on whom we depend, and would, if necessary, ascertain the moments of the enemy, however distant, had we but a few horses.

In this extremity I will assure you, that as far as our strength goes, we will, till reinforced, use it both in spy service, and if drawn within the walls, will defend the garrison to the last.

I beg leave to subscribe myself,

Your obedient servant
J. C NEILL,
Lieutenant-colonel, commanding.

P.S.—The bearer of this takes a requisition to the chairman and members of the committee of safety, at Gonzales, to assist me with as many men and horses as possible, until I can receive reinforcements through orders of the government, from some other quarter, for which I have applied, and hope to receive soon, at the same time putting them in possession of my situation, and my cause of apprehension.

I shall not again make application for aid, as considering it superfluous, but wait the result of either receiving aid or an attack before it should arrive; in which case I will do the best I can with the small force I have,

Understanding that my commanding officer was under marching orders, and not knowing his destination, I have been induced to make my situation known to you, supposing it the chance through which I, as well as the country, may receive most immediate assistance.

J.C.N.
L't-col.com.

4.5.12.   Amos Pollard, letter, January 16, 1836.

Pollard, Amos, to Gov. Henry Smith. January 16, 1836. Adjutant General (RG-401), Army Papers, TSLA.

This letter was written by the doctor who was in charge of the medical department during the siege the following month. He died in its fall.

Bejar J<u>an</u> 16<u>th</u> 1836

Excellent Sir

I have but moment to write you as I am so busy in regulating the Hospital—Things have been in the worst possible state here as you are aware—I hope and have reason to believe they will soon become much better—I ought to have written by the express but know not when it started—I have only to say that we are much in want of money and that some could be collected in goods that are being brought into this place and the Commandant will do it yet he is ignorant of the rate of duties established by the government—When he in possession of that knowledge he would avail himself of it now as there are goods here and he talks of charging but four percent—I am interested in this you will see [?] for the Hospital is in great want of a little money.—We shall endeavor to elect as many of our countrymen as possible from this jurisdiction—What the prospect is I have not yet been able to learn—I think we have now an excellent ["to" crossed out] opportunity to completely conquor [sic] our most formidable foe—our internal enemy—[hole in paper; a word like "the" missing?] mexican tory party of the country—I hope every friend of his country will be diligent at his post and from the righteousness of our cause we cannot but succeed.—

I am your Excellencys
humble servant
Amos Pollard

4.5.13.   Houston, Samuel, letter, January 17, 1836.

Yoakum, Henderson. 1855. *History of Texas from Its First Settlement in 1685 to Its Annexation to the United States in 1846.* 2:58–59. New York: Redfield.

This is support for Gen. Sam Houston's claim that he ordered the Alamo blown up.

General Houston, having reached Goliad on the 16th of January, ordered the command of Major R. C. Morris to take up the line of march for the mission of Refugio on the next day at ten o'clock. On the 17th, he despatched Colonel Bowie, with thirty men, to Bexar, with a letter to Colonel Neill, desiring him to demolish the fortifications at that place and bring off the artillery, as it would be impossible to hold the town with the force there.* "In an hour," says Houston, in a letter to Governor Smith of the 17th of January, "I will take up the line of march for Refugio mission, with a force of about two hundred effective men, where I will await orders from your excellency. I do not believe that an army of such small force should advance upon Matamoras, with a hope or belief that the Mexicans will co-operate with us. I have no confidence in them. The disaster of Tampico should teach us a lesson to be noted in our future operations......I would myself have marched to Bexar, but the 'Matamoras fever' rages so high, that I must see Colonel Ward's men. You can have no idea of the difficulties I have encountered. Patton has told you of the men that make the trouble. Better materials never were in ranks. The government and all its officers had been mis-represented to the army."

It may be proper to state that the order to Colonel Neill to demolish the Alamo, and retire with the artillery, was induced by the information received from that officer on the 17th, advising of the approach of one thousand of the enemy to reduce the place. The commander-in-chief not only despatched Bowie to that point, but relieved Captain Dimit from the command at Goliad, and ordered him to raise a hundred men, if practicable, and repair to San Antonio. Captain Wyatt was left in command at Goliad until he could be relieved by the regulars, when he was ordered to proceed to headquarters with the force under him.

The letter to Colonel Neill was duly received by that officer; and, in reply, he stated that he could not remove the artillery for want of teams, and therefore did not demolish the fortifications of the place. [*Yoakum continues with Neill's complaints about his men not getting paid, as per documents above.*]

---

* Order to Bowie, January 17, 1836.

4.5.14.   Houston, Samuel, letter, January 17, 1836.

Houston, Samuel, to Henry Smith. January 17, 1836. State Department Record Book, no. 3, p. 236, RG-307, TSLA.

A copy of the damaged original with some words missing is also in the TSLA. An edited version appears in Johnson 1916.

Head Quarters
Goliad Jany 17, 1836.

To His Excellency
Henry Smith

I have the honor to enclose for your information a communication from Lt Col. JC Neill, under date of the 14th Inst. Col. Bowie will leave here in a few hours for Bexar, with a detachment of from twenty to fifty men. Capt. Patton's company, it is believed, are now there. I have ordered the fortifications in the town of Bexar to be demolished, and, if you should think fit of it, I will remove all the cannon and other munitions of war to Gonzales and Copano, blow u[p] the Alamo, and abandon the place, as it will be impossible to keep up the station with volunteers. Th[e] sooner that I can be authorized the better it will be for the country. In an hour I will take up the line of March for Refusio Mission, with about 209 effective men, where I will await orders from your Excellency, believing that the Army should not advance with a small force upon Matamoras, with a hope or belief that the Mexicans will co-operated with us. I have no confidence in them, and the disaster at Tampico shoul[d] teach us a lesson to be noted in our future operations. I have learned that Col Iszates [?] is somewhere on the escuces [?] with 170 men, but accounts vary as to their actual numbers. They are to co-operate in the Eastern [Con]fedracy I'm told. [*Houston continues with other actions and requests to Smith.*]

4.5.15.   J. C. Neill, letter, January 23, 1836.

Neill, J. C., to Henry Smith. January 23, 1836. Adjutant General (RG-401), Army Papers, TSLA.

This letter and the next should be compared with Neill's third letter of this same date (4.5.17) in their low-key approach to routine business despite the pending invasion of Texas by the Mexican Army.

Commandancy of Bexar
23<u>rd</u> January 1836

To
His Excellency Henry Smith
Dear Sir

I wrote the Commander in chief on the 16th Inst., recommending Mʳ Gerald Navan as a fit and Suitable person for the office of Sutler to the army of this place, and now beg to recommend him to your notice, and to State that Such an appointment would be of infinite Service to the army now here, when we are So distressed for want of money.

Mr. Navan has been in the army for Some three months at this place, he is a suitable and capable person, and has funds whereby he can conduct the office with great effect to the army, and has at all times been of great utility to the army, to the Engineer department, as well as to the Commandancy

Should the above nomination be confirmed the Sooner he is advised of it through me the better, that he might make the necessary preparations without loss of time that the nature of the department requires.

Trusting that you will use your influence in the above request I Remain Respectfully

Your obServt
J.C Neill Let Coln
Comd Bexar

4.5.16.   J. C. Neill, letter, January 23, 1836.

Neill, J. C., to Henry Smith. January 23, 1836. Secretary of State (RG-307), Records of the Governor, TSLA.

Private   Bexar Jaury 23^d 1836
To His Excellency Henry Smith
Dear Sir

I ask the privilege of you to send to me here at this place a Writ of Election for the Volunteer Army now under my command to authorize them to Elect two delegates to the Convention to be held in Washington. The reasons I request this is that not a man here under my command will or can have a voice in an Election only by and through that method they are all volunteers they are all in favor of Independence.

Such men Should be represented in the council of their Country and that too by men chosen from among themselves. The Citizens have all declared for us and will on the 1st day of next Month take the oath to support the provisional Govt̲ You have the highest regards of the whole Army and you Shall be sustained for your firmness and Philanthropy[.] Yours in hast[e] Verry Respectfully

J. C Neill Let Coln
Comd Bexar

4.5.17.   J. C. Neill, letter, January 23, 1836.

Neill, J. C., to Governor and Council. January 23, 1836. Secretary of State (RG-307), Executive Record Book (Consultation, General Council 11/7/1835–3/16/1836), 155–56, TSLA.

The original manuscript of this letter is in Secretary of State (RG-307), Communications Received, TSLA. It has been seriously damaged and stained, and thus is missing pieces or is completely unreadable over about a third of the document; therefore, this transcript is from the official copy in the Executive Records Book, with some minor revisions based on the readable portions of the original. Someone also made some corrections directly in the Executive Records Book accomplishing the same purpose. Clearly this is an important document in giving solid intelligence of Santa Anna and the threat to Bexar. "Buoy" refers to James Bowie.

Commandancy of Bexar
To The Governor & Council   January 23rd 1836
San Felipe de Austin
Sirs

I hasten to inform you that a Courrier [*sic*] has arrived here last night in Twenty days from St. Louis Potosi dispatched by Eugene Navaro to his brother bringing inteligence that Santa Anna has arrived at Saltillio with Three thousand troops, also that there are at the Town of Rio Grande Sixteen hundred more and that he makes Saltillio [*sic*] his head quarters for the present, and further that he is instructed by the Government to raise forthwith Ten Thousand in such manner as he may think proper and proceed against Texas, which he says he will reduce to the State it originally was in 1820. I was also or at least Col. Buoy was informed yesterday confidentially by the Priest of this place who is a staunch Republican that it was the intention of Santa Anna to attack Copano and Labahia first and send but a few hundred cavalry against this place at the same time.

If teams could be obtained here by any means to remove the Cannon and Public Property I would immediately destroy the fortifications and abandon the place, taking the men I have under my command here, to join the Commander in chief at Copanoe, of which I informed him last night immediately on the above information being Communicated to me.

The foregoing information is received thr'u such a channel that the most implicit reliance may be given to its correctness and veracity, as the parties are personally Known to Col.ⁿ Buoy and he says deserving the utmost confidence.

> Respectfully
> Your obt. Servt.
> J.C Neill
> Lieut Colⁿ. Commanding

4.5.18.   David Crockett, claim, January 23, 1836.

Crockett, David. January 23, 1836. Historical Research Materials: General Texas Revolution Research: Notes from Texas Comptroller's Military Service Records. Williams (Amelia Worthington) Papers, CAH.

The original of this document, possibly the last signature of David Crockett, should be found in the Republic Claims files of the TSLA but is missing.

CMSR. Series II

170-730

1407–1835

(1836)

Washington 23rd Jan, 1836.

#

13.

This is to certify that John Lott furnished myself and four other volunteers on our way to the army with accomodations [*sic*] for ourselves and horses and the government will pay him $7⁵⁰

> (signed) David Crockett

No 10

This is to certify that Jno Lott furnished myself and horse for one night for which the government will settle, 1^{\underline{25}}$

Jany 24, 1835 [*sic*]

> B.A.M. Thomas
> one of
> (signed) D. Crockett's Co.

4.5.19.   Citizens' Meeting, January 26, 1836.

Bonham, James B., et al. January 26 (or 24?), 1836. Secretary of State (RG-307), Communications Received, TSLA.

A major confrontation occurred between the Council and Gov. Henry Smith, with Smith being deposed on January 11. The forces in Béxar were obviously concerned. This is a stained and faded document, and the best reading possible was made. Probable readings of uncertain words are noted by [?]. It appears to have been written by a single scribe, as all the names except the final signature by Neill are in the same hand as the text. It was transmitted by Neill on January 27 in the next document (4.5.20), which includes background details clarifying items in this resolution. The cover is dated Jan. 26, 1836, in a different hand, but in all cases in both documents the date could also be read as the twenty-fourth.

At a large and respectable meeting of the citizens & soldiers of this place, held this 26th [*or 24th, typical*] day of January 1836, to take into consideration the recent movements at San Felipe, J. C. Neill was called to the chair, and [*letter unclear*] J. ["*C.*" *crossed out*] Williamson appointed secretary. The [*word unclear; "intent"?*] of the meeting having been stated by the chair, On motion of J.B. Bonham [?] a committee of Seven was appointed to draft a preamble [?] and resolutions for the consideration of the meeting where upon the following gentlemen were appointed by the chair.

Chairman of Com   J. B. Bonham
                   Jas Bowie
                   G.B Jamison
                   Doctor Pollard
                   Jesse Badgett
                   J. N. Seguin.
                   Don Gasper Flores

Preamble

Whereas we have been informed from an undoubted messenger, that the executive council and its president, a subordinate and auxiliary department of the government, have usurped the right of impeaching the governor, whom if we would imitate the wise institutions of the land of Washington, can only be impeached by a body set forth in the Constitution, which constitution must have been established by the people through their representatives assembled in general Convention. Although [?] the said Council and its President, whose powers are defined to aid the governor to fulfilling the measures and objects adopted by the general consultation, have taken it upon themselves to annul [?] the offices [?] of the Said general Consultation. They are about to open the said offices, which were temporarily closed until a general convention of the people should take place, thereby opening a door to private Speculation, at the expense of the men who are serving their country in the field. Moreover, the said council have improperly used, and appropriated to their own purposes, a Five Hundred Dollar Loan, from a generous and patriotic citizen of the United States, intended to pay the Soldiers in the garrison of Bexar. Moreover, that private and designing [*words unclear; perhaps "Foes are,"*] and have been embarrassing the governor, the legitimate officer of the government, by usurping, contrary to all notions of good order and good government, the right of publicly and formally instructing and advising the governor and the people, on political, civil and institutional matters subject. Moreover, that a particular individual [?] has gone so far as to issue a proclamation on the State of public affairs, and to invite volunteers to join him as the Commander of the Matamoros Expedition, when that particular individual must have known that General Houston, the Commander in Chief of all the land forces in the service of Texas, has been ordered by the government to take command of that expedition. This particular individual is also fully aware that all officers under the commander in chief are elected by the volunteers themselves, and that therefore there was neither room nor necessity for another appointment by the Council. Still, in the possession of these facts, he has issued his proclamation and continues to aid all those who are embarrassing the Executive. Therefore be it Resolved 1st.

That we will support his Excellency Gov. Smith, to his [*word uncertain; "unending"?*] and patriotic efforts to fulfill the duties and to preserve the dignity of his office, while promoting the best interests of the people, against all usurpations and the designs of selfish and interested individuals.

Resolved 2nd. That all attempts of the president and members of the executive council to desist [?] the actions [?] to embarrass the officer appointed by the general consultation and decried by this meeting and end [?] anarchical assumption of power to which we will not submit.

Resolved 3rd. That we invite a similar expression of sentiment in the army under Genl. Houston and throughout the country generally.

Resolved 4th That the conduct of the president and members of the executive council in relation to the Five Hundred Dollar Loan, for the liquidation of the claims of the soldiers in Bexar, is in the highest degree criminal and unjust; Yet under the [?] [*word unclear; "moment"?*] however illiberal and ungrateful, we cannot be driven from the post of honor—and the sacred cause of Freedom.

Resolved 5th. That we do not recognize the illegal appointment of agents and officers, made by the president and members of the executive council, in relation to the Matamoros Expedition; Since their power does not extend [?] further than to take measures and to make appointments for the public, unless [?] with the Sanction of the governor.

Resolved 6th. That the Governor Henry Smith will [?] please to accept the gratitude of the army at this station, for his firmness in the execution of his trust, as well as for his patriotic exertions in our behalf.

Resolved 7th That [?] the editors of the Brazoria Gazette, the Nacogdoches Telegraph, and the San Felipe Telegraph be requested, and they are hereby requested, to publish the proceedings of this meeting.

Bexar. January 26th 1836.

Signed   J. C Neill Pes [*Presiding?*]

4.5.20.   J. C. Neill, letter, January 27, 1836.

Neill, James C., to Council. January 27, 1836. Adjutant General (RG-401), Army Papers, TSLA.

This is the transmittal of the previous document, and has several misspellings.

                                                            Bejar Jan 27th 1836

Prst & Memb[s]. of
the Executive Council
of Texas
Gent.

I have receivd your despatches per express and are truly astonished to find your body in such a disorganisd situation—Such Interuptions in the General Council of Texas have bad tendancies, they create distrust & alarm and at this critical Period of our History are much to be lamented—I do hope however to hear of a reconciliation of matters. Our Govt. sufferss [*unclear; "to be"?*] without a legitimate head, and unanimity of action is certainly necessary to answer the ends and to effect the objects contemplated by the consultation,—

I enclose to you a copy of the proceedings of a meeting held in this place 26th [*or 24th?*] Ult. which will convey to you some idea of the feeling of the Army on the subject.

I also Enclose to you the Address of the Commandant of the Post [?] of Saltillio to his Subalterns—Every Courier from the west seems to corroborate the previous statements in relation to the preparation of the Mexican for War—

I remain Yr O[bst]

                                        J. C Neill Lt
                                        Coln Comd Bexar

4.5.21.   J. C. Neill, letter, January 27, 1836.

Neill, J. C., to Henry Smith. January 27, 1836. Adjutant General (RG-401), Army Papers, TSLA.

Pieces of the paper in the original are gone, hence there are missing words. These have been supplied as italicized words in brackets from the official copy in the Secretary of State (RG-307), Executive Records Book, 250.

Commandancy of Bexar Jany 27th 1836

To His Excellency
Henry Smith
Governor of Texas
Dr Sir

I have received a copy of resolutions enacted by the Council & approved by James W. Robinson Acting Governor as signed, empowering me (as said therein) without giving me the means to do Sundry acts to my own relief as Commander of this place. In my communications to the Executive I did not ask for pledges & resolves but for money provisions & Clothing—There has been money given or loaned by private individuals expressly for the use of this army & none has been [*recei*]ved—Mr Clay from Ala gave or Loaned 500$ (in the presence of [*long dash in Exec. Rec. Book*]) express and on his pledge that, that sum would keep the Army here for the present—[*word unclear; not in Exec. Rec. Book*] to the Council for the use of this garrison Expressly—My Express after having been detained two days to receive that 500$ was told by the Committee that they had appropated it otherwise.—We cannot be fed & clothed on paper pledges—My Men cannot nor will not stand this [*course*] of things much longer—But it appears that [*the*] ligitimate Executive has not had my return by express before him—I wish to be advised. I wish to keep up a correspondence with you publick or private. Enclosed are our resolves they speak their import. Certain inteligence in confirmation of the fact that 1400 troops of the Central Army are on the Rio Grande making every preparation to attack us was receid this morning.

Enclosed is a transcript of an address of the Com-in Chief of the Central Army to his Subalterns.

I am Sir, Respectfully
Your obt. Svt
J.C Neill Let Coln
Comd Bexar

4.5.22.   Amos Pollard, letter, January 27, 1836.

Pollard, Amos, to Henry Smith. January 27, 1836. Adjutant General (RG-401), Army Papers, TSLA.

Bejar Jan 27th 1836

Most excellent Sir

I perceive that the tory party have bought up your council and intend of being an assistant to you as intended they have usurped the government to themselves;—but the people will not stand this—You will see by our resolutions here that we are determined to support you at all hazards.—I did hope that the provisional government would continue till we could establish another and a ["f" in manuscript] more firm one—This we shall endevor [sic] to do in March and God grant that we may create an independent government— Though we be previously invaded I hope that A council will come back from its corrupt course and meet the exigencies of the country—Reports say that troops are now on their way.——

Rely my Dear Sir on every support that my feeble efforts can give you in endeavoring to secure the liberties and establish the Independence of our adopted country.

I am your obt. Servt.
Amos Pollard

4.5.23.   J. C. Neill, letter, January 28, 1836.

Neill, J. C., letter to General Council and Governor. January 28, 1836. Executive Record Book, 150–52, TSLA.

The original of this letter is also in the TSLA but has been heavily damaged by fire and water and is nearly illegible. This copy was also unclear in some spots, and the reading by Jenkins 1973, 4:174–75 was also used for checking this transcript.

Communications to General Council and Governor.
Refered to the Council—
Per Express
To the Provisional Government of Texas, San Felipe de Austin
San Antonio de Bexar, Thursday 6 A.M.
January 28th. 1836

Gentlemen

A friend to the cause of Texas who arrove yesterday from the Presidio de Rio Grande, which place he left 9 days [few letters unclear] back communicated to me the following intelligence of the enemies movements which I deem sufficient important to transmit by Express to the Provisional Government as derived from a source entitled to credit.

The Commander in Chief, General Ramirez y Sesma, of the army of the centralists destined to operate against Texas, had assembled at Rio Grande, 1600 infantry and 400 cavalry of the Presidial [?] companies, 80 waggons and 400 mules with supplies and baggage, including 3000 mules loads of flour, 300 <u>fanegas</u> of biscuit &c. &c. two mortars and 6 pieces of artillery supposed to be twelves and had sent to Dr Beales' colony of <u>dolores</u> for two boats wherein to pass the infantry &c, for the purpose of taking up their march into the colonies, which in Ramirez y Sesma' [*sic*] language are to be Exterminated if they offer any resistance. A forced loan of one per cent had been imposed upon all property and hires made of horses, mules, oxen waggons corn &c in order to fit out the Expedition, even women had been compelled to grind the corn and prepare the bread for the invading army, and the country presented a scene of extortion and oppression, which when inflicted upon friends and countrymen, we may expect to behold inflicted with double rigor upon ourselves. Extraordinary measures of severity were adopted towards those guilty of distortion [*extortion?*] of which some symptoms had been manifested, and on the day of my informants departure these were to be shot for that offense. The roads between this and the Rio Grande, which is fordable, are now good as the season there has been a dry one.

As I expect the Enemy to be on the point of commencing their march, I intend sending out tomorrow a spy to reconoiter [*sic*] and on the arrival of Col. Travis and his men I shall also dispatch them to cut off their supplies, a policy I conceive to be at this juncture most expedient as by depriving the enemy's troops of their provisions & of the means of progressing they will become discouraged and be induced to return. The first misfortune that may happen to them, far from this place will be productive of the best effects. I shall instruct Col. Travis to cut down the bridges over the Leona and Nueces to embarrass the enemy in crossing those streams, with the men, say 25, under that officers command the force of this garrison will consist of 130 Americans and with 600 to 1000 men, I can oppose an effectual resistence [*sic*].

On my Couriers arrival from San Felipe minds became excited and the Resolutions sent out were the result. But Fellow citizens, the time has now arrived and a second <u>epocha</u> is to be from this day dated in the affairs of our adopted country in which domestic dissentions should be hushed and reason [*word uncertain*] should be the watchword. United, the attempts of the Enemy can be baffled even if Sant [*sic*] Anna with his 3000 men do come on. Texas ought and must again arouse to action, another victory will secure us forever from the attack of Tryany [*sic*] and our Existence will no longer be doubtful but prosperous and glorious to attain so desirable an end. I am ready to sacrifice my all, and if as I expect every citizen of the country and our colabrators [*sic*] from the United States are animated by the same spirit, Destiny will be compeled [*sic*] to acknowledge us as her favorites, from the time of my taking the field in the defence of Texas liberties up to the present moment, my labours and watchfulness have been unremitting and they shall continue to be so until I see the land of my adoption free.

I have respectfully to advise that the efforts of the Government be all concentrated and directed to the support and preservation of this town, that supplies of Beef, pork, hogs, salt &c be forthwith forwarded, and if waggons cannot be procured let as much as possible come by hand, men, money, rifles and cannon powder are also necessary. I shall consult with some of the influential Mexicans known to be attached to our cause, about obtaining the effectual assistence of these citizens of whom I judge that 4/5 would join us if they entertained reasonable expectations of reinforcements.

> I remain Respectfully
> Gentlemen
> Your mo: obd. humble Serveant
> J. C. Neill Lt Col.
> Comd. Bexar

4.5.24.   Sam Houston to Henry Smith, letter, January 30, 1836.

Yoakum, Henderson. 1855. *History of Texas from Its First Settlement in 1685 to Its Annexation to the United States in 1846*. 2:460–62. New York: Redfield.

This is a key letter illustrating the chaos in the command of the Texas Army and the actions of the Council in deposing Gov. Henry Smith, resulting in the lack of preparedness for the coming invasion.

MUNICIPALITY OF WASHINGTON, JANUARY 30, 1836.

Sir: I have the honor to report to you that, in obedience to your order under the date of the 6th., I left Washington on the 8th, and reached Goliad on the night of the 14th. On the morning of that day I met Captain Dimit, on his return home with his command, who reported to me the fact that his *caballada* of horses (the most of them private property) had been pressed by Dr. Grant, who styled himself acting commander-in-chief of the federal army, and that he had under his command about two hundred men. Captain Dimit had been relieved by Captain P. S. Wyatt, of the volunteers from Huntsville, Alabama. I was also informed by Major R. C. Morris that breadstuff was wanted in camp; and he suggested his wish to remove the volunteers farther west. By express, I had advised the stay of the troops at Goliad until I could reach that point.

On my arrival at that point, I found them destitute of many supplies necessary to their comfort on a campaign. An express reached me from Lieutenant-Colonel Neill, of Bexar, of an expected attack from the enemy in force. I immediately requested Colonel James Bowie to march with a detachment of volunteers to his relief. He met the request with his usual promptitude and manliness. This intelligence I forwarded to your excellency, for the action of the government. [*Houston gives more details on his actions relating to the situation in*

Refugio and Goliad, then continues with the following.] I found much difficulty in prevailing on the regulars to march until they had received either money or clothing; and their situation was truly destitute. Had I not succeeded, the station at Goliad must have been left without any defence, and abandoned to the enemy, whatever importance its occupation may be to the security of the frontier. Should Bexar remain a military post, Goliad must be maintained, or the former will be cut off from all supplies arriving by sea at the port of Copano.

On the evening of the 20th, F. W. Johnson, Esq., arrived at Refugio, and it was understood that he was empowered, by the general council of Texas, to interfere in my command. On the 21st, and previous to receiving notice of his arrival, I issued an order to organize the troops so soon as they might arrive at that place, agreeably to the "ordinance for raising an auxiliary corps" to the army. A copy of the order I have the honor to enclose herewith. Mr. Johnson then called on me, previous to the circulation of the order, and showed me the resolutions of the general council, dated 14th of January, a copy of which I forward for the perusal of your excellency.

So soon as I was made acquainted with the nature of his mission, and the powers granted to J. W. Fannin, jr., I could not remain mistaken as to the object of the council, or the wishes of individuals. I had but one course left for me to pursue (the report of your being deposed had also reached me), which was, to return, and report myself to you in person—inasmuch as the objects intended by your order were, by the *extraordinary* conduct of the council, rendered useless to the country; and, by remaining with the army, the council would have had the pleasure of ascribing to me the evils which their own conduct and acts will, in all probability, produce. I do consider the acts of the council calculated to protract the war for years to come; and the field which they have opened to insubordination, and to *agencies* without limit (unknown to military usage), will cost the country more useless expenditure than the necessary expense of the whole war would have been had they not transcended their proper duties. Without integrity of purpose, and well-advised measures, our whole frontier must be exposed to the enemy. All the available resources of Texas are directed, through *special* as well as *general agencies*, against Matamoras; and in all probability, prove as unavailing to the interest as they will to the honor of Texas. [*Houston goes on in this lengthy letter to review the background and situation in Texas, essentially to document his actions and the negative impact by the establishment of separate authority for Johnson, Fannin, and Grant—in particular, for conducting an attack on Matamoros. This overview of earlier activities includes this statement about Jim Bowie: "My reason for ordering Colonel Bowie on the service was, his familiar acquaintance with the country, as well as the nature of the population through which the troops must pass, as also their resources; and to this I freely add that there is no man on whose forecast, prudence, and valor, I place a higher estimate than Colonel Bowie."*]

Sam Houston
Commander-in-Chief of the Army

4.5.25.   Edward Gritten, letter, February 2, 1836.

Gritten, Edward, to acting governor of Texas James W. Robinson. February 2, 1836. Secretary of State (RG-307), Records of the Governor, TSLA.

Bexar—2^d. February 1836
Tuesday 4 P.M.

Sir,

Since the P.S. of my letter to you of this day, it appears that the Army has decided on sending separately the two members to the Convention, which will leave the representation of the mexican citizens as before, viz. four members.—

Respectfully,
Your Exc.^{y's} ob^t.hum.Servant
Edward Gritten
H. E.
James W. Robinson, act. Gov.^{or} of Texas
San Felipe de Austin

4.5.26.   John W. Smith, financial report, February 3, 1836.

Smith, John W. February 3, 1836. Republic Claims, AU-Smith, John W.; 4; R130 Fr: 0214–0216, TSLA.

The table of the original document was in a landscape format; here the columns and rows have been reversed to fit the portrait style page. Originally the item descriptions to the left were on top, and the ditto marks to the right in this table are underneath in the original.

Report of the Public Stores and the maner [sic] in which the Articles contain'd in my report of the 31st December 1835. were disposed of.

[*The column (row in the original) headings are as follows: (1) Report of 31st. Decr. 1835, (2) Deliver'd to Master of ordinance as p^r. Order, (3) To Co^l. Nails order, (4) To Quarter Masters order, (5) Capt Blazeby's D^o., (6) " Fapete . . D^o., (7) Dickinson . . D^o., (8) Deliver'd*]

[*Column headings per above list*]

	1	2	3	4	5	6	7	8
Muskets Carabins &ce	357	368	"	"	"	"	"	368
Barrels of Carabins &ce	5	8	"	"	"	"	"	8
Blunderbuses	1	1	"	"	"	"	"	1
Bayonets	420	451	"	"	"	"	"	451

Cartridges	19300	19300	"	"	"	"	"	19300
Aparajor [?]	12	12	"	"	"	"	"	12
Lances	7	7	"	"	"	"	"	7
Boxes Musket Balls &ce	1	1	"	"	"	"	"	1
Camp hornes.	1	1	"	"	"	"	"	1
Doubletrees	1	1	"	"	"	"	"	1
Troughs or Canale,	18	18	"	"	"	"	"	18
Leather Stocks	11	11	"	"	"	"	"	11
Round Bushes	12	12	"	"	"	"	"	12
Cases Instruments	3	3	"	"	"	"	"	3
Boxes Buckels [?] &ce	1	1	"	"	"	"	"	1
Lots of Cartridge boxes	1	1	"	"	"	"	"	1
Dram Hoops	11	12	"	"	"	"	"	12
Case bottles	46	46	"	"	"	"	"	46
Chunck bottles	3	3	"	"	"	"	"	3
Trails	6	6	"	"	"	"	"	6
Flag Staffs	1	1	"	"	"	"	"	1
Bullet Moales	3	3	"	"	"	"	"	3
Balls for Canon	22	45	"	"	"	"	"	45
Small Shells	4	4	"	"	"	"	"	4
Small bags of powder	7	7	"	"	"	"	"	7
Old Hoes	3	"	"	1	"	"	"	1
Frames for Lamps	1	1	"	"	"	"	"	1
Boxes Gun Locks	1	1	"	"	"	"	"	1
Swords	1	1	"	"	"	"	"	1
Pices Iron & Steel	4	4	"	"	"	"	"	4
Iron in square bars	4	"	"	4	"	"	"	4
Iron in round bars.	5	"	2	3	"	"	"	5
Bundles round bars of Iron	1	"	"	1	"	"	"	1
Bags Salt	1	"	"	1	"	"	"	1
Wool Hats	5	"	3	2	"	"	"	5
Socks	44	"	47	"	"	"	"	47
Kegs powder	1/2	1	"	"	"	"	"	1
Shoes	102	"	90	3	3	"	1	97
Shirts	11	"	13	"	"	"	"	13
Pieces Domestic distributed by yards/96 yds	3	"	81	4	"	34	"	119
Frying pans	4	"	4	"	"	"	"	4
pounds of Thread	5	3	1	"	"	1	"	5
Spades	33	4	"	31	"	"	"	35
Axes	12	5	7	"	"	"	"	12
Bags Coffee	2	"	1	1	"	"	"	2
Lances	57	57	"	"	"	"	"	57

Pigs of Lead	1	1	"	"	"	"	"	1
Bars of Lead	"<0?>	36	"	"	"	"	"	36
Bags of Flints	2	2	"	"	"	"	"	2
Rifles.	"<0?>	"	1	"	"	"	"	1

Note the deficiency in the Shoes of five pair will be accounted for When M[r]. Fetche Returns from San Felipe where he is now gone

Bejar 3rd February 1836.   John W. Smith P.S.K.

Further note the difference in the account of [*last three words inserted*] muskets Bayonets & Canon balls arrises from my having gethered all reaturing ones after Johnson left this for Matemores. Smith

---

4.5.27.   J. C. Neill, et al., letter, c. February 5, 1836.

Neill, James C., et al., to Convention. c. February 5, 1836. Historical Research Materials: Alamo Research: Correspondence relating to Alamo Defense. Williams (Amelia Worthington) Papers, CAH.

Wrote Jenkins (1973, 4:263–65): "Travis arrived in San Antonio on February 3, Crockett on February 7 or 8, and Neill left on February 11. Since Neill and Travis both signed and Crockett did not, the date of this document is probably between February 3 and 7, 1836. Maverick and Badgett were both seated by the Convention." The apparent original, complete with signatures, including those of Neill, Travis, Bowie, Jameson, Dickinson (sp?), and several others, now resides in the Secretary of State (RG-307), Private Manuscripts, TSLA. The first page, about ten inches wide, is intact, but the second page, starting where the break is noted, has been cut to about seven inches, eliminating text on both margins. Williams and Jenkins both filled in the missing portions with reasonable readings of the text. For signatures, this has to be one of the most remarkable documents in the Texas State Archives.

A Memorial, of the Undersigned, Officers in and over the army stationed at Bejar, to the President and members of the Convention of Texas to be held at Washington on the 1st day of March next, respectfully showeth that;

Whereas it is evident, as well from the Resolution of the Consultation which provides for the calling of a Convention of all Texas, as from the clear equity of the case, that an equal representation of all persons & interests was aimed at and intended: and whereas the volunteer and regular Soldiers in the actual service of the country, are, by the same Consultation, declared to be citizens, and raised to the right of suffrage: and whereas it is but right on the grounds of population, and appears, from the early date of the aforesaid Resolution, to be intended, that the resident Mexican Citizens of Bejar should have four representatives in the Convention: and whereas our officers perceived that impediments were put in the way of our men voting, such as requiring an oath of actual citizenship in this Municipality before the vote wold [*sic*] be taken; and

furthermore they wished to prevent any, the least, breach in the good understanding which has so happily existed between the Citizens and our garrison
And Whereas no facilities and insufficient time was afforded to such individuals in the army as live in a certain Municipality, to send their votes; and at the
same time a large portion of this army, whilst they possess the declared right of
voting for members of this Convention, do not yet possess any local habitation
whatsoever; and whereas it is of great importance that this [*start of second page*]
army should have representation in the convention who understand their
wants and their wishes, and are participants of their feelings; and of importance
also to all Texas, since she would proceed with less hesitation on any great measures whilst having the voice of all and whereas if the army here, could so far
neglect their interests and their duty, as not to send members of their own
choice, it is evident the wants of the army and the necessity of maintaining &
supplying this important garrison in a manner required by the public safety,
might be forcibly or seasonably urged on the attention of the Government—
inasmuch as the members sent from this municipality, though they have the
best intentions, are yet unable, from difference of language & habits, to represent the Anglo American and Army interest: and whereas the reasonableness as
well as the particular advantage of such a representation has gained the hearty
good wishes of the Mexicans as well as the Americans at this place: And
Whereas by general wish, under the influence of these powerful reasons, an
order was issued to three respectable gentlemen, who are Captains in this service, to hold an election for two members to the Convention, the certificate of
whom, with the return of the votes taken, is transmitted with this memorial:
And whereas on the election being held at the time and in the manner prescribed by law, and in strict conformity with common usage, it appeared on
summing up the votes, as the result of the election that, by a vote which was
almost unanimous, Samuel A Maverick, and Jesse B Badgett, Esquires, were
elected as members of the Convention:

Therefore, for these and other good reasons it is the united petition of ourselves and of the army under our command that the said Samuel A Maverick
and the said Jesse B Badgett shall receive seats as members of your honorable
body and be admitted to a full participation in all the rights, powers, privileges
and immunities enjoyed by the other members: All which, your memorialists
very respectfully submit to the president and members of your honorable body,
& will ever pray

J. C. Neill Lt Col^n.
Comd Bexar

R White capt of
the Bejar Guards.

W^m A Irwin 1st Lieut.

Wᵐ B Carey Capt of
the Artillery

W C W Baker Capt

Saml C. Blair Capt

Geo Evins Most Orde

Wᵐ Blazeley Captain of
the Orleans Greys.

W. Barret Travis
Lt. Col. of Cavalry

James Bowie

G. B. Jameson

E. Melton Q M

Almeron Dickinson Lut

W H Patton Capt

[Endorsed:] Memorial Citizens & Soldiers of Bexar, asking a seat in Convention for Maverick & Jesse B Badgett
[Source:] Consulatation Papers, Archives, Texas State Library.

4.5.28.   Amos Pollard, letter, February 13, 1836.

Pollard, Amos, to Henry Smith. February 13, 1836. Adjutant General (RG-401), Army Papers—Correspondence, TSLA.

Hospital Bexar Feb. 13ᵗʰ 1836

Excellent Sir

I am glad to learn that you are in good health and spirits.—Be assured Sir that the country will sustain you.—We are unanimous in your favor here and determined to have nothing to do with that corrupt council.—It is my duty to inform you that my department is nearly destitute of medicine and in the event of a siege I can be of very little use to the sick under such instances.—I have a plenty of instruments with the exception of a treppining-case—some catheters and and [*sic*] injection syringe which would complete this station.—I write you this because I suppose the Surgeon general not to be in the country and we are threatened with a large invading army.—Four mexicans are to represent this jurisdiction in the convention although we might with great ease have sent the same number of mexicans had it not have been that a few of our people through mexican policy perfectly hood-winked head-Quarters making them believe that it was unjust to attempt to send any other then [*sic*] mexicans thereby exerting all that influence to the same end.—Perhaps I have said enough however I intend that those representatives shall distinctly understand previously to their-leaving that if they vote against <u>independence</u> they will have to be very careful on returning here.—I wish Ge<u>nl</u> Houston was now on the frontier to help us to crush at once both our external and internal ene-mies.—Let us show them how republicans can and will fight

I am your o<u>bt</u> Ser<u>vt</u>

Amos Pollard M.D.
Surgeon

P.S. Some method should be obvious to neutralize Fannin's influence.——
A. P.

4.5.29.   Baugh, John J., letter, February 13, 1836.

Baugh, John J., to Henry Smith. February 13, 1836. Adjutant General (RG-401), Army Papers—Correspondence, TSLA.

Garrison of Bexar Feb 13/36

Sir,

Lt. Col. J. C. Neill being suddenly called home, in consequence of the illness of some of his family, requested Col. Travis, as the Senior Officer, to assume the command of the Post during his absence.—Col. Travis, informed the Volunteers in the Garrison, that they could, if not satisfied with him as a commandant, <u>Pro Tem</u>, elect one such of their own body—The volunteers being under a wrong impression, and ever ready to catch at any popular excitement objected to Col. Travis upon the grounds of his being a Regular Officer, and immediately named Col. Bowie as their choice.

An Election was consequently ordered by Col. Travis and Bowie was Elected.—without opposition none but the volunteers voted & in Fact, not all of them—The consequence was, a split in the Garrison. Col. Travis, as a matter of course, would not submit to the control of Bowie, and he (Bowie) availing him-self of his popularity among the volunteers seemed anxious to arrogate to him-self the entire control.—

Things passd on in this way yesterday & to-day until at length they have
become intolerable—Bowie as Commandant of the volunteers, has gone so far
as to stop carts Laden with the Goods of private families removing into the
Country. He has ordered the Prison door to be opened for the release of a Mexican convicted of Theft who had been tried by a jury of 12 men, among which
was Col. Travis and Col. Bowie himself—

He has also ordered, and effected,—the release of D. H. Barre a private in
the Regular Army attachd to the Legion of Cavalry, who had been tried by a
court-martial and found Guilty of mutiny, and actually liberated him from
Prison with a Corporals Guard with Loud Hurras.—

But the most extraordinary step of all, & that which sets aside all Law, civil
& military, is that which follows——

> Commandancy of Bejar
> Feby 13th 1836—
> Capts of Co^ys

You are hereby required to release such Prisoners as may be under your
direction, For labor, or [*word unclear; looks like "ashriuibe"; Jenkins's probably correct reading is "otherwise"*]

> James Bowie
> Commands of the
> volunteer forces of Bejar

Under this order, the Mexicans who had been convicted by the civil authorities, and the Soldiers, convicted by Court-martials, & some of whom had been
placed in the Alamo, on the public works, were released.

Antonio Fuentes who had been released as above presented himself to the
judge under the Protection of Capt. Baker of Bowie^s volunteers & demanded his
Clothes which were in the Calabash, Stating that Col Bowie had set him at Liberty, whereupon the Judge (Seguin) orderd him to be remanded to prison,
which was accordingly done.—As soon as this Fact was reported to Bowie, he
went, in a furious manner, and demanded of the judge, a release of the Prisoner,
which the Judge refusd, saying that "he would open up his office & let the military appoint a Judge"—Bowie immediately sent to the Alamo for troops and
they immediately paraded in the Square, under Arms, in a tumultuously and
disorderly manner. Bowie, himself, and many of his men, being drunk—which
has been the case [*unclear word; "while" or "since"?*] he has been in command —
—

Col. Travis protested against the proceedings So the Judge, and others, and
as a friend to good order, and anxious to escape the stigma which must
inevitably Follow, held, as a last resort, draws off his Troops to the Medina,
where he believes he may be as useful as in the Garrison, at all events, save
himself from implication in this disgraceful business—

I have venturd to give you a hasty sketch of passing events, in justice to myself and others who have had no hand in these transactions.—

Yo^r ob^t S^t.
P. P. Baugh
Adjt of the Post
of
Bejar

4.5.30. David Cummings, letter, February 14, 1836.

Cummings, David P. Court of Claims File C-1936. Archives and Records Division, Texas General Land Office, Austin.

Cummings would fall as an Alamo defender three weeks after he wrote this letter. The file has an earlier letter of January 20 as well.

San Antonio de Bexar
February 14th 1835 [*sic*]

Dear Father

I wrote you from Gonzales and soon after left there for this place, yet under different views from what I stated in as a sudden attack was expected on our Garrison here and were Called on for assistance.

It is however fully ascertained that we have nothing of the kind to apprehend before a month or Six weeks as the Enemy have not yet crossed the Rio Grande 180. m distant from this place nor are they expected to make any movement this way until the weather becomes warm or until the grass is sufficiently up to support their horses we conceive it however, important to be prepared as a heavy attack is expected from Sant Ana himself in the Spring as no doubt the despot will use every possible means and Strain every nerve to Conquer and extermenate [*sic*] us from the land—in this we have no fear and are confident that Texas cannot only sustain what she now holds but talk [*sic; "take"*] Mexico itself did She think on Conquest.

The northern Indians have joined to our assistance and the volunteers from the United States are every day flocking to our ranks which from the liberal promises of the Government and desirable resources of the Country Seem determined to Sustain themselves or Sinke in the attempt. Many it is true have left the country and returned home to their friends and pleasures but of such Texas has no use for and her Agents in the U. States should be careful whom they Send us for assistance we want men of determined Spirits, that can undergo hardships and deprivation Otherwise they are only a pest and expense to their fellow Soldiers—to the first Class (tho I would be the last to advise in any case), I Say come on, there is a fine field open to you all no matter how you are situated or what may be your circumstances. At least come and See the country, as a farmer, mechanic or a Soldier you will do well—I believe no Country Offers such Strong inducements to Emmigration, affording all the Convieniencies [*sic*] of life that man can devise—what I write is from my own observation and from what I hear from those who have resided for years in the Country I am to leave this to return to the Cibilo creek in Company with 10 Others to take up, our lands we get as citizens which in more than 1100 acres for single men, man of family 4428 acres and Volunteer pay is 20$s pr month & 640 acres at close of the war.

Any Communication to San Felipe de Austin you may make with postage paid to the Boundary line I will get or Send to Stiles Duncan Natchitoches, he could mail it to San Felipe as I would be very glad to hear from you all.

It might be that I might be of some benefit to you here provided any of you could have a mind to come out and indeed to speak Sincearly [*sic*] this would be the Country for us all, nothing could induce me from my determination of Settling here, tho my disposition may not be like most Others. I should like you could once see it—a visit by Jonathan would improve his health I have been very healthy since I have been here and am improving

Yours Affectionately,
D. P. Cummings

PS

There is one thing might be proper for me to add Members have been elected to a Convention of All Texas t[o] meet on 1st March, which will make an immediate declaration of independence—upon the faith of this event great Speculation is going on in Lands, tho the Office for the disposal of the public lands is not yet opened but is expected will be in a Short time. The price of Land has risen greatly Since the commencement of the war. And a declaration of Independence will bring them to vie with those of the U. States tho—they can be purchased from 50 cts to 5$ pr acre by the League depending on their improvement Or convenience to Settlements—No Country is now settling faster—As I will most probably be engaged in surveying of public lands I might be of Service to some of our friends in procuring desireable or Choice locations.

D. P. Cummings

Commentary

Pre-siege Correspondence (4.5)

This section presents a collection of letters written from San Antonio between the capture of the city and the Alamo from General Cós in December 1835 and the start of the siege at the end of February 1836. An in-depth analysis of this material is not given, as those documents of more direct significance to the siege and battle have already been presented. The documents of this section give considerable background information, which helps one understand the context, anticipation, and preparation prior to the siege, and something about a few of the personalities important in this pre-siege period as well as a few of the defenders.

Francis W. Johnson, as described in the historical December 11, 1835, letter (4.5.1), was the first commander of the Alamo after its capture from General Cós. The three (apparently unpublished) memos of December 17 (4.5.2–4.5.4) raise general questions on how logistics were handled in the early Texas Army, and what supplies Travis had on hand a couple months later. Did he fight only with the weapons and ammunition that had been seized from General Cós? If not, might the extent of material captured have been such that an inventory was made? Did the rather disorganized government actually have some capability to resupply its field commanders? Was anything ever sent to Travis? One family oral tradition indicates that a Sampson Connell did, in fact, bring in supplies to Commander Neill.[1] An article by Eugene Barker reviews the Texas Army, but the practical details of logistics are not discussed in any depth.[2] Albert Curtis was one of the first researchers to systematically examine the Republic Claims files. He noted several documents relating to logistics and what they can reveal about the situation in Béxar—for example, when Bowie arrived.[3] A detailed study of the Texas archives on this topic of logistics would be an interesting addition to the scholarship of this era.

John W. Smith provided considerably more details on an inventory of military stores in San Antonio for December 1835 updated February 3, 1836 (4.5.26). William Davis has also found some particularly useful records in the Mexican archives on the amount of armaments and munitions captured after the fall (2.4.3, 2.4.4).

Meanwhile, the response (4.5.5) to the requests for supplies from the actual field commander Johnson by the Committee on Military Affairs for the Provisional Government of Texas should give pause to those who like to believe that bureaucracy is a creation of current and/or long-established governments. One could be more amused if the situation in less than two months were not so deadly.

J. C. Neill succeeded Johnson as the commander in Béxar, likely due to some internal maneuvering, as implied in his January 1 and 6, 1836, letters (4.5.6, 4.5.7). He referred to the Matamoras campaign led by Grant and Johnson, which pulled men away from San Antonio, thus weakening the defenses, and later turned into a disaster, as alluded to in various documents above and below (e.g., Houston in 3.5.6, 4.5.14, and 4.5.24).[4] Williams followed Johnson and his editor Barker in attributing the January 6 letter as the trigger for the Council desposing Henry Smith as governor.[5] Chariton, however, reviews the correspondence of Neill and Houston in this period to strongly argue that an unknown letter of around January 1 was the culprit.[6] Neill's count of 104 men on January 6 is interesting, as this would rise to about 150 plus by the time the siege started at the end of February, and this letter also confirms the Jameson plans for improving Alamo defenses (4.2.1.1). Meanwhile, it is clear from Neill's reports later in January that no supplies or money had yet been received (4.5.10, etc.). On January 14 (4.5.10, 4.5.11), he blamed a lack of horses for his inability to send out a spy party to gather information on the Mexican Army, thus demonstrating that a lack of intelligence was already a problem before Travis arrived (e.g., 3.2.1, 4.2.1.1).

Chariton used the January 14 letter (4.5.11) to raise an interesting possibility concerning executed prisoners after the fall of the Alamo.[7] Citing a number of documents, he argued the real possibility that the reason some defenders survived the battle only to be executed by Santa Anna was that they were simply too sick to fight.

Neill was also positive about support by the local Tejanos in his January 14 and 28 (4.5.23) letters, also echoed by Bowie on February 2 (1.1.1.6) and in contrast to Travis's letter of March 3 (1.1.6).

Neill's letter of January 8 (4.5.8) concerning a possible threat from the Comanche Indians was a partial justification for Houston's visit to the Cherokee in late February to negotiate a peace treaty, making him unavailable to respond to Travis's initial calls for help. This concern about a threat from the Comanche is also recorded in the *Brazoria Texas Republican* for March 7, 1836.[8]

Along with the Jameson letters already seen (section 4.2.1), letters from future Alamo defenders are naturally of considerable human interest in addition to setting the stage. The ones included in this collection are mostly limited, however, to those that directly relate to the situation in Béxar. Three letters of Amos Pollard (4.5.12, 4.5.22, 4.5.28), the Alamo surgeon, report on the lack of hospital supplies and some of the politics in Béxar. The letter of David Cummings of February 14 (4.5.30, also note 1.2.3) gives a sense of how the non-Texans among the Alamo defenders found themselves in Béxar. He was a surveyor, hence his interest in the land distribution. One wonders about the source for the intelligence that "fully ascertained" that an attack was at least four to six weeks away.

The Crockett letter of January 9 (4.5.9) stretches the limitations of the documents selected for this work, being those related directly to the events of the siege and fall of the Alamo. There are, in fact, several other letters by Alamo defenders prior to February 1836 not included here but of human interest concerning those men.[9] As for the Crockett letter from Texas, the warmth, friendliness, and high human interest are all the apology offered for including it here. Of more specific interest is the receipt Crockett signed on January 23 at Washington-on-the-Brazos (4.5.18).[10] This document, from the Williams Papers, CAH, is Williams's transcript recording what might have been the last signature of David Crockett in a document no longer to be found in the Republic Claims files of the Texas State Library, possibly stolen. The document is also significant in locating a specific time and place Crockett was on his way to San Antonio.

Another question discussed by historians concerns the number and identities of the men who accompanied Crockett to San Antonio.[11] An anonymous source from Bastrop, not quoted here, claimed five years later that he was one of at least six men who departed from Nacogdoches with Crockett, and was one of two who did not complete the trip due to sickness.[12] He did not reflect on what might have happened to him had he not gotten sick. The John Swisher memoirs record a delightful account of a young Gonzales man who returned home from hunting to find the former congressman staying with them before going on to San Antonio.[13]

The letters of Sam Houston of January 17 and 30 (4.5.13, 4.5.24) give a sense of his activities in the pre-siege period and the difficulties caused by the Matamoros campaign. His letter of the thirtieth is the best overview of the leadership situation with Governor Smith being deposed; Johnson, Fannin, and Grant given independent authority to support the attack on Matamoros; and the consequent departure of Houston from Goliad to return east. This left the Béxar area without a strong senior leader to meet the coming invasion. Along with the apparent lack of response per their letters, one might wonder why people like Neill and Travis didn't just give up and go home.

Of special interest for Alamo studies is the statement in the January 17 letter that both Neill and Bowie were ordered to blow up the Alamo and retire with the artillery. Documents above have already introduced Houston's claim to this effect (3.5.6, 4.4.2; also in 5.2.2 below). That the original orders have not been found resulted in something of a controversy over whether Houston did in fact issue such orders. Yoakum (4.5.13) cited the orders to Bowie, but Houston's letter to Smith talks only of abandoning the town, with the destruction of the Alamo conditional upon Smith's support. The January 23 letter of Neill (4.5.17) talks as if destroying the Alamo were up to his discretion. Of course, if Neill had been disobeying orders, one could not expect him to admit it in writing. Chariton gives a documented argument that Houston's claim was made with twenty-twenty hindsight.[14] At any rate, had Houston had sent the orders as Yoakum described, one is struck by the appeal of the Alamo to Neill, Bowie, and later Travis when they resolved to defend it to the last.[15] One can also ask the unresolvable "what-might-have-been" question of what would have happened had Houston gone to Béxar and seen to it that the Alamo was blown up.

The crisis in San Felipe with the removal of Governor Smith had an immediate reaction among the soldiers, regular and volunteer, on the front line (4.5.19). The most physically obvious component of the January 26 meeting resolution by Bonham, Neill, et al. is that the "Five Hundred Dollar Loan" is in significantly larger script. That implies it was the most prominent in their own minds. A second point of special interest is the extent of support for Governor Smith and General Houston among the Béxar military leaders. It also helps make clearer why Houston might rather have been off negotiating with the Cherokee nation the next month (Commentaries for 4.4.2, 4.5.8) than dealing with the Texas government. Perhaps, however, the most significant aspect of this resolution in the ultimate outcome of the upcoming battle at the Alamo was the choosing of sides in the San Felipe political fight. The result might

have been that acting Governor Robinson or the Executive Council had little motivation to send any support or assistance in the month remaining till the arrival of Santa
Anna. This possibility has some additional suppport from a letter of January 31 from
an advisory committee to Robinson, which, while advising him to countermand Houston's order to abandon Béxar, states the opinion that "no further necessity exists of
increasing the number of troops now at Bejar."[16]

Returning to Neill, there are several further letters to consider. The January 23
group of three letters from Neill (4.5.15–4.5.17) is a bit curious, as the first two have
a very low-key approach to routine business, while the third gives the solid intelligence of Santa Anna's pending invasion and the threat to Béxar. One possibility is
that even though Neill stated that the courier arrived the previous night, he might not
have actually talked to the informant until after the first two letters were written. With
the shock of this news of the pending invasion, Neill now expressed a desire to
destroy the Alamo and retreat, in contrast to his attitude on January 14 (4.5.11).
Then, in two letters on January 27 (4.5.20, 4.5.21), he was further concerned with the
actions of the council in replacing Gov. Henry Smith with James Robinson. The letter
to Henry Smith of this date, with the frustration he expressed, is particularly interesting
to compare with his initial letters in command (4.5.6, 4.5.7), where he blamed the lack
of money and provisions on prior commanders and was optimistic that the governor
and council would quickly accommodate the needs of his post. But on January 28
(4.5.23), Neill was again ready to fight even Santa Anna and his three thousand
troops. As Travis was officially part of the Texas cavalry, Neill also assumed that he
would add mobility in the form of horses to the Béxar defense.[17]

There are two documents, Gritten's of February 2 (4.5.25) and that of Neill et al.
of February 5 (4.5.27), that primarily relate to the selection of representatives to the
Convention to be held March 1 (and which would declare independence on March 2).
The latter is additionally important in dating the arrivals of Travis and Crockett to
Béxar, as Travis was there to sign the document but Crockett was not.[18]

The Audited Claims files (4.5.26) provide a detailed inventory from John W.
Smith, in his role as military store keeper for the Alamo, on the various supplies and
materials held by the army in San Antonio.[19] One of the most striking observations on
this list is that, with the exception of muskets and cartridges, there do not seem to be
enough stores for 190 or so men to maintain a siege for thirteen days. A conclusion is
that this list of "Public Stores" is not all that was available to Travis later in February.
Certainly the cannons known to be in the Alamo are not listed, so they, as well as
powder, food, and other supplies, might well have been separate "military stores"
under the direct control of the commander of the Alamo. This is reinforced by the
items and quantities in Johnson's list of December 17, 1835 (4.5.2). A considerable
number of rifles and some additional powder were likely personal property as well.

Finally, there is an exceptionally interesting February 13 letter of Baugh (4.5.29)
recording the departure of Neill, the assumption of command by Travis, and the initial
tension with Jim Bowie. This constitutes strong support for Travis's version of the
events (1.1.1.8) and says something for his ability to work around the problems of the

joint command. It might also be noted that several historians have stated that Bowie was normally temperate, and therefore his described drunkenness was unusual.[20]

Both Stephen Hardin and Wallace Chariton further studied Neill's actions and career. Chariton in particular used several documents to demonstrate the efforts Neill made to reinforce the Alamo when the siege began.[21]

One of the most curious aspects of this collection is what is missing. There is not a single letter from Henry Smith, James Robinson, Sam Houston, or anyone else of senior authority that was sent to Béxar. Of course, any originals would have been in the Alamo and seized by Santa Anna after the fall, but it is not clear why they would have been destroyed, as they might have given useful propaganda to Mexican audiences similar to the Williamson letter (4.3.4). Nor is it clear why some sort of letter book wouldn't have been maintained by the Texans in official positions and survived somewhere. A partial explanation is that Henry Smith's papers were destroyed when San Felipe burned during the invasion by Santa Anna.[22] This appears to be one of the major gaps in the Alamo story, and it is hoped that overlooked files or documents might still be located.

A final comment is on the patriotic spirit expressed in these soon-to-be-famous letters. Certainly the expressions of these authors would form a foundation for the attitudes of Texans in the future, and they have had a significant effect on American attitudes in general toward the Alamo.

---

1. Jackson 1997, 131–32.
2. Barker, 1906.
3. Curtis 1961a, 13, also note Sutherland claim, 1.7.1.4.
4. There is also a summary in Williams in *SWHQ* 36:258–64(1933); Filisola 1987, 2:266 on; and Davis 1998, 491 on.
5. Williams in *SWHQ* 36:262–63; Johnson 1916, 1:369–70.
6. Chariton, 107–15.
7. Chariton's citations include documents 4.5.7, 4.2.1.1, 1.2.11, 1.2.8, 4.3.10, and 4.3.7 in this work.
8. For contrary viewpoints, see Lindley 1995, 30–31, and Davis 1998, 518, who labels the trip "near-pointless."
9. Other letters close to the siege, most of which can be found in Gronemans 1990a, were written by Micajah Autry (January 13, December 13, December 7, 1835); Richard W. Ballentine and Cleveland F. Simmons (December 9, 1835); James R. Bonham (December 1, 1835); William R. Carey (January 12, 1836); Daniel W. Cloud (December 26, 1835); David Cummings (January 20, 1836); John H. Forsyth (January 3, 1836); John C. Goodrich (November 28, 1835); Joseph M. Hawkins (January 20, January 24, 1836); Charles A. Parker (November 20, 1835); and John M. Thurston (December 18, 1835). Still another possibly unpublished letter is one from Gonzales by John W. Smith of January 23, 1836 (Don Carlos Barett Papers, CAH).
10. Williams in *SWHQ* 37:105 n. 1.
11. See also Davis 1998, 416–17.
12. In the *Austin City Gazette* for April 14, 1841.
13. Swisher, 18–23.
14. Chariton 1992, 1–17. Houston's side of the story, from two speeches in 1845 and 1859, is in Williams and Barker 1941, 6:5–13; 1942, 7:306–36. Lindley 1995 goes fur-

ther in using these and other documents to give a characteristically negative viewpoint on the actions of his subject, Houston in this case.

15. E.g., Williams *SWHQ* 36:277–78; Davis 1998, 493–501.
16. Jenkins 1973, 4:204–6.
17. Davis 1998, 496, describes well how Grant and Johnson had stripped Béxar of horses as well as men.
18. See Davis 1998, 717 nn. 44 and 46, which make a case for the petition to date from February 4.
19. There are additional documents in Republic of Texas/Audited Claims R:098 Fr:0009-0019, TSLA.
20. E.g., per Williams *SWHQ* 37:103 n. 52.
21. Hardin 1989, and Chariton, 95–105.
22. Smith 1910, 24.

CHAPTER 5

Later Sources

Understanding the events of the siege and fall of the Alamo also depends on later sources, which, despite the lapse of years from 1836, still have valuable information. These include both sources already excerpted earlier for specific participants and those histories that were major secondary sources forming common perceptions in later years. Also included are important historical studies of a more general and analytical scope.

The first selection is of those later accounts that still had at least the possibility of access to primary sources, and also demonstrate how additional dramatic details sometimes got added to earlier accounts. The first such account is a town resolution from Nacogdoches on March 26, 1836. Excerpted next is one of the very first books printed on the Texas Revolution, that by Joseph Field (1836). Next are relevant sections of histories already quoted in part above: Rev. Chester Newell (1838), William Kennedy (1841), Henderson Yoakum (1855), and James Morphis (1874). Following is the most careful and comprehensive nineteenth-century study of the Alamo: "The Fall of the Alamo," by Reuben Potter (1878). The last set of documents of this group gives the evidence relating to James Bonham's dash into the Alamo on March 3, as narrated by John Henry Brown (1889). All these documents claimed they had firsthand information about the events of the Alamo.

The second group selected is from portions of some important twentieth-century research or sources. These include additional excerpts from Amelia Williams's thesis (1934); the appendix summarizing the "Riddles of the Alamo" from Walter Lord's *A Time to Stand* (1961); two excerpts by Anne Fox et al. (1976), and Jack Eaton (1980), as a sample of the modern archeology studies in the Alamo Plaza; a detailed review by Susan Schoelwer (1988) of pictorial representations of the Alamo; and a study of Tejano sources for the Alamo, by Timothy Matovina (1995). These documents represent some of the newer directions and the value that modern researchers and scholars bring to the understanding of this century-old event.

5.1.1.   Town resolution, March 26, 1836.

Raguet, Henry. March 26, 1836. "Meeting of the citizens of Nacogdoches." Carson (Sam P.) Letters, TSLA.

This document was published in Jenkins 1973, 9:159–61, but was not found as per Jenkins's citation in the *Austin Statesman*. What must be the original was located as cited. The Jenkins version is mostly very accurate in content, though a couple of lines were missed in the second paragraph. There are numerous misspellings in the original.

At a meeting of the citizens of Nacogdoches on the 26th of March 1836, the following preamble and [*"volunteers" crossed out*] resolutions were unanimously adopted, and ordered to be published.

The citizens of this municipality in common with all Texas, feeling the profoundest grief for the loss of their gallant countrymen in the storming of the Fort Alimo, at St Antonio de Bexar on the 6th of the present month, and entertaining the highest admiration for their heroism, cannot refrain from a public expression of there sentiments. Brave men struggling for liberty in distant lands receive the sympathy of generous and liberal minds of all nations, but when their achievements are in our own immediate defence they arouse the Strongest sensations of the heart. The reflection comes home to our bosoms that valuable lives have been offered up a willing sacrifice for our safty and protection. We emblam it with our tears and give utterance to our gratitude and praise. The tongue of eulogy shall bestow its tribute and the record of history emblazon their fame.

It is due to the occasion that we give a summary of facts. Colonels Travis and Bowie with 187 Volunteers, and only 150 effective, for fourteen days maintained an extensive fortress against a Mexican Army of eight thousand strong commanded by the famous General Santa Anna! During this period they repulsed the enemy in repeated asalts by day and night, repaired successive breaches in the fortification, made a terrible slaughter of the assailants and remained almost unhurt, on the morning of the 6th worn out by incessant toil, exhausted nature would endure no longer; and during a temporary suspension of the bombardment they sought repose: The enemy became apprised of their situation by the supposed treachery of a Mexican in the Fort and surrounded it with their whole force of infantry and cavelry they were roused from their sleep by the cry that "the enemy [*is*] on the walls," and as giants they arose to the fight and thrice drove them back. Before undaunted courage the whole host covered [*sic; probably "cowered"*] and were forced again to the charge at the point of the lance. They came on thousands, and as a herd of Cattle overrun a handfull of men. But the gallant band remained undaunted to the last, and the conflict was terrible & almost superhuman. Five hundred and twenty one of the

enemy were slain and as many wounded. In previous encounters they had sustained an equal loss. This statement is estimable from the fact that the fort contained cannon & musket to a very large amount captured by the Gallant Milam
at the Surrender of Gen'l Coss, and that each man was armed with from five to
ten loaded pieces for every assault on the 6th. Capt. Jamison is said to have discharged the artilery under his command thirty times. The generous Bonham,
who with thirty-three brave fellows had entered the Fort during the siege, was
found apart from his [*"commanders" crossed out*] comrades with eighteen Mexicans dead around him. David Crocket (now rendered immortal in Glory) had
fortyfied himself with sixteen guns well charged, and a monument of slain foes
encompassed his lifeless body. These few details are evidence of the feats of all.
They were determined to conquer or die. From a merciless enemy they had no
quarters to expect, and resolved to ask none. Every man fought to his last
breath and <u>not one survives.</u> The chivalric Travis fell in the breach, and prostrate with wounds, grasped his sword, and with the last ebb of life felled to the
earth the officer who first entered the Fort and they both were extended lifeless
corpses.

The tongue of every noble Spirit of whom we speak is silent in death and
we anticipate in a succinct [*word crossed out*] imperfect narrative the future
Glory of their fame. They Died Martyrs to liberty; and on the alter of there sacrifice will be made many a vow that shall break the shackles of tyranny. Thermopylae is no longer without a paralel: and [*"where" crossed out*] when time
shall consecrate the deeds of the Alimo, Travis and his companions will be
named in rivalry with Leonidas his Spartan band.

The Impotent revenge of the Mexicans in mutilating the dead bodies of
these brave men, and in denying them the rites of the sepulchre by burning
them in heaps, we cannot forbear to mention as deserving the excercation of all
mankind, and as evidence of their deep rooted ferocity. It was indeed an
appalling sight to the usurper Santa An[*na missing in tear*] to behold such hav-
ock of his [*something missing in tear; possibly "megalomania by"*] a handful of
[*"men" crossed out*] intrepid volunteers, and we are told he stood agast at the
spectacle! He might truly had exclaimed "A few more such victories and I am
destroyed." And that he will be destroyed the whole country has every confidence.

Resolved—1st that we entertain the highest admiration for the sublime and
noble defence of Fort Alimo by our Commented countrymen; and that we will
ever venerate their memory.

2nd that we call upon the Government of Texas to obtain a correct list of the
names of these patriots and preserve it in the archives for the future award [*partial word crossed out*] of appropriate honors.

3. That we offer our deepest sympathy to the relatives of these distinguished worthies.

4.That we will continue to maintain the good cause in which we have embarked, and adopt the Motto of the Alamo.

Victory or Death
Henry Raguet
Chairman

5.1.2.   Dr. Joseph Field, narrative, 1836.

Field, Joseph E. 1836. *Three Years in Texas. Including a View of the Texan Revolution, and an Account of the Principal Battles* . . . 11–12, 36. Greenfield, MA: Justin Jones.

In giving a history of the battle of San Antonio, the obstacles which always obtrude themselves upon the narrators of military operations in the field, present peculiar difficulties in the present instance in consequence of the great irregularity of the town and country adjacent, where the bloody scenes I am about to describe were acted.

The village of San Antonio stands on the west bank of the river, of the same name, at a place where the stream by a sudden turn leaves a point of land in shape resembling a horse shoe. Upon this peninsula it is said that David Crockett killed the first Mexican soldier, at the distance of two hundred yards. It was here that Crockett and Dickinson burned some houses that stood in the way of their artillery. That part of the town, which is more particularly important to be understood on account of its having been the centre of the military operations, is a square, enclosed on all sides by stone houses, with streets running, from all the corners, parallel and at right angles with the sides of the square.—At the entrance of every street, with the exception of that leading to the Alamo, a ditch was dug ten feet wide, five feet deep, raised on the inner side, so as to make an elevation of ten feet. Over this was erected a breast-work of perpendicular posts, with port holes for muskets, and one in the centre for cannon. These slight outlines may be a sufficient introduction to the details, which are to assist the reader in tracing the contest, which ended in the evacuation of San Antonio by the Mexicans, and its occupation by the friends and defenders of Texas.

[*In addition to his narrative of his own experiences, Dr. Field's closing includes the following.*]

It is said and generally believed in Texas of Col. Crockett, that when Gen. Santa Anna was surveying the Alamo for the purpose of informing himself of the best method of arranging an attack, he made so good a shot at him as to come near taking his life, which so much enraged the General, that he resolved to storm the fort the next day and he kept his resolution.

It is also reported, as coming from Mrs. Dickinson, who was in the Alamo during the storm, that Col. Crockett came into her apartment, fell upon his knees, committed himself to his God, went out and was soon killed.

5.1.3.   Chester Newell, narrative, 1838.

Newell, Rev. Chester. 1838. *History of the Revolution in Texas* . . . 89–91. New York: Wiley & Putnam.

This narrative quotes letters of Travis and the diary of Almonte (2.2.1) and was the source for the interview with Ben (2.12.1). This is the end of his chapter on the Alamo that has his unattributed sources.

On other authority we have it, that at day-break on the morning of the 6th, the enemy surrounded the fort with their infantry, with the cavalry forming a circle outside, to prevent the escape of the Texans. The number of the enemy was at least 4000, opposed to 140! Gen. Santa Anna commanded in person, assisted by four generals and a formidable train of artillery. The Texans were greatly exhausted by incessant toils and watchings, having sustained, for several days, a heavy bombardment and several real and feigned attacks. But American valor and love of Liberty displayed themselves to the last: they were never more conspicuous. Twice did the enemy apply to the walls their scaling ladders, and twice did they receive a check; for the Texans were resolved to verify the words of the immortal Travis, that he would make a "victory worse to the enemy than a defeat." A pause ensued after the second attack, which, by the exertions of Santa Anna and his officers, was again renewed, and the assailants poured in over the walls "like sheep." The struggle, however, did not end here. Unable, from the crowd and want of time, to load their guns and rifles, the Texans made use of the butt ends of the latter, and continued the fight till life ebbed out of their wounds, and the enemy had conquered the fort; but not its brave, its matchless defenders. They perished, but yielded not. Only one remained to ask quarter, which was denied by the ruthless enemy. Total extermination succeeded, and the darkness of death closed upon the scene! Spirits of the mighty had fallen; but their memory shall brighten the page of Texan history; and they shall be hailed, like the demi-gods of old, as the founders of new institutions, and the patterns of virtue!

The storming of the fort had lasted less than an hour. Col. Travis had stood on the walls cheering his men, and exclaiming "Hurra, my boys!" till he received the shot of which he fell. A Mexican officer then rushed upon him, and lifted his sword to destroy his victim, who, collecting all his expiring energies, directed a thrust at his inhuman foe, which changed their fortunes,—for the victim became the victor; and the remains of both descended to eternal sleep—but not alike to everlasting fame.

The end of David Crocket, of Tennessee, the great hunter of the West, was as glorious as his career in life had been conspicuous. He and his companions were found with heaps of dead around them, whom they had immolated on the altar of Texan Liberty. His countenance was unchanged, and as fresh as when in his wonted exercise of the chase in the forest, or on the prairie. Texas, with pride, numbers him among the martyrs to her cause.

Major Evans, of the artillery, was shot when in the act of setting fire to a train of powder to blow up the magazine, agreeably to the previous orders of Travis. In the magazine was near a ton of powder, which, had it exploded, might have put an end to the career of Santa Anna, and blown to a more timely destruction the minions of his power, destined to whiten with their bones the plains of San Jacinto or the prairies of the West. Santa Anna, when the body of Evans was pointed out to him, drew his dirk and stabbed it twice in the breast.*

James Bowie, who was lying sick, was murdered in his bed, and his body mutilated.

The bodies of the Texans were denied the right of burial: stripped, thrown in a pile, and burned! Thus was bigotry added to cruelty. But revenge had already been taken: fifteen hundred Mexicans lay weltering in their blood!

---

* The account of this act was subsequently verified by the discovery of a shirt on a Mexican prisoner, which was recognized as having belonged to Evans, and which had in the bosom two cuts like those of a dirk.

5.1.4.   William Kennedy, narrative, 1841.

Kennedy, William. 1841. *Texas: The Rise, Progress, and Prospects of the Republic of Texas* . . . 2:180–81, 186–88. London: R. Hastings.

This narrative uses Almonte's journal (2.2.1) and Newell (5.1.3) extensively. Footnotes from the source material are given in brackets and italicized within the text.

General Santa Anna moved from the Rio Grande in the afternoon of the 16th, and at half-past twelve o'clock on the 23rd halted on the heights of the Alasan, near San Antonio de Bexar. [*Footnote: Manuscript Journal of the Campaign, by Colonel Almonte found on the battle-field of San Jacinto by Dr. Anson Jones.*] The whole of the invading army was ordered to concentrate at the place, with the exception of a division under General Urrea, which had marched from Mata-moros for San Patricio, the Irish settlement on the river Nueces. At two o'clock, according to Colonel Almonte's Journal, the Mexican army resumed its march—

[*Kennedy quotes extensively from Almonte's journal, interspersed with para-phrases or quotes of Travis's letters. He then continues his account.*]

Reinforcements were arriving daily to Santa Anna, until the force at Bexar amounted to more than 4,000 men, with all the means and appliances of war. For Travis and his little band, cooped within the walls of what one of the Mexican generals (Filisola) aptly termed the barrack *(del cuartel)* of the Alamo, there came no succour. Real and feigned attacks, a heavy bombardment, and the necessity of procuring wood and water outside the fort, wore down the physical energies of the garrison, but did not subdue their spirit. Soon after midnight on the 6th of March, the Mexican army, commanded by Santa Anna in person, surrounded the fort, for the purpose of taking it by storm, cost what it might. The cavalry formed a circle around the infantry, for the double object of pricking them on, and preventing the escape of the Texans. Long before daylight, the Mexicans advanced towards the Alamo, amidst the discharge of musketry and cannon. Twice repulsed in their attempt to scale the walls, they were again impelled to the assault by the exertions of their officers, until, borne onward by the pressure from behind, they mounted the walls, and, in the expressive language of an eye-witness, "tumbled over like sheep." Then commenced the last struggle of the garrison. Travis received a shot and fell as he stood on the walls, cheering on his men. When he dropped, a Mexican officer rushed forward to despatch him. Summoning up his powers for a final effort, Travis met his assailant with a thrust of his sword, and both expired together. The brave defenders of the fort, overborne by multitudes, and unable in the throng to load their fire-arms, continued the combat with the but-end [*sic*] of their rifles, until only seven were left, and these were refused quarter. Of all the persons in the place, no more than two were spared—Mrs. Dickerson and the negro servant of the Commandant. Major Evans, of the artillery, was shot while in the act of firing a train, to blow up the magazine, by order of Travis. Colonel James Bowie, who had been confined seven days by sickness, was butchered in his bed and his remains savagely mutilated. The rudest form of a sepulture was denied the dead. Their bodies were stripped, thrown into a heap, and burnt, after being subjected to brutal indignities, in the perpetration of which General Santa Anna has been charged with being a leading instrument. [*Footnote quotes Newell's story of Santa Anna stabbing the body of Major Evans. Kennedy continues with a discussion of the casualties on both sides and a review of the career of David Crockett.*]

5.1.5.   Henderson Yoakum, narrative, 1855.

Yoakum, Henderson. 1855. *History of Texas from Its First Settlement in 1685 to Its Annexation to the United States in 1846.* 2:75–82. New York: Redfield.

Yoakum was a personal friend of Sam Houston. He footnoted many of his sources, including Almonte's journal, original letters, Mrs. Dickinson, and Antonio Peréz. These footnotes are included in the text here in brackets and italicized. Yoakum additionally had access to several documents now lost, such as some Houston letters, and so is the primary source remaining for these documents. As a consequence, his early history is one of the most well researched and important of Texas. Since his sources are traceable, most have already been included earlier in this work in their original form, and hence there is little new material. At the time of publication, this was not the case, and this was a principal history for generations of Texans.

It is proper that we now return to the operations of the enemy. It will be remembered that Santa Anna reached the Alazan at noon, on the 23d day of February; and Urrea arrived at San Patricio before dawn on the morning of the 27th. At two o'clock in the afternoon, Santa Anna marched into San Antonio. [*Footnote: Almonté's Journal*] The Texan guard in the town retired in good order to the Alamo. Colonel Travis, in anticipation of an attack, had done what he could to strengthen the walls, and provide means for defence. The Alamo, though strong, was built for a mission, and not for a fortress. The walls are thick, but of plain stone-work, and without a redoubt or bastion to command the lines of the fort. The main wall is a rectangle, one hundred and ninety feet long, and one hundred and twenty-two feet wide. On the southeast corner was attached the old church, a large building, and containing the magazine and soldiers' quarters. Adjoining this on the east side was the stone *cuartel* for horses. About midway of the east side of the main wall, but within it, was a two-story stone building; the upper story being used for a hospital, and the lower one for an armory, soldier's quarters, &c. There were four pieces of artillery mounted on the side toward the town, and a like number facing the north; two on the side of the church, and four to defend the gate which looked toward the bridge across the San Antonio river. The place was supplied with water from two aqueducts running on either side of the walls. [*Letter of G. B. Jameson, with plot and description of the Alamo, January 18, 1836.*] But Travis was greatly deficient in men, provisions, and ammunition.

Santa Anna immediately demanded a surrender of the Alamo and its defenders, without terms. The demand was answered by a shot from the fort. The enemy then hoisted a blood-red flag in the town, and commenced an attack. It was intended to be by slow approaches, for at first the bombardment was harmless. Travis sent off an express with a strong appeal for aid, declaring that *he would never retreat.* [*Travis's letter of February 24 is quoted in full in the footnote. A map of the Alamo in 1835–36, 4.2.3.2, is on the facing page.*] Early on the 25th, Santa Anna in person crossed the river with the battalion de Cazadores of Matamoras, with a view of erecting a battery in front of the gate of the Alamo.

Travis made a strong resistance, and the Mexicans were reinforced by the battalion of Ximines. The enemy, according to their own account, lost in this action, which continued until the afternoon, eight in killed and wounded. [*Almonté's Journal. Travis's account of this action, directed to General Houston, seems to have been lost, or cut off by the enemy.*] They, however, succeeded that night in erecting their battery, being protected by some old houses between the gate of the Alamo and the bridge. It was three hundred years south of the place. They also erected another, the same night, near the powder-house, or *Garita*, a thousand yards to the southeast; and posted their cavalry at the old *Casa Mata* on the Gonzales road, toward the east. At night, Travis burnt the straw and wooden houses in the vicinity of the fort.

Early in the morning of the 26th, there was a slight skirmish between a portion of the Texans and the enemy's cavalry stationed east of the fort. A *norther* having sprung up on the previous night, the thermometer fell to thirty-nine degrees above zero. Meanwhile, Santa Anna had received reinforcements, and now enlarged his guard, the sentinels being placed nearer the fort. The Texans sallied out for wood and water, without loss; and at night they succeeded in burning some old houses northeast from the fort, and near a battery erected by the enemy on the Alamo ditch, about eight hundred yards distant. [*Almonté's Journal. Travis to President of the Convention, March 3, 1836.*]

During all this time the Mexicans kept up a constant firing, but with little effect. On the 28th, they erected another battery at the old mill, eight hundred yards north, and attempted to cut off the water from the fort. The Texans were engaged in strengthening their works, by throwing up earth on the inside of the walls.

It is proper here to state that Travis wrote on the 23d to Colonel Fannin, then at Goliad, making known his position, and requesting him to march to his relief. The letter reached Goliad on the 25th. Fannin set out on his march for Bexar on the 28th, with three hundred men and four pieces of artillery, leaving Captain Westover in command at Goliad, with about a hundred men. But he had only proceeded two hundred yards, when one of his wagons broke down, and, having but one yoke of oxen to each piece of artillery, he was compelled to double his teams in order to get them, one at a time, across the river. Besides, his only provisions consisted of a tierce of rice and a little dried beef. A council of war was therefore held, when it was determined to return to Goliad, [*Fannin to Lieutenant-Governor Robinson, February 29, 1836*] which was accordingly done.

The intelligence of Fannin's departure for Bexar was received by the enemy at the latter place the same day on which he started; and, before the council of war, above alluded to, was closed, on the 29th, General Sesma, with detachments of cavalry and infantry, was on his march to meet him.

On the morning of the 1st of March, thirty-two gallant men from Gonzales were safely conducted by Captain John W. Smith into the Alamo, making the effective force under Travis one hundred and eighty-eight men. The bombardment of the fort still continued. The Texans, being short of ammunition, fired but seldom. In the evening, however, they struck the house occupied by Santa Anna in Bexar with a twelve-pound shot. On the 2d, the attack was still maintained. The Texans continued to the fight as their means and strength would allow. On the 3d, the enemy erected a battery on the north of the fort, and within musket-shot. Travis addressed a last appeal to the president of the convention, setting forth fully his position and determination. He stated that the "blood-red banners which waved on the church at Bexar, and in the camp above him, were tokens that the war was one of vengeance against rebels." Perhaps by the same courier he sent the affecting note to his friend in Washington county: "Take care of my little boy. If the country should be saved, I may make him a splendid fortune; but if the country should be lost, and I should perish, he will have nothing but the proud recollection that he is the son of a man who died for his country." [*Travis's letter of March 3 to Jesse Grimes is quoted here.*] On that day, J. B. Bonham, who had gone as express to Fannin for aid, returned and made his way safely into the fort at eleven o'clock in the morning. At night the Texans made a sally, and had a skirmish with the Mexican advance.

The enemy continued the fire on the 4th; but few shots were returned from the fort. In the afternoon, Santa Anna called a council of war, to advise on the question of assaulting the place. After much discussion, "Cos, Castrillon, and others, were of the opinion that the Alamo should be assaulted *after* the arrival of the two twelve-pounders expected on the 7th. The president, General Ramirez, Sesma, and Almonté, were of opinion that the twelve-pounders should not be waited for, but the assault made." [*Almonté's Journal*] Santa Anna, without making a public decision, determined upon an assault, and made his preparations accordingly. His troops then in Bexar exceeded four thousand in number, the most of whom had been refreshed during the time they had spent there. The Texans, on the contrary, were worn down by incessant watching and labor within their walls.

On Sunday morning, the 6th of March, a little after midnight, the Alamo was surrounded by the entire Mexican army. The cavalry were placed without the infantry, to cut them down if they offered to give way. The latter were provided with scaling-ladders. The enemy, thus forming a circle facing the fort, advanced rapidly under a tremendous fire from the Texan rifles and artillery. Just at daylight the ladders were placed against the walls, and an attempt made by the enemy to enter the fort, but they were driven back by the stern defenders within. Again the charge was sounded, and a second effort made to reach the top of the walls, but again the assailants were repulsed. For a few minutes there was a pause. By the presence, threats, and promises, of Santa Anna, a third assault was made, and with more fatal success. The enemy, reaching the tops of the ladders, wavered and fell; but their places were supplied by the hundreds pressing onward and behind them on each ladder. At length, killed, cut down, and exhausted, the Texan defenders did not retreat, but ceased to keep back the Mexicans. Instantly the fort was filled by the latter. The survivors within the walls still continued to do battle. They clubbed their guns, and used them till they were nearly all cut down. It is said that a few called for quarter, but the cry was unheeded. One would suppose that admiration for such unequalled heroism would have saved these few. Travis and Crockett fell—the former near the western wall, the latter in the corner near the church—with piles of slain around them. It had been previously agreed on by the besieged that the survivor should fire a large quantity of damaged powder in the magazine. Major Evans, the master of ordnance, was shot as he attempted to perform that last high duty to his country. Colonel Bowie, who had been for some days sick in his bed, was there butchered and mutilated!

Thus fell the Alamo and its heroic defenders; but before them lay the bodies of five hundred and twenty-one of the enemy, with a like number wounded. At an hour by sun, on that sabbath morning, all was still; yet the crimson waters of the aqueduct around the fort resembled the red flag on the church at Bexar! The defenders of Texas did not retreat, but lay there in obedience to the command of their country; and in that obedience the world has witnessed among men no greater moral sublimity.

Those in the fort that survived were, Mrs. Dickinson (wife of Lieutenant Dickinson, who fell in the defence), her child, negro-servant of Colonel Travis, and two Mexican women of Bexar. [*Account furnished by Mrs. Dickinson. Telegraph, March 24, 1836. Statement of Antonio Perez, on the evening after the battle. Perez gives the number of the Mexican killed and wounded as stated: it seems to be most reliable, as he remained several hours after the storming. He says Travis killed himself. This is hardly credible.*] The bodies of the Texans, after being stripped and subjected to brutal indignities, were thrown into heaps and burnt! The most of them were Americans, many of them colonists, who emigrated to Texas under the assurance of the colonization laws that their rights and liberties should be protected. The Mexicans in Bexar were mostly hostile: only three of them were among the defenders of the Alamo.

5.1.6.   James Morphis, narrative, 1874.

Morphis, James M. 1874. *History of Texas from Its Discovery and Settlement . . .* 168–69. New York: United States Publishing Co.

Morphis's account primarily consists of letters of Travis that have already been quoted, along with the interview with Susan Hannig (1.2.7). For completeness, the following is included to show the structure of his narration.

On the 23d of February, 1836, Santa Anna, crossing the *Alazan,* where, in 1813, the Republicans under the gallant Perry gained a signal victory over the forces of the viceroy under Elisondo, entered San Antonio without opposition, and having demanded the surrender of the *Alamo,* which was refused, commenced a furious bombardment of that *devoted* place! When it was invested, the Alamo was defended by one hundred and fifty-six men, commanded by the gallant captor of Anahuac, Colonel W. B. Travis, and included Colonel James Bowie, the hero of *Concepcion,* Colonel Davy Crockett, the celebrated ex-member of Congress from Tennessee, Colonels J. B. Bonham and J. Washington, with others less famous.

On the 24th, Colonel Travis sent the following letter by express to his people:

[*Document 1.1.4 is quoted here.*]

On the 1st of March he was joined by thirty-two men from Gonzales, who increased his force to 188 soldiers. On the 3d of March he wrote to the President of the Convention at Washington:

[*Morphis goes on to quote Travis letters 1.1.6 and 1.1.8, and gives the original of Dickinson 1.2.5. After some poetic asides, he quotes Zuber 1.8.1.1.*]

5.1.7. Reuben Potter, narrative, 1878.

Potter, Reuben M. January 1878. The fall of the Alamo. *Magazine of American History* 2:1–21.

Reuben Potter's account is perhaps the most carefully researched and balanced version of the siege and fall of the Alamo from the nineteenth century, and it cites sources not already quoted in this work. A more recent edition has been published with an introduction and notes by Charles Grosvenor (Hillsdale, NJ: Otterden Press, 1977). This edition also includes a number of pictures and drawings of participants and area views. Potter's original version of 1860, the one used by Sutherland (section 1.7.1), was not found.

THE FALL OF THE ALAMO

The fall of the Alamo and the massacre of its garrison, which in 1836 opened the campaign of Santa Anna in Texas, caused a profound sensation throughout the United States, and is still remembered with deep feeling by all who take an interest in the history of that section, yet the details of the final assault have never been fully and correctly narrated, and wild exaggerations have taken their place in popular legend. The reason will be obvious when it is remembered that not a single combatant of the last struggle from within the fort survived to tell the tale, while the official reports of the enemy were neither circumstantial nor reliable. When horror is intensified by mystery, the sure product is romance. A trustworthy account of the assault could be compiled only by comparing and combining the verbal narratives of such of the assailants as could be relied on for veracity, and adding to this such lights [*sic*] as might be gathered from military documents of that period, from credible local information, and from any source more to be trusted than rumor. As I was a resident at Matamoros when the event occurred, and for several months after the invading army retreated thither, and afterwards resided near the scene of action, I had opportunities for obtaining the kind of information referred to better perhaps than have been possessed by any person now living outside of

Mexico. I was often urged to publish what I had gathered on the subject, as thereby an interesting passage of history might be preserved. I consequently gave to the San Antonio *Herald* in 1860 an imperfect outline of what is contained in this article, and the communication was soon after printed in pamphlet form. Subsequently to its appearance, however, I obtained many additional and interesting details, mostly from Colonel Juan N. Seguin of San Antonio, who had been an officer of the garrison up to within six days of the assault. His death, of which I have since heard, no doubt took away the last of those who were soldiers of the Alamo when it was first invested. I now offer these sheets as a revision and enlargement of my article of 1860.

[*Potter gives a diagram and four paragraphs describing the Alamo, based in part on his personal observations and measurements from 1841 and 1860. He then continues with the narrative.*]

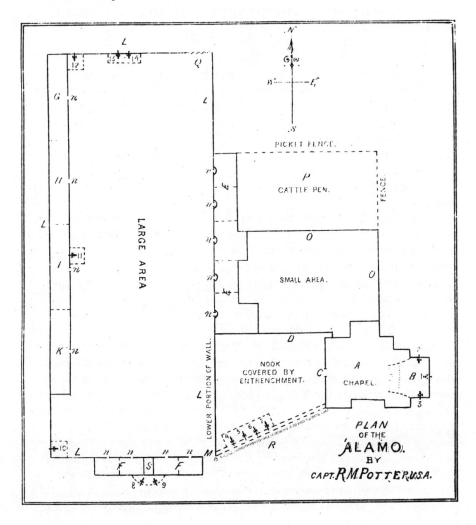

In the winter of 1835–6 Colonel Neill, of Texas, was in command of San Antonio, with two companies of volunteers, among whom was a remnant of New Orleans Greys, who had taken an efficient part in the siege and capture of the town about a year before. At this time the Provisional Government of Texas, which, though in revolt, had not yet declared a final separation from Mexico, had broken into a conflicting duality. The Governor and Council repudiated each other, and each claimed the obedience which was generally not given to either. Invasion was impending, and there seemed to be little more than anarchy to meet it. During this state of affairs Lieutenant-Colonel Wm. B. Travis, who had commanded the scouting service of the late campaign, and had since been commissioned with the aforesaid rank as an office of regular cavalry, was assigned by the Governor to relieve Colonel Neill of the command of his post. The volunteers, who cared little for either of the two governments, wished to choose their own leader, and were willing to accept Travis only as second in command. They were, therefore, clamorous that Neill should issue an order for the election of a Colonel. To get over the matter without interfering with Travis' right, he prepared an order for the election of a Lieutenant-Colonel, and was about to depart, when his men, finding out what he had done, mobbed him, and threatened his life unless he should comply with their wishes. He felt constrained to yield, and on the amended order James Bowie was unanimously elected a full Colonel. He had been for several years a resident of Texas, and had taken a prominent part in the late campaign against Cos. His election occurred early in February, 1836, about two weeks before the enemy came in sight; and Travis, who had just arrived or came soon after, found Bowie in command of the garrison, and claiming by virtue of the aforesaid election the right to command him and the re-enforcement he brought. They both had their headquarters at the Alamo, where their men were quartered, and there must have been a tacit understanding on both sides that conflict of authority should as far as possible be avoided. This, however, could not have continued many days but for the common bond of approaching peril.

Travis brought with him a company of regular recruits, enlisted for the half regiment of cavalry which the Provisional Government had intended to raise. J. N. Sequin, a native of San Antonio, who had been commissioned as the senior Captain of Travis' corps, joined him at the Alamo, and brought into the garrison the skeleton of his company, consisting of nine Mexican recruits, natives, some of the town aforesaid and others of the interior of Mexico. The aforesaid company and squad of enlisted men and the two companies of volunteers under Bowie formed the garrison of the Alamo, which then numbered from a hundred and fifty-six to a hundred and sixty. Of these the volunteers comprised considerably more than half, and over two-thirds of the whole were men who had but recently arrived in the country. Seguin and his nine recruits were all that represented the Mexican population of Texas. Of that nine, seven fell in the assault, the Captain and two of his men having been sent out on duty before that crisis. David Crockett, of Tennessee, who had a few years before represented a squatter constituency in Congress, where his oratory was distinguished for hard sense and rough grammar, had joined the garrison a few weeks before, as had also J. B. Bonham, Esq., of South Carolina, who had lately come to volunteer in the cause of Texas, and was considered one of the most chivalrous and estimable of its supporters. I pair them, a rough gem and a polished jewel, because their names are among the best known of those who fell; but I am not aware that either of them had any command.

The main army of operation against Texas moved from Laredo upon San Antonio in four successive detachments. This was rendered necessary by the scarcity of pasture and water on certain portions of the route. The lower division commanded by Brigadier-General Urrea, moved from Matamoros on Goliad by a route near the coast, and a short time after the fall of the Alamo achieved the capture and massacre of Fannius' [sic; Fannin's] command.

The advance from Laredo, consisting of the Dragoon Regiment of Delores and three battalions of infantry, commanded by Santa Ana in person, arrived at San Antonio on the afternoon of February 22d. No regular scouting service seems to have been kept up from the post of Bowie and Travis, owing probably to division and weakness of authority, for, though the enemy was expected, his immediate approach was not known to many of the inhabitants till the advance of his dragoons was seen descending the slope west of the San Pedro. A guard was kept in town with a sentinel on the top of the church, yet the surprise of the population was so nearly complete that one or more American residents engaged in trade fled to the Alamo, leaving their stores open. The garrison, however, received more timely notice, and the guard retired in good order to the fort. The confusion at the Alamo, which for the time being was great, did not impede a prompt show of resistance. In the evening, soon after the enemy entered the town, a shot from the 18-pounder of the fort was answered by a shell from the invaders, and this was followed by a parley, of which different accounts have been given. According to Santa Ana's official report, after the shell was thrown, a white flag was sent out by the garrison with an offer to evacuate the fort if allowed to retire unmolested and in arms, to which reply was made that no terms would be admitted short of unconditional surrender. Seguin, however, gave me a more reliable version of the affair. He related that after the firing a parley was sounded and a white flag raised by the invaders. Travis was not inclined to respond to it; but Bowie, without consulting him, and much to his displeasure, sent a flag of truce to demand what the enemy wanted. Their General, with his usual duplicity, denied having sounded a parley or raised a flag and informed the messenger that the garrison could be recognized only as rebels, and be allowed no other terms than a surrender at discretion. When informed of this, Travis harangued his men and administered to them an oath that they would resist to the last.

The officers obtained a supply of corn, and added to their stock of beef after the enemy entered the town. On the same day a well, which a fatigue party had been digging within the walls, struck a fine vein of water. This was fortunate; for the irrigating canal, which flowed past the foot of the wall, was shortly after cut off by the enemy. The investment had not yet commenced, nor was the firing, I think, renewed that evening, and the few citizens who had taken refuge in the fort succeeded in leaving it during the night, if not earlier.

On the night of the 22d of February the enemy planted two batteries on the west side of the river, one bearing west and the other southwest from the Alamo, with a range with no houses then obstructed. They were the next day silenced by the fire of the 18-pounder of the fort, but were restored to activity on the following night. On the 24th another body of Mexican troops, a regiment of cavalry and three battalions of infantry arrived; and then the fort was invested and a regular siege commenced, which, counting from that day till the morning of the 6th of March, occupied eleven days. By the 27th seven more besieging batteries were planted, most of them on the east side of the river, and bearing on the northwest, southwest and south of the fort; but there were none on the east. As that was the only direction in which the garrison would likely to attempt retreat, Santa Ana wished to leave a temptation to such flitting, while he prepared to intercept it by forming his cavalry camp on what is now called the Powder House Hill, east of the Alamo.

During the first few days occasional sallies were made by the garrison to obstruct the enemy's movements and burn houses which might cover them. The operations of the siege, which, omitting the final assault, are probably given correctly in Yoakum's History of Texas, consisted of an active but rather ineffective cannonade and bombardment, with occasional skirmishing by day and frequent harassing alarms at night, designed to wear out the garrison with want of sleep. No assault was attempted, though it has been so asserted, till the final storming took place. The enemy had no siege train, but only light field pieces and howitzers; yet a breach was opened in the northern barrier, Q [on Potter's map], near the northeast angle, and the chapel was the only building that withstood the cannonade firmly, as the balls often went clean through the walls of the others. Yet, when I saw them unrepaired five years later, they seemed less battered than might have been expected.

The stern resistance which had sprung up in the demoralized band within, and the comparative unity and order which must have come with it, were ushered in by a scene which promised no such outcome. The first sight of the enemy created as much confusion with as little panic at the Alamo as might be expected among men who had known as little of discipline as they did of fear. Mr. Lewis, of San Antonio, informed me that he took refuge for a few hours in the fort when the invaders appeared, and the disorder of the post beggared description. Bowie with a detachment was engaged in breaking open deserted houses in the neighborhood and gathering corn, while another squad was driving cattle into the enclosure east of the long barrack. Some of the volunteers, who had sold their rifles to obtain the means of dissipation, were clamoring for guns of any kind; and the rest, though in arms, appeared to be mostly without orders or a capacity for obedience. No "army in Flanders" ever swore harder. He saw but one officer, who seemed to be at his proper post and perfectly collected. This was an Irish Captain, named Ward, who though generally an invet-

erate drunkard, was now sober, and stood quietly by the guns of the south battery, ready to use them. Yet amid the disorder of that hour no one seemed to
think of flight; the first damaging shock, caused by the sight of the enemy, must
have been cured by the first shell that he threw; and the threat conveyed by
Santa Ana's message seems to have inspired a greater amount of discipline than
those men had before been thought capable of possessing. The sobered toper
who stood cooly by his guns was the first pustule which foretold a speedy inoc-
ulation of the whole mass with the qualification.

The conflict of authority between Bowie and Travis, owing probably to the
caution in which neither was deficient, had luckily produced no serious colli-
sion; and it was perhaps as fortunate that, at about the second day of the siege,
the rivalry was cut short by a prostrating illness of the former, when Bowie was
stricken by an attack of pneumonia, which would probably have proved fatal,
had not its blow been anticipated by the sword. This left Travis in undisputed
command.

The investment was not so rigid to admit of the successful exit of couriers
by night, and one or two had been sent out, since the enemy appeared, with letters to Colonel Fannin at Goliad, asking for aid. On the 29th of February it was
resolved to send an officer, who, in addition to bearing despatches, might make
his own influence and information available to accomplish the object of his mission. Captain Seguin was recommended by most of the officers; for, as he was of
Spanish race and language, and well acquainted with the surrounding country,
it was thought that he would be more likely than any one of his rank to succeed
in passing the enemy's lines. Travis wished to retain him in the garrison; but at a
council of war, held on the night of the 29th, he yielded to the wishes of the
majority. That night Seguin and his orderly, Antonio Cruz Oroche, prepared for
the sally. Another of his Mexican recruits, named Alexandro de la Garza, had
already been sent as a courier to the Provisional Government. Having no horse
or equipments for himself, the Captain requested and obtained those of Bowie,
who was already so ill that he hardly recognized the borrower. To him and the
rest Seguin bade what proved to be a last adieu, and sallying from the postern
on the northern side, took the high road to the east. As might be expected, the
rank and file had begun to look with jealousy on any departure from within,
though of but one or two; and when Seguin produced the order which was to
pass him and his orderly out, the sentinel at the postern began a rude comment;
but a few words from the Captain, intimating that his errand was one which
might bring safety, at once soothed the rough soldier, who bade him God-speed.

The road which the two horsemen took passed near the cavalry camp of the
enemy, and where it crossed their lines was stationed a guard of dragoons, who
were then resting dismounted. Seguin and his man rode leisurely up towards
them, responding in Spanish to the hail of their sentinel that they were countrymen. They were doubtless taken for Mexican rancheros of that neighborhood,
and seemed to be riding up to report, but when near enough for a bold start,
they dashed past the guard at full speed. The hurried fire of the troopers was

ineffective, and before they were in the saddle the fugitives, who were both well mounted, were far ahead. The latter then took to the bush and made good their escape. The next day Seguin met an officer from Fannin's post, who informed him that his mission would be wholly unavailing, and advised him to join the camp then forming at Gonzales, which he did.

On the following night, the 1st of March, a company of thirty-two men from Gonzales made its way through the enemy's lines, and entered the Alamo never again to leave it. This must have raised the force to 188 men or there-about, as none of the original number of 156 had fallen.

On the night of the 3d of March, Travis sent out another courier with a let-ter of that date to the government, which reached its destination. In that last despatch he says: "With a hundred and forty-five men I have held this place ten days against a force variously estimated from 1,500 to 6,000, and I shall con-tinue to hold it till I get relief from my countrymen, or I will perish in the attempt. We have had a shower of bombs and cannon-balls continually falling among us the whole time, yet none of us have fallen. We have been miracu-lously preserved." As this was but two days and three nights before the final assault, it is quite possible that not a single defender was stricken down till the fort was stormed. At the first glance it may seem almost farcical that there should be no more result from so long a fire, which was never sluggish; but if so, this was a stage on which farce was soon to end in tragedy, and those two elements seem strangely mingled through the whole contest. But the fact above referred to was not really farcical, however singular, and it serves merely to illustrate the mysterious doctrine of chance. It must have tended to uphold the determination of men in a situation where the favor of luck is so apt to be accepted as the shielding of Providence. Travis, when he said, "We have been miraculously preserved," no doubt expressed a sincere feeling, in which his companions shared; for such fancies are apt to take a strong contagious hold of men who stand day after day unharmed within a step of death, it is a time when the fierce, profane and dissolute often begin for the first time to look upward. It is worthy of note that, although the readiness of couriers to go out indicates a consciousness that the chance of life was at least as good without as within, we know not of a single case of night flitting. Brute bravery or reckless despair would hardly have produced this without some exceptions. The inci-dent of the sentinel at the postern probably showed what were prevailing traits—scorn of desertion with readiness for hope. In many a rough bosom that hope had probably a new and half-comprehended faith under it. Though the hope was disappointed, I trust that the faith was not all in vain.

In stating the force of the garrison during the previous ten days, Travis did not include the little re-enforcement which had come in only two days before; yet, as he mentions but 145, while the garrison is known to have numbered 156 when the enemy appeared, he must have rated eleven as ineffective or absent. A part of them may have been counted as departed couriers, and the rest had perhaps sunk under fatigue of duty. Had there been any wounded, he would probably have referred to them.

On the 4th of March Santa Ana called a council of war, and fixed on the morning of the 6th for the final assault. The besieging force now around the Alamo, comprising of all the Mexican troops which had yet arrived, consisted of the two dragoon regiments of Dolores and Tampico, which formed a brigade, commanded by General Andrade, two companies or batteries of artillery under Colonel Ampudia, six battalions of infantry, namely, Los Zapadores (engineer troops), Jimenes, Guerrero, Matamoros, Toluca, and Tres Villas. These six battalions of foot were to form the storming force. The order for the attack, which I have read, but have no copy of, was full and precise in its details, and was signed by General Amador, as Chief of Staff. The infantry were directed at a certain hour between midnight and dawn to form at convenient distances from the fort in four columns of attack and a reserve. These dispositions were not made by battalions, for the light companies of all were incorporated with the Zapadores to form the reserve, and other transpositions were made. A certain number of scaling ladders, axes and fascines were to be borne by particular columns. A commanding officer, with a second to replace him in case of accident, was named, and a point of attack designated for each column. The cavalry were to be stationed at suitable points around the fort to cut off fugitives. From what I have learned from the men engaged in the assault, it seems that these dispositions were modified before it was carried out so as to combine the five bodies of infantry, including the reserve, into only three columns of attack, thus leaving no actual reserve but the cavalry. The immediate direction of the assault seems to have been intrusted to General Castrillon, a Spaniard by birth and a brilliant soldier. Santa Ana took his station, with a part of his staff and all the bands of music at a battery about 500 yards south of the Alamo and near the old bridge, from which post a signal was to be given by a bugle-note for the columns to move simultaneously at double-quick time against the fort. One, consisting of Los Zapadores, Toluca, and the light companies, and commanded by Castrillon, was to rush through the breach on the north; another, consisting of the battalion of Jimenes and other troops, and commanded by General Cos, was to storm the chapel; and a third, whose leader I do not recollect, was to scale the west barrier. Cos, who had evacuated San Antonio a year before under capitulation, was assigned to the most difficult point of attack, probably to give him an opportunity to retrieve his standing. By the timing of the signal it was calculated that the columns would reach the foot of the wall just as it should become sufficiently light for good operation.

When the hour came, the south guns of the Alamo were answering the batteries which fronted them; but the music was silent till the blast of a bugle was followed by the rushing tramp of soldiers. The guns of the fort opened upon the moving masses and Santa Ana's bands struck up the assassin note of *deguello,* or no quarter. But a few and not very effective discharges of cannon from the works could be made before the enemy were under them, and it was probably not till then that the worn and wearied garrison was fully mustered. Castrillon's column arrived first at the foot of the wall, but was not the first to enter. The guns of the north, where Travis commanded in person, probably raked the breach, and this or the fire of the riflemen brought the column to a disordered halt, and Colonel Duque, who commanded the battalion of Toluca, fell dangerously wounded; but, while this was occurring, the column from the west crossed the barrier on that side by escalade at a point north of the centre, and, as this checked resistance at the north, Castrillon shortly after passed the breach. It was probably while the enemy was thus pouring into the large area that Travis fell at his post, for his body, with a single shot in the forehead, was found beside the gun at the northwest angle. The outer walls and batteries, all except one gun, of which I will speak, were now abandoned by the defenders. In the mean time Cos had again proved unlucky. His column was repulsed from the chapel, and his troops fell back in disorder behind the old stone stable and huts that stood south of the southwest angle. There they were soon rallied and led into the large area by General Amador. I am not certain as to his point of entrance, but he probably followed the escalade of the column from the west.

This all passed within a few minutes after the bugle sounded. The garrison, when driven from the thinly manned outer defenses, whose early loss was inevitable, took refuge in the buildings before described, but mainly in the long barrack, and it was not till then, when they became more concentrated and covered within, that the main struggle began. They were more concentrated as to space, not as to unity of command, for there was no communicating between buildings, nor, in all cases, between rooms. There was little need of command, however, to men who had no choice left but to fall where they stood before the weight of numbers. There was now no retreating from point to point, and each group of defenders had to fight and die in the den where it was brought to bay. From the doors, windows, and loopholes of the several rooms around the area the crack of the rifle and the hiss of the bullet came fierce and fast; as fast the enemy fell and recoiled in his first efforts to charge. The gun beside which Travis fell was now turned against the buildings, as were also some others, and shot after shot was sent crashing through the doors and barricades of the several rooms. Each ball was followed by a storm of musketry and a charge; and thus room after room was carried at the point of the bayonet, when all within them died fighting to the last. The struggle was made up of a number of separate and desperate combats, often hand to hand, between squads of the garrison and bodies of the enemy. The bloodiest spot about the fort was the long barrack and the ground in front of it, where the enemy fell in heaps.

Before the action reached this stage, the turning of Travis' gun by the assailants was briefly imitated by a group of the defenders. "A small piece on a high platform," as it was described to me by General Bradburn, was wheeled by those who manned it against the large area after the enemy entered it. Some of the Mexican officers thought it did more execution than any gun which fired outward; but after two effective discharges it was silenced, when the last of its cannoneers fell under a shower of bullets. I cannot locate this gun with certainty, but it was probably the twelve-pound carronade which fired over the centre of the west wall from a high commanding position. The smallness assigned to it perhaps referred only to its length. According to Mr. Ruiz, then the Alcalde of San Antonio, who, after the action, was required to point out the slain leaders to Santa Ana, the body of Crockett was found in the west battery just referred to, and we may infer that he either commanded that point or was stationed there as a sharpshooter. The common fate overtook Bowie in his bed in one of the rooms of the low barrack, when he probably had but a few days of life left in him; yet he had enough remaining, it is said, to shoot down with his pistols more than one of his assailants ere he was butchered on his couch. If he had sufficient strength and consciousness left to do it, we may safely assume that it was done.

The chapel, which was the last point taken, was carried by a *coup de main* after the fire of the other buildings was silenced. Once the enemy in possession of the large area, the guns of the south could be turned to fire into the door of the church, only from fifty to an [sic] hundred yards off, and that was probably the route of attack. The inmates of this last stronghold, like the rest, fought to the last, and continued to fire down from the upper works after the enemy occupied the floor. A Mexican officer told of seeing one of his soldiers shot in the crown of the head during this mélée. Towards the close of the struggle Lieutenant Dickenson, with his child in his arms, or, as some accounts say, tied to his back, leaped from the east embrasure of the chapel, and both were shot in the act. Of those he left behind him, the bayonet soon gleaned what the bullet had left; and in the upper part of that edifice the last defender must have fallen. The morning breeze which received his parting breath probably still fanned his flag above that fabric, for I doubt not he fell ere it was pulled down by the victors.

The Alamo had fallen; but the impression it left on the invader was the forerunner of San Jacinto. It is a fact not often remembered that Travis and his band fell under the Mexican Federal flag of 1824, instead of the Lone Star of Texas, although Independence, unknown to them, had been declared by the new Convention four days before at Washington, on the Brazos. They died for a Republic of whose existence they never knew. The action, according to Santa Ana's report, lasted thirty minutes. It was certainly short, and possibly no longer time passed between the moment the enemy entered the breach and that when resistance died out. The assault was a task which had to be carried out quickly or fail. Some of the incidents which have to be related separately occurred simultaneously, and all occupied very little time. The account of the assault which Yoakum and others have adopted as authentic is evidently one which popular tradition has based on conjecture. By a rather natural inference it assumes that the enclosing walls, as in the case of regular forts, were the principal works, and that in storming these the main conflict took place. The truth was, these extensive barriers formed in reality nothing more than the outworks, speedily lost, while the buildings within constituted the citadel and the scene of sternest resistance. Yoakum's assertion that Santa Ana, during the height of the conflict, was under the works, urging on the escalade in person, is exceedingly fabulous. Castrillon, not Santa Ana, was the soul of the assault. The latter remained at his south battery, viewing the operations from the corner of a house which covered him, till he supposed the place was nearly mastered, when he moved up towards the Alamo, escorted by his aides and bands of music, but turned back on being greeted by a few shots from the upper part of the chapel. He, however, entered the area towards the close of the scene, and directed some of the last details of the butchery. It cannot be denied that Santa Ana in the course of his career showed occasional fits of dashing courage, but he did not select this field for an exhibition of that quality. About the time the area was entered, a few men, cut off from inward retreat, leaped from the barriers, and attempted flight, but were all sabred or speared by the cavalry except one, who succeeded in hiding himself under a small bridge of the irrigating ditch. There he was discovered and reported a few hours after by some laundresses engaged in washing near the spot. He was executed. Half an hour or more after the action was over a few men were found concealed in one of the rooms under some mattresses. General Houston, in his letter of the 11th, says as many as seven; but I have generally heard them spoken of as only four or five. The officer to whom the discovery was first reported entreated Santa Ana to spare their lives; but he was sternly rebuked, and the men ordered to be shot, which was done. Owing to the hurried manner in which the mandate was obeyed, and the confusion prevailing at the moment, a Mexican soldier was accidentally killed with them. A negro belonging to Travis, the wife of Lieutenant Dickenson, who at the time was *enceinte,* and a few Mexican women with their children were the only inmates of the fort whose lives were spared. The massacre involved no women and but one child. Lieutenant Dickenson commanded the gun at the east embrasure of the chapel. His family was probably in one of the small vaulted rooms of the north projection, which will account for his being able to take his child to the rear of the building when it was being stormed. An irrigating canal ran below the embrasure, and his aim may have been to break the shock of his leap by landing in the mud of that waterless ditch, and then try to escape, or he may have thought that so striking an act would plead for his life; but the shower of bullets which greeted him told how vain was the hope. The authenticity of this highly dramatic incident has been questioned, but it was asserted from the first, and was related to me by an eye-witness engaged in the assault.*

It was asserted on the authority of one of the women that, while the church was being stormed, Major Evans, the Master of Ordnance, rushed with a torch or burning match towards the magazine of the fort to fire it, when he was shot down before his object was accomplished. It may seem unlikely that any of the women would be in a position to witness such an incident, but they may have been put into the magazine as a place most sheltered from the enemy's shots. The powder was probably stored in the little vaulted room on the north of the chapel which I have just referred to.**

There were two officers of the name just mentioned in the garrison of the Alamo, Major Robert Evans, Master of Ordnance, and Irishman, and Captain J. B. Evans, of Texas, a nephew of General Jacob Brown, who formerly commanded the United States army.

[*Potter goes on to analyze the Mexican casualty count, about five hundred killed or wounded, some of the military lessons learned, and the burial place of the ashes of the defenders. An excerpt on the Mexican casualties from an earlier version is given in document 3.4.4. The two footnotes for the above follow.*]

---

* I had for several years in Texas as a servant one of the Mexican soldiers captured at San Jacinto, Sergeant Becero, of the battalion of Matamoros. He was in the assault, and witnessed Dickenson's leap. He also saw the body of Bowie on his bed, where he had been killed, and witnessed the execution of the few men who were found in concealment after the action was over. He did not know the names of Bowie or Dickenson, and related the circumstances, not in reply to inquiries, but in a natural way as recollections in narrating his experience. Many absurd stories about the admissions made by Mexicans touching the force of the assailants and the amount of their loss at the Alamo are based on sycophantic statements, drawn by leading questions from prisoners of the lower class.

** In 1841 the husband of one of the Mexican women who were with the garrison during the siege and assaults pointed out to me the vaulted room referred to, and observed, "During the fight and massacre five or six women stood in that room all in a huddle." He was an intelligent man, but so given to embellishing whatever he related that I did not then rely much on his information; but I have since called it to mind in connection with what is above said. This man did not refer to Evans' attempt, nor did he say that the cell referred to was used for storing powder, but, according to my recollection, it was the most fitting place for a magazine which I saw about the Alamo.

5.1.8.1.   Milledge Luke Bonham (probable), biography, n.d.

Anon. (Milledge Luke Bonham). N.d. (before 1889?). "COL. JAS. BUTLER BONHAM," in the Brown (John Henry) Papers, CAH.

This is a typed manuscript without author or date noted. The potential identification, date, and significance of this as well as the other Bonham-related documents following, tied to historian John Henry Brown, are analyzed in the Commentary. The identification is that the author was Milledge Luke Bonham, the younger brother of James. The idiosyncratic typing is replicated in these transcripts, as it has significance in comparing them with the typed letters of Milledge also in the Brown papers. As this essay was most probably written by the brother of James Bonham, the manuscript as a whole is of the highest importance as a biography of a major Alamo figure.

COL. JAS. BUTLER BONHAM

[*Four paragraphs give the early life of James Bonham.*]

In the spring of '38 the writer met in Houston,Tex. Col.Augustus Maverick,who was born in Pendleton,S.C. and was an intimate personal frien[*d*] of Col.Bonham's. Frm [*from*] himself,Gen.Greene of Texas and Mrs Dickinson,the widow of Lieut.Dickinison of Travis's command,was received substatially the information hereinafter contained.

Col. Bonham was but ashort time in the Alamo,with Travis,who had but(I50)one hundred and fifty men in his command,when he volunteered to go out and make an effort to get reinforcements. Between his departure and return a company of 32 succeeded in entering the Fort He visited several commands where he hoped he might obtain reinforcements,but failing he returned to San Antonio. The writer understood Col.Maverick,that he accompanied Col.Bonham to near that place and finding the Mexican Army had closely invested the works,and the prospect of a successful defense so hopeless,he presented to Col.Bonham the view that it was useless to sacrifice himself by reentering again the beleagured works-That he could be of no benefit to his comrades; Col.Bonham replied substantially,that he could not reconcile it to himself not to return;That he would take the fate of his comrades. It was also stated about that period that Mr.Smith a Texan also endeavored to dissuade him from reentering the works,for the same reason. The enemy's lines were then closing in around the works ,and it was not easy to get through them. A white handerkerchief displayed from an adjacent mountain had been pre-arranged as the signal of Col.Bonham's return. He rode a magnificent dove colored horse. About midday on the 3d of March,approaching as near as he could unperceived by the enemy , he turned his horse's head towards the gate of the Alamo and drawing his cloak close sbout him,he laid down on the neck of his noble steed, and dashed through the enemy's lines. The gate flew open on his approach and he passed in to the Alamo. A great many shots were fired at him as he passed thorough the lines into the works.

Mrs.Dickinson who was met also in Houston Tex.in the spring of '38told the writer that Col.Bonham on the evening of the 5th of March(the evening before the fall of the works) took tea with Lieut Dickinson and herself and their mess. She never saw him afterwards. She and her infant were the only white survivors of the fall of the Alamo. After quarter was refused the defenders of the Fort and the last one was ruthlessly butchered , she was put on a horse with her infant in her arms,and sent to the interior of Texas.

[*Another two paragraphs give information on the Bonham family. Milledge L. Bonham—referred to in the third person—was a U.S. Congressman in 1857, a brigider general in the Confederate army, and governor of South Carolina in 1863 and 1864. At the time of writing, he was the chairman of the board of Railroad Commissioners of South Carolina.*]

5.1.8.2.   Milledge Luke Bonham (probable), notes, n.d.

Anon. (Milledge Luke Bonham). N.d. (before 1889?). "TOASTS &. EDITORI-ALS," in the Brown (John Henry) Papers, CAH.

This is a four-page manuscript, also typed. It is physically separated from the prior biography (5.1.8.1) in the Brown Papers, but as noted in the Commentary, it appears to be an addendum. The excerpt presented here is only one of several testimonials and quotations apparently accumulated from various sources.

TOASTS &. EDITORIALS

By Col.Augustus Maverick,(it is supposed) in the Pendleton Messenger. [*The phrase after "Maverick" is a handwritten addition; the reading of the possible newspaper is probable but not certain.*]

"All speak in raptures of Bonham. He was sent to obtain aid for Travis at the Alamo-returned without-again went to implore Fannin to spare 20 or 50 men-again returned wi thout and on approaching a Mr.Smith who had been sent with him , said'It is useless Bonham to attempt to enter';the Alamo is surrounded'. 'I must said Bonham: 'You are a braver man than I',said Smith,I cannot;' and Bonham pushed in under a fire of 30 muskets and perished with his friends."

5.1.8.3.   John Henry Brown, article, early 1889.

Brown, John Henry. Early 1889. "HERO OF THE ALAMO," reprinted in the *Newberry (South Carolina) News and Herald*. Brown (John Henry) Papers, CAH.

This is a newspaper clipping transmitted by a handwritten letter, which is also quoted.

[*Transmittal:*]

Newberry S.C
March 11. 1889

Dear Col

Permit me to return my thanks as a South Carolinian to you for your article giving to Col Bonham due credit for what was claimed for another—Enclosed I send an extract from the Newberry S.C. News and Herald republishing your article—Do see that Texas has a Bonham County others have been remembered why not him

Yours Truly
S.Pope

[*Newspaper clipping:*]

THE HERO OF THE ALAMO

LET THE TRUTH OF HISTORY BE PRESERVED!

The Respective Claims of Travis, Bonham and Crockett—The First was the Soul of the Defense—The Last was a Faithful and Brave Private soldier—Col James Butler Bonham, of South Carolina, Performed the Most Distinguished Feat of Personal Heroism Connected with the Siege.

[John Henry Brown, in the Texas Farm and Ranch.]

I ask to correct certain recent erroneous publications reciting assumed historical facts and appearing in the public press of the day, and desire to do so in Texas Farm and Ranch because many persons in the Dixie [*unclear word in copy; possibly "South"*] preserve its files, which is not often the case with regards to our daily and weekly papers. I have recently, through the St Louis Republic, and the Times-Herald of this city, corrected respectively two different errors with regard to the late Samuel A. Maverick, of San Antonio.

[*The next paragraph is a critique of an obituary of William Young in the* Dallas News, *not related to the Alamo.*]

But the most unjust historical statement of current publications is in a poem published in the Dallas News of January 13, on the Fall of the Alamo. While most of the facts are correctly given in verse, the following lines occur:

> But once again the foemen gaze in wonderment and fear
> To see a stranger break their lines and hear the Texans cheer.
> God! how they cheered to welcome him, those spent and starving men!
> For Davy Crockett by their side was worth an army then.
> The wounded once forgot their wounds, the dying drew a breath
> To hail the king of border men, then turned to laugh at death.
> For all knew Davy Crockett, blithe and generous as bold.
> And strong and ragged as the quartz that hides its heart of gold.

It is inconceivable to imagine a more incorrect and unjust statement than is embodied in the lines quoted. David Crockett, a private soldier in the Alamo, was there some weeks before the siege began, and never left it till his spirit took its flight on the fall of the fort. But the character presented as pertaining to Crockett rightfully belongs to the memory of Col James Butler Bonham, a native South Carolinian, who was born, reared and educated within five miles of Travis, his friend from infancy and his schoolmate, who came to the rescue of Texas the moment he heard of the revolution. He joined Travis in San Antonio, and at his request, when the bravest might have shrunk from the hazard, on the approach of the cohorts of Santa Anna, he bore a message from Travis to Fannin, in Goliad; then, in fulfilment of a further trust he hurried to Gonzales, beseeching aid. Finding that thirty-two men under Capt. Albert Martin, had left two days before to reinforce Travis he tarried not, but hastened back to San Antonio, accompanied by his South Carolina friend Samuel A. Maverick. They approached San Antonio and found it encircled by thousands of Mexicans. Maverick, by his own manly statement afterwards, considered the case hopeless, refused to seek an entrance and tried to persuade Bonham to retire to Gonzales. This Bonham refused to do, saying he would hazard life and everything else rather than fail to report to his loved old friend and schoolmate, Travis, the result of his mission. An obligation rested upon him which did not attach to Maverick, chivalrous as the latter was ever known to be. Maverick retired—wisely, all will admit. Bonham, at 11 o'clock on the 3d of March, and the ninth day of the siege, only two days and seventeen hours before all in the Alamo were dead, passed through the Mexican lines and staked his life with that of the hundred and eighty-one in the doomed fortress. He it was, and not the heroic Crockett, already battling among them, who was received with shouts of welcome by the beleaguered garrison, and well he might be, for he had performend an act of personal heroism and self-immolation unsurpassed in the world's history. It was a glory to Gonzales and DeWitt's colony, when, at dawn on the 1st of March, and the seventh day of the siege, thirty-two of their citizens (some of whom I knew when a child,) fought their way into the Alamo to swell the total number of its defenders to one hundred and eight-one. But it was immeasurably a greater glory in Bonham, the lone Carolinian, to enter two and a half days later, and thus make the number one hundred and eighty-two.

All honor to Crockett, and to every man who fell in the Alamo; but thrice honored among the children of men by the memory of the peerless Bonham! After Travis come the names of Bonham, Bowie and Crockett. The recent suggestion to crown the proposed Alamo monument with a statue of Crockett would be, negatively speaking, a crowning act of injustice to the memory of Travis, the master spirit of the matchless defence—the commander and director—the cultured and refined gentleman—the embodiment of patriotism, and the exemplar of all that is grand and glorious in chivalric heroism!

These reflections spring from the historic injustice set forth in the poem referred to, and the suggestion last mentioned. While revering the memory of all who consecrated their lives to liberty in the Alamo, and thereby gave Houston time to save Texas at San Jacinto, my heart revolts at the perversion of historic justice involved in the two cases.

5.1.8.4.   Milledge Luke Bonham, letter, 1889.

Bonham, Milledge Luke, to John Henry Brown. April 4? (numeral unclear), 1889. Brown (John Henry) Papers, CAH.

In addition to the three typed letters transcribed in this and the next two documents, the Brown Papers have handwritten letters or notes from March and April 1889 from Milledge Bonham to Brown.

Columbia, S.C.
April 4[?] 1889

Hon.John Henry Brown,
Dallas, Tex.
My.Dear Sir:-

You have perceived that I write a bad hand and with great labor. My sixteen year old son uses a typewriter for me in these communications.

I have given you briefly what I could as to my brother and Travis. The latter left South Carolina when I was a child. I sent to the St.Louis Republican a brief correction of some misstatements in that paper. Perhaps you saw my article if it was published . No copy was sent me and I dont think I preserved one.

I have endeavored to comply with your request and am sorry I cannot be more satisfactory. Hope the unavoidable delay may not in commode you.

I have given youan account of my father's family for your own satisfaction.

The toasts and editorials I transcribe as part of the history of the times. We have never had a likeness of my brother Jas.Butler Bonham,nor have I yet laid my hand on a specimen of his autograph.

He was over 6ft. 2in. Weighed about I75 lbs-was sinewy and very strong.

I sent you two photographs at different periods of my life but have not heard if you received them

[*The remainder is a handwritten addition on the back side.*]

There seem to be some discrepancies between the different statements; and my own communications as to my fathers family is rather bunglingly [?] put.

Yours very Truly
M.L.Bonham

5.1.8.5.   Milledge Luke Bonham, letter, 1889.

Bonham, Milledge Luke, to John Henry Brown. April 19, 1889. Brown (John Henry) Papers, CAH.

Columbia,S.C.April 19th.1889.

Col.John Henry Brown,

Dallas,Texas.

My dear sir:

The enclosed medal and circular were handed to me this morning by my son Gen.[*sic*]M.L.Bonham Jr.who had just received them,and I send them to you as you are vindicating the truth of Texas history. They are unaccompanied by anything more than as enclosed. You need not trouble to return them—they possess no interest to us as now presented.

This must be the veritable Historian whom you have so fully exposed in the Farm and Ranch.

I think, from Col.Maverick or Mrs.Dickinson herself,I heard in Texas in 1838,that she and her infant were the only white persens in the Alamo left alive by the Mexicans.

Travis was not born in North Carolina,nor Bowie in Georgia,I think.

[*Bonham goes on to describe an inkstand he received that was cut from a stone from the Alamo, then concludes:*] I am much gratified at your just vindication of that gallant gentleman,James Bowie.

Yours very truly,

M.L. Bonham

5.1.8.6.   Milledge Luke Bonham, letter, 1889.

Bonham, Milledge Luke, to John Henry Brown. May 13, 1889. Brown (John Henry) Papers, CAH.

Columbia,S.C.May 13th.1889.

Col.John Henry Brown,

Dallas,Texas.

Dear sir:-

Your letters of May Ist & 5th,the latter covering Gen.Bee's letter to you,which I return as requested,have been received. I had not supposed the Medal or Narrative accompanying it had been issued by the authority of the Monumental Association. I felt confirmed in that belief,when I received from Gen.Bee,an old friend of mine,a letter in reference to Capt. Schramm's Mission.

Possibly I may have made a mistake,as to Maverick being with my brother near San Antonio: He may have recounted the remarks,which it seems Col.Bonham made to a Mr.Smith also,as he was abotu [*sic*] to enter the Alamo. I think I could not have been mistaken as to Col.M averick's having had an interview with my brother and endeavored to dissuade him from returning to the Fort for the reasons given. Perhaps Mrs.Maverick can throw some light on it. Mrs.Dickinson if alive can give her own account,and it would seem strange to me if she has not put in writing her statement. The last I heard of her,she was living in Austin,and,if alive,may be too old to give her account of what occurred

Mrs.Dickinson told me she was the only white person,with her baby,that was left alive. The Mexican women recently reported as being in the Alamo,I never heard of till lately. They may have been there,but certainly could not have been on the Texan side.

My hand is not a good one and I therefore use a type writer.

Yours truly
M.L. Bonham

5.1.8.7.   Milledge Luke Bonham, letter, 1889.

Bonham, Milledge Luke, to John Henry Brown. May 22, 1889. Brown (John Henry) Papers, CAH.
Unlike the preceding letters, this is a handwritten postcard.

Columbia May 22/89

I have just read in the herald of the Comp. Genl. a copy of your Article in the Farm & Ranch of the 15ʰ on the Alamo, sent them by a friend [?] in Texas. I am sure you have sent me a copy as you said you would, But it has Miscarried. This a very interesting piece of History

M.L.Bonham

5.1.8.8.   John Henry Brown, narrative, 1889.

State. April 26, 1914. Columbia, South Carolina.
This is a reprint of an article by John Henry Brown reputed to be published in the *Texas Farm and Ranch,* May 15, 1889. This is the account of Bonham that has been incorporated into numerous versions of the Alamo story. The article is titled "Bonham and the Alamo" and gives a general biography of James Butler Bonham, but without references except those included internally. The excerpt here covers the actual events of the Alamo starting in January 1836. The original *Farm and Ranch* article was not located.

. . . Wild schemes not untinged with selfishness, and consequent demoralization, were in the air. Gov. Smith sent Col. Travis to take command at San Antonio, after Johnson, Grant and their self-organized expedition to take Matamoros had depleted San Antonio of its military supplies and left it as a defenseless outpost. Travis hastened to his post of duty, preceded a short time by the friend of his youth, Bonham. Travis, grand in intellect, unselfish in spirit and noble in heart, organized his force as best he could, determined to hold the advancing enemy in check until Gen. Houston could collect and organize a force sufficient to meet and repel him on the open field. He trusted that Fannin, with over 400 thoroughly equipped men at Goliad, would march to his relief.

He sent appeals to him to that effect, and finally, after Santa Ann's cohorts had encircled his position in the Alamo, he sent Bonham for a last appeal for aid, with instructions also to his lifetime friend to proceed from Goliad to Gonzales in search of aid. This mission was full of peril from both Mexicans around San Antonio and Indians on the entire route of his travel. As things were then, none but a man oblivious of danger would have undertaken the mission. James Butler Bonham, then just 29 years of age, assumed its hazards. He presented the facts to Fannin, but the latter failed to respond. Thence Bonham, through the wilderness, without a human habitation between the points, hastened from Goliad to Gonzales, just as a few volunteers began to collect there. In response to the appeals of Travis 32 citizens of that colony had left a day or two before, under Capt. Albert Martin, to succor the 150 defenders of the Alamo. The siege had begun on the 23rd of February. These 32 men had fought their way in at daylight on the 1st of March. Bonham, supplied with all the information he could gather, and satisfied he could get no further present recruits, determined to return to Travis. He was accompanied by Samuel A. Maverick and John W. Smith. When they reached the heights overlooking San Antonio and saw that the doomed Alamo was encircled by Santa Anna's troops, Smith and Maverick deemed it suicidal to seek an entrance. That was the ninth day of the siege and the doom of the garrison was inevitable. Smith and Maverick, by their own honorable statements afterwards, to both Gen. Sam Houston and ex-Governor Milledge L. Bonham, in Houston, in 1838, urged Bonham to retire with them; but he sternly refused, saying: "I will report the result of my mission to Travis or die in the attempt." Mounted on a beautiful cream-colored horse, with a white handkerchief floating from his hat (as previously agreed with Travis) he dashed through the Mexican lines, amid the showers of bullets hurled at him— the gate of the Alamo flew open, and as chivalrous a soul as ever fought and died for liberty entered—entered to leave no more, except in its upward flight to the throne of God. . . .

Commentary

Possible Primary Sources—Nineteenth Century (5.1)

Later in the nineteenth century, a number of histories covering the Texas Revolution included accounts of the Alamo that may have had additional interviews with participants not already covered in the materials transcribed. The first selection of documents in this section is of those that might have included or did include such possible additional primary sources.

In some cases, there is a significant problem in that the nineteenth-century writers frequently did not credit their sources and also indulged in extensive paraphrasing. Therefore one often has little basis on which to judge how valid their additional sources were, or how much the narrative was rewritten and distorted for the purposes of the later author. It seems to be an unfortunate trend in recent years by some journalists and popular writers to revert to this practice, which makes their work of significantly less value to the future.

The account/resolution of a meeting in Nacogdoches (5.1.1) has details not otherwise recorded, and also gives a sense of the immediate impact of the defense and fall of the Alamo on the rest of Texas. The participants certainly had access to some authentic information for some details, as judged by the Houston letters (section 3.5) and the *Telegraph and Texas Register* account (4.1.1). These details include the casualties on both sides and the sudden attack on the exhausted, sleeping garrison. The death of Travis and, to a lesser extent, the death of Crockett are reflected in some of the stories circulating early. The date is rather early for the specifics to have come from the *Telegraph and Texas Register* account, as the San Felipe newspaper would not likely have reached Nacogdoches by the twenty-sixth. This is reinforced by the different wording in the general manner of description and many of the details. Thus this account probably serves as an independent comparison with the newspaper on the stories in immediate circulation in Texas. The details of the three attacks on the Alamo, which were first reported in the *Telegraph and Texas Register,* show up here as well and therefore were unlikely to have been invented in San Felipe. New details are the treachery of someone in the fort, a report on Captain Jamison's efforts, and the death of Bonham. However, these details are not supported by any other sources and should be treated skeptically. My conclusion is that this resolution is an independent reflection and check on early battle stories, but it does not have a reliable source for new details.

Joseph Field (5.1.2) circulated outside of Texas the story of Crockett's marksmanship. He also added two more unsupported Crockett items: Santa Anna being nearly shot, and Crockett visiting Mrs. Dickinson during the storming. These are basically unsupported otherwise. It seems fair to conclude that Field was merely repeating rumors current in Texas later in 1836 rather than having eyewitness sources of his own.

Newell (5.1.3) certainly culled the accounts available to him. For example, he used about half of Almonte's journal entries (2.2.1) for February 27 to March 4. All of the items in this portion of unattributed details have been seen elsewhere—especially in the accounts originating with Joe. The narratives of the Alamo's fall and the death of Crockett are nearly verbatim from the *Telegraph and Texas Register* (4.1.1), with a few embellishments added. The one new item, related to Evan's attempt to blow up the power supply, is Santa Anna stabbing the body. Once again, here is an unsupported detail that seems suspiciously like an addition for dramatic effect, and it is therefore questionable. So this unattributed portion of Newell's history (as opposed to the attributed recording of Ben's account, 2.12.1) does not appear to add new information on the Alamo events.

William Kennedy (5.1.4) extensively used Travis's letters and Newell's history, with some additional dates from Almonte's journal. A few details of the Mexican Army, a reference to Filisola and the cavalry forming a circle around the Alamo and the attacking army, strongly suggest that Kennedy had access to some information from the Mexican side. This is curious, as most of the Mexican sources were not published until much later than Kennedy. However, there are no details from this later work that have not already been presented in earlier documents, so for the Alamo, his information has been supplanted.

Henderson Yoakum (5.1.5), a true historian in the modern sense of the word, deserves a lot of credit for the extent to which he attributed his sources. As a consequence, in those cases where original written accounts were nonexistent or are now lost, one can still evaluate and judge the accuracy of his information. The most valuable detail in this portion of his history is the statement of Antonio Peréz. This tells much more explicitly than Houston's letters (section 3.5) that Peréz was the source for the figures of Mexican casualties and the early accounts that Travis committed suicide.[1] One also learns about Peréz getting his information by remaining several hours after the storming. The greatest debt owed to Yoakum is for the documents presented earlier with him as the source. Without Yoakum's history, all that information would be less known, at best, and in most cases lost forever.

Morphis has already been reviewed (5.1.6) as a source for Susanna Dickinson (1.2.7). There is little additional information in this remaining portion, and thus little to add to what has already been said critiquing his history.

The selection by Reuben Potter (5.1.7) is likely the most widely disseminated and influential account of the Alamo written in the nineteenth century. On reviewing it, one can conclude that this rightfully should have been especially significant. A large number of details are given; in most cases, the sources for these items can be attributed to documents already presented, and these can be used to verify that he did a reliable report on what was said. It should be clear that he reviewed original and secondary material available at his time carefully, and made mostly reasonable selections of details for his narration; in this respect, he is the forerunner of Meyers, Tinkle, and Lord. As many of these details have already been given in the original sources, as well as others not available to Potter, his overall narrative composition will not be explored much further here. Those interested in studying Potter in greater depth should refer to the annotated edition of 1977 published by Charles Grosvenor.

Of more focused interest for the purposes of this study is to note those items that show up here for the first time or seem inconsistent with other documents: Travis being ordered to relieve Neill (per documents 1.1.1.5 and 1.1.1.8, he was ordered to Béxar, but not explicitly to relieve Neill of command); Bowie being in command when Travis arrived (an error, see 1.1.1.8 and 4.5.27); the siege starting on February 22 (an error for the twenty-third, i.e., 1.1.1.16 on); Mexican reinforcements arriving on February 24 (unsupported by 2.2.1 and 2.6.1); Crockett being found at the west battery, according to Ruiz (a paraphrase of 3.1.1), and Bowie in the low barracks (discussed in detail in Appendix C); and a few details of the battle from a Mexican officer. The errors in Potter's map have already been noted in Schoelwer (4.2.4).

Most important are Potter's attributed interviews with sources not otherwise available. Foremost in this category is the vivid account by Mr. Lewis of the disorder in the Alamo during the first few hours of the siege. Another important description is that of General Bradburn of the turning of a cannon by the defenders to fire on the attackers *inside* the outer walls.[2] There is also a comment recorded in a footnote by a husband of one of the women inside the Alamo during the siege, likely to have been Horace Alsbury.

Potter can also be compared against those sources for which we do have other documents. For example, he made it clear that Juan Seguín was an important source (though he was wrong in believing Seguín was dead by 1878). Potter's version of Seguín's departure from the Alamo is quite consistent with that in the latter's memoirs (1.7.2.2), and thus serves as verification that Seguín's story was consistent between the two interviews. Another important contribution from Seguín via Potter is the identities of nine of his men. Potter glossed over them in his published account, but Williams elaborated on the information available from Potter in letters to William Steele in July 1874, particularly one of July 10 (1.11.2).[3]

Because the two narratives do not match well, Potter's Sergeant Becero is not likely to be Ford's Becerra (2.10.1). It also seems that Potter never interviewed Susanna Dickinson. Those items related to her are from the newspaper accounts then circulating (e.g., 4.1.1); the especially bizarre story of the Dickinson leap circulated right after the battle (e.g., 3.5.2).

Potter gave a number of military details on the fall of the Alamo, which are briefly considered in Appendix B. Although Potter did not meet modern standards for source attribution, I would acknowledge him as a careful historian with a genuine desire to understand the truth of what happened at the Alamo, rather than trying to make the story fit what he wanted to believe.

One of the most dramatic, even astonishing, personal stories of the Alamo has so far been poorly represented by the primary sources in this collection of documents. From Travis, it is known that James Butler Bonham entered the Alamo on the morning of March 3 (1.1.6), the tenth day of the siege. He is likely to have known there would be no immediate help coming from Fannin or Houston. Therefore, it is widely believed that he would have concluded prior to his last ride that the garrison was doomed and that by entering, so was he. Most historians believe that Travis sent Bonham to Fannin, and when he realized Fannin would not come to reinforce the Alamo, Bonham thought it vital to return and report this fact to Travis. It is both curious and frustrating that there is only one firsthand reference by someone—Williamson (4.3.4)—who met Bonham while he was outside the Alamo.

The final published account by John Henry Brown (5.1.8.8) is likely the major source for all subsequent narratives of Bonham's dash into the Alamo. In addition to the letters by Travis and Williamson, the only other reference to his movements found in known primary sources is in Sutherland (1.7.1.1, p. 31).[4]

A number of issues surrounding the Bonham story are raised by the documents in this section. First is to attempt to verify the sources Brown had to work with, and to assess how much of the story is from those sources or from Brown himself. A particularly important part of that issue is whether, via James Bonham's brother Milledge Luke Bonham, we have a testimonial from someone—Samuel Maverick, John W. Smith, both, or neither—who was with James Bonham on the outskirts of San Antonio before he took his final ride. We might also have another secondhand account from Susanna Dickinson. Still other questions are whether Bonham took one trip or two as Travis's messenger, and whether Milledge Bonham got his information from a different source, such as Sam Houston or Benjamin Highsmith. This is one of the more confusing pieces of the Alamo story.

An examination, not exhaustive, of the John Henry Brown Papers in the CAH located various correspondence and material Brown received from Milledge Bonham. These have been partially transcribed here. The most important and immediate question is whether one can be sure the first two anonymous manuscripts in this section (5.1.8.1, 5.1.8.2) were written by Bonham rather than Brown or somebody else. Fortunately, a very definite answer is possible. The solid evidence based on content is that Bonham's letter of around April 4 (5.1.8.3) explicitly refers to the "toasts and editorials I transcribed," while his letter of April 19 (5.1.8.5) states, consistent with the author of the biography: "I think, from Col. Maverick or Mrs. Dickinson herself, I heard in Texas in 1838 . . ." Therefore we have the latter two documents directly referring to information in the first two.

The idiosyncratic typing in the manuscripts and some of the letters is equally solid evidence. Overall, there are many apparent consistencies between the first two manuscripts and the letters of April 4 and May 13, two of which I consider definitive. The first is reflected in the transcripts given here: The typist (Bonham's sixteen-year-old son, per the April 4 letter) frequently and consistently neglected to put spaces between words and punctuation marks. The second is that in four documents, the letter "o" is distinctly below the rest of the letters in a line of typing. This is nearly certain proof that the same typewriter was used for the various attributed and unattributed documents. The letter of April 19, however, does not share this trait; it appears to have been typed on a different machine by a different person. Taking content and physical characteristics as a whole, the identification of the first two manuscripts as being by Milledge Bonham seems positive.

There are several characteristics to this Milledge Bonham account to look for in the evolution of the story. The most important is the statement that in 1838 he interviewed Sam Maverick, who became the main source for the account of Bonham's last dash. A Mr. Smith was also reputed to have given the same advice, though the narrative doesn't say where Smith was when he talked to Bonham—presumably it could have been at a significantly different time and place. On the same 1838 trip, Mrs. Dickinson also gave some information. Still another detail is that a white handkerchief was tied to a nearby height to signal to the Alamo defenders that Bonham was coming in.

In comparing the Milledge Bonham summary with the first Brown *Farm and Ranch* article (5.1.8.3), written prior to March 11, 1889, it is clear that the specific details are basically consistent. Brown added Albert Martin as the leader of the Gonzales party of thirty-two that entered the Alamo on March 1, along with a few other general details, but did not modify the details of the story significantly. Sam Maverick was still Milledge Bonham's primary source. Therefore, it is likely Brown already had the Bonham account in hand when this was written early in 1889.

Soon, however, an issue arose over Sam Maverick's identification and apparently was discussed between Bonham and Brown. In the "Toasts and Editorials," (Samuel) Augustus Maverick said it was Smith who was with Bonham's brother rather than himself. This statement was thirdhand hearsay at best, but it is worth noting that Samuel Augustus Maverick was born in Pendleton, South Carolina, where the quoted newspaper was reputed to be from.[5] In the letter of May 13, 1889 (5.1.8.6), Bonham allowed the possibility, but didn't outright concede that he might have made a mistake about Maverick having been with his brother.

Soon thereafter, presumably in the *Farm and Ranch* for May 15, 1889 (5.1.8.8), Brown rewrote the Milledge Bonham story into a narrative of the James Bonham story.[6] In addition to biographical details, the narrative has both Samuel A. Maverick and John W. Smith trying to discourage James Bonham from his suicidal mission. Sam Houston is now included as another source for the story. With a white handkerchief floating from his hat, James proceeds to ride into the Alamo and his fate.

Who really was the source for the story? Per later information, on March 3 Samuel Maverick was supposed to be on his way to Washington-on-the-Brazos as a delegate to the Convention (4.5.27). Down to 1932, when Williams was researching the subject (see 5.2.1.2), Maverick's family insisted he hadn't been near San Antonio.[7]

John W. Smith is universally reported by historians to have been the guide who led the Gonzales reinforcements into the Alamo on March 1, and then left the Alamo after Bonham's arrival with the letters of March 3. Yoakum (5.1.5) so reported in 1855, supported in detail in Sutherland's account. It is worth noting that Yoakum wrote not only before 1860, when Sutherland started writing (in response to Potter's original account), and so was uninfluenced by the latter, but also while a number of other direct participants were still alive. These were people, including Yoakum's friend Sam Houston, who must have known whether his statements on John W. Smith were accurate. It is clear that Smith would not have been on the hills outside San Antonio trying to dissuade Bonham from riding into the Alamo on the morning of March 3 if he was already inside to bring Travis's letters out later the same day.

John Sutherland added another twist in his account (1.7.1.1, p. 31) by reporting that Bonham was in the vicinity of San Antonio on February 23 at the start of the siege, heard the cannons, and rode to the Alamo to report to Travis.[8] Thus, if this story is correct—presumably coming via Smith from Travis or Bonham himself before Smith left the Alamo on March 3—Bonham was twice sent as a messenger. The first was fourteen days before Travis's letter of March 3, the second after the siege began. The possibility was also suggested by Brown (5.1.8.8). Williams accepted the story and speculated that the second trip began around February 26 or 27.[9] Sutherland did not claim personal knowledge of this story.

The fundamental problem remains that neither Maverick nor Smith appears to have been the source for Milledge Bonham's account. This might have bothered Brown himself, because in 1892, he did not include the story in his major *History of Texas*. Williams noted similarities between the Milledge Bonham (via Brown) account and the account of Benjamin Highsmith (section 1.7.6). Her idea, accepted by her thesis advisor, Eugene Barker, was that perhaps Highsmith was the source. Therefore, sixty years later, either Milledge Bonham forgot he had heard the story from Highsmith or Maverick was repeating the story secondhand (5.2.1.2).[10]

The grandson of Bonham, Milledge L. Bonham, Jr., wrote another version of the story that was eventually published.[11] This is a major summary of the biographical information known on James Bonham. For the story of James at the Alamo, he appears to have had some family papers available, but most of his details are attributed to published works.[12] Thus there is not much new from this article.

Much later, Thomas Lindley did a survey of the known documents to try to place the movements of James Bonham during the siege of the Alamo.[13] By a careful look at the letters and documents that indicate the times and places for those people Bonham most likely met, such as Fannin and Houston, he came up with a reasonable chronology. In particular, he noted that the Williamson letter (4.3.4) of March 1 states that Fannin had been on the way for three days—from February 27—establishing that Bonham could not have visited Fannin more recently to learn that the Goliad force had turned back. Thus the second trip implied by Sutherland and Brown, and speculated on by Williams, to have started February 26 or 27 must have been wrong, and Bonham was not riding to Travis to report on the failure of Fannin to come fight the besiegers. Lindley also added another interesting idea: that Bonham's message from Travis fourteen days prior to March 3 (and thus prior to the siege) was to ask Fannin to come and take command of the defense. There is nothing in the materials presented in this book to make this possibility far-fetched.[14]

Further research is warranted. Perhaps a truly thorough review of John Henry Brown's Papers might reveal other relevant documents. If available, papers from the Bonham or Maverick family could be significant. Or perhaps a letter or expense claim from someone who met Bonham during the siege—pinpointing where he was and when—might still be found.

---

1. E.g., 3.5.5, Williams in *SWHQ* 37:262–63 n. 13.
2. General Bradburn was not in Béjar. He is briefly discussed in the portion not transcribed here; see Potter 1977, 46.

3. Williams *SWHQ* 37:242–43.
4. The Audited Claims files of the Republic Claims records, TSLA, were examined for obvious names without any new material of the crucial period being discovered.
5. Reference the biography of Samuel Maverick in Webb, 1952.
6. Here, "presumably" means that an actual copy of the May 15 *Farm and Ranch* was not located, only the 1914 reprinted article in the *Columbia (South Carolina) State.* It is possible that this resulted from confusion by the Bonham family per the note of May 22 (5.1.8.7) that does not specify what was in the May 15 issue.
7. See also the biography of Samuel Augustus Maverick in Wharton. Per granddaughter Rena Maverick Green (1952, x–xi, 48), Maverick reached the Convention in Washington-on-the-Brazos on March 3. Biographer Paula Marks (1989, 51–52, 56–58) has Maverick remaining in the Alamo during the earlier part of the siege until March 2, though I don't find her evidence cited very compelling, then escaping through the Mexican lines and reaching the Convention on March 5.
8. First widely disseminated in DeShields 1911.
9. Williams in *SWHQ* 37:20–21 n. 52; 37:25–26 n. 58.
10. Also Williams in *SWHQ* 37:25–26 n. 58.
11. Bonham 1931. An earlier version copied by Williams was sent to her April 22, 1925, and is in the General Correspondence files of the Williams Papers, CAH.
12. For example, he cites Brown's *Farm and Ranch* of May 15, 1889; Brown 1892; Bancroft 1889; and Sheppard c. 1898. The article does not account for the possibility that Bancroft and especially Sheppard could be largely derivative from the first source. It is also possible that he got the *Farm and Ranch* reference from Milledge Bonham's papers (e.g., 5.1.8.7) rather than an original article.
13. Lindley, 1988.
14. Hardin (c. 2000) also pointed out that the lack of specifics in the Travis letter makes the second trip unlikely, as implied by Sutherland and Brown and accepted by Williams. Hardin's discussion is limited, because he did not review the second Williams reference, *SWHQ* 37:25–26 n. 58, which was Williams's main justification for accepting this piece of Sutherland's account. Also, Hardin noted that due to the basic "hold-on" optimism of the Williamson letter, Bonham's return to the Alamo was not as obviously suicidal as commonly thought. On the other hand, I believe the sight of a few thousand troops surrounding the Alamo on the tenth day of the siege and the lack of any reinforcements in sight immediately behind should have given a clearer picture of the actual situation to Bonham than anything in his saddlebags. The article is posted (2003) on the Internet at http://Alamo-de-parras.welkin.org/archives/feature/bonham/bonham.html.

5.2.1.1.   Amelia Williams, dissertation, 1931.

Williams, Amelia W. January 1934. A critical study of the siege of the Alamo and of the personnel of its defenders. *Southwestern Historical Quarterly* 37:179–82.

These two sections were Appendix V and IV, respectively, of Williams's original (1931) dissertation.

---

9. The Flag of the Alamo

No official document, or statement can be found concerning the flag of the Alamo, but there is considerable discrepancy in the statements of the various Texas historians in referring to it. Kennedy, *Texas*, II, 180–181, says that the flag used by Travis and his men, was the Mexican tricolor—red, white, green—with two blue stars on the white bar. Bancroft, *North Mexican States and Texas*, II, 208, and others who follow Kennedy as authority, make the same statement. The flag they describe was the Coahuila-Texas flag. Yoakum, Potter, McArdle, and other more recent students agree that the Alamo flag was the Mexican tricolor with the numerals *1824* on the white bar. The tenet is logical. The hated union with Coahuila was one cause of the Texas Revolution, and it is hardly likely that the Texans would fight under a flag which symbolized that union. When they began the Revolution they did not immediately declare for independence, but for liberal government as a state of the Mexican republic, according to the terms of the Mexican constitution of 1824. Hence, it was but logical that they should adopt as their flag a modification of the Mexican national standard, so instead of the eagle, they decided to imprint 1824 on the white bar of the tricolor. This flag was almost certainly the one used at the Alamo.

But from what part of the fortress did it float? The earlier writers did not venture to say, but R. M. Potter, "The Texas Revolution," *Magazine of American History*, January, 1878, states that the flag was over the church. H. A. McArdle and a half dozen or more other writers accept his statement as authority. But a few others—seemingly a minority in both numbers and authority—say that the flag was over the southwest corner of the main building of the fort, the building designated "long barracks" in the plats. Not one of all these writers takes the pains to give any authority for his statements concerning the flag, nor has research on the subject revealed unquestionable information, still I am convinced, that in this case, the minority authority has reached the correct conclusion. Their conclusion, at any rate, is logical, for the flag of a fortress would normally fly from that portion of the structure that was, and that had throughout the history of the building, been the stronghold.

In the mission days of the Alamo, the south end of the main building—then the tower—had guarded the entrance to the mission, and from this tower the flag had floated. In 1827 Juan Sanchez Estrada made a rough sketch of the Alamo [*Sánchez Navarro, per Schoelwer (5.2.4)*]. In that picture the Coahuila-Texas flag is conspicuous. It floats from this same southwest corner of the main building.[47] In Estrada's sketch the church is scarcely noticeable; it is merely a square block in the background. We must remember that since 1763 the church of the Alamo had been in a ruined condition, the roof and twin towers having fallen in during that year. We must remember, also, that the irregular facade of the church, with which we are so familiar today, is a form given to the old building for the first time in 1848, when the old ruin was repaired by the authority of the United States government. At the time of the siege in 1836, the church was roofless except for flat covers over the small anterooms at the west entrance and on the north side. The towers were gone, the roof was gone, and the walls of the church were lower than were the flat roof of the main building only 50 feet away. The south end of this main building, as has been previously stated, served, on its first floor, as the armory of the fort, while its second floor was the hospital. It seems, then, far more reasonable to think that the flag of the fortress should fly over the armory—the real stronghold—than over the decadent chapel. Especially is this thinking logical, since over the armory—the south end of the main building—had been the location of the flag staff during the mission days, and evidently, also, during the times (Estrada's sketch) the Mexicans had used the building to house their soldiery.

---

[47] Appendix III of the thesis of which these chapters are a part shows nine pictures of the Alamo. The second picture of that collection is the Estrada drawing. It was sketched from the roof of the Verramendi house. The original sketch is in the *Wagner Collection of Materials for Southwestern and Mexican History,* and is now the property of Yale University.

The *Star-Telegram* (Fort Worth) of November 12, 1933, prints an article, written by B. C. Utecht (Staff Correspondent), under the title, *Flag that Waved Over Alamo's 180 Defenders Is Discovered by a Texan in a Mexican Museum.* This article is about two columns in length, and carries a picture of the so-called discovery. It also states that the discovery of this flag, and the materials relative to it, collected by the former Attorney General W. A. Keeling, has opened a new chapter in Texas history.

The entire article makes it clear to any student of Texas history—especially of the history of the Alamo episode—that the newly discovered flag in the Mexican museum is not the flag that floated from the Alamo's fortress tower in 1836, but is merely a company flag of the first company of New Orleans Grays. There is little doubt that the Mexicans did acquire that flag, they now have in their museum, when they took possession of the Alamo after the massacre of its defenders on March 6, 1836, but historical facts almost certainly prove that it could not have been the flag used by Travis as the general flag of his fort.

Some of these conclusive historical facts are: (1) There were two well-organized companies of New Orleans Grays. The flag, pictured in the *Telegram* was presented to the first company of the New Orleans Grays as it left Nacogdoches in November, 1835. Both these companies of troops, organized at New Orleans for Texas service, participated in the "Storming of Bexar," December 5–10, 1835. Most of the men of both companies remained at San Antonio after General Cos evacuated the place, but by the first of January, 1836, all of them, except some half dozen, had deserted the Alamo, led away by Francis W. Johnson and James Grant. Indeed, only six men from these New Orleans companies—two from the first, and four from the second—died with Travis at the Alamo. (2) Colonel J. C.

Neill, the commander of the Alamo after Johnson left, bitterly resented the deple-
tion of the Alamo fortress by Johnson, Grant, and their men. Bowie and Travis
who became the commanders of the San Antonio troops after Neill's departure
on February 12, 1836, felt this same bitterness, and there is little probability that
any of these three leaders at the Alamo would have tolerated as their banner the
flag of a company, all members of which, except *two*, had deserted and depleted
the fortress. (3) We know definitely (see C.M.S.R, State Library) that Travis
advanced money from his private purse with which to buy a flag and other supplies for the company that he carried to the Alamo. If any *company* flag was to fly
from the fortress tower it would surely have been that of Travis's own company. I
am sure that all who know Travis will readily concede this. We have no description of the flag of Travis's company. (4) A goodly number of Texans, contemporary with the fall of the Alamo, tell us that the flag used by the Texan soldiers in
1835 and early part of 1836, was the Mexican tri-color with the figures *1824* on
the white bar. (See McArdle's Alamo Book, Texas State Library, for a good summary of these authoritative statements.)

10. El Deguello

All authentic accounts of the fall of the Alamo state that the signal for the final
attack was given by "a long clear blast from a bugle, followed by the notes of
the dreadful deguello."

This old bugle call has an interesting history of its own, a history that is
much older than that of Texas, or even of Mexico itself, for it is known to extend
back through the centuries of Spanish annals to the wars against the Moors.
Always its notes have meant wanton destruction of property and death without
mercy, and for this reason it is often designated as "the fire and death call." In
fact, the very word *deguello* in the Spanish language signifies the act of behead-
ing or throat cutting—utter destruction and ruin. Throughout its history this
old call has always been the relentless signal of no quarter, no mercy to the foe.

Like all long-used music, the *deguello* has many variants.[48] Three versions of
this old *toque* have been found during this study, the one used by Villa's band,
the one the Professor Asbury discovered, and finally, the official version of
1836.[49] Although the arrangement of the music differs in all three of these versions, it is interesting to note that they are all written in the key of *C*, and all
extend through the octave to *G* of the lower octave. Separated from its aged significance, the music within itself is not especially harsh or discordant. There is
little doubt that the *deguello* here presented is the call that was sounded at the
Alamo on the morning of March 6, 1836.

[*The music for the* deguello *is reproduced in* SWHQ 37:183.]

---

[48] I am indebted to Professor Samuel E. Asbury of the Texas A. and M. College for
initiating my research concerning this old bugle call.

[49] Credit for finding the official *deguello* belongs to Mr. Luis Chavez Orosco of Mexico City. In 1926, Mr. Orosco was employed by the Mexican government to write
a history of the Texas Revolution of 1836. While working in the Garcia Library of
the University of Texas, he was amused at, and became interested in the difficulties I was having in my search for this old Mexican bugle call. He kindly offered

to help find it. At his request the Mexican War Department sent many books of martial music, tactics, toques, and orders, but in none of them could the *deguello* be found. However, upon Mr. Orosco's return to Mexico, he himself searched through the archives of the War Department, and succeeded in finding a copy of the *deguello* used by the Mexican armies from 1830 to 1845 and later. Its official use is now obsolete.

5.2.1.2.   Amelia Williams, letter, 1932.

Williams, Amelia, to Samuel Asbury. February 1, 1932. Williams (Amelia Worthington) Papers, CAH.

Williams, in this letter written soon after the completion of her dissertation, summarized some of the oral traditions she heard, which have not all been otherwise recorded.

Box 804
Austin, Texas
Feb.1, 1932.

Dear Mr. Asbury:

At last I have finished the job that I had hold of with both hands and couldn't turn loose until it was finished. Now, let me acknowledge your letters and the copies of letters relative to Amos Pollard. Let me also state that as soon as I can dig out the material from among my <u>mess</u> of notes I shall send what I have concerning Green Benito Jameson, copies of the Pollard letters to be found among the <u>Army</u> <u>Papers</u>, and as soon as I can, I'll have some copies made of the <u>1836</u> <u>degnello</u> [*deguello*] and send one to Miss Mixon, because you ask it. In the meanwhile why not send her your degnello; she—like Dr. Dieust [?]—may prefer to use it.

Now, for answers to some of your questions. Don't take these answers for absolutely correct ones—only my opinion concerning them. First, I want to have this to say about Dr. Bonham and his writing. I think there are several blunders in the paper you read for him before the Association and that is now printed in the <u>Quarterly</u>. I think the Mavericks are over sensitive about the thing but Dr. Bonham's sources for his story—Texas part of it, are rather thin. I do not believe that it was Jno. W. Smith, at all who accompanied Bonham on his return from Fannin on March 3, but Benjamin High Smith, Maverick was possibly along, too, as there seem to have been three or four in the crowd, but the Mavericks say not and I believe they are truthful about it. I have had several long talks with Mr. Samuel A. Maverick, son of the man of 1836. I know Mrs. Sammons, Mr. S. A. Maverick's daughter well, also Mrs. Miller, another daughter. They are women of intelligence, as is also Mr. S. A. Maverick. (Mr. Maverick was educated at University of Edinburg, Scotland.) Mr. S. A. Maverick affirms that his father left Bexar on the day of the arrival of the Mexicans, Feb. 23. He was not exactly a messenger from the Alamo because he did not belong to the army, then, but rode by the fortress and talked with Travis—he sitting on his horse—and Travis standing on top [*of*] the outer walls. Maverick agreed to ride through out the country, spread the alarm and get together whatever troops and supplies possible. They, the Mavericks, say that Maverick did not return until he went with the company sent out on March 6, from Washington—the one that reached the Cibola and not hearing guns sent scouts ahead. Maverick was one of the scouts who went ahead and was chased by Mexican sentinels. But that, as you know, was after the fall of the fortress. I believe this is [*a*] true account. Just who accompanied Bonham to Bexar on March 3, I did not succeed in definitely establishing. I think, however, B. Highsmith was one. He had been sent out with a message. I work this explanation out in my theses. Dr. Barker thinks my solution of the problem and my interpretation of the story about Bonham's dash on the "snow-white" horse etc., very highly probable. This is one of the things, however, that I believe will never be known with absolute certainty. I think that Fannin, certainly, and probably many others urged Bonham not to return to San Antonio, arguing that it was certain death, but this advice was, no doubt, at Goliad and not before the walls of San Antonio. Travis, himself, says in letter of Mar. 3, that "My messenger, Col. Bonham, got in this morning without molestation". That doesn't sound much like the dramatic dash on the snow-white horse, does it? I think most of that dramatic story was "fixed up" by Jno. H. Brown. The related materials just won't substantiate it.

The line that Travis drew is another unsolved problem, but, I think, there may be some truth back of it. I know that most careful students discredit it. But the doing of a thing like that just fits the character of Travis as I have come to know him. But I did not prove it. Here are my grounds for believing it may be true. Remember in my master's thesis I definitely stated that I believed the story untrue—but Dr. Ramsdell assured me I could trust implicitely [*sic*] what ever his father-in-law, Mr. A. D. Griffeth [*sic*] might tell me. That is Dr. R. said I might trust that Mr. Griffith believed everything he told me. (This is getting ahead of myself on the story of Mr. Griffith but it will come later.) I mean to say Dr. R- vouched in strongest terms for the truthfulness of Mr. Griffith. Well, Mr. Griffith says when he was a small boy just after the Civil War, he was wont to sit around and listen to his uncle, H. A. Griffith, and Captain Frank Dupree talk about wars and battles. He says he first heard the Rose story from them. This was down near Matagorda [*sic*]—in the Old Caney country. He is quite sure this was before the story was published by Zuber. Mrs. Sterling says that she heard her grand mother (Mrs. Dickinson) tell it many times. At first she was positive that she had heard it prior to 1873, but upon several weeks consideration she said she could not be certain whether she heard her grandmother tell the story before 1873 or not. Mr. Griffith's story robs me of my cock-sure opinion that the whole story was hatched in Zuber's mind, still I must forever doubt it in a way because had it been true why didn't Mrs. D- tell it when she reached Gonzales? And had she told it there the dramatic thrill of it would have taken hold of the minds of the people, and it would have been on every tongue, where as we can

find no trace of it in print, or in <u>MS</u>. until after 1873. So there you are. A <u>truthful</u>
man says he heard the story before 1873. The man we know Travis to have been
would have done just such a thing—on the other hand, had it been true it must
have created some attention, it certainly would have been told again and again.
Some one must have put the story into writing. Joe would have told it—Gray
would have recorded it. Work it out is [as] you can. I almost went crazy trying
to do it, but must confess I don't know. I'll tell you what I said in my theses, and
Dr. Barker thinks I disposed of the problem wisely. I told the Rose story briefly. I
stated that all of the most careful students and investigators had discredited the
story, but that there was some evidence that the story had been told before 1873.
In a foot note I told about Mr. Griffith and of his having heard the story during
his boyhood.

Now, about Mrs. Dickinson. During the early days of my investigation of
the Alamo story, you wrote me that Mrs. Ramsdell was a great-grand daughter
of Mrs. Dickinson's, I went immediately to Dr. R- for information. He was gracious and kind as Dr. R. always is. He told me his father-in-law, and his sister
were both living in Austin, that they were very poor, and that both were more
than eighty years old, but that they would be glad to know me and would tell
me all they knew about their grandmother and mother. He himself took me to
see them first. After that I went to see them several times.

[*The letter continues with what Williams had learned about the biographies of*
Susanna and Angelina, not directly relevant to the Alamo story. She also returns to the
writings of Dr. Bonham referred to at the start, reiterating her opinion that he had not
done enough research with Texas sources.]

But, please, don't send this letter or copies of it to folks. It is rather poorly
written, and most of it is merely my opinion of things—<u>undocumented</u>—you
know. But you asked me for my opinion, and I think I owe it to you to give it to
you concerning these problems. For the most part I can document what I have
said, I think, but I do not seek a controversy.

I shall send the materials you want soon.

Sincerely,
Amelia Williams.

5.2.2.   Lord, analysis, 1961.

Lord, Walter. 1961. *A Time to Stand*. New York: Harper & Row. Reprint, 1978. 198–212. Lincoln: University of Nebraska Press.

This is among the more well-researched narratives of the siege and fall of the Alamo. Lord's appendix tackles some of the most interesting issues, which are also the hardest to resolve.

Riddles of the Alamo

"You know," the old Texan gently admonished, "legend is often truer than history and always more lasting." And yet the haunting questions remain—did Travis *really* draw the line, did Crockett *really* fall fighting, and so on.

The answers come hard, even when someone wants to know the facts. Traces of the frontier are few today in terms of towns, wild game, Indians, lawlessness, almost everything—except research. Here the frontier is still very much alive, for the pioneer's impatience with dates, spelling and record-keeping lingers on to plague anyone digging into the past.

Dates alone are a nightmare in the story of the Alamo. Ramón Caro had an exasperating way of saying things happened on February 30. Juan Seguin gave at least four different dates as the day he left the fort—February 26 (letter to W. W. Fontaine, 1890); the 28th (*Memoirs*, 1858); the 29th (talk with R. M. Potter, about 1878); March 2 (affidavit on behalf of Andreas Nava, about 1860). Actually, it appears he left on February 25. Seguin was almost certainly the man who carried Travis' message of the 25th to Houston, and was seen at Gonzales on the morning of the 28th by Dr. John Sutherland.

Under frontier conditions, dates could also get mixed up in putting them down. Foote's 1841 history of Texas contains a letter from Colonel Fannin describing his abortive march to relieve the Alamo. Because the letter is dated February 29 and Fannin speaks of marching "yesterday," readers have understandably assumed he started out on the 28th.

Yet Fannin's letter is either misdated, miscopied or misprinted. At least seven other letters conclusively show that he actually marched February 26, and the letter in Foote should be dated the 27th. But because Foote is widely read, the error lingers on and Fannin becomes even slower than he was.

Names are another problem. Fannin ended his signature with such a fancy rubric that early historians often spelled his name "Fanning." In early documents Almeron Dickinson's name was sometimes spelled "Dickerson," and through the years a debate of medievalist proportions developed over which version was correct. At the time, of course, people didn't care as long as they knew who was meant. This book follows the spelling in his marriage certificate and application for headright land—but he would not have minded the other.

Place names are almost as complicated. People rarely saw a map and used the names they picked up from others, who perhaps used some personal description of association. Hence the same general spot on the Brazos is variously called Thompson's Ferry, Orozimbo, Old Fort and Fort Bend. In a later better-organized day it became the town of Richmond.

Finally, so little was written down at all. Texas was acutely aware of the Alamo's importance, yet nobody had time to make a serious study until twenty-four years later, when Captain Reuben M. Potter issued his first little pamphlet in 1860. Potter, incidentally, was the first to add a fall to Bowie's various ailments. Later he changed his mind, wrote Henry Arthur McCardle [McArdle] in 1874 that Bowie had not been injured. But the story was now launched and still sails on, even though denied by the person who started it.

It is, then, a rash man indeed who claims he has the final answer to everything that happened in the Alamo. The best that can be done is to offer some careful conclusions—always subject to correction—that might throw new light on a few of the many intriguing riddles. . . .

Did Houston Order the Alamo Blown Up?
He later said he did, but his critics (of whom there were many) always maintained that this was just another example of Houston taking credit where no credit was due.

Actually, the evidence indicates that Houston did indeed try to avert the siege by ordering the Alamo destroyed and the garrison withdrawn. His orders to Bowie of January 16 have not been preserved, but a letter of the 17th to Governor Smith says, "I have ordered the fortifications in the town of Bexar to be destroyed, and if you think well of it, I will remove all the cannon, and other munitions of war to Gonzales and Copano, blow up the Alamo, and abandon the place. . . ."

While final action was apparently contingent on the Governor's approval, other evidence suggests that Houston—feeling sure of his grounds—had already given the necessary orders to Bowie. The Provisional Council certainly thought so and on January 30 angrily complained that Houston had ordered the destruction of all defenses at Bexar and the abandonment of the post.

Nor was this a case where Houston gained his foresight long after the event. Writing James Collinsworth on March 15—only two days after Mrs. Dickinson reached Gonzales—the General declared: "Our forces must not be shut up in forts, where they can neither be supplied with men nor provisions. Long aware of this fact, I directed, on the 16th of January last, that the artillery should be removed, and the Alamo blown up. . . ."

Did Travis Draw the Line?
[This section was presented under Louis Rose as document 1.8.3.2.]

Who Was the Last Messenger from the Alamo?
John W. Smith gets all the glory and deserves much of it, for he carried Travis's last dispatch to the Convention on the night of March 3. But another messenger left later with a final appeal to Fannin. This man reached Goliad on

March 8, and his arrival is noted in two different letters—Burr H. Duval to William P. Duval, March 9, 1836; and John Sowers Brooks to James Hagerty, same date.

The courier to Goliad evidently left the Alamo considerably after Smith, for his report is much more gloomy. On March 3 the walls were "generally proof against cannon balls"; now "every shot goes through, as the walls are weak." Clearly, the later report was sent after the Mexicans erected their new battery on March 4 just to the north of the Alamo.

The evidence indicates that this last courier was 16-year-old James L. Allen and that he rode from the Alamo "after nightfall" on March 5. He left no written account, but through the years he told his story to others. At least three of these listeners have independently set down his story, and none seem to doubt his word. Allen himself was a responsible citizen—later tax assessor, justice of the peace, and Mayor of Indianola.

Did Travis Wear a Uniform?

No, despite all the portraits. He had ordered one from McKinney & Williams, but judging from his letter of January 21, 1836 to Captain W. G. Hill, it wasn't very far along. Since he left for the Alamo on the 23rd, there's little chance it caught up with him before the siege. Sergeant Felix Nuñez, who appropriated Travis's coat after the battle, said that it was of homemade Texas jeans.

Where Was Bowie Killed?

A wide variety of sources give six different places. The favorites: a small room on the north side of the church; the second floor room in the southwest corner of the long barracks; a small room in the low barracks. Of these choices, the best evidence points to the low barracks. Authorities: Mrs.. Alsbury, who was Bowie's sister-in-law; Captain Sánchez Navarro, Sergeant Loranca, and Sergeant Nuñez, all of the attacking force; Francisco Ruiz, who had the job of identifying Bowie's remains for Santa Anna. On Sánchez Navarro's plan of the Alamo, Bowie's room is clearly marked in the low barracks, just to the east of the main gate.

Did Travis Commit Suicide?

According to Antonio Pérez, one of the first friendly Mexicans to reach Gonzales after the massacre, Travis stabbed himself to avoid capture. Houston believed the story, and it was widely circulated. But late and more reliable evidence indicates that the Colonel was killed by enemy gunfire.

This certainly is the opinion of those who were there. Travis' slave Joe is emphatic on the point, and he was standing beside his master on the north battery. Captain Sánchez Navarro and Colonel José Enrique de la Peña, who wrote detailed firsthand accounts from the Mexican side, both agree that Travis fell fighting.

Much has been made of the report by Francisco Ruiz, who identified Travis' body for Santa Anna. In her celebrated thesis on the Alamo, Miss Amelia Williams pointed out that Ruiz said Travis' only wound was "a pistol shot through the forehead." But Ruiz never mentioned a pistol, and to one observer at least, there seems nothing remarkable about a soldier being shot in the head during battle.

Did David Crockett Surrender?

It's just possible that he did. A surprising number of contemporary sources suggest that Crockett was one of the six Americans who gave up at the end, only to be executed on Santa Anna's orders.

Colonel Peña flatly said so in his *Diario,* first published in September, 1836. Colonel Almonte told a similar story, according to a letter from Sergeant George M. Dolson in the Detroit *Democratic Free Press* of September 7, 1836. So did an unidentified Mexican officer (who sounds suspiciously like Ramón Caro), according to a letter appearing in the Frankfort, Kentucky, *Commonwealth* of July 27, 1836. A similar account also came from Captain Fernando Urizza after San Jacinto, according to Dr. N. D. Labadie. Urizza said the prisoner's name was "Cocket," but Labadie had no doubts whom he meant.

Nor are all the sources Mexican. Passengers on the schooner *Comanche,* arriving in New Orleans on March 27 with first details of the massacre, also reported how Crockett and others had tried to surrender "but were told there was no mercy for them." The New Orleans *Post-Union* picked up the story, and it quickly spread to the *Arkansas Gazette* and elsewhere. Even Mary Austin Holley [sic], that most loyal of Texans, finally included it in her 1836 guidebook.

But it must be stressed that most early Texan accounts declared that Crockett fell in battle. "Fighting like a tiger," to use Andrew Briscoe's words. Both Joe and Mrs. Dickinson also believed he was killed in action, although neither saw him till after he was dead.

So there's a good chance Crockett lived up to his legend, and in some circles it remains dangerous even to question the matter. A few years ago when *The Columbia Encyclopedia* ventured the opinion that Crockett surrendered, an angry retort in the *Southwestern Historical Quarterly* declared that Texas would need better authority than "a New York publication." Next edition, the New York editors meekly changed their copy.

How Many Survivors?

At least fourteen people in the Alamo lived through the siege. Three were Americans: Mrs. Dickinson, her daughter Angelina, and Travis' slave Joe. Some early sources also listed a slave belonging to Bowie (variously called "Sam" and "Ben"), but this was actually Almonte's cook Ben, detailed to escort the others to Gonzales. Mrs. Dickinson, Joe and Houston are all firm that only three Americans came out alive.

A minimum of ten Mexican women and children also survived: Mrs. Alsbury and her baby, her sister Gertrudis Navarro, Mrs. Gregorio Esparza and her four children, Trinidad Saucedo, and Petra Gonzales. There were probably others, but the evidence is conflicting. On the other hand, Madam Candelaria—one of the better-known claimants—definitely was not in the Alamo.

One member of the garrison almost certainly survived—Brigido Guerrero, who talked himself free by claiming to have been a prisoner of the Texans. Both Almonte and Gregorio Esparza mention him, and he later made a good enough case to get a pension from Bexar County in 1878.

There is also evidence that Henry Warnell lived through the assault but soon died from his wounds. A sworn statement in a land claim filed in 1858 declares Warnell "at the massacre but made his escape to Port Lavacca, where he died in less than three months from the effects of said wound." (General Land Office, Court of Claims Application No. 1579, File W to Z, July 30, 1858.) This document seems stronger than an unsupported story that Warnell was fatally wounded while serving as a courier to Houston.

Finally, there is the bare possibility of two other survivors. The *Arkansas Gazette* of March 29, 1836—when it was still generally believed that the Alamo was safe—carried an intriguing item about two men (one badly wounded) turning up in Nacogdoches, "who said San Antonio had been retaken by the Mexican, the garrison put to the sword—that if any others escaped the general massacre besides themselves, they were not aware of it." The item appeared a week before the *Gazette* carried Houston's "express" reporting the defeat. In the thirty-one other newspapers examined, the General's announcement was invariably the first word received.

None of these possibilities seem strong enough to detract from the Alamo as a genuine example of a group of men who knowingly sacrificed their lives rather than yield to their enemy.

How Many Texans Fell in the Alamo?

Figures range from 180 to Santa Anna's ludicrous 600. Best estimate seems to be 183. This is the final figure given by Ramón Caro, the Mexican general's secretary. Also by Jesse Badgett, one of the first Texans to supply details to the U.S. press (*Arkansas Gazette*, April 12, 1836). Francisco Ruiz, in charge of burning the bodies, listed 182—but he missed Gregorio Esparza, the only defender Santa Anna allowed to be buried.

How Many Mexican Casualties?

Nineteen different sources give nineteen different answers—ranging from 65 killed and 223 wounded (Colonel Almonte) to 2,000 killed and 300 wounded (Sergeant Francisco Becerra). Most Texan sources claimed a thousand Mexicans killed and wounded, while General Andrade's official report acknowledged 311 casualties. Both probably reflect wishful thinking, and the problem is complicated by the Mexican's tendency after San Jacinto to say absolutely anything that might please a Texan—until they got back south of the border.

Best estimate seems about 600 killed and wounded. This is in line with figures worked out by Captain Reuben M. Potter, a contemporary Texan authority with firsthand knowledge of Santa Anna's army; also with a Mexican study made in 1849, when enough time had passed for a little perspective. In addition, it fits figures reported by Dr. Joseph H. Barnard, a Texan physician captured by the Mexicans and sent to San Antonio to tend their injured. He was told that 400 men were wounded in the assault; an additional 200 killed would be about right, or 600 casualties altogether.

The estimate goes with what is known of the Mexican Army. Judging from Filisola's battle order figures and Santa Anna's attack order of March 5, there were no more than 2,400 Mexicans in San Antonio, or 1,800 in the actual assault. A casualty rate of 33 per cent is a stiff price, even if 600 seems a modest figure. No Texan need feel cheated.

What Was the Alamo Flag?
Traditionally the Alamo flew a modified Mexican flag, but the best evidence indicates that this was not the case.

The early Texan sources mention no specific flag, but in 1860 Captain R. M. Potter remedied the omission. In the first of several accounts he did on the subject, Captain Potter declared that the Alamo flag was the regular Mexican tricolor, but with the date 1824 substituted for the usual golden eagle. This was based on no evidence but on Potter's theory that the Texans were fighting for the Mexican Constitution of 1824, until the Declaration of Independence was formally passed on March 2, 1836. Since the Alamo defenders knew nothing of this event, the theory ran, they went down still fighting for a liberal Mexico. The irony of Potter's theory was appealing; others backed it up and it lingers on.

But the theory does not jibe with the facts. Actually, Texas had stopped fighting for the Constitution of 1824 long before the Alamo. The old Constitution had been a good enough goal for many during the fall and December, but early in 1836 popular opinion swung violently and overwhelmingly for independence. In the elections to the Convention, the independence candidate won a smashing victory in every Texas municipality.

As loyalty to Mexico ceased, so did the trappings. Down came the old 1824 flags; up went new, strange banners—each designed according to the maker's whim, but all proclaiming the idea of independence. There was the flag with the azure blue star raised at Velasco . . . another based on the stars and stripes at Victoria . . . a hodgepodge of red, white, blue and green at San Felipe. There was no time to wait—events had outstripped such formalities as conventions, declarations and official flags.

The men in the Alamo were no different. By February only Seguin's handful of local Mexicans seemed hesitant; the rest wanted no part of 1824. "All in favor of independence," Colonel Neill assured Governor Smith on January 23. The men's letters bore him out. "Every man here is for independence," wrote Private M. Hawkins. "God grant that we may create an independent government," prayed Amos Pollard.

These men, like the rest of Texas, had their improvised flags. The New Orleans Greys carried their azure blue. Travis' regulars had the five-dollar flag he bought en route to San Antonio (no description remains). Seguin's nine men might well have carried a Mexican tricolor with two stars standing for Coahuila and Texas as separate states—but the Anglo-Americans remained all for independence.

Santa Anna's arrival only strengthened the men's resolve. Writing Jesse Grimes on March 3, Travis stated, "If independence is not declared, I shall lay down my arms and so will the men under my command. But under the flag of independence we are ready to peril our lives a hundred times a day . . ."

Such a man was not likely to be flying any kind of Mexican flag three days later. Judging from Colonel Almonte's diary, only one Texan banner was taken on March 6; and judging from the Mexican archives, this was the azure emblem of the New Orleans Greys. Full details on its capture were uncovered in 1934 by Dr. Luis Castrillo Ledon, Director of the Mexican National Museum of Archaeology, and there's no reason to doubt his findings. So the Greys' flag was the one Santa Anna sent home, complete with its boast of New Orleans help. As he pointed out, it clearly showed the designs of "abettors, who came from the ports of the United States of the North."

The flag remains in Mexico City today, still with Santa Anna's faded victory message attached to it. Kept at Chapultepec, it is not on exhibit but buried in the files . . . crumbling to pieces in brown wrapping paper. Thanks to the courtesy of the Mexican government, it was recently brought out once again, and enough of it pieced together to identify it beyond any doubt.

5.2.3.1. Fox et al., research report, 1976.

Fox, Anne A., Feris A. Bass, Jr., and Thomas R. Hester. 1976. *The Archaeology and History of Alamo Plaza*. Archaeological Survey Report no. 16, 51–53. Center for Archaeological Research, University of Texas at San Antonio.

This report includes a comparison of early maps to the actual remains in the vicinity of the original main gate on the south side of the outer walls or low barracks, as revealed by excavations in 1975. This excerpt gives only a brief example of the report on the excavations, and the paper has both figures and references that are not included here. Trenches A and B were roughly parallel to each other about seven meters apart in the area of the main gate at the low barracks, now in a traffic island southwest of the chapel.

Discussion of Features

Although many maps have been drawn of the compound of Mission San Antonio de Valero, the two most dependable, given the training of the artist and reasons for the execution of the map, were done by Francois Giraud, City Engineer and architect for Samuel Maverick in 1849, and by Theodore Gentilz, artist and architect, as background study for a painting probably in 1849 or 1850. These agree rather closely in the important details, and have been extensively used on this project in evaluating the architectural remains uncovered.

In Trench A two intrusive masses of rubble consisting of large irregular chunks of limestone set in a grey-brown, pebbly soil, were encountered at approximately 115 cm depth. The southernmost one measures 190 cm across and extends downward to a level of 186 cm. The northern one measures 135 to 140 cm across and extends to 189 cm. The distance between the outside faces of these features is approximately 615 meters (17 feet). The location of these features in relation to the buildings still standing and in relation to wall locations on the maps of Giraud and Gentilz, plus the fact that they are unquestionably intrusions into the subsoil, lead to the conclusion that these are the footings of the south wall and the building constructed within it.

In Trench B, near the south end, a smaller intrusion of limestone chunks surrounded by friable, brown soil may be the continuation of the south wall footing to the west, toward the gate. If this is so, Giraud's map may not have been completely accurate in the angle of this wall, either by accident of drafting or measurement. It is interesting to speculate upon the effect which alteration of this angle by a few degrees could have on the location of the northwest corner of the mission, which falls within the former property of Samuel Maverick, for whom the map was drawn.

The absence of a definite footing to the north in Trench B can be explained by the amount of earth-moving which has been done in the areas since 1870. There is evidence of disturbance of the subsoil in the general areas where it should lie, however. The fact that the Gentilz and Giraud maps are so close to agreement on the angle of the wall makes it seem likely that the stone found in Trench B was slightly displaced during later clearing activities. Certainly it is not sufficient evidence to suggest any drastic revision of the present estimate of the locations of the wall.

It appears from archaeological evidence that considerable earth moving and leveling was done on the plaza in the late 19th century. Apparently, the grade was lowered below the level of the floors and base of the walls of the building on the south wall, since no trace of floors was found in either trench and no recognizable building stone or mortar debris above the footings still remains. The grey layer which intermittently covers the site is evidently all that remains of the original floors and plaza surface, which was scraped and churned up and redeposited during the leveling process. The brown soil containing middle-to-late 19th century artifacts was then probably hauled in from elsewhere to create the park, and was later covered with black gumbo during landscaping operations.

The ditch at the south end of Trench B appears to be part of the fortification of the gate, illustrated variously on the maps of Potter, Berlandier and a composite map of those done by participating Mexican officers. No two observers agree exactly on the size, shape and location of a ditch and parapet arrangement within which were mounted two or three cannon for protection of the gateway. The location of the ditch appears quite far from the actual gate until one realizes that there must be room behind it for a parapet, behind which the cannon required at least double their length to allow for the recoil on firing, and behind this there must be enough room to pass through the gate.

Apparently the ditch was dug carefully (the walls are straight and uniform) and may have been refilled not too long after the battle, since pick marks are still visible in the west wall. The fact that fragments of several objects were found to occur in several different zones in the fill suggests that this material accumulated in a pile somewhere nearby and was dug up and redeposited in the ditch on a single occasion. The location of a wine glass manufactured before 1830 within Zone VI made it appear, on first examination, that the ditch was filled soon after the 1836 battle. However, the presence of two later artifacts elsewhere in the fill suggest[s] a later date for the operation. A metal button of a type found by South in Florida in an 1837 to 1865 context and a percussion cap which probably would not have arrived in Texas until after 1840 suggest that the ditch may have been filled by U.S. troops when the Army restored the south wall structure in 1848–1849.

The importance of the fill, however, is that its contents indicate there was a Spanish colonial mission trash dump somewhere in the vicinity. Such dumps are known to exist outside of gates of mission establishments of this period, including both San Juan Capistrano and San José. This suggests that the south wall and main gate of the mission could have been located here from at least the mid-18th century, if not before.

One explanation which came to mind for the hurried refilling of the ditch is possible use as a burial pit for Mexican casualties after the 1836 battle. A careful watch was kept during excavation, but no indications were found of such usage. However, this does not mean that there may not be burials elsewhere in the section of the ditch which is as yet unexamined.

Artifacts

In general, artifacts are ordered according to the materials from which they are made, avoiding where possible categories such as Indian, Spanish, Colonial, or grouping according to use. In many cases origins and/or uses are not definitely known, and such grouping would reflect a purely subjective decision on the part of the author. The majority of the artifacts found in the ditch are identical to or closely related to ones found in other Texas mission sites, or are known to have been made in the 18th century and are therefore probably mission-connected. Sources for this information include published excavation reports for mission San Juan Capistrano, San José y San Miguel de Aguayo, Rosario, Valero, the San Xavier missions, and Presidio Ahumada, as well as the author's personal observation of collections from numerous other Spanish colonial sites in Texas and Northeastern Mexico.

The columns at the right side of each page indicate the number of fragments or objects found in the grey stratum which overlay the early footings, and those found in the fortification ditch. A description of more precise location within the ditch will be found in Table 1. An inventory of artifacts recovered from the park fill is included as Appendix 1.

Identification and dating of the artifacts has been done with as much care and precision as possible, and the author of this section takes full responsibility for any inadvertent errors. . . .

5.2.3.2.   Jack Eaton, research report, 1980.

Eaton, Jack D. 1980. *Excavations at the Alamo Shrine (Mission San Antonio de Valero)*. Special Report no. 10: 24–26, 47. Center for Archaeological Research, University of Texas at San Antonio.

This report is on archeological research examining the area where the palisade wall (defended by Davy Crockett) abutted the Alamo chapel at its southwest corner. It is extensively footnoted, and references to figures and tables are not included in this selection; the original of this important document should be referred to by those with special archeological interests.

Basal Caliche

Roughly 50 cm below the dark brown clay surface and lying just below the reddish brown clay, a level of grayish brown granulated sterile caliche was encountered. This deposit is about 15 cm in depth and rests upon hard white basal caliche. This is the basal footing upon which the church foundation was set. In other words, the foundation footing trench had been dug approximately 65 cm below the mission ground surface to reach suitable caliche base.

The term <u>caliche</u> is of Spanish origin, from Latin <u>calx</u>, meaning lime, and is commonly applied in North America to a porous, earthy calcium carbonate containing impurities of soil, sand, and gravel, which occurs widely at the surface or at shallow depth in the soil or penetrating porous rock outcrops in the zone of weathering. In a broad sense, caliche is used as a generic term for all types of soil-mineral accumulations. Here we will be referring to <u>calcareous caliche</u>, the accumulating of calcium carbonate in the soil processes which occur abundantly in south Texas.

Palisade Trench

During the excavations, a section of backfilled palisade trench dating to the famous battle of 1836 was uncovered and tested. This was first discovered in Unit 8, which was dug against the building wall and followed by means of Units 10 and 11 extending out from the wall.

The old backfilled trench was first noted as a slight depression and soil color change within the upper level white caliche. The trench began about 65 cm out from the building wall and extended southwest (250° magnetic) to as far as the old sidewalk curb, located three meters from the wall (Figs. 3, 11). The trench did not follow beyond the curb since that was the area of the old street and was very much disturbed. The trench averaged ca. 70 cm in width and ca. 45 cm in depth. The fill consisted of mixed soil types including caliche, but generally dark gray to brown in color with inclusions of artifacts and many animal bones. The artifacts included a variety of lead and bronze balls, ranging from pistol and musket balls to large canister shot. Two large fragments of 8-inch howitzer spherical shells (bronze), one exhibiting part of a fuse hole, were also found. Other artifacts include metal and bone buttons, square nails and other objects of metal, fragments of bottle and window glass, and a variety of pottery sherds. These and other objects collected will be discussed in more detail in the chapter on artifacts.

Also during excavations, traces of what appears to have been the edge of a second palisade trench were uncovered in Units 7 and 12 (Fig. 3). The remnant of this second probable trench is located 1.90 m (6 ft.) south of the first trench, extending parallel with it, and is of the same orientation.

The temporary fortification installed here, probably in preparation for battle, is described as consisting of two rows of cedar piles six feet apart, with the space between filled with earth from a ditch dug in front.

The Alamo Shrine Foundation

Excavations against the building wall exposed sections of the foundation which provided a view of the construction and its condition. The foundation wall which supports the large church structure is nearly four feet in width and is very sturdy. The foundation, at least in our limited tests, was found to be dry and in excellent condition, and is the reason the building stands firm today.

The base of the church wall, which rests upon the foundation, is 24 cm below the present flagstone paved surface. At this level, there appears to have been older flagstone paving possibly dating to the mission period. Some flagstone fragments were found to butt against the wall base. These earlier flagstones were possibly either part of an old walkway extending along the building wall or remnants of church courtyard paving.

The building foundation wall is thicker by several centimeters than the church wall it supports, and it extends down 60 cm to where it rests upon a wall footing of the same thickness. This level is coincidental with the top of the dark brown clay, which evidently was the original construction-period ground surface. The foundation wall is constructed of large, load-bearing irregular stones and slabs which are roughly dressed on the facings and maintain fairly even coursing and alignment. These stones, which are generally around 10 to 20 cm in height and roughly 20 to 40 cm in length, are laid in rough horizontal coursing, using gray to occasionally pink sandlime mortar and many spalls to fill the larger mortar joints and to aid in setting the stones.

The footing upon which the foundation wall rests is not as carefully built, and uses rubble stones and slabs set without coursing in yellowish sandlime mortar. It appears that the footing trench had been dug through the dark brown clay to the underlying base caliche, a depth of more than a meter. Stones and mortar had been placed into the trench to provide the footing. These were not merely dumped into the trench but were carefully set to bear the load. It seems possible that the footing had been installed some years prior to the construction of the foundation and might be the footing which supported the original stone church that subsequently collapsed. The construction of the foundation footing is remarkably similar to the technique recorded at Missions San Juan Bautista and San Bernardo.

In building the church, there seems to have been three distinct construction phases: (1) a foundation footing resting upon basal caliche which was placed within a footing trench; (2) a foundation wall installed upon this which rose above the old ground surface; and (3) the church walls, slightly less in thickness, which rest upon the foundation. The building walls above the foundation are described in the chapter on architecture.

[*The report has extensive and detailed observations on artifacts and architecture. The following is particularly interesting for our subject.*]

The double palisade wall, which extended between the old church southwest corner and the quadrangle, was described as having been installed by the Texans prior to the 1836 battle. Although this is the generally accepted view, it seems possible that this fortification might in fact have been installed during the occupation by General Cos in 1835, when he had the place put in "fort fashion" and ordered other similar palisade defenses erected at the Alamo complex. The Texans were not trained military engineers, and they had little time and materials to do more than hastily patch up breaches in the walls, rig scaffolding, and mount cannons before the Mexican forces arrived. The procurement of materials and construction of the double palisade, and digging the deep fronting ditch which provided the wall core fill, was a formidable task to undertake on short notice.

It is interesting to note that, contrary to established view, the palisade wall evidently did not butt against the old church wall as usually depicted, but instead there was a space left, easy to defend or block off, but wide enough to allow a person to pass. Perhaps this way was used to allow messengers and others to pass in and out of the fortifications unnoticed. The palisade walls were torn down after the 1836 battle, and the ditches backfilled.

A section of backfilled ditch which once supported the inner row of palisades was discovered and excavated during the current study. The mixed soils of the trench fill contained equally mixed cultural materials, since the ditch had cut through the subsurface stratified soil levels already described. Collected artifacts included materials from all occupation periods, as well as military artifacts from the 1836 battle (see Table 1) [*these include a fragment of a musket and lead and brass balls*].

In addition, there was much animal bone, mostly cow, but also goat and chicken, and many unidentified fragments. The many cow bones in the backfilled ditch aid in support of the statement that the Alamo defenders brought numerous cows into the complex for their subsistence during the siege.

The Alamo Shrine, although never completed and subjected to repeated attempts to demolish it, has been standing for well over 200 years. There are no serious structural problems, such as shifting or wall cracking due to faulty construction. The sturdy condition can be attributed largely to setting the foundation on firm footing and doing good stonemasonry, all of this adhering to sound planning. . . .

5.2.4.   Susan Schoelwer, analysis, 1988.

Schoelwer, Susan Prendergast. April 1988. The artist's Alamo: A reappraisal of pictorial evidence, 1836–1850. *Southwestern Historical Quarterly* 91:403–4, 409, 411–13, 415–20, 424–26.

This modern review is an example of useful research topics still available, even with a subject as widely discussed as the Alamo. The article has extensive footnotes not included here, and this excerpt focuses only on analysis of documents already presented or that were especially close to the siege. There are a number of other plans and elevations not included in this work.

Pictorial materials constitute a rich but generally untapped vein in Alamo research. Ranging from period military plans to modern movie scenes, from picturesque Victorian sketches to bicentennial cigarette advertisements, from real-estate surveys to souvenir postcards, pictorial materials can provide extensive insights into the historic place, the battle, and the legend subsequently

evolving around them. For Texans, the Alamo has become a preeminent symbolic landscape, a cultural icon, and, as geographer Donald W. Meinig has suggested, "part of the shared set of ideas and memories and feelings which bind a
people together." The symbolic landscape and the real landscape are not the
same, however, and the Alamo we find is frequently not the one we expect. As
journalist Bob Greene discovered in 1984, the Alamo is not a "lonely sentry" on
the "high desert"; instead, it lies just across the street from Woolworth's.

There are, in fact, at least three landscapes of the Alamo: the actual contemporary landscape, the historic landscape of 1836, and the symbolic landscape,
selectively idealized and imprinted in the public consciousness by the media of
popular culture. [*Schoelwer's analysis continues, not just of the actual structure itself,
but also with some discussion of portraits of the defenders. She continues with analyses
of documents already presented earlier.*]

BATTLEFIELD OBSERVERS
[*Two paragraphs concern the Jameson plat(s), presented as document 4.2.4*]

The Mexican army also had its "official" map of the fortifications [*document
2.8.1*], drawn by Col. Ygnacio de Labastida, commander of engineers for the
Army of the North, and dated March, 1836. The Labastida map differs from its
Texan counterpart in several notable aspects. First, while the missing Jameson
manuscripts make verification of published versions impossible, Labastida's
original drawing, executed in ink and watercolors, survives in the collections of
the Barker Texas History Center, University of Texas at Austin. Second, while
Jameson's drawing is an unmeasured schematic diagram, rather amateur in its
draftsmanship and limited to the Alamo compound itself, the Labastida map is
a more sophisticated cartographic effort, with graphic scale and compass rose
suggesting the hand of a trained draftsman. Finally, the focus of the Labastida
map is not on the mission fortress alone but on the fortress and its environment.
Thus the map provides a topographical study of the immediate locale, depicting in considerable detail the San Antonio River and the arrangement of streets
and buildings in San Antonio proper and in La Villita, the quarter immediately
adjoining the Alamo on the east side of the river. Individual trees are indicated
(including the lone pecan, noted by Jameson and later observers, at the Alamo's
northwest corner), as well as cultivated fields to the east and rising ground
leading up from the river to the Texas position. The Alamo itself is depicted in
considerably less detail than on the Jameson plat.

Although dated only to the month of March, 1836, Labastida's map has
generally been presumed to have been drawn during the five days before the
battle, as an aid to planning artillery emplacements and other elements of the
Mexican advance. In this case, Labastida could not have had firsthand knowledge of Texan preparations inside the walls; he would have had to rely on the
reports of scouts, civilian informants, and officers previously assigned there. In
several points of fact, Labastida's sketch of the Alamo proper shows inaccuracies, which are easily explained if the map was prepared from secondhand

information: (1) it assumes the outer compound to be a true rectangle when it was actually an irregular trapezium; (2) it orients the compound slightly off-axis to the west of north, whereas it was actually oriented slightly to the east of north; (3) it depicts only three artillery pieces inside the fort, two at locations not matched by Jameson (at the earthworks southwest of the church and along the southern section of the west wall facing west toward the town); and (4) the various buildings of the *convento* and outer yard are incorrectly arranged and mislabeled. In the case of several exterior fortification details, however, which the Mexicans would have been in better position to observe, the Labastida map may indicate the actual state of the Alamo more accurately than Jameson's plans. Specifically, Labastida shows only a small semicircular battery outside the south entrance—nothing approaching Jameson's grandiose half-moons that were to have encompassed the entire end walls.

[*The possibility of a later date for the plat is then discussed, as well as its survival and provenance.*]

A final revolutionary-era plan of the Alamo [*document 2.7.1*] comes from the pen of José Juan Sánchez Navarro, a Mexican army officer who was also the creator of the earliest known elevation of the Alamo. According to his memoirs, Sánchez Navarro, adjutant inspector of the departments of Nuevo León and Tamaulipas, was stationed in San Antonio during the siege of Béxar in the fall of 1835. He departed with the retreating forces of Gen. Martín Perfecto de Cós and did not arrive back until March 2, only four days before the battle of the Alamo and March 6. A former classmate of Santa Anna, Sánchez Navarro was apparently well connected within the Mexican army; he reported having spent March 3 and 4 touring the fortifications in the company of Cós and other generals. He was also evidently an unusually perceptive and introspective officer who sketched, wrote poetry, and kept a personal diary on the blank pages of an index to his official records.

As published in 1938 by a family descendant, Carlos Sánchez Navarro y Peón, Juan Sánchez Navarro's papers contain not one but two variations of the same Alamo plan. Although neither is dated, their slight differences suggest a sequence of production. Version A, illustrated here [2.7.1], from the front flyleaf of volume two of the officer's manuscript index, encompasses the San Antonio River and Mexican batteries as well as the fortress itself. Stylistically, this version has a sketch quality, while the studied look of version B (not shown), with heavily inked lines, precisely delineated features, and neat compass rose, suggests that it may have been reworked from version A, possibly at a time considerably after the campaign. Both diagrams are quite clearly postbattle records rather than prebattle plans. Sánchez Navarro's annotations on version A include numerous details of the final assault and its immediate aftermath; his caption title refers to the destruction of the fort by retreating Mexican troops on May 22, 1836; and his memorial verse, inscribed on a tablet at the lower right, urges patriotic Mexicans to "return to Texas" and assuage the wounded national honor.

Of the three Revolutionary-era Alamo plans, Sánchez Navarro's diagram and annotations provide the most extensive information. His is the only plan, for example, to depict the locations, firing lines, and movements of Mexican artillery and assault forces. Unfortunately, he does not cite his sources of information, apparently a combination of observation, official contacts. and local gossip. Some of his features, such as the death sites of various defenders, are conspicuously at odds with other sources. Sánchez Navarro's plan lacks the topographical features of the Labastida map and omits any references to the buildings of Béxar or La Villita. His configuration of the Alamo proper is also seriously flawed. The compound is once again idealized as a true rectangle, the church facade is placed on a line with the *convento* (instead of being set back to the east), and the enclosures behind the *convento* have erroneously been extended all the way to the north wall. Sánchez Navarro shows a total of six ramped batteries (most in locations agreeing with Jameson and Labastida), but he does not record a cannon atop the *convento*, which had long been a strongly defended area of the compound, equipped with a gun by 1793 and retaining one, according to Jameson, as late as the opening weeks of 1836. Instead, Sánchez Navarro comments that this building, with its gallery and yard behind, was "the high fortification and the principal part of the fort"; had the Texans "made it into a second line of defense it would have been very difficult to have taken it from them or to have driven them out of it."

At the main entrance, Sánchez Navarro depicts a fortification similar to that on Labastida's map, but equipped with two cannons (not shown by the latter) and reinforced by another two guns behind a trench or barricade (as originally proposed by Jameson). Other exterior fortifications shown by Sánchez Navarro include a second line of pickets protecting the breastworks between church and south outer wall (this has been verified by recent archaeological work) and three semicircular breastworks located at the northeast corner of the compound and along the west wall. The latter defenses are not mentioned by Jameson and are corroborated only by Sánchez Navarro's own contemporary elevation of the fort (fig. 5). Interior fortifications, according to Sánchez Navarro, consisted principally of a ditch and "poorly constructed banquette, with which the colonists, thinking they were reenforcing part of the fort, weakened it." His location of this ditch along the northern edge of the rear yards exactly corresponds with the Labastida map, although, again, Jameson does not indicate this feature in his plans.

There are also numerous discrepancies between the three plans as to the number and placement of artillery pieces inside the fort: Jameson shows seventeen guns; Sánchez Navarro, eighteen, plus three unmounted barrels found inside the main plaza by Mexican troops. Labastida shows only three guns, plus five ramped batteries on which others were positioned; presumably he did not attempt to provide as exact a count as the others did. Instead of seeing the Jameson, Labastida, and Sánchez Navarro plans as conflicting versions of the same situation, it is more instructive to consider them as sequential versions of an evolving defense, each reflecting the limitations and biases of its particular creator. While Jameson and Labastida prepared their maps in the course of military duty, Sánchez Navarro seems to have created his on his own initiative and with a conscious eye toward posterity. Buried in the pages of his index, however, his plan had received relatively little attention until recent years.

Even less well known than Sánchez Navarro's plan is his view of the Alamo, the earliest identified elevation of the site and the only period view of its prebattle appearance. It is also the only known period vista encompassing the entire compound. Although it was previously misattributed, the correct authorship of this important drawing is established by the 1938 edition of Sánchez Navarro's papers, *La guerra de Tejas*. Shown together as plate 2 in *La guerra* are this view and Sánchez Navarro's plan (version B), which are identified as "Vista y plano del Fuerte del Alamo, por José Juan Sánchez-Navarro." Despite the very poor graphic quality of the reproduction, it is barely possible to decipher, below the south end of the compound, the artist's signature and date: "José Juan Sánchez 1836 del [?]." As a family descendant, the compiler of *La guerra* evidently had access to materials that were not included with the two-volume manuscript index acquired by the University of Texas; at any rate, the original elevation published in 1938 cannot presently be located and is not known to have appeared in any other publications.

The version of the Sánchez Navarro drawing seen in American publications (notably the works of San Antonio historian Frederick C. Chabot) is a fair copy preserved in one of the Berlandier sketchbooks acquired by Yale University from the Wagner collection. [*Schoelwer continues with a discussion of earlier misattributions and internal evidence supporting attribution of this elevation to Sánchez Navarro, as well as indicating that it was compiled from memory or rough sketches rather than being a field sketch.*]

PILGRIMS AT THE SHRINE
The Mexican army departed from San Antonio on May 24, 1836, setting the Alamo's wooden fortifications afire in hopes of destroying the site as a future military threat. Smoke from these fires still hung in the air as the first Texas pilgrims arrived: a party including John Shackelford and Joseph H. Barnard, Anglo-Texan surgeons who had been captured at Goliad and sent to San Antonio to tend the Mexican wounded there; Béxar alcalde Francisco Ruiz; and "some other of the [Hispanic] citizens." Although there is no visual record of the scene witnessed by these early visitors, Barnard's journal provides a vivid verbal account:

> We found the fire proceeding from a church, where a platform had been built extending from the great door to the top of the wall on the back side for the purpose of taking up the artillery to the top of the church. This was made of wood, and was too far consumed for any attempt to be made to extinguish it. The walls of the church being built

of solid masonry, of course would be but little injured by the fire. The
Alamo was completely dismantled, all the single walls were leveled,
the fossee [trench] filled up, and the pickets torn up and burnt.

Like many later visitors, Barnard was greatly moved by the scene:

After looking at the spot where it is said Travis fell and Crockett closed
his mortal career, we went to visit the ashes of those brave defenders of
our country, a hundred rods from the fort or church to where they were
burnt. The bodies had been reduced to cinders; occasionally a bone of a
leg or arm was seen almost entire. Peace to your ashes! Your fame is
immortal!

Although the ashes of the Alamo dead were gathered up in February, 1837,
and reinterred with military honors at a ceremony led by Béxar commander
Col. Juan N. Seguín, there is little evidence to suggest that the scene at the
Alamo had otherwise changed measurably by the fall of 1838, when the first
known view of the ruins, by Mary Ann Adams Maverick, was probably pro-
duced. The bride of Texas Revolution veteran Samuel A. Maverick, Mary Maverick had arrived in San Antonio in June, 1838, and was consequently reputed
to have been the first Anglo-American woman to settle permanently in the
Tejano community of Béxar. According to her memoirs, Maverick visited the
Alamo grounds during the fall of 1838, accompanied by Juana de Navarro
Pérez Alsbury, one of the local Tejano women who had been present in the
Alamo during the siege, and the latter's husband, Dr. Horace A. Alsbury,
another veteran of the Revolution. Although Maverick's sketch is undated and
not mentioned in her memoirs, it seems likely to have been made about the
time of her 1838 visit. It was subsequently sent to the artist's father-in-law in
South Carolina, where it remained among the family papers, unknown to
Alamo scholars until published by a descendant in 1952.

[*Schoelwer continues with a detailed discussion of the Maverick view, other views
by Bissett (c. 1838–39), Ikin publication (c. 1841), Falconer (1841), Bollaert (1843),
Gentilz (c. 1844–), and later "Military Romantics," including Everett (1847). She also
identifies the Yoakum plan as being from François P. Giraud in 1849 and not Jameson's
1836 plan, and ends with the Potter plan (c. 1860–78).*]

5.2.5. Timothy Matovina, analysis, 1995.

Matovina, Timothy M. 1995. *The Alamo Remembered: Tejano Accounts and Perspectives.* 8-9, 121–22, 124. Austin: University of Texas Press.

Matovina addressed the need for a comprehensive review of the Tejano sources. In his preface, he noted that Williams cited only half of the Tejano sources, and later authors less than a third. Most footnotes in this selection are not included, and should be referred to for more detailed study.

Tejano Accounts and Historical Studies of the Alamo

Like other Alamo accounts, Tejano accounts require critical assessment. Historians must bear in mind that petitions for land claims, pensions, and other government compensation are legal documents that reflect their author's purposes of procuring their claims. Statements like those of Andrés Barcena, Anselmo Bergara, and José Antonio Navarro were based on second-hand information and could reflect inaccurate renderings of eyewitness testimony. Furthermore, third parties recorded their statements, removing extant documents one step further from the original sources. Some Tejano testimony may also suffer from mistakes in translation. Anglo Americans interviewed many witnesses in Spanish, at times with the help of an interpreter. Significant observations and details could easily have been lost or misunderstood in the process.

Published Tejano accounts merit the most critical attention, since the majority of them were based on interviews conducted at least fifty years after the recorded events and many of the witnesses were children at the time of the battle. The published accounts also tend to provide far more detail than other Tejano testimony. Such detailed accounts are more prone to inaccuracies than the general observations contained in earlier statements. The position from which eyewitnesses viewed the siege and battle is yet another consideration in assessing the veracity of their accounts, since the precision of their descriptions is contingent on how clearly they saw these events.

Interviewer bias also undoubtedly influenced how reporters recorded Tejano testimony. In a 1902 article, for example, a *San Antonio Express* reporter asserted that Enrique Esparza "tells a straight story. Although he is a Mexican, his gentleness and unassuming frankness are like the typical old Texan." The presumption that Mexicans tend not to tell "straight stories" reveals the racial bias of this reporter, a bias that easily could have influenced an interview of Esparza or other Tejanos.

While a comprehensive analysis of the historical accuracy in Tejano Alamo accounts is beyond the scope of this work, the possibilities of errant observation, alterations in original testimony by second or third parties, faulty translation, memory lapse, and interviewer bias indicate the need for critical assessment in studies that utilize Tejano (and other) sources. Despite this need, extant Tejano accounts remain a significant and often untapped resource for historical studies of the Alamo.

[*Following is the beginning of Matovina's thoughtful concluding essay.*]

TEJANO ALAMO ACCOUNTS: COLLECTIVE LEGACY

In a recent essay, anthropologist Richard Flores recounted his first visit to the Alamo. Accompanied by his third grade classmates, Flores was filled with awe as he imagined the heroic deeds of Texas legends like Bowie, Travis, and Crockett, whom he had learned were martyrs for freedom. These musings were abruptly interrupted after leaving the mission church, however, when Flores' best friend Robert nudged him and whispered, "You killed them! You and the other 'mes'kins'!" Flustered, the young Flores retorted that he had never killed anyone, nor had his grandfather, whom he perceived as the most likely contemporary of the Alamo battle among his relatives. But this defense did not shield him from the enduring influence of his friend's accusation. Flores concluded: "I don't know what I lost that day, if it was innocence, certitude, identity, or some other existentially derived nine-year old sense-of-self. Whatever it was, it was gone."[1]

Flores' experience during his first visit to the Alamo reflects that of other Mexican Americans. The popular perception of the Alamo battle as a conflict between barbaric Mexican savages and heroic Anglo-American martyrs is amazingly persistent. Fortunately, this perception is fading in light of the historical fact that women and men of Mexican heritage served within the Alamo during the siege and final assault. Yet, even for Mexican Americans who are enlightened about Tejano defenders of the Alamo, the famous battle can remain an ambiguous historical event. Historian Rodolfo Acuña, for example, stated upon resigning from the advisory board of a 1982 Public Broadcasting Service program on Texas Revolutionary hero Juan Nepomuceno Seguín: "To make heroes of the Mexican people defending the Alamo is like making heroes of the Vichy government . . . *Seguín* represents an accommodationist point of view that promotes the wrong kind of assimilation."[2]

The statements of Flores and Acuña reveal the dilemma which many Mexican Americans face with regard to the Alamo. To identify with the victorious Mexican army leaves Mexican Americans open to the false accusation Flores' friend Robert leveled at him: that they descend from a race of murderous butchers who are the enemies of liberty. But to identify with Tejano Alamo defenders implies that their ancestors rejected their own people and heritage to ally themselves with Anglo-American aspirations and ideals.

Tejano accounts of the Alamo are important records for Mexican Americans who face this dilemma. While various historical works examine the Mexican and Texan viewpoints on the famous battle, extant Tejano accounts suggest a third perspective. Unlike African Americans, Anglo Americans, European immigrants, and Mexican soldiers who fought at the Alamo, San Antonians of

Mexican heritage were hometown residents caught between two opposing armies. Like many of today's Mexican Americans, nineteenth-century Tejanos felt pressured to choose between their Texas homeland and their Mexican cultural motherland. Collectively, their accounts are a legacy of the hometown Tejano perspective often forgotten in our remembrance of the Alamo.

The diverse vantage points from which San Antonio Tejanos observed the Alamo battle reflect their response to the dilemma of choosing sides in the conflict between Mexico and Texas. . . .

---

[1] Richard R. Flores, "Memory-Place, the Alamo, and the Construction of Meaning," *American Journal of Semiotics*, forthcoming.

[2] As cited in Susan Prendergast Schoelwer with Tom W. Glaser, *Alamo Images: Changing Perceptions of a Texas Experience*, with a forward by Clifton H. Jones and an introduction by Paul Andrew Hutton (Dallas: De Golyer Library and Southern Methodist University Press, 1985), 7. For a further treatment of contemporary Tejano response to the Alamo, see . . . [*several more sources given*].

Commentary

Later (20th Century) Sources (5.2)

Twentieth-century scholars continue to add to our understanding of the events of the Alamo battle as well as the broader picture of the Texas Revolution with its role in American history.

The foremost of these scholars, Amelia Williams, whose thesis has been extensively referred to and quoted in this work, studied the documents on the Alamo as carefully as anyone. Her original thesis had six chapters and five appendixes. Most of it was published in the *Southwestern Historical Quarterly*, in a somewhat restructured form.[1] Of the unpublished remainder, the original chapter 1, "Introductory Background" (document 1.0), and the first two portions of appendix II, on "Plans of the Alamo" (4.2.3.1, 2.8.2), are given in this collection. Still unpublished are the balance of appendix II (the plans of Everett, Potter, Corner, and the Alamo as of 1931), appendix III (Pictures of the Alamo), and the Bibliography. These remaining appendixes were not included here primarily because the full article of Schoelwer excerpted in 5.2.4 has essentially superseded Williams's earlier work on this topic.[2] One exception to this statement on Schoelwer is that Williams did review the eighteenth-century descriptions, which would still be useful reference for those interested in the early mission-era history of the Alamo.[3]

Her letter of February 1, 1932, to Samuel Asbury (5.2.1.2) gives us her opinions about some of the more open issues, questions, and uncertainties in the Alamo documents that she felt were not resolved in her dissertation.

The two selections of Williams's dissertation reproduced here (5.2.1.1), "The Flag of the Alamo" and "El Deguello," add interesting sidelights on a couple of the specific details.[4] In both cases, the conclusions are more speculative, based on something being "logical." She pointed out the lack of primary sources to help answer the questions of "what flag flew where" and "the use of the *deguello* as a bugle call" the morning of the final attack. There is, of course, no fundamental restriction against historians speculating on topics for which documentation is lacking—provided the lack is made clear, as it is in this case, and any conclusion is based on arguments derived from what is (reasonably) known.

On the specific topics, Williams drew the conclusion that the flag of the New Orleans Greys, now in Mexico, was likely to have been found in the Alamo though not actually flying. This possibility has been unanswered in other discussions, such as Lord's (5.2.2). Lord pointed out the weaknesses in Williams's argument that a tricolor with "1824" flew at the Alamo.[5] Almonte (2.2.1) mentioned the initial use of a tricolor with two stars, for Coahuila and Texas, in Béxar before the defenders retreated into the Alamo.[6] Other possible eyewitnesses were Pablo Díaz (3.7.2), who described it as "the flag of Mexico under the Constitution and prior to the usurpation . . . by Santa Anna," and Juan Chávez (3.7.5), who recorded essentially the same information. Crompton (3.6.3) remembered the Lone Star Flag, but he also included a lot of later material in his narrative, which could have influenced his account on this detail. C. D. Huneycutt believed there were three flags: Travis's two-star flag, the New Orleans Greys', and the Gonzales "Come and Take It" flag brought to the Alamo by Almeron Dickinson.[7] Chariton pointed out that Almonte located the flag in the town of San Antonio rather than the Alamo. He also noted that the Travis account book had a January 21, 1836, entry of $5.00 for a flag.[8] What this flag was or whether it was at the Alamo can only be guessed.

On the other side of the battle, the flag of the "Batallon Matamoros Permanente," present at the storming of the Alamo and captured at San Jacinto, is now in the Texas State Archives and has recently been restored.[9] Some Mexican sources state that three standard bearers of the Jiménez Battalion were killed trying to pull down the defenders' flag and raise a Mexican one, and identify José María Torres of the Zapadores Battalion as being the one who succeeded prior to also being killed.[10]

Concerning the use of the *deguello,* it was a surprise to me how little documented this widely reported detail really is. Potter (5.1.7) was apparently the first source to claim it was used.

What is striking about the Williams citations in this book is that despite the length of time that has passed, the material still yields a lot of good information and useful analysis. By and large, later scholars have added to specific issues or details of the event, primarily from more recently discovered material, while not supplanting the value of her accomplishment through the material she located. All later scholarship remains heavily indebted to her dissertation, directly or indirectly, because of her major compilation of sources. But apparently not everyone agrees with my assessment. Several of the more recent scholars, including some cited in this book, have expressed negative, even harsh, judgments on her work.[11] I think they are unjust.

Usually these critics have made broad negative comments without specifying the basis for stating such general assertions. I will therefore address what I think their objections are, because these objections usually are not explicitly stated. First, and least significant in my mind, is disagreements with Williams's conclusions. Second is that her evidence is not sufficiently thorough. The third, and by far the most serious, criticism is that her citations are inaccurate.

Before addressing these objections, I want to note that Williams's intent was to reference as carefully as possible what she wrote. Consequently, she made it easy to find errors in her statements and conclusions, because she was exceptionally clear about on what she based those statements and conclusions. She takes second place to no one in this regard.[12] Some critics attack her cited information without bothering to present their own citations for independent assessment, and therefore apply a double standard.

The first apparent objection by later critics is that they disagree with Williams's conclusions.

I have not hesitated to cite specific conclusions of Williams, and others, with which I disagree, sometimes enthusiastically. Such disagreements, when based primarily on the same documents, arise because each scholar places different emphasis or weight on the validity of the same sources. Such disagreements are also due to different perspectives of the commentators. That people don't agree on conclusions based on the same sources is not a reason in itself to invalidate the fundamental contributions that another researcher with differing opinions has made in locating and identifying those sources in the first place. As more information is discovered, it is only natural that earlier conclusions based on less information are supplanted. It can become trivially easier to see the weakness of a conclusion when new data contradicts the basis for that conclusion. Williams can be at a significant disadvantage simply because she did her work at a much earlier time.

The second apparent objection concerns the thoroughness of her work.

There have been numerous discoveries by dozens of professional and lay historians in the six decades since Williams did her research, I submit that well over half of *all* relevant citations—those covering the same ground as the core of her dissertation—of original source material by *any* scholar was identified by Williams. That statement applies to this work as well as any earlier, and it is the basis for saying that all her successors—whether or not they know it or acknowledge it explicitly—had a major proportion of their research time saved because, in the majority of cases, they knew exactly what to look for and where.

Williams did not have a similar advantage. Prior to her dissertation, there was not a single comprehensive study that referenced a tenth of the source materials she found or cited. To take one particular case, Yoakum—the first, and rare, example of a nineteenth-century Texas historian to explicitly reference his documents—cited only one or two dozen sources for his narrative of the Alamo, whereas Williams cited hundreds, possibly thousands. In addition, I have found *no one* prior to Williams that even considered the value of the General Land Office records. The Williams Papers in the Center for American History preserve criticism of her thesis that fault her by giving more weight to the material—again, materials that no one had used previously—than to the muster rolls that were commonly used in the nineteenth century.[13] One can refer to her evaluation of problems with the nineteenth-century lists, or spend time in the reading room of the Texas General Land Office, to appreciate the value of her highly original approach and its permanent value to the study of Texas history. I believe it is one of her major and permanent contributions that this body of material is now so widely used and appreciated.

Williams said in her concluding statement that she considered her work in identifying and documenting the defenders as her most important contribution.[14] The identity of the defenders is the most neglected part of Alamo scholarship in this book, in part because Williams did such a major job in her dissertation, which, along with more recent updates noted in the Bibliography, can be referred to by the interested reader. Her work in this area has remarkably stood the test of time. Over six decades, her list of 188 names has been, or was proposed to be, modified by no more than the possible deletion of nine or ten names and the addition of four, including one she provided after her dissertation was published. Some other possible names have been discussed by scholars, but based on weaker evidence than the standards she applied. There are generic arguments that perhaps as many as 250 defenders fell, but no one has provided additional names to go along with the arguments. I do not think there are many works that have stood the test of time as well.

The third, harsher, apparent objection is that her citations are inaccurate. Some claim grossly inaccurate.

The claims, implied or explicit, of Williams's inaccuracy are a serious reflection on a professional scholar. I have noted cases in this work where she (or typists) made errors in citations. I am convinced that she would be the first to appreciate the corrections. But these claims need further consideration because additional, usually implied, reasons are given by these critics that the cited documents do not say what she said they say, or that they do not exist.

I have indeed found documents that I think say something different from what Williams wrote. In an era before copiers, without which my work would have been impossible, the restricted time in archives or libraries would have limited the ability to make perfectly accurate notes. Williams's papers are full of examples of long, tedious, labor-intensive transcripts and notes of documents. These papers are now being mined, even by her critics, for still additional discoveries. Errors could far more readily be expected under those circumstances than from more recent authors, with some of whom I have also disagreed about a reading of a document. Later researchers will no doubt draw similar conclusions where I paraphrased a source rather than directly quoted it, did not include additional text that another feels is significant, or made an outright mistake. So I accept the existence of such problems. The real question is whether the extent of such "misreadings" is excessive.

There are numerous cases where Williams's sources could not be located by later researchers. I, too, have had that difficulty. I have also had the same difficulty with every other major work *since* Williams. One reason is that perhaps I didn't look hard enough, or in the right places, or spend enough time to review files more carefully. Another is that documents have disappeared, perhaps due to theft, from some of the archives. In many cases, perhaps the majority, major reorganizations of the various archives may have resulted in the originals being filed somewhere not now obvious. Prior to the 1960s, the files of the Archives Department of the Texas General Land Office were filed in the rather illogical fashion by how they arrived or how they were used in the nineteenth-century offices. Today the files are alphabetized by name. But especially considering the eccentric spelling of names during the early nineteenth century, how many documents might have ended up in different files due to problems with spelling, legibility, or simple error? Another example of missing material is an important set of Alamo documents (section 4.2.3) cited by Williams that was in a separate box in the secretary of state's office prior to 1931. Upon recent inquiry, neither this office nor the Texas State Library Archives was able to locate the material. This should not surprise anyone. My guess is that some of the material could well be there, but with a file name that makes locating it difficult, or perhaps the documents were split up and put in different locations. Thus, there are numerous problems and discrepancies in Williams's citations, but the question remains, is the number excessive?

No. I do not consider the number of problems in the Williams citations excessive relative to those of other scholars, when the amount of original material is considered. I repeat, I have found the same problem with essentially every major work in the field. But, I return to my original assertion that the number of first-located or first-cited documents by Williams significantly exceeds that of every other relevant work (or appropriate section of a work). I don't find as many problems in these more recent works as a gross number. But this is an unfair comparison since, as a percentage of the total quantity of documents discovered, Williams is quite comparable.

Put more explicitly, I submit that Williams's first-time discovery and use of original material relevant to the subject is on an order of magnitude greater than *any* other scholar and far exceeds that of many critics. Her errors do not proportionally exceed those of other scholars. Furthermore, few have matched and no one has exceeded her in explicitly documenting the basis of any conclusion drawn, and therefore she makes it easy for critics with twenty-twenty hindsight to find the weaknesses. With the sheer volume of material and the difficulties of working in her day, I assert that Williams did an outstanding job and has contributed significantly more than anyone else to our understanding of the siege and fall of the Alamo.

As a short analysis of the "Riddles of the Alamo," Walter Lord's Appendix (5.2.2, along with 1.8.3.2) is exceptional. Most of his major topics are considered in the relevant commentaries where the original documents have been presented. These are Houston's order to blow up the Alamo (3.5), Travis drawing the line (1.8), the last messenger (1.7.4), Travis's uniform (2.14.1), the number of survivors (1.10.1), and the Alamo flag (5.2.1.1). Appendixes B and C address Texan and Mexican casualties and the deaths of Bowie, Travis, and Crockett. Minor riddles such as dates and the name Dickerson versus Dickinson are also covered in the various documents.

There have been three relatively modern narrative accounts of the events at the Alamo, by John Meyers, Lon Tinkle, and Walter Lord. All of these are well done and make good reading. Lord's bibliographical information, for which this work owes considerable debt, is also particularly valuable. More recently, Stephen Hardin (1994) published an account of the military aspects of the Texas Revolution and the political situation only introduced here in the pre-siege documents (section 4.5). Recently published (1998) is the William Davis book, which adds considerable flesh to the characters of Crockett, Bowie, and Travis.

The two archeological reports add some independent data to our knowledge. That by Fox et al. (5.2.3.1) gives a sense of where a portion of the south wall/low barracks was located, as well as some details of the constructed fortifications. The report of Eaton (5.2.3.2) reveals a number of details relating to the palisade and associated trench, the defensive fortification defended by Crockett and his Tennessee boys (Sutherland, 1.7.1), and the construction of the Alamo chapel itself. These two documents are only samples of the several archeological investigations and discoveries made over the years by the Center for Archaeological Reseach at the University of Texas at San Antonio. Though not quoted here, others especially relevant to the Alamo battle are *La Villita Earthworks* and *Archaeological and Historical Investigations at the Alamo North Wall . . .*[15] *La Villita Earthworks* relates to the discovery of some of the Mexican siege works to the south of the main gate, along with an extraordinary collection of military and other artifacts, and includes useful summaries of the types of fortifications and weapons in use at the time of the battle. The investigation at the north wall of the current Alamo property located a defensive trench in the corral area of the mission, shown on the Labastida plat (2.8.1), along with a skull that may have been from a casualty, side unknown, of the battle.

Several further studies and analyses based on the archeological discoveries as well as archival material have been done or are in progress by James (Jake) Ivey.[16] These combine specific knowledge of the physical information obtained, the historical records, and vivid drawings to create a thoughtful projection of the nature and appearance of the fortifications at specific locations.

The Schoelwer article (5.2.4) brings modern scholarship as well as a broader, more interdisciplinary look at the subject. Such a study indicates the limitations that a simple presentation of only original documents can have. The Alamo is not just an event, but also a visual subject that is internationally recognized. In addition to pulling together and evaluating all prior research, such a study is valuable in broadening our interests and perceptions.[17]

Finally, Matovina (5.2.5) at last seriously tackled the project of identifying and reproducing the available documents from the perspective of the local Tejano population. As he pointed out in his Introduction, the narrations from these vicinity sources was significantly underrepresented in the earlier works. He made up for this lack by publishing transcripts of the relevant documents, finally making such key accounts as Alsbury (1.4.1) commonly available for probably the first time. He also noted important issues such as the influence of interviewers and the possible impact on how they reported the Tejano testimony. But these accounts are only an introduction to far broader questions of the meaning of the event to the Tejano population of that time and ours. And so, in that respect, Matovina brings us full circle to Williams's Introduction (1.0) and the broader issues she too raised.

A compilation such as this one is only the beginning of a major story. First we have asked ourselves, to the best of our abilities, what happened. But the questions keep arising: Why did it happen? How and why did the participants arrive there? What social factors were significant? What were the consequences? At the broadest level, the meaning of any significant event is an unending question that keeps being reasked as people themselves change. A related question often raised with the Alamo, as evidenced by the selection here from Matovina, is to what extent is it appropriate or even useful to judge historical figures by the criteria of a later time? And finally, even a seemingly obvious question at the end of such a work as this will be left for the reader's consideration: To what extent does one need to understand what happened before one can understand its meaning?

---

1. *SWHQ* volumes 36:251–87 and 37:1–45, 79–184, 237–312 (April 1933 to April 1934).
2. Schoelwer *SWHQ* 91:403+.
3. Williams 1931, 419–25, plus a reconstructed image by De Zavala. Also, Nelson 1998 gives a number of plans, inventories, and reports of this early period.
4. Published in *SWHQ* from the original thesis appendixes V and IV.
5. Also Williams in *SWHQ* 37:27 n. 62.
6. Also Hardin 1994,113.
7. Huneycutt, 1986, 37–38.
8. Chariton 1992, 230, on Almonte, 89–93, on Travis's account book. This account book is recorded by Ruby Mixon in her papers at the CAH.
9. *Austin American-Statesman,* June 30, 1999, B-1.
10. See Borroel 1997a, 61–63, and 1998a, 23–24.
11. E.g., Lord 1968, 19; Paul Hutton in the Introduction to Schoelwer 1985, 4; Lindley 1988, 8–9; Lindley 1993; Lindley in Curtis 1993; Lindley 1996; Davis 1998, 682 n. 74, 732 n. 99, 733–34 n. 102, 753; Lindley 1999.
12. Checking her original notes, for example, clearly establishes that between her original research and the final publication in *SWHQ,* "Jun" became "Jan" and so "January" for a newspaper citation of 4.5.9, and the source for a letter of E. M. Pease to William Steele, July 14, 1876, was transposed from the Texas State Library to an Austin paper. Original notes can be found respectively in the Williams Papers, CAH in Box 2N503/Folder 2, and Boxes 4N494/Folder 1; the transposition resulted from her note "What was Austin Newspaper 1876?" Published references are in *SWHQ* 37:110 n. 9, and 237–38 n. 1.
13. Muster Rolls and Other Lists of Defenders/Folder 10. Also see references per section 1.11.
14. Williams in *SWHQ* 37:312.
15. Labadie 1986 and Ivey and Fox 1997. Also see Fox 1992 and Hard 1994.
16. Ivey 1981a, 1981b, 2000, 2001, and manuscript in preparation 2002.
17. See Jackson and Ivey 2001 for an update and critique of the Sánchez documents. Another recent look at the visual side of the Alamo story, with reproductions of additional images, is Nelson 1998, which reprints numerous visuals and descriptive details of the Alamo from the mission era as well as giving a later photo history.

Special Commentary

The Life of Amelia Williams

In 1989, I began my research on Alamo documents by tracking down the references in Amelia Williams's 1931 thesis. A year later, as I was winding up my initial research, I realized it was possible that if she had received her doctorate at a typical age of twenty-six or so, she could now be in her eighties. My then fiancée, now my wife, who claims I'm mostly interested in people who have been dead a hundred years, encouraged me to see if Dr. Williams might still be alive. I quickly discovered, however, on checking the library files, that she had died August 14, 1958. I decided to pay my respects, and one weekend I drove to the Little River Cemetery, a rural location about an hour northeast of Austin, and located the Williams family plot. Discovering the birth and death dates for her, her parents, and her sisters, I conjectured that her biography must have been dramatically different from the typical academic career. Years later, especially with the help of her niece Jane Smoot, I have the following story.

Amelia Worthington Williams was born March 25, 1876, in Maysfield, Texas, to Thomas Herbert and Emma Massengale Williams. Her father, a Confederate veteran, emigrated from South Carolina and established a two thousand-acre spread in Milam County. He returned to his original home in South Carolina to recruit ex-slaves to help work as sharecroppers on his new land. Amelia was followed by four sisters: Harriet Emily (later Mrs. Hubert Atkinson), South Carolina (Mrs. George Peets), Julia Emma (Mrs. Lawrence Kelly Smoot), and Virginia Kentucky (Mrs. Andrew C. Freeman). Thomas wanted to name all his children after the states in the Confederacy, but recent deaths of aunts gave Emma sufficient excuse to give more normal names to three of the five sisters. Thomas Williams died in 1890, when his daughters ranged from age fourteen (Amelia) to three (Virginia).

Amelia attended Stuart Seminary in Austin and graduated in 1895 with a mistress of liberal arts degree from Ward Seminary (later Ward-Belmont) in Nashville. But further sorrow followed, with the death of her mother in 1898. She was left at age twenty-two the sole manager of the family plantation, with four younger sisters. She stayed at the country home to raise the sisters and manage the spread, with the support and assistance of the original sharecroppers and their families, "proving herself adept in all home-making skills of cooking, sewing, gardening, preserving fruit, and even the more rigorous routines of meat-dressing after hog killing."[1] She also ensured that all her sisters graduated from college and that their futures were secure. She further earned teaching certificates during this period, and a diploma from the Southwest Texas State Normal in 1910.

Her brother-in-law Atkinson eventually took over the management of the family spread around 1910, but flooding limited the family finances. She spent nearly fifteen years as a grammar school teacher in the rural schools of Milam County and in the county seat of Cameron. Through continuous summer schooling, she eventually earned a bachelor of arts degree from Southwest Texas State Normal in 1922.

It was not until about 1925 that she had the personal freedom to move to her sister Julia's home in Austin and enroll at the University of Texas, earning a bachelor and a master of arts simultaneously in June 1926. She had been interested in history well before this time, and now, while working on her master's thesis, she developed a fascination with the Alamo. For her doctoral dissertation, she expanded her master's thesis much further. For this research, she drove a Model-T around central and coastal Texas, visiting libraries and individuals in search of original source materials. Many people she spoke to had letters, diaries, and other materials in attic trunks, which they never thought were of much importance. One indirect but significant contribution she made during this period was to encourage people to donate these materials to libraries or otherwise preserve them.

Amelia Williams was fifty-five years old when she completed her dissertation on the Alamo, receiving her doctorate of philosophy on June 8, 1931.

Difficulties did not go away after she received her doctorate. It was the height of the Great Depression, and her papers in the Center for American History include numerous letters regarding the difficulties of getting a position. One San Antonio letter from 1932 holds little hope even for a position in the high schools, noting that seven hundred teachers had moved into the area and were competing for such jobs. Policy against hiring someone of her age was also given.

Remarkably, at a time when many people are considering retirement, she embarked on still another career of teaching and research at the University of Texas. She wound up staying there, although job security even into the 1940s was not insured, for another twenty years, before retiring in 1951. Her hopes to continue researching and writing on her own time were disappointed almost immediately by ill health, which continued until her death.

I do not imagine very much of her career was easy, and I consider her a powerful example that age should not prevent one from seeking further development or growth.

---

1. Smoot 1985. Many other details are from personal communications with Jane Smoot, who donated her aunt's papers to the CAH for the use of all.

Special Commentary

Military Details

Numerous statements have been given on the military details of the siege and fall of the Alamo. The question to address now is to what extent one can understand the battle based on consistent or reasonable interpretation of the mixed information supplied. To do so requires cross-comparison of sources.

MAPS AND LAYOUT

The first thing to consider is the physical layout and defenses of the Alamo as given in maps and descriptive sources. A number of maps of the Alamo have been discussed in isolation; let's now compare them to see what more can be learned of the military activities of the siege and fall. The maps for consideration are as follows:

> Jameson plat(s) in two versions: De Zavala (4.2.1.4) and Looscan/Williams (4.2.3.4)
>
> Giraud plat in five versions: original (4.2.2.1), Texas Title Company (4.2.2.2), *San Antonio Light* (4.2.2.3), Yoakum (4.2.3.2), and McArdle (4.2.3.3)
>
> Labastida (2.8.1)
>
> Sánchez (2.7.1)
>
> Sutherland (1.7.1.2, 1.7.1.3)
>
> Potter (5.1.7)

Only brief discussion points of some of the more obvious comparisons will be given here; this is not intended to be an in-depth study. The full article by Schoelwer (ref. 5.2.4) is a much more thorough, documented review for those interested in further study. Williams (1931) and Schoelwer also reviewed additional maps done by the U.S. Army around the same time as the Giraud plat.

The surviving versions of the Jameson plats include contemplated improvements to the southern defenses around the main gate, such as the half-moon battery to the south, which do not show on any later maps, including Giraud, Labastida, and Sánchez. The actual extent of the trenching at the main gate defenses has been partially mapped by archeologists.[1] The positions of the trenches are shown only on Sánchez, and the scale is approximately correct.

As for the main gate itself, Sutherland, who would have known, drew and indexed an arched entrance. The maps are consistent in showing the palisade wall running from the southwest corner of the church to the southeast corner of the plaza wall/low barracks, famous for its defense by Crockett.

On the west of the plaza, maps indicate that there were some buildings behind the wall nearly the entire length, with the Jameson versions and Potter indicating a break where the stream had run through. A significant exception is Labastida, but this is natural consequence of the external perspective of the besieging army looking toward the walls and not inside (see Commentary for 2.8). In the Commentary for 1.7.1, the possible significance of Sutherland's two structures along this wall was noted. A curious addition to Sánchez's west wall is the indication of two "circular saps with moat and stockade" outside the wall toward the southern end (J on his index).

The north side is shown fairly consistently, with the platform and cannon shown where Travis would fall (by most accounts). Sánchez shows another circular sap with moat on this side as well.

On the east side of the plaza, the convent/long barracks is shown by all the maps, as it remained standing. Furthermore, some buildings apparently extended behind the wall to the north and continued a short distance along the north wall.

Extending south from the convent was a low wall, shown only in the earliest elevations by Wells/1837 and Maverick/1839, which formed a sort of enclosure or mini-plaza in front of the church.[2] The Giraud map is unique in showing that the entire east plaza line was not straight, but had a slight angle at the north of the convent before continuing to the plaza's northeast corner.

The corrals behind the convent are shown as double, extending to about the middle of the chapel on the east, in all the Texan maps. Sánchez shows them as double, but extending all the way to the north wall in that direction, while on the east side there is a jog between the corrals, and the southerly one goes to the backside of the chapel. Labastida shows only one of the two corrals, which, being visible from the exterior and probably having cannons per Sánchez, one might have expected to be more complete.

Not surprisingly, the chapel itself is shown with a more explicit floor plan on the Texan maps than the Mexican. The most detailed plan is the De Zavala version of the Jameson plat, which supports the speculation (in the Commentary for 4.2) that De Zavala may have modified her version to more closely match the modern appearance.

The most surprising detail of all these maps is Sánchez's mislocation of the chapel and its mini-plaza in front with respect to the eastern line of the plaza, including the convent/long barracks. He shows this line as being continuous with the front of the chapel, so the mini-plaza is forced to be a bite out of the southeast corner of the plaza. He may have neglected to note this alignment in whatever field notes he made in preparation for drawing the maps, and inaccurately remembered it later when he did the actual drawing. Since he made the map after May 22, per the caption, which is when the Mexican Army retreated from Béxar, he would not have been able to check his notes at the actual location.

A comparison at this level of the Potter map with the earlier source material does not reveal any significant inconsistencies or additional information. He does show the northeastern corral as enclosed by a picket fence, but it is shown in Giraud's map, while the southern palisade is not indicated.[3] This implies that the corral fence was more substantial than just a simple picket fence, while all traces of the palisade wall, which had been deliberately destroyed when the Mexican Army retreated from Bexar in 1836, had vanished by Giraud's time.

Only the Mexican sources were concerned with the details of the surrounding area of the Alamo. Labastida shows the town, exterior shacks in the west and south to La Villita, which became part of the action during the siege, the battery to the northeast, and some of the topography in the area. Sánchez shows the batteries in the northeast and in town, some of the troop movements during the final assault, and the location where the defenders were cremated to the southeast of the church.

In addition to these visual representations, Filisola provided a verbal map (2.6.1). Though not entirely clear, his account is a good descriptive complement to the maps. It gives the clearest description of the ramp and cannons in the interior of the church, and also describes the weakness of the north wall and the location of the platforms constructed for cannons.

The cannons in the Alamo, being mobile objects, are inconsistent in number and location on the few maps that show them. The two Jameson versions show about 18: 3 on the north, 6 on the west, 2 at the entrance, 4 in the interior, 3 in the church. Labastida shows only 4 total. Sánchez gives 20: 5 on the north, 4(?) on the west, 2 at the entrance, 4 at the palisade, 3 in the church, and 2 at corrals on the east. Potter shows 14: 3 on the north, 2 on the west, 2 at the entrance, 4 at the palisade, 3 in the church. Of the written sources, Sutherland (1.7.1.1) said that the defenders had 30 or 40 guns of various calibers (not necessarily all mounted or functioning), including an 18-pounder, with the powder kept in a small room in the southwest corner of the church (however, where Dickinson was located per 1.2.11). Dickinson (1.2.7, 1.2.8) stated that there were 18 cannons in service. Santa Anna (2.1.1.10) said that 21 pieces were used with perfect accuracy. De la Peña (2.9.1) said the enemy had 15 pieces of artillery, not all mounted, with an 18-pounder and 8-pounder pointed toward town.

The detailed studies on the cannons in the files of the DRT (mentioned briefly in the Commentary for 4.4) identify 21 cannons that have a traceable history, about 9 of which survived.[4] The military reports by the Mexican Army (2.4.3, 2.4.4) confirm that about 20 cannons were left by Cós, along with considerably more details on the other armaments and munitions.

NUMBERS OF COMBATANTS

The various estimates on the numbers of combatants range widely: the Alamo defenders from 130 (Almonte) to 600 (Santa Anna), and the Mexican Army from 1,300 (Santa Anna) to 13,000 (Dickinson/*San Antonio Express*). Perhaps the best way to get an overview is to review the material from the various sources in tabular format.

NUMBERS OF COMBATANTS

Source	Doc. #	Date	Comments
Travis	1.1.3	2/23	Had 146 defenders.
Travis	1.1.6	3/3	Mexican Army 1,500–3,000 under command of Siezma and Batres.
Santa Anna	2.1.1.10	3/6	Force 1,400 infantry; 600 corpses of enemy.
Almonte	2.2.1	2/23	Travis had about 130 men.
Almonte	2.2.1	3/6	Enemy had 250 killed.
Sesma	2.3.1	3/11	Over 50 defenders killed outside the walls.
Cós	2.4.2	2/23	Three battalions (Zapadores, Aldama, Toluca) had 899 soldiers plus 62 officers prior to arrival at Béxar.

NUMBERS OF COMBATANTS *(continued)*

Source	Doc. #	Date	Comments
Caro	2.5.1	1837	Enemy numbered 156. Four attack columns and reserve, consisting of 1,400 men. Later stated 183 defenders killed.
Filisola	2.6.1	1849	About 202 enemy dead.
Sánchez	1.7.1. 2, 1.7.1.3	3/1836	257 defenders.
de la Peña	2.9.1	c. 1837–39	Total of 1,100. Reserve of 400. 253 defenders counted.
Garza	2.9.3.6	1955	Zapadores Battalion had 195 officers and men.
Becerra	2.10.1	—	250 Americans in Alamo.
Soldana/Taylor	2.11.1	—	Had about 3,000 men at Alamo.
San Luis Potosi	2.9.3.7	—	230 enemy dead.
Joe	1.3.4	3/1836	Told 6,000 troops, believed only half that in Béxar.
Dickinson	1.2.7	1874	1,600 Mexican, 182 defenders.
Dickinson	1.2.8	1876	Besieged included 50 or 60 wounded men from Cós fight.
Dickinson	1.2.11	c. 1881	Mexican 10–13,000. 75 defenders already wounded in Cós fight killed.
Sutherland	1.7.1.1	c. 1860?	Defenders 186.
Ruiz	3.1.1	1860	182 defenders cremated. Santa Anna's loss estimated at 1,600.
Bergara & Barsena	3.5.2	3/1836	2,300 attacked. 250 Mexican soldiers killed and equal number wounded. Travis had only 150 effective men out of 187.
Pablo Díaz	3.7.2	1906	10,000 in Santa Anna's force.
Telegraph and Texas Register	4.1.1	3/1836	4,000 against 140.
Commercial Bulletin	4.1.2	3/1836	6,000 attached after two days of bombardment.
Briscoe	4.1.3	3/1836	2,000 attacked.
Brooks	4.3.5.2	3/1836	1,800 attacked 2/24, 300 joined later.
Arkansas Gazette	2.17.1	3/1836	Formed evening before with 3,400 men and 2,000 cavalry under Gen. Moro.
Sabia	2.17.3	~5/1836	200 or 250 defenders.

NUMBERS OF COMBATANTS *(continued)*

Source	Doc. #	Date	Comments
Nuñez (doubtful source)	2.14.1	1889	4,500 men.
de la Peña/ Borroel 1997b, 104–6	—	1836	Total Texas campaign had 5,046 soldiers, given in the de la Peña papers—Garza's Annexo 20.
Filisola/ Castañeda 1928, 196	—	1836	Total strength of army on April 24 (i.e., after San Jacinto) was 4,078.
Filisola 1987, 2:152	—	1849	Total army assembled was 6, 019.

The counts of Alamo defenders in these sources are primarily of historical interest, reflecting the knowledge available in the nineteenth century. All such estimates have been supplanted by the documentation-based count of 187 done by Williams (1.11.1), modified by later historians to the current total of 189 identified defenders (1.11.2 and section 1.11 Commentary). A number of accounts were very close to this documented number. The lower figures of 130 or 140 may have accounted only for effective men, as a sizable number were recovering from wounds in the Cós fight of December. By his own account, Ruiz should have been the most accurate, at 182 plus one for Esparza being buried, which exactly matches Caro's count as well. One possible reason Ruiz's count is a little low was that some bodies may not have been recovered and cremated. In 1979, a skull of a possible battle participant was discovered by archeologists in the fill of a defensive trench near the north part of the corrals.[5] The documented count of 189 could be low as well. Williams gave another 12 names as probable and possible, and some defenders may not have been listed in the later records.

There is some speculation, based particularly on Almonte's March 6 entry and also on the accounts of Sesma, Sánchez, and de la Peña, that higher figures up to 250 might be correct.[6] De la Peña in particular was positive about the higher figure, his diary stating, "but according to the number counted by us it was 253," while his papers are more personally explicit: "and to us, 253 was the number I counted."[7] His accounts also give a higher number— "about 60"—as entering the Alamo after the siege began, but neither he nor any other Mexican source stated that more than one group broke through the siege to enter the Alamo. The higher number of 250-plus defenders does contradict Travis (1.1.3), who must be a more definitive source through his last letters of March 3. Past that date, beyond the 32 Gonzales reinforcements on March 1, no additional force of 60 or so men that might have reached the Alamo was documented as entering by the Mexican side or as missing on the Texan side. Such a high number is also inconsistent with Caro, Filisola, and Ruiz.

As for the estimate of the number of Mexican troops, clearly Travis, who estimated 1,500 to 3,000, would have taken this question more seriously than any historian. Williams reviewed the accounts of Filisola and Santa Anna, which give a total of 6,000 and 8,000 troops respectively for the entire Texas campaign.[8] As some were not sent to Bexar and others arrived after the fall, a mean of Travis's estimate is reasonable—and 2,300 is what Bergara and Barsena (3.5.2) reported to Sam Houston later that same week. Santa Anna (2.1.1.10, fairly consistent with de la Peña 2.9.1) reported 1,400 infantry actually attacking, apparently not including Sesma's cavalry of several hundred posted to the east.

These early secondhand counts on the Mexican forces can now be checked against the formal report by General Cós (2.4.2). The Zapadores, Aldama, and Toluca battalions were three of the six that participated in the March 6 battle (along with the Matamoros, Jiménez, and St. Luis), and thus Cós's report provides an official count of about half the attacking forces. On February 23, when they were starting across the Texas plains following the advance forces under Santa Anna and Sesma, the Zapadores battalion had 182 men and 11 officers, Aldama 393 men and 27 officers, and Toluca 324 men and 24 officers, making a total of 961. Also likely to have been in the battle was Cós's squad of the St. Luis battalion, with 33 total. The Queretaro and Guanajuato battalions, which did not reach Béxar prior to the battle, totaled 312 and 313, respectively. Considering the later complaints that Santa Anna did not wait a few more days for the heavy artillery to arrive in Béxar, the artillery force of 67 men and officers was probably with the last two battalions. If one assumes that the Matamoros, Jiménez, and St. Luis battalions had similar numbers, then more than 1,900 were in these six key battalions—not counting a battalion of engineers, five companies of grenadiers, and Sesma's cavalry, which were also in San Antonio on March 6. There must have been several hundred in these additional forces. As Santa Anna stated (2.1.1.8), not all were in the actual attack. Therefore, he might have been giving accurate information when he said there were 1,400 infantry in the actual attack (2.1.1.10).

Filisola gave a count of 1,541 for the entire vanguard forces, including 369 cavalry, under Sesma, which includes these additional forces as well as the three battalions.[9] Interestingly, he understated the count for the battalions reported by Cós—especially the Aldama, which he gave as only 280 men. If nothing else, it is clear that Filisola did not use the report of Cós.

Some other information and possible qualifications should be considered as well. Losses to the battalions in reaching Béxar were not considered in this averaging, which could reduce the counts. On the other hand, the Zapadores battalion was significantly below strength compared with the other four on Cós's list. If the three battalions with Santa Anna had similar numbers to four of the five with Cós, the count for the six battalions could easily have been 100 or 200 more than the 1,900.

The force of the St. Luis battalion also could be estimated if it were assumed that the squad of 33 with Cós was a reasonable average for the whole battalion. In a modern army, a battalion has six companies, two platoons per company, and two squads per platoon.[10] A force of 33 times 24, or 792, is clearly much too high, so it is likely there were two squads per company or twelve per battalion in Santa Anna's Texas campaign. This would give 396 for the St. Luis battalion, a figure quite consistent with the Aldama and Toluca battalions. The necessary assumptions to reach this figure, though, are a bit of a reach. In comparison, Filisola gave 460 men for the St. Luis battalion.[11]

Regardless of the qualifications, the figure of 2,300 officers and men total on the Mexican side (not all of whom participated in the attack of March 6), as reported to Houston by Bergara and Barsena on March 11, is very realistic.

DETAILS OF THE SIEGE

To do a cross-comparison of the details recorded concerning the siege, the table below presents the information from a representative sample of the sources, following as closely as possible the day-to-day chronology. An informal prioritization by significance of the source has been done for each day's entry.

SIEGE CHRONOLOGY, FEBRUARY 23–MARCH 5, 1836

Source	Doc. #	Date	Comments
Travis	1.1.1.16	2/23	Enemy in sight at 3 P.M.
Bowie	1.1.2	2/23	Parley attempted.
Travis	1.1.5	2/23	Parley answered with cannon shot.
Santa Anna	2.1.1.3	2/23	Occupied Béjar 2/23 with Sesma's division, composed of permanent battalions of Matamoros and Jiménez, the active battalion of San Luis Potosi, regiment of Dolores, and 8 pieces of artillery.
			Surprise attack prevented by heavy rain 2/22.
			Casualties: a corporal and a scout killed, 8 wounded.
			Response to message from Bowie ordered by Santa Anna.
			Seized 50 rifles.
Almonte	2.2.1	2/23	Sesma arrived (at hills of Alazan) 7 A.M.; did not advance due to spy's report of enemy.
			Division arrived at hills at 12:30 P.M.
			Advanced into city at 2 P.M. with Santa Anna.
			Fired 4 grenades at Alamo.
			Small battery set up near house of Veremende that night.
			Texans hoisted tricolored flag with two stars.
			Fled into Alamo at 3 P.M.

SIEGE CHRONOLOGY, FEBRUARY 23–MARCH 5, 1836 *(continued)*

Source	Doc. #	Date	Comments
			Jameson messenger desired honorable conditions. Second messenger (Martin) from Travis.
Filisola	2.3.1	2/23	Occupied Béxar without difficulty.
Sutherland	1.7.1.1	2/23	Travis hears of Mexicans 8 miles away at 11 A.M.
			Sutherland and Smith discover cavalry a short distance from Bexar.
			Sutherland sent to Gonzales.
			Crockett assigned to picket fence.
			Beeves and corn found and brought into Alamo.
			Well dug within walls.
			Smith and Sutherland went south, then turned east, crossing Gonzales road before Powderhouse Hill (1 mile east of town).
			Parley with Maj. Morris and Capt. Martin. Answered with shot.
			Almonte stationed main force on hill east of Alamo about 1,000 yds.
			Siege opened with considerable vigor, then tapered. Frequent skirmishes toward night.
			Several jueahes or huts near SW corner of wall torn down.
Esparza	1.5.2	2/23	Saw Santa Anna arrive about sundown.
Oury	1.7.5.3	2/23	Bowie active first day.
Santa Anna	2.1.2	2/23	Ordered Béjar taken, but officer (Sesma) stopped outside city at 10 A.M. awaiting new orders. Offered life to defenders.
Santa Anna	2.1.3.2	(2/23)	Travis and defenders refused to surrender.
de la Peña	2.9.1	2/23	Sesma advanced at dawn toward Béjar. Should have continued into town and did not. Rest of division arrived between 12 and 1 P.M. at Alazan hill, 2 miles from town.
			Santa Anna entered about 2 P.M. with companies under Morales, Romero, two mortar pieces, and Sesma's cavalry. Rest marched with Mora to Mission Concepción. Alamo fired 18-pounder, 2 howitzers fired 4 grenades.

SIEGE CHRONOLOGY, FEBRUARY 23–MARCH 5, 1836 *(continued)*

Source	Doc. #	Date	Comments
			White flag raised, and Bowie sent written communication. Santa Anna replied only unconditional surrender.
San Luis Potosi	2.9.3.7	2/23	Col. Minon ordered to take Mission Concepción, ignorant of its being abandoned. Alamo raised white flag for parley after howitzers fired from Mexican side.
Caro	2.5.1	2/23 (2/26)	Entered city.
Soldana/Taylor	2.11.1	2/23? (2/22)	Entered Béxar. Night before, spies from Santa Anna and Cós's soldiers from town exchanged visits.
Becerra	2.10.1	2/23	Becerra under Sesma's division. Col. Mora ordered to take Mission Concepción. A few shots fired by each side.
Nuñez (doubtful source)	2.14.1	2/23	Santa Anna ordered Texans to surrender. They answered with cannon shot. Santa Anna ordered a charge, which was repulsed with heavy loss.
Loranca (doubtful source)	2.13.1	2/23?	Santa Anna arrived 9 A.M. Defenders raised a red flag.
Almonte	2.2.1	2/24	New battery set up on bank of river, 350 yds. from Alamo. 18-pounder and another dismounted. 4 defenders killed, 30 men arrived from Gonzales per spy [*though this might be an entry after the fact?*].
Filisola	2.6.1	2/24	Reconnoitering Alamo and river crossings. At night, 2 batteries set up.
Caro	2.5.1	(2/24)	Battery of 2 cannons at 600 yds. began bombardment. Took possession of small houses to left (from Béxar viewpoint), with loss of several killed and wounded.
Sutherland	1.7.1.1	2/24	Fighting more vigorous.
Oury	1.7.5.3	2/24	Bowie injured by gun carriage. [*Not from Oury? Tinkle?*]
de la Peña	2.9.1	2/24	Frontal advance toward Alamo, battery of 2 8-pounders and howitzer began bombardment.

SIEGE CHRONOLOGY, FEBRUARY 23–MARCH 5, 1836 *(continued)*

Source	Doc. #	Date	Comments
San Luis Potosi	2.9.3.7	2/24	Frontal assault ordered, no casualties.
Soldana/Taylor	2.11.1	2/24	Preparation for siege and reconnoitering Alamo. Two batteries planted.
Becerra	2.10.1	2/24?	Mora ordered to north and east of Alamo to prevent escape. Santa Anna waited for Gen. Tolza with 2,000. First movement by Matamoros battalion under Castrillón, crossing river and taking possession of some houses below the Alamo. Texans fired on them. Santa Anna and Mino went to spot.
Brooks	4.3.5.2	2/24	1,800 made assault, repulsed with loss.

Travis	1.1.5	2/25	Attack of 200–300 across river under cover of houses. Grape, canister, and small arms repulsed attack. Many attackers injured.
			  Good service by Lt. Simmons; Capts. Carey, Dickinson, Blair, and Crockett.
			  Charles Despallier and Robert Brown sallied and set fire to houses under enemy fire.

Almonte	2.2.1	2/25	Battalion de Cazadores with Santa Anna crossed river to houses. New fortification near house of McMullen. Enemy wounded 6 and killed 2. 2 batteries erected other side of river in Alameda with battalion of Matamoros. Cavalry posted on hills to east and road to Gonzales at the Casa Mata Antigua. Enemy burned straw and houses in their vicinity.
Filisola	2.6.1	2/25	Batteries opened fire at dawn, fire returned. Santa Anna with chasseurs from Jiménez and Matamoros crossed river and took position in houses and huts to south of the Alamo, about half a rifle shot from Alamo. Trench dug near Mr. Mullen's house. 2 killed and 6 wounded. Order to Gen. Ganona issued. Two trenches dug in cottonwood grove. Cavalry posted on hills to east on road to Gonzales and vicinity of former Casa Mata. Enemy burned hay and wooden houses near them. North side still open.

SIEGE CHRONOLOGY, FEBRUARY 23–MARCH 5, 1836 *(continued)*

Source	Doc. #	Date	Comments
de la Peña, also Potosi	2.9.1, 2.9.3.7	2/25	Santa Anna with column of chasseurs San Luis and Matamoros battalion marched to other side of river. Fought within pistol range; lost 2 dead and 2 wounded. At night, line in La Villita under Morales protected.
Soldana/Taylor	2.11.1	2/25	2 batteries opened fired. Brisk fire whole day from both sides. 2 entrenchments constructed along Alameda. 9 Americans came over from Alamo.
Becerra	2.10.1	2/25?	2 companies made reconnaissance, many killed. Firing from Alamo continued all day. Battalion Matamoros sent to reinforce Mora, replaced (in south) by Romero's command. Small work commenced above Alamo (north?).
Almonte	2.2.1	2/26	Slight skirmish with Sesma's division to east. Only occasional firing from Alamo. Enemy burnt small houses near battalion of San Luis. Sentinels advanced. Enemy sallied out for wood and water, opposed by marksmen.
Filisola	2.6.1	2/26	Small skirmish with Sesma's men on east. Other straw huts burnt at night.
Becerra	2.10.1	2/26?	Matamoros sent to reoccupy position in front (south). Another work to north constructed closer to Alamo. Heavy fire on it from Alamo all day.
Loranca (doubtful source)	2.13.1	2/26 (2/23)	Batres conferred with Bowie and Travis, to surrender on discretion but lives spared.
Santa Anna	2.1.1.4	2/27	Need resupply in food, money, and salt.
Almonte	2.2.1	2/27	Lt. Menchaco sent to raid ranches of Seguín and Flores. Tried to cut off water at old mill. Little firing from either side. Enemy worked hard to repair entrenchments. Santa Anna fired at in P.M.
Filisola	2.6.1	2/27	Fire from both sides. Lt. Menchaca sent to Seguín and Flores for corn, cattle, and hogs. Unsuccessful attempt made to cut off water at

SIEGE CHRONOLOGY, FEBRUARY 23–MARCH 5, 1836 *(continued)*

Source	Doc. #	Date	Comments
			Old Mill. Enemy working on interior ditch to support parapet; no walkway, so exposed to fire on 3/6.
Loranca (doubtful source)	2.13.1	2/27	Bombardment effectually commenced.
Almonte	2.2.1	2/28	Intelligence that reinforcement of 200 coming from La Bahia not true [*after the fact?*].
Filisola	2.6.1	2/28	Report of 200 men from Goliad due to arrive. Cannon fire almost all day long.
Santa Anna	2.1.1.5	2/29	Sesma ordered out with Jiménez battalion to search for enemy. No prisoners.
Almonte	2.2.1	2/29	Battalion of Allende posted east of Alamo. One soldier killed in night. Sesma left at midnight with cavalry of Dolores and infantry of Allende to meet reinforcements.
Filisola	2.6.1	2/29	Jiménez ordered to right of cavalry, or left of road to Gonzales. Sesma moved in at night. Also marched with detachment of Jiménez battalion and Dolores regiment toward Goliad.
San Luis Potosi	2.9.3.7	2/29	Soldier of first company killed.
Travis	1.1.6	3/1	32 Gonzales reinforcements arrived 3 A.M.
Almonte	2.2.1	3/1	Sesma wrote from Mission de la Espador that no reinforcements. Cavalry and infantry returned. Col. Ampudia commissioned to construct more trenches. In P.M., 2 12-pound shots fired at house of president, one hit.
Filisola	2.6.1	3/1	Sesma returned.
Sutherland	1.7.1.1	3/1	Smith entered Alamo with 32 men; Mexican officer tried to mislead them.
		(3/1)	Mexicans allowed Gonzales 32 and Bonham into Alamo?
Caro	2.5.1	(3/1)	2 sets of reinforcements from Gonzales, 4 at night and 25 in day. 2 messengers left fort, including Seguín.
de la Peña	2.9.1	(3/1)	About 60 men entered Alamo one night.

SIEGE CHRONOLOGY, FEBRUARY 23–MARCH 5, 1836 *(continued)*

Source	Doc. #	Date	Comments
Sánchez	2.7.2	3/1	Map V. Battery set up in City.
Almonte	2.2.1	3/2	Orders to Col. Duque to arrive next day. Lt. Menchaca sent to Seguín farm for corn. Santa Anna discovered covered road within pistol shot of Alamo; battalion of Jimenez posted there.
Sánchez	2.7.3	3/2	Sánchez arrived in Béjar at 11 P.M.
Travis	1.1.6	3/3	Bonham arrived 11 A.M. Reinforcements arrived under Santa Anna?
Travis	1.1.7	3/3	Bonham arrived, coming between powder house and upper encampment.
Sutherland	1.7.1.1	3/3	Cheers of "Santa Anna" from town, thought to be arriving. All but three Tejanos left the Alamo.
Santa Anna	2.1.1.6	3/3	No prisoners.
Santa Anna	2.1.1.10	(3/3)	Waited until battalions of Engineers, Aldama, and Toluca arrived.
Almonte	2.2.1	3/3	Enemy fired a few cannons and musket shot at city. Battery erected on north of Alamo within musket shot. Urrea announcement on defeat at San Patricio cause for celebration. Battalions of Zapadores, Aldama, and Toluca arrived. Enemy repulsed in a sally at night at the sugar mill.
de la Peña	2.9.1	3/3	Sapper battalions from Aldama and Toluca arrived. De la Peña with this group.
Sánchez	2.7.3	3/3	2 batteries to West and Northeast of Alamo; no sign they caused serious damage. Santa Anna risked life.
Becerra	2.10.1	3/3	Gen. Tolza arrived.
Almonte	2.2.1	3/4	One or two shots fired in P.M. by enemy. Meeting with Gens. Cós, Sesma, and Castrillón; Cols. Duque/Toluca, Orisnuela/Aldama, Romero/Matamoros, Arnat/Zapadores, a Major/San Luis. Assault supported by Cós, Castrillón, Orisnuela, and Romero after arrival

SIEGE CHRONOLOGY, FEBRUARY 23–MARCH 5, 1836 *(continued)*

Source	Doc. #	Date	Comments
			of 2 12-pounders on Monday. Santa Anna, Ramírez, Almonte for not waiting. At night, north parapet advanced toward enemy through watercourse.
Caro	2.5.1	3/4	Companies from General Gaona arrived.
Sánchez	2.7.2	3/4	Map R. Battery constructed by Amador, manned by Zapadores, did not go into action. Commanded by Santa Anna.
Sánchez	2.7.3	3/4	Santa Anna risked life again. No change in tactics.
de la Peña	3.9.1	3/4	Council of War. Castrillón, Almonte, and Romero in favor of a breach being made, with fieldpieces coming up.
Joe	1.3.4	3/5	Bombardment suspended day and night prior to attack. Garrison worked late repairing and strengthening position.
Sutherland	1.7.1.1	3/5	Artillery ceased about 10 P.M. Defenders fell asleep.
Almonte	2.2.1	3/5	Brisk fire from north battery, only occasionally answered. Santa Anna determined to make assault. 4 Columns commanded by Cós, Duque, Romero, and Morales; seconds Castrillón, Amador, and Minon. Muster at 12 midnight, attack at 4 A.M.
Filisola	2.6.1	3/5	4 columns leave city in silence for surprise attack. Several officers in favor of waiting for 12-caliber pieces to arrive 3/7 or 3/8. Travis reported to ask for surrender provided lives spared. Answer was must be unconditional.
Sánchez	2.7.3	3/5	Troops labored through night; trench abandoned in morning. Santa Anna decided to attack.

SIEGE CHRONOLOGY, FEBRUARY 23–MARCH 5, 1836 *(continued)*

Source	Doc. #	Date	Comments
de la Peña	2.9.1	3/5	Travis promised if no help arrived, they would surrender the next day or try to escape. Per lady from Béjar, a male Negro, and several women rescued by Cols. Morales and Minon.
Becerra	2.10.1	3/5	Preparation for assault.
			Comments over a range of dates
Travis	1.1.5	2/23–25	Continuous bombardment commenced with 5-inch howitzer and heavy cannonade. No disabling injuries inside Alamo.
Travis	1.1.6	2/23–3/3	Entrenching inside and strengthening walls. 200 shells fell inside without injuries. Killed many of the enemy. Bombardment with 5½-inch and 8-inch howitzer, heavy cannonade from 2 long 9-pounders in battery on opposite side of river at 400 yds. Encircled with entrenched encampments: Béjar/400 yds. west, La Villita/300 yds. south, Powder House/1,000 yds. east by south (ESE), ditch/800 yds. northeast, old mill/800 yds. north.
Sutherland	1.7.1.1	2/23–3/3	Bombardment increased.
Caro	2.5.1	2/29–30	Orders to General Gaona to send picked companies of his brigade.
Ehrenberg	4.3.9	2/24–3/3	Several assaults successfully repulsed.
			Undatable general comments
Telegraph and Texas Register	4.1.1	—	Defenders much fatigued and harassed by night watching and incessant toils, heavy bombardment, and several real and feigned attacks.
Esparza	1.5.2	—	Cannons fired repeatedly during nights. Fighting intermittent, defenders fell. Travis spent most of his time directing fire from roof of church and the convent.
Ourey	1.7.5.3	—	Sleepless nights. "We were all tired . . ." Erected parapets on north wall and palisade during day, "dragging guns around."

SIEGE CHRONOLOGY, FEBRUARY 23–MARCH 5, 1836 *(continued)*

Source	Doc. #	Date	Comments
Sutherland	1.7.1.1	—	Assaults small, 100 to 200 men. (Used Ruiz, Yoakum, and Potter as sources.)
de la Peña	2.9.1	—	Townspeople made clear the limited strength and supplies of the Alamo.
Soldana/Taylor	2.11.1	—	Constant, almost hourly alarms in night used to harass and weaken defenders.
Nuñez (doubtful source)	2.14.1	—	Sapas dug north, south, and east of Alamo. No one could escape; Seguín allowed to leave. Further heavy losses on second and third day of siege.
Soldana/Taylor	2.11.1	—	[*Post-battle*] Gen. Gaona's division arrived 3/8; Woll 3/10; Filisola, Arago, and Andrade 3/19.

Comparing the details from the different sources on a day-by-day basis shows that basically, most of the sources tend to give some sort of consistent viewpoint, whereas accounts already considered doubtful, such as Nuñez and Loranca, continue to demonstrate their divergence from the rest. One should be cautious, though, in placing too much weight on this consistency, as many of these accounts were derived from others. Similarities in a number of incidences between Almonte and Filisola, for example, might suggest that Filisola either had Almonte's diary (published in English in the United States in 1836) available when he wrote his account in 1840, or had a comparably detailed daily account to pull from.

It is not the intent of this work to duplicate the narrative day-to-day accounts by previous writers such as Potter, Tinkle, Lord, Hardin, and Davis, but to allow the reader to understand the basis for such narratives. Hardin (1994) in particular approached the battle from a military tactics point of view.[12] Huffines (1999) took the sort of tabulation done above a step further, excerpting quotations in chronological order and making a serious effort to document the issues raised. Consequently, this comparison of sources will not be reviewed in greater depth, other than to note that the general trend of the siege is clear: a gradual tightening of the encirclement, placing the artillery on different sides and pushing them closer to the fort, fairly continual bombardment and alarms from the Mexican side, and occasional return fire and skirmishes from the Texan side.

DETAILS OF THE FALL OF THE ALAMO

This section will use the tabulation approach to compare representative selections from the sources on the fall of the Alamo.

CHRONOLOGY OF THE ALAMO'S FALL, MARCH 6, 1836

Source	Doc. #	Date	Comments
Santa Anna	2.1.1.8	3/5	Attack to start 4 A.M., starting at musket-shot distance from entrenchments, signaled by bugle from northern battery.

First column commanded by Cós, alternate Santa Anna. Consisting of permanent battalion of Aldama (except company of grenadiers) and three companies of the active battalion of San Luis.

Second column commanded by Duque, alternate Castrillón. Composed of active battalion of Toluca (except company of grenadiers) and the three remaining companies of the active battalion of San Luis.

Third column by Romero, alternate Salas, composed of permanent battalions of Matamoros and Jiménez.

Fourth column by Morales, alternate Minon, composed of light companies of battalions of Matamoros and Jiménez, and active battalion of San Luis.

Reserve commanded by Santa Anna, assembled by Arnat, composed of battalion of engineers and the five companies of grenadiers of the permanent battalions of Matamoros, Jiménez, and Aldama, and the active battalions of Toluca and San Luis.

First column would carry 10 ladders, 2 crowbars, and 2 axes; the second, 10 ladders; the third, 6 ladders; and the fourth, 2 ladders. Men carrying ladders slung their guns, 6 packages cartridges for grenadiers, 2 packages for central companies. No overcoats or blankets, chinstraps down, wore shoes or sandals.

Troops to sleep at dark, ready to move at 12 midnight. Active battalion of San Luis to abandon current position when moon raised to prepare.

CHRONOLOGY OF THE ALAMO'S FALL, MARCH 6, 1836 *(continued)*

Source	Doc. #	Date	Comments
			Cavalry under Sesma to be stationed at the Alameda, saddling up at 3 A.M. to scout country to prevent escape.
Santa Anna	2.1.1.10	3/6	Force divided into 4 columns of attack and a reserve. 8 A.M., triumph completed. Attack commenced at 5 A.M. Stubborn resistance, lasted more than an hour and a half, reserve brought into action. Enemy used 21 pieces of artillery with perfect accuracy. One flag of enemy's battalions sent.
Santa Anna	2.1.2	3/6	Imprudent soldiers' huzzas spoiled surprise attack.
Santa Anna	2.1.3.2	1874	Struggle lasted more than 2 hours.
Almonte	2.2.1	c. 3/6	5 A.M., columns in position. Attack made at 5:30, continued to 6 A.M. Some attempted to flee, put to the sword. 5 women, a Mexican soldier (prisoner), and a black slave escaped.
Sesma	2.3.1	3/11	2 groups of defenders, 50 men in second group, retreated into brush to east of Alamo, cut down by cavalry.
Filisola	2.6.1	3/6	Shouts from one column awakened Texans. Fire played terrible havoc in ranks. Columns became disorganized, Santa Anna sent in reserves. Army in place at 4 A.M. Fatal trumpet sounded, reckless shouting. 3 columns on west, north, and east drew back. Attacked again, west and east, moved to north into nearly a single mass. Gen. Amador one of first over parapet. In south, Col. Minon and Morales used small jacales, seized cannon on platform. Gen. Amador used enemy's own artillery on doors of small inner rooms where rebels had taken cover.
Caro	2.5.1	3/6	Attack at daybreak with agreed signal. First charge wavered, Col. Duque of Toluca battalion wounded. Reserve ordered to advance. Amador, Ampudia, Mora, and Aguirre gained

CHRONOLOGY OF THE ALAMO'S FALL, MARCH 6, 1836 *(continued)*

Source	Doc. #	Date	Comments
			foothold on north side, where strife bitterest. Enemy took refuge in inside rooms. Alamo guns used to demolish interior defenses. Opposite side (south) gained by Morales and Minon.
Sánchez	2.7.2, 2.7.3	3/6	5 A.M., assault made. 4 columns commanded by Cós, Duque, Romero, and Morales; reserves by Santa Anna. Firing lasted half hour. By 6:30, not an enemy left. Woman and children saved. Troops permitted to pillage. 21 fieldpieces, many arms, and munitions captured.
			Map E. Palisade where a few colonists tried in vain to escape when all was lost.
			Map F. Barracks through which Matamoros and Ximenex battalions with Romero attacked and entered.
			Map G. Where Toluca and Zapadores battalions with Duque and Castrillón entered.
			Map H. Aldam Cazadores and fusiliers with Cós attempted, annoyed by firing of Toluca battalion, ordered oblique movement to right, entered plaza by postern at asterisk.
			Map S. Position of first column under Cós from 3 A.M. till 5 A.M.
Joe	1.3.2	3/6	Pickets posted 100 yds. out.
Joe	1.3.4	3/6	Garrison much exhausted by hard labor and incessant watching and fighting.
			Adjutant Baugh, officer of the day, only one not asleep at start of attack.
			3 picket guards supposed asleep, gave no alarm.
			Ladders against walls before garrison aroused.
			Dickinson said 3 attacks.
			Dickinson(?) said Mexicans poured over "like sheep."
			Fighting became melee, hand-to-hand with gun butts, swords, pistols, knives.

CHRONOLOGY OF THE ALAMO'S FALL, MARCH 6, 1836 *(continued)*

Source	Doc. #	Date	Comments
Dickinson	1.2.7	3/6	2 assaults repulsed before the final one. Battle lasted 2 hours.
Dickinson	1.2.8	3/6	Attack announced with signal rocket. Army attacked and were repulsed. Second assault with scaling ladders, first thrown up on east side of fort. Walker only man she saw killed.
Dickinson	1.2.11	3/6	Army in semicircle from Northeast to Southwest. Strongest attack from Military Plaza and by division from Villita. 3 times repulsed.
Dickinson	1.2.12	3/6	Saw no fighting, only noise of battle.
Esparza	1.5.2	3/6	Mexican fire slackened and ceased, all asleep. Mexican cannons fired, then soldiers swarmed over walls. Hand-to-hand fighting with knives at end.
Sutherland	1.7.1.1	3/6	Sentinel gave alarm. Two charges under walls unsuccessful. Third successful. Outer walls overrun, retreat to church and barracks. Fight lasted a half hour.
Telegraph and Texas Register	4.1.1	3/6	Twice repulsed. Third time got over walls, fought with butt end of rifles. Storming lasted an hour.
Bergara & Barsena	3.4.1	3/6	Attacked at daybreak, planted ladders against the 4 walls. Great loss of infantry.
Arkansas Gazette	2.17.1	3/6	Mexican Army formed evening before led by Gen. Moro. Signal given between 3 and 4 A.M. by rockets.
de la Peña	2.9.1	3/6	4 columns: Aldama and 3 companies from San Luis contingent under Cós from west; Duque's battalion and 3 other companies from San Luis from north; 2 companies of fusiliers from Matamoros and Jiménez battalions under Romero from east, which was strongest; fourth under Morales of chasseurs from south. Reserve was the Sapper battalion and 5 grenadier companies, under Santa Anna, though Amat actually led it into combat.

CHRONOLOGY OF THE ALAMO'S FALL, MARCH 6, 1836 *(continued)*

Source	Doc. #	Date	Comments
			1–3 A.M. Approached Alamo. "Terrible bugle call of death" aroused the men at dawn. Half company of chasseurs from Toluca and Capt. Herrera killed. De la Peña with Col. Duque. Ladders poorly put together, didn't arrive at walls. Cós's column joined other two, reserve sent in, half of its officers wounded. Torres died inside fort after taking flag. Struggle continued 15 minutes until sufficient numbers reached parapet. Defenders withdrew into quarters. Some Mexicans fell from friendly fire. Enemy cannon brought down doors. Attempted signal to stop firing ignored. About 50,000 cartridges used up. Some defenders tried to surrender, others tried to escape. Extermination lasted about an hour, till 6 A.M.
de la Peña	2.9.3.2, 2.9.3.3		Testimonials of de la Peña's brave actions in climbing the wall (Ampudia), carrying messages (Amat) during the fighting.
San Luis Potosi	2.9.3.7	3/6	Bugle sounded at 5:35. Attack lasted 20 minutes. All defenders dead by 8:30.
Becerra	2.10.1	3/6	3 A.M., Matamoros marched near river and above Alamo. In their rear were 2,000 under Cós, Castrillón in overall command. Gen. Tolza held ground below Alamo. Attack to be signaled by bugle. 4 A.M., bugle sounded. Castrillón moved in silence, planted ladders. After half hour, made lodgment in outwork. Doors of Alamo barricaded, hand-to-hand fighting inch-by-inch. Gen. Tolza command forced church door. Long room on first floor [*probably the long barracks rather than church*] identified as the hospital had bitter fighting. Fired their cannon with grape and canister. Top of church defended by 11 Texans with artillery.
Soldana/Taylor	2.11.1	3/6	Per Dickinson, fight lasted more than two hours. Soldana in Tampico battalion.

CHRONOLOGY OF THE ALAMO'S FALL, MARCH 6, 1836 *(continued)*

Source	Doc. #	Date	Comments
El Mosquito	2.16.1	3/6	4 columns under Cós, Morales, Romero. Source under Cós. In position 3 A.M. on north side, 300 paces from fort. Waited till 5:30, signal given, charge made. Walls scaled at once, (but) took ¾ hour to get inside. Terrible hand-to-hand fighting.
Loranca (doubtful source)	2.13.1	3/6	Morales on north with battalion "Firmas" of San Luis Potosi, Salas on west with battalion of Aldama, Minon on south with battalion of infantry, Serna [*sic, Sesma*] with squadron of lancers. Took place 3:30, time only to discharge 4 of 18 cannons. Signal from fort to east with Santa Anna. 63 defenders killed outside walls by Sesma.
Nuñez (doubtful source)	2.14.1	3/6?	Wednesday, 3/6, fourth day of siege. Filisola attacked from east, Castrillón from south, Sesma supposed to have commanded west but arrested and sent back, so Woll commanded, Santa Anna commanded north and northeast. Final battle all at church. [*See Commentary for 2.14.1.*]

Again, only a few general observations will be made concerning the relatively consistent picture drawn by these sources. The interested reader can turn to Potter, Williams, Tinkle, Lord, Hardin, Davis, or any of the other numerous narrative accounts to see how the detailed material was used and accepted or rejected. Hardin (1994) diagrammed the movement of Mexican forces during the fall of the Alamo. Ivey (2001) also gave a detailed analysis of the movements of the Mexican Army during the attack.

Per Santa Anna's order, and taking the directions from the other sources, the general flow of the battle is clear. From the west, Cós attacked with the permanent battalion of Aldama and three companies from the active battalion of San Luis. On the north, Duque and Castrillón attacked with the active battalion of Toluca and the three remaining companies of the active battalion of San Luis. From the east, Romero and Salas attacked with the permanent battalions of Matamoros and Jiménez. From the south, Morales and Minon attacked with the light companies of the battalions of Matamoros and Jimenez, and active battalion of San Luis. Santa Anna was probably on the north with the reserves, led into battle by Amat, which included the battalion of engineers and the five companies of grenadiers from the various battalions. The cavalry under Sesma was stationed to the east to scout the country to prevent escape.

The artillery bombardment had stopped early the night before, and most of the defenders fell asleep. The attack apparently started between 5 and 5:30 A.M. and lasted no longer than two hours (with 5 to 6:30 per Santa Anna being the most likely). The initial attacks were repulsed at least once, probably twice. The fierceness of the fighting and artillery fire forced both Cós in the west and Romero in the east to the north, merging with Duque in a confused but concentrated attack. This confusion caused Santa Anna to order in the reserves. The plaza walls were initially overrun on the north and south, then the defenders retreated to the buildings—especially the convent/long barracks. The Alamo's own cannons were used to blow in defensive works at the doors to these buildings, and the fighting ended in vicious hand-to-hand melees. The church door was also blown open, and the final fighting inside the Alamo occurred there. After the plaza walls were overrun, some defenders retreated outside the Alamo walls to the east, where they were run down by the lancers of Sesma's cavalry.

MEXICAN CASUALTIES
One of the most widely variable details of the Alamo is the number of Mexican troops killed in the siege and fall. Again a cross-comparison will aid in the analysis.

MEXICAN CASUALTIES

Source	Doc. #	Date	Comments
Santa Anna	2.1.1.10	3/6	600 enemy slain, lost 70 killed and 300 wounded, including 25 officers.
Santa Anna	2.1.3.3	1874	1,000 died and wounded.
Almonte	2.2.1	3/6	250 enemy killed, and 17 pieces of artillery, a flag, muskets, and firearms taken. Mexican losses 60 soldiers and 5 officers killed, 198 soldiers and 25 officers wounded. Battalion of Toluca lost 98 men between wounded and killed.
Filisola	2.6.1	1849	Losses 70 dead, 300 wounded. A greater number of Mexicans died than Texans.
			Losses great and deplorable. Col. Duque one of first who fell. Most of dead and wounded from friendly fire. Enemy cannons and parapets poorly positioned. Per Gen. Andrade, 60 dead and 311 wounded, large number of latter died due to poor care. Only one old woman and a Negro slave left alive. Defenders dead were 150 volunteers, 32 from Gonzales (arrived 3/3), and about 20 townspeople. There were "atrocious authorized acts."

MEXICAN CASUALTIES *(continued)*

Source	Doc. #	Date	Comments
Andrade/Filisola	2.6.1	1836	60 dead, 251 wounded.
Caro	2.5.1	1837	300 killed outright, 100 died of wounds. 183 defenders killed. 6 women captured and set at liberty. 5 defenders discovered by Castrillón, executed per Santa Anna. Caro source for 600 defenders killed per Santa Anna orders.
Ben	2.12.2	—	Heard officer say loss was 1,200 men (dead and wounded?).
Dickinson	1.2.7	1876	Texans killed 8–9 Mexicans each, total 1,600
Dickinson	1.2.8	1876	No one hurt till final assault.
Sutherland	1.7.1.1	c. 1860	1,540 Mexicans slain.
Sánchez	2.7.2, 2.7.3	3/6	257 of enemy killed. Mexicans 121 killed and 266 wounded. No hospitals.
de la Peña	2.9.1	c. 1837–38	Mexicans lost over 300.
Moro	2.9.3.4	8/1836	200 wounded in assault.
Andrade	2.9.3.5	4/1836	Still 150 wounded (with another 40 sick) in April.
Garza	2.9.3.6	1955	3 Zapadores killed, 24 wounded in battle.
San Luis Potosi	2.9.3.7	1836	230 defenders killed. Mexican dead and wounded were 21 officers and 295 men.
de la Peña/Borroel 1997b, 104–6	—	1836	Total losses of Mexican Army in Texas were 1,220 (including ~550 captured at San Jacinto, ~530+ killed at San Jacinto).
El Mosquito	2.16.1	3/6	257 defenders. Lost many, with 200 wounded.
Becerra	2.10.1	pre-1882	Mexican losses 2,000 killed, over 300 wounded.
Soldana/Taylor	2.11.1	—	About half attacking force, 1,600 to 2,000, fell.
Ben	2.12.3	—	1,200 Mexicans lost.
Loranca (doubtful source)	2.13.1	1878	283 defenders died, 400 Mexicans.
Rabia	2.17.3	—	Defenders "200, 50[?] Americans, 4 women," dead and wounded Mexican troops 500 men.
Mexico Archives	2.4.5	1836	456 Mexicans in hospital from March 6 to August 1.

MEXICAN CASUALTIES *(continued)*

Source	Doc. #	Date	Comments
Peréz	3.4.1	3/6	500 Mexicans killed.
Bradburn	3.4.4	pre-1868	300 lost (killed or permanently disabled).
Bergara	3.4.4	pre-1868	521 killed and as many wounded.
Bergara & Bargana	3.5.2	3/6	520 killed.
Commercial Bull.	4.1.2	1836	533 killed, 600 mortally wounded.
Briscoe	4.1.3	1836	Repulsed with loss of 450 to 600.
Bernard	4.3.10	1836+	~500 in hospital immediately after fall; in April, 100 in hospital and 200–300 recovering in town; 300–400 died.
Arkansas Gazette	2.17.1	1836	183 defenders. 881 Mexicans killed and 700 wounded during siege. 521 killed in assault.
Ruiz	3.1.1	1860	Lost 1,600 men. Defenders, 182.
Pablo Díaz	3.7.2	1906	6,000 fallen.
Potter	5.1.7	1878	500 killed and wounded.
Williams	5.2.1	1931	1,544 (i.e., follows Sutherland account).
Lord	5.2.2	1961	About 200 killed and 400 casualties.

I do not believe that the senior Mexican sources can be accepted at face value regarding the number of their casualties, although the Texan sources as a whole are not much more reliable.

As noted by Lord, estimates of Mexican casualties range from Almonte's 65 killed (or 60 per Andrade in Filisola 2.6.1) and 223 wounded to Becerra's 2,000 killed and 300-plus wounded. The most careful analyses are those of Potter, Williams, and Lord (5.2.2).[13] Potter took his number of 500-plus from Bergara and Bargana (3.4.4), with the proviso that the figure should have been killed *and* wounded rather than just killed. His earlier version explicitly cited General Bradburn as saying the loss was 300 killed and permanently disabled. Lord basically concurred with Potter's analysis, while Williams believed Potter was too conservative and, after some discussion, concluded that Sutherland's 1,544 and Ruiz's 1,600 were the best figures—emphasizing that a number of these casualties were from "friendly fire." The lack of medical facilities as recorded would have led to serious losses among the wounded.

My opinion is that a casualty rate of approximately 25 percent of the attacking troops would be a maximum possible figure, and that rate—if 1,544 to 1,600 by Sutherland and Ruiz was correct—means that some 6,000 troops had to have attacked. I've already indicated above the evidence that such a number is far too high—rather, that the upper limit is around 2,300. Consequently, I largely concur with Potter's and Lord's analyses.

With this in mind, Dr. Bernard's account (4.3.10) deserves more attention. He reported that the Mexican Army surgeon told him about 500 wounded were brought in on the morning of the attack. In late April, the townspeople said there were 300 or 400 killed, and he observed 100 still in the hospital and 200 to 300 recovering wounded around town. Questions on Dr. Bernard's account are whether it was influenced by later published figures and how accurate his estimated numbers were.

These figures are very close to the numbers given by Caro (2.5.1): 300 killed and 100 wounded. Though Filisola's actual numbers followed Andrade, he contradicted this report by also stating that a greater number of their men died than of the enemy (2.6.1).

Direct data from the Mexican archives shows that 456 men were treated in the Béxar hospital from March 6 to August 1, 1836 (2.4.5). Davis (1998) noted that about 50 were probably the wounded and sick from Cos's surrender in December. Bernard's account is reasonably consistent with these figures. Undoubtedly many other sick were treated during the period covered. If these soldiers represented about half the total number treated, likely a conservative guess, then at least 200 to 300 were wounded on March 6. Neither this source nor Bernard gives a number of troops killed outright. Davis (1997) believed, though he did not give a complete argument, that no more than 75 to 100 died outright in the assault.

The material in the de la Peña Papers tends to follow Andrade's report of lower numbers, approximately 300 killed and wounded. There is not an explicit statement as the number who were killed outright or who died within a day or so of the attack. Borroel put the outright killed at 137.[14] The Andrade report says 60, but it is uncertain whether this document was prepared for military or Santa Anna's political purposes, and therefore I give it less weight than Borroel. From the numbers of defenders alone, it is clear that Santa Anna must have lied in his report by maximizing the number of defenders killed (600 per 2.1.1.10), and Caro stated that he was ordered to misreport the number (2.5.1). So the possibility must be considered that he lied, minimizing his losses, and that the other Mexican sources are derivative of his instructions. This possibility is weakened, though, by the fact that Caro explicitly noted that the number of defenders killed was exaggerated without saying anything about the casualties on their side.

Still, it seems to me that the original figure of 500-plus from Bergara and Barsena, as used by Potter as killed and wounded, is realistic and could even be a little low. This is said recognizing that Bergara and Barsena may have only been repeating thirdhand information circulating in the Mexican camp after the battle. Using Bernard's figures, the Mexican Army would have had about 300 killed, half outright and half later, and another 300 wounded but not mortally. These figures are basically in agreement with the Mexican sources on the number wounded (about 250 to 300), and the discrepancy is limited to the number killed outright or who died right away.

Everyone agrees that the fighting was hard fought. The defenders fired several cannons into massed groups of attackers. Filisola emphasized the number of deaths due to "friendly fire." Santa Anna had not bothered with preparing his medical services. Consequently, I feel that the figure of about 65 killed seems too low—and too helpful for Santa Anna's purposes—to be believed.

The higher figures would mean that the attack was remarkably costly. Santa Anna would have had about a quarter of his actual attacking forces killed or wounded. Even if the lower Andrade figure of 311 killed and wounded is accepted, the casualties were still more than 12 percent of the attacking force.

OTHER AREAS OF BROADER STUDY

A number of more general areas of study, particularly for a broader understanding of the Texas Revolution, are not addressed in the specific Alamo topics reviewed here. Nofi has interesting mini-studies on the financing of the war for Texas and weapons of the Texas Revolution, as well as appendixes on the Texas Revolution at sea, description and structure of the Mexican Army, and the Mexican order of the battle in Texas.[15] Pohl and Hardin 1986 gives an overview of the military history of the Texas Revolution that studies and critiques the strategic thinking and military planning on both sides of the war. Hardin 1994 also gives a comprehensive overview of the political aspects of the Texas Revolution, only briefly alluded to in this work, which probably had as significant an effect on the military response (or lack thereof) by the Texans as any of the actual moves by the soldiers. This work also includes a good set of maps of the Mexican movements during the March 6 battle. DePalo 1997 is a substantive study of the Mexican Army, and one of the few works in English that makes a major application of Mexican sources.[16]

---

1. Fox 1992, see especially figs. 6 and 10, pp. 21 and 27.
2. Wells/1837 is in Hard 1994, 46, and Maverick/1839 in Schoelwer 1988, 425.
3. Details notes for Giraud are also reflected in the unreproduced Everett map of 1846 in Schoelwer 1988, 446.
4. Nofi 1982, 72–73, gives a summary of printed sources consistent with a count of 18 to 21 but doesn't use the DRT research papers.
5. Hard 1994, 54.
6. E.g., Huffines 1999, 197 n. 102; 206 n. 108.
7. Borroel 1997d, 10; 1997a, 36.
8. Williams *SWHQ* 37:7–9.
9. Williams in *SWHQ* 37:8; Filisola 1987, 2:149–51.
10. E.g., *Encyclopedia Britannica*.
11. Filisola 1987, 2:149. Another list deserving of more attention is Filisola's comment in Castañeda 1928, 196, of the forces with him in Texas on April 24, just after he consolidated troops after San Jacinto. His gross total of 4,078 as the total strength of the army is likely not comparing "apples-to-apples" with that of his total count in 1849 of over 6,000 in Filisola 1987, 2:152, or of over 5,000 in the de la Peña papers per Borroel 1997b. Still, for example, the list in Castañeda has one battalion explicitly in Cos's document 2.4.2—the Zapadores. On February 22, they had 193 men including officers. On April 24, Filisola says there were 144. The implication is the missing count of 49 men and officers could be the killed and hospitalized due to the Alamo attack.
12. Also, Huneycutt 1986 gives a detailed, though uncritical, study, especially on the military aspects of the campaign and battle.

13. Potter 1878, 15–17, Williams in *SWHQ* 37:35 n. 72 and 175–78.
14. E.g., Borroel 1997b, 104–6. Also see Borroel 2000, e.g., 66–67 and especially 81–82, where he began a roll call of the Mexican losses by specific individual; and Borroel 2001, 4:53–56, which includes an update of the individual list.
15. Nofi 1982; however, he did not use footnotes, and therefore his sources are not apparent. Subjects include financing, 96–97; weapons, 100–106; appendixes, 181–206.
16. A somewhat notorious book by Long 1990 is a very different type of overview, portraying the figures of the Texas Revolution such as Travis and Houston in a highly negative fashion with no redeeming qualities to be found. My opinion is that Long uses his sources very selectively. His book has numerous footnotes, but on close examination they are either sources already known and used by others (including myself) who see different meanings or significance in them, or are secondary analyses that are much more statements of opinion. Thus, for the main purpose of this book, Long's work was basically useless.

Special Commentary

Deaths of Travis, Bowie, and Crockett

Nearly every source was asked, or thought he or she had to answer, how the leaders of the Alamo died. And nearly every source—or pretended source—had an answer.

It is reasonable to suppose that this was a central interest of the later Texans, and that the real or reputed participants felt the pressure to supply answers. These answers might have been based on real incidents, with an identity added, or on no more than a perception of what the questioners wanted to hear.

There is also the possibility that some participant did observe and record reasonably accurately the death of one of the Alamo leaders.

In considering this possibility, one must ask several questions. First, what is the likelihood of authentic observations of specific individuals during the battle? As the appendix on military details demonstrates, the fall of the Alamo had an abundance of the typical battlefield confusion and chaos. In addition, much of the fighting took place in the dark or low light before sunrise. Furthermore, practically no Mexican soldier would have had reason to know Travis, Bowie, or Crockett by sight, although Bowie likely would have been recognized by some officers, such as Sánchez, who were in Béxar with Cos in December 1835. The chances of one of these rare few happening to be in the vicinity when an Alamo leader fell (if during the actual fighting), and being able to recognize the individual and what was happening, must be close to nil.

Joe, with respect to Travis, is the only individual for whom the above discussion would not apply. Otherwise, virtually the only authentic information possible is that based on observations after the fall when bodies were identified. As a result, the selection of sources cited in this discussion will in general be first concerned with where the individual was found, followed by those that address how the individual died, with more specific issues pooled separately, such as Travis's reported suicide, Bowie's sickness, and Crockett's reported execution.

With these general comments in mind, following is a tabulated study of who said what concerning the events of each man's death. The reliability of the sources, as reviewed in the commentaries throughout this book, is rated here in three categories: *good* if the specific narrative seemed reliable (as reviewed in the respective commentaries) and the source had a reasonable chance to have observed what was claimed; *marginal* if there was evidence that the source was less reliable or unlikely to be in position to observe directly what was stated; and *poor* or *rejected* if the source has been evaluated as of little or no value. Those in the last category, such as Candelaria, Loranca, and Nuñez, are included only for completeness and to support the earlier conclusions that they are useless. This reliability rating is, of course, highly subjective, and others will not concur completely with my assessment.

WILLIAM BARRETT TRAVIS

TRAVIS

Source	Doc. #	Reliability	Where Travis was found
Joe	1.3.4	good	Body found with many bayonet stabs.
Ben	2.12.1, 2.12.2	good	Pointed out body.
Sánchez	2.7.2	good	Map G. In esplanade of battery, Travis died like a soldier.
Ruiz	3.1.1	good	Body found on north battery, shot in head.
Dickinson	1.2.8	marginal	Joe forced to point out bodies after fall.
El Mosquito	2.16.1	marginal	Died with carbine in hand, back to cannon.
			How Travis died
Joe	1.3.4	good	Shot almost immediately, before attackers got over the wall. Travis wounded, killed General Mora before dying.
Telegraph and Texas Register	4.1.1	good	Shot while cheering men. Stated Gen. Mora rushed on him and Travis killed him with sword.
Sánchez	2.7.2, 2.7.3	good	"Died like a hero."
Dickinson	1.2.7	marginal	Killed working a cannon, on top of church.
Nacogdoches	5.1.1	marginal	Fell at breach in wall, killed first officer to enter.
Arkansas Gazette	2.17.1	marginal	Killed in first hour, after he killed commander Gen. Moro with his own hand.

TRAVIS *(continued)*

Source	Doc. #	Reliability	Where Travis was found
			Suicide accounts
Bergara & Bargana	3.4.2	marginal	Killed himself (source actually Peréz per Yoakum).
Houston	3.5.5	marginal	Stabbed himself.
Briscoe	4.1.3	marginal	Shot himself.
Commercial Bulletin	4.1.4.1	marginal	Stabbed himself.
Yoakum	5.1.5	marginal	Peréz source of Travis suicide report.
Williams	5.2.1	—	Analysis in *SWHQ* 37:41–42 n. 88. Accepted Travis's shooting himself.
Lord	5.2.2	—	Analysis.
			More marginal accounts
Esparza	1.5.4	marginal	Directed fire from roof of church? (or during siege).
Sutherland	1.7.1.1, 1.7.1.2 (map)	marginal	Fought with Joe to near northeast corner of church in corral, where he was shot.
Bergara & Barsena	3.4.3	marginal	Last words of Travis, "No rendirse muchachos!"
de la Peña	2.9.1	marginal	Some remained in open, . . . Travis was seen to hesitate, . . . take a few steps and stop, turning his proud face toward us to discharge his shots.
Becerra	2.10.1	marginal	Gen. Cós, Gen. Almonte, Gen. Tolza entered the room. As soon as Gen. Cós saw the gentleman . . . told the other it was Travis . . . the other man was Col. Crockett . . . commander-in-chief . . . with Gen. Castrillón . . . 'Soldiers killed them.' I do not know the names of two Texians, only as given by Gen. Cós.
			Poor or rejected accounts
Loranca	2.13.1	poor	Corpse with Bowie in room to right of gate.
Nuñez	2.14.1	poor	Killed at front door of chapel by cannon fire.
Candelaria	1.9.4	rejected	Fell on southeast side near Menger hotel location.

Travis's is the most straightforward of the death accounts to analyze. A clear description of his end came from the one individual likely to have been next to him: Joe, whose account has already been strongly supported in the Commentary for section 1.3. Both Ruiz and Sánchez support Joe in placing Travis's body at the northern battery, and *El Mosquito* at least places him at one of the cannons with a carbine in hand.

As to the manner of death, again Sánchez supports Joe that Travis died fighting. The same thing was also reported right away in Nacogdoches and in the *Advocate*, though these are weak support, as they were likely to have originated with Joe.

Davis speculated that the story that Travis killed a General Mora originated with a Mexican officer telling Susanna Dickinson, who passed it on.[1] Considering the camp rumors and journalistic license perceived in the relevant accounts, it seems just as likely that the story was "improved" in Gonzales or San Felipe without needing any help from someone closer to the battle.

The earliest accounts, however, said Travis shot himself. Yoakum demonstrated that these stories all originated with Antonio Peréz, who might well have reported an immediate post-battle story in good faith. Williams accepted this version, mostly because Sánchez was not known to her, so the initial story of Peréz was given more weight than the slightly later story of Joe. If Sánchez is accepted, then as a participating Mexican officer, his version supporting Joe has more weight than Peréz. But even if Sánchez's version is not accepted, that Travis commited suicide in the violent and chaotic fighting is unlikely and uncharacteristic of the individual. Therefore, it is reasonable to take Peréz's story as only an unverified rumor that he passed on.

That someone observed Travis as described in de la Peña, who may only have been passing along another camp rumor ("marginal" reliability here means only the death account, not the whole work of de la Peña), falls under the general assessment above of being nearly impossible. The Becerra account appears to be a garbled account of the Crockett execution stories with Travis thrown in purely for added dramatic effect.

JAMES BOWIE

BOWIE

Source	Doc. #	Reliability	Where Bowie was found
Ruiz	3.1.1	good	Found in bed, in room on south side (low barracks, per Potter).
Sánchez	2.7.2	good	Map L. Hospital. In inner room located in fore part toward the main gate, the braggart James Wuy [Bowie] died . . .
Alsbury	1.4.1	good	Moved to low barracks for quarantine.
Dickinson	1.2.14	good	Carried to small room of low barracks on the south side, per Susan Sterling.

BOWIE *(continued)*

Source	Doc. #	Reliability	Where Bowie was found
Dickinson	1.2.8	good	Sick, saw him before and after his death.
Ben	2.12.1, 2.12.2	good	Pointed out body.
Telegraph and Texas Register	4.1.1	good	Murdered in bed.
Bergara & Bargana	3.4.2, 3.5.2	marginal	Killed lying sick in bed.
Esparza	1.5.4	marginal	Placed in smaller room on north side of church. Esparza said saw his corpse before others were taken out of building.
Sutherland	1.7.1.1, 1.7.1.2 (map)	marginal	Shot in bed at "K" on map at west-central wall.
Oury	1.7.5.3	marginal	Oury only explicitly noted him being "sick in the little room by the main gate."
Sterling	4.3.4.4	marginal	In Alamo Church with Susanna Dickinson and nurse in "room known as the baptismal room."
Baker/Fulton	Brown	marginal	South corner room of long barracks. [*In Brown 1892, see Commentary.*]

			Bowie's sickness
Alsbury	1.4.1	good	Had typhoid fever.
Dickinson	1.2.14	good	Had typhoid-pneumonia.
Oury	1.7.5.3	marginal	Active first day, injured by gun carriage (from Tinkle/Potter?).
Esparza	1.5.1	marginal	Ill with fever. Wounded and . . .

			How Bowie died
Joe	1.3.4	good	Fired through door, found in his bed.
Sánchez	2.7.2	good	At hospital "L" to east of main gate, "the braggart son-in-law of Beraméndi [died] like a coward" without resisting.
Dickinson	1.2.7	marginal	Sick in bed, he killed two with pistols before they killed him with sabers.
Esparza	1.5.4	marginal	Fired pistol and rifle, then killed another with knife as shot by a second.

BOWIE (continued)

Source	Doc. #	Reliability	Where Bowie was found
Sutherland	1.7.1.1, 1.7.1.2 (map)	marginal	Too sick to fight.
El Mosquito	2.16.1	marginal	Died hiding under a mattress.
Soldana/Taylor	2.11.1	marginal	Died in room with Mrs. Dickinson, fighting from cot to the end.
Houston	3.5.5	marginal	Shot himself as soldiers approached bed.
Commercial Bulletin	4.1.4.1	marginal	First said to have shot himself, later article states murdered in bed, sick and helpless.
Memphis Enquirer	4.1.5	marginal	Lying in bed, discharged pistols and gun, then killed last assailant with knife.
Becerra	2.10.1	marginal	"In the main building, on the ground-floor, . . . man lying in bed . . . shot the sergeant . . . and a soldier . . . I then fired and killed him. "He seemed too weak to use [*a rifle*]."
Brown/ DeZavala	4.2.1.4	marginal	P. 23 note, not in quoted section. Killed in upper floor of main barracks, having shot one or more of enemy as they entered the room.
Poor/rejected accounts			
Alsbury/ Maverick	1.4.5	poor	Located on second floor of long barracks; bayoneted and died in plaza.
Loranca	2.13.1	poor	Corpse with Travis in room to right of gate.
Nuñez	2.14.1	poor	Sick man in room to left of chapel door, died without fighting.
Saldigua	2.17.2	poor	Survived fall, tongue cut out and burned alive.
Memphis Enquirer	4.1.5	poor	Bowie and six others burnt to death.
Candelaria	1.9.1	rejected	Died few minutes before attackers entered.
Candelaria	1.9.2	rejected	In Alamo church with typhoid, died in her arms.
Candelaria	1.9.3	rejected	Died of pneumonia on 3/5 before battle.
Candelaria	1.9.4	rejected	In little room on north side, next to Crockett. Killed two with pistols before being bayoneted.
Analysis			
Potter	5.1.7	—	In low barracks, reputed he shot down more than one of assailants.

BOWIE *(continued)*

Source	Doc. #	Reliability	Where Bowie was found
Williams	SWHQ	—	Analysis in *SWHQ* 37:16–17 nn. 42–44, Alsbury primary source for Bowie having typhoid-pneumonia. Also from Dickinson's granddaughter Susan Sterling. 37:43–44. Accepts being in church. 43:90–92. Analysis of Bowie's death.
Dobie/Rohrbough	—	—	1939, 48–58, not quoted. General review including Saldigua; no final conclusion.
Lord	5.2.2	—	Low barracks, Alsbury noted his move there.
Davis 1998	544, 561	—	Low barracks left of main gate, too sick to put up any resistance.

Analyzing the accounts of where and how Bowie died is more problematical than with Travis. All the sources agree he was killed in bed; there is more variation on where that took place. An important consensus is that it was in the low barracks behind the south wall, probably in a room just to the right of the main gate. Ruiz and Sánchez put him there, Alsbury says he was moved there to avoid spreading his illness to others, and this location is supported by the possibly independent sources of Dickinson's granddaughter Susan Sterling (1.2.14) and Oury (though the latter excerpt comes from a book that has Tinkle as a source and therefore may not have been independent). On the other hand, Esparza (also note affidavit of Sterling, 4.4.4.9) puts him in a room on the north side of the church. This is mildly supported by the Dickinson interview for the adjutant general (1.2.8), in which she said that she saw him after his death. The church was the only structure of which she was likely to have seen the inside after the fall, so if she did see him where he was killed, that is the only reasonable place. The accounts are consistent if she saw his body in the plaza after it was dragged out of his sickroom. A third location was given by Sutherland, who put him in a room on the west wall. While one should take the Sutherland account seriously, this unsupported statement should be considered misinformation he received from local residents a few years after the battle. Another reasonable possibility is that Bowie was located there at the time Sutherland left on February 23, and was moved later to the low barracks as per Alsbury's account, so Sutherland was misled when he returned to the scene later.

Another possible source not included in this book is a statement in Brown's *History of Texas* that in August 1837, Judge Baker, chief justice of Béxar County, showed Col. George Fulton the upper-floor south corner room of the main barracks (the convent/long barracks) as Bowie's location.[2] This account also has Crockett falling just outside the northeast corner of the low barracks. As the account is at least three times removed through nonparticipants, it does not seem to carry much weight. It does have some interest, however, as De Zavala used it in her book around the time she was try-ing to save the long barracks from destruction.[3]

As to the nature of his illness, there is no apparent reason to doubt Alsbury's statement that it was typhoid fever. A story that he was injured moving a cannon the second day of the siege was picked up by later works such as Tinkle and Oury, but this is unsupported by the original documents.

A central highlight of numerous accounts of the fall of the Alamo is a final fight of Bowie, where he lifts himself from his sickbed and manages to shoot and/or stab a couple attackers before expiring with his famous knife in his last opponent. There are several early versions of this story, and the appropriateness of such an ending for this great fighter makes them nearly irresistible. However, the evidence is not so good. The story is supported in the Dickinson account per Morphis (1.2.7), for example, but Morphis had a tendency to "improve" Susanna's narrative when describing something she would not have personally seen. Most of the other Bowie accounts are compara-bly weak.

Only two accounts have a real possibility of being based on good information: those of Joe and Sánchez. It was reported that Joe had to point out the bodies after the battle, and therefore he could have observed something of Bowie's final struggle, such as that he fired through the door at his assailants. But the account does not directly attribute the observation to Joe, saying, "Bowie is said to have fired through the door of his room." This statement in fact implies that the information was *not* from Joe, and the Bowie knife is missing. Sánchez said Bowie died without resisting, adding with obvious prior dislike that he died like a coward. Bowie was the best known of the Texan leaders to the Mexican community in Bexar, and as an opponent to Cos and Sánchez in December, it is to be expected that he would have been an object of contempt to the soldiers associated with Béxar. Therefore, it is reasonable that Sánchez was reporting a story circulating immediately after the fall, and that Bowie's illness was misinterpreted as cowardliness, especially as he was fit and func-tional when the townspeople last saw him thirteen days before.

If one accepts the Rose/Zuber story (1.8.1.1), then shortly before March 6, Bowie was strong enough to understand what was happening and to take some ini-tiative in a characteristic manner.

Five important scholars examined the stories of Bowie. Potter was cautious and apparently used Joe's version: that Bowie was in the low barracks and was "reputed" to have shot down more than one of his assailants ("If he had sufficient strength . . . we may safely assume that it was done"). Williams gave the most weight to Dickin-son/Morphis, Dickinson/Sterling, and Esparza as eyewitnesses, so she placed him in the church. To address the discrepancy with Alsbury, Williams had Bowie being moved into the church for better care a day or so before the fall. Edward G. Rohrbough gave a useful descriptive synopsis of the numerous versions, but he did not analyze their discrepancies or make final conclusions.[4] Lord gave Alsbury and Sánchez the most weight and put Bowie in the low barracks. Davis did likewise, adding the *El Mosquito* account.[5] He concluded—not unreasonably, considering the evidence—that Bowie was too weak to even remove his blanket and might not have known what was happening. As he was not placed in the hospital to avoid contagion, his condition was even more readily interpreted as simply an attempt to hide due to cowardice.

I too believe that Sánchez, in complement to Alsbury, has the most weight in placing Bowie in the low barracks, but that there is no consistent, compelling information available as to whether Bowie was strong enough at the end to take any action.

DAVID CROCKETT

CROCKETT

Source	Doc. #	Reliability	Where Crockett was found
Dickinson	1.2.7	good	Lying dead and mutilated between church and two-story barracks, with peculiar cap at his side.
Ruiz	3.1.1	good	Found toward west, in small fort opposite the city. [*Potter makes this the west battery in interior of plaza.*]
Sutherland	1.7.1.1, 1.7.1.2 (map)	marginal	Found near picket wall with 25 dead.
Baker/Fulton	Brown	marginal	Just outside northeast corner of low barracks (*see comments earlier under Bowie*).

			How Crockett died
Dickinson	1.2.8	good	He was killed, she believed [*sense?*]. Joe forced to point out bodies after fall.
Joe	1.3.4	good	Surrounded with 24 dead enemy.
Ben	2.12.2	good	Pointed out body. 16 dead Mexicans around, one with Crockett's knife in bosom. "Had the biggest pile."
Ben (or Joe)	2.12.3	good	"Had the biggest pile."
Sánchez	2.7.2, 2.7.3	good	"Horrified by some cruelties, among others, the death of an old man named Cochran and of a boy about fourteen."
Esparza	1.5.4	marginal	Crockett slew many with rifle, pistol, and knife. Clubbed with rifle until overwhelmed. Fell in front of large double doors, which he defended with force by his side. Surrounded by a heap of slain.

CROCKETT *(continued)*

Source	Doc. #	Reliability	Where Crockett was found
Yorba	3.7.1	marginal	Saw Crockett lying dead, coat and shirt soaked with blood due to ball or bayonet thrust to chest.
Mexican Capt./ Taylor	2.11.1	marginal	Crockett last man slain, fought like infuriated lion. In small room with gun in hand, brained Mexicans at door. Shot broke right arm, fought with knife before being bayoneted.
Soldana/Taylor	2.11.1	marginal	Killed in room to left of door using knife. Shot broke right arm, then used gun as club until shot. Last defender.
Telegraph and Texas Register	4.1.1	marginal	Found surrounded by piles of assailants.
Nacogdoches	5.1.1	marginal	Crockett had 16 guns, slain foes surrounded him.
Field	5.1.2	marginal	Came into Dickinson's apartment, fell on knees, committed himself to God, went out and was soon killed.
Commercial Bulletin	4.1.2	marginal	Killed 20 using breech of gun before falling.
Briscoe	4.1.3	marginal	Fell fighting like a tiger.
			Execution accounts
Bergara & Barsena	3.4.1,	good	7 executed on orders of Santa Anna.
Caro	2.5.1	good	5 defenders discovered by Castrillón, executed per Santa Anna.
Filisola	2.6.1	good	There were "atrocious authorized acts."
Cruz y Arocha	3.6.1	maginal	A few tried to surrender, Santa Anna made signal, and they were executed.
Commercial Bulletin	4.1.2	marginal	7 asked for quarter, continued fighting when refused.
Dickinson	4.1.6	marginal	Of the 5 who survived for a moment, 2 were pursued into Dickinson's room and killed.
			Crockett as one of executed
Commonwealth	4.1.8	marginal	6 surrendered to Castrillón, including Crockett. Executed by orders of Santa Anna.

CROCKETT *(continued)*

Source	Doc. #	Reliability	Where Crockett was found
Dolson/ Connelly	4.3.7	marginal	6 surrendered to Castrillón, including Crockett. Executed by orders of Santa Anna.
de la Peña	2.9.1	marginal	7 surrendered, including naturalist David Crockett. Santa Anna ordered executions.
Becerra	2.10.1	marginal	Gens. Cós, Almonte, and Tolza entered room. Cós identified men there as Travis and Crockett. Soldiers killed them.
Arkansas Gazette	4.1.4.2	marginal	With Bonham, asked to surrender, continued fighting when told no terms would be given.
Urissa	2.15.1	poor	Old man, single surviving prisoner of Castrion [*Castrillón*], shot on orders of Santa Anna.
Poor/rejected accounts			
Dickinson	1.2.13	poor	Found in confessional room in northeast corner with pile of dead Mexicans around him.
Cós/Patrick	1.8.1.7	rejected	Cós took him, tried to stab Santa Anna.
Candelaria	1.9.4	rejected	Fell at door in heap of attackers.
Nuñez	2.14.1	poor	Killed inside front door, kept shooting with gun, knocked down by saber, then bayoneted.
Analysis			
Potter	5.1.7	—	Found in west battery in plaza behind central part of wall, per Ruiz.
Zuber	1.8.1.7	—	Cós described execution, but as example of how Alamo stories were invented.
Williams	SWHQ	—	SWHQ 37:43. Per Dickinson/Morphis, between church and long barracks. Tennessee boys defended palisade per Kennedy, *Telegraph and Texas Register*, Gray.
Lord	5.2.2	—	It's possible de la Peña described execution, but also possible Crockett went down fighting.
Kilgore	—	—	Analysis, not quoted. Executed.
Groneman 1994	2.9.2	—	Analysis, not quoted (n. 45). Died fighting.
Crisp 1994	—	—	Analysis, not quoted. Executed.
Davis	—	—	1998, 562–63. No definite conclusion.

The death of David Crockett has exercised more emotions than any other single aspect of the Alamo story. The heart of the issue is whether Crockett fell fighting or survived the battle and then surrendered or was captured and executed. The sources themselves are more divergent on this topic than most and can support any of these versions. This topic is taken seriously enough by some that a scholar has actually gotten hate mail and threatening phone calls (see the Special Commentary on de la Peña, 2.9) for publishing something contrary to popular perceptions. Two full books, Dan Kilgore's *How Did Davy Die?* and Bill Groneman's *Defense of a Legend* (1994), have been published in recent decades to argue alternative sides. The only sure guarantee for this short review is that it will not end the arguments.

In trying to physically locate Crockett after his death, most of the sources I consider "good" for such information place him near his originally assigned position (Sutherland, 1.7.1.1) at the palisade wall in the mini-plaza in front of the church. Many of these sources also have him surrounded by dead assailants. Dickinson, in one of the strongest pieces given by Morphis, was said to have even remembered his peculiar cap (not to be taken as a coonskin) lying by his side. She also noted in the adjutant general interview that Joe was forced to point out bodies after the fall, which supports Joe's descriptions that he saw him surrounded by fallen foes. These descriptions are also supported by Ben, a source I give considerable weight. Two important secondary sources, the *Telegraph and Texas Register* and Sutherland, follow suit. The major discrepancy is Ruiz, who said he found Crockett "toward the west, and in the small fort opposite the city," which Potter clarified as the battery behind the center of the west wall (clearly shown on De Zavala's and Potter's maps). These sources are the core basis for believing that Crockett died fighting.

When sources go a little further and describe the final scene, there are immediately problems with accounts that are otherwise useful and acceptable. Esparza in 1907 had Crockett right at the front double doors of the chapel; the Mexican captain and Soldana placed him in a little room, presumably inside the church; and Field included a bit of drama unsupported by any of the more authentic Dickinson accounts. I do not think these descriptions carry much weight. An opinion on why they were included in otherwise fairly valid accounts will be discussed shortly.

The next set of documents consists of several accounts of the execution of a small group of defenders, about six or seven, who were captured or surrendered.[6] In these accounts, General Castrillón is credited with accepting their surrender (if the account states that they surrendered rather than being captured) and taking them to Santa Anna with a request to spare their lives; Santa Anna contemptuously demands to know why enemies are still alive; and the prisoners are then immediately executed in front of Santa Anna. This basic story circulated so soon after the fall, and was given by so many different sources, that I, like most scholars, believe it reflects an actual incident.

Davis argued the possibility that it was only one story that went from Barsena and Bergara to Houston to New Orleans to Mexico and back to the Mexican prisoners in Galveston after San Jacinto. They in turn reinforced the story as a way of attacking Santa Anna and making points with their jailers. He also noted the possibility that Dolson might have been the source for the Caro account of this execution.[7]

C. D. Huneycutt gave an interesting speculation that the executed prisoners were Mexicans who had collaboratored with the Texans, which would explain some of the reluctance shown by the soldiers present.[8]

But several accounts take the story one step further, maintaining that Crockett was one of the prisoners. Looking at my reliability assessment given for the documents in this group, it is obvious that I consider support for this possibility weaker than for the earlier questions. But deeper analysis is warranted.

Regarding the scholars who studied these accounts, Potter believed Ruiz's was the most significant (though Potter wrote long before some of the relevant accounts were discovered). Williams gave the most weight to the Dickinson/Morphis account, adding that the idea that Crockett's Tennessee boys fell defending their assigned post at the palisade fence was quickly picked up and spread by the *Telegraph and Texas Register,* Gray, and Kennedy. Lord hedged, indicating the importance of de la Peña and Dolson on one hand, and Joe and Dickinson on the other. Davis, probably with more sense than the rest of us, reviewed the ambiguities in the sources and saw no reason to put forth any account as strongest.[9] William Zuber (1.8.1.7) gave a story attributed to Cos to show "how easily the lies of idle talkers may find their way into history."

Dan Kilgore used the de la Peña diary as a central document in a collection of material supporting the execution of Crockett. He gave primary weight to Caro, Urriza, and Becerra, but I consider the last two to be more than usually questionable.

Chariton gave the most weight to Dickinson, Joe, Soldana, and Nuñez and believed Crockett died fighting.[10] He also argued that Kilgore's quotations were incomplete and that the full quotes weakened Kilgore's arguments.

Groneman (1994) rejected the de la Peña diary, with its Crockett execution story, as a fraud. As discussed in the Special Commentary (section 2.9), I believe that most of the diary might be valid, with the Crockett account and that of Travis's death unwarranted insertions based on camp rumor or later information he obtained in Mexico.

James Crisp countered Groneman and added important external evidence in support of the basic validity of de la Peña.[11] He joined Kilgore in giving the most weight to de la Peña and therefore thought Crockett was executed.

I rate de la Peña to be of "marginal" reliability *on this and the Travis death accounts only.* In particular, the "naturalist" description of Crockett seems to me hearsay information that de la Peña added to flesh out the story.[12] But this does not mean that the mostly firsthand information in his account is not of the highest importance. As with numerous other sources cited in this work, Esparza for example, personal experiences in an account can be of high reliability and value while the additional inserted secondhand material is not.

Those who wish to explore the debate on the death of Crockett further might start with chapter 16, "Crockett's Many Deaths," in Groneman 1994 for an excellent bibliographical survey. Another analysis missed there and worth attention is Todd Harburn's commentary (1991) reacting to a book by Jeff Long. A recent continuation of the debate is by Michael Lind with responses by James Crisp and Groneman (1998 for all three).

We are left asking why did such divergent stories circulate. Not surprisingly, I have some opinions.

The 1950s Disney television show "Davy Crockett, King of the Wild Frontier," has been cited repeatedly as a reason why the execution story is hard to accept. This viewpoint holds that the Hollywood image of Crockett, (played by Fess Parker on TV and John Wayne in the 1960 movie), has created an image of heroism that cannot stand up to alternate scenarios. I think this charge has been overused, and it is time to question how fragile people's psyches can be from the influence of a TV show over forty years ago that is rapidly becoming irrelevant as increasingly fewer people even remember the show.[13]

More serious is the observation that practically *every* source felt the pressure of public interest regarding the demise of the leaders of the Alamo. Travis's end was described right away by Joe and widely disseminated. Bowie's illness was well documented and accepted, though for a fitting closure on his life, details about the Bowie knife or some other fighting weapon in the bosom of an enemy could easily have been added to embellish the story. That left Crockett with only a less personal observation in the *Telegraph and Texas Register* of being found surrounded by dead enemy. Because of the pressure of constant questioning, any source that did not explicitly cover the subject of Crockett, in addition to Travis and Bowie, had something added—often vague enough that it might have been based on a real incident and attributed to Crockett—by either the original individual in later years or the assistance of a newswriter or editor. This would explain why otherwise fairly consistent accounts do not match up in this case.

The other essential factor revolves around the battle of San Jacinto, with the capture of Santa Anna and his attempted release by Sam Houston in return for a secret agreement to accept Texas independence. The significance of the *Commonwealth* account (4.1.8) and the Dolson letter (4.3.7) is the hatred they reveal in the Texas Army toward Santa Anna ("Such are the monsters we have had to deal with . . .") and the desire to see him executed.[14] After the Alamo and Goliad, this attitude is not surprising, but it gave a powerful ulterior motive for describing the death of Crockett as an execution ordered by Santa Anna. What better way to ensure Santa Anna's execution than to make him directly responsible for the execution of a Texan leader? Clearly the Mexican general was not involved in the direct attack at the north wall of the Alamo with Travis, or in the sickroom of Bowie, or even in Goliad with Fannin. But he had already been reported as responsible for the execution of six or seven prisoners at the Alamo, and the famed Crockett was still available.

An argument that this is not mere speculation is that not one of the Crockett execution sources is truly confirmed as being attributable *prior* to San Jacinto. Lord (5.2.2) cited a possible exception in the *New Orleans True American,* but no copy of that newspaper has been located, and there is strong evidence (4.1.4.1, 4.1.4.2, and associated commentary) that the Crockett attribution might have been done in the *Arkansas Gazette* as an editor's distortion of the original story. Therefore, such stories would be highly useful to the end—made explicit by Dolson—of justifying and forcing the execution of Santa Anna. I submit that little further reason is necessary to understand the creation and dissemination of this story, even into Mexico and into such accounts as that of de la Peña, who could well have observed or known of an execution of some prisoners.

Thus I give the heaviest weight to the accounts that place Crockett in the mini-plaza in front of the Alamo church and behind the palisade fence he was assigned to defend. Had he stayed in that assigned position, after the Mexican troops poured into the plaza, they would have swept over the low wall and confronted Crockett just where most sources placed his corpse. It is also practically the only area that Susanna Dickinson must have walked through on the way out from the chapel through the main gate in the low barracks after the fall. Even the Ruiz account might be a misinterpretation or misremembrance of the low wall separating the plaza from the front of the church.[15]

The one source that ties both parts of this argument together is the low-keyed account of Ben. His matter-of-fact statement about being asked to identify the bodies and seeing Crockett surrounded by foes directly supports Dickinson's and Joe's accounts. Indirectly, it is also a significant denial of the Crockett execution stories, as Santa Anna and Almonte would have had no need for Ben (or Joe, or Ruiz) to point out the body of Crockett if the *Commonwealth* and Dolson stories were correct. For these reasons, I accept the evidence of those documents that have him falling close to his assigned post during heavy fighting.

But a more fundamental point should also be made. I agree with Groneman's comments that "Crockett's life was more important than the manner of his death" and that there is "nothing dishonorable in surrender in the face of overwhelming odds after a battle becomes hopeless."[16] I think no less of the six or seven defenders for having still been alive at the end of the attack, regardless of whether Crockett was one of them, or of the others who fled the Alamo after it was overrun, to be hunted down by Sesma's cavalry. Who can answer for how hard they fought or how they initially survived the assault? Should some surprise discovery tomorrow truly prove that David Crockett was an executed prisoner in reversal of my assessment, my opinion of him would not change one iota. All the defenders of the Alamo defined and proved their courage just by being there the morning of March 6, 1836.

1. Davis 1998, 732–34 n. 102, gives a general analysis of the death of Travis. Earlier, Hardin 1987 also gives an overview of the various accounts.
2. Brown 1892, 1:581–82.
3. De Zavala 1917, 23.
4. Rohrbough in Dobie, 48–58.
5. Davis 1998, 725 n. 31; 728 n. 78; 734–36 n. 104.
6. Kilgore 1978, 47, notes the distinction.
7. Davis 1997, 16, 21–25, 34. Dolson note, 27–28.
8. Huneycutt 1986, 99–100.
9. Davis 1997, 1998, 737–38 n. 108. (One could hope a letter on the Alamo by Castrillón might still be found in Mexico.)
10. Chariton 1992, 43–48.
11. Crisp 1994, 1996, 1998.

12. Note there is different, less explicit wording on Crockett in the de la Peña papers per Borroel 1997a, 33 and 1997c, 9–10.
13. Though, true, this editor did have a "coonskin cap" at the time! I didn't keep it, however.
14. See Henson 1990 for a detailed study of the situation with prisoners after San Jacinto.
15. For an alternate opinion, see Durham (1997), who takes Ruiz much more literally.
16. Groneman 1994, 85, 88.

One of the first concluding comments that can be made, and one of the initial surprises to me, is that much research remains to be done on the Alamo. There is archival material still not closely examined or incorporated into Alamo scholarship, and detailed analyses of many important sources have not yet been performed. Many issues and questions have yet to be resolved, though with some topics, like the death of Crockett, such a goal is no doubt unrealistic. This work has been an effort to understand what happened in a particular historical event, and to set forth the basis for that understanding.

One issue about historical research, alluded to in specific cases and worth discussing more generally, is that very different understandings can be derived from the same set of information. The same collection of sources can be used to "prove" very different hypotheses, or to draw very different conlusions. Some writers use sources selectively either to state as established fact something that is not, or to present only such evidence that supports their claim while ignoring conflicting reports.

A significant market exists that emphasizes supplying validation to satisfy existing perceptions, instead of adding to understanding or balancing judgments. Thus, our own (e.g., segments of the public's) interests are reflected rather than the reputed subject matter. For example, there is a regular industry generating publications on Kennedy assassination conspiracies. Both indicators noted above are present in abundance. The vast bulk of quoted material used to "prove" this or that conspiracy was part of the Warren Commission documentation and readily available. Selected pieces are presented in isolation, along with asserted "facts" to make the case. Numerous books claim to prove many different—or even outright contradictory—scenarios. That essentially the same sources of information are so used can be an immediate indication that the analyses are biased.

Why are such publications so common? Clearly, money is a prime motivation for many, but there are also those who are truly passionate about their subjects. Perhaps the sense of being an "insider"—the knowledgable member of an elite or exclusive group with access to more information than the general public—is another important impetus. Whatever the motivation, however, it is necessary that we recognize the extent to which these motivations can influence our own perceptions.

Tabloid history is another example that purports misused or neglected information as fact. Biographies are particularly susceptible. The dilemma facing this style of history is that the negatives are emphasized, and this can undermine our efforts to achieve balanced understanding. For example, should the significance of Alexander the Great or Genghis Khan be dismissed because of their unpleasant characteristics or misdeeds?

With any history, we must be careful that we not are learning more about the author or editor than about the subject. Because history is about humans, we should focus our attention on whether there is a lesson to be learned from the actions of others. Do we learn more about who we are? Do we discover more about what we are capable of—bad and good, or both?

What do we know about the siege and fall of the Alamo, and how do we know it? My stated goal in the Preface was to study the "facts" as given by the sources for a particular sequence of events in 1836, and to rationally assess them and their logical consistency with each other. Along the way, the study also represented the need for critical thinking and evaluation of a complex circumstance.

What is the appeal of the Alamo story? Why is it important to understand the reality of those thirteen days in 1836—or, for that matter, any event or personage from the past?

Historical events are no more unambiguous or clear than the events and decisions of our own lives. Does this ambiguity and lack of clarity make the event less significant or irrelevant? I think not. Because of their applicability to deeper issues of our lives, the lessons we can learn from the Alamo are too important to ignore.

The Alamo is about courage. Nearly two hundred people decided to die rather than surrender at the Alamo. This courage won the immediate and lasting respect of all, even the Mexican opponents including Santa Anna. Who among us can claim that we wouldn't, given the choice, surrender in a hopeless situation or take a practical, sensible way out? We can always say, with Rose, "I was not ready to die," or, in less dramatic situations, not be ready to take serious risks.

The Alamo defenders were a random collection of real human beings who reflected characteristics of all of us. Any one of them could have gone over the wall and gotten out of there. Yet all but one chose not to surrender or flee, but to die. We all are faced with real choices, and hard ones at that. We all wonder whether we can, and will, respond to the challenges and crises imposed on us. The Alamo suggests that we can. And deeper still, history gives us the most reliable and relevant insights into our own human behavior and actions and capabilities. The irresistible draw of the Alamo story in particular, and history in general, is what we might learn about our own potential.

ACKNOWLEDGMENTS

For the assistance I have received over the years, I am extremely grateful to a considerable number of the staff, not all of whom I can acknowledge by name, of libraries, archives, other agencies, and organizations. I especially wish to recognize the help of Ralph Elder of the Center for American History, whose enthusiasm and professionalism initiated and strongly encouraged my numerous faltering steps toward this book. I also want to express a special gratitude for the late Lon Tinkle, whose book first "turned me on" to the Alamo story when I was in my young teens.

I would like to thank the following, in roughly chronological order: the Center for American History at the University of Texas at Austin, including Ralph Elder, William Richter, Stefanie Wittenbach, Alison Beck, and Ned Brierley; the Archives Divisions of the Texas State Library, especially Michael Green, Sergio Velasco, and Donaly Brice; the Texas General Land Office, especially John Molleston; the Daughters of the Republic of Texas Library at the Alamo, including Evelyn Belcher, Cathy Herpich, Martha Utterback, Warren Strickler, Jeanette Phinney, Sally Koch, and Nancy Skokan; the Bancroft Library at the University of California at Berkeley, including David Kessler, Baiba Strods, Teri Rinne, Wayne Silka, and Walter Brem; the Beinecke Rare Book and Manuscript Library of Yale University, including Bridget Burke, Jessica McLaughlin, Lynn Braunsdorf, and Kevin Glick; the Center for Archaeological Research at the University of Texas at San Antonio, including Robert Hard, Donna Edmondson, Anne Fox, and Raymond Mauldin; the General Libraries of the University of Texas at Austin, including Susan Macicak; Patricia Bozeman of the University of Houston; the Arizona Historical Society, including Rose Byrne and Riva Dean; Courtney Page of Tulane University Libraries; Gloria Williams of the Parker County District Clerk Office, Weatherford, Texas; Office of the Nacogdoches County Clerk; the Mississippi Department of Archives and History; the Louisiana Division of the New Orleans Public Library; the DeGolyer Library of Southern Methodist University; Lic. Claudia Constantine Roca of the Archivo General de la Nacion in Mexico; Millie Reynolds of the Greene County District Library in Ohio; B. K. Brennan and Amy Kyte of the Youngstown State University; Amy Bolt of the Library of Michigan; George Ward of the Texas State Historical Association; the

Corporations and the Statutary Documents Sections of the Secretary of State Office in Austin; Edward Privino of the Central Mapping Office, City of San Antonio; Mendell Morgan and Warren Strickler of the University of the Incarnate Word, San Antonio; Jane Smoot; Mark Lambert of the San Jacinto Museum of History; Cornelius C. Smith, Jr.; Mary Waters of the South San Francisco Public Library; William C. Davis; Christine Colburn of the Newberry Library; Roger Meyers of Special Collections, University of Arizona; Roger Borroel, La Villita Publications; John Wheat; Shirley Rodnitzky of the University of Texas at Arlington; Alfred Rodriguez and John Leal of the Office of the County Clerk, Bexar County; Jake Ivey; Stephen Hardin; Gladys Filizola and Susan Lewis; James Crisp; H. Perry Driggs, Jr.; Fernando Cordova; and Gen. Juan Manuel de La O Gonzales of the Direccion General De Archivo E Historia, Secretaria De La Defensa Nacional, Mexico. Any conclusions or opinions I derived from anyone's information or assistance is my sole responsibility.

An extensive number of copyright permissions were required for this work, and I would like to acknowledge the following publishers, archives, libraries, and individuals for granting permissions to publish or reprint documents, as explicitly cited in the bibliographical references in the header of each document:

Arizona Historical Society, Tuscon

Association for the Study of Afro-American Life and History, Inc., Washington, D.C.

The Bancroft Library, University of California, Berkeley

Borroel, Roger (La Villita Publications, E. Chicago, IN)

Center for American History, The University of Texas at Austin

Center for Archaeological Research, The University of Texas at San Antonio

Daughters of the Republic of Texas Library, San Antonio

Davis Bros. Publishing Company (Texian Press), Waco

Direccion General De Archivo E Historia, Secretaria De La Defensa Nacional, Mexico

Driggs, H. Perry

Eakin Press, Sunbelt Media, Inc.

Filizola, Mrs. Gladys

HarperCollins Publishers (Appendix "Riddles of the Alamo," 198–212 of *A Time to Stand*, by Walter Lord. Copyright (c) 1961 by Walter Lord. Reprinted by permission of HarperCollins Publishers, Inc.)

Library Chronicle of the University of Texas

Lifshey, Adam

Presidial Press, Austin

Southern Historical Association

Smith Jr., Cornelius C.

Smoot, Miss Jane

Texas A&M University Press

Texas Folklore Society

Texas General Land Office
Texas State Historical Scociety *(Southwestern Historical Quarterly)*
Texas State Library and Archives Commission
Tulane University, Special Collections
University Libraries of the University of Tennessee in Knoxville
University of Houston Libraries, courtesy of Special Collections
University of Oklahoma Press
University of Texas Press (From *The Alamo Remembered: Tejano Accounts and Perspectives,* by Timothy M. Matovian, Copyright © 1995. By permission of the University of Texas Press.)
Wheat, John (for Work for Hire © Todd Hansen)
Wordware Publishing Company, Plano, TX
Yale University, Beinecke Rare Book & Manuscript Library
Additional thanks are due to the highly professional assistance from Stackpole Books, particularly Leigh Ann Berry, Judith Schnell, Ryan Masteller, Christopher Evans, with exceptional copyediting by Joyce Bond.

Last, but certainly not least, is special gratitude also to those others who have helped me as a personal effort, especially Jane Smoot for her enthusiasm and encouragement, Ronald Larson, Esq., for his orientation on the legal aspects, the late John Picardi for serving as my "in-house" translator, and my sister Allene for—among very many things—articulating the legacy of our father per the dedication. Finally, to my wife, Lonny, go thanks and love for her editing skills, for being my best and most helpful critic, and for her patience and support through the long incubation.

BIBLIOGRAPHY

This Bibliography is not intended to be comprehensive on everything written on the Alamo. I doubt such a project is feasible. There is a vast literature on the subject, but a considerable proportion of it is derivative of the source materials rather than a direct contribution to finding or understanding that material. Numerous works do not clearly reference the origin of specific information and therefore are of limited help toward accomplishing the purpose of this book. Other works are included here that are not explicitly cited in this book but are of real value in understanding some of the secondary topics only touched upon. Also included are many thoughtful analyses of the documents, even if not specifically used.

For identifying and locating source documents, Amelia Williams's dissertation and the Bibliography in Walter Lord's *A Time to Stand* were the ideal starting places. Despite my effort to use the original documents, or versions as close to the originals as possible, the earlier compilations of source material, particularly John H. Jenkins's *Papers of the Texas Revolution* and Timothy Matovina's *The Alamo Remembered . . .* , are still of considerable value.

For the reader interested in a continuous narrative of events—the product of an author's or editor's having evaluated and selected from among the source materials—there are several conscientious works. Especially thorough are John Myers Myers's *The Alamo,* Lon Tinkle's *Thirteen Days to Glory,* and Walter Lord's *A Time to Stand.* More recent works, which include the account of the Alamo siege and fall as part of a larger effort, are Steven Hardin's *Texas Iliad,* covering the military history of the Texas Revolution, and William Davis's *Three Roads to the Alamo,* consisting of interwoven biographies of Crockett, Bowie, and Travis.

Without the existence of the archives and libraries, and the staff waiting to help all comers, writers would have no chance to accomplish any meaningful study.

Archival Collections

Texas State Library, Archives Division (TSLA).
Adjutant General (RG-401), Army Papers.
Adjutant General (RG-401), General Correspondence.
Adjutant General (RG-401), Miscellaneous Papers.
Adjutant General (RG-401), Strays—Alamo Dead and Monument.
Alamo Papers, Claimants to Property.
Alsbury, Juana Navarro. November 1, 1857. Petition to Senate and House of Representatives.
Biographical and Historical Files, Travis, W. B.
Carson (Sam P.) Letters.
Companion Battle Paintings. Vol. 1, Dawn at the Alamo (also McArdle, HA).
Dickenson, Susanna. October 16, 1836. Petition to the Honorable House of Representatives of the Republic of Texas.
Ford (John Salmon) Papers.
Hearne, Madge, Collection. Letters, Sam Houston, 1835–June 1836.
Home Papers.
Houston, A. J., Collection.
Indian Affairs Papers (RG-005).
Lamar, Mirabeau Buonaparte, Papers.
Manuscript collections, Juan N. Seguín.
Memorial files: Juana Alsbury, John Sutherland.
McArdle, H. A. *Companion Battle Paintings.* Vol. 1, *Dawn at the Alamo.*
Republic Claims: Allen, James; Benites, Miguel; Bernal, Agustin; Bonham, James; Bowie, James; Criswell, William; Cruz, Antonio; Diaz, Julian; Dickerson (Dickinson), Almeron and Susanna; George, James; Guerrero, Brigido; Nash, J. H.; Neill, James; Rose, Lewis; Smith, John W.; Smith, Joshua G.; Sutherland, John; Travis, William; Tumlinson, George W.; Ware, Joseph; Xaimes, Felipe. (Not all files for all names.)
Republic Claims, Pension Claims: Guerrero, Brigidio.
Secretary of State (RG-307), Communications Received.
Secretary of State (RG-307), Consultation, General Council.
Secretary of State (RG-307), Executive Record Book.
Secretary of State (RG-307), Memorials.
Secretary of State (RG-307), Private Manuscripts.
Secretary of State (RG-307), Records—Domestic Correspondence.
Secretary of State (RG-307), Records of the Governor.
Secretary of State (RG-307), Series 64/ Proceedings.

Center for American History (including the Eugene C. Barker Texas History Center), University of Texas at Austin (CAH).
Almonte (Juan Nepomuceno) Papers.
Archivo General de Mexico, Secretaria de Guerra y Marina. Vols. 334, 335.
Barett (Don Carlos) Papers.
Biographical Files, Allen, James L.
Biographical Files, Dickenson Family.
Biographical Files, Dickenson, Almeron.
Biographical Files, Dickenson, Suzanna A. Wilkinson.
Biographical (General) Files, Ford, John S.
Biographical Files, Sutherland, John.
Blake (Robert Bruce) Collection. N.d. (1940).
Brown (John Henry) Papers.
Colquitt (Oscar Branch) Papers.
De Zavala (Adina) Papers.
Dimitt (Philip) Papers.
Fontaine (W. W.) Papers.
Ford (John S.) Papers.
Hassell Family Papers.
Holly (Mary Austin) Papers. Notes and items. . . .
Index of Texas Newspapers.
Kemp (Louis Wiltz) Papers.
Labastida Plat. N.d. (c. 1836).
Mixon (Ruby) Papers.
Peña (José Enrique de la) Collection. 1835–40, 1857.
Republic of Texas, General File.
Sanchez-Navarro (José Juan) Papers. Translation of Sanchez Navarro Papers.
Sanchez-Navarro Capt. José Juan. N.d. (c. 1836). "Ayudentía de inspección de
    Nuevo León y Tamaulipas, vol. 2.
Seguín (Juan N.) Papers.
Sutherland (John) Papers.
Williams (Amelia Worthington) Papers.
Zuber (William P.) Papers. "Biographies of Texas Veterans."

Archives and Records Division, Texas General Land Office, Austin.
Cummings, David P. File C-1936.
Esparza, Gregorio. File C-2558.
Guerrera, Jose Maria. File RV-1384.
Guerrero, Brigidio. File C-3416.
Losoya, Toribio. File C-5027 (or 5026).
Moore, Willis A. File C-5893.
Muster Rolls.
Nava, Andres. File C-6073.

Rose, James M. File C-7115.
Rose, Lewis (or Louis?). Nacogdoches First Class #312.
Warnell, Henry. File C-8490.

Daughters of the Republic of Texas Library at the Alamo (DRT).
Alamo Defenders/Alamo/Historic Sites/San Antonio Clipping files, for James Tylee, William Wills.
Biography/Esparza, Enrique.
Bissel (or Bissett), William. 1912. Painting by V. Chaskey "From original painting of the Alamo made in 1839 by William Bissel a Scotsman."
Curtis, Albert, Papers.
Gentilz-Fretelliere Family Papers. 1793–1962.
Haythornthwaite, Philip, and Kevin R. Young. N.d. Some thoughts on Alamo artillery, Part 2. Typed article without date in DRT files: Historic Sites/Alamo/Cannon.
Historic Sites/Alamo/Alamo Defenders/Dickinson, Almeron.
Historic Sites/Alamo/Alamo Defenders/Dickinson, Susanna.
Historic Sites/Alamo/Alamo Defenders/Esparza, Gregorio.
Historic Sites/Alamo/Cannon.
Historic Sites/Alamo/Defenders Burial Site.
Historic Sites/Alamo/Maps.
Historic Sites/Alamo/Survivors.
Jackson, Ron. N.d. (c. 1997). In the Alamo's shadow: Black participants. Typescript in DRT Library. (Published as edited version without footnotes: Jackson, Ron. February 1998. In the Alamo's shadow. In *True West*, edited by Stillwater, OK: Western Publications.)
Kemp, L. W. (probable author). N.d. (c. 1939). Dickinson-Almeron. Typed manuscript in Historic Sites/Alamo/Alamo Defenders/Dickinson, Almeron.
Lindley, Thomas Ricks. 1989. The revealing of Dr. John Sutherland. Typed manuscript.
Long, Charles. Copies of various correspondence in DRT files: Historic Sites/Alamo/Cannon.
Orbelo, William R. N.d. Guns of interest. *The Artilleryman.* 21–23. Copy without date in DRT files: Historic Sites/Alamo/Cannon.
Rabia, Santiago, Papers. N.d. (c. 1838).
Scott, Etna Rhoades. February 6, 1984. Information—Enrique Esparza: Evidence that he was born in 1828. In Biography/Esparza, Enrigue.
Siegmund, Col. Walter F. September 1, 1947. History of the Dickert rifle used in defense of the Alamo.
Smith, John W. Vertical files.
Young, Kevin R. N.d. Some thoughts on Alamo artillery. Typed article noted "for Alamo News" in DRT files: Historic Sites/Alamo/Cannon.

Bancroft Library, University of California, Berkeley.
Archivo Historico Militar; Archivo de la Secretaria de la Defensa Nacional. Microfilm collection. Expediente 1149, 1897, 1899, 1900, 1904.
Documents for the History of Texas, 1824–38 (BANC MSS P-O 110). Alphonse Louis Pinert Collection of Bancroft Manuscripts (P-O 110, #2).

Other
Arizona Historical Society, Tucson. Smith Sr., Cornelius C. N.d. (c. 1930). A history of the Oury Family.
Béxar County, Deeds/Vital Records Section, Office of the County Clerk. Headright Books nos. 1 and 2, also Book A.
Houston, University of, Special Collections, Letter (reputed) of Isaac Millsap.
Incarnate Word, University of, San Antonio, Texas. Adina De Zavala Papers.
Ivey, James E. N.d. (2002). "Mapping the Alamo." Manuscript in preparation. Courtesy of the author.
Nacogdoches County, County Clerk's Office, "Proceedings of the Board of Land Commissioners."
Newberry Library, Chicago. William Bollaert. Sketches from journey to Texas, 1843.
Parker County, Texas. Deposition in the case of Malone et al. v. Moran et al. No. 3644.
San Antonio, City of. Central Mapping Office.
Santa Anna (Antonio López de) Papers. García Collection. 1874. Benson Latin American Collection, University of Texas at Austin.
Smoot, Jane, to Thomas W. Cutrer. November 26, 1985. Draft of entry on Dr. Amelia W. Williams for the *Handbook of Texas*. Courtesy of Jane Smoot.
Smoot, Jane. Prior to April 26, 1959. Amelia Worthington Williams. Written for celebration ceremony of the United Daughters of the Confederacy at the tomb of Gen. Albert Sidney Johnston in the State Cemetery. Courtesy of Jane Smoot.
Tennessee, University of, Special Collections Library, Knoxville.
Tulane University Library, New Orleans. Special Collections. Mrs. Mason Barrett Collection of the Papers of Albert Sidney Johnston.
Yale University Library, Beinecke Rare Book and Manuscript Library, New Haven, Thomas W. Streeter Collection.
Yale University Library, Beinecke Rare Book and Manuscript Library, New Haven, Connecticut. Wagner Collection, Western Americana Collection.

Newspapers and Similar Periodicals and Journals

Advocate. April 15, 1836. Little Rock, Arkansas.
Arkansas Gazette. March 29, April 5, 12, 19, 1836. Little Rock.
Austin American-Statesman. April 19, 1950; August 27, 1961; March 12, 1996; December 5, 1998; June 30, 1999.

Austin City Gazette. April 14, 1841.

Broome Republican. April 21, 1836. Binghamton, New York.

Clarksville (Texas) Standard. March 4, 1887.

Columbia (Tennessee) Observer. April 14, 1836.

Commercial Bulletin. April 9, 11, 1836. New Orleans.

Commonwealth. May 25, July 27, 1836. Frankfort, Kentucky.

Dallas News or *Dallas Morning News.* February 5, 12, 1911; June 1, 1913; January 12, March 12, 1930; March 8, 1931.

Democrat. April 16, 1836. Goshan, New York.

Democratic Free Press. September 7, 1836. Detroit.

Dennison (Texas) Daily News, October 4, 1878.

El Correo Atlantico. April 11, June 13, 1836. New Orleans.

El Mosquito Mexicano. March 22, April 5, September 30, 1836; February 28, 1837.

El Nacional, Suplemento al Numero 79. 1836. Mexico.

Express News. September 13, 1986; June 9, 1991. San Antonio.

Galveston Daily News. April 25, 1909.

Gazette. July 12, 1889. Fort Worth, Texas.

Gentleman's Magazine. 1839.

Greene County (Ohio) Gazette. April 14, April 21, May 26, June 16, 23, 30, 1836.

Houston Chronicle. March 6, 1999.

Louisville Daily Journal. June 30, July 11, 1836.

Memphis Enquirer. March 29, April 5, 12, 1836.

Metropolitan. July 19, 1836. Washington, D.C.

Mississippi Free Trader and Natchez Gazette. April 8, 29, 1836.

National Intelligencer. April 30, 1836. Washington, D.C.

New Orleans Bulletin. March 28, 1836.

New Yorker. April 16, 1836.

Northern Standard. March 11, 18, 1848. Clarksville, Texas.

Port Gibson (Mississippi) Correspondent. April 23, 1836.

Republic Daily. June 28, 1852. Washington, D.C.

San Antonio Express or *San Antonio Daily Express.* June 23 (or 18 or 28), 1878; April 28, 1881; March 6, 1887; June 30, August 1, 2, 1889; March 6, 1892; April 12, 1896; February 11, 1899; October 27, 1900; November 24, 1901; November 22, 1902; March 7, August 28, 1904; May 28, 1905; July 1, October 28, November 11, 1906; May 12, 19, July 19, December 15, 22, 1907; March 26, 1911; February 18, September 8, 1912; September 28, 1913; December 21, 1917; June 21, 1927; February 24, 1929; December 10, 1933.

San Antonio Light. February 19, 1899; November 10, 1901; September 1, 1907; July 25, 1908; April 3, 1910; November 26, 1911; February 4, 12, 1912; February 4, 1917.

Southern Messenger. February 16, 1899.

Star-Telegram. February 28, 1932; November 12, 1933. Fort Worth, Texas.

State. April 26, 1914. Columbia, South Carolina.

Telegraph and Texas Register. January 23, February 27, March 12, 24, October 11, 1836; March 28, 1837; March 23, 1842; July 26, 1843. San Felipe and Houston.

Texas Almanac. 1859, 1860, 1868, 1870, 1873.
Texas Monument. March 31, 1852. La Grange.
Texas Mute Ranger. April 1882.
Texas Republican. March 2, March 9, 1836. Brazoria.
Texas State Gazette. September 15, October 13, 1849. Austin.
United States Magazine and Democratic Review. October 1838.

Published or Authored Works

Ables, L. Robert. 1967. The second battle for the Alamo. *Southwestern Historical Quarterly* (hereafter *SWHQ*) 70 (3):372–413.

Alsbury, Juana. December 1981. *Alamo Lore and Myth Organization.* 3–4:37.

Andrade, Juan José de. 1836. *Documentos Que el General Andrade.* 5–6. Monterey, Mex.: Imprenta de Nivel, propiedad de Lorenzo A. De Melo (printing shop of Nivel, ownership of Lorenzo A. De Melo).

Asbury, Samuel. 1944. The private journal of Juan Nepomuceno Almonte, February 1–April 16, 1836. *SWHQ* 48:10–32.

Bancroft, Hubert Howe. 1889. *North American States and Texas.* 2:201–37. Vol. 16 of *The Works of Hubert Howe Bancroft.* San Francisco: History Company, Publishers.

Barker, Eugene C. April 1906. The Texas revolutionary army. *Texas Historical Association Quarterly* (hereafter *THAQ*) 9:227.

———, ed. 1929. *Readings in Texas History.* 262–64. Dallas: Southwest Press.

Barrett, D. C., to Robinson. January 31, 1836. In John H. Jenkins, ed. and trans. 1973. *The Papers of the Texas Revolution, 1835–1836.* 4:204–6. Austin: Presidial Press.

Bassett, John Spencer, ed. 1931. *Correspondence of Andrew Jackson, 1833–1838.* Vol. 5 Washington, DC: Carnegie Institute.

Becerra, Francisco. 1980. *A Mexican Sergeant's Recollections of the Alamo and San Jacinto.* Austin: Jenkins Publishing Co.

Bernard, J. H. In Dudley G. Wooten, ed. 1898. *A Comprehensive History of Texas, 1685 to 1897.* 1:608–30. Dallas: William G. Scarff.

Binkley, William C. 1936. *Official Correspondence of the Texan Revolution, 1835–1836.* 2 Vols. New York: D. Appleton-Century Co.

———. 1952. *The Texas Revolution.* Louisiana State University Press. Reprinted 1979. Austin: Texas State Historical Association.

Biographical Directory of Texan Conventions and Congresses. 1941.

Blake, Robert B. 1939. A vindication of Rose and his story. *In the Shadow of History.* 27–41. Austin: Texas Folk-Lore Society Publications, no. 15.

Bonham, Milledge L., Jr. July 1931. James Butler Bonham: A consistent rebel. *SWHQ* 35:124–36.

Borroel, Roger. 1997a. *The Papers of Colonel José Enrique de la Peña: Selected Appendixes from His Diary, 1836–1839.* East Chicago, IN: La Villita Publications.

———. 1997b. *The Papers of Colonel José Enrique de la Peña: The Last of His Appendixes,* Vol. 2. East Chicago, IN: La Villita Publications.

———. 1997c. *After the Battle of the Alamo: Documents Published by General Juan José Andrade on the Evacuation of San Antonio de Béjar, Texas, May 1836.* East Chicago, IN: La Villita Publications.

———. 1997d. *The Concordance of Lieutenant Colonel José Enrique de la Peña's Diary and Appendixes: A Comparative Critical Analysis.* East Chicago, IN: La Villita Publications.

———. 1998a. *The J. Sanchez Garza Introduction to the Rebellion of Texas: The Diary of Lt. Col. José Enrique de la Peña.* East Chicago, IN: La Villita Publications.

———. 1998b. *Mexican Accounts of the Battle of the Alamo: A Collection and Critical Analysis.* East Chicago, IN: La Villita Publications.

———. 1999a. *Mexican Battalion Series at the Alamo.* Vol. 1. East Chicago, IN: La Villita Publications.

———, trans. 1999b. *The Diary of Lt. Col. Nicola de la Portilla, March 18th–April 23rd 1836.* East Chicago, IN: La Villita Publications.

———, trans. and ed. 2000–2001. *Field Reports of the Mexican Army during the Texan War of 1836.* Vols. 1–4. East Chicago, IN: La Villita Publications.

———, trans. 2001a. *Field Reports of the Mexican Army during the Texan War of 1836.* Vol. 2. East Chicago, IN: La Villita Publications.

———, trans. 2001b. *Field Reports of the Mexican Army during the Texan War of 1836.* Vol. 3. East Chicago, IN: La Villita Publications.

———, trans. 2001c. *Field Reports of the Mexican Army during the Texan War of 1836.* Vol. 4. East Chicago, IN: La Villita Publications.

———, trans. 2002. *The Texas Revolution of 1836: A Concise Historical Perspective Based on Original Sources.* Second Revised/Expanded Edition. East Chicago, IN: La Villita Publications.

Bradburn, Juan Davis, biography. 1880. *Biographical Encyclopedia of Texas.* 262–63. New York: Southern Publishing Co.

Brady, Cyrus T. 1905. *Conquest of the Southwest.* New York: D. Appleton & Co.

Brierley, Ned F., trans. 1997. *The Journal of Sergeant Santiago Rabia.* 9. Austin, TX: Texian Army Investigations. Copyrighted Thomas Ricks Lindley.

Brogan, Evelyn. 1922. *James Bowie: A Hero of the Alamo.* San Antonio: Theodore Kunzman.

Brown, John Henry. 1887. *Life and Times of Henry Smith.* Dallas: A. D. Aldbridge & Co.

———. 1890. *Indian Wars and Pioneers of Texas.* Austin: I. E. Daniell. Reprinted 1988, Austin: State House Press.

———. 1892. *History of Texas from 1685 to 1892.* 2 vols. St. Louis: I. E. Daniell.

Brown, Mary M. 1895. *A Condensed History of Texas.* Dallas: Published by author.

Burleson, Georgia J., comp. 1901. *The Life and Writings of Rufus C. Burleson, D.D., LL.D.* 735–41. Published privately.

Canales, J. T. 1957. *Bits of Texas History in the Melting Pot of America.* Part 2:11–49. San Antonio: Artes Graficas.

Carleton, Don. June 25, 2000. Post-mortem of a hero. *Texas: Houston Chronicle Magazine.* 8–12.

Caro, Ramón. A true account of the first Texas campaign and the events subsequent to the battle of San Jacinto, by Ramón Martinez Caro. In Carlos Castañeda, trans. 1928. *The Mexican Side of the Texan Revolution.* 93–94, 99–104, 107. Dallas: P. L. Turner Company.

Casso, Raul, IV. July 1992. Damacio Jimenez: The lost and found Alamo defender. *SWHQ* 96:87–92.

Castañeda, Carlos, trans. 1928. *The Mexican Side of the Texan Revolution, by the Chief Mexican Participants.* Dallas: P. L. Turner Company.

Castañeda, Carlos E., and Jack Autrey Dabbs. 1939. *Guide to the Latin American Manuscripts in the University of Texas Library.* Austin: Committee on Latin American Studies, American Council of Learned Societies. Miscellaneous Publication no. 1.

Chabot, Frederick C., 1931. *The Alamo: Altar of Texas Liberty.* San Antonio: Naylor Publishing Co.

———, 1937. *With the Makers of San Antonio.* San Antonio: Arte Graficas.

———, ed. 1940. *Texas Letters* 146–47. San Antonio: Yanaguana Society Publications no. 5.

Chariton, Wallace O. 1992. *Exploring the Alamo Legends.* Plano, TX: Woodware Publishing.

Chemerka, William R. June 1987. Damacio Jimenes: A new name to the Alamo's roll call. *Alamo Journal* 56:10.

———. 1997. *Alamo Almanac and Book of Lists.* Austin: Eakin Press.

Colquitt, Gov. Oscar B. 1913. *Message of Gov. Oscar B. Colquitt to the Thirty-third Legislature Relating to the Alamo Property.* Austin: Van Boeckman-Jones Co.

Connelly, Thomas, ed. 1960. "Notes and Documents: Did David Crockett Surrender at the Alamo? A Contemporary Letter." In *Journal of Southern History* 26:368–76.

Corner, William, ed. 1890. *San Antonio de Bexar: A Guide and History.* 117–19. San Antonio: Bainbridge & Corner.

———, ed. July 1897. John Crittenden Duval: The last survivor of the Goliad massacre. *Texas Historical Association Quarterly.* 1:48–49.

Costeloe, Michael. April 1988. The Mexican press of 1836 and the battle of the Alamo. *SWHQ* 91:533–43.

Crawford, Ann, ed. 1988. *The Eagle: The Autobiography of Santa Anna.* Austin, TX: State House Press.

Crisp, James E. October 1994. The little book that wasn't there: The myth and mystery of the de la Peña diary. *SWHQ* 98:260–96.

———. Fall 1995. When revision becomes obsession: Bill Groneman and the de la Peña diary. *Military History of the West* 25:143–56.

———. March 1996. Back to basics: Conspiracy, common sense, and Occam's razor. *Alamo Journal* 100: 15–23.

————. Winter 1998. *Wilson Quarterly*. Response to Michael Lind's article posted on Internet.

Crockett, David (reputed), Richard Penn Smith (putative author). 1836. *Col. Crockett's Exploits and Adventures in Texas . . . Written by Himself*. Philadelphia: T. K. and P. G. Collins. Reprinted 1955. New York: Citadel Press.

Curtis, Albert. N.d. James Butler Bonham: Alamo Hero. Typed manuscript. Albert Curtis Papers, DRT.

————. 1961a. *Remember the Alamo*. San Antonio: Clegg Co.

————. c. 1961b. *Remember the Alamo: Alamo Heroes*. San Antonio: Clegg Co.

Curtis, Gregory. March 1989a. Highly suspect. *Texas Monthly* 109.

————. March 1989b. Forgery, Texas style. *Texas Monthly* 105–8, 178–85.

————. December 1993. Seer and scholar. *Texas Monthly*.

Daughters of the Republic of Texas. 1986a. *The Alamo Long Barrack Museum*. Dallas: Taylor Publishing Co.

————. 1986b. *Muster Rolls of the Texas Revolution*. Lubbock, TX: Craftsman Printers.

Davis, Robert H. February 28, 1932. Bob Davis uncovers an untold story about the Alamo. *Star-Telegram*. Oils, Auto and Features: 16. Fort Worth.

Davis, William C. Fall 1997. How Davy probably didn't die. *Journal of the Alamo Battlefield Association* 2:3–35.

————. 1998. *Three Roads to the Alamo: The Lives and Fortunes of David Crockett, James Bowie, and William Barret Travis*. New York: HarperCollins Publishers.

DePalo, William A. 1997. *The Mexican National Army, 1822–1852*. College Station: Texas A&M University Press.

DeShields, James T. February 5, 12, 1911. Fall of the Alamo, *Dallas News*.

————, ed. 1935. *Tall Men with Long Rifles . . . as Told by Captain Creed Taylor . . .* 152–67. San Antonio: Naylor Company.

De Zavala, Adina Emilia. N.d. (c. 1911). *The Story of the Siege and Fall of the Alamo*. San Antonio: Privately published.

————. 1917. *History and Legends of the Alamo and Other Missions in and around San Antonio*. 26–30. San Antonio: Privately published by author.

Dobie, J. Frank, ed. 1939a. *In the Shadow of History*. Austin: Texas Folk-Lore Society Publications no. 25.

————. 1939b. The line that Travis drew. *In the Shadow of History*. 9–16. Austin: Texas Folk-Lore Society Publications no. 15.

Drake, David. 1981. "Joe": Alamo hero. *Negro History Bulletin*. April–May–June:34–35.

Driggs, Howard R., and Sarah S. King. 1936. *Rise of the Lone Star*. 199–231. New York: Frederick A. Stokes Co.

Durham, Robert L. March 1997. Where did Davy die? *Alamo Journal* 104:3–6.

Eaton, Jack D. 1980. *Excavation at the Alamo Shrine (Mission San Antonio de Valero)*. Special Report no. 10. Center for Archaeological Research, University of Texas at San Antonio.

Eberstadt, Edward. April 1957. The Thomas W. Streeter collection. *Yale University Library Gazette* 31:147–53.

Ehrenberg, Herman. 1935. *With Milam and Fannin: Adventures of a German Boy in Texas' Revolution.* Translated by Charlotte Churchill. 154–55. Dallas: Tardy Publishing Co.

Field, Joseph. 1836. *Three Years in Texas. Including a View of the Texas Revolution, and an Account of the Principal Battles . . .* 11–12, 36. Greenfield, MA: Justin Jones. Reprinted 1936. 16–17, 57–58. Austin: Steck Co. with different pagination.

Filisola, Gen. Vicente. 1849a. *Memorias Para la Historia de la Guerra de Tejas.* Mexico: Imprenta De Ignacio Cumplido.

———. 1849b. *Memorias Para la Historia de la Guerra de Tejas.* Mexico: Tipografia de R. Rafael.

———. 1985–1987. *Memoirs for the History of the War in Texas.* Edited and translated by Wallace Woolsey. 2 Vols. Austin, TX: Eakin Press.

———. Representation to the supreme government with notes on his operations as general-in-chief of the army of Texas, by General Vicente Filisola. In Castañeda, Carlos., trans. 1928. *The Mexican Side of the Texan Revolution.* 169, 170–71. Dallas: P. L. Turner Company.

Filizola, Umberto, ed. and trans. August 1939. Correspondence of Santa Anna during the Texas campaign, 1835–1836. 3–4, 30, 70–75. Master's thesis, University of Texas at Austin.

Folmsbee, Stanley J., and Anna Grace Catron. 1958. David Crockett in Texas. *East Tennessee Historical Society Publications* 30:48–74.

Foote, Henry Stuart. 1841. *Texas and the Texans.* 2:224–26. [Philadelphia]: Thomas, Cowperthwait & Co.

Ford, John S. Col. Ford's Memoirs: The Fighting of the Alamo. In William Corner ed. 1890. *San Antonio de Bexar: A Guide and History.* 119–23. San Antonio: Bainbridge & Corner.

———. 1896. "Origin and Fall of the Alamo." San Antonio: No publisher.

Fox, Anne A. 1992. *The Archaeological Investigations in Alamo Plaza, San Antonio, Bexar County, Texas, 1988 and 1989.* Center for Archaeological Research, University of Texas at San Antonio, Archaeological Survey Report no. 205.

Fox, Anne A., Feris A. Bass, Jr., and Thomas R. Hester. 1976. *The Archaeology and History of Alamo Plaza.* Archaeological Survey Report no. 16. Center for Archaeological Research, University of Texas at San Antonio.

Gaddy, Jerry J. 1973. *Texas in Revolt.* 49. Fort Collins, CO: Old Army Press.

Garza, J. Sánchez, ed. 1955. *La Rebelion de Texas, Manuscrito Inedito de 1836 por un Oficial de Santa Anna.* Mexico, D.F.: A. Frank de Sánchez.

Gentilz, Jean Louis Theodore. 1844 on. Fall of the Alamo. In Mary Ann Noonan Guerra. 1983. *The Alamo.* San Antonio: Alamo Press.

Giraud, François P. 1849. Central Mapping Office, City of San Antonio. Microfilm. Book 1, 114.

Gould, Stephen. 1882. *The Alamo City Guide, San Antonio, Texas. Being a Historical Sketch of the Ancient City of the Alamo and Business Review* . . . 21–22. New York: Macgowan & Slipper, Printers.

Gracy, David B., II. October 2001. "Just as I have written it": A study of the authenticity of the manuscript of José Enrique de la Peña's account of the Texas campaign. *SWHQ* 105:254–91.

Gray, William F. 1909. *From Virginia to Texas, 1835, Diary of Col. Wm. F. Gray* . . . 136–42. Houston: Gray, Dillaye & Co. Reprinted 1965. Houston: Fletcher Young Publishing Co.

Green, Michael., ed. April 1988. To the people of Texas and all Americans in the world. *SWHQ* 91:483–508.

Green, Rena Maverick, ed. 1921. *Memoirs of Mary A. Maverick, Arranged by Mary A. Maverick and Her Son Geo. Madison Maverick.* 135–36. San Antonio: Alamo Printing Co.

———. 1952. *Samuel Maverick, Texan, 1803–1870: A Collection of Letters, Journals and Memoirs.* x–xi, xvii–xviii, 48, 55, 420. San Antonio: Privately published.

Greer, James K., ed. July 1928. Journal of Ammon Underwood, 1834–1838. *SWHQ* 32:142–43.

Gregg, Josiah. 1941. *Diary and Letters of Josiah Gregg.* Edited by Maurice Garland Fulton. 1:231–32. Norman: University of Oklahoma Press.

Groneman, Bill. 1985. The death of Davy Crockett. In Phil Rosenthal and Bill Groneman *Roll Call at the Alamo.* 29–37. Ft. Collins, CO: Old Army Press.

———. 1990a. *Alamo Defenders, A Genealogy: The People and Their Words.* Austin: Eakin Press.

———. Spring 1990b. Anthony Wolf: Tracing an Alamo defender. *Journal of South Texas* 3:24–35.

———. 1994. *Defense of a Legend: Crockett and the de la Peña Diary.* Plano, TX: Republic of Texas Press, Wordware Publishing Co.

———. 1996. *Eyewitness to the Alamo.* Plano, TX: Republic of Texas Press, Wordware Publishing Company.

Groneman, William. Fall 1995a. The controversial alleged account of José Enrique de la Peña. *Military History of the West* 25: 129–42.

———. Fall 1995b. A rejoinder: Publish rather than perish—regardless: Jim Crisp and the de la Peña diary. *Military History of the West* 25:157–66.

———. Winter 1998. *Wilson Quarterly.* Response to Michael Lind's article posted on Internet.

Grosvenor, Charles, ed. (Reuben M. Potter). 1977. *The Fall of the Alamo.* Hillsdale, NJ: Otterden Press.

Guerra, Mary Ann. 1983. *The Alamo.* San Antonio: Alamo Press.

Gulick, Charles Adams, et al., eds. 1968. *Papers of Mirabeau Buonaparte Lamar.* Vol. 1. Austin: Pemberton Press.

Hanford, Albert. 1878. *Albert Hanford's Texas State Register for 1878.* 29–30. Galveston.

Harburn, Todd. April 1991. The Crockett death controversy. *Alamo Journal* 76:5–8.

Hard, Robert J., ed. 1994. *A Historical Overview of Alamo Plaza and Composento.* Center of Archaeological Research, University of Texas at San Antonio. Special Report no. 20.

Hardin, Stephen L. December 1987. A volley from the darkness: Sources regarding the death of William Barret Travis. *Alamo Journal* 59:3–10.

———. May 1989. J. C. Neill: The forgotten Alamo commander. *Alamo Journal* 66:5–11.

———, ed. July 1990. The Felix Nuñez account and the siege of the Alamo: A critical appraisal. *SWHQ* 94, no. 1:65–84.

———. 1994. *Texas Iliad: A Military History of the Texas Revolution, 1835–36.* Austin: University of Texas Press.

———. Efficient in the cause. In Gerald E. Poyo, ed. 1996. *Tejano Journey, 1770–1850.* 49–71. Austin: UT Press.

———, ed. Fall 1998. J. H. Kuykendall's recollections of William B. Travis. *Journal of the Alamo Battlefield Association* 3–1:31–36.

———. N.d. (c. 2000). Where was Bonham? Copy from the author. Posted on the Internet at alamo-de-parras.

Harris, Dilue. October 1900. The reminiscences of Mrs. Dilue Harris, Part I. *Quarterly of the Texas State Historical Association* 4:88.

Hart, Katherine, and Elizabeth Kemp, eds. July 1964. E. M. Pease's account of the Texas revolution. Notes and documents. *SWHQ* 68:85–86.

Helm, Mary S. 1884. *Scraps of Early Texas History.* 56. Austin: B. R. Warner & Co.

Henson, Margaret Swett. October 1990. Politics and the treatment of the Mexican prisoners after the battle of San Jacinto. *SWHQ* 94:189–230.

Hizar, W. R., and J. T. Guthrie. 1967. Study of Weapons in the Alamo Collection. Typed manuscript (two volumes). DRT Library at the Alamo.

Hollon, W. Eugene, and Ruth Lapham Butler, eds. 1956. *William Bollaert's Texas.* Norman: University of Oklahoma Press.

Huffines, Alan C. 1999. *Blood of Noble Men: The Alamo Siege and Battle: An Illustrated Chronology.* Illustrated by Gary S. Zaboly. Austin: Eakin Press.

Hughes, W. J. 1964. *Rebellious Ranger: Rip Ford and the Old Southwest.* Norman: University of Oklahoma Press.

Huneycutt, C. D. 1986. *The Alamo: An In-depth Study of the Battle.* 99–100. New London, NC: Gold Star Press.

———, trans. 1988. *At the Alamo: Memoirs of Capt. Navarro.* New London, NC: Gold Star Press.

Hunnicutt, Helen. Summer 1951. A Mexican view of the Texas war: Memoirs of a veteran of the two battles of the Alamo. *Library Chronicle of the University of Texas* 4:59–74.

Hunter, Robert. c. 1936. *Narrative of Robert Hancock Hunter.* Austin: Cook Printing Co.

Huntford, Roland. 1984. *The Last Place on Earth.* Originally published as *Scott and Admundsen.* New York: Macmillan Publishing Co.

Hutton, Jim. June 9, 1991. *Express-News*. Insight, 1-M. San Antonio. Re Esparza's story.

Ivey, James. N.d. (c. 1978). General Notes on the History of the Alamo Plaza: Ivey Papers. Manuscript. Center for Archeological Research, University of Texas at San Antonio.

Ivey, James (Jake). September 1981a. Southwest and northwest wall gun emplacements. *Alamo Lore and Myth Organization* 3–3:1–5.

———. December 1981b. South gate and its defenses. *Alamo Lore and Myth Organization* 3–4:1–6.

———. March 1982a. The Losoyas and the Texas revolution. *Alamo Lore and Myth Organization* 4–1:1–2.

———. March 1982b. The problem of the two Guerreros. *Alamo Lore and Myth Organization* 4–1:10–2.

———. June 2000. Archaeological evidence for the defenses of the Alamo. *Alamo Journal* 117:2–8.

———. March 2001. Another look at storming the Alamo walls. *Alamo Journal* 120:9–16.

Ivey, James E. N.d. (2002). Mapping the Alamo. Manuscript in preparation. Courtesy of the author.

Ivey, James E., and Anne A. Fox. 1997. *Archaeological and Historical Investigations at the Alamo North Wall, San Antonio, Bexar County, Texas*. Center for Archaeological Research. University of Texas at San Antonio. Archaeological Survey Report no. 224.

Jackson, Jack, and James E. Ivey. October 2001. Mystery artist of the Alamo: José Juan Sánchez. *SWHQ* 105:207–53.

Jackson, Ron. 1997. *Alamo Legacy: Alamo Descendants Remember the Alamo*. Austin: Eakin Press.

———. February 1998. In the Alamo's shadow. *True West*. Stillwater, OK: Western Publications. Note also the manuscript in DRT Library above.

James, Marquis. 1929. *The Raven: A Biography of Sam Houston*. Indianapolis: Bobbs-Merrill. Reprinted 1988. Austin: University of Texas Press.

Jenkins, John H., ed. and trans. 1973. *The Papers of the Texas Revolution, 1835-1836*. 10 Vols. Austin: Presidial Press.

Johnson, Francis. 1916. *A History of Texas and Texans*. Edited by Eugene Barker. 398. Chicago: American Historical Society.

Kemp, Louis. c. 1936. The Life of Creed Taylor. Williams (Amelia Worthington) Papers, Muster Rolls, and Other Lists of Defenders, CAH.

———. N.d. (c. 1937). The Burial Places of the Alamo Heroes. Typescript. Williams (Amelia Worthington) Papers, Historical Research Material: Alamo research: Burial of Alamo dead information, CAH.

Kendall, Dorothy Steinbomer, and Carmen Perry. 1974. *Gentilz: Artist of the Old Southwest*. Austin: University of Texas Press.

Kennedy, William. 1841. *Texas: The Rise, Progress, and Prospects of the Republic of Texas*. 2:180–93. London: R. Hastings.

Kielman, Chester. 1967. *The University of Texas: A Guide to the Historical Manu-scripts Collections in the University of Texas Library.* Austin: UT Press.

Kilgore, Dan. 1978. *How Did Davy Die?* College Station: Texas A&M Press.

King, C. Richard. 1976. *Susanna Dickinson: Messenger of the Alamo.* Austin: Shoal Creek Publishers.

Labadie, Joseph H., comp. 1986. *La Villita Earthworks: A Preliminary Report of Investigations of Mexican Siege Works at the Battle of the Alamo.* Center for Archaeological Research, University of Texas at San Antonio. Archaeological Survey Report no. 159.

Labadie, N. D., ed. 1859. Urissa's account of the Alamo massacre. *Texas Almanac* 61–62.

Lamego, Miguel A. Sanchez. 1943. *Apuntes para la Historia del Arma de Ingenieros en Mexico, Hisoria del Batallon de Zapadores.* Mexico, D.F.: Secretaria de la Defensa Nacional, Taller Autografico.

Lanier, Sidney. 1899. *Retrospects and Prospects.* New York: Charles Scribner's Sons.

Lind, Michael. Winter 1998. The death of David Crockett. *Wilson Quarterly* 22:50. Posted on Internet.

Lindley, Thomas Ricks. August 1988. James Butler Bonham, October 17, 1835–March 6, 1836. *Alamo Journal.* 62:3–10.

———. 1989. The Revealing of Dr. John Sutherland. Typed manuscript. DRT.

———. July 1992. Alamo artillery: Number, type, caliber and concussion. *Alamo Journal* 82:1–8.

———. December 1993. A correct list of Alamo patriots. *Alamo Journal* 89:2–7.

———. December 1994. A new Alamo account. *Alamo Journal* 94:4–7.

———. September 1995. Drawing truthful deductions. *Journal of the Alamo Battle-field Association* 1:19–42.

———. March 12, 1996. 160 years later, historians ask: Who died at the Alamo? By David McLemore. *Austin American Statesman.*

———. March 6, 1999. Scholar says Alamo's numbers don't add up. By Bob Tutt. *Houston Chronicle.*

———. June 2000. Storming the Alamo walls. *Alamo Journal.* 117:11–18.

Linn, John J. 1883. *Reminiscences of Fifty Years in Texas.* 141. New York: D. & J. Sad-lier & Co.

Long, Jeff. 1990. *Duel of Eagles: The Mexican and U.S. Fight for the Alamo.* New York: William Morrow and Company.

Lord, Walter. 1961. *A Time to Stand.* New York: Harper & Row, Publishers. Reprinted 1978. Lincoln: University of Nebraska Press (Bison Book).

———. Myths and realities of the Alamo. In Stephen B. Oates, ed. 1968. *The Republic of Texas.* 18-25. Palo Alto, CA: American West Publishing Co.

Lozano, Ruben Rendon. 1985. *Viva Tejas: The Story of the Tejanos, the Mexican Patri-ots of the Texas Revolution, with New Material Added by Mary Ann Noonan Guerra.* Reprint. San Antonio: Alamo Press.

Marks, Paula Mitchell. 1989. *Turn Your Eyes toward Texas: Pioneers Sam and Mary Maverick.* 51–52, 56–58. College Station: Texas A&M University Press.

Matovina, Timothy M. 1995. *The Alamo Remembered: Tejano Accounts and Perspectives.* Austin: University of Texas Press.

Maverick, Mary A. N.d. (1898). *The Fall of the Alamo.* N.p.

———. 1921. *Memoirs of Mary A. Maverick arranged by Mary A. Maverick and Her Son Geo. Madison Maverick.* Edited by Rena Maverick Green. 133-34. San Antonio: Alamo Printing Co.

McArdle, H. A. N.d. Companion Battle Paintings. Per above under TSLA manuscripts.

McCall, G. A. April 1911. William T. Malone. *Texas Historical Quarterly.* 14:325–26.

McDonald, David, trans., and Kevin Young, ed. Fall 1998. The siege of the Alamo: A Mexican army journal. *Journal of the Alamo Battlefield Association* 3–1:31–6.

Memorial and Genealogical Record of Southwest Texas. 1894. 402–3. Chicago: Goodspeed Bros.

Menchaca, Antonio. 1937. *Memoirs.* Edited by James P. Newcomb. San Antonio: Yanaguana Society.

Milam County Heritage Preservation Society. 1985. *Matchless Milam: History of Milam County, Texas.* 236. Dallas: Taylor Publishing Co.

Miller, Randall M. March 1971. After San Jacinto: Santa Anna's role in Texas independence. *East Texas Historical Journal* 9:50–59.

Miller, Thomas Lloyd. Spring 1964. The roll of the Alamo. *Texana* 2:54–64.

———. 1967. *Bounty and Donation Land Grants of Texas, 1835–1888.* Austin: University of Texas Press. Includes Thomas Hendrick.

———. Fall 1971. Mexican-Texans at the Alamo. *Journal of Mexican American History* 2:33–38.

Mixon, Ruby. August 1930. William Barrett Travis: His Life and Letters. Master's thesis, University of Texas at Austin.

Moore, Francis. 1840. *Map and Description of Texas.* Philadelphia: H. Tanner, Jr.

Morphis, James M. 1874. *History of Texas from Its Discovery and Settlement . . .* 168–77. New York: United States Publishing Company.

Muir, Andrew, ed. 1958. *Texas in 1837: An Anonymous Contemporary Narrative.* 113. Austin: UT Press.

Myers, John Myers. 1948. *The Alamo.* New York: E. P. Dutton & Co., Reprinted 1973. Lincoln: University of Nebraska Press (Bison Book).

Nelson, George. 1998. *The Alamo: An Illustrated History.* Dry Frio Canyon, TX: Aldine Press.

Newell, Rev. Chester. 1838. *History of the Revolution in Texas, Particularly of the War of 1835 and '36 . . .* 87–91. New York: Wiley & Putnam.

Nichols, James L. April 1959. Book review of *Thirteen Days to Glory,* by Lon Tinkle. *SWHQ* 62:403-5.

Niles, John N., and L. M. Pease. 1837. *History of South America and Mexico.* Hartford, CT: H. Huntington, Jr.

Nofi, Albert A. 1982. *The Alamo and the Texas War for Independence.* Conshohocken, PA: Combined Books. Reprinted 1994. New York: Da Capo (Plenum Publishing Corp).

Notes and fragments. April 1902. *Texas Historical Association Quarterly* 5:355. Re Benjamin Highstreet.

Pease, E. M. Letter of January 8, 1837. In Hart, Katherine, and Elizabeth Kemp, eds. July 1964. E. M. Pease's account of the Texas revolution. *SWHQ* 68:85–86.

Peña, José de la. 1955. See J. Sánchez Garza, ed.

Pennybacker, Anna J. 1888. *A New History of Texas.* Tyler, TX: Published for the author. Revised ed. 1895. Palestine, TX: Percy V. Pennybacker.

Perry, Carmen, trans. and ed. 1975. *With Santa Anna in Texas: A Personal Narrative of the Revolution, by José Enrique de la Peña.* xi, xiii–xiv, 38–58. College Station: Texas A&M University Press.

Pohl, James W., and Stephen L. Hardin. January 1986. The military history of the Texas revolution: An overview. *SWHQ* 89:269–308.

Potter, Reuben. 1868. The fall of the Alamo: A reminiscence of the revolution of Texas. *Texas Almanac* 36.

———. January 1878. The fall of the Alamo. *Magazine of American History* 2:1–21.

———. 1977. *The Fall of the Alamo.* Edited by Charles Grosvenor. Hillsdale, NJ: Otterden Press.

Poyo, Gerald E., ed. 1996. *Tejano Journey, 1770–1850.* Austin: UT Press.

Presley, James. April 1959. Santa Anna in Texas: A Mexican viewpoint. *SWHQ* 62:489–512.

Ragsdale, Crystal Sasse. 1994. *The Women and Children of the Alamo.* Austin, TX: State House Press.

Ramsdell, Charles. N.d. The women in the Alamo. *San Antonio Express Magazine* 10. Historic Sites/Alamo/Survivors. DRT.

Rios, John F., comp. 1987. *Readings on the Alamo.* New York: Vantage Press.

Roberts, Randy, and James S. Olson. 2001. *A Line in the Sand: The Alamo in Blood and Memory.* New York: Free Press.

Rodriguez, J. M. 1913. *Rodriguez Memoirs of Early Texas.* 7–10. San Antonio: Passing Show Printing Co.

Rohrbough, Edward G. How Jim Bowie died. In J. Frank Dobie. 1939. *In the Shadow of History.* 48–59. Austin: Texas Folk-Lore Society.

Roller, Gen. John E., ed. January 1906. Capt. John Sowers Brooks. *Texas Historical Association Quarterly.* 9:190–94.

Ruiz, Francis. 1860. Fall of the Alamo, and massacre of Travis and his brave associates. *Texas Almanac* 80–82.

Sanchez Lamego, Gen. Miguel A. 1968. *The Siege and Taking of the Alamo.* Sante Fe: Press of the Territorian.

Sánchez-Navarro y Peón, Carlos. 1938. *La Guerra de Tejas: Memorias de un Soldado.* Foldout opposite p. 94. Mexico City: Editorial Polis.

Sánchez-Navarro, Carlos. 1960. *La Guerra De Tejas: Memorias de un Soldado.* Mexico: Editorial Jus.

Sánchez-Navarro, José Juan. N.d. *A Mexican Officer's Report of the Fall of the Alamo.* Unattributed pamphlet with reprint and translation of the Alamo plan. CAH.

Santa Anna, Antonio López de. Manifesto relative to his operations in the Texas campaign and his capture. In Castañeda, Carlos, trans. 1928. *The Mexican Side of the Texan Revolution.* 5–6, 10–15. Dallas: P. L. Turner Company.

Santos, Richard G. 1968. *Santa Anna's Campaign against Texas, 1835–1836: Featuring the Field Commands Issued to Major General Vicente Filisola.* 66-68. Salisbury, NC: Documentary Press (Texian Press).

Schoelwer, Susan Prendergast. April 1988. The artist's Alamo: A reappraisal of pictorial evidence, 1836–1850. *SWHQ* 91:403–56.

Schoelwer, Susan, with Tom Glass. 1985. *Alamo Images: Changing Perspection of a Texas Experience.* Dallas: DeGolyer and Southern Methodist University Press.

Shackford, James A. 1956. *David Crockett: The Man and the Legend.* 273–81. Chapel Hill: University of North Carolina Press.

Shackford, James A., and Stanley J. Folmsbee. 1973. Introduction. *A Narrative of the Life of David Crockett of the State of Tennessee by David Crockett.* Knoxville: University of Tennessee Press.

Sheppard, Seth. N.d. (c. 1898). The Siege and Fall of the Alamo. In Dudley G. Wooten, ed. 1898. *A Comprehensive History of Texas, 1685 to 1897.* Vol. 1, 637–48. Dallas: William G. Scarff.

Shiffrin, Gale Hamilton. September 1992. Journey of the Travis ring from the Alamo and back. *Senior Sentinel.* San Antonio.

Sibley, Marilyn McAdams. October 1966. The burial place of the Alamo heroes. *SWHQ* 70:272–80.

Smith, Cornelius C., Jr. 1967. *William Sanders Oury: History-Maker of the Southwest.* 19–27. Tucson: University of Arizona Press.

Smith, Cornelius C., Sr. N.d. (c. 1930). A History of the Oury Family. 8–12. MS 738. Arizona Historical Society, Tucson, and CAH.

Smith, Henry. July 1910. Reminiscences of Henry Smith. *Quarterly of the Texas State Historical Association.* 14:24–73.

Smith, Richard Penn (putative author). 1836. *Col. Crockett's Exploits and Adventures in Texas . . . Written by Himself.* Philadelphia: T. K. and P. G. Collins. Reprinted 1955. New York: Citadel Press.

Smoot, Jane, to Thomas W. Cutrer. November 26, 1985. Draft of entry on Dr. Amelia W. Williams for *Handbook of Texas.* Courtesy of Jane Smoot.

Smoot, Jane. Prior to April 26, 1959. Amelia Worthington Williams. Written for celebration ceremony of the United Daughters of the Confederacy at the tomb of Gen. Albert Sidney Johnston in the State Cemetery. Courtesy of Jane Smoot.

Solomon, Susan. 2001. *The Coldest March.* New Haven: Yale University Press.

Sowell, A. J. 1884. *Rangers and Pioneers of Texas.* San Antonio: Shepard Bros. & Co.

———. 1900. *Early Settlers and Indian Fighters of Southwest Texas.* Austin: Ben C. Jones & Co.

Stiff, Edward. 1840. *The Texan Emigrant.* 312–15. Cincinnati: George Conclin.

Streeter, Thomas W. 1955–60. *A Bibliography of Texas.* 5 vols. Cambridge: Harvard University Press.

Sutherland, John. 1936. *The Fall of the Alamo*. Edited by Annie B. Sutherland. San Antonio: Naylor Company.

Swisher, John M. 1932. *The Swisher Memoirs*. 18–23, 31. San Antonio: Sigmund Press.

Teja, Jesús F. de la. 1991. *A Revolution Remembered: The Memoirs and Selected Correspondence of Juan N. Seguín*. Austin: State House Press.

Templeton, Frank. 1907. *Margaret Ballentine; or, The Fall of the Alamo*. 66. Houston: State Printing Co.

Tinkle, Lon. 1958. *Thirteen Days to Glory*. New York: McGraw-Hill Book Co. Reprinted as *The Alamo*. New York: Signet New American Library.

Todish, Tim J., and Terry S. Todish. 1998. *Alamo Sourcebook, 1836*. Austin, TX: Eakin Press.

Tornel y Mendívil, José María. In Carlos Castañeda, trans. 1928. *The Mexican Side of the Texan Revolution*. 204–378. Dallas: P. L. Turner Company.

Turner, Martha Ann. 1972. *William Barret Travis: His Sword and His Pen*. Waco: Texian Press.

Tyler, Ron, et al., eds. 1996. *The New Handbook of Texas*. Austin: Texas State Historical Association.

Urrea, José. 1838. *Diario Militar del General Jose Urrea Durante la Primera Campana de Tejas*. 54–55. Victoria de Durango, Mexico: Manuel Gonzalez.

———. Diary of the military operations . . . In Carlos Castañeda, trans. 1928. *The Mexican Side of the Texan Revolution*. 207–8. Dallas: P. L. Turner Company.

Watkins, Willye Ward, trans. 1922. Memoirs of General Antonio López de Santa Anna. 90–93. Master's thesis, University of Texas Austin.

Webb, Walter Prescott, et al., eds. 1952. *The Handbook of Texas*. Austin: Texas State Historical Association.

Whitfield, John, and Rex Dalton. August 8, 2002. Ink analysis raises storm over Viking map. *Nature* 418:574.

Williams, Amelia W. 1931. A critical study of the siege of the alamo and of the personnel of its defenders. Ph.D. diss., University of Texas at Austin.

———. July 1933, October 1933, January 1934, April 1934. A critical study of the siege of the Alamo and of the personnel of its defenders. *Southwestern Historical Quarterly*. Vol. 36 (Part 4) through vol. 37.

———. April 1946. *SWHQ* 49:634–37.

Williams, Amelia, and Eugene Barker, eds. 1938–42. *The Writings of Sam Houston, 1835–1836*. 1:364–80, 2:22, 4:17–19, 6:5–13, 7:306–36. Austin: University of Texas Press.

Winkler, Ernest, ed. 1911. *Secret Journals of the Senate, Republic of Texas, 1836–1845*. Austin: Austin Printing Company, for the Texas Library and Historical Commision.

Woolsey, Wallace, ed. and trans. 1987. *Memoirs for the History of the War in Texas, by Gen. Vicente Filisola*. 82–84, 167–81. Austin: Eakin Press.

Wooten, Dudley G., ed. 1898. *A Comprehensive History of Texas, 1685 to 1897*. Dallas: William G. Scarff.

Wright, Ione William (Mrs. S. J.). 1916. *San Antonio de Bexar.* 56. Austin: Morgan Printing Co.

Yoakum, Henderson. 1855. *History of Texas from Its First Settlement in 1685 to Its Annexation to the United States in 1846.* 2:58–59, 75–82, 46–62. New York: Redfield. Revised edition 1856 with appendixes.

Zaboly, Gary S. March 2001. Once more unto the breach! *Alamo Journal* 120:1–8.

Zuber, William P. July 1901. The escape of Rose from the Alamo. *The Quarterly of the Texas State Historical Association.* 5:1–11.

———. October 1901. Letter in "Notes and Fragments." *The Quarterly of the Texas State Historical Association* 5:164.

———. January 1902. Notes and fragments: Last messenger from the Alamo. *Texas Historical Association Quarterly* (later *SWHQ*) 5:263–66.

———. July 1902. Rose's escape from the Alamo. *Texas Historical Association Quarterly* 6:67–69.

———. An escape from the Alamo. In J. Frank Dobie. 1939. *In the Shadow of History.* 17–27.

———. 1971. *My Eighty Years in Texas.* Edited by Janis Boyle Mayfield. Austin: University of Texas Press.

Zuber, W. P., to Charlie Jeffries. August 17, 1904. Inventing stories about the Alamo. In J. Frank Dobie. 1939. *In the Shadow of History.* 42–47. Austin: Texas Folk-Lore Society Publications no. 25.

Zuber, William P., and Mary Ann. 1873. An escape from the Alamo. *Texas Almanac.* 80–85.

INDEX

Page numbers in italics indicate illustrations and tables.